Notable Women Scientists

Pamela Proffitt Editor

GALE GROUP

Detroit
San Francisco
London
Boston
Woodbridge, CT

Editor

Pamela Ann Proffitt

Assistant Editors

Annie Balocating

Suzanne Sessine

Contributing Editor

Kristine Krapp

Managing Editor

Christine B. Jeryan

Editorial Technical Consultant

Mary Fyke

Production Director

Mary Beth Trimper

Assistant Production Manager

Evi Seoud

Buyer

Wendy Blurton

Image Permissions

Margaret Chamberlain

Art Director

Cynthia Baldwin

Product Design Manager

Martha Schiebold

Imaging Supervisor

Randy Bassett

Image Coordinator

Pamela Reed

Imaging Specialist

Mike Logusz

ISBN 0-7876-3900-1
Printed in the United States of America by Gale Group
Gale Group and Design is a trademark used herein under license.

Library of Congress Cataloging-in-Publication Data

Notable women scientists / Pamela Proffitt, editor.
p. cm.
Includes bibliographical references and index.
ISBN 0-7876-3900-1
Summary: Biographical profiles of 500 women around the world who have made significant contributions to the field of science, from antiquity to the present.
ISBN 0-7876-3900-1 (hardcover)
1. Women scientists Biography Juvenile literature.
[1. Scientists. 2. Women Biography.]
I. Proffitt, Pamela, 1966-
Q141.N736 1999 500'.82' 092 dc21

99-35741
[B] CIP

Contents

Introduction vii

Advisory Board and Contributors ix

Entry List xi

Timeline xxi

Entries 1

Subject Index 639

Field of Specialization Index 659

Nationality/Ethnicity Index 665

Introduction

Notable Women Scientists provides narrative biographical profiles of 485 women from around the world who have made significant contributions to science. The book covers women from antiquity to present in a wide range of scientific disciplines including agriculture, astronomy, biology, botany, chemistry, computer science, earth science, ecology, engineering, mathematics, medical science, physics, technology, and zoology. *Notable Women Scientists* includes well-known scientists like Marie Curie and Jane Goodall, as well as lesser-known figures like Evelyn Boyd Granville and Marjorie Lee Browne, who were the first African-American women to receive doctorates in mathematics.

It is important to highlight the achievements of women scientists apart from male scientists because in so many cases they have gone unrecognized or simply ignored. The stories that emerge over and over from this book are of women being denied education, tenure, jobs, and recognition simply because they were women. Most of the women in this book had to face, at some point in their careers, resistance or outright hostility because they sought to work in the male-dominated field of science. Many of the women in this book worked equally with men who took credit for their ideas and discoveries. It is important, however, to recognize the men who overcame their own biases and potential ridicule or censure to help women scientists in their careers.

A quick glance at the timeline will show that times are changing and that women are being increasingly recognized for their work. There are more women Nobel Laureates, professors, industry leaders, and inventors than ever before. For many of the scientists featured here, almost no information has been published previously about their lives or their scientific achievements. Similarly, images of most of the women were extremely difficult to obtain. The difficulty in finding information about these women demonstrates the need for this book. It is the editor's hope that these stories will inspire young women to choose careers in science and that readers in general will be inspired by the remarkable accomplishments of these women.

Selection Process and Criteria

A preliminary list of scientists was compiled from a wide variety of sources, including science indices, other biographical collections, periodical articles, and awards lists. The list was reviewed by an advisory board, and final selection was made by the editor. An effort was made to include a variety of disciplines and a variety of ethnicities and nationalities. An effort was also made to include lesser-known women scientists, including women who were considered skilled amateurs. Coverage includes those in all of the natural, physical, social, and applied sciences. Selection criteria include:

- Discoveries, inventions, awards, overall contributions, influence, and/or impact on scientific progress

- Notable "first" achievements, including degrees earned, positions held, or organizations founded

- Involvement or influence in education, organizational leadership, or public policy

Features of this product

For easy access, entries are arranged alphabetically according to the entrant's last name.

• **Timeline**—includes scientific milestones of the book's entrants, as well as significant events in the history of women in science.

• **Entry head**—lists basic information on each scientist, including name, birth and death dates, nationality, and occupation/field of specialty.

• **Biographical essay**—offers 400–2,000 words on the scientist's life and professional accomplishments. Scientific principles are explained in terminology that readers without a scientific background can understand. **Bold-faced** names within entries indicate an entry on that person.

• **Selected Writings** by the Scientist section— lists publications written or edited by the entrant, including important papers, textbooks, autobiographies, etc.

• **Further Reading** section—provides a list of resources the reader may access to seek additional information on the scientist.

• **Indices**—allow the reader to access the entrants by nationality/ethnicity or field of specialization. A general subject index with cross references offers additional access.

Acknowledgments

The editor would like to thank advisors Margaret Alic and Phyllis Holman Weisbard for their invaluable help in compiling the entry list and suggesting resources. The editor would also like to thank the contributing writers of this book for their outstanding work in locating information about the entrants. Many of the entrants who were still living at the time of publication were personally interviewed by our contributors. To obtain information on those who had died, several writers talked to family members, colleagues, or archivists who had access to unpublished personal information. As many thanks are due to those entrants, friends, or family members who answered questions, provided written information, and generously contributed photos for the book. Without their kind assistance, this book could not have been written.

Advisory Board

Margaret Alic
Author of *Hypatia's Heritage: A History of Women in Science from Antiquity through the Nineteenth Century*

Phyllis Holman Weisbard
Women's Studies Librarian
The University of Wisconsin System
Madison, Wisconsin

Contributors

Margaret Alic, Ethan E. Allen, Kyra Anderson, Olga K. Anderson, Denise Adams Arnold, Karl Leif Bates, Nicole Beatty, Maurice Bleifeld, Barbara Boughton, Barbara A. Branca, Leonard C. Bruno, Jill Carpenter, Chris Cavette, Miyoko Chu, Jane Stewart Cook, Tom Crawford, Margaret DiCanio, Mindi Dickstein, John Henry Dreyfuss, Marianne Fedunkiw, Jerome P. Ferrance, David E. Fontes, Bridget K. Hall, Loretta Hall, Lauri R. Harding, Elizabeth Henry, Fran Hodgkins, Roger Jaffe, Corrine Johnson, J. Sydney Jones, Lee Katterman, Evelyn B. Kelly, Janet Kieffer Kelley, Helene Barker Kiser, Michael Kiser, Geeta Kothari, Jennifer Kramer, Marc Kusinitz, Benedict A. Leerburger, Linda Lewin, Pamela O. Long, Jacqueline L. Longe, C. D. Lord, David E. Newton, Gail B. C. Marsella, Liz Marshall, Mike McClure, Kimberlyn McGrail, George A. Milite, Zoran Minderovic, Carol L. Moberg, Sally M. Moite, Patrick Moore, A. Mullig, M. C. Nagel, Margo Nash, Laura Newman, Joan Oleck, Donna Olshansky, Kristin Palm, Daniel Pendick, Anne M. Perusek, David Petechuk, Annette Petrusso, Karl Preuss, Pamela Proffitt, Barbara Proujan, Lewis Pyenson, Leslie Reinherz, Kelley Reynolds-Jacquez, Francis Rogers, Shari Rudavsky, Kathy Sammis, Joel Schwarz, Laurel M. Sheppard, Michael Sims, Monica Stevens, Julian A. Smith, Linda Wasmer Smith, Sharon F. Suer, Peter H. Taylor, Sebastian Thaler, Cynthia Washam, Karen Wilhelm, Katherine Williams, Karen Withem, Alexandra Witze

Entry List

A

Abella 1

Sophie Bledsoe Aberle 1

Agamede 2

Elizabeth Cabot Cary Agassiz 3

Aglaonice 4

Maria Gaëtana Agnesi 5

Agnodice 6

Fay Ajzenberg-Selove 6

Hattie Alexander 8

Angeles Alvariño 10

Betsy Ancker-Johnson 11

Gloria L. Anderson 13

Mary Ann Anning 14

Virginia Apgar 15

Esther Richards Applin 17

Charlotte Auerbach 18

Mary Ellen Avery 19

Hertha Ayrton 20

B

Florence Augusta Merriam Bailey 23

Nina Bari 24

Eileen Barnes 26

Ida Barney 27

James Miranda Stuart Barry 27

Florence Bascom 28

Laura Maria Catarina Bassi 30

Eleanor Baum 31

Elise Jenny Bäumgartel 32

Aphra Behn 33

Jocelyn Susan Bell Burnell 34

Ruth Fulton Benedict 37

Ruth Mary Roan Benerito 38

Marie Catherine Biheron 39

Isabella Lucy Bird 40

Anna Blackburne 41

Elizabeth Blackwell 42

Elizabeth Blackwell 43

Mary Adelia Blagg 44

Marietta Blau 45

Katharine Burr Blodgett 47

Dorotea Bocchi 49

Rachel Littler Bodley 50

Marie Anne Victorine Gillain Boivin 51

Alice Middleton Boring 52

Louyse Bourgeois 53

Sylvia Trimble Bozeman 54

Sophie Brahe 55

Jenny Eugenia Rosenthal Bramley 56

Yvonne Claeys Brill 58

Elizabeth Gertrude Knight Britton 59

Harriet T. Brooks 60

Dorothy Lavinia Brown 61

Rachel Fuller Brown 63

Marjorie Lee Browne 64

Margaret Bryan 66

Mary Morland Buckland 66

Mary Alice Bunting-Smith 67

Eleanor Margaret Burbidge 69

Augusta Ada Byron, Countess of Lovelace 71

C

Alexa I. Canady 75

Annie Jump Cannon 76

E. Eleanor Carothers 77

Emma Perry Carr 78

Rachel Louise Carson 81

Margaret Cavendish, Duchess of Newcastle 83

Sun-Yung Alice Chang 85

Mary Agnes (Meara) Chase 86

Gabrielle-Émilie Le Tonnelier de Breteuil, the marquise du Châtelet 88

May Edward Chinn 90

Cornelia Maria Clapp 91

Jamie Rappaport Clark 92

Edith Clarke 93

Edith Jane Claypole 94

Cleopatra the Alchemist 95

Agnes Mary Clerke 95

Geraldyn Cobb 97

Jewel Plummer Cobb 99

Mildred Cohn 101

Theodora E. Colborn 102

Jane Colden 104

Eileen Marie Collins 105

Margarita Colmenares 106

Anna Comnena 107

Anna Botsford Comstock 108

Anne Finch Conway 109

Rita R. Colwell 111

Gerty Theresa Cori 112

Gertrude Mary Cox 115

Elizabeth Caroline Crosby 116

Elizabeth Bragg Cumming 118

Clara Eaton Cummings 119

Maria Cunitz 120

Marie Curie 121

D

Maria Dalle Donne 125

Marie M. Daly 126
Ingrid Daubechies 126
Margaret Oakley Dayhoff 128
Frederica Annis de Laguna 129
Maude Jane Delap 130
Gladys (Henry) Dick 131
Amalie Dietrich 132
Irene Diggs 133
Allie Vibert Douglas 134
Mary Anna Palmer Draper 135
Mildred Spiewak Dresselhaus 136
Jeanne Dumée 138
Helen M. Dyer 138

E

Sylvia Alice Earle 141
Annie J. Easley 142
Alice Eastwood 143
Tilly Edinger 144
Cecile Hoover Edwards 145
Helen T. Edwards 147
Tatiana Ehrenfest-Afanaseva 147
Rosa Smith Eigenmann 149
Mileva Einstein-Marić 150
Minnie Joycelyn Elders 151
Gertrude Belle Elion 153
Elizabeth of Bohemia 156
Gladys Anderson Emerson 157
Dorothea Christiana Leporin Erxleben 158
Katherine Esau 159
Thelma Estrin 159
Alice Evans 160

F

Sandra M. Faber 163
Etta Zuber Falconer 164
Marilyn G. Farquhar 166
Wanda K. Farr 166
Anne Fausto–Sterling 168
Jacoba Felicie 169
Catherine Clarke Fenselau 170
Angella Dorothea Ferguson 171
Margaret Clay Ferguson 172
Adele Marion Fielde 173
Mary Peters Fieser 174
Elizabeth F. Fisher 176
Perrenelle Lethas Flammel 177
Williamina Paton Stevens Fleming 177
Alice Cunningham Fletcher 179
Irmgard Flügge-Lotz 181
Katherine A. Foot 182
Dian Fossey 183
Melissa Franklin 186
Rosalind Elsie Franklin 187

Helen M. Free 189
Charlotte Friend 190
Elizabeth Fulhame 192
A. Oveta Fuller 193

G

Julia Anna Gardner 195
Margaret Joan Geller 196
Sophie Germain 197
Lillian Evelyn Gilbreth 199
Alessandra Giliani 201
Gloria Ford Gilmer 202
Ruth Ann Bobrov Glater 203
Catherine Anselm Gleason 204
Ellen Gleditsch 206
Maria Goeppert–Mayer 208
Winifred Goldring 211
Adele K. Goldstine 212
Jane Goodall 213
Temple Grandin 215
Evelyn Boyd Granville 217
Mary Jane Guthrie 219

H

Dorothy Anna Hahn 221
Julia Brainerd Hall 222
Alice Hamilton 223
Anna Jane Harrison 225
Ethel Browne Harvey 226
Margaret Harwood 227
Harriet Ann Boyd Hawes 228
Ellen Amanda Hayes 229
Elizabeth Lee Hazen 230
Olive Clio Hazlett 231
Beulah Louise Henry 232
Herrad of Landsberg 233
Caroline Lucretia Herschel 234
Elisabetha Koopman Hevelius 236
Jacqueline N. Hewitt 236
Hope Hibbard 238
Beatrice Hicks 239
Hildegard of Bingen 240
Gladys Lounsbury Hobby 242
Dorothy Crowfoot Hodgkin 243
Ellen Dorrit Hoffleit 245
Helen Sawyer Hogg 247
Mary Jane Hogue 248
Mary Emilee Holmes 250
Erna Schneider Hoover 250
Lou Henry Hoover 251
Grace Murray Hopper 252
Dorothy Millicent Horstmann 255
Ruth Hubbard 256
Marie Aimee Lullin Huber 257

Margaret Lindsay Murray Huggins 258
Ellen Hutchins 259
Ida H. Hyde 260
Libbie Henrietta Hyman 261
Hypatia of Alexandria 263

I

Valentina Ivanovna Iveronova 265

J

Shirley Ann Jackson 267
Mary Corinna Putnam Jacobi 268
Aletta Henriette Jacobs 270
Sof'ja Aleksandrovna Janovskaja (also transliterated as Sofia Yanovskaya) 271
Mae Carol Jemison 272
Sophia Jex-Blake 274
Irène Joliot-Curie 275
Mary Ellen Jones 277
Lynda Jordan 278
Madeleine M. Joullié 279

K

Isabella Karle 281
Joyce Jacobson Kaufman 282
Elizabeth Keller 284
Evelyn Fox Keller 285
Frances Oldham Kelsey 286
Helen Dean King 288
Mary Henrietta Kingsley 289
Maria Margaretha Winkelmann Kirch 290
Vera Kistiakowsky 282
Flemmie Pansy Kittrell 293
Margaret Knight 294
Eleanora Bliss Knopf 295
Mimi A. R. Koehl 296
Marian Elliot Koshland 297
Sonya Vasilievna Kovalevskaya (Also transliterated as Sofia Vasilevna Kovalevskaia) 298
Mathilde Krim 300
Stephanie Louise Kwolek 302

L

Elise Depew Strang L'Esperance 305
Marie-Louise Dugès Lachapelle 306
Christine Ladd–Franklin 307
Elizabeth Rebecca Laird 309
Marie-Jeanne Lalande 310
Bertha Aranelle Lamme 311
Rebecca Craighill Lancefield 312
Marie Lavoisier 314
Mary Leakey 316
Henrietta Leavitt 319
Esther Miriam Zimmer Lederberg 320
Inge Lehmann 322
Nicole-Reine Étable de la Brière LePaute 323
Iulya Isevolodovna Lermontova 324

Rita Levi-Montalcini 325
Graceanna (or Grace Anna) Lewis 327
Margaret Adaline Reed Lewis 329
Leona Woods Marshall Libby 330
Ruth Smith Lloyd 331
Martha Daniell Logan 332
Cynthia Evelyn Longfield 332
Kathleen Lonsdale 333
Jane Lubchenco 335
Shannon Ann Lucid 337
Mary Elizabeth Horner Lyell 339
Mary Mason Lyon 340

M

Madge Thurlow Macklin 343
Grace MacLeod 344
Icie Gertrude Macy Hoobler 345
Ada Isabel Maddison 347
Michelle Anne Mahowald 349
Maud Worcester Makemson 350
Harriet Florence Mylander Maling 351
Vivienne Malone-Mayes 352
Margaret Eliza Maltby 353
Ines Mandl 355
Hilde Proescholdt Mangold 356
Anna Morandi Manzolini 357
Jane Haldimand Marcet 357
Lynn Margulis 359
Maria the Jewess 360
Sagrario Martinez-Carrera 362
Ursula Bailey Marvin 364
Anne L. Massy 365
Sybilla Masters 366
Mildred Esther Mathias 367
Annie Russell Maunder 368
Antonia Caetana de Paiva Pereira Maury 369
Carlotta Joaquina Maury 370
Martha Dartt Maxwell 371
Barbara McClintock 372
Margaret Sumwalt McCouch 375
Elizabeth McCoy 376
Marcia Kemper McNutt 377
Mary Alice McWhinnie 379
Margaret Mead 380
Lise Meitner 382
Dorothy Reed Mendenhall 385
Maud Leonora Menten 386
Maria Sibylla Merian 388
Helen Abbot Merrill 389
Marie Meurdrac 390
Ynes Mexia 391
Helen Abbott Michael 392
Cynthia Dominka Millis 393

Beatrice Mintz 394
Maria Mitchell 395
Helen Swift Mitchell 397
Mary Wortley Montagu 398
Agnes Mary Claypole Moody 400
Ruth Ella Moore 401
Emmeline Moore 401
Cathleen Synge Morawetz 403
Ann Haven Morgan 404
Margaretta Hare Morris 405
Maria Eimmart Müller 406
Sandra Murray 407
Mary Esther Murtfeldt 407

N

Prudence Hero Rutherford Napier 409
Elizabeth F. Neufeld 410
Hanna Neumann 412
Mary Frances Winston Newson 413
Margaret Morse Nice 414
Dorothy Virginia Nightingale 416
Ida Tacke Noddack 417
Amalie Emmy Noether 418
Marianne North 420
Antonia Coello Novello 421
Christiane Nüsslein-Volhard 422
Zelia Maria Magdalena Nuttall 425

O

Ellen Ochoa 427
Ida H. Ogilvie 428
Jane Marion Oppenheimer 429
Eleanor Anne Ormerod 430

P

Katherine Evangeline Hilton (Van Winkle) Palmer ...433
Barbara F. Palser 434
Ivy May Parker 434
Edith Marion Patch 436
Jennie R. Patrick 437
Ruth Patrick 438
Flora Wambaugh Patterson 440
Cecilia Payne-Gaposchkin 441
Louise Pearce 443
Annie Smith Peck 444
Elizabeth Gifford Peckham 445
Florence Peebles 446
Mary Engle Pennington 447
Marguerite Catherine Perey 449
Candace Dorinda Bebe Pert 450
Mary Locke Petermann 451
Rózsa Péter 453
Almira Hart Lincoln Phelps 454
Lucy Weston Pickett 456
Susan LaFlesche Picotte 457

Elizabeth Lucas Pinckney 458
Elena Lucrezia Cornaro Piscopia 459
Dorothy Riggs Pitelka 460
Margaret Pittman 461
Julia Barlow Platt 462
Agnes Pockels 463
Pelageya Yakovlevna Polubarinova-Kochina 465
Judith Graham Pool 466
Helen Beatrix Potter 467
Helen Walter Dodson Prince 469
Mary Proctor 470
Margie Profet 471

Q

Edith H. Quimby 473

R

Estelle R. Ramey 475
Kamal Jayasing Ranadive 476
Marie Gertrude Rand 477
Mary Jane Rathbun 478
Sarah Ratner 479
Dixy Lee Ray 480
Mina S. Rees 481
Maria Reiche 482
Ellen Swallow Richards 484
Sally Ride 485
Dorothea Klumpke Roberts 488
Edith Adelaide Roberts 489
Lydia Jane Roberts 490
Julia Robinson 491
Daisy Maude Orleman Robinson 493
Emily Warren Roebling 494
Elizabeth Roemer 495
Nancy Grace Roman 496
Mary Swartz Rose 498
Clemence Augustine Royer 498
Vera Cooper Rubin 500
Augusta Rucker 502
Mary Ellen Rudin 502
Dorothea Rudnick 504
Anna Worsley Russell 505
Elizabeth Shull Russell 506

S

Florence Rena Sabin 509
Ruth Sager 512
Grace Adelbert Sandhouse 514
Ethel Sargant 514
Lucy Way Sistare Say 515
Alice T. Schafer 516
Berta Scharrer 517
Dorothea Schlözer 519
Charlotte Angas Scott 520
Mary Sears 522

Florence B. Seibert 524
Susan Wyber Serjeantson 525
Kate Olivia Sessions 527
Lydia White Shattuck 527
Jennie Arms Sheldon 529
Althea Rosina Sherman 529
Patsy O'Connell Sherman 530
Mary Lura Sherrill 531
Lora Mangum Shields 532
Vandana Shiva 533
Odette Louise Shotwell 534
Justine Dittrichin Siegemundin 535
Ellen Kovner Silbergeld 536
Dorothy Martin Simon 537
Joanne Malkus Simpson 538
Charlotte Emma Moore Sitterly 540
Maud Slye 541
Erminnie Adele Platt Smith 542
Emilie Snethlage 543
Mary Fairfax Somerville 543
Queen Sonduk (or Sondok) 545
Effie Almira Southworth Spalding 546
Dolores Richard Spikes 547
Thressa Campbell Stadtman 549
Louise Stanley 550
Genevieve Stearns 550
Joan Steitz Argetsinger 551
Nettie Maria Stevens 553
Sara Yorke Stevenson 554
Susan Smith McKinney Steward 555
Alice M. Stewart 558
Grace Anne Stewart 559
Lucille Farrier Stickel 560
Alice M. Stoll 561
Isabelle Stone 562
Alicia Boole Stott 562
Ella Church Strobell 562
Agnes Naranjo Stroud-Lee 563
Henrietta Hill Swope 564
Paula Szkody 565

T

Mignon Talbot 567
Helen Brooke Taussig 568
Olga Taussky-Todd 570
Charlotte de Bernier Scarbrough Taylor . 572
Valentina Tereshkova 573
Giuliana Cavaglieri Tesoro 574
Marie Tharp 575
Theano 577
Marie Thiroux d'Arconville 578
Caroline Burling Thompson 579
Shirley Marie Caldwell Tilghman 580

Beatrice Muriel Hill Tinsley 581
Mary Lua Adelia Davis Treat 583
Trotula of Salerno 584
Elizabeth Truswell 585
Helen Alma Newton Turner 586

U

Karen Uhlenbeck 589

V

Florence Wilhelmina van Straten 591
Argelia Velez-Rodriguez 592
Birgit Vennesland 592
Lydia Villa-Komaroff 594
Marjorie Jean Young Vold 596
Hilda Geiringer von Mises 597

W

Priscilla Bell Wakefield 599
Mary Ward 600
Margaret Floy Washburn 601
Katharine Way 602
Karen Elizabeth Wetterhahn 604
Anna Johnson Pell Wheeler 605
Sarah Frances Whiting 607
Mary Watson Whitney 608
Sheila Evans Widnall 609
Jane Anne Russell Wilhelmi 611
Cicely Delphin Williams 612
Emma T. R. Williams 613
Heather Williams 614
Lee Anne Mordy Willson 615
Elizabeth Armstrong Wood 617
Geraldine Pittman Woods 617
Jane Cooke Wright 618
Dorothy Maud Wrinch 620
Chien-Shiung Wu 622
Y. C. L. Susan Wu 624
Hildegarde Howard Wylde 625
Rosemary Frances Gillian Wyse 626

X

Xie Xide 627

Y

Rosalyn Sussman Yalow 629
Anne Sewell Young 632
Grace Chisholm Young 632
Judith Sharn Rubin Young 634
Roger Arliner Young 635

Timeline

c. 2350 B.C. **En Hedu'anna** Babylonian priestess of the Moon Goddess conducts astronomical work, including observing stars and following moon cycles.

c. 520 B.C. Greek philosopher **Theano**, student and later wife of Greek philosopher Pythagoras, writes treatises on mathematics, physics, and medicine. She is also credited with writings on the Pythagorean concept of the "golden mean," or moderation.

c. 350 B.C. Greek philosopher and teacher **Arete of Cyrene** succeeds her father, Aristippus, as head of the Cyrenaic school of philosophy where she teaches natural philosophy.

Neopythagorean natural philosopher **Perictione** is active; scholars credit her with the authorship of *Harmony and Woman.*

c. 300 B.C. Greek physician **Agnodice** is brought to trial in Athens for treating women; she is acquitted when influential Athenian women intercede on her behalf.

c. First century B.C. Egyptian alchemist known as **Cleopatra the Alchemist** describes the process of making gold in her *Chrysopoiea.*

c. 50 Egyptian chemist **Maria the Jewess** invents her water bath, the *balneum mariae* or "Maria's bath," which is similar to a double-boiler. It was used to maintain a constant temperature, or to slowly heat a substance.

c. 200 Roman Empress and philosopher **Julia Domna** leads a circle of noted philosophers and scientists.

c. 400 Greek Neoplatonic philosopher and mathematician **Hypatia of Alexandria** writes commentaries on *Diophantus* and *Apollonious.* She is noted as the only woman scholar of ancient times and the first woman mentioned in the history of mathematics.

c. 1050 Italian physician **Trotula** writes *Passionibus mulierum curandorum*, translated and published in English as *Diseases of Women*, which discusses obstetrics and neonatal care.

c. 1150 German scientist, physician, musician, and spiritual leader **Hildegard of Bingen** writes *Physica*, a natural history encyclopedia that includes descriptions of plants and animals, stones and metals, with German as well as Latin terms, and medical applications.

1322 French physician **Jacoba Felicie** is taken to court for practicing medicine; despite testimony in her favor, the court fines her.

1702 German astronomer **Maria Margaretha Winkelmann Kirch** discovers a new comet.

1705 German zoologist and scientific illustrator **Maria Sybylla Merian** publishes her acclaimed *Metamorphosis insectorum surinamensium (Metamorphosis of the Insects of Surinam).*

1733 Italian physicist **Laura Bassi** receives a professorship at the University of Bologna, becoming the first female professor of physics in Europe.

1749 French mathematician, physicist, philosopher, and translator **Gabrielle-milie Le Tonnelier de Breteuil du Chtelet** completes, just shortly before her death, her translation of Isaac Newton's *Principia mathematica.*

1760 Italian anatomist **Anna Morandi Manzolini** becomes professor of anatomy at the University of Bologna.

1786 German-born English astronomer **Caroline Lucretia Herschel** discovers her first comet.

1801 French mathematician and philosopher **Marie-Sophie Germain** presents a partial proof of Fermat's Last Theorem

1843 English mathematician and writer **Augusta Ada Byron, Countess of Lovelace**, publishes *Sketch of the Analytical Engine*, which includes many important insights about the programming of calculating machines.

1848 American astronomer **Maria Mitchell** is the first female member of the American Academy of Arts and Sciences.

1849 English-born American **Elizabeth Blackwell** is the first woman to receive an M.D. degree in the United States.

1854 English nurse **Florence Nightingale** takes charge of a barracks hospital when the Crimean War breaks out. She goes on to create a female nursing service and a nursing school at St. Thomas's Hospital (1860).

1865 American astronomer **Maria Mitchell** is appointed professor of astronomy at the newly formed Women's College, Vassar.

1879 American chemist **Ellen Henrietta Swallow Richards**, noted for her work in metal analysis, is the first woman to join the American Institute of Mining and Metallurgical Engineers.

1889 Russian mathematician and writer **Sofya Vasilyevna Kovalevskaya**, known for her extraordinary work in partial differential equations, rotating bodies, and other fields of mathematics, accepts a permanent professorship at the University of Stockholm.

1894 American microbiologist **Anna Wessels Williams** discovers a strain of bacteria which becomes the standard source of diphtheria toxin production. Her discovery becomes known as the Park-Williams Strain, despite the fact that laboratory director W.H. Park did not participate in the discovery.

1896 American physiologist **Ida Henrietta Hyde** is the first woman to earn a Ph.D. at the University of Heidelberg.

1898 Polish-born French chemist and physicist **Marie Skodowska-Curie** discovers a new radioactive element, which she names *polonium*, in honor of her native Poland.

1901 Canadian physicist **Harriet Brooks** publishes her findings on radioactivity, including the discovery that an element can change into another element.

1903 Polish-born French chemist and physicist **Marie Skodowska-Curie** shares the Nobel Prize in physics with Pierre Curie and Henri Becquerel, becoming the first woman to win the Nobel Prize.

1905 German physicist **Lise Meitner** is the first woman to earn a Ph.D. in physics from the University of Vienna.

American geneticist **Nettie Maria Stevens** publishes her discovery that an individual organism's gender is determined by a particular chromosome.

1906 English physicist, engineer, and inventor **Hertha Ayrton** is the first woman to receive the Hughes Medal from the Royal Society for her work on electric arcs.

Polish-born French chemist and physicist **Marie Skodowska-Curie** takes up the chair of Physics at the Sorbonne that had been occupied by her late husband Pierre. She is the first woman to teach at the Sorbonne.

1911 Polish-born French chemist and physicist **Marie Skodowska-Curie** receives her second Nobel Prize, this time in chemistry, becoming the first scientist to win the Nobel Prize twice.

c. 1912 American astronomer **Henrietta Swan Leavitt** develops a method for measuring the brightness of stars.

1917 American microbiologist **Alice Catherine Evans** publishes the results of her pioneering work on the bacterial etiology of a serious disease (later named brucellosis) transmitted in milk.

Austrian physicist **Lise Meitner**, working with her colleague Otto Hahn, discovers the radioactive element protactinium.

1918 Austrian physicist **Lise Meitner** is the first woman named a full professor of physics in Germany.

German mathematician **Emmy Noether** discovers the mathematical nature of the conservation laws of physics.

1920 American physiologist **Ida Henrietta Hyde** invents the micro electrode, a fundamental instrument for the study of nerve cells.

1921 German-American mathematician **Emmy Noether** publishes her studies on abstract rings and ideal theory, an important development in modern algebra. She is considered to be the greatest of all women mathematicians.

1923 American microbiologist **Gladys Rowena Dick**, working with husband George Frederick Dick, identifies the bacterial cause of scarlet fever.

1924 American medical researcher **Florence Rena Sabin** is the first woman elected president of the American Association of Anatomists.

1925 American astronomer **Annie Jump Cannon**, known for her extraordinary work in spectral analysis of stars, is the first woman to a receive an honorary doctorate from Oxford University.

American medical researcher **Florence Rena Sabin** is the first woman to join the National Academy of Sciences (U.S.).

1926 American industrial physicist **Katharine Burr Blodgett** is the first woman to earn a Ph.D. degree from Cambridge University.

1927 American geneticist **Barbara McClintock**, working with Harriet Creighton, performs experiments on maize, providing the definitive proof for the chromosome theory of heredity.

1928 American microbiologist **Alice Catherine Evans** is the first woman president of the American Society for Microbiology.

American anthropologist **Margaret Mead** publishes *Coming of Age in Samoa.*

1929 American zoologist **Florence Augusta Merriam Bailey** becomes the first female member of the American Ornithological Union.

Czech-born American biochemist **Gerty Cori**, working with her husband, Carl Cori, discovers how organisms process carbohydrates. The "Cori cycle," as it was later named, is regarded as one of the fundamental discoveries in modern biochemistry.

1931 American astronomer **Annie Jump Cannon** receives the Henry Draper Medal for investigations in astronomical physics from the National Academy of Sciences (U.S.).

1933 French physicist and chemist **Irène Joliot-Curie**, working with husband Frédéric Joliot-Curie, discovers the first radioisotope.

1934 American anthropologist **Ruth Fulton Benedict** publishes *Patterns of Culture*, a landmark work on cultural anthropology.

1935 French physicist and chemist **Irène Joliot-Curie** and husband Frédéric Joliot-Curie share the Nobel Prize in Chemistry for their discovery of the first radioisotope.

1937 American organic chemist **Emma Perry Carr** is the first recipient of the Francis Garvan Medal given by the American Chemical Society. This medal was established to recognize distinguished service to chemistry by women chemists.

1938 Austrian-born Swedish physicist **Lise Meitner** provides the crucial theoretical insight that explains the revolutionary phenomenon of nuclear fission.

c. 1940 American geneticist **Barbara McClintock** begins her studies of the genes in maize, eventually discovering transposable or "jumping genes." Her work baffles the genetics community for nearly three decades before her observations are confirmed.

American pediatrician **Helen Taussig**, working with surgeon Alfred Blalock, develops a surgical procedure to treat "blue babies," children suffering from a lack of oxygen due to a heart defect.

1946 English crystallographer **Dorothy Crowfoot Hodgkin**, working with Barbara Rogers-Low, determines the molecular structure of penicillin, which enables scientists to produce synthetic penicillin.

1947 Czech-born American biochemist **Gerty Cori** is the first American woman to receive a Nobel Prize in science. She received the Nobel Prize in physiology or medicine (with Carl Cori and Bernardo Houssay) for her pioneering work on sugar metabolism.

1948 American medical researchers **Elizabeth Lee Hazen** and **Rachel Fuller Brown** discover a powerful antibiotic that provides the basis for the versatile drug antifungal drug *Nystatin*.

English anthropologist and paleontologist **Mary Nicol Leakey**, working at Rusinga, Lake Victoria, Kenya, discovers the skull of *Proconsul africanus*, a hominid ape which lived approximately 1.8 million years ago.

German-born American physicist **Maria Gertrude Goeppert-Mayer** develops a theory explaining the arrangement of particles in an atom's nucleus.

1949 American meteorologist **Joanne Malkus Simpson** is the first woman to earn a Ph.D. in meteorology.

1950 American chemist **Gertrude Belle Elion** develops 6-mercaptopurine, a powerful anti-cancer drug.

1951 Austrian chemist and physicist **Erika Cremer** is named professor at the University of Innsbruck, in recognition for her pioneering work in gas chromatography during World War II.

1952 American physician **Virginia Apgar** introduces her method, later named the Apgar Score System, for quickly determining a newborn's health status.

English chemist **Rosalind Elsie Franklin** makes x-ray photographs of DNA. Despite the crucial importance of her work for the discovery of the structure of DNA, Watson and Crick refuse to acknowledge her contribution.

Italian medical researcher **Rita Levi-Montalcini** identifies a substance she calls "the nerve-growth promoting agent" and later labels it nerve growth factor (NGF).

1953 English crystallographer **Dorothy Crowfoot Hodgkin** determines the molecular structure of vitamin B_{12}.

1957 American computer scientist and Navy officer **Grace Hopper** designs Flowmatic, the computer language that later provides the foundation for COBOL.

Japanese chemist and geologist **Katsuko Saruhashi** is the first woman to receive a Ph.D. in chemistry at the University of Tokyo.

1959 American computer scientist and Navy officer **Grace Hopper** and colleagues design COBOL (Common Business-Oriented Language).

English anthropologist and paleontologist **Mary Nicol Leakey**, working at Olduvai Gorge, Tanzania, discovers the fossils remains of a hominid, 17.5 million years old, named *Zinjanthropus,* and later classified as *Australopithecus*.

American physicist and medical researcher **Rosalyn Sussman Yalow** and collaborator Solomon A. Berson describe their radioimmunoassay, a revolutionary diagnostic technique which uses radioisotopes to tag individual molecules.

1962 American ecologist, marine biologist, and writer **Rachel Carson** publishes *Silent Spring*.

French chemist and physicist **Marguerite Perey**, discoverer of the radioactive element francium, becomes the first female member of the French Academy of the Sciences.

1963 German-born American physicist **Maria Goeppert-Mayer** wins, along with Hans D. Jensen and Eugene Wigner, the Nobel Prize in physics. She received the prize for her work on nuclear structures.

Soviet cotton-mill worker and parachutist **Valentina Vladimirovna Tereshkova** becomes the first woman in space as she flies in *Vostok 6*. She remains in orbit for three days.

1964 English crystallographer **Dorothy Crowfoot Hodgkin** receives the Nobel Prize in chemistry, becoming the first woman in Britain to earn a Nobel Prize for science.

American pediatrician **Helen Taussig** is the first female president of the American Heart Association.

Austrian-born Swedish physicist **Lise Meitner** is the first female recipient of the Enrico Fermi Award. This award, given in recognition of scientific and technical achievement in atomic energy, is presented by the president of the United States.

1967 English radio astronomer **Jocelyn Bell Burnell** discovers pulsars, but Anthony Hewish, leader of Bell's radio astronomy project, gets the 1974 Nobel Prize in physics for the discovery.

1969 American mathematician **Mina Rees** is the first woman to become president of the American Association for the Advancement of Science.

1972 American medical researcher **Candace Pert** identifies opiate receptors in animal brain tissue.

1973 American physician **Shirley Ann Jackson** is the first African-American woman to earn a Ph.D. at the Massachusetts Institute of Technology (MIT).

1975 American mathematician **Julia Bowman Robinson** is the first female mathematician to join the National Academy of Sciences.

1976 English-born American astronomer **Eleanor Burbidge**, known for her work on the chemical composition of stars, is the first woman to assume the presidency of the American Astronomical Society.

English anthropologist and paleontologist **Mary Leakey**, working near Olduvai Gorge, Tanzania, a discovers fossilized hominid footprints, which indicate that hominids walked in an upright position some 3.5 million years ago.

American geneticist **Barbara McClintock's** pioneering work is finally acknowledged at a symposium, where scientists introduce the term "transposon" to describe the controlling genes that she had discovered.

American physicist and medical researcher **Rosalyn Sussman Yalow** is the first woman to receive the Albert Lasker Basic Medical Research Award.

1977 American physicist and medical researcher **Rosalyn Sussman Yalow** shares the Nobel Prize in physiology or medicine with Roger Guillemin and Andrew Victor Schally.

1980 Japanese chemist and geologist **Katsuko Saruhashi** is the first woman to join the Science Council of Japan.

1983 American mathematician **Julia Bowman Robinson** is the first female president of the American Mathematical Society.

American geneticist **Barbara McClintock** receives the Nobel Prize for Physiology or Medicine, the first woman to win the entire prize.

1984 American medical researcher **Candace Pert** discovers that certain immune system cell receptors can also be found in the brain.

Chinese-born American geneticist **Flossie Wong-Staal** is the first scientist to clone HIV genes.

1986 Italian medical researcher **Rita Levi-Montalcini** shares the Nobel Prize in physiology or medicine with Stanley Cohen.

1988 American chemist **Gertrude Belle Elion** shares the Nobel Prize in physiology or medicine with James Black and George Hitchings.

1990 American marine biologist **Sylvia Alice Earle** is the first female Chief Scientist of the National Oceanic and Atmospheric Administration.

American geneticist **Mary-Claire King** identifies the breast cancer gene, which she names BRCA1.

American physicist **Mildred Dresselhaus** receives the National Medal of Science (U.S.).

American physician **Antonia Novello** becomes the first female Surgeon General of the United States.

1991 American chemist **Gertrude Belle Elion** is the first woman to earn a place in the Inventors' Hall of Fame.

1992 American physician **Mae Jemison** is a crew-member of the space shuttle *Endeavor*, becoming the first female African- American astronaut.

1995 German geneticist **Christiane Nüsslein-Volhard** wins the Nobel Prize in physiology or medicine for her discoveries concerning the genetic control of early embryonic development.

Canadian-born American physicist **Melissa Eve Bronwen Franklin** and her research team discover the top quark, regarded as the last undiscovered subatomic particle.

American physicist **Shirley Ann Jackson** is the first woman, and the first African-American, to head the Nuclear Regulatory Commission.

1998 Turkish-born American archeologist **Kutlu Aslihan Yener** develops a new x-ray technique for determining the chemical make-up of ancient objects.

A

Abella
1380–?
Italian teacher of medicine

Abella studied medicine and lectured at the medical school of Salerno in southern Italy. She wrote about women's health and the role of bile in the human body. She published two treatises on these subjects: *De atrabile* and *De natura seminis humani*. None of her writings exist today. She is mentioned by Renatus Moreau in the book *Schola Salernitano de Valetudine* (1625) as having written her works in verse.

Women in antiquity have always practiced some form of medicine, as it fell to them to nurse and care for the sick—whether family, friends or neighbors. Often, their instruction came by way of the Church. For example, the convent during the early Middle Ages was a place of intellectual advancement for women. Although much of the learning at that time centered on literature and history, by the twelfth century astronomy and geography books were being written to instruct convent students. By the late twelfth century, a nun, **Hildegard of Bingen**, was writing on scientific topics as well as practical medicine.

Medical training for women was not, however, confined to convents. Italian medical schools connected to universities also instructed women in the healing arts. The School of Salerno was a prime example of this, as records show women attended classes there beginning about the eleventh century. (The medical school in Bologna was another. **Alessandra Giliani** was trained as an anatomist at this school. She has the distinction of being the only woman recorded in medieval history to have performed dissections.) Abella most likely trained at Salerno sometime in the early fourteenth century. The School of Salerno was the first medical school in medieval times independent of the Church. Its reputation as a place of scientific study qualified it as the first European university, and it influenced the development of other medical schools throughout Europe.

The "Ladies of Salerno"

Women attended the medical school in Salerno from its opening—thus the term, "the Ladies of Salerno." **Trotula** (eleventh century), Abella, Rebecca Guarna, Francesca de Romana, and Mercuriade (fourteenth century), all graduates of Salerno, were known and revered during their time as medical scientists and scholars. As might be expected, obstetrics and gynecology were specialties for many women aspiring to the medical profession, although they were not restricted in their choice.

Unlike other European women, Italian women were accepted in this traditionally male profession because of educational opportunities afforded to them from Roman times through the Renaissance period. Italian universities in general were open to women who wished to gain an education. Both women students and women professors were fairly common. In teaching and in practice, Abella and the other "Ladies of Salerno" helped bring about a "medical Renaissance," advancing medicine as a science throughout Europe.

FURTHER READING

Books

Alic, Margaret. *Hypatia's Heritage, A History of Women in Science from Antiquity through the Nineteenth Century*. Boston: Beacon Press, 1986.

Hughes, Muriel Joy. *Women Healers in Medieval Life and Literature*. Freeport, NY: Books for Libraries Press, 1968.

Mozans, H. J. *Women in Science*. New York: D. Appleton and Co., 1913.

Ogilvie, Marilyn Bailey. *Women in Science, Antiquity through the Nineteenth Century*. Cambridge: MIT Press, 1986.

Siraisi, Nancy G. *Medieval & Early Renaissance Medicine, An Introduction to Knowledge and Practice*. Chicago: University of Chicago Press, 1990.

Sketch by Jane Stewart Cook

Sophie Bledsoe Aberle
1899–?
American anthropologist and nutritionist

Sophie Bledsoe Aberle was a Native American anthropologist and nutritionist whose multi-faceted career included many years of research into the culture of the Pueblo tribe of New Mexico. Her groundbreaking work as physician, nutritionist, psychiatrist, and anthropologist marks her as one of the few Native American women scientists to earn professional recognition in the early twentieth century.

As an advocate for the Pueblo people, she held various committee and board positions, both at the regional and national level, that served to advance the Pueblos' health, education, and living conditions. These included the Rio Grande drainage basin committee; New Mexico Nutrition Committee; Committee of Maternal and Infant Mortality; health committee of the All Indian Pueblo Council; White House Conference on Children in Democracy; Southwest Field Training School for Federal Service; and Commission on Rights, Liberties, and Responsibilities of American Indians. She also served as consultant to the All Indian Pueblo Council on computer–assisted instruction; Stanford University's study of Indian Education; and the Bernalillo School District's bilingual/bicultural project. Her scholarly achievements and her committee work earned her recognition at the national level. When the United States National Science Foundation was formed in 1950, she became the first women to serve on its policy–making board, and remained on the National Science board until 1957.

Aberle was born in Schenectady, New York, on July 21, 1899. She married in 1940. She earned undergraduate and graduate degrees from Stanford University (A. B.,1923; M. A., 1925). Her Ph.D. in genetics was awarded in 1927. In 1930, she also earned a medical degree from Yale University in 1930. She remained at Stanford until 1934, holding various teaching and research positions, and was a Sterling fellow for the Yale School of Medicine from 1930–1931.

More Than 50 Years of Field Work and Research

In 1935, Aberle became general superintendent of the United Pueblo Agency for the Bureau of Indian Affairs, Department of the Interior. She held this position until 1944. She then worked for the National Research Council until 1949, when she became special research director for the University of New Mexico at Albuquerque. Her anthropological research, some of which was funded by a grant from the Carnegie Foundation, helped her to understand how the civil organization and cultural practices of the Pueblo were used to strengthen their economic circumstances.

In 1948, the American Anthropological Association published her work based on that research, entitled *The Pueblo Indians of New Mexico, Their Land, Economy and Civil Organization*. In it, she looks at how retaining ownership of their lands was a major factor for the Pueblo in strengthening their economic position. That factor, combined with a scientific approach to livestock raising, the formation of sheep and cattle business associations, and tribal cohesion and common purpose, helped the modern Pueblo adapt to changing economic conditions with a high degree of success. She also discusses how important the land is to the Pueblo way of life—indeed to all Native Americans—definitively stating, "Land in the eyes of the Indian is his most precious possession." The acquisitiveness of white Americans, as with the Spanish and Mexicans of earlier times, was a danger to the Pueblo's way of life. In order to protect their land, the Pueblo "adopted the only method he knew how to use—that was, his own version of the "iron curtain." This attitude of secretiveness characterizes the Pueblo today," she wrote.

In her concern for improving the physical and mental health of the Pueblo, Aberle became chief nutritionist of the Bernalillo County Indian Hospital in 1953, and, in 1966, a staff member of the Department of Psychiatry at the Medical School of the University of New Mexico. From 1970 until her retirement, she was on staff at the university's law school. Aberle was a member of the American Association for the Advancement of Science, American Medical Association, and the American Anthropological Association.

SELECTED WRITINGS BY ABERLE:

Books

The Pueblo Indians of New Mexico, Their Land, Economy and Civil Organization. New York: American Anthropological Association, Kraus Reprint Co., 1969.

FURTHER READING

Books

American Men and Women of Science. Vol. 1, 17th ed. New York: R.R. Bowker, 1989.

Bailey, Martha J. *American Women in Science: A Biographical Dictionary.* Santa Barbara: ABC/CLIO, 1994.

O'Neill, Lois Decker. *The Women's Book of World Records and Achievements.* Garden City: Anchor Press/Doubleday, 1979.

Sketch by Jane Stewart Cook

Agamede
c. 12th century B.C.
Greek physician

Much of what is known about Agamede is derived from myth. Still, some facts are known. Agamede was born at Elis in ancient Greece. The name of her mother is not known but her father was Augeas, King of the Epeans. She married Mulius, a warrior. Physicians of Agamede's time typically were skilled in the use of hellebore, iron-rust, pain killers, burned sulphur, and the use of mandrake. Given the violent nature of the time, the physicians were also adept at removing spear heads and arrows from human flesh as well as treating wounds. Agamede is attributed with a broad knowledge of the medicinal properties of various plants and is widely considered one of the first female physicians, along with Helen of Troy. In the *Iliad*, an ancient collection of Greek mythology, Homer describes Agamede as one who "understood as many drugs as the wide earth nourishes."

FURTHER READING

Books

Hurd–Mead, Kate Campbell. *A History of Women in Medicine from the Earliest Times to the Beginning of the Nineteenth Century*. Haddam, CT: Haddam Press, 1938. Reprint, Boston: Mildford House, 1973.

Ogilvie, Marilyn Bailey. *Women in Science: Antiquity through the Nineteenth Century*. Cambridge: MIT Press, 1993.

Sketch by Kristin Palm

Elizabeth Agassiz (The Granger Collection, New York. Reproduced by permission.)

Elizabeth Cabot (Cary) Agassiz
1822–1907
American naturalist

The founder and first president of Radcliffe College, Elizabeth Agassiz was a naturalist who worked in close association with her famous husband, Jean Louis Agassiz. She was the author of several popular natural history and travel books and a champion of education for women.

Born in 1822, the second of seven children in an intellectual Unitarian upper-class Boston family, Elizabeth Cabot Cary was the daughter of Thomas Graves and Mary Ann Cushing (Perkins) Cary. Agassiz was often ill as a child and, unlike her brothers and sisters, did not attend school. She studied at home, on her own or with a governess. In 1849, at the age of 27, she moved in with her older sister, who was married to a Harvard College faculty member. This was to be an important move to Agassiz, because her sister also introduced her to her future husband, Louis Agassiz.

Marries Louis Agassiz

A Swiss zoologist, geologist and paleontologist, Louis Agassiz was famous for his studies on fossil fish. A widower with three children, Agassiz came to America in 1846 to join the Harvard faculty. In 1850, a short time after meeting, Elizabeth Cary and Agassiz were married. The couple shared a passion for promoting education. They both believed in the importance of teaching, the popularization of science, and in the education of women. Although lacking in scientific training, Agassiz initially became her husband's assistant, learning natural history and editing his English scientific publications. Her notes on his lectures provided much of his published material.

The Agassizes established a marine laboratory on Sullivan Island, South Carolina, and as a result of their work, Agassiz published her *Actaea, a First Lesson in Natural History* in 1859, under a pseudonym. This was followed by *Seaside Studies in Natural History*, written in collaboration with her adopted son Alexander, in 1866. Both of these works proved to be popular manuals.

To help support the family financially, Agassiz founded a high school for 80 girls in her Cambridge home. She ran the school for the next 80 years. She also was instrumental in the development of Agassiz's Museum of Comparative Zoology at Harvard and the Anderson Natural History School on Penikese Island in Buzzards Bay, off the coast of Cape Cod. Although short-lived, the Anderson School, where high school and college teachers studied research problems using the latest biological techniques, was the first introduction to laboratory biology for American women.

The Agassizes made a number of scientific expeditions, including an ocean survey. During 1865 and 1866, they traveled to Brazil by way of Cape Horn. Agassiz learned Portuguese, kept all of their field notes, and published her literary and scientific chronicle of the journey in 1867, with her husband as coauthor. *A Journey in Brazil* proved a popular success. Following their expedition through the Straits of Magellan in 1872, Agassiz published her husband's new discoveries on the process of glaciation in articles in *The Atlantic Monthly*.

Agassiz's scientific contributions were overshadowed by those of her famous husband, who died in 1873. Eight days later, her adopted son also died. Agassiz assumed responsibility for her three young grandsons.

Founds Radcliffe College

In 1879, Agassiz helped to found the "The Society for the Collegiate Instruction of Women," commonly called the Harvard Annex, which provided courses for women taught by Harvard professors. She became its president in 1882 and, when Harvard Annex became Radcliffe College in 1893, Agassiz became its first president, serving until her retirement in 1903. From its beginnings, the college included scientific laboratories, and Agassiz demanded that her students receive Harvard degrees. During her tenure, a scholarship and a building were endowed in her honor.

In addition to publishing scientific articles, Agassiz edited Alexander's publications, wrote a biography of her husband, and edited his correspondence. A cerebral hemorrhage in 1904 left her an invalid, and Agassiz died following a second stroke in 1907.

SELECTED WRITINGS BY AGASSIZ:

Books

(With Alexander Agassiz) *Seaside Studies in Natural History*. Boston: Houghton Mifflin, 1865.

(With Louis Agassiz) *A Journey in Brazil*. Boston: Ticknor and Fields, 1868.

Louis Agassiz: His Life and Correspondence. 2 vols. Boston: Houghton Mifflin, 1886.

Periodicals

"The Hassler Glacier in the Straits of Magellan." *The Atlantic Monthly* 30 (October 1872): 472–78.

FURTHER READING

Books

Hawkins, Hugh. "Elizabeth Cabot Cary Agassiz." In *Notable American Women 1607–1950: A Biographical Dictionary*, edited by Edward T. James, Janet Wilson James, and Paul W. Boyer. Vol. 1. Cambridge: Harvard University Press, 1971.

Paton, Lucy Allen. *Elizabeth Cary Agassiz: A Biography*. Boston: Houghton Mifflin, 1919.

Tharp, Louise Hall. *Adventurous Alliance: The Story of the Agassiz Family of Boston*. Boston: Little Brown, 1959.

Sketch by Margaret Alic

Aglaonice

fl. 5th century B.C. (?)

Greek astronomer

Aglaonice was known in her time as a sorceress who possessed the ability to make the moon disappear. In fact, Aglaonice's powers appear to have been the result of her ability to understand and accurately calculate the times and locations of lunar eclipses. As such, she can be considered one of the first women astronomers.

Agalonice, sometimes spelled Aglaonike, is believed to have lived in the fifth century B.C., although the exact dates of her birth and death are not known. She was probably born in Thessaly in the northern part of what is now known as Greece. Her father is believed to be Hegetor of Thessaly, according to one source, or Hegemon, according to another, but neither name appears in other writings of the period. Nothing is known of her childhood or other family members.

Very little is known about Aglaonice or her life. Popular belief of the time held that certain Thessalian women had the power to make the moon disappear at will, and several of the most learned men of ancient Greece seemed to believe this ancient superstition. Plato described these women as " . . . Thessalian enchantresses, who, as they say, bring down the moon from heaven at the risk of their own perdition." Aglaonice was reputed to have this power and was much feared. Several centuries later, the Greek biographer Plutarch seemed to have a better understanding of Aglaonice's skills, when he wrote that "she, through being thoroughly acquainted with the periods of the full moon when it is subject to eclipse, and, knowing beforehand the time when the moon was due to be overtaken by the earth's shadow, imposed upon the women, and made them all believe that she was drawing down the moon."

The ability to predict lunar eclipses was not new, even in ancient Greece, and Aglaonice may have learned it from someone else. It did require a knowledge of the lunar cycle, however, and an ability to calculate the position of the moon relative to Earth over a period of several decades. Apparently Aglaonice was skillful enough to make these calculations with great accuracy and used her predictions to astound and terrify her followers. Because of her gender and her Thessalian heritage, her skills were attributed to sorcery, rather than scientific ability. In a belated recognition of her role as an astronomer, a crater on the planet Venus is named in her honor.

FURTHER READING

Books

Ogilvie, Marilyn Bailey. *Women in Science.* Cambridge: MIT Press, 1986.

Other

"Aglaonike." *4,000 Years of Women in Science.* http://www.astr.ua.edu/4000WS/AGLAONIKE.html (20 Mar 1999).

Sketch by Chris Cavette

Maria Gaëtana Agnesi
1718–1799
Italian mathematician and philosopher

One of the great figures of Italian science, Maria Gaëtana Agnesi was born and died in Milan, an Italian city under Habsburg rule. In early childhood, she demonstrated extraordinarily intellectual abilities, learning several languages, including Greek, Latin, and Hebrew.

While still a child, Agnesi took part in learned discussions with noted intellectuals who visited her parents' home. Agnesi's father, who taught mathematics at the University of Bologna, hired a university professor to tutor her in mathematics. Her knowledge encompassed various fields of science, and to any foreign visitor who was not a Latinist (the discussions were held in Latin), she spoke fluently in his language. Her brilliance as a multilingual and erudite conversationalist was matched by her fluency as a writer. When she was 17 years old, Agnesi wrote a memoir about the marquis de l'Hospital's 1687 article on conic sections. Her *Propositiones philosophicae*, a book of essays published in 1738, examines a variety of scientific topics, including philosophy, logic, and physics. Among the subjects discussed is Isaac Newton's theory of universal gravitation.

Following her mother's death, Agnesi wished to enter a convent, but her father decided that as the oldest child, she should supervise the education of her numerous younger siblings. As an educator, Agnesi recognized the educational needs of young people, and eloquently advocated the education of women.

Witch of Agnesi

Agnesi's principal work, *Instituzione analitiche ad uso della gioventu' italiana* (1748), known in English as her *Analytical Institutions*, is a veritable compendium of mathematics, written, as the Italian title indicates, for the edification of Italian youth. The work introduces the reader to algebra and analysis, providing elucidations of both and of integral and differential calculus. Praised for its lucid style, Agnesi's book was translated into English by John Colson, Lucasian Professor of Mathematics at Cambridge University. Colson, who learned Italian for the express purpose of translating Agnesi's book, had already translated Newton's *Principia mathematica* into English. Among the prominent features of Agnesi's work is her discussion of a curve, subsequently named the "Witch of Agnesi," due in part by a confusion of terms. (The Italian word *versiera*, derived from the Latin *vertere*, meaning *to turn*, became associated with *avversiera*, which in Italian means *devil's wife*, or *witch*.) Studied previously by Pierre de Fermat and by Guido Grandi, the "Witch of Agnesi" is a cubic curve represented by the Cartesian equation $y\ (x2 + a2) = a3$, where a represents a parameter, or constant. For $a = 2$, as an example, the maximum value of y will be 2. As y tends toward 0, x will tend, asymptotically, toward $\pm\infty$.

Receives Papal Recognition and Accepts Religious Vocation

In 1750, Pope Benedict XIV named Agnesi professor of mathematics and natural philosophy at the University of Bologna. As David M. Burton explains, it is not quite clear whether she accepted the appointment. Considering the fact that her father was gravely ill by 1750, there is speculation that she would have found the appointment difficult to accept. At any rate, after her father's death in 1752, Agnesi apparently lost all interest in scientific work, devoting herself to a religious life. She directed charitable projects, taking charge of a home for the poor and infirm in 1771, a task to which she devoted the rest of her life.

SELECTED WRITINGS BY AGNESI:

Propositiones philosophicae, quas crebris disputationibus domi habitis coram clarissimis viris explicabat extempore, 1738 (Translated in 1801 as *Analytical Institutions* by John Colson)

FURTHER READING

Books

Alic, Margaret. *Hypatia's Heritage: A History of Women in Science from Antiquity through the Nineteenth Century.* Boston: Beacon Press, 1986.

Burton, David M. *Burton's History of Mathematics: An Introduction.* Dubuque, IA: Wm. C. Brown, 1995.

Kramer, Edna E. "Maria Gaetana Agnesi," in *Dictionary of Scientific Biography*. Volume I. Edited by Charles Coulston Gillispie. New York: Charles Scribner's Sons, 1970.

Olsen, Lynn M. *Women in Mathematics*. Cambridge: MIT Press, 1974.

Sketch by Zoran Minderovic

Agnodice
fl. 4th Century B.C.
Greek physician

Agnodice was a Greek woman who, at about 300 B.C., disguised herself as a man and traveled to Alexandria, in Egypt, to study medicine. She returned to Athens and, still posing as a man, began to practice medicine among the women of the aristocracy. When her identity was revealed and she faced prosecution, the women of Athens rose up in support of her, and the laws forbidding women to practice medicine were abolished.

At the time of Agnodice (Agnodike), women in Athens were barred from practicing medicine, ostensibly because they were performing abortions, an operation which periodically was declared illegal. The story of Agnodice appeared in the *Fabulae* of Hyginus, a Roman historian and the librarian of Emperor Augustus in the first century B.C. It was repeated in a letter published in 1687 by Elizabeth Celleor, a famous English midwife, and quoted by **Sophie Jex-Blake** in her history of women in medicine: "Among the subtle Athenians a law at one time forbade women to study or practice medicine or physick on pain of death, which law continued some time, during which many women perished, both in child-bearing and by private diseases, their modesty not permitting them to admit of men either to deliver or cure them."

In Alexandria, the center of Greek science, Agnodice studied medicine and midwifery with Herophilus, one of the greatest anatomists of the ancient world. In one version of her story, the physicians of Athens became jealous of Agnodice's successful medical practice and, believing her to be a man, accused her of taking advantage of women patients. They were embarrassed to learn that she was a woman and decided to prosecute her for illegally practicing medicine. As Jex-Blake quotes from Elizabeth Celleor: "she was like to be condemned, to death, for transgressing the law. . . which, coming to the ears of the noble women, they ran before the Areopagites, and the house being encompassed by most women of the city, the ladies entered before the judges, and told them they would no longer account them for husbands and friends, but for cruel enemies that condemned, her to death, who restored to them their health, protesting they would all die with her if she were put to death."

After this incident, Agnodice was allowed to resume her medical practice and to dress as she wished. The laws were changed and, subsequently, freeborn women were allowed to study medicine and treat women patients, even earning a stipend from the state. Eventually the influence and knowledge of Greek medical women spread over the Roman Empire.

FURTHER READING

Books

Jex-Blake, Sophia. *Medical Women: A Thesis and a History*. 2d ed. 1886. Reprint, New York: Source Book Press, 1970.

Mozans, H. J. [John Augustine Zahm]. *Women in Science*. 1913. Reprint, Cambridge: MIT Press, 1974.

Periodicals

Hurd-Mead, Kate C. "An Introduction to the History of Women in Medicine." *Annals of Medical History* NS 5 (1933).

McMaster, Gilbert. "The First Woman Practitioner of Midwifery and the Care of Infants in Athens, 300 BC." *American Medicine* 18 (1912): 202–205.

Sketch by Margaret Alic

Fay Ajzenberg-Selove
1926–
German-born American nuclear physicist

Fay Ajzenberg-Selove is known as an internationally recognized expert on nuclear structure and an authority on characteristics of light nuclei. She is a professor of physics at the University of Pennsylvania and advocate for women in the sciences. Her greatest contribution to physics has been to review, evaluate, and compile experimental work on the structure and decay of light nuclei with mass numbers from 5–20. Mass numbers are integers that approximate the mass of an isotope and designate the number of nucleons in the nucleus.

Fay Ajzenberg-Selove was born in Berlin, Germany, on February 13, 1926, the second daughter of Russian parents Moisei (Misha) Abramovich Ajzenberg and Olga Naiditch. Her father, although born in Warsaw to poor Jewish parents, won a scholarship to attend the St. Petersburg Mining Academy, an unheard-of opportunity for a Jew in Tsarist Russia. Ajzenberg-Selove's mother studied at the Academy of Music but gave it up to marry the young graduate in mining.

After the Communist revolution in 1917, the Ajzenbergs sought refuge in Germany. Getting there was not easy, however. Misha purportedly hijacked a train to get his wife and daughter out of the country. In Berlin he left engineering behind and became a successful banker. Ajzenberg-Selove was born into comfortable circumstances in the family villa in Neubabelsberg. With the Depression, her father left the banking business to became a chemical engineer and partner in the family sugar beet business in France where Ajzenberg-Selove spent her formative years, from 1930–1940. She went to school at the Lycée Victor Duruy and at Le Collège Sevigné in Paris. Growing up, she was encouraged to think for herself and pursue all subjects that interested her. Believing strongly in the education of women, her parents discouraged her from playing with dolls, giving her books instead, and on one memorable occasion, an erector set. Her father was the primary influence in her life, and because of him, she planned to study engineering.

Solves Difficult Physics Problem

With Europe in turmoil and the Germans marching on Paris, the Ajzenbergs once again became refugees, this time passing through Portugal to the United States where they finally settled in New York. After graduating from Julia Richman High School in Manhattan in 1943, Ajzenberg-Selove majored in engineering at the University of Michigan, the sole female in a class of 100. In 1946 she earned her B.S. degree and went on to graduate studies at Columbia University. Her studies proved so difficult for her that she left them to teach physics and mathematics to veterans at the University of Illinois. The break allowed her to finally master basic physics and she returned to graduate studies at the University of Wisconsin a year later, determined to become a physicist.

As a graduate student, she proved to herself that she really had a career in physics by solving a difficult problem. She identified excited states of certain boron nuclei as uneven, disproving an earlier theory by Thomas Lauritsen and others that they were harmonic. She earned her Ph.D. in 1952, basing her dissertation on energy levels and classification of light nuclei. Lauritsen was so impressed by her work that he invited her to work with him at the California Institute of Technology where she began the work on light nuclei for which she is best known. Part of her work involved helping Lauritsen edit the fourth edition of *Energy Levels of Light Nuclei*.

Battles for a Place in Academe

After her summer at the California Institute of Technology Ajzenberg-Selove accepted a lecturer's position at Smith College, during which time she also held a position as visiting research fellow at the Massachusetts Institute of Technology (MIT). In 1953 she was offered an assistant professorship at Boston College, but at a salary 15% below that of male faculty. Because she'd been offered a position at MIT, she rejected the offer. Boston College promptly reissued the contract at the standard salary. The following year she attended a lecture given by Harvard physicist Walter Selove. at the University of Pennsylvania. But when she applied for a tenured position in 1972, she was turned down because she was considered too old and not active enough in her field. Ajzenberg-Selove appealed these decisions to the state of Pennsylvania and was granted a full professorship in 1973, a position she continues to hold.

Continues Research Into Light Nuclei and Nucleic Structure

Denying Ajzenberg-Selove tenure on the grounds of inactivity in her field was particularly wrong taking her work on light nuclei into account. She and Lauritsen published the fifth edition of *Energy Levels of Light Nuclei* in 1955 and she has continued to work on that publication since 1973. Light nuclei include isotopes of hydrogen, helium, lithium, beryllium, boron, carbon, nitrogen, oxygen, fluorine, neon, and sodium. These elements are particularly important for basic nuclear research and also for understanding the nucleosynthesis (the production of a chemical element from simpler nuclei) of elements in stars. Her experimental work in nuclear spectroscopy, or the ways in which light nuclei absorb and emit energy, is invaluable in her peer review of the some 1,200 scientific papers written annually. She has also worked at the major particle accelerators in the United States and in England, studying characteristics of light nuclei, research that has important applications in fusion, the dating of artifacts, and in nuclear medicine.

Ajzenberg-Selove is a fellow of the American Physical Society, whose division of nuclear physics she chaired from 1973–1974, and of the American Association for the Advancement of Science, where she was a member of the governing council from 1974–1980. She has also chaired the Commission on Nuclear Physics of the International Union of Pure and Applied Physics (1978–81), and served as a member of the Department of Energy/National Science Foundation, Nuclear Science Advisory Committee (1977–1980). In 1991 she was awarded the Christian and Mary Lindback Foundation Award for Distinguished Teaching and also holds honorary doctorates from Smith College (1995) and from Michigan State University (1997).

SELECTED WRITINGS BY AJZENBERG-SELOVE:

Books

"Nuclear Spectra." In *McGraw-Hill Encyclopedia of Science and Technology*. New York: McGraw-Hill, 1992.

A Matter of Choices: Memoirs of a Female Physicist. New Brunswick: Rutgers University Press, 1994.

Periodicals

(With R. E. Brown, E. R. Flynn, and J. W. Sunier) "Experimental Location of Gamow–Teller Strength for Astrophysical Calculations in the Region of A = 54–58." *Physics Review* C30 (1984): 1850–1854.

(With R.E. Brown, E.R. Flynn, and J.W. Sunier) "(t, —3He) Reactions on Fe56, Fe58, and Ni58." *Physics Review* C31 (1985): 777–786.

"Energy Levels of Light Nuclei, A = 16–17, A = 18–20, A = 5–10, A = 11–12, A = 13–15." *Nuclear Physics* (1986–1991).

FURTHER READING

Books

American Men and Women of Science. 20th ed. New York: R.R. Bowker, 1998.

Bailey, Martha J. *American Women in Science, 1950 to the Present: A Biographical Dictionary*. Santa Barbara: ABC–CLIO, 1998.

McLane, Victoria. "Fay Ajzenberg-Selove." In *Women in Chemistry and Physics: A Biobibliographic Sourcebook*. Westport, CT: Greenwood Press, 1993.

Smith, Roger. *Biographies of Scientists: An Annotated Bibliography*. Metuchen, NJ: Scarecrow Press, 1998.

Other

Hanson, Erik. "Faye Ajzenberg-Selove." http://dept.physics.upenn.edu/gradute/facultyinfo/ajzenberg.html.

Sketch by J. Sydney Jones

Hattie Alexander
1901–1968
American microbiologist and pediatrician

Dr. Hattie E. Alexander (Corbis-Bettmann. Reproduced by permission.)

Hattie Alexander, a dedicated pediatrician, medical educator, and researcher in microbiology, won international recognition for deriving a serum to combat influenzal meningitis, a common disease that previously had been nearly always fatal to infants and young children. Alexander subsequently investigated microbiological genetics and the processes whereby bacteria, through genetic mutation, acquire resistance to antibiotics. In 1964, as president of the American Pediatric Society, she became one of the first women to head a national medical association.

Hattie Elizabeth Alexander was born on April 5, 1901, in Baltimore, Maryland. She was the second of eight children born to Elsie May (Townsend) Alexander and William Bain Alexander, a merchant. Alexander attended Baltimore schools and then enrolled in Goucher College in Baltimore on a partial scholarship. There, she excelled at sports but was an average student in her course work, which included bacteriology and physiology. Alexander graduated from Goucher with an A.B. degree in 1923. For the next three years she worked as a bacteriologist for the U.S. Public Health Service laboratory in Washington, D.C., and at a branch laboratory of the Maryland Public Health Service. Impressed with her research experience, Johns Hopkins University in Baltimore admitted her to their medical program. Alexander performed exceptionally at Johns Hopkins, earning her M.D. in 1930.

As an intern at the Harriet Lane Home of Johns Hopkins Hospital from 1930 to 1931, Alexander became interested in influenzal meningitis. The source of the disease was *Hemophilus influenzae*, a bacteria that causes inflammation of the meninges, the membranes surrounding the brain and spinal cord. In 1931, Alexander began a second internship at the Babies Hospital of the Columbia–Presbyterian Medical Center in New York City. There, she witnessed first–hand the futility of medical efforts to save babies who had contracted influenzal meningitis.

Beginning in 1933, with her medical training complete, Alexander held a series of pediatric, teaching, and research positions at the Babies Hospital, the Vanderbilt Clinic of the Columbia–Presbyterian Medical Center, and Columbia University's College of Physicians and Surgeons. She was appointed an adjunct assistant pediatrician in 1933 and an assistant attending pediatrician in 1938 by the Babies Hospital, and held parallel posts at the Vanderbilt Clinic; she would be promoted to attending pediatrician at the Babies Hospital and the Vanderbilt Clinic in 1951. At Columbia, she held a fellowship in children's diseases from 1932 to 1934 and became an assistant in children's diseases in 1933 and an instructor in children's diseases in 1935. Known as a gifted teacher who disliked lecturing but excelled at clinical instruction, she rose steadily through the teaching ranks, becoming associate professor in 1948 and full professor in 1958 and retiring as professor emeritus in 1966.

Develops Anti-Influenzal Rabbit Serum

Alexander's early research focussed on deriving a serum (the liquid component of blood, in which antibodies are contained) that would be effective against influenzal meningitis. Serums derived from animals that have been exposed to a specific disease–producing bacterium often contain antibodies against the disease and can be developed for use in immunizing humans against it. Alexander knew that attempts to develop an anti–influenzal serum from horses had been unsuccessful. The Rockefeller Institute in New York City, however, had been able to prepare a rabbit serum for the treatment of pneumonia, another bacterial disease. Alexander therefore experimented with rabbit serums, and by 1939 was able to announce the development of a rabbit serum effective in curing infants of influenzal meningitis.

In the early 1940s, Alexander experimented with the use of drugs in combination with rabbit serum in the treatment of influenzal meningitis. Within the next two years, she saw infant deaths due to the disease drop by eighty percent. With improvements in diagnosis and the standardization of treatment, the mortality rate fell still further in later years. In recognition of her research on influenzal meningitis, Alexander received the E. Mead Johnson Award for research in pediatrics from the American Academy of Pediatrics in 1942 and the Elizabeth Blackwell Award from the New York Infirmary in 1956, and in 1961, she became the first woman recipient of the Oscar B. Hunter Memorial Award of the American Therapeutic Society.

Researches Microbiological Genetics

Alexander's research in supplementary drug treatment for influenzal meningitis led her to the study of antibiotics (antibacterial substances generally produced by a bacterium or a fungus). As was evident from the cultures of influenza bacilli utilized in Alexander's research, antibiotics do not provide a permanent defense against bacteria. Alexander was among the first to recognize that it was through genetic mutation that bacteria are able to develop resistance to antibiotics, and she became a pioneer in research on DNA, the nucleic substance that bears an organism's genetic blueprint. By 1950, due to lab work conducted in association with Grace Leidy Alexander was able to alter the genetic code of *Hemophilus influenzae* by manipulating its DNA. Alexander subsequently extended this line of research to other bacteria and to viruses.

In addition to her hospital service, research, and teaching duties, Alexander also served on the influenza commission under the United States Secretary of War from 1941 to 1945, served as consultant to the New York City Department of Health from 1958 to 1960, and joined the medical board of the Presbyterian Hospital of the Columbia–Presbyterian Medical Center in 1959. After chairing the governing council of the American Pediatric Society from 1956 to 1957 and serving as vice president from 1959 to 1960, she became president of the society in 1964.

In addition to her affiliation with the American Pediatric Society, Alexander was a member of several other pediatric associations as well as the Society for Experimental Biology and Medicine, the American Association for the Advancement of Science, the New York Academy of Medicine, and other professional and scientific bodies. During her career she published some 150 papers as well as chapters in textbooks on microbiology and pediatrics and delivered many honorary lectures at medical and academic institutions. Alexander lived with her companion, Dr. Elizabeth Ufford, in Port Washington, N.Y. In her spare time, Alexander enjoyed music, boating, travel, and growing exotic flowers. She died from cancer on June 24, 1968, at the age of 67.

SELECTED WRITINGS BY ALEXANDER:

Periodicals

(With Grace Leidy) "Experimental Investigations as a Basis for Treatment of Type–B Hemophilus Influenzae Meningitis in Infants and Children." *Journal of Pediatrics* (December 1943): 640–655.

(With Michael Heidelberger and Leidy) "The Protective or Curative Element in Type B H. Influenzae Rabbit Serum" *Yale Journal of Biology and Medicine* (May 1944): 425–434.

"A Broad Horizon" (1965 Presidential Address of the American Pediatric Society). *Journal of Pediatrics* (November 1965): 993–999.

(With Leidy and Iris Jaffee) "Genetic Modifiers of the Phenotypic Level of Deoxyribonucleic Acid–Conferred Novobiocin Resistance in Haemophilus." *Journal of Bacteriology* (November 1966): 1464–1468.

FURTHER READING

Books

Sicherman, Barbara, Carol Hurd Green with Ilene Kantrov, and Harriette Walker. *Notable American Women: The Modern Period.* Cambridge, MA: Belknap Press, 1980.

Periodicals

New York Times, June 25, 1968, p. 41.

Rustin, McIntosh. "Hattie Alexander." *Pediatrics* 42 (1968): 554.

Sketch by Miyoko Chu

Angeles Alvariño
1916–
Spanish-born American marine biologist

For more than four decades, fishery research biologist and marine scientist Angeles Alvariño has made an immense contribution to knowledge about the ecology and geographic distribution of marine zooplankton (small drifting animal life in the ocean) and other marine organisms. During the course of her work, Alvariño discovered twenty–two new ocean species.

Alvariño was born on October 3, 1916 in El Ferrol, Spain, to Antonio Alvariño Grimaldos and Maria del Carmen González Diaz–Saavedra de Alvariño. An intelligent, curious child, Alvariño often enjoyed her physician–father's library, especially his volumes on natural history. She aspired to become a physician herself, but her father discouraged such a choice. He did not want her to experience, as he had, the pain associated with patients whose suffering could not be alleviated.

Alvariño studied a wide range of courses in physical and natural sciences, social science, and humanities during her undergraduate years at the Lycée. After passing final examinations and completing two dissertations for baccalaureate degrees in both science and letters, she graduated *summa cum laude* in 1933 from the University of Santiago de Compostela, Spain. During the next year, Alvariño's desire to study medicine persisted, but her father's viewpoint remained unchanged. Therefore, she entered the University of Madrid in 1934 to study natural sciences. Her studies were interrupted when the university closed from 1936–1939 as a result of the Spanish Civil War.

In 1940 Alvariño married Sir Eugenio Leira Manso, Captain of the Spanish Royal Navy and Knight of the Royal and Military Order of Saint Hermenegild. Alvariño continued her studies at the University of Madrid and in 1941 was awarded a master's degree in natural sciences. From 1941–1948, she taught biology, zoology, botany, and geology at various colleges in El Ferrol.

In order to do active research, Alvariño left teaching in 1948 to become a research biologist with the Spanish Department of Sea Fisheries in Madrid. In spite of a ban against women, she began to conduct research and study oceanography at the Spanish Institute of Oceanography in Madrid. The quality of her work persuaded officials to admit her as a student researcher in 1950. Academic work at the University of Madrid led in 1951 to a doctoral certificate in experimental psychology, chemistry, and plant ecology.

Studies Aquatic Life Forms

Alvariño's success in a competitive examination resulted in an appointment as a marine biologist–oceanographer with the Spanish Institute of Oceanography in 1952. In 1953 a British Council Fellowship enabled her to work on zooplankton at the Marine Biological Laboratory in Plymouth, England. At the Plymouth lab, she met English marine biologist Frederick Stratten Russell, an expert on jellyfish, who directed her attention to chaetognaths (arrowworms), hydromedusae (jellyfish), and siphonophores (small, free–swimming water organisms). In the 1950s, these animals had received such little study that Alvariño designed and made plankton nets, which she provided to captains of Spanish fishing vessels and research ships so they could collect zooplankton samples for her research.

In 1956, Alvariño was granted a Fulbright Fellowship, allowing her to conduct research in Massachusetts at the Woods Hole Oceanographic Institute. Impressed by her work, Mary Sears, president of the first U.S. Oceanographic Congress, recommended Alvariño to Dr. Roger Revelle, the director of the Scripps Institute of Oceanography at La Jolla, California. He offered Alvariño a position as a biologist and she accepted. Alvariño's years of research at Scripps produced a significant body of knowledge about chaetognaths, siphonophores, and hydromedusae. Her Scripps research also contributed toward completion of work toward her doctoral degree at the University of Madrid (now known as the University Complutense), which awarded her a doctor of sciences degree in 1967, *summa cum laude.*

To further expand her research opportunities, Alvariño in 1970 accepted a position as a fisheries biologist with the Southwest Fisheries Science Center (SWFSC) in La Jolla, a division of the newly–formed National Marine Fisheries Service. There she continued research on predatory chaetognaths, siphonophores, and hydromedusae and their relationship to larval fish survival.

Although officially retired in 1987, Alvariño continues her work, adding to the body of knowledge about zooplankton. She has shed light on how zooplankton relate to the dynamics of the oceanic environment and about which ones are "indicator species," those species associated with specific currents or concentrations of other aquatic life, including spawning fish and their eggs and larvae.

On July 25, 1993, Alvariño was awarded the Great Silver Medal of Galicia by King Juan Carlos I and Queen Sophia of Spain. She participated in numerous expeditions aboard research vessels of several countries, and was the first woman to serve as a scientist aboard a British research vessel.

Angeles Alvarino (Arte Publico Press Archives, University of Houston. Reproduced by permission.)

Alvariño and her husband live in La Jolla. Their only child, Angeles Leira–Alvariño, is an architect and city planner. In addition to her first love, marine science, Alvariño enjoys classical music, literature, and art.

SELECTED WRITINGS BY ALVARIÑO:

Books

Atlantic Chaetognatha, Distribution and Essential Notes of Systematics, Travaux Spanish Institute of Oceanography, 1969.

Siphonophores of the Pacific; with a Revision of the World Distribution, University of California Press, 1971.

"Chaetognatha. Oogenesis, Ovopostion, and Oosorption.," In *Reproductive Biology of Invertebrates,* Volume 1, edited by K. G. and R. G. Adiyodi. Wiley & Sons, 1983.

"Chaetognatha. Spermatogenesis and Sperm Function." In *Reproductive Biology of Invertebrates,* Volume 2, edited by K. G. and R. G. Adiyodi. Wiley & Sons, 1983.

"Fertilization, Development and Parental Care in Chaetognatha." In *Reproductive Biology of Invertebrates,* Volume 4, edited by K. G. and R. G. Adiyody, Oxford & IBH Publishing, 1990.

"Sexual Differentiation and Behavior in Chaetognatha. Hermaphroditi." In *Reproductive Biology of Invertebrates,* Volume 5, edited by K. G. and R. G. Adiyody. Oxford & IBH Publishing, 1992.

Periodicals

"The Relation Between the Distribution of Zooplankton Predators and *Engraulis Mordax* (Anchovy) Larvae."*California Cooperative Oceanic Fisheries Investigations Reports* (1980): 150–60.

"The Depth Distribution, Relative Abundance and Structure of the Population of the Chaetognatha *Sagitta Scrippsae* Alvariño 1962, in the California Current off California and Baja California." *Anales del Instituto de Ciencias del Mar y Limnologia,* Universidad Nacional Autonoma de Mexico (1983): 47–84.

"Abundance of Zooplankton Species, Females and Males, Eggs and Larvae of Holoplanktonic Species. Zooplankton Assemblages and Changes in Zooplankton Communities Related to *Engraulis mordax* Spawning and Survival of the Larvae," *Mem. III Encontro Brasileiro de Plancton.* (1989): 63–149.

FURTHER READING

Alvariño, Angeles, interviews conducted by Susan Smith and Connie Blair of the Southwest Fisheries Science Center Public Information staff.

Sketch by Margaret DiCanio

Betsy Ancker-Johnson
1929–
American physicist

In her far-ranging career, Betsy Ancker-Johnson has been the first woman to hold a vice-presidency in the American auto industry, held management posts in government and private industry, and has also made significant contributions in solid state physics, microwave and molecular electronics, and ferromagnetism and nonreciprocal effects. The author of more than 80 scientific papers, Ancker-Johnson also holds a handful of patents and also designed 50 devices and techniques in solid-state physics.

Ancker-Johnson was born on April 27, 1929, in St. Louis, Missouri, the daughter of Clinton James and Fern (Lalan) Ancker. She earned her BA degree in physics with high honors from Wellesley College in 1949, and later described it as her best educational experience, because her interest in physics had been supported there. During graduate classes at Harvard and the Massachusetts Institute of Technology, however, she was told that she would not find a husband if she studied physics. Ancker-Johnson ignored such negative comments and continued her studies at Tübingen University in Germany, in part because she was also interested in having a cultural experience.

At Tübingen, professors and students alike declared that women could not think analytically, and insisted that she was shopping for a husband, not studying for a career. There were not even any women's bathrooms in the buildings that housed her classes. Ancker-Johnson did not dwell on such obstacles, however, an attitude that served her well throughout her career. As she wrote in *Women & Success: The Anatomy of Achievement,* "It seems that a woman in physics must be at least twice as determined as a man with the same competence, in order to achieve as much as he does." Ancker-Johnson went on to earn her Ph.D degree *magna cum laude* from Tübingen University in 1953.

After graduation, shen decided to pursue a career in research, but she a hard time finding the kind of positions she wanted. She found many opportunities to help male scientists, but few to work independently. Finally, she took a job as a junior research physicist and lecturer in physics at the University of California at Berkeley from 1953–54, receiving a lower salary than her male colleagues.

In 1956, she moved to the private sector, working at the Microwave Physics Lab at Sylvania Electric Products, Inc., as a senior research physicist. Two years later, on March 15, 1958, she met mathematics professor Harold Hunt Johnson. They married and eventually had four children: Ruth P., David H., Paul A., and Marti H. That same year,She was hired by RCA (Radio Corporation of America) as a technical staff member at the David Sarnoff Research Center.

In 1961, Ancker-Johnson went to Boeing Aerospace Company and became a research specialist at the Electronic Science Laboratory. Here she enjoyed a fruitful career resulting in numerous patents, one of which was "the pinch effect" the use of high temperatures to create pathways in a semiconductor. She also developed a method of extracting high–grade aluminum from low–grade ore. By 1970, she was named supervisor of solid state and plasma electronics at Boeing.

A year later, Ancker-Johnson made a huge career change. In 1971 she became the first woman to break into middle management at Boeing. Of her decision, she told *Newsweek,* "I was just getting restless. I guess I wanted a bigger playpen." She managed Boeing's advanced energy systems two years. In retrospect, she believed that this was the hardest employment experience of her career, at least in part because unlike her male counterparts, she had no mentor.

In 1973, Ancker-Johnson was named assistant secretary for science and technology for the U.S. Department of Commerce. She was the first woman to hold this position, but she knew she had been hired just for her gender. With a budget of $230 million, Ancker-Johnson managed six organizations and 7,500 employees. She brought researchers involved with recombinant DNA research in line with National Institute of Health guidelines in a resourceful way: Corporations that cooperated with her had their patent processes handled more quickly. By 1977, Ancker-Johnson became the associate lab director of physics research for the Argonne National Laboratory.

Ancker-Johnson made arguably the biggest jump of her career in 1979 when she became the vice–president for the environmental activities staff at the General Motors Tech Center, the first woman to hold a vice–presidency in the automobile industry. Overseeing a 200–person staff, her duties included controlling pollution from factories, limiting pollution and increasing fuel economy and safety in automobiles, and working with government agencies and GM contacts on areas such as auto emissions, fuel economy, and product safety. Ancker-Johnson told Executive Female, "The best part of my position is that I play a significant role in policies that are important to this corporation."

Though Ancker-Johnson retired from GM in 1992, she continues to be active in numerous professional organizations. She also retained several committee chairs for such groups as the U.S. Environmental Protection Agency. Over the course of her career, Ancker-Johnson received several honorary degrees, but wrote in *Women & Success,* "I should like to be known, if I'm known at all, for my contributions to physics research, teaching and management, and not for being 'a woman in physics.'"

SELECTED WRITINGS BY ANCKER-JOHNSON:

Books

"Physicist." *Women and Success: The Anatomy of Achievement.* New York: William Morrow and Company, Inc., 1974.

FURTHER READING

Books

Rossiter, Margaret W. *Women Scientists in America: Before Affirmative Action, 1940–1972.* Baltimore: Johns Hopkins University Press, 1995.

Stanley, Autumn. *Mothers and Daughters of Invention: Notes for a Revised History of Technology.* Metuchen, NJ: Scarecrow Press, Inc., 1993.

Vare, Ethlie Ann, and Greg Ptacek. *Mothers of Invention: From the Bra to the Bomb: Forgotten Women and Their Unforgettable Ideas.* New York: William Morrow and Company, Inc., 1988.

Who's Who of America Women: 1999–2000. New Providence: Marquis Who's Who, 1998.

Periodicals

Sheils, Merrill et al. "Three Who Made It to the Top." *Newsweek* (September 14, 1981): 67.
Watts, Patti. "Policy Driver." *Executive Female* (May–June 1991): 21.

Sketch by Annette Petrusso

Gloria L. Anderson
1938–
American chemist

Gloria L. Anderson is a distinguished chemist, educator, and college administrator. Her scientific research has involved industrial, medical and military applications of fluorine–19 chemistry. As an educator, she has served as the Callaway professor of chemistry, chair of the chemistry department, and dean of academic affairs at Morris Brown College in Atlanta. Anderson, in addition, has been a board member and vice–chair of the Corporation for Public Broadcasting, for which she has lectured nationally on issues related to minorities and women in mass media and public television.

Anderson was born in Altheimer, Arkansas, on November 5, 1938, the daughter of Charley Long and Elsie Lee Foggie. She enrolled at the Arkansas Agricultural, Mechanical and Normal College (now the University of Arkansas at Pine Bluff), where she was awarded a Rockefeller Scholarship from 1956 to 1958. Anderson received her B.S. degree summa cum laude in 1958. She married Leonard Sinclair Anderson on June 4, 1960; they have one son, Gerald. In 1961, Anderson was awarded her M.S. degree from Atlanta University. For the next year, she worked as a chemistry instructor at South Carolina State College in Orangeburg. From 1962 to 1964, she held an instructorship at Morehouse College in Atlanta, then went on to take a position as a teaching and research assistant at the University of Chicago, where she received her doctorate in organic chemistry in 1968.

Dr. Gloria L. Anderson (AP/Wide World Photos, Inc. Reproduced by permission.)

Researches Fluorine–19 Chemistry

Anderson's dissertation and aspects of her subsequent research have related to fluorine–19 chemistry. (The '19' following fluorine refers to a particular isotope of fluorine that, like other elements with odd numbered masses, has magnetic properties.) Fluorine–19 chemistry became an important field of research shortly before World War II when many commercial uses for fluorine compounds were discovered. Much of Anderson's research has involved nuclear magnetic resonance (NMR) spectroscopy, a method of investigating organic compounds by analyzing the nucleic responses of molecules subjected to radio–frequency radiation within a slowly changing magnetic field. NMR spectroscopy, which has been widely exploited for chemistry, biochemistry, biophysics, and solid–state physics research, enables extremely sophisticated analysis of the molecular structures and interactions of various materials. The small size, low reactivity, and high sensitivity of fluorine–19 make it particularly suited for NMR spectroscopy. Since the late 1960s, fluorine NMR spectroscopy has been applied to a range of biochemical problems, including the study of the human metabolism and the formulation of new pharmaceuticals.

Anderson joined the faculty of Morris Brown College in Atlanta in 1968 as associate professor and chair of the chemistry department. From 1973 to 1984, Anderson was the Fuller E. Callaway professor of chemistry at Morris Brown, and continued her service as the chemistry department chair. Anderson left the chemistry department to serve as dean of academic affairs at Morris Brown for the years 1984–89. In 1990, Anderson resumed her post as the Callaway professor of chemistry. In 1976, Anderson was recognized as an Outstanding Teacher at Morris Brown, and received a Scroll of Honor award from the National Association of Negro Business and Professional Women. In 1983, she received a Teacher of the Year award and was voted into the Faculty/Staff Hall of Fame at Morris Brown. In 1987, she received an Alumni All–Star Excellence Award in Education from the University of Arkansas at Pine Bluff.

In addition to her work at Morris Brown, Anderson has conducted research through a number of independent and government facilities. Beginning in 1971 she continued her investigations of fluorine–19 chemistry—first in association with the Atlanta University Center Research Committee, then under the National Institutes of Health, the National Science Foundation, and the Office of Naval Research. She also conducted research on amantadines (a drug used to prevent viral infection) under the Minority Biomedical Support Program of the National Institutes of Health. She held a faculty industrial research fellowship with the National Science Foundation in 1981, and with the Air Force Office of Scientific Research in 1984. In 1985, Anderson investigated the synthesis of potential antiviral drugs as a United Negro Fund Distinguished Scholar. In that same year, she conducted research on the synthesis of solid rocket propellants under the Air Force Office of Scientific Research. Since 1990, she has been affiliated with BioSPECS of The Hague, Netherlands, as a research consultant.

In 1972, Anderson was appointed to a six–year term on the board of the Corporation for Public Broadcasting (CPB). At the CPB, Anderson chaired committees on Minority Training, Minorities and Women, and Human Resources Development; she was vice–chair of the CPB board from 1977–79. She is a member of the American Institute of Chemists, the American Chemical Society, the National Institute of Science, the National Science Teachers Association, the Association of Computers in Mathematics and Science Teaching, the Georgia Academy of Science, and the Atlanta University Science Research Institute, among other scientific and professional bodies. She has served as a proposal review panel member, contract reviewer, or field reader for the Department of Health, Education and Welfare's Office of Education, the National Science Foundation's Women in Science Program, the Nation Cancer Institute, the Department of Education, and the National Institute of Drug Abuse.

SELECTED WRITINGS BY ANDERSON:

Periodicals

(With L. M. Stock) "$_{19}$F Chemical Shifts for Bicyclic Fluorides." *Journal of the American Chemical Society* 90 (1968): 212.

(With L. M. Stock) "$_{19}$F Chemical Shifts for Bicyclic and Aromatic Molecules." *Journal of the American Chemical Society* 91 (1969): 6804.

(With R. C. Parish and L. M. Stock) "Transmission of Substituent Effects, Acid Dissociation Constants of 10–Substituted–9–Anthroic Acids." *Journal of the American Chemical Society* 93 (1971): 6984.

(With Issifu I. Harruna) "Synthesis of Triflate and Chloride Salts of Alkyl *N, N* –Bis (2, 2, 2–Tri–Fluoroethyl) Amines." *Synthetic Communications* 17 (1987): 111–114.

(With Winifred A. Burks and Issifu I. Harruna) "Novel Synthesis of 3–Fluoro–1–Aminoadamantane." *Synthetic Communications* 18 (1988): 1967–1974.

(With Betty J. Randolph and Issifu I. Harruna) "Novel Synthesis of Some 1–N–(3–Fluoroadamantyl) Ureas." *Synthetic Communications.* 19 (1989): 1955–1963.

FURTHER READING

Periodicals

"Atlanta's Best and Brightest Scientists." *Atlanta Magazine* April, 1983.

New York Times, December 1, 1973, p. 39.

Sketch by M. C. Nagel

Mary Ann Anning
1799–1847
British paleontologist

Although Mary Anning had little education, her determination and keen scientific interest in fossils led to several significant discoveries that advanced the field of paleontology. Most of her work was done as a source of income to support her family at a time when the excavation of fossils was considered as much a commercial venture as it was a scientific discovery. Many of the fossils she found were purchased by noted paleontologists of the day, who, in turn, donated them to museums and were given the credit for their discovery.

Mary Ann Anning was born on May 21, 1799, in the rural seaside town of Lyme Regis in Dorset County on the southern coast of England. She was named after her mother, Mary Anning, who had as many as ten children. Only two of these children, Mary and her brother Joseph, lived to maturity. Her father was Richard Anning, a cabinet maker with a passion for fossil collecting. As a child, Mary would often accompany her father on his explorations of the nearby cliffs along the beach. She was educated in the local parish school, but her knowledge of fossils was derived primarily from the time spent with her father, as well as her own studies. In 1810, when Anning was only 11 years old, her father was killed on one of his fossil-hunting trips when an unstable cliff collapsed and buried him. His death left the family destitute, and they relied on charity to survive.

Makes Important Discovery at Age 12

Anning made her first significant fossil discovery in 1811, when she found a complete skeleton of a mysterious beast projecting from the face of a cliff in the same area where her father was killed. The fossil, often dubbed Mary's Monster or the Lyme Crocodile, was in fact an *Ichthyosaurus*, a porpoise-like marine dinosaur from the Jurassic period. The discovery caught the attention of London's scientific community, who had never before seen a specimen of a dinosaur species. This resulted in a modest tourist trade for the town and brought Anning a source of income when she sold the bones to the British Museum. Her family joined her in her fossil–hunting activities, and they managed to earn a modest living from their excavations.

In 1817, or possibly the early 1820s, the family gained a benefactor when they met Lieutenant-Colonel Thomas Birch, a wealthy fossil collector, who was impressed with their work. Birch was distressed by the family's limited financial situation and sold his extensive collection of fossils to help support them. Anning continued to find new and unusual fossils, including a *Plesiosaurus* skeleton in 1823 and the skeleton of a flying reptile known as *Pterodactylus macronyx* in 1828. She is also credited with discovering a *Squaloraja* fish fossil, which established an important link between modern sharks and rays.

Fossil Expertise Finally Acknowledged

Despite her impressive finds, Anning was initially regarded by many as simply a talented amateur without any scientific credentials. Her gender and lack of formal education reinforced this view. However, her seemingly innate understanding of fossils, including the scientific skills necessary to find and carefully uncover them, gradually won her recognition by many in the field. After visiting Anning in 1824, Lady Harriet Silvester [Sivester] noted in her diary that Anning regularly corresponded with "professors and other clever men on the subject, and they all acknowledge that she understands more of the science than anyone else in this kingdom."

In 1838, Anning was granted a small annual income from the British Association for the Advancement of Science in recognition of her work. The Geological Society of London also gave her a small stipend, and she was named the first Honorary Member of the Dorset County Museum. Anning died of breast cancer in her hometown of Lyme Regis on March 9, 1847, just short of her 48th birthday. The Quarterly Journal of the Geological Society published her obituary, even though it wasn't until 1904 that they admitted women. Unfortunately, the hard-won recognition she achieved during her life seemed to fade after her death. Inadequate records left Anning forgotten by today's scientific community and historians. Credited or not, her work and discoveries were important contributions to the developing field of paleontology.

FURTHER READING

Books

The Europa Biographical Dictionary of British Women. London: Europa Publications, Ltd, 1983.

Ogilvie, Marilyn Bailey. *Women in Science.* Cambridge: MIT Press, 1986.

Periodicals

Torrens, Hugh. "Presidential Address: Mary Anning (1799–1847) of Lyme; 'The Greatest Fossilist the World Ever Knew'." *British Journal of the History of Science* 28 (1995): 257–284.

Other

Simison, W. Brian, and Ben Waggoner. "Mary Anning (1799–1847)." http://www.ucmp.berkeley.edu/history/anning.html

Maisel, Merry and Laura Smart. "Mary Anning, Finder of Fossils." http://www.sdsc.edu/ScienceWomen/anning.html

Sketch by Chris Cavette

Virginia Apgar
1909–1974
American physician

Within minutes of birth, virtually every child today receives an Apgar Score from a delivery nurse or midwife. This simple but crucial test devised in 1952 by Virginia Apgar evaluates infants immediately after birth and is able to identify babies that may be at risk during their first few minutes and hours of life. As an anesthesiologist who attended over 17,000 births, Apgar felt the need to act on her conviction that birth is the most hazardous time of life. Apgar's own life and achievements ranged far beyond her internationally recognized test of newborn health, resulting in the 1997 release of a U. S. postage stamp commemorating her many accomplishments.

Virginia Apgar was born in Westfield, New Jersey, to a very musical family. Her father, Charles Emory Apgar, a businessman and automobile salesman, was an amateur musician. Her mother, Helen May, shared the family's interest in music as did Virginia's brother. Apgar began studying the violin at six and soon was able to join in the family's living room concerts. Apgar eventually became a member of the local Amateur Chamber Music Players, performing with the Teaneck (N.J.) Symphony, and even learned how to build her own stringed instruments. Despite her love of music, Apgar set her sights on a career in medicine as early as high school. After graduating from Westfield High School in 1925, she entered Mount Holyoke College, majoring in zoology and undertaking a rigorous premedical curriculum. During her college years, she

Virginia Apgar (The Mount Holyoke Archives and Special Collections. Reproduced by permission.)

demonstrated her abilities and versatility by working as both a librarian and waitress, while still having time to earn a letter in athletics, work as a reporter for the school paper, and play the violin in the school orchestra. After graduating in 1929, she entered Columbia University College of Physicians and Surgeons in New York and was awarded a degree in medicine in 1933.

Apgar First Encounters Gender Bias

As one of very few female medical students at Columbia during the early 1930s and one of the first women to graduate from its medical school, Apgar knew that her goal of becoming a surgeon would not be achieved easily in a male–dominated profession. Nonetheless, her record of excellence enabled her to become a surgical intern at Columbia Presbyterian Medical Center—only the fifth woman to be awarded that coveted internship. Yet after laboring for two years as an intern and performing many successful operations, she realized that the advice given to her by a professor of surgery, that a female surgeon would never have enough patients to make a living, was unfortunately true. Apgar herself summed up the situation realistically, saying that "even women won't go to a woman surgeon. Only the Lord can answer that one."

Switches to Anesthesiology

Although she reluctantly switched her medical specialty to anesthesiology, she embraced her new field with typical intelligence and energy. At this time, anesthesiology was a relatively new field, having been left by the doctors mostly to the attention of nurses. Apgar realized immediately how much in need of scientifically trained personnel was this significant part of surgery, and she set out to make anesthesiology a separate medical discipline. By 1937, she had become the fiftieth physician to be certified as an anesthesiologist in the United States. The following year she was appointed director of anesthesiology at the Columbia–Presbyterian Medical Center, becoming the first woman to head a department at that institution. It was mostly due to Apgar's hard work, excellent credentials, and growing national reputation that anesthesiology was established at Columbia–Presbyterian as an entirely new academic department. In 1949, when Columbia made her a full professor, she became the first full professor of anesthesiology ever.

Develops the Apgar Score System

As the attending anesthesiologist who assisted in the delivery of thousands of babies during these years, Apgar noted two post–delivery habits that she came to realize were sometimes detrimental to the health and survival of newborns. The first of these was the inclination of most medical staff to focus their immediate attention on the mother's condition and needs, leaving examination of the infant to be done later in the nursery. Second, she noticed that unless the newborn had suffered some obvious trauma during birth, its condition was assumed to be good. Many a time she realized that an infant had died from respiratory or circulatory complications that early treatment could have prevented. These endangered but seemingly normal babies were failing to receive the immediate medical care that could save their lives simply because no one knew enough to give their vital functions a quick, routine check.

Apgar then decided to bring her considerable research skills to this childbirth dilemma, and her careful study resulted in her publication of the Apgar Score System in 1952. Designed to assure that correctable problems are discovered immediately and addressed on the spot, her system enables the attending nurse or doctor to take a quick reading of a newborn's pulse, respiration, muscle tone, color, and reflexes. The Apgar System rates an infant from 0 to 2 in each of these five areas, with the test being performed from one minute to five minutes after birth. For each vital sign, 0 means no response, 1 is marginal, and 2 is normal or the best response. A newborn that is doing well would receive between 8 and 10, with lower scores suggesting that the baby might need some attention. A score of 4 or below would alert a physician to possible risk factors.

Apgar's quick and easy assessment soon was adopted worldwide, and medical schools adopted Apgar's own name as an acronym for teaching her test: Appearance (skin color), Pulse (heart rate), Grimace (reflex irritability), Activity (muscle tone), and Respiration (breathing). For her work in obstetrical anesthesia and for her development of the Apgar score, she is credited with laying the foundation for the new science called perinatology.

Becomes Director of Birth Defects Research

Although Apgar later published a book titled *Is My Baby All Right?*, she made no money from her test. She did, however, become well–known internationally, and in 1959, after 30 years at Columbia, teaching, administering, and assisting in the birth of some 20,000 babies, she became director of birth defects research for the March of Dimes Foundation. As the head of its division of clinical malformations, her work focused on birth defects and prenatal care.

Part of her responsibilities as director included the distribution of more than $5 million annually in research grants. She also realized that to be really effective, she herself would have to preach the gospel of good prenatal care. So Apgar, a woman of science who nonetheless was afraid of elevators, took to traveling a hundred thousand miles a year lecturing mothers–to–be about the benefits of seeking early prenatal care. She also warned of the dangers of drugs and radiation to the developing fetus. Today's awareness and emphasis on avoiding preventable birth defects owes much to the programs initiated by Apgar. She also proved to be more than a popular and visible proselytizer, as she doubled the annual March of Dimes income. Remaining with the Foundation until her death in 1974, she became vice–president and director of basic research in 1967. In 1973, she was elevated to senior vice–president in charge of medical affairs.

Although she had become internationally known and respected, Apgar remained a modest and unassuming individual. Despite never marrying—"I haven't found a man who can cook," — and living in an apartment in Tenafly, New Jersey, where she cared for her mother, she was by no means a one–dimensional person. She took up flying lessons when she was well over 50 and had as her goal being able to fly under New York City's George Washington Bridge. Described by many as a warm and compassionate person, she died in New York City of cirrhosis of the liver. The recipient of numerous awards and honors, Apgar is today silently acknowledged by the countless (and still–growing) numbers of individuals around the world who owe their lives and well–being to the physician who regarded birth as "the most hazardous time of life."

SELECTED WRITINGS BY APGAR:

Books

(With Joan Beck) *Is My Baby All Right? A Guide to Birth Defects.* New York: Trident Press, 1972.

FURTHER READING

Books

Bailey, Brooke. *The Remarkable Lives of 100 Woman Healers and Scientists.* Holbrook, MA: Bob Adams, Inc., 1994, pp. 10–11.

Forbes, Malcolm. *Women Who Made A Difference.* New York: Simon and Schuster, 1990, pp. 17–19.

Periodicals

"Newborn Care: Starting with the Apgar Score, Modern Medicine Offers Babies the Best Start in Life." *American Baby* (May 1988): 55–58.

Sketch by Leonard C. Bruno

Esther Richards Applin
1895–1972
American geologist and paleontologist

Esther Richards Applin was a pioneer in the field of micropaleontology. For nearly half a century, Applin conducted surveys, published papers, consulted, and taught. She spearheaded the study of microfossils embedded in the strata (layers of soil and rock deep within the Earth's crust) to identify faunal zones (periods of animal life) in subsurface geological subsurface geologic formations. In this way, she expanded the understanding of the coastal region of the Gulf of Mexico, and established valuable criteria for successful oil and gas exploration.

Applin was born to Gary F. and Jennie (DeVore) Richards, in Newark, Ohio, on November 24, 1895. She and her sister, Helen, lived with their parents in Newark and other Ohio cities until the early 1900s, when the family moved to Fort Des Moines, Iowa. There her father worked as a civil engineer for the Quartermaster Corps of the U.S. Army. In 1907, Mr. Richards was transferred to Alcatraz Island in California to oversee the construction of the prison. For the next 12 years, Applin lived on the island and took the ferry to San Francisco and the University of California Berkeley to attend school.

Applin received an A.B. from Berkeley in 1919, graduating with honors in paleontology. , She earned her masters in geology, physiography, and micropaleontology in 1920. She was employed as a paleontologist in the intervening summer at the Rio Bravo Oil Company in Houston, Texas, returning to study fossils from oil well sites in the Gulf Coast until 1927.

Established Field of Applied Micropaleontology

Applin discovered early in her work that macrofossils, her subject of study at Berkeley, became too damaged from the well cutting process to allow for accurate species identification, so she directed her attention to microfossils, specifically Foraminifera. These single–celled organisms form the microscopic shells found in high concentrations in sediment. With female colleagues Alva Ellisor and Hedwig

Kniker, Applin invented a way to separate and mount the microfossils for study and identification, creating a new and highly effective method for stratigraphic correlation, and establishing the field of applied micropaleontology.

While at Rio Bravo, Applin consulted for other oil companies and sat on a committee to organize the antecedent to the Society of Economic Paleontologists and Mineralogists (SEPM). She married fellow geologist Paul L. Applin in 1923. In 1926 the couple's first child, Louise was born. A son, Paul Jr., was born in 1927, the same year the Applins moved to Forth Worth, Texas. From 1927 until 1944, Applin consulted as a paleontologist and subsurface geologist, and began a two year assistant professorship of geology at The University of Texas at Austin in 1942. The Applins then moved to Tallahassee, Florida to join the U.S. Geological Survey in 1944, where they worked as one of the most compelling research teams of their time, concentrating on the surface and subsurface stratigraphy of the southeastern United States.

Throughout her career, Applin published numerous definitive papers on micropaleontology, coauthoring many with her husband, Paul. When she retired from the Geological Survey on December 31, 1962, she received a Citation for Meritorious Service from the United States Department of the Interior. After retirement, she continued to work and publish many papers, among them the exemplary professional papers on *The Comanche Series* in 1965, and *The Gulf Series* in 1967.

Applin was a charter and honorary member of the SEPM and the Mississippi Geological Society, a member of the American Association of Petroleum Geologists, and a fellow of the Geological Society of America. In 1960, E. H. Rainwater presented her with The Gulf Coast Association of Geological Society award for outstanding contributions to Gulf Coast geology, saying Applin contributed "more to the knowledge of gulf coast stratigraphy than any other person." Applin died in Jackson, Mississippi on July 23, 1972.

SELECTED WRITINGS BY APPLIN:

Periodicals

"Memorial to Laura Lane Weinzierl." *Journal of Paleontology* 2, no. 4 (1928): 383.

(With Ellisor, A.E., and H.T. Kniker) "Subsurface stratigraphy of the Coastal Plain of Texas and Louisiana."*American Association of Petroleum Geologists Bulletin* 9, no. 1 (1925): 79–122.

"The Comanche Series and associated rocks in the subsurface in central and south Florida," *U. S. Geological Society Professional Paper 447* 84 (1965).

FURTHER READING

Books

American Men and Women of Science. Vol. 1, 12th ed. New Providence: R.R. Bowker, 1971.

American Association of Petroleum Geologists Bulletin 57 (1973): 596–597.

Periodicals

Berdan. "Memorial to Esther Richards Applin." *Memorials—Geological Society of America* 4 (1975): 14–18.

Maher. "Memorial To Esther Richards Applin." *Journal of Paleontology* 47, no. 2 (1973): 340–342.

Sketch by Kyra Anderson

Charlotte Auerbach
1899–
German geneticist

Charlotte Auerbach is a German-born geneticist best known for her work on chemical mutagenesis, that is, the use of chemicals to induce genetic mutations in living things. Notable among her research efforts are her study of mutagens and other genes on the fruit-fly, or *Drosophila.* While her work was part of an ongoing research effort to discover the nature of genetic mutation, Auerbach made important contributions to the study of mutagenesis and was highly decorated for her efforts.

Auerbach was born in Krefeld, Germany, on May 14, 1899, to a scientifically inclined German-Jewish family. Her own father was a chemist and one of her uncles a physicist. Her grandfather, an anatomist, identified the Auerbach's plexus in the human intestine. After being educated in Germany, Auerbach had to flee Germany in 1933 with the rise of Nazism. She went to Scotland and joined the Institute of Animal Genetics in Edinburgh, where she obtained her Ph.D. in 1935. She remained here throughout her career except for several sabbaticals taken in the United States and Japan.

Begins Studies on Mutagenesis

In 1938 Auerbach became familiar with the research of Hermann Joseph Muller, an American geneticist who spent a year at the Institute of Animal Genetics. In 1927 Muller had shown how x rays could be used to induce mutations in the fruit fly *Drosophila melanogaster.* Mutations are changes or breakage in parts of the chromosomes, the cell organelles that contain deoxyribonucleic acid (DNA), the source of genetic information and inheritance. Mutations spontaneously occur in nature, giving rise to different characteristics. However, when an organism is exposed to a mutagenic agent, the mutation rate increases dramatically. Many mutations can be lethal for the organism.

At the University of Edinburgh, Auerbach was asked to research the effects of mustard gas on *Drosophila.* Mustard gas, a compound used in chemical warfare during World War I and then outlawed, appeared to have pharmacological effects similar to x rays, so it was thought that its mutagenic effects might be similar. To this end, Auerbach designed and executed many experiments, the results of which were more dramatic than expected. Although other mutagens were being discovered in Germany, Switzerland, and the Soviet Union at about the same time, Auerbach's research on chemical mutagenesis was conducted with greater depth. Rarely hypothesizing, and carefully progressing from one conclusion to another, Auerbach discovered the relationship between chromosome breakage and gene mutation by experimenting on fruit flies. She noted how chemical mutagens have a slower action than the immediate effect of x rays. Auerbach also conducted experiments using yeast to try to explain replication of unstable genes. She also used yeast in experiments to study how one-strand lesions in DNA are changed into two-strand mutations.

While visiting the United States at one time, Auerbach visited the national laboratory in Oak Ridge, Tennessee. There she began experimenting on the bread mold *Neurospora;* she wished to show that spontaneous mutations can happen without DNA replication. Her work on fungi also focused on the analysis of mutagen specificity–that is, the selective action of certain mutagens on certain genes. This line of research on the metabolic and physiological influence on the action of mutagens was carried out by her successor, B. J. Kilbey.

During the early 1950s, when DNA was discovered as the compound that carries the genetic code, Auerbach was able to explain how chemical mutagenesis is a process that occurs in many steps, the first of which is a chemical change in DNA. Because of her expertise on the effects of chemical mutagens, Auerbach has been involved in the detection and analysis of environmental mutagens. She served as a member of a government committee, honorary president of the second International Congress on Environmental Mutagen Research, and acted as sponsor and advisor to the European Economic Community Program.

For her outstanding work, Auerbach won several honorary degrees from such institutions as the universities of Leiden, Cambridge, and Dublin. She received the Keith Medal from the Royal Society of Edinburgh in 1947 and the Darwin Medal from the Royal Society of London in 1977. The University of Edinburgh awarded her a D.Sc. in 1947, and in 1967 gave her a personal chair. Other honors received by Auerbach include election to the Genetical Society of Japan in 1966, the Danish Academy of Science in 1968, and an appointment as foreign associate of the U.S. National Academy of Sciences in 1970. She has also won awards of the Environmental Mutagen Society of the United States (1972) and Europe (1974).

SELECTED WRITINGS BY AUERBACH:

Books

Genetics in the Atomic Age. Illustrated by I. G. Auerbach. Oliver and Boyd, 1956.

The Science of Genetics. Illustrated by I. G. Auerbach. Harper, 1962.

Sketch by Barbara A. Branca

Mary Ellen Avery
1927–
American pediatrician

Mary Ellen Avery is most known for discovering the main cause of respiratory distress syndrome (RDS) in premature infants. Avery found that premature babies with immature lungs lack a substance called pulmonary surfactant, which normally lines the tiny air sacs in the lungs and keeps them from closing. Without this substance, the lungs cannot properly expand and take in oxygen. The result is the severe breathing impairment called RDS. Once the problem was identified, Avery also led the search for life–saving therapies. In 1970, there were about 10,000 infant deaths a year in the United States from RDS. By 1995, that number had been slashed to only 1,460 deaths a year. Much of the credit for this dramatic drop goes to Avery.

Avery was born on May 6, 1927, in Camden, New Jersey. Her parents were William Clarence Avery, the owner of a manufacturing company in Philadelphia, and Mary Catherine Miller Avery, the vice principal of a high school in Newark, New Jersey. Avery was the younger of two sisters. While growing up, she was lucky enough to have a role model living right next door, a pediatrician named Emily Bacon. As Avery later recalled in a November 7, 1997, telephone interview with writer Linda Wasmer Smith. "She used to talk to me about medicine and take me into the hospital occasionally. Actually, she showed me the first premature baby I ever saw. There weren't many women in pediatrics in those days, and I greatly admired her."

After high school, Avery attended Wheaton College in Norton, Massachusetts, where she graduated summa cum laude with a bachelor's degree in chemistry in 1948. From there, Avery went to the Johns Hopkins University School of Medicine in Baltimore, where she received her M.D. degree in 1952. Up until this point, Avery had not been especially interested in respiratory problems. Soon after graduation from medical school, however, she was diagnosed with tuberculosis, which kept her at home in bed for six months. When Avery finally recovered her health, she had a newfound fascination with the workings of the lungs.

Mary Ellen Avery (Reproduced by permission of Mary Ellen Avery.)

Landmark Research on Respiratory Distress Syndrome

Avery stayed at Johns Hopkins for her internship and residency in pediatrics, during which she grew interested in newborns. Next came a research fellowship at Harvard Medical School, where Avery made a crucial observation. Upon comparing the lungs of infants who had died of RDS to those of healthy experimental animals, she noticed that the latter contained a foamy substance that looked like egg white. Since the lungs of the dead infants lacked this foam, Avery deduced that it must play a critical role. As it turned out, the foam was the result of what came to be called pulmonary surfactant. Avery's observation formed the basis of a breakthrough paper published in the *American Journal of Diseases of Children* in 1959.

Avery also spearheaded the effort to find better therapies for RDS. She and her coworkers showed that giving glucocorticoid hormones to fetal lambs sped up the development of their lungs. This led to the use of glucocorticoids in pregnant women who are at risk for premature birth. In addition, Avery and her colleagues laid much of the groundwork for the introduction of replacement surfactant in 1991. A pamphlet published the next year by the American Lung Association noted, "The availability of surfactant, a key to the survival of thousands of babies gasping for their first breath, is an achievement that owes a great deal to Mary Ellen Avery."

In 1960, Avery joined the faculty at Johns Hopkins University as an assistant professor of pediatrics. At Johns Hopkins Hospital, she also assumed the role of pediatrician in charge of newborn nurseries. In 1969, she moved to McGill University in Montreal, where she served as professor and chairman of the department of pediatrics. Then in 1974, Avery began a long stint as a pediatrics professor at Harvard Medical School. While at Harvard, she simultaneously served as physician–in–chief at Children's Hospital in Boston. Over the years, Avery has also traveled widely as a guest speaker and visiting professor in countries including Canada, Mexico, Japan, Korea, Singapore, Pakistan, New Zealand, Australia, Argentina, Chile, Brazil, Cuba, Portugal, Finland, France, Italy, Switzerland, and the United Kingdom.

Pioneering Work in Newborn Medicine

Avery made her mark not only as a researcher but also as an educator. She established a joint program in neonatology, the branch of pediatrics that deals with the diseases and care of newborns, at Harvard Medical School, Children's Hospital, and two other hospitals. At least 10 of her trainees in this program and elsewhere went on to head neonatology divisions at various hospitals around the United States and Canada. Avery's textbook *The Lung and Its Disorders in the Newborn Infant*, first published in 1964, is considered a classic in the field.

Avery has received numerous honors in a long and distinguished career. In 1991, she was presented the National Medal of Science by President George Bush. The citation recognized her contributions to the understanding, treatment, and prevention of RDS. In addition, it stated that "Avery is one of the founders of neonatal intensive care, and a major advocate of improving access to care for all premature and sick infants." Avery's other awards include the 1984 Edward Livingston Trudeau Medal from the American Lung Association, the 1991 **Virginia Apgar** Award from the American Academy of Pediatrics, and the 1997 Medical Alumnus Award from Johns Hopkins Medical School. Avery is a member of the National Academy of Sciences. She has received honorary degrees from a dozen colleges and served on a number of national and international committees.

Avery, who never married, lives in Wellesley, Massachusetts. She enjoys regular visits to her vacation home on a lake in Maine, where she fishes, swims, boats, and eats lobster. However, in an interview at age 70, the still very busy pediatrician told Smith that "work is really my relaxation."

SELECTED WRITINGS BY AVERY:

Books

(With B.D. Fletcher and R. Williams) *The Lung and Its Disorders in the Newborn Infant*. 4th ed. Philadelphia: W.B. Saunders, 1981.

(Editor with A.J. Schaffer) *Diseases of the Newborn.* 4th ed. Philadelphia: W.B. Saunders, 1977.
(Editor with H.W. Taeusch Jr.) *Schaffer's Diseases of the Newborn.* 5th ed. Philadelphia: W.B. Saunders, 1984.
(Editor with H.W. Taeusch Jr. and R.A. Ballard) *Schaffer and Avery's Diseases of the Newborn.* 6th ed. Philadelphia: W.B. Saunders, 1991.
(Editor with H.W. Taeusch Jr. and R.A. Ballard) *Avery's Diseases of the Newborn,* 7th ed. Philadelphia: W.B. Saunders, to be published 1998.
(With Georgia Litwack) *Born Early: The Story of a Premature Baby.* Boston: Little Brown, 1982.
(Editor with Lewis R. First) *Pediatric Medicine.* 2nd ed. Baltimore: Williams and Wilkins, 1994.

Periodicals

(With J. Mead) "Surface Properties in Relation to Atelectasis and Hyaline Membrane Disease." *American Journal of Diseases of Children* (1959): 517–523.

FURTHER READING

Books

Harvey, A. McGehee. *Adventures in Medical Research: A Century of Discovery at Johns Hopkins.* Baltimore: Johns Hopkins University Press, 1976.
May, Hal, ed. *Contemporary Authors.* Vol. 188. Detroit: Gale Research, 1986, pp. 29–30.

Other

National Medal of Science, citation dated August 21, 1991.
"Profile of a Researcher: Mary Ellen Avery, M.D." American Lung Association, 1992.

Sketch by Linda Wasmer Smith

Hertha Ayrton
1854–1923
English physicist

Hertha Ayrton (The Library of Congress. Reproduced by permission.)

Hertha Ayrton's contributions to science in the early twentieth century included research on areas as diverse as electrical engineering and wave formation. Her inventions included the Ayrton Fan that dispelled poison gases from the trenches in World War I and refinements to early model film projectors. A leading expert on electric arc lamps, she wrote *The Electric Arc,* which became a standard textbook in the field. She became the first woman elected to the Institution of Electrical Engineers and was involved in the suffrage and peace movements.

Hertha Ayrton was born Phoebe Sarah Marks in Portsea, England, the third of Alice Moss Marks' and Levi Marks' five children. Her father was a clock maker and jeweler. After his death in 1861, Alice Marks supported the family by selling her needlework. In spite of the family's limited finances, young Sarah attended the school her aunt ran in London. When she became a teenager, Sarah changed her name to Hertha as an expression of her independence. Although she remained proud of her Jewish heritage, she regarded herself as an agnostic.

At the age of 16 Ayrton left school to become a governess in order to help support her family. In 1873 she met Barbara Bodichon, a philanthropist who supported women's causes and had helped found Girton College at Cambridge. With Bodichon's financial assistance, Ayrton entered Girton in 1874 after passing the Cambridge University Examination for Women with honors in mathematics and English. She exhibited an aptitude for science by inventing the sphygmograph, a device that charts pulse beats, before discovering that a similar machine had already been developed. Although her studies were interrupted by illness, Ayrton passed her Cambridge baccalaureate honors examinations in 1881 but did not receive a degree because Cambridge did not offer degrees to women at that time.

Following her graduation, Ayrton taught high school mathematics and later became a private tutor. In 1884 Ayrton invented and patented her line divider, an instrument that could immediately divide a line into any given number of equal parts. This inspired her to launch a career in science, and she enrolled in Finsbury Technical College in London, again with Bodichon's financial assistance. At Finsbury, she worked with W. E. Ayrton, a professor of physics and a pioneer in electrical engineering whom she had first met while she was a teacher. Ayrton was a widower who strongly supported women's rights. The couple married in 1885; their only child, Barbara Bodichon Ayrton, was born in 1892. In 1893 Ayrton took over her husband's electric arc experiments while he was lecturing in Chicago. Electric arc lamps, which were widely used for lighting at the time, were much in need of improvement: they hissed, hummed, and burned unsteadily. Her experiments solved many of these problems, and she published the results in a series of articles for *The Electrician* in 1895 and 1896. Her conclusions regarding humming arcs led to later discoveries concerning the musical arc—an important step in the development of radio. She also presented several papers on the arc to the British Association, and in 1899 she was invited to read her paper on the cause of the hissing arc to the Institution of Electrical Engineers. She became a recognized authority on the arc and with support from the organization's president was the first woman elected to membership in the Institution of Electrical Engineers. In 1902 Ayrton published a compilation of her findings, *The Electric Arc,* which became the standard text in the field.

By 1901 her husband's health was deteriorating, and they moved to the seaside town of Margate where Ayrton became interested in the action of the ocean's waves and the formation of sand ripples. Her writing on the topic proved noteworthy to the scientific community, and although she had been refused admittance to the Royal Society in 1902, two years later she became the first woman to read her own paper before the group. In 1906 the Society awarded Ayrton its Hughes Medal for her work on the electric arc and sand ripples. The following several years she spent working with the British Admiralty on standardizing types and sizes of carbon for searchlights, and later research involved air currents. In 1912 she developed improved lamp house designs for movie projectors, and during World War I she invented the Ayrton Fan to drive poison gas out of the trenches. She became a founding member of the National Union of Scientific Workers in 1920.

After the war Ayrton continued her research on the fan principles and became active in the suffrage movement, participating in many demonstrations along with her daughter. For a time during these years, Ayrton also provided a home for the ailing **Marie Curie**, whom she had known since 1903. Ayrton died in North Lancing, Sussex, on August 27, 1923.

SELECTED WRITINGS BY AYRTON:

Books

The Electric Arc, [London], 1902.

FURTHER READING

Books

Abir-Am, Pnina G., and Dorinda Outram, editors, *Uneasy Careers and Intimate Lives: Woman in Science 1789–1979.* New Brunswick: Rutgers University Press, 1989, pp.115–123.

Dictionary of Scientific Biography, Volume 17, supplement II, Scribner's, 1990, pp. 40–42.

Ogilvie, Marilyn Bailey. *Women in Science: Antiquity through the Nineteenth Century.* Cambridge: MIT Press, 1986, pp. 32–34.

Periodicals

Armstrong, Henry E. "Mrs. Hertha Ayrton." *Nature* (December 1, 1923): 800–801.

Mather, T. "Mrs. Hertha Ayrton." *Nature* (December 29, 1923): 939.

Trotter, A.P. "Mrs. Ayrton's Work on the Electric Arc." *Nature* (January 12, 1924): 48–49.

Sketch by Kathy Sammis

B

Florence Augusta (Merriam) Bailey (The Library of Congress. Reproduced by permission.)

Florence Augusta (Merriam) Bailey
1863–1948
American naturalist and ornithologist

Florence Augusta (Merriam) Bailey is best known for her observant, accessible publications about birds and nature. A skilled observer of birds in their natural habitat, Bailey was able to balance the scientific and the popular in her writing. She authored 12 books and more than 120 articles in her lifetime. Bailey popularized natural history in the late nineteenth century, and was the most important female nature writer of her time.

Bailey was born on August 8, 1863 in Locust Grove, New York, the daughter of Clinton Levi and Caroline (Hart) Merriam. Clinton Merriam was a businessman who had retired by the time of Bailey was born. Upon his retirement he moved the family to Homewood, the family estate in Locust Grove. He also served as a Congressional Representative from 1871–75. Caroline Merriam was fascinated by gardening and astronomy and passed her daughter, the youngest of her four children. Clinton Merriam had some knowledge of natural history and shared this with Bailey and her elder brother, Clinton Hart Merriam. The siblings became very close, in part because of their common interest in natural history. Their parents encouraged them in these endeavors.

Bailey was educated primarily at home as a child because of a lengthy illness, probably tuberculosis. This disease would strike Bailey again later in life. When she was older, Bailey attended Mrs. Piatt's School, a preparatory school in Utica, New York. In 1882, Bailey was admitted to the newly founded Smith College as a special student. Because her education did not qualify her for a degree program, she could take any classes she wanted and did not receive a degree when she left Smith in 1886. Many years later, in 1921, Smith College would grant her an honorary A.B.

Publishes First Book

While a student at Smith College, Bailey became interested in ornithology (the study of birds) and studied natural history in depth. Bailey began publishing articles—first in local publications, then in *Audubon Magazine*. In 1885, she became the first woman to be made a member of the American Ornithologists' Union (AOU), which had been founded in 1883. However, she was only given associate status, not a full membership. That year she also founded one of the first chapters of the Audubon Society at Smith College. Bailey continued to write and in 1889, published her first book, *Birds Through an Opera Glass*, a collection of her articles.

Birds were not Bailey's only interest. Raised in a religious family, Bailey was also active in social reform. In 1887 she worked in Brooklyn, New York, as a social worker for social reformer Grace Dodge. Several years later, in 1891, Bailey spent the summer in Chicago at a school for working girls, and that winter did similar work in New York City, again for Dodge.

In 1893, Bailey's tuberculosis returned and she spent the next three years in the West and Southwest for her health. As she traveled, she continued to expand her knowledge of birds. To that end, she attended lectures at Stanford University and continued to write books on birds based on her observations in their natural habitat. At the time, many scientists studied birds by killing them then examining them. Bailey also continued to publish articles in both general interest and ornithological publications, including *Auk*, the magazine of the AOU. In some of her writings, Bailey railed against a fashion trend in women's hats that used feathers and, on occasion, entire stuffed birds. Bailey found the killing of birds for ornamentation offensive.

In 1896, when Bailey had sufficiently recovered, she moved to Washington, D.C., to live with her brother Clinton who was working as the first chief of survey at the United States Biological Survey. Bailey founded a chapter of the Audubon Society in Washington, D.C., in 1897, where she taught the basics of ornithology. The following year Bailey published *Birds of Village and Field*, which was among the first popular bird guides published in America. She also published a definitive beginner's guide to ornithology.

On December 16, 1899 Bailey married Vernon Bailey, a naturalist who worked with her brother and with whom she had been acquainted with for 10 years. The couple had no children.

Vernon Bailey's work often took him on the road and Bailey usually accompanied him. They traveled all over the West Coast to California, New Mexico, Arizona, Texas, and the Pacific Northwest. She occasionally contributed to her husband's books, writing chapters for books such as *Cave Life of Kentucky*, published in 1933. However, she primarily wrote on her own. In 1902, she published *Handbook of Birds in the Western United States*, a standard bird watching text that went through many editions.

Bailey published *Birds of New Mexico* in 1928, a hefty 800 page text that examined a subject that had never received such coverage before. This book won Bailey national acclaim and in 1929 she became the AOU's first woman fellow. The organization also awarded her the Brewster Medal for *Birds* in 1932. She was the first woman to win this honor. Two years later, the University of New Mexico bestowed her with an honorary degree for *Birds*.

Bailey died in Washington, D.C., on September 22, 1948 of myocardial degeneration. As Harriet Kofalk wrote in *No Woman Tenderfoot: Florence Merriam Bailey, Pioneer Naturalist*, "Florence claimed no breakthroughs, but in the firm foundation for studying live birds in the field she certainly laid the bricks that lasted for half a century before others refined the study to its present terms."

SELECTED WRITINGS BY BAILEY:

Books

Birds Through an Opera Glass. Boston: Houghton Mifflin, 1890.

Handbook of Birds of the Western United States. Boston: Houghton Mifflin, 1902.

Birds of New Mexico. Santa Fe: New Mexico Department of Game and Fish, 1928.

Among the Birds in the Grand Canyon National Park. Washington, D.C.: National Park Service, 1939.

FURTHER READING

Books

Bailey, Martha J. *American Women in Science: A Biographical Dictionary*. Denver: ABC–CLIO, 1994.

Brooks, Paul. *Speaking for Nature: How Literary Naturalist from Henry Thoreau to Rachel Carson Have Shaped America*. Boston: Houghton Mifflin, 1980.

Grinstein, Louise S. et al, eds. *Women in the Biological Sciences: A Biobibliographic Sourcebook*. Westport, CT: Greenwood Press, 1997.

James, Edward T., ed. *Notable American Women, 1607–1950: A Biographical Dictionary*. Vol. 1. Cambridge, Mass.: Belknap Press, 1980.

Kofalk, Harriet. *No Woman Tenderfoot: Florence Merriam Bailey—Pioneer Naturalist*. College Station, TX: Texas A&M University Press, 1989.

Mainiero, Lina, ed. *American Women Writers: A Critical Reference Guide from Colonial Times to the Present*. Vol. 1. New York: Frederick Ungar, 1979.

McHenry, Robert, ed. *Famous American Women: A Biographical Dictionary from Colonial Times to the Present*. New York: Dover Publications, 1980.

Ogilvie, Marilyn Bailey. *Women in Science: Antiquity through the Nineteenth Century*. Cambridge: MIT Press, 1986.

O'Neill, Lois Decker, ed. *The Women's Book of World Records and Achievements*. Garden City: Anchor Press, 1979.

Rossiter, Margaret W. *Women Scientists in America: Struggles and Strategies to 1940*. Baltimore: Johns Hopkins Press, 1982.

Siegel, Patricia Joan and Kay Thomas Finley. *Women in the Scientific Search: An American Bio–bibliography, 1724–1979*. Metuchen, NJ: The Scarecrow Press: 1985.

Sterling, Keir B. et al, eds. Biographical Dictionary of American and Canadian Naturalist and Environmentalists. Westport, CT: Greenwood Press, 1997.

Sketch by Annette Petrusso

Nina Bari
1901–1961
Russian mathematician and educator

Nina Bari's work focused on trigonometric series. She refined the constructive method of proof to prove results in function theory, and her work is regarded as the foundation of function and trigonometric series theory.

Nina Karlovna Bari was born in Moscow on November 19, 1901, the daughter of Olga and Karl Adolfovich Bari, a physician. In the Russia of her youth, education was segregated by gender and the best academic opportunities reserved for males only. Bari attended a private high school for girls, but in 1918 she defied convention and sat for—and passed—the examination for a boy's high school graduation certificate.

In 1917, Russia's political and social structure was shattered by the Russian Revolution. The power vacuum left the country at the mercy of the czarists, socialist revolutionaries, and Bolsheviks. While many of Russia's universities closed at the beginning of the Revolution, the Faculty of Physics and Mathematics of Moscow State University reopened in 1918, and began accepting applications from women. Records show that Bari was the first woman to attend the university and was probably the first woman to graduate from it. Russia's educational institutions were in the same turmoil as the society around them. Graduation exams were scheduled on a catch–as–can basis, and Bari took advantage of the disorder to sit for her examinations early. She graduated from Moscow State in 1921—just three years after entering the university.

Finds a Mentor and a Movement

After graduation, Bari began her teaching career. She lectured at the Moscow Forestry Institute, the Moscow Polytechnic Institute, and the Sverdlov Communist Institute. Bari applied for and received the only paid research fellowship awarded by the newly created Research Institute of Mathematics and Mechanics. (Ten postgraduate students were accepted at the Research Institute; Bari won the stipend because her name appeared first on the alphabetically arranged list. According to a colleague, she shared the stipend with her fellow students.)

As a student, Bari was drawn to an elite group nicknamed the Luzitania—an informal academic and social organization. These scholars clustered around Nikolai Nikolaevich Luzin, a noted mathematician who rejected any area of mathematical study but function theory. With Luzin as her inspiration, Bari plunged into the study of trigonometric series and functions. She developed her thesis around the topic and presented the main results of her research to the Moscow Mathematical Society in 1922—the first woman to address the society. In 1926, she defended her thesis, and her work earned her the Glavnauk Prize.

In 1927, Bari took advantage of an opportunity to study in Paris at the Sorbonne and the College de France. She then attended the Polish Mathematical Congress in Lvov, Poland; a Rockefeller grant enabled her to return to Paris to continue her studies. Bari's decision to travel may have been influenced by the disintegration of the Luzitanians. Luzin's irascible, demanding personality had alienated many of the mathematicians who had gathered around him. By 1930, all traces of the Luzitania movement had vanished, and Luzin left Moscow State for the Academy of Science's Steklov Institute.

Gains Recognition at Home and Abroad

Bari returned to Moscow State in 1929 and in 1932 was made a full professor. In 1935, she was awarded the degree of Doctor of the Physical–Mathematical Sciences, a more prestigious research degree than the traditional Ph.D.

In 1936, during the dictatorship of Josef Stalin, Bari's mentor, Luzin, was charged with ideological sabotage. For some reason—possibly Stalin's preoccupation with more important enemies of the state—Luzin's trial was canceled. Luzin was officially reprimanded and withdrew from academia.

Bari managed to avoid the taint of association. She and D.E. Men'shov took charge of function theory work at Moscow State during the 1940s. In 1952, she published an important piece on primitive functions, and trigonometric series and their almost everywhere convergence. Bari also presented works at the 1956 Third All–Union Congress in Moscow and the 1958 International Congress of Mathematicians in Edinburg.

Mathematics was the center of Bari's intellectual life, but she enjoyed literature and the arts. She was also a mountain hiking enthusiast and tackled the Caucasus, Altai, Lamir and Tyan'shan' mountain ranges in Russia. Bari's interest in mountain hiking was inspired by her husband, Viktor Vladmirovich Nemytski, a Soviet mathematician, Moscow State professor and an avid mountain explorer. There is no documentation of their marriage available, but contemporaries believe the two married later in life.

Bari's last work—her 55th publication—was a 900–page monograph on the state of the art of trigonometric series theory, which is recognized as a standard reference work for those specializing in function and trigonometric series theory.

Bari died July 15, 1961, when she fell in front of a train at the Moscow Metro. Colleagues, however, suspect her death was suicide; they speculate she was despondent over the death of Luzin in 1950, who some believe had been not only her mentor but her lover.

SELECTED WRITINGS BY BARI:

Books

A Treatise on Trigonometric Series. Translated by Margaret F. Mullins, 1964

Periodicals

"Sur l'uncite du developpement trigonometrique." *Comptes rendus hebdomadaires des seances de l'Academie des Sciences* 177 (1923): 1195–1197.

"Sur la nature diophantique du probleme d'uncite du developpement trigonometrique." *Comptes rendus hebdomadaires des seances de l'Academie des Sciences* 202 (1936): 1901–1903.

"The Uniqueness Problem of the Representation of Functions by Trigonometric Series." *Uspekhi Matematicheskikh Nauk* 3, no. 31, (1949): 3–68. Supplement, 7 (1952): 193–196. (Translation: American Mathematical Society Translation no. 52, (1951.)
"On primitive functions and trigonometric series converging almost everywhere" (in Russian). *Matematicheskii Sbornik* 31, no. 73, (1952): 687–702.
"Trigonometric Series" (in Russian). *Trudy III Vzesoyuznogo Matematicheskoga S'ezda* 2 (1956): 25–26.
"Trigonometric Series" (in Russian). *Trudy III Vzesoyuznogo Matematicheskoga S'ezda* 3 (1957): 164–177.
(With D. E. Men'shov) "On the International Mathematical Congress in Edinburgh" (in Russian). *Upsekhi Matematicheskikh Nauk,* 14, no. 2, (1959): 235–238.
"Subsequences converging to Zero Everywhere of Partial Sums of Trigonometric Series" (in Russian). *Izvestiya Akademii Nauk SSSR. Seriya Matematika* 24 (1960): 531–548.

FURTHER READING

Books

Fang, J. *Mathematicians From Antiquity to Today.* Memphis State University: Paideia, 1972, p. 185.
Spetich, Joan and Douglas E. Cameron. "Nina Karlovna Bari," in *Women of Mathematics: A Bibliographic Sourcebook.* Edited by Louise S. Grinstein and Paul J. Campbell. Westport, CT.: Greenwood Press, 1987, pp. 6–12.
Zdravkovska, Smilka and Peter L. Duren, editors. *Golden Years of Moscow Mathematics, History of Mathematics,* Volume 6, Providence, RI: American Mathematical Society, 1993, pp. 35–53.

Other

Soublis, Giota. "Nina Karlvona Bari." *Biographies of Women Mathematicians.* June 1997. http://www.scottlan.edu/lriddle/women/chronol.htm (July 22, 1997).

Sketch by A. Mullig

Eileen Barnes
?–1960?
Irish botanical artist

Eileen Barnes's name has been all but forgotten, but among her botanical drawings are several that are considered the definitive examples of specific plants, notably *sedums* (stonecrops) and *sempervivums* (house leeks). During her years as an illustrator, she was highly regarded for her thoroughness and accuracy.

Almost nothing is known about Barnes outside of her illustrations. She was probably born in Dublin sometime before 1890, and likely got her initial artistic training at the Dublin Metropolitan School of Art. The careful details of both her drawings and her clay and wax models indicate that she studied anatomy. For example, she made wax and clay models of slugs, the idea being that farmers who saw the models would recognize these crop-destroying animals.

Barnes spent most of her career at the Natural Museum of Ireland, where she worked as a craft–worker and artist. The earliest references to Barnes are in the Museum's 1911 annual report, and few other actual records of her employment exist. She worked in the museum's natural history division and antiquities division. She worked with scientists such as the botanist Matilda Knowles and the naturalist Robert Lloyd Praeger, illustrating their works and making models of various artifacts for museum exhibits. She also painted the habitat backgrounds for the museum's mammal and bird showcases. A number of these models are still on display at the museum.

Barnes's drawings of plants, which are included in numerous books and monographs, demonstrate her firm grasp of botany, even though she herself probably received no training as a scientist. The drawings she did for Praeger over a period of nearly 20 years are still regarded today as uncommonly accurate. This was particularly challenging, because *sedums* and *sempervivums* (the plants that Praeger primarily studied) included so many species and hybrids that it was often difficult to distinguish one from another.

Praeger, who died in 1953, acknowledged Barnes's skill in his writings and even named one of the plants he studied *Sedum barnesiannum* in her honor. But Barnes's life remained quiet, and her work gained little recognition. Although her drawings are still regarded as the definitive examples of certain plant species, the artist herself seems to have quietly faded out of existence. She was at the museum during the 1950s, when she retired, although she continued on a part-time basis for several years thereafter. She kept a small garden at her home in the south of Dublin. Even though little known is known about her as a person, her work speaks eloquently to her knowledge, skill, and commitment to scientific illustration.

FURTHER READING

Books

Stars, Shells, and Bluebells: Women Scientists and Pioneers. Dublin: Women in Technology and Science, 1997.

Sketch by George A. Milite

Ida Barney
1886–1982
American astronomer

Yale astronomer Ida Barney was responsible for the cataloguing of some 150,000 stars during a period of more than 30 years. Trained as a mathematician, she spent many years doing painstaking calculations. By the time she retired in 1955, she had introduced ways at streamline the process while actually making the measurements more accurate.

Barney was born in New Haven, Connecticut on November 6, 1886, the daughter of Samuel Eben and Ida (Bushnell) Barney. She distinguished herself early as an outstanding student and attended Smith College where she received her bachelor of arts degree in 1908. She returned to New Haven to do her graduate work at Yale where, in 1911, she was awarded her Ph.D. in mathematics. For the next several years she taught mathematics at the college level at Rollins College in Winter Park, Florida; Lake Erie College in Plainsville, Ohio; and at Smith.

In 1922, Barney left teaching to join the staff of the Yale Observatory. At that time, scientists were almost rushing to make astronomical measurements, in part because of improvements in telescopic and photographic techniques and in part because increased interest in astronomy had also led to increased funding for projects. Barney's solid background in mathematics made her ideally suited for the work being conducted at Yale, and she was named a research assistant.

Mapping the Night Sky

Working with astronomer Frank Schlesinger, Barney made calculations based on the positions of stars as seen on special photographic plates. It was her responsibility to measure the images and to conduct and supervise the mathematical calculations that were needed to match their positions to their celestial coordinates. Much of this work was tedious—the calculations had to be done by hand, and the positioning of the plates had to be done visually (which was excessively tiring to the eyes). Barney may have seen ways to streamline the system even in her early days, but Schlesinger was not forward-thinking enough to believe that women should contribute anything significant but practical labor at the observatory.

Schlesinger, however, did make innovations that both reduced eyestrain and allowed for more accurate measurements. Moreover, it was under Schlesinger that the Yale Observatory began using punch card machines manufactured by IBM. These early "computers" were crude and slow by today's standards, but in the 1930s they were a breakthrough for researchers such as Barney. Schlesinger retired in 1941 and, under Barney's tenure, the photographic plates were measured by an automatic image-centering device at IBM Watson Scientific Laboratory.

Barney continued her work on cataloguing stars for an additional 14 years after Schlesinger left. She became a research associate in 1959. Even with the new technological innovations, the process was still long and often tedious, but Barney persisted. Her persistence is the reason she was able to catalogue more than 150,000 stars during her career. The Yale Catalogues are still considered one of the most important undertakings of the school's astronomy department. The American Astronomical Society recognized that what Barney was doing, however tedious, was critically important for mapping outer space as accurately as possible. In 1952, the AAS awarded Barney the Annie J. Cannon Prize, given out only once every three years. Barney retired in 1955, but several of the star catalogues were still being complied at the time, so her name appears as editor until 1959. Barney remained in New Haven after retirement, dying there at the age of 95 on March 7, 1982.

SELECTED WRITINGS BY BARNEY:

Books

Barney, Ida. *Catalogue of the Positions and Proper Motions of. . . Stars.*Transactions of the Astronomical Observatory of Yale University, Vols. 16–27. New Haven, CT, The Observatory, 1945–59.

FURTHER READING

Books

Shearer, Benjamin F. and Barbara S, Shearer, eds. *Notable Women in the Physical Sciences: A Biographical Dictionary.* Westport, CT: Greenwood Press, 1997.

Sketch by George A. Milite

(James) Miranda Stuart Barry
1795–1865
British physician

Like **Agnodice** in fourth-century B.C. Greece, who dressed as a man in order to study and practice medicine, James Barry disguised herself as a man in order to become a doctor. Unlike Agnodice, Barry, who had a long and successful career as an army surgeon, never revealed her sex.

Born in 1795, as Miranda Stuart or Miranda Stuart Barry, Barry may have been orphaned as a child. It also is possible that she was the daughter of a Mrs. Bulkeley, who chaperoned her during her first year at university. Barry's mentor was James Barry, probably her uncle, a well–known Irish painter and a follower of the feminist writer Mary Wollstonecraft. Another family friend was General Francisco de Miranda, who made his London medical library available to Barry. James Barry entered the Edinburgh School of Medicine in 1809 disguised as a man and graduated in 1812, nearly a century before **Sophie Jex–Blake** led the "Battle of Edinburgh," which finally resulted in women's admission to the medical school. Barry took many extra courses at the university and went on to study surgery in London with Sir Astley Cooper. At the university and later in her career, she apparently was helped in her masquerade by people in high positions, including members of the army command.

Barry entered the British military in 1813, and in 1816 she was stationed to Cape Town, South Africa, where she soon was promoted to Colonial Medical Inspector and Physician to the Governor's Household. She became famous for having performed one of the first caesarean operations in which both mother and infant survived. However, after protesting conditions in prisons, leper colonies, and asylums, and publicly attacking her close friend, the governor, Barry's job was fired. She accepted a staff surgeon's position in Mauritius in the Indian Ocean. Later, she served in the British colonies of the Caribbean, Malta, and the Crimea. In Trinidad, her assistant–surgeon discovered her secret when she was very ill with yellow fever, but Barry swore him to secrecy. Although she was often in trouble with the authorities, and was once sent back to England under armed guard, Barry was always reprieved, apparently due both to her competence and her well–placed supporters. In 1857, she was appointed Inspector–General of Hospitals for Upper and Lower Canada. There, she traveled in furs in a red sleigh, accompanied by her manservant, a uniformed footman, a coachman, and her small white dog.

Barry was only five feet tall with a tiny frame, beardless, and with a high–pitched voice. She avoided the camaraderie of the army men, and she was extremely outspoken, often going over the heads of her army superiors. She responded to ridicule with anger and fought several duels. Nevertheless, she was considered to be a brilliant physician and surgeon and a progressive, reformist administrator who stressed sanitary conditions and proper diets in the hospitals and army barracks. She prepared a significant scientific report on a South African plant that was useful for treating syphilis and gonorrhea.

In 1859 Barry became ill and she returned to England. The trip back from Canada was grueling. She even may have been shipwrecked. Nevertheless, she bitterly contested her forced retirement at age 65. It was not until Barry's death of diarrhea in 1865 that she was discovered to be a woman and perhaps to have had a child. The rumors at the time were that she was hermaphroditic, part man and part woman. Apparently these rumors began because it was assumed that no woman could have carved out such successful career for herself. Barry's life inspired a play and two novels.

FURTHER READING

Books

Hacker, Carlotta. *The Indomitable Lady Doctors*. Toronto: Clarke, Irwin & Co., 1974.

Rae, Isobel. *The Strange Story of Dr. James Barry*. London: Longmans, 1958.

Periodicals

Russell, M. P. "James Barry–1792(?)–1865, Inspector-General of Army Hospitals." *Edinburgh Medical Journal* 50 (1943), 558–67.

Sketch by Margaret Alic

Florence Bascom
1862–1945
American geologist

Florence Bascom was a pioneer in expanding scientific career opportunities for women. She was the first woman to receive a Ph.D. in geology from an American university, the first female to receive a Ph.D. of any kind from the Johns Hopkins University (1893), and the first woman to join the United States Geological Survey as an assistant geologist (1896). She began teaching at Bryn Mawr College in 1895, turning one course into a full major in less than a decade. Bascom was a widely known (her students came from all over the world) and respected geologist whose work mapping the crystalline rock formations in the Pennsylvania, New Jersey, and Maryland region became the basis for many later studies of the area.

Bascom was born on July 14, 1862, in Williamstown, Massachusetts, home of prestigious Williams College, where her father, Dr. John Bascom was professor of oratory and rhetoric. Both Professor Bascom and his wife Emma (Curtiss) Bascom actively supported women's rights issues and held strong avocational interests in the natural sciences. In 1874, John Bascom accepted the presidency of the University of Wisconsin, and his family left Williamstown. Florence Bascom was less than fifteen years old when she graduated high school in Madison, Wisconsin. She then obtained, in 1882, two degrees—a Bachelor of Arts and a Bachelor of Letters—from the university of which her father was president. Two years later she earned a Bachelor of Science degree, and in 1887 completed a Master of Arts in geology.

Roland D. Irving and Charles R. Van Hise were Bascom's mentors at the University of Wisconsin. Both were eminent geologists, and it was under their tutelage that

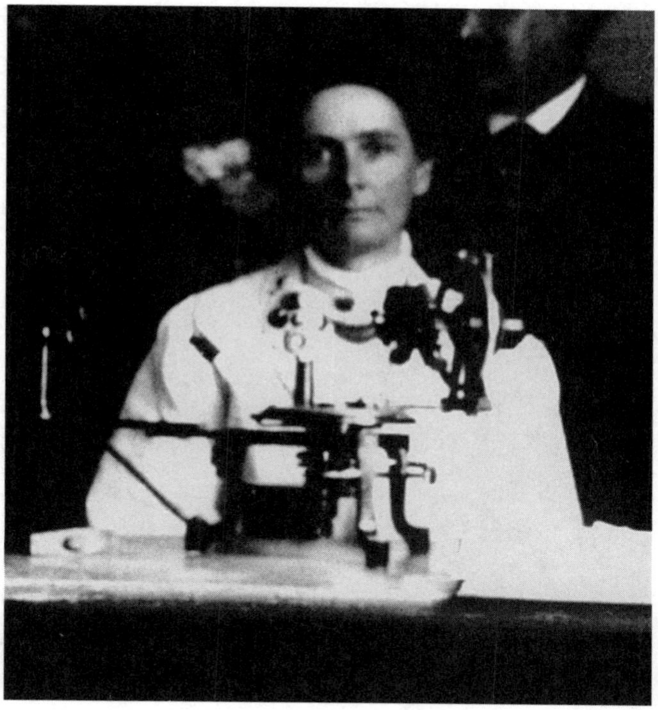

Florence Bascom (The Sophia Smith Collection. Reproduced by permission.)

Bascom learned the techniques of an emerging field of geology—the analysis of thin, translucent rock sections using microscopes and polarized light. These methods had only recently been developed in Germany, and there existed no textbook from which to learn them. Instead, Bascom studied directly from the original research papers, written in German.

As president of the University of Wisconsin, John Bascom was instrumental in instituting coeducation. Conversely, Florence Bascom faced immense obstacles in applying for a doctoral program. She hoped to study with George H. Williams, a professor at the Johns Hopkins University renowned for his use of microscopic geological techniques. The Johns Hopkins, however, had not yet allowed a woman to officially complete a degree program. Bascom applied for admission to the Geology Department at the university in September of 1890. Seven months later, the executive committee concluded that Bascom could attend without being officially enrolled as a student, and charged only for her laboratory fees. During classes, Bascom's seat was located in the corner of the classroom—and hidden behind a screen. Undaunted, Bascom applied formally to the doctoral program in 1892. She was accepted secretly. By intrepidly completing difficult and often solitary field work, Bascom produced a dissertation that a writer in *American Mineralogist* later described as "brilliant." For this, Bascom earned in 1893 the first Ph.D. in geology ever awarded to a woman by an American university.

After receiving her Ph.D., Bascom taught for two years at Ohio State University. In 1895, she accepted an invitation to join the faculty of Bryn Mawr College in Pennsylvania as a Reader in Geology. She was hired to teach a single course, and the college had no plans to create a new department of geology. Because of her success, however, within a few years the single course grew into an entire major. Bascom was granted full professorship in 1906. Bascom's specialty was petrology, the study of how present–day rocks were formed. Much of her research focused on the mid–Atlantic Piedmont region, and she wrote approximately 40 publications.

Bascom retired from Bryn Mawr in 1928. She had been editor of *The American Geologist,* a Fellow of the Geological Society of America (1894), and vice–president of that organization (1930). Through her research and teaching, Bascom left an important scientific legacy. In 1937, a total of eleven women were Fellows of the Geological Society of America; eight of them were Bryn Mawr College graduates. Never married, Bascom lived after retirement in her farmhouse atop Hoosac Mountain in northwestern Massachusetts. For several winters, she traveled to Washington, D.C., to complete work for the United States Geological Survey. Despite being shy, concise, and serious–minded, Bascom maintained close ties to her academic family of students and colleagues. She died of cerebral hemorrhage in Williamstown, Massachusetts, on June 18, 1945, and was buried next to her family in a small Williams College cemetery. According to former student Eleanora Bliss Knopf writing in *American Mineralogist,* Bascom's death left "to her colleagues, her students, and her friends the inspiring memory of a scholarly and brilliant mind combined with a forceful and vigorous personality."

SELECTED WRITINGS BY BASCOM:

Periodicals

"The New Geology." *Journal of the National Institute of Social Sciences* (January 1917).

FURTHER READING

Books

Arnold, Lois Barber. *Four Lives in Sciences.* Schocken Books, 1984.

Smith, Isabel F. *The Stone Lady: A Memoir of Florence Bascom.* Bryn Mawr College, 1981.

Periodicals

American Mineralogist. 31 (1946): 168–172.

Bryn Mawr Alumnae Bulletin (November 1945): 12–13; (spring 1965): 111–4.

Science (September 1945): 320–321.

University of Wisconsin Department of Geology and Geophysics Alumni Newsletter (1991): 61–63.

Sketch by Peter H. Taylor

Laura Maria Catarina Bassi
1711–1778
Italian physicist and teacher

Laura Maria Catarina Bassi was the world's first female professor of physics. During her lifetime, she was famous throughout Europe for her scholarship and her achievements.

Few details are known of Bassi's life and work. She was a child prodigy from a middle-class family who studied French and Latin, mathematics, philosophy, natural history, and anatomy with the medical professor Dr. Gaetano Tacconi. At age 21, encouraged by her family and friends, Bassi participated in a public debate with five renowned philosophers. Instead of the university hall, the debate was held in the great hall of the Palace of the Senators in order to accommodate the crowds that came to witness the spectacle. Cardinal Lambertini, Archbishop of Bologna, who later became Pope Benedict XIV, was among those who came to hear Bassi. He visited her the following day at her home to congratulate and encourage her to continue her studies. Shortly thereafter, the University of Bologna awarded Bassi a doctorate, in philosophy at the Hall of Hercules in the Communal Palace. The Bologna senate granted her a stipend to continue her studies.

In contrast to the rest of Europe, there had been women at the universities of Italy, as students and professors, since as early as the tenth century. In particular, the University of Bologna was known for its liberal attitude toward women scholars. Following a public examination by a committee of five professors, Bassi became the first woman professor of physics at that university. Her name appeared on the registry of the university for the years 1732 through 1778, and she became well known as a teacher. Bassi continued to study Greek and mathematics, and she published papers on the works of René Descartes and Isaac Newton. She designed and constructed apparatus for her experiments. Her dissertations on mechanics and hydraulics were published in Latin in *Commentaries of the Bologna Institute* and manuscripts of her physics lectures still exist. She also published poetry.

Bassi was a member of the Academy of Science of Bologna, and she presented papers there each year; for example: "On the Compression of Air" in 1746, "On the Bubbles Observed in Freely Flowing Fluid" in 1747, and "On the Bubbles of Air that Escape from Fluids" in 1748. In 1774, after the French philosopher Voltaire was denied admission to the French Academy, he asked Bassi to arrange for his election to the Bologna Academy, and she complied. In 1776, Bassi succeeded Paolo Balbi as professor of physics at the Institute of Bologna.

Laura Maria Catarina Bassi (Photo Researchers, Inc. Reproduced by permission.)

In 1738, Bassi married Giuseppe Veratti, a physician and professor at the Institute, and reportedly became the mother of 12 children. Bassi's renown led to numerous visits from scholars and a voluminous correspondence. Her cousin, Lazzaro Spallanzani, who became one of the founders of experimental biology, studied mathematics with her at the University of Bologna.

Bassi died in 1778 of a respiratory disease. The senate of Bologna coined a medal in her honor.

FURTHER READING

Books

Mozans, H. J. [John Augustine Zahm]. *Women in Science*. 1913. Reprint, Cambridge: MIT Press, 1974.

Schiebinger, Londa. *The Mind Has No Sex? Women in the Origins of Modern Science*. Cambridge: Harvard University Press, 1989.

Sketch by Margaret Alic

Eleanor Baum (Photograph by Richard Termine. Reproduced by permission of Eleanor Baum.)

Eleanor Baum
1940–
American electrical engineer

Dr. Eleanor Baum is internationally recognized for her outstanding efforts in advancing engineering education and promoting engineering as a career to minorities and women. Baum was the first woman dean of a college of engineering and the first woman president of the American Society for Engineering Education (ASEE).

Baum was the only child of Anna (Berkman) and Sol Kushel. She was born on February 10, 1940, on the border between Poland and Lithuania. Her parents emigrated to Brooklyn, New York when she was young. Baum developed a strong interest in math, science, and literature while attending Midwood High School, taking advanced math and science at a time when women were not encouraged to do so. Because her parents pressured her to become a high school math teacher, Baum chose engineering "as a form of rebellion, my way of shocking my parents and teachers," she said in an interview in *U.S. Woman Engineer.*

Becomes Only Female Engineer in Her Class

In 1955, Baum enrolled in the City College of New York in electrical engineering. Other schools she applied to would not admit women. As the only female in her class, she received little support and felt very isolated. However, she persevered, earned her Bachelor's degree in 1959, and went to work in the aerospace industry on Long Island. "Again, I was the only woman engineer," she said in the 1991 Stuckenberg Lecture. "Most people assumed I was one of the secretaries."

When Baum returned to graduate school on a fellowship from the Polytechnic Institute of New York, she taught a class. "I was really excited about the process of transmitting knowledge and seeing students' faces light up with understanding," she said in *U.S. Woman Engineer.*

From Industry to Academia

After earning her master's degree and Ph.D. in 1961 and 1964 respectively, she joined the engineering faculty at Pratt Institute and was once again the only woman. She was promoted to chair of the electrical engineering department in 1971 and dean in 1984. She created opportunities for disadvantaged minority youth, significantly increased enrollment, and established outreach programs to community colleges. In 1973, the Institute of Electrical and Electronic Engineers recognized her with the Outstanding Faculty Award and, in 1981, she received the Outstanding Professor Award from the National Society of Black Engineers.

Advances Engineering Education for Women

In 1987, Baum became dean of The Cooper Union Albert Nerken School of Engineering and a fellow of the Society of Women Engineers (SWE). She increased the number of women enrolled in engineering at Cooper Union from about 5% to more than 30% (double the national average); modernized laboratories; encouraged innovative ways to educate students; expanded the curriculum to include leadership skills, entrepreneurship, and ethics; and upgraded curriculums by encouraging interaction between government, industry, and academia.

Baum also established the SWE student section at Pratt Institute, has organized numerous career days, given many speeches on engineering careers for women, and sponsored national surveys on female student and professional engineers. She was a member of the first advisory board for Women in Engineering Program Advocates Network, and is a member of the National Research Council's Commission on Engineering and Technical Systems. As chair of the New York Academy of Sciences, she explores how different science and engineering disciplines can work together, and is applying this approach at Cooper Union since she believes major advances are made in areas where disciplines intersect.

Takes a Global View of Engineering

Through her roles as president of the ASEE and the accreditation board for Engineering and Technology, and as chair of the National Engineering Deans Council, Baum has helped American engineering education gain international visibility. "Engineering is now global in nature," Baum said in an interview with Sheppard. Baum is exploring areas of cooperation between universities in several countries through the National Science Foundation, National Research Council, and the Accreditation Board for Engineering and Technology. Baum has presented keynote addresses around the world, and chairs the Washington Accord—an agreement between English speaking nations dealing with equivalency of academic credentials for engineers.

Baum received the 1988 Emily Warren Roebling Award from National Women's Hall of Fame, the 1990 Upward Mobility Award from SWE, and the 1990 Woman of Distinction Award from the National Association of Student Leaders. In 1996, she was a founding inductee in the Women in Technology International Hall of Fame, received the Townsend Harris medal from the City College of New York and the Gruenwald Award from the Institute of Electronic and Electrical Engineers in 1997, and has been granted honorary doctorate degrees from a number of universities, including Notre Dame, Union College, the New Jersey Institute of Technology, Trinity College, and the Colorado School of Mines. She is a director of Allegheny Energy Inc., the United States Trust Company, and Avnet Corporation—the world's largest distributor of electrical components.

Baum is married to Paul Baum, a physics professor at Queens College, and has two daughters, Elizabeth and Jennifer. Baum, who credits her husband's support for being able to combine her career with motherhood, wants to change the perception of engineering from "nerdy" to one that helps solves society's problems. "Making life better for people is what engineering is all about," she emphasized in an interview with Sheppard.

SELECTED WRITINGS BY BAUM:

Other

Women in Engineering: Creating a Professional Workforce for the 21st Century, The Second Annual Elvera and William Stuckenberg Lecture in Technology and Human Affairs, Washington University in St. Louis, April 23, 1991.

Keynote Address: "Engineering Education for the 21st Century," UNESCO Conference on Engineering Education, Paris, 1996

Keynote Address: "New Paradigms for U.S. Engineering Education," Siemens International Symposium on Research and Engineering Education in a Global Society, Berlin, 1997

Chair and Presenter, "Desired Attributes of Engineering Graduates," International Conference on Engineering Accreditation, San Francisco, 1998

Keynote Address: "U.S. Engineering Accreditation," Latin American Conference on Engineering Education, Rio Dejanero, Brazil 1998

Keynote Address: "Importance of Workforce Technological Ability," IEEE Conference on Technological Literacy, Baltimore, 1998

Keynote Address: "Advances in Outcomes–based Educational Evaluation," Indian Conference on Trends in Engineering, Bangalore, 1998

"Distance Education and Professions," CHEA Conference on Education, San Diego, 1999

"Corporate Universities," College Industry Education Conference, Palm Springs, 1999

FURTHER READING

Periodicals

"Eleanor Baum Appointed Dean of Engineering." *U.S. Woman Engineer* (January/February 1985): 42–43.

"Eleanor Baum: Upward Mobility Award." *U.S. Woman Engineer* (September/October 1990): 24

West, Arlene. "Feminist at Work" *Woman Engineer* (winter 1991): 26–27

Baldwin, Joyce. "Training Engineers That Defy Stereotypes." *The New York Times* (June 4, 1989).

Other

Sheppard, Laurel. Interview with Eleanor Baum, conducted March 22, 1999.

Sketch by Laurel M. Sheppard

Elise Jenny Bäumgartel
1892–1975
German-born British archaeologist

Elise Jenny Bäumgartel is best remembered for her work on the earliest phases of Egyptian society and her penetrating critiques of the work of other archaeologists.

Born Elise Jenny Goldschmidt in 1892 to a prominent Berlin family, Bäumgartel was educated at home by a French governess, and then entered the University of Berlin with the intention of studying medicine. Instead, she switched to Egyptology, and became a student of the highly influential Professor Kurt Sethe, whose achievements included translations of pyramid texts and New Kingdom historical documents. In 1914, she married art historian Hubert Bäumgartel and subsequently had three daughters. The daughters occupied a central place in her life, but the marriage itself did not last.

Bäumgartel went on to the University of Königsberg, where she received a doctorate in 1927. Her thesis was on the Neolithic period in Tunis, Algiers, and neighboring countries. Upon completing her Ph.D., she worked in Berlin and traveled to excavations in Egypt, Italy, and Palestine. In the early years of her career, she focused on establishing that Egyptian funerary architecture of the first dynasties was a fusion of the native single-grave tradition with megalithic influences from the West. By doing so, she challenged some of the prevailing views of the day.

In 1934 she left Germany with her daughters. First she went to Paris, where she studied flints, and then on to London. Encouraged by Professor Sir John L. Myers to stay in England, she took a position in the Egyptology Department of University College, London, succeeding the trailblazing Margaret Murray. For the next 20 years, Bäumgartel struggled against financial instability, depending on grants and dividing her time between University College, Manchester Museum, and Oxford.

At University College, Bäumgartel began cataloguing the extensive collection of artifacts in the university's Neolithic collection, most of which was from Sir William Flinders Petrie's 1896 excavations at Naqada. The overwhelming majority of Petrie's findings, significant as they were, had never been published. When World War II broke out in the fall of 1939, the university was forced to close and pack up the collection for safekeeping. The London blitzes partially destroyed University College, and the flooding that ensued damaged some of the artifacts.

Bäumgartel left London for Oxford and entered what was to become a long-term working relationship with the Griffith Institute in the University of Oxford. While waiting out the war, she decided it was imperative to publish the results of her research at University College. She obtained funding from the Griffith Institute, and in 1947 *The Cultures of Prehistoric Egypt, I* was published. The volume was revised in 1954, and a companion piece, *The Cultures of Prehistoric Egypt, II,* was published in 1960. Her work was enthusiastically received and sparked much debate. She questioned Petrie's dating and its resulting implications. The book also critiqued the work of her former teacher, Kurt Sethe, and dispelled his theory of the origins and sequence of pharaonic civilization and the dating of the Neolithic period. In *The Cultures of Prehistoric Egypt, II*, she also examined the rise of urban life.

In 1957, Bäumgartel left England to join her family in the United States. For several years, she stayed in the States, concentrating on the family business and working at the Oriental Institute in Chicago. In 1964, she returned to Oxford in 1964. Serendipitiously, a lost box of Petrie's papers known as "the London box" was discovered under a telephone at University College, and so began her last book, *Petrie's Naqada Excavations, A Supplement.*

Bäumgartel's remaining years were spent at Oxford, where she continued her research and writing. The latter period of her life remained fruitful and productive, with her work still regarded as penetrating and insightful. Her final publication, "Some Remarks on the Origins of the Titles of the Archaic Egyptian Kings," appeared in 1975, the same year as her death.

SELECTED WRTINGS BY BÄUMGARTEL:

Books

The Cultures of Prehistoric Egypt, 1. London: Oxford University Press, 1947.

The Cultures of Prehistoric Egypt, 1. Revised edition. London: Oxford University Press, 1955.

The Cultures of Prehistoric Egypt, 2. London: Oxford University Press, 1960.

Petrie's Naqada Excavation: A Supplement. London: Quartich, 1970.

Periodicals

"The Flint Quarries of Wady Sheykh." *Ancient Egypt,* [15], (1930): 103–108.

"The Cire Perdue Process." *Antiquity,* 37, (1963): 295–96.

"The Predynastic Cemetery at Naqada," *Antiquity,* 39, (1965): 299.

"Some Remarks on the Origins of the Titles of the Archiac Egyptian Kings." *JEA*, 61, (1975): 28–32.

FURTHER READING

Books

Hoffman, Michael A. *Egypt Before The Pharaohs.* New York: Barnes & Noble Books, 1993.

Winstone, H.V.F. *Uncovering The Ancient* World. New York: Facts on File, 1986.

Periodicals

Donohue, V.A. "A Bibliography of Elise Jenny Bäumgartel." *Journal of Egyptian Archaeology,* 63, (1977): 48–51.

Payne, Joan Crowfoot, "Appreciation." *Journal of Egyptian Archaeology* 62, (1976): 3–4.

Sketch by Anne M. Perusek

Aphra Behn
1640–1689
English writer and translator

Aphra Behn is best known as a playwright and novelist, and one of the first women to make a living as a professional writer. Her significance to science is her translation of *Entretiens sur la pluralité des mondes,* a book about an enlightened woman's astronomy education. Her

Aphra Behn

novel *Oroonoko, or the History of the Royal Slave* is considered to be a useful anthropological study of the practice of slavery.

She was born around July 1640 in Wye, Kent, probably as Aphra Johnson. Her parents were Amy and John Johnson. Although accounts differ as to her childhood and youth, apparently she spent several years with her family in Surinam, which was then a British colony. (Her father may have been the lieutenant general there.) Following her return to England (sometime between 1658 and 1663) she married a merchant named Behn who died not long afterwards.

Behn somehow made a connection with the court of King Charles II, who sent her to Antwerp, Belgium as a spy against the nearby Dutch (with whom England was at war). Upon her return, she was apparently engaged in a number of adventures that brought her into contact with several of the better known writers of the day. Partly to give herself a steady income, and partly because she was a good writer and observer of her surroundings, she became a professional writer, penning some 45 works, including novels, poems, and plays.

In addition to original writing, Behn also translated the works of other writers. One such work was Fontenelle's *Entretiens sur la Pluralité des Mondes (A Plurality of Worlds)*, which was a treatise that detailed a woman's study of astronomy. Behn's 1686 translation was well received; she noted in her preface to the work that she would have preferred to do original research on astronomy, were it not for her lack of "health and leisure."

Oroonoko, which she wrote in 1688, tells the story of an African prince who is enslaved and taken to South America. The novel provided a vivid picture of the slave trade and its effects on both the enslaved and the enslavers. In later years, some scholars have questioned whether Behn actually went to Surinam (which is where she claimed to have gotten her information for the book) or whether she merely read books on South America. Most scholars do believe that Behn did spend time in South America. But even during her lifetime, her unique status as a female professional writer opened her up to numerous criticisms and rumors. Despite the uncertainty about her life and works, she remains an important figure in the history of women in science. After her death on April 16, 1689, she was given the honor of burial in Westminster Abbey.

SELECTED WRITINGS BY BEHN:

Books

Oroonoko and other writings. Oxford: Oxford University Press, 1998.

FURTHER READING

Books

Drabble, Margaret, ed. *The Oxford Companion to English Literature.* Oxford: Oxford University Press, 1985.

Goreau, Angeline, *Reconstructing Aphra: A Social Biography of Aphra Behn.* The Dial Press, 1980.

Oglivie, Marilyn Bailey. *Women in Science: Antiquity through the Nineteenth Century.* Cambridge: MIT Press, 1986.

Other

"Aphra Behn." *Britannica Online.* http://www.eb.com:195 (July 14, 1999).

Sketch by George A. Milite

Jocelyn Susan (Bell) Burnell
1943–
Irish astronomer

Jocelyn Susan Bell Burnell is the astronomer who discovered stars that release regular bursts of radio waves, known as pulsars, while working under Antony Hewish at Cambridge University. Hewish was awarded the

Jocelyn Bell Burnell (Photograph by Jonathan Blair. Corbis-Bettmann. Reproduced by permission.)

Nobel Prize in 1974 for this discovery and Bell Burnell was not included in the citation. She has been Senior Research Fellow at the Royal Observatory in Edinburgh, Scotland, since 1982, and following the discovery of pulsars her work has concentrated on gamma-ray and infrared astronomy, as well as millimeter wave astronomy.

Bell Burnell was born in Belfast, Northern Ireland, on July 15, 1943. Her father was an architect who designed the Armagh Observatory, an astronomical observatory which was close to their home, and her early interest in astronomy was encouraged by the observatory staff. Bell Burnell attended the Mount School in York and then the University of Glasgow in Scotland, where she earned her B.S. degree in 1965. That same year, she began work on her Ph.D. under Hewish at Cambridge.

Discovers Pulsars While Looking for Quasars

Bell Burnell chose to do her doctoral work on recently discovered quasars—star formations the size of galaxies that are so distant from Earth that they appear to be single stars. She worked in radio astronomy, as opposed to optical astronomy, and she spent her first two years as a graduate student building a special radio telescope designed by Hewish to pick up and record rapid variations in radio signals. Radio telescopes have an advantage over visible-light telescopes in that they can pick up radiation in the form of long wavelength radio waves from objects in deep space that cannot be seen using an optical telescope.

In 1964 astronomers had discovered that the radio signals given off by sources in spaces were not always steady, just as light from stars (visible wavelengths of radiation) appears to twinkle. This twinkling of radio signals, called scintillation, could be used to calculate the size of radio source, if it were known how much the signal varied as its radio waves passed through the wispy gas between planets. The radio telescope which Hewish had designed was able to record time variations in the strength of radio sources. The telescope had over 2,000 separate receivers spread out over four acres. It was constantly receiving and recording signals onto rolls of paper, producing some 400 feet of charts every week. Once the telescope was operating in July of 1967, it was Bell Burnell's job to make sense out of the signals recorded by the instrument.

The month after the receivers were in place, in August of 1967, Bell Burnell noticed some curious variations in signals which had been recorded at about midnight the night before. They came from the direction opposite the sun, between the stars Vega and Altair. This seemed odd, because strong changes in signals from quasars occur as a result of the solar wind and thus are usually weak during the night. This source gave off short bursts of energy, lasting less than one hundredth of a second and occurring very rapidly, though at precise intervals.

Bell Burnell approached Hewish with the problem, and he thought there was a problem with the equipment. If it was not a problem with the new telescope, he believed it was a ham radio, car ignition, or some other local radio wave or electrical transmission causing interference. No one realized at the time that stars could emit radio waves that began and ended so quickly, and there was a good reason why they believed stars could not do such a thing: A star giving off a signal that rapid would have to be very, very small, and if it were that small it could not possibly have enough energy to travel so far. Hewish had her check out the instruments many more times to eliminate any possible source of interference.

No interference or problems with the telescope were found. The scintillating star continued to wink at her through the radio telescope, and the signals grew earlier and earlier each night, just as stars appear to do. After a month of precise observation, Bell Burnell was able to establish that the signals continued and remained fixed with respect to the stars—which meant they were coming from somewhere other than the earth or the sun. By November, Bell Burnell measured some strong signals. The rapid set of pulses occurred regularly every 1.3373013 seconds and lasted for only 0.016 of a second.

This extraordinary regularity was perhaps the most compelling aspect of these signals. The research team felt obliged, at least initially, to consider the possibility that the source of the signals was a beacon from some extraterrestrial civilization. Initially, the source of the signals was jokingly named LGM 1, for Little Green Men 1. Hewish wanted to be sure that LGM 1 was not an anomaly, and searching through miles and miles of charts recorded in previous months, Bell Burnell found three other sources with similar signals. Soon other members of the team found other sources of these signals. Hewish named the sources "pulsating stars," and the term was soon contracted to pulsars, because they pulsated at regular intervals. He announced the discovery on February 9, 1968. Some British tabloid newspapers distorted the nature of the discovery and claimed scientists had made contact with alien civilizations.

The pulsars were named for the observatories where they were found: CP for the Cambridge Pulsar, HP for Harvard, and so on, followed by four numbers that indicated their location in the sky. The biggest theoretical problem with all of these signals was the short duration of the burst and their rapid repetition. Calculations based on what was known about the radio emissions from other stars continued to indicate a source which, by astronomical standards, was extremely small. The pulsars had to be less than ten miles in radius, when the radius of an average star is hundreds of thousands of miles. Furthermore, a star like our sun could not turn on and off in less than two seconds. Hewish initially speculated that they were either white-dwarf stars or perhaps even neutron stars—stars that had been predicted but never seen.

It was an astrophysicist named Thomas Gold who solved this problem. Working across the Atlantic at Cornell University in New York, Gold hypothesized that the pulsars must be neutron stars that resulted from the explosion of a supernova. The existence of neutron stars had been predicted by Russian theorist and Nobel Prize winner Lev Davidovich Landau. When a star is dying, the outer parts explode, causing a bright light known to astronomers as a supernova. But what happens to its inner core is a compression: Rather than exploding, it implodes. The star's inner mass squeezes so tightly together that it actually overcomes the forces that hold atoms together. It pulls the electrons right into the nuclei, and the electrons and protons of the matter join, forming neutrons. Furthermore, all of this mass close to the center of the imploded star causes it to spin very fast.

Neutron stars would be very small in diameter, but incredibly dense with matter, 1015 times the density of water. (The one Bell Burnell found could only be about ten miles in diameter.) Gold argued that the LGM signals were from neutron stars; these stars would be small, very dense spheres spinning rapidly, which would cause an intense magnetic field. Ionized atomic particles rotating within the field would create a narrow beam of radiation that would turn around rapidly, and the radio waves would appear through the radio telescope as a beam similar to a lighthouse beacon flashing periodically in our direction.

Gold's theory was almost completely ignored at first, and this interpretation of the Bell Burnell's data obviously needed some support. The support came late in 1968 when two other astronomers, David Staelin and Edward Reifenstein at the National Radio Astronomy Observatory at Green Bank, West Virginia, found a pulsar which they named NP 0532. It was located right at the center of the Crab Nebula, the remains of an exploded supernova. The scientific community acknowledged that pulsars were indeed neutron stars.

After the discovery of pulsars and the completion of her doctorate, Bell Burnell accepted a position at the University of Southampton and began working on gamma–ray astronomy. Like radio astronomy, gamma–ray astronomy involves detecting signals from space. The difference is the length of the waves involved: Along the radio spectrum, radio signals have the longest wavelengths and gamma rays have the shortest. The visible spectrum, the light used in an optical telescope, lies somewhere in between these extremes. From 1974 to 1982 Bell Burnell worked at the Mullard Space Science Laboratory in X–ray astronomy using signals from the British satellite Ariel V. Along the spectrum, X rays are longer in wavelength than gamma rays, but still shorter than the visible spectrum. In 1982 Bell Burnell was appointed Senior Research fellow at the Royal Observatory in Edinburgh, Scotland. Her research there has continued in detecting and analyzing spectra that come from different parts of the sky using a variety of techniques, including optical astronomy, infrared astronomy, and millimeter wave astronomy.

Bell Burnell was awarded the Michelson Medal from the Franklin Institute in Philadelphia in 1973. She won the J. Robert Oppenheimer Memorial Prize in 1978, the Beatrice M. Tinsley Prize from the American Astronomical Society in 1987, and the Herschel Medal from the Royal Astronomical Society in 1989. She is a member of the Royal Astronomical Society and the International Astronomical Union. Bell Burnell is married and has one child.

FURTHER READING

Books

Branley, Franklyn M. *Black Holes, White Dwarves, and Supernovas.* Crowell, 1976, pp. 78–82.

Fisher, David E. *The Origin and Evolution of Our Own Particular Universe.* Atheneum, 1988, pp. 94–99.

Halperin, Paul. *Cosmic Wormholes: The Search for Interstellar Shortcuts.* Dutton, 1992, pp. 45–48.

Shipman, Harry L. *Black Holes, Quasars, and the Universe.* Houghton Mifflin, 1976, pp. 51–53.

World of Scientific Discovery. Detroit: Gale, 1994, p. 72–73.

Sketch by Barbara A. Branca

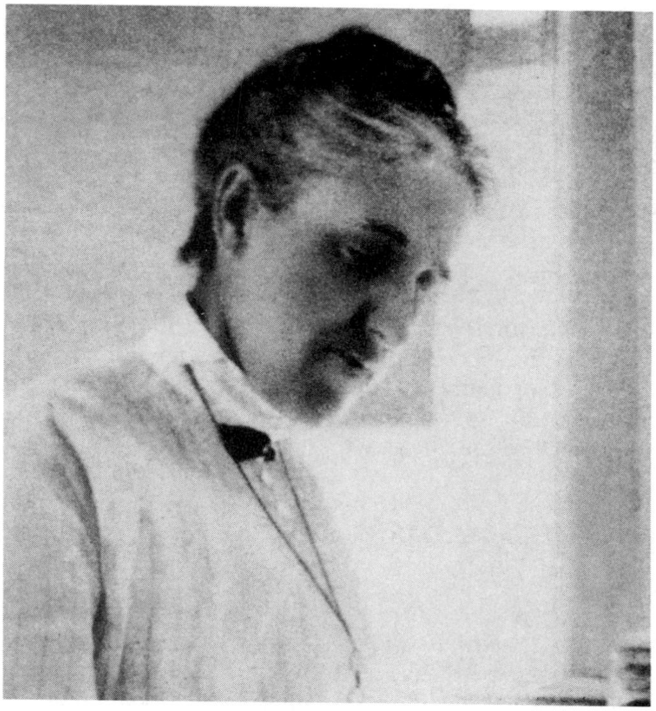

Ruth Fulton Benedict (The Library of Congress. Reproduced by permission.)

Ruth Fulton Benedict
1887–1948
American anthropologist

Ruth Fulton Benedict was America's first woman anthropologist and, for many years, the country's leading specialist in the field. Benedict was best known for her "patterns of culture" theory that combined philosophy, sociology, psychology, and anthropology to explain, in part, how all human behavior and thought is culturally relative and distinct.

Benedict was born in New York, New York, on June 5, 1887, to Frederick Samuel Fulton, a surgeon, and Beatrice Joanna (Shattuck) Fulton. Benedict did not have a happy childhood; when she was not quite three years old and her sister, Margery, was an infant, their father died of a fever. Their mother Beatrice, distraught with what Benedict would later call a "cult of grief," moved with her children to her parents' central New York farm. A Vassar College graduate, Benedict's mother was able to find work teaching school in Missouri and Minnesota and working at the Buffalo Public Library, supporting her family on a meager $60 a month. After a bout with the measles, the young Benedict lost most of her hearing. Of her childhood, Benedict later said in her autobiography, "Happiness was a world I lived in all by myself, and for precious moments."

Benedict attended Vassar College on a scholarship, graduating Phi Beta Kappa in 1909, with a degree in English literature. She traveled to Europe before moving back in with her mother and doing charity work in Buffalo. In 1911 she moved to California to teach at two girls' schools until 1914. Because she disliked the work and feared becoming a spinster like so many other teachers, she agreed to marry Stanley Rossiter Benedict, a biochemist about whom she had mixed feelings.

The couple married on June 18, 1914 and afterwards moved to New York where Stanley Benedict became a professor at Cornell Medical School. The Benedicts wanted children, but Ruth unable to conceive. Feeling hopeless and without focus, Benedict turned to her love of reading and writing in order to find meaning in her life. She wrote poetry, later published under the pseudonym Anne Singleton in several literary journals, and began work on a book about three female writers, of which only the section on Mary Wollstonecraft was ever completed. She also began doing charity work again, but soon became dissatisfied.

Finds Calling in Anthropology

Writing and charity work did not fulfill Benedict, so she enrolled at Columbia University's New School for Social Research in 1919. She discovered the field of anthropology, and received her Ph.D. in 1923, after studying with Franz Boas, the leader in the field at that time. She had also served as his teaching assistant at Barnard where **Margaret Mead** was her student. In 1923, Benedict became a lecturer at Columbia University, a position she held until 1930. Benedict was also appointed editor of *Journal of American Folklore* in 1923, which she worked on until 1940. She also served as president of the American Anthropological Society and the American Ethnological Association from 1927–1929. Although she and her husband were separated, and her work with students and on the distribution of grant money for field work was very important, Boas paid Benedict very little money because she was married.

Much of an anthropologist's education comes from field trips—observing cultures at work. Benedict's field trips involved observing Native American tribes in the summers. In 1922 she observed the Serrano tribe in California; from 1924–1926 she observed the Zuni and Pirma tribes in New Mexico; in 1931 she observed the Mescalaro Apaches, also in New Mexico; and in 1939 she observed the Blackfoot tribe in Montana. Because she was hard of hearing, field work was especially difficult for Benedict. She had to rely on interpreters and her time in the field was always short. Margaret Mead later said that she thought Benedict enjoyed working with her students' field notes and work in preference to her own field work.

Evolves Patterns of Culture Theory

In 1931 Boas appointed Benedict to assistant professor at Columbia. By this time she and her husband were completely separated and Boas realized that her financial situation had changed. During this time she began to work on the ideas which would become her groundbreaking book *Patterns of Culture*. Her view of culture was holistic and she believed that each culture had its own personality and distinct identity. Consequently, one culture's values and personality should never be imposed on another's, no matter what the intention. In her theory she proposed that a culture's personality made it emphasize certain characteristics in the members of that culture. She believed, for example, that the most valued personality in Western culture was the wealthy, social–climbing male. Benedict felt that this personality, although emphasized and encouraged by Western culture, could be that society's downfall, because of the pathology of the personality type. Her theories explained why certain personality types would be outcasts in one society and preferred in another. In every culture, she believed, the members of society are made to fit in, to conform, to become part of the whole. While ideals varied by culture, the pattern never did.

When *Patterns of Culture* was published in 1934, Benedict's theory was controversial, not only in the anthropological community, but also in society as a whole. Translated into 14 languages, the book revolutionized anthropological study and was still used as the standard introduction to anthropology 25 years after it was published. That same year she was named a fellow at the New York Academy of Sciences. Two years after the publication of *Patterns* Benedict was promoted to associate professor, the same year she became editor of *Columbia University Contributions to Anthropology* and acting executive officer of the anthropology department. In 1937, she was named executive officer.

Speaks Out Against Racism and War in Publications

In the 1930s, during Hitler's rise to power, Benedict began to believe that anthropologists were obligated to educate the public on race in society. With this in mind, she wrote *Race: Science and Politics*, which spoke out heavily against racism. This book was somewhat eclipsed by a pamphlet she wrote with anthropologist Gene Weltfish in 1943 titled "The Races of Mankind." A furor was caused when the U.S. Army's Morale Division proposed distributing the pamphlet and this was opposed by southern congressman. However, instead of suppressing the pamphlet, the opposition only resulted in private organizations copying and distributing it. Following this, Benedict was invited to work in Washington's Office of War Information to observe and learn about foreign cultures during World War II. During this time she traveled to Europe, Thailand, and Japan.

In 1945 she left government service and took a leave of absence from Columbia to write *The Chrysanthemum and the Sword: Patterns of Japanese Culture*. This book was a culmination of her patterns of culture theory, her work at Columbia, and her experiences overseas. It explored the intricacies and balance of power in Japanese society and attempted to explain complex issues of war. After the book's publication, Benedict's fame and respect grew. She was offered a grant by the Office of Naval Research to create and direct a program of research called "Contemporary Cultures" at Columbia. The university promoted her to full professor soon after. In 1946 she served as vice president of the American Psychopathological Association and was president of the American Anthropological Association from 1947 until her death. Benedict did not have long to enjoy her new position or the recognition that came from her publications. On September 17, 1948, she died of coronary thrombosis (heart attack), only a few short months after her appointment to professor. At the time of her death, Benedict was the premiere American anthropologist after Boas and before Mead.

SELECTED WRITINGS BY BENEDICT:

Books

The Chrysanthemum and the Sword. New York: Houghton Mifflin, 1946.
Race: Science and Politics. New York: Modern Age Books, 1940.
Patterns of Culture. New York: Houghton Mifflin, 1934.
Zuni Mythology. New York: Columbia University Press, 1935.

FURTHER READING

Books

Bailey, Martha J. *American Women in Science*. Denver, CO: ABC–CLIO, 1994.
James, Edward T. et al, eds. *Notable American Women 1607–1950*. Cambridge: Belknap Press, 1971.
Mead, Margaret. *An Anthropologist at Work*. Cambridge: Houghton Mifflin, 1959.
Mead, Margaret. *Ruth Benedict*. New York: Columbia University Press, 1974.

Sketch by Helene Barker Kiser

Ruth Mary Roan Benerito
1916–
American physical chemist

Wrinkle-free, drip-dry cotton may not seem like a scientific discovery, but it was the work of the chemist Ruth Benerito that led to its development. More germane to science, perhaps, she also developed glasslike cotton fibers that became important in the development of laboratory equipment. Not surprisingly, she has been honored several times by both the American Chemical Society and the U.S. Department of Agriculture.

Ruth Mary Roan was born in New Orleans on January 12, 1916 to John Edward and Bernadette Elizardi Roan. Her father was a civil engineer and her mother was an artist, so young Ruth and her five brothers and sisters grew up in intellectually stimulating environment. Ruth proved to be an outstanding student; she graduated from high school at 14 and entered Sophie Newcomb College (then the women's college of Tulane University) a year later. Science was her chief interest; she majored in chemistry and minored in physics and mathematics. She received her bachelor of science degree at age 19 in 1935, and from there went on to do graduate work for a year in Pennsylvania at Bryn Mawr College.

She returned to New Orleans, but the U.S. in 1936 was in the middle of the Great Depression and job opportunities were almost nonexistent. She worked briefly without pay as a lab technician in a hospital, and then secured a position as a social worker with the U.S. Works Progress Administration. She also taught science and math in the public school system. At the time "science" was a bit more broadly based a discipline; one of the courses Benerito was required to teach was driver's education.

During this time, she was also taking courses at Newcomb, from which she received her master's degree in 1938. In 1940 she then took a teaching position at Randolph–Macon Women's College in Lynchburg, Virginia. She returned to New Orleans in 1943 and taught physical chemistry at Newcomb (and at Tulane) for the next 10 years. During these years she worked part–time on her doctorate at the University of Chicago, which she was awarded in 1948. Two years later she married Frank Benerito, a marriage that lasted until his death in 1970.

From Chlorine Scorch to Solar Energy

In 1953, Benerito left Newcomb–Tulane (although she remained an adjunct professor) to join the U.S. Department of Agriculture's Southern Research Center in New Orleans. For her first five years there she worked with the Intravenous Fat Program, in which she studied triglycerides to discover new ways to analyze proteins and fats. Her work was useful in determining the caloric intake necessary for people who were being fed intravenously.

Benerito also studied cotton during this time, and in 1958 she became research leader in the USDA's Cotton Chemical Reactions Laboratory. It was while studying cotton that Benerito made some of her most important contributions to science.

Some of her research was important primarily from a commercial standpoint. Her findings helped create a fabric with crease resistance in other words, minimal wrinkling. These finding also helped eradicate the problem of chlorine scorch, which could ruin cotton clothing. In the late 1950s, the cotton industry was facing stiff competition from the manufacturers of synthetic fabrics, which did not wrinkle or stain. Now that cotton was more versatile, it could compete with artificial materials.

Other research had a more direct impact on scientific technique. Benerito found that cotton soaked with sodium plumbite (a lead compound) produced a glassy substance when heated. This substance, which could be molded to fit around glass or porcelain lab containers, turned out to be electroconductive. It was important not only in the development of specialized lab equipment, but to electronic and solar energy research as well. Additional research on cotton fibers also led to breakthroughs in the development of flame–retardant fabric.

Benerito remained with the USDA until her retirement in 1986, and continued to serve as adjunct professor at Tulane, where she later was named professor emerita. The USDA awarded her its Distinguished Service Award twice (1964 and 1970) and its Outstanding Professional Award in 1986. In addition to several regional awards from the American Chemical Society, she also won the Garvan Medal in 1970.

FURTHER READING

Books

Shearer, Benjamin F. and Barbara S, Shearer, eds. *Notable Women in the Physical Sciences: A Biographical Dictionary.* Westport, CT: Greenwood Press, 1997.

Who's Who in Government. 1st ed. Chicago: Marquis Who's Who, 1972.

Sketch by George A. Milite

Marie Catherine Biheron
1719–1786
French anatomist

Marie Catherine Biheron was famous throughout eighteenth-century Europe for her anatomically precise wax models of the human body. These models included moveable parts that could be used for demonstrations in classes. Her collection of models eventually was sent to Catherine the Great of Russia to add to the collection of the Academy of Sciences in St. Petersburg.

Born in Paris in 1719, Biheron, of Anglo-French ancestry, was the daughter of an apothecary, or pharmacist. Despite her relatively impoverished background, she was able to obtain a good education and studied illustration with Madeleine Basseporte, a botanical artist at the Paris Royal Gardens. Little is known of Biheron's life, although she is mentioned in the memoirs of the French philosopher Denis Diderot, his friend Baron Melchior von Grimm, and the playwright Comtess de Genlis. Basseporte encouraged Biheron, who never married, to study anatomy as a way to support herself. Since cadavers for dissections were difficult to obtain, there was a demand for wax anatomical models to be used in medical and midwifery schools. It is unclear how Biheron obtained her anatomical knowledge, but it has been said that she hired men to steal cadavers from the military and that she kept them stored in a glass case in her garden.

Biheron became famous for the accuracy and precision of her models. As Londa Schiebinger quoted from Sir John Pringle, the physician-general of Britain and later president of the Royal Society, her models were so life-like that "They want nothing but the smell." The chemical formula of the material she used in her models was a secret. Some did not believe she used wax, since her models didn't melt when heated.

Biheron sold her models and supported herself by opening her collection to the public, for a small fee, every Wednesday for 30 years. She also taught anatomy in her home, and Diderot, and Genlis were among her pupils. At one point, she was censured by the physicians and surgeons of Paris for interfering with their trade. Apparently, they were particularly upset that she was attracting male students away from their classes. Twice, Biheron traveled to London to look for work, without success. However after viewing her models, the physicians William and John Hunter were inspired to open their own museum of comparative anatomy.

In 1759, the anatomist Jean Morand invited Biheron to display her work at the Académie Royale des Sciences. As Schiebinger quoted from the records of the presentation, whereas the leading wax modeler of the past "showed only the position and color of the different parts of the human body, Biheron has reproduced exactly the consistency, suppleness, and weight of the brain, kidneys, intestine, and other parts of the human body."

Women anatomists usually specialized in models of the female body and the stages of fetal development. Biheron was invited to the Académie in 1770 to display her moveable model of a pregnant woman, which exactly reproduced the stages of birth, including a cervix which dilated and an infant which could be removed. The model was designed to teach students methods for dealing with difficult deliveries. The following year, Biheron was invited back to demonstrate her models for Crown Prince Gustavus of Sweden. She was accompanied by the famous chemist Antoine Lavoisier, and even women of the court were allowed to attend this special session. Gustavus reportedly offered Biheron a position as demonstrator of anatomy at the University of Sweden.

In 1830, Biheron's models were still being cited in the proceedings of the Académie. The only record left by Biheron was a four–page advertisement for her collection.

SELECTED WRITINGS BY BIHERON:

Other

Anatomie Artificielle. (advertisement for her collection) Paris, 1761.

FURTHER READING

Books

Mozans, H. J. [John Augustine Zahm]. *Women in Science.* 1913. Reprint, Cambridge: MIT Press, 1974.

Schiebinger, Londa. *The Mind Has No Sex? Women in the Origins of Modern Science.* Cambridge: Harvard University Press, 1989.

Sketch by Margaret Alic

Isabella Lucy Bird
1831–1904
British travel writer and naturalist

Isabella Bird was an intrepid Victorian explorer who traveled the world on her own, studying natural history and geography. Her accounts of her adventures remain popular to this day.

Isabella Lucy Bird was born in 1831, at Boroughbridge Hall in Yorkshire, England, the daughter of Dora (Lawson) and Edward Bird. Her father was an evangelical Anglican clergyman and her mother was a clergyman's daughter. Bird suffered from a spinal disease as a child, and she suffered from backaches, headaches, and depression. She traveled for her health and, indeed, her symptoms were much less severe when she found herself in an exotic locale.

After an operation in 1854, her father gave her money to make a voyage. Bird spent several months in North America and published her first book about her experiences there. In 1858, after her father's death, Bird moved with her mother and sister Henrietta to Edinburgh, Scotland. She made several shorter journeys in the following years.

In 1872, at the advice of Dr. John Bishop, her sister's physician, Bird traveled to Australia and New Zealand. Disappointed in those places, she headed for California in a leaky paddle steamer that barely made it to Honolulu. She spent six months in the frontiers of the Hawaiian Islands, and the 31 letters she wrote to her sister constituted the bulk of her book on this adventure, augmented with chapters on the Molokai leper colony, native life and the natural history of the islands, and Hawaiian history. Her horsemanship

Isabella Lucy Bird (The Granger Collection, New York. Reproduced by permission.)

served her well, allowing her to visit remote locales that were unexplored by Europeans.

Returning via the United States, Bird recounted the story of her relationship with the trapper "Rocky Mountain Jim" Nugent, as well as the geology and natural history of the Rocky Mountains, in her book *A Lady's Life in the Rockies*. Again, the book was an edited version of letters she wrote to her sister, which was originally serialized in *Leisure Hour* magazine. It was published in the United States and Great Britain, and translated into French. The work clearly established her as an early conservationist. Unwilling to marry Jim, she returned to Scotland and then journeyed to Japan, Indonesia, and the Middle East.

Bird married John Bishop in 1881. Following his death five years later, she studied medicine in London and then traveled to India as a medical missionary. She established hospitals in the Punjab and Kashmir and then traveled through Afghanistan and Persia (Iran) to the Black Sea. Returning to England, she lectured at the British Association, became the first woman Fellow of the Royal Geographical Society, and spoke out against the atrocities being committed against the Armenians in the Middle East.

Bird's last journey, from 1894 to 1897, took her to Canada, Japan, Korea, and China. In China, she traveled 8,000 miles (12,872 km) alone, through Szechwan Province to Tibet. Bird's books were extremely popular, going through many editions and revisions. She died in 1904 in Edinburgh, after a long illness.

SELECTED WRITINGS BY BIRD:

Books

The Englishwoman in America. 1856. Reprint, Madison: University of Wisconsin Press, 1966.

The Hawaiian Archipelago. Six Months Among the Palm Groves, Coral Reefs and Volcanoes of the Sandwich Islands. 7th ed. 1875. Reprint, Rutland, VT: Charles E. Tuttle,1974.

Unbeaten Tracks in Japan; an Account of Travels on Horseback in the Interior, including Visits to the Aborigines of Yezo and the Shrines of Nikkô and Isé. New York: G. P. Putnam's Sons, 1881.

A Lady's Life in the Rockies. Edited by Ernest S. Bernard. Norman: University of Oklahoma Press, 1999.

FURTHER READING

Books

Barr, Pat. *A Curious Life for a Lady: The Story of Isabella Bird, A Remarkable Victorian Traveller*. Garden City, NY: Doubleday, 1970.

Middleton, Dorothy. *Victorian Lady Travellers*. New York: Dutton, 1965.

Stoddart, Anna. *The Life of Isabella Bird*. London: John Murray, 1906.

Sketch by Margaret Alic

Anna Blackburne
1726–1793
British naturalist

Anna Blackburne was a highly regarded naturalist and prominent collector of plants and animals. She maintained gardens and a museum that served as sources of reference specimens for other naturalists.

Anna Blackburne, born in 1726, was fifth of nine children of Katherine Ashton (or Assheton) and John Blackburne of Orford Hall, near Warrington, in Lancashire, England. Her father was a wealthy botanist who maintained a famous garden of exotic plants, and her father and brother both were local government officials. Her mother died in 1740 and eventually her siblings died or left Orford Hall, leaving Blackburne as mistress of the estate. Blackburne's interest in botany was encouraged by her family, and she collaborated with her father on many projects.

Blackburne's concerns expanded from botany into other areas of natural history. She studied insects with Johann Reinhold Forster, while he was a natural history tutor at the Warrington Academy. He was the naturalist on James Cook's second voyage to the Pacific, and he named the *Blackburnia* genus of plants after Blackburne, based on *B. pinnata* from the south Pacific. The name was later changed to *Zanthoxylum blackburnia*.

Blackburne collected specimens from America, sent to her by her brother Ashton. Beginning in 1771, she carried on a correspondence with the Swedish taxonomist, Carl Linnaeus, who was developing the modern system of biological classification. Blackburne taught herself Latin in order to utilize the Linnaean system. Coincidentally, Linnaeus had observed her in the gardens at Oxford, England in 1769 and had been impressed with her botanical knowledge. She forwarded to Linnaeus several birds and insects that her brother had sent from New York and which had not been described previously. In her letters, she referred to herself as "Mrs. Blackburne," as was the custom for unmarried women. Linnaeus's student, Johann C. Fabricius, visited Orford Hall to study her insect collection and he named a new species of beetle, *Scarabaeus blackburnii* (now *Geotrupes blackburnii*), after her.

Blackburne's collections were among the best in England. She collected birds, shells, fish, and fossils and traded many specimens with Peter Simon Pallas, a German naturalist who worked for the Russian government. Blackburne sent him minerals from England and he sent her birds, minerals from Russia, seeds from Siberia, and an occasional mammal. The eminent naturalist, Thomas Pennant, named the North American Blackburnian warbler, *Dendroica fusca*, after Blackburne. It had been sent from New York by her brother for classification. Pennant made extensive use of Blackburne's museum for the North American birds, insects, fish, a mammal, and a salamander described in his *Arctic Zoology*. He included more than 100 New York birds from her collection.

Blackburne remained at Orford Hall until her father's death in 1787, at which time she moved, with her collections, to Fairfield, a newly built house closer to Warrington. There she intended to construct new gardens based on the Linnaean system of classification. However, poor health prevented her from completing this project. She died in December of 1793. Her nephew, John Blackburne, a member of Parliament, inherited her collection.

FURTHER READING

Books

Todd, Janet, ed. *A Dictionary of British and American Women Writers 1660–1800*. Totowa, NJ: Rowman and Allanheld, 1985.

Periodicals

Wystrach, V. P. "Anna Blackburne (1726–1793) – A Neglected Patroness of Natural History." *Journal of the Society for the Bibliography of Natural History* 8 (May, 1977): 148–68.

Sketch by Margaret Alic

Elizabeth Blackwell
1712–1770
British medicinal botanist

Elizabeth Blackwell wrote and illustrated one of the most famous herbals of all time. Her comprehensive and accurate descriptions of plants and their medicinal properties made this an exceptionally useful book for medical practitioners and lay people alike.

Very little is known of Elizabeth Blackwell, outside her work as an herbalist. She apparently was the daughter of a wealthy merchant in Aberdeen, Scotland, who left her an inheritance. She married Alexander Blackwell, a physician and a graduate of Aberdeen University. She studied botany and anatomy with her husband and with James Douglas, a famous anatomist, physician and surgeon. Her husband gave up his medical practice to start a printing business in London. However since he had not completed the appropriate apprenticeship, his business failed, and he found himself in debt and in prison.

During the seventeenth and eighteenth centuries, many English women acted as their own physicians. Since chemists, or apothecaries, often prescribed expensive or harmful remedies, and physicians would not treat those who could not pay, medical cookery, as it was called, was a necessity. Women experimented with various chemical and botanical remedies, and they often compiled and published their medicinal recipes. Blackwell learned of the need for a new comprehensive medicinal herbal and saw this as a way to rescue her husband from prison. Blackwell moved to lodgings near Chelsea Botanical Garden and began work on the 500 drawings and copper plate engravings for her book of medicinal plants. She hand–colored the prints herself. Her imprisoned husband helped her with the text, as did Isaac Rand, an apothecary, the garden's curator, and a Fellow of the Royal Society. Blackwell published *A Curious Herbal* in two volumes in 1737 and 1739. The first volume was dedicated to Dr. Richard Mead, "Physician to Kings," who apparently served as an advisor. The second volume was dedicated to Rand.

One of the title pages to *A Curious Herbal* included the following endorsement from a group of physicians and botanists, as quoted by Myra Reynolds: "We whose names are underwritten, having seen a considerable Number of the Drawings from which the Plates are to be engraved, and likewise some of the Coloured Plants, think it a Justice done the Publick to declare our Satisfaction with them, and our good Opinion of the Capacity of the Undertaker." The book was so financially successful that Blackwell was able to obtain her husband's release from prison.

Later her husband went to Sweden, where he was involved in a plot against the Swedish monarchy and was beheaded. To support herself, Blackwell apparently studied obstetrics and became a successful and wealthy general practitioner.

A Curious Herbal was enlarged and republished by Dr. Trew in Nuremberg, Germany in 1757 as the *Herbarium Nurenbergianum*. Blackwell died in 1770. The *Blackwellia* genus of plants was named for her.

SELECTED WRITINGS BY BLACKWELL:

Books

A Curious Herbal, Containing Five Hundred Cuts of the Most Useful Plants, which are now used in the Practice of Physick, Engraved on Folio Copper Plates, after Drawings Taken from the Life. To which is added, a short Description of the Plants and their common Uses in Physick. London: John Nourse, 1739.

FURTHER READING

Books

Blunt, Wilfrid. *The Art of Botanical Illustration.* 2d ed. London: Collins, 1951.

Hurd–Mead, Kate Campbell. *A History of Women in Medicine, from the Earliest Times to the Beginning of the Nineteenth Century.* Haddam, CT: Haddam Press, 1938. Reprint. Boston: Milford House, 1973.

Reynolds, Myra. *The Learned Lady in England: 1650–1760.* Boston: Houghton Mifflin, 1920.

Sketch by Margaret Alic

Elizabeth Blackwell
1821–1910
English–American physician

Elizabeth Blackwell was the first woman to obtain a medical degree in the United States. A vocal activist in the opening up of the medical profession to women, Blackwell's life work increased both the number of women physicians and their acceptance by the public, and resulted in a marked improvement in medical education for both men and women.

Elizabeth Blackwell, M.D. (Archive Photos. Reproduced by permission.)

Blackwell was born in Bristol, England, February 3, 1821, the third of nine surviving children in a family of social reformers and religious dissenters. Her parents, Samuel and Hannah (Lane) Blackwell, hired private tutors to educate their daughters with the same high standards as their sons. After Samuel Blackwell, a sugar refiner, experienced business failures, the family emigrated to the United States. They settled in New York City, in 1832 and became actively involved in the abolitionist movement. Five years later the family moved again, to Cincinnati, Ohio, where Samuel Blackwell died the following year. To support themselves, Blackwell, her mother, and sisters established a private school.

First Woman M.D. in United States

Blackwell's decision to pursue a medical degree was influenced by many factors. It was partly motivated by financial need, but the desire to avoid marriage, as well as a strong belief in the struggle for women's rights and education, also played into the decisions. It was a surprising choice for a woman who, as a child, became violently ill at the sight of dissected animals. Nevertheless, Blackwell began studying science and medicine with private tutors, while supporting herself by teaching, an occupation that she disliked. With the help of Quakers who believed in her cause, she began applying to numerous medical schools, none of which had ever admitted a woman. Her acceptance by the small Geneva Medical College (now Hobart College) in Geneva, New York was something of a fluke: the faculty was opposed to admitting a woman, but rather than appear close–minded on the subject, they asked the students to vote on her application. Apparently treating the matter as a joke, the male students voted unanimously to accept Blackwell. Blackwell more than proved her education was no joke and she received her M.D. degree in 1849, graduating at the head of her class with a thesis dealing with the relationship between typhus and hygiene. Although the National Medical Association had censured Geneva College for admitting Blackwell, they reversed their position after her thesis was presented at a medical convention. The awarding of her degree was widely–hailed, both in the United States and in Europe, as a milestone for the advancement of women. Ironically, several years later, Geneva College refused to admit Blackwell's sister Emily.

Thwarted in her attempts to seek further training as a surgeon, both in the United States and after moving to Paris, Blackwell turned to gynecology and obstetrics, studying at La Maternité in Paris. Despite her M.D., she was forced to enroll as a student midwife. While working there, she contracted an eye disease from an infant infected with gonorrhea and Blackwell lost sight in one eye. Eventually her eye was removed, putting an end to her surgical ambitions. Despite this setback, the following year she was able to train under the famous doctor, James Paget, at St. Bartholomew's Hospital in London.

Establishes Hospital

Blackwell returned to New York City in 1851 and, unable to find a hospital post, tried to set up a private medical practice. Since few patients were willing to see a woman doctor, she established a free infirmary for poor women and children. This proved so successful that Blackwell obtained a state charter for a small hospital. In partnership with her sister Emily and Marie Elizabeth Zakrzewska, who had obtained their medical degrees at Western Reserve Medical School in Cleveland in 1854 and 1856, respectively, Blackwell opened the New York Infirmary for Indigent Women and Children in 1857. The Blackwell sisters' other interest was in opening a medical school for women. But the Civil War would find them training burses, and it wasn't until 1868 that the Blackwell sisters were able to open the Women's Medical College of New York, in conjunction with the Infirmary. It was one of the first of a number of women's medical colleges that flourished until after the turn of the twentieth century, when more established medical schools began admitting women. Throughout its existence, the Women's Medical College of New York was highly respected and many of the important women physicians and medical scientists of the late nineteenth century received training there.

As a Professor of Hygiene at the Women's Medical College, Blackwell's primary interest was in preventative medicine, and she lectured and published on this subject. Throughout her career, she was a vocal opponent of vaccinations and of all animal experimentation. Despite her interest in sanitation, she believed that the new science of bacteriology was without merit.

Blackwell was the first woman to be placed on the British Medical Register. In 1869 she returned to England where she founded the National Health Society of London and helped establish the London School of Medicine for Women, where she was head of the Gynecology Department until poor health forced her retirement in 1879.

Blackwell travelled in illustrious company. Among her friends and associates were the mathematician and founder of the nursing profession, Florence Nightingale, and the novelists Harriet Beecher Stowe and George Eliot. Her younger brother, Henry Brown Blackwell, worked for women's suffrage and was married to suffragist Lucy Stone. Her brother Samuel married Antoinette Brown, an activist for women's rights and the first female ordained minister in the United States. Like her four sisters, Blackwell never married. However, in 1854 she adopted a seven–year–old Irish orphan, Kitty Barry, who lived with her until her death on May 31, 1910 in Hastings, England.

SELECTED WRITINGS BY BLACKWELL:

Books

Pioneer Work in Opening the Medical Profession to Women: Autobiographical Sketches. 1895. Reprint, New York: Source Book Press, 1970.

Essays in Medical Sociology. London: Ernest Bell, 1902.

(With Emily Blackwell) "Medicine as a Profession for Women." In *The Feminist Papers*, edited by Alice Rossi. New York: Columbia University Press, 1974.

FURTHER READING

Books

Sahli, Nancy. *Elizabeth Blackwell, M.D. (1821–1910): A Biography.* New York: Arno Press, 1982.

Wilson, Dorothy Clarke. *Lone Woman; the Story of Elizabeth Blackwell, the First Woman Doctor.* Boston: Little, Brown, 1970.

Sketch by Margaret Alic

Mary Adelia Blagg
1858–1944
British astronomer

Self-taught astronomer Mary Blagg used her inquisitive mind, love of mathematics, and fascination with astronomy to become a recognized expert on the names of lunar formations. Over a period of 13 years she worked for the International Association of Academies and the newer International Astronomical Union, collating and standardizing lunar terminology. Her work earned her election to the Royal Astronomical Society; a small lunar crater was named for her after her death.

Blagg was born in Cheadle, North Staffordshire. Her father was a lawyer. She was educated at a private boarding school in London, and as was customary for women of her time and station, she involved herself in numerous worthy causes. Seeking to take her education to a higher level, she taught herself mathematics using her brother's textbooks. Her inquiring mind was challenged by the sciences and she soon brought herself to a level of competence that allowed her to understand the basics of astronomy.

Self-Taught Amateur Assists Leading Astronomers

A lecture by British astronomer J. A. Hardcastle inspired Blagg and convinced her to continue her study of astronomy, particularly the task of collating all lunar nomenclature from astronomical maps then in use throughout the world. In 1920, working on a subcommittee of the Lunar Commission for the recently established International Astronomical Union, she helped adopt a standard for lunar nomenclature that was later published by the union in a definitive work.

During this period Blagg continued to advance her knowledge of astronomy, assisting astronomer H. H. Turner in preparing a study of variable stars. Their work, published in a series of 10 papers, improved on the earlier studies of Joseph Baxendell's research on variable stars. Blagg also identified new elements for the stars Lyrae, RT Cygni, V Cassiopeiae, and U Persei. She also contributed by building on the work of other astronomers to harmonically analyze light waves.

Mary Blagg was an amateur in the best sense of the word: she pursued knowledge for the love of it. She was respected for her originality, abilities, and dedication. It is important to note that many women astronomers of Blagg's era and before were unpaid assistants to professional astronomers—that being the only way they could participate and gain knowledge. Although increasing educational opportunities for women in the sciences in early years of the twentieth century began to see more women astronomers employed as lecturers, teachers, "computers," and author/translators, this progress came too late for Blagg. Her contributions as an amateur place her among the professionals of her day.

SELECTED WRITINGS BY BLAGG:

Books

(Editor) *Collected List of Lunar Formations Names or Lettered in the Maps of Nelson, Schmidt, and Madler*. Edinburgh: Neill, 1913.

(With K. Muller) *Named Lunar Formations*. London: Percy Lund Humphries, 1935.

Periodicals

(With H. H. Turner) Series of ten papers. *Monthly Records*. Vols. 73–78. (1912–1918).

FURTHER READING

Books

Ogilvie, Marilyn Bailey. *Women in Science: Antiquity through the Nineteenth Century*. Cambridge: MIT Press, 1986, pp. 156–157.

Periodicals

Kidwell, Peggy Aldrich. "Women Astronomers in Britain, 1780–1930." *Isis* 75 (September 1984): 534–546.

Sketch by Jane Stewart Cook

Marietta Blau
1894–1970
Austrian physicist

Marietta Blau was a pioneer in the filed of particle physics. During her work of nearly half a century, she created a photographic method to study cosmic rays, a method that was simpler and more accurate than any other method of study up to that time. Blau's method founded what became known as emulsion physics, the use of photograph emulsion to track cosmic rays, which became essential to early nuclear research. In the early stages of the method's use, Blau and her colleague Herta Wambacher observed star-like tracks that were actually fragments from disintegrated atoms. This discovery became known as "Blau-Wambacher Stars."

Blau was born on April 29, 1894, in Vienna, Austria. Her parents, Dr. Mayer (Markus) Blau and Florentine Goldenzweig, headed the comfortable Jewish family which included Marietta's brother, Otto. In addition to being an attorney, Dr. Blau founded the most important music publishing company in Europe, issuing the works of many well-known composers. Yet despite the family's prosperity, as history would later show, it was a difficult time for Jews in Vienna.

Blau attended the private Girl's High School for Continued Education of Women, graduating in 1915. At the University of Vienna, Blau became interested in physics, particularly in gamma ray absorption. She graduated from the university in 1919 with a Ph.D., after which she worked for a time at Vienna's Central X–Ray Institute and then at the Radium Institute. In 1921, she moved to Berlin, Germany, to make x-ray tubes for commercial use, until she was offered work on x-ray absorption at the University of Frankfort am Main. Here, Blau's task was to explain radiology to physicians.

Her work in Frankfort was cut short in 1923 when family called Blau back home to Vienna. She was able to obtain work at the Radium Institute and at the University of Vienna, studying Radium A, proton ray ionization, and observing radiation tracks using photographic emulsion. By 1925, Blau had sufficiently perfected her emulsion method to successfully detect radiation tracks, atom fragments, and the rarely detected proton tracks. Although her work was voluntary, and she was financially supported by her family, her success prompted her to request a paid position at the Institute. She was told that because she was Jewish and a woman, a position was impossible.

Although discouraged, Blau continued her work. She was awarded a grant from the Austrian Association of University Women in 1932 which enabled her to work at the University of Göttingen on crystal physics, and then at Curie Institute where she was provided with powerful radioactive sources in order to study artificial atom disintegration using the emulsion technique.

Discovers "Blau-Wambacher Stars"

When she returned to Vienna, Blau began working to improve the emulsion method in order to study cosmic rays. Blau's new method allowed for greater film exposure time, which led to the recording of rare processes. Her method became the most important advancement in nuclear research, allowing her to study cosmic ray-produced nuclear and alpha tracks which had rarely been observed.

Herta Wambacher, a young woman uncertain about her educational path despite studies in law, was invited by Blau to help conduct her emulsion research, which was being carried out on Hafelekar Mountain. There, the pair exposed photographic plates at 7,500 feet (2,300 meters). When the plates were developed, Blau and Wambacher observed a particle track longer and higher in energy than any seen before. Further research on the mountain revealed similar tracks with up to twelve branches—the Blau-Wambacher "stars." They discovered these tracks had been caused by the collision of the cosmic rays with elements in the emulsion and that the "stars" were actually fragments from the disintegrating atoms. This discovery would pave the way for the study and understanding of nuclear physics. For their work, in 1937 Blau and Wambacher were awarded the Ignaz L. Lieben prize of the Austrian Academy of Sciences. Though the women were honored jointly, it was common knowledge at the university that Blau was the scientist and Wambacher her helper.

Blau and Wambacher were anxious to try the photographic emulsions at greater altitudes, and were awarded a grant from the Academy of Sciences which would fund balloon flights for the research. However, in 1938, the research was cut short when Austria was occupied by Nazi forces.

Flees the Nazis

Unknown to Blau, she had already been surrounded by Nazi supporters. Wambacher and Georg Stetter, an institute head, were early and ardent members of the secret and illegal Nazi party years before Austria's invasion. In fact, all of the emulsion researchers were Nazi supporters who, headed by Stetter, tried to make Blau leave her work at the institute and turn her research over to Wambacher. When the Nazis occupied Vienna, Blau fled first to Copenhagen then to Oslo to work with chemist **Ellen Gleditsch**. Not only did she have to leave her home and family behind, she, in effect, left her emulsion research and her career, as well.

However, she was able to continue working on some photographic plates she brought from Austria. On these she discovered the new phenomena of short tracks. She was, however, unable to stay in Oslo because there were no more refugee places available. Blau desperately turned to other researchers for help. Albert Einstein, who had respected Blau's groundbreaking work on emulsions, wrote on her behalf to the American Association of University Women and helped her secure a position as physics professor at the Technical University of Mexico. But she was not yet free. Desperate to leave by the quickest means, Blau boarded a German airship which would stop in Hamburg. During the brief stop, German officials boarded the airship to bring Blau and her baggage out of the cabin. Terrified, Blau complied. After removing Blau's research papers and plans, they allowed her to reboard. Stetter and Wambacher's later studies were remarkably similar to Blau's confiscated plans.

Wins Schrödinger Prize

During her time in Mexico, Blau studied radioactivity and lectured. She impressed the rector of a school in Morelia so much that he invited her to set up a laboratory for him with equipment just purchased. Anxious to return to her research, Blau eagerly accepted. However, when she arrived, the laboratory equipment had been pawned. In 1944, Blau moved to New York to work for the International Rare Metals Refinery, then the Gibbs Manufacturing and Research Corporation, and later the Canadian Radium and Uranium Corporation. Her successful work prompted the Atomic Energy Commission (AEC) to invite her to use her photographic emulsions in research at Columbia University. In 1950, the AEC asked Blau to work with the Cosmotron, a high energy accelerator, at Brookhaven, which would produce the particles previously only observed in cosmic rays. This was a highly successful time for Blau.

In 1955, Blau accepted an associate professorship at the University of Miami where she studied measurement in photographic emulsions and constructed a measuring device. Because of her field expertise, she was asked to write the photographic emulsion chapter of the book *Methods of Experimental Physics—Nuclear Physics.*

During her time at the University of Miami, Blau's health began to deteriorate. Her eye had developed a cataract which made her work impossible. The operation to remove the cataract was too expensive in the United States, as her meager Social Security income barely covered her living expenses. She decided to return to Austria, but the Austrian eye surgeon felt Blau's operation would have to wait until she was in better health. Blau was forced to wait for years, unable to pursue her research work. She was only well enough to work part time on a volunteer basis, supervising dissertations. Although she had serious financial difficulties, she wasn't interested in a paid position at the Vienna Institute, primarily because Stetter was again in power.

When she was unable to gain reparations from the government for her forced exile, her remaining friends rallied to help. The Nobel laureate Erwin Schrödinger, who had twice nominated her for the Nobel Prize for her emulsion research and the Blau-Wambacher stars discovery, awarded her, in 1962, the highest Austrian honor, the Schrödinger Prize. Subsequently, Blau's and Wambacher's names were engraved on the University of Vienna's "honor board."

In 1962, the cataract operation was successful. Despite a heart condition, Blau felt ready to work again. Sadly, she was unable to obtain a paid position, and her financial difficulties increased. Additionally, because her work had been volunteer, she had no claim to an Austrian pension. Refusing to ask her brother for help, she continued looking for work. One company which had benefitted from her emulsion production sent her a small compensation on the urging of Otto Frisch. Eventually, her health became so poor that any work she might have found was impossible.

In 1969 Blau was placed under the hospital's intensive care. She died on January 27, 1970, impoverished and obscure to the scientific community. Although the length of her work, her list of publications, and the "portability" of her emulsions were impressive, Blau remained virtually unknown. Because she was forced to move so many times after such short durations, her work and research never had a chance to become well known. Dropping her groundbreaking work to flee from the Nazis and constantly searching for a permanent position and financial stability all took their toll on Blau. Despite all her hardships, Blau was remembered by friends as kind, understanding, and forgiving.

SELECTED WRITINGS BY BLAU:

Periodicals

"The Photographic Effect of Natural H-Rays." (in German) *SBAWW (Sitzungsberichte Akademie der Wissenscaften in Wien)* IIa, 134 (1925): 427–436.

"Disintegration Processes by Cosmic Rays with the Simultaneous Emission of Several Heavy Particles." *Nature* 140 (1937): 585.

"Photographic Tracks from Cosmic Rays" *Nature* 142 (1938): 613.

FURTHER READING

Books

Galison, Peter. *Image and Logic: A Material Culture of Microphysics.* Chicago: The University of Chicago Press, 1997.

Grinstein, Louise S., Rose K. Rose, and Miriam H. Rafailovich, eds. *Women in Chamistry and Physics:A Bibliographic Sourcebook.* Westport: Greenwood Press, 1993.

Marelene F. and Geoffery W. Rayner-Canham. *A Devotion to Their Science: Pioneer Women of Radioactivity.* Philadelphia: Chemical Heritage Foundation, 1997.

Sketch by Helene Barker Kiser

Katharine Burr Blodgett

1898–1979

American chemist

Katharine Burr Blodgett, the first woman to become a General Electric (GE) scientist, made several significant contributions to the field of industrial chemistry. The inventor of invisible, or non–reflecting, glass, Blodgett spent nearly all of her professional life working in the Schenectady, New York, GE plant. Although Blodgett's name has little household recognition, some of the techniques in surface chemistry that she and her supervisor and mentor Irving Langmuir developed are still used in laboratories; in addition, Blodgett's invisible glass is used extensively in camera and optical equipment today.

Blodgett was born on January 10, 1898 in Schenectady, New York, the town in which she spent most of her life. Her parents had moved to Schenectady earlier in the decade from their native New England when Blodgett's father, George Bedington Blodgett, became the head of the patent department at the GE plant opening up in town. Blodgett never knew her father, who died a few weeks before she was born. Left widowed with two small children, Blodgett's mother, Katharine Buchanan Burr, decided to move back east to New York City; three years later, she moved the family to France so that her children would be bilingual. After a few years of French schooling, Blodgett spent a year

Katherine Burr Blodgett (UPI/Corbis-Bettmann. Reproduced by permission.)

at an American school in Saranac Lake, New York, followed by travel in Germany. While in her mid–teens, Blodgett returned with her family to New York City where she attended the now–defunct Rayson School. Blodgett later won a scholarship to the all–women's Bryn Mawr College, where she excelled at mathematics and physics.

After college, Blodgett decided that a career in scientific research would allow her to further pursue both of these academic interests. During Christmas vacation of her senior year, she traveled to upstate New York to explore employment opportunities at the Schenectady GE plant. Some of George Blodgett's former colleagues in Schenectady introduced his daughter to research chemist Irving Langmuir. After conducting to a tour of his laboratory, Langmuir told eighteen–year–old Blodgett that she would need to broaden her scientific education before coming to work for him.

Hired As First Woman Researcher at General Electric

Taking Langmuir's advice, Blodgett enrolled in the University of Chicago in 1918 to pursue master's degree in science. Since she knew thata job awaited her in industrial research, Blodgett picked a related thesis subject: the chemical structure of gas masks. Upon graduating, Blodgett returned to GE, where Langmuir hired her as his assistant (the first female research scientist the company had ever employed). At the time, Langmuir who had worked on vacuum pumps and light bulbs early in his GE career had turned his attention to studying current flow under restricted conditions. Blodgett soon started working with Langmuir on these studies; between 1918 and 1924, the two scientists wrote several papers about their work. Blodgett's collaboration with the 1932 Nobel winner lasted until Langmuir's death in 1957.

Blodgett soon realized that she would need a doctoral degree if she wanted to further her career at GE. Six years after Blodgett started working for him, Langmuir arranged for his associate to pursue doctoral studies in physics at the Cavendish Laboratory at England's Cambridge University. Blodgett needed her mentor's help to gain admission to Cavendish because laboratory administrators hesitated to give one of their few open spots to a woman. With Langmuir's endorsement, however, Blodgett was able to persuade the Cambridge physicists including Nobel winner Ernest Rutherford to allow her entrance. In 1926, Blodgett became the first woman to receive a doctorate in physics from Cambridge University.

When Blodgett returned to Schenectady, Langmuir encouraged her to embellish some of his earlier discoveries. First, he set her to work on perfecting tungsten filaments in electric lamps (the work for which he had received a patent in 1916). Langmuir later asked his protege to concentrate her studies on surface chemistry. In his own long–standing research on the subject, Langmuir had discovered that oily substances formed a one–molecule thin film when spread on water. By floating a waxed thread in front of stearic acid molecules, the scientist showed that this layer was created by the molecules' active ends resting on the water's surface. Blodgett decided to see what would happen if she dipped a metal plate into the molecules; attracted to the metal, a layer of molecules formed similar to that on the water. As she inserted the plate into the solution again and again, Blodgett noticed that additional layers all one molecule formed on top of one another. As the layers formed, different colors appeared on the surface, colors which could be used to gauge how many layers thick the coating was. Because this measurement was always constant, Blodgett realized she could use the plate as a primitive gauge for measuring the thickness of film within one micro–inch.

Not long after Blodgett's discovery, GE started marketing a more sophisticated version of her color gauge for use in scientific laboratories. The gauge was comprised of a sealed glass tube that contained a six–inch strip on which successive layers of molecules had formed. To measure the thickness of film few millionths of an inch thick, the user need only compare the color of film with the molecular grades. The gauge could measure the thickness of a transparent or semi–transparent substances within one to twenty millionths of an inch as effectively as much more expensive optical instruments, a very effective device for physicists, chemists, and metallurgists.

Work Leads to Development of Invisible Glass

Blodgett continued working in the field of surface chemistry. Within five years, she had found another practical application that stemmed from Langmuir's original studies: non–reflecting, or invisible, glass. Blodgett discovered that coating sheets of ordinary glass with exactly forty–four layers of one–molecule thick transparent liquid soap rendered the glass invisible. This overall layer of soap four–millionths of an inch thick and one quarter the wave length of white light neutralized the light rays coming from the bottom of the glass with those coming from the top so that no light was reflected. Since the transparent soap coating blocked only about one percent of the light coming in, invisible glass was perfect for use in optical equipment such as cameras and telescopes in which multiple reflecting lenses could affect performance.

Blodgett did not hold sole credit for creating invisible glass. Two days after she announced her discovery, two physicists at the Massachusetts Institute of Technology (MIT) publicized that they had found another method of manufacturing non–reflecting glass using calcium fluoride condensed in a vacuum. Both groups of scientists, however, were concerned that their coatings were not hard and permanent enough for industrial use. Using some Blodgett's insights, the MIT scientists eventually found a more appropriate method of producing invisible glass. Today, the fruits of Blodgett's discovery can be found in almost all lenses used in cameras and other optical equipment, as well as automobile windows, showcases, eyeglasses, picture frames, and submarine periscopes.

During World War II, GE moved away from studies such as the one that lead to invisible glass in favor of tackling problems with more direct military applications. Following suit, Blodgett temporarily shelved her glass research, but did not move far from the field of surface chemistry. Her wartime experiments lead to breakthroughs involving plane wing deicing; she also designed a smoke screen that saved numerous lives during various military campaigns.

Receives Garvan Medal for Women Chemists

When the war ended, Blodgett continued doing research that had military ramifications. In 1947, for example, she worked with the Army Signal Corps, putting her thin film knowledge to use by developing an instrument that could be placed in weather balloons to measure humidity in the upper atmosphere. As Blodgett worked, plaudits for her research continued to pour in. Along with receiving numerous honorary degrees, Blodgett won the 1945 Annual Achievement Award from the American Association of University Women for her research in surface chemistry. In 1951, she accepted the Francis P. Garvan Medal from the American Chemical Society; that same year, Blodgett also had the distinction of being the only scientist honored in Boston's First Assembly of American Women in Achievement. To top off the year, Schenectady decided to honor its own by celebrating Katharine Blodgett Day.

Blodgett spent all of her adult life in the home she bought overlooking her birthplace. She was active in civil affairs in her beloved Schenectady, serving as treasurer of the Travelers Aid Society. Blodgett summered in a camp at Lake George in upstate New York, where she could pursue her love of gardening. She also enjoyed amateur astronomy, collecting antiques, and playing bridge with her friends. Blodgett died at her home on October 12, 1979, at the age of eighty–one.

FURTHER READING

Books

Golemba, Beverly. *Lesser Known Women: A Biographical Dictionary.* Lynne Rienner, 1992.

O'Neill, Lois Decker, ed. *Women's Book of World Records and Achievements.* Anchor Press, 1979.

Rothe, Anne, and Evelyn Lohr, eds. *Current Biography.* H. W. Wilson, 1952, pp. 55–57.

Yost, Edna. *American Women of Science.* Frederick A. Stokes, 1943.

Periodicals

Clark, Alfred E. "Katharine Burr Blodgett, 81, Developer of Nonreflecting Glass." *New York Times* (October 19, 1979): 24.

McLaughlin, Kathleen. "Creator of 'Invisible Glass' Woman of Many Interests." *New York Times* (September 24, 1939): 4.

Sketch by Shari Rudavsky

Dorotea Bocchi
1390–1436
Italian philosopher and teacher of medicine

Dorotea Bocchi was professor of moral philosophy and practical medicine at the University of Bologna in 1390. A respected professor, her tenure didn't end until 40 years later in 1430. One of the learned woman of the Renaissance, Bocchi succeeded her father.

Though there are few records of Bocchi's teaching or training still in existence today, it's probable that Bocchi was trained in arts and sciences by humanist scholars or her prominent father. Most Italian woman physicians of the time were allowed to practice through licenses obtained by passing a special exam. To prepare, they studied with a private teacher. Many women like Bocchi also studied medicine with a relative, helping the family keep up a respected medical practice and shielding their healing secrets from outsiders.

Although the Renaissance period is known for male intellectuals, learned female professors like Bocchi had similar stature to men. Indeed two writers of the day,

Ariostoto and Bocaccio mention that people in Italian centers of culture, such as Bologna, regularly consulted female doctors and surgeons as well as their male counterparts.

The University of Bologna, where Bocchi taught, was founded in 425 A.D. by Theodosius II. It steadily developed into a world-renowned center of learning. At the end of the eleventh century it was reorganized so that it could grant both bachelor and doctoral degrees. Both women and men were admitted to all examinations. Women and men often studied together and had equal access to degrees conferred by the university. Unfortunately, most physicians and midwives who practiced during the Renaissance, such as Bocchi, left very few medical writings. Thus, from the mid–1400s until the early 1700s, most of the famed women in Italy were known as experts in arts and literature, not science.

FURTHER READING

Books

Alic, Margaret. *Hypatia's Heritage: A History of Women in Science from Antiquity through the 19th Century*. Boston: Beacon, 1986.

Periodicals

Hurd-Mead, Kate Campbell. "The Bologna Medical School." *Quarterly Bulletin of the Medical Women's National Association*. (October, 1927): 8.

Sketch by Barbara Boughton

Rachel Littler Bodley
1831–1888
American chemist and botanist

Rachel Bodley was dean of the Woman's Medical College of Pennsylvania. Her professional activities helped to establish science as a career for American women, and she improved the educational opportunities for women physicians.

Rachel Bodley was born in Cincinnati, Ohio, in 1831, the eldest daughter of Rebecca Wilson (Talbott) and Anthony Prichard Bodley. She had two older brothers and two younger sisters. Her father was a carpenter and later a pattern maker, and her mother ran a private school in Cincinnati where Bodley was educated until she was 12. Bodley then attended Wesleyan Female College in Cincinnati, graduating in 1849, and teaching there for the next 10 years. In 1860 she returned to school, studying natural sciences at the Polytechnic College in Philadelphia. In 1862 Bodley returned to teach science at the Cincinnati Female Seminary. The seminary had inherited a large plant collection, and Bodley began her first major research project, the classifying and mounting of the herbarium.

In 1865, Bodley was named as the first chemistry professor at the Female Medical College in Philadelphia, which, in 1868, was renamed the Woman's Medical College. She continued botanical research, making an original study of saltwater plants. She spent her summers traveling the United States, lecturing and collecting botanical specimens.

Bodley was invited to give a series of lectures on "household chemistry" to the Franklin Institute, and she was active in a number of scientific societies. She was elected to the Academy of Natural Sciences of Philadelphia in 1871 and became a corresponding member of the New York Academy of Sciences in 1876. In 1874, Bodley wrote to the *American Chemist* and suggested that the 100th anniversary of Joseph Priestley's discovery of oxygen be commemorated with a meeting at Priestley's former home in Pennsylvania. At that meeting, the American Chemical Society was established, and Bodley was elected honorary vice-president of the interim committee, the only woman so honored by the society for another 100 years. Bodley, however, did not attend the convention, preferring to spend the summer in Colorado studying botany with friends. The only woman member of the Chemical Society until the 1890s, Bodley dropped out in 1880, because of the sexist attitudes of the member.

In 1874, Bodley was chosen to succeed Emeline Cleveland as dean of the Woman's Medical College. During the 14 years of her tenure, she made major improvements in the course of medical training, including lengthening it to three years, increasing clinical experience and constructing a surgical amphitheater, and attracting distinguished new faculty. She aggressively promoted the college, attracting students from around the world. Since childhood, Bodley, a Presbyterian, had supported medical missionaries, and she encouraged her students to pursue this vocation. In 1881, she conducted a large statistical study of the college's graduates, published as a pamphlet, which demonstrated that most of the alumnae were engaged in successful medical practices. It was a vindication of medical education for women. Two of her lectures at the college were also published.

In addition to her academic activities, Bodley was an elected director for the public school system and held an appointment from the state to inspect charitable institutions. She was awarded an honorary medical degree by the Woman's Medical College of Pennsylvania in 1879.

Bodley never married. She lived with her mother near the college and died in 1888, at age 56, of a heart attack.

SELECTED WRITINGS BY BODLEY:

Books

Catalogue of Plants, Contained in the Herbarium of Joseph Clark. National Agricultural Library, 1865.

Introductory Lectures to the Class of the Woman's Medical College of Pennsylvania: Delivered at the Opening of the Nineteenth Annual Session, October 15, 1868. Philadelphia: Merrihew and Son, 1868.

FURTHER READING

Books

Alsop, Gulielma Fell. "Rachel Littler Bodley." In *Notable American Women 1607–1950: A Biographical Dictionary*, edited by Edward T. James, Janet Wilson James, and Paul W. Boyer. Vol. 1. Cambridge: Harvard University Press, 1971.

Ogilvie, Marilyn Bailey. *Women in Science, Antiquity through the Nineteenth Century: A Biographical Dictionary with Annotated Bibliography*. Cambridge: MIT Press, 1991.

Rossiter, Margaret W. *Women Scientists in America: Struggles and Strategies to 1940*. Baltimore: Johns Hopkins University Press, 1982.

Sketch by Margaret Alic

Marie Anne Victorine (Gillain) Boivin
1773–1841
French midwife and medical writer

One of the most important gynecologists and obstetricians of nineteenth–century France, Marie Boivin made original anatomical discoveries, invented medical instruments, and wrote widely used medical texts.

Marie Anne Victorine (Gillain) Boivin was born in 1773 in Montreuil, France, and was educated by nuns at a hospital in Étampes. She married Louis Boivin, a government bureaucrat, in 1897 and they had one daughter. Widowed, with a baby daughter, Boivin became a student of the famous midwife and researcher, **Marie Louise Lachapelle** at the Hospice de la Maternité, or Maison d'Accouchements, receiving her diploma in midwifery in 1800. She then moved to Versailles after her daughter was killed. She returned to La Maternité as Lachapelle's assistant, where she remained for the next 11 years. After quarrelling with Lachapelle, Boivin resigned and accepted a position at a servant's salary at a hospital for unmarried mothers. Although she turned down an offer from the Empress of Russia, Boivin did become the director of several hospitals, including the General Hospital for Seine and Oise in 1814, a temporary military hospital in 1815, the Hospice de la Maternité in Bordeaux, and the Maison Royale de Santé.

Boivin's first important writing was her *Art of Obstetrics*, published in 1812. It was in its third edition by 1824 and was translated into several European languages. The work received a commendation from the general council of the city hospitals of Paris, and the Minister of the Interior chose it as the text for medical students and midwives. Boivin also translated works on gynecology from English into French. Her treatise, *One of the Most Frequent and Least Known Causes of Abortion*, was awarded a commendation from the Royal Society of Medicine of Bordeaux.

Boivin's most significant medical writing, published in 1833, on diseases of the uterus, also became a popular medical school textbook. It included 41 plates and 116 figures, which she colored herself. Her writings were all well documented with the medical literature of the time. Boivin also made original anatomical discoveries. She invented a vaginal speculum for dilating the vagina and examining the cervix, and she was one of the first physicians to use a stethoscope to listen to the heart of a fetus.

Boivin was awarded the Order of Merit from the King of Prussia in 1814, and in 1827 she received an honorary medical degree from the University of Marburg in Germany. Although she was a member of several medical societies, she was disappointed that she was never accepted into the Academy of Medicine in Paris. She died in poverty, of paralysis, in 1841.

SELECTED WRITINGS BY BOIVIN:

Books

Mémorial de l'Art des Accouchements: Ou Principes Fondés sur la Pratique de l'Hospice de la Maternité de Paris et sur celles des Célèbres Praticiens Nationaux et Étrangers. Suivis des Aphorismes de Mauriceau et de ceux d'Orazio Valota. 2nd ed. Paris: Méquignon, 1817.

Nouveau Traité des Hemorragies de l'Uterus. 1818.

(With A. Dugès)*Traité Pratique des Maladies de l'Utérus et de ses Annexes, Fondé sur un Grand Nombre d'Observations Cliniques*. Paris: Baillière, 1833.

FURTHER READING

Books

Hurd–Mead, Kate Campbell. *A History of Women in Medicine, from the Earliest Times to the Beginning of the Nineteenth Century*. Haddam, CT: Haddam Press, 1938. Reprint, Boston: Milford House, 1973.

Jex–Blake, Sophia. *Medical Women: A Thesis and a History*. 2d ed. Edinburgh, 1886. Reprint, New York: Source Book Press, 1970.

Periodicals

Loomis, Metta May. "The Contributions Which Women Have Made to Medical Literature." *New York Medical Journal* 100 (1914): 522–24.

Sketch by Margaret Alic

Alice Middleton Boring
1883–1955
American zoologist, cytologist, and geneticist

Although born and educated in the United States, Alice Middleton Boring spent the bulk of her career in China, where she contributed greatly to science education through her work at Yenching University. She also brought numerous new species of Chinese reptiles and amphibians to the attention of Western science through her work in studying their taxonomy and in providing assistance to visiting researchers.

Alice Middleton Boring was born in Philadelphia, Pennsylvania, in 1883, one of four children of Edwin, a pharmacist, and Elizabeth (Truman) Boring. Alice graduated from the Friends' Central School in Philadelphia in 1900, and went on to college at Bryn Mawr, one of the few women's colleges where pioneering scientific work was being conducted.

During her time at Bryn Mawr, she studied with Thomas Hunt Morgan, a noted geneticist, and published the first of her 36 professional papers as Morgan's junior co–author. Boring received her bachelor's degree in 1904 and her master's in 1905, both from Bryn Mawr.

Boring then spent a year at the University of Pennsylvania, where she began a lifelong friendship with the biologist Edwin Conklin. She then returned to Bryn Mawr to complete her doctorate. At the suggestion of faculty member and cytogeneticist **Nettie Stevens**, who had also studied with Morgan, Boring's doctoral subject was on the course of spermatogenesis (the process of male gamete formation) in certain species of insects.

While completing her doctoral research, Boring worked as a biology instructor in at Vassar from 1907–1908. After receiving her doctorate in 1910, taught biology at the University of Maine in 1911 and remained there until 1918, holding the posts of assistant professor (1911–1913) and associate professor (1913–1918) of zoology.

Work Moves to China

During her years at Vassar and Maine, Alice Boring's work added valuable information to the data available to researchers, although she had made no original contributions. However, the course of her career changed in 1918, when she accepted a job in China.

She spent the next two years as an assistant biology professor at Peking Union Medical College, as part of its premedical division. Her return to the States after the two years ended proved to be only temporary. She taught biology at Wellesley from 1920–1923, but when the chance to return to China came up, she jumped at the opportunity.

She asked for a two–year sabbatical from Wellesley, but the two years would expand into a career, interrupted only by brief returns to the United States and encompassing invasion, imprisonment, and revolution.

She would serve as a professor of zoology at Peking (later Yenching) University from 1923–1950. During those years, Dr. Boring acquainted many Chinese students with Western science, and also successfully introduced Chinese reptiles and amphibians to Western taxonomists. Not only did she help visiting taxonomists when they arrived to collect specimens, but she herself collected and provided to American universities and museums specimens of reptiles and amphibians from areas previously unsurveyed.

Dr. Boring's interest in China extended beyond its unique fauna: she was also involved in Chinese political concerns. She disliked the involvement of foreign powers in Chinese affairs, and believed that sometimes social concerns should come before science.

An Interrupted Career

The political climate of China, and the world, was changing as World War II approached. In 1937 the Japanese invaded China. Although the university was largely untouched for several years after the invasion, a pall hung over much of everyday life as finances grew tight and communication with the world outside became difficult. Many foreign nationals made plans to leave, but Dr. Boring stayed. For her, China had become home.

In 1941, the Japanese shut down Yenching University, and Dr. Boring and other British and American faculty members were sent to a concentration camp in Shantung. There she remained for more than a year. Finally, in 1943 she was sent back to the United States, along with several other faculty members. During her brief return to the United States, she worked at Columbia University's College of Physicians and Surgeons as an histology instructor, and then in 1945 and 1946 served as visiting professor of zoology at Mount Holyoke.

Despite having been held in a concentration camp, Boring still loved China. In 1946, she returned to Yenching University and while she was there, war broke out between the Chinese Communist Party and the Nationalists . However, family concerns, rather than politics brought her back to the United States for the last time. Her sister had fallen ill, so Dr. Boring settled in Cambridge, Massachusetts to take care of her. She obtained a part–time professorship at Smith College.

Alice Middleton Boring died in 1955 in Cambridge, Massachusetts, of cerebral arteriosclerosis (hardening of the arteries). Although her contributions through original research may have been few, Alice Middleton Boring had a tremendous impact on science by training several generations of Chinese scientists. Her students went on to distinguish themselves in teaching and in the study of reptiles and amphibians as well.

SELECTED WRITINGS BY BORING:

Periodicals

"A Study of the Spermatogenesis of Twenty–Two Species of Membracidae, Jassidae, Cercopidae, and Fulgoridae, with Especial Reference to the Behavior of the Odd Chromosome." *Journal of Experimental Zoology* 4, no. 4 (October 1907).

"A Checklist of Chinese Amphibia with Notes on Geographical Distribution." *Peking Natural History Bulletin* 4 (December 1929).

FURTHER READING:

Books

Ogilvie, Mary Bailey. *Women in Science: Antiquity through the Nineteenth Century.* Cambridge: MIT Press, 1986.

Rossiter, Marilyn. *Women Scientists in America: Struggles and Strategies to 1940.* Baltimore: Johns Hopkins University Press, 1982.

Sketch by Fran Hodgkins

Louyse Bourgeois
1563–1636
French obstetrician

The observations and writings of Louyse Bourgeois helped to establish the science of obstetrics. One of the most important medical writers of the scientific revolution, she authored the first textbook on obstetrics that discussed anatomy. Her common sense approach to medicine and her treatment of the underlying causes of disease, rather than the symptoms, were new innovations in medical writing.

Although little is known of Bourgeois's background, she was born in 1563 and grew up in a middle-class family in the wealthy Paris suburb of Saint-Germain. She apparently received a good education. Ambroise Paré, who had invented important new surgical techniques and had written works on anatomy, lived nearby. He shared his house with his student and assistant, the surgeon Martin Boursier. When Bourgeois was still very young, she married Boursier.

Louyse Bourgeois (The Granger Collection, New York. Reproduced by permission.)

In May of 1588 there was a popular insurrection against King Henry III, known as "the Day of the Barricades," and in retaliation, the king had the Paris suburbs ransacked. Bourgeois was forced to flee with her mother and her three young children. Boursier was serving as an army surgeon at the time and Bourgeois barely managed to feed her family by selling her embroidery.

When peace returned, the family settled in Paris and Bourgeois set out to learn anatomy and midwifery from her husband and from Paré's books. For five years she was a midwife to the poor. Later, she joined the Paris midwifery guild and became midwife to the gentry and nobility. By 1609 she had participated in more than 2,000 deliveries. As midwife to Queen Marie de Medici, wife of King Henry IV, Bourgeois delivered seven royal infants. She was paid 1,000 ducats for delivering a royal son and 600 for a royal daughter.

Bourgeois was a successful midwife, but came under attack from male obstetricians after the Duchess of Orleans died of childbed fever while under her care. Male obstetricians were a relatively new phenomena in the seventeenth century and in order to establish themselves, they attempted to wipe out the female midwives. Bourgeois responded to the attack by publishing a pamphlet criticizing male physicians who practiced obstetrics. However her pamphlet had the adverse effect of advertising the male midwives, who were beginning to attend the nobility, and Bourgeois's own practice suffered.

In 1608, Bourgeois published a comprehensive obstetrics text. Dedicated to Marie de Medici, Queen of Henry IV of France, it was the first new work on the subject in centuries. It included her own observations and discoveries, as well as information from Paré's writings. Bourgeois introduced new methods of delivery and discussed female anatomy, as well as all aspects of normal and abnormal pregnancy and labor, and she was one of the first to suggest the induction of labor under certain conditions. Bourgeois was ahead of her time in censuring the improper use of bleeding and strong medicines, as well as in recognizing poor nutrition as a cause of premature birth, birth defects, and anemia. She was the first physician to treat anemia with iron. Most importantly, Bourgeois stressed the importance of anatomical studies for midwives and entreated physicians to allow midwives to attend their lectures and dissections.

Bourgeois's book went through many revised editions over the next century and was translated into German, Latin, English, and Dutch. Later editions included general medicine as well as obstetrics. The second edition, published in 1617, featured a long list of clinical cases, an account of Bourgeois's education entitled "How she became a Midwife," "A true Description of the Births and Baptisms of the Children of France," and "Advice to my Daughter" who was training to be a midwife. The latter was republished separately in 1626. The sixth edition, published in 1634, included many of her remedies under the title "A Collection of the Secrets of Louyse Bourgeois."

In 1635 the midwives of Paris petitioned the Faculty of Medicine to allow Bourgeois to give them a public course in obstetrics, but the petition was denied. However one of Bourgeois's students, Marguerite du Tertre de la Marche, became head midwife at the Hôtel Dieu and reorganized the training of midwives. In addition to obstetrics, Bourgeois practiced surgery and wrote poetry. She died in 1636, without receiving the pension that the king had promised her after she had saved the lives of several royal infants.

SELECTED WRITINGS BY BOURGEOIS:

Books

Divers Observations on Sterility, Loss of the Ovum after Fecundation, Fecundity and Childbirth, Diseases of Women and of Newborn Infants. Paris, 1617.

FURTHER READING

Books

Goodell, William. *A Sketch of the Life and Writings of Louyse Bourgeois: Midwife to Marie De' Medici, the Queen of Henry IV of France.* Philadelphia: Collins, 1876.

Hurd–Mead, Kate Campbell. *A History of Women in Medicine, from the Earliest Times to the Beginning of the Nineteenth Century.* 1938. Reprint, Boston: Milford House, 1973.

Periodicals

Robb, Hunter. "Remarks on the Writings of Louyse Bourgeois." *Johns Hopkins Hospital Bulletin* 4 (1893): 75–81.

Sketch by Margaret Alic

Sylvia Trimble Bozeman
1947–
American mathematician

Sylvia Trimble Bozeman is a professor of mathematics whose dedication to teaching women and minorities has brought her great recognition. In addition to her teaching skills, she has conducted important research in the fields of functional analysis and image processing.

Bozeman was born on August 1, 1947, in Camp Hill, Alabama, the daughter of Horace Edward Trimble, Sr. and Robbie L. (Jones) Trimble. She had one brother, Horace Edward Trimble, Jr. Bozeman's father was employed as an insurance agent. Her mother, a housewife, encouraged Sylvia in her interest in math. Both parents instilled in their daughter the sense that she could accomplish anything. Bozeman attended segregated public schools in Camp Hill. While attending Edward Bell High School, her interest in mathematics was further encouraged by her math teacher Frank Holley. Holley taught Bozeman and other interested students trigonometry on his own time because it was not offered in school.

Bozeman entered Alabama A&M University in Huntsville, in 1964, and found more mentors for her mathematics goals. Through the efforts of a professor, she was able to work on a computer-based project for the National Aeronautics and Space Administration (NASA). She also spent a summer conducting research at Harvard, learning the early computer programming language FORTRAN. Sylvia earned her B.S. in math in 1968, graduating second in her class. She was also vice president of student government during her senior year. Soon after graduation, she married Robert Edward Bozeman on May 25, 1968. Robert Bozeman was a fellow mathematics student who also became a mathematician and professor. The couple eventually had two children together, Kizzie Renate and Robert Okang.

The Bozemans moved to Tennessee soon after their marriage, and both entered Vanderbilt University's graduate program. Sylvia earned her M.A. in math from Vanderbilt in 1970, as did her husband. Her thesis dealt with group theory, a specialty within algebra. While her husband worked on his Ph.D., Bozeman worked as an instructor of mathematics at Vanderbilt from 1971 to 1972. In 1972, she was hired by Nashville's Tennessee State University for a year as an instructor of math for the Upward Bound Program.

Begins Teaching at Spelman College

After her husband completed his Ph.D., the family moved to Atlanta, Georgia, where he was hired as a professor at Morehouse College. In 1974, Sylvia was hired by the historically black Spelman College as a math instructor. Her interview was conducted by **Etta Falconer**, who was the chair of the math department at that time. Falconer was a mentor to Bozeman while she taught at Spelman and continues to be a professional guide.

Even though teaching math to black women was satisfying work, Bozeman knew she had to get her Ph.D. if she wanted to truly succeed as a college teacher. She took a leave of absence and began the Ph.D program in mathematics at Emory University. She returned to Spelman full–time after finishing her preliminary exams. Bozeman earned her Ph.D. in 1980. Her work focused on functional analysis, an advanced area of mathematics combining ideas from algebra and a kind of geometry known as topology. Her dissertation was titled "Representations of Generalized Inverses of Fredholm Operators." In 1982, Bozeman was named chair of the math department at Spelman, which she held through 1993. By 1983, Bozeman was promoted to associate professor, and in 1991, full professor.

While teaching at Spelman, Bozeman continued her interest in functional analysis and was awarded several prestigious grants, including one from the National Science Foundation. From 1981 through 1984, the U.S. Army Research Office funded her research. In 1986, she received a grant from NASA, funding her new research in the area of image processing, which involves the manipulation and analysis of pictures on a computer screen. For her work, Bozeman was recognized with the White House Initiative Faculty Award for Excellence in Science and Technology in 1988. That same year, she was honored by the Tenneco United Negro College Fund with an Excellence in Teaching Award.

Throughout her career, Bozeman has been active in several professional organizations, including the National Association of Mathematicians. She served as that organization's vice president from 1984–88. Bozeman also participated in the Mathematics Association of America. She was a member of its board of governors from 1989–92 and served as co-chair of its Committee on Minority Participation in Mathematics, hoping to increase the strength and number of minorities in math.

In 1993, Bozeman became Project Director for the Center for Scientific Applications of Mathematics (CSAM). Through a grant from the Kellogg Foundation, Spelman College received three million dollars to set up a center to increase African American students' exposure to the sciences. Bozeman was the natural choice to direct this program. CSAM also works to expose high school teachers to new trends in math and teaching through a summer program called the Spelman Summer Science and Mathematics Institute. In the late 1990s, Bozeman was given another promotion to Associate Provost for Science and Mathematics at Spelman. In her spare time, Bozeman is active in her church and plays English handbells.

SELECTED WRITINGS BY BOZEMAN:

"Black Women Mathematicians: In Short Supply." *Sage* (Fall 1989).

FURTHER READING

Books

Hine, Darlene Clark, ed. *Black Women in America: An Historical Encyclopedia, Volume1.* Brooklyn: Carlson Publishing, 1993.

———. *Black Women in America: Science, Health, and Medicine.* New York: Facts on File, Inc., 1997.

Morrow, Charlene and Teri Perl. *Notable Women in Mathematics: A Biographical Dictionary.* Westport, CT: Greenwood Press, 1998.

Other

"1998 Edge Program." http://www.brynmawr.edu/Acads/Math/edge/bozeman.html (11 March 1999).

Williams, Scott. "Black Women in Mathematics." http://www.math.buffalo.edu/mad/PEEPS/bozemansylviat.html (11 March 1999).

Sketch by Annette Petrusso

Sophie Brahe
1556–1643
Danish astronomer

Sophie Brahe collaborated closely with her brother, the famous astronomer Tycho Brahe. As both a scientist and a writer, she was a major contributor to the scientific and artistic renaissance in sixteenth-century Denmark.

Born at the family seat of Kuntstorp, Scania (later a part of Sweden) in 1556, Brahe was the youngest of five daughters and five sons in a prominent Danish family. Her mother, Beate Bille, was from a noble family, and her father, Otto Brahe, was Royal Counsel to King Christian III of Denmark and later, the governor of Helsingborg Castle. A talented and gifted child, Brahe received the best possible education. She became an expert in classical literature and a self-taught astrologer and alchemist. At the time, astrology was considered be a legitimate subdivision of astronomy, and Brahe shared these interests with her brother Tycho, who was 10 years her senior. By the age of 17, she was frequently assisting him with his astronomical observations.

Brahe's first husband, the nobleman Otto Thott of Eriksholm, whom she had married in Scania when she was 19 or 20, died in 1588, leaving her with one son, Tage Thott. Brahe managed the Eriksholm estate until her son reached adulthood and devoted herself to horticulture and to the study of genealogy, astrology, chemistry, botany, and medicine. She practiced medicine among the poor. She also began to collaborate with her brother Tycho at his observatory, Uraniborg, on Hven Island in the Danish Sound. The observatory had been built for him by Queen Sophia and King Frederick II of Denmark and Norway. Queen Sophia herself was an enthusiastic student of astronomy, chemistry, and other sciences.

Brahe worked closely with her brother and, since he received the credit for their work, her specific contributions are not known. However over the course of their collaboration, the Brahes made crucial observations that enabled Johannes Kepler to determine the elliptical orbits of the planets. Their accurate measurements of the positions of the sun, moon, stars, and planets helped lead astronomy into the modern era.

Brahe met Erik Lange of Engelsholm-Solvig, a young nobleman, when he came to Hven to study with Tycho Brahe. Lange and the Brahes experimented with alchemy; however Lange lost much of his family's fortune in pseudoscientific attempts to make gold and to find the "Stone of Wisdom." When Brahe announced her engagement to Lange in 1590, the entire Brahe family, with the exception of her brother, objected strongly. Shortly thereafter, Lange left for Germany to escape his creditors and to continue his alchemical pursuits.

Brahe's major writing was a long poetic Latin letter to Lange, "Urania Titani" or "Urania to Titan," written in 1594. She also wrote a long love song to Lange in Danish, a long letter written from Eckernforde, Germany in 1602 to her sister Margrethe Brahe, works of genealogy, and a 900–page study of the Danish nobility. These writings are considered to be major works of Danish literature.

Brahe finally married Lange in 1602 in Eckernforde. By that time, Lange was destitute and he died in Prague in 1613. Brahe disclaimed his debts and relinquished claims on his inheritance, returning to Helsing, Denmark in 1616. There she continued writing on genealogy and astrology until her death in 1643.

SELECTED WRITINGS BY BRAHE:

Books

"Urania Titani: Urania til Titan," translated by Johan Ludvig Heiberg in "Rensenii Inscriptiones hafniensis." In *Sophie Brahe. En hverdagshistorie fra det 16de og 17de Aarhundrede.* Urania, 1846.

FURTHER READING

Books

Dreyer, J. L. E. *Tycho Brahe, a Picture of Scientific Life and Work in the Sixteenth Century.* 1890. Reprint, New York: Dover, 1963.

Isaacson, Lanae Hjortsvang. "Sophie Brahe." In *An Encyclopedia of Continental Women Writers,* edited by Katharina M. Wilson. Vol. 2. New York: Garland, 1991.

Sketch by Margaret Alic

Jenny Eugenia (Rosenthal) Bramley
1910–1997
Russion-born American laser physicist

Dr. Jenny Rosenthal Bramley, a governmental scientist in laser and radar research, co–discovered the Breit–Rosenthal effect, otherwise known as the hyperfine structure anomaly. She invented the microwave–pumped high efficiency lamp, whose brightness far exceeded that of the more conventional high–power xenon arc lamps. She was also the first woman to receive a doctorate in physics in the United States, receiving her degree in 1929 from New York University at the age of 19. Bramley became the second woman to become a fellow of the Institute of Electrical and Electronical Engineers (IEEE) which cited her "for achievement in spectroscopy, optics, mathematical techniques and their application for electronic tubes, displays and light sources to engineering." These achievements included the development of mathematical techniques that were used successfully in the design of storage devices for high–speed photoconductor switches and research into the spectra of polyatomic molecules.

Jenny Eugenia Rosenthal was born in Moscow on July 31, 1909 to Lazar and Elizabeth Vishnial Rosenthal, natives of Lithuania. Her physician father was well known for his work in antibiotics research and also served as a colonel during World War I. Initially, Bramley received her education from tutors and her parents. After the war, she moved with her parents to Lithuania under a hostage exchange agreement with the Soviet Union and attended high school at the Bismarck Lyzeum in Berlin. Another move to Paris allowed Bramley to earn her bachelor's degree at the age of 16 from the University of Paris in 1926.

Shortly thereafter, the family emigrated to New York, where Bramley's father took a research position at Maimonides Hospital in Brooklyn. At age 17, Bramley entered the doctoral program in physics at New York University, receiving her degree two years later. After graduation, she was granted a National Research Council fellowship at Johns Hopkins University in Baltimore from 1929–1931. She also did post–doctoral work for several well known scientists Enrico Fermi at the University of Michigan and Nobel Laureate Harold Urey, discoverer of heavy water. After Johns Hopkins, she went back to New York University as a research associate until 1933. She was a staff member at Harvard Observatory in 1934 and then received a two–year fellowship from the American Association of University Women at Columbia University. From 1937–1942, she taught graduate physics courses at Brooklyn College.

A Career in Government and Private Industry

Bramley joined the U.S. Army's Signal Corps Engineering Laboratories in Belmar/Ft. Monmouth, New Jersey in 1942 as a mathematics consultant and as a supervisor of Signal Corps research and development contracts. Here, she met her future husband, Dr. Arthur Bramley, a well–known physicist who had worked on the Manhanttan Project, which developed the first atomic bomb. They had three children Nora, Alan and Timothy. Arthur Bramley died in 1971.

Her government career spanned more than 20 years. She worked at Signal Corps until 1950 on electronics projects involving pulse networks and vacuum–tube design, and as a consulting physicist until 1953. From 1953–1958, she ran the U.S. Navy's project on Dynamic Range of Persistent Screens as a project engineer at Du Mont Labs, and helped design and develop cathode ray and image tubes.

In 1958, she formed her own consulting firm, providing advice on display systems and various types of opto–electronic devices until 1962 when she was hired as a section head at Melpar, Inc. Bramley worked there until 1967, in charge of optical radar projects involving light sources of high brightness, infrared, and visible wavelengths, when she returned to government work.

At the Engineer Topographic Laboratories (Fort Belvoir, Virginia), she developed and decipheredcodes to allow the transmission of top secret pictorial information, as well as other special projects. Bramley's last position with the government as a supervisory physicist at the Night Vision and Electro–Optics Laboratory in Fort Belvoir ended in 1985. She also worked on her own projects involving gas lasers and display units, obtaining 18 patents on devices including tubes for early color televisions and computer screens. Her government service earned her the Lifetime Achievement Award in 1985 from the InterAgency Committee on Women in Science and Engineering "as the most outstanding woman scientist in the federal government." After leaving the laboratory, she went back to academia to become a professor of physics at the University of Oregon in Eugene. She remained there until 1988.

Author, Translator, and Women in Science Advocate

Throughout her career, Bramley authored 54 scientific papers. Besides Russian and English, she was also fluent in French and German, which allowed her to gain extensive experience in translating technical papers for publication and as a translator at professional meetings.

In addition, Bramley was involved in recruiting women into science, speaking at high school career nights and to high school guidance counselors while in New Jersey. She demonstrated her leadership skills in several professional associations, running local chapters or chairing major conventions. In 1972, she was chair of the IEEE's international convention.

Bramley died in 1997 at the age of 87. The legacy of Bramley's research in laser and optics technology lives on. The Breit–Rosenthal effect is still being cited in the literature more than 40 years after it was first published and is a required text for graduate students studying nuclear physics at New York University. In the Fall of 1999, the university dedicated the Jenny Rosenthal Bramley Laser Laboratory.

SELECTED WRITINGS BY BRAMLEY (UNDER ROSENTHAL):

Periodicals

"Vibrations of Tetrahedral Pentatomic Molecules, Parts I and II." *Physics Review* 45 (1934): 538.

"Vibrations of Tetrahedral Pentatomic Molecules, Parts III and IV." *Physics Review* 46 (1934): 730.

"Vibrations of Tetrahedral Pentatomic Moleculars, Part V." *Physics Review* 49 (1936): 535.

(with G.M. Murphy) "Group Theory and the Vibrations of Polyatomic Molecules." *Review of Modern Physics* 8 (1937): 317.

"Mechanism of Conductivity in Semiconducting Phosphors." *Journal of Chemistry and Physics* 20 (1952): 1946.

"Physical Optics of Coherent Radiation Systems." *Applied Optics* 1 (1962): 169.

"Display Devices in Image Processing." *Applied Optics* 14 (1975): 2971.

FURTHER READING

Books

Kass–Simon, G., and Patricia Farnes, eds. *Women in Science: Righting the Record.* Bloomington: Indiana University Press, 1990

Sketch by Laurel M. Sheppard

Yvonne Claeys Brill
1924–
Canadian-born American aerospace engineer

Yvonne Claeys Brill developed new rocket propulsion systems for communications satellites. Her innovative hydrazine resistojet, a single propellant rocket system she developed in the 1970s and for which she holds the patent, is still in use today. Brill served with the National Aeronautics and Space Administration's (NASA) space shuttle program office from 1981 to 1983, and she played a role in developing the propulsion system design for the International Maritime Satellite Organization (INMARSAT).

A native of Winnipeg, Canada, Brill was born on December 30, 1924. Her family discouraged her ambition to pursue science but she prevailed, earning her B.S. degree in mathematics at the University of Manitoba in 1945. Unable to find work in Canada, she relocated to Santa Monica, California, where she accepted a position as a mathematician for the Douglas Aircraft Company. At Douglas, Brill initially assisted with studies of aircraft propeller noise. Seeking more challenging work, she began graduate studies in chemistry at the University of Southern California.

At the end of World War II, Brill transferred to Douglas' aerodynamics department, where she remained for a short time before accepting a position as a research analyst with the RAND think tank in Santa Monica. During her association with RAND, a mentor helped her to obtain a promotion to the propellant department. During the day, Brill researched rocket and missile designs and propellant formulas, while continuing to pursue her graduate degree at night. When her association with RAND ended, her work became more theoretical. Dissatisfied, Brill joined Marquardt, a small firm, as a group leader, performing more applied work on super propellants and experimental ramjets.

Moves to East Coast

Brill earned her M.S. degree in chemistry in 1951, the same year she met and married her husband, a research chemist. In 1952 the couple moved to Connecticut, where Brill took a position as a staff engineer with United Aircraft Research Laboratory in East Hartford. During her tenure there, she resumed her study of rocket and ramjet engines and evaluated proposals for new projects. In 1955, Brill joined Wright Aeronautical Division of Curtiss–Wright Corporation where, as a project engineer, she directed corporate development of high energy fuels and studied state–of–the–art turbojet and turbofan engines adapted for advanced aircraft. Following the birth of her first child in 1957, Brill served as a part–time consultant on rocket propellants to FMC Corporation in Princeton. She had two more children before returning to full–time work in 1966.

Contributes to Mars Spacecraft

Brill accepted a position as Senior Engineer with RCA Astro–Electronics (now GE Astro) in 1966, and was named manager of NOVA Propulsion in 1978. She found her work at RCA challenging, and it was here that she made the most significant contributions of her career. She developed a hydrazine/hydrazine resistojet thruster, for which she later received a patent; the thruster was a monumental advance for single propellant rockets and is still used today. In addition, Brill performed preliminary work on the Mars Observer spacecraft, which was launched in 1992. She also tracked launch vehicle performance on the Scout, Delta, Atlas and Titan spacecrafts. In 1970, Brill received RCA's Astro–Electronics Engineering Excellence Award.

Brill left RCA in 1981 to serve as the director of the Solid Rocket Motor program in the Office of Space Flight (Shuttle Program) at NASA, a post she held for two years. Brill later remarked that while she missed the "hands–on work" she had performed at RCA, she found her experience with NASA valuable, having gained greater understanding of the interplay between the space program and federal political and budgetary processes.

Returning to RCA Astro–Electronics in 1983, Brill was disappointed to find that reorganization had changed management philosophy. She found herself simply writing proposals. In 1986, she accepted the position of space segment engineer with INMARSAT in London, where she worked until retiring from that project in 1991. That same year, Brill participated in the creation of two studies commissioned by the National Research Council. She subsequently was employed as a consultant for Telespace, Ltd., in Skillman, New Jersey, while monitoring propulsion system activities for all of the INMARSAT–2 spacecraft communication satellites which were in orbit in 1994.

Brill's many honors include the 1993 Resnik Challenger Medal for her "innovative concepts for satellite propulsion systems and her breakthrough engineering solutions (which) have designated her as a pioneer in expanding space horizons." She also received the Society of Women Engineers (SWE) Achievement Award in 1986; the Diamond Super Woman Award from *Harper's Bazaar* and DeBeers Corporation; and the American Institute of Aeronautics and Astronautics' (AIAA) National Capitol Section Marvin C. Demler Award for Outstanding Service, 1983, having previously been elected a fellow of the AIAA. She is also a fellow of the SWE, and a member of the National Academy of Engineering, the British Interplanetary Society, and the scientific societies Sigma Xi and Tau Beta Pi. She has authored 40 publications.

SELECTED WRITINGS BY BRILL:

Periodicals

"Going for the Assignments." *Aerospace America* (November 1984): 88.

FURTHER READING

Periodicals

Parsons, Susan V. "1993 Resnik Challenger Medal Recipient: Yvonne C. Brill." *SWE* (September/October 1993): 18–20.

Sharp, Daisy. "When Not Propelling Satellite, Enjoys Cooking and Concerts." *Trenton Advertiser* (December 8, 1968).

Sketch by Karen Withem

Elizabeth Gertrude (Knight) Britton
1858–1934
American botanist

The pre–eminent American woman botanist of the late nineteenth and early twentieth centuries, Elizabeth Gertrude Knight Britton specialized in bryology, the study of mosses. She made important contributions to the taxonomy of mosses throughout the world. In addition, she was a founder of the New York Botanical Garden and a pioneer conservationist.

Although born in New York City in 1858, Britton spent much of her childhood in Cuba, where her grandfather and her parents, James and Sophie Anne (Compton) Knight, owned a sugar plantation and furniture factory. One of five sisters, she attended a private elementary school until 1869 when she returned to New York to live with her maternal grandmother. There she attended Dr. Benedict's private school and later, Normal College (now Hunter College). Britton graduated in 1875 at age 17, and immediately joined the teaching staff of Normal College. Her interest in botany and natural history dated back to her childhood in Cuba and in 1883 she became an assistant in natural science at the college, a position she held until her marriage to Nathaniel Lord Britton in 1885.

Although no longer teaching, Britton stayed connected to science by joining the famous Torrey Botanical Club in 1879 as its first woman member. She edited the *Bulletin of the Torrey Botanical Club,* one of the major botanical journals in America, and served as the Club's curator in 1884 and 1885. Her first scientific paper, on albinism in plants, was published in 1883 and was followed within a few months by the first of many publications on mosses. By 1930, Britton had published 346 scientific papers and reviews, the majority of them on mosses.

Britton's husband, although originally a geology assistant at Columbia College in New York City, switched his field to botany shortly after their marriage. The Brittons had no children and together they went on numerous botanical expeditions to the West Indies. Britton also embarked alone on major plant–collecting expeditions in wilderness areas of the Adirondacks. The unofficial curator of the moss collection at Columbia, she greatly enlarged it with her own field collections. In 1893 she raised the money to purchase a large moss herbarium, which is a collection of dried plants, from the Swiss bryologist August Jaeger and move it to Columbia.

A visit to the Royal Botanic Gardens at Kew, near London, made a great impression on Britton and she determined that New York City should have its own botanical garden. Along with her husband, who was now a world–famous botanist, and fellow members of the Torrey Botanical Club, she was the driving force in the establishment of the New York Botanical Garden in the Bronx. The original 250 acre garden was incorporated in 1891 and her husband became its first director, a position he held for the next 33 years. Although Britton did not hold a salaried position at the Garden, she worked closely with her husband throughout his tenure. After 1899, when the Botanical Garden collections, along with the Columbia College herbarium, were moved to the Museum Building at the Garden, Britton worked as a full–time volunteer for the moss herbarium. Finally, in 1912, she was appointed Honorary Curator of Mosses, a position she held until her death from a stroke in 1934. She was responsible for greatly enlarging the moss herbarium by acquiring and incorporating other large collections. In addition, she identified the specimens sent to the Garden from around the world and supervised at least one doctoral student, Abel Joel Grout, who went on to become a leading bryologist.

Britton's later years were devoted to conservation. She helped found the Wild Flower Preservation Society of America in 1902 and served as its secretary and treasurer. Through publications, lectures, and correspondence, Britton raised public interest in conservation issues and promoted legislation for the protection of endangered native plants. In 1925, as chair of the conservation committee of the Federated Garden Clubs of New York, Britton successfully fostered a national boycott of the use of wild American holly in Christmas decorations, saving the native plant and promoting the use of cultivated holly.

Britton was the only woman charter member of the American Botanical Society when it was founded in 1893. She also was founder and president of the Sullivant Moss Chapter, which became the American Bryological Society, and she founded and edited the society's journal, the *Bryologist.* Although lacking both a college degree and a paid academic position after her early years at the Normal School, Britton nevertheless taught and inspired a new generation of bryologists. As a member of the National Science Club, Britton encouraged other women to take up the collection and study of mosses. Fifteen species of plants and the moss genus *Bryobrittonia* were named for her.

SELECTED WRITINGS BY BRITTON:

Periodicals

"The Jaeger Moss Herbarium." *Bulletin of the Torrey Botanical Club* 20 (1893): 235–36.

"A Trip to Jamaica." *Torreya* 8 (January 1908): 9–12.

FURTHER READING

Books

Slack, Nancy G. "Nineteenth–Century American Women Botanists: Wives, Widows, and Work." In *Uneasy Careers and Intimate Lives: Women in Science 1789–1979*. Edited by Pnina G. Abir–Am and Dorinda Outram. New Brunswick: Rutgers University Press, 1987.

Steere, William Campbell. " Elizabeth Gertrude Knight Britton." In *Notable American Women 1607–1950: A Biographical Dictionary* Edited by Edward T. James, Janet Wilson James, and Paul W. Boyer. Vol. 1. Cambridge: Harvard University Press, 1971.

Sketch by Margaret Alic

Harriet T. Brooks

1876–1933

Canadian physicist

Harriet Brooks was a pioneer in the field of nuclear physics, whose discoveries helped to unravel the mysteries of radioactivity and, eventually, of the atomic nucleus. The first Canadian nuclear scientist, she collaborated with the Nobel Prize winners Ernest Rutherford and **Marie Curie**. Since her scientific work spanned a period of only about seven years, her contributions to nuclear physics have been largely overlooked.

Born in Exeter, Ontario, in 1876, Brooks was the third of nine children in a family of very limited income. Her parents, George and Elizabeth Agnes (Worden) Brooks, moved the family to Montreal for three years and then returned to Seaforth, Ontario, in 1888, where Brooks attended high school. Financial support was available for women students at McGill University in Montreal and, an excellent student, Brooks graduated with a bachelor's degree in mathematics and natural philosophy in 1898, having received a number of scholarships and awards.

Joins Rutherford's Laboratory

Brooks' academic success caught the attention of physicist Ernest Rutherford, who invited her to work in his McGill laboratory as his first graduate student. Brooks entered a world where exciting new scientific discoveries were revolutionizing ideas about the nature of matter. Rutherford recently had discovered alpha radiation and in 1908 he would receive the Nobel Prize for his discoveries on the nature of radioactivity. Throughout his life, Rutherford promoted the careers of women physicists and Brooks was no exception. Brooks's master's thesis, on the magnetization of steel needles, was presented to the Royal Society of Canada in 1899 and published in the Society's *Transactions*. In 1901, Brooks became the first woman to receive a master's degree in physics from McGill.

In 1899, Brooks accepted a teaching position at the Royal Victoria College, while continuing her research with Rutherford. In this work, she identified the "emanation" given off by the element thorium as radon, a radioactive gas of lower molecular weight than thorium. This was a crucial step toward Rutherford and Frederick Soddy's discovery that one radioactive element can change into another. The following year, Brooks and Rutherford demonstrated that, in addition to alpha radiation, uranium and radium emitted beta radiation which was deflected in a magnetic field. They concluded that beta radiation was a negatively–charged particle, now known as the electron.

In 1901, Brooks was awarded a graduate student scholarship from Bryn Mawr College in Pennsylvania, the first women's college to emphasize graduate education. After one year of graduate study, she received the Bryn Mawr President's European fellowship to study at the prestigious Cavendish Laboratory at Cambridge University in England, where she worked with J. J. Thomson, the discoverer of the electron. There she continued her work on radium and thorium radiation and recognized that half of the radon gas from thorium disappeared in about one minute. This was one of the first observations of radioactive half–life.

Resuming her position at the Royal Victoria College, Brooks went back to work with Rutherford. There she identified polonium as the decay product of radon and was the first person to observe the phenomenon of radioactive recoil, the deflection of alpha radiation by thin metal foil. Eventually, this observation provided a means for separating radioactive isotopes. Between 1901 and 1905, Brooks continued to study the disintegration of the elements radium and actinium into other isotopes. She was also able to isolate various radioactive isotopes of radium.

In 1904 Brooks accepted a teaching position in physics at Barnard College in New York City. After two years of teaching, Brooks informed the Barnard dean of her plans to marry Bergen Davis, a physicist at Columbia University, whom she had met when they both worked at Cavendish. Knowing that she would be told to resign if she married, Brooks wrote to the dean, asking to keep her job. In her letter to the dean, as quoted by Margaret Rossiter, Brooks wrote: "I think also it is a duty I owe to my profession and

Harriet Brooks (Photo Researchers, Inc. Reproduced by permission.)

to my sex to show that a woman has a right to the practice of her profession and cannot be condemned to abandon it merely because she marries." **Margaret Maltby**, chair of the Barnard physics department, also pleaded with the dean to allow Brooks to stay. Nevertheless, Brooks was told that she would have to resign if she married. In the end, Brooks resigned even though she broke off her engagement.

Brooks spent the summer at Summerbrook, a socialist Utopian community in the Adirondack Mountains. There she met the Russian revolutionary writer, Maxim Gorky, and accompanied his entourage to Europe. In Paris, she went to work at the Sorbonne, in the laboratory of Marie Curie, continuing her research on the transmutation of radioactive elements. However, marriage plans once again interfered with her work. Frank Henry Pitcher, whom Brooks had met as an undergraduate at McGill, followed her to Europe and persuaded her to marry him in London in 1907 and return with him to Montreal.

Brooks never resumed her scientific career. Instead, she devoted herself to her three children and to horticulture. Two of her children died as teenagers. Brooks herself died in 1933, at the age of 56, from leukemia or a similar radiation–induced disease, as did many of the early nuclear researchers, including Marie Curie and her daughter **Irène Joliot-Curie**. Although Rutherford stated that, next to Marie Curie, Brooks was the greatest woman scientist working in the field of radiation, her contributions have never been fully recognized. As crucial as her discoveries were to the struggle to understand radioactivity and the nature of the atomic nucleus, they were not fully appreciated for many years, until a better understanding of the transmutation of radioactive elements was achieved.

SELECTED WRITINGS BY BROOKS:

Periodicals

(With E. Rutherford) "The New Gas from Radium." *Transactions of the Royal Society of Canada* 3 (1901): 21.

(With E. Rutherford) "Comparison of the Radiations from Radioactive Substances." *Philosophical Magazine* 6 (1902): 1.

"Volatile Product from Radium." *Nature* 70 (1904): 270 .

FURTHER READING

Books

Rayner–Canham, Marelene F. and Geoffrey W. Rayner–Canham. *Harriet Brooks: Pioneer Nuclear Scientist.* Montreal: McGill–Queen's University Press, 1992.

Rossiter, Margaret W. *Women Scientists in America: Struggles and Strategies to 1940.* Baltimore: Johns Hopkins University Press, 1982.

Other

Wong, C. W. , ed. "Brooks, Harriet." *CWP.* 1996. http://www.physics.ucla.edu/~cwp

Sketch by Margaret Alic

Dorothy Lavinia Brown
1919–
American surgeon

Dorothy Lavinia Brown was the first black female surgeon in the South. She was also the first black woman admitted to the American College of Surgeons, the first black woman to serve in the Tennessee State Legislature, and the first single woman to adopt a child in Tennessee.

Brown was born on January 7, 1919, in Philadelphia, Pennsylvania, to Edna and Kevin Thomas Brown. Her mother took her to Troy, New York, within weeks of her birth, and Brown did not meet her father until she was an

Dorothy Lavinia Brown (The Meharry Medical College Archives. Reproduced by permission.)

adult. Unable to care for her daughter, Brown's mother left her at Troy Orphanage when she was about five months old. Brown spent the next 12 years of her life there. She decided to become a doctor after having surgery to remove her tonsils when she was five years old.

When Brown was 13, her mother reclaimed her from the orphanage, hoping to prevent her daughter from being put in domestic service. Brown was not happy with her mother, who was a virtual stranger. She ran away at least five times, returning to Troy Orphanage each time. At the age of 15, Brown returned again to Troy and enrolled in Troy High School. With the help of the school's principal, Brown was placed with Samuel and Lola Redmon, who became her foster parents. With their support, she graduated near the top of her high school class. A local organization, the Women's Division of Christian Service of the Methodist Church, arranged a scholarship for her to attend Bennett College in Greensboro, North Carolina.

Brown's first year at Bennett was difficult; college administrators initially told the Methodist Women's Division that she was not suitable for Bennett. But Brown held on to her scholarship and completed her bachelor's degree in 1941. While attending Bennett, Brown took as many science courses as possible, though school officials discouraged her from entering medical school. They thought she should set her sights on being a schoolteacher instead. After graduation, she worked as an inspector in the Rochester Army Ordinance Department, during World War II.

In 1944, Brown entered Meharry Medical College in Nashville, Tennessee. She graduated with her medical degree in 1948 and worked a year–long internship at Harlem Hospital in New York City. She decided she wanted to pursue surgery but was discouraged by her superiors at Harlem Hospital. Brown returned to Meharry Medical College and did her surgical residency at George W. Hubbard Hospital. In the course of her residency, Brown was the first woman to be chief resident in general surgery at Meharry. She completed her surgical residency in 1954 and in 1955 became an assistant professor of surgery. Eventually, Brown became a clinical professor of surgery at Meharry. Brown also maintained her own private practice. In 1956, Brown took advantage of changes in state laws to adopted an infant, Lola Denise; she was the first single mother to adopt in Tennessee. Three years later, in 1959, Brown became the first black female surgeon to become a fellow of the American College of Surgeons.

By 1960, Brown was the chief of surgery and educational director at Riverside Hospital in Nashville, a position she held until the hospital closed in 1983. Brown also was an attending surgeon at Nashville Memorial Hospital and Metro General Hospital, as well as student health services director at Meharry Medical College and Fisk University. In 1966, while maintaining her professional responsibilities, Brown was elected to the Tennessee State Legislature, the first black woman to achieve this position. Her two years in the legislature were controversial. She authored and sponsored an abortion rights bill which could, she believed, save many women's lives. Though Brown initially intended to only serve one term, she decided to run for the Tennessee State Senate. The furor over the abortion bill, and other controversies, led to Brown's defeat in 1968.

While juggling teaching and medicine with motherhood, Brown served as a trustee for several universities, including Philander Smith College, Bennett College, and Russell Sage College in Troy, New York. Russell Sage College honored her in 1972 with an honorary doctorate of science, one of several honorary doctorates Brown received over the course of her career. Brown also held important committee memberships. In 1976, she served on the Joint Committee on Opportunities for Women in Medicine, sponsored by the American Medical Association. Brown was also a sought–after public speaker, both nationally and internationally.

Throughout her career, Brown maintained memberships in numerous professional and civic organizations. In addition to being a fellow of the American College of Surgeons and of the American College of Medicine, Brown is a member of the Nashville Academy of Medicine, the R.F. Boyd Medical Society, and the National Medical Association. She is also a life member of the National Association for the Advancement of Colored People (NAACP). Brown has been recognized many times for her professional and civic work. These honors include the 1970 renaming of the Women's Building at Meharry Medical College to the Dorothy L. Brown Building.

FURTHER READING

Books

Organ, Claude H. and Margaret M. Kosiba, eds. *A Century of Surgeons: The U.S.A. Experience, Volume II.* Norman, OK: Transcript Press, 1987, pp. 591–93.

Sammons, Vivian Ovelton. *Blacks in Science and Medicine.* New York: Hemisphere Publishing, 1990.

Periodicals

"Bachelor Mother." *Ebony* (September 1958): 92–96.

"Meharry Gets Woman Chief of Surgery." *Afro–American* (July 25, 1953).

Sketch by Annette Petrusso

Rachel Fuller Brown (The Library of Congress. Reproduced by permission.)

Rachel Fuller Brown
1898–1980
American biochemist

Rachel Fuller Brown, with her associate **Elizabeth Hazen**, developed the first effective antibiotic against fungal disease in humans; the most important biomedical breakthrough since the discovery of penicillin two decades earlier. The antibiotic, called nystatin, has cured sufferers of life-threatening fungal infections, vaginal yeast infections, and athlete's foot. Nystatin earned more than $13 million in royalties during Brown's lifetime, which she and Hazen dedicated to scientific research.

Brown was born in Springfield, Massachusetts, on November 23, 1898, to Annie Fuller and George Hamilton Brown. Her father, a real estate and insurance agent, moved the family to Webster Groves, Missouri, where she attended grammar school. In 1912, her father left the family. Brown and her younger brother returned to Springfield with their mother, who worked to support them. When Brown graduated from high school, a wealthy friend of the family financed her attendance at Mount Holyoke College in Massachusetts.

At Mount Holyoke, Brown was initially a history major, but she discovered chemistry when fulfilling a science requirement. She decided to double–major in history and chemistry, earning her A.B. degree in 1920. She subsequently went to the University of Chicago to complete her M.A. in organic chemistry. For three years, she taught chemistry and physics at the Francis Shimer School near Chicago. With her savings, she returned to the University to complete her Ph.D. in organic chemistry, with a minor in bacteriology. She submitted her thesis in 1926, but there was a delay in arranging her oral examinations. As her funds ran low, Brown took a job as an assistant chemist at the Division of Laboratories and Research of the New York State Department of Health in Albany, New York. Seven years later, when she returned to Chicago for a scientific meeting, Brown arranged to take her oral examinations and was awarded her Ph.D.

Discovers Fungal Antibiotic

Brown's early work at the Department of Health focused on identifying the types of bacteria that caused pneumonia, and in this capacity she helped to develop a pneumonia vaccine still in use today. In 1948, she embarked on the project with Hazen, a leading authority on fungus, that would bring them their greatest acclaim: the discovery of an antibiotic to fight fungal infections. Penicillin had been discovered in 1928, and in the ensuing years antibiotics were increasingly used to fight bacterial illnesses. One side effect, however, was the rapid growth of fungus that could lead to sore mouths or upset stomachs. Other fungal diseases without cures included infections attacking the central nervous system, athlete's foot, and ringworm. Microorganisms called actinomycetes that lived in soil were known to produce antibiotics. Although some killed fungus, they also proved fatal to test mice. Hazen ultimately narrowed the search down to a microorganism taken from soil near a barn on a friend's dairy farm in Virginia, later named streptomyces norsei. Brown's chemical analyses revealed that the microorganism produced two antifungal substances, one of which proved too toxic with test animals to pursue for human medical use. The other, however, seemed to have promise; it wasn't toxic to test animals and attacked both a fungus that invaded the lungs and central nervous system and candidiasis, an infection of the mouth, lungs, and vagina.

Brown purified this second antibiotic into small white crystals, and in 1950 Brown and Hazen announced at a meeting of the National Academy of Sciences that they had found a new antifungal agent. They patented it through the nonprofit Research Corporation, naming it "nystatin" in honor of the New York State Division of Laboratories and Research. The license for the patent was issued to E. R. Squibb and Sons, which developed a safe and effective method of mass production. The product called Mycostatin became available in tablet form in 1954 to patients suffering from candidiasis. Nystatin has also proved valuable in agricultural and livestock applications, and has even been used to restore valuable works of art.

In 1951, the Department of Health laboratories promoted Brown to associate biochemist. Brown and Hazen, in continuing their research, discovered two additional antibiotics, phalamycin and capacidin. Brown and Hazen were awarded the 1955 Squibb Award in Chemotherapy. Brown won the Distinguished Service Award of the New York State Department of Health when she retired in 1968, and the Rhoda Benham Award of the Medical Mycological Society of the Americas in 1972. In 1975, Brown and Hazen became the first women to receive the Chemical Pioneer Award from the American Institute of Chemists. In a statement published in the *Chemist* the month of her death, Brown hoped for a future of "equal opportunities and accomplishments for all scientists regardless of sex."

On retirement, Brown maintained an active community life, and became the first female vestry member of her Episcopalian church. By her death on January 14, 1980, she had paid back the wealthy woman who had made it possible for her to attend college. Using the royalties from nystatin, more importantly, she helped designate new funds for scientific research and scholarships.

SELECTED WRITINGS BY BROWN:

Periodicals

"Rachel Fuller Brown, Retired Scientist, New York State Department of Health." *Chemist* (January, 1980): 8.

FURTHER READING

Books

Baldwin, Richard S. *The Fungus Fighters: Two Women Scientists and Their Discovery.* Cornell University Press, 1981.

Vare, Ethlie Ann and Greg Ptacek *Mothers of Invention:From the Bra to the Bomb: Forgotten Women and Their Unforgettable Ideas.* New York: Morrow, 1988, pp. 124–126.

Yost, Edna. *Women of Modern Science.* Greenwood, 1959, pp. 64–79.

Periodicals

New York Times (June 29, 1957) p. 22–26; (January 16, 1980): D19.

Sketch by Miyoko Chu

Marjorie Lee Browne
1914–1979
American mathematician

Marjorie Lee Brown, along with **Evelyn Boyd Granville**, was one of the first African–American women to earn a doctorate in mathematics, graduating with a Ph.D. degree from the University of Michigan in 1949. Both a noted educator and a respected mathematician who focused on topology, Browne was the recipient of National Science Foundation fellowships as well as the W.W. Rankin Memorial Award for Excellence in Mathematical Teaching.

Browne was born on September 9, 1914, in Memphis, Tennessee, the daughter of Mary Taylor Lee and Lawrence Johnson Lee. Browne's mother died when she was only two years old and she was raised primarily by her father, a railway postal clerk who had finished two years of college. Browne's father had an abiding love for mathematics, a passion he passed on to his children. Browne attended public school in Memphis and then went to the private LeMoyne High School, where she was a tennis star. After graduation she attended Howard university, graduating *cum laude* in 1935.

A Lonely Subject

Browne once reported to Patricia Clark Kenschaft in *Black Women in America* that she "always, always liked mathematics As far back as I can remember, I like mathematics because it was a lonely subject." Browne turned this "lonely subject" into a career that touched hundreds of students. Out of Howard, she first taught school in New Orleans, then returned to earn a master's in mathematics at the University of Michigan in 1939. Thereafter she took a position at Wiley College in Marshall, Texas, and worked toward her doctorate in mathematics during the summers. In 1947 she became a teaching fellow at Michigan, and earned her Ph.D. degree two years later, with a dissertation on "The One Parameter Subgroups in Certain Topological and Matrix Groups."

Marjorie Lee Browne

Browne was acutely aware of the obstacles that women and minorities faced in pursuing scientific careers. Shortly after receiving her doctorate in 1949 she sought, unsuccessfully, to obtain an instructorship at several major research institutions. After receiving many polite letters of rejection, she decided to remain in the South and resolved that her greatest contributions would be directing programs designed to strengthen the mathematical preparation of secondary school mathematics teachers and to increase the presence of minorities and females in mathematical science careers.

For the next 30 years, Browne taught at North Carolina Central University (NCCU). She became the chair of the mathematics department in 1951, a position she held until 1970. She won a Ford Foundation fellowship to study combinational topology at England's Cambridge University from 1952–1953, as well as National Science Foundation faculty fellowships to study numerical analysis at UCLA and differential topology at Columbia University. Under her stewardship, NCCU, a predominantly black college, won a National Science Foundation grant for a summer institute for secondary teachers, a $60,000 IBM grant to fund a digital computer for academic computing, and a Shell grant to recognize outstanding students in mathematics. At NCCU's summer institutes, Browne authored the notes for mathematical studies, including "Sets, Logic, and Mathematical Thought," in 1957, "Introduction to Linear Algebra," in 1959, "Elementary Matrix Algebra." in 1969, and "Algebraic Structures," in 1974.

For her work in mathematics education, Browne was awarded the first W. W. Rankin Memorial Award from the North Carolina Council of Teachers of Mathematics in 1974. During her acceptance speech, she described herself as "a pre–sputnik mathematician," referring to the purist nature of her advanced mathematical preparation and the practice of many American industries and businesses, prior to the launching of the first Russian satellite in 1957, to allow scientists and mathematicians to pursue research projects that had no immediate real world or job–related applications. Browne served as the advisor for 10 master's theses in mathematics. Her publications include "A Note on Classical Groups," published in *American Mathematical Monthly.*

Browne retired in 1979 and died shortly thereafter, on October 19, 1979, of a heart attack. She was 65 years old. Browne was a pioneer in opening up academia to black students. In the latter part of her career, Browne personally helped to finance gifted young mathematicians in the pursuit of their doctorates. Browne was a generous humanitarian who believed that no good student should go without an education simply because he or she lacked financial resources. Thus, it was not uncommon for her to assume the financial responsibilities for many students whose families were unable to provide tuition, books, board, or transportation. To continue the philanthropic legacy she began, four of her former students established the Marjorie Lee Browne Trust Fund at North Carolina Central University in 1979. This fund supports two major activities in the mathematics and computer science department: the Marjorie Lee Browne Memorial Scholarship and the annual Marjorie Lee Browne Distinguished Alumni Lecture Series.

SELECTED WRITINGS BY BROWN:

Periodicals

"A Note on Classical Groups." *American Mathematical Monthly* 62 (1955): 424–27.

FURTHER READING

Books

Kenschaft, Patricia Clark. "Marjorie Lee Browne." *Black Women in America: An Historical Encyclopedia.* Edited by Darlene Clark Hine. Brooklyn, New York: Carlson Publishing, 1993, pp. 186–87.

Periodicals

Giles–Giron, Jacqueline. "Black Pioneers in Mathematics: Brown [sic], Granville, Cox, Claytor, and Blackwell." *American Mathematical Society Focus* (January–February 1991): 18.

Other

Fogg, Erica, Cecilia Davis, Jennifer Sutton, et al. "Marjorie Lee Browne." http://www.scottlan.edu/lriddle/women/brown.htm.

Williams, Scott. "Profile of Marjorie Lee Browne." http://www.math.buffalo.edu/mad/PEEPS/brownemarjorielee.html.

Sketch by J. Sydney Jones

Margaret Bryan
c. 1760–?
English teacher and natural philosopher

Margaret Bryan was a teacher and mistress of a girls' boarding school. Enormously successful in her time, Bryan emphasized scientific inquisitiveness and knowledge in conjunction with traditional religion.

Little is known about Margaret Bryan's early life, and nearly all that is known about her is gleaned from her own books. She was given eight years of science education, and spent seven years experimenting and researching the practical application of her scientific knowledge. She was the mother of two daughters. Toward the end of the 1700s, Bryan opened a girls' boarding school in Blackheath. It changed addresses several times over the years, each time to a wealthier neighborhood and larger quarters.

Bryan's school taught both mathematics and science to young women. Within the science courses, Bryan taught physics, chemistry, and mechanics. She stated that her lessons were not just "infusions of science, but also, and more particularly . . . leading to all that is lovely, dignifying, and noble." Because she taught science as a subject given by God for spiritual revelation, her classes were often inextricable from religious ideas.

Bryan's work garnered the praise and support of Charles Hutton, an important scientist at the time, who helped her publish her scientific writing. In addition to her book *Lectures in Natural Philosophy*, which contained chapters on matter, mechanics, pneumatics, acoustics, water and hydrostatics, magnetism, electricity, optics, and astronomy, Bryan wrote *A Compendious System of Astronomy*, and *An Astronomical and Geographical Class Book for Schools*. The book, *Conversations on Chemistry*, is sometimes attributed to Bryan, but it was actually written and published anonymously by English science writer, **Jane Marcet**. Her books contained the course lectures given to the young women at her school.

Bryan evidently loved her work, claiming that she "rejoiced" in her profession and that her "heart is deeply interested in the results of my labours." Her work was widely known and discussed, both in the general populace and in the scientific community.

SELECTED WRITINGS BY BRYAN:

Books

Lectures in Natural Philosophy. London: Thomas Davison, 1806.

FURTHER READING

Books

Ogilvie, Marilyn Bailey. *Women in Science: Antiquity through the Nineteenth Century*. Cambridge: MIT Press, 1986.

Phillips, Patricia. *The Scientific Lady*. New York: St. Martin's Press, 1990.

Stephen, Leslie, and Sidney Lee, eds. *The Dictionary of National Biography*. London: Oxford University Press, 1917.

Sketch by Helene Barker Kiser

Mary Morland Buckland
1797–1857
English geologist

Mary Buckland, the wife of William Buckland, one of the founders of modern geological science, was an accomplised fossil geologist. She collaborated closely with her husband, and her contributions have often been overlooked in favor of her husband's accomplishments.

Mary Morland Buckland was born in 1797, at Sheepstead House, near Abingdon, in Berkshire, England. Her mother died when she was an infant, and her father, Benjamin Morland, remarried and subsequently had a large family. For much of her childhood, Buckland lived in Oxford with Sir Christopher Pegge, a physician, and his wife. The Pegges encouraged Buckland's interests and fascination with natural science.

In the early nineteenth century, geology was developing into an important scientific discipline, in part because of the activities of amateur and professional fossil hunters. Many of these early geologists were English women who have been largely overlooked. Mary Morland Buckland was already an accomplished naturalist when she married the Reverend William Buckland in 1825. They had met on a coach while traveling in Dorsetshire. They had noticed that they were both reading the new book by the French biologist Georges Cuvier, who had sent Mary Buckland a copy.

The Bucklands went on geological expeditions together, and Mary Buckland became an accomplished fossil geologist. She identified and reconstructed the fossils they collected, made leather models of their discoveries, and recorded their observations. In addition, she edited and illustrated several of her husband's works, including his famous "Bridgewater Treatise" in *Geology and Mineralogy Considered with Reference to Natural Theology*. As H. J. Mozans quoted from the introduction to this work, written by Buckland's son Francis: "her natural talent in the use of her pencil enabled her to give accurate illustrations and finished drawings . . . She was also particularly clever and neat in mending broken fossils. There are many specimens in the Oxford Museum, now exhibiting their natural forms and beauty, which were restored by her perseverance to shape from a mass of broken and almost comminuted fragments. It was her occupation also to label the specimens." After long nights working with her husband, Buckland spent her mornings supervising the education of her five children. Buckland also contributed drawings to a work by the geologist William Conybeare.

It is difficult to evaluate Buckland's scientific contributions, since all of her work was published under her husband's name. Shortly after their marriage, her husband became one of the first presidents of the new British Association for the Advancement of Science (BAAS). Although Buckland attended BAAS meetings, her husband, at least initially, was opposed to women attending the presentations of scientific papers. Buckland died in 1857, a year after her husband. Apparently they both died from the long–term effects of injuries sustained in a carriage accident in Germany 30 years previously.

FURTHER READING

Books

Cannon, Walter F. "William Buckland." In *Dictionary of Scientific Biography*, edited by Charles Coulston Gillispie, New York: Charles Scribner's Sons, 1970.

Fox, Caroline. *Memories of Old Friends, Being Extracts from the Journals and Letters of Caroline Fox, of Penjerrick, Cornwall, from 1835 to 1871.* Edited by Horace M. Pym. Philadelphia: J. B. Lippincott, 1882.

Mozans, H. J. [John Augustine Zahm]. *Women in Science*. 1913. Reprint, Cambridge: MIT Press, 1974.

Ogilvie, Marilyn Bailey. *Women in Science, Antiquity through the Nineteenth Century: A Biographical Dictionary with Annotated Bibliography*. Cambridge: MIT Press, 1991.

Sketch by Margaret Alic

Mary Alice Bunting-Smith
1910–1998
American geneticist

Mary Bunting-Smith was a pioneer in bacterial genetics and the effects of radiation on microorganisms. As dean of Douglass College and president of Radcliffe College, she used innovative approaches to increase educational and professional opportunities for women.

Mary Bunting–Smith was born in 1910, in Brooklyn, New York, the oldest of four children. Her father, Henry Ingraham, was a lawyer, and her mother, Mary Shotwell Ingraham, a graduate of Vassar College, was involved in a number of groups advocating women's rights and other women's issues. Due to a series of childhood illnesses, Bunting–Smith had little formal education prior to high school. Rather, she was tutored by her maternal grandmother on their farm in Northport, Long Island. In 1923, she entered Packer Collegiate Institute.

Bunting–Smith attended Vassar College, graduating Phi Beta Kappa in 1931 with a degree in physics. After studying chemistry at Cornell University summer school, she received a Nancy Skinner Clark Fellowship from Vassar College for graduate studies in agricultural bacteriology at the University of Wisconsin. She studied bacteriology with **Elizabeth McCoy** and minored in biochemistry, receiving her master's degree in 1932. Bunting–Smith then conducted research in agricultural bacteriology and was awarded an Annie Gorham Fellowship to apply towards her doctorate. After receiving her Ph.D. in 1934, Bunting–Smith worked as a research assistant to Harry Steenbock in agricultural chemistry. In 1936, she began teaching physiology and genetics at Bennington College, a new, progressive women's school in Vermont.

In 1937, Bunting–Smith married Henry Bunting, whom she had previously met at the University of Wisconsin, where they were both taking his father's pathology course. While her new husband completed his medical internship at Johns Hopkins University, Bunting–Smith taught physiology and hygiene at Goucher College in Baltimore. The following year, the couple moved to Yale University, where Bunting–Smith worked as a researcher with Leo Roetger and her husband completed a residency in pathology. Bunting–Smith continued to do her own research and presented her findings at a Cold Spring Harbor Symposium on Quantitative Biology. With the birth of her first child, she left the laboratory and had four children over the next six years. While her husband pursued postdoctoral research in Boston, Bunting–Smith taught bacteriology at Wellesley College. Returning to Yale in 1948, she obtained a research assistant position, followed by a lectureship position in microbiology held until 1955. She also received

Mary Bunting-Smith (Archive Photos. Reproduced by permission.)

a research grant from the American Tuberculosis Association to study the genetics of the mycobacterium that causes tuberculosis. Later, she obtained a grant from the Atomic Energy Commission to study the effects of radiation on the genetics of bacteria.

Appointed Dean of Douglass College

In 1954, Bunting–Smith's husband died. Needing to support four young children, she found a better job opportunity in 1955 becoming dean of Douglass College, the state college for women, and professor of bacteriology at Rutgers University, in New Brunswick, New Jersey. Her extensive involvement with community activities and public education, while raising her children, provided Bunting–Smith with the expertise she needed for her new position.

Becoming concerned with the decreasing opportunities of science education for girls and young women, Bunting–Smith introduced a program of part–time study for married women. Additionally, in 1957, she joined the National Science Foundation's Divisional Committee for Scientific Personnel and Education, which better informed her of these issues. Bunting–Smith became a leader in promoting fellowships and part–time opportunities for women and in the movement for the reentry of women into higher education, subsequent to starting their families.

Initiates Reforms at Radcliffe College

In 1960, Bunting–Smith became the fifth president of Radcliffe College, a position held until 1972, while continuing to teach a small freshman research seminar on microbial genetics. Her goal was to fully integrate Radcliffe with Harvard University. She replaced the Radcliffe dormitories with Harvard–style residence halls that included faculty and graduate students. She oversaw the merger of the Radcliffe Graduate School with that of Harvard and the opening of the Harvard Business School to women which enabled Radcliffe students to receive Harvard degrees for the first time. Bunting–Smith also established the Radcliffe Institute for Independent Study, now the Bunting Institute, to assist women with families to continue to work toward their career goals, and to provide resident fellowships for gifted women. This experiment was a resounding success and served as a model for innumerable programs to encourage the professional careers of women. Bunting–Smith took a one year leave–of–absence from Radcliffe in 1964, to serve as the first woman member of the Atomic Energy Commission. In 1972, she resigned from Radcliffe to serve as assistant for special projects at Princeton University, a position she held until her retirement in 1975.

Following her retirement, Bunting–Smith continued to serve on the boards of various industrial and public institutions. She remarried in 1979 to Dr. Clement A. Smith. Bunting–Smith died in1998 at her home in Hanover, New Hampshire.

SELECTED WRITINGS BY BUNTING-SMITH:

Books

(Moderator) "Panel Discussion: The Commitment Required of a Woman Entering a Scientific Profession." In *Women and the Scientific Professions: The M.I.T. Symposium on American Women in Science and Engineering*. Edited by Jacquelyn A. Mattfeld and Carol G. Van Aken. Cambridge: MIT Press, 1965.

Periodicals

(With M. A. Ingraham) "The Bacteriostatic Action of Gentian Violet and its Dependence on the Oxidation–Reduction Potential." *Journal of Bacteriology* 26 (1933): 573–98.

(With C. A. Bauman) "The Relation of Microorganisms to Carotenoids and Vitamin A." *Journal of Bacteriology* 28 (1934): 31–40.

"The Inheritance of Color in Bacteria, with Special Reference to *Serratia marcescens*." *Cold Spring Harbor Symposium on Quantitative Biology* 11 (1945): 25–32.

"From *Serratia* to Women's Lib and a Bit Beyond." *American Society for Microbiology News* 37 (1971): 46–52.

"Education: A Nurturant if not a Determinant of Professional Success." *Annals of the New York Academy of Sciences* 208 (1973): 194–99.

FURTHER READING

Books

O'Hern, Elizabeth Moot. *Profiles of Pioneer Women Scientists.* Washington, D.C.: Acropolis Books, 1985.

Rossiter, Margaret W. *Women Scientists in America: Before Affirmative Action 1940–1972.* Baltimore: Johns Hopkins University Press, 1995.

Other

Hopkins, Nancy Doe. "A Cornerstone of Our Thinking." *Harvard Magazine.* 1998. http://www.harvard–magazine.com/ma98/jhj.bunting.html.

"Mary Bunting–Smith Dies as 87." *The Harvard University Gazette.* 1998. http://www.news.harvard.edu/gazette/1998/01.29/MaryBunting–Smi.html.

Sketch by Margaret Alic

Margaret Burbidge (UPI/Corbis-Bettmann. Reproduced by permission.)

Eleanor Margaret Burbidge
1919–
English-born American astrophysicist

Eleanor Margaret Burbidge gained recognition for producing the first accurate estimates of galactic masses, for her discoveries concerning quasars, and for her work on the metal content of stars. Burbidge also served on the scientific committees that planned and outfitted the Hubble Space Telescope, an instrument designed to provide the clearest snapshots of distant galaxies yet produced. Despite initial difficulties, United States astronauts successfully made repairs to the Hubble Telescope in December, 1993.

Burbidge was born Eleanor Margaret Peachey in Davenport, England, on August 12, 1919, the daughter of Stanley John and Marjorie (Stott) Peachey. Her father was a lecturer in chemistry at the Manchester School of Technology and her mother was a chemistry student there. When Burbidge was only a year and a half old, her father, after obtaining patents in rubber chemistry, set up a laboratory in the London, where the family relocated. There, Burbidge's budding interest in science was encouraged by her parents. "I'd been interested in astronomy but only from the point of view of thinking it would be an amateur interest," Burbidge told Joan Oleck in an interview. "I first got interested in the stars when I was a small child. . . I had to make do with my father's binoculars."

Later, at the University of London, Burbidge took First Class Honors with her bachelor's degree in science in 1939. In the ensuing years, Burbidge stayed on at the University Observatory for her graduate education. World War II, which was raging across Europe, oddly aided her studies. As Burbidge explained, the lenses of the Observatory's double refracting telescope were buried in its concrete pier for safekeeping against bombing raids, but the twenty–four inch reflector was left intact. At night, Burbidge could use the telescope for her Ph.D. work. "The director had been called to the Admiralty for classified War work," she recalled. "The first assistant had gone in the Army and the mechanic was in the Air Force repairing airplanes. So, in a junior fashion, I was appointed general caretaker and looker–after of everything there." Burbidge's duties included repairing damage to the telescope's dome caused by shrapnel. As the War continued, Burbidge was awarded her Ph.D. in 1943 for her studies of the physics of hot stars.

Her coursework curtailed because of the War, Burbidge returned to the classroom once peace was established. There, in 1947, she met fellow graduate student Geoffrey Burbidge, whom she married in April, 1948 (they would later have a daughter). In the late 1940s, Burbidge worked as assistant director and acting director of the Observatory. In 1951, she was invited to Harvard University's Yerkes

Observatory on a fellowship with Fulbright funds; her husband traveled with her on an Agassiz fellowship of his own to Harvard. Though the Burbidges liked life in the United States, they were obliged under the terms of their fellowships to return to England, which they did in 1953. Burbidge dove into an analysis of the data she had collected in the U.S. while working at the University of Chicago's telescope in southwest Texas and her husband took a job at Cambridge University's Cavendish Laboratory. It was at Cambridge in 1954 that the Burbidge first teamed up with the English astronomer Fred Hoyle and American physicist William A. Fowler to study the content of stars.

Works on Metal Content of Stars

Throughout the late 1950s, between Burbidge's stints as a research fellow and associate professor at the University of Chicago and California Institute of Technology, the Cambridge foursome delved into the evolution of stars, continuing the astronomical spectroscopy and analysis of the surface layers of stars Burbidge had engaged in for her doctoral thesis. Together the four looked at star evolution by studying star interiors; they concluded that stars can generate nearly every known metal but that only the lightest elements could have been created during the special conditions incredible density and heat of the universe's first moments. Stars can, however, use the metal, created by earlier stars, that exists in the interstellar gas to create increasingly heavier metals. Therefore, the four scientists determined, the metal content of stars and interstellar gas grows as stars build on the metals derived from previous stars.

"It added up to starting with the outside of stars and understanding what you actually observed from the surface of stars, then going on to the study of the interior of stars," Burbidge recalled. "It had been known since 1938 what the nuclear energy source of stars was so as they use up their hydrogen and convert it to helium, structural changes occur in the stars. [Our work consisted of] understanding those [conversions] and looking at stars of different ages and seeing that the heavy element content of stars was a function of the age of the stars. So, that led to the idea that there must have been production of the elements in the interior of stars. . . .

"We found out a way to produce all of the elements heavier than hydrogen starting with hydrogen, assuming that a first generation of stars was made up of just hydrogen. We actually know now that it was hydrogen and a little bit of helium. How you can get nuclear energy by nuclear reactions that cause our sun to shine that builds helium out of hydrogen and then a star that is older than our sun or has gone through its life faster than our sun will start further reactions, like building carbon out of helium and so on, through heavier elements. And you can go on getting energy from nuclear reactions up until you build elements as heavy as iron."

Studies Galaxy Rotation and Quasars

During the late 1950s and early 1960s, Burbidge contributed pioneering work to the rotation of galaxies. Burbidge explained: "Galaxies rotate around an axis. Why they don't collapse is because of centrifugal force [which she likens to swinging a stone on a string; if the string is cut, the stone flies off into space]. For our galaxy, the force of gravity holds the material in place and the rotational speed counterbalances this. So a galaxy takes up a structure in which gravitational pull is equated to centrifugal force." Therefore, Burbidge explained, if one wishes to calculate a galaxy's weight and the distribution of its mass, one must measure rotational speed.

In the late 1960s, Burbidge turned her attention to quasars, celestial objects more distant than stars that emit excessive amounts of radiation. By this time, she and her husband were settled in at the University of California at San Diego, having moved there in 1962 (her presidency of the American Astronomical Society from 1976 to 1978 prompted Burbidge to obtain U.S. citizenship). Burbidge became a full professor in 1964 and directed the University's Center for Astrophysics and Space Sciences from 1979 to 1988. Burbidges's work on quasars included measuring their redshifts. When moving objects emit light, the light waves in front of them are closer together than if the object were standing still, a phenomenon evidenced by the light's frequency "shifting" to the blue end of the color spectrum. Conversely, objects moving away have light waves that are farther away from each other, shifting the light toward the red end of the spectrum. (The same phenomenon also occurs with moving objects emitting sound, known as the Doppler effect.) It had been known that all galaxies except those nearest to earth emit redshifted light. "You can measure speed looking at variations of the elements and measuring their shifts," Burbidge explained. "By a simple relationship you can tell how fast the galaxy is moving away. And this was done for quasars." Burbidge continues her work in spectroscopy and the ultraviolet spectrum of quasars, the latter of which the repaired Hubble Telescope greatly aids.

Burbidge became a professor emeritus in 1990. Over the years she has collected a number of awards, including a National Medal of Science in 1984 and twelve honorary doctoral degrees. She shared the 1959 Warner Prize from the American Astronomical Society with her husband, was elected a fellow of the Royal Society of London in 1964 and the American Academy of Arts and Sciences four years later, was made Abby Rockefeller Mauze Professor of the Massachusetts Institute of Technology in 1968, was elected into the National Academy of Science in 1978, received a Catherine Wolfe Bruce Medal from the Astronomical Society of the Pacific in 1982, and was awarded the Albert Einstein World Award of Science Medal in 1988.

SELECTED WRITINGS BY BURBIDGE:

Books

Lectures on Radio Galaxies and Quasi–Stellar Objects. Tata Institute of Fundamental Research, 1968.

Periodicals

(With Barlow T. A., Cohen R. D., Junkkarinen Volume T. and Womble D. S.) "Extent of Warm Haloes around Medium–Redshift Galaxies." *Astronomy and Space Science* 157 (1989): 263–269.

FURTHER READING

Other

Burbidge, E. Margaret, telephone interview with Joan Oleck conducted on January 20, 1994.

Sketch by Joan Oleck

Augusta Ada Byron, Countess of Lovelace
1815–1852
English applied mathematician

Augusta Ada Byron, Countess of Lovelace (Doris Langley Moore Collection.)

Ada Byron, Countess of Lovelace is best known for her early contributions to the field of computing. A friend and devotee of Charles Babbage, she published detailed descriptions of his calculating machines. Byron is credited with having written the world's first computer program, a set of instructions for Babbage's Analytical Engine. She was a visionary who speculated on how calculating machines might someday be put to practical use.

Byron was born in London, December 10, 1815, to an aristocratic family. Named Augusta Ada Byron, she was the only legitimate daughter of George Gordon, Lord Byron, the English poet. Her mother, Lady Byron, was born Anne Isabella Milbanke, a wealthy intellectual and eccentric, who had been tutored in mathematics. According to historians, Lord Byron was unprepared for the commitments of marriage and fatherhood. In the hours before his daughter's birth he threw furniture around the room. When Ada Byron was only a month old, her mother took her and fled from his household. The young Byron never again saw her father, who died of fever when she was eight years old. Byron was raised by her mother, maternal grandparents, and nannies. Her mother was strongly opinionated about child–rearing practices. While she encouraged Byron's formal education, uncommon among the wealthy during the era, she also believed in such practices as teaching young children to lie perfectly still for long periods of time. Byron spent many hours of her childhood lying flat on a wooden plank, forbidden to move even a finger. She was a precocious child, able to add six rows of numbers and spell two–syllable words at the age of five. Her mother decided science and mathematics should be emphasized in her education, believing these disciplines would counter the romanticism and lack of self–control Byron had supposedly inherited from her father. Byron was tutored in science and mathematics by William Frend, a controversial peace advocate, William King, the family's physician, and **Mary Somerville**, an astronomer and the first female to be elected to Britain's prestigious scientific group, the Royal Society. Byron also studied and excelled in drawing, music, and foreign languages. Her fluency in French would play a role in her contribution to computer history.

In the spring of 1833, Byron attended a party at the home of Charles Babbage, inventor of several steam–driven calculating machines that were to become the precursors of modern computers. Byron quickly took interest in a small working model of Babbage's first Difference Engine, a contraption that could mechanically compete values of quadratic functions. She studied Babbage's plan for the construction of his Analytical Engine, a machine that received instructions and numerical data from punched cards and could make and analyze mathematical calculations. Babbage became a close friend and intellectual mentor to Byron, directing her in 1840 to Augustus de Morgan, a professor of mathematics at the University of London. Under De Morgan's tutelage Byron began advanced studies in mathematics, equivalent to what men were receiving at the time from Cambridge University. De Morgan was reportedly impressed by Byron's intellect, but feared her studies might strain her delicate female nervous system.

Writes "First" Computer Program

The same year that Byron began her advanced studies, Babbage traveled to Turin, Italy, to give a presentation about his Analytical Engine. In attendance was a young military engineer, Luigi Federico Manabrea. Manabrea, who would eventually become prime minister of Italy, was impressed with Babbage's invention, and described its operation for a Swiss journal. His article, written in French, was published in October of 1842. Babbage, who had been so preoccupied with the development and fund–raising for construction of his engines, had never bothered to publish his own descriptions. Charles Wheatstone, pioneer of the telegraph, read Manabrea's article and convinced Byron to translate the article for the British journal *Taylor's Scientific Memoirs*. Wheatstone was a close family friend and aware of Byron's facility in both French and mathematics. When Byron discovered the original article described only the mathematical concepts by which the engine would work, she decided to append a series of notes to the translation. The notes were remarkable in that she not only produced the first clear mechanical explanation of Babbage's Analytical Engine, but provided illustrations of how it might be instructed to perform particular tasks. In so doing, Byron created the world's first computer program. She invented the idea of asubroutine, a set of instructions that are used repeatedly in a variety of contexts. Byron also anticipated the process she called "backing," which is equivalent to the modern day concept of looping, and she described the notion of a conditional jump, in which the machine responds to "if–then" statements. In her final note, Byron produced a diagram which showed how Bernoulli numbers could be derived through mechanical computation. Her program provided instructions on where to set and how to display calculations in the engine. Byron's eight lengthy notes were written in just under a year, during which time she corresponded heavily with Babbage. In July of 1843 the translation and notes, titled "Sketch of the Analytical Engine Invented by Charles Babbage, Esq.," appeared in print. Although the publication was to constitute Byron's most important contribution to mathematics, she chose to sign her work with only the initials A.A.L., for Augusta Ada Lovelace. It has been speculated she did so to preserve the image of a modest and proper Victorian lady. Many of her friends knew nothing of her intense interest in mathematics.

Creates Scandal for Her Family

While some aspects of Byron's lifestyle did conform to the expectations placed on her by Victorian society, in the end her behavior brought scandal to her family. In 1835 Byron had met and married William King, unrelated to her childhood tutor of the same name. King took a seat in the House of Lords in 1838 and adopted the title first earl of Lovelace. Byron became countess of Lovelace. The couple shared a love of horses and spent considerable time riding on their estates. Their social circle, in addition to Charles Babbage, included physicist Michael Faraday, astronomer Sir John Herschel, and inventor of the kaleidoscope, Sir David Brewster. They were also close friends with Charles Dickens. The couple had three children: Byron, Anne Isabella, and Ralph. In 1837, shortly after giving birth to Anne Isabella, Byron developed cholera. Although she survived, her health never fully recovered. She suffered from asthma and digestive problems, and was prescribed laudanum, opium, and morphine, which she took with wine. Historians believe that Byron was unaware of an addiction, but her personal letters reveal that she experienced the symptoms of withdrawal. She became known for her bizarre mood swings and reportedly had hallucinations. In the decade before her death Byron also took up gambling. An avid fan of horse–racing, she squandered much of the family fortune on a flawed betting scheme. This, and an alleged affair with a gambling accomplice, John Crosse, were the subject of gossip among her social peers. In 1851 Byron was diagnosed with uterine cancer. She died on November 27, 1852, and was laid to rest in a church near Newstead, next to her father, Lord Byron.

Honored Posthumously

In 1953, after digital computing had become a reality, Byron's notes were rediscovered. They appeared in a volume by B.Y. Bowden, titled *Faster Than Thought: A Symposium on Digital Computing Machines*. The computer revolution underway, her contribution to the field would finally receive public recognition. In 1974, the U.S. Defense Department decided to standardize its computer operations by choosing a single computer language for all its tasks. In 1980, on what would have been Byron's 165th birthday, the Ada Joint Program Office was created for the purpose of introducing the Ada language. Three years later, the American National Standards Institute approved Ada as a national all–purpose standard. It was given the code name MIL–STD–1815, the last four digits honoring her birth year.

FURTHER READING

Books

Baum, Joan. *The Calculating Passion of Ada Byron.* Hamden CT: Archon Books, 1986.

Moore, Doris Langley–Levy. *Ada, Countess of Lovelace: Byron's Legitimate Daughter.* New York: Harper and Row, 1977.

Stein, Dorothy. *Ada: A Life and a Legacy.* Cambridge: MIT Press, 1985.

Toole, Betty Alexandra, ed. *Ada, the Enchantress of Numbers: A Selection from the Letters of Lord Byron's Daughter and Her Description of the First Computer.* Mill Valley, CA: Strawberry Press, 1992.

Wade, Mary Dodson, *Ada Byron Lovelace: The Lady and the Computer*. New York: Dillon Press, & Toronto: Maxwell Macmillan Canada, 1994.

Other

Toole, Betty. "Ada Byron." *Biographies of Women Mathematicians*. June 1997. http://www.scottlan.edu/lriddle/women/chronol.htm (July 22, 1997).

Sketch by Leslie Reinherz

C

Alexa I. Canady
1950–
American neurosurgeon

Alexa I. Canady is the first African American woman to become a neurosurgeon in the United States. Honored with numerous professional and academic awards, she has since held several teaching posts and is the director of neurosurgery at Children's Hospital of Michigan in Detroit.

Alexa Irene Canady was born November 7, 1950, in Lansing, Michigan, to Elizabeth Hortense Golden Canady, an educational administrator, and Clinton Canady, Jr., a dentist. She has three brothers: Clinton III, Alan, and Mark. As the only black girl in her elementary school, Canady experienced racism at an early age. In an interview with Brian Lanker in *I Dream a World: Portraits of Black Women Who Changed the World,* she stated: "During the second grade I did so well on the California reading test that the teacher thought it was inappropriate for me to have done that well. She lied about what scores were mine, and ultimately, she was fired." By the time Canady was in high school in the 1960s, however, she was recognized as a National Achievement Scholar.

While pursuing a mathematics degree at the University of Michigan, Canady attended a minority health careers program and subsequently redirected her studies, receiving a B.S. in 1971 and an M.D. in 1975. As a student, she was elected to Alpha Omega Alpha honorary medical society and received the American Medical Women's Association citation. Canady's internship was spent at the Yale–affiliated New Haven Hospital in 1975–76. After completing the internship, she gained her landmark residency in neurosurgery at the University of Minnesota from 1976 to 1981. Afterward, Children's Hospital in Philadelphia awarded Canady a fellowship in pediatric neurosurgery in 1981–82. Besides treating patients directly, Canady served as an instructor in neurosurgery at the University of Pennsylvania College of Medicine.

In 1982, she moved back to Michigan and took a post in neurosurgery at Henry Ford Hospital in Detroit. The following year, she transferred to pediatric neurosurgery at Children's Hospital of Michigan. She became the assistant director of neurosurgery at Children's Hospital three year's later, and director in 1987. She was named Teacher of the Year there in 1984, the same year she was certified by the American Board of Neurological Surgery. Canady was honored as Woman of the Year by the Detroit chapter of the National Association of Negro Business and Professional Women's Club in 1986 and received the Candace Award from the National Coalition of 100 Black Women in the same year. She began teaching at Wayne State University School of Medicine as a clinical instructor in 1985 and assumed a clinical associate professorship in 1987. Canady married George Davis in June 1988.

SELECTED WRITINGS BY CANADY:

Periodicals

(With J. Donders and B. P. Rourke) "Psychometric Intelligence after Infantile Hydrocephalus: A Critical Review and Reinterpretation." *Childs Nervous System* (May 1990): 148–154.

(With S. Sood, S. Kim, and others) "Useful Components of the Shunt Tap Test for Evaluation of Shunt Malfunction." *Childs Nervous System* (June 1993): 157–162.

(With R. D. Fessler and M. D. Klein) "Ultrasound Abnormalities in Term Infants on ECMO." *Pediatric Neurosurgery* (July–August 1993): 202–205.

FURTHER READING

Books

Lanker, Brian. *I Dream a World: Portraits of Black Women Who Changed the World.* Stewart, Tabori, 1989, p. 128.

Smith, Jessie Carney, ed. *Notable Black American Women.* Detroit: Gale, 1992, pp. 155–156.

Periodicals

Ross–Flanigan, Nancy. "Hall of Fame Inductees Followed Their Hearts: Canady Is at Home with Neurosurgery." *Detroit Free Press* (October 17, 1989): 1C.

Sketch by Linda Lewin

Annie J. Cannon (UPI/Corbis-Bettmann. Reproduced by permission.)

Annie Jump Cannon
1863–1941
American astronomer

Annie Jump Cannon was the best-known American woman astronomer of her time. Educated at Wellesley College, Cannon spent her professional life at the Harvard College Observatory. Her most lasting contribution is the cataloging system she developed that rationally arranges stars by their temperatures and compositions. In her lifetime she classified the spectra of hundreds of thousands of stars, filling ten volumes. In recognition of this achievement, the National Academy of Sciences awarded Cannon the Henry Draper Medal in 1931.

Cannon was born on December 11, 1863, in Dover, Delaware, eldest of the three children of Wilson Lee Cannon, a shipbuilder, farm owner, and state senator, and his second wife, the former Mary Elizabeth Jump. Annie also had four siblings from her father's first marriage. Her mother, who had been educated at a school run by Quakers near Philadelphia, taught Annie the constellations. As a child, Cannon observed the night sky through an attic window, reading her astronomical guidebook by candlelight.

Cannon received her early education at local schools. She graduated from the Wilmington Conference Academy (Methodist) in 1880 and continued her education at Wellesley College in Massachusetts. At Wellesley, she studied with **Sarah Frances Whiting**, a professor of physics and astronomy. Cannon also delved into spectroscopy, the measurement of the various wavelengths that make up light.

After receiving her bachelor's degree from Wellesley in 1884 Cannon returned to the family home in Dover, where she lived for ten years. Her interest in astronomy persisted, however, and she visited Italy and Spain to observe a solar eclipse. She also pursued her interest in photography. In 1894, following her mother's death, Cannon returned to Wellesley for post–graduate studies. There she worked as a teaching assistant in physics for professor Whiting and participated in experiments to confirm Wilhelm Conrad Röntgen's discovery of X rays. Her interest soon turned to stellar spectroscopy, however, and in 1895 she enrolled at Radcliffe College as a special student in astronomy.

Cataloguing the Stars

In 1896, Cannon became an assistant at the Harvard College Observatory through the support of Edward Pickering, director of the observatory and a leader in the field of spectroscopy. There she began a study of variable stars (stars whose light output varies because of internal fluctuations or because they are eclipsed by another star) and stellar spectra (the distinctive mix of radiation every star emits). She worked for a time at Harvard's astronomical station in Arequipa, Peru, which had been established by Pickering and his brother, William.

Using a hybrid scheme that combined the classification systems developed by **Antonia Maury** and **Williamina P. Fleming**, Cannon classified 1,122 bright stars whose spectra had been photographed at Arequipa. Cannon's system arranged stars according to the color of the light they emit, which is determined by their temperature. She classified as types O, B, and A the hot, white or blue stars. The type F and G stars, like our own sun, are yellow. Type K stars are orange, and type M, R, N, and S are reddish and therefore relatively cool. This system made possible the easy classification of all stars in relatively few, rationally related categories. In 1910 the astronomical community adopted her new method, known as the "Harvard system." In 1911 Cannon was promoted to curator of astronomical photographs. At this time she began one of the most extensive collections of astronomical data ever achieved by a single observer, the Henry Draper Catalogue of stellar spectra. Published by the Harvard College Observatory in 10 volumes from 1918 to 1924, the catalogue lists the spectral types of 225,300 stars, their positions in the sky, their visual and photographic magnitudes, and includes notes on the eccentricities of particular stars. As soon as Cannon finished this survey, she began enlarging the catalogue to include fainter stars in the Milky Way, the Large Magellanic Cloud, and other selected regions of the cosmos. In all, Cannon classified the spectra of some 400,000 stars in her lifetime.

During the same period Cannon pursued her interest in variable stars. In 1903 she issued a catalogue of the 1,227 variable stars known at the time. Subsequently, she published a second catalogue of variable stars (1907), with precise data and notes on 2,000 stars. In the course of her work, she discovered 300 previously unknown variables and five novae.

Highly esteemed by her colleagues, Cannon was active in professional activities such as the annual meeting of astronomical societies. Astronomers from all over the world visited her at Star Cottage, her home in Cambridge, Massachusetts. She received a number of honorary degrees and awards, including election to the American Philosophical Society (1925). Cannon was the first woman to receive the Henry Draper Gold Medal of the National Academy of Sciences (1931), the first woman to receive an honorary doctoral degree from Oxford University, and the first woman elected to an office of the prestigious American Astronomical Society (treasurer, 1912–1919). In 1929, the National League of Woman Voters listed her as one of the twelve greatest living American women. In 1938 she was appointed William Cranch Bond Astronomer at Harvard University.

Cannon's achievements came at a time in the history of science when the roles for women in astronomy and other male–dominated disciplines were severely limited by prevailing social attitudes and prejudices about women's abilities. Writing about this period, scholars John Lankford and Rickey L. Slavings observe: "Although the field took in large numbers of women, gender dictated who collected data, who reduced it, who analyzed it and who published the results. The assignment of roles reflected the perceptions male astronomers had of females, and those perceptions in turn mirrored the values of American culture."

An incident involving the National Academy of Sciences (NAS) illustrates the extent to which the reward system of science, traditionally held to be based on merit, was influenced by gender. In 1923, two prominent members of the NAS discussed the possibility of electing Cannon to the ranks of the academy, an honor which no women had at that time received. Despite the support of several distinguished fellow astronomers and Cannon's recognized contributions to science, her candidacy received little support, and she was not elected into the academy.

Cannon held her position at Harvard University until her retirement in 1940. She continued observing until shortly before she died in Cambridge on April 13, 1941, at the age of 77.

SELECTED WRITINGS BY CANNON:

Books

Henry Draper Catalogue. In *Annals of the Harvard Observatory.* Vols. 91–99. 1918–1924.

FURTHER READING

Books

Rossiter, Margaret W. *Women Scientists in America: Struggles and Strategies to 1940.* Baltimore: Johns Hopkins University Press, 1982.

Periodicals

Lankford, John, and Slavings, Rickey L. "Gender and Science: Women in American Astronomy, 1859–1940." *Physics Today* (March, 1990): 58–65.

New York Times (April 14, 1941): 17.

Sketch by Daniel Pendick

Estella Eleanor Carothers
1882–1957

American zoologist and cytologist

Eleanor Carothers focused her scientific endeavors in cytology, the study of cells and their inner workings. Particularly concerned with the relationship between cytology and genetics, and the effect x rays have on cells, she was most noted for her precise research methodologies. Carothers contributed much data on the subject and published prolifically in many prestigious journals.

Estella Eleanor Carothers was born on December 4, 1882, in Newton, Kansas. Her parents were Z. W. Carothers and Mary E. (Bates) Carothers. Carothers attended the Kansas–based Nickerson Normal College, a teacher's school, then several years after graduating, entered the University of Kansas. Carothers earned her undergraduate degree at age 28 in 1911, and her Masters at the same institution a year later. Carothers attended University of Pennsylvania for the remainder of her graduate work, and was awarded her Ph.D. in 1916.

While still a graduate student, Carothers worked as an assistant in the zoology department at the University of Pennsylvania. In 1926, she was promoted to a lecturer position. While at the University of Pennsylvania, Carothers was part of two scientific expeditions conducted in the south and southwestern United States, in 1915 and 1919.

Carothers was afforded many honors from the time she was a graduate student and onward. In Thomas Morgan's 1915 book, *The Mechanism of Mendelian Heredity*, she was named as a primary investigator, one of only seven women to be so cited. She won the 1921 Ellen Richards Research Prize (sponsored by the Naples Table Association) for her work. Her name was starred in the 1926 edition of the *American Men of Science*, meaning that she was considered one of the United States' 1,000 most distinguished scientists.

The reason for the many honors bestowed upon Carothers was the thoroughness of her research in cytology. In focusing on the genetics of the order Orthoptera (which includes crickets and grasshoppers), Carothers answered many questions concerning cytological heredity. Carothers published her findings in many leading journals such as the *Journal of Morphology*, *The Biological Bulletin*, *Quarterly Review of Biology*, and *Proceedings of the Entomolgocial Society*. As befitting such a honored scientist, Carothers was a member of the National Academy of Sciences and the Academy of Natural Sciences of Philadelphia, as well as many related organizations.

Carothers left the University of Pennsylvania in 1933 to become a research associate in zoology at the University of Iowa. She retired in 1941. Carothers loved outdoor activities like horseback riding, hiking, and canoeing. She died in 1957 at the age of 75.

SELECTED WRITINGS BY CAROTHERS:

Books

The Segregation and Recombination of Homologous Chromosomes as Found in Two Genera of Acrididae (Orthoptera). Baltimore: Waverly Press, 1917.

FURTHER READING

Books

Bailey, Martha J. *American Women in Science*. Denver: ABC–CLIO, 1994, p. 55.

Ogilvie, Marilyn Bailey. *Women in Science: Antiquity through the Nineteenth Century*. Cambridge: MIT Press, 1986, pp. 52–53.

Siegel, Patricia Joan, and Kay Thomas Finley. *Women in the Scientific Search: An American Bio–Bibliography, 1724–1979*. Metuchen, NJ: The Scarecrow Press, Inc., 1985, pp. 363–64.

Sketch by Annette Petrusso

Emma Perry Carr
1880–1972
American chemist and educator

Emma P. Carr (Mt. Holyoke College Archive. Reproduced by permission.)

Emma Carr was perhaps the most renowned chemical educator of the first half of the twentieth century. She was known not only for the chemistry program she established at Mount Holyoke College, which became a model for group research, but also for her groundbreaking work on the structure of unsaturated hydrocarbons. Employing absorption spectroscopy and later, far ultraviolet vacuum spectroscopy, Carr and her faculty and student collaborators made significant contributions to the understanding of the make–up of certain organic compounds.

Carr was the first recipient of the Francis Garvan Medal to honor an outstanding woman in American chemistry. In addition to her research and teaching skills, she also proved to be a formidable administrator, making Mount Holyoke College one of the premier chemistry schools in the nation at the time. At her instigation, Mount Holyoke became one of the first institutions in the United States to use ultraviolet spectrophotometry to illuminate the structure of complex organic molecules. Her 33 years as head of the chemistry department, from 1913 to 1946, were marked by her personal approach to teaching and to her rigorous techniques in research. Active in both community and college, Carr became a much sought–after speaker following her retirement from teaching, and lived until the age of 92, mostly on or near the campus of Mount Holyoke, the center of both her public and private life.

Emma Perry Carr was born on July 23, 1880, in Holmesville, Ohio, the third of five children to Anna Mary (Jack) Carr and Edmund Cone Carr. Her father and grandfather were both highly respected doctors, as was her brother, and Carr followed in this scientific tradition. Carr's mother was a devout Methodist, active in church and community affairs, and this also heavily influenced the young Carr. Raised in Coshocton, Ohio, and dubbed the "Emmy the smart one" in high school, Carr went on to Ohio State University for her freshman year in college, one of very few women attending that institution in 1898. There she studied chemistry with William McPherson, but decided at the end of her freshman year to transfer to Mount Holyoke College in South Hadley, Massachusetts.

After successfully completing two years of college there, she worked as an assistant in the Mount Holyoke chemistry department for three years, and then completed her B.S. degree at the University of Chicago in 1905. Thereafter, she returned to Mount Holyoke to teach for another three years until taking up graduate studies in 1908. During her graduate studies in physical chemistry at the University of Chicago, she received the Mary E. Woolley and the Lowenthal fellowships, working and studying with Alexander Smith and Julius Stieglitz, the latter being her primary advisor in her Ph.D. work on aliphatic imido esters. Carr was only the seventh woman to be awarded a doctorate from the University of Chicago.

Carr of Mount Holyoke

The name of Emma Carr and Mount Holyoke College are indelibly connected, for it was at that institution where she did her major work and it was that institution which benefited so greatly from her teaching and administrative skills. Returning there to teach in 1910, she was made full professor and head of the Department of Chemistry in 1913, a position she retained until her retirement in 1946. Under her guidance, this department became one of the strongest at Mount Holyoke and one of the premier chemistry departments in the country. Though a liberal arts institution, Mount Holyoke had a strong science tradition from the time of its founding by **Mary Lyons** in 1837. Lyons herself taught chemistry, and subsequent directors of the college continued this emphasis. Carr, however, attracted top–notch instructors to the program such as **Dorothy Hahn** and Louisa Stephenson, establishing a curriculum every bit as challenging as those found at Ivy League schools. Known as a charismatic teacher, Carr was intimately involved with her students, and was a staunch believer in having the best instructors teach introductory courses so as to interest young students in the sciences. Moreover, she involved her students in active research, developing important research projects for the college to pursue.

From her survey of the literature, Carr came to see that British and European researchers were increasingly intrigued with the relationship between ultraviolet absorption spectra and the electronic configurations of organic molecules. Carr had been searching for some manner in which she could apply physical chemistry to organic problems, and this seemed the perfect project, for very little research on the subject was being conducted in North America at the time. In 1913 she initiated work on the project, working with Hahn to synthesize hydrocarbons. Students also participated in the research project as part of their hands–on training, an innovative approach then. These organic compounds were subsequently analyzed, using a Fery spectrograph which Carr had persuaded the college to purchase. Initial research results, published in 1918 under the title of "The Absorption Spectra of Some Derivatives of Cyclopropane," established the college as a research institution of note and solidified research in the educational curriculum.

To gain further knowledge of spectroscopic techniques, Carr studied at Queen's University, Belfast, Northern Ireland, in 1919. These studies, and her expertise in spectroscopy, led to an invitation in 1925 to participate in the preparation of the *International Critical Tables* (ITC), an authoritative compilation of chemical data, including spectroscopic information. Carr traveled to Europe in 1925, taking a 12–month leave to complete her work on this project in the laboratories of two co–compilers, Jean Becquerel of the Collège de France in Paris and Victor Henri of the University of Zurich. Carr returned to Zurich after receiving the 1929 recipient of the Alice Freeman Palmer Fellowship to study vacuum spectroscopy with Henri.

Wins Fame for Ultraviolet Spectrographic Measurements

Carr and her research colleagues began to understand limitations to their work by the late 1920s. Specifically, they could not answer why certain molecular atomic groups absorbed some wavelengths of light, nor could they explain what mechanics were at play within the molecule when such light was absorbed. To answer these questions, Carr determined that simpler molecules with fewer variables needed to be studied. Again, undergraduates, graduate students, and professors teamed up in 1930 to prepare highly purified hydrocarbons with known positions of the carbon–carbon double bond in the molecule. These then were employed in the measurement of the absorption spectra in the far ultraviolet spectrum, employing vacuum spectroscopic techniques Carr had learned in Europe. Funds from the National Research Council aided in this research which shed new light on the spectra of aliphatic hydrocarbons, or those organic compounds in which the carbon atoms form open chains, especially the olefins. Carr and her students used these techniques to attempt to understand the causes of selective absorption of radiant energy in these simple structures.

While Carr's theories on the spectral absorption and heats of combustion of hydrocarbons did not gain widespread acceptance, her work with vacuum spectrographic analysis of purified hydrocarbons altered the understanding of the carbon–carbon double bond and also resulted in a better theoretical understanding of energy relationships in ehtylenic unsaturation. Carr's further work on this project, partly funded by the National Science Foundation and the Rockefeller Foundation, continued throughout the 1930s and into the 1940s and had lasting import, especially for the petroleum industry. Her research was later expanded upon by the Nobel laureate, Robert S. Mulliken, in developing theories about energy relationships in organic compounds.

A Life for Science

Carr continued to live in college dorms until 1935, when she and another researcher at Mount Holyoke, **Mary L. Sherrill**, began sharing a house on campus. Internationally recognized as a first class researcher, Carr continued to maintain close contact with her students, putting as much emphasis on the classroom as the lab. In 1937, she was awarded the first Francis Garvan Medal by the American Chemical Society to honor an outstanding woman in American chemistry. As part of the selection committee, she was embarrassed to find herself nominated while absent from one of the meetings.

During the Second World War, Carr and her students worked on a project to synthesize quinine, and though there were many near misses, her team was unable to come up with a successful synthetic form of the anti-malaria drug. In 1944, she gave a series of seminars at the fledgling Institute of Chemistry in Mexico City. Honorary degrees were conferred on Carr from Allegheny College in 1939, from Russell Sage College in 1941, and from Mount Holyoke in 1952.

Though she retired in 1946, Carr's professional life was far from over. She continued to speak at colleges and clubs well into her seventies, promoting the scientific ethos as well as her beloved baseball. In 1957, she shared the James Flack Norris Award for outstanding achievement in the teaching of chemistry with her friend and collaborator, Sherrill. When Sherrill retired in 1954, the two traveled extensively. A lover of music, Carr played the organ in the Methodist church and also played the cello until arthritis, which developed in her later years, forced her to become a listener rather than player. With failing health, Carr had to leave Mount Holyoke, moving to the Presbyterian Home in Evanston, Illinois, where she died on January 7, 1972 of heart failure. It is a lasting tribute to this renowned woman of science that the chemistry building at Mount Holyoke College bears her name.

SELECTED WRITINGS BY CARR:

Books

(With L. W. Pickett, G. E. Hall, et al.) *Absorption Spectra and Chemical Reactivity of Selected Unsaturated Hydrocarbons, Amines, and Ethers*. Final Report, ONR Project NR–055–160 (Oct. 1, 1949 June 30, 1951).

Periodicals

(With C. P. Burt) "The Absorption Spectra of Some Derivatives of Cyclopropane." *JACS* 40 (1918): 1590–1600.

(With M. Dobbrow) "Absorption Spectra of Some Derivatives of Anisalhydantoin." *JACS* 47 (1925): 2961–2965.

(With M. L. Sherrill) "Absorption Spectra of a Series of Dienes." *International Critical Tables* MGH 5 (1929):326–358.

(With M. K. Walker) "The Ultraviolet Absorption Spectra of Simple Hydrocarbons. I and II." *JCP* 4 (1936): 751–760.

(With L. W. Pickett and H. Stücklein) "The Absorption Spectra of a Series of Dienes." *RMP* 14 (1942): 260–264.

"Electronic Transitions in the Simple Unsaturated Hydrocarbons." *ChemR* 41 (1947): 293–299.

(With D. Semenow and A. J. Harrison) "Absorption Intensities of the Isomeric Pentenes in the Vacuum Ultraviolet." *JCP* 22 (1954): 638–642.

FURTHER READING

Books

Atkinson, Edward R. "Emma Perry Carr." *American Chemists and Chemical Engineers*. Edited by Wyndham D. Miles. Washington: American Chemical Society, 1976, pp. 66–67.

Bailey, Martha J. *American Women in Science: A Biographical Dictionary*. Santa Barbara: ABC–CLIO, 1994, pp. 55–56.

Banville, Debra L. "Emma Perry Carr." *Women in Chemistry and Physics*. Westport, CT: Greenwood Press, 1993, pp. 77–84.

"Carr, Emma P(erry)." *Current Biography*. Edited by Charles Moritz. New York: H. W. Wilson, 1959, pp. 55–57.

Rayner–Canham, Marelene, and Geoffrey Rayner–Canham. *Women in Chemistry: Their Changing Roles from Alchemical Times to the Mid–Twentieth Century*. Washington: American Chemical Society, 1998, pp. 187–192.

Verbrugge, Martha H. "Carr, Emma Perry." *Notable American Women: The Modern Period*. Edited by B. Sicherman and C. H. Green. Cambridge: Belknap Press, 1980, pp.136–138.

Periodicals

Burt, C. P. "Emma Perry Carr." *Nucleus* 34 (June 1957): 214– 216.

"Dr. Emma P. Carr, 91 Chemist at Holyoke." *New York Times* 121 (8 January 1972): 32.

Hallock, Grace Taber, editor. "Emma Perry Carr: Professor Emeritus of Chemistry." *Mount Holyoke Quarterly* 30 (August 1946): 53–55.

Sketch by J. Sydney Jones

Rachel Carson (AP/Wide World Photos. Reproduced by permission.)

Rachel Louise Carson
1907–1964
American marine biologist

Rachel Carson is considered one of America's finest science and nature writers. She is best known for her 1962 book, *Silent Spring,* which is often credited with beginning the environmental movement in the United States. The book focused on the uncontrolled and often indiscriminate use of pesticides, especially dichlorodiphenyltrichloroethane (commonly known as DDT), and the irreparable environmental damage caused by these chemicals. The public outcry Carson generated by the book motivated the U.S. Senate to form a committee to investigate pesticide use. Her eloquent testimony before the committee altered the views of many government officials and helped lead to the creation of the Environmental Protection Agency (EPA).

Rachel Louise Carson, the youngest of three children, was born on May 27, 1907, in Springdale, Pennsylvania, a small town twenty miles north of Pittsburgh. Her parents, Robert Warden and Maria McLean Carson, lived on 65 acres and kept cows, chickens, and horses. Although the land was not a true working farm, it had plenty of woods, animals, and streams, and here, near the shores of the Allegheny River, Carson learned about the interrelationship between the land and animals.

Carson's mother was the daughter of a Presbyterian minister, and she instilled in her a love of nature and taught her the intricacies of music, art, and literature. Carson's early life was one of isolation; she had few friends besides her cats, and she spent most of her time reading and pursuing the study of nature. She began writing poetry at age eight and published her first story, "A Battle in the Clouds," in *St. Nicholas* magazine at the age of 10. She later claimed that her professional writing career began at age eleven, when *St. Nicholas* paid her a little over three dollars for one of her essays.

Focuses on Career in the Sciences

Carson planned to pursue a career as a writer when she received a four–year scholarship in 1925 from the Pennsylvania College for Women (now Chatham College) in Pittsburgh. Here she fell under the influence of Mary Scott Skinker, whose freshman biology course altered her career plans. In the middle of her junior year, Carson switched her major from English to zoology, and in 1928 she graduated magnum cum laude. "Biology has given me something to write about," she wrote to a friend, as quoted in *Carnegie* magazine. "I will try in my writing to make animals in the woods or waters, where they live, as alive to others as they are to me."

With Skinker's help, Carson obtained first a summer fellowship at the Marine Biology Laboratory at Woods Hole in Massachusetts and then a one–year scholarship from the Johns Hopkins University in Baltimore. While at Woods Hole over the summer, she saw the ocean for the first time and encountered her first exotic sea creatures, including sea anemones and sea urchins. At Johns Hopkins, she studied zoology and genetics. Graduate school did not proceed smoothly; she encountered financial problems and experimental difficulties but eventually managed to finish her highly detailed master's dissertation, "The Development of the Pronephoros during the Embryonic and Early Larval Life of the Catfish (*Inctalurus punctaltus*)." In June 1932, she received her master's degree.

Begins Her Writing Career in Federal Government

Carson was entering the job market at the height of the Great Depression. Her parents sold their Pennsylvania home and moved to Maryland to ease some of her financial burdens. She taught zoology at Johns Hopkins during the summers and on a part-time basis at the University of Maryland during the regular school year. While she loved teaching, the meager salaries she earned were barely enough to sustain herself, and, in 1935, her financial situation became even more desperate when her father died unexpectedly, leaving her solely responsible for supporting her fragile mother.

Before beginning her graduate studies at Johns Hopkins, Carson had arranged an interview with Elmer Higgins, who was head of the Division of Scientific Inquiry at the U.S. Bureau of Fisheries. Carson wanted to discuss her job prospects in marine biology, and Higgins had been encouraging, though he then had little to offer. Carson contacted Higgins again at this time, and she discovered that he had an opening at the Bureau of Fisheries for a part-time science writer to work on radio scripts. The only obstacle was the civil service exam, which women were then discouraged from taking. Carson not only did well on the test, she outscored all other applicants. She went on to become only the second woman ever hired by the bureau for a permanent professional post.

At the Bureau of Fisheries, Carson wrote and edited a variety of government publications—everything from pamphlets on how to cook fish to professional scientific journals. She earned a reputation as a ruthless editor who would not tolerate inconsistencies, weak prose, or ambiguity. One of her early radio scripts was rejected by Higgins because he found it too "literary." He suggested that she submit the script in essay form to the *Atlantic Monthly,* then one of the nation's premier literary magazines. To Carson's amazement, the article was accepted and published as "Undersea" in 1937. Her jubilation over the article was tempered by personal family tragedy. Her older sister, Marian, died at age forty that same year, and Carson had to assume responsibility for Marian's children, Marjorie and Virginia Williams.

The *Atlantic Monthly* article attracted the notice of an editor at the publishing house of Simon & Schuster, who urged Carson to expand the four–page essay into book form. Working diligently in the evenings, she was able to complete the book in a few years; it was published as *Under the Sea-Wind.* Unfortunately, the book appeared in print in 1941, just one month before the Japanese attacked Pearl Harbor. Despite favorable, even laudatory reviews, it sold fewer than 1,600 copies after six years in print. It did, however, bring Carson to the attention of a number of key people, including the influential science writer William Beebe Beebe published an excerpt from *Under the Sea-Wind* in his 1944 compilation *The Book of Naturalists,* including Carson's work alongside the writings of Aristotle, Audubon, and Thoreau.

The poor sales of *Under the Sea–Wind* made Carson concentrate on her government job. The Bureau of Fisheries merged with the Biological Survey in 1940 and was reborn as the Fish and Wildlife Service. Carson quickly moved up the professional ranks, eventually reaching the position of biologist and chief editor after World War II. One of her postwar assignments, a booklet about National Wildlife Refuges called *Conservation in Action,* took her back into the field. As part of her research, she visited the Florida Everglades, Parker River in Massachusetts, and Chincoteague Island in the Chesapeake Bay.

Attracts National Notice with Science Writing

After the war, Carson began work on a new book that focused on oceanography. She was now at liberty to use previously classified government research data on oceanography, which included a number of technical and scientific breakthroughs. As part of her research, she did some undersea diving off the Florida coast during the summer of 1949. She battled skeptical administrators to arrange a deep-sea cruise to Georges Bank near Nova Scotia aboard the Fish and Wildlife Service's research vessel, the *Albatross III.*

Entitled *The Sea around Us,* her book on oceanography was published on July 2, 1951. It was an unexpected success; abridged in *Reader's Digest,* it was a Book-of-the-Month Club alternative selection and it remained on the *New York Times* bestseller list for 86 weeks. The book brought Carson numerous awards, including the National Book Award and the John Burroughs Medal, as well as honorary doctorates from her alma mater and Oberlin College. Despite her inherent shyness, Carson became a regular on the lecture circuit. Money was no longer the overarching concern it had been; she retired from government service and devoted her time to writing.

Freed from financial burdens, Carson began work on another book, focusing this time on the intricacies of life along the shoreline. She took excursions to the mangrove coasts of Florida and returned to one of her favorite locations, the rocky shores of Maine. She fell in love with the Maine coast and in 1953 bought a summer home in West Southport on the shore of Sheepscot Bay. *The Edge of the Sea* appeared in 1955 and earned Carson two more prestigious awards, the Achievement Award of the American Association of University Women and a citation from the National Council of Women of the United States. The book remained on the bestseller list for 20 weeks, and RKO Studios bought the rights to it. In typical Hollywood fashion, the studio sensationalized the material and ignored scientific fact. Carson corrected some of the more egregious errors but still found the film embarrassing, even after it won an Oscar as the best full-length documentary of 1953.

From 1955 to 1957, Carson concentrated on smaller projects, including a telescript, "Something about the Sky," for the *Omnibus* series. She also contributed a number of articles to popular magazines. In July 1956, Carson published "Help Your Child to Wonder" in the *Woman's Home Companion.* The article was based on her own real-life experiences, something rare for Carson. She intended to expand the article into a book and retell the story of her early life on her parent's Pennsylvania farm. After her death, the essay reappeared in 1965 as the book *The Sense of Wonder.*

Investigates Pesticide Use

In 1956, one of the nieces Carson had raised died at age 36. Marjorie left her son Roger; Carson now had to care for him in addition to her arthritic mother, who was now 88. She legally adopted Roger that same year and began looking for a suitable place to rear the child. She built a new winter home in Silver Spring, Maryland, on an uncultivated tract of land, and she began another project shortly after the home was finished. The luxuriant setting inspired her to turn her thoughts to nature once again. Carson's next book grew out of a long-held concern about the overuse of pesticides. She had received a letter from Olga Owens Huckins, who related how the aerial spraying of DDT had destroyed her Massachusetts bird sanctuary. Huckins asked her to petition federal authorities to investigate the widespread use of such pesticides, but Carson thought the most effective tactic would be to write an article for a popular magazine. When her initial queries were rejected, Carson attempted to interest the well-known essayist E. B. White in the subject. White suggested she write the article herself, in her own style, and he told her to contact William Shawn, an editor at the *New Yorker.* Eventually, after numerous discussions with Shawn and others, she decided to write a book instead.

The international reputation Carson now enjoyed enabled her to enlist the aid of an array of experts. She consulted with biologists, chemists, entomologists, and pathologists, spending four years gathering data for her book. When *Silent Spring* first appeared in serial form in the *New Yorker* in June 1962, it drew an aggressive response from the chemical industry. Carson argued that the environmental consequences of pesticide use underscored the futility of humanity's attempts to control nature, and she maintained that these efforts to assume control had upset nature's delicate balance. Although the message is now largely uncontroversial, the book caused near panic in some circles, challenging the long-held belief that humans could master nature. The chemical companies, in particular, attacked both the book and its author; they questioned the data, the interpretation of the data, and the author's scientific credentials. One early reviewer referred to Carson as a "hysterical woman," and others continued this sexist line of attack. Some chemical companies attempted to pressure Houghton Mifflin, the book's publisher, into suppressing the book, but these attempts failed.

The general reviews were much kinder and *Silent Spring* soon attracted a large, concerned audience, both in America and abroad. A special CBS television broadcast, "The Silent Spring of Rachel Carson," which aired on April 3, 1963, pitted Carson against a chemical company spokesman. Her cool-headed, commonsensical approach won her many fans and brought national attention to the problem of pesticide use. The book became a cultural icon and part of everyday household conversation. Carson received hundreds of invitations to speak, most of which she declined due to her deteriorating health. She did find the strength to appear before the Women's National Press Club, the National Parks Association, and the Ribicoff Committee—the U.S. Senate committee on environmental hazards.

In 1963 Carson received numerous honors and awards, including an award from the Izaak Walton League of America, the Audubon Medal, and the Cullen Medal of the American Geographical Society. That same year, she was elected to the prestigious American Academy of Arts and Sciences. She died of heart failure on April 14, 1964, at the age of 56. In 1980, President Jimmy Carter posthumously awarded her the President's Medal of Freedom. A Rachel Carson stamp was issued by the U.S. Postal Service in 1981.

SELECTED WRITINGS BY CARSON:

Books

Under the Sea-Wind, Dutton, 1941.
The Sea around Us, Oxford University Press, 1951.
The Edge of the Sea, Houghton Mifflin, 1955.
Silent Spring, Houghton Mifflin, 1962.
A Sense of Wonder, Harper and Row, 1965.

Periodicals

"Undersea," *Atlantic Monthly* (September, 1937).
"The Bat Knew It First," *Colliers* (November 18, 1944).
"Help Your Child to Wonder," *Woman's Home Companion* (July, 1956).
"Rachel Carson Answers Her Critics," *Audubon Magazine* (September, 1963).

FURTHER READING

Books

Brooks, Paul. *The House of Life: Rachel Carson at Work.* Houghton Mifflin, 1972.
Gartner, Carol B. *Rachel Carson.* Ungar, 1983.
McKay, Mary A. *Rachel Carson.* Twayne, 1993.

Periodicals

Brooks, Paul. "The Courage of Rachel Carson," *Audubon 89* 12 (January, 1987): 14–15.
McKibben, Bill. "The Mountain Hedonist." *New York Review of Books* (April 11, 1991): 29–32.
Wareham, Wendy. "Rachel Carson's Early Years." *Carnegie* (November/December, 1986): 20–34.

Sketch by Tom Crawford

Margaret Cavendish, Duchess of Newcastle
1623–1673
English natural philosopher

Margaret Cavendish was one of the first prolific female science writers. As the author of approximately 14 scientific or quasi-scientific books, she helped to popularize some of the most important ideas of the scientific

Margaret Cavendish (Corbis/Bettmann. Reproduced by permission.)

revolution, including the competing vitalistic and mechanistic natural philosophies and atomism. A flamboyant and eccentric woman, Cavendish was the most visible of the "scientific ladies" of the seventeenth century.

Margaret Lucas was born into a life of luxury near Colchester, England, in 1623, the youngest of eight children of Sir Thomas Lucas. She was educated informally at home. At the age of eighteen, she left her sheltered life to become Maid of Honor to Queen Henrietta Maria, wife of Charles I, accompanying the queen into exile in France following the defeat of the royalists in the civil war. There she fell in love with and married William Cavendish, the Duke of Newcastle, a 52 year-old widower, who had been commander of the royalist forces in the north of England. Joining other exiled royalists in Antwerp, the couple rented the mansion of the artist Rubens. Margaret Cavendish was first exposed to science in their informal salon society, "The Newcastle Circle," which included the philosophers Thomas Hobbes, René Descartes and Pierre Gassendi. She visited England in 1651–52 to try to collect revenues from the Newcastle estate to satisfy their foreign creditors. It was at this time that Cavendish first gained her reputation for extravagant dress and manners, as well as for her beauty and her bizarre poetry.

Publishes Original Natural Philosophy

Cavendish prided herself on her originality and boasted that her ideas were the products of her own imagination, not derived from the writings of others. Cavendish's first anthology, *Poems, and Fancies*, included the earliest version of her natural philosophy. Although English atomic theory in the seventeenth century attempted to explain all natural phenomena as matter in motion, in Cavendish's philosophy all atoms contained the same amount of matter but differed in size and shape; thus, earth atoms were square, water particles were round, atoms of air were long, and fire atoms were sharp. This led to her humoral theory of disease, wherein illness was due to fighting between atoms or an overabundance of one atomic shape. However in her second volume, *Philosophical Fancies*, published later in the same year, Cavendish already had disavowed her own atomic theory. By 1663, when she published *Philosophical and Physical Opinions*, she had decided that if atoms were "Animated Matter," then they would have "Free-will and Liberty" and thus would always be at war with one another and unable to cooperate in the creation of complex organisms and minerals. Nevertheless, Cavendish continued to view all matter as composed of one material, animate and intelligent, in contrast to the Cartesian view of a mechanistic universe.

Challenges Other Scientists

Cavendish and her husband returned to England with the restoration of the monarchy in 1660 and, for the first time, she began to study the works of other scientists. Finding herself in disagreement with most of them, she wrote *Philosophical Letters: or, Modest Reflections upon some Opinions in Natural Philosophy, maintained by several Famous and Learned Authors of this Age, Expressed by way of Letters* in 1664. Cavendish sent copies of this work, along with *Philosophical and Physical Opinions*, by special messenger to the most famous scientists and celebrities of the day. In 1666 and again in 1668, she published *Observations upon Experimental Philosophy*, a response to Robert Hooke's *Micrographia*, in which she attacked the use of recently-developed microscopes and telescopes as leading to false observations and interpretations of the natural world. Included in the same volume with *Observations* was *The Blazing World* was a semi-scientific utopian romance, in which Cavendish declared herself "Margaret the First."

Invited to the Royal Society

More than anything else, Cavendish yearned for the recognition of the scientific community. She presented the universities of Oxford and Cambridge with each of her publications and she ordered a Latin index to accompany the writings she presented to the University of Leyden, hoping thereby that her work would be utilized by European scholars.

After much debate among the membership of the Royal Society of London, Cavendish became the first woman invited to visit the prestigious institution, although the controversy had more to due with her notoriety than with her sex. On May 30, 1667, Cavendish arrived with a large retinue of attendants and watched as Robert Boyle and Robert Hooke weighed air, dissolved mutton in sulfuric acid and conducted various other experiments. It was a major advance for the scientific lady and a personal triumph for Cavendish.

Cavendish published the final revision of her *Philosophical and Physical Opinions*, entitled *Grounds of Natural Philosophy*, in 1668. Significantly more modest than her previous works, in this volume Cavendish presented her views somewhat tentatively and retracted some of her earlier, more extravagant claims. Cavendish acted as her own physician, and her self-inflicted prescriptions, purgings and bleedings resulted in the rapid deterioration of her health. She died in 1673 and was buried in Westminster Abbey.

Although her writings remained well outside the mainstream of seventeenth-century science, Cavendish's efforts were of major significance. She help to popularize many of the ideas of the scientific revolution and she was one of the first natural philosophers to argue that theology was outside the parameters of scientific inquiry. Furthermore, her work and her prominence as England's first recognized woman scientist argued strongly for the education of women and for their involvement in scientific pursuits. In addition to her scientific writings, Cavendish published a book of speeches, a volume of poetry, and a large number of plays. Several of the latter, particularly *The Female Academy*, included learned women and arguments in favor of female education. Her most enduring work, a biography of her husband, included as an appendix to her 24 page memoir, was first published in 1656 as a part of *Nature's Pictures*. This memoir is regarded as the first major secular autobiography written by a woman.

SELECTED WRITINGS BY CAVENDISH:

Books

Poems, and Fancies. 1653. Reprint, Menston, England: Scolar, 1972.

Philosophical Fancies. London, 1653.

Plays. London: Martyn, Allestry and Dicas, 1662.

Philosophical and Physical Opinions. London: William Wilson, 1663.

Philosophical Letters. London, 1664.

Observations upon Experimental Philosophy: To which is added, the Description of a New Blazing World.. 2d ed. London: Maxwell, 1668.

Grounds of Natural Philosophy. London: Maxwell, 1668.

Nature's Pictures Drawn by Fancies Pencil to the Life. 2d ed. London: Maxwell, 1671.

The Life of the (1st) Duke of Newcastle and Other Writings. Edited by Ernest Rhys. London: J. M. Dent, 1916.

FURTHER READING

Books

Alic, Margaret. *Hypatia's Heritage: A History of Women in Science from Antiquity through the Nineteenth Century*. Boston: Beacon Press,1986.

Battigelli, Anna. *Margaret Cavendish and the Exiles of the Mind*. Lexington: University Press of Kentucky, 1998.

Grant, Douglas. *Margaret the First: A Biography of Margaret Cavendish, Duchess of Newcastle, 1623–1673*. Toronto: University of Toronto Press, 1957.

Kargon, Robert Hugh . *Atomism in England from Hariot to Newton*. Oxford: Clarendon, 1966.

Meyer, Gerald Dennis. *The Scientific Lady in England 1650–1760: An Account of her Rise, with emphasis on the Major Roles of the Telescope and Microscope*. Berkeley: University of California Press, 1955.

Schiebinger, Londa. *The Mind Has No Sex? Women in the Origins of Modern Science*. Cambridge: Harvard University Press, 1989.

Periodicals

Mintz, Samuel I. "The Duchess of Newcastle's Visit to the Royal Society." *Journal of English and Germanic Philology* 51 (April 1952): 168–76.

Sketch by Margaret Alic

Sun-Yung Alice Chang
1948–
Chinese-born American mathematician

Sun–Yung Alice Chang, working with Paul Yang, Tom Branson, and Matt Gursky, has produced what the American Mathematical Society has termed "deep contributions" to the study of partial differential equations in relation to geometry and topology.

Sun–Yung Alice Chang was born in Ci–an, China, on March 24, 1948, and studied for her bachelor's degree at the National University of Taiwan, which she received in 1970. Chang emigrated to the United States for graduate work and a series of teaching jobs. In 1974, Chang earned her Ph.D. from the University of California at Berkeley. She has served as assistant professor at SUNY–Buffalo, the University of California at Los Angeles, and the University of Maryland. Chang returned to UCLA as an associate professor, and she became a full professor in 1980. Her

Sun-Yung Alice Chang (Mathematisches Forschungsinstitut, Oberwolfach. Reproduced by permission.)

most visible performance was as a speaker at the International Congress of Mathematicians, held in Berkeley in 1986.

Wins Satter Prize

In 1995, Chang was awarded the third the Ruth Lyttle Satter Prize at the American Mathematical Society's 101st annual meeting in San Francisco (the previous two recipients were Lai–Sung Young and Margaret McDuff). Young was on the selection committee that recommended Chang for that year's prize. In her acceptance speech, Chang acknowledged her debt to her collaborators and promised to "derive further geometric consequences" in various problems currently under study.

Reflecting momentarily on her own school years, Chang admitted that it had been important for her to have role models and female companionship. However, she stated, the deciding factor in the future will be to have more women proving theorems and contributing to mathematics as a whole. To that end, she has joined with a number of steering committees and advisory panels at the national level. After being a Sloan Fellow for the National Academy of Sciences in 1980, she returned ten years later as a member of their Board of Mathematical Sciences. Chang also advised the National Science Foundation and the Association for Women in Mathematics throughout the early 1990s.

Chang always finds time to involve her students in the sometimes arcane world of her specialty. At the University of Texas, she took part in their Distinguished Lecturer Series of 1996–97, a program that successfully targets an audience of young graduate students. She has been most active with the American Mathematical Society, working on a range of committees and speaking at a number of their meetings. Chang's most current professional positions include a three–year term on the Editorial Boards Committee of the AMS, expiring in 1998. Chang was married in 1973 and has two children.

FURTHER READING

"1995 Ruth Lyttle Satter Prize in Mathematics." *Notices of the AMS* (April 1995) http://e–math.ams.org/notices/199504/prize–satter.html

"Sun–Yung Alice Chang." *Biographies of Women Mathematicians.* http://www.scottlan.edu/lriddle/women/chronol.htm (July 1997).

Sketch by Jennifer Kramer

Mary Agnes (Meara) Chase
1869–1963
American botanist

Although she had only a grammar-school education, botanist Agnes Chase became one of the most important researchers to ever work in agrostology, the study of grasses. She cataloged more than 10,000 members of the grass family, discovered many previously unknown species, and added immeasurably to the world's knowledge of this important plant family.

Born Mary Agnes Meara on April 20, 1869, in Iroquois County, Illinois, she was the second–youngest child of Martin Meara, from Tipperary, Ireland, and Mary (Cassidy) Brannick Meara, from Louisville, Kentucky. Martin Meara, a railroad blacksmith, died in 1871. Mrs. Meara moved her five surviving children to Chicago (the youngest child had died in infancy). There they lived with Mary Agnes's maternal grandmother.

Mary Agnes completed grammar school and then went to work to help support the family. Among her jobs was proofreading and setting type at the *School Herald*, a periodical for rural school teachers edited by William I. Chase. They married on January 21, 1888. Mary Agnes was not quite 19; her new husband was 34. Chase, ill with tuberculosis, died several weeks short of their first anniversary. His death left his young widow with considerable debt.

The tiny woman—she stood less than five feet tall and weighed about 98 pounds—threw herself into work to pay off the bills. She worked as a proofreader at Chicago's *Inter–Ocean* newspaper while living on a diet of beans and oatmeal. Briefly, she worked at her brother–in–law's general store—a job that was to be a turning point in her life.

Discovers Her Interest in Botany

While working at the store, Chase became very fond of her nephew Virginius Chase. The boy enlisted his aunt's help in using a manual to identify some local plants. Chase was fascinated and continued her botany studies whenever she could. She began to collect in the field and record her observations. On one collecting trip, she met the Rev. Ellsworth Hill, who studied mosses. They became fast friends. Hill recognized Chase's talent as a botanical illustrator, and enlisted her help in illustrating some of his scientific papers. He introduced her to Charles Millspaugh of the Field Museum of Natural History in Chicago, who then hired her to illustrate two museum publications.

Hill also taught Chase how to use a microscope. He encouraged her to take a position as a meat inspector in the Chicago stockyards, where she used her newly acquired skill. She worked there from 1901 to 1903, when she applied—reluctantly, but at Hill's urging—for the position of botanical illustrator at the United States Department of Agriculture (USDA) Bureau of Plant Sciences in Washington D.C. To her surprise, she got the job.

At the USDA, she illustrated publications, and after hours studied grasses in the herbarium. These after–hours studies culminated in the publication of her first scientific paper in 1906.

A Lifelong Partnership

In 1905 Chase began what was to be a lifelong collaboration with Albert Spear Hitchcock, the principal scientist in systematic agrostology. In 1907, she became his assistant. Hitchcock and Chase worked well together, and their professional friendship lasted 30 years until Hitchcock's death. Without her, "it is doubtful if Hitchcock could have accomplished as much as he did," wrote Dr. Jason R. Swallen in *Taxon*. Indeed, the thousands of specimens she gathered on her many collecting trips added immeasurably to the value of Hitchcock's book, *A Manual of Grasses of the United States*, published in 1935, shortly before his death.

A Traveling Woman

Chase financed her collecting trips out of her own pocket (even when she was earning $720 a year) and donated her specimens to the herbarium. Her horizons spread beyond America's borders. In 1913, she made her first overseas collecting trip to Puerto Rico, where she discovered a new species of fern. While she was in Europe visiting herbaria in 1922, Chase's book, *A First Book of Grasses*, was published; a year later, she was promoted to assistant botanist.

In 1924, at age 56, she made the first of her two trips to Brazil. She explored areas botanists had never researched, searching jungles and climbing mountains in pursuit of specimens. After six months in Brazil, she returned home with 20,000 specimens, including 500 grasses. She was named associate botanist when she returned. Four years later she went back to Brazil, doing much of her exploring alone, and returning with 10 new species. All together, Chase brought 4,500 grass specimens back from Brazil, many of which had been previously unknown to exist in that country. The trips earned her the title "Uncle Sam's chief woman explorer." In 1936, she became senior botanist, succeeding her friend and mentor Hitchcock.

Although grasses were her consuming passion, they were not the only thing she cared about. She was active in the suffragist movement in 1918 and 1919, and was even arrested and force–fed. She supported prohibition and socialism and contributed to such organizations as the National Association for the Advancement of Colored People (NAACP) and the Woman's International League for Peace and Freedom.

Agnes Chase retired officially from the USDA in 1939, but "retired" was just a word to her. She continued working as a herbarium research associate. At 71, she traveled to Venezuela at the government's invitation to help develop its range management program. In 1950, she updated Hitchcock's *Manual*. She fostered the careers of many young botanists, urging them to come to the United States to study and even allowing some to board at her home.

She was recognized for her contributions to science by the Botanical Society of America, which awarded her a certificate of merit in 1956; the University of Illinois, which gave her an honorary Doctor of Science degree in 1958; the Smithsonian Institution, which named her an honorary fellow in 1958; and the Linnean Society, by which she was made a fellow in 1961.

Time finally caught up with this tireless investigator. On September 24, 1963, her first day in Bethesda, Maryland, nursing home, Mary Agnes Chase died. She was 94.

SELECTED WRITINGS BY CHASE:

Books

A First Book of Grasses: The Structure of Grasses Explained for Beginnners. New York: Macmillian, 1922. (Revised in 1937 and 1968, and reissued in 1977.)

(With Cornelia D. Niles) *Index to Grass Species*. 1962.

Periodicals

"Eastern Brazil Through an Agrostologist's Spectacles." *in Annual Report of the Smithsonian Institution*, 1926.

Other

Chase's papers are collected in the Albert S. Hitchcock and Mary Agnes Chase Papers, Hunt Institute for Biological Documentation, Carnegie Mellon University. Other materials, including her field notebooks, are part of the Hitchcock–Chase Library at the Smithsonian.

FURTHER READING

Books

Bonta, Marcia Myers. *Women in the Field: America's Pioneering Women Naturalists.* 1991.

Periodicals

Fosberg, F.R., and J.R. Swallen. "Agnes Chase." *Taxon* 8 (June 1959): 145–51.

Furman, Bess. "Grass Is Her Liferoot." *The New York Times* (June 12, 1956): 37.

Hillenbrand, Liz. "87–Year–Old Grass Expert Still Happy with Subject." *The Washington Post and Times Herald* (April 30, 1956): 7.

Sketch by Fran Hodgkins

Gabrielle–Émilie Le Tonnelier de Breteuil, the marquise du Châtelet
1706–1749
French physicist, chemist, and translator

Marquise du Chatelet (The Granger Collection, New York. Reproduced by permission.)

Gabrielle–Émilie Châtelet had a major role in the scientific revolution of the eighteenth century. By popularizing the theories of Isaac Newton she brought them more widespread acceptance in Europe where most people still followed the ideas of René Descartes. Châtelet's scientific work has been ignored and overshadowed by her relationship with the philosopher Voltaire.

Born Gabrielle–Émilie Le Tonnelier de Breteuil in Paris on December 17, 1706 into an aristocratic family, the marquise du Châtelet received an exceptional education at home, which included scientific, musical, and literary studies. In 1725, she married the marquis du Châtelet, who was also the count of Lomont. It was a marriage of convenience, but she nevertheless had three children with him. After spending some years with her husband, whose political and military career kept him away from Paris, Châtelet returned to the capital in 1730.

Initially leading a busy social life, Châtelet became the lover of the philosopher François–Marie Arouet de Voltaire in 1733. One of the greatest intellectual figures of 18th–century France, Voltaire recognized her exceptional talent for science, and encouraged her to develop her intellect. Châtelet consequently embarked on a study of mathematics, taking private lessons from the prominent French philosopher and scientist Pierre–Louis Moreau de Maupertuis. Both Voltaire and Maupertuis were enthusiastic supporters of Isaac Newton's scientific theories and world view, and it seems that the marquise was, as a result, immersed in Newtonian philosophy.

Creates Intellectual Center at the Chateau de Cirey

In 1734, Voltaire, who faced arrest because of his criticism of the monarchy, was offered sanctuary at Châtelet's chateau at Cirey, in Lorraine, where they spent many productive years. The two welcomed Europe's intellectual elite, thus creating a remarkable cultural center away from Paris. Châtelet was involved in a variety of literary and philosophical projects, eventually concentrating on the study of Newton's philosophy. She assisted Voltaire in the preparation of his 1738 book, *Elements of Newton's Philosophy*.

In 1737, Châtelet, like many other 18th–century scientists, attempted to explain the nature of combustion, submitting an essay entitled *Dissertation sur la nature et la propagation du feu*, as an entry for a contest organized by the Académie Royale des Sciences. Voltaire also participated in the contest, but was unaware of her work. When Leonhard Euler and two other scientists were declared the winners, Voltaire arranged that Châtelet's essay be published with the winning entries. In her study, she correctly argued that heat was not a substance, a view defended by the proponents of the phlogiston theory, which the great French chemist Antoine–Laurent Lavoisier empirically disproved in 1788. Furthermore, Châtelet put forth the original idea that light and heat were essentially the same substance.

Incorporates Leibniz's Ideas into Work on Newtonian Physics

While writing her *Institutions de physique*, a work on Newtonian physics and mechanics, Châtelet became acquainted with the ideas of Gottfried Leibniz, particularly his conception of *forces vives*, which she accepted as true. While René Descartes described the physical world geometrically as extended matter, to which force can be applied as an external agent, Leibniz defined force as a distinctive quality of matter. In view of Châtelet's general Newtonian orientation as a scientist, her passionate interest in Leibnizian metaphysics, which essentially contradicts the Newtonian world view, may seem odd. However, as Margaret Alic argues, the marquise sought a synthesis of the two world views. "*Institutions*," Alic has written, "remained faithful to Newtonian physics, but Newton's purely scientific, materialistic philosophy did not completely satisfy the marquise. She believed that scientific theory demanded a foundation in metaphysics and this she found in Leibniz. . . She never doubted that Leibnizian metaphysics was reconcilable with Newtonian physics, as long as the implications of the Newtonian system were limited to empirical physical phenomena." Châtelet's acceptance of the metaphysical foundations of science was an implicit rejection of any mechanistic world view, Cartesian or Newtonian. Naturally, French scientists, most of whom tacitly accepted the Cartesian scientific paradigm, found the marquise's ideas offensive. For example, the eminent Cartesian physicist and mathematician Jean–Baptist Dortous de Mairan, whom she had singled out for criticism, responded sharply in 1741, representing a majority view which Châtelet was unable to refute alone.

Translates Newton's Masterpiece into French

Retreating from the philosophical war between the Cartesians and the Leibnizians, Châtelet focused on her Newtonian studies, particularly the huge task of translating Newton's *Principia mathematica* into French, an undertaking which she devoted the rest of her life. An excellent Latinist with a deep understanding of Newtonian physics, she was ideally suited for the project. Despite many obstacles, which included a busy social life and an unwanted pregnancy at the age of 42, Châtelet finished her translation. On September 4, 1749, she gave birth to a daughter, and died of puerperal fever shortly thereafter. Her translation of Newton's work remains one of the monuments of French scientific scholarship.

SELECTED WRITINGS BY THE MARQUISE DU CHÂTELET:

Books

Dissertation sur la nature et la propagation du feu, 1739

Institutions de physique, 1740

Principes mathématiques de la philosophie naturelle, 1759 (Translation of *Principia mathematica*, by Isaac Newton)

Periodicals

"Lettre sur la philosophie de Newton." *Journal des sçavans.* (September 1738): 534–41.

FURTHER READING

Books

Alic, Margaret. *Hypatia's Heritage: A History of Women in Science from Antiquity through the Nineteenth Century.* Boston: Beacon Press, 1986.

Copleston, Frederick. *Modern Philosophy: From Descartes to Leibniz.* Vol. 4: *A History of Philosophy.* New York: Image Books, 1960.

Klens, Ulrike. *Mathematikerinnen im 18. Jahrhundert: Maria Gaëtana Agnesi, Gabrielle–Émilie du Châtelet, Sophie Germain.* Pfaffenweiler: Centaurus–Verlagsgesellschaft, 1994.

Mitford, Nancy. *Voltaire in Love.* New York: Greenwood Press, 1957.

Olsen, Lynn M. *Women in Mathematics.* Cambridge: MIT Press, 1974.

Smelding, Anda von. *Die göttliche Emilie.* Berlin: Schlieffen Verlag, 1933.

Vaillot, René;. *Madame du Châtelet.* Paris: Albin Michel, 1978.

Wolf, A. *A History of Science, Technology, and Philosophy in the Eighteenth Century.* 2d ed. London: George Allen & Unwin, 1952.

Sketch by Zoran Minderovic

May Edward Chinn
18961980
American physician

May Edward Chinn was a committed and determined black woman physician at a time in American history when both color and gender were barriers to advancement in the medical profession. In spite of these obstacles, her productive career spanned more than 50 years, and she was recognized by both the white medical establishment and black doctors for her many accomplishments. She was the first black woman physician to graduate from Bellevue Hospital Medical College, and the first black intern at Harlem Hospital (where she was also the first woman doctor to go on emergency calls with the ambulance squad). She called herself a "family doctor," and preferred to care for women, children and babies. Her efforts in cancer research led her to work with George Papanicolaou, the inventor of the "Pap" test for cervical cancer.

Chinn was born on April 15, 1896, in Great Barrington, Massachusetts, the only child of Lula Ann (Evans) and William Lafayette Chinn. Her father was born a slave in Virginia and escaped to the North as a young boy. Her mother was an African–American/ Native American of the Chickahominy tribe. The family moved to New York City when Chinn was three years old. She received her early education in the City's public school system and at the Bordentown Manual Training and Industrial School in New Jersey. (In Chinn's elementary years, an inflammatory bone disease in her jaw forced her to leave school. She received prolonged medical treatment for her condition.) She attended Morris High School, but did not graduate. Her mother—unlike her father—recognized the value of education for her daughter and encouraged her to strive for a college degree. Although she did not have a high school diploma, Chinn was able to pass the entrance exam for the Columbia University Teacher's College. She began her college education there in 1917.

From Music to Medicine

Chinn was a talented musician and her talent had been nurtured by the Tiffany family of jeweler fame. While living with the Tiffany family (her mother was employed as a housekeeper there), she was taken to concerts and given piano lessons. She began her college studies as a music major. It was during this time that she became the accompanist of the black singer, Paul Robeson, a rising star of the stage and screen. However, she soon changed her major to science. One source says the reason for this was that she was uncomfortable being the only black and the only woman in her music classes; another says only that she was persuaded to change by Jean Broadhurst, one of her teachers at Columbia. Whatever the reason, she graduated from Columbia with a bachelor of science degree in 1921. She entered Bellevue Medical College, where in 1926, she became the first black woman graduate. She subsequently was accepted as an intern at Harlem Hospital—again the first black woman to intern there.

A serious obstacle to Chinn's career as a doctor was the inability of black physicians to have admitting privileges at regular hospitals and access to postgraduate education. For this reason, in 1928, she joined a group of black doctors at Edgecombe Sanitarium, an alternative hospital in New York City. Here, many patients came to her in advanced stages of disease, when there was little she could do for them. Her cancer research work began at this time, and was an effort to diagnose and treat cancer in its early stages. In connection with her research, she was allowed, on an informal basis, to work with resident doctors at Memorial Hospital. It was at this time that she studied cell pathology with Dr. Papanicolaou. Her concern for the health of her patients also led her to acquire a master's degree in public health in 1933. Her work at Memorial Hospital eventually brought her a staff appointment to the Strang Clinic in 1944. She was to remain on staff at Strang until 1974.

A Harlem Legend

For 52 years, Chinn broke new ground in medicine. Educational and professional barriers were overcome and the path made smoother for others to follow. She also co–founded the **Susan Smith McKinney Steward** Medical Society to help black women who aspired to become physicians achieve their goals. In addition to her private practice, she was on staff at the New York Infirmary for Women and Children from 1945 to 1956, and served as a clinician and medical consultant to New York City day care centers from 1960 to 1977. Even after her retirement at the age of 81, she continued to work at three Harlem day care centers.

Chinn was elected a member of the New York Academy of Sciences; honored by the New York City Cancer Committee of the American Cancer Society; elected to the Society of Surgical Oncology, the American Geriatrics Society, and the American Society of Cytology; and made a Life Member of the American Academy of Family Physicians. The year she died, she was honored with a Teachers' College Distinguished Alumnus Award from Columbia University, and an honorary doctor of science degree from New York University. Chinn died in New York City on December 1, 1980, while attending a reception at Columbia University.

SELECTED WRITINGS BY CHINN

Other

Papers of May Edward Chinn are in Schomburg Center for Research in Black Culture, New York City.

Manuscript of her autobiography is in Special Collections of Fisk University Library.

FURTHER READING

Books

Garraty, John A., and Mark C. Carnes, eds. *American National Biography.* Vol. 4. New York: Oxford University Press, 1999, pp. 816–817.

Hine, Darlene Clark, ed. *Black Women in America, An Historical Encyclopedia.* Brooklyn: Carlson Publishing, 1993, pp. 235–236.

O'Neill, Lois Decker, ed. *The Women's Book of World Records and Achievements.* Garden City: Anchor Press/Doubleday, 1979, p. 207.

Smith, Jessie Carney, ed. *Notable Black American Women.* Detroit: Gale Research, Inc., 1992, pp. 183–185.

Other

Dammond, Ellen Craft. "Interview with May Edward Chinn, M. D." *The Black Women's Oral History Project.* Schlesinger Library, Radcliffe College, 1979.

"May Edward Chinn." *Distinguished Women of the Past and Present.* http://www.netsrq.com/~dbois/ and http://www.sdsc.edu/sciencewomen/chinn.html

Sketch by Jane Stewart Cook

Cornelia Maria Clapp

1849–1934

American zoologist

Cornelia Clapp was the first American woman to become a professional research zoologist. She conducted her research at the Woods Hole Biological Laboratory in Massachusetts and was a faculty member at Mount Holyoke, where she introduced the first laboratory courses and was instrumental in Mount Holyoke's transition from a female seminary to a prestigious women's college.

Cornelia Clapp was born in 1849 in Montague, Massachusetts. Her parents, Richard C. and Eunice Amelia (Slate) Clapp, were school teachers and her father was a farmer. Clapp was the oldest of six children. She was educated in local schools and then attended Mount Holyoke Seminary in South Hadley, Massachusetts, graduating in 1871. She spent the following year teaching Latin to boys in Andalusia, Pennsylvania, and then joined the Mount Holyoke faculty where she remained until he retired.

Clapp originally taught mathematics and gymnastics, but **Lydia Shattuck**, Mount Holyoke's science teacher and herself also a protéegée of Mount Holyoke founder **Mary Lyon**, inspired Clapp to study natural history. The two women began to do field studies together. In the summer of 1874, Shattuck arranged for Clapp to attend the new Anderson School of Natural History, which the zoologist Louis Agassiz and his wife, the naturalist **Elizabeth Agassiz,** had established on Pekinese Island, which is off the coast of Cape Cod. The Agassizes had a profound influence on Clapp, as they did on many other women educators. Consequently, Clapp returned to Mount Holyoke determined to establish a modern zoology laboratory for her students. One of her first projects was to rent a hen and place a new egg under the hen each day for 21 days. At the end of that time, she had samples of each stage of each chick's embryo development. She charged admission to see the display and earned back the cost of the hen.

Clapp went on several major collecting trips, first in the White Mountains in New Hampshire where she collected insects, and later to the southern United States, Switzerland, and northern Italy. The latter trips were led by the famous naturalist David Starr Jordan who, like Agassiz, had a major impact on the careers of women biologists.

Clapp was involved with the Marine Biological Laboratory at Woods Hole, Massachusetts, a successor to the Anderson School, since its opening in 1888, and continued to work there for the rest of her life. She was part of a summer research group that included the geneticist Thomas Hunt Morgan, and the famous biologists Jacques Loeb and E. B. Wilson. In addition to her research in the fields of marine biology and embryology, she taught at Woods Hole, acted as the librarian between 1893 and 1907, and also served as a trustee. She encouraged many of her Mount Holyoke students to study at Woods Hole there as well.

During this period, Clapp continued her education and research. She studied the embryology of chickens at the Massachusetts Institute of Technology and earthworms at Williams College. Passing her examinations, she received a Ph.B. degree in 1888 and a Ph.D. in 1889 from Syracuse University. Taking a three-year leave of absence from Mount Holyoke, Clapp, along with some of her students, did graduate work at the University of Chicago. There, Clapp earned her second Ph.D. on her doctoral thesis on the toadfish in 1896, which was later published in 1899.

In 1904, Clapp was named professor of zoology after establishing the zoology department at what had become Mount Holyoke College. Although she retired from Mount Holyoke in 1916 and moved to Florida, she continued to spend her summers working at Woods Hole.

Although Clapp published very little during her career, she was recognized as one of the important zoologists of her day. She was also considered to be one of the finest teachers of her generation. She was involved in the Association to Aid Scientific Research by Women which financially supported a "woman's table" or laboratory bench for American women researchers at the Naples Zoological Station in Italy, where Clapp became a fellow in 1901. In 1921, she received an honorary doctor of science degree

Cornelia Clapp (Mt. Holyoke College Archive. Reproduced by permission.)

from Mount Holyoke. The laboratory building at Mount Holyoke that she had worked so hard to build, was named in her honor. In 1906, Clapp became one of only six women named in the first edition of *American Men of Science*. She died in Florida in 1934 following a cerebral thrombosis.

SELECTED WRITINGS BY CLAPP:

Books

The Lateral Line System of Batrachus tau. Boston: Ginn, 1899.

Periodicals

"Some Recollections of the First Summer at Woods Hole." *Collecting Net* 2, no. 4 (1927): 2–10.

FURTHER READING

Books

Haywood, Charlotte. "Cornelia Maria Clapp." In *Notable American Women 1607–1950: A Biographical Dictionary* Edited by Edward T. James, Janet Wilson James, and Paul W. Boyer. Cambridge: Harvard University Press, 1971.

Shmurak, Carole B. "Cornelia M. Clapp." In *Notable Women in the Life Sciences: A Biographical Dictionary*. Edited by Benjamin F. Shearer and Barbara S. Shearer. Westport, CT: Greenwood Press, 1996.

Sketch by Margaret Alic

Jamie Rappaport Clark
1957?–
American wildlife biologist and administrator

Jamie Rappaport Clark was confirmed as director of the U.S. Fish and Wildlife Service on July 1, 1997, the second woman to hold that position. A wildlife biologist and ecologist by training, Clark has helped develop national policy on wetlands, endangered species, and environmental contaminants.

A self–confessed "Army brat," Clark moved continually in her youth, following her father's various postings in the Army Corp of Engineers. "That certainly brought many challenges," Clark told the Senate Committee on Environment and Public Works during her confirmation hearings. "But it also gave me opportunities to see many areas of the United States. I fondly remember exploring spectacular open spaces on horseback, seeing new birds and other wildlife, and discovering unique habitats."

From Amateur Naturalist to Professional Environmentalist

Clark turned her love for the outdoors into a career. Attending Maryland's Towson State Univesity, she studied wildlife biology, focusing on the reintroduction of peregrine falcon populations in northern Maryland. Graduating with a B.S. degree in 1979, she worked for two years as a wildlife biologist for the National Institute for Urban Wildlife. At the same time she was also studying toward an M.S. degree in wildlife ecology at Towson. Her graduate thesis involved working with hunters to determine optimum levels of white–tailed–deer herd density. "I learned first hand the role of hunting as an effective wildlife management tool," Clark told senators during her confirmation hearing. "I share with hunters, anglers, and other outdoor enthusiasts an appreciation of wildlife that comes from long hours in the field observing nature." Clark also completed a master's degree in environmental planning at the University of Maryland.

From the National Institute for Urban Wildlife Clark became a research biologist for the U.S. Army Medical Research Institute manager for the National Guard Bureau. In 1988 she served as the fish and wildlife administrator for the Department of the Army, acting as lead technical authority for fish and wildlife management on Army installations around the world. Then in 1989 she joined the U.S. Fish and Wildlife Service.

An Organic Approach to Wildlife Management

Clark early on demonstrated a varied approach to species and habitat conservation, attempting to include all parties in the debate: state wildlife agencies, local governments, conservationists, and sportsmen's groups alike. She even incorporated environmental matters into her private life, marrying a wildlife biologist. Joining the service provided Clark with new scope for her work, charged as it is with conserving, protecting, and enhancing fish and wildlife in their natural habitats, managing 65 national fish hatcheries and 511 wildlife refuges covering 92 million acres. The service also administers the Endangered Species Act, manages migratory bird populations, and conserves wildlife habitat.

With the service, Clark began as the senior staff biologist for the endangered species division, with responsibilities in the Pacific Northwest. From there she took on the position of deputy assistant regional director for the Southwest region, including Arizona, New Mexico, Oklahoma, and Texas, acting as principal advisor on all aspects of the Endangered Species Act. Thereafter she became chief of the endangered species, responsible for the overall direction and management of programs for threatened and endangered species. In 1994, she was named assistant director for ecological services, overseeing the Endangered Species Act, wetland and upland habitat restoration, environmental contaminants, and a host of other environmental issues. Her rise in the service was rapid: within five years she was taking the lead in developing and implementing national policy regarding wetlands, endangered species, and environmental contaminants. At this same time, Vice–President Al Gore and the Office of Environmental Policy (OEP) were setting a new agenda for environmental conservation to fit alongside sustainable economic growth; Clark represented the Service in interagency talks with the OEP. When then director Mollie Beattie of the service was diagnosed with incurable brain cancer in 1995, Clark was designated to carry on congressional battles for her. With the Beattie's death in 1996, Clark was nominated by President Clinton and confirmed as director in 1997, making her the nation's lead official in wildlife management and has since continued her all–encompassing approach to the issues of the day.

FURTHER READING

Other

"Biographical Sketch of the Director, U.S. Fish and Wildlife Service: Jamie Rappaport Clark." http://www.fws.gov/who/dirbio.html.

"Jamie Clark Confirmed Director of U.S. Fish and Wildlife Service." http://www.fws.gov/r9extaff/pr/jamie.html, August 1, 1997.

"Testimony before the Senate Committee on Environment and Public Works by Jamie Rappaport Clark, Nominee for Director of the U.S. Fish and Wildlife Service, July 16, 1997." http://gos.sbc.edu/clark.html.

Sketch by J. Sydney Jones

Edith Clarke
1883–1959
American engineer

Edith Clarke is chiefly recognized for her contributions to simplifying and mechanizing the calculations required in power systems analysis. A pioneering female engineer, Clarke was the first woman granted an M.S. in electrical engineering from the Massachusetts Institute of Technology (MIT) and later became the first woman to deliver a technical paper before the American Institute of Electrical Engineers (AIEE).

Clarke was born on a farm near Ellicott City, Maryland, one of nine children of Susan Dorsey (Owings) and John Ridgely Clarke, a lawyer. She attended a nearby school until 1897, when she entered boarding school after the deaths of her parents. She returned home two years later with no ambition for a career. Clarke decided to study languages with a tutor, however, and entered Vassar College in 1904. There she studied mathematics and astronomy, graduating with an A.B. in 1908.

Clarke taught math and science in San Francisco and later in Huntington, West Virginia, before renewing her studies in 1911 at the University of Wisconsin. After one year of course work in civil engineering, she joined the American Telephone and Telegraph company (AT&T) in New York as a computing assistant to research engineer George A. Campbell. At the time, computing mathematical problems for engineers was considered an appropriate profession for women with advanced training in mathematics. During World War I, Clarke led a group of women who made calculations for the Transmission Department at AT&T. Concurrently, she studied radio at Hunter College and electrical engineering at Columbia University in the evenings.

Awarded Landmark Degree from MIT

In 1919 Clarke became the first woman to graduate from the Massachusetts Institute of Technology (MIT) with an M.S. degree in electrical engineering. Even with such credentials, however, she was unsuccessful in acquiring a position as an engineer. She worked briefly as a computor for General Electric (GE) before accepting a post teaching physics at Constantinople Women's College (now Istanbul

American College) in 1921. The following year, Clarke returned to GE—this time as an engineer. She analyzed electric power systems and researched special problems related to power–system operations.

Clarke remained with GE for twenty–six years. Chief among her contributions there were innovations in long–distance power transmission and the development of the theory of symmetrical component and circuit analysis. Her method of regulating the voltage on power transmission lines was patented in 1927. In 1932 she became the first woman to present a paper before the AIEE and garnered recognition for her work as the best paper of the year in the northern district. Her paper explored the use of multiple conductor transmission lines to increase power line capacity. While at GE, Clarke also published a textbook which covered circuit analysis of alternating–current power systems. Prior to World War II, Clarke devised calculating charts which greatly streamlined the computation process.

Clarke retired to Maryland in 1945 but was drawn back to engineering within a year, this time accepting an associate professorship in electrical engineering at the University of Texas. Gaining full professorship in 1947, Clarke also served on numerous committees and was a graduate student advisor, providing special assistance to foreign students. Clarke was elected a fellow of the AIEE (now the Institute for Electrical and Electronics Engineers, known as the IEEE) in 1948, the first woman to be so named. In 1957, at age 74, Clarke retired a second time. She died two years later in Baltimore.

SELECTED WRITINGS BY CLARKE:

Books

Circuit Analysis of A–C Power Systems, Volume 1, 1943.

FURTHER READING

Books

Goff, Alice C., *Women Can Be Engineers,* Edwards Brothers, 1946, pp. 50–65.

Periodicals

Brittain, James E., "From Computor to Electrical Engineer: The Remarkable Career of Edith Clarke," *IEEE Transactions on Education,* November, 1985, pp. 184–89.

"Edith Clarke Dies, 1954 SWE Award Winner," *Society of Women Engineers Newsletter,* December, 1959, p. 3.

Sketch by Karen Withem

Edith Jane Claypole
1870–1915
American physiologist and pathologist

Although still a young woman when she died, Edith Claypole managed to make a name for herself as a noted researcher whose findings led to a better understanding of diseases such as typhoid fever. She was the twin sister of **Agnes Mary Moody**, who also distinguished herself as a scientist.

Edith Claypole was born in Bristol, England, in 1870, the daughter of Edward Waller and Jane Trotter Claypole. Edward Claypole was a scientist, and in 1879 he took a position at Buchtel College in Akron, Ohio. Edith and Agnes were educated at home by their father. Both girls (no doubt at least partly influenced by their home life) showed an early interest in science, and both attended Buchtel.

After graduating from Buchtel in 1892, Claypole went to Cornell, where she received her master's degree in science the following year. She took a position as an instructor in histology and physiology at Wellesley College in 1894 and remained there for five years. (Between 1896 and 1898 she was acting head of the zoology department.) In 1899, she returned to Cornell to continue her education and then went to southern California in 1900 to help take care of her ailing mother (who was then living in Pasadena). Claypole picked up her studies at UCLA, where she received her M.D. in 1904.

She had started working part-time as a pathologist in Pasadena in 1902, and upon completion of her degree she continued her work, now on a full-time basis. At first, she was relegated to fairly basic tasks, but her talents, especially as a researcher, began to surface quickly. One of her colleagues said that she was "fitted as few women and men have been" to work as a researcher. It was not until 1912, however, that she devoted herself exclusively to research. She signed on as a volunteer at UCLA and was soon appointed research associate.

During her years at UCLA Claypole did extensive research on blood and tissue histology and pathology, focusing primarily on the lung. Her work was well known in the scientific community, and she began research on the typhoid bacillus. Even today one of the dangers of working with lethal samples is accidental exposure, and in 1915 the safeguards were much less sophisticated. Claypole contracted typhoid fever as a result of her work, and it led to her early death later that year in Berkeley, California.

SELECTED WRITINGS BY CLAYPOLE:

Books

Human Streptotrichosis and Its Differentiation from Tuberculosis. American Medical Association, 1914.

FURTHER READING

Books

Bailey, Martha J. *American Women in Science: A Biographical Dictionary.* Denver: ABC-Clio, 1994.

Oglivie, Marilyn Bailey. *Women in Science: Antiquity through the Nineteenth Century.* Cambridge: MIT Press, 1986.

Sketch by George A. Milite

Cleopatra the Alchemist
fl. First century (?)
Egyptian alchemist

Cleopatra, an alchemist who probably lived in Alexandria, Egypt, left two surviving works which are among the earliest alchemical writings and among the earliest scientific works by a woman.

Almost nothing is known about Cleopatra. She often has been confused with the famous Queen Cleopatra, who may have been interested in alchemy as well. Ancient alchemists often ascribed their work to famous, or infamous, people, both to ensure acceptance of their work, and also because of the traditional concern with alchemical secrecy. Cleopatra was associated with the teachings of **Maria the Jewess**, and like Maria, she may have worked in Alexandria in the first century.

Cleopatra's surviving treatise, "A Dialogue of Cleopatra and the Philosophers," dating from the second century, was a work of allegorical poetry. In her "Dialogue," Cleopatra is taught by the high priest and philosopher Komarios, and she transmits his teachings to later philosophers. Jack Lindsay called her treatise "the most imaginative and deeply-felt document left by the alchemists." Although the ultimate goal of the alchemist was to transmute common metals into silver and gold, these ancient alchemists were scientists who also examined chemical processes and the nature of life. They believed that metals were living males and females and that the products of their laboratory experiments were the result of sexual generation. The early alchemists also believed that the base metals were evolving toward the perfect metal gold and that by transferring the "spirit" or vapor of gold to a base metal, as measured by the transfer of color, alchemists saw themselves as encouraging a natural process. Cleopatra used the imagery of conception, birth, renewal, and transformation to describe these alchemical processes.

Cleopatra's single surviving sheet of papyrus, with alchemical symbols and diagrams, dates from the third century, and is considered to be one of the major sources for ancient alchemy. The papyrus sheet, called the "Chrysopoeia" or "Gold-making" of Cleopatra, included the Egyptian symbol of the cosmos or eternity, called the "Ouroboros," a snake eating its tail. It also included an inscribed double ring with the symbols for gold, silver, and mercury, the earliest known use of symbols for these elements; a diagram of a two–armed still; and a type of chemical apparatus called a "kerotakis." These may be the earliest surviving drawings of chemical apparatus.

Cleopatra was an experimentalist as well as a theorist. She was interested in weights and measurements for quantifying alchemical experiments and apparently wrote a treatise on this subject. She also is said to have studied the dissolving action of vinegar on pearls.

By the third century, the alchemists of Alexandria were being persecuted and their texts were destroyed. Much of this work was rescued by the Arabs; however, when alchemy was rediscovered in medieval Europe, it was primarily in the form of charlatanism. Today, the work of these ancient alchemists are recognized as the forerunner of modern chemistry.

SELECTED WRITINGS BY CLEOPATRA:

Books

"A Dialogue of Cleopatra and the Philosophers." In *Collection des Anciens Alchimists Grecs.* Vol. 3. Edited by M. Berthelot. Paris, 1888.

FURTHER READING

Books

Alic, Margaret. *Hypatia's Heritage: A History of Women in Science from Antiquity through the Nineteenth Century.* Boston: Beacon Press,1986.

Lindsay, Jack. *The Origins of Alchemy in Graeco-Roman Egypt.* New York: Barnes & Noble, 1970.

Miller, Jane A. "Women in Chemistry." In *Women of Science: Righting the Record.* Edited by G. Kass–Simon and Patricia Farnes. Bloomington: Indiana University Press, 1990.

Taylor, F. Sherwood. *The Alchemists: Founders of Modern Chemistry.* New York: Henry Shuman, 1949.

Sketch by Margaret Alic

Agnes Mary Clerke
1842–1907
Irish-English astronomer

In the latter half of the nineteenth century, astronomy had progressed from an amateur science to a professional field with many specializations. Masses of data were being collected by new techniques and instruments and it was becoming increasingly difficult for astronomers to keep up with these developments. Agnes Clerke digested, collated, and synthesized this new science, publishing books on astronomy for both professional and amateur scientists. In the process, she invented a new type of science writing.

Born in Skibbereen, County Cork, Ireland, in 1842, Clerke grew up in a wealthy Anglo-Irish family during the time of the Irish famine. She was one of three children educated at home in music, modern languages, and science by their parents, Catherine (Deasy) and John Clerke. Her father, a bank manager, was also a classical scholar and an amateur astronomer. He had both a chemistry laboratory and a telescope and he encouraged his children's scientific pursuits. Clerke taught herself mathematics and astronomy, making use of her father's library.

Between 1870 and 1877, after time in Dublin and Queenstown, the Clerke family resided in Italy. In her final year there, Clerke submitted an article, "Copernicus in Italy," to the *Edinburgh Review*. It was the first of many articles on astronomy that she would write for that journal.

In 1877, the family settled in London where Clerke, who never married, would remain for the rest of her life. In 1885, she published her first book, *A Popular History of Astronomy during the Nineteenth Century*, which went through several English editions and a German translation. It is still considered to be a standard of astronomical history and its success brought Clerke recognition in scientific circles. She became close friends with the astronomer **Margaret Huggins** and many other prominent scientists of her day. An American astrophysicist considered her to be so influential among scientists, that he often announced his discoveries to Clerke before publishing them.

Clerke spent the summer of 1888 at the Royal Observatory at the Cape of Good Hope on the southern tip of Africa, in order to gain practical experience in observational astronomy. This experience led to *The System of the Stars*, published in 1890. These first two books won her the Actonian Prize of the Royal Institution. Although women were barred from membership in the Royal Astronomical Society, Clerke was elected an honorary member in 1903.

Clerke always used primary sources for her information and wrote in a literary, but objective, style that appealed to popular audiences as well as scientific ones. She was viewed by her contemporaries as not just an historian and popularizer of astronomy, but also as an expert in the field, a critic of new theories, and an originator of new ideas. Indeed, she was able to make new and original connections between isolated discoveries in different specializations. As a devout Catholic, Clerke also stressed a reconciliation between religion and the new astronomy.

Clerke was a prolific author. Her books and wide array of articles covered everything from the history of astronomy to the most recent developments in astrophysics. Her most famous books included *The Herschels and Modern Astronomy*, published in 1895, and *Modern Cosmogonies*, published in 1906. Many of her books became best-sellers, appealing to popular audiences as well as professional scientists. She also authored two sections of "Concise Astronomy" for the *Concise Knowledge Library* in 1898 and wrote a great many scientific biographies for reference books. In addition, Clerke studied Greek and wrote a popular book on the Greek poet Homer.

Clerke's older sister Ellen Mary Clerke, who shared her interest in astronomy, remained her companion throughout her life. Ellen Mary Clerke was also a writer who published poetry, a novel, and translations of Italian poetry, as well as articles on popular astronomy. Agnes Clerke died of pneumonia in her home in South Kensington, London in 1907.

SELECTED WRITINGS BY CLERKE:

Books

A Popular History of Astronomy during the Nineteenth Century. 1885. Reprint. London: Adam and Charles Black, 1908.

The Herschels and Modern Astronomy. London: Cassell, 1895.

Problems in Astrophysics. London: Adam and Charles Black, 1903.

Modern Cosmogonies. London: Adam and Charles Black, 1905.

The System of the Stars. London: Adam and Charles Black, 1905.

FURTHER READING

Books

Lightman, Bernard. "Constructing the Victorian Heavens: Agnes Clerke and the 'New Astronomy.'" In *Natural Eloquence: Women Reinscribe Science*. Edited by Barbara T. Gates and Ann B. Shteir. Madison: University of Wisconsin Press, 1997.

Periodicals

Davis, Herman S. "Women Astronomers (400A.D.–1750)." *Popular Astronomy* 6 (1898): 129–38.

Sketch by Margaret Alic

Jerrie Cobb (Reproduced by permission of Jerrie Cobb.)

Geraldyn "Jerrie" Cobb
1931–
American pilot

Geraldyn "Jerrie" Cobb was the first woman to pass astronaut testing during NASA's Mercury program in 1954. Although she passed all tests successfully, NASA refused to accept women as astronauts. She later became known as the "Flying Angel of Amazonia" for her humanitarian efforts over three decades as a missionary pilot in the Amazon and was nominated for the Nobel Peace Prize in 1981 for this work. Cobb earned her commercial pilot's license, airline transport rating, flight instructor, and ground instructor certifications in navigation, meteorology, aircraft, and engines early in her career. In 1973, she was awarded a Harmon Trophy, honoring her as the world's best woman pilot. While Cobb is not a scientist, her pioneering work as a pilot and lobbying efforts to include women in the space program opened up opportunities for future women astronauts.

Not limiting her skills to fixed wing aircraft, she soloed in a helicopter after only 83 minutes of dual instruction, something that usually takes eight hours, which earned her a commercial helicopter license in 1961. For her flying accomplishments—she has flown over 56,000 hours during her career—she was inducted into the Oklahoma Hall of Fame in 1976 as the most outstanding aviatrix in the United States.

Cobb was born on March 5, 1931 in Norman, Oklahoma to Harvey and Helena (Stone) Cobb, the younger of two daughters. By 1943, the family was living in Wichita Falls, Texas, where Cobb's father was stationed at Sheppard Army Air Base. In contrast to her older sister Carolyn, Cobb was somewhat of a tomboy, riding horses, studying pictures of military planes, and making paper gliders. She did not enjoy school, partly because she was shy and had a lisp, which even the teachers made fun of. School became something to be endured until she was old enough to fly on her own.

Learns to Fly

Cobb fell in love with flying at age 12 when she got her first ride in her father's airplane, a 1936 Waco bi–wing. He had bought the airplane so he could gain enough hours to fly for the Air Force. "I had the wondrous feeling of being truly free for the first time," Cobb says in her autobiography. "The sky was the only place I felt really at home." Her father began teaching her how to fly, but her instruction was interrupted when the plane was sold after he was transferred to Lowrey Air Field in Colorado.

For the next four years, Cobb spent all her free time working at small country airports to earn short flights around the field and to learn everything she could about airplanes. She later finished her lessons with the high school football coach who was also a flight instructor, earning her pilot's license on her 16th birthday with already 400 hours of flying time. During the summer of that year, Cobb went barnstorming across the Great Plains in a circus Piper J–3 Cub, dropping flyers announcing the upcoming circus and giving plane rides.

After World War II ended and military pilots returned home, there were few flying jobs available, especially for women. A professional pilot at 18, Cobb was forced to take a variety of other jobs, including waitress, typist, and horse trainer, to continue her flying lessons. To help pay for her multi–engine and instrument ratings, she even played three seasons with a semiprofessional women's softball team (the Oklahoma City Queens) in the spring and summer of 1949. In the fall of that same year, she enrolled at Oklahoma College for Women at Chickasaw but only stayed a year so she could return to flying. In 1950, she was hired part–time by an oil company to inspect its pipelines in Oklahoma and Kansas.

By the time she turned 19 in 1950, Cobb had earned all her professional pilots licenses, as well as flight instructor and ground instructor ratings. By this time she had more than 3,000 hours flying time in 41 different airplanes. That same year, she was hired as a flight and ground school instructor. Later she worked as a charter pilot out of Downtown Airpark in Oklahoma City, ferrying passengers to cities in Texas, Kansas and Colorado.

International Ferry Pilot

In 1953, Cobb went to Florida to apply for a co–pilot job at a new airline called Trans–International. She was turned down no airline passenger will ever fly with a woman pilot, she was told—despite her experience. Cobb then found a job as a typist/file clerk at Miami International Airport, typing work orders on airplanes. About six months later, she met Jack Ford, President of Fleetway, Inc., who eventually offered her a job as an international ferry pilot. Her first flight was piloting a T–6 military fighter to Lima, Peru. Before she completed her flight, Cobb was arrested in Ecuador during a refueling stop, accused as a Peruvian spy. The countries had begun fighting while she was en route, and Cobb spent 13 days in a military prison before she was released.

In 1953, Cobb made her first ferry flight across the Atlantic in a B–17 four-;engine bomber. This required a stop in Greenland to refuel, which involved a treacherous landing and liftoff in bad weather, and a near mid-air collision with some jet fighters. That same year Cobb had to make an emergency landing in Jamaica during another flight. In one ferrying mission, she was requested by Paraguayan officials to fly to Buenos Aires to pick up an important official. Since had received no official orders to do so, she agreed to teach one of their military pilots to fly the plane. The next day, Cobb discovered that the official was the exiled Argentinean leader, Juan Peron, who had been rescued by the pilot she had trained.

Record Breaker and Astronaut Candidate

After she left Fleetway in 1955, Cobb returned to her family in Ponca City, Oklahoma, for a much needed rest. She then took a job as chief pilot for the Executive Aircraft Company in Kansas City. From 1957–1960, she flew as a test pilot, setting three world aviation records for speed, distance, and altitude. Her world records broke the records previously held by male Russian Air Force officers in Yak–II military fighters.

When she was selected as America's first woman to undergo astronaut testing in 1959 by NASA, Cobb was only 28, and had more than 10,000 hours of flight time, twice as many as any of the male astronauts. She also was one of the few women executives in American aviation as manager for Aero Design and Engineering Company of Oklahoma City, Oklahoma, (which later became the Aero Commander Company, a subsidiary of Rockwell International). That same year Cobb had been named Pilot of the Year by the National Pilots' Association, and the Woman of the Year in Aviation from the Women's National Aeronautic Association. She also had earned the Gold Wings from the Federation Aeronautique Internationale, and the Amelia Earhart Gold Medal from the 99s—a woman's pilot association.

During her Mercury astronaut tests which began in February 1960 at Lovelace Clinic in Albuquerque, New Mexico, Cobb underwent three phases of tests involving a total of 124 different physical and psychological tests, passing every one. She broke the record for the water tank test, which measured a person's ability to spend long periods alone without any sensory stimulation. Cobb remained in the tank for nine hours, nearly a third longer than the previous record. She had also completed her first run in the Multi–Axis Spin Test Inertia Facility, which simulated a spacecraft tumbling wildly out of control, without hitting the "chicken" switch. Alan Shepard hit this switch his first run.

In 1961, Cobb was appointed a consultant in manned space flight to NASA's Office of the Administrator. She recommended that the Mercury program should include women on subsequent flights. Despite her lobbying efforts and the successful Phase I testing of 12 other women candidates, NASA refused to include women as astronauts (they had not expected a woman to pass) and canceled testing of women later that year. In 1962, Cobb testified at a Congressional hearing to examine the qualifications of astronaut candidates after Senator Philip Hart and his wife (one of the 13 women tested) urged Congress to do so. Despite her testimony, NASA refused to accept women as astronauts. After the hearing, Cobb continued to write letters and give speeches promoting women as astronauts but her efforts were fruitless.

A Humanitarian Pilot in the Amazon

After the testing program was discontinued in 1963 (the same year the Russians launched the first woman into space), a discouraged Cobb turned to more humanitarian activities and became a missionary pilot, bringing seeds, medical supplies, and hope to the indigenous people of the Amazon headwaters. For 35 years, Cobb has dedicated her life to this mission, learning more than 16 dialects and surviving encounters with unfriendly guerrilla forces. Her mission has served six million people living in Amazonia, covering parts of Brazil, Colombia, Bolivia, Peru, Venezuela, and Ecuador. She has been honored by the governments of these countries, as well as France, for her humanitarian flying missions. Awards for this effort include the Pioneer Woman Award, the Bishop Wright Air Industry Award, and the Lady Hay Drummond–Jessie R. Chamberlin Trophy.

In February 1995, Cobb and six other women who tested with her during the Mercury program, attended the launch of the STS-63 Space Shuttle mission, which was the first Space Shuttle flight to be piloted by a woman: **Eileen Collins.** Three years later, Cobb returned from the Amazon to begin campaigning to finally get her chance to fly in space and follow in John Glenn's footsteps. Supporters have included the National Women's History Project; the American Association of University Women of California, Michigan and Minnesota; the Business and Professional Women Organization; the National Organization of Women, and senators from both Oklahoma and California.

SELECTED WRITINGS BY COBB:

Books

(With Jane Riecker). *Woman into Space: The Jerrie Cobb Story, Prentice–Hall*, 1962.

Jerrie Cobb, Solo Pilot, Florida: Jerrie Cobb Foundation, Inc., 1997.

FURTHER READING

Books

Haynsworth, Leslie, and David Toomey. *Amelia Earhart's Daughters*, New York: William Morrow and Company, Inc., 1998.

Holden, Henry. *Ladybirds: The Untold Story of Women Pilots in America*, Mt. Freedom: Black hawk Publishing Co., 1993.

Periodicals

Coffey, Ivy. "The Girl Who Excels in Loneliness." *Guideposts* (August 1961): 1–4.

Dunn, Marcia. "Thirty-eight Years Later, Jerrie Cobb Wants Her Shot at Space." *The Associated Press* (July 13,1998).

Other

Shepler, John. "Astronaut Jerrie Cobb, Our Other American Legend," http://www.execpc.com/~shepler (8 November 1998).

http://www.jerrie-cobb.org

Sketch by Laurel M. Sheppard

Jewel Plummer Cobb
1924–
American cell biologist

Jewel Plummer Cobb (Reproduced by permission of Jewel Plummer Cobb.)

Jewel Plummer Cobb is known for her contributions to the field of cell biology and for promoting minority involvement in the sciences. She has focused much of her research on melanin, a brown or black skin pigment, and the factors that affect the causes and growth of normal and cancerous pigment cells. Her research into the effects of drugs on cancer cells was important to future work in the field of chemotherapy. As an educator, Cobb initiated a number of programs to encourage ethnic minorities and women in the sciences.

Born in Chicago on January 17, 1924, Cobb was the only child of Frank V. Plummer, a doctor and graduate of Cornell University, and Carriebel (Cole) Plummer, who taught dance in public schools and participated in the Works Projects Administration (WPA) efforts. Cobb's family had a history in the sciences: not only was her father a doctor, but her paternal grandfather was a pharmacist who had graduated from Howard University in 1898.

As an upper–middle–class African American, Cobb was exposed to a variety of African American professionals through her parents, all accomplished in their fields. She also socialized with well–off peers during her summers at a northern Michigan resort. Although the schools in Chicago were largely segregated, Cobb received a solid public school education, bolstered by her exposure to her father's library at home. Her interest in biology was sparked in her sophomore year by her first look through the lens of a microscope.

A member of her high school's honor society, Cobb attended the University of Michigan after graduation. She was drawn there partly by the knowledge that some of her summer friends would be there and by the university's nationally known football team. The segregation she had experienced in public schools continued in college, however: all the African American students had to live in one house. After three semesters at Michigan, Cobb transferred to Alabama's Talladega College, and in 1944 she graduated with a bachelor of arts degree in biology. She then accepted a teaching fellowship at New York University, which had at first turned her down. Her poise and credentials finally tipped the scales in her favor. She maintained her fellowship for five years and undertook graduate studies in cell physiology.

Pursues Career as Cell Biologist

By 1950 Cobb had completed her master's degree and doctorate. Because she enjoyed research and a theoretical approach to biology, Cobb decided to become a cell biologist. As a cell biologist, her focus was the action and interaction of living cells. She was particularly interested in tissue culture, in which cells are grown outside of the body and studied under microscopes. Among her most important work was her study with Dorothy Walker Jones of how new cancer–fighting drugs affected human cancer cells.

As a researcher, Cobb has held a series of positions at various colleges and research facilities throughout the United States. She was a fellow at the National Cancer Institute for two years after receiving her doctorate, and from 1952 to 1954 she was the director of the Tissue Culture Laboratory at the University of Illinois. At the end of this period Cobb married, and in 1957 she and her husband had a son, Roy Jonathan Cobb. After leaving Illinois, Cobb worked at several universities, including New York University and Hunter College in New York, and in 1960 she was appointed professor of biology at Sarah Lawrence College. There Cobb taught and continued her research into skin pigment. She was particularly interested in melanoma, or skin cancer, and melanin's ability to protect skin from damage caused by ultraviolet light.

Establishes Programs for Minority Students

In 1969, two years after she and her husband divorced, Cobb was appointed dean of Connecticut College and professor of zoology. In addition to teaching and continuing her research, she established a privately funded premedical graduate program and a pre–dental program for minority students. Numerous other colleges used these programs as models for their own, but after she left in 1976, the programs at Connecticut were discontinued. From 1976 to 1981 Cobb served as dean and professor of biological sciences at Douglass College. Although she had to give up her research in order to fulfill her administrative and teaching obligations, she continued to press for the advancement of minorities and women in the sciences.

Cobb wrote about the difficulties women face in scientific fields in a 1979 paper, "Filters for Women in Science," published in the book *Expanding the Role of Women in the Sciences,* which was edited by Anne M. Briscoe and Sheila M. Pfafflin. In this piece, Cobb argued that various pressures, particularly in the educational system, act as filters that prevent many women from choosing science careers. The socialization of girls has tended to discourage them from pursuing math and the sciences from a very early age, and even those women who got past such obstacles have struggled to get university tenure and the same jobs (at equal pay) as men.

In 1981 Cobb was named president at California State University (CSU) in Fullerton. She was extremely active in initiating improvements for the campus, notably in obtaining state funding for a new engineering and computer science building and a new science building. In addition, she built an apartment complex for students (later named in her honor), ending the university's years as a commuter campus, and established the president's opportunity program for ethnic students. Her work also extended to the community, for which she founded a privately funded gerontology center.

Cobb became a trustee professor at California State College in Los Angeles in 1990, and in 1991 she was made principal investigator for Southern California Science and Engineering ACCESS Center and Network. A trustee of several colleges, with numerous honorary degrees, Cobb worked with a consortium of six colleges to raise private funds to replace diminishing government grants and fellowships for minorities in science and engineering. The group worked to motivate minorities in the sciences, to bring more of them into the field. Over the years, Cobb had become increasingly aware of the disparity between the number of black men in sports and those in the lab, for instance. As part of her group's effort, faculty members tutored students on an individual basis in order to solidify their math skills, which Cobb felt were a crucial foundation for a career in the sciences. President emeritus of CSU since 1990, Cobb continues to use her skill as an educator, administrator, and scientist to promote the educational needs and careers of minorities in the sciences.

SELECTED WRITINGS BY COBB:

Periodicals

(With D. G. Walker) "Studies on Human Melanoma Cells in Tissue Cultures. I. Growth Characteristics and Cytology." *Cancer Research* 20 (1960): 858–67.

(With Walker) "Cytologic Studies on Human Melanoma Cells in Tissue Culture after Exposure to Five Chemotherapeutic Agents." *Cancer Chemotherapy Reports* 51 (1968): 543–52.

"I Am Woman, Black, Educated." *Hartford Courant Sunday Supplement,* February 4, 1973.

"Filters for Women in Science." *Expanding the Role of Women in the Sciences.* Edited by Anne M. Briscoe and Sheila M. Pfafflin. New York Academy of Sciences, 1979, pp. 236–48.

"The Role of Women Presidents/Chancellors in Intercollegiate Athletics." *Women at the Helm.* Edited by J. A. Sturnick, J. E. Milley, and C. A. Tisinger. AASCU Press, 1991, pp. 42–50.

FURTHER READING

Books

Hine, Darlene Clark, ed. *Black Women in America: An Historical Encyclopedia.* Carlson Publishing Inc., 1993, pp. 257–58.

Notable Black American Women. Detroit: Gale, 1992, pp. 195–98.

Sketch by Geeta Kothari

Mildred Cohn
1913–
American biochemist and biophysicist

Mildred Cohn overcame both gender and religious prejudice to have a profound impact on biochemistry and biophysics. Her research contributed to the scientific understanding of the mechanisms of enzymatic reactions and the methods of studying them. Cohn authored numerous papers that are considered classics and received many honors, including the 1982 National Medal of Science presented by President Ronald Reagan. She was a member of the National Academy of Sciences, the American Academy of Arts and Sciences, and the American Philosophical Society.

Cohn was born on July 12, 1913, to Isidore M. and Bertha (Klein) Cohn, the second of their two children. Her parents were both immigrants from Sharshiv, a small town in Russia. Her father was a businessman who did linotype work for the printing trade and published a journal on printing. Cohn attended public schools in New York City, demonstrating an interest in mathematics and chemistry by the time she reached high school. In 1928, at age fourteen, she enrolled at Hunter College in New York to study chemistry and physics. She received her B.A. *cum laude* little more than three years later, at age seventeen. Cohn was determined to pursue a graduate education in the physical sciences in spite of the many barriers raised against her.

Overcomes Obstacles to Attain Career

Cohn entered the doctoral program at Columbia University but was not accepted as a teaching assistant, because the positions were awarded only to men. She worked as a babysitter to help pay for her first year of education in thermodynamics, classical mechanics, molecular spectroscopy, and physical chemistry. In 1932, after being awarded an M.A., she accepted a job in the laboratory at the National Advisory Committee for Aeronautics at Langley Field, Virginia. She was initially assigned computational work and later a research position in the engine division. The project was to develop a fuel–injection, spark–ignition airplane engine that operated on the diesel cycle. Cohn believed that her positions at Langley impressed upon her the importance of attacking problems on many levels, including the practical and theoretical.

Mildred Cohn (Corbis/Bettmann-UPI. Reproduced by permission.)

In 1934, Cohn decided that her opportunities for scientific advancement had declined at Langley and she returned to Columbia to seek a Ph.D. She worked under Harold Clayton Urey, separating stable isotopes. She was not successful in trying to separate the isotopes but learned experimental and theoretical methods from which she benefited throughout her career. Cohn wrote her Ph.D. dissertation in 1937 and published it with Urey under the title “Oxygen Exchange Reactions of Organic Compounds and Water.” Upon graduation, she considered applying for an industrial position, as many of the other graduates did. Due to her sex and Jewishness, however, she was not even granted interviews with large corporations, including Du Pont and Standard Oil.

Cohn was eventually offered and accepted a postdoctoral position with Vincent du Vigneaud, professor of biochemistry at George Washington University Medical School. He wanted to introduce isotopic tracers into his research on sulfur–amino acid metabolism. Isotopic tracers are forms of chemical elements; because of their difference in nuclear structure, either mass or radioactivity, they can be observed as they progress through a metabolic pathway. By following an isotope, Cohn was able to understand more clearly the mechanisms of chemical reactions in animals. For example, one study, which Cohn told contributor John Henry Dreyfuss was "the most elegant tracer experiment done in du Vigneaud's lab," involved what she called "doubly labeled" methionine. The researchers used the labeled methionine—a large, complicated molecule to which two isotopes had been added—to observe the mechanism by which methionine was converted to the amino acid cystine in a rat.

Contributes Advances in Medicine

Cohn married Henry Primakoff, a physicist, on May 31, 1938. During World War II, Cohn and the draft–exempt men in du Vigneaud's lab continued their research, while du Vigneaud and the others supported the war effort. In 1946, her husband accepted a position in the physics department at Washington University in St. Louis. Cohn took a position in the biochemistry department, where she worked with the Nobel Prize–winning husband and wife team of **Gerty T. Cori** and Carl Ferdinand Cori. One of her major objectives at Washington University was to study the mechanisms of enzyme–catalyzed reactions. Cohn used an isotope of oxygen to gain insight into the enzyme–catalyzed reactions of organic phosphates and in 1958 initiated work with nuclear magnetic resonance (NMR) toward the same goal.

Two years later, her husband was named Donner Professor of Physics at the University of Pennsylvania, and Cohn joined the biophysics department there. At Pennsylvania, Cohn pursued her research on energy transduction within cells and cellular reactions in which adenosinetriphosphate (ATP) is utilized using NMR. Cohn told Dreyfuss that she began to look more deeply into the structure and function of enzymes by studying manganese–enzyme–substrate complexes, utilizing "every technically feasible aspect of magnetic resonance." Cohn performed other important collaborative studies, including NMR of transfer ribonucleic acid (RNA), a key chemical in cellular protein synthesis. Cohn's work with nuclear magnetic resonance of various types of molecules, structures, and reactions was probably her most important contribution to science and medicine.

Cohn and Primakoff had three children. Besides her scientific work, she enjoyed the theater, hiking, writing, and reading. In 1958, after nearly twenty–one years as a research associate, she was promoted to associate professor; she was a Career Investigator of the American Heart Association for fourteen years after 1964. In 1982, she was named Benjamin Bush Professor in Biochemistry and Biophysics at the University of Pennsylvania. From 1982 to 1985, she was a senior scientist at the Fox Chase Cancer Center. In 1982, she was awarded the National Medal of Science and in 1987 the Distinguished Award of the College of Physicians. From 1978 to 1979, she was president of the American Society of Biological Chemistry. Cohn was also elected to the American Academy of Arts and Sciences and American Philosophical Society.

SELECTED WRITINGS BY COHN:

Periodicals

(With Harold Clayton Urey) "Oxygen Exchange Reactions of Organic Compounds and Water." *Journal of the American Chemical Society* 60 (1938): 679–87.

"Atomic and Nuclear Probes of Enzyme Systems." *Annual Review of Biophysics and Biomolecular Structure* 21 (1992): 1–24.

FURTHER READING

Cohn, Mildred, interview with John Henry Dreyfuss.

Sketch by John Henry Dreyfuss

Theodora Emily Colborn
1927–
American environmentalist

Theodora Emily Decker Colborn, better known as Theo Colborn, is a leading proponent of the theory of endocrine disruption. This theory states that some synthetic chemicals interfere with the ways that hormones work in humans and animals. Colborn argues that such disruption can have profound adverse effects, especially when a mother passes a contaminating agent to a growing fetus, and the contamination interferes with the hormonal signals used by the fetus to direct its growth. Colborn says the possible adverse effects, which in some cases are not apparent until adulthood, include impaired ability to reproduce, diminished intelligence, altered behavior, and reduced ability to resist disease. Colborn, along with journalist Dianne Dumanoski and zoologist John Peterson Myers, presented her argument in a controversial 1996 book titled *Our Stolen Future: Are We Threatening Our Fertility, Intelligence, and Survival?—A Scientific Detective Story.*

Colborn was born on March 28, 1927, in Plainfield, New Jersey. Her parents were Theodore Decker and Margaret L. DeForge Decker. As a girl, Colborn was fascinated by water, spending many hours playing in the river by the farm where her family lived. This early love for the outdoors laid the groundwork for an enduring commitment to the environment. However, it was many years before Colborn found her calling as a professional environmental activist. Her bachelor's degree, earned from Rutgers University in 1947, was in pharmacy.

While studying at Rutgers, Colborn met Harry R. Colborn, and the couple married on January 20, 1949. Colborn and her new husband took over his father's drugstore in Newton, New Jersey. Over the years, they added two more stores to their business. At the same time, their family expanded with the births of their children, Harry, Christine, Susan, and Mark. By 1962, the demands of running three drugstores and raising four children had become so overwhelming that the couple felt they needed a change. They sold their New Jersey business and moved to Colorado, where they sought a simpler lifestyle in a sunnier climate.

Colborn and her husband owned pharmacies and raised sheep in western Colorado. It was during this period that Colborn first began to champion environmental causes. Her farm was located in a valley that was rich in coal. During the oil shortage of the 1970s, the coal began to be mined on a massive scale. Combined with the mining of other minerals, this led to significant damage of the local river, the Gunnison's North Fork. Colborn became active as a volunteer on western water issues. However, she felt hampered by the lack of official credentials. As she and her coauthors later wrote in *Our Stolen Future*, "Without a degree behind you, it was easy for opponents to dismiss you as a do–gooder, a 'little old lady in tennis shoes,' even though she was tall, middle–aged, and shod in cowboy boots."

In 1978, at age 51, Colborn entered the graduate program at Western State College of Colorado. For her master's degree in freshwater ecology, completed in 1981, she studied whether aquatic insects such as stone flies and mayflies could serve as indicators of river and stream health. For her doctoral work, Colborn moved to the University of Wisconsin at Madison, where she earned a Ph.D. degree in zoology in 1985. Her children were now grown, and her husband had died in 1983. Colborn was ready to embark upon a new stage of her life.

Promotes the Theory of Endocrine Disruption

In 1985, Colborn began a two–year stint with the Office of Technology Assessment of the U.S. Congress. As a congressional fellow and science analyst there, Colborn worked on studies of air pollution and water purification. Then in 1987, she joined the research team at the Conservation Foundation, a think tank in Washington, D.C. There, in the breakthrough assignment of her career, Colborn studied the environmental health of the Great Lakes. Her job involved sifting through hundreds of papers, trying to determine how well the Great Lakes were recovering from decades of acute pollution. At first, Colborn looked for a link between toxic chemicals in the lakes and cancer among people living in the region, but this proved to be a dead end. Yet she was still convinced that something was wrong. Colborn gradually came to believe that a disruption in hormones was the key to understanding the ill health effects seen in a long list of animals across the Great Lakes basin.

In 1988, Colborn accepted a position at the World Wildlife Fund in Washington, D.C., where she now serves as a senior scientist and director of the Wildlife and Contaminants Program. On sabbatical from 1990–1993, she served as a senior fellow of the W. Alton Jones Foundation, a private philanthropic trust. By this point, dozens of scientists around the world had begun collecting isolated pieces to the puzzle of hormonal disruption, but their work still had not been assembled into a single, coherent picture. In July 1991, Colborn helped bring together 21 key researchers from various disciplines for the Wingspread Conference in Racine, Wisconsin. Participants issued the Wingspread Statement, which warned that hormone–disrupting chemicals could jeopardize the future of humanity.

Not everyone agrees with Colborn's theory or her method of communicating it. For example, in a review of *Our Stolen Future* for *Scientific American*, Michael A. Kamrin wrote: "The authors present a very selective segment of the data that have been gathered about chemicals that might affect hormonal functions. They carefully avoid evidence and interpretations that are not in accord with their thinking." Even the critics admit, however, that Colborn has been remarkably successful at raising public awareness of her theory. *Our Stolen Future* has been debated in publications ranging from *Environmental Science and Technology News* and *Science* to the *New York Times Book Review* and *Business Week*.

Colborn is in heavy demand as a speaker on environmental health issues. Her honors include the Women Leadership in the Environment Award from the United Nations Environment Programme in 1997 and the National Conservation Achievement Award in Science from the National Wildlife Federation in 1994. In her leisure time, Colborn enjoys bird–watching, a lifelong passion that has undoubtedly contributed to her choice of career path.

SELECTED WRITINGS BY COLBORN:

Books

(With Dianne Dumanoski and John Peterson Myers) *Our Stolen Future: Are We Threatening Our Fertility, Intelligence, and Survival?—A Scientific Detective Story*. New York: Dutton, 1996.

Periodicals

(With Dianne Dumanoski and John Peterson Myers) "Hormone Impostors." *Sierra* (January/February 1997): 28–35.

FURTHER READING

Periodicals

Carey, John. "A Scary Warning—Or Scare Story?" *Business Week* (April 8, 1996): 18.

Cortese, Anthony D. "Endocrine Disruption." *Environmental Science and Technology News* 30, no. 5 (1996): 213A–215A.

Frazier, Deborah. "Drugstore Curiosity Pays Off: Colorado Pharmacist Learns about Chemicals' Effect on Reproduction." *Rocky Mountain News* (May 30, 1996): 50A.

Hertsgaard, Mark. "A World Awash in Chemicals." *New York Times Book Review* (April 7, 1997): 25.

Hirshfield, Anne N., Michael F. Hirshfield, and Jodi A. Flaws. "Problems Beyond Pesticides." *Science* (June 7, 1996): 1444–1445.

Kamrin, Michael A. "The Mismeasure of Risk." *Scientific American* (September 1996): 178, 180.

Wapner, Kenneth. "Chemical Sleuth." *The Amicus Journal* (Spring 1995): 18–21.

Other

"Follow the Facts . . . About Endocrine Disruption and *Our Stolen Future*." http://www.osf–facts.org/ (November 14, 1997). This site contains extensive information about Colborn's book and endocrine disruption.

Sketch by Linda Wasmer Smith

Jane Colden
1724–1766
American botanist

Jane Colden is considered to be the first woman American botanist. During her career, she catalogued, by descriptions, drawings, and the Linnaean system of classification, over 300 species of flowers and plants. Farquhar was also the first person to "discover" and name the gardenia.

Colden was born in New York City on March 27, 1724. She was the fifth child and second daughter in a family of ten, raised by her parents Cadwallader and Alice (Christie) Colden. Both parents came from families of Scottish clergymen, who placed a high value on education. Her father first practiced as a physician before becoming a surveyor general for New York. He also was a politician, becoming lieutenant governor of the state in 1761 and serving as acting governor on many occasions. Cadwallader Colden was also a naturalist who shared his enthusiasm for botany with his daughter. Colden's mother taught her children at home, and she tried to give them a broad education.

Colden grew up on her parents' estate, Coldengham, near Newburgh, New York. Though many well known and important visitors spent time on the estate, Coldengham did not provide the cultural and education opportunities of city life. However, Colden's parents worked hard to stimulate and educate their children. While she was growing up, Colden loved to read, and she exhibited the same interest in botany as her father early in life.

Corresponds with Leading Scientists

When Colden was in her twenties, her father took her under his wing. He wrote a "textbook" for her that explained botanical principles. He also provided her with an English translation of botanical Latin and the Linnaean classification system. Additionally, he ordered books from England for her to use in her work. Colden learned how to use printer's ink for the recording of leaf impressions during this time. Soon she was able to take over much of her father's international correspondence with leading scientists of the day, a list that included Linnaeus himself, as well as Alexander Garden (after whom she named the gardenia), and John Ellis (who suggested that Linnaeus name a new plant after her). Because there were no scientific journals at the time, correspondence was the chief method of sharing information with other scientists.

Colden's botanical work included a study, with her father, of Orange County flora. In the 1750s, she classified the flora of the Hudson River Valley, and by 1957, she had classified over 300 species. Although she was also interested in insects and shells, she worked mainly with seeds and plants, many of which she described in her correspondence. In addition to cataloguing plant species, Colden sketched the plants and took leaf impressions. Although the sketches she made are considered amateurish by modern standards, her descriptions are thought to be exceptionally accurate.

Colden was never accorded the respect of her male counterparts, despite her extensive work and knowledge. Her botany career was apparently cut short when she married Scottish physician William Farquhar on March 12, 1759. Colden died on March 10, 1766, which was the same year her only child died. Her work on New York flora is housed by the British Museum.

SELECTED WRITINGS BY COLDEN:

Periodicals

"Description." *Essays and Observations, Physical and Literary.* Edinburgh Philosophical Society (2), 1770.

FURTHER READING

books

Bailey, Marth J. *American Women in Science.* Denver: ABC–CLIO, 1994.

James, Edward T., et al, eds. *Notable American Women 1607–1950.* Cambridge: Belknap Press, 1971.

Johnson, Allen and Malone, Dumas, eds. *Dictionary of American Biography*. New York: Charles Scribner's Sons, 1930.

Ogilvie, Marilyn Bailey. *Women in Science: Antiquity Through the Nineteenth Century*. Cambridge: MIT Press, 1986.

Rossiter, Margaret W. *Women Scientists in American: Struggles and Strategies to 1940*. Baltimore: The John Hopkins University Press, 1982.

Sketch by Helene Barker Kiser

Eileen Marie Collins
1956–
American astronaut and pilot

Eileen Collins was the first woman to pilot the Space Shuttle and the first to command a Space Shuttle mission. A lieutenant colonel in the United States Air Force, she has logged over 419 hours in space, and over 5,000 hours in 30 different types of aircraft. She's been honored with several Air Force service awards and the NASA Space Flight Medal. She was inducted into the National Women's Hall of Fame in 1998, the same year that the National Soaring Museum established a special aviation summer day camp for teenagers in her name. Her community college's observatory has also been named in her honor.

Collins was born on November 19, 1956, in Elmira, New York, to James and Rose Marie Collins, the second of four children. As a child she dreamed of flying and at 14 wrote a letter to NASA expressing her desire to become an astronaut.

After graduating from Elmira Free Academy in 1974, Collins put herself through community college with grants, loans, and minimum–wage jobs. She earned an associate degree in mathematics and science from Corning Community College in 1976. When she was 20, she learned to fly, paying for lessons with a variety of jobs. On her first solo flight, the plane door came open, but she managed to remain calm and kept flying. She attended Syracuse University on an Air Force ROTC scholarship, earning a bachelor of arts degree in mathematics and economics in 1978.

Becomes Military Pilot and Instructor

A year later Collins graduated from undergraduate pilot training at Vance Air Force Base, Oklahoma, one of four women in a class of 320 men. She remained at the base until 1982, working as the Air Force's first female flight instructor. From 1983 to 1985, she was a C–141 aircraft commander and instructor pilot at Travis Air Force Base, California, where she also met her future husband and fellow instructor, Pat Youngs. She spent 1986 as a student

Eileen Collins (Photograph by Larry Downing. Archive Photos. Reproduced by permission.)

with the Air Force Institute of Technology, while also earning a master of science degree in operations research from Stanford University.

In the same year, Collins was assigned to the U.S. Air Force Academy in Colorado as an assistant professor in mathematics and a T–41 instructor pilot. She married Youngs, who later became an airline pilot, in 1987. Collins earned a master of arts degree in space systems management from Webster University in St. Louis, Missouri, in 1989, then became only the second woman to attend the Air Force Test Pilot School at Edwards Air Force Base, California. Before graduating in 1990, Collins was selected for the astronaut program.

Collins finally realized her dream of becoming an astronaut in July 1991. Initially assigned to Orbiter engineering support, she has also served on the astronaut support team responsible for Orbiter prelaunch checkout, final launch configuration, crew ingress/egress and landing/recovery. She also worked in Mission Control as a spacecraft communicator (CAPCOM) for numerous shuttle missions and served as the Astronaut Office Spacecraft Systems Branch Chief.

Becomes First Female Shuttle Pilot and Commander

Collins became the first woman to pilot the Space Shuttle during February 2–11, 1995. As a pilot, she was second only to the shuttle commander. The STS-63 mission was the first flight of the new joint Russian–American Space Program, included the rendezvous with the Russian Space Station Mir, the deployment and retrieval of an astronomy satellite, and a space walk. In the mission's 129 orbits, Collins traveled over 2.9 million miles in 198 hours, 29 minutes. "This mission marks the first baby steps in international space cooperation," she declared at her induction to the National Women's Hall of Fame. Less than a year after her first space flight, her daughter Bridget was born.

In 1996, Collins received the President's Medal from the New York Institute of Technology. A year later she flew a second shuttle mission to rendezvous and dock with the Russian Space Station Mir. During the flight, the crew conducted a number of secondary experiments and transferred nearly four tons of supplies and experiment equipment between Atlantis and the Mir station. In this nine-day mission, Collins traveled 3.8 million miles in 145 orbits of the Earth logging a total of 221 hours and 20 minutes in space.

Collins became the first female shuttle commander during July 23–27, 1999. Collins' extensive experience paid off when five seconds into *Columbia's* flight, a damaged electrical wire short-circuited and knocked out the primary computers for two of the three main engines. The backup computers came on, but a worse problem was happening at the same time. A pin had come loose during takeoff and damaged some tubes in one of the engines. Over 2,500 pounds of hydrogen leaked during the climb to orbit, causing the engines to shut down and leaving the shuttle seven miles short of its orbital mark. Collins would have had to attempt an emergency landing if more hydrogen had leaked or if the backup engine computers had failed. However, Collins and her four crewmates were able to correct the problem and continue the five day orbit. The *Columbia* crew deployed the Chandra X-Ray Observatory, the world's most powerful x-ray telescope. This telescope will allow scientists to study phenomena such as quasars and black holes, providing more insights about the beginning, the evolution, the current structure, and possibly even the fate of the universe. When she spoke at the White House after her promotion to commander, Collins said, ". . . it's my hope that all children, boys and girls, will see this mission and be inspired to reach for their dreams, too, because dreams do come true."

Collins is grateful to the pioneering women who proceeded her, and acknowledged her debt during her White House remarks: "I didn't get here alone. There are so many women throughout this century that have gone before me and have taken to the skies. From the first barnstormers through the women military Air Force pilots. . .[in] World War II, the Mercury women. . .the first women who entered the Air Force and navy military pilot training in the mid 1970s, and most important, the first women astronauts. . .all these women have been my role models and inspiration and I couldn't be here today without them."

FURTHER READING

Books

Haynsworth, Leslie and Toomey, David. *Amelia Earhart's Daughters.* William Morrow and Company, Inc., 1998

Periodicals

Calkins, Laurel Brubaker, O'Neill, Anne–Marie, and Podesta, Jane Sims. "On the Top: Command Performance Astronaut Eileen Collins Takes Charge in Space." *People* (May 11, 1998): 225.

Dunn, Marcia. "First Female Shuttle Commander Likes Stress, Dislikes Fuss." AP Online, March 16, 1998

Holland, Steve. "Collins to be First Woman to Command Space Shuttle," Reuters, March 5, 1998

Suriano, Robyn. "NASA's First Woman Pilot to Become First Woman Shuttle Commander." Gannett News Service, March 4, 1998

Other

Biography on NASA's web site. www.jsc.nasa.gov/bios/htmlbios/collins.html. July 1999.

"Troubled shuttle launch makes Collins more celebrated." FLORIDA TODAY Space Online. http://www.flatoday.com/space/today/081699d.htm. August, 16, 1999.

Sketch by Laurel M. Sheppard

Margarita Colmenares
1957–
American environmental engineer

Margarita Colmenares was the first Hispanic engineer to be selected for a White House fellowship, and she was also the first woman to be elected national president of the Society of Hispanic Professional Engineers (SHPE). Employed by Chevron USA since 1981 and presently an air–quality specialist in its office for environmental affairs, she has in her short career established herself as a national leader in the fields of both education and engineering.

Margarita Hortensia Colmenares was born in Sacramento, California, on July 20, 1957, the eldest of five children. Her parents, Luis S. Colmenares and Hortensia O. Colmenares, had emigrated from Oaxaca, Mexico, and her childhood world was bicultural and bilingual. Her parents believed strongly in the importance of a good education and sacrificed to send their children to private Catholic schools. In high school, Colmenares founded an organization for Mexican–American students in her all–girls school. She began her college career at California State University in Sacramento studying business, but she realized in her freshman year that engineering was the field she really wanted to pursue. She returned to junior college for more chemistry, physics, and calculus courses, and she also accepted a part–time engineering job with the California Department of Water Resources. Funded by five different scholarships, she entered Stanford University and graduated with a B.S. in civil engineering in 1981.

Begins Association with Chevron Corporation

Between her junior and senior years at Stanford, Colmenares entered the Chevron Corporation's Co–Op Education Program, and after graduation she joined that company as a field construction engineer. By 1982 she had founded the San Francisco chapter of SHPE. After serving Chevron as a recruiting coordinator, she took on a field construction position whose duties led her to Colorado, Utah, Idaho, and Nevada. Her upward path at Chevron continued as she became a foreign trade representative in 1983 and subsequently won promotion to compliance specialist. It was in this position that she first became involved with environmental issues. In 1986, she was the lead engineer for an eighteen million dollar environmental cleanup project at the Chevron refinery in El Segundo, near Los Angeles. Following this experience with environmental engineering, Colmenares was promoted in 1989 to air–quality specialist at the El Segundo plant.

In that same year, she was elected SHPE's first woman president. As president of this national society, Colmenares achieved a platform from which she could address many of the issues facing the engineering community in general and Hispanics in particular. Her agenda was based on the importance of education, and she stressed to the society's members that they should seek election to positions that could have an impact on education, engineering, or policy making. Following her term as society president, she applied for a White House fellowship and was chosen as one of the sixteen members of the class of 1991–1992. Colmenares became the first Hispanic engineer selected since the program was established in 1964. As part of this program, she chose to work at the Department of Education and became special assistant to David T. Kearns, the department's deputy secretary.

Colmenares has received many honors and awards during her career. In 1989 she was named Outstanding Hispanic Woman of the Year by *Hispanic* magazine, as well as Hispanic Role Model of the Year by SHPE. That same year she also received *Hispanic Engineer* magazine's Community Service Award. In 1990 and 1992, *Hispanic Business* magazine named her one of the one hundred most influential Hispanics in the United States, and in 1991 she was the youngest recipient ever to receive the California Community College League's Outstanding Alumni Award. Her career was also profiled on the Public Broadcasting Service (PBS) series "Choice for Youth."

Colmenares plans to continue her education, possibly in the area of public policy, and she would like to continue working for the betterment of the educational system in the United States. One of her many avocations is an interest in Mexican folk dance and during college she taught, directed, and performed with the Stanford Ballet Folklorico.

FURTHER READING

Books

Telgen, Diane and Jim Kamp, eds. *Notable Hispanic American Women.* Detroit: Gale, 1993, pp. 104–07.

Periodicals

"The 1989 Hispanic Engineer National Achievement Awards." *Hispanic Engineer* Conference Issue (1989): 43–46.

Sketch by Leonard C. Bruno

Anna Comnena
1083–1148
Byzantine medical writer

Princess Anna Comnena was the most famous of the Byzantine women scholars. She studied the complete medieval course of scientific education: geometry, arithmetic, astronomy, and music. Her book, *The Alexiad*, a history of the reign of her father, the Emperor Alexius I Comnenus, is considered to be one of the major works of medieval history, and it marked a literary revival in the Byzantine Empire. The book also includes Comenena's medical theories and advice.

Anna Comnena was born in 1083, two years after her father came to power. The daughter of Irene Dukas, Comnena was well educated in Greek science and mathematics. She was well versed in the works of Plato and Aristotle and well-acquainted with geography and meteorology. This was typical for members of the royal families of the eastern Byzantine Empire; for example, the Empress Zoe, who died in 1050, enjoyed studying science so much that she turned her private apartments into a chemistry laboratory. Above all, however, Comnena was knowledgeable about medicine. She was familiar with the medical theories of Galen, the famous Roman physician, and she may have studied, taught, and practiced at the medical school in Constantinople.

Comnena married Nicephorus Bryennius, a historian from a prominent Byzantine family, in 1097. With her mother, she made an unsuccessful attempt to seize the royal succession by having her father name her husband, rather than her brother John, as his heir. As a result, she was forced to retire from the court after her father's death, when her brother took the throne in 1118.

With her husband's death in 1137, Comnena moved to a convent in Constantinople, founded by her mother, and devoted herself to completing the work that her husband had just begun on the history of her father's reign. *The Alexiad* was a fifteen–book prose poem that was devoted primarily to military technology, with detailed descriptions of weapons and tactics. However she also included a great deal of medical theory and advice. She wrote: "The infirmities of the body, it seems to me, are sometimes aggravated by external causes, but there are also occasions when the reasons for sickness emanate from the organs themselves; often we blame the vagaries of climate and certain qualities of food for the onset of fevers, even sometimes putrid humours." Her husband's tumor, she said, was caused by the rigors of military life, climate, and worry for his family. Her father's gout, she attributed, not to heredity or intemperate habits, but to a knee injury incurred while playing polo, to anxiety, to the Germans who monopolized his attention, and to the constant presence of an intimate enemy. When her father was dying, she chose among the treatments suggested by three different physicians.

Comnena was also very interested in the physical sciences, and she gave an accurate description of a solar eclipse. She discussed astrology, but did not believe that the stars influenced human affairs. Comnena wrote in Greek and considered Latin to be a barbaric language. She died in 1148. The first English translation of *The Alexiad* was made in 1928 by Elizabeth Dawes.

SELECTED WRITINGS BY COMNENA:

Books

The Alexiad, translated by E. R. A. Sewter. Middlesex, England: Penguin, 1969.

FURTHER READING

Books

Buckler, Georgina. *Anna Comnena. A Study*. 1929. Reprint, London: Clarendon, 1968.

Hughes, Muriel Joy. *Women Healers in Medieval Life and Literature*. Oxford: Oxford University Press, 1943. Reprint, Freeport, N.Y.: Books for Libraries Press, 1968.

Mitchison, Naomi. *Anna Comnena*. London: G. Howe, 1928.

Sketch by Margaret Alic

Anna Botsford Comstock
1854–1930
American entomologist and nature writer

Anna Botsford Comstock, an entomologist who collaborated with her husband in the study of insects, was the first woman professor at Cornell University. Her primary vocation was the training of school teachers in science, but she was also a prolific author and scientific illustrator of popular nature study books. She was the leader of the "nature-study movement," a forerunner of the ecology movement, which encouraged teachers and their students to learn about nature in the field.

Born in 1854, Comstock was the only child of Phoebe (Irish) and Marvin S. Botsford. Growing up on her family's prosperous farm in southwestern New York state, her early interest in natural history was encouraged by her mother, a Quaker and a naturalist herself. After graduating from the village elementary school, Comstock attended a private Methodist boarding school, the Chamberlain Institute and Female College in Randolph, New York. Encouraged by her friend and teacher Ann French Allen to attend college, Comstock entered Cornell University, in Ithaca, New York, in 1874 as one of the first female students.

After two years of studying languages and literature, Comstock took a zoology course with the entomology professor John Henry Comstock. Soon they had become the closest of friends and even although she had left school without a degree and returned to her parents' home, she stayed in contact with him and began illustrating his publications. They would eventually marry in 1878.

During the years 1879–1881, John Comstock was acting chief entomologist at the United States Department of Agriculture in Washington D. C. Anna Comstock worked with him, doing clerical work, writing, editing and illustrating his reports, and directing the laboratory. Together, the Comstocks worked out the classification of the scale insects of America.

With John Comstock's stint as acting chief entomologist completed, the Comstocks returned to Ithaca determined to continue their collaborative work. Comstock resumed her university studies, receiving her Bachelor of Science degree from Cornell in 1885, with a thesis on "The Fine Anatomy of the Interior of the Larva of *Corydalus cornutus*," the dobsonfly. She also took up wood engraving, studying with the artist John P. Davis in New York City, in order to illustrate her husband's entomological texts. Although she was acknowledged as "Junior Author" in the preface to her husband's major work, *A Manual for the Study of Insects*, Comstock wrote much of the text and created all of the engravings from nature. It was Anna Comstock's readable prose that made the book a popular, as well as a scientific, success.

In response to the agricultural depression of the early 1890s, the New York state government initiated a program designed to encourage children to stay on the farms and off the New York City welfare rolls. The agricultural college at Cornell took over this program, using nature study in rural schools to interest students in farming. Comstock began developing a home nature study course for rural teachers in 1895, and ran the program from 1903 until 1911, providing monthly lessons and pamphlets for school teachers, most of whom had little or no training. In 1911, Comstock published her *Handbook on Nature Study*, based on her monthly lessons. The book is nontechnical, with an emphasis on individual organisms and how they are adapted to their environments. Although initially afraid that it would lose money, the book became Cornell University's all-time best-seller. It went through 25 editions and was translated into eight languages. The book, and Comstock's efforts with teachers and community leaders, launched the "nature study movement" and in 1913 she became president of the American Nature Study Society.

Although Comstock was appointed assistant professor of nature study in the Cornell University Extension Division in 1899, the university trustees objected to a woman professor and she was demoted to lecturer. Nevertheless, she developed the department of nature studies and finally, in 1913, she was appointed assistant professor. She was finally made a full professor in 1919. In addition to writing, teaching, and traveling the lecture circuit, Comstock helped establish William Smith College in Geneva, New York.

Comstock wrote for *Nature Study Reviews* from its founding in 1905 and began editing the journal in 1917. Alone, and in collaboration with her husband, she wrote and illustrated several books on insects, which included many of her original observations. She also wrote books on spiders and bee-keeping and authored a series of field notebooks for school children. Her works for children also include a children's book on the care of domestic and wild pets. In addition, Comstock wrote an extended prose poem *Trees at Leisure* and edited poetry for the magazine *Country Life in America*. In 1906, she wrote a novel, *Confessions to a Heathen Idol*, under the name Marian Lee, since she thought it would seem improper for a woman of science to publish novels. However, the second edition was published under her own name. Many of the Comstocks' books were published by their own small company, Comstock Publishing, a forerunner of the Cornell University Press.

Much to their disappointment, the Comstocks remained childless. In 1888 Comstock became one of the first four women elected to Sigma Xi, the national honor society of science. In 1923, the League of Women Voters named her one of the 12 greatest American women. Just a few weeks before her death from cancer in 1930, she was awarded an honorary doctorate from Hobart College.

SELECTED WRITINGS BY COMSTOCK:

Books

Ways of the Six-Footed. Boston: Ginn, 1903. Reprint, Ithaca: Cornell University Press, 1977.

Handbook of Nature Study. Ithaca: Comstock, 1911. 25th ed. Ithaca: Cornell University Press, 1986.

Trees at Leisure. Ithaca: Comstock, 1916.

(With G. W. Herrick and Ruby Green Smith) *The Comstocks of Cornell: John Henry Comstock and Anna Botsford Comstock, an Autobiography*. Ithaca: Cornell University Press, 1953.

Periodicals

"Insect Communities." *Chautauquan* 26 (1898): 479–83.

"How to Begin Bee-Keeping." *Country Life in America* 7 (1905): 636–38.

"Geography and Life." *Nature Study Review* 16 (1920): 75–80.

"Bird Study in Honolulu." *Nature Magazine* 6 (1925): 52–53.

FURTHER READING

Books

Bonta, Marcia Myers. "Anna Botsford Comstock." In *American Nature Writers*. Edited by John Elder. New York: Charles Scribner's Sons, 1996.

Henson, Pamela M. "'Through Books to Nature:' Anna Botsford Comstock and the Nature Study Movement." In *Natural Eloquence: Women Reinscribe Science*. Edited by Barbara T. Gates and Ann B. Shteir. Madison: University of Wisconsin Press, 1997.

Jacklin, Kathleen. "Anna Botsford Comstock." In *Notable American Women 1607–1950: A Biographical Dictionary*. Edited by Edward T. James, Janet Wilson James, and Paul W. Boyer. Vol. 1. Cambridge: Harvard University Press, 1971.

Sketch by Margaret Alic

Anne Finch Conway
1631–1679
English natural philosopher

Anne Conway was a scholar who devoted her life to the study of natural philosophy. Her only published work, *Principles of the Most Ancient and Modern Philosophy*, described her philosophical system. This treatise had a profound influence on the natural philosopher Gottfried Wilhelm von Leibniz, who proposed that the universe was composed of elemental particles called *monads,* which were endowed with a vital life force. Conway was the originator of this concept, which vied with Isaac Newton's proposition of the mechanistic universe as the major scientific paradigm, or the theoretical framework that the universe's operation is based on motion and its causes. Vitalism, as it came to be known, influenced the development of modern biology and has continued to influence scientific thought in the twentieth century.

Anne Finch was born into the large aristocratic family of Sir Heneage Finch, who died a week before her birth, and Elizabeth Cradock Finch, on December 14, 1631, in Kensington House (now Kensington Palace), London. By a very early age, she had mastered French and Latin and embarked on the serious study of science and philosophy. However, at the age of 12, a serious illness precipitated migraine attacks, which became increasingly frequent and severe during her adult life. As was typical in the seventeenth-century fashion, the Finch family blamed her illness on overzealous study. Although Conway lacked formal education, her older brother John Finch provided her with books and directed her studies. At Cambridge University, he studied with the platonist Henry More, who was introducing the ideas of René Descartes to the English intelligensia. Finch, in turn, introduced his sister to the works of Descartes.

Initiates Scholarly Relationship with Henry More

About 1650, John Finch was preparing to leave for the Continent, where he first became an anatomy professor at the University of Padua, and later ambassador to Constantinople. At the loss of her tutor, Conway wrote to More herself, requesting assistance with her studies. This was the beginning of a relationship that would last almost 30 years. More's early letters to Conway were treatises on Cartesian philosophy, and he began translating Descartes for her scholarly purposes.

At about the same time, Conway's family arranged her marriage to Edward, Viscount Killultagh, first Earl of Conway, a politician, statesman, and early member of the Royal Society of London. Because her new husband was often away on business or at his estate in Ireland, Conway remained at Kensington, pursuing her studies. She taught herself astronomy and mathematics, studied Euclidean geometry with a tutor, and continued her scholarly correspondence with More.

Several years later, the Conways moved to Ragley Hall in Warwickshire, and More became a frequent visitor and eventually a semi–permanent resident of their home. As she searched for the organic unity of nature, Conway and More began to study ancient alchemy together, as well as the *Kabbala*, the traditional medieval mystical texts derived from Hebrew scriptures. These works, with their emphasis on the equality of male and female principles, were major influences on Conway's developing philosophy.

Van Helmont the Alchemist Arrives at Ragley Hall

In 1660, Conway contracted smallpox, and her only child, two–year–old Heneage, died of the disease. Conway's health never recovered, and she suffered from debilitating pain that frequently interfered with her work. Although attended by the most famous physicians and healers of the day, she was pronounced incurable and nearly died twice from poisonous mercury treatments. In 1654, John Finch had begun to write to his sister about Francis Mercury van Helmont, the famous gypsy scholar. As the son of a famous alchemist-physician, van Helmont was believed to possess a universal panacea that Finch hoped would cure Conway's migraines. Van Helmont was also a student of the *Kabbala*. Van Helmont arrived at Ragley Hall in 1670 with letters for Henry More from Princess Elizabeth of Bohemia. Intending to stay in England for only one month, van Helmont spent almost 10 years at Ragley Hall, which became an intellectual center presided over by Conway. It also became the home of van Helmont and More's chemistry laboratory. Although unable to cure her headaches, van Helmont introduced Conway to new areas of intellectual inquiry.

Conway and van Helmont developed an interest in Quakerism, in part because of the similarities of Quaker tenets to those of the *Kabbala*, including the Quaker belief in the equality of the sexes. By 1677, Conway and van Helmont had both converted. The religious leaders George Fox and George Keith became frequent visitors to Ragley Hall, and Conway corresponded with William Penn. Over a four-year period, she collaborated with van Helmont and Keith on a treatise entitled *Two Hundred Queries . . . Concerning the Doctrine of the Revolution of Humane Souls*, which was published in 1684.

Conway Develops Her Philosophy of Nature

Conway was one of the first scientists to challenge the mechanistic universe of Descartes, in which organisms are made up of soulless matter in motion. Conway hoped to reconcile her religious beliefs with the new scientific theories and, in contrast to Descartes, she viewed matter and spirit as indivisible and interchangeable. Rather than a machine, she saw nature as a living entity. In this theory, the monad is the elemental particle, endowed with vital force, and integrated and organized by the Cosmic Order. Although Conway believed in the hierarchy of nature known as the Great Chain of Being, she also believed that matter could undergo monadic transformation, with lower forms becoming higher forms, an idea that was to influence the development of later evolutionary theories.

When Conway died in 1679 of unknown causes, van Helmont returned to Europe, taking with him many of her papers, including the notebook she kept between 1671 and 1675 on her philosophical system. Van Helmont arranged to have a Latin translation of the notebook published in Amsterdam in 1690. It was translated back into English and published in London two years later. Since it was considered improper for a woman to be identified as an author, Conway's name did not appear on the title page; however, in the preface, the work was attributed to "a certain English Countess."

Nevertheless, errors in scholarship in the nineteenth century resulted in the treatise being attributed to its editor, van Helmont. In 1696, van Helmont personally introduced

Leibniz to the work of Anne Conway, at a time when Leibniz was first developing his philosophy of nature. Although in his writings Leibniz repeatedly acknowledged the "Countess of Kennaway" as the source of his "monadology," Conway's contributions to the development of modern science have gone mostly unrecognized.

SELECTED WRITINGS BY CONWAY:

Books

The Principles of the Most Ancient and Modern Philosophy. Edited by Allison P. Courdert and Taylor Corse. Cambridge: Cambridge University Press, 1996.

The Conway Letters: The Correspondence of Anne, Viscountess of Conway, Henry More, and their Friends, 1642–1684. Edited by Majorie Hope Nicolson. Oxford: Clarendon Press, 1992.

FURTHER READING

Books

Alic, Margaret. *Hypatia's Heritage: A History of Women in Science from Antiquity through the Nineteenth Century*. Boston: Beacon Press,1986.

Merchant, Carolyn. *The Death of Nature: Women, Ecology, and the Scientific Revolution*. San Francisco: Harper and Row, 1980.

Sketch by Margaret Alic

Rita Rossi Colwell
1934–
American marine microbiologist

Rita R. Colwell is a leader in marine biotechnology, the application of molecular techniques to marine biology for the harvesting of medical, industrial and aquaculture products from the sea. As a scientist and professor, Colwell has investigated the ecology, physiology, and evolutionary relationships of marine bacteria. As a founder and president of the University of Maryland Biotechnology Institute, she has nurtured a vision to improve the environment and human health by linking molecular biology and genetics to basic knowledge scientists had gleaned from life and chemistry in the oceans.

Rita Rossi was born in Beverly, Massachusetts, November 23, 1934, the seventh of eight children to parents Louis and Louise Di Palma Rossi. Her father was an Italian immigrant who established his own construction company, and her mother was an artistic woman who worked to help ensure her children would have a good education. She died when her daughter was just thirteen years old, but she had been proud of her success in school. In the sixth grade, after Rossi had scored higher on the IQ exam than anyone in her school's history, the principal asked sternly whether she understood that she had the responsibility to go to college. Rossi had answered, "Yes, ma'am," and eventually received a full scholarship from Purdue University. She earned her bachelor of science degree with distinction in bacteriology in 1956. Although she had been accepted to medical school, Rossi chose instead to earn a master's degree so that she could remain at the same institution as graduate student Jack Colwell, whom she married on May 31, 1956. Colwell would have continued her studies in bacteriology, but the department chairman at Purdue informed her that giving fellowship money to women would have been a waste. She instead earned her master's degree in the department of genetics. The University of Washington, Seattle, granted her a Ph.D. in 1961 for work on bacteria commensal to marine animals, which is the practivce of an organism obtaining food or other benefits from another without either harming or helping it. Colwell's contributions included establishing the basis for the systematics of marine bacteria.

In 1964, Georgetown University hired Colwell as an assistant professor, and gave her tenure in 1966. Colwell and her research team were the first to recognize that the bacterium that caused cholera occurred naturally in estuaries. They isolated the bacterium from Chesapeake Bay and in ensuing years sought to explain how outbreaks in human populations might be tied to the seasonal abundance of the host organisms in the sea, particularly plankton. In 1972, Colwell took a tenured professorship at the University of Maryland. Her studies expanded to include investigations on the impact of marine pollution at the microbial level. Among her findings was that the presence of oil in estuarine and open ocean water was associated with the numbers of bacteria able to break down oil. She studied whether some types of bacteria might be used to treat oil spills. Colwell and her colleagues also made a discovery that held promise for improving oyster yields in aquaculture—a bacterial film formed on surfaces under water attracted oyster larvae to settle and grow.

In the spirit of using knowledge gained from the sea to benefit humans and the environment, Colwell prepared a seminal paper on marine biotechnology published in the journal *Science* in 1983. It brought attention to the rich resources of the ocean that might be tapped for food, disease–curing drugs, and environmental clean–up by the applications of genetic engineering and cloning. In order to realize the potential of marine biotechnology as originally outlined in her 1983 paper, Colwell helped foster the concept and growth of the University of Maryland Biotechnology Institute, established in 1987. As president of the U.M.B.I., she has formed alliances between researchers and industry and has succeeded in raising funds to develop the center as a prestigious biotech research complex.

In addition, Colwell has held numerous professional and academic leadership positions throughout her career and is a widely published researcher. At the University of Maryland, Colwell was director of the Sea Grant College from 1977 to 1983. She served as president of Sigma Xi, the American Society for Microbiology, and the International Congress of Systematic and Evolutionary Biology, and was president–elect of the American Association for the Advancement of Science. Colwell has written and edited more than sixteen books and over four hundred papers and articles; she also produced an award–winning film, *Invisible Seas.* Her honors included the 1985 Fisher Award of the American Society for Microbiology, the 1990 Gold Medal Award of the International Institute of Biotechnology, and the 1993 Phi Kappa Phi National Scholar Award.

Colwell is the mother of two daughters who pursued careers in science. She is an advocate for equal rights for women, and one of her long–standing aspirations is to write a novel about a woman scientist. Her hobbies include jogging and competitive sailing.

SELECTED WRITINGS BY COLWELL:

Books

(With L. H. Stevenson) *Estuarine Microbial Ecology.* University of South Carolina Press, 1973.

(Editor) *Biomolecular Data: A Resource in Transition.* Oxford University Press, 1989.

(Editor, with others) *Biotechnology of Marine Polysaccharides,* Hemisphere, 1985.

Periodicals

"Biotechnology in the Marine Sciences." *Science* (October 7, 1983): 19–24.

FURTHER READING

Periodicals

Andrews, Joan Kostick. "Lady With A Mission." *Natural Science* (May, 1991): 304–310.

Henderson, Randi. "Scientist Plays Many Roles." *The Baltimore Sun* (October 13, 1991).

Sherman, Scott L. "The Long Road From the Laboratory." *Warfield's* (August 1990).

Sketch by Miyoko Chu

Gerty Theresa Cori
1896–1957
Czech–born American biochemist

Gerty T. Cori made significant contributions in two major areas of biochemistry, which increased understanding of how the body stores and uses sugars and other carbohydrates. For much of her early scientific career, Cori performed pioneering work on sugar metabolism (how sugars supply energy to the body), in collaboration with her husband, Carl Ferdinand Cori. For this work they shared the 1947 Nobel Prize in physiology or medicine with Bernardo A. Houssay, who had also carried out fundamental studies in the same field. Cori's later work focused on a class of diseases called glycogen storage disorders. She demonstrated that these illnesses are caused by disruptions in sugar metabolism. Both phases of Gerty Cori's work illustrated for other scientists the importance of studying enzymes (special proteins that permit specific biochemical reactions to take place) for understanding normal metabolism and disease processes.

Gerty Theresa Radnitz was the first of three girls born to Otto and Martha Neustadt Radnitz. She was born in Prague, then part of the Austro–Hungarian Empire, on August 15, 1896. Otto was a manager of sugar refineries. It is not known if his work helped shape his eldest daughter's early interest in chemistry and later choice of scientific focus. However, her maternal uncle, a professor of pediatrics, did encourage her to pursue her interests in science. Gerty was first taught by tutors at home, then enrolled in a private girls' school. At that time, girls were not expected to attend a university. In order to follow her dream of becoming a chemist, Gerty first studied at the Tetschen Realgymnasium. She then had to pass a special entrance exam (*matura*) that tested her knowledge of Latin, literature, history, mathematics, physics, and chemistry.

In 1914 Gerty Radnitz entered the medical school of the German University of Prague (Ferdinand University). There she met a fellow classmate, Carl Ferdinand Cori, who shared her interest in doing scientific research. Together they studied human complement, a substance in blood that plays a key role in immune responses by combining with antibodies. This was the first of a lifelong series of collaborations. In 1920 they both graduated and received their M.D. degrees.

Shortly after graduating, they moved to Vienna and married. Carl worked at the University of Vienna's clinic and the University of Graz's pharmacology department, while Gerty took a position as an assistant at the Karolinen Children's Hospital. Some of her young patients suffered from a disease called congenital myxedema, in which deposits form under the skin and cause swelling, thickening, and paleness in the face. The disease is associated with

Gerty T. Cori (The Library of Congress.)

severe dysfunction of the thyroid gland, located at the base of the neck, which helps to control many body processes, including growth. Gerty's particular research interest was in how the thyroid influenced body temperature regulation.

Immigrates to United States

In the early 1920s, Europe was in the midst of great social and economic unrest in the wake of World War I, and in some regions, food was scarce; Gerty suffered briefly from malnourishment while working in Vienna. Faced with these conditions, the Coris saw little hope there for advancing their scientific careers. In 1922 Carl moved to the United States to take a position as biochemist at the New York State Institute for the Study of Malignant Diseases (later the Roswell Park Memorial Institute). Gerty joined him in Buffalo a few months later, becoming an assistant pathologist at the institute.

Life continued to be difficult for Gerty Cori. She was pressured to investigate malignant diseases, specifically cancers, which were the focus of the institute. Both she and Carl did publish studies related to malignancies, but studying cancer was not to be the focus of either Gerty's or Carl's work. During these early years in the United States, the Coris' publications covered topics from the biological effects of X rays to the effects of restricted diets on metabolism. Following up on her earlier work on the thyroid, Gerty published a report on the influence of thyroid extract on paramecium population growth, her first publication in English.

Colleagues cautioned Gerty and Carl against working together, arguing that collaboration would hurt Carl's career. However, Gerty's duties as an assistant pathologist allowed her some free time, which she used to begin studies of carbohydrate metabolism jointly with her husband. This work, studying how the body burns and stores sugars, was to become the mainstream of their collaborative research. During their years in Buffalo, the Coris jointly published a number of papers on sugar metabolism that reshaped the thinking of other scientists about this topic. In 1928 Gerty and Carl Cori became naturalized citizens of the United States.

In 1931 the Coris moved to St. Louis, Missouri, where Gerty took a position as research associate at Washington University School of Medicine; Carl was a professor there, first of pharmacology and later of biochemistry. The Coris' son, Carl Thomas, was born in 1936. Gerty become a research associate professor of biochemistry in 1943 and in 1947 a full professor of biochemistry. During the 1930s and 1940s the Coris continued their work on sugar metabolism. Their laboratory gained an international reputation as an important center of biochemical breakthroughs. No less than five Nobel laureates spent parts of their careers in the Coris' lab working with them on various problems.

For their pivotal studies in elucidating the nature of sugar metabolism, the Cori's were awarded the Nobel Prize for physiology or medicine in 1947. They shared this honor with Argentine physiologist Bernardo A. Houssay, who discovered how the pituitary gland functions in carbohydrate metabolism. Gerty Cori was only the third woman to receive a Nobel Prize in science. Previously, only **Marie Curie** and **Irène Joliot–Curie** had been awarded such an honor. As with the previous two women winners, Cori was a corecipient of the prize with her husband.

Research Yields Understanding of Significant Physiological Processes

In the 1920s, when the Coris began to study carbohydrate metabolism, it was generally believed that the sugar called glucose (a type of carbohydrate) was formed from another carbohydrate, glycogen, by the addition of water molecules (a process known as hydrolysis). Glucose circulates in the blood and is used by the body's cells in virtually all cellular processes that require energy. Glycogen is a natural polymer (a large molecule made up of many similar smaller molecules) formed by joining together large numbers of individual sugar molecules for storage in the body. Glycogen allows the body to function normally on a continual basis, by providing a store from which glucose can be broken down and released as needed.

Hydrolysis is a chemical process that does not require enzymes. If, as was believed to be the case in the 1920s, glycogen were broken down to glucose by simple hydrolysis, carbohydrate metabolism would be a very simple, straightforward process. However, in the course of their work, the Coris discovered a chemical compound, glucose–1–phosphate, made up of glucose and a phosphate group (one phosphorus atom combined with three oxygen atoms—sometimes known as the Cori ester) that is derived from glycogen by the action of an enzyme, phosphorylase. Their finding of this intermediate compound, and of the enzymatic conversion of glycogen to glucose, was the basis for the later understanding of sugar metabolism and storage in the body. The Coris' studies opened up research on how carbohydrates are used, stored, and converted in the body.

Cori had been interested in hormones (chemicals released by one tissue or organ and acting on another) since her early thyroid research in Vienna. The discovery of the hormone insulin in 1921 stimulated her to examine its role on sugar metabolism. Insulin's capacity to control diabetes lent great clinical importance to these investigations. In 1924 Gerty and Carl wrote about their comparison of sugar levels in the blood of both arteries and veins under the influence of insulin. At the same time, inspired by earlier work by other scientists (and in an attempt to appease their employer), the Coris examined why tumors used large amounts of glucose.

Their studies on glucose use in tumors convinced the Coris that much basic research on carbohydrate metabolism remained to be done. They began this task by examining the rate of absorption of various sugars from the intestine. They also measured levels of several products of sugar metabolism, particularly lactic acid and glycogen. The former compound results when sugar combines with oxygen in the body.

The Coris measured how insulin affects the conversion of sugar into lactic acid and glycogen in both the muscles and liver. From these studies, they proposed a cycle (called the Cori cycle in their honor) that linked glucose with glycogen and lactic acid. Their proposed cycle had four major steps: (1) blood glucose becomes muscle glycogen, (2) muscle glycogen becomes blood lactic acid, (3) blood lactic acid becomes liver glycogen, and (4) liver glycogen becomes blood glucose. Their original proposed cycle has had to be modified in the face of subsequent research, a good deal of which was carried out by the Coris themselves. For example, scientists learned that glucose and lactic acid can be directly inter–converted, without having to be made into glycogen. Nonetheless, the Coris' suggestion generated much excitement among carbohydrate metabolism researchers. As the Coris' work continued, they unraveled more steps of the complex process of carbohydrate metabolism. They found a second intermediate compound, glucose–6–phosphate, that is formed from glucose–1–phosphate. (The two compounds differ in where the phosphate group is attached to the sugar.) They also found the enzyme that accomplishes this conversion, phosphoglucomutase.

By the early 1940s the Coris had a fairly complete picture of carbohydrate metabolism. They knew how glycogen became glucose. Rather than the simple non–enzymatic hydrolysis reaction that, twenty years earlier, had been believed to be responsible, the Coris' studies painted a more elegant, if more complicated picture. Glycogen becomes glucose–1–phosphate through the action of one enzyme (phosphorylase). Glucose–1–phosphate becomes glucose–6–phosphate through the action of another enzyme (phosphoglucomutase). Glucose–6–phosphate becomes glucose, and glucose becomes lactic acid, each step in turn mediated by one specific enzyme. The Coris' work changed the way scientists thought about reactions in the human body, and it suggested that there existed specific, enzyme–driven reactions for many of the biochemical conversions that constitute life.

Resumes Early Interest in Pediatric Medicine

In her later years, Cori turned her attention to a group of inherited childhood diseases known collectively as glycogen storage disorders. She determined the structure of the highly branched glycogen molecule in 1952. Building on her earlier work on glycogen and its biological conversions via enzymes, she found that diseases of glycogen storage fell into two general groups, one involving too much glycogen, the other, abnormal glycogen. She showed that both types of diseases originated in the enzymes that control glycogen metabolism. This work alerted other workers in biomedicine that understanding the structure and roles of enzymes could be critical to understanding diseases. Here again, Cori's studies opened up new fields of study to other scientists. In the course of her later studies, Cori was instrumental in the discovery of a number of other chemical intermediate compounds and enzymes that play key roles in biological processes.

At the time of her death, on October 26, 1957, Cori's influence on the field of biochemistry was enormous. She had made important discoveries and prompted a wealth of new research, receiving for her contributions, in addition to the Nobel Prize, the prestigious Garvan Medal for women chemists of the American Chemical Society as well as membership in the National Academy of Sciences. As the approaches and methods that she helped pioneer continue to result in increased scientific understanding, the importance of her work only grows greater.

SELECTED WRITINGS BY CORI:

Periodicals

(With Carl F. Cori) "Glycogen Formation in the Liver from d– and l–Lactic Acid." *Journal of Biological Chemistry* 81 (1929): 389–403.

(With C. F. Cori and S. P. Colowick) "The Enzymatic Conversion of Glucose–1–Phosphoric Ester to 6–Ester in Tissue Extracts." *Journal of Biological Chemistry* 124 (1938): 543–55.

"Glycogen Structure and Enzyme Deficiencies in Glycogen Storage Disease." *Harvey Lectures* 48 (1952–53): 145–71.

FURTHER READING

Books

Cori, Carl F. "Gerty Theresa Cori." In *American Chemists and Chemical Engineers.* American Chemical Society, 1976, pp. 94–5.

Dictionary of Scientific Biography. Vol. 3. Scribner, 1971, pp. 415–16.

Magill, F. N., ed. *The Nobel Prize Winners, Physiology or Medicine.* Vol. 2. Salem Press, 1991, pp. 550–59.

Sketch by Ethan E. Allen

Gertrude Mary Cox
1900–1978
American statistician

Gertrude Mary Cox organized and directed several agencies dedicated to research and teaching in statistics. "By her missionary zeal, her organizational ability and her appreciation of the need for a practical approach to the statistical needs of agricultural, biological and medical research workers she did much to counter the confused mass of theory emanating from mathematical statisticians, particularly in the United States, who had little contact with scientific research," eulogized Frank Yates in the *Journal of the Royal Statistical Society.*

Cox was born in Dayton, Iowa, on January 13, 1900, to John William Allen and Emmaline (Maddy) Cox. After graduating from Perry (Iowa) High School in 1918, she devoted several years to social service and training for the role of deaconess in the Methodist Episcopal Church. She spent part of that time caring for children in a Montana orphanage. By 1925, however, she had decided on different career goals. She entered Iowa State College in Ames, earning a B.S. in mathematics in 1929, and registered for graduate work under the direction of George Snedecor, a proponent of the research methods of British statistician and geneticist Ronald A. Fisher. Cox and Fisher became friends when he worked at Iowa State during the summers of 1931 and 1936. In 1931, Cox earned Iowa State's first M.S. degree in statistics. For the next two years, she worked as a graduate assistant at the University of California at Berkeley, studying psychological statistics.

Snedecor asked Cox to return in 1933 to work at Iowa State's new statistical laboratory, where she gained a reputation for expertise in experimental design. By 1939, she had become an assistant professor at Iowa State, although her teaching and consulting activities did not allow her time to write a doctoral dissertation. Eventually, in 1958, she was awarded an honorary doctor of science degree by Iowa State.

When Snedecor was asked to recommend nominees to head the new department of experimental statistics being formed at the North Carolina State College School of Agriculture, he showed his list to Cox, who asked why her name was not included. So he added a footnote to his letter: "Of course if you would consider a woman for this position I would recommend Gertrude Cox of my staff," as quoted by R. L. Anderson in *Biometrics.* Cox was hired in 1940, becoming the first woman to head a department at North Carolina State.

In 1944, Cox assumed additional duties as director of the North Carolina State Institute of Statistics, which she had organized. By 1946, the University of North Carolina joined the institute, taking responsibility for teaching statistical theory while North Carolina State provided courses in methodology. Cox saw the institute's mission as developing strong statistical programs throughout the South.

Cox helped create the Biometrics Society in 1947 and edited *Biometrics Bulletin* and *Biometrics* from 1945–1955. In 1949, she became the first female member of the International Statistical Institute. Seven years later, she was elected president of the American Statistical Association. In 1950, Cox and her colleague William G. Cochran published *perimental Designs,* which was intended to be a reference book for research workers with little technical knowledge; in fact, the work became a widely used textbook, which Yates described nearly 30 years later as "still the best practical book on the design and analysis of replicated experiments," as cited in the *Journal of the Royal Statistical Society.* In her own experimental design classes, Cox taught by focusing on specific examples gleaned from her years of consulting experience.

Cox played an integral role in planning what would become the Research Triangle Institute for consulting and research, uniting the resources of the University of North Carolina, North Carolina State, and Duke University. In 1960, she retired from North Carolina State and became the first director of Research Triangle Institute's statistics section. After retiring a second time in 1964, Cox spent a year in Egypt establishing the University of Cairo's Institute of Statistics. She had always loved world travel, making 23 trips to various international destinations. On five different occasions she worked on statistical assistance programs in Thailand. At age 76, she toured Alaska and the Yukon Territory by bus, train, and boat.

Although she received numerous honors, including her 1975 election to the National Academy of Sciences, Cox was particularly pleased with the dedication of the statistics building at North Carolina State University as "Cox Hall" in 1970, and the establishment by her former students of the $200,000 Gertrude M. Cox Fellowship Fund for outstanding students in statistics at North Carolina State in 1977.

Cox died of leukemia on October 17, 1978, at Duke University Medical Center in Durham. During the preceding year, she had kept meticulous records of her treatment and response, making herself the subject of her final experiment.

SELECTED WRITINGS BY COX:

Books

(With William G. Cochran) *Experimental Designs.* Wiley, 1950, 2d ed., 1957.

Periodicals

"The Multiple Factor Theory in Terms of Common Elements." *Psychometrika* 4 (1939): 59–68.

"Enumeration and Construction of Balanced Incomplete Block Configurations." *Annals of Mathematical Statistics* 11 (1940): 72–85.

(With William G. Cochran) "Designs of Greenhouse Experiments for Statistical Analysis." *Soil Science* 62 (1946): 87–98.

(With W. S. Connor) "Methodology for Estimating Reliability." *Annals of the Institute of Statistical Mathematics* 16 (1964): 55–67.

FURTHER READING

Books

Grinstein, Louise S., and Paul J. Campbell, eds. *Women of Mathematics* Greenwood Press, 1987, pp. 26–29.

Periodicals

Anderson, R. L., R. J. Monroe, and L. A. Nelson. "Gertrude M. Cox—A Modern Pioneer in Statistics." *Biometrics* (March 1979): 3–7.

Cochran, William G. "Gertrude Mary Cox, 1900–1978." *International Statistical Review* (April 1979): 97–98.

Cochran, William G. "Some Reflections." *Biometrics* (March 1979): 1–2.

Monroe, Robert J., and Francis E. McVay. "Gertrude Mary Cox, 1900–1978." *American Statistician* (February 1980: 48.

Yates, Frank. "Gertrude Mary Cox, 1900–1978." *Journal of the Royal Statistical Society* 142, Part 4, (1979): 516–517.

Sketch by Loretta Hall

Elizabeth Caroline Crosby
1888–1983
American neuroanatomist

Elizabeth Caroline Crosby was the first woman to be appointed a full professor at the University of Michigan's medical school. In 1980 she received the federal government's highest honor for scientists, the National Medal of Science. Her descriptive studies of reptilian and other vertebrate brains provided insight into their evolutionary history and helped lay the foundation for the science of comparative neuroanatomy. During a career spanning more than six decades, Crosby made important contributions to the male-dominated areas of science and medicine. Between 1920 and 1958 she taught neuroanatomy to an estimated 8,500 students and became known as the "angel of the medical school." Following her official retirement, Crosby continued her energetic pace, applying her comprehensive knowledge of the human brain to help neurosurgeons map brain surgery.

Crosby was born in Petersburg, Michigan, on October 25, 1888, the only child of Lewis Frederick and Frances Kreps Crosby. In the log house on their homestead, Crosby read adult books before she went to school. When she graduated from high school, her father promised her four years of college as a graduation present. Majoring in mathematics at nearby Adrian College, she completed the four–year program in three years, graduating in 1910. With one year left of her father's gift, she applied to C. Judson Herrick's anatomy program at the University of Chicago. At that time her only background for the course was one undergraduate course in zoology. Crosby was a diligent student. She stayed so late in the laboratory studying that, at one point, Herrick took away her key to force her to get some rest. When he saw her making her way home with her heavy reference books, microscope, and box of slides in her arms, however, he returned the key.

She received a master's degree in 1912 and was given a fellowship in the anatomy department. Her Ph.D. degree followed in 1915, and her dissertation, *The Forebrain of Alligator mississippiensis,* became an influential work. Prior to Crosby's study, little was known about reptilian brains. In 1918, Crosby and Herrick published *A Laboratory Outline of Neurology* with detailed instructions for brain dissection. Throughout her career, she received ten honorary doctorates, and her honorary M.D. from the University of Groningen in The Netherlands allowed her to add that designation behind her name.

With her parents' health failing, Crosby returned home to Petersburg, where she taught zoology, mathematics, and Latin in the high school, and coached the local boys' basketball team. She became principal of the school in 1916 and superintendent of schools in 1918. Her mother died that

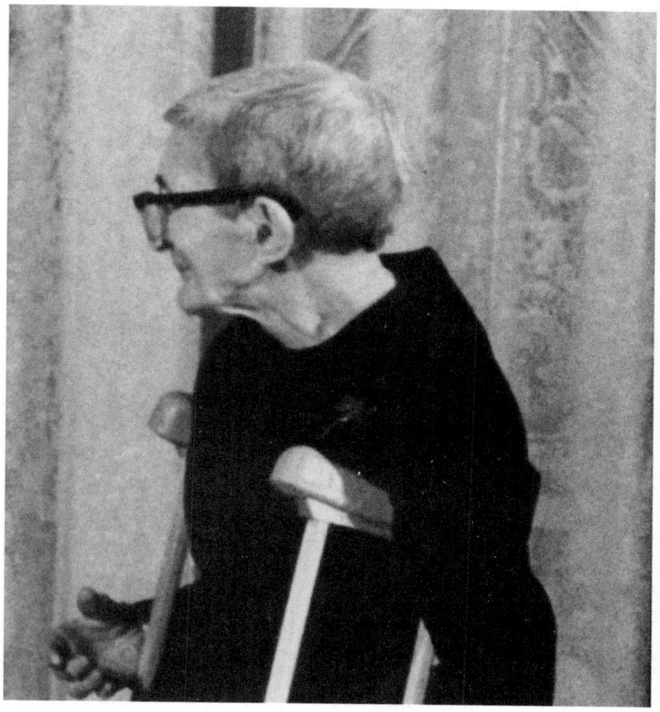

Elizabeth Crosby (Corbis/Bettmann-UPI. Reproduced by permission.)

year, and in 1920, Crosby secured a job as junior instructor at the University of Michigan in Ann Arbor, 30 miles from Petersburg. There she taught histology and assisted G. Carl Huber, head of the anatomy department, with the neuroanatomy course. Crosby and Huber developed a close personal and working relationship. They continued her work on the alligator brain, then turned to descriptive studies of the brains of birds. After her father died in 1923, Crosby took several leaves to study at the University of London and the Central Institute for Brain Research in Amsterdam, The Netherlands.

Publishes Comparative Anatomy Text

C. U. Ariens Kappers, Crosby's colleague in Amsterdam, had published a comparative neurology textbook in German, and Huber and Crosby agreed to join him in preparing an English translation that incorporated more recent material. But because so much new descriptive information had accumulated, the book was almost a new effort; it ultimately became a ten–year project. Huber died of leukemia in 1934, and Crosby produced the book with little assistance. Although the two volumes of *The Comparative Anatomy of the Nervous System of Vertebrates, Including Man* list Crosby as the third author after Ariens Kappers and Huber, it is essentially her work. The book was published in 1936, the same year that Crosby achieved the rank of full professor.

Spending the school year of 1939 to 1940 at Marischal College of the University of Aberdeen, Scotland, Crosby helped to organize the school's first course in histology and neuroanatomy. There she met a young girl, Kathleen, whom she later sent for and legally adopted.

The graduate research program at Michigan grew rapidly, and Crosby determined to continue the programs that she and Huber had begun. When she retired in 1958, 38 students had received Ph.D. degrees under her direction, and many visiting scientists had come to Ann Arbor to work with her. Crosby often published with students and colleagues, and often deferred first authorship to them even when her contribution was great. Each year, the University of Michigan presents the Elizabeth C. Crosby Award to an outstanding medical student in the basic sciences.

Her work in comparative anatomy was fundamental. Prior to the intense descriptive period in which she worked, scientists had only crude knowledge of the interior of the brain. By the time Crosby had retired, she had gathered, according to *Time* magazine, "the largest collection of submammalian and mammalian brains in the world." In addition to her research she had also taught an estimated 8,500 students; she was well-loved and known as an excellent teacher. In 1957, the Galens Society of the medical school established the Elizabeth C. Crosby Award for outstanding teaching in the basic sciences. According to a University of Michigan press release, Crosby believed that teachers "must do research. Teaching keeps you alert to the unanswered questions and by doing research you get your students interested. I learned a great deal from what my students needed to know."

Turns to Clinical Work, Assisting Surgeons

As practicing physicians and neurologists brought their patients' problems to her, Crosby became more clinically oriented. She conferred on the wards, discussed cases at bedside, and consulted in operating rooms. In 1955 she collaborated with Edgar A. Kahn, Richard C. Schneider, and James A. Taren on *Correlative Neurosurgery.* In 1962, she published *Correlative Anatomy of the Nervous System* with Tryphena Humphrey and Edward Lauer.

In 1963 Humphrey, one of Crosby's first graduate students, took a position in the department of anatomy at the University of Alabama in Birmingham. As they continued their friendship and collaboration, Crosby became a frequent visitor to Alabama, sharing her talents with that school's faculty and students. The relationship was formalized with Crosby's appointment as professor emeritus of anatomy at Alabama's medical school. For eighteen years she commuted between Alabama and her consultantship at the University of Michigan, whose neurosurgery section named its research laboratories after her in 1982, the same year *Comparative Correlative Neuroanatomy of the Vertebrate Telencephalon* was published, co–edited with H. N. Schnitzlein of the University of South Florida. Crosby was inducted into both the Alabama and Michigan Women's Hall of Fame.

Over the years, numerous other honors were bestowed upon Crosby. In 1950, she received the Achievement Award of the American Association of University Women. She was the first non–neurosurgeon to be named an honorary member of the American Association of Neurological Surgeons, and was named the first woman nonclinician to become an honorary member of the Harvey Cushing Society. The University of Michigan honored her in 1946 with its Henry Russel Lectureship, and in 1956 with its Distinguished Faculty Achievement Award; in both cases she was the first woman to receive the award. In 1980, President Jimmy Carter awarded her the federal government's highest honor for scientists, the National Medal of Science.

Although Crosby never married, she took pleasure in her adopted daughter's five children, whom she called her "pseudograndchildren," and to whom she was "auntie–grandma." She also considered her students her family, and former students passing through often contacted "Ma Crosby." She died on July 28, 1983, at age 94.

SELECTED WRITINGS BY CROSBY:

Books

The Forebrain of Alligator mississippiensis. [Philadelphia], 1917.

(With C. U. Ariens Kappers and G. Carl Huber) *The Comparative Anatomy of the Nervous System of Vertebrates, Including Man.* Volume I and II, Macmillan, 1936.

(Editor with H. N. Schnitzlein) *Comparative Correlative Neuroanatomy of the Vertebrate Telencephalon.* Macmillan, 1982.

FURTHER READING

Books

Rossiter, Margaret W. *Women Scientists in America: Struggles and Strategies to 1940.* Baltimore: Johns Hopkins University Press, 1982, pp. 185, 188–89.

Periodicals

"Elizabeth Crosby: Laying the Foundations of Neuroscience." *The Research News* University of Michigan (August/September 1983): 3–13, 16–17.

"Goodbye, Messrs. Chips." *Time* (July 21, 1958): 64.

Ryan, Virginia. "Dr. Elizabeth Crosby Champions Good Teaching." *The Ann Arbor News* (September 11, 1964).

"The Strange Case of the Whodunit She Didn't Do." *The Michigan Alumnus* (May 1966): 14–15.

Woodburne, Russell T. "Elizabeth Caroline Crosby, 1888–1983." *The Anatomical Record* (September 1984): 175–77.

Other

University of Michigan press release, August 17, 1978.

Sketch by Jill Carpenter

Elizabeth Bragg Cumming
1859–1929
American engineer and educator

Elizabeth Bragg Cumming was the first woman to receive an engineering degree from an American university. She was also the first woman to graduate in civil engineering from the University of California at Berkeley. Braving a male-dominated field, Cumming joined the less than 1% of women engineers of that time. As the first female engineering graduate at Berkeley, according to Karen Holtermann of the University of California at Berkeley, she "represents a unique landmark in the engineering education at Berkeley."

Enters Berkeley Without High School Diploma

Not much is known about Cumming's early childhood. According to her grandson Bruce Cumming, in a letter he wrote to the College of Engineering, Cumming became dissatisfied with high school at the age of 14, so she decided to take an exam that would allow her to enter the University of California, Berkeley without a high school diploma. She passed the exam and subsequently enrolled in the College of Engineering. Bruce Cumming believes she chose civil engineering because of an "aptitude in mathematics and the challenge it presented."

Certainly, Cumming had to have such an aptitude because math courses required at the time included algebra, trigonometry (plane and spherical), and analytical geometry. In addition to these classes, a civil engineering student was expected to have a well–rounded education by taking French or German, history, geography, and chemistry. Later, physics, mechanics, zoology and one term of astronomy were required. Engineering courses included land surveying, road and railroad surveying, masonry construction, and strength of building materials. Cumming must have had a mechanical aptitude as well, since the principles and practice of framing, bridge, and truss building had to be learned.

Cumming was only 18 when she graduated, and was one of only three women to graduate in the Class of 1876. According to her grandson, after graduation Bragg returned to her first love—small children—and taught school in San Francisco at the elementary level. As was true for many women at that time, it may also be possible that she could not find a job in her field, or jobs that were offered did not provide enough challenge. Cumming continued teaching until her marriage to George Marion Cumming, a civil engineer, who graduated from Berkeley in 1881.

Although Cumming never practiced engineering, her husband was an engineer for the Southern Pacific Railroad Company and it is possible she helped him in his work. However, it is not known whether Cumming contributed in any way to her husband's work, since women at the time were often not credited for their contributions. It is more likely that Cumming's time was devoted to taking care of her four sons. Cumming was also known for her participation in civic work in San Francisco. She attended her 50th class reunion in 1926.

Bragg died on November 10, 1929 at the age of 53 of unknown causes. She was a rarity for her time, proving that women could have the aptitude to earn a technical degree, despite popular belief to the contrary. Two of her sons followed in her footsteps and received degrees in electrical engineering at Berkeley in 1910 and 1914.

FURTHER READING

Books

Farnes, Patricia and G. Kass–Simon. *Women of Science: Righting the Record.* Bloomington, IN: Indiana University Press, 1990.

Periodicals

Register of the University of California. 1872–73, 1874–75, 1875–76.

Other

College of Engineering Home Page, The University of California, Berkeley, http://engnewscoe.berkeley.edu/.

Personal letter from Bruce Cummings to Karen Holtermann, Director, Engineering Public Affairs, College of Engineering, University of California, Berkeley.

Sketch by Laurel Sheppard

Clara Eaton Cummings
1855–1906
American botanist

Clara Cummings was one of the foremost authorities in cryptogamic botany, the science of spore–producing plants. She was known worldwide as an expert in lichens, as well as a dedicated naturalist.

Born in Plymouth, New Hampshire, to Noah and Elmira Cummings, Clara Cummings spent her early years at the Plymouth Normal School. She attended Wellesley College from 1876 to 1878, and although she never earned a degree, Cummings spent nearly her entire professional career at Wellesley, first as curator of the botanical museum, then as instructor associate professor, retiring in 1906 as Hunnewell Professor of Cryptogamic Botany.

During the years of 1886 and 1887, Cummings studied at the University of Zurich, where she created charts illustrating her chosen specialty in botany. She spent time visiting gardens in Geneva, Paris, and Brussels, and was able to bring seed specimens back with her to Wellesley, where she planted and tended them. Her time abroad allowed her to meet many other botanists of the day, with whom she would exchange information and specimens for the rest of her career.

Much of Cummings's research was devoted to lichens and to identifying species for other researchers and gardeners. She took several field trips to collect lichens and mosses from Alaska and Labrador. In 1885 Cummings published a catalogue of studies on North American liverworts and mosses. She also published *Decades of North American Lichens* and *Lichenes Boreali–Americani* in 1892 and 1894, respectively, which spurred a specimen exchange program among collectors. Later publications focused on what was then the new branch of science—ecology. Cummings also served as associate editor of *Plant World.*

Cummings was a member of the Wellesley College Faculty Science Club, the Boston Mycological Club, the Torrey Botanical Club, the American Association for the Advancement of Science, the Boston Society of Natural History, and served as vice president of the Society of Plant Morphology and Physiology.

Cummings was patient and thorough in her research and classification. She was remembered as a dedicated professional, an involved teacher, was loyal to Wellesley College, and an affectionate personality who loved nature and mountain climbing. She died on December 28, 1906.

SELCTED WRITINGS BY CUMMINGS:

Books

Catalogue of Musci and Hepaticae of North America, North of Mexico. Natick, Massachusetts: Howard and Stiles, 1885.

FURTHER READING

Books

Bailey, Martha J. *American Women in Science.* Denver: ABC–CLIO, 1994.

Ogilvie, Marilyn Bailey. *Women in Science: Antiquity through the Nineteenth Century.* Cambridge: MIT Press, 1986.

Siegel, Patricia Joan and Kay Thomas Finley. *Women in the Scientific Search*. Metuchen, NJ: The Scarecrow Press, 1985.

Other

Special Collections Archives. Wellesley College.

Sketch by Helene Barker Kiser

Maria Cunitz
1610–1664
German astronomer

Maria Cunitz, a major seventeenth-century German astronomer, attempted to correct the orbital calculations of the planets as determined by Johannes Kepler. As one of the few early women astronomers who was not also the daughter or wife of an astronomer, Cunitz is often cited in histories of astronomy for her own accomplishments.

Born in Schweidnitz, in Silesia in central Europe, in 1610, Cunitz was the eldest daughter of Heinrich Cunitz, a physician and lord of the estates of Kunzendorf and Hoch Giersdorf. As a child, Cunitz developed an interest in science. She was educated by her father and by tutors, including Eliae von Löwen, a physician and amateur astronomer in Pitschensis. She was taught medicine, mathematics, history, poetry, music, and painting. From her father, she learned Hebrew, Greek, Latin, Italian, French, and Polish. However her major interest was astronomy. At the age of 20, she married von Löwen.

Modern observational astronomy was in its infancy during the early seventeenth century, and this exciting new science was very popular among German amateurs. With her husband's encouragement, Cunitz set about making new calculations of older observations, in order to simplify the "Rudolphine Tables" of planetary motion, which were used for calculating the positions of the planets. However, Cunitz was delayed in her studies because Silesia was in the midst of the Thirty Years' War between France and Germany, which lasted from 1618 until 1648. The family fled to Poland, and Cunitz and her husband eventually were forced to take refuge in a convent. It was not until 1648 that Cunitz was able to resume her studies and her correspondence with other scholars.

Cunitz lacked both observational instruments and the necessary financial resources to carry out original observations. Therefore she was limited to performing manual calculations. Although she corrected a number of errors in the original sources and simplified the tables, she ignored small terms in the formulae and thereby introduced new errors. Nevertheless, during these years of turmoil, she compiled the *Urania Propitia*, which included the theory and art of astronomy, as well as her calculations, and a guide to astronomy for nonscientists. According to Cunitz, there were four components to astronomy: carefully recorded observations, the construction of astronomical instruments, theory, and the calculations or tables of predictions.

Cunitz wrote *Urania Propitia* in both German and Latin and published it in Frankfurt, Germany, in 1650. Although she published it under her maiden name, most believed that it was her husband's work, since she acknowledged his assistance in the preface. In later editions, her husband added a preface stating that the work was hers alone.

Cunitz was widowed in 1662. She died in 1664, in Pitschensis, Silesia, while fleeing from the ravages of another war. In the years following her death, and throughout the eighteenth century, attempts were made to discredit Cunitz, including accusations that she neglected her household by watching the stars all night.

SELECTED WRITINGS BY CUNITZ:

Books

Urania Propitia, sive Tabulae Astronomica mirè faciles, vim hypothesium physicarum à Kepplero proditarum complexae; facillimo calculandi compendio, sine ulla Logarithmorum mentione, phenomenis satisfacientes. Olsnae Silesiorum, 1650.

FURTHER READING

Books

Ogilvie, Marilyn Bailey. *Women in Science: Antiquity through the Nineteenth Century: A Biographical Dictionary with Annotated Bibliography*. Cambridge: MIT Press, 1991.

Schiebinger, Londa. *The Mind Has No Sex? Women in the Origins of Modern Science*. Cambridge: Harvard University Press, 1989.

Periodicals

Davis, Herman S. "Women Astronomers (400 A.D.–1750)." *Popular Astronomy* 6 (1898): 129–38.

Schiebinger, Londa. "Maria Winkelmann at the Berlin Academy: A Turning Point for Women in Science." *Isis* 78 (1987): 174–200.

Sketch by Margaret Alic

Marie Curie
1867–1934
Polish-born French physicist and radiation chemist

Marie Curie was the first woman to win a Nobel Prize, and one of very few scientists ever to win that award twice. In collaboration with her physicist–husband Pierre Curie, Marie Curie developed and introduced the concept of radioactivity to the world. Working in very primitive laboratory conditions, Curie investigated the nature of high energy rays spontaneously produced by certain elements, and isolated two new radioactive elements, polonium and radium. Her scientific efforts also included the application of xrays and radioactivity to medical treatments.

Marie Curie (The Library of Congress. Reproduced by permission.)

Curie was born to two schoolteachers on November 7, 1867, in Warsaw, Poland. Christened Maria Sklodowska, she was the fourth daughter and fifth child in the family. By the age of five, she had already begun to suffer deprivation. Her mother Bronislawa had contracted tuberculosis and assiduously avoided kissing or even touching her children. By the time Curie was eleven, both her mother and her eldest sister Zosia had passed away, leaving her an avowed atheist. Curie was also an avowed nationalist (like the other members in her family), and when she completed her elementary schooling, she entered Warsaw's "Floating University," an underground, revolutionary Polish school that prepared young Polish students to become teachers.

Curie left Warsaw at the age of seventeen, not for her own sake but for that of her older sister Bronya. Both sisters desired to acquire additional education abroad, but the family could not afford to send either of them, so Marie took a job as a governess to fund her sister's medical education in Paris. At first, she accepted a post near her home in Warsaw, then signed on with the Zorawskis, a family who lived some distance from Warsaw. Curie supplemented her formal teaching duties there with the organization of a free school for the local peasant children. Casimir Zorawski, the family's eldest son, eventually fell in love with Curie and she agreed to marry him, but his parents objected vehemently. Marie was a fine governess, they argued, but Casimir could marry much richer. Stunned by her employers' rejection, Curie finished her term with the Zorawskis and sought another position. She spent a year in a third governess job before her sister Bronya finished medical school and summoned her to Paris.

In 1891, at the age of 24, Curie enrolled at the Sorbonne and became one of the few women in attendance at the university. Although Bronya and her family back home were helping Curie pay for her studies, living in Paris was quite expensive. Too proud to ask for additional assistance, she subsisted on a diet of buttered bread and tea, which she augmented sometimes with fruit or an egg. Because she often went without heat, she would study at a nearby library until it closed. Not surprisingly, on this regimen she became anemic and on at least one occasion fainted during class.

In 1893, Curie received a degree in physics, finishing first in her class. The following year, she received a master's degree, this time graduating second in her class. Shortly thereafter, she discovered she had received the Alexandrovitch Scholarship, which enabled her to continue her education free of monetary worries. Many years later, Curie became the first recipient ever to pay back the prize. She reasoned that with that money, yet another student might be given the same opportunities she had.

Marries Pierre Curie and Two Begin Radiation Research

Friends introduced Marie to Pierre Curie in 1894. The son and grandson of doctors, Pierre had studied physics at the Sorbonne; at the time he met Marie, he was the director of the École Municipale de Physique et Chimie Industrielles. The two became friends, and eventually she accepted Pierre's proposal of marriage. Their Paris home was scantily furnished, as neither had much interest in housekeeping. Rather, they concentrated on their work. Pierre Curie accepted a job at the School of Industrial Physics and Chemistry of the City of Paris, known as the EPCI. Given lab space there, Marie Curie spent eight hours a day on her investigations into the magnetic qualities of steel until she became pregnant with her first child, Irene, who was born in 1897.

Curie then began work in earnest on her doctorate. Like many scientists, she was fascinated by French physicist Antoine–Henri Becquerel's discovery that the element uranium emitted rays that contained vast amounts of energy. Unlike Wilhelm Röntgen's x rays, which resulted from the excitation of atoms from an outside energy source, the "Becquerel rays" seemed to be a naturally occurring part of the uranium ore. Using the piezoelectric quartz electrometer developed by Pierre and his brother Jacques, Marie tested all the elements then known to see if any of them, like uranium, caused the nearby air to conduct electricity. In the first year of her research, Curie coined the term "radioactivity" to describe this mysterious force. She later concluded that only thorium and uranium and their compounds were radioactive.

While other scientists had also investigated the radioactive properties of uranium and thorium, Curie noted that the minerals pitchblende and chalcolite emitted more rays than could be accounted for by either element. Curie concluded that some other radioactive element must be causing the greater radioactivity. To separate this element, however, would require a great deal of effort, progressively separating pitchblende by chemical analysis and then measuring the radioactivity of the separate components. In July, 1898, she and Pierre successfully extracted an element from this ore that was even more radioactive than uranium; they called it polonium in honor of Marie's homeland. Six months later, the pair discovered another radioactive substance—radium—embedded in the pitchblende.

Although the Curies had speculated that these elements existed, to prove their existence they still needed to describe them fully and calculate their atomic weight. In order to do so, Curie needed an abundant supply of pitchblende and a better laboratory. She arranged to get hundreds of kilograms of waste scraps from a pitchblende mining firm in her native Poland, and Pierre Curie's EPCI supervisor offered the couple the use of a laboratory space. The couple worked together, with Marie performing the physically arduous job of chemically separating the pitchblende and Pierre analyzing the physical properties of the substances that Marie's separations produced. In 1902 the Curies announced that they had succeeded in preparing a decigram of pure radium chloride and had made an initial determination of radium's atomic weight. They had proven the chemical individuality of radium.

Pierre Curie's father had moved in with the family and assumed the care of their daughter, Irene, so the couple could devote more than eight hours a day to their beloved work. Pierre Curie's salary, however, was not enough to support the family, so Marie took a position as a lecturer in physics at the École Normal Supérieure; she was the first woman to teach there. In the years between 1900 and 1903, Curie published more than she had or would in any other three–year period, with much of this work being coauthored by Pierre Curie. In 1903 Curie became the first woman to complete her doctorate in France, summa cum laude.

Receives Her First Nobel

The year Curie received her doctorate was also the year she and her husband began to achieve international recognition for their research. In November the couple received England's prestigious Humphry Davy Medal, and the following month Marie and Pierre Curie—along with Becquerel—received the Nobel Prize in physics for their efforts in expanding scientific knowledge about radioactivity. Although Curie was the first woman ever to receive the prize, she and Pierre declined to attend the award ceremonies, pleading they were too tired to travel to Stockholm. The prize money from the Nobel, combined with that of the Daniel Osiris Prize—which she received soon after—allowed the couple to expand their research efforts. In addition, the Nobel bestowed upon the couple an international reputation that furthered their academic success. The year after he received the Nobel, Pierre Curie was named professor of physics of the Faculty of Sciences at the Sorbonne. Along with his post came funds for three paid workers, two laboratory assistants and a laboratory chief, stipulated to be Marie. This was Marie's first paid research job.

In December, 1904, Marie gave birth to another daughter, Eve Denise, having miscarried a few years earlier. Despite the fact that both Pierre and Marie frequently suffered adverse effects from the radioactive materials with which they were in constant contact, Eve Denise was born healthy. The Curies continued their work regimen, taking sporadic vacations in the French countryside with their two children. They had just returned from one such vacation when on April 19, 1906, tragedy struck; while walking in the congested street traffic of Paris, Pierre was run over by a heavy wagon and killed.

A month after the accident, the University of Paris invited Curie to take over her husband's teaching position. Upon acceptance she became the first woman to ever receive a post in higher education in France, although she was not named to a full professorship for two more years. During this time, Curie came to accept the theory of English physicists Ernest Rutherford and Frederick Soddy that radioactivity was caused by atomic nuclei losing particles, and that these disintegrations caused the transmutation of an atomic nucleus into a different element. It was Curie, in fact, who coined the terms disintegration and transmutation.

In 1909, Curie received an academic reward that she had greatly desired: the University of Paris drew up plans for an Institut du Radiumthat would consist of two branches, a laboratory to study radioactivity—which Curie would run—and a laboratory for biological research on radium therapy, to be overseen by a physician. It took five years for the plans to come to fruition. In 1910, however, with her assistant André Debierne, Curie finally achieved the isolation of pure radium metal, and later prepared the first international standard of that element.

The First Scientist to Win a Second Nobel

Curie was awarded the Nobel Prize again in 1911, this time "for her services to the advancement of chemistry by the discovery of the elements radium and polonium," according to the award committee. The first scientist to win the Nobel twice, Curie devoted most of the money to her scientific studies. During World War I, Curie volunteered at the National Aid Society, then brought her technology to the war front and instructed army medical personnel in the practical applications of radiology. With the installation of radiological equipment in ambulances, for instance, wounded soldiers would not have to be transported far to be x–rayed. When the war ended, Curie returned to research and devoted much of her time to her work.

By the 1920s, Curie was an international figure; the Curie Foundation had been established in 1920 to accept private donations for research, and two years later the scientist was invited to participate on the League of Nations International Commission for Intellectual Cooperation. Her health was failing, however, and she was troubled by fatigue and cataracts. Despite her discomfort, Curie made a highly publicized tour of the United States in 1921. The previous year, she had met Missy Meloney, editor of the *Delineator,* a woman's magazine. Horrified at the conditions in which Curie lived and worked (the Curies had made no money from their process for producing radium, having refused to patent it), Meloney proposed that a national subscription be held to finance a gram of radium for the institute to use in research. The tour proved grueling for Curie; by the end of her stay in New York, she had her right arm in a sling, the result of too many too strong handshakes. However, with Meloney's assistance, Curie left America with a valuable gram of radium.

Curie continued her work in the laboratory throughout the decade, joined by her daughter, **Irène Joliot-Curie**, who was pursuing a doctoral degree just as her mother had done. In 1925, Irene successfully defended her doctoral thesis on alpha rays of polonium, although Curie did not attend the defense lest her presence detract from her daughter's performance. Meanwhile, Curie's health still continued to fail and she was forced to spend more time away from her work in the laboratory. The result of prolonged exposure to radium, Curie contracted leukemia and died on July 4, 1934, in a nursing home in the French Alps. She was buried next to Pierre Curie in Sceaux, France.

SELECTED WRITINGS BY CURIE:

Books

Recherches sur les substances radioactives. 2d ed., [Paris], 1904.
La Radiologie et la Guerre. Librarie Felix Alcan, 1921.
Pierre Curie. Macmillan, 1923.
Radioactivite. Herman, 1935.
Oeuvres de Marie Sklodowska–Curie. Edited by Irène Joliot–Curie, [Warsaw], 1954.

Periodicals

"Les mesures en radioactivitéet l'étalon du radium," *Journal de physique* 2 (1912): 715.

FURTHER READING

Books

Curie, Eve. *Madame Curie: A Biography by Eve Curie.* Translated by Vincent Sheean, Doubleday, 1937.
Pflaum, Rosalynd. *Grand Obsession: Madame Curie and Her World.* Doubleday, 1989.
Reid, Robert William. *Marie Curie.* Dutton, 1974.
Rossiter, Margaret W. *Women Scientists in America: Struggles and Strategies to 1940.* Baltimore: Johns Hopkins University Press, 1982.

Sketch by Shari Rudavsky

D

Maria Dalle Donne
1778–1842
Italian physician and professor of obstetrics

Maria Dalle Donne is known for her skills as a teacher of obstetrics who trained midwives in more enlightened and less superstitious birthing practices. She was so well regarded as a professor that a chair of obstetrics at the University of Bologna was set up for her by Napoleon.

Dalle Donne was born in 1778, the daughter of a poor family who lived near Bologna, in northern Italy. Her uncle, a priest, noticed her intellectual abilities and assumed the responsibility of providing for her education. After studying with tutors, Dalle Donne was encouraged by her uncle and her teachers to seek further education. To persuade doubters of her intellectual abilities they organized a public examination. After a brilliant performance, she entered the University of Bologna to study medicine. Dalle Donne's abilities were noticed by a patron of the sciences, Prospero Ranuzzi, who underwrote her tuition and made a gift to her of his medical instruments and books. She graduated with highest honors from the University of Bologna in 1799 with a doctorate in medicine and philosophy. H. J. Mozans, a Roman Catholic priest who wrote a history titled *Women in Science*, remarks that Clothilde Tambroni, an eminent woman professor and accomplished Greek scholar at the University, delivered the graduation address. Also teaching at Bologna just a year before Dalle Donne's graduation was the famed **Laura Bassi**, who held the chair of physics.

Begins Medical Career

In 1802, Napoleon's conquests brought Bologna into the French Empire. On the recommendation of a learned man named Caterzani, Napoleon established a chair of obstetrics at the Bologna University for Dalle Donne. She also was appointed head of a school for midwives there. Most likely, Dalle Donne taught many of the principles laid down by **Trotula**, a woman professor of obstetrics and gynecology, who taught at the medical school in Salerno during the eleventh century. Trotula wrote the first European book on women's health, *On Diseases of Women*. Over the intervening years, her knowledge of obstetrics was forgotten. As a result, much to the patients' detriment, obstetrics was practiced by untrained and ignorant midwives. With the rise of the Italian medical schools, and teachers like Dalle Donne, obstetrical training again began to advance.

At her school for midwives, Dalle Donne's students received a strict education. She set high standards of training and was determined that women in the surrounding country villages would receive competent care from the midwives she was sending out to attend them. Through her efforts, she was to correct many crude and superstitious practices and obstetrical patients received the benefit of her enlightened and skilled teaching.

In *Women in Science* Mozan calls Maria Dalle Donne "a worthy link between that long line of women doctors, beginning with Trotula, who have so honored their sex in Italy and those still more numerous practitioners in the healing art who shortly after her death, began to spring up in all parts of the civilized world." He also credits the University of Bologna as nurturer of the female scholar: ". . . no seat of learning can point to such a long list of eminent scholars and teachers among the gentler sex as is to be found on the register of Bologna's famous university."

In 1829, Dalle Donna was recognized for her accomplishments and awarded the title of *Academic* by the Academia Benedettina. She remained at the University of Bologna as director of obstetrics until her death in 1842, distinguishing herself as an excellent teacher and physician.

FURTHER READING

Books

Alic, Margaret. *Hypatia's Heritage: A History of Women in Science from Antiquity through the Nineteenth Century*. Boston: Beacon Press, 1986.

Mozans, H. J. *Women in Science*. New York: D. Appleton and Co., 1913.

Ogilvie, Marilyn Bailey. *Women in Science, Antiquity through the Nineteenth Century*. Cambridge: MIT Press, 1986, p 72.

Schiebinger, Londa. *The Mind Has No Sex?* Cambridge: Harvard University Press, 1989.

Sketch by Jane Stewart Cook

Marie Maynard Daly
1921–
American biochemist

Marie M. Daly was the first African American woman to earn a Ph.D. in chemistry. Throughout her career, her research interests focused on areas of health, particularly the effects on the heart and arteries of such factors as aging, cigarette smoking, hypertension, and cholesterol. In addition to research, she taught for 15 years at Yeshiva University's Albert Einstein College of Medicine.

Marie Maynard Daly was born in Corona, Queens, a neighborhood of New York City, on April 16, 1921. Her parents, Ivan C. Daly and Helen (Page) Daly, both valued learning and education and steadily encouraged her. Her father had wanted to become a chemist and had attended Cornell University, but was unable to complete his education for financial reasons and became a postal clerk. Daly attended the local public schools in Queens and graduated from Hunter College High School in Manhattan. She credits her interest in science to both her father's scientific background and to influential books such as Paul DeKruif's *The Microbe Hunters.*

Daly enrolled in Queens College as a chemistry major, graduating with a B.S. degree in 1942. The following year she received her M.S. from New York University and then went to Columbia University where she entered the doctoral program in biochemistry. In 1948 she made history at that university, becoming the first African American woman to earn a Ph.D. in chemistry.

Daly began teaching during her college days as a tutor at Queens College. She began her professional career a year before receiving her doctorate, when she accepted a position at Howard University in Washington, D.C., as an instructor in physical sciences. In 1951 she returned to New York first as a visiting investigator and then as an assistant in general physiology at the Rockefeller Institute. By 1955 she had become an associate in biochemistry at the Columbia University Research Service at the Goldwater Memorial Hospital. She taught there until 1971 when she left Columbia as an assistant professor of biochemistry to become associate professor of biochemistry and medicine at the Albert Einstein College of Medicine at Yeshiva University in New York.

Daly conducted most of her research in areas related to the biochemical aspects of human metabolism (how the body processes the energy it takes in) and the role of the kidneys in that process. She also focused on hypertension (high blood pressure) and atherosclerosis (accumulation of lipids or fats in the arteries). Her later work focused on the study of aortic (heart) smooth muscle cells in culture.

During her career, she held several positions concurrently with her teaching obligations, such as investigator for the American Heart Association from 1958 to 1963 and career scientist for the Health Research Council of New York from 1962 to 1972. She was also a fellow of the Council on Arteriosclerosis and the American Association for the Advancement of Science, a member of the American Chemical Society, a member of the board of governors of the New York Academy of Science from 1974 to 1976, and a member of the Harvey Society, the American Society of Biological Chemists, the National Association for the Advancement of Colored People, the National Association of Negro Business and Professional Women, and Phi Beta Kappa and Sigma Xi. In 1988 Daly contributed to a scholarship fund set up at Queens College to aid African American students interested in the sciences. Daly, who married Vincent Clark in 1961, retired from teaching in 1986.

SELECTED WRITINGS BY DALY:

Books

(With Q. B. Deming and H. Wolinsky) "Hypertension: A Precursor of Arteriosclerosis." *Hypertension: Mechanisms and Management.* Edited by Gaddo Onesti, Kwan Eun Kim, and John H. Moyer. New York: Grune and Stratton, 1973.

FURTHER READING

Books

Grinstein,Louise S., Rose K. Rose, and Miriam H. Rafailovich, eds. *Women in Chemistry and Physics.* Westport, CT: Greenwood Press, 1993, pp. 145–149.

Periodicals

Prestwidge, K. J., "Scientifically Speaking . . . !" *New York Voice,* February 4, 1984.

Sketch by Leonard C. Bruno

Ingrid Daubechies
1954–
Belgian-born American applied mathematician

Ingrid Daubechies was born August 17, 1954, in Houthalen, Belgium. Her father, Marcel Daubechies, is a retired civil engineer and her mother, Simone, is a retired criminologist. Daubechies credits her parents with giving her a love of learning and her mother with teaching her by example to be her own person. Her father always encouraged her to pursue her interest in science. She has one brother.

As a small child, Daubechies displayed an insatiable interest in how things worked and in making things with her hands. She took up the hobbies of weaving and pottery at a young age and continues to produce *objets d'art* in both crafts. At the age of eight or nine Daubechies' favorite hobby was to sew clothes for her dolls because it fascinated her that flat pieces of material could be worked into curved surfaces that fit the angles of the doll's body. But she also fascinated with machinery and mathematical axioms. Daubechies used to lie in bed and compute the powers of two, or test the mathematical law that any number divisible by nine produces another number divisible by nine when the digits are added together. Reading has been a lifelong hobby.

Daubechies spent her entire childhood and school years in Belgium. She was educated at the Free University Brussels, earning a B.S. degree in 1975 and a Ph.D. in 1980, both in physics. Her thesis was entitled "Representation of Quantum Mechanical Operators by Kernels on Hilbert Spaces of Analytic Functions." Between 1978 and 1980 Daubechies wrote ten articles based on her own original research. While pursuing her own studies, she taught at the Free University Brussels a total of 12 years. Daubechies first visited the United States in 1981, staying for two years, then returned to Belgium believing she would not come back to America.

In 1984, Daubechies was the recipient of the Louis Empain Prize for physics. The prize is given every five years to a Belgian scientist for scientific contributions done before the age of 29. She returned to the United States in 1987 and joined AT&T Bell Laboratories, where she was a technical staff member for the Mathematics Research Center. During her employment with AT&T, she concurrently took leaves of absences to teach at the University of Michigan and later at Rutgers University. In 1993, Daubechies became a full professor at Princeton University in the Mathematics Department and Program in Applied and Computational Mathematics, where she has remained to date. Daubechies is the first woman to obtain this position at Princeton. Her responsibilities include teaching both undergraduate and graduate courses, directing Ph.D. students in thesis work, and collaborating with postdoctoral fellows in research. She has also devoted much time to creating mathematics curriculums for grades kindergarten through 12th grade that reflect present–day applications of mathematics.

The Physicist Who Became a Mathematician

Daubechies' original intent was to become a physicist (particularly in the field of engineering). But she involved in mathematical work which was very theoretical in nature. She soon found herself caught up in mathematical applications. Her designation as a mathematician was sealed through her brilliant and innovative work in wavelet theory.

In 1987, Daubechies made one of the biggest breakthroughs in wave analysis in the past two hundred years. Prior to the development of Daubechies' theorem, signal processing was accomplished by using French mathematician Jean–Baptiste Fourier's series of trigonometric functions, breaking down the signal into combinations of sine waves. Sine waves can measure the amplitude and frequency of a signal, but they can't measure both at the same time. Daubechies changed all that when she discovered a way to break signals down into wavelets instead of breaking them down into their components; a task thought by most mathematicians to be impossible.

This discovery has changed the image–processing techniques used by the Federal Bureau of Investigation for transmitting and retrieving the information contained in their massive database of fingerprints. With more than 200 million fingerprints on file, the technique also allows for data compression without loss of information, and eliminates extraneous data that slows or clutters the procedure. Of more significance to Daubechies is the application of her discovery to the field of biomedicine. She likens a wavelets transform to "a musical score which tells the musician which note to play at what time," and this is of particular importance to medical science. Through the analysis of signals used in electrocardiograms, electroencephalograms, and other processes used in medical imaging, the medical world hopes to employ Daubechies' development to detect disease and abnormalities in patients much sooner than is presently possible. The development and implementation of wavelet imagery in medicine would improve the ability of an ECG from a simple recording of a heartbeat to a digitized record of complete heart function.

Other applications for wavelets still in the research stage include video and speech compression, sound enhancement, statistical analysis, and partial differential equations involving shock waves and turbulence, to name only a few.

Leaving a Legacy in Her Own Time

Daubechies' work has not gone unnoticed by her peers. She has been a fellow of the John D. and Catherine T. MacArthur Foundation from 1992 to 1997 and an elected member of the American Academy of Arts and Sciences since 1993. She was the recipient of the American Mathematical Steele Prize for Exposition for her "Ten Lectures on Wavelets" in 1994, and received the Ruth Lyttle Satter Prize in 1997. Daubechies is also a member of the American Mathematical Society, the Mathematical Association of America, the Society for Industrial and Applied Mathematics, and the Institute of Electrical and Electronics Engineers.

Daubechies has written more than 70 articles and papers during her career, more than 20 of them dealing with the nature, application, and interdisciplinary use of wavelets. She has held memberships in more than 17 professional organizations and committees, including her current memberships with the United States National Committee on Mathematics and the European Mathematical Society's Commission on the Applications of Mathematics. Daubechies has been a guest editor or member of the editorial board for ten professional journals and has served as editor–in–chief for the publication *Applied and Computation Harmonic Analysis.*

Daubechies married A. Robert Calderbank, a mathematician, in 1987 and has two children.

SELECTED WRITINGS BY DAUBECHIES:

"Ten Lectures on Wavelets." CBMS–NSF Lecture Notes, no. 61, *SIAM*, 1992.

(With S. Maes) "A Nonlinear Squeezing of the Continuous Wavelet Transform Based on Auditory Nerve Models." *Wavelets in Medicine and Biology*. Edited by A. Aldroubi and M. Unser, 1996.

"Where Do Wavelets Come From? A Personal Point of View." *Proceedings of the IEEE Special Issue on Wavelets* 84, no. 4 (April 1996): 510–13.

FURTHER READING

Periodicals

Von Baeyer, Hans Christian. "Wave of the Future." *Discover* (May 1995): 69–74.

What's Happening in the Mathematical Sciences 2 (1994): 23.

Other

Daubechies, Ingrid with Kelley Reynolds Jacquez conducted May 16, 1997.

Sketch by Kelley Reynolds Jacquez

Margaret Oakley Dayhoff
1925–1983
American biochemist

Margaret Oakley Dayhoff developed a widely used database of protein structures and was a pioneer in the use of computers in medicine. One of the first women elected as both president and secretary of the international Biophysical Society, Dayhoff has an award named after her presented annually by that body.

Born in Philadelphia on March 11, 1925, Dayhoff graduated from New York University in 1945, then went on to Columbia University, where she earned her Ph.D. in quantum chemistry in 1948, at an age when many young men and women are just earning their bachelor's or master's degrees. That same year she became a research assistant at the Rockefeller Institute and also married Edward Samuel Dayhoff, a physicist involved in military systems. The Dayhoffs would have two daughters, both of whom became doctors.

Dayhoff had a highly respected career in research and academia, becoming a resident fellow at the University of Maryland from 1957 to 1959 and associate director of National Biomedical Research Foundation in Washington, DC in 1960, a position she held until her death in 1983. Additionally, at Georgetown University, she became the head of the Department of Biochemistry in 1962 and associate professor of biophysics at the School of Medicine in 1970, earning a full professorship there in 1978. She held both these positions until her death.

Work in Protein Structure Wins Accolades

Dayhoff pioneered the use of high-speed computer programs to determine protein and nucleic acid structures and sequencing, establishing and maintaining a large computer database of protein structures. Her multi-volume reference work, *Atlas of Protein Sequence and Structure,* updated regularly between 1965 and 1983, became a bible for other researchers in the fields of genetic engineering and in medical research.

Involved also in the study of evolution and the origin of life, Dayhoff made lasting contributions to the understanding of the evolutionary process by showing the correlation between proteins and living organism in schematic evolutionary "trees." Among other breakthroughs made by Dayhoff and her staff at the National Biomedical Research Foundation was the discovery or similarities between certain genes found in cancer cells and in healthy body tissue cells.

A member of the International Society for the Study of the Origin of Life, Dayhoff also belonged to the American Society of Biological Chemistry and of the American Chemistry Society, in addition to her work with the Biophysical Society, where she was secretary from 1971–79, and president from 1980–81. Following her death of a heart attack in Silver Spring, Maryland, on February 8, 1983 at age 57, Dayhoff was recognized for her work by an award named in her honor. The Margaret Oakley Dayhoff Award, presented by the Biophysical Society, honors notable women in the physical sciences.

SELECTED WRITINGS BY DAYHOFF:

Books

(Editor) *Atlas of Protein Sequence and Structure*. Silver Spring, Maryland: National Biomedical Research Foundation, 1965–83.

FURTHER READING

Books

American Men and Women of Science. 15th ed. New York: R.R. Bowker, 1982.

"Margaret Oakley Dayhoff, 57; Expert on Protein Structures." *New York Times* (February 9, 1983): B12.

Sketch by J. Sydney Jones

Frederica Annis de Laguna
1906–?
American anthropologist and archaeologist

Frederica de Laguna was an archaeologist and anthropologist who gained fame for her work in the northwest region of the North American continent. She was responsible for leading the first study of Pacific cultures, specifically the Eskimos of the region.

The daughter of intellectuals and academics, Frederica Annis Lopez de Leo de Laguna was born on October 3, 1906. She and her younger brother Wallace grew up in a family that placed a strong emphasis on education; both of her parents were teachers at Bryn Mawr College. Her father was especially involved in the children's lives, providing educational enrichment at every turn in his children's schooling. During his youth, de Laguna's father had taught English in the Philippines and traveled throughout Japan, and his experiences there sparked in de Laguna an early interest in other cultures.

In 1923, de Laguna accepted a scholarship to Bryn Mawr, where she studied economics and learned to be both student and daughter of faculty members. de Laguna was awarded the Bryn Mawr European Fellowship at her graduation, but at the urging of her parents, she first went to Columbia University to study anthropology with Franz Boas. The de Lagunas felt that anthropology would suit their daughter's academic interests, as well as accommodate her enjoyment of the outdoors. In addition to her scholarly and academic writing, de Laguna wrote and published mysteries. At Columbia, Boas suggested she focus her research on Eskimo and Upper Paleolithic art.

Discovers New Culture

After her year at Columbia, de Laguna accepted her European fellowship, traveling to England and France in 1928. To continue the research Boas had suggested, she contacted the archaeologist Therkel Mathiassen, an expert in the Arctic area. He invited her to help him as an assistant archaeologist on an excavation in Greenland, the first excavation to take place in that region. de Laguna loved the work so much that she broke off her engagement to an Englishman in order to pursue a career in anthropology. A lover of the area and its people since childhood, de Laguna experienced a dream come true when she and Mathiassen were able to excavate sites from a Norse culture previously unknown to scientists, the Inugsuk.

De Laguna returned to Columbia, leaving each year on excavation trips to Alaska, where she spent much time in Cook Inlet and Prince William Sound. In addition to her school work and field work, de Laguna worked as an assistant in the American section and as a research associate of the University of Pennsylvania Museum from 1931–1935. She used the money to fund her trips, and also received grants from the Danish government, the Rockefeller Foundation, and the Viking Fund. She completed her Ph.D. in anthropology in 1933, and her book on the Alaskan findings was published in 1934.

After graduation, de Laguna continued her field work in the Yukon and the Pima Indian Reservation in Arizona, where she worked as an associate soil conservationist for the United States Department of Agriculture. In 1938, de Laguna returned to Bryn Mawr as a lecturer from 1938–1941, assistant professor from 1941–1942, associate professor from 1942–1949, and professor from 1949–1975. At the college, de Laguna created the Anthropology Department. She believed that anthropologists should not overspecialize, and that the science was holistic, the only one in which human experience could be closely studied. As one of the few Americans with Arctic experience and knowledge, de Laguna was asked to join the United States Naval Reserve during World War II as a lieutenant commander.

De Laguna continued her field trips while at Bryn Mawr. She also served as president of the American Anthropological Association, editing its publications and bring the group out of financial crisis. At her retirement as Emeritus Professor, de Laguna was also made Kenan Professor, which allowed research funding, won the Lindback teaching award, and was elected member of the National Academy of Science. At her retirement, de Laguna continued publishing and doing field work. Her work was so accurate and important that her Alaskan book was republished over 40 years after its first printing.

SELECTED WRITINGS BY DE LAGUNA:

Books

The Archaeology of Cook Inlet, Alaska. Philadelphia: University of Pennsylvania Press for the University Museum, 1934.

Selected Papers from the American Anthropologist 1888–1920. Evanston, IL: Row, Peterson, and Company, 1960.

Periodicals

"A Comparison of Eskimo and Paleolithic Art." *American Journal of Archaeology.* 36(4) and 38(1), 1922–1923.

FURTHER READING

Books

Bailey, Martha J. *American Women in Science*. Denver: ABC–CLIO, 1994.

Gacs, Ute, et. al., eds. *Women Anthropologists: A Biographical Dictionary*. New York: Greenwood Press, 1988.

Sketch by Helene Barker Kiser

Maude Jane Delap
1866–1953
Irish naturalist

Before the latter half of the twentieth century, many of the most productive scientists actually had no formal training. They attended no formal classes, held no advanced degrees, and were not produced by the rigorous university system that now produces all scientists. However, amateur scientists, as they would be called today, made many important contribtions. Maude Jane Delap is one of these valuable people. Science is in her debt for her study of the life cycle of the jellyfish.

Maude Jane Delap was born December 7, 1866, in County Donegal, Ireland. She was the fifth daughter of the 10 children born to the Reverend Alexander Delap and his wife. Delap spent the early years of her life at Templemore Rectory, and in 1876 the family moved to Valentia Island in County Kerry. The island would be her home for the rest of her long life; she did not even leave it to attend school. Instead, her father, who was interested in natural history, taught her himself.

Studies Island Flora and Fauna

The island presented an array of flora and fauna to investigate, and the sea's constant presence in all aspects of island life made it only natural that Delap's interests would include the study of its creatures. In fact, a number of her published papers would focus on the plankton and other creatures found in the island's harbor.

In addition to her father, naturalist E.T. Browne encouraged her in her scientific interests, particularly in the study of marine biology and jellyfish, or medusae. Under Browne's tutelage, she contributed greatly to the understanding of these animals' life cycle. In addition to studying planktonic forms, she also successfully reared jellyfish in an aquarium, including rearing the jellyfish *Dipurena ophiogaster* from a previously unknown hydroid. From her aquarium studies, she determined that *Dipleurosoma typicum* and *Laodicea undulata* hydroids were in fact species of *Cuspidella*. She also studied *Cuanea larmacki, Crysaora isoceles, Aurelia aurita* and *Pelagia peria*. Delap published a paper on these last two species jointly with her sister Constance.

In recognition of her remarkable work, Delap was offered a position at the Marine Biological Station in Plymouth, England. However, her father did not want her to leave home, and she declined the opportunity. Instead, she remained on the island with him and her two sisters. Despite what would appear to be a huge setback, Maude Delap continued her research.

Delap's work was much appreciated by the naturalist community of Ireland and Britain. In addition to being offered the Plymouth post, she was mentioned in the book *British Sea–Anemones* in a citation that read: "Miss Delap's skill and persistence in collecting rare species are indefatigable." At least one species was named after her: *Edwardsta delapsiae*. In 1936, the Linnean Society named her an Associate, "a signal honor and not lightly bestowed," wrote N.F. McMillan and W.J. Rees in her obituary in *The Irish Naturalists' Journal*.

Delap provided invaluable assistance to other researchers, including much of the material for the book *The Flora of County Kerry*. She also published a number of papers herself on jellyfish, as well as papers concerning fulmars (a seabird of cold, Northern seas), swans, seals, and plankton.

In addition to a productive scientific career, Delap enjoyed a fulfilling home life. She never married, or had children of her own, but she was greatly attached to her nieces and nephews. Even into her seventies she worked in her garden and rowed out in a small boat to conduct her studies. She also ran the local cottage hospital for years.

Delap died July 23, 1953. A warm tribute to her appeared in *The Irish Naturalists' Journal* in January, 1958. It concluded, "Although she long out–lived her sisters, and saw everything she loved and respected sinking into disrepute, she remained cheerful, serene and intensely interested in world affairs until the very end."

SELECTED WRITINGS BY DELAP:

Periodicals

"Notes on the Rearing of *Chrysaora isoceles* in an Aquarium." *The Irish Naturalists' Journal* X (1901): 25–28.

"Seal Caught on a Handline." *The Irish Naturalists' Journal* XII (1904): 49.

"Notes on the Plankton of Valencia Harbour, 1902–1905." *Fisheries, Ireland, Sci. Invest.1905* VII (1906).

"New Localities for *Geomalacus maculosus*." *The Irish Naturalists' Journal* XV (1906):190.

FURTHER READING

Periodicals

McMillan, N.F., and W.J. Rees, "Obituary: Maude Jane Delap." *The Irish Naturalists' Journal* XII (January 1958): 221–223.

Sketch by Fran Hodgkins

Gladys (Henry) Dick
1881–1963
American medical researcher and physician

Before 1922, not much was known about the then–endemic disease of scarlet fever, which primarily affected children in Europe and North America, killing about 25% of the children who contracted it. Additionally, scarlet fever had many complications, some of which were severe and could be crippling. Gladys Dick, with her husband, George Dick, successfully isolated the bacteria which caused scarlet fever, developed a test for human vulnerability to the disease, and devised preventive methods. The couple patented their findings, specifically the way their scarlet fever toxin and antitoxin were prepared, although this decision was controversial at the time.

Dick was born Gladys Rowena Henry in December 18, 1881, in Pawnee City, Nebraska, to William Chester Henry, a grain dealer and banker who also raised carriage horses, and Azelia Henrietta (Edson) Henry. She had one older brother and one older sister. Dick was raised in Lincoln, Nebraska, where her family moved when she was an infant. She graduated in 1900 from the University of Nebraska, earning a Bachelor of Science degree. Dick wanted to study medicine, but could not persuade her mother to agree to such a radical notion. In the interim, Dick taught biology at a high school in Carney, Nebraska, and took some graduate courses at her alma mater.

When Dick's mother finally granted permission, Dick enrolled at the Johns Hopkins University School of Medicine, and graduated in 1907. She practiced medicine for several years at Johns Hopkins, first as an intern, and later as a staff physician. She then traveled to Berlin to do a year of postgraduate work, which was completed in 1910. While in medical school, Dick became interested in biomedical research. Blood chemistry and experimental cardiac surgery were her first experiences in research, and her studies in Berlin reinforced this interest.

Teamed with George Dick

After returning from Berlin, Dick moved to Chicago in 1911, where her mother then lived. She began working at the University of Chicago on the pathochemistry of kidneys and scarlet fever etiology. Dick was teamed with George F. Dick, her future husband, in the etiological research. They married on January 28, 1914. After returning from their honeymoon, Dick went into private practice and was employed as Evanston Hospital's pathologist, while her husband went to work at the University of Chicago–affiliated John R. McCormick Institute for Infectious Diseases. Dick began working at the Institute a short time later.

Most of Dick's research on scarlet fever (always in conjunction with her husband) was accomplished at McCormick. In 1923, the Dicks published papers in which they proved that scarlet fever was caused by hemolytic streptococcus. Within a few years, the Dicks also published papers on how to prevent, test, diagnose, and treat scarlet fever. Their ground–breaking work insured that the disease was finally understood and brought under control.

Dick and her husband announced the development of what came to be known as the Dick test in 1924. This skin test showed whether the patient was susceptible or immune to scarlet fever. The test involved injecting a toxin–containing substance in the arm and determining if the skin around the area became inflamed. If it did, the patient was vulnerable to scarlet fever. This test was also useful in predicting if pregnant women would develop puerperal infection during childbirth.

The essence of the Dicks' discovery—the toxin and antitoxin—became controversial because the couple took a patent out on their preparation and manufacture methods. They patented these processes in the United States in 1924 and in Great Britain two years later. The controversy revolved around accusations of commercial opportunism; the health organization of the League of Nations argued as late as 1935 that the patent forced unnecessary restrictions on research and prevented biological standardization. Another aspect of contention was the issue of whether the discovery was original and/or an invention. The Dicks defended their actions, asserting that they did so to ensure that quality standards would be met and not for financial gain. In fact, Dick did bring suit against a manufacturer, Lederle Laboratories, in the late 1920s for negligent production procedures and patent infringement. After a long court battle, she won the lawsuit.

Nominated for Nobel Prize

With her husband, Dick was nominated for the 1925 Nobel Prize in Medicine for her work on scarlet fever, but no prize was awarded that year. The couple did receive the University of Edinburgh's 1933 Cameron Prize and the University of Toronto's 1926 Mickel Prize for their success. Their work remained important for the next 20 years until the discovery of antibiotics during World War II. The new treatments became the preferred standard, and the Dicks' work became outdated.

Scarlet fever research was not Dick's sole accomplishment, however. She began investigating polio, and worked as a bacteriologist for the United States Public Health Service during World War I. Dick also maintained a lifelong interest in children and their welfare. She founded what is arguably the first professional adoption organization in the United States, the Cradle Society, headquartered in Evanston, Illinois. She worked with the Cradle Society from 1918 until 1953. Dick took this issue quite personally, and in 1930, she and her husband adopted two children, Roger Henry Dick and Rowena Henry Dick.

In addition to the honors with her husband, Dick received numerous accolades during her lifetime. Honorary degrees were conferred on her by the University of Nebraska (1925) and Northwestern (1928). Dick retired in 1953, and the couple moved to Palo Alto, California. During the last years of her life, Dick suffered from cerebral arteriosclerosis, which had severely limited her activities. She died of a stroke on August 21, 1963, in Menlo Park, California.

SELECTED WRITINGS BY DICK:

Books

(With George Dick) *Scarlet Fever.* 1938.

Periodicals

(With George Dick) "Scarlet Fever." *Edinburgh Medical Journal* (1934): 1–13.

FURTHER READING

Books

Bailey, Martha J. "Gladys Rowena Henry Dick." *American Women in Science: A Biographical Dictionary.* Denver: ABC–CLIO, 1994, p. 86.

Rubin, Lewis P. "Gladys Rowena Henry Dick." In *Notable American Women, 1607–1950: A Biographical Dictionary.* Edited by Edward T. James. Cambridge, MA: Belknap Press, 1971, pp. 191–2.

Siegel, Patricia Joan and Kay Thomas Finley. "Gladys Rowena Henry Dick." *Women in the Scientific Search: An American Bio–bibliography, 1724–1979.* Metuchen, NJ: The Scarecrow Press, Inc., 1985, pp. 246–48.

Periodicals

"Deaths. Dick, Gladys Rowena Henry." *Journal of the American Medical Association* (December 28, 1963): 120.

"Gladys Dick, Scarlet Fever Expert, Dies." *Chicago Tribune* (August 23, 1963): 2A.

Sketch by Annette Petrusso

Amalie Dietrich
1821–1891
German naturalist

Although Amalie Dietrich was like many nineteenth century naturalists who collected specimens, she differed in her lack of formal education and the many hardships she endured to make her living. She spent 10 years in Australia and New Guinea collecting plants and mammal specimens for a natural history museum and this work contributed to knowledge of Pacific flora and fauna.

She was born Amalie Nelle in the Saxon village of Siebenlehn in 1821. Her parents, Gottlieb and Cordel Nelle, were uneducated, but they sent their children to school. Young Amalie became a voracious reader and proved to be a quick learner.

As a young woman she married Wilhelm Dietrich, a naturalist, and the couple had one daughter, Charitas. Almost from the beginning the marriage was a disaster. Wilhelm was domineering and dictatorial to both wife and daughter. He was also unfaithful. More than once during their marriage, Amalie took her child and left; often she worked as a maid to earn money. There were reconciliations, but eventually this tumultuous marriage came to an end.

Wilhelm may have been a bad husband and father, but he was a good teacher. Early in their marriage, he had taught Amalie the Latin names for various plants; he also taught her how to collect and prepare specimens. Amalie decided to parlay this meager knowledge into a career. She tried at first to collect and sell specimens. This proved an auspicious step, because she soon met a businessman named R.A. Meyer, who was keenly interested in plants. He and his family bought Amalie's collections, educated her daughter, and introduced her to Caesar Godeffroy, who was creating a museum based on the natural history of the South Pacific.

This meeting led to a 10-year stay (1863–73) in Australia and New Guinea for Dietrich. She spent her time collecting specimens of plants and mammals. Often this was not delicate work; commonly the way to get animal specimens was to shoot the animals. This was a minor problem in comparison to others Dietrich faced. She contracted a tropical illness that left her seriously ill for a long time; later, a fire destroyed much of her work. Still, she continued her studies, making remarkable progress.

When Dietrich returned to Europe, living in Hamburg, she maintained her interest and involvement in natural science. Despite her accomplishments, being a woman in a man's field of study made it difficult for her to be taken seriously. However, there were small but significant victories: Toward the end of her life, Dietrich went to Berlin, where an anthropological conference was being held. Women were not allowed to participate, but she asked a doorkeeper whether she could stand in the back of the gallery to listen. The doorkeeper mentioned her name to one of the officials, who took the unprecedented step of walking the elderly naturalist into the proceedings and introducing her to the other committee members. Dietrich died at the age of 70 in 1891.

SELECTED WRITINGS BY DIETRICH:

Books

Australische Briefe. Edited by Augustin Lodewyck. Melbourne and London: Melbourne University Press, 1943.

FURTHER READING

Books

Ogilvie, Marilyn Bailey. *Women in Science: Antiquity through the Nineteenth Century.* Cambridge: MIT Press, 1986.

Sketch by George A. Milite

Irene Diggs
1906–
American anthropologist

Irene Diggs focused her anthropological work on the comparative ethnohistorical sociology of the descendants of Africans in the Americas. Her scholarship was influenced by her work with W. E. B. DuBois, a black scholar, educator, and leader. She later wrote about him and his work with original insight because of this experience. In addition to much international research and travel, Diggs was also one of the founders of *Phylon: A Journal of Race and Culture.*

She was born Ellen Irene Diggs on April 13, 1906, in Monmouth, Illinois, to Charles Henry and Alice Diggs. She was an intelligent and imaginative child who read extensively and dreamed of travelling all over the world. Her working-class parents encouraged and supported her scholarly and worldly ambitions. After spending a year at Monmouth College on scholarship, from 1923–24, she transferred to the University of Minnesota. While at Minnesota, Diggs experienced overt racism for the first time. This experience showed Diggs that there was a need for black role models, which in turn influenced her to pursue her education further. She earned her B.A. from Minnesota in 1928.

Diggs began graduate work at Atlanta University in 1932 and also started what would become a fruitful association with W. E. B. DuBois. It was a mutually beneficial relationship. Diggs assisted DuBois in the research and publication of some of his most important writings, including *The Dusk of Dawn,* and DuBois gave Diggs freedom and support in her own developing scholarship. Also while at Atlanta, Diggs co-founded *Phylon,* a scholarly journal published by Atlanta University, which published articles on race and culture.

In the early 1940s Diggs began to fulfill her dreams of traveling. A vacation to Cuba inspired her to return there to study. She received a Roosevelt Fellowship from the Institute for International Education at the University of Havana. There she worked with Fernando Ortiz, an ethnographer with an international reputation, and learned fieldwork skills collecting information on local cultures. In 1945 she earned her Ph.D. in anthropology from the University of Havana. After graduation and the end of World War II, she spent several years traveling throughout Central and South America; researching and writing popular travel articles. Diggs spent part of 1946 in Montevideo, Uruguay, as an exchange scholar. She continued to travel and research in South America, Europe, and the Middle East. The newspaper articles she wrote about these travels were syndicated by the Associated Negro Press.

Diggs became a professor of sociology and anthropology at Morgan State University in Baltimore, Maryland, in 1947. While maintaining a heavy and varied teaching load, Diggs traveled throughout the world, both to engage in research and write travel literature. Because of her experiences in Havana, she also has contributed significant work on blacks in Central and South America, as well as the Caribbean. In the 1950s, she published a series of articles on the Brazilian phenomenon of *quilombos,* communities formed by runaway slaves. Diggs's most important publication is the book *Black Chronology,* which, as the subtitle proclaims, outlines the contribution of black people to the world from 4000 B.C. to the abolition of slavery.

Diggs was associated with a number of professional anthropological associations, including the American Anthropological Association and the American Association for the Advancement of Science. Though she retired from Morgan State in 1976, she continued to conduct research and held an emeritus professorship at the University of Maryland. In 1978, she was honored by the Association of Black Anthropologists for her many years of service as a scholar as well as mentor to black students.

SELECTED WRITINGS BY DIGGS:

Books

Black Chronology from 4000 B.C. to the Abolition of the Slave Trade. G.K. Hall & Company, 1983.

Periodicals

"Argentine Diptych: Meliton and Schimu." *Crisis* (June–July 1953).

"DuBois and Marcus Garvey." *A Current Bibliography on African Affairs* (Spring 1973).

FURTHER READING

Books

Deegan, Mary Jo, ed. "(Ellen) Irene Diggs (1906–)." *Women in Sociology: A Bio–bibliographic Source Book.* New York: Greenwood Press, 1991, pp. 124–30.

Sketch by Annette Petrusso

Allie Vibert Douglas
1894–1988
Canadian astrophysicist

Allie Vibert Douglas (Corbis/Bettmann-UPI. Reproduced by permission.)

Allie Douglas was the first Canadian woman to earn a Ph.D. in astrophysics. In addition to her scientific research, Douglas was a proponent of education for women and for public education in her field.

Born December 15, 1894, in Montreal, Canada, Allie Douglas Vibert and her brother George lived with their grandmother, Maria Bolton Pearson Douglas, in London, England, during the early years of their lives. Both their parents, John Arthur Vibert and Allie Douglas Vibert, died of Bright's Disease—the father in 1904 and the mother only a week after Douglas was born. The Vibert children returned to Canada in 1904 and lived with their mother's sister, Mina Elizabeth Douglas. The family was a very close one and in 1914, Allie and George legally changed their names to Douglas.

Despite the fact that science was not a discipline open to women at the time, Douglas's interest was keen and aided by her brother, she was able to eavesdrop on a student discussion group. She went on to graduate from Westmount High School in 1912 as valedictorian, and accepted a McGill University entrance scholarship to study mathematics and physics in the honors program.

But in 1915 the family relocated to London, where George was to be stationed during World War I. Douglas worked in the War Office's Department of Recruiting as Chief of Women Clerks, a position that would earn her the Member of the Order of the British Empire's silver cross in 1918. That same year, she began work as a registrar for Khaki University, a correspondence school, while auditing courses at the Royal College in South Kensington. Douglas returned to McGill to finish her studies and graduated with a bachelor's degree in 1920. Douglas graduated with honors, which earned her the Anne Molson Gold Medal.

Remaining at McGill for her master's of science degree, Douglas worked as a physics demonstrator while completing her thesis research, entitled "Beta Rays from Radium E." Upon graduation in 1921, Douglas won the Imperial Order Daughters of the Empire Overseas Fellowship, for which she would travel to Cavendish Laboratory at Cambridge University, bringing her aunts with her. At the Cavendish lab she worked with the Nobel Prize winning physicist Ernest Rutherford who assigned her a project researching radioactivity.

At this time Douglas became concerned that she would be unable to get her Ph.D. and become a physicist. She saw women who had passed all the requirements for a Ph.D. being denied a Cambridge degree. This was discouraging for Douglas who had taken all the Ph.D. prerequisites herself. She began taking different classes, one of which was a practical astronomy course. This class proved to be her savior academically and highlighted her true talents and interests. She resigned from Rutherford's lab and began researching stellar velocity. She provided physical proof for one of astronomer Arthur Eddington's theories about star motion and her results were submitted to the Royal Astronomical Society. In addition to this work, Douglas was analyzing pelagic (relating to the sea) sediment samples that her brother George brought back from his work as a geologist on the Antarctic expedition *Quest.* Allie and

George's findings were so impressive that Rutherford himself presented them to the Royal Society of Edinburgh.

It now seemed entirely possible for Douglas to get a Ph.D. She returned to McGill in 1923, where she lectured and researched cloud chambers until 1925 when the opportunity to study at Yerkes Observatory in Wisconsin arose. There she worked as an unpaid research assistant in return for access to the I-prism spectrograms held by Yerkes. Her research formed the basis for her Ph.D. dissertation in 1926, "Spectroscopic Absolute Magnitudes and Parallaxes of Class A Stars."

Douglas was never offered a tenured position at McGill University. Therefore, in 1939 she accepted a position as dean of women and full professor of astronomy and physics at Queen's University in Kingston, Ontario where she would remain until her retirement. At Queen's, Douglas helped many women in the sciences and published both scholarly and popular articles. An extraordinary speaker, Douglas was invited to speak by many organizations. She also attended many astronomy conventions and more meetings of the International Astronomical Union than any other Canadian astronomer. With her speaking engagements and conference participation, Douglas traveled to every country in the world except for six.

Douglas was involved with several professional organizations, including the Royal Astronomical Society, the International Astronomical Union, and the International Federation of University Women, and she served as a UNESCO delegate. Her awards include honorary doctorates from the University of Queensland, McGill University, and Queen's University. She was named a "Woman of the Century" by the National Council of Jewish Women in 1967. Douglas died on July 2, 1988. That same year, astronomers named a new planet *Vibert Douglas* in her honor.

SELECTED WRITINGS BY DOUGLAS:

Books

Meteors. Toronto: University of Toronto Press, 1932.

The Life of Arthur Stanley Eddington. London: Thomas Nelson and Sons, 1956.

FURTHER READING

Books

Shearer, Benjamin F. and Barbara S. Shearer, eds. *Notable Women in the Physical Sciences.* Westport, CT: Greenwood Press, 1997.

Other

Special Collections, Queen's University Archives.

Sketch by Helene Barker Kiser

Mary Anna (Palmer) Draper
1839–1914
American astronomer

The wife of a pioneering astronomical photographer Henry Draper, Mary Anna Palmer Draper collaborated with her husband throughout their marriage. After his death, Palmer endowed the Harvard College Observatory, enabling their work to be carried on by a new generation of astronomers.

Born in Stonington, Connecticut, in 1839, Draper was the daughter of Mary Ann (Suydam) and Courtlandt Palmer. Little is known of her early life, prior to her 1867 marriage to Henry Draper. However her father, a merchant and real estate investor, left his daughter and three sons a large fortune at his death in 1874.

Henry Draper was a physician and professor of chemistry and physiology at the University of the City of New York (later New York University). He also was an early experimental photographer and an amateur astronomer. He stimulated his wife's interest in astronomy and they became collaborators. At the time of their marriage, Draper was constructing a large telescope at his observatory at Hastings–on–Hudson, New York, near their summer home in Dobbs Ferry. Here, the Drapers made the first photographs of the spectrum of a star, showing the unique pattern of bands and lines created when the light from a star is passed through a prism. For the next fifteen years, Draper assisted her husband in all of his observations, photography, and laboratory work. In 1878 they traveled to Rawlins, Wyoming, to observe a solar eclipse.

The Drapers spent their winters in New York City, where they maintained a laboratory connected to their Madison Avenue home and where Anna Draper housed her extensive collection of archeological artifacts. Intelligent and talented, she presided over New York scientific society.

Following her husband's death in 1882, Draper abandoned the idea of continuing her astronomical research. However after visiting the Harvard College Observatory, where astronomers were building on the Drapers' pioneering photography of star spectra, she donated some of her husband's astronomical instruments to the Observatory and endowed the Henry Draper Memorial to continue the research. This grant enabled the Observatory to undertake a massive program that supported the work of many women. Among these women astronomers were **Williamina Fleming**, **Annie Jump Cannon**, **Henrietta Leavitt**, and Draper's niece, **Antonia Maury**. Draper visited the observatory regularly, following the detailed progress of the research and personally examining the star spectra.

Draper also endowed the Henry Draper Medal of the National Academy of Sciences, to be awarded for original research in astronomical physics, and she was instrumental in the establishment of the Mount Wilson Observatory in California. She turned her laboratory into a scientific lecture and exhibition hall and continued to be at the center of scientific events until her death of pneumonia in 1914.

FURTHER READING

Books

Wright, Helen. "Mary Anna Palmer Draper." In *Notable American Women 1607–1950: A Biographical Dictionary.* Edited by Edward T. James, Janet Wilson James, and Paul W. Boyer. Vol. 1. Cambridge: Harvard University Press, 1971.

Periodicals

Cannon, Annie J. "Mrs. Henry Draper." *Science* 41 (1915): 380–82.

Sketch by Margaret Alic

Mildred Spiewak Dresselhaus
1930–
American physicist

Mildred Dresselhaus (Photograph by Rick Wilking. Reuters/ Archive Photos. Reproduced by permission.)

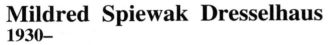

Born during the Depression to a poor immigrant family, Mildred S. Dresselhaus possessed a natural intelligence and love of science that brought her recognition in the field of solid state physics. She has contributed a great deal of new knowledge about the electronic properties of many materials, particularly semimetals such as graphite, and was the recipient of the National Medal of Science in 1990. Dresselhaus is currently Institute Professor of Electrical Engineering and Physics at Massachusetts Institute of Technology, as well as consultant to Lawrence Livermore National Laboratory in California and Treasurer of the National Academy of Sciences. Her public service includes work on behalf of the National Research Council and the National Science Foundation.

Mildred Spiewak Dresselhaus was born on November 11, 1930, in Brooklyn, New York; her father was a journalist. As a child, she worked in sweatshops and factories to help with family expenses. At age eleven, she spent one year teaching a mentally retarded child how to read and write. In helping the child, she found her first insight into her future—in education. Dresselhaus' ambition then was to become an elementary school teacher. Her other love was music, and she and her talented brother received free violin lessons from philanthropic organizations which served as an introduction to the world of education.

Dresselhaus' parents encouraged her natural love of learning, and she studied diligently for an entrance exam for Hunter College High School—a girls' preparatory school associated with Hunter College in New York. She not only passed the exam, she did so with a perfect score in mathematics. Dresselhaus struggled at the school initially because her prior education was meager. She also had a difficult time socially among upper-middle-class schoolmates and their families. But her drive, intelligence and wit carried her through these early challenges. She excelled in high school and, with the help of a state scholarship, entered Hunter College, where she was graduated with highest honors in 1951. By that time, she was preparing for a career in physics.

Earns Scholarship to Cambridge

Dresselhaus then accepted a Fulbright Fellowship and performed graduate studies at Newnham, the women's college of Cambridge University. After returning from England, where she had benefitted from her studies as well as the new friendships she formed, she earned a master of science degree in physics from Radcliffe College in Massachusetts. Upon her graduation from Radcliffe in 1953, Dresselhaus entered the prestigious doctoral program in physics at the University of Chicago. Solid state physics, the specialty which addresses matter in a condensed state, was in its infancy. The transistor had just been developed, and pioneers in the field were researching practical applications of semiconductors. In her graduate research, Dresselhaus explored the activities of superconductors. She found that some materials are excellent conductors of current at extremely low temperatures. She wrote two papers, "Magnetic Field Dependence of High-Frequency Penetration into a Super-Conductor" and "Magnetic Field Dependence of the Surface Impedance of Superconducting Tin," in 1958 and 1959, respectively, which were significant contributions to an area that few had begun to investigate.

Soon after receiving her doctorate degree, she married a colleague, solid state physicist Gene Dresselhaus. In 1958, she accepted a postdoctoral appointment as a National Science Foundation Fellow at Cornell University, while he became a junior faculty member there. Two years later, following the birth of her first child, Dresselhaus accepted a staff position at Lincoln Laboratory, a part of Massachusetts Institute of Technology that at that time specialized in semiconductors. Her husband also obtained a position there. Around that same time, a revolutionary development occurred in physics: the invention of integrated circuits, which would later be used in computers, automobile electronics, and entertainment systems. Dresselhaus began focusing on this area, examining the transport of electrons in high magnetic fields.

Studies Superconductors and Semimetals

While at Lincoln Laboratory, where she remained until 1967, Dresselhaus resumed her study of low temperature superconductors. She researched the behavior of various materials at temperatures as low as negative 250 degrees Celsius—the point at which hydrogen gas liquifies. She inquired into why semiconductors carry electricalcurrent at room temperature, and applied what she discovered to further study. Dresselhaus also embarked on a study of semimetals—materials such as arsenic and graphite. These semimetals were shown to have properties in common with semiconductors and even superconductors. Dresselhaus' work on the structure of graphite(a form of pure carbon) was extremely original and earned her the respect of her colleagues. Apart from her academic life, Dresselhaus had three more children during the 1960s.

Dresselhaus was named Abby Rockefeller Mauze Visiting Professor in 1967, and the following year received a full professorship at MIT. She served as Associate Department Head of Electrical Science and Engineering from 1972 to 1974, and Director of the Center of Material Science and Engineering from 1977 to 1983. In 1973, she became permanent holder of the Abby Rockefeller Mauze Chair, and in 1983, she was named Professor of Physics. Two years later, she was named Institute Professor, a lifetime honor conferred on no more than twelve active professors at MIT. Beginning in the 1980s she and her associates investigated the properties of carbon, finding it to harbor hollow clusters, each containing sixty atoms. Today scientists are experimenting with these clusters—known as Buckminster Fullerenes, or "Buckyballs," on account of their shape—for their potential use as a delivery system for drugs, and as an extremely strong form of wire tubing.

Champions Women in Science

The challenges Dresselhaus faced as a prominent physicist and mother of four children caused her to become an advocate of women scientists. When her children were small, she had met with a lack of support from her male colleagues, and as a result she worked with other female colleagues at MIT to expand the admission opportunities for women at the Institute. She also began a Women's Forum to explore solutions for difficulties faced by working women. Her initiative in this forum led to her appointment to the Committee on the Education and Employment of Women in Science and Engineering, part of the National Research Council's Commission on Human Resources.

Concurrent with her work at MIT, Dresselhaus has held numerous advisory and service positions. She was a member of the National Academy of Sciences' Executive Committee of Physics and Math Sciences from 1975 to 1978. She chaired the Steering Committee Evaluation Panels of the National Bureau of Standards from 1978 to 1983. She served as President of the American Physical Society in 1984. She chaired the English Section of the National Academy of Sciences from 1987 to 1990, and is a member of the National Academy of Engineering, as well as a senior member of the Society of Women Engineers.

Dresselhaus has received many honors. In 1977, she received the Society of Women Engineers Annual Achievement Award "for significant contributions in teaching and research in solid state electronics and materials engineering." In addition, she was a visiting Professor at the University of Campinas in Brazil in 1971, and at the Technion Israel Institute of Technology in Haifa. She also was Hund–Klemm Lecturer at the Max Planck Institute in Stuttgart, Germany, and received the Ann Achievement Award from the English Societies of New England, both in 1988. In 1990, Dresselhaus was awarded the prestigious National Medal of Science.

Her lifetime of achievements in the field of solid state physics might have surprised some who knew of her early circumstances, but Dresselhaus has no regrets. "All the hardships I encountered," she has said, as quoted in Iris Noble's *Contemporary Women Scientists of America,* "provided me with the determination, capacity for hard work, efficiency, and a positive outlook on life that have been so helpful to me in realizing my professional career."

SELECTED WRITINGS BY DRESSELHAUS:

Books

(With Gene Dresselhaus, K. Sugihara, I. L. Spain, and H. A. Goldberg) *Graphite Fibers and Filaments.* Springer-Verlag (Berlin), 1988.

(With G. Dresselhaus and P. C. Eklund) *Physical Properties of Fullerenes.* Academic Press, 1993.

FURTHER READING

Books

Noble, Iris. *Contemporary Women Scientists of America.* Julian Messner, pp. 138–51.

Periodicals

Lear's (March 1994): 56–61, 82–83.

Uglow, Jennifer S., ed. *The Continuum Dictionary of Women's Biography.* New York: Continuum, 1989.

Sketch by Karen Withem

Jeanne Dumée
fl. 1680
French astronomer

Jeanne Dumée was born in Paris in the seventeenth century and was widowed by the age of 17. Interested in astronomy since she was a child, she pursued studies in this field following her husband's death. She focused on the theories of Nicolaus Copernicus (1473–1543), the Polish astronomer who advanced the notion that the Sun, and not the Earth, was the center of the solar system and that the rotation of the Earth accounted for what appeared to be the movement of heavenly bodies viewed from Earth. In 1687, she published a book–length work entitled *Entretiens sur l'opinion de Copernic touchant la mobilité de la terre,* which sought to explain the Copernican system. The book included an apologia in which Dumée pardoned herself for writing on subject matter usually not touched upon by women. She went on to explain that she wished to prove to other women "that they are not incapable of study, if they wish to make the effort, because between the brain of a woman and that of a man there is no difference." She also noted that she did not seek to defend Copernicus and his theories but, rather, to discuss the arguments used by students of Copernicus in defense of their work.

In setting forth these arguments, Dumée concluded that the idea of a celestial body circumnavigating a stationary Earth was impossible. Her work was critically lauded for its clear explanation of the "three motions of the Earth." *Entretiens* was never published in its entirety. It is mentioned, however, in an edition of the *Journal des scavans* and the manuscript is archived at the Bibliothèque Nationale in Paris.

FURTHER READING

Books

Ogilvie, Marilyn Bailey, *Women in Science: Antiquity through the Nineteenth Century.* Cambridge, MA: MIT Press, 1993.

Sketch by Kristin Palm

Helen M. Dyer
1895–1998
American biochemist

The word "pioneer" is often overused when describing scientists, but Helen Dyer's invaluable work as a cancer researcher was truly pioneering. Her research had a direct impact on the treatment of cancer and other diseases, and she was the first person to compile an index on tumor chemotherapy. In addition to her research work, she was also a dedicated teacher who strove to inspire her students in the science of biochemistry. Dyer knew from personal experience the importance of being inspired by teachers; two of her high school teachers encouraged her to pursue a career in science.

The youngest of four children, Helen Marie Dyer was born in Washington, D.C., on May 26, 1895, to Joseph Edwin and Florence Robertson Dyer. She attended public schools, where she excelled both as a student and as an athlete. Despite her talent as a science student, she had no strong leaning toward a scientific course of study. It was on the recommendation of two teachers that she attended Goucher College in Baltimore, where she majored in biology and minored in physiology.

Dyer was planning to go to China to teach biology after her graduation from Goucher, but she changed her plans when the United States entered the First World War. She went home to Washington and did war-related work for the American Red Cross and the U.S. Civil Service Commission. In 1919, she took a position at Mount Holyoke College as an instructor in physiology. She enjoyed her work there and was able to take courses in chemistry. She soon realized that she would need a graduate degree if she wanted to move ahead.

Embarks on Career in Cancer Research

In 1920 Dyer returned once more to Washington, planning to do graduate work at George Washington University. Initially, however, she took a position at the Hygienic Laboratory of the U.S. Public Health Service. Working with pharmacologist Carl Voegtlin in the lab's chemotherapy section, Dyer studied the effects of arsenic-based compounds in fighting diseases such as syphilis and cancer. Dyer and Voegtlin also studied the effects of lead-based compounds on tumors. Their work on establishing the effectiveness and toxicity of these substances were instrumental in the later development of chemotherapy drugs.

In 1927, Dyer at last began her graduate work at George Washington, earning her master's degree in 1929. She stayed on for her doctorate, working with Vincent du Vigneaud (who would later win a Nobel Prize) on sulfur compounds. She received her Ph.D. in 1935 and remained at George Washington for seven years as an assistant professor of biochemistry. She was known as a thorough teacher, but she also managed to continue her research work.

Dyer made a breakthrough discovery in 1938 when she synthesized a form of the amino acid methionine, which had medical and nutritional uses. Unfortunately, she found that this synthesized substance was in fact toxic. Her discovery was nonetheless important, because it helped researchers better understand the composition of amino acids. Dyer's research had an indirect influence on the later development of sulfa drugs.

Dyer left George Washington in 1942 to work again with Voegtlin, who was now head of the National Cancer Institute. Over the next several years, she made a number of important discoveries about the role of vitamins and minerals in the development and treatment of cancer. She also developed new methods of isolating proteins found in tumors.

Compiles Groundbreaking Cancer Index

In 1949, Dyer put together the first comprehensive index of tumor chemotherapy. This was a critically important achievement, because it gave researchers information on chemical treatments from earliest times to the present, and also described more than 5,000 therapeutic tests. It also included a comprehensive index on available literature. The National Cancer Institute regarded Dyer's index as one of its most important tools in developing its cancer chemotherapy program.

Over the next several years Dyer worked with other scientists at the Institute to determine the effects of even more substances on cancer. Her work resulted in an increasingly better understanding about the role of nutrition in cancer treatment. Dyer's achievements were recognized by both her alma maters; Goucher gave her an award in 1954 and George Washington in 1958. (Goucher later awarded her an honorary doctorate.) In 1962, Dyer was awarded the American Chemical Society's prestigious Garvan Medal.

Dyer retired from the Institute in 1965, but remained active in research for a number of years thereafter. From 1965 to 1967 she was a research biochemist with the Federation of American Societies for Experimental Biology. In that capacity, she compiled data that was used by the U.S. Environmental Protection Agency. Throughout her career and into retirement she was also active with the Goucher Alumni Association and also with her local church. She died in Washington D.C. on September 20, 1998, not long after her 103rd birthday.

SELECTED WRITINGS BY DYER:

Books

Dyer, Helen M. *An Index of Tumor Chemotherapy: A Tabulated Compilation of Data from the Literature on Clinical and Experimental Investigation.* Washington, D.C.: Federal Security Agency, Public Health Service, 1949.

FURTHER READING

Books

O'Neill, Lois Decker, ed. *The Women's Book of World Records and Achievements.* New York: Anchor Press/Doubleday, 1979.

Shearer, Benjamin F. and Barbara S, Shearer, eds. *Notable Women in the Physical*Westport, Conn.: Greenwood Press, 1997.

Periodicals

Roscher, Nina M. and Chinh K. Nguyen. "Helen M. Dyer, A Pioneer in Cancer Research." *Journal of Chemical Education* 63 (1986): pp. 253–5.

Sketch by George A. Milite

E

Sylvia A Earle (AP/Wide World Photos. Reproduced by permission.)

Sylvia Alice Earle
1935–
American marine biologist and oceanographer

Sylvia A. Earle is a former chief scientist of the National Oceanic and Atmospheric Administration (NOAA) and a leading American oceanographer. She was among the first underwater explorers to make use of modern self–contained underwater breathing apparatus (SCUBA) gear, and identified many new species of marine life. With her former husband, Graham Hawkes, Earle designed and built a submersible craft that could dive to unprecedented depths of 3,000 feet.

Sylvia Alice (Reade) Earle was born in Gibbstown, New Jersey on August 30, 1935, the daughter of Lewis Reade and Alice Freas (Richie) Earle. Both parents had an affinity for the outdoors and encouraged her love of nature after the family moved to the west coast of Florida. As Earle explained to *Scientific American,* "I wasn't shown frogs with the attitude 'yuk,' but rather my mother would show my brothers and me how beautiful they are and how fascinating it was to look at their gorgeous golden eyes." However, Earle pointed out, while her parents totally supported her interest in biology, they also wanted her to get her teaching credentials and learn to type, "just in case."

She enrolled at Florida State University and received her Bachelor of Science degree in the spring of 1955. That fall she entered the graduate program at Duke University and obtained her master's degree in botany the following year. The Gulf of Mexico became a natural laboratory for Earle's work. Her master's dissertation, a detailed study of algae in the Gulf, is a project she still follows. She has collected more than 20,000 samples. "When I began making collections in the Gulf, it was a very different body of water than it is now—the habitats have changed. So I have a very interesting baseline," she noted in *Scientific American.*

In 1966, Earle received her Ph.D. from Duke University and immediately accepted a position as resident director of the Cape Haze Marine Laboratories in Sarasota, Florida. The following year, she moved to Massachusetts to accept dual roles as research scholar at the Radcliffe Institute and research fellow at the Farlow Herbarium, Harvard University, where she was named researcher in 1975. Earle moved to San Francisco in 1976 to become a research biologist at and curator of the California Academy of Sciences. That same year, she also was named a fellow in botany at the Natural History Museum, University of California, Berkeley.

Although her academic career could have kept her totally involved, her first love was the sea and the life within it. In 1970, Earle and four other oceanographers lived in an underwater chamber for fourteen days as part of the government–funded Tektite II Project, designed to study undersea habitats. Fortunately, technology played a major role in Earle's future. A self–contained underwater breathing apparatus had been developed in part by Jacques Cousteau as recently as 1943, and refined during the time Earle was involved in her scholarly research. SCUBA equipment was not only a boon to recreational divers, but it also dramatically changed the study of marine biology. Earle was one of the first researchers to don a mask and oxygen tank and observe the various forms of plant and animal habitats beneath the sea, identifying many new species of each. She called her discovery of undersea dunes off the Bahama Islands "a simple Lewis and Clark kind of observation." But, she said in *Scientific American,* "the presence of dunes was a significant insight into the formation of the area."

Creates Deep-Sea Technology

Though Earle set the unbelievable record of freely diving to a depth of 1,250 feet, there were serious depth limitations to SCUBA diving. To study deep–sea marine life would require the assistance of a submersible craft that could dive far deeper. Earle and her former husband, British–born engineer Graham Hawkes, founded Deep Ocean Technology, Inc., and Deep Ocean Engineering, Inc., in 1981, to design and build submersibles. Using a paper napkin, Earle and Hawkes rough–sketched the design for a submersible they called *Deep Rover,* which would serve as a viable tool for biologists. "In those days we were dreaming of going to thirty–five thousand feet," she told *Discover* magazine. "The idea has always been that scientists couldn't be trusted to drive a submersible by themselves because they'd get so involved in their work they'd run into things." *Deep Rover* was built and continues to operate as a mid–water machine in ocean depths ranging 3,000 feet.

In 1990, Earle was named the first woman to serve as chief scientist at the National Oceanic and Atmospheric Administration (NOAA), the agency that conducts underwater research, manages fisheries, and monitors marine spills. She left the position after eighteen months because she felt that she could accomplish more working independently of the government.

Earle, who has logged more than 6,000 hours under water, is the first to decry America's lack of research money being spent on deep–sea studies, noting that of the world's five deep–sea manned submersibles (those capable of diving to 20,000 feet or more), the U.S. has only one, the *Sea Cliff.* "That's like having one jeep for all of North America," she said in *Scientific American.* In 1993, Earle worked with a team of Japanese scientists to develop the equipment to send first a remote, then a manned submersible to 36,000 feet. "They have money from their government," she told *Scientific American.* "They do what we do not: they really make a substantial commitment to ocean technology and science." Earle also plans to lead the $10 million deep ocean engineering project, Ocean Everest, that would take her to a similar depth.

In addition to publishing numerous scientific papers on marine life, Earle is a devout advocate of public education regarding the importance of the oceans as an essential environmental habitat. She is currently the president and chief executive officer of Deep Ocean Technology and Deep Ocean Engineering in Oakland, California, as well as the coauthor of *Exploring the Deep Frontier: The Adventure of Man in the Sea.*

SELECTED WRITINGS BY EARLE:

Books

(With Al Giddings) *Exploring the Deep Frontier: The Adventure of Man in the Sea.* National Geographic Press, 1980.

FURTHER READING

Periodicals

Brownlee, Shannon. "Explorers of the Dark Frontiers." *Discover* (February 1986): 60–67.

Holloway, Marguerite. "Fire in Water." *Scientific American* (April 1992): 37–40.

Sketch by Benedict A. Leerburger

Annie J. Easley
1933–
American computer scientist

Annie Easley was a key member of the National Aeronautics and Space Administration team (NASA) that developed computer software for the Centaur, a high–energy rocket used to launch space vehicles and communication satellites.

Easley was born in Birmingham, Alabama. She attended Xavier University in New Orleans and worked as a substitute teacher in Jefferson County, Alabama, before moving to Ohio. In 1955, Easley joined the staff of NASA's Lewis Research Center in Cleveland. At that time, the United States was on the verge of the space age, and a tense competition with the former Soviet Union had just begun. The Soviet Union dedicated much of its resources—including many of its most capable scientists—to the race for space. But support in the United States for the fledgling space program was not as strong; Americans were dismayed by military action in Korea and reluctant to continue in the role of international guardian of democracy. They were also disturbed by the allegations of Communism that had been part of the much–publicized McCarthy hearings. Most people focused their efforts on striving to succeed in the post–World War II economy and were uninterested in visionary quests.

The mood changed abruptly in 1957, when the Soviet Union launched Sputnik, the first satellite to be placed in orbit around the Earth. American pride was pricked (and American fears of a possible Soviet military advantage were awakened) by the feat. In that year, the Air Force studied a proposal for a high–energy space booster with a new propulsion system that mixed liquid hydrogen and oxygen. Dubbed the Centaur, the booster's development was authorized by the United States government in 1958.

Easley was assigned to the Flight Software Section at the Lewis Research Center. The space race pushed forward the development of computer hardware and software because complex, miniaturized systems were required to monitor and run space vehicles. Easley developed and helped implement computer programs used to determine solar wind and solve numerous energy monitoring and conversion problems. Easley also worked on projects related to energy while at Lewis. She studied the life use of storage batteries that powered electric utility vehicles and the efficiency of energy conversion systems. While at the Lewis Research Center, Easley attended Cleveland State University and completed a bachelor of science degree in mathematics in 1977.

Easley's work with NASA's Centaur developed the technological foundations for today's shuttle launches, as well as for the launches of communication, weather, and military satellites. Easley retired in 1991, but her work contributed to the 1997 flight to Saturn of the Cassini—launched on its way by the Centaur.

SELECTED WRITINGS BY EASLEY:

Other

"Effect of Turbulent Mixing on Average Fuel Temperatures in a Gas–Core Nuclear Rocket Engine." *NASA–TN–D–4882* (November 1968).

"Performance and Operational Economics Estimates for a Coal Gasification Combined–Cycle Cogeneration Powerplant." *NASA Technical Memo 82729* (March 1982).

FURTHER READING

Books

Sammons, Vivian O. *Blacks in Science and Medicine.* New York: Hemisphere Publishing Company, 1990.

Other

Brown, Mitchell C. *Faces of Science: African Americans in the Sciences* http://www.lib.lsu.edu/lib/chem/display/easley.html

NASA *Centaur: America's Workhorse in Space* http://www.lerc.nasa.gov/WWW/PAO/html/centaur.htm

Sketch by A. Mullig

Alice Eastwood
1859–1953
Canadian-born American botanist

Alice Eastwood (Special Collections Library/California Academy of Sciences. Reproduced by permission.)

Alice Eastwood's life was her work as a systematic botanist, specializing in flowering plants indigenous to the California coast and Colorado Rocky Mountains. Despite a limited formal education, Eastwood's position as curator of botany at the California Academy of Sciences spanned 50 years and established the Academy's vast botanical collections. Eastwood eagerly collected and classified area plant species. She passionately shared her botanical knowledge through her work with clubs and her journal and book publications. Her many accomplishments did not go unnoticed in her lifetime.

Alice Eastwood was born to Eliza Jane (Gowdey) and Colin Skinner Eastwood, on January 19, 1859, in Toronto, Canada. She was the eldest of three children. Her mother died when Eastwood was six, and she and her siblings were sent to live with relatives while their father struggled financially. For a period of time, Eastwood lived with her uncle, William Eastwood, a doctor, and it was during this period that her interest in flora was piqued. Eastwood was educated at the Oshawa convent near Toronto, where a like–minded priest also encouraged her budding curiosity in plants. At age 14, Eastwood rejoined her father in Denver, Colorado. She graduated valedictorian from the East Denver High School in 1879, despite having to continually work to support her family. Though Eastwood's formal education ended after her high school graduation, she continued to study botany on her own.

Because of her family's financial difficulties, Eastwood was compelled to teach high school in Denver for the next 11 years. While teaching, she continued to collect and identify plant species in the nearby Rocky Mountains. By saving her money, she was able to expand her library of botany texts. Eventually, she became locally recognized for her growing botanical knowledge and collection. Such recognition led to the recommendation that she guide the famous naturalist Alfred Russel Wallace, who was visiting the area, on an expedition of Gray's Peak.

In 1890, after she and her father made a modest profit in Denver real estate, Eastwood was finally able to leave her teaching position and pursue botany full time. She visited San Francisco, California, where she met Katharine Brandegree, the curator of botany at the California Academy of Sciences. Brandegree hired Eastwood to contribute to their botanical magazine, *Zoe*, and work in the Academy's herbarium.

Eastwood returned to Denver briefly, where she finished her self–published book, *A Popular Flora of Denver, Colorado* (1893). In 1892, Brandegree offered Eastwood an assistantship position at the Academy, which she accepted. During this time, Eastwood founded the California Botanical Club, an organization in which she would remain active for many years. Eastwood became the editor of *Zoe* and the curator when Brandegree and her husband left the Academy in 1893. Eastwood continued to improved the Academy's collection through her own collecting and acquisition efforts. Eastwood published *A Handbook of the Trees of California* in 1905.

When an earthquake hit San Francisco on April 18, 1906, Eastwood chose to save as much of the Academy's botanical specimens as she was able, rather than save any personal possessions from the fires that followed. Eastwood later went on to rebuild the collection she had so carefully organized, visiting and sometimes working at other collections and herbariums in the United States and Europe. Between 1912, when the Academy reopened with Eastwood back as curator, and her retirement in 1950, Eastwood collected some 340,000 specimens and built up the Academy's library of botanical literature. The herbarium is now officially known as the Alice Eastwood Herbarium of the California Academy of Sciences.

In 1932, she founded a forum for botanical research called the *Leaflets of Western Botany* with her assistant John Thomas Howell. Eastwood is credited with over 300 published articles on botany. Such a prolific bibliography garnered her an international reputation. Because she lacked a university education, Eastwood refused all honorary degrees offered to her. In 1950, at the age of 91, the Seventh International Botanical Congress in Stockholm, Sweden, asked Eastwood to serve as their honorary president. Active until the end, Eastwood died of cancer in San Francisco on October 30, 1953. She was 95 years old.

SELECTED WRITINGS BY EASTWOOD:

Books

Eastwood, Alice. *A Popular Flora of Denver, Colorado*. San Francisco: Zoe Publishing Co, 1893.

FURTHER READING

Books

Bailey, Martha J. "Alice Eastwood." In *American Women in Science: A Biographical Dictionary*. Denver: ABC–CLIO, Inc., 1994, pp. 95–96.

Bonta, Marcia Myers. "Alice Eastwood: Grand Old Botanist of the Academy." In *Women in the Field: America's Pioneering Women Naturalists*. College Station, TX: Texas A & M University Press, 1991, pp. 93–102.

Ewan, Joseph. "Alice Eastwood." In *Notable American Women, The Modern Period: A Biographical Dictionary*. Barbara Sicherman and Carol Hurd Green, eds. Cambridge, MA: The Belknap Press of Harvard University Press, 1980, pp. 216–17.

Ogilvie, Marilyn Bailey. "Alice Eastwood." In *Women in Science: Antiquity through the Nineteenth Century*. Cambridge: MIT Press, 1986, pp. 79–80.

Other

Eastwood, Alice. *Science Magazine* publication of a letter discribing the 1906 San Francisco earthquake. (May 7, 1906). http://www.kqed.org/fromKQED/Cell/Calhist/afterstory.html (October 5, 1997).

Sketch by Annette Petrusso

Tilly Edinger
1897–1967
German-born American paleontologist

Tilly Edinger is credited as one of the originators of the field of paleoneurology, the study of the brain through fossil remains. She conducted the first systematic studies of the brain in fossil vertebrates, which led her to challenge the then popular conception of evolution as a unilinear process modeled upon the eighteenth- and nineteenth-century concept of a chain of being. Edinger made an important contribution to the notion of a branching process of evolution that is generally accepted today.

Tilly Edinger was born Johanna Gabrielle Ottelie in Frankfurt am Main, Germany, November 13, 1897, to independently wealthy parents, Ludwig E. and Anna Goldschmidt Edinger. She was the youngest of three children. Her parents were both prominent citizens of Frankfurt. Her father was a respected medical researcher who was key in developing the field of comparative neurology, and had a street, Edingerstrasse, named in his honor. Her mother, from a line of bankers, was active in social welfare groups, and was honored by the town with a bust in the town park. Edinger grew up with a respect for geology and comparative neurology, both of which were to influence her own career in the sciences.

Edinger attended the Universities of Heidelberg and Munich from 1916 to 1918. In 1921, she received her doctorate in natural philosophy from University of Frankfurt, for studies in geology, zoology, and psychology, with her dissertation on the cranium (brain) of the fossil reptile Nothosaurus. She then worked as a research assistant in paleontology there, from the year she earned her degree until 1927.

Edinger's remaining years in Germany—1927 to 1938—were spent as the curator of fossil vertebrates at the Senckenberg Museum in Frankfurt. Edinger received no pay for this work. She published the groundbreaking study, *Die fossilen Gehirne* ("Fossil Brains") in 1929. Because of the increasingly hostile climate in Germany with the rise of the Nazis, Edinger, who was Jewish, left Germany in May of 1939 to go to London, where she worked as a translator.

Re–examines Evolution

Edinger came to the United States in 1940 and became a naturalized citizen in 1945. At that time, Harvard University had set aside funds to provide employment for displaced European scholars. Edinger took advantage of this opportunity; she settled in Massachusetts and joined the staff of Harvard's Museum of Comparative Zoology as a research associate. She continued her studies of the fossil brain, and began to challenge the commonly held notion that evolution consisted of a linear progression from "lower" animals, such as rats and mice, up to the "highest" creatures, human beings. Edinger instead developed and advanced the idea of evolution as a complex branching process. She left Harvard to serve as an instructor in zoology at Wellesley College from 1944 to 1945. Then she resumed her work at Harvard, producing the major work, *Evolution of the Horse Brain,* and becoming a full–fledged research paleontologist, both in 1948. She would remain at the Museum for the rest of her life.

Edinger established the need for direct study of fossil brains by using casts made from the cranial cavities of mammals, since brain tissue cannot fossilize. Casts of the inside of the skull allow experts to reconstruct a reasonable facsimile of the brain, which ultimately impacted the study of the evolution of intelligence. Edinger's studies of the enlargement of the forebrain in the horse established that the rate of evolution varies for different lineages, and that as mammals adapt to different environments, the parts of the brain interact differently. Edinger's was the first strong voice in favor of a branching model of evolution, and the prototype she advanced is generally accepted today.

Both the Guggenheim Foundation and the American Association of University Women assisted Edinger in her work through fellowships. She received many honorary degrees, including doctorates from Wellesley College in 1950, the University of Giessen in 1957, and the University of Frankfurt in 1964. From 1963 to 1964 she also served as president of the Society of Vertebrate Paleontology.

Edinger died on May 27, 1967, after being struck by an automobile near her home in Cambridge the day before.

SELECTED WRITINGS BY EDINGER:

Books

Die fossilen Gehirne, Verlag, 1929.

Evolution of the Horse Brain, Geological Society of America, Memoir 25, 1948.

(With A. S. Romer, N. E. Wright, and R. Frank) *Bibliography of Fossil Vertebrates, Exclusive of North America, 1509–1927.* 2 vols. Geological Society of America, Memoir 87, 1962.

Periodicals

"Paleoneurology, 1804–1966: An Annotated Bibliography," *Advances in Anatomy, Embryology and Cell Biology* 49 (1975):parts 1–6.

FURTHER READING

Books

Gould, S. J. *Notable American Women: The Modern Period.* Edited by B. Sicherman and C. H. Green. Cambridge: Harvard University Press, 1980, pp. 218–219.

Kass–Simon, G., and P. Farnes, *Women of Science: Righting the Record.* Bloomington: Indiana University Press, 1990, p. 60.

Periodicals

Romer, A. S. "Tilly Edinger." *Society of Vertebrate Paleontology News Bulletin* no. 81 (1967): 51–53.

Sketch by Sharon F. Suer

Cecile Hoover Edwards
1926–
American nutritional researcher

Cecile Hoover Edwards, a nutritional researcher and educator, devoted her career to improving the nutrition and well–being of disadvantaged people. In recognition of her achievements, she was cited by the National Council of Negro Women for outstanding contributions to science and by the Illinois House of Representatives for "determined devotion to the cause of eliminating poverty through the creation of a quality environment."

Edwards was born in East St. Louis, Illinois, on October 26, 1926. Her mother, Annie Jordan, was a former schoolteacher and her father, Ernest Hoover, was an insurance manager. Edwards enrolled at Tuskegee Institute, the college made famous by Booker T. Washington and George Washington Carver, at age fifteen, and entered a home economics program with minors in nutrition and chemistry. "I knew from the first day that I had no interest in dietetics," Edwards told Laura Newman in an interview. "My real interest was in improving nutrition through research." Edwards was awarded a bachelor of science degree with honors from Tuskegee in 1946. With a fellowship from Swift and Co. she conducted chemical analyses of an animal source of protein. In 1947, she earned a master's degree in chemistry from Tuskegee. Edwards received a Ph.D. in nutrition from Iowa State University in 1950. Edwards's doctoral dissertation was a study of methionine, an essential amino acid that she said has "not only the good things needed to synthesize protein, but also has sulfur, which can be given to other compounds and be easily released." Edwards wrote at least twenty papers on methionine.

Appointed Head of Tuskegee's Food and Nutrition Department

After completing her doctorate, Edwards returned to Tuskegee as a faculty member and a research associate of the Carver Foundation, remaining there for six years. "Staying in nutrition at Tuskegee seemed like an opportunity," said Edwards. "I felt obligated to pay back the opportunity Tuskegee had given me." In 1952 she became head of Tuskegee's department of foods and nutrition. Edwards's nutritional research later expanded to studies of the amino acid composition of food, the utilization of protein from vegetarian diets, and the planning of well–balanced and nutritious diets, especially for low–income and disadvantaged populations in the United States and developing countries.

Develops Human Ecology Curriculum at Howard University

Designing a new curriculum for the School of Human Ecology at Howard University, Washington, D.C., in the 1970s was a high point of Edwards's career. Just before she came to Howard, in 1969, Arthur Jensen had argued in his paper, "How Much Can We Boost IQ," that blacks were inherently inferior, and that providing education, nutrition, and other resources could not bring them equality. Disproving the Jensen hypothesis became a major goal for Edwards. Howard's School of Human Ecology conducted research and evaluated work in providing resources for low–income people so that they could help themselves. It taught parenting, childcare, nutrition, budgeting, job skills, and other skills useful in overcoming obstacles. In 1974, Edwards was appointed Dean of the School of Human Ecology, a position she held until 1987.

In 1985 Edwards became director of a five–year project sponsored by the National Institute of Child Health and Human Development to study the nutritional, medical, psychological, socioeconomic, and lifestyle factors which influence pregnancy outcomes in low–income women. In 1994 she served as editor of the *Journal of Nutrition* May supplement on "African American Women and Their Pregnancies." A humanitarian and prolific writer who published numerous scientific papers, Edwards helped to establish a family resource development program in her birthplace, East St. Louis, Illinois.

SELECTED WRITINGS BY EDWARDS:

Books

(Editor) *Current Knowledge of the Relationships of Selected Nutrients, Alcohol, Tobacco, and Drug Use, and Other Factors to Pregnancy Outcomes,* School of Human Ecology, Howard University, 1988.

(Editor with others) *Human Ecology: Interactions of Man with His Environments,* Kendall–Hunt, 1991.

Periodicals

"Utilization of Methionine by the Adult Rat, Distribution of the alpha–carbon of DL–methionine–2–C14 in Tissues, Tissue Fractions, Expired Carbon Dioxide, Blood and Excreta." *Journal of Nutrition* 72 (1960): 185.

(With L. K. Booker, C. H. Rumph, and S. N. Ganapathy) "Utilization of Wheat by Adult Man: Vitamins and Minerals." *American Journal of Clinical Nutrition* 24 (1971): 547.

"Low Income Black Families: Strategies for Survival in the 1980s." *Journal of Negro Education* 51 (1982): 85–89.

"Quality of Life: Black Families." *Human Ecology Monograph* School of Human Ecology, Howard University, 1991.

FURTHER READING

Edwards, Cecile Hoover, interview with Laura Newman conducted March 12, 1994.

Sketch by Laura Newman

Helen T. Edwards
1936–
American physicist

Helen T. Edwards is an accelerator physicist, who has helped to design and build the Tevatron accelerator at Fermilab in Batavia, Illinois, and headed up the accelerator systems division for the U.S. Superconducting Super Collider until the project was canceled in 1993. Her work on accelerators, particularly the systems that produce collisions between protons and antiprotons at Fermilab, have led to major advances in particle physics.

Helen Thom Edwards was born in Detroit, Michigan, on May 27, 1936. She received her B.A. from Cornell University in Ithaca, New York, in 1957. A master's degree and Ph.D. in physics from the same university followed in 1963 and 1966. Edwards stayed on at Cornell as a research associate until 1970, when she moved on to Fermi National Accelerator Laboratory to become Associate Head of the Booster Group. She stayed at Fermilab until 1989, eventually becoming head of the Accelerator Division.

Builds Tevatron Accelerator

In 1978 Fermilab began work on building a superconducting proton accelerator. Protons are positively charged elementary particles. Edwards was put in charge of the design of the new accelerator, called the Tevatron. When the design phase was completed, she became responsible for directing the technical aspects of building the Tevatron, which became the first successful superconducting proton accelerator and is the most powerful accelerator presently in operation. The Tevatron accelerates particles to about 1 TeV, or 1 trillion electron volts (whence the name of the accelerator), so that collisions occur in the Tevatron's detectors at about 2 TeV. These are energy levels similar to those that reigned in the universe a fraction of a second after the big bang, the explosion thought to have created the universe we live in. As a consequence, particles are thought to replicate early atomic behavior.

Not long after the Tevatron was completed, the accelerator was fitted out with the equipment to produce and store antiprotons for use in collisions with protons. Antiprotons are the antimatter equivalents of protons; that is to say, they are identical to protons except for a negative charge. Antiprotons are produced by collisions between electrons, negatively charged elementary particles, and their antimatter equivalents, positrons. High–energy collisions of protons and antiprotons, it was hoped, would yield the first observations of the hypothetical particles called top quarks. Quarks are the basic building–blocks of which particles such as protons and electrons are thought to be composed. Although a facility for producing and storing antiprotons was in operation in Geneva, Switzerland, Fermilab's capacity to generate antiprotons was to exceed that of the Swiss facility by far. Again, Edwards was in charge of design and construction. She is particularly notable for her design of a system that transfers protons and antiprotons from different sources into the Tevatron detectors almost simultaneously, so that very high energy collisions can be obtained. So far the top quark has not been detected, leading scientists to speculate that it has much greater mass than previously suspected.

In 1986 Edwards received one of the Ernest O. Lawrence Awards from the U.S. Department of Energy in recognition of her work in accelerator design and construction. She also received a MacArthur Foundation Fellowship for outstanding contributions in particle physics in 1988. The following year she was awarded the National Medal of Technology and accepted a position as Head of the Accelerator Division of the Superconducting Super Collider (SSC) to be built at Waxahachie, Texas. The SSC was designed to produce collisions at 40 TeV (40 trillion electron volts) and was hoped to yield more data on quarks and a hypothetical particle called the Higgs boson. Budget cutting in Congress, however, led to the cancellation of the SSC in 1993.

FURTHER READING

Books

Lederman, Leon and Dick Teresi. *The God Particle.* Houghton Mifflin, 1993.

Periodicals

"Five Physicists Receive Lawrence Awards." *Physics Today* (October 1986): 137.

"MacArthur Foundation Confers Five Physics–Related Fellowships." *Physics Today* (March 1989): 123.

Sketch by Olga K. Anderson

Tatiana Ehrenfest-Afanaseva
1876–1964
Russian–born Dutch theoretical physicist

Tatiana Ehrenfest–Afanaseva was one of the most accomplished theoretical physicists of the twentieth century. Together with her husband, Paul Ehrenfest, Ehrenfest–Afanaseva authored a critique of statistical thermodynamics which centered on a newer, statistical treatment of the behavior of gas molecules. Their work in articulating the ergodic hypothesis helped illuminate how microscopic particles in an unbalanced state could explain the overall macroscopic balance of matter.

Tatiana Alexeyevna Ehrenfest–Afanaseva (sometimes spelled Afanassjewa) was born in Kiev, Ukraine, on

November 19, 1876. Her father, a civil engineer of Russian–Orthodox faith, died when she was a child, and she went to live with a childless uncle, who was a professor at the Polytechnical Institute in St. Petersburg. During the generation leading up to World War I, St. Petersburg offered special university–level institutions for women, notably in engineering, medicine, and teaching. The institution that shadowed the imperial university (reserved for men) was the Women's Curriculum, which offered courses in arts, sciences, and law. Afanaseva attended the women's pedagogical (teaching) school and then the Women's Curriculum, among whose physics professors was Orest D. Chvolson, author of an introductory text used widely in Europe. She excelled in mathematics.

In 1902 Afanaseva, accompanied by her aunt Sonya, traveled to the University of Göttingen in Germany, then renowned for mathematics and physics. There she met and fell in love with Paul Ehrenfest, a Jewish physics student from Vienna. The couple married in 1904, shortly after Paul Ehrenfest completed his doctorate under Ludwig Boltzmann at the University of Vienna. They lived in Vienna at first, then moved to Göttingen, and in 1907 settled in St. Petersburg, Russia, living on inherited income. As Russian law prohibited marriages between Jews and Christians, they were allowed to live as husband and wife only by declaring themselves to be without religion—a risky step in view of the power of the Russian theocracy. In St. Petersburg, Ehrenfest–Afanaseva raised two daughters and also took care of her mother and her aunt. The household was vegetarian, teetotal, and non–smoking.

Ehrenfest–Afanaseva published her first paper in theoretical physics in 1905, and she continued issuing published work during her Russian years, both in Russian and in German. Paul Ehrenfest also published theoretical papers—rather more frenetically than his wife. Paul's most important work, a magisterial critique of statistical thermodynamics written for a mathematical encyclopedia edited by Felix, was written jointly with his wife. The monograph centered on the so–called H–theorem—by which Boltzmann had provided a statistical proof of the second law of thermodynamics, which concerns the conservation of entropy, or available energy within a system. In the monograph, the Ehrenfests brought out the newer, statistical treatment of gas molecules, and they emphasized the importance of the ergodic hypothesis (in which a portion of a process represents the whole) for understanding how the disequilibrium, or imbalance, of microscopic particle dynamics may account for the macroscopic equilibrium of matter—how, for example, a cup of hot tea slowly cools to room temperature.

Following the work of the Ehrenfests, the ergodic problem occupied the attention of a number of mathematicians. Ehrenfest–Afanaseva's role in writing the monograph, she recalled, was a critical one: While Paul collected the literature and organized the structure, she discussed all the problems with her husband, a number of which she clarified. She was the critical logician, while he provided physical intuition. This type of collaboration, familiar to those who have studied Albert Einstein's interaction with his mathematician–physicist wife Mileva Marić, contributed to Paul Ehrenfest's call, in 1912, to succeed Hendrik Antoon Lorentz in the chair of theoretical physics at the University of Leiden in the Netherlands.

At Leiden, Ehrenfest–Afanaseva expanded her horizons by publishing in Dutch and English. She designed a new house for the family which was completed in July 1914. Her family grew—sons were born in 1915 and 1918. The Ehrenfests had firm ideas about training young minds, and they educated their children at home. Ehrenfest–Afanaseva took a professional interest in questions of education, publishing a number of monographs and articles in German, Russian, and Dutch that discussed such issues as axiomatization, randomness and entropy, geometrical intuition and physical reality, and teaching method. Her output slowed after the suicide of her husband in 1933, but it resumed in the 1950s, when she wrote two major monographs. Her last work, published at age 84 in 1960, was a 164–page treatise on the teaching of mathematics. Although Ehrenfest–Afanaseva neither completed a doctorate nor held a regular university teaching position, her writings substantially enriched physics in the Netherlands. She died on April 14, 1964, in Leiden.

SELECTED WRITINGS BY EHRENFEST-AFANASEVA:

Books

Die Grundlagen der Thermodynamik, [Leiden], 1956.

(With Paul Ehrenfest) *The Conceptual Foundations of the Statistical Approach in Mechanics,* translated by Michael J. Moravcsik, Cornell University Press, 1959.

Wiskunde: Didactische opstellen, [Zutphen], 1960.

Periodicals

"On the Use of the Notion 'Probability' in Physics," *American Journal of Physics,* Volume 26, 1958, pp. 388–392.

FURTHER READING

Books

Frankfurt, Yu. I., *P. Ehrenfest* (in Russian), Nauka (Moscow), 1972.

Klein, Martin, *Paul Ehrenfest: The Making of a Theoretical Physicist,* North Holland, 1970.

Tropp, Eduard A., Viktor Y. Frenkel, and Artur D. Chernin, *Alexander A. Friedmann: The Man Who Made the Universe Expand,* translated by Alexander Dron and Michael Burov, Cambridge University Press, 1993.

Periodicals

Sviridonov, M. N., "Razvitiye ponyatiya entropii v rabotakh T. A. Afanas'yevoy–Erenfest," *Istoriya i metodologiya yestestnevvykh nauk: Fizika,* Volume 10, 1971, p. 77–111.

Visser, C., "In memoriam T. Ehrenfest–Afanassjewa," *Viernieuwing van opvoeding en onderwijs,* Volume 22, 1964, p. 217.

Sketch by Lewis Pyenson

Rosa Smith Eigenmann
1858–1947
American ichthyologist

Rosa Smith Eigenmann was the first prominent woman ichthyologist—a zoologist specializing in fish. Her studies on the taxonomy, or classification, of North and South American fish were important contributions to this field of knowledge.

Born in Monmouth, Illinois in 1858, Rosa Eigenmann was the youngest of nine children of Lucretia (Gray) and Charles Kendall Smith. Her father was a printer who founded the first newspaper in the area. Eigenmann developed her interest in natural history, particularly in collections of spiders and plants, at an early age. In 1876, her father moved the family to San Diego, California, where he became a school board clerk. There, Eigenmann attended Point Loma Seminary. She attended business college in San Francisco and then became a newspaper reporter for the *San Diego Union* in 1886, when her brother and brother-in-law took over the publication. Her interest in fish developed when she was living in San Diego.

Eigenmann delivered her first paper—on a new species of fish she had discovered—in 1880 at a meeting of the San Diego Society of Natural History, of which she was the first woman member, as well as recording secretary and librarian. Professor David Starr Jordan, an important naturalist and ichthyologist at Indiana University and, later, president of Stanford University, was impressed with her work and invited her to come study with him in Indiana. Jordan, who encouraged the scientific careers of a number of nineteenth-century American women, including Mount Holyoke zoologist **Cornelia Clapp**, became Eigenmann's mentor. She worked with him at Indiana from 1880 until 1882 and participated in his survey of West Coast fisheries for the United States Fish Commission. She became one of "Jordan's tramps," a group of students who hiked through Europe with Jordan in the summer of 1881. In 1887, she married another of Jordan's students, the German ichthyologist Carl H. Eigenmann.

Rosa Smith Eigenmann (Special Colletions, California Academy of Sciences. Reproduced by permission.)

The Eigenmanns moved to Boston to study the large collection of South American fish at Louis Agassiz's Harvard Museum of Comparative Zoology, and Rosa Eigenmann became a special student of Harvard's William G. Farlow, studying cryptogamic botany, the lower study of plants such as ferns and mosses.

When her husband became curator of the San Diego Society of Natural History in 1888, the Eigenmanns established a biological station there, where they continued their joint research. Between 1888 and 1893, Eigenmann published 20 papers on the fish of San Diego, and coauthored with her husband another 15 papers, including important monographs on the fresh water fish of South America and western North America. With Joseph Swain, Eigenmann published a monograph on the fish of Johnson Island in the central Pacific. In addition to taxonomy, these publications dealt with embryological development and evolution.

In 1891, Carl Eigenmann succeeded Jordan as professor of zoology at Indiana University and, later, dean of the graduate school. Rosa Eigenmann retired from research in 1893 to care for their five children, two of whom were handicapped. She continued to edit her husband's scientific manuscripts. In 1926, the Eigenmanns returned to San Diego, where Carl Eigenmann died the following year. Rosa

Eigenmann died of chronic myocarditis (inflammation of the middle layer of muscle in the heart wall) in 1947.

SELECTED WRITINGS BY EIGENMANN:

Periodicals

(With J. Swain) "Notes on a Collection of Fishes from Johnson Island, including Descriptions of Five New Species." *Proceedings, U. S. National Museum* 5 (1883): 119–43.

"Women in Science." *Proceedings of the National Science Club* 1 (January 1895): 13–17.

FURTHER READING

Books

Elliot, Clark A. *Biographical Dictionary of American Science: The Seventeenth Through the Nineteenth Centuries*. Westport, CT: Greenwood Press, 1979.

Hubbs, Carl L. "Rosa Smith Eigenmann." In *Notable American Women 1607–1950: A Biographical Dictionary*, edited by Edward T. James, Janet Wilson James, and Paul W. Boyer, Cambridge: Harvard University Press, 1971.

Irwin, Margaret A. "Rosa Smith Eigenmann." In *Notable Women in the Life Sciences: A Biographical Dictionary*, edited by Benjamin F. Shearer and Barbara S. Shearer. Westport, CT: Greenwood Press, 1996.

Ogilvie, Marilyn Bailey. *Women in Science, Antiquity through the Nineteenth Century: A Biographical Dictionary with Annotated Bibliography*. Cambridge: MIT Press, 1991.

Sketch by Margaret Alic

Mileva Einstein-Marić
1875–1948
Austrian-born Hungarian-Serbian physicist

Mileva Einstein-Marić (Corbis/Bettmann-UPI. Reproduced by permission.)

Although Mileva Marić never authored a scientific paper, Russian physicist Abraham F. Joffe recalled that the manuscripts of three of Einstein's famous papers of 1905 bore both Einstein's and Marić's names. She also worked with Einstein and scientist Paul Habicht to patent an instrument for measuring small electrical voltages, although her name did not appear as a coinventor or coauthor. Marić also corrected the proofs of at least some of Einstein's papers. She also formed friendships with other women physicists who were her contemporaries, **Marie Curie** and **Tatiana Ehrenfest-Afanaseva**.

Mileva Marić (or in Hungarian, Marity), wife of Albert Einstein, was born in Titel, a small town north of the Danube ruled at the time of her birth by Austria. Her father, Miloš Marić, was a soldier under Austrian command on the so-called Banat Military Frontier—the easternmost part of the southern line of Austrian defense against Bosnia and Serbia. (Titel passed to the civil jurisdiction of Hungary with the abolition of the Military Frontier in 1882, and it later formed part of the new state of Yugoslavia.) The Banat, north of the Danube in southeastern Hungary, was peopled by a mosaic of Austrians, Romanians, Hungarians, Slavonians, and Serbs. Marić's parents belonged to the latter community, which was seen by Austria as a buffer against invasion. Miloš Marić knew German well, from the time of his youth, but his wife Marija Ružić (whom he married in 1867) spoke only Serbian to her oldest child, Mileva. From birth Marić suffered from a displaced hip joint, giving her a lifelong limp.

In 1882 Marić's father joined the Hungarian civil service, which moved him and his family about the southern part of the kingdom. Mileva attended elementary school in Ruma and in 1886 began secondary school in Novi Sad (Neusatz) at the Serbian Girls' School; she transferred to the Kleine Realscule in Sremska Mitrovica (Syrmia), an old school that had until 1881 taught only in German. Since at that time girls in Austria-Hungary could not attend the classical secondary schools that prepared students for university studies, Miloš Marić sent Mileva to the Royal Serbian Gymnasium in Šabac in 1890. There she deepened her knowledge of German and acquired a knowledge of French. Then she followed her father to a new posting in Zagreb. By special arrangement, Mileva was the only female student in Zagreb's all-male Köningliche Obergymnasium, and there in 1894 she received the best grade in mathematics and physics.

Living conditions were poorer in Zagreb than in Novi Sad, and Miloš Marić decided to send his daughter to complete her secondary education in Switzerland—where the physical conditions would not as readily compromise her health and where women were encouraged to attend universities. From 1894 to 1896 Marić attended the Höhere Töchtershcule in Zurich, and the school's diploma (which she obtained in 1896) allowed her to enter the Swiss universities.

In 1896 Marić began studying medicine at the University of Zurich, altogether after a semester she transferred to the scientific-pedagogical division of the Federal Institute of Technology (ETH), also in Zurich, which was then one of Europe's finest science and engineering schools. The ETH dated from the early part of the nineteenth century. Marić was the fifth woman to pass through its portals as a student. There she met Albert Einstein, also at the beginning of his scientific studies.

The two attended classes together for four years (she spent a semester at the University of Heidelberg in 1897–1898), although they did not become a couple until 1898–1999. Einstein graduated in 1900. Marić tried twice to obtain a diploma from the ETH (in 1900 and 1901), and twice failed. But like Einstein, she began working on a doctorate, in her case at the University of Zurich under Heinrich Friedrich Weber. After two and a half lean years of living together, during which Einstein took odd jobs, they married, over the objections of their parents. Einstein's father had died (thus removing one objector), and Einstein had received a position as a patent examiner in Berne, establishing a steady family income.

In 1902 Marić gave birth to Einstein's daughter, Lieserl, of whom there is no trace after 1903. The couple later had two sons, Hans Albert and Eduard; Hans Albert Einstein became a professor at the California Institute of Technology. Evidence in the form of letters suggests that during the years leading up to 1905, when Einstein was composing his epoch-making physics, he and his physicist wife discussed all his ideas. Although Marić never authored a scientific paper, Russian physicist Abraham F. Joffe recalled that the manuscripts of three of Einstein's famous papers of 1905 bore both Einstein's and Marić's names (Joffe worked with a professor who then coedited the journal that published the papers). Marić's biographer reports that in 1907–08 she worked with Einstein and Paul Habicht to patent an instrument for measuring small electrical voltages and describe the instrument in a published article; again, her name did not appear as a coinventor or coauthor. Marić corrected the proofs of at least some of Einstein's papers. She formed friendships with other women physicists who were her contemporaries, Marie Curie and Tatiana Ehrenfest-Afanaseva.

Marić raised Einstein's family and kept his house until 1914, when the couple separated—he to occupy one of the highest-paid physics positions in the world at Berlin, she to live in Zurich with her two sons. At first it was temporary arrangement, but with the beginning of the First World War (and Einstein's progressively intimate friendship with his first cousin Elsa Einstein, whom he later married) Einstein cut himself off from Marić. His support for Marić and the children was inconsistent. In 1919 Marić, whose health was uncertain, accepted a divorce from Einstein on the condition that he give her any Nobel Prize money that came his way. Einstein won the Nobel Prize in Physics soon after the divorce, and Marić did indeed receive its tangible reward.

FURTHER READING

Books

Stachel, John, et al. *The Collected Papers of Albert Einstein. Volume 1: the Early Years, 1879–1902.* Princeton University Press, 1987.

Periodicals

Pyenson, Lewis. "Einstein's Natural Daughter," *History of Science* 28 (1990): 365–79.

Troemel–Ploetz, Senta. "Mileva Einstein-Marić: The Woman Who Did Einstein's Mathematics," *Women's Studies International Forum* 13 (1990): 415–532.

Sketch by Lewis Pyenson

Minnie Joycelyn Elders
1933–
American physician, former U.S. Surgeon General

Joycelyn Elders' controversial ideas about health care education have won her stalwart admirers and fierce critics. But neither her supporters nor her foes probably know that this pediatric endocrinologist, medical professor, and former U.S. Surgeon General did not visit a doctor until she was 15 years old. Where Elders grew in rural Arkansas, medical care was only for emergencies. By the time she became "the nation's doctor," Elders had become quite

Jocelyn Elders (AP/Wide World Photos. Reproduced by permission.)

practiced in fighting stereotypes and defending unpopular causes—something she has never shied away from doing.

Minnie Joycelyn Jones was born on August 13, 1933 in Schaal, Arkansas. She was the oldest of eight children. Her parents, Haller and Curtis Jones, eked out a living as sharecroppers, supplementing their meager cotton income by trapping raccoons. Minnie Jones grew up in a loving but destitute environment. Her home had no electricity or running water. She and her brothers and sisters worked in the cotton fields with their parents.

However, Elders was also a studious child—so studious that at age 15 she received a scholarship from the United Methodist Church to go to Philander Smith College in Little Rock, Arkansas. It was as a college student that the young woman first saw a doctor. It was also then that she became interested in medicine. She met Edith Irby Jones, the first black woman to attend the University of Arkansas Medical School, and Jones inspired Elders to strive for a medical degree.

Enters Medical School

Elders worked her way through college and graduated with a B.A. in three years. She was just 19 at the time. She joined the U.S. Army, attaining the rank of first lieutenant. She trained to become a physical therapist while in the Army, and upon her discharge she went to the University of Arkansas Medical School, assisted by the G.I. Bill. She received her M.D. in 1960, the only woman graduate in her class. That same year she married Oliver Elders, a high school teacher and basketball coach. The couple had two sons.

Elders' internship was spent in Minneapolis at the University of Minnesota Hospital, and she served as a resident at the University of Arkansas Medical Center in Little Rock. In 1963 she was named chief pediatric resident, and a year later she was named a pediatric research fellow. Over the next several years her career continued to build momentum. She enrolled in the master's program in biochemistry at the University of Arkansas, from which she graduated in 1967. Soon after her graduation she was named an assistant professor of pediatrics. In 1971 she became an associate professor, and in 1976 she was made a full professor. In 1978 she was board certified as a pediatric endocrinologist.

Impresses Governor Clinton

A tragedy during the 1970s led to a meeting that would prove important in Elders' career. Her brother was murdered in Arkansas in a much publicized case. Among those who attended the funeral was the governor of Arkansas—Bill Clinton. The two got to know each other, and Clinton saw in Elders a pragmatic and dedicated physician.

Clinton was so impressed, in fact, that in 1987 he selected Elders to serve as the chief public health director for the state of Arkansas. In this capacity, she oversaw a staff of 2,600 employees across the state. In five years, Elders made significant strides in improving health care for Arkansans. She initiated a childhood immunization program that nearly doubled the number of immunized toddlers. The number of early childhood screenings rose from 4,000 to 45,000. Elders expanded the state's prenatal care program, which cut down the infant mortality rate. She made it easier for poor women to get mammograms, and she increased home–care options for the chronically or terminally ill.

Elders also tackled such difficult issues as teenage pregnancy and AIDS (acquired immune deficiency syndrome). Under her tenure, HIV (human immunodefiency virus, which causes AIDS) testing and counseling services were serving nearly twice as many people. She also worked to cut down the state's teenage pregnancy rate, which was then the second highest in the United States. Her advocacy of sex education and contraception rankled many political and religious conservatives, but she refused to cave in. A portent of the outspokenness that was to cut short her career as Surgeon General revealed itself at a 1987 press conference; asked whether she would distribute condoms to students, she replied, "Well, I'm not going to put them on their lunch trays, but yes."

When Clinton became President in 1993, he nominated Elders to replace **Antonia Novello** as U.S. Surgeon General. If confirmed, Elders would be second woman, and the first black, to serve in that office. Not surprisingly, her nomination faced enormous opposition, especially from conservative members of Congress who saw her views on contraception and abortion rights as too liberal. After an often bitter fight, Elders was finally confirmed to the position by the Senate in September, 1993.

An Opponent of Ignorance

Elders proved to be as outspoken as ever in her new role, which she saw as a "bully pulpit." She called for higher taxes on both tobacco and alcohol, citing the harm both substances could do. She also supported a physician's right to use marijuana medicinally, and even suggested that perhaps the legalization of marijuana and other drugs should be explored. In an interview co–sponsored by the American Civil Liberties Union and America Online in June 1995, Elders elaborated on her views: "Our present policy of locking [marijuana offenders] up and throwing away the key without treatment, without consideration of the nature of the offense, is not doing anything but promoting the prison industry and costing this country billions of dollars."

Increasingly, high officials in the government—even allies of the President—questioned whether Elders' candor was helpful to her or to her causes. But Elders continued to speak out, convinced that the only way to deal with important issues was to confront them. Eventually, the pressure became too much for the Clinton administration, and Elders resigned in December 1994. She returned to the University of Arkansas. In 1995 she was named to the national board of the American Civil Liberties Union, and she published her autobiography in 1996. Today she continues to speak out frequently on controversial issues; her belief in the importance of combating ignorance with education remains unshaken.

SELECTED WRITINGS BY ELDERS:

Books

Elders, M. Joycelyn, with David Chanoff. *Joycelyn Elders, M.D. From Sharecropper's Daughter to Surgeon General of the United States of America.* New York: Morrow, 1996.

FURTHER READING

Books

Jones, Chester R. *Dancing With the Bear and Other Facts of Life: The Story of M. Joycelyn Elders.* Pine Bluff, Arkansas: Delta Press, 1995.

Periodicals

Popkin, James. "A Case of Too Much Candor." *U.S. News and World Report* (December 19, 1994): 31.

Rosellini, Lynn. "Joycelyn Elders is Master of Her Own Domain." *U.S. News and World Report* (November 3, 1997): 65.

"What I Would Say." *Time.* (December 9, 1996): 30.

Sketch by George A. Milite

Gertrude Belle Elion
1918–
American biochemist

Gertrude Belle Elion's innovative approach to drug discovery furthered the understanding of cellular metabolism and led to the development of medications for leukemia, gout, herpes, malaria, and the rejection of transplanted organs. Azidothymidine (AZT), the first drug approved for the treatment of AIDS, came out of her laboratory shortly after her 1983 retirement. One of the few women who has held a top post at a major pharmaceutical company, Elion worked at Wellcome Research Laboratories for nearly five decades. Her work, with colleague George H. Hitchings, was recognized with the Nobel Prize for physiology or medicine in 1988. Her Nobel award was notable for several reasons: few winners have been women, few have lacked a Ph.D., and few have been industrial researchers.

Elion was born on January 23, 1918, in New York City, the first of two children, a daughter and a son, of Robert Elion and Bertha Cohen. Robert, a dentist, immigrated to the United States from Lithuania as a small boy. Bertha came to the United States from Russia at the age of 14. Elion, an excellent student who was accelerated two years by her teachers, graduated from high school at the height of the Great Depression. As a senior in high school, she had witnessed the painful death of her grandfather from stomach cancer and vowed to become a cancer researcher. She was able to attend college only because several New York City schools, including Hunter College, offered free tuition to students with good grades. In college, she majored in chemistry because that seemed the best route to her goal.

In 1937 Elion graduated Phi Beta Kappa from Hunter College with a B.A. at the age of 19. Despite her outstanding academic record, Elion's early efforts to find a job as a chemist failed. One laboratory after another told her that they had never employed a woman chemist. Her self–confidence shaken, Elion began secretarial school. That lasted only six weeks, until she landed a one–semester stint teaching biochemistry to nurses and then took a position in a friend's laboratory. With the money she earned from these jobs, Elion began graduate school. To afford tuition, she continued to live with her parents and to work as a substitute science teacher in the public schools. In 1941, she graduated summa cum laude from New York University with a M.S. degree in chemistry.

Upon her graduation, Elion again faced difficulties finding work appropriate to her experience and abilities. The only job available to her was as a quality control chemist in

Gertrude Elion (UPI/Corbis-Bettmann. Reproduced by permission.)

a food laboratory, checking the color of mayonnaise and the acidity of pickles for the Quaker Maid Company. After a year and a half, she was finally offered a job as a research chemist at Johnson & Johnson. Unfortunately, her division closed six months after she arrived. The company offered Elion a new job testing the tensile strength of sutures, but she declined.

Seeks Opportunity at Wellcome Research Laboratories

As it did for many women of her generation, the start of World War II ushered in a new era of opportunity for Elion. As men left their jobs to fight the war, women were encouraged to join the workforce. "It was only when men weren't available that women were invited into the lab," Elion told the *Washington Post.*

For Elion, the war created an opening in the research lab of biochemist George Herbert Hitchings at Wellcome Research Laboratories in Tuckahoe, NY, a subsidiary of Burroughs Wellcome Company, a British firm. When they met, Elion was 26 years old and Hitchings was 39. Their working relationship began on June 14, 1944, and lasted for the rest of their careers. Each time Hitchings was promoted, Elion filled the spot he had just vacated, until she became head of the Department of Experimental Therapy in 1967, where she was to remain until her retirement 16 years later. Hitchings became vice president for research. Over the years, they have written many scientific papers together.

Settled in her job and thrilled by the breakthroughs occurring in the field of biochemistry, Elion took steps to earn a Ph.D., the so–called "union card" that all serious scientists are expected to have as evidence that they are capable of doing independent research. Only one school offered night classes in chemistry, the Brooklyn Polytechnic Institute (now Polytechnic University), so that's where Elion enrolled. Attending classes meant taking the train from Tuckahoe into Grand Central Station and transferring to the subway to Brooklyn. Although the hour–and–a–half commute each way was exhausting, Elion persevered for two years, until the school accused her of not being a serious student and pressed her to attend full–time. Forced to choose between school and her job, Elion had no choice but to continue working. Her relinquishment of the Ph.D. haunted her, until her lab developed its first successful drug, 6–mercaptopurine (6MP).

In the 1940s, Elion and Hitchings employed a novel approach to fighting the agents of disease. By studying the biochemistry of cancer cells, and of harmful bacteria and viruses, they hoped to understand the differences between the metabolism of those cells and normal cells. In particular, they wondered whether there were differences in how the disease–causing cells used nucleic acids, the chemicals involved in the replication of DNA, to stay alive and to grow. Any dissimilarities discovered might serve as a target point for a drug that could destroy the abnormal cells without harming healthy, normal cells. By disrupting one crucial link in a cell's biochemistry, the cell itself would be damaged. In this manner, cancers and harmful bacteria might be eradicated.

Elion's work focused on purines, one of two main categories of nucleic acids. Their strategy, for which Elion and Hitchings would be honored by the Nobel Prize 40 years later, steered a radical middle course between chemists who randomly screened compounds to find effective drugs and scientists who engaged in basic cellular research without a thought of drug therapy. The difficulties of such an approach were immense. Very little was known about nucleic acid biosynthesis. Discovery of the double helical structure of DNA still lay ahead, and many of the instruments and methods that make molecular biology possible had not yet been invented. But Elion and her colleagues persisted with the tools at hand and their own ingenuity. By observing the microbiological results of various experiments, they could make knowledgeable deductions about the biochemistry involved. To the same ends, they worked with various species of lab animals and examined varying responses. Still, the lack of advanced instrumentation and computerization made for slow and tedious work. Elion told *Scientific American,* "if we were starting now, we would probably do what we did in 10 years."

Discovers Drug That Fights Leukemia

By 1951, as a senior research chemist, Elion discovered the first effective compound against childhood leukemia. The compound, 6–mercaptopurine (6MP) (trade name Purinethol), interfered with the synthesis of leukemia cells. In clinical trials run by the Sloan–Kettering Institute (now the Memorial Sloan–Kettering Cancer Center), it increased life expectancy from a few months to a year. The compound was approved by the Food and Drug Administration (F.D.A.) in 1953. Eventually 6MP, used in combination with other drugs and radiation treatment, made leukemia one of the most curable of cancers.

In the next two decades, the potency of 6MP prompted Elion and other scientists to look for more uses for the drug. Robert Schwartz, at Tufts Medical School in Boston, and Roy Calne, at Harvard Medical School, successfully used 6MP to suppress the immune systems in dogs with transplanted kidneys. Motivated by Schwartz and Calne's work, Elion and Hitchings began searching for other immunosuppressants. They carefully studied the drug's course of action in the body, an endeavor known as pharmacokinetics. This additional work with 6MP led to the discovery of the derivative azathioprine (Imuran), that prevents rejection of transplanted human kidneys and treats rheumatoid arthritis. Other experiments in Elion's lab intended to improve 6MP's effectiveness led to the discovery of allopurinol (Zyloprim) for gout, a disease in which excess uric acid builds up in the joints. Allopurinol was approved by the F.D.A. in 1966. In the 1950s, Elion and Hitchings's lab also discovered pyrimethamine (Daraprim and Fansidar) a treatment for malaria, and trimethoprim (Bactrim and Septra) for urinary and respiratory tract infections. Trimethoprim is also used to treat Pneumocystis carinii pneumonia, the leading killer of people with AIDS.

Launches Antiviral Program

In 1968, Elion heard that a compound called adenine arabinoside appeared to have an effect against DNA viruses. This compound was similar in structure to a chemical in her own lab, 2,6–diaminopurine. Although her own lab was not equipped to screen antiviral compounds, she immediately began synthesizing new compounds to send to a Wellcome Research lab in Britain for testing. In 1969, she received notice by telegram that one of the compounds was effective against herpes simplex viruses. Further derivatives of that compound yielded acyclovir (Zovirax), an effective drug against herpes, shingles, and chicken pox. An exhibit of the success of acyclovir, presented in 1978 at the Interscience Conference on Microbial Agents and Chemotherapy, demonstrated to other scientists that it was possible to find drugs that exploited the differences between viral and cellular enzymes. Acyclovir (Zovirax), approved by the F.D.A. in 1982, became one of Burroughs Wellcome's most profitable drugs. In 1984 at Wellcome Research Laboratories, researchers trained by Elion and Hitchings developed azidothymidine (AZT), the first drug used to treat AIDS.

Although Elion retired in 1983, she continued at Wellcome Research Laboratories as scientist emeritus and keeps an office there as a consultant. She also accepted a position as a research professor of medicine and pharmacology at Duke University, where she works with a third–year medical student each year on a research project. Since her retirement, Elion has served as president of the American Association for Cancer Research and as a member of the National Cancer Advisory Board, among other positions. Hitchings, who retired in 1975, also remains active at Wellcome Research Laboratories.

In 1988, Elion and Hitchings shared the Nobel Prize for physiology or medicine with Sir James Black, a British biochemist. Although Elion had been honored for her work before, beginning with the prestigious Garvan Medal of the American Chemical Society in 1968, a host of tributes followed the Nobel Prize. She received a number of honorary doctorates and was elected to the National Inventors' Hall of Fame, the National Academy of Sciences, and the National Women's Hall of Fame. Elion maintained that it was important to keep such awards in perspective. "The Nobel Prize is fine, but the drugs I've developed are rewards in themselves," she told the *New York Times Magazine*.

Elion never married although she was engaged once. Sadly, her fiance died of an illness. After that, Elion dismissed thoughts of marriage. She is close to her brother's children and grandchildren, however, and on the trip to Stockholm to receive the Nobel Prize, she brought with her 11 family members. Elion has said that she never found it necessary to have women role models. "I never considered that I was a woman and then a scientist," Elion told the *Washington Post*. "My role models didn't have to be women—they could be scientists." Later in life, her interests included photography, travel, and music, especially opera. Elion continued working through the World Health Organization, honorary university lectureships, and providing assistance to students in medical research until her death on February 21, 1999, at the age of 81.

SELECTED WRITINGS BY ELION:

Periodicals

"The Quest for a Cure." *Annual Review of Pharmacology and Toxicology* 33 (1993): 1–23.

FURTHER READING

Books

Bertsch, Sharon McGrayne. *Nobel Prize Women in Science: Their Lives, Struggles, and Momentous Discoveries*. Carol Publishing Group, 1992.

McGuire, Paula, ed. *Nobel Prize Winners: 1987–1991 Supplement*. H. W. Wilson, 1992, pp. 77–78.

Periodicals

Altman, Lawrence K. "3 Drug Pioneers Win Nobel in Medicine." *New York Times* (October 18, 1988): 1.

Bouton, Katherine. "The Nobel Pair." *New York Times Magazine,* (January 29, 1989.)

Colburn, Don. "Pathway to the Prize." *Washington Post* (October 25, 1988.)

"Drug Pioneers Win Nobel Laureate." *New Scientist* (October 22, 1988): 26–27.

Holloway, Marguerite. "The Satisfaction of Delayed Gratification."*Scientific American* (October, 1991): 40–44.

Marx, Jean L. "The 1988 Nobel Prize for Physiology or Medicine."*Science* 242 (October 28, 1988): 516–517.

"Tales of Patience and Triumph." *Time* (October 31, 1988): 71.

Sketch by Liz Marshall

Elizabeth of Bohemia
1618–1680
German natural philosopher

Elizabeth of Bohemia, the exiled Princess of Palatine, dedicated her life to mathematics and philosophy. She is best known for her voluminous correspondence with the French philosopher René Descartes and the influence she had on his work.

Born in Heidelberg, Germany, in 1618, Princess Elizabeth was the eldest daughter of Frederick V, elector of the Rhine Palatinate from 1610 to 1623 and King of Bohemia in 1619 and 1620. Her mother was Elizabeth, daughter of King James I of England. After her father was deposed in 1620, Elizabeth spent the rest of her life in exile. She lived in the Hague in the Netherlands, where her mother maintained a court. The children in the family all received excellent educations, and Elizabeth was tutored along with her brothers. She was exceptionally adept at mathematics and natural philosophy.

The Marquis de Dohna introduced Elizabeth to Descartes in 1641. She became the philosopher's closest friend and colleague. Although Descartes may have been her teacher, she had a profound influence on him as well, and she apparently lectured on his Cartesian philosophy at the University of Heidelberg. Their correspondence, which began in 1643 and continued until Descartes' death in 1650, was filled with philosophical and mathematical discussions, much of which concerned the nature of matter versus spirit. Elizabeth always voiced her disagreements. Her questions and objections were addressed in Descartes' *Principles of Philosophy*, published in 1644, which he dedicated to Elizabeth and in which he expressed his admiration for her talents. Their letters evolved into Descartes' *Treatise on the Passions*, which he dedicated to his student Queen Christine of Sweden. Descartes tried to foster an intellectual relationship between Elizabeth and Queen Christine, but Christine rebuffed these attempts.

Elizabeth also carried on a correspondence with Francis Mercury van Helmont, the famous "gypsy scholar," and with the English philosopher Henry More, the mentor and associate of the natural philosopher **Anne Conway**, another student of Cartesian philosophy. Conway's long philosophical collaboration with van Helmont first began when he arrived at her home in England, with Elizabeth's letters to More. Like Elizabeth's influence on Descartes, Conway's writings had a major influence on Gottfried Wilhelm von Leibniz, whose philosophical system, along with that of Isaac Newton, would supersede the natural philosophy of Descartes in the next century. Elizabeth's younger sister, the Electress Sophia of Hanover, another learned woman, was Leibniz's closest associate, both intellectually and politically, from the 1670s until her death in 1714, the same year her son, Elizabeth's nephew, became King George I of Great Britain. Sophia's daughter, Sophia Charlotte, Elizabeth's niece, also studied with Leibniz and was responsible for the establishment of the Berlin Academy of Sciences. Elizabeth studied with Leibniz as well, but she never wavered in her allegiance to Descartes' philosophy.

Elizabeth, a protestant Calvinist, never married, and in 1667 she became abbess of the Lutheran abbey of Hervorden in Westphalia, in northwestern Germany. Anna Maria van Schurman of Utrecht, an artist, philosopher, and early feminist who spoke out for the scientific education of women, also took refuge there. She had been a close friend of both Elizabeth and Descartes and was being persecuted for her involvement with Labadism, a strict Protestant sect founded by Jean de Labadie. Elizabeth died at her convent in 1680. Unfortunately, historians of mathematics have attempted to discount and even ridicule Elizabeth's intellectual achievements, and her contributions to the development of natural philosophy have never been fully appreciated.

FURTHER READING

Books

Alic, Margaret. *Hypatia's Heritage: A History of Women in Science from Antiquity through the Nineteenth Century*. Boston: Beacon Press,1986.

Descartes, René. *Philosophical Letters*, translated and edited by Anthony Kenny. London: Clarendon, 1970.

Haldane, Elizabeth S. *Descartes: His Life and Times.* London: John Murray, 1905.

Schiebinger, Londa. *The Mind Has No Sex? Women in the Origins of Modern Science* Cambridge: Harvard University Press, 1989.

Ward, Adolphus William. *Electress Sophia and the Hanoverian Succession* 2d ed. London: Longmans, Green, and Co., 1909.

Sketch by Margaret Alic

Gladys Anderson Emerson
1903–
American biochemist and nutritionist

Gladys Anderson Emerson was a landmark biochemist who conducted valuable research on vitamin E, amino acids, and the B vitamin complex. She later studied the biochemical bases of nutrition and the relationship between disease and nutrition. An author and lecturer, Emerson helped establish dietary allowances for the United States Department of Agriculture.

Emerson was born in Caldwell, Kansas, on July 1, 1903, the only child of Otis and Louise (Williams) Anderson. When the family moved to Texas, Emerson attended elementary school in Fort Worth. She later graduated from high school at El Reno, Oklahoma, where she excelled in debate, music, languages, and mathematics. In 1925 she received a B.S. degree in chemistry and an A.B. in English from the Oklahoma College for Women.

Following graduation, Emerson was offered assistantships in both chemistry and history at Stanford University and earned an M.A. degree in history in 1926. She eventually became head of the history, geography, and citizenship department at an Oklahoma City junior high school, then a short time later accepted a fellowship in biochemistry and nutrition at the University of California at Berkeley, where she received her Ph.D. in animal nutrition and biochemistry in 1932. That same year Emerson was accepted as a postdoctoral fellow at Germany's University of Gottingen, where she studied chemistry with the Nobel Prize–winning chemist Adolf Windaus and Adolf Butenandt, a prominent researcher who specialized in the study of hormones.

In 1933 Emerson returned to the United States and began work as a research associate in the Institute of Experimental Biology at the University of California at Berkeley. She remained there until 1942, conducting pioneering research on vitamin E; using wheat germ oil as a source, Emerson was first to isolate vitamin E. In 1942 she joined the staff of Merck and Company, a pharmaceutical firm, eventually heading its department of animal nutrition. Staying with Merck for fourteen years, Emerson directed research in nutrition and pharmaceuticals. In particular, she studied the structure of the B vitamin complex and the effects of B vitamin deprivation on lab animals; she found that when vitamin B6 was withheld from rhesus monkeys, they developed arteriosclerosis, or hardening of the arteries.

Gladys A. Emerson (Corbis/Bettmann-UPI. Reproduced by permission.)

During World War II Emerson served in the Office of Scientific Research and Development. From 1950 to 1953 she worked at the Sloan Kettering Institute, researching the link between diet and cancer. From 1962 to her retirement in 1970, she was professor of nutrition and vice–chairman of the department of public health at the University of California at Los Angeles.

In 1969 President Richard M. Nixon appointed Emerson vice president of the Panel on the Provision of Food as It Affects the Consumer (the White House Conference on Food, Nutrition, and Health). In 1970 she served as an expert witness before the Food and Drug Administration's hearing on vitamins and mineral supplements and additives to food. A photography enthusiast who won numerous awards for her work, Emerson was also a distinguished board member of the Southern California Committee of the World Health Organization and was active on the California State Nutrition Council.

SELECTED WRITINGS BY EMERSON:

Periodicals

"Agnes Fay Morgan and Early Nutrition Discoveries in California." *Federation Proceedings* 36: 1911–1914.

FURTHER READING

Books

Haber, Louis. *Women Pioneers of Science.* Harcourt, 1979.

Siegel, J. P., and R. T. Finley. *Women in the Scientific Search.* Scarecrow, 1985.

Vare, Ethlie Ann, and Greg Ptacek. *Mothers of Invention: From the Bra to the Bomb: Forgotten Women and Their Unforgettable Ideas.* New York: William E. Morrow, 1988.

Sketch by John Henry Dreyfuss

Dorothea Christiana Leporin Erxleben
1715–1762
German medical scientist

Dorothea Erxleben wrote a book on the value of education for women and was the first woman to obtain a medical degree from a German university.

Erxleben was born into a middle–class family in the small town of Quedlinburg, Germany, in 1715. She was the daughter of Anna Sophia (Meinecken) and Christian Polycarpus Leporin, a physician. Her father believed that the talents of women were wasted in the kitchen, and he taught Erxleben and her brother Christian together. Erxleben found that she could read books as she completed her household chores. When Christian studied Latin with the rector from the high school, he brought his sister's lessons home to her, since it was not proper for her to go to the instructor's house. Later, the Latin teacher wrote to Erxleben of **Laura Bassi**, who had received her doctorate at the University of Bologna. He urged Erxleben to do the same. At 16, she began studying medicine with her brother as he prepared for the university exams.

In 1740, Erxleben petitioned Frederick the Great of Prussia to allow her to study at the new University of Halle with her brother. Amazingly, her petition was granted in 1741. The public response was both positive and negative. Johann Rhetius wrote a pamphlet arguing that since it was unlawful for women to practice medicine, it was silly to allow them to earn a university degree. At her father's urging, Erxleben responded with her book *Inquiry into the Causes Preventing the Female Sex from Studying,* which she published in 1742. Her father wrote a long introduction to the book, arguing for university education for women. The book was pirated in 1749 and published under a different title, without Erxleben's name. However it then disappeared for many years and even Erxleben's stepson, a professor, was unable to locate a copy some years after her death.

When war broke out with Austria, Erxleben's brother was forced into the military. Instead of attending the university on her own, she married Johann Christian Erxleben, a clergyman and a widower with several children. Together they had four more children. Erxleben continued her medical studies at home. Six years later her father died, leaving large debts, and her husband became ill. To support the family, Erxleben began practicing medicine. In 1753, after one of her patients died, three physicians accused her of practicing medicine illegally. Erxleben responded by offering to take a medical exam, if her accusers did the same. The physicians refused. The officials told Erxleben that she had three months to take an examination at Halle. However she was nine months pregnant at the time. Once again, she appealed to Frederick II for permission to take the exam at a later date.

Erxleben obtained her medical doctorate in 1754, defending and publishing her thesis, based on original research, in which she argued that physicians often provided their patients with unnecessary treatments. There were so many requests for copies of her thesis that she translated it from Latin into German. As Londa Schiebinger quoted from the university rector concerning Erxleben's performance on the final examinations, she "proved herself a man." There was a public celebration in Halle, on the day she was awarded her degree and the legal right to practice medicine.

Erxleben practiced medicine for only eight years before dying of breast cancer in Quedlinburg in 1762. It was not until 1901 that another woman graduated from the School of Medicine at the University of Halle.

SELECTED WRITINGS BY ERXLEBEN:

Books

(As Dorothea Leporinin) *Gründliche Untersuchung der Ursachen, die das weibliche Geschlecht vom Studieren abhalten.* Berlin, 1742.

Academische Abhandlung von der gar zu geschwinden und angenehmen aber deswegen öfters unsichern Heilung der Krankheiten. Halle, 1755.

FURTHER READING

Books

Chaff, Sandra L., et al., eds. *Women in Medicine: A Bibliography of the Literature on Women Physicians.* Metuchen, NJ: Scarecrow, 1977.

Ogilvie, Marilyn Bailey. *Women in Science, Antiquity through the Nineteenth Century: A Biographical Dictionary with Annotated Bibliography.* Cambridge: MIT Press, 1991.

Schiebinger, Londa. *The Mind Has No Sex? Women in the Origins of Modern Science.* Cambridge: Harvard University Press, 1989.

Sketch by Margaret Alic

Katherine Esau
1898–
Russian-born American botanist

Botanist Katherine Esau is best known for her research into the effects of viruses upon plant tissues, and her studies of plant tissue structures and physiology. Esau's definitive work, *Plant Anatomy,* was published in 1953 and revised in 1965. She received the National Medal of Science in 1989.

Esau was born in Ekaterinoslav, Russia, on April 3, 1898, and spent her formative years in that industrial city. She completed her first year of college before political events within the country led her parents to emigrate. Escaping from the Russian Revolution and the ensuing civil war, the Esaus left Russia in 1919 to take up residence in Germany. Katherine was able to complete her baccalaureate degree in Germany in 1922 before European political events following the first World War led her parents to move again. The family arrived in America in 1922 and settled in California. Esau obtained work with the Spreckels Sugar Company in the agricultural Salinas Valley, where she became a member of the experiment station staff trying to develop a strain of sugar beet resistant to a virus called "curly top." The disease caused the leafy bloom of the sugar beet plant to wilt, diminishing the size of the valuable white root. She worked in Salinas for six years before the company's experiment station staff was transferred to the campus of the University of California in Davis. Esau moved to Davis and continued her experimental work at the station, now under the aegis of the university's School of Agriculture. In 1928, she enrolled in the graduate department of botany at the university and three years later was awarded her doctorate degree.

In 1931 Esau became an instructor of botany and junior botanist at the University of California, Davis. She became a full professor of botany in 1949. In 1963, Esau transferred to the University of California's Santa Barbara campus, where she was named emeritus professor in 1965. She was a special lecturer at the Botanical and Plant Research Institute of the University of Texas in 1956, the Prather Lecturer at Harvard University in 1960, a national lecturer for Sigma Xi in 1965 and 1966, a lecturer at the J. C. Walker Conference on Plant Pathology at the University of Wisconsin, Madison, in 1968, and the John Wesley Powell Lecturer at the American Academy of Art and Science in 1973. Esau was a Guggenheim fellow in 1940.

Esau's research into plant viruses focused on how viruses effect the structure and development of a plant's food–conducting tissue known as the phloem. This research enabled her to distinguish between primary and secondary viral symptoms, allowing studies of viral damage to specific plant tissues to be conducted. In addition, Esau clarified the development phases of plant tissues, particularly the sieve tubes which serve to move solutes throughout a plant. Her research provided an impetus to phloem study in America.

Esau has published more than 160 papers and five books. In 1971, she was elected to both the National Academy of Sciences and the Swedish Royal Academy. She belonged to many organizations, including the American Philosophical Society, the American Academy of Art and Science, the International Society of Plant Morphologists, and the Botanical Society of America, where she served as the organization's president in 1951. Esau died at her Santa Barbara, California, home on June 4, 1997, at the age of 99.

SELECTED WRITINGS BY ESAU:

Books

Plant Anatomy. 2d ed. Wiley, 1965.
Anatomy of Seed Plants, Wiley, 1960.
Plants, Viruses and Insects. Cambridge: Harvard University Press, 1961.

Sketch by Benedict A. Leerburger

Thelma Estrin
1924–
American engineer

Thelma Estrin has contributed to science through her endeavors in the application of computer technology to neurophysiological research. She is currently Professor Emerita at the University of California at Los Angeles (UCLA), having retired in 1991 as Assistant Dean of the School of Engineering and Applied Sciences. Until 1990, she also served as Director of the Department of Engineering and Science at the UCLA School of Continuing Education. Estrin developed methods of utilizing the brain's electrical signals, as measured by computers, to study information processing in humans and animals. Her innovations have been further developed by medical researchers, and are widely used in the delivery of health care. Applications include the creation of internal brain maps of patients based on external imaging prior to surgery, and the identification of epileptic foci in the brain. For this work she received the 1981 Society of Women Engineers Achievement Award, which cited her "outstanding contributions to the field of biomedical engineering, in particular neurophysiological research through application of computer science."

Estrin was born in New York City on February 21, 1924. She received all of her higher education at the University of Wisconsin, earning a bachelor of science degree in 1948, a master of science the following year, and her doctorate degree in electrical engineering in 1951. Her association with UCLA began in 1960, when she accepted a position as Resident Engineer with the Health Sciences Center at the University. She held this position for a decade. In 1970, she was named Director of the Data Processing Laboratory of the Brain Research Institute. Ten years later, Estrin received a full professorship at UCLA's Computer Sciences Department.

In 1982, Estrin was appointed Director of the Division of Electronics, Computer and Systems Engineering at the National Science Foundation, a position she held for two years. She then was named Assistant Dean of the School of Engineering and Applied Sciences, and Director of the Department of Engineering and Sciences. Both of these appointments occurred in 1984. Estrin was a Fulbright Fellow with the Weizmann Institute of Science in Rehovot, Israel in 1963.

She was also a member of the Board of Trustees for the Aerospace Corporation from 1979 to 1982 (the first woman to hold that position), and served on the Army Sciences Board from 1980 to 1982; the National Institutes of Health Biotechnology Resources Review Committee from 1981 to 1986; the National Research Council (NRC) Board of Telecommunications and Computer Applications in 1982; and the NRC Energy Engineering Board from 1984 to 1989.

Promotes Advancement of Women Scientists

In addition, Estrin has served as President of the Biomedical Engineering Society and Executive Vice President of the Institute for Electrical and Electronics Engineers. She was the first woman to be certified as a Clinical Engineer. Estrin has been a leader in the application of engineering to neurophysiology. She also helped build the first computer in the Middle East in 1954. She continues to actively promote the inclusion and advancement of women in scientific and technological fields. "Most of the decisions we make today are based on technology. Women have to be able to contribute to technology and be leaders in the field," Estrin said in an interview. She also believes women generally approach and solve problems differently than men. "Women take more of a system view. They are more concerned with how their work is related to that of others, and how their work affects society."

FURTHER READING

Estrin, Thelma, interview with Karen Withem conducted March 23, 1994.

Sketch by Karen Withem

Alice Evans (UPI/Corbis-Bettmann. Reproduced by permission.)

Alice Evans
1881–1975
American microbiologist

The eminent bacteriologist Alice Evans was a pioneer both as a scientist and as a woman. She discovered that brucellae bacteria, contracted from farm animals and their milk, was the cause of undulant fever in humans, and responded by fighting persistently for the pasteurization of milk, eventually achieving success. She was the first woman president of the Society of American Bacteriologists (now American Society of Microbiology). Although marginalized early in her career, Evans overcame many obstacles and lived to see her discoveries repeatedly confirmed. She had a major impact on microbiology in the United States and the world and received belated honors for her numerous achievements in the field.

Alice Catherine Evans was born on January 29, 1881, in the predominantly Welsh town of Neath, Pennsylvania, the second of William Howell and Anne Evans' two children. William Howell, the son of a Welshman, was a surveyor, teacher, farmer, and Civil War veteran. Anne Evans, also Welsh, emigrated from Wales at the age of 14. Evans received her primary education at the local district school. She went on to study at the Susquehanna Institute at

Towanda, Pennsylvania. She wished to go to college but, unable to afford tuition, took a post as a grade school teacher. After teaching for four years she enrolled in a tuition–free, two year course in nature study at the Cornell University College of Agriculture. The course was designed to help teachers in rural areas inspire an appreciation of nature in their students, but it changed the path of Evans' life and she never returned to the schoolroom.

Begins Research on Bacteria

At Cornell Evans discovered her love of science and received a B.S. degree in agriculture. She chose to pursue an advanced degree in bacteriology and was recommended by her professor at Cornell for a scholarship at the University of Wisconsin. She was the first woman to receive the scholarship, and under the supervision of E. G. Hastings she studied bacteriology with a focus on chemistry. In 1910 she received a Master of Science degree in bacteriology from Wisconsin. Although encouraged to pursue a Ph.D., Evans accepted a research position with the University of Wisconsin Agriculture Department's Dairy Division and began researching cheese–making methods in 1911. In 1913 she moved with the division to Washington, DC, and served as bacteriological technician in a team effort to isolate the sources of contamination of raw cow's milk which were then believed to be external.

On her own, Evans began to focus on the intrinsic bacteria in raw cow's milk. By 1917 she had found that the bacterium responsible for undulant or "Malta" fever was similar in important respects to one associated with spontaneous abortions in cows, and that the two bacteria produced similar clinical effects in guinea pigs. Prevailing wisdom at the time held that many bovine diseases could not be transmitted to humans. That year she presented her findings to the Society of American Bacteriologists; her ideas were received with skepticism that seems to have been more due to her gender and level of education than her data.

In 1918 Evans was asked to join the staff of the U.S. Public Health Service by director George McCoy. There she was absorbed in the study of meningitis. Although she was unable to continue her milk studies during this time, support for Evans' findings was trickling in from all over the world. By the early 1920s it was recognized that undulant fever and Malta fever were due to the same bacteria, but there was still resistance to the idea that humans could contract brucellosis by drinking the milk of infected cows. Because the symptoms of brucellosis were so similar to those of influenza, typhoid fever, tuberculosis, malaria, and rheumatism, it was not often correctly diagnosed. Evans began documenting cases of the disease among humans in the U.S. and South Africa, but it was not until 1930, after brucellosis had claimed the lives of a number of farmers' children in the U.S., that public health officials began to recognize the need for pasteurization.

In 1922, Evans herself, like many others who researched these organisms, became ill with brucellosis. Her condition was chronic, plaguing her on and off for almost 23 years, and perhaps providing her with new insight into the disease. As the problem of chronic illness became widespread, Evans began surveying different parts of the U.S. to determine the numbers of infected cows from whom raw milk was sold, and the numbers of chronic cases resulting from the milk.

Argues for Pasteurization

In 1925 Evans was asked to serve on the National Research Council's Committee on Infectious Abortion. In this capacity Evans argued for the pasteurization of milk, a practice that later became an industry standard. In recognition of her achievements, Evans was in 1928 elected the first woman president of the American Society of Bacteriologists. In 1930 she was chosen, along with Robert E. Buchanan of Iowa State University, as an American delegate to the First International Congress of Bacteriology in Paris. She attended the second Congress in London in 1936 and was again able to travel widely in Europe. She returned to the United States and eventually was promoted to senior bacteriologist at the Public Health Service, by then called the National Institute of Health. By 1939 she had changed her focus to immunity to streptococcal infections and in 1945 she retired. Evans, who never married, died at the age of 94 on September 5, 1975, in Alexandria, Virginia, following a stroke.

FURTHER READING

Books

Kass–Simon, G., and P. Farnes. *Women of Science.* Bloomington: Indiana University Press, 1990, p. 278.

O'Hern, Elizabeth M.. *Profiles of Pioneer Women Scientists.* Acropolis, 1985, pp. 127–138.

Siegel, J. P., and R. T. Finley. *Women in the Scientific Search.* Scarecrow, 1985, pp. 67–70.

Periodicals

"Alice Evans, 94, Bacteriologist, Dies." *Washington Post* (September 8, 1975): B4.

MacKaye, Milton. "Undulant Fever." *Ladies Home Journal* (December, 1944): 23, 69–70.

O'Hern, Elizabeth M. "Alice Evans, Pioneer Microbiologist." *American Society for Microbiology News* (September 1973).

Sketch by John Henry Dreyfuss

F

Sandra Moore Faber
1944–
American astronomer

Sandra M. Faber, an astronomer and professor at the Lick Observatory of the University of California, Santa Cruz, has made significant contributions to the big bang theory, a model of cosmic evolution which states that the universe was created in a giant explosion of a super–dense nucleus of matter some fifteen billion years ago. Faber's work in defining and developing theories of the evolution of galaxies has resulted in a number of discoveries relating to this model of the universe, including the Faber–Jackson relation. In 1984, working with theoretical physicists George Blumenthal and Joel Primack at Santa Cruz, Faber further hypothesized that the universe was now composed largely of cold, dark matter, rather than the hot, neutrino–based matter scientists had earlier supposed. In 1990, working with a group of six other astronomers, Faber participated in identifying the great attractor, a concentration of matter whose gravitational pull on galaxies as distant as 150–million light years away seems to defy previously accepted laws of expansion.

Faber was born Sandra Moore in Boston on December 28, 1944, the only child of Donald Edwin and Elizabeth Mackenzie (Borwick) Moore. Her father was an insurance executive with an interest in science; her mother was a homemaker with an interest in medicine. Raised in the Midwest, Faber gained an interest in astronomy through star gazing with her father. In an interview with Alan Lightman and Roberta Brawer in *Origins,* she observed: "I was born when my mother was 42 and my father was [43]. . . . Their education came from the beginning of this century rather than the middle of the century, as it would have had the age gap been more normal." As a result, Faber found herself influenced by early twentieth–century scientific literature, including James Jeans' *The Stars in Their Courses* and Hoyle's *Frontiers of Astronomy,* which espoused the steady–state theory, in which the universe has neither a beginning or an end. Although Faber ceased subscribing to the theory as an adult, the intellectual experiences of her youth left her left a strong influence on her.

Faber attended Swarthmore College in Pennsylvania and obtained her bachelor's degree in physics in 1966. While at Swarthmore, she met Andrew Leigh Faber, whom she married on June 9, 1967. They have two daughters, Robin Leigh and Holly Ilena. Faber's mentor at Swarthmore was Sarah Lee Lippincott, an astronomer who was not a member of the university faculty. Observing that Lippincott's career had been limited by the lack of a Ph.D., Faber became determined to obtain one for herself.

Faber attended Harvard University, where she completed a Ph.D. in astronomy in 1972. Further graduate work was affected by the fact that Faber's husband took a position at the Naval Research Laboratory in Washington, DC. To continue her research there, Faber obtained an office at the lab among astronomers who were "doing things like measuring the temperature of Venus and studying water masers," she reported in *Origins.* A year–and–a–half later, she was offered a residency at the Department of Terrestrial Magnetism, where she worked alongside astronomers **Vera Cooper Rubin** and Kent Ford.

Research Leads to Faber-Jackson Relation

When she completed her doctoral thesis, a study of elliptical galaxies, Faber accepted a position as assistant professor and astronomer at the Lick Observatory at the University of California, Santa Cruz. Her early work at Lick led her to study further the formation, structure and evolution of galaxies, and postulate that the outer regions of certain small galaxies had been stripped away by massive companion galaxies. In 1975 she developed, with graduate student Robert Jackson, the Faber–Jackson relation. This was the first of many galactic "sealing laws" and related the size of elliptical galaxies to the internal orbital speeds of their component stars. It was later developed into an important formula used to calculate distances between galaxies.

In 1977 Faber was promoted to associate professor and astronomer at Lick, and made full professor in 1979. That same year, with colleague John Gallagher, she wrote a review concluding that galaxies are surrounded by enormous pockets of invisible matter, an idea that led Faber and her colleagues to predict that the galaxies themselves had been formed from this invisible matter. This resulted in the 1984 theory of dark matter, which suggested that invisible, or dark, matter is cold and lightless, a series of weakly interacting particles that eventually cluster together to form galaxies.

In the early 1980s Faber collaborated with six other astronomers in the Seven Samurai project to measure the distances and velocities of elliptical galaxies, those collections of stars arranged in an elliptical pattern that seemingly have no internal structure. The project led to the 1990 discovery of the great attractor, a concentrated "galaxy of clumped galaxies" and matter which exerts a steady gravitational pull on an area of space approximately 100 million light years across, which includes our own Milky Way. The astronomers have also identified over 250 galaxies of two types, spiral and elliptical, that are moving toward the great attractor at an average rate of 400 miles per second. Some believe that the existence of the great attractor has weakened proof of the big bang theory and that it contradicts Faber's own theory of dark matter. But Faber believes the discovery will not make the older theory obsolete. On the contrary, her latest theory proposes that dark matter consists of two new particles, one of which is massive, the other which is light. A computer model of this theory shows that such a mix of matter would, in fact, predict such clumping.

In 1985 Faber was presented the Dannie Heineman Prize for astrophysics by the American Astronomical Society and the American Institute for Physics, in recognition of "her spirited observational approach" and for her insights into and advancement of "the theory of galaxy evolution." The following year she received an honorary doctorate of science from Swarthmore College, and is one of the few women to have been extended membership in the National Academy of Sciences. In 1990 she helped establish the Keck Observatory on the summit of Mauna Kea in Hawaii, where she is co–chair of the science committee. She is also a member of the wide–field camera design team for the Hubble Space Telescope.

"I think of myself now in terms of the ancient Greeks," she stated in *Origins:* "What they saw in the universe was the sun, the planets, and the earth. And they might have said, 'Well, why is the earth the way it is, or why is the sun the way it is?' . . . The earth is the way it is because we happen to be on it. This is the old anthropic way of answering cosmological questions. I really think that we will probably find that our universe is the way it is to some extent just because we're in it."

SELECTED WRITINGS BY FABER:

Books

(Editor) *Near Normal Galaxies: From the Planck Time to the Present: The Eighth Santa Cruz Summer Workshop in Astronomy and Astrophysics, July 21 –August 1, 1986, Lick Observatory,* Springer–Verlag, 1987.

Periodicals

"Variations in Spectral–Energy Distributions and Absorption–Line Strengths Among Elliptical Galaxies." *Astrophysical Journal* no. 179 (1973): 731.

"Ten–Color Intermediate–Band Photometry of Stars." *Astronomy and Astrophysics Supplement* no. 10 (1973,): 201.

(With Robert E. Jackson) "Velocity Dispersions and Mass–to–Light Ratios for Elliptical Galaxies." *Astrophysical Journal* no. 204 (1976,): 668.

FURTHER READING

Books

Lightman, A. and Brawer, R., "Interview with Sandra Faber." *Origins* Cambridge: Harvard University Press, 1990, pp. 324–40.

Pasachoff, J. "Interview with Sandra Faber." *Journey Through the Universe.* Saunders, 1992.

Periodicals

Bagne, Paul. "Interview with Sandra Faber." *Omni* (July 1990): 62–92.

"Faber Receives Heineman Prize for Work in Astrophysics." *Physics Today* (March 1986): 119.

Hilts, Philip J. "Far Out In Space, A Giant Discovery." *New York Times* (January 12, 1990): 22.

Wilford, John Noble "Astronomers Say Proof of Black Hole Theory is Almost Within Their Grasp." *New York Times* (January 17, 1992): 17.

Wilford, John Noble. "Star Clusters Astonish Astronomers." *New York Times* (January 21, 1992): 6.

Sketch by Mindi Dickstein

Etta Zuber Falconer
1933–
American mathematician

Etta Zuber Falconer has encouraged hundreds of young people, particularly African American women, to study mathematics and the sciences through her classroom teaching and program work at Spelman College in Atlanta, where, she told author Fran Hodgkins in an interview, she "was able to crystallize my desire to change the prevailing pattern of limited access and limited success for African American women in mathematics." Falconer received the Louise Hay Award for her contributions to mathematics education in 1995.

Falconer was born in Tupelo, Mississippi, in 1933, the younger of two daughters of Dr. Walter A. Zuber and Zadie L. (Montgomery) Zuber. She attended Tupelo public schools and graduated from George Washington High School in 1949. At Fisk University in Nashville, she found two of her three life mentors: Dr. **Evelyn Boyd Granville** and Dr. Lee Lorch. Granville taught just one year at Fisk. For Falconer, seeing an African American woman teaching at the college level was inspiring; most instructors were men. She had intended to teach high–school mathematics after graduation, but Lorch, who served as chair of the mathematics department, encouraged her to go on to

Etta Falconer (Reproduced by permission of Etta Falconer.)

graduate school. Falconer graduated *summa cum laude* with a bachelor of science degree in mathematics in 1953, and went on to earn her master's degree in mathematics from the University of Wisconsin in 1954.

From 1954 to 1963, she taught mathematics at Okolona Junior College in Okolona, Mississippi. While teaching there, she met and married her husband, Dolan Falconer. They would have three children, Dolan Jr., an engineer; Alice (Falconer) Wilson, a physician; and Walter, also a physician.

In 1963, Falconer left Okolona to teach at Chattanooga Public School. Two years later, she joined the faculty of Spelman College in Atlanta as an instructor. In 1969, she earned her Ph.D. in mathematics from Emory University, where she studied under her third mentor, Trevor Evans, who encouraged her growth in algebra and her study of quasigroups and loops. Her dissertation was titled "Quasigroup Identities Invariant Under Isotopy." Out of her dissertation came two published papers, "Isotopy Invariants in Quasigroups" and "Isotopes of Some Special Quasigroup Varieties." After receiving her doctorate, Falconer held an associate professorship at Norfolk State College from 1971 to 1972. She received a master's degree in computer science from Atlanta University in 1982, and also attended the National Science Foundation Teacher Training Institute at the University of Illinois from 1962 to 1965.

Falconer has spent most of her professional career at Spelman College, her mother's alma mater. She has held the positions of instructor/associate professor (1965–71), professor of mathematics and chair of the mathematics department (1972–82), chair of the division of natural sciences (1982–90), director of science programs and policy (1990), and associate provost for science programs and policy (1991–present). Falconer has been Spelman's Fuller E. Callaway Professor of Mathematics since 1990.

Falconer has devoted her career to encouraging African American students, particularly women, to study mathematics and the sciences. She is the director of Spelman College's NASA Women in Science and Engineering Scholars program (WISE), which fosters promising women students and encourages them to continue into graduate school. Among students' fields of study are applied mathematics, chemistry, and industrial engineering. Approximately 150 women have taken part in the program since its inception in 1987, and the program will soon celebrate the first of its alumnae receiving her Ph.D. Falconer also coordinates the university's NASA Undergraduate Scholar Awards program, which, like WISE, allows undergraduate students to conduct research at NASA facilities. In addition, she is one of the founders of the National Association of Mathematicians, which promotes the concerns of African American students and mathematicians, and the Atlanta Minority Women in Science Network.

Falconer has received many awards in recognition of her work on behalf of the next generation of scientists. In addition to the Louise Hay Award from the Association for Women in Mathematics (AWM), she also received the Giants in Science Award from the Quality Education for Minorities Network (1995). Her other honors include: Spelman College Presidential Faculty Award for Distinguished Service (1994); Spelman College Presidential Award for Excellence in Teaching (1988); United Negro College Fund Distinguished Faculty Award (1986–87); Achievement and Service Award, presented by the Atlanta Minority Women in Science Network and the Auxiliary to the Atlanta Medical Association; and the National Association of Mathematicians' Distinguished Service Award (1994). Falconer also received an honorary doctor of science degree from the University of Wisconsin at Madison in 1996. She is a member of Phi Beta Kappa, Pi Mu Epsilon (honorary mathematics fraternity), and Beta Kappa Chi (honorary scientific society). In addition, she has served in a variety of roles in the following organizations: the American Association for the Advancement of Science, the American Mathematical Society, the AWM, the Mathematical Association of America, the National Association of Mathematicians, and the National Science Foundation.

SELECTED WRITINGS BY FALCONER:

"Isotopy Invariants in Quasigroups." *Transactions of the American Mathematical Society*151 (1970): 511–526.

"Isotopes of Some Special Quasigroup Varieties." *Acta Mathematica* 22 (1971): 73–79.

"Women in Science at Spelman College." *Signs* 4 (1978): 176–177.
"A Story of Success: The Sciences at Spelman College." *SAGE* 6 (1989): 36–38.
"Views of an African American Woman on Mathematics Meetings." *A Century of Mathematics Meetings*. Edited by Bettye Anne Case. American Mathematical Society, 1996.

FURTHER READING

Bailey, Lakiea. "Etta Falconer." *Biographies of Women Mathematicians*. June 1997. http:/www/scottlan.edu/lriddle/women/chronol.htm (July 21, 1997).
Falconer, Etta Zuber, interview with Fran Hodgkins conducted May 1, 1997.

Sketch by Fran Hodgkins

Marilyn Gist Farquhar
1928–
American cell biologist and experimental pathologist

Marilyn G. Farquhar was a influential cell biologist who struggled from humble beginnings to leave an indelible impression on her field. Farquhar greatly advanced scientific knowledge of the mechanisms of renal disease and protein trafficking within cells. She published numerous papers and received various honors in her career, such as election by her peers to the National Academy of Sciences.

Marilyn Gist Farquhar was born July 11, 1928, in Tulare, California, the second of Brooks DeWitt and Alta Gertrude Green Gist's two children. A pediatrician friend of Alta's was an early catalyst for Farquhar's interest in medicine and biology. Farquhar grew up in Tulare and completed her early schooling there. She attended a country school from grades one through four and completed her elementary education at Wilson School in Tulare. She later went to Tulare Union High School, where her interest in biology was further sparked by an inspiring science teacher.

Although few of Farquhar's high school classmates attended college, her parents saw to it that she would not miss the opportunity. She attended the University of California at Berkeley, where she received an A.B. in zoology in 1949. In 1951 she entered her first marriage, which produced two sons, Bruce and Douglas. At the University of California at San Francisco (UCSF) Farquhar received an M.A. in 1953 and a Ph.D. in 1955. Her first project at UCSF was to begin the operation of one of the first electron microscopes in the Bay Area. That project led directly to the subject of her Ph.D. dissertation, which was electron microscopy of secretory processes in the front part of the pituitary gland.

Farquhar did her postdoctoral work at Rockefeller University with the Nobel Prize–winning biologist George Palade, whom she eventually married on June 7, 1970. After her postdoctoral work she returned to UCSF and took a post as an assistant research pathologist. She researched cellular and molecular mechanisms of renal disease (disease involving the kidneys and their surroundings) and the secretory processes of various systems including the liver and pancreas. Farquhar considered her work in these two areas to be her most important contributions to her field.

After eight years with UCSF as a researcher and teacher, Farquhar became a professor of cell biology and pathologist at Yale University's medical school in 1973. She became Sterling Professor of Cell Biology there in 1987, and in the same year she was awarded the Wilson Medal of the America Society of Cell Biology for her work on secretion and membrane trafficking. Farquhar also received the Homer Smith Award of the American Society of Nephrology for her study of the cellular and molecular mechanisms of renal disease in 1987. The next year, 1988, she was honored for career achievements in her field by election to the prestigious National Academy of Sciences. Farquhar returned to California in 1990 to be professor of pathology at the medical school of the University of California in San Diego.

Farquhar is a passionate lover of nature and music. She is especially fond of the chamber and orchestral works of J. S. Bach, Ludwig van Beethoven, Johannes Brahms, and Franz Schubert. She and Palade have often taken long walks on Del Mar beach in California. They have also vacationed in Colorado, hiking in the mountains and attending classical music festivals there.

FURTHER READING

Other

Dreyfuss, John Henry. Interview with Marilyn Farquhar, conducted on March 1, 1994.

Sketch by John Henry Dreyfuss

Wanda Margarite (Kirkbride) Farr
1895–1983
American biochemist

Wanda K. Farr solved a major scientific mystery in botany by showing that the substance cellulose, an important compound found in all plants, is made by tiny, cellular structures called plastids. The discovery was all the

Wanda K. Farr (AP/Wide World Photos. Reproduced by permission.)

more notable because the process of cellulose synthesis had been obscured by the very techniques that previous researchers were using to study the phenomenon under the microscope.

Farr was born Wanda Margarite Kirkbride in New Matamoras, Ohio, on January 9, 1895, the daughter of C. Fred and Clara M. Kirkbride. Although Farr's father died of tuberculosis when she was a child, her budding interest in living things was nurtured by her great-grandfather, Samuel Richardson, who was a prominent local physician. Farr had initially decided to attend medical school, but her family insisted she not become a doctor, fearing she too would be exposed to tuberculosis. Farr enrolled at Ohio University in Athens, where she received her B.S. in botany in 1915. She did graduate work in botany at Columbia University, earning her M.S. in 1918. It was there she met her future husband, Clifford Harrison Farr, who was completing work for a Ph.D. in botany.

When Clifford went to the Agricultural and Mechanical College of Texas to teach plant physiology, Farr accepted a position as instructor of botany at Kansas State College in 1917 to be closer to him. After they were married, the young couple moved to Washington, where Clifford Farr worked at the Department of Agriculture during World War I. Here, their son Robert was born, and Farr completed her research for her master's degree from Columbia.

After the war, they moved back to Texas A & M and then to Iowa in 1919, where Clifford became a faculty member of the University of Iowa's botany department. There, the two botanists continued to pursue their research on root hair cells—the tiny, fine hairs on plant roots that absorb water and nutrients from the soil. In 1925 Clifford accepted a position at Washington University in St. Louis, and the couple again moved. It was there, in February, 1928, that her husband died from a long–standing heart condition. Farr was later remarried to E. C. Faulwetter.

Begins Research on Cotton

After her husband's death, Farr abandoned her plan to return to Columbia to finish her doctorate and she remained at Washington University to teach her late husband's classes. She also became a research assistant at the Barnard Skin and Cancer Clinic in St. Louis from 1926 to 1927, where she learned new techniques for growing animal cells in culture dishes. After the school year ended, the Bache Fund of the National Academy of Sciences awarded her a grant to continue her studies of root hairs. Her work led in 1928 to a position with the U.S. Department of Agriculture working as a cotton technologist at the Boyce Thompson Institute, which was at that time located in Yonkers, New York.

The cotton industry was eager to learn more about cotton so it could train their employees to be better judges of the quality of this crop. Farr's work centered on the origin of cellulose, which makes up most of the cell walls of cotton fibrils and provides its form and stiffness. Though she and her coworkers studied the chemical content and other characteristics of the fibrils, they were confounded—as were scientists before them—by the origin of cellulose. Researchers knew that sugar was made in tiny structures called plastids, which capture the sun's energy during the process of photosynthesis. Molecules of cellulose, however, seemed to spring into existence fully formed within the cytoplasm of cells.

The problem, Farr discovered, was that plastids seemed to disappear into the cytoplasm when mounted in water for study under the microscope. Normally, light waves refract or bend when traveling from one medium, such as air, into another medium, such as water. (This refraction of light waves is what makes a spoon placed into a glass of water seem to bend.) The cellulose plastids, however, do not do this; rather, light passes directly through them, and they are rendered indistinguishable from the liquid medium. When these plastids fill with cellulose, the pressure within the structures makes them explode, spilling the cellulose molecules into the cytoplasm, where they are then visible. Thus, when viewed through a microscope, these molecules appear to arise suddenly, fully formed.

In 1936, during her studies of cotton cellulose, Farr was appointed Director of the Cellulose Laboratory of the Chemical Foundation at the Boyce Thompson Institute, and she later worked for the American Cyanamide Company (1940–1943) and the Celanese Corporation of America (1943–1954). In 1954 she was the twelfth annual **Marie Curie** lecturer at Pennsylvania State University. In 1956 she established her own laboratory, the Farr Cytochemistry Lab, in Nyack, New York. She also taught botany and cytochemistry at the University of Maine from 1957 to 1960, later serving as an occasional lecturer. At the time, she was one of the few women to become director of a research laboratory.

In a 1940 *New York Times* article about Farr, she was described as "versatile, chic, vivacious, [and] as modern as tomorrow." Her versatility included using her knowledge of cellulose to analyze the sheets from a 3,500-year-old Egyptian tomb for New York's Metropolitan Museum of Art to determine if they were made of cotton or linen (she determined they were linen). Among the organizations Farr belonged to were the American Association for the Advancement of Science; the American Chemical Society; the New York Academy of Science; the Royal Microscope Club (London); the American Institute of Chemists; Phi Beta Kappa; Sigma Xi; and Sigma Delta Epsilon. Almost nothing is known about Farr's activities later in her life. She died in April of 1983, in Rockland, Maine.

SELECTED WRITINGS BY FARR:

Periodicals

(With S. H. Eckerson) "Formation of Cellulose Membranes by Microscopic Particles of Uniform Size in Linear Arrangement." *Contributions of the Boyce Thompson Institute* 6 (1934): 189.

"Microscopical and Microchemical Analysis of Material of Plant Origin from Ancient Tombs." *American Journal of Botany* 31 (1944): 9.

FURTHER READING

Books

Yost, Edna. *American Women of Science.* Frederick A. Stokes Company, 1943.

Periodicals

"Cellulose Explained." *Time* (November 25, 1935): 54.

"Cellulose Factory Located in Plants." *New York Times* (December 27, 1939): 10.

"Challenging Approach to Study Brings Rewards to Scientist." *New York Times* (January 14, 1940): section 2, p. 8.

Sketch by Marc Kusinitz

Anne Fausto-Sterling
1944–
American biologist and author

Anne Fausto-Sterling, a highly regarded biologist, publishes scientific papers in the disparate and specialized fields of developmental genetics and social science. She has written and lectured on theories about women, gender, race and science, and is an considered an expert on the biological bases of sexual expression. Her early research was on the genetic mutation in *Drosophila*; since 1990, her laboratory has analyzed the regenerative capabilities of a group of flat worms called *Planaria.*

Fausto–Sterling was born in New York City on July 30, 1944 to Marxist parents whose orientation had a strong and lasting influence. She and her brother were indoctrinated into a scientific method of observation, and dialectics, and invited to think globally in analytical, theoretical frameworks. Exposure to her parents' cultural and historical studies on blacks and women, and her mother's natural science writing for children planted the seeds for her later work.

In 1965, Fausto–Sterling graduated with a major in zoology from the University of Wisconsin. Her marriage to a researcher the following year took her to Brown University, where she pursued graduate studies in developmental genetics. She earned her Ph.D. in 1970 and accepted a faculty position at Brown. For the next 15 years, she published widely on the molecular genetics of *Drosophila.* This work led to her tenure at Brown, and she was named Professor of Medical Science in the Department of Molecular, Biochemical, and Cellular Biology.

Writes *Myths of Gender*

As the field of molecular genetics ballooned, Fausto–Sterling gradually lost interest. She claimed in an essay in *Journeys of Women in Science and Engineering* that is "became highly competitive, very macho, and quite unpleasant to be in, because I don't do well under high–pressure, competitive situations." She took a leave of absence to write *Myths of Gender:Biological Theories about Women and Men*, published in 1985. This critical analysis of research on biological bases for differences between men and women has won international acclaim.

Since then, Fausto–Sterling has continued her compelling and controversial work on the social construction of science. She writes extensively and critically on the role of gender and race. She questions both the techniques used in the experimental process, and the objectivity of the scientist using them. Her ground–breaking article on "The Five Sexes" published in 1993 in the journal *The Sciences* received honorable mention in *The Best American Essays of 1994*, and has been reprinted in many publications, including *The New York Times.*

After finishing her book, Fausto–Sterling began new research on *Planaria*, an organism long–studied for its regenerative abilities. She returned to her laboratory, invigorated by the simplicity of her research projects and the low technology needed to make necessary observations. She joins developmental and evolutionary disciplines, examining and analyzing the regenerative differences in populations of *Planaria* according to methods of reproduction, and environmental factors.

A workshop leader and guest lecturer in high demand at universities, conferences, and panels, Fausto–Sterling also reviews manuscripts, and advises on academic curricula. She is a member of the Society of Developmental Biology, the International Society of Developmental Biology, the National Women's Studies Association; a fellow of the History of Science Society, and the American Association for Women in Science. In 1990, the American Association for the Advancement of Science elected her as a member. Fausto–Sterling, divorced in 1988, lives with her life partner, Paula Vogel, a playwright and professor in the graduate writing program at Brown.

In her essay in *Journeys of Women in Science and Engineering* she encourages young people to "see science as an enormously diverse set of worlds in which it is possible to find a comfortable place [and to] look around and find the field and style that is compatible with who you are, how you are, and how you work best."

SELECTED WRITINGS BY FAUSTO–STERLING:

Books

Myths of Gender: Biological Theories About Women and Men. New York: Basic Books, 1985; 2nd Edition with added chapters, 1992.

Periodicals

"The Five Sexes:Why Male and Female are Not Enough."*The Sciences* (March/April, 1993).

"Polyembryony in the Flatworm *Dugesia tigrina*: A Life History Approach." *American Zoologist* (1997):110A.

"Interactions between *Fused* and *Engrailed* Two Mutations Affecting Pattern Formation in *Drosophila melanogaster*. *Genetics* (1982): 71–80.

"Anatomy." *Encyclopedia of African American Culture and History*. Edited by Hamilton, Charles V., and Salzman, Jack. New York: Macmillan, 1995

FURTHER READING

Books

Ambrose, Susan, and Kristin L. Dunkle, et al., eds. *Journeys of Women in Science and Engineering; No Universal Constants*. Philadelphia: Temple University.

American Men and Women of Science 1998–99. 20th ed. New Providence: R.R. Bowker, 1998, p. 1210.

Sketch by Kyra Anderson

Jacoba Felicie
1280(?)–?
Italian physician

In 1220, the Faculty of Medicine of the University of Paris prohibited the practice of medicine by anyone who had not received a Masters degree from the Faculty and been approved by the Chancellor. Women were not admitted to the university. Although the edict was widely ignored, in the fourteenth century Jacoba Felicie, a successful physician, was brought to trial for the illegal practice of medicine.

The only surviving information about Jacoba (or Jacobe or Jacobina) Felicie comes from the records of her trial. She apparently was of noble birth, since the record refers to her as "Lady Jacoba." Born c.1280, she originally may have been from Florence, Italy, the only European country at the time where a woman could receive formal medical training. Apparently she did receive specialized training in medicine before becoming a practicing physician in Paris. However, neither Felicie herself, nor the patients who testified on her behalf at the trial, ever referred to her as a physician. Referring to a woman as a physician may have been enough to convict her of breaking the law. Felicie used sophisticated methods of diagnosis and she successfully treated patients whose illnesses had been declared hopeless by recognized male physicians. She accepted payment only after the patient was cured and she often treated the poor who could not afford to pay her. Interestingly, the Royal Chancellor and his family were reported to be among her patients.

Despite Felicie's successes, or perhaps because of them, the Faculty of Medicine, determined to preserve its monopoly on medical practice, singled her out for prosecution. Felicie was one of four women and two men who were tried in Paris in 1322 for illegally practicing medicine. Because Felicie had received a warning not to practice medicine, and because several of her patients testified on her behalf, her trial became a noteworthy event. The Dean and Masters of the Faculty of Medicine brought seven distinct charges against her in the Paris Court of Justice. The charges were based on her diagnoses, treatments, and aftercare of patients in Paris and its suburbs. As quoted by Eileen Power, one of her defense witnesses had "heard it said by several that she was wiser in the art of surgery and medicine than the greatest master doctor or surgeon in Paris." Felicie also testified in her own defense, arguing that the 1220 law was aimed at charlatans and ignorant folk, not practitioners with her training and expertise. Furthermore, she argued that women needed to be treated by women doctors. As Muriel Hughes quoted from Felicie's self defense: "It is better and more honest that a wise and expert woman in this art visit sick women, and inquire into the secret nature of their infirmity, than a man . . . this is the cause of many women and also men dying of their infirmities, not wishing to have doctors see their secret parts." Nevertheless, Felicie was forced by the Paris court to pay a large fine and was prohibited from practicing medicine under threat of excommunication from the Church. It was not until 1868 that the medical school in Paris began admitting women students.

FURTHER READING

Books

Hughes, Muriel Joy. *Women Healers in Medieval Life and Literature*. Oxford: Oxford University Press, 1943. Reprint, Freeport, NY: Books for Libraries Press, 1968.

Periodicals

Power, Eileen. "Some Women Practitioners of Medicine in the Middle Ages." *Proceedings of the Royal Society of Medicine, Section of the History of Medicine* 15 (1921): 20–23.

Sketch by Margaret Alic

Catherine Clarke Fenselau
1939–
American chemist

Catherine Fenselau is a preeminent chemist in the specialized field of mass spectrometry (a method for identifying a substance's chemical composition). This work with determining molecule charge and mass has enabled Fenselau to research drug metabolism and cancer therapies. In 1985 she was awarded the Garvan Medal from the American Chemical Society for her important work.

Fenselau was born April 15, 1939, in York, Nebraska, to businessman Lee Keckley Clarke, and Muriel (Thomas) Clarke, a teacher in both high schools and colleges. Fenselau's interest in science started early in her life, inspired by several family trips to Mesa Verde, and the launch of the Russian satellite *Sputnik*, in the late 1950s. As a sophomore in high school, Fenselau determined to study science in college and, encouraged by a family friend to attend a women's college, she decided on Bryn Mawr, from which she graduated *magna cum laude* in 1961 with a degree in chemistry.

Begins Mass Spectrometry Work

Fenselau married Allan H. Fenselau the following year, and during their 18-year marriage, they had two sons. The couple accepted appointments to the Johns Hopkins School of Medicine in 1967 and, during the intervening years, Fenselau completed her Ph.D. at Stanford University where she worked with Carl Djerassi on mass spectrometry. At the time, this was a brand new discipline in organic chemistry. Fenselau would eventually make it her specialty. Her post-doctoral work took place at Berkeley and the National Aeronautics and Space Administration's (NASA) space science laboratory, where Fenselau used mass spectrometry to study lunar rocks.

For 20 years, Fenselau remained at Johns Hopkins in the department of pharmacology, first as an instructor, in 1969 as an assistant professor, in 1973 as an associate professor, and in 1982 as full professor—the first woman to become professor in a pre-clinical department. In the mid-1980's, Fenselau's work on acylinked glucoronides opened up a new world of study and research.

Fenselau's work as an analytical chemist during these years led to important discoveries about anti-cancer drugs She and her colleagues were able to gain a better understanding of such drugs as cyclophosphamide, including the ways in which it was toxic to certain cells. Fenselau did research on the controversial substance laetrile, which during the late 1970s was hailed by some as a breakthrough in cancer treatment, and reviled by others as a blatant product of quackery. Fenselau and her colleagues did not determine whether laetrile was as successful as its proponents claimed, but they were able to establish a legal definition of the substance. Later in her career, the World Health Organization asked her to study the anti-leprosy drug clofazamine.

Fenselau has been the recipient of a number of prestigious awards. In 1972, she was presented with the Research Career Development Award from the National Institutes of Health; in 1978, the National Science Foundation awarded her a grant for the establishment of the Mass Spectrometry Regional Center for the Middle Atlantic; and, in 1985, the same year she married her second husband, Robert J. Cotter, she was presented with the Garvan Medal from the American Chemical Society. In later years, she received the Maryland Chemist Award from the American Chemical Society, the Distinguished University Scholar Award from the University of Maryland, the Merit Award from the National Institutes of Health, and the Pittsburgh Spectroscopy Award.

In addition to her university work, from 1973 to 1989, Fenselau was founding editor-in-chief of *Biomedical and Environmental Mass Spectrometry*, and since, 1990, has edited *Analytical Chemistry*. Fenselau enjoys her editing duties and active participation on a number of scientific advisory boards because, she says, she is "kept informed both about current research and current scientists."

Becomes Professor and Chair of Chemistry Department at Maryland

Anxious to return to teaching, in 1987 Fenselau left Johns Hopkins to accept the position of professor and chair of the department of chemistry at the University of Maryland, Baltimore County, where she also became the first permanent woman on the faculty. She later took on the position of interim dean of the graduate school and associate vice president for research.

Since 1998, Fenselau has been professor and chair of the chemistry department at the University of Maryland, College Park, where she heads a research strategy and discussion group and teaches a special topics course in mass spectrometry. Recognized as a leader in the field, she has been a visiting professor in several foreign countries, and is often invited to lecture across the globe. In her free time, she enjoys traveling, hiking, and bicycling on the banks of the Potomac River.

SELECTED WRITINGS BY FENSELAU:

Periodicals

"The New Mass Spectrometry: Desorption Ionization." *Chemtech* , 18 (1988): pp. 616–619.

"Mass Spectrometric Analysis of Proteins." *Current Opinion in Biotechnology*, 4 (1993): pp. 14–19.

FURTHER READING

Books

Shearer, Benjamin F. and Barbara S., eds. *Notable Women in the Physical Sciences.* Westport: Greenwood Press, 1997.

Other

Kiser, Helene Barker, interviews with Catherine Fenselau, conducted June 29, 1999 and July 20, 1999.

Sketch by Helene Barker Kiser

Angella Dorothea Ferguson
1925–
American pediatrician

Angella Ferguson is both a pediatrician and a well–respected researcher in the area of sickle–cell anemia. While in medical school, she began studying sickle–cell anemia, an illness that mainly strikes people of African descent. Ferguson drew up guidelines to identify the disease and established procedures for treating it. She also did research work in the area of growth and development in infants and children, especially African Americans. In the 1960s, Ferguson became involved in health and hospital administration. She oversaw the construction of the Howard Medical Center before her retirement in 1990.

Ferguson was born on February 15, 1925, in Washington, D.C. She was one of eight children born to George Alonzo and Mary (Burton) Ferguson. Ferguson's father worked several jobs; he was a schoolteacher, an architect, and a lieutenant colonel in the Army Reserves, but Ferguson and her family lived in poverty. Ferguson attended Washington's Cordoza High School, and while a sophomore, she became interested in chemistry and mathematics. Ferguson decided to attend college to study science, and upon her high school graduation in 1951, she enrolled in Howard University.

While attending Howard, Ferguson became more interested in biology. Her experiences with other biology students influenced her decision to become a doctor. Ferguson earned her bachelor of science degree from Howard in 1945 and then entered the medical school at Howard that same year. While a medical student, Ferguson took a class in pediatrics with Roland Scott, who became her mentor. Ferguson graduated with her medical degree in 1949. After graduation, Ferguson did a year–long internship in general medicine at Freedmen's Hospital, the teaching hospital attached to Howard. As part of her rotation, she worked in pediatrics, and this experience helped her decide on a specialty. She was admitted to a two–year residency program in pediatrics at Freedmen's Hospital. She later did postgraduate training at Bethesda Naval Hospital in radioisotopes and their clinical uses; she also held a fellowship at Cornell University Hospital in hematology. In 1951, she married Charles M. Cabanis, who was also a doctor. Together they would have two daughters, Carla Victoria and Caryn Leota.

When her residency was completed and her board examinations were passed, Ferguson opened her own private pediatric practice. The developmental questions that came up in the course of treating infants and children intrigued her. Most of the available information about child development focused on those of European, not African, descent. With the help of Scott, Ferguson studied the developmental physiology of African American children as a research associate at Howard's medical school. While conducting this research, Ferguson noticed the large number of black children suffering from sickle–cell anemia. This is a usually nonfatal though potentially serious condition; in sickle–cell anemia, red blood cells are sickle shaped rather than donut shaped as healthy red blood cells are, and this creates painful blockages in small blood vessels.

Throughout the 1950s and early 1960s, Ferguson continued to study sickle–cell anemia. In 1953, she became an instructor in the pediatric department of Howard University's school of medicine and an assistant pediatrician at Freedmen's. By 1959, she was promoted to assistant professor in the medical school. In her sickle–cell research, she first devised guidelines for identifying the illness in children under 12 years of age, since symptoms were difficult to distinguish from other childhood maladies. She promoted the use of a blood test in infants to check for the condition, something that had not been done before her time. After accomplishing this goal, she turned to treatment methods. For small active children, about five years of age, Ferguson recommended drinking at least one extra glass of water with some baking soda dissolved in it each day to relieve any extreme symptoms. Drinking water adds more volume to the blood, increasing its flow. When a patient suffering from sickle–cell anemia underwent surgery, symptoms of the disease would increase because of the strain from the operation. Ferguson recommended that doctors give such patients extra oxygen as they emerge from the anesthetized state to reduce the symptoms.

As a result of this research, Ferguson was awarded two certificates of merit from the American Medical Association. In 1963, she became an associate professor at Howard and an associate pediatrician at Freedmen's. She was also hired as member of the attending staff at D.C. General Hospital that year.

In 1965, Freedmen's Hospital was being torn down so that a new hospital could be built in its place. Ferguson was initially involved in the development of the children's wing but became director of programs and facilities for the entire hospital in 1970. That year, she was promoted to director of the University Office of Health Affairs at Howard Medical School. In addition to facility development, she oversaw student health services, research, and instruction in the medical school's advanced degree programs. Ferguson continued to supervise the planning and construction of the new hospital building. She also dealt with the United States Congress and their budgetary restrictions, eventually persuading them to increase funding. When the hospital, named the Howard University Medical Center, was completed in 1975, Ferguson became the associate vice–president of health affairs. She continued to be involved in new building development, including projects such as Howard College of Medicine's Seeley G. Mudd Building, the Animal Research Center, and the renovation of the College of Allied Health and Sciences and the College of Nursing.

Throughout her career, Ferguson was active in professional societies including the Society for Pediatric Research, the Society for Nuclear Medicine, and the National Medical Association. She also served on the board of directors for the Association for Sickle–Cell Anemia Research. Ferguson retired in 1990.

FURTHER READING

Books

Hayden, Robert C. *Eleven African–American Doctors.* Frederick: 1992.

Kessler, J.H., et al. *Distinguished African American Scientists of the 20th Century.* Phoenix: Oryx Press, 1996.

Sammons, Vivian Ovelton. *Blacks in Science and Medicine.* New York: Hemisphere Publishing, 1990.

Periodicals

Ebony. (August 1960): 44.

Ebony. (May 1964): 70.

Sketch by Annette Petrusso

Margaret Clay Ferguson
1863–1951
American botanist

Margaret Clay Ferguson, the first woman president of the Botanical Society of America, made important scholarly and educational contributions to the field of botany. As a scholar, her early work focused on the life history of plants, especially the reproductive process. Her study of the North American pine became a standard for plant life histories used by countless other botanists. Ferguson's later work concerned plant genetics. In addition to her productive work as a botanist, Ferguson's role as an educator, mostly at Wellesley College, was equally influential. She improved the curriculum for undergraduate botany education, and welcomed an unparalled number of female botanists to the field.

Ferguson was born on August 29, 1863, in Orleans, New York, to Robert Bell and Hannah (Warner) Ferguson. Her parents were farmers, and she had five siblings. From the age of 14, Ferguson taught in local public schools while continuing her own education at the Genesee Wesleyan Seminary in Lima, New York. She graduated from the Seminary in 1885. Ferguson was a special student at Wellesley College, where she studied botany and chemistry, from 1888 until 1891.

From 1891–93, Ferguson served as the head of the science department in the Gambier, Ohio, Harcourt Place Seminary. Though Ferguson earned no degree while at Wellesley, department head Susan Hallowell was so impressed with her work that she invited Ferguson to be an instructor there in 1893. Ferguson later earned both her B.S. and Ph.D. from Cornell University in botany. Her thesis began her life's academic work concerning the life history and reproductive process of plants. After earning her Ph.D. in 1901, Ferguson rose through the ranks at Wellesley from instructor to associate professor to full professor, and finally to head of the botany department in 1930.

The first focus of Ferguson's scholarly achievements concerned the physiology of the spores of fungi. Next, she expanded on her thesis, exploring native pine and its functional morphology and cytology. Her detailed analysis in these areas was vital, especially to fellow botanists who used her work as a standard for their own. By the mid–1920s, Ferguson moved on to plant genetics and inheritance. She found the genus *Petunia* useful for a higher plant genetics study. Through this study Ferguson proved that plant flower color and pattern are variable in that they do not follow Mendelian laws of inheritance, which state that the hybridized offspring of plants have a statistically determined appearance.

Ferguson's work as an educator was equally important. She modernized Wellesley's botany facilities and improved the course of study, molding Wellesley into an important institution for undergraduate education in plant sciences. As a teacher, Ferguson believed in the then–radical idea that botanists should study other sciences—such as chemistry, zoology, and physics—because of their relevance to botany. Ferguson also introduced lab work in the greenhouse as an important part of botony education. Her efforts included raising funds and designing a new botany building and greenhouses. In 1943, the greenhouses were named in her honor.

After stepping down from her administrative position in 1930, Ferguson spent two years as a research professor at Wellesley before retiring in 1932. She continued to receive accolades, such as an honorary degree from Mount Holyoke in 1937; and in 1943, she was named a fellow of the New York Academy of Sciences. Ferguson ended her research in 1938, when she moved to Seneca Castle, New York, to be near family. She later moved to Florida, then San Diego, California. Ferguson, who never married, suffered a heart attack and died on August 28, 1951 in San Diego.

SELECTED WRITINGS BY FERGUSON:

Periodicals

"Contributions to the Knowledge of the Life History of *Pinus* with Special Reference to Sporogenesis, the Development of the Gametophytes and Fertilization." *Proceedings of the Washington Academy of Sciences* (1906): 101–02.

FURTHER READING

Books

Bailey, Martha J. *American Women in Science: A Biographical Dictionary*. Denver: ABC–CLIO, 1994, pp. 112–13.

Hirsch, Ann M. and Lisa J. Marroni. *Notable American Women, The Modern Period*. Edited by B. Sicherman and C.H. Green. Cambridge: Belknap Press, 1980, pp. 229–30.

Ogilvie, Marilyn Bailey. *Women in Science: Antiquity through the Nineteenth Century*. Cambridge: MIT Press, 1986, pp. 84–85.

Siegel, Patricia Joan, and Kay Thomas Finley. *Women in the Scientific Search: An American Bio–bibliography, 1724–1979*. Metuchen, NJ: The Scarecrow Press, Inc., 1985, pp. 96–97.

Sketch by Annette Petrusso

Adele Marion Fielde
1839–1916
American entomologist

Adele Fielde was an well-traveled nineteenth-century entomologist, who was an expert on ants and butterflies. She also was a well-known missionary, author, and suffragette.

Fielde was born in 1839 in East Rodman, New York, the daughter of Leighton and Sophia (Tiffany) Fielde. She graduated from Albany Normal College in 1860. For the next 45 years, Fielde was employed intermittently as a teacher and principal in the New York City public schools and served as a Baptist missionary in China and Siam (now Thailand).

Fielde made her first trip to Siam in 1865, and she first went to Swatow, China in 1873. There she established schools for boys and Chinese women. In 1883 she took an obstetrics course at the Woman's Medical College of Philadelphia, and two years later, after turning down the job of president of Vassar College, Fielde returned to China to teach obstetrics. She circled the globe three times during her life, traveling extensively in Asia, Africa, and Europe during the years 1889–1892, following her retirement as a missionary. At the age of 69, she journeyed to Alaska and the Yukon Territory. Fielde wrote books on politics and Chinese culture and folklore, and she published a dictionary of the Swatow Chinese dialect. She also wrote several works in Chinese.

Determined to learn about biological evolution, in 1883 Fielde convinced the scientists at the Academy of Natural Sciences in Philadelphia to take her on as their only student. She spent two winters at the Academy, studying and dissecting animals and performing original research on the regeneration of nerve tissues. She spent the summers at Annisquam Biological Laboratory and at Nantucket with Dr. Benjamin Sharp and his family. Subsequently, she served as a delegate to the World Congress of Scientists in New York City, where she lectured on Chinese science. Back in China, she carried on her scientific correspondence, sending specimens of trees and shells and a new species of insect to various scientists.

Between 1894 and 1907, Fielde was a researcher and lecturer at the Marine Biological Laboratory at Woods Hole, Massachusetts. In her summers at Woods Hole, she carried out research and helped to train a generation of American women biologists. Field's primary research interest was insect behavior. Her 20 papers of original research on ants and butterflies, published between 1900 and 1907, appeared in various publications, including *The Biological Bulletin* and the *Proceedings* of the Academy of Natural Sciences of Philadelphia. Her publications in the latter journal were collected and reprinted as *Ant Studies.* She discovered that ants could remember a smell for at least three years and that they could see only ultraviolet light. Fielde was a member of the American Association for the Advancement of Science and an honorary member of the Philadelphia Geographical Society.

An ardent feminist, Fielde lectured for the League for Political Education in New York City between 1894 and 1907. She published pamphlets and gave public speeches on women's rights until she was well into her 70s. Fielde moved to Seattle in 1907 because of respiratory problems. There she continued to work for women's suffrage, until Washington State women were granted voting rights in 1910. She also campaigned for prohibition and improved child welfare. In 1912, Fielde was appointed a trustee of the Seattle Public Library, becoming the first woman in that city to hold a public office. She died in Seattle in 1916.

SELECTED WRITINGS BY FIELDE:

Books

Pagoda Shadows: Studies from Life in China. Boston: W. G. Corthell, 1885.

Chinese Nights Entertainment; Forty Stories Told by Almond-Eyed Folk Actors in the Romance of the Strayed Arrow. New York: G. P. Putnam's Sons, 1893.

Ant Studies. Philadelphia: Academy of Natural Sciences, 1901–07.

Parliamentary Procedure; a Compendium of its Rules Compiled from the Latest and Highest Authorities, for the Use of Students and for the Guidance of Officers and Members of Clubs, Societies, Boards, Committees, and all Deliberative Bodies. Seattle: Helen N. Stevens, 1914.

FURTHER READING

Books

Bailey, Martha J. *American Women in Science: A Biographical Dictionary.* Denver: ABC–CLIO, 1994.

Bonta, Marcia Myers. *Women in the Field: America's Pioneering Women Naturalists.* College Station: Texas A & M University Press, 1991.

Leonard, John William, ed. *Woman's Who's Who of America: A Biographical Dictionary of Contemporary Women of the United States and Canada.* New York: The American Commonwealth Co., 1914–1915.

Sawyer, Helen Norton. *Memorial Biography of Adele M. Fielde.* New York: Fielde Memorial Committee, 1918.

Sketch by Margaret Alic

Mary Peters Fieser
1909–1997
American research chemist and writer

Mary Peters Fieser, along with her husband and research partner, Louis F. Fieser, were so important to textual organic chemistry and student development in the chemical sciences, that in 1995, Harvard University dedicated its undergraduate chemistry laboratory in their memory. In addition to co–authoring several influential chemistry textbooks with her husband, Fieser also co–produced and edited the significant 17–volume reference series, *Reagents for Organic Synthesis*, the last volume of which she completed after her husband's death. Both Fiesers were known for their work in the area of natural products and the structural examination and ultimate synthesis of quinones and steroids. They achieved significant research and development in the synthesis of the hormone cortisone and Vitamin K, and also developed an important antimalarial drug, lapinone, which became a viable substitute where quinine (a standard drug to treat malaria) was in shortage.

Mary Fieser was especially appreciated as mentor to thousands of Harvard chemistry students, inspiring them to study science with passion and without hindrance. Professionally, Fieser held the position of research associate in Harvard's Department of Chemistry and Chemical Biology for more than 60 years, continuing the work of her husband after his death in 1977. In 1971, Fieser was the American Chemical Society's honored recipient of the prestigious Garvan Medal, a national award for women scientists who have performed distinguished service in the field of chemistry.

Born to Robert and Julia (Clutz) Peters in 1909, young Fieser was one of three children raised in a family of academic excellence and service to others. Her father (an English professor) was the son of the president of Midland College and her mother had a degree in English from Goucher College. The family moved from Atchison, Kansas to Harrisburg, Pennsylvania, where her father had accepted a teaching position with what is now Carnegie–Mellon University. Fieser's mother, having herself done graduate work, was also owner–manager of a local bookstore in

Harrisburg. The family encouraged personal and professional achievement, especially for the female members. Fieser's sister was a mathematics professor, and her maternal grandmother taught all seven of her children until they were of college age.

Fieser herself was educated in private schools, then went on to earn her bachelor's degree in chemistry from Bryn Mawr College in 1930. She had intended a career in medicine, inspired as a youth by a female family doctor. While at Bryn Mawr, Fieser met her future husband, Louis, who was a chemistry instructor at the college. She became particularly interested in his approach to the field of chemistry, more experimental than disciplined or theoretic, and she decided to team with him, switching majors from premed to chemistry. They married in 1932. When he later accepted a teaching position at Harvard, Fieser went with him and became his research chemist while earning her master's degree in organic chemistry from Harvard in 1936.

Overcomes Gender Bias to Achieve Success

Having thus allied herself with her husband professionally, Fieser spared herself the continued humiliation and subprofessional treatment she had received in undergraduate work because of bias toward women scientists at that time. For example, Fieser was ostracized from laboratory experiments and had to conduct her own in the basement of another building. (Sadly, even Harvard failed to pay her a salary, and she was not granted the title of Research Fellow at Harvard until 29 years after she began her research there.) For this reason, Fieser deferred pursuit of her doctoral degree in chemistry, in favor of remaining on her husband's research team. (Fieser received an honorary Sc.D. from Smith College in 1969, in recognition for her outstanding contributions to the field of chemistry.)

Moreover, Fieser complimented her husband professionally: in addition to being regarded as a top research chemist, Fieser possessed extraordinary writing skills. This allowed her not only to communicate complex technical data in precise terms to others, but also helped her formulate results from the joint research she and her husband completed on significant projects, such as the development of synthesized cortisone, an important steroid for the treatment of rheumatoid arthritis. She and her husband, himself an accomplished writer, often engaged in good–natured argument over the particular spelling, form, or placement of a word or symbol. Their textbooks were methodically instructive as well as interesting, for example, *Organic Chemistry* contained 454 biographical sketches to lighten up the subject matter. Fieser completed the 17th volume of *Reagents* in 1994 at the age of 85.

A consummate achiever, both professionally and personally, Fieser enjoyed organizing competitive games among her husband's research team members, such as badminton, horse shoes or table tennis. She also developed a caring interest and professionally–maternal attitude toward countless undergraduate and graduate students, prodding them to achieve and helping them when they were overwhelmed by the complexity of science and studies in general. In her personal life, Fieser enjoyed cats, many photographs of which appeared in her/their published works. She died at her Belmont home in 1997, at the age of 87. There were no immediate survivors.

SELECTED WRITINGS BY FIESER:

Books

(With Louis Fieser) *Organic Chemistry.* New York: John Wiley and Sons, 1944.

(With Louis Fieser) *Style Guide for Chemists.* New York: Reinhold, 1959.

(With Louis Fieser) *Advanced Organic Chemistry.* New York: Reinhold, 1963.

(With Louis Fieser) *Topics in Organic Chemistry.* New York: Reinhold, 1963.

(With Louis Fieser) *Reagents for Organic Synthesis.* New York: John Wiley & Sons (17 volumes), 1967, 1980, 1994.

FURTHER READING

Books

McMurray, Emily J., ed. *Notable Twentieth–Century Scientists.* New York: Gale Research Inc., 634.

O'Neill, Lois Decker, ed. *The Women's Book of World Records and Achievements.* New York: Double–day, 1979.

Shearer, Benjamin F. and Barbara S. Shearer, eds. *Notable Women in the Physical Sciences.* Westport, CT: Greenwood Press, 1997.

Periodicals

Pramer, Stacey. "Mary Fieser: a Transitional Figure in the History of Women." *Journal of Chemical Education.* March 1985.

Other

"Awards in Chemistry." http://www.meduniv.lviv.ua/chemistry1.html (22 June 1999)

"C&EN's Top 75." *Chemical & Engineering News.* 1998. http://pubs.acs.org/hotartcl/cenear/980112/top.html (22 June 1999).

"Mary Fieser, Researcher, Writer in Organic Chemistry, Dies at Age 87." *The Harvard University Gazette.* 27 March 1997. http://www.news.harvard.edu.hno.subpages/gazarch/hno.gazette.march.27.htm (22 June 1999).

"Memorial Service." *The Harvard University Gazette,* 12 June 1997. http://www.news.harvard.edu/gazette/1997/06.12/MemorialService.html (22 June 1999).

"Smith College Honorary Degrees." http://www.smith.edu/collegerelations/history/hon.html (22 June 1999).
Strategian. at http://www.strategina.com/chemistry.html (22 June 1999).

Sketch by Lauri R. Harding

Elizabeth F. Fisher
1873–1941
American geologist

Elizabeth F. Fisher was one of the first women field geologists in the United States. A professor at Wellesley College for thirty–two years, she taught geology, geography, and resource conservation. In 1918, Fisher helped locate oil wells in Texas as the first female geologist hired by an oil company.

Fisher was born in Boston, Massachusetts, on November 26, 1873, to Charles and Sarah Cushing Fisher. In 1894, while still a student at the Massachusetts Institute of Technology, she began teaching courses in geology and geography at Wellesley College; in 1896 she earned her S.B. degree from MIT. The next year, she traveled to Russia with the International Geological Congress; during her four–month stay, she and other foreign geologists visited the famous oil wells of Baku on the shores of the Caspian Sea.

She was an instructor at Wellesley College until 1906, when she was made an associate professor of geology and mineralogy there. In 1909, she became professor and head of the department of geology and geography. She also taught extension courses at Harvard and Radcliffe. In her lectures, Fisher addressed agricultural issues such as soil erosion and fertilization, as well as water supply and water power, advocating the reclamation of deserts and swamplands for agricultural use. Fisher's main research interests were river terraces, shorelines, and natural resource conservation. When World War I caused shortages of fuels and metals, Fisher also advocated the economic efficiency of mining. She wrote a textbook for junior high schools on natural resources; the book, *Resources and Industries of the United States,* described the position of the United States in world commerce and the natural and economic factors that stimulated its industrial growth. It also emphasized the dependence of the industries on natural resources and the critical need for conservation.

Hired to Scout Oil Fields

During a nationwide oil shortage in 1918, an oil company in Kansas hired Fisher to help locate oil wells in their north central Texas fields. She was the first woman sent out by an oil company to do such a survey. In 1926, Fisher became professor emeritus at Wellesley College. After her retirement she participated in a geographical survey of coastal Florida. On the shores of the twenty–seven–mile–wide Lake Okeechobee, she noted that drainage canals had lowered the level of the lake by about four feet. She is quoted in a Wellesley College news release as saying that "This uncovered about 80,000 acres of the richest muck land one would care to see; land so rich that weeds were growing ten feet high." She described the farmers growing radishes there that were as big as beets, and she calculated that further drainage of the lake could add nearly one million acres of arable land, on which Florida farmers might raise all the nation's sugar.

After her retirement, Fisher filled out a Wellesley College questionnaire, now preserved in the Wellesley College Archives. She noted her travels to national parks in Alaska in 1900 and a trip she took with twelve geology students to camp and ride horseback in Glacier National Park in 1919. At the bottom of the questionnaire, which Fisher filled out by hand, she had written, "At present I am studying and getting well." She died on April 25, 1941, in Los Angeles, California, after what the Wellesley College Office of Publicity described as a long illness. Fisher was a fellow of the American Association for the Advancement of Science and the American Geographical Society. She was also an active member of the Appalachian Mountain Club and the Boston Society of Natural History.

SELECTED WRITINGS BY FISHER:

Books

Resources and Industries of the United States. Ginn & Co., 1919.

FURTHER READING

Books

Who Was Who in America. Marquis, 1973.

Periodicals

"Conservation Work by Professor Elizabeth Fisher." *Wellesley Alumnae Quarterly* (January 1919).
"Elizabeth Fisher, Geologist, Dies." *The Boston Herald* (May 2, 1941).

Other

"Wellesley Geologist, on Survey of Florida Everglades, Finds Fountain of Eternal Sweetness in Reclaimed Land," news release, Wellesley College Archives.
Wellesley College Questionnaire for Faculty and Officers of Administration, Wellesley College Archives.

Sketch by Miyoko Chu

Perrenelle Lethas Flammel
?–1397
French alchemist

Perrenelle Flammel and her husband were famous alchemists in fourteenth–century Paris. It was a time when the knowledge of the ancient Greek alchemists, which had been rescued from oblivion by the Arabs during the Dark Ages, was being rediscovered in medieval Europe and entering the popular culture.

Nothing is known of Flammel prior to her marriage to Nicholas Flammel, a wealthy scribe, or copyist. She had been widowed twice and, reportedly, the Flammels lived a simple, religious life until Nicholas Flammel came upon an ancient alchemical manuscript, the "Book of Abraham." Although the Flammels admired the book for its beautiful cover and elaborate illustrations, they had no idea what the writing meant. For 21 years, they consulted various authorities about possible interpretations, and they began trying alchemical experiments. Finally, Nicholas Flammel journeyed to Spain, where he conferred with a Jewish physician named Canche about the meaning of the text and figures. Canche was returning to Paris with Flammel when he died; the Flammels spent the next three years carrying out new experiments with the information they had learned from him. On Monday, January 17, 1382, Nicholas Flammel announced that he and his wife had turned a half–pound of mercury into pure silver.

Several months later, as F. S. Taylor quotes from Nicholas Flammel's account: "I made projection of the red stone upon the like quantity of mercury, in the presence likewise of Perrenelle only. . . which I transmuted truely into almost as much pure gold, better assuredly than common gold, more soft and pliable. I may speak it with truth, I have made it three times, with the help of Perrenelle, who understood it as well as I because she helped me with my operations, and without doubt, if she would have enterprised to have done it alone, she had attained the end and perfection thereof."

Most likely, the Flammels had succeeded in repeating some of the ancient alchemists experiments in gilding or forming alloys of base metals to simulate gold and silver. Nevertheless, in carrying out such experiments Perrenelle Flamel had rediscovered ancient chemical techniques for working with metals and elements. Such techniques were the forerunners of modern experimental chemistry. Nicholas Flammel wrote an account of their experiments that was very popular and was reprinted numerous times in the fifteenth through seventeenth centuries. Their experiments made the Flammels rich, and they reportedly used their wealth for charitable purposes, endowing hospitals and churches. Their activities improved the reputation of medieval alchemists. Perennelle Flammel died in 1397.

FURTHER READING

Books

Alic, Margaret. *Hypatia's Heritage: A History of Women in Science from Antiquity through the Nineteenth Century.* Boston: Beacon Press,1986.

Taylor, F. Sherwood. *The Alchemists: Founders of Modern Chemistry.* New York: Schuman, 1949.

Sketch by Margaret Alic

Williamina Paton Stevens Fleming
1857–1911
Scottish-born American astronomer

The first of the famous women astronomers at the Harvard College Observatory, Williamina Fleming helped to revolutionize astronomy in the late nineteenth and early twentieth centuries. She discovered ten novae, or exploding stars, and more than 200 variable stars. She also developed a new star classification system. Fleming was considered to be the leading female astronomer of her day and her achievements opened up astronomy as a scientific field for women.

Born in Dundee Scotland in May,1857, Williamina (known as Mina) Fleming was the daughter of Robert and Mary (Walker) Stevens. Her father had a profitable carving and gilding business and was well known for his picture frames. He was also one of the first in Dundee to experiment with photograph. He died when his daughter was seven. Fleming attended public schools in Dundee until she was 14 and then worked as a student–teacher until her marriage to James Orr Fleming at age 20. In 1878, the couple emigrated to the United States, settling in Boston, Massachusetts, where her husband promptly deserted her. To make matters worse, she was pregnant. Fleming then had to go to work as a domestic to support herself. Her choice of employers would change her life

From Housekeeper to Astronomer

In 1879 Fleming went to work as a domestic for Edward C. Pickering, an astrophysicist and the new director of the Harvard College Observatory. She returned briefly to Scotland that fall to give birth to her son. Presumably, she wanted to be with her family for the birth. Pickering must have made an impression on her in the brief time they knew one another, because she named her son Edward Pickering Fleming.

Pickering was an advocate of higher education for women and an exacting employer. Frustrated with the inefficiencies of his male assistant, the story goes that he proclaimed that even his Scottish maid could do a better job and he set out to prove it. Soon, the 24–year–old Fleming had progressed from housework to astronomical observations.

The major work of the Harvard Observatory, made possible by the Draper Memorial established by **Mary Anna Palmer Draper** in 1886, was to use photographs to analyze the spectra, brightness, positions, and motions of stars. Photographs revealed wavelengths of light that were invisible to the human eye and therefore had never been seen with telescopes. The photographs of star spectra, the pattern of bands and lines that form when a star's light is dispersed through a prism, provided an entirely new way of classifying and analyzing stars. Nettie A. Farrar, an assistant at the Observatory who was leaving to marry, trained Fleming to analyze the spectra. Fleming's most important contribution to astronomy was her classification of 10,351 stars into 17 categories for the *Draper Catalogue of Stellar Spectra*, published in 1890. Her system of classification, known as the Pickering–Fleming System, supplanted the original classification system devised by Pickering.

In the course of her career, Fleming examined nearly 200,000 photographic plates, made at Cambridge and at Harvard's southern observatory in Arequipa, Peru, and supervised their classification. Fleming's studies of these photographic plates of star spectra led to her discoveries of ten of the 24 novae that were known at the time of her death in 1911. Novae are stars whose light suddenly increases dramatically and then fades. She also discovered 59 gaseous nebulae. Gaseous nebulae are high density interstellar dust or clouds, belonging to two groups of nebulae—planetary and diffuse. One of her most important discoveries concerned long–period variable stars, which were thought to be very rare, since their brightness changed so slowly that the magnitude of brightness was not observed to vary. Fleming discovered that variable stars could be identified by certain spectral characteristics. This enabled her to identify and analyze 222 of these of stars. Furthermore, she selected comparison stars that enabled the brightness of the variable stars to be determined with accuracy. This was the first photographic standard for determining the magnitude of star brightness. Of the 107 unusual Wolf–Rayet stars known at the time, Fleming discovered 94. In 1891, Fleming discovered spectral variations corresponding to changes in the light from the star Beta Lyrae, indicating that it was a double star. The latter discovery is usually credited to Pickering. Fleming's early work was published under Pickering's name, although by 1890, "M. Fleming" was appearing on the reports as Pickering's coauthor.

Directs the Women of the Harvard College Observatory

Fleming's work at the observatory was so outstanding that Pickering put her in charge of hiring and supervising a team of women to sort and study the immense collection of photographs of star spectra. Over the next 15 years, Fleming hired some 20 women. Some of the them were college graduates who had majored in astronomy and went on to become famous astronomers in their own right. Among these women were **Antonia Maury**, **Henrietta Leavitt**, and **Annie Jump Cannon**. In 1893, Fleming gave a speech on women's work in astronomy at the Chicago World's Fair, and following this, astronomy as a scientific profession for women became a subject for the popular press. As a result, other observatories around the United States began hiring women.

In 1898, Fleming was made Curator of Astronomical Photographs at the Observatory, the first woman appointed by the Harvard Corporation. She directed the work of the other women, assisted Pickering at the Observatory, and prepared the work of other astronomers for publication. Much of her time was occupied with editing the *Annals of the Harvard College Observatory*, which she resented because this distracted her from her own astronomical research. Fleming worked 60–hour weeks for a salary of $1,500 per year, which was far below what the newest male assistant at the Observatory received. Her recently discovered journals from 1900 reveal her frustration with this situation, particularly because she was putting her son through the Massachusetts Institute of Technology at the time. She had to struggle to make ends meet, but she was even more indignant at having her work and expertise undervalued.

Fleming was awarded honorary memberships in the Royal Astronomical Society and the French and Mexican astronomical societies. The latter presented her with a gold medal for her discovery of new stars. She was one of 11 women charter members of the American Astronomical Society and an honorary fellow of Wellesley College. After her death from pneumonia at the age of 54, Fleming was succeeded as curator by her protégée, Annie Jump Cannon.

SELECTED WRITINGS BY FLEMING:

Periodicals

"A Field for Woman's Work in Astronomy." *Astronomy and Astrophysics* 12 (1893): 683–89.

"A Photographic Study of Variable Stars." *Annals of the Harvard College Observatory* 47 (1907).

"Stars Having Peculiar Spectra."*Annals of the Harvard College Observatory* 56 (1912).

FURTHER READING

Books

Hoffleit, Dorrit. "Williamina Paton Stevens Fleming." In *Notable American Women1607–1950: A Biographical Dictionary*. Edited by Edward T. James, Janet Wilson James, and Paul W. Boyer. Cambridge: Harvard University Press, 1971.

Jones, Bessie Z. and Lyle Boyd. *The Harvard College Observatory: The First Four Directorships, 1839–1919.* Cambridge: Harvard University Press, 1971.

Rossiter, Margaret W. *Women Scientists in America: Struggles and Strategies to 1940.* Baltimore: Johns Hopkins University Press, 1982.

Periodicals

Cannon, Annie J. "Williamina Paton Fleming." *Science* 33 (June 30, 1911): 987–88.

Sketch by Margaret Alic

Alice Cunningham Fletcher
1838–1923
American anthropologist and ethnologist

Alice Cunningham Fletcher was a pioneer ethnographer, anthropologist, and reformer, best known for her field work in recording and preserving the music and religious ceremonies of many Native American tribes. Her studies advanced understanding of Native American culture, and her reform work for the United States government brought her recognition as an expert in tribal ways of life.

Fletcher was born in Havana, Cuba, on March 15, 1838, to Lucia Adeline (Jenks) and Thomas Gilman Fletcher. Her parents moved to Cuba because her father, a New York City attorney suffering from tuberculosis, thought the climate would benefit his health. This proved not to be the case and he died a little over a year after her birth. Fletcher grew up in New York, but left home as a teenager to escape ill treatment by her stepfather. She was taken in by a wealthy businessman, Claudius Conant, whose daughters had attended the Packer Collegiate Institute with her. She served as a tutor to his younger children and taught in private schools. Conant also helped her to strike out on her own.

After touring Europe, Fletcher returned to New York and became involved in educational and reform issues for women. In order to support herself she decided to give a series of lectures on "Ancient America." While researching at the Peabody Museum at Harvard University for her lecture series, she met the man whom she would call her "godfather in science," Frederic W. Putnam, the museum's director. His influence and guidance led to her pioneering work in the newly emerging science of anthropology.

Begins Career as Ethnographer

Fletcher began studying ethnology, the study of cultures, and archaeology. She helped Putnam raise money

Alice Cunningham Fletcher (The Granger Collection, New York. Reproduced by permission.)

for the museum and conducted field work in Florida. After meeting a group of Omaha who were touring the East, her fascination with Native American life began, and she decided to learn first hand about tribal cultures. In 1881, she left New York for the West, stopping in Dakota Territory for six weeks to camp with the Sioux, and then continuing on to Nebraska to the Omahas. Her careful observations, recorded in "Five Indian Ceremonies," were published in the 1884 annual report for the Peabody Museum. She was one of the first ethnographers to conduct field work for scientific study.

Fletcher studied the Sioux, Pawnee, Alaskan, Winnebago, and Nez-Percé tribes, but the Omahas retained a special place in her heart. She lived with them for more than a year intent on scientifically recording their culture. However, in living with the tribe, she became caught up in their difficulties and her work turned toward social reform. She championed their struggle to avoid transfer to a reservation in Indian Territory (Oklahoma). In 1881 she helped the tribe petition the federal government for individual ownership of and title to their lands in Nebraska. When the plea went unanswered, Fletcher went to Washington herself to press the Omaha's case.

Once in the capital she mounted a vigorous personal lobbying campaign and the bill to apportion the Omaha's tribal lands among its members passed. Fletcher herself was made an agent of the Bureau of Indian Affairs and was sent back to Nebraska to oversee the allotment. This work actually allowed her to observe native life more closely and introduced her to the Joseph LaFlesche family, whose son, Francis, became her field assistant, and a noted ethnologist in his own right. Fletcher regarded him as her adopted son and he lived with and cared for her in her later years in Washington, D. C. Their collaboration produced many works, the best known of which is *The Omaha Tribe*, published in 1911, which included previously unknown details of religious rites and ceremonies.

Works to Pass Dawes Act

Fletcher believed that Native American tribes should be assimilated into white society and given the benefit of citizenship and education, and she worked actively to dismantle the agency system. In 1887 the Dawes Act, for which Fletcher had been a vocal advocate, extended the Omaha allotment system to all tribes. Fletcher was placed in charge of seeing that the Dawes Act was carried out on the Winnebago and Nez-Percé reservations. Unfortunately, the tribes did not benefit as she hoped. Many Native Americans were unable to adjust to a settled life and others were tricked out of their land. Fletcher and other reformers were criticized, especially by tribal leadership, for the negative results of the act. Fletcher was deeply disappointed and disillusioned by the failure of the Dawes Act to improve the lot of the tribes, but she never admitted this in public. She did remove herself from working with the federal government after this failure and turned again to anthropological study.

Fletcher's anthropological work has been overshadowed by her work in helping Native Americans. It was, however, her humanitarian work that allowed her such close contact with the Omaha and therefore access to ceremonies and cultural artifacts that she otherwise wouldn't have had access to. Fletcher wrote more than 115 papers and books on Native American culture. She was one of the first anthropologists to study Native American music and she remained the leading expert until her death. Her interest in preserving Native American artifacts and monuments was responsible in great part for the establishment of the School of American Archaeology, opened in Santa Fe, New Mexico, in 1909. For the majority of her professional life she was associated with the Peabody Museum at Harvard University. She was appointed a research fellowship in 1891, and retained that fellowship until her death. The fellowship was the first ever given to a woman by Harvard University. Fletcher died in Washington, D. C., on April 6, 1923.

SELECTED WRITINGS BY FLETCHER:

Monographs

The Hako: A Pawnee Ceremony. Washington: Twenty-second Annual Report of the Bureau of American Ethnology, 1904. Reprint, University of Nebraska Press, 1996.

(With Francis La Flesche) *'The Omaha Tribe'*. Washington: Twenty–seventh Annual Report of the Bureau of American Ethnology, 1911. Reprint, University of Nebraska Press, 1992.

Periodicals

"Five Indian Ceremonies." *16th Annual Report, Peabody Museum of American Archaeology and Ethnology* (1884): 260–888.

(With James R. Murie) "A Study of Omaha Indian Music." *Archaeological and Ethnological Papers, Peabody Museum of American Archaeology and Ethnology* 1 (1893): 237–87.

FURTHER READING

Books

Bailey, Martha J. *American Women in Science, A Biographical Dictionary*. Santa Barbara: ABC–CLIO, 1994, pp. 117–118.

Garraty, John A and Mark C. Carnes, eds. *American National Biography*. Vol. 8. New York: Oxford University Press, 1999.

James, Edward T. ed. *Notable American Women, 1607–1950*. Vol. I. Cambridge: Belknap Press, 1971, pp. 630–633.

Johnson, Allen and Dumas Malone, eds. *Dictionary of American Biography*. Vol. III. New York: Charles Scribner's Sons, 1930–31, pp. 463–464.

Ogilvie, Marilyn Bailey. *Women in Science, Antiquity through the Nineteenth Century*. Cambridge: MIT Press, 1986, pp. 86–87.

Rossiter, Margaret W. *Women Scientists in America, Struggles and Strategies to 1940*. Baltimore: Johns Hopkins University Press, 1986, pp. 58–59; pp. 80–81.

Winters, Christopher, ed. *International Dictionary of Anthropologists*. New York: Garland Publishing, 1991, pp. 202–203.

Other

Boland, Patrick. "Alice Cunningham Fletcher." 4000 Years of Women in Science. http://vms.www.uwplatt.edu/˜nicols/fletcher.html

Sketch by Jane Stewart Cook

Irmgard Flügge-Lotz
1903–1974
German-born American engineer

Irmgard Flügge–Lotz conducted pioneering studies of aircraft wing lift distribution, making significant contributions to modern aeronautic design. She became an advisor to the National Aeronautics and Space Administration (NASA), as well as to German and French research institutes. During an era when few women engaged in engineering as an occupation, she became Stanford University's first female professor in its College of Engineering.

The eldest daughter of a journalist, Irmgard Flügge–Lotz was born on July 16, 1903, in Hameln, Germany. Her interest in engineering began during her childhood as members of her mother's family worked in the construction business. Flügge–Lotz became intrigued with the science as she visited various family building sites. In her teens she took on much responsibility in providing for her family. Her father, Oskar Lotz, had left his newspaper job when he was drafted into the German Army during World War I. To assist with family finances, Flügge–Lotz began tutoring fellow students. She continued to work after her father returned from the war in ill health.

Upon graduation from high school, she opted to further her education in applied mathematics and engineering. After six years of classwork, she received the German equivalent of a Ph.D. in engineering from the Technical University of Hanover. The topic of her dissertation concerned the mathematical theory of circular cylinders and heat conduction.

Wins Supervisory Position

Despite her advanced degree, Flügge–Lotz had difficulty finding a level of employment that was on par with her education. Her first professional position reflected the limited opportunities available to women in engineering during that time. Obtaining a job with the Aerodynamische Veruchsanstalt (AVA) research institute in Gottingen, she was to spend half of her time as a cataloguer.

Perceptions of Flügge–Lotz's abilities changed dramatically when she applied herself to a problem which had daunted two leading aerodynamicists, including the director of the institute. A decade earlier, one of her colleagues had developed an equation for his theory about the lift distribution of an airplane wing. However, the equation was not successful consistently. When Flügge–Lotz tackled the problem, she solved the equation for the general case. Continuing to work with the equation, she developed it so that it had widespread practical applications. Her brief career as a cataloguer ended as she was named supervisor of a group of engineers who researched theoretical aerodynamics within the AVA.

While in this position, she deciphered a method of calculating the lift distribution on aircraft wings known as the "Lotz–method"—a technique that is still in use today. She issued her findings for publication. Continuing to delve into wing theory, she added to the knowledge of the effects of control surfaces, propeller slipstream, and wind–tunnel wall interference.

The course of Flügge–Lotz's career changed in 1938 when she married Wilhelm Flügge, a civil engineer. The husband and wife team began work at Berlin's Deutsche Versuchsanstalt für Luftfahrt (DVL), a German agency similar to the U.S. government's NASA. Beginning work as a consultant in flight and aerodynamics, Flügge–Lotz conducted groundbreaking research in automatic control theory, especially pertaining to on–off controls. Subsequently, these controls, being reliable and inexpensive to build, came into widespread use.

By 1944 the Flügges had relocated to the small town of Saulgau, continuing work for the DVL there. After Germany's loss of World War II, the Flügges joined the staff of French National Office for Aeronautical Research, called ONERA, in Paris. Flügge–Lotz headed a research group in theoretical aerodynamics, continuing her studies of automatic control theory. In 1948 the Flügges left Paris to join the staff at Stanford University in California.

Creates Seminar for Students

Her husband obtained work as a professor at the university, while Flügge–Lotz began as a lecturer. She was prohibited from a similar position due to nepotism regulations. She found time to further her research and established graduate coursework in mathematical hydro– and aerodynamics. She also designed a weekly seminar in fluid mechanics. The course was attended by Stanford students as well as by young engineers from the National Advisory Committee for Aeronautics—NASA's predecessor. The seminar has continued to serve as an important arena for faculty and students of varying specializations to share their findings.

Flügge–Lotz was not offered a full professorship until 1960. Her promotion occurred after she attended the First Congress of the International Federation of Automatic Control in Moscow as the only female delegate from the United States. Upon her return from that congress, she was named professor of aeronautics and astronautics as well as of engineering mechanics. She was the first woman to achieve such status at Stanford.

During her tenure at Stanford, Flügge–Lotz used computers in the development of aerodynamic theory. Working with her students, she helped solved numerous problems in compressible boundary–layer theory. The results of her automatic control research were published in book form as *Discontinuous Automatic Control* and *Discontinuous and Optimal Control.*

Of the numerous awards and honors she received during her career were the Society of Women Engineers

Achievement Award in 1970. She was also the first female chosen by the American Institute of Aeronautics and astronautics (AIAA) to deliver the prestigious annual von Karman Lecture in 1971. The AIAA also elected her as its first woman fellow.

Flügge–Lotz retired from teaching in 1968. She maintained her research activities, however, studying heat transfer and the control of satellites. She died on May 22, 1974.

SELECTED WRITINGS BY FLÜGGE-LOTZ:

Books

Discontinuous Automatic Control. Princeton University Press, 1953.

Discontinous and Optimal Control. McGraw–Hill, 1958.

Periodicals

(With A. F. Johnson) "Laminar Compressible Boundary Layer Along a Curved, Insulated Surface." *Journal of the Aeronautical Sciences* 22 (1955): 445–454.

(With M. D. Maltz) "Attitude Stabilization Using a Contactor Control System with a Linear Switching Criterion." *Automatica* 2 (1963): 255–274.

(With T. K. Fannelöp) "Viscous Hypersonic Flow over Simple Blunt Bodies: Comparison of the Second–order Theory with Experimental Results." *Journal de Mécanique* 5 (1966): 69–100.

(With Jose L. Garcia Almuzara) "Minimum Time Control of a Nonlinear System." *Journal of Differential Equations* 4 (1968): 12–39.

(With T. A. Reyhner) "The Interaction of a Shock Wave with a Laminar Boundary Layer." *International Journal of Nonlinear Mechanics* 3 (1968): 173–199.

Sketch by Karen Wilhelm

Katherine A. Foot
1852–1944 (?)
American cytologist

Katherine Foot was a cytologist, one who studies the structures of cells using a microscope. In particular, she studied the chromosomes in maturating egg cells. Although her conclusions about chromosomes were incorrect, she revolutionized microscopic technology by her use of photography.

There is almost no biographical information about Katherine Foot, other than that she was born in Geneva, New York, in 1852, and was educated at private schools. Foot first studied at the Marine Biological Laboratory at Woods Hole, Massachusetts, in 1892, and she returned to Woods Hole each summer until 1897 to conduct research. She continued as a regular member of the Marine Biological Laboratory until 1921. During this period, her address was listed variously as Denver, Colorado, Evanston, Illinois, and New York City. Foot apparently never married; nor did she obtain a doctoral degree.

Foot began collaborating with **Ella Church Strobell** in 1896, a partnership that continued until Strobell's death between 1918 and 1920, at which time she may have left Foot an inheritance to continue their research. Apparently both women worked independently, without academic or industrial affiliation, a highly unusual arrangement in twentieth–century science.

Most of Foot's published research was in collaboration with Strobell. They were interested in genetics and in cytological studies of chromosomes. Foot and Strobell argued that the chromosomes were too variable in size and shape to be individual structures that carried the genetic material. They used photographs made through the microscope of maturing and fertilized eggs or oocytes of the earthworm, *Allolobophora foetida* to try to demonstrate their contention. Foot noted that the very first photomicrographs of developing eggs were taken by her friend Dr. Charles G. Fuller of Chicago, using her microscopic sections. Foot and Strobell published hundreds of photomicrographs. Later, Foot also worked on the development of sperm and eggs in certain insects. This new technology reproduced the features of cells with clarity and accuracy. Previously, researchers had relied on their drawings of what they saw in the microscope. For the first time, the inaccuracies and biases of the human observer and the human hand were eliminated from cytological research.

In addition to working out the multiple technical problems of photomicroscopy, Foot and Strobell developed a method for using low temperatures to make extremely thin biological preparations for microscopic observations. They were among the first to develop these types of techniques.

Although Foot and Strobell were on the wrong side of the debate concerning the nature of the genetic material, they were highly regarded by other biologists. Foot was a "starred" scientist in the first edition of *American Men of Science* in 1906, indicating that she had been judged by her peers to be one of the 1,000 most distinguished scientists in the country at the time. She continued to be starred until the 1944 edition, the final listing for her. In 1915, the famous geneticist Thomas Hunt Morgan identified Foot as one of the seven principle female investigators in genetics. From 1927 to 1938, Foot's address was listed as London, England. Subsequently she was listed as working for a company in Paris. Foot was last listed as a member of the Marine Biological Laboratory Corporation at Woods Hole in 1943, and her final address was listed as Camden, South Carolina.

SELECTED WRITINGS BY FOOT:

Periodicals

(With Elizabeth Strobell) "Further Notes on the Egg of *Allolobophora foetida*." *Zoological Bulletin* 2 (1898): 130–51.

(With E. Strobell) "Sectioning Paraffine at a Temperature of 25°F." *Biological Bulletin* 9 (1905): 281–86.

FURTHER READING

Books

Cattell, Jaques. *American Men of Science*. 7th ed. Lancaster, PA: Science Press, 1944.

Cattell, J. McKeen, ed. *American Men of Science*. New York: Science Press, 1906.

Chadwell, Faye A. "Katherine Foot." In *Notable Women in the Life Sciences: A Biographical Dictionary*. Edited by Benjamin F. Shearer and Barbara S. Shearer. Westport, CT: Greenwood Press, 1996.

Kass-Simon, G. "Biology is Destiny." In *Women of Science: Righting the Record*. Edited by G. Kass-Simon and Patricia Farnes. Bloomington: Indiana University Press, 1990.

Sketch by Margaret Alic

Dian Fossey
1932–1985
American primatologist

Dian Fossey is remembered by her fellow scientists as the world's foremost authority on mountain gorillas. But to the millions of wildlife conservationists who came to know Fossey through her articles and book, she will always be remembered as a martyr. Throughout the nearly 20 years she spent studying mountain gorillas in central Africa, the American primatologist tenaciously fought the poachers and bounty hunters who threatened to wipe out the endangered primates. She was brutally murdered at her research center in 1985 by what many believe was a vengeful poacher.

Fossey's dream of living in the wilds of Africa dates back to her lonely childhood in San Francisco. She was born in 1932, the only child of George, an insurance agent, and Kitty, a fashion model, (Kidd) Fossey. The Fosseys divorced when Dian was 6 years old. A year later, Kitty married a wealthy building contractor named Richard Price. Price was a strict disciplinarian who showed little affection for his stepdaughter. Although Fossey loved animals, she was allowed to have only a goldfish. When it died, she cried for a week.

Fossey began her college education at the University of California at Davis in the preveterinary medicine program. She excelled in writing and botany, she failed chemistry and physics. After two years, she transferred to San Jose State University, where she earned a bachelor of arts degree in occupational therapy in 1954. While in college, Fossey became a prize–winning equestrian. Her love of horses in 1955 drew her from California to Kentucky, where she directed the occupational therapy department at the Kosair Crippled Children's Hospital in Louisville.

Book Inspires Career Choice

Fossey's interest in Africa's gorillas was aroused through primatologist George Schaller 1963 book, *The Mountain Gorilla: Ecology and Behavior.* Through Schaller's book, Fossey became acquainted with the largest and rarest of three subspecies of gorillas, *Gorilla gorilla beringei.* She learned that these giant apes make their home in the mountainous forests of Rwanda, Zaire and Uganda. Males grow up to six feet tall and weigh 400 pounds or more. Their arms span up to eight feet. The smaller females weigh about 200 pounds.

Schaller's book inspired Fossey to travel to Africa to see the mountain gorillas in their homeland. Against her family's advice, she took out a three–year bank loan for $8,000 to finance the seven–week safari. While in Africa, Fossey met the celebrated paleoanthropologist Louis Leakey, who had encouraged **Jane Goodall** in her research of chimpanzees in Tanzania. Leakey was impressed by Fossey's plans to visit the mountain gorillas.

Those plans were nearly destroyed when she shattered her ankle on a fossil dig with Leakey. But just two weeks later, she hobbled on a walking stick up a mountain in the Congo (now Zaire) to her first encounter with the great apes. The sight of six gorillas set the course for her future. "I left Kabara (gorilla site) with reluctance but with never a doubt that I would, somehow, return to learn more about the gorillas of the misted mountains," Fossey wrote in her book, *Gorillas in the Mist.*

Her opportunity came three years later, when Leakey was visiting Louisville on a lecture tour. Fossey urged him to hire her to study the mountain gorillas. He agreed, if she would first undergo a preemptive appendectomy. Six weeks later, he told her the operation was unnecessary; he had only been testing her resolve. But it was too late. Fossey had already had her appendix removed.

The L.S.B. Leakey and the Wilkie Brothers foundations funded her research, along with the National Geographic Society. Fossey began her career in Africa with a brief visit to Jane Goodall in Tanzania to learn the best methods for studying primates and collecting data.

Dian Fossey (AP/Wide World Photos. Reproduced by permission.)

She set up camp early in 1967 at the Kabara meadow in Zaire's Parc National des Virungas, where Schaller had conducted his pioneering research on mountain gorillas a few years earlier. The site was ideal for Fossey's research. Because Zaire's park system protected them against human intrusion, the gorillas showed little fear of Fossey's presence. Unfortunately, civil war in Zaire forced Fossey to abandon the site six months after she arrived.

She established her permanent research site September 24, 1967, on the slopes of the Virunga Mountains in the tiny country of Rwanda. She called it the Karisoke Research Centre, named after the neighboring Karisimbi and Visoke mountains in the Parc National des Volcans. Although Karisoke was just five miles from the first site, Fossey found a marked difference in Rwanda's gorillas. They had been harassed so often by poachers and cattle grazers that they initially rejected all her attempts to make contact.

Theoretically, the great apes were protected from such intrusion within the park. But the government of the impoverished, densely populated country failed to enforce the park rules. Native Batusi herdsmen used the park to trap antelope and buffalo, sometimes inadvertently snaring a gorilla. Most trapped gorillas escaped, but not without seriously mutilated limbs that sometimes led to gangrene and death. Poachers who caught gorillas could earn up to $200,000 for one by selling the skeleton to a university and the hands to tourists. From the start, Fossey's mission was to protect the endangered gorillas from extinction—indirectly, by researching and writing about them, and directly, by destroying traps and chastising poachers.

Fossey focused her studies on some 51 gorillas in four family groups. Each group was dominated by a sexually mature silverback, named for the characteristic gray hair on its back. Younger, bachelor males served as guards for the silverback's harem and their juvenile offspring.

Experiences Historic Touch with Gorilla

When Fossey began observing the reclusive gorillas, she followed the advice of earlier scientists by concealing herself and watching from a distance. But she soon realized that the only way she would be able to observe their behavior as closely as she wanted was by "habituating" the gorillas to her presence. She did so by mimicking their sounds and behavior. She learned to imitate their belches that signal contentment, their barks of curiosity and a dozen other sounds. To convince them she was their kind, Fossey pretended to munch on the foliage that made up their diet. Her tactics worked. One day early in 1970, Fossey made history when a gorilla she called Peanuts reached out and touched her hand. Fossey called it her most rewarding moment with the gorillas.

She endeared laymen to Peanuts and the other gorillas she studied through her articles in National Geographic magazine. The apes became almost human through her descriptions of their nurturing and playing. Her early articles dispelled the myth that gorillas are vicious. In her 1971 *National Geographic* article she described the giant beasts as ranking among "the gentlest animals, and the shiest." In later articles, Fossey acknowledged a dark side to the gorillas. Six of 38 infants born during a 13–year–period were victims of infanticide. She speculated the practice was a silverback's means of perpetuating his own lineage by killing another male's offspring so he could mate with the victim's mother.

Three years into her study, Fossey realized she would need a doctoral degree to continue receiving support for Karisoke. She temporarily left Africa to enroll at Cambridge University, where she earned her Ph.D. in zoology in 1974. In 1977, Fossey suffered a tragedy that would permanently alter her mission at Karisoke. Digit, a young male she had grown to love, was slaughtered by poachers. Walter Cronkite focused national attention on the gorillas' plight when he reported Digit's death on the CBS Evening News. Interest in gorilla conservation surged. Fossey took advantage of that interest by establishing the Digit Fund, a non–profit organization to raise money for anti–poaching patrols and equipment.

But the money wasn't enough to save the gorillas from poachers. Six months later, a silverback and his mate from one of Fossey's study groups were shot and killed defending their three–year–old son, who had been shot in the shoulder. The juvenile later died from his wounds. It was rumored that the gorilla deaths caused Fossey to suffer a nervous breakdown, although she denied it. What is clear is that the deaths prompted her to step up her fight against the Batusi poachers by terrorizing them and raiding their villages. "She did everything short of murdering those poachers," Mary Smith, senior assistant editor at National Geographic, told contributor Cynthia Washam in an interview. A serious calcium deficiency that causes bones to snap and teeth to rot forced Fossey to leave Africa in 1980. She spent her three–year sojourn as a visiting associate professor at Cornell University. Fossey completed her book, *Gorillas in the Mist,* during her stint at Cornell. It was published in 1983. Although some scientists criticized the book for its abundance of anecdotes and lack of scientific discussion, lay readers and reviewers received it warmly.

When Fossey returned to Karisoke in 1983, her scientific research was virtually abandoned. Funding had run dry. She was operating Karisoke with her own savings. "In the end, she became more of an animal activist than a scientist," Smith said. "Science kind of went out the window."

Brutal Murder Remains a Mystery

On Dec. 27, 1985, Fossey, 54, was found murdered in her bedroom at Karisoke, her skull split diagonally from her forehead to the corner of her mouth. Her murder remains a mystery that has prompted much speculation. Rwandan authorities jointly charged American research assistant Wayne McGuire, who discovered Fossey's body, and Emmanuel Rwelekana, a Rwandan tracker Fossey had fired several months earlier. McGuire maintains his innocence. At the urging of U.S. authorities, he left Rwanda before the charges against him were made public. He was convicted in absentia and sentenced to die before a firing squad if he ever returns to Rwanda.

Farley Mowat, the Canadian author of Fossey's biography, *Woman in the Mists,* believes McGuire was a scapegoat. He had no motive for killing her, Mowat wrote, and the evidence against him appeared contrived. Rwelekana's story will never be known. He was found dead after apparently hanging himself a few weeks after he was charged with the murder. Smith, and others, believe Fossey's death came at the hands of a vengeful poacher. "I feel she was killed by a poacher," Smith said. "It definitely wasn't any mysterious plot."

Fossey's final resting place is at Karisoke, surrounded by the remains of Digit and more than a dozen other gorillas she had buried. Her legacy lives on in the Virungas, as her followers have taken up her battle to protect the endangered mountain gorillas. The Dian Fossey Gorilla Fund, formerly the Digit Fund, finances scientific research at Karisoke and employs camp staff, trackers and anti–poaching patrols.

The Rwanda government, which for years had ignored Fossey's pleas to protect its mountain gorillas, on September 27, 1990, recognized her scientific achievement with the Ordre (sic) National des Grandes Lacs, the highest award it has ever given a foreigner. Gorillas in Rwanda are still threatened by cattle ranchers and hunters squeezing in on their habitat. According to the Colorado–based Dian Fossey Gorilla Fund, by the early 1990s, fewer than 650 mountain gorillas remained in Rwanda, Zaire and Uganda. The Virunga Mountains is home to about 320 of them. Smith is among those convinced that the number would be much smaller if not for Fossey's 18 years of dedication to save the great apes. "Her conservation efforts stand above everything else (she accomplished at Karisoke)," Smith said. "She single–handedly saved the mountain gorillas."

SELECTED WRITINGS BY FOSSEY:

Books

Gorillas in the Mist. Houghton Mifflin Company, 1983.

Periodicals

"Making Friends With Mountain Gorillas." *National Geographic* (January 1970): 48–67.

"More Years With Mountain Gorillas." *National Geographic* (October 1971) 574–585.

"The Imperiled Mountain Gorilla" *National Geographic* (April 1981): 501–522.

FURTHER READING

Books

Current Biography Yearbook. H.W. Wilson Company, 1985, pp. 121–123.

Hayes, Harold T.P. *The Dark Romance of Dian Fossey.* Simon and Schuster, 1990.

Mowat, Farley.*Woman in the Mists.* Warner Books, 1987.

Schoumatoff, Alex. *African Madness.* Alfred A. Knopf, 1988, pp. 5–42.

Periodicals

Brower, Montgomery. "The Strange Death of Dian Fossey." *People* (February 17, 1986): 46–54.

Hayes, Harold. "The Dark Romance of Dian Fossey." *Life* (November, 1986): 64–70.

New Yorker, (January 27, 1986): 26–27.

Other

Smith, Mary, interview with Cynthia Washam conducted July 23, 1993.

Sketch by Cynthia Washam

Melissa Franklin
1956–
Canadian physicist

Melissa Franklin is something of a contradiction: a high school dropout with a Ph.D. in physics, a deadpan comic who is intensely serious about her work, and the first tenured female professor in the otherwise all–male physics department at Harvard University. In 1995, she was part of a team of researchers who discovered the top quark, a subatomic particle whose existence helps scientists better understand the past and present nature of the universe.

Melissa Franklin was born in Edmonton, Canada, on September 30, 1956. Her mother was a television producer and her father was a journalist. She grew up in Toronto with her brother, Havoc, and her sister, Jodi. Franklin accelerated through school and graduated from the ninth grade at age 13. She briefly attended high school, but dropped out. "It was boring," she told Cavette in an interview. With some friends she met on the street, Franklin started a free school, which she attended for two years taking whatever classes interested her. When she was 15, she went to England and attended school there for two more years. While living in England, Franklin read a book on quantum physics, the study of the energy associated with atomic and subatomic particles, and became interested in particle physics. She returned to Canada and talked her way into the University of Toronto, despite the fact that she never officially graduated from high school.

Focus on Particle Physics

While at the University of Toronto, Franklin began working at the Fermi Laboratory in Batavia, Illinois, near Chicago, where she often stayed up all night working on projects involving particle physics. She focused so intensely on this particular subject that she didn't take many of the other required courses for physics majors, ending up with a B.S. in Science in 1977, rather than a B.S. in Physics.

Now fully committed to particle physics, Franklin did her postgraduate work at the Stanford Linear Accelerator at Stanford University in Palo Alto, California, where she studied a subatomic particle named the charm quark. She received her Ph.D. from Stanford in 1982, and went to work at the Lawrence Berkeley Laboratories in Berkeley, California from 1983 to 1987. In 1988, she took a position as an assistant professor of physics at the University of Illinois, Champaign–Urbana campus, for a year.

The Road to Harvard

Franklin had always wanted to return to Canada, and in 1986 she applied for a position as an assistant professor of physics at the University of Toronto, where she had done her undergraduate work. Although she was told she was the leading candidate, the job was given to a man. When she applied again in 1988, the university offered her a lower position instead. By the time the university upgraded their offer, Franklin had accepted a position as a junior fellow in the Society of Fellows at Harvard University in Cambridge, Massachusetts, where she did research in particle physics.

Franklin's personality may have been one of the reasons she was initially rebuffed by the University of Toronto. "I think that they didn't want me there because I'm female and because I'm aggressive," she said in MacLean's magazine in 1992. She is also prone to off–the–wall behavior, such as making faces at her colleagues as she passes them in a hallway or walking up to strangers and commenting on their clothes. One photo of her, taken for a Women in Science and Technology Month web page, shows her with close–cropped hair and sun glasses, prying the cap off a bottle with her teeth. When she's not trying to coax some all–but–undetectable particle to reveal itself, she plays jazz saxaphone and listens to Frank Zappa music.

Search for the Top Quark

She is also "an unusually talented physicist," Professor Howard Georgi, chairman of Harvard's physics department, said in an article in *MacLean's* magazine in 1992. This was the same year Franklin accepted a position as the first tenured female physics professor at Harvard. If anyone doubted Georgi's remark then, Franklin proved them wrong three years later when she and her colleagues, working with the Fermilab's powerful Tevatron particle accelerator, discovered the first verifiable existence of the top quark in 1995. The top quark has proven to be elusive because it takes a lot of energy to hold it together and it is therefore very unstable compared to other particles. Even in a powerful machine like the Tevatron, the top quark only pops into existence for about a trillionth of a trillionth of a second before it disintegrates into smaller, more mundane particles. It joins a family of other subatomic particles that make up the most basic level of matter now known. These particles, and the forces and energies involved with them, may help scientists in their search to understand the past and present nature of the universe. It is a search that Melissa Franklin relishes.

FURTHER READING

Books

Who's Who of American Women. 20th edition, 1997–1998. New Providence: Marquis Who's Who, 1996.

Periodicals

Freedman, D.H. "Over the Top." *Discover* (February 1995): 74–81.

Nichols, M. "Brain–Drained." *MacLean's* (July 20, 1992): 44.

Other

"Melissa Franklin." *Harvard University High Energy Physics Faculty.* 6 Oct 1998. http://www.physics.harvard.edu/facstaff/highenergy.html (3 Apr 1999).

"Melissa Franklin." *WITI Museum and Hall of Fame: Women in Science and Technology Month, June 1996.* 12 Jun 1996. http://www.witi.com/Center/Museum/Special/Wistmonth/96/mfrankli.html (31 Mar 1999).

Cavette, Christopher J., interview with Melissa Franklin conducted April 6, 1999.

Sketch by Chris Cavette

Rosalind Elsie Franklin
1920–1958
English molecular biologist

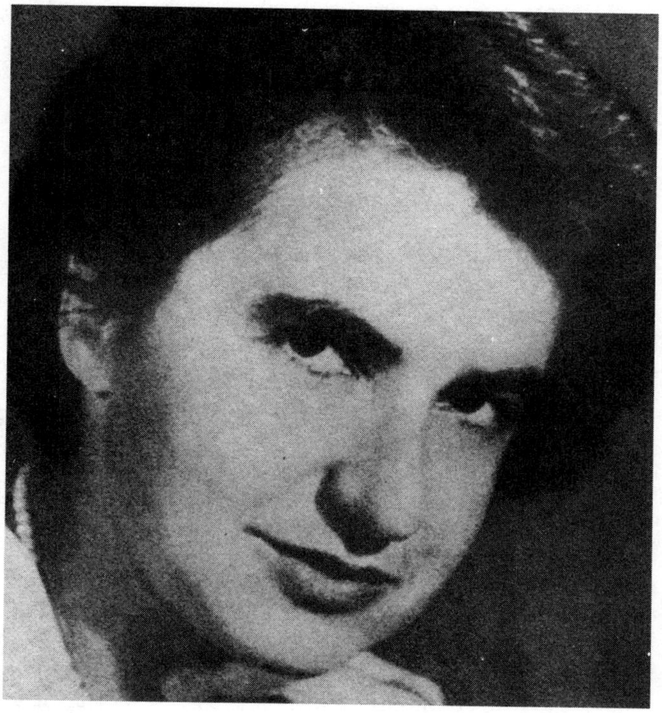

Rosalind Franklin (Photo Researchers, Inc. Reproduced by permission.)

The story of a great scientific discovery usually involves a combination of inspiration, hard work, and serendipity. While all these ingredients play a part in the discovery of DNA, the relationships between the four individuals who pieced together the double–helix model of the master molecule provides a subplot tainted by controversy. At the center of this quartet stands British geneticist Rosalind Franklin, who made key contributions to studies of the structures of coals and viruses, in addition to providing the scientific evidence upon which James Watson and Francis Crick based their double–helix model. Compounding the irony that Franklin died four years before Watson, Crick and Maurice Wilkins shared the Nobel Prize for this discovery (the Nobel Committee honors only living scientists), is James Watson's characterization of Franklin in his personal chronicle of the search for the double–helix as a competitive, stubborn, unfeminine scientist. Despite his account, Franklin has been depicted elsewhere as a devoted, hard–working scientist who suffered from her colleagues' reluctance to treat her with respect.

Franklin was born in London on July 25, 1920, to a family with long–standing Jewish roots. Her parents, who were both under the age of twenty–five when she was born, were avowed socialists. Ellis Franklin devoted his life to fulfilling his socialist ideals by teaching at the Working Men's College, while his wife, Muriel Waley Franklin, cared for their family, in which Rosalind was the second of five children and the first daughter. From an early age, Franklin excelled at science. She attended St. Paul's Girls' School, one of the few educational institutions that offered physics and chemistry to female students. A foundation scholar at the school, Rosalind decided at the age of fifteen to pursue a career in science, despite her father's exhortations to consider social work. In 1938, Franklin enrolled at Newnham College, Cambridge, the second youngest student in her class.

She graduated from Cambridge in 1941 with a high second degree and accepted a research scholarship at Newnham to study gas–phase chromatography with future Nobel Prize winner Ronald G. W. Norrish. Finding Norrish difficult to work with, she quit graduate school the following year to accept a job as assistant research officer with the British Coal Utilization Research Association (CURA). At CURA, she applied the physical chemistry experience she had garnered at Cambridge to studies concerning the microstructures of coals, using helium as a measurement unit. From 1942 to 1946, she authored five papers, three of them as sole author, and submitted her thesis to Cambridge. Franklin moved to Paris in 1947 to take a job with the Laboratoire Central des Services Chimiques de l'Etat. There she became fluent in French and, under the tutelage of Jacques Mering, learned the technique known as X–ray diffraction. Using this technique, Franklin was able to describe in exacting detail the structure of carbon and the changes that occur when carbon is heated to form graphite. In 1951, she left Paris for an opportunity to try her new skills on biological substances. As a member of Sir John T. Randall's Medical Research Council at King's College, London, Franklin was charged with the task of setting up an X–ray diffraction unit in the laboratory to produce diffraction pictures of DNA.

Begins Work on Structure of DNA

Eager to apply Franklin's X–ray diffraction skills to the problem of DNA structure, Randall had lured her to his lab with a Turner Newall Research Fellowship and the promise that she would be working on one of the more pressing research problems of the era—puzzling out the structure and function of DNA. When she arrived in Randall's research unit, she started working with a student, Raymond Gosling, who had been attempting to capture pictures of the elusive DNA. No stranger to the sexism rife in science at that time, Franklin made no apologies for the fact she was a woman. Maurice Wilkins, already well ensconced in the lab and working on the same problem as Franklin, took a disliking to her the first time they met. Franklin's biographers have difficulty ascertaining exactly why Wilkins and Franklin did not find common ground. Anne Sayre has suggested that the discomfort might have stemmed from the fact that Wilkins, only four years older than Franklin, may have misinterpreted her presence in his lab as a subordinate, whereas she considered herself an equal. Their mutual dislike of one another was not helped by the fact that the staff dining room was open only to the male faculty. In addition, she was the only Jew on staff. But the animosity between the two did not detract Franklin from her work, and shortly after arriving at King's, she started x–raying DNA fibers that Wilkins had obtained from a Swiss investigator.

Within a few months of joining Randall's team, Franklin gave a talk describing preliminary pictures she had obtained of the DNA as it transformed from a crystalline form, or A pattern, to a wet form, or B pattern, through an increase in relative humidity. The pictures showed, she suggested, that phosphate groups might lie outside the molecule. In the audience that November day sat James Watson, a twenty–four–year–old American who was also working on unraveling the molecular structure of DNA. Working with Francis Crick at Cambridge, Watson was even more disinclined than Wilkins to like and respect Franklin. Compounding his dislike for her was Franklin's refusal to set aside hard crystallographic data in favor of model building. Perhaps for that reason, Franklin remained publicly scornful of the notion gradually gaining adherents that perhaps the DNA molecule had a helical structure. In her unpublished reports, however, she suggested the probability that the B form of DNA exhibited such a structure, as did, perhaps, the A form. Throughout the spring of 1952, she continued studying the A form, which seemed to produce more readable X–ray photographs. This presumed legibility proved deceptive, however, because the A form does not show the double–helical structure as clearly as the B form.

Research Provides Evidence of DNA's Double–Helical Structure

In the late spring of 1952, Franklin traveled to Yugoslavia for a month, where she visited coal research labs. When she returned, she and Gosling continued to investigate the A form, to no avail. In January 1953, she started model building, but could think of no structure that would accommodate all of the evidence she had gleaned from her diffraction pictures. She ruled out single and multi–stranded helices in favor of a figure–eight configuration. Meanwhile, Watson and Crick were engaged in their own model building, hastened by the fear that the American scientist Linus Pauling was nearing a discovery of his own. Although Watson had not befriended Franklin in the past two years, he had grown quite close to Wilkins. In *The Double–helix,* Watson recalls how Wilkins showed him the DNA diffraction pictures Franklin had amassed (without her permission), and immediately he saw the evidence he needed to prove the helical structure of DNA. Watson returned to Crick in Cambridge and the two began writing what would become one of the best–known scientific papers of the century: "A Structure for Deoxyribose Nucleic Acid." Franklin and Gosling, who had been working on a paper of their own, quickly revised it so that it could appear along with the Watson and Crick paper. Although it is unclear how close Franklin was to a similar discovery—in part because of the misleading A form—unpublished drafts of her paper reveal that she had deduced the sugar–phosphate backbone of the helix before Watson and Crick's model was made public.

On April 25, 1953, Watson and Crick published their article in the British science journal *Nature,* along with a corroborative article by Franklin and Gosling providing essential evidence for the double–helix theory. In July of 1953, she and Gosling published another paper in *Nature* that offered "evidence for a 2–chain helix in the crystalline structure of sodium deoxyribonucleate." But Franklin's interest in the world of DNA research had already begun to wane by the spring of 1953. Despite all the excitement surrounding the double–helical structure, she had decided to move on to a lab that she hoped would offer a more congenial working environment. When she informed Randall of her intention to leave King's College for J. D. Bernal's unit at Birkbeck College, he made it clear that the DNA project was to stay in his lab. Although Gosling had been warned against further associating with Franklin, they continued to meet in private and finish their DNA work. She also continued to work on coal, but devoted the bulk of her efforts to applying crystallographic techniques to uncover the structure of the tobacco mosaic virus (TMV).

Franklin did, in fact, find the Birkbeck lab more to her liking, even though she complained to some of her friends that Bernal, a strong Marxist, attempted to foist his political views on anyone who would listen. In comparison to the situation at King's College, however, she found this bearable. She did not even complain about her lab situation. At Birkbeck she worked in a small lab on the fifth floor while her X–ray equipment sat in the basement. Because there was no elevator in the building, she made frequent treks up and down the stairs. The roof leaked, and she had to set up pots and pans to catch the water. But Franklin didn't mind adversity. In fact, she told friends she preferred the challenge it presented, whether at work or even while travelling. She loved to travel and once journeyed to Israel in the steerage of a slow boat sheerly for the adventure of it. She said she preferred to travel with little money "because then you need your wits," an attitude that stood her in good stead in 1955 when the Birkbeck lost its backing from the Agricultural Research Council, in part, Franklin thought, because they did not approve of a project headed by a woman. Franklin successfully sought funding from another government source—the U.S. Public Health Service. The year after Franklin began at Birkbeck, the South African scientist Aaron Klug joined the laboratory. By 1956, Franklin had obtained some of the best pictures of the crystallographic structure of the TMV and, along with her colleagues, disproved the then–standard notion that TMV was a solid cylinder with RNA in the middle and protein subunits on the outside. While Franklin confirmed that the protein units did lay on the outside, she also showed that the cylinder was hollow, and that the RNA lay embedded among the protein units. Later, she initiated work that would support her hypothesis that the RNA in theTMV was single–stranded.

Franklin spent the summer of 1956 in California with two American scientists, learning from them techniques by which to grow viruses. Upon returning to England, Franklin fell ill, and friends began to suspect she was in pain a great deal of the time. That fall, she was operated on for cancer and, the following year, she had a second operation, neither of which stopped either her work or the disease. Franklin knew she was dying, but did not let that impede her progress. She began working on the polio virus, even though people warned her it was dangerous and highly contagious. She died of cancer at the age of 37 on April 16, 1958. Four years later, Watson, Crick, and Wilkins won the Nobel Prize in medicine or physiology, and Watson penned his potboiler account of the discovery of DNA. Although he vilifies her throughout his account, he tones down his earlier depiction of her as the mad, feminist scientist in an epilogue: "Since my initial impressions of her, both scientific and personal (as recorded in the early pages of this book), were often wrong, I want to say something here about her achievements." He continues that he and Crick "both came to appreciate greatly her personal honesty and generosity, realizing years too late the struggles that the intelligent woman faces to be accepted by a scientific world which often regards women as mere diversions from serious thinking."

SELECTED WRITINGS BY FRANKLIN:

Periodicals

"Evidence for 2–Chain Helix in Crystalline Structure of Sodium Deoxyribonucleate." *Nature* 172 (1953): 156–57.

(With Aaron Klug) "Order–Disorder Transitions in Structures Containing Helical Molecules." *Discussions of the Faraday Society* 25 (1958): 104–10.

FURTHER READING

Books

Judson, Horace Freeland. *The Eighth Day of Creation: Makers of the Revolution in Biology.* Simon and Schuster, 1980.

Sayre, Anne. *Rosalind Franklin and DNA.* Norton, 1975.

Watson, James D. *The Double–Helix: A Personal Account of the Discovery of the Structure of DNA.* Norton, 1980.

Periodicals

Klug, A. "Rosalind Franklin and the Discovery of the Structure of DNA." *Nature* 219 (1968).

Sketch by Shari Rudavsky

Helen Murray Free
1923–
American chemist

Helen Free has distinguished herself as a chemist, but she has also been particularly active in making science topics more accessible to a general audience. As a longtime active member of the American Chemical Society, she has used that organization's resources to help demystify science to students, teachers, and public officials. As a researcher, her contributions to diagnostic testing methods have made the tests less cumbersome, more streamlined, and much faster.

She was born in Pittsburgh, Pennsylvania, on February 20, 1923 to James Summerville and Daisy Piper Murray. She attended the College of Wooster in Wooster, Ohio, graduating with a bachelor of science degree in 1944. She then took a job with the pharmaceutical firm Bayer (whose American subsidiary was known until 1995 as Miles Laboratories) in Elkhart, Indiana. Beginning as a chemist, she worked her way up over the years to new products manager, director of clinical lab reagents, and director of marketing services in the research division. In 1947 she married a fellow chemist at Bayer, Alfred H. Free, with whom she would collaborate on research projects during their careers. The couple also raised six children.

Research Leads to New Diagnostic Tests

Free's major work during her years at Bayer was in the development of clinical and medical testing procedures. In particular, she developed new methods of urinalysis that were quicker and less expensive (using tablets and "dip–and–read" sticks). Urinalysis is an extremely important diagnostic procedure because it can successfully detect the presence of chemicals that signal the presence of disease. Diabetics, for example, test urine samples to determine their glucose samples. Free has filed seven patents for her clinical tests; among her numerous writings is the book (co–authored with her husband) *Urinalysis in Clinical Laboratory Practice*, considered one of the definitive studies of the subject.

Later in her career, Free decided to return to school; she received her master's degree in laboratory management from Central Michigan University in 1978. After retiring from Bayer in 1983, she became a consultant for the company; in 1977 she became an adjunct professor at Indiana University–South Bend.

A Leader on Public Outreach

In addition to her work as a chemist and researcher, Free has been consistently active in efforts to bring science to the public. Believing that often even teachers are misinformed about science, she has been instrumental in furthering science education beginning at the grade–school level. She has devoted much of her long association with the American Chemical Society to this; she headed ACS' committee on Public Affairs and Public Relations and urged members to communicate the importance of science to the general public. In 1993, she served as ACS president. Free explained her rationale in an article that appeared in *Chemical and Engineering News* in 1994: "Public outreach is not a luxury. Only a small percentage of Americans know the basic facts of science. Many teachers, intimidated by a subject they know little about, avoid or abbreviate science lessons." Free has not only urged others to promote science in the schools; she has taken an active role herself by going into schools and working directly with students and teachers.

Among the awards that Free has received over the years is ACS's Garvan Medal, which she was awarded in 1980. She has won numerous other awards (including several that she shared with her husband), and was awarded honorary Doctor of Science degrees from both the College of Wooster and Central Michigan University. An award named in her honor, the Helen M. Free Public Outreach Award was established in 1995 by ACS; appropriately, she was the award's first recipient.

SELECTED WRITINGS BY FREE:

Books

Free, Alfred H. and Helen M. *Urinalysis in Clinical Laboratory Practice.* Cleveland, OH, CRC Press, 1975.

Periodicals

Free, Helen M. "Changing Public Perceptions." *Chemical and Engineering News* 14 (November 1994): 44.

FURTHER READING

Books

Shearer, Benjamin F. and Barbara S. Shearer, eds. *Notable Women in the Physical Sciences: A Biographical Dictionary.* Westport, CT: Greenwood Press, 1997.

Other

"Helen M. Free." *American Chemical Society.* 1998. http://www.acs.org/elections/free.html (July 22, 1999).

Sketch by George A. Milite

Charlotte Friend
1921–1987
American microbiologist

As the first scientist to discover a direct link between viruses and cancer, Charlotte Friend made important breakthroughs in cancer research, particularly leukemia. She was successful in immunizing mice against leukemia and also in pointing a way toward new methods of treating the disease. Because of Friend's work, medical researchers developed a greater understanding of cancer and how it can be fought.

Friend was born on March 11, 1921, in New York City to Russian immigrants. Her father died of endocarditis (heart inflammation) when Charlotte was three, a factor that may have influenced her early decision to enter the medical field; at age ten she wrote a school composition entitled, "Why I Want to Become a Bacteriologist." Her mother's job as a pharmacist also exposed Friend to medicine. After graduating from Hunter College in 1944, she immediately enlisted in the U.S. Navy during World War II, rising to the rank of lieutenant junior grade.

After the war, Friend entered graduate school at Yale University, obtaining her Ph.D. in bacteriology in 1950. Soon afterward, she was hired by the Sloan–Kettering Institute for Cancer Research, and in 1952 became an associate professor in microbiology at Cornell University, which had just set up a joint program with the institute. During that time Friend because interested in cancer, particularly leukemia, a cancer of blood–forming organs that is a leading killer of children. Her research on the cause of this disease led her to believe that, contrary to the prevailing medical opinion, leukemia is caused by a virus. To confirm her theory, Friend took samples of leukemia tissue from mice and, after putting the material through a

Charlotte Friend (The Library of Congress. Reproduced by permission.)

filter to remove cells, injected it into healthy mice. These animals developed leukemia, indicating that the cause of the disease was a substance smaller than a cell. Using an electron microscope, Friend was able to discover and photograph the virus she believed responsible for leukemia .

However, when Friend presented her findings at the April, 1956, annual meeting of the American Association for Cancer Research, she was denounced by many other researchers, who refused to believe that a virus was responsible for leukemia. Over the next year support for Friend's theory mounted, first as Dr. Jacob Furth declared that his experiments had confirmed the existence of such a virus in mice with leukemia. Even more importantly, Friend was successful in vaccinating mice against leukemia by injecting a weakened form of the virus (now called the "Friend virus") into healthy mice, so they could develop antibodies to fight off the normal virus. Friend's presentation of a paper on this vaccine at the cancer research association's 1957 meeting succeeded in laying to rest the skepticism that had greeted her the previous year.

In 1962, Friend was honored with the Alfred P. Sloan Award for Cancer Research and another award from the American Cancer Society for her work. The next year she became a member of the New York Academy of Sciences, an organization that has members from all fifty states and more than eighty countries. In 1966 Friend left Sloan–Kettering to become a professor and director at the Center for Experimental Cell Biology at the newly formed medical school of New York's Mount Sinai Hospital. During this time she continued her research on leukemia, and in 1972 she announced the discovery of a method of altering a leukemia mouse cell in a test tube so that it would no longer multiply. Through chemical treatment, the malignant red blood cell could be made to produce hemoglobin, as do normal cells.

Although the virus responsible for leukemia in mice has been discovered, there is no confirmation that a virus causes leukemia in humans. Likewise, her treatment for malignant red blood cells has limited application, because it will not work outside of test tubes. Nonetheless, Friend had pointed out a possible cause of cancer and developed a first step toward fighting leukemia (and possibly other cancers) by targeting specific cells.

In 1976, Friend was elected president of the American Association for Cancer Research, the same organization whose members had so strongly criticized her twenty years earlier. Two years later, she was chosen the first woman president of the New York Academy of Sciences. Friend was long active in supporting other women scientists and in speaking out on women's issues. During her later years, she expressed concern over the tendency to emphasize patient care over basic research, feeling that without sufficient funding for research, new breakthroughs in patient care would be impossible. Friend died on January 13, 1987, of lymphoma.

SELECTED WRITINGS BY FRIEND:

Periodicals

"Cell–Free Transmission in Adult Swiss Mice of a Disease Having the Characteristic of Leukemia." *Journal of Experimental Medicine* 105 (1957): 307–318.

"Immunological Relationships of a Filterable Agent Causing a Leukemia in Adult Mice." *Journal of Experimental Medicine* 10 (1959): 217–221.

(With J. G. Holland, William Scher, and Toru Sato) "Hemoglobin Synthesis in Murine Virus–Induced Leukemia Cells In–Vitro: Stimulation of Erythroid Differentiation by Dimethyl Sulfoxide." *Proceedings of National Academy of Sciences* Volume 68, pp. 378–382.

FURTHER READING

Books

Beattie, Edward, *Towards the Conquest of Cancer,* Crown Publishing, 1988.

Marget, Madeline, *Life's Blood,* Simon & Schuster, 1992.

Noble, Iris, *Contemporary Women Scientists,* Julian Messner, 1979.

Periodicals

Diamond, Leila, and Sandra Wolman, "Viral Oncogenesis and Cell Differentiation: The Contributions of Charlotte Friend." *Annals of the New York Academy of Sciences* 567 (August 4, 1989).

Schmeck, Harold M., Jr., "Charlotte Friend Dies at 65; Researched Cancer Viruses," *New York Times,* January 16, 1987.

"Science Academy Installs First Female President." *Newsday* (December 9, 1977).

Thomas, Emy, "Cancer Award Honors Woman," *New York World–Telegram and Sun,* May 9, 1962.

Other

Papers of Charlotte Friend. Mount Sinai Medical Center (1993).

Sketch by Francis Rogers

Elizabeth Fulhame

fl. 18th century

British chemist

British chemist Elizabeth Fulhame made several significant contributions to her field, the most important of which was an original (if erroneous) theory of combustion. Because of the social pressures of the time, Fulhame nearly did not publish her work.

All that is known of Fulhame's background is that she was married to a doctor, probably named Thomas Fulhame, and lived primarily in London. For several years, beginning in 1780, she explored the idea of using light or chemical processes to convert gold, silver, platinum, and other metals into a form usable as cloth and/or as a paint to be used on cloth as a decoration. Through many experiments, she showed that gold salts could be reduced by the heat caused by light. This was arguably one of the earliest examples of photoimaging.

Fulhame's experiments also led her to several conclusions on the nature of combustion. In 1793, she met Joseph Priestly, famed scientist and discoverer of oxygen, with whom she discussed her experiments. In 1794 Fulhame published at her own expense *An Essay on Combustion, with a View to a New Art of Dying and Painting: Wherein the Phlogistic Antiphlogistic Hypotheses Are Proved Erroneous* in 1794. Other scientists in her field praised her work, and it was widely discussed into the early nineteenth century. It was also translated into German.

In the piece, Fulhame put forth several key theories. She argued that water is needed for many oxidation reactions, because both of its components hydrogen and oxygen are used in this process. This was a bold statement for the time and later recognized as one of the first concepts of catalysts, 40 years before Eduard Buchner. Fulhame also speculated on particular reaction mechanisms, though her arguments in the book are not supported fully by the experiments she described. Fulhame's experiment using light to produce the reduction of gold salts were later replicated by Count Rumford, another British scientist.

An Essay on Combustion was also published in the United States in 1810. Fulhame was elected an honorary member of the Philadelphia Chemical Society after the book's American debut. As Rayner–Canham notes in *Education in Chemistry,* one of the society's members was so impressed by her work that he was moved to declare: "Mrs. Fulhame has now laid such bold claims to chemistry that we can no longer deny the sex the privilege of participating in this science also."

SELECTED WRITINGS BY FULHAME:

Books

An Essay on Combustion with a View to a New Art of Dying and Painting: Wherein the Antiphlogistic Hypotheses Are Proved Erroneous. 1794. Reprint, London: J. Cooper, 1974.

FURTHER READING

Books

Alic, Margaret. *Hypatia's Heritage: A History of Women in Science from Antiquity to the late Nineteenth Century.* Boston: Beacon Press, 1986.

Laidler, Keith J. *The World of Physical Chemistry.* New York: Oxford University Press, 1993, pp. 250–52.

Laidler, Keith J. and Athel Cornish–Bowden. "Elizabeth Fulhame and the Discovery of Catalysis: 100 Years before Buchner." In *New Beer in an Old Bottle: Eduard Buchner and the Growth of Biochemical Knowledge.* Valencia: Universitat de Valencia, 1997, pp. 123–26.

Ogilvie, Marilyn Bailey. *Women in Science: Antiquity through the Nineteenth Century.* Cambridge: MIT Press, 1986.

Partington, J.R. *A History of Chemistry.* Vol. 3. New York: St. Martin's Press, 1962, pp. 708–09.

Pledge, H.T. *Science Since 1500: A Short History of Mathematics, Physics, Chemistry, Biology.* New York: Harper Torchbooks, 1959, p. 214.

Wheeler, T.S. and J.R. Partington. *The Life and Work of William Higgins, Chemist (1763–1825).* New York: Pergamon Press, 1960, pp. 121–22.

Periodicals

Cornish–Bowden, Athel. "Two Centuries of Catalysis." *Journal of Biosciences* (1998): 87–92.

Houlihan, Sheridan and John H. Wotiz. "Women in Chemistry before 1900." *Journal of Chemical Education* (June 1975): pp. 362–64.

Rayner-Canham, G.W. "Two British Women Chemists." *Education in Chemistry* (July 1983): 140–41.

Sketch by Annette Petrusso

A. Oveta Fuller
1955–
American microbiologist

A. Oveta Fuller is a research scientist who primarily studies viruses and how they attach to the cells they infect. Her research has two main objectives: to better understand the interaction between viruses and cells in order to gain insight into the control of viral diseases; and to explore the possibility of using certain viruses as a means of facilitating genetic engineering.

Oveta Fuller was born on August 31, 1955 in Mebane, North Carolina. She grew up on the family farm operated by her father, Herbert R. Fuller. Her mother, Deborah Woods Fuller, worked as a junior high school teacher to help supplement the family's income.

While her parents were working, young Oveta spent a great deal of time with her paternal grandmother, Lillie Willis Fuller Graves, who lived on the farm. Oveta had an early experience with the powers of medicine when her grandmother was bitten by a water moccasin. Oveta was worried when her grandmother was rushed to the hospital, but relieved when she returned safely, having been treated with a medicine known as antivenin.

Fuller moved further along the path to becoming a scientist in high school, where she had inspiring biology teachers, and was able to attend the North Carolina Governor's School, a highly regarded summer school, following her junior year. The program focused on mathematics, but also involved a range of topics from music to literature.

Following high school, Fuller was awarded a full four–year scholarship to the University of North Carolina (UNC) at Chapel Hill, where she majored in biology. She did not follow a strict premedical curriculum and greatly enjoyed classes in English literature, composition, and journalism. She also worked for one of the college newspapers.

Following her junior year, Fuller took a summer job at a local health clinic, where she discovered the job she most enjoyed was working in the laboratory. She began to consider a career as a research scientist. Nevertheless, she still had a strong interest in writing, and after graduating, she worked for a summer with a large publishing company in Louisiana, where she marketed children's reference books. Her scientific inquisitiveness soon took hold, however, and she decided to return to UNC for graduate studies in biology.

Fuller's doctoral research at UNC involved the biological actions of plant toxins, but she became increasingly interested in the study of viruses and cell surface chemistry. Following her graduation in 1983, she joined the research team of Professor Patricia G. Spear at the University of Chicago, where she studied the behavior of the herpes virus.

Fuller spent nearly five years at the University of Chicago, during which time she helped to identify certain molecules found in cell walls which appear to bring about at least a partial immunity to the herpes virus. In 1987, Fuller received a fellowship from the Ford Foundation, which enabled her to soon become a independent research scientist.

She joined the faculty of the medical school at the University of Michigan in 1987, where she has continued to pursue her research interests. She also teaches in the medical, dental, and graduate schools, and is a mentor to several graduate students and part–time undergraduates who are a part of her research team. Her team continues to report new information on the interactions between viruses and the cells they infect.

FURTHER READING

Kessler, James H., J. S. Kidd, Renée A. Kidd, and Katherine A. Morin. "A. Oveta Fuller" In *Distinguished African American Scientists of the 20th Century*. Phoenix: Oryx Press, 1996.

Sketch by David E. Fontes

G

Julia Anna Gardner
1882–1960

American geologist and stratigraphic paleontologist

Julia Anna Gardner's work as a stratigraphic paleontologist was an important addition to the study of geology, especially throughout the Western Hemisphere. Stratigraphy is concerned with the geographical origin, composition, disposition, and succession of sedimentary rock or earth. In the early 1900s, Gardner began a study of mollusks found in strata that dated back to Mesozoic and Cenozoic eras. Her study of mollusks was to continue throughout her career, and contributed to national and international advancements in both paleontology and geology. In addition, her work made substantial contributions to the area of economic geology, most notably in the petroleum sector. Petroleum geologists were able to use her stratigraphic data when searching for oil deposits, particularly in Texas and the southern rim of the Caribbean.

Born in Chamberlain, South Dakota, on January 26, 1882, Gardner was the only child of Charles Henry Gardner and Julia M. (Brackett) Gardner. Her mother was a teacher, originally from Dixon, Illinois. Her father, a physician, died when she was four months old. When Gardner was thirteen years old, she and her mother returned to Dixon. They later moved to North Adams, Massachusetts, where she attended Drury Academy. An inheritance from her grandmother allowed her to enter Bryn Mawr College in 1901, where she studied geology and paleontology. She graduated in 1905 and taught at the elementary–school level before returning to Bryn Mawr to receive a master's degree in 1907. She began doctoral studies at Johns Hopkins that same year, receiving her Ph.D. in 1911. Her dissertation was titled *On Certain Families of Gasteropoda from the Miocene and Pliocene of Virginia and North Carolina.*

Becomes Affiliated with the United States Geological Survey

Gardner was to teach from time to time at Johns Hopkins University, but for most of her career she worked for the United States Geological Survey (USGS). The USGS was involved with strata mapping projects throughout the United States, Mexico, and the Caribbean area. She began field work with them in 1908, while pursuing her doctoral degree. In 1914, she investigated the taxonomy of Oligocene mollusks found in northern and western Florida. When World War I began, her desire to help alleviate the suffering brought on by the war led her to serve as a Red Cross volunteer in France. After the war was over, she remained in France with the American Friends Service Committee until 1920.

She then returned to the United States, where she was hired by the USGS to work on a geologic mapping project on the lower Rio Grande. It was while working on this project that she was made associate geologist and then geologist. During this period, Gardner also spent time in Europe promoting the exchange of ideas and geological data with European colleagues. With the outbreak of World War II, she joined the military geology unit of the USGS. By analyzing maps and aerial photographs, this unit supplied the United States with strategic and tactical information concerning the movements of the Japanese military. At the end of the war, Gardner was sent to Japan to map the West Pacific islands. While there, she also was able to extend her knowledge of the island's fossils through a study of the area's animal life. Gardner retired in 1952. She received a Distinguished Service Award from the Interior Department for her work with the USGS. That same year, she served as president of the Paleontological Society, and in 1953, was elected a vice president of the Geological Society of America. Even though retired, Gardner continued to do contract work for the USGS for several years. In 1954, she was involved in writing, along with L. R. Cox, the gastropod volume for a book entitled *Treatise on Invertebrate Paleontology,* when she suffered cerebral paralysis and was unable to continue her work. Her condition grew progressively worse over the years, and on November 15, 1960, she died of a stroke at her home in Bethesda, Maryland.

SELECTED WRITINGS BY GARDNER:

Books

The Molluscan Fauna of the Alum Bluff Group of Florida. U.S. Government Printing Office (Washington, D.C.), 1926–1950.

On Certain Families of Gasteropoda from the Miocene and Pliocene of Virginia and North Carolina. U.S. Government Printing Office (Washington, D.C.), 1943–1948.

Mollusca of the Tertiary Formations of Northeastern Mexico. [New York], 1945.

FURTHER READING

Books

Sicherman, Barbara, and Carol Hurd Green, eds. *Notable American Women, the Modern Period.* Cambridge: Belknap Press, 1980, pp. 260–262.

Sketch by Jane Stewart Cook

Margaret Joan Geller
1947–
American astronomer

Margaret Joan Geller, an astronomy professor at Harvard University and a senior scientist at the Smithsonian Astrophysical Observatory, helped discover a "Great Wall" of galaxies in space stretching at least 500 million light–years. The existence of this structure, the largest ever seen in the universe, presents a conundrum for theorists dealing with the early universe.

Geller was born in Ithaca, New York, on December 8, 1947, to Seymour Geller and Sarah Levine Geller. She received her bachelor's degree at the University of California at Berkeley in 1970, and was a National Science Foundation fellow from 1970 to 1973. Her M.A. followed at Princeton University in 1972, and her Ph.D. thesis, entitled "Bright Galaxies in Rich Clusters: A Statistical Model for Magnitude Distributions," was received at Princeton University in 1975. She was a fellow in theoretical physics at the Harvard–Smithsonian Center for Astrophysics from 1974 to 1976, and a research associate at the center from 1976 to 1980. She was a senior visiting fellow at the Institute for Astronomy in Cambridge, England, from 1978 to 1982, and an assistant professor at Harvard University from 1980 to 1983. Geller became an astrophysicist with the Smithsonian Astrophysical Observatory in 1983 and a professor of astronomy at Harvard University in 1988.

Since 1980 Geller has collaborated with astronomer John P. Huchra on a large–scale survey of galaxies, using redshifts to measure the galaxies' distance. (A redshift is a shift toward the red or longer–wavelength end of the visible spectrum that increases in proportion to distance.) Cosmologists have long predicted that galaxies are uniformly distributed in space, despite recent evidence of irregularities. Geller and Huchra hypothesized that three–dimensional mapping of galaxies beyond a certain brightness over a large–enough distance—500 million light–years—would confirm the predictions of uniformity. In January 1986 Huchra and Geller published their first results. But instead of the expected distribution, their "slice" of the cosmos (135 degrees wide by 6 degrees thick) showed sheets of galaxies appearing to line the walls of bubblelike empty spaces.

Discovers Largest Structure Known in Universe

Geller and Huchra's so–called Great Wall is a system of thousands of galaxies arranged across the universe—its full width was indeterminable because it fell off the edges of the survey map. The wall contains about five times the average density of galaxies; but "what's striking," Geller told M. Mitchell Waldrop of *Science Research News* in 1989, "is how incredibly *thin* [fifteen million light-years] the bubble walls are." Large structures such as the Great Wall pose a problem for astronomers—they are too large to have formed as a result of gravity since the big bang (a cosmic explosion that the universe was born out of and expanded from over time), unless a significant amount of clumpiness was present at the origin of the cosmos. This theory, however, is contradicted by the smoothness of the cosmic microwave background, or "echo" of the big bang. Dark matter, invisible elementary particles left over from the big bang and believed to constitute 90 percent of the mass of the universe, is another possible explanation. But even dark matter may not be capable of producing so large an object as the Great Wall. "There is something fundamentally missing from our understanding of the way things work," Geller told Waldrop. Between January 1986 and November 1989, Geller and Huchra published four maps (including the first), and in each found the same line of galaxies perpendicular to our line of sight. Geller and Huchra's survey will eventually plot about 15,000 galaxies.

Geller won a MacArthur fellowship—also known as a "genius award"—in 1990 for her research. She received the Newcomb–Cleveland Prize of the American Academy of Arts and Sciences that same year. In addition to galaxy distributions, Geller is interested in the origin and evolution of galaxies and x-ray astronomy. She is a member of the International Astronomical Union, the American Astronomical Society, and the American Association for the Advancement of Science.

SELECTED WRITINGS BY GELLER:

Books

(With A. C. Fabian and A. Szalay) *Large Scale Structures in the Universe.* Geneva Observatory, 1987.

Periodicals

(With Antonaldo Diaferio and Massimo Ramella) "Are Groups of Galaxies Viralized Systems?" *Astronomical Journal* (June 1, 1993): 2035.

(With Ann I. Zabludoff and John P. Huchra) "The Kinematics of Dense Clusters of Galaxies." *Astronomical Journal* (October 1, 1993): 1301.

FURTHER READING

Periodicals

Bartusiak, Marcia. "Mapping the Universe." *Discover* (August 1990): 60–63.

Powell, Corey S. "Up against the Wall." *Scientific American* (February, 1990): 18–19.
Waldrop, M. Mitchell. "Astronomers Go up against the Great Wall." *Science Research News* (November 17, 1989): 885.

Sketch by Sebastian Thaler

Sophie Germain
1776–1831
French mathematician

Sophie Germain's foundational work on Fermat's Last Theorem, a problem unsolved in mathematics into the late 20th century, stood unmatched for over 100 years. Though published by a mentor, Adrien–Marie Legendre, it is still referred to in textbooks as Germain's Theorem.

Germain worked alone, which was to her credit, yet contributed in a fundamental way to her limited development as a theorist. Her famed attempt to provide the mystery of Chladni figures with a pure mathematical model was made with no competition or collaboration. The three contests held by the Paris Académie Royale des Sciences from 1811 to 1816, regarding acoustics and elasticity of vibrating plates, never had more than one entry—hers. Each time she offered a new breakthrough: a fundamental hypothesis, an experimentally disprovable claim, and a treatment of curved and planar surfaces. However, even her final prizewinning paper was not published until after her death.

Sophie Germain (The Granger Collection, New York. Reproduced by permission.)

Teaches Herself Mathematics

Marie–Sophie Germain was born April 1, 1776, in Paris to Ambroise–François Germain and Marie–Madeleine Gruguelu. Her father served in the States–General and later the Constituent Assembly during the tumultuous Revolutionary period. He was so middle class that nothing is known of his wife but her name. Their eldest and youngest daughters, Marie–Madeleine and Angelique–Ambroise, were destined for marriage with professional men. However, when the fall of the Bastille in 1789 drove the Germains' sensitive middle daughter into hiding in the family library, Marie–Sophie's life path diverged from them all.

From the ages of 13 to 18 Sophie, as she was called to minimize confusion with the other Maries in her immediate family, absorbed herself in the study of pure mathematics. Inspired by reading the legend of Archimedes, purportedly slain while in the depths of geometric meditation by a Roman soldier, Germain sought the ultimate retreat from ugly political realities. In order to read Leonhard Euler and Isaac Newton in their professional languages, she taught herself Latin and Greek as well as geometry, algebra, and calculus. Despite her parents' most desperate measures, she always managed to sneak out at night and read by candlelight. Germain never formally attended any school or gained a degree during her entire life, but she was allowed to read lecture notes circulated in the École Polytechnique. She passed in her papers under the pseudonym "Le Blanc."

Correspondence School

Another tactic Germain used was to strike up correspondences with such successful mathematicians as Carl Gauss and Legendre. She was welcomed as a marvel and used as a muse by the likes of Jean B. Fourier and Augustin–Louis Cauchy, but her contacts did not develop into the sort of long–term apprenticeship that would have compensated for her lack of access to formal education and university–class libraries. Germain did become a celebrity once she dropped her pseudonym, however. She was the first woman not related to a member by marriage to attend Académie des Sciences meetings, and was also invited to sessions at the Institut de France—another first.

Some interpret Gauss' lack of intervention in Germain's education and eventual silence as a personal rejection of her. Yet this conclusion is not borne out by certain facts indicating Gauss took special notice. In 1810, Gauss was awarded one of his many accolades, a medal from the Institut de France. He refused the monetary component of this award, accepting instead an astronomical clock Germain and the institute's secretary bought for him with part of the prize. Gauss' biographer, G. Waldo Dunnington, reported that this pendulum clock was used by the great man for the rest of his life.

Gauss survived her, expressing at an 1837 celebration that he regretted Germain was not alive to receive an honorary doctorate with the others being feted that day. He alone had lobbied to make her the first such honored female in history. A hint of why Gauss valued her above the men who joined him in the Académie is expressed in a letter he sent to her in 1807, to thank her for intervening on his behalf with the invading French military. A taste for such subjects as mathematics and science is rare enough, he announced, but true intellectual rewards can only be reaped by those who delve into obscurities with a courage that matches their talents.

Germain was such a rarity. She outshone even Joseph–Louis Lagrange by not only showing an interest in prime numbers and considering a few theorems, about which Lagrange had corresponded with Gauss, but already attempting a few proofs. It was this almost reckless attack of the most novel unsolved problems, so typical of her it is considered Germain's weak point by twentieth century historians, that endeared her to Gauss.

Germain's one formal prize, the Institut de France's Gold Medal Prix Extraordinaire of 1816, was awarded to her on her third attempt, despite persistent weaknesses in her arguments. For this unremedied incompleteness, and the fact that she did not attend their public awards ceremony for fear of a scandal, this honor is still not considered fully legitimate. However, the labor and innovation Germain had brought to the subjects she tackled proved of invaluable aid and inspiration to colleagues and other mathematical professionals as late as 1908. In that year, L. E. Dickson, an algebraist, generalized Germain's Theorem to all prime numbers below 1,700, just another small step towards a complete proof of Fermat's Last Theorem.

Germain died childless and unmarried, of untreatable breast cancer on June 27, 1831 in Paris. The responsibility of preparing her writings for posterity was left to a nephew, Armand–Jacques Lherbette, the son of Germain's older sister. Her prescient ideas on the unity of all intellectual disciplines and equal importance of the arts and sciences, as well as her stature as a pioneer in women's history, are amply memorialized in the École Sophie Germain and the rue Germain in Paris. The house on the rue de Savoie in which she spent her last days was also designated a historical landmark.

SELECTED WRITINGS BY GERMAIN:

Books

Recherches sur la theorie des surfaces elastiques, 1821

Remarques sur la nature, les bornes et l'etendue de la question des surfaces elastiques, 1826

Oeuvres philosophiques de Sophie Germain, (edited by H. Stupuy), 1879

Periodicals

"Examen des principes qui peuvent conduire a la connaissance des lois de l'equilibre et du mouvement des solides elastiques." *Annales de chimie et de physique* 8 (1828): 123–131.

"Memoire sur la courbure des surfaces." *Journal fur die reine und angewandte Mathematik* 7 (1831): 1–29.

"Memoire sur l'emploi de l'epaisseur dans la theorie des surfaces elastiques." *Journal de Mathematiques pures et appliques* 6 (1880) Supplement: S5–S64.

Other

Cinq lettres de Sophie Germain et C. F. Gauss. Berlin: B. Boncompagni–Ludovici, 1880.

FURTHER READING

Books

Bucciarelli, Louis L., and Nancy Dworsky. *Sophie Germain: An Essay in the History of the Theory of Elasticity.* Dordrecht, Holland: D. Reidel Publishing Company, 1980.

Dunnington, G. Waldo. *Carl Friedrich Gauss: Titan of Science.* New York: Exposition Press, 1955, pp. 66–69, 93, 192.

Gray, Mary W. "Sophie Germain (1776–1831)," in *Women of Mathematics.* Edited by Louise S. Grinstein and Paul J. Campbell. New York: Greenwood Press, 1987, pp. 47–56.

Kramer, Edna E. "Sophie Germain," in *Dictionary of Scientific Biography.* Volume V. Edited by Charles Coulston Gillispie. New York: Charles Scribner's Sons, 1972, pp. 375–76.

Mozans, H. J. *Woman in Science.* New York: D. Appleton & Co., 1913, pp. 154–57.

Ogilvie, Marilyn Bailey. *Women in Science.* Cambridge: MIT Press, 1986, pp. 16, 90–92.

Osen, Lynn M. "Sophie Germain." *Women in Mathematics.* Cambridge: MIT Press, 1992, pp. 83–93.

Perl, Teri. *Math Equals: Biographies of Women Mathematicians.* Menlo Park, NJ: Addison–Wesley Publishing, 1978.

Periodicals

Dalmedico, Amy Dahan. "Sophie Germain." *Scientific American* (December 1991): 117–122.

Dauben, Joseph W. "Reviews: Sophie Germain." *American Mathematical Monthly* 92 (1985): 64–70.

Gray, Mary. "Sophie Germain: A Bicentennial Appreciation." *Association for Women in Mathematics Newsletter* 6 (September–October 1976): 10–14.

Ladd–Franklin, Christine. "Sophie Germain: An Unknown Mathematician." *Century* 48 (1894): 946–49.
Sampson, J. H. "Sophie Germain and the Theory of Numbers." *Archive for History of Exact Science* 41 (1990–91): 157–61.

Other

Caldwell, Chris K. "The Ten Largest Known Sophie Germain Primes." *The Largest Known Primes.* (1995–96). http://www.utm.edu/research/primes/largest.html#Sophie.
O'Connor, John J. and Edmund F. Robertson. "Sophie Germain." *MacTutor History of Mathematics Archives.* (December 1996). http://www–groups.dcs.st–and.ac.uk/~history/index.html
Swift, Amanda. "Sophie Germain." *Biographies of Women Mathematicians.* June 1997. http://www.scottlan.edu/lriddle/women/chronol.htm (July 22, 1997).

Sketch by Jennifer Kramer

Lillian Gilbreth (The Library of Congress.)

Lillian Evelyn Gilbreth
1878–1972
American engineer

Lillian Gilbreth was one of the founders of modern industrial management. She brought psychology to the study of management in the early twentieth century and then brought them both to the forefront of the business world. She broke new ground with her book *The Psychology of Management,* which concerned the health of the industrial worker. An outstanding academician who developed new curricula for major universities throughout the United States, Gilbreth became widely known for making human relations an integral part of management theory and practice.

Gilbreth was born Lillian Evelyn Moller on May 24, 1878, in Oakland, California. She was the oldest of nine children of William and Annie Delger Moller, who ran a devout household of strong German influence. Her mother was the daughter of a prominent Oakland businessman, and her father was a dedicated husband who had sold his New York business to buy into a partnership in the hardware industry in California. Because of her mother's poor health, Gilbreth's public school education did not begin until she was nine, but she progressed quickly and was academically successful in high school. Her passions at the time were literature and music, which she studied with composer John Metcalfe. She was well traveled as a high school student, visiting New York, Boston, and Chicago with her father.

Although very proud of his daughter's talents, Gilbreth's father did not believe that women should attend college. She convinced him, however, to let her enter the University of California and live at home, continuing to care for her sisters. She studied modern languages and philosophy, and her goal was to teach English. Gilbreth was the first woman in the university's history to speak on commencement day in 1900, when she received her B.A. in literature. After graduation, Gilbreth entered Columbia University to pursue a master's degree in literature, but illness forced her to return home in her first year. She reentered the University of California, finished her master's degree in literature in 1902, and began work on a Ph.D.

In 1903, Gilbreth took a break from her studies to travel abroad. She stopped first in Boston, where she met Frank Gilbreth. Ten years her senior, he owned a construction business and was working on the development of motion–study techniques—methods to minimize wasted time and energy and increase productivity in industry. They corresponded through the mail for ten months after they met, and they were married on October 19, 1904. They would have twelve children, two of whom would later record their humorous memories of family life in the popular books *Cheaper by the Dozen* and *Belles on Their Toes.*

Begins Work on Time-and-Motion Studies

Work was the focus of Frank Gilbreth's life. He wanted a complete partnership with his new wife and began to teach her about construction. He saw that her interest in the human aspects of industry complemented his ideas and he encouraged her to work with him. Their goals and their personalities influenced each other so strongly that both of their careers were redirected into new areas. The mental and physical health of workers was then largely neglected, and Lillian Gilbreth became increasingly interested in her husband's work as she recognized her potential contribution. Her doctoral studies shifted from literature to psychology.

Lillian Gilbreth's marriage began with several major responsibilities—her academic work, starting a large family, and becoming acquainted with the business world. She started as a systems manager in her husband's consulting business and was soon acknowledged as an expert in the study of worker fatigue and production. Her reputation was partially due to her precise measurements when collecting data. Among her contributions were the analysis of machinery and tools, the invention of new tools and the methods to simplify their use, and the standardization of tasks. Most importantly, her work led to a greater understanding of the importance of the welfare of individual in business operations. This was instrumental in broadening acceptance of her husband's work on increasing productivity.

In 1910, the Gilbreths moved their growing family to Providence, Rhode Island, where Lillian Gilbreth entered Brown University to continue her doctoral studies in psychology. She began writing about industrial management from a scientific and psychological perspective. A lecture she delivered at the Dartmouth College Conference on Scientific Management in 1911 on the relationship between management and psychology became the basis for her doctoral dissertation.

In 1913, Frank and Lillian Gilbreth started the Summer School of Scientific Management. The school trained professionals to teach new ideas about management, and it emphasized the study of motion and psychology. Tuition was free, admission was by invitation, and classes were well attended by professors and business people from the United States and abroad. The Gilbreths ran the summer school for four years. Lillian Gilbreth received her Ph.D. from Brown in 1915. Her dissertation had already been published as a book, *The Psychology of Management,* in 1914. She was the first theorist in industrial management to emphasize and document the importance of psychological considerations in management.

After Frank Gilbreth's death in 1924, Lillian Gilbreth moved her family to her home state of California, where she provided a new home and college educations for her children, maintained a consulting business, and continued teaching and researching on efficiency and health in industry. Gilbreth became a well respected businesswoman; Johnson & Johnson hired her consulting firm to train their employees, and Macy's in New York had her study the working conditions of their salespeople to investigate techniques to reduce fatigue. The Dennison Co. and Sears & Roebuck were also clients, among many others. She started a new school called Gilbreth Research Associates, which catered to retail interests and went international in 1926. But by 1929, several universities were modeling motion in their engineering schools, using laboratories complete with photographic devices and movement measurement tools. Convinced that her ideas would now be carried on, she closed Gilbreth Research Associates. That same year she traveled to Tokyo to speak at the First World Power Congress. Gilbreth was now lecturing at universities such as Stanford, Harvard, Yale, and the Massachusetts Institute of Technology. She joined the Purdue University faculty in 1935 as a professor of management, becoming the first woman professor in the engineering school.

When America entered World War II, Gilbreth consulted at the Arma Plant in Brooklyn, New York, which handled huge Navy contracts. The staff at the plant grew from a few hundred to eleven thousand men and women, and she managed the personnel restructuring and worker training for this enormous expansion. Especially notable was her development of an exercise program for the women; although white–haired and over sixty years old, she kept up with the younger women.

In 1948, Gilbreth began teaching at the Newark College of Engineering in New Jersey. She was the first woman professor in this school of engineering as well, and she stayed there for two years. She went on to teach in Formosa from 1953 to 1954 and at the University of Wisconsin in 1955. Gilbreth remained active professionally well into her eighties, speaking and writing on management issues. She also became a widely sought speaker on human relations problems in management. Gilbreth received over a dozen honorary degrees. She was the recipient of the Hoover Medal from the American Society of Civil Engineers in 1966, and other engineering and management professional organizations around the world bestowed many awards upon her for her pioneering work. She died in Phoenix, Arizona, on January 2, 1972.

SELECTED WRITINGS BY GILBRETH:

Books

The Psychology of Management. Sturgis and Walton, 1914.

(With Frank Gilbreth) *Fatigue Study: The Elimination of Humanity's Greatest Unnecessary Waste.* Sturgis and Walton, 1916.

(With Frank Gilbreth) *Applied Motion Study.* Sturgis and Walton, 1917.

The Quest of the One Best Way: A Sketch of the Life of Frank Bunker Gilbreth. Society of Industrial Engineers, 1926.

FURTHER READING:

Books

Carey, Ernestine G., and Frank B. Gilbreth, Jr. *Cheaper by the Dozen.* Crowell, 1948, expanded edition, 1963.

Carey, Ernestine G., and Frank B. Gilbreth, Jr. *Belles on Their Toes.* Crowell, 1950.

Haas, Violet B. and Carolyn C. Perrucci, eds. *Women in Scientific and Engineering Professions.* University of Michigan Press, 1984.

Spriegel, W. R. and C. E. Meyers, eds. *The Writings of the Gilbreths.* Richard D. Irwin, 1953.

Yost, Edna. *Frank and Lillian Gilbreth, Partners for Life.* New Brunswick: Rutgers University Press, 1949.

Periodicals

"Lillian Moller Gilbreth: Remarkable First Lady of Engineering." *Society of Women Engineers Newsletter* 24 (1978).

Trescott, M. M. "A History of Women Engineers in the United States, 1850–1975: A Progress Report." *Proceedings of the Society of Women Engineers 1979 National Convention,* New York Society of Women Engineers, 1979.

Sketch by David N. Ford

Alessandra Giliani
1307(?)–1326
Italian anatomist

Alessandra Giliani was an assistant to Mundinus (Mondino) de Luzzi, who was a renowned surgeon and anatomist practicing in Bologna, Italy. Under his guidance, she became skilled in philosophy, and eventually in anatomy. Her skill was recognized, and she became a prosector (one who makes dissections for anatomic demonstrations). She has the distinction of being the only medieval female prosector recorded in history. She also pioneered anatomical injection. This valuable discovery allowed her to draw blood from arteries and even the most minute of veins. The process further involved refilling veins and arteries with various colored dyes. By this method, she was able to show the workings of the circulatory system. This proved to be a valuable teaching tool in training anatomists of the day.

Science of Dissection Begins in Thirteenth Century

Nancy G. Siraisi, writing in *Medieval & Early Renaissance Medicine*, says that dissection of human cadavers seems to have begun near the end of the thirteenth century. Mondino de Luzzi, later mentor to Giliani, wrote a handbook in 1316 (*Anatomia corporis humanis*), which developed the methods of dissection. The handbook had illustrations of anatomists seated on platforms directing their assistants in the performance of a dissection. At that time, bodies used for this purpose were those of executed criminals. It is said the bodies were supplied by local authorities, thus giving the practice a legality that it did not possess previous to that time. (Grave robbing for the purpose of cadaver dissection did occur. However, this was a sacrilegious act, and anyone caught could be prosecuted.) For more than 100 years, de Luzzi's handbook served as the standard textbook in medical schools. The knowledge gained through human dissection from the fourteenth through the sixteenth centuries was to advance the science of anatomy and lead to improved surgical techniques.

It is not known how Giliani became associated with de Luzzi, the so–called "father of anatomy." According to James Walsh, quoting from *The History of the Anatomy School in Bologna in his Medieval Medicine*, de Luzzi considered her "a most valued dissector and assistant." From all indications, she worked as an equal with the male practitioners. When she died, Otto Agenius, a fellow anatomist and possibly her fiance, had a plaque placed in the Church of San Pietro e Marcellino, enscribed with the following: *In this urn enclosed, the ashes of the body of Alessandra Giliani, a maiden of Periceto, skillful with the brush in anatomical demonstrations and a disciple, equalled by few, of the most noted physician, Mondinus of Luzzi, await the resurrection. She lived nineteen years; she died consumed by her labours March 26, in the year of grace 1326. Otto Agenius Lustrulanus, by her loss deprived of his better part, his excellent companion deserving of the best, has erected this tablet.*

FURTHER READING

Books

Alic, Margaret. *Hypatia's Heritage: A History of Women in Science from Antiquity through the Nineteenth Century.* Boston: Beacon Press, 1986.

Hughes, Muriel Joy. *Women Healers in Medieval Life and Literature.* Freeport, New York: Books for Libraries Press, 1968.

Mozans, H. J. *Women in Science.* New York: D. Appleton and Company, 1913.

Ogilvie, Marilyn Bailey. *Women in Science, Antiquity through the Nineteenth Century.* Cambridge: MIT Press, 1986, pp. 8–13; p. 92.

Siraisi, Nancy G. *Medieval & Early Renaissance Medicine.* Chicago: University of Chicago Press, 1990.

Sketch by Jane Stewart Cook

Gloria Ford Gilmer
?–
American mathematician and educator

Gloria Ford Gilmer is a leader in the field of ethnomathematics, which describes the mathematical practices of identifiable cultural groups, including small–scale indigenous societies, national societies, labor communities, religious groups, and professional classes. Evidence now shows that people in all societies devise their own way of doing mathematics, independently of their technological level or what they may have learned in school.

In 1956, Gilmer became the first African American woman to publish two (non–Ph.D. thesis) mathematics research articles. She was also the first African American female on the board of governors of the Mathematical Association of America (1980–82) and is currently president of Math–Tech, a consulting firm that seeks better ways to teach math. From 1980–1982, she was national director of the Blacks and Mathematics Program of the Mathematical Association of America. In this capacity, she traveled around the country, encouraging African American students to pursue mathematics.

Shows Early Interest in Math

Gilmer was born in Baltimore, Maryland to James and Mittie Ford. She became interested in math from working in her father's grocery store, doing shop arithmetic. Gilmer's teachers also encouraged her interest in math. Gilmer became a teacher herself at an early age; since fourth grade she has tutored her classmates in math and other subjects.

Gilmer earned a B.S. in mathematics from Morgan State University where she was a student of Clarence Stephens. Then she earned an M.A. in mathematics from the University of Pennsylvania. After graduation she was employed at the U.S. Army's Aberdeen Proving Grounds in Baltimore, Maryland, conducting ballistics research, before spending a year in the doctoral program in mathematics at the University of Wisconsin–Madison. In 1957 she married Jay Gilmer, a native of Milwaukee, and they had two children.

Several years later, Gilmer earned a Ph.D. in curriculum and instruction from Marquette University's School of Education, the first African American woman to do so. Gilmer believes in the two laws of teaching: "The first law is to know your subject, the second law is to know how to teach," she said to the contributor in an interview.

Much of Gilmer's early career has been spent in education. During 1957 she was a math teacher at Lockport High School, a western New York public school, because she thought it was a good opportunity to learn what public education was like. She moved to Milwaukee, Wisconsin in 1958 to join her husband and began teaching math in the public school system a year later, the first African American to do so. Gilmer also became the first African American to lecture in the math department at both the University of Wisconsin–Milwaukee (as a part–time adjunct professor in 1963) and Milwaukee Area Technical College as a full–time instructor in 1965.

In 1979 Gilmer left Milwaukee to accept a position at Atlanta University (Atlanta, Georgia and now Clark Atlanta University) as associate professor of mathematics education and grantsperson. In 1980 she became an associate professor in mathematics at Morehouse College (an all–male college), part of the Atlanta University center. These schools are two of the six historically black universities she has taught at. The others are Hampton University, Hampton, VA (her first university teaching job), Virginia State University (Petersburg, VA), Morgan State University (Baltimore, Maryland), and Coppin State University (Baltimore, Maryland).

Pioneers Research in Math Education

In 1981, Gilmer became a research associate at the National Institute of Education. She remained there until 1984, investigating the use of microcomputers for the teaching of mathematics. During this period she was a member of the U.S. Mathematics Delegation to the People's Republic of China and National Science Fellow to the Fifth International Congress on Mathematical Education in Adelaide, Australia. She left in 1984 to return to Milwaukee and to form her own company, Math–Tech, Inc.

In 1985, Gilmer co–founded the International Study Group on Ethno–mathematics. She also became Chair of the AMS–MAA–AAAS Committee on Opportunities in Mathematics for Underrepresented Minorities (COMUM), a position she remained in until 1996. Gilmer believes that this is one of her most important contributions to mathematical education. COMUM initiated support from the Mathematical Sciences Education Board of the National Research Council, who established a nation–wide series of workshops called Making Math Work for Minorities on how best to attract minorities to mathematics–based fields. This culminated in a summit meeting at the National Academy of Sciences.

Gilmer also moved to Baltimore, Maryland in 1984 to become Professor of Mathematics & Director of the Center for Mathematics Teaching and Learning at Coppin State College, remaining in that position until 1986. That same year she again returned to Milwaukee where she established the Family Math Center at the Carter Child Development Center, becoming the first person to create a family math program in that city.

In the following years, Gilmer became an international expert in education issues. In 1988, she gave a speech on worldwide development in ethnomathematics at the Sixth International Congress on Mathematical Education in Budapest, Hungary. She also was a member of the Mathematics Educators Study Tour of the Soviet Union that same year. During the early 90s Gilmer gave numerous speeches on ethnomathematics and curriculum development. More recently, in 1997, she traveled with a diocesan committee to Jeanette, Haiti to examine educational issues there.

Gilmer is passionate about her field and makes time to be involved in various professional organizations, as well as civic service. She has been a judge for the National Mathcounts Competition for junior high school students, participated in several committees and panels related to undergraduate mathematics and minorities, and is a member of seven professional math associations. Gilmer also served on several committees of the Episcopal Church (including chairing the Commission of Racial Justice for the Episcopal Diocese of Milwaukee), the National Urban Coalition, and the National Urban League.

Gilmer is currently Chair of the Commission on Education of the National Council of Negro Women, which she has held since 1985. In this position she guided the national Excellence in Teaching Awards program, sponsored by Shell Oil, which selects eight outstanding teachers every year that teach in schools with minority students. "This is very important since we can also identify the best practices used to teach math to African American students effectively," she explained in an interview with Sheppard. Gilmer recently accepted a two–year appointment as President of the Alumni Association of Marquette University's Graduate School.

SELECTED WRITINGS BY GILMER:

Books

Building Bridges to Cultural Connections. New York: Addison–Wesley Publishing Company, Inc., 1993.

"Afterword" in *Ethnomathematics: Challenging Eurocentrism in Mathematics Education.* Edited by Powell and Frankenstein. New York: State University of New York Press, 1997.

"Computers in the Remedial Mathematics Curriculum" in *Computers and Mathematics.* David Smith, et al, editors. The Mathematical Association of America, 1988.

Periodicals

(As Ford, with Luna I. Mishoe) "On the Limit of the Coefficients of the Eigenfunction Series Associated with a Certain Non–self–adjoint Differential System." *Proc. Amer. Math. Soc.* 7 (1956): 260–66.

(As Ford, with Luna I. Mishoe) "On the Uniform Convergence of a Certain Eigenfunction Series." *Pacific J. Math.* 6 (1956): 271–78.

"Socio–Cultural Influences on Learning." American Perspective on the Fifth International Congress on Mathematical Education, Mathematical Association of America, 1985.

"An Ethnomath Approach to Curriculum Development." *Newsletter of the International Study Group on Ethnomathematics* 5, no. 2 (May 1990).

Other

"Ethnomathematics Coming of Age." NCTM Annual meeting, Salt Lake City, Utah, April 1990.

"Status of Ethnomathematics in the U.S." Seventh International Congress on Mathematical Education, Quebec, Canada, August 1992.

FURTHER READING

Books

Hine, Darlene Clark, ed. *Black Women in America: An Historical Encyclopedia, Volume I, A–L.* Carlson Publishing Inc., 1993.

Other

Sheppard, Laurel M., interview with Gloria Gilmer conducted May and June 1999.

Sketch by Laurel M. Sheppard

Ruth Ann (Bobrov) Glater
1919–
American botanist

Ruth Ann Bobrov Glater is recognized for her work on the effects of pollution on plants. Her groundbreaking research continues to affect the lives of the residents of Los Angeles county, and has impacted science's understanding of air quality and its importance to plants, animals, and humans.

Ruth Ann Bobrov, called Ruthie, was born August 11, 1919, in the kitchen of her parents' tenement in the Bronx. Her father, Jacob, and her mother, Jennie, had immigrated separately to the United States from Russia, and Glater and her older brother Solly learned Yiddish and English, not Russian, because of their parents' hatred for Russia. The Bobrovs were Orthodox Jews, and Jacob worked as a kosher butcher. Early on, Glater was drawn to the beauty of plants and flowers as a foil to the dirty and ugly world of the tenement where she lived.

Her mother taught Glater to read at four, and she was an excellent student, skipping first grade and later scoring the highest grade in the state on the standardized geometry test. Glater knew as a child that she wanted to be a doctor or a scientist, because her uncle was a doctor, and she used to amuse herself by reading his medical books.

Glater graduated from high school at 15, and attended Hunter College. Her education was virtually free since the city paid her tuition. There were no scholarships for women to go to medical school, and Glater could not afford to pay her own way, so she felt obligated to study to teach high school science. At Hunter, she became intrigued by botany, specifically, mycology, and said in her autobiography, "I was captivated by the diversity and perfection of the fungi, beauty that could be detected only when using the high power of a fine microscope." This experience led her to change her plans and study botany instead of natural science and education.

When she graduated Hunter in 1939, she had received scholarships to both Boston University and the University of Arizona, but was unable to attend because of financial and family considerations. That summer she worked as a nature–study camp counselor and matriculated to Columbia University in the fall, where she was the only full–time Jewish student. Her thesis work was done with almost no guidance or help, so Glater was forced to learn quickly and independently. She isolated several forms of fungi and described one new to the literature. After graduation, Glater was unable to find a salaried position, and volunteered at the Bronx Botanical Gardens, where she learned about plant pathology.

Finally, Glater accepted a position with the census, which led her to join the Navy for the war effort. She served in the Navy from 1943 to 1945, and married an old acquaintance, Ronald Cramer, in 1944. The marriage did not last long.

Begins Work on Pollution

After her discharge from the Navy, Glater went on to UCLA to complete her Ph.D. in botany and medical mycology, her education paid for by the GI Bill. She was the only female in the department, and although an excellent student, could not find a university position after graduation in 1951. Finally, the Los Angeles County Air Pollution Control District asked Glater to join their work in discovering why crops were dying or becoming damaged. Glater studied air pollution, including that caused by ever increasing motor vehicle use, and published several groundbreaking studies describing how pollution destroys leaves from the interior out. On her first day of work, she met Bud Glater, and they married on December 31, 1953. They had two daughters before divorcing in 1977.

In 1955, Glater applied for a grant from the United States Public Health Service to continue research on pollution, and she worked in the lab at UCLA as a research botanist. When her grant expired, she was rehired by UCLA, but was expected to work wherever she was needed, and could no longer direct the research. Glater did receive a measure of recognition, however, and was invited to lecture on several occasions. In 1972, she discovered the cause of lead poisoning in plants.

Glater's health began to steadily deteriorate, and in 1969 she underwent open heart surgery. A few years later, she was told she would need a second operation, but with the help of the Pritikin diet, was able to avoid the surgery a second time. She worked for Pritikin's clinic for a while before teaching adult education courses in nutrition at Santa Barbara City College. Glater remained at the college until 1982, when her health problems forced her to retire. Glater continues to live in Santa Barbara, California.

SELECTED WRITINGS BY GLATER:

Periodicals

"The Effect of Smog on the Anatomy of Oat Leaves." *Phytopathology* (42), 1952.

"Smog Damage to Ferns in the Los Angeles Area." *Phytopathology* (46), 1956.

"Use of Plants as Biological Indicators of Smog in the Air of Los Angeles County." *Science* (12), 1955.

FURTHER READING

Books

Glater, R.A.B. *Slam the Door Gently*. Santa Barbara: Fithian Press, 1997.

Sketch by Helene Barker Kiser

Catherine Anselm Gleason
1865–1933
American mechanical engineer

Catherine "Kate" Gleason became a legend for her achievements in the construction and machine-tool industries, was the first woman member of the American Society of Mechanical Engineers, pioneered the development of low–cost housing, and became the first woman member of the American Concrete Institute, earning the nickname "Concrete Kate".

Gleason was born to William Gleason and Ellen McDermot Gleason on November 24, 1865 in Rochester, New York, the first of four children. Her father, an Irish immigrant, owned Gleason Works, a machine-tool factory he had founded that same year. Her mother was a good friend of the suffragist, Susan B. Anthony, who probably influenced the Gleason family regarding the role of women in society. Growing up, Gleason was a tomboy and very competitive.

Enters the Family Business

In 1877, Gleason's half-brother Tom died at the age of 18, leaving her father without an assistant to run his company. Gleason, only 11 at the time, took it upon herself

Kate Gleason (Rochester Institute of Technology. Reproduced by permission.)

to help. By the age if 14, Gleason was the company's bookkeeper. Four years later she became the first woman to enter Cornell University's engineering program. She also briefly attended the Sibley College of Engraving and the Mechanics Institute (now the Rochester Institute of Technology).

Gleason did not finish her degree because her father could no longer afford to pay her replacement. He asked her to return home before her first year was completed. Though disappointed, Gleason applied her talents to the company operations and by 1890 (at age 24), she was both the secretary-treasurer and chief sales representative.

Gleason decided to expand the company's markets overseas and made her first trip to Europe three years later. She returned from a tour of England, Scotland, France, and Germany with orders from some of the most prestigious companies in Europe. Her trip represented one of the earliest attempts by an American manufacturer to establish overseas markets and it was made by a woman. Gleason machines are now installed in more than 50 countries and between 65–70% of its products are shipped outside the United States.

Switches to Banking and Construction

Gleason's strong will and forceful personality led to clashes with her siblings about the business. Her family may also have been jealous about her fame from incorrectly being identified as the inventor of the bevel gear planar (which eliminated hand cutting), that was actually her father's invention. Henry Ford is quoted to have said that the gear planer was "the most remarkable machine work ever done by a woman", although Kate herself never claimed to have had a large role in the invention. So, in 1913, Gleason left the company to pursue another career. That same year, Verein Deutscher Ingenieure elected her to membership, the first woman to be so honored. In 1914 Gleason became the first woman to be appointed receiver by a bankruptcy court in New York State regarding the Ingle Machine Co.

Gleason then applied her business skills to the banking industry, becoming one of the first American women presidents of a bank (the First National Bank of East Rochester). While at the bank, Gleason helped launch eight new businesses and conceived and promoted large-scale development of low-cost tract housing.

Her first development was Concrest, a subdivision of 100 poured-concrete houses (using a method she had developed), a country club, a golf course, and a park. She applied the technique of standardization and mass production of homes after being inspired by a visit to an automotive factory assembly line.

Immediately following World War I, Gleason applied her construction knowledge in Europe, restoring most of the French village of Septmonts. She purchased some of the buildings in the project, including twelfth-century battlements, hired villagers in the restoration project, and returned one building to the town after converting it into a library and movie theater.

During the 1920s, Gleason brought her affordable housing concept to other areas of the United States, including Sausalita, California, and Beaufort County, South Carolina. In Beaufort, she started a writers' and artists' colony resort, which her sister, Eleanor, continued after Kate's death. Gleason was ahead of her time, developing beach property, a golf course and clubhouse—all in her vision of Beaufort County as a center for tourism. The Kate Gleason Memorial Park at Beaufort Memorial Hospital now remains a tribute to her generosity and creativity. In 1924, Gleason acted as advisor to Berkeley on rebuilding the city after a major fire. In 1930, she served as ASME's representative to the World Power Conference in Germany.

Gleason died January 9, 1933 of pneumonia at the age of 68. She gave away the bulk of her wealth before her death, but still left an estate of $1,400,000 that benefitted medical, educational, and charitable institutions. In 1998, the Rochester Institute of Technology's College of Engineering was named after her, the first American engineering college to be named after a woman.

SELECTED WRITINGS BY GLEASON:

Periodicals

"How a Woman Builds Houses to Sell at a Profit for $4,000." *Concrete* (January 1921): 9–14.

FURTHER READING

Books

Farnes, Patricia and G. Kass–Simon. *Women of Science: Righting the Record.* Bloomington: Indiana University Press, 1990

McHenry, Robert, ed. *Her Heritage: A Biographical Encyclopedia of Famous American Women.* Cambridge, MA" Pilgrim New Media, Inc., 1994.

Vare, Ethlie Ann and Greg Ptacek. *Mothers of Invention: From the Bra to the Bomb: Forgotten Women & Their Unforgettable Ideas.* New York: William E. Morrow, 1988

Other

Bartels, Nancy. "The First Lady of Gearing." *Gear Technology* http://www.geartechnology.com/mag/gt–kg.htm

Bois, Danuta. "Kate Gleason." *Distinguished Women of Past and Present.* www.netsrq.com/~dbois/gleason.html.

Gleason, Janis. Correspondence with Laurel Sheppard, April 2, 1999.

Lindsley, Kathy. Press release and correspondence. Rochester Institute of Technology. March 15, 1999.

Sketch by Laurel M. Sheppard

Ellen Gleditsch
1879–1968
Norwegian chemist

Ellen Gleditsch (Archive Photos. Reproduced by permission.)

Ellen Gleditsch began her long career in chemistry as **Marie Curie**'s assistant, but quickly grew to prominence in her own right. She pioneered the field of chemical radioactivity, becoming one of the first specialists. Gleditsch established the half-life of radium and aided in proving the existence of isotopes. In addition, Gleditsch was in contact with many prominent scientists of the time, and her friendship and work connected them all.

Ellen Gleditsch was born on December 29, 1879, in Mandal, Norway, the first of 10 children born to Karl Kristian Gleditsch, a teacher, and Petra Birgitte (Hansen) Gleditsch. Although poor, the Gleditsch family was an exceptionally happy and close one. Both Karl and Petra were intellectual and politically liberal. The children were exposed to cultural, musical, and natural activities in addition to their regular studies. Gleditsch's mother was an advocate of women's rights.

Gleditsch graduated from high school in 1895 as valedictorian, with her highest grades in science and mathematics. She could not enter the university because it was not open to women at the time, so she began training as a pharmacologist in Tromso, and completed her nonacademic degree in pharmacology in 1902.

Because her studies involved chemistry and her degree qualified her to take courses at Oslo University, chemist Eyvind Bodtker invited her to study at the university laboratory. In 1903, she was an assistant in the chemistry lab, and in 1906 she was permitted to take the university entrance exam, which she passed. Bodtker, who became a lifelong friend—as did most who came into contact with sociable Gleditsch—suggested she continue her training at Marie Curie's laboratory in Paris and personally saw to her appointment there in 1907.

Becomes Curie's Assistant

Gleditsch received a grant from philanthropic funds made available by Josephine, the dowager queen of Norway and Sweden, for her Paris studies. Although students normally paid to work in Curie's laboratory, Curie needed a chemist and gave Gleditsch responsibility for purifying radium salts in exchange for exemption from fees. Curie also asked Gleditsch to help her reproduce a recent study in which British scientists claimed that copper changed to lithium when exposed to radium, a study Curie doubted. Their findings did, indeed, prove the first study wrong. Gleditsch worked closely with Curie and became a family friend to Curie and her children. Most of her work in Curie's lab involved analyzing uranium and radium in radioactive minerals.

Establishes Half-Life of Radium

Gleditsch returned to Norway periodically to visit her family and, in 1912, returned to stay after receiving her *Licencée ès Sciences* from La Sorbonne in Paris. She was offered a fellowship at the University of Oslo, where she supervised the laboratory and lectured on radioactivity. The university's most experienced radiochemist, she continued her study of radium's half-life, but became discouraged by isolation and the lack of equipment. Hope for better opportunities came in 1913 in the form of a scholarship from the American-Scandinavian Foundation to study the United States. That same year, both her parents and a brother died within weeks of each other and Gleditsch then took in two of her brothers to care for them.

In 1914 Gleditsch wrote to Theodore Lymann at Harvard and Bertram Boltwood at Yale, asking to work in their laboratories. Lymann informed her that no woman had ever worked in his lab and he did not intend to change that. Boltwood was more polite, trying to discourage her with claims of minimal space. Undeterred, Gleditsch went to Yale anyway and spent a year there where she established the half-life of radium: 1,686. Her number remained the standard for many years until it was adjusted to 1,620 years. Half-life refers to the amount of time it takes for half the atoms of a radioactive substance to decay, or decrease in amount. Measuring the half-life of radium was important in the study of radioactivity because it could be used as a constant to study other elements. This work brought her acclaim and respect in the scientific community. Smith College awarded her a honorary Doctor of Science degree, and Lyman changed his mind about having women in his lab. Boltwood even helped her to publish her results in the *American Journal of Science.*

Helps to Confirm Existence of Isotopes

Gleditsch's other significant contribution to chemistry was her part in confirming the existence of isotopes. Isotopes are two or more atoms of an element that have the same atomic number and chemical behavior, but different atomic mass and physical properties. British chemist Frederick Soddy had suggested that an element's atoms could have different atomic weights, but most scientists maintained that atomic weight was fixed within an atom and evidence otherwise was hard to find. American chemist Theodore Richards was considered the expert in the field at the time, so like many other scientists trying to prove the existence of isotopes, Gleditsch sent a lead sample to him to analyze. Gleditsch's sample was so free of errors that it was the only one that proved the existence of isotopes.

Her work finally gained her respect and she was appointed a reader in chemistry at the University of Oslo in 1916. Although it was not a tenure track position, it was an improvement over the low-paying fellowship she had before. In 1917, Gleditsch coauthored two chemistry textbooks, one of which was the first of its kind written by Scandinavians. That same year, she became a member of Oslo's Academy of Science, only the second woman to be elected.

Gleditsch was always active in promoting the reputation of women in academics. In 1919, Gleditsch cofounded the Norwegian Women Academics Association, for which she acted as president from 1924–1928. She also served as president of the International Federation of University Women from 1926–1929, a position that allowed her to travel and lecture extensively. She began a radio lecture series and wrote biographies and research papers in several languages, in order to keep the public and other scientists informed in scientific research and breakthroughs. During the 1920s Gleditsch also traveled to Curie's laboratory many times to supervise experiments and once the entire lab while Curie was in South America.

Gleditsch continued her isotope research during this time, sometimes working with her chemist sister. She published a book on isotopes which was translated into English and sold so well it had to be reprinted in a year after it's publication. In 1929, the University of Oslo finally appointed her professor of chemistry, making her only the second woman at Oslo to be appointed to that level.

Provides Safe Haven for Scientists

During the 1930s, Gleditsch began work at a new laboratory she had helped to plan. Soon after, the Nazis came into power. Gleditsch, always the "mother," took in her brother's child during the war, and offered her laboratory space in Oslo as a kind of "safe house" for scientists, including **Marietta Blau**, who were fleeing Nazi persecution in other countries. By 1940, Norway was under German occupation as well. Even though part of the university had been taken control of by Nazis, Gleditsch continued her work. She and a few of her colleagues secretly became "guerrilla scientists," working with an underground organization to defy Nazi power. Gleditsch aided the university community, sometimes hiding people in her own home. They planted gardens because food was scarce, and took turns guarding them from thieves. She went undercover, pretending to be a needleworker making national costumes, so she could relay messages to people about the underground resistance movement.

In 1943, the laboratory was raided by the Germans, and all of the men were arrested. Gleditsch and the other women worked quickly to clear the lab of anything valuable, and Gleditsch hid valuable minerals in a suitcase under her bed. When she was finally arrested, her scientific knowledge and fluent German helped her to negotiate her release.

After the war and her retirement, Gleditsch worked for the newly established United Nations organization UNESCO, only to resign several years later in protest to fascist

Spain becoming a member. She was granted an honorary doctorate by the University of Strasbourg in 1948 and by La Sorbonne in 1962. She was the first woman to receive the award at La Sorbonne, and it was her proudest achievement.

After her retirement, Gleditsch continued her research and wrote papers on scientific history. She still kept an office at the laboratory and continued to advise and inspire students. She gave a dinner party at her country house for her students less than a week before her death of a stroke on June 5, 1968. That same year, the Ellen Gleditsch Scholarship Foundation was established in Norway to support aspiring scientists in their education.

SELECTED WRITINGS BY GLEDITSCH:

Books

Contributions to the Study of Isotopes. Oslo: Dybwad, 1925.

Periodicals

"The Life of Radium." *American Journal of Science* 41 (1916):112.

"Ratio Between Uranium and Radium in the Radioactive Minerals." *Comptes Rendus* 149 (1909): 267.

FURTHER READING

Books

Shearer, Benjamin F., and Barbara S. Shearer, eds. *Notable Women in the Physical Sciences.* Westport, CT: Greenwood Press, 1997.

Rayner-Canham, Marelene F., and Geoffrey W., eds. *A Devotion to Their Science: Pioneer Women of Radioactivity.* Philadelphia: Chemical Heritage Foundation, 1997.

Sketch by Helene Barker Kiser

Maria Goeppert-Mayer
1906–1972
German-American physicist

Maria Goeppert–Mayer (UPI/Corbis–Bettmann. Reproduced by permission.)

Maria Goeppert–Mayer was one of the inner circle of nuclear physicists who developed the atomic fission bomb at the secret laboratory at Los Alamos, New Mexico, during World War II. Through her theoretical research with nuclear physicists Enrico Fermi and Edward Teller, Goeppert–Mayer developed a model for the structure of atomic nuclei. In 1963, for her work on nuclear structure, she became the first woman awarded the Nobel Prize for theoretical physics, sharing the prize with J. Hans D. Jensen, a German physicist. The two scientists, who had reached the same conclusions independently, later collaborated on a book explaining their model.

An only child, Goeppert–Mayer was born Maria Göppert on July 28, 1906, in the German city of Kattowitz in Upper Silesia (now Katowice, Poland). When she was four, her father, Dr. Friedrich Göppert, was appointed professor of pediatrics at the University at Göttingen, Germany. Situated in an old medieval town, the university had historically been respected for its mathematics department, but was on its way to becoming the European center for yet another discipline—theoretical physics. Maria's mother, Maria Wolff Göppert, was a former teacher of piano and French who delighted in entertaining faculty members with lavish dinner parties and providing a home filled with flowers and music for her only daughter.

Dr. Göppert was a most progressive pediatrician for the times, as he started a well–baby clinic and believed that all children, male or female, should be adventuresome risk–takers. His philosophy on child rearing had a profound effect on his daughter, who idolized her father and treasured her long country walks with him, collecting fossils and learning the names of plants. Because the Göpperts came from several generations of university professors, it was unstated but expected that Maria would continue the family tradition.

When Maria was just eight, World War I interrupted the family's rather idyllic university life with harsh wartime deprivation. After the war, life was still hard because of postwar inflation and food shortages. Maria Göppert attended a small private school run by female suffragists to ready young girls for university studies. The school went bankrupt when Göppert had completed only two of the customary three years of preparatory school. Nonetheless, she took and passed her university entrance exam.

From Quantum Mechanics to the Bomb

The University of Göttingen that Göppert entered in 1924 was in the process of becoming a center for the study of quantum mechanics—the mathematical study of the behavior of atomic particles. Many well–known physicists visited Göttingen, including Niels Bohr, a Danish physicist who developed a model of the atom. Noted physicist Max Born joined the Göttingen faculty and became a close friend of Göppert's family. Göppert, now enrolled as a student, began attending Max Born's physics seminars and decided to study physics instead of mathematics, with an eye toward teaching. Her prospects of being taken seriously were slim: there was only one female professor at Göttingen, and she taught for "love," receiving no salary.

In 1927 Göppert's father died. She continued her study, determined to finish her doctorate in physics. She spent a semester in Cambridge, England, where she learned English and met Ernest Rutherford, the discoverer of the electron. Upon her return to Göttingen, her mother began taking student boarders into their grand house. One was an American physical chemistry student from California, Joseph E. Mayer, studying in Göttingen on a grant. Over the next several years, Maria and Joe became close, going hiking, skiing, swimming and playing tennis. When they married, in 1930, Maria adopted the hyphenated form of their names. (When they later moved to the United States, the spelling of her family name was anglicized to "Goeppert.") Soon after her marriage she completed her doctorate with a thesis entitled "On Elemental Processes with Two Quantum Jumps."

After Joseph Mayer finished his studies, the young scientists moved to the United States, where Mayer had been offered a job at Johns Hopkins University in Baltimore, Maryland. Goeppert–Mayer found it difficult to adjust. She was not considered eligible for an appointment at the same university as her husband, but rather was considered a volunteer associate, what her biographer Joan Dash calls a "fringe benefit" wife. She had a tiny office, little pay, and no significant official responsibilities. Nonetheless, her position did allow her to conduct research on energy transfer on solid surfaces with physicist Karl Herzfeld, and she collaborated with him and her husband on several papers. Later, she turned her attention to the quantum mechanical electronic levels of benzene and of some dyes. During summers she returned to Göttingen, where she wrote several papers with Max Born on beta ray decay—the emissions of high–speed electrons that are given off by radioactive nuclei.

These summers of physics research were cut off as Germany was again preparing for war. Max Born left Germany for the safety of England. Returning to the states, Goeppert–Mayer applied for her American citizenship and she and Joe started a family. They would have two children, Marianne and Peter. Soon she became friends with Edward Teller, a Hungarian refugee who would play a key role in the development of the hydrogen bomb.

When Joe unexpectedly lost his position at Johns Hopkins, he and Goeppert–Mayer left for Columbia University in New York. There they wrote a book together, *Statistical Mechanics,* which became a classic in the field. As Goeppert–Mayer had no teaching credentials to place on the title page, their friend Harold Urey, a Nobel Prize-winning chemist, arranged for her to give some lectures so that she could be listed as "lecturer in chemistry at Columbia."

In New York, Goeppert–Mayer made the acquaintance of Enrico Fermi, winner of the Nobel Prize for physics for his work on radioactivity. Fermi had recently emigrated from Italy and was at Columbia on a grant researching nuclear fission. Nuclear fission—splitting an atom in a way that released energy—had been discovered by German scientists Otto Hahn, Fritz Strassmann, and **Lise Meitner**. The German scientists had bombarded uranium nuclei with neutrons, resulting in the release of energy. Because Germany was building its arsenal for war, Fermi had joined other scientists in convincing the United States government that it must institute a nuclear program of its own so as not to be at Hitler's mercy should Germany develop a nuclear weapon. Goeppert–Mayer joined Fermi's team of researchers, although once again the arrangement was informal and without pay.

In 1941, the United States formally entered World War II. Goeppert–Mayer was offered her first real teaching job, a half–time position at Sarah Lawrence College in Bronxville, New York. A few months later she was invited by Harold Urey to join a research group he was assembling at Columbia University to separate uranium–235, which is capable of nuclear fission, from the more abundant isotope uranium–238, which is not. The group, which worked in secret, was given the code name SAM—Substitute Alloy Metals. The uranium was to be the fuel for a nuclear fission bomb.

Like many scientists, Goeppert–Mayer had mixed feelings about working on the development of an atomic bomb. (Her friend Max Born, for instance, had refused to work on the project.) She had to keep her work a secret from her husband, even though he himself was working on defense–related work, often in the Pacific. Moreover, while she loved her adopted country, she had many friends and relatives in Germany. To her relief, the war in Europe was over early in 1945, before the bomb was ready. However, at Los Alamos Laboratory in New Mexico the bomb was still being developed. At Edward Teller's request, Goeppert–Mayer made several visits to Los Alamos to meet with other physicists, including Niels Bohr and Enrico Fermi, who were working on uranium fission. In August of 1945 atomic bombs were dropped on the Japanese cities of Hiroshima and Nagasaki with a destructive ferocity never before seen. According to biographer Joan Dash, by this time Goeppert–Mayer's ambivalence about the nuclear weapons program had turned to distaste, and she was glad she had played a relatively small part in the development of such a deadly weapon.

The "Madonna of the Onion" Wins the Nobel Prize

After the war, Goeppert–Mayer returned to teach at Sarah Lawrence. Then, in 1946, her husband was offered a full professorship at the University of Chicago's newly established Institute of Nuclear Studies, where Fermi, Teller, and Urey were also working. Goeppert–Mayer was offered an unpaid position as voluntary associate professor; the university had a rule, common at the time, against hiring both a husband and wife as professors. However, soon afterwards, Goeppert–Mayer was asked to become a senior physicist at the Argonne National Laboratory, where a nuclear reactor was under construction. It was the first time she had been offered a position and salary that put her on an even footing with her colleagues.

Again her association with Edward Teller was valuable. He asked her to work on his theory about the origin of the elements. They found that some elements, such as tin and lead, were more abundant than could be predicted by current theories. The same elements were also unusually stable. When Goeppert–Mayer charted the number of protons and neutrons in the nuclei of these elements, she noticed that the same few numbers recurred over and over again. Eventually she began to call these her "magic numbers." When Teller began focusing his attention on nuclear weapons and lost interest in the project, Goeppert–Mayer began discussing her ideas with Enrico Fermi.

Goeppert–Mayer had identified seven "magic numbers:" 2, 8, 20, 28, 50, 82, and 126. Any element that had one of these numbers of protons or neutrons was very stable, and she wondered why. She began to think of a shell model for the nucleus, similar to the orbital model of electrons spinning around the nucleus. Perhaps the nucleus of an atom was something like an onion, with layers of protons and neutrons revolving around each other. Her "magic numbers" would represent the points at which the various layers, or "shells," would be complete. Goeppert–Mayer's likening of the nucleus to an onion led fellow physicist Wolfgang Pauli to dub her the "Madonna of the Onion." Further calculations suggested the presence of "spin–orbit coupling:" the particles in the nucleus, she hypothesized, were both spinning on their axes and orbiting a central point—like spinning dancers, in her analogy, some moving clockwise and others counter–clockwise.

Goeppert–Mayer published her hypothesis in *Physical Review* in 1949. A month before her work appeared, a similar paper was published by J. Hans D. Jensen of Heidelberg, Germany. Goeppert–Mayer and Jensen began corresponding and eventually decided to write a book together. During the four years that it took to complete the book, Jensen stayed with the Goeppert–Mayers in Chicago. *Elementary Theory of Nuclear Shell Structure* gained widespread acceptance on both sides of the Atlantic for the theory they had discovered independently.

In 1959, Goeppert–Mayer and her husband were both offered positions at the University of California's new San Diego campus. Unfortunately, soon after settling into a new home in La Jolla, California, Goeppert–Mayer suffered a stroke which left an arm paralyzed. Some years earlier she had also lost the hearing in one ear. Slowed but not defeated, Goeppert–Mayer continued her work.

In November of 1963 Goeppert–Mayer received word that she and Jensen were to share the Nobel Prize for physics with Eugene Paul Wigner, a colleague studying quantum mechanics who had once been skeptical of her magic numbers. Goeppert–Mayer had finally been accepted as a serious scientist. According to biographer Olga Opfell, she would later comment that the work itself had been more exciting than winning the prize.

Goeppert–Mayer continued to teach and do research in San Diego, as well as grow orchids and give parties at her house in La Jolla. She enjoyed visits with her granddaughter, whose parents were daughter Marianne, an astronomer, and son–in–law Donat Wentzel, an astrophysicist. Her son Peter was now an assistant professor of economics, keeping up Goeppert–Mayer's family tradition of university teaching.

Goeppert–Mayer was made a member of the National Academy of Sciences and received several honorary doctorates. Her health, however, began to fail. A lifelong smoker debilitated by her stroke, she began to have heart problems. She had a pacemaker inserted in 1968. Late in 1971, Goeppert–Mayer suffered a heart attack that left her in a coma. She died on February 20, 1972.

SELECTED WRITINGS BY GOEPPERT-MAYER:

Books

(With Joseph E. Mayer) *Statistical Mechanics,* Wiley, 1940.

(With J. Hans D. Jensen) *Elementary Theory of Nuclear Shell Structure,* Wiley, 1955.

Periodicals

"Nuclear Configurations in the Spin–orbit Coupling Model: I. Empirical Evidence, and II. Theoretical Considerations." *Physical Review* (April, 1950).

Other

Goeppert–Mayer's papers are collected at Central University Library, University of California, San Diego.

FURTHER READING

Books

Dash, Joan. *The Triumph of Discovery: Women Scientists Who Won the Nobel Prize,* Messner, 1991.

Opfell, Olga S. *The Lady Laureates: Women Who Have Won the Nobel Prize.* Scarecrow, 1978, pp. 194–208.

Sach, Robert G. *Maria Goeppert–Mayer, 1906–1972: A Biographical Memoir,* National Academy of Science of the United States, 1979.

Sketch by Barbara A. Branca

Winifred Goldring
1888–1971
American paleontologist

Winifred Goldring pursued a career in paleontology at a time when it was difficult for a woman to advance and succeed as a scientist. She did both, becoming a respected figure in her profession. Goldring was associated with the New York State Museum for forty years, rising to the position of state paleontologist, a post she held for fifteen years. In 1949 she became the first woman to be elected president of the Paleontological Society. A year later, Goldring became a vice president of the Geological Society of America, an organization that had elected her as a fellow in 1921.

Goldring was born February 1, 1888, just outside of Albany in Kenwood, New York. She was one of seven daughters and one son born to Frederick Goldring, an orchid grower and operator of a floral business, and Mary Grey Goldring, a one–time school teacher. When she was two, the family moved to Slingerlands, New York, southeast of Albany, to a home that Winifred lived in, on and off, for nearly 81 years. She attended local schools, graduating as valedictorian of her class in 1905.

Much of Goldring's college education was concentrated at Wellesley College in Massachusetts, where she studied geology and geography, developing her interest in paleontology. She earned her B.A. in 1909 and her M.A. in 1912. She took additional graduate level courses at Harvard, Columbia, and Johns Hopkins universities. Goldring began her career as a geology instructor at Wellesley and at the Teacher's School of Science in Boston from 1912 to 1914.

Focuses on New York Fossils and Geology

In 1915 Goldring began her long association with the New York State Museum when she was hired as an assistant paleontologist. In subsequent years she was promoted to associate paleontologist, paleobotantist, assistant state paleontologist, and provisional state paleontologist. In 1939 Goldring was named state paleontologist, a position she filled with distinction and considerable energy until her retirement in 1950.

At the museum, and as a paleontologist, Goldring was particularly interested in the fossils and geology of New York state, especially those of the Devonian period, which flourished 345 to 395 million years ago. While her duties at the state museum required her to do much administrative work, she still found time to contribute to museum displays and engage in paleontological research. She enjoyed the process of creating museum displays, and her creation of a Devonian fossil forest diorama at the New York museum drew nationwide acclaim. As a researcher and educator, Goldring produced more than 40 papers and books for journals and the general public. These ranged from paleontology handbooks for laypersons to a detailed 670–page book on the crinoids, a sea urchin–like animal, of New York.

For her achievements, Goldring was awarded an honorary doctor of science degree from Russell Sage College and Smith College in 1937 and 1957, respectively. In addition, she was a member of the American Association for the Advancement of Science, the New York Academy of Sciences, and the American Geophysical Union. Goldring remained single throughout her life and died in Albany on January 30, 1971.

SELECTED WRITINGS BY GOLDRING:

Books

The Devonian Crinoids of the State of New York, New York State Museum, 1923.

Handbook of Paleontology for Beginners and Amateurs; Part 1, The Fossils, New York State Museum, 1929.

Handbook of Paleontology for Beginners and Amateurs, Part 2, The Formations, New York State Museum, 1931.

Geology of the Berne Quadrangle, New York State Museum, 1935.

Geology of the Coxsackie Quadrangle, New York State Museum, 1943.

FURTHER READING

Books

Memorials, Volume 3, Geological Society of America, 1974, pp. 96–101.

Sketch by Joel Schwarz

Adele Katz Goldstine
1920–1964
American mathematician

Adele Goldstine left a lasting legacy in the world of computing by writing one of the first computer manuals, a gargantuan task for the equally gargantuan ENIAC, the world's first electronic digital computer, completed in 1946. She was also instrumental in revamping the ENIAC, developing a stored program that obviated the necessity of reconfiguring the entire system for each new task.

Born on December 21, 1920, Goldstine was one of two daughters born to William Katz, a successful retail businessman. Growing up in New York City, Goldstine attended Hunter College High School and received her B.A. from Hunter College. From there she went on to the University of Michigan, where she graduated with a master's degree in mathematics. It was also at the University of Michigan that she met her future husband, Herman Goldstine. The couple was married in 1941.

Trains Human Computers

Goldstine's husband also worked in mathematics and in the fledgling field of computer science. Entering the military during World War II, he was assigned as a first lieutenant to the Ballistic Research Laboratory at the Aberdeen Proving Grounds in Maryland to prepare firing and bombing tables. Such tables, involving complex mathematical calculations, were needed for each weapon, and allowed gunners in the field to make sighting adjustments for distance and angle to the target, weight of shell, wind speed, and other variables. When Herman Goldstine was sent to the Moore School of Engineering at the University of Pennsylvania, to set up a training program for Aberdeen, Adele Goldstine also became active in the war effort.

Beginning in the fall of 1942 at the Moore School, Adele Goldstine began training women to calculate firing and bombing tables, using mechanical desk calculators. Known as computers, the women selected for the program ultimately could perform the complex series of mathematical calculations in about one or two days. Ultimately some 75 women were working at the Moore School, and the talent pool of Philadelphia had virtually been drained. Adele Goldstine thereafter went out recruiting at colleges and universities all over the Northeast. Finally, with the formation of the WACS, the Women's Army Corps, many more women were made available for the tabular calculations. However, something faster was still needed.

Begins Programming the ENIAC

Beginning in 1943, the Army funded a program at the Moore School to construct an electronic computer that could take over some of the calculating work. Working with Pres Eckart and John Mauchly at the University of Pennsylvania, Herman Goldstine helped to develop the ENIAC computer, or Electronic Numerical Integrator and Computer, an advance over all other forms of computing. The ENIAC took advantage of the introduction of vacuum tubes, which sped the computing process. Until that time, such processes had been performed by mechanical relays. The ENIAC was an imposing machine, consisting of 18,000 vacuum tubes, 70,000 resistors, and five million soldered joints. It was a room-sized computer that had a voracious appetite, consuming more than 160 kilowatts of electrical power. (The lights of an entire section of Philadelphia dimmed when it was running.) It also had a calculating speed 1,000 times greater than any machine at the time.

Adele Goldstine's task was to write the manual for the ENIAC, something that her mathematics training only partially prepared her for. "At first I thought I would never be able to understand the workings of the machine since this involved a knowledge of electronics that I did not have at all, "Adele Goldstine wrote in a diary she later kept for her children." But gradually as I lived with the job and the engineers helped to explain matters to me, I got the subject under control. Then I began to understand the machine and had such masses of facts in my head I couldn't bring myself to start writing." Goldstine overcame all such obstacles, however, finally finishing her extensive report in 1946.

Thereafter, when John von Neumann was brought on board the project, he and the Goldstines worked on converting the ENIAC to a stored program computer, one that could retain instructions. Up to this time, a program was set manually by plugging in cables and setting switches for each function to be run. Starting in 1947, Adele Goldstine was instrumental in programming ENIAC to permanently understand a vocabulary of about 50 instructions, which could be introduced to the machine by punched cards. During the postwar years, she was von Neumann's primary programmer, working at Los Alamos preparing problems to be fed to ENIAC.

Adele Goldstine had two children, one in 1953, and a second in 1960. By 1962 she was diagnosed with cancer, and died in November, 1964. Her work with first-generation computers made a lasting contribution to the field of computer science.

SELECTED WRITINGS BY GOLDSTINE:

Books

Report on the ENIAC, Technical Report I. 2 vols. Philadelphia: Government Printing Office, 1946.

Periodicals

(With Herman Goldstine) "The Electronic Numerical Integrator and Computer (ENIAC)." *Mathematical Tables and Other Aids to Computation* 2 (1946): 97–110.

(With A. H. Taub) "Reflections of Plane Shock Waves." *Physical Review* 72 (1947): 51–60.

FURTHER READING

Books

Goldstine, Herman H. *The Computer: From Pascal to von Neumann.* Princeton: Princeton University Press, 1972.

Periodicals

"Looking Back at ENIAC: Computers Hit Half–Century Mark." *The Scientist* 9 (1995).
IEEE Annals of the History of Computing. 18/1, 1996.

Other

Goldstine, Adele K., diary entries supplied by Herman Goldstine, May 22, 1999.

Sketch by J. Sydney Jones

Jane Goodall (AP/Wide World Photos. Reproduced by permission.)

Jane Goodall
1934–
English ethologist

Jane Goodall is known worldwide for her studies of the chimpanzees of the Gombe Stream Reserve in Tanzania, Africa. She is well respected within the scientific community for her ground–breaking field studies and is credited with the first recorded observation of chimps eating meat and using and making tools. Because of Goodall's discoveries, scientists have been forced to redefine the characteristics once considered as solely human traits. Goodall is now leading efforts to ensure that animals are treated humanely both in their wild habitats and in captivity.

Goodall was born in London, England, on April 3, 1934, to Mortimer Herbert Goodall, a businessperson and motor–racing enthusiast, and the former Margaret Myfanwe Joseph, who wrote novels under the name Vanne Morris Goodall. Along with her sister, Judy, Goodall was reared in London and Bournemouth, England. Her fascination with animal behavior began in early childhood. In her leisure time, she observed native birds and animals, making extensive notes and sketches, and read widely in the literature of zoology and ethology. From an early age, she dreamed of traveling to Africa to observe exotic animals in their natural habitats.

Meets Leakey in Africa

Goodall attended the Uplands private school, receiving her school certificate in 1950 and a higher certificate in 1952. At age 18 she left school and found employment as a secretary at Oxford University. In her spare time, she worked at a London-based documentary film company to finance a long-anticipated trip to Africa. At the invitation of a childhood friend, she visited South Kinangop, Kenya. Through other friends, she soon met the famed anthropologist Louis Leakey, then curator of the Coryndon Museum in Nairobi. Leakey hired her as a secretary and invited her to participate in an anthropological dig at the now famous Olduvai Gorge, a site rich in fossilized prehistoric remains of early ancestors of humans. In addition, Goodall was sent to study the vervet monkey, which lives on an island in Lake Victoria.

Leakey believed that a long-term study of the behavior of higher primates would yield important evolutionary information. He had a particular interest in the chimpanzee, the second most intelligent primate. Few studies of chimpanzees had been successful; either the size of the safari frightened the chimps, producing unnatural behaviors, or the observers spent too little time in the field to gain comprehensive knowledge. Leakey believed that Goodall had the proper temperament to endure long-term isolation in the wild. At his prompting, she agreed to attempt such a study. Many experts objected to Leakey's selection of Goodall because she had no formal scientific education and lacked even a general college degree.

While Leakey searched for financial support for the proposed Gombe Reserve project, Goodall returned to England to work on an animal documentary for Granada Television. On July 16, 1960, accompanied by her mother and an African cook, she returned to Africa and established a camp on the shore of Lake Tanganyika in the Gombe Stream Reserve. Her first attempts to observe closely a group of chimpanzees failed; she could get no nearer than 500 yards before the chimps fled. After finding another suitable group of chimpanzees to follow, she established a nonthreatening pattern of observation, appearing at the same time every morning on the high ground near a feeding area along the Kakaombe Stream valley. The chimpanzees soon tolerated her presence and, within a year, allowed her to move as close as 30 feet to their feeding area. After two years of seeing her every day, they showed no fear and often came to her in search of bananas.

Chimpanzee Research Yields Numerous Discoveries

Goodall used her newfound acceptance to establish what she termed the "banana club," a daily systematic feeding method she used to gain trust and to obtain a more thorough understanding of everyday chimpanzee behavior. Using this method, she became closely acquainted with more than half of the reserve's 100 or more chimpanzees. She imitated their behaviors, spent time in the trees, and ate their foods. By remaining in almost constant contact with the chimps, she discovered a number of previously unobserved behaviors. She noted that chimps have a complex social system, complete with ritualized behaviors and primitive but discernible communication methods, including a primitive "language" system containing more than 20 individual sounds. She is credited with making the first recorded observations of chimpanzees eating meat and using and making tools. Tool making was previously thought to be an exclusively human trait, used, until her discovery, to distinguish humans from animals. She also noted that chimpanzees throw stones as weapons, use touch and embraces to comfort one another, and develop long-term familial bonds. The male plays no active role in family life but is part of the group's social stratification. The chimpanzee "caste" system places the dominant males at the top. The lower castes often act obsequiously in their presence, trying to ingratiate themselves to avoid possible harm. The male's rank is often related to the intensity of his entrance performance at feedings and other gatherings.

Ethologists had long believed that chimps were exclusively vegetarian. Goodall witnessed chimps stalking, killing, and eating large insects, birds, and some bigger animals, including baby baboons and bushbacks (small antelopes). On one occasion, she recorded acts of cannibalism. In another instance, she observed chimps inserting blades of grass or leaves into termite hills to lure worker or soldier termites onto the blade. Sometimes, in true toolmaker fashion, they modified the grass to achieve a better fit. Then they used the grass as a long–handled spoon to eat the termites.

Finds Audience through Television and Books

In 1962 Baron Hugo van Lawick, a Dutch wildlife photographer, was sent to Africa by the National Geographic Society to film Goodall at work. The assignment ran longer than anticipated; Goodall and van Lawick were married on March 28, 1964. Their European honeymoon marked one of the rare occasions on which Goodall was absent from Gombe Stream. Her other trips abroad were necessary to fulfill residency requirements at Cambridge University, where she received a Ph.D. in ethology in 1965, becoming only the eighth person in the university's long history who was allowed to pursue a Ph.D. without first earning a baccalaureate degree. Her doctoral thesis, "Behavior of the Free-Ranging Chimpanzee," detailed her first five years of study at the Gombe Reserve.

Van Lawick's film, *Miss Goodall and the Wild Chimpanzees,* was first broadcast on American television on December 22, 1965. The film introduced the shy, determined Goodall to a wide audience. Goodall, van Lawick (along with their son, Hugo, born in 1967), and the chimpanzees soon became a staple of American and British public television. Through these programs, Goodall challenged scientists to redefine the long-held "differences" between humans and other primates.

Goodall's fieldwork led to the publication of numerous articles and five major books. She was known and respected first in scientific circles and, through the media, became a minor celebrity. *In the Shadow of Man*, her first major text, appeared in 1971. The book, essentially a field study of chimpanzees, effectively bridged the gap between scientific treatise and popular entertainment. Her vivid prose brought the chimps to life, although her tendency to attribute human behaviors and names to chimpanzees struck some critics being as manipulative. Her writings reveal an animal world of social drama, comedy, and tragedy where distinct and varied personalities interact and sometimes clash.

Advocates Ethical Treatment of Animals

From 1970–1975 Goodall held a visiting professorship in psychiatry at Stanford University. In 1973 she was appointed honorary visiting professor of Zoology at the University of Dar es Salaam in Tanzania, a position she still holds. Her marriage to van Lawick over, she wed Derek Bryceson, a former member of Parliament, in 1973. After attending a 1986 conference in Chicago that focused on the ethical treatment of chimpanzees, she began directing her energies toward educating the public about the wild chimpanzee's endangered habitat and about the unethical treatment of chimpanzees that are used for scientific research.

To preserve the wild chimpanzee's environment, Goodall encourages African nations to develop nature-friendly tourism programs, a measure that makes wildlife into a profitable resource. She actively works with business and local governments to promote ecological responsibility. Her efforts on behalf of captive chimpanzees have taken her around the world on a number of lecture tours. She outlined her position strongly in her 1990 book *Through a Window:* "The more we learn of the true nature of nonhuman animals, especially those with complex brains and corresponding complex social behaviour, the more ethical concerns are raised regarding their use in the service of man—whether this be in entertainment, as 'pets,' for food, in research laboratories or any of the other uses to which we subject them. This concern is sharpened when the usage in question leads to intense physical or mental suffering—as is so often true with regard to vivisection."

Goodall's stance is that scientists must try harder to find alternatives to the use of animals in research. She has openly declared her opposition to militant animal rights groups who engage in violent or destructive demonstrations. Extremists on both sides of the issue, she believes, polarize thinking and make constructive dialogue nearly impossible. While she is reluctantly resigned to the continuation of animal research, she feels that young scientists must be educated to treat animals more compassionately. "By and large," she has written, "students are taught that it is ethically acceptable to perpetrate, in the name of science, what, from the point of view of animals, would certainly qualify as torture."

Goodall's efforts to educate people about the ethical treatment of animals extends to young children as well. Her 1989 book, *The Chimpanzee Family Book,* was written specifically for children, to convey a new, more humane view of wildlife. The book received the 1989 Unicef/Unesco Children's Book–of–the–Year award, and Goodall used the prize money to have the text translated into Swahili. It has been distributed throughout Tanzania, Uganda, and Burundi to educate children who live in or near areas populated by chimpanzees. A French version has also been distributed in Burundi and Congo.

In recognition of her achievements, Goodall has received numerous honors and awards, including the Gold Medal of Conservation from the San Diego Zoological Society in 1974, the J. Paul Getty Wildlife Conservation Prize in 1984, the Schweitzer Medal of the Animal Welfare Institute in 1987, the National Geographic Society Centennial Award in 1988, and the Kyoto Prize in Basic Sciences in 1990. Many of Goodall's endeavors are conducted under the auspices of the Jane Goodall Institute for Wildlife Research, Education, and Conservation, a nonprofit organization located in Ridgefield, Connecticut.

SELECTED WRITINGS BY GOODALL:

Books

(Under name Jane van Lawick-Goodall; with Hugo van Lawick) *Innocent Killers,* Collins, 1970.
(Under name Jane van Lawick–Goodall) *In the Shadow of Man,* Houghton Mifflin, 1971.
(Under name Jane van Lawick–Goodall; with Hugo van Lawick) *Grub: The Bush Baby,* Houghton, 1972.
The Chimpanzees of Gombe: Patterns of Behavior, Harvard University Press, 1986.
My Life with Chimpanzees, Simon and Schuster, 1988.
The Chimpanzee Family Book, Picture Book Studio, 1989.
Jane Goodall's Animal World: Chimpanzees, Macmillan, 1989.
Through a Window: My Thirty Years with the Chimpanzees of Gombe, Houghton, 1990.

Periodicals

"Life and Death at Gombe." *National Geographic* 155, no. 5 (1979): 592–621.
"Mountain Warrior: Dian Fossey and Her Research on Mountain Gorillas." *Omni* (May, 1986): 132.
"A Plea for the Chimpanzee." *American Scientist* 75, no. 6 (1987): 574–577.

FURTHER READING

Books

Green, Timothy. *The Restless Spirit: Profiles in Adventure,* Walker, 1970.
Montgomery, Sy. *Walking with the Great Apes: Jane Goodall, Dian Fossey, Biruté Galdikas.* Houghton Mifflin, 1991.

Periodicals

Smith, Wendy. "The Wildlife of Jane Goodall." *USAir* (February, 1991): 42–47.

Sketch by Tom Crawford

Temple Grandin
1947–
American animal behaviorist

Temple Grandin, the world's leading authority on livestock handling, devotes her study and research to the humane treatment of animals. A pioneer in research on livestock behavior, Grandin designs cattle chutes and slaughterhouses, and consults with animal handlers all over the world. She has written hundreds of articles on animal handling and behavior, as well as the design of facilities. She owns Grandin Livestock Handling Systems Incorporated, consulting on issues involving the care and treatment of livestock.

Temple Grandin was born on August 29, 1947, the oldest of four children. Her father, Richard McCurdy Grandin, was a realtor, and her mother, Eustacia (Purves) Grandin, a writer and actress. One grandfather was a farmer, and the other invented the automatic pilot control, and these influences contributed to Grandin's later interests and skills.

Coping with Autism

Appearing normal until six months of age, Grandin was diagnosed with autism at two and a half. Little was known about autism during Grandin's childhood. Scientists now know that autism causes the person to process sensory information differently from those without the disorder. Some stimuli can be overwhelming, while others seem not to affect the person at all. Because of this, the autistic person continually withdraws fearfully into his or her own world, cut off from normal human experience and emotion. Grandin's parents were told that their daughter would likely never be able to live alone and to function in the world. Although her mother knew Grandin's problems better than anyone, she never gave up, always working with her daughter on reading and exposing her to as many normal experiences as possible, such as summer camp. But Grandin had uncontrollable reactions to her own frustrations, and would physically lash out. In addition, she did poorly in school, failing every subject except for subjects learned visually and with hands-on work like art or biology.

Until seventh grade, Grandin attended Valley County Day School, a small school with, for the most part, caring teachers who tried to work with Grandin despite her problems. The following year, she attended Cherry Hill Girls School, which expelled her after two and a half years for throwing a book at a girl who taunted her. She next went to Mountain Country School, a small girls' boarding school, where she remained until graduation. Here, Grandin's problems were dealt with sympathetically but firmly. Her physical aggressiveness ended completely after she had to suffer the punishment of going without riding horses for a week. At Mountain Country School, the teachers were able to see past Grandin's autism to her intellectual capacity (her IQ scores were 137) and encouraged her in her interests. The psychology teacher fueled her interest in animal behavior, and William Carlock, the science teacher, taught her how to do scientific library research in addition to motivating her, in general, to learn.

Grandin's next turning point was in the summer between her junior and senior year. She went to stay with her rancher aunt to help with the animals and other farm chores. Grandin became fascinated with the cattle chute—a device to restrain the animals for vaccination, branding, or castration. Noticing how the excited animals would immediately grow calm while in the chute, she wondered if it might help her too, and tried it out. The pressure felt like a hug from which Grandin was unable to withdraw, and it calmed her so much that she became obsessed with it. Back at school, she constructed a model for her own use with scrap wood. But the school authorities feared that Grandin was regressing, and tried to take it away from her. She insisted that the calming effect was not merely her imagination, and Carlock challenged her to prove it. After many trials and models, Grandin later perfected her chute and, in college, she did a study with "normal" students that showed a majority found it relaxing and therapeutic. The device is now used to help other autistic people, as well as those with attention-deficit hyperactivity disorder and other disorders.

Grandin went to Franklin Pierce College, where she studied sensory interaction in relation to the chute. Graduating in 1970 as salutatorian with a B.A. in psychology, Grandin then went on the Arizona State University. Although she began work in psychology, Grandin soon switched her major to animal science, and she was able to turn her autism into an asset in her work as an animal scientist. She worked for a feedlot as a chute operator and also for a farm equipment company selling equipment. Her research centered on chute design, one of the first research projects ever done on livestock behavior. In 1973, she became the livestock editor for the magazine *Arizona Farmer Ranchman,* and for several years was able to visit facilities all over the state. Before she graduated with her M.S. in animal science in 1975, Grandin began designing equipment for a cattle company, but she soon started her own consulting business, Grandin Livestock Handling Systems Incorporated.

In Tune With the Animals

In her consulting work, Grandin researches the handling and welfare of the animals, which in turn increases meat quality and productivity. She soon discovered her ease with and understanding of the animals, a quality she lacked in human relationships. Because an autistic person is plagued by fear, Grandin understands that same fear in animals, which is caused by loud noises or sudden movements. Able to feel an animal's nervousness, she learned to calm them by firm touch. Grandin believes that animals are owed humane treatment in life and death and works to design equipment that will not startle or frighten them. Her designs remove all distractions to insure that an animal about to be slaughtered has a calm and peaceful death.

A visual thinker, Grandin is able to design every piece of equipment in her head. Running simulations in her mind from every angle, working out problems as she goes, no blueprints are made until the design is perfectly completed in her mind. In this manner, Grandin pioneered the design of curved chutes and ramps with high walls and double-rail restrainers, eliminating the animals' fear and distractions in addition to going along with their natural circling behavior. Her designs are now in the majority of American and Canadian facilities. In addition, her educational background in psychology has helped to reform the slaughterhouse and feedlot workers by promoting efficient and humane practices. Grandin has also consulted for game parks, veterinarians, stockyards, zoos, and dozens of other animal facilities in most of the United States and many other countries, from Mexico to China.

Grandin received her Ph.D. in animal science from the University of Illinois in 1989, and went on to become an assistant professor at Colorado State University, where she teaches and conducts her research. Her dissertation focused on how different environments affect swine development. This and other research in animal science has offered many theories on autism and its development and treatment, which has improved the care of many human patients.

Because of her skills and knowledge in animal behavior and equipment design, Grandin is the world's leading authority on livestock management. Due to her renown, in 1991 the American Meat Institute asked her to write the guidelines for their book on animal handling for use by meat packers. She has been honored with the Industry Innovation Award in the Meat Industry, the Livestock Conservation Institute Award for Meritorious Service, the Alumni Achievement Award from Franklin Pierce College, and the Tramell Crow Award of the Autism Society of America.

SELECTED WRITINGS BY GRANDIN:

Books

(With Margaret Scarino) *Emergence: Labeled Autistic.* Novato: Arena Press, 1986.

Other

"Dr. Temple Grandin's Web Page: Livestock Behavior, Design of Facilities and Humane Slaughter." http://www.grandin.com

FURTHER READING

Books

Ambrose, Susan A., et al. *Journeys of Women in Science and Engineering*. Philadelphia: Temple University Press, 1997.

Graham, Judith, ed. *Current Biography Yearbook*. New York: H. H. Wilson Company, 1994.

Sacks, Oliver. *An Anthropologist on Mars*. New York: Alfred A. Knopf, 1995.

Sketch by Helene Barker Kiser

Evelyn Granville (The University of Texas at Tyler. Reproduced by permission.)

Evelyn Boyd Granville
1924–
American applied mathematician and educator

In 1949, Evelyn Boyd Granville at Yale University and **Marjorie Lee Browne** at the University of Michigan became the first African–American women to receive doctoral degrees in mathematics. Granville's specialty is complex analysis and her career has encompassed both college teaching and applied work in the United States space program during its formative years.

Granville was born in Washington, D.C., on May 1, 1924. Her father, William Boyd, worked as a custodian in their apartment building. He did not stay with the family, however, and Granville was raised by her mother, Julia Walker Boyd, and her mother's twin sister, Louise Walker, both of whom worked as examiners for the U.S. Bureau of Engraving and Printing. Granville and her sister Doris, who was a year and a half older, often spent portions of their summers at the Linden, Virginia, farm of a family friend.

The public schools of Washington, D.C., were racially segregated when Granville attended them. However, Dunbar High School (from which she graduated as valedictorian) maintained high academic standards. Several of its faculty held degrees from top colleges, and they encouraged the students to pursue ambitious goals. With the encouragement of her family and teachers, Granville entered Smith College with a partial scholarship from Phi Delta Kappa, a national sorority for Black women. During the summers, she returned to Washington to work at the National Bureau of Standards. Granville majored in mathematics and physics, and in 1945 she graduated summa cum laude and was elected to Phi Beta Kappa.

Granville undertook graduate studies at Yale University, earning an M.A. in mathematics and physics in one year. Her doctoral studies were supported by an Atomic Energy

Commission Predoctoral Fellowship and a Julius Rosenwald Fellowship that was offered to help promising Black Americans develop their research potential. Granville's research concentrated on functional analysis, and her advisor, Einar Hille, was a former president of the American Mathematical Society.

Granville spent a year doing postdoctoral research at New York University's Institute of Mathematics and Science. Apparently because of *de facto* housing discrimination, she was unable to find an apartment in New York City, so she moved in with a friend of her mother. Despite attending segregated schools, Granville had not encountered discrimination based on race or gender in her professional preparation. Only years later would she learn that her 1950 application for a teaching position at a college in New York City was turned down for such a reason. Biographer Patricia Kenschaft reported in *The American Mathematical Monthly* that, according to two different sources, Granville's application was rejected because of either her race or her gender. Whichever version was true, it is clear that an exemplary academic record and a Ph.D. from a prestigious school, earned under a renowned mentor, were not enough to overcome such entrenched biases. In 1950, Granville accepted the position of associate professor at Fisk University, an historically black college in Nashville, Tennessee. She was a popular teacher and at least two of her female students credited her with inspiring them to earn doctorates in mathematics in later years.

After two years of teaching, Granville went to work for the Diamond Ordnance Fuze Laboratories as an applied mathematician. Subsequently, from 1956–1960, she worked for IBM on the Project Vanguard and Project Mercury space programs, analyzing orbits and developing computer procedures. Her job included making "real–time" calculations during satellite launchings. "That was exciting, as I look back, to be a part of the space programs—a very small part—at the very beginning of U.S. involvement," Granville told Loretta Hall in an interview.

On a summer vacation in southern California, Granville met the Reverend Gamaliel Mansfield Collins, a minister in the Community Church. They were married in 1960 and made their home in Los Angeles. They had no children, although Collins' three children occasionally lived with them. In 1967, the marriage ended in divorce.

Upon moving to Los Angeles, Granville took a job at the Computation and Data Reduction Center of the U.S. Space Technology Laboratories, studying rocket trajectories and methods of orbit computation. In 1962, she became a research specialist at the North American Aviation Space and Information Systems Division, working on celestial mechanics, trajectory and orbit computation, numerical analysis, and digital computer techniques for the Apollo program. The following year, Granville returned to IBM as a senior mathematician.

In 1967, not wanting to leave Los Angeles during a restructuring phase at IBM, Granville took a teaching position at California State University in Los Angeles. Although she found the job enjoyable and rewarding, she was disappointed in the mathematics preparedness of her students. Granville began working to improve mathematics education at all levels. She taught an elementary school supplemental mathematics program part–time in 1968–1969 through the State of California Miller Mathematics Improvement Program. The following year, Granville directed a mathematics enrichment program that provided after–school classes for kindergarten through fifth grades, teaching grades two through five herself. She also taught at a National Science Foundation Institute for Secondary Teachers of Mathematics summer program at the University of Southern California in 1972. In 1975, Granville coauthored *Theory and Application of Mathematics for Teachers*, which was used as a textbook at over 50 colleges.

In 1970, Granville married Edward V. Granville, a real estate broker. After her 1984 retirement from California State University in Los Angeles, they moved to a 16 acre farm in Texas, where they sold eggs produced by their 800 chickens. From 1985–1988, Granville taught mathematics and computer science at Texas College in Tyler. In 1990, she accepted an appointment to the Sam A. Lindsey Chair at the University of Texas at Tyler, and in subsequent years continued teaching there as a visiting professor. Smith College awarded Granville an honorary doctorate in 1989, making her the first Black woman mathematician to receive such an honor from an American institution.

Throughout her career, Granville has shared her energy with a variety of professional and public service organizations and boards. For example, she has been involved with the National Council of Teachers of Mathematics, the American Association of University Women, and the Psychology Examining Committee of the Board of Medical Examiners of the State of California. When asked to summarize her major accomplishments, Granville told Hall, "First of all, showing that women can do mathematics." Then she added, "Being an African–American woman, letting people know that we have brains too."

SELECTED WRITINGS BY GRANVILLE:

(With Jason L. Frand) *Theory and Applications of Mathematics for Teachers.* 2d ed. 1978.

FURTHER READING

Books

Kenschaft, Patricia Clark. "Evelyn Boyd Granville." *Women of Mathematics: A Biobibliographic Sourcebook.* Edited by Louise S. Grinstein and Paul J. Campbell. Westport, CT: Greenwood Press, 1987, pp. 57–>61.

Hine, Darlene Clark, editor. *Black Women in America.* Volume I. Brooklyn NY: Carlson, 1993, pp. 498–99.

Perl, Teri, and Joan M. Manning. *Women, Numbers and Dreams.* Santa Rosa, CA: National Women's History Project, 1982.

Periodicals

Kenschaft, Patricia C., "Black Women in Mathematics in the United States." *The American Mathematical Monthly* (October 1981): 592–604.

Other

"Evelyn Boyd." *Biographies of Women Mathematicians.* June 1997. http://www.scottlan.edu/lriddle/women/chronol.htm (July 21, 1997).

Granville, Evelyn Boyd, interview with Loretta Hall conducted January 11, 1994.

Sketch by Loretta Hall

Mary Jane Guthrie
1895–1975
American zoologist

Mary Jane Guthrie was an expert in cytology (cell biology). Within cytology, Guthrie was interested in the cytoplasm of the female reproductive system. Guthrie also did research into endocrinology, specifically the cytoplasm of the endocrine glands; experimental pathology; and organ culture.

Mary Jane Guthrie was born on December 13, 1895, in Bloomfield, Missouri, to George Robert Guthrie and his wife Lula Ella Loyd. She earned her undergraduate degree (A.B.) at the University of Missouri in 1916 and her A.M. in 1918 at the same institution. Guthrie attended Bryn Mawr College for her Ph.D., which she was awarded in 1922. While engrossed in her doctoral studies, she was a demonstrator in the biology department from 1918 until 1920, then worked as an instructor from 1920–21.

In 1922 Guthrie returned to the University of Missouri to teach. She moved through the ranks in the zoology department, spending nearly 30 years at Missouri. She was named an assistant professor in 1922; an associate professor in 1927; and finally a full professor in 1937. Like many female scientists of her generation, Guthrie had problems getting funding for her research projects. Though she was respected as a scientist, for example, she was told in 1934 by a Rockefeller Foundation official that women scientists had to have more confirmation of their scientific prowess than men to get grants.

Guthrie did not lack for employment, however. While at the University of Missouri, she collaborated with several other scientists on textbooks for Zoology. With Winterton Conway Curtis, she wrote the *Textbook of General Zoology.* With John M. Anderson, she wrote two books of note: *General Zoology* and *Laboratory Directions in General Zoology.*

In 1951 Guthrie moved to Detroit, Michigan, and was first associated with the Detroit Institute of Cancer Research as research associate. She also did research at Wayne State University (in Detroit), until four years later, in 1955, when Guthrie became a professor at Wayne State, while retaining her position at the Institute of Cancer Research. She retired from both posts in 1960.

Guthrie belonged to numerous professional societies over the course of her career. They included the American Society of Zoologists, the American Association of Anatomists, Genetics Society, American Society of Mammologists, Tissue Culture Association, American Association for the Advancement of Science, and the American Society of Naturalists.

Guthrie had many interests outside of science. She enjoyed collecting stamps and furniture, reading, theater, golf, and horseback riding. Guthrie died in 1975 at the age of 80.

SELECTED WRITINGS BY GUTHRIE:

Books

(With John M. Anderson) *General Zoology.* New York: Wiley and Sons, 1957.

(With John M. Anderson) *Laboratory Directions in General Zoology.* New York: Wiley and Sons, 1958.

(With Winterton Conway Curtis) *Textbook of General Zoology.* 3d ed. New York: Wiley & Sons, 1938.

FURTHER READING

Books

Bailey, Martha J. "Guthrie, Mary Jane." *American Women in Science: A Biographical Dictionary.* Denver: ABC–CLIO, 1994, p. 145.

Sketch by Annette Petrusso

H

Dorothy Anna Hahn (Mt. Holyoke College Archive. Reproduced by permission.)

Dorothy Anna Hahn
1876–1950
American chemist

As an instructor in chemistry at Mount Holyoke College, Dorothy A. Hahn helped to turn that institution into a premier training ground for young women scientists in the first half of the twentieth century. Like her contemporary at Mount Holyoke, **Emma Perry Carr,** Hahn blended instruction with a hands-on curriculum, in which students actively participated in original research projects. Mount Holyoke's chemistry department fed promising young female scientists to such prestigious centers as Yale and MIT. Not only a talented and dedicated educator, Hahn was also a noted researcher, working in ultraviolet spectroscopy. In the course of her researches, she was able to confirm the ring structure of organic compounds such as Vitamin B, called hydantoins. She also explicated the relationship between electrons and chemical valence. Additionally, Hahn was coauthor of *Theories of Organic Chemistry* as well as dozens of articles in professional journals.

Born on April 9, 1876 in Philadelphia, Pennsylvania, Hahn was the younger of two daughters of Mary Beaver Hahn of Pennsylvania, and Carl J. Hahn, German by birth. Hahn's father, a man of many trades, worked mostly as a clerk or bookkeeper, but was also variously listed as a seller of artificial flowers and as a linguist. Hahn attended school primarily in Pennsylvania, going to the Philadelphia Girl's High School and graduating from Miss Florence Baldwin's School, now called the Baldwin School. In 1895 she went to Bryn Mawr College, graduating with degrees in chemistry and biology in 1899. Of a generation in which there were few females in the professions, Hahn, like other educated women of her time, had difficulty finding a job after graduation.

Career in Education Leads to Mount Holyoke

After college, Hahn first found a teaching position at Pennsylvania College for women, later known as Chatham College. She remained at this post until 1906; from 1904 to 1906 she also concurrently held the position of professor of biology at Kindergarten College in Pittsburgh. A sabbatical year took her to Germany, where she studied organic chemistry under Professor Arthur Hantzch at the University of Leipzig from 1906 to 1907. Returning to the United States, she continued her graduate studies in organic chemistry with E. P. Kohler at her alma mater, Bryn Mawr. In 1908 she became a member of the faculty at Mount Holyoke College, in South Hadley, Massachusetts, where she would remain for the rest of her professional life.

At Mount Holyoke, Hahn was quickly promoted to associate professor, and then to full professor of chemistry in 1918, a position she held until 1941. During the two decades at Mount Holyoke, Hahn was either the author of or adviser for a score of papers published in the *Journal of the American Chemical Society.* She, like Carr, was influential in attracting bright young women into the sciences, and Hahn favored the collaborative approach to education, teaming up with her students on original research projects. Her first publication a confirmation of the ring structure of hydantoins—came in 1913, and was the result of cooperative work with one of her Mount Holyoke graduate students.

Synthesizes Organic Molecules

Hahn attended Yale University on a fellowship in 1915–16, receiving her Ph.D. there in 1916. Hahn's year of study at Yale had two lasting effects. First, having studied with Treat B. Johnson, she began researching in the area of cyclic polypeptide hydantoins. At Mount Holyoke, she continued this work, utilizing the newly developed techniques of ultraviolet spectroscopy to aid in her research. Carr, a physical chemist, also collaborated on such studies, though there was a degree of rivalry between the two divisions of the chemistry department. For over a decade, Hahn, Carr, and various students synthesized complex organic molecules and then analyzed their structures using absorptive spectroscopy and other techniques. Secondly, Hahn's year at Yale provided her with a graduate and post-graduate department where she could place promising young chemists from Mount Holyoke.

Hahn also collaborated with Treat Johnson on a translation and enlargement of *Theories of Organic Chemistry* by Ferdinand Heinrich, and on studies of pyrimidines. She was involved in industrial research as well, specifically dealing with coal-tar products. A gifted and conscientious teacher, Hahn built her life around Mount Holyoke. She lived in South Hadley even after retirement in 1941, spending her summers on the coast of Connecticut, where she loved to sail. Hahn was also something of an intrepid traveler, touring Europe on sabbaticals. As one of her biographers, Alice G. Renfrew noted, Hahn "possessed imagination, humor, a fine capacity for terse and apt comment, and a sense of realism later tempered by keen insight and sympathy." After her death, from a heart ailment, her ashes were scattered on a hillside near Mount Holyoke, and a seminar room in the new chemistry building was furnished in her honor.

SELECTED WRITINGS BY HAHN:

Books

(With Arthur M. Comey) *A Dictionary of Chemical Solubilities, Inorganic.* New York: Macmillan, 1921.

(With Treat B. Johnson) *Theories of Organic Chemistry.* New York: John Wiley, 1922.

(With Treat B. Johnson) *Pyrimidines: Their Amino and Aminooxy Derivatives.* Monograph in *Chemical Reviews,* 1933.

Periodicals

(With Angie Allbee) "Saturated Delta–Ketonic Esters and Their Derivatives." *American Chemical Journal* 49 (1913): 171–79.

(With M. E. Holes) "The Valence Theory of I. Stark from a Chemical Standpoint." *Journal of the American Chemical Society* 37 (1915): 2611–26.

(With Treat B. Johnson) "Researches on Hydantoins." *Journal of the American Chemical Society* 39 (1917): 1257–66.

(With Margaret K. Seikel) "The Isomerization of Certain Saturated and Unsaturated Hydantoins." *Journal of the American Chemical Society* 47 (1936): 647–49.

FURTHER READING

Books

Renfrew, Alice G. "Dorothy Anna Hahn." *Notable American Women, 1607–1950: A Biographical Dictionary.* Edited by Edward T. James. Cambridge, MA: Belknap Press, 1971, pp. 108–09.

Shmurak, Carole B. "Dorothy Anna Hahn." *Notable Women in the Physical Sciences: A Biographical Dictionary.* Edited by Benjamin F. Shearer and Barbara S. Shearer. Westport, CT: Greenwood Press, 1997, pp. 163–66.

Periodicals

Renfrew, Alice G. "Dorothy A. Hahn, Scientist and Teacher." *Mount Holyoke Alumnae Quarterly* (February 1951).

Sketch by J. Sydney Jones

Julia Brainerd Hall
1859–1925
American aluminum scientist

Julia Brainerd Hall is responsible for aiding her brother, Charles Martin Hall, develop an inexpensive method of manufacturing aluminum. Hall gave her brother scientific and technical support as he conducted his experiments. Without her help, Charles Hall probably would not have been credited with revolutionalizing the aluminum industry.

Hall was born on November 11, 1859, in Jamaica, the British West Indies. Her parents, Heman and Sophronia (Brook) Hall, were missionaries who worked for American Missionary Association. While Hall was still an infant, the family relocated to Thompson, Ohio. Heman Hall found employment as a minister in the Congregational Church. Hall had four sisters and two brothers; she and her brother Charles were very close, and they shared a life–long love of science.

In 1873, the Hall family moved to Oberlin, Ohio. Like the rest of her siblings and parents, Hall attended Oberlin College and was enrolled in the women's literary course. She focused on science classes as well as mathematics and economics, though most women were directed to study liberal arts at the time. Hall graduated with a diploma in 1881. Upon graduation, Hall returned home and took over housekeeping from her mother, who was seriously ill. Her mother subsequently died on May 7, 1885. Hall never left home or married, taking care of her siblings and father.

While still attending Oberlin in 1882, Charles Hall began experiments in a woodshed near the family home. His goal was to become a rich inventor by developing a process to cheaply manufacture aluminum. Hall helped her brother by taking daily detailed notes on the progress of his quest. She also gave him her ideas on the subject, because she had taken more science courses at Oberlin than her brother. From the beginning, Hall collaborated with her brother on how to market his work, how to get investors involved, and to whom he might sell his work. Hall also sought advice on obtaining patents and ensured that every step was properly documented for future reference.

By February 1886, Charles Hall had perfected his electrolytic process. Using carbon electrodes, Charles Hall dissolved aluminum oxide in cryolite, a molten mineral. This produced aluminum. After this event, Charles Hall was often gone from home, but the siblings continued to work together by mail. Hall saved their voluminous correspondence, chiding her brother to be careful about what he included in his letters, and where he left her letters in case they fell into the wrong hands. For her part, Hall self–censored letters so that they would provide documentation, but not reveal anything of importance.

Hall's attention to detail paid off in 1887 when Charles Hall had to go to court over the rights to the patent for his process. Charles Hall applied for a patent several months after another scientist, a Frenchman named Heroult, was granted a patent for the same work. Heroult had developed the same process, but in a different way. Charles Hall won his case, mostly because of Hall's testimony, meticulous documentation, and a six–page history she wrote of his work entitled "History of C.M. Hall's Aluminum Invention." Without Hall's efforts, Charles Hall probably would have lost his case. Heroult did win something, however: this manufacturing process is still known as the Hall–Heroult Process.

Charles Hall formed the Pittsburgh Reduction Company on July 31, 1888. This company later became ALCOA (Aluminum Company of America), an extremely successful manufacturing venture on which an entire industry was based. Hall continued to advise him on scientific and technical matters after the company was formed, though Charles Hall moved from Oberlin permanently in 1890. Charles Hall had given his sister, as well as other members of the family, stock in the company in 1889. These shares supported Hall for the rest of her life. However, Charles Hall became extremely wealthy, and did not publicly credit his sister for her contributions to his work. Still, Hall continued to advise her brother on his other scientific experiments, including his work related to windmills. Hall died in 1925 at the age of 66. At her death, she held about 1,200 shares of ALCOA stock, earning about $7,000–$8,000 per year off the interest.

FURTHER READING

Books

Asimov, Issac. *Asimov's Biographical Encyclopedia of Science and Technology: The Lives and Achievements of 1195 Great Scientists from Ancient Times to the Present Chronologically Arranged.* Garden City, NY: Doubleday & Co., 1972, p. 522.

Kass–Simon, G., and Patricia Farnes, eds. *Women of Science: Righting the Record.* Bloomington: Indiana University Press, 1990, pp. 173–76.

Trescott, Martha Moore. "Julia B. Hall and Aluminum." *Dynamos and Virgins Revisited: Women and Technological Change in History.* Metuchen, NJ: The Scarecrow Press, Inc., 1979, pp. 149–79.

Vare, Ethlie Ann and Greg Ptacek. *Mothers of Invention: From the Bra to the Bomb: Forgotten Women & Their Unforgettable Ideas.* New York: William Morrow and Company, 1988, pp. 239–40.

Sketch by Annette Petrusso

Alice Hamilton
1869–1970
American pathologist

Alice Hamilton was a pioneer in correcting the medical problems caused by industrialization, awakening the country in the early twentieth century to the dangers of industrial poisons and hazardous working conditions. Through her untiring efforts, toxic substances in the lead, mining, painting, pottery, and rayon industries were exposed and legislation passed to protect workers. She was also a champion of worker's compensation laws, and was instrumental in bringing about this type of legislation in the state of Illinois. A medical doctor and researcher, she was the first woman of faculty status at Harvard University, and was a consultant on governmental commissions, both domestic and foreign.

Alice Hamilton was born on February 27, 1869, in New York City, the second of five children born to Montgomery Hamilton, a wholesale grocer, and Gertrude (Pond) Hamilton. Alice Hamilton grew up in secure material surroundings. Her mother encouraged the children to follow their minds and inclinations, and this approach proved beneficial. Her sister, Edith, later became a noted Greek scholar and the editor of well–known books on Greek myths and literature. Alice was educated at home and for a few years at a private school.

Hamilton's decision to pursue a career in medicine came, in part, because it was one of the few professional

Alice Hamilton (The Library of Congress. Reproduced by permission.)

fields open to women of her day. She earned a medical degree from the University of Michigan in 1893, without having completed an undergraduate degree and taking surprisingly few science courses. Realizing that she wanted to pursue research rather than medical practice, Hamilton went on to do further studies both in the United States and abroad: from 1895–1896 at Leipzig and Munich; 1896–1897 at Johns Hopkins; and 1902 in Paris at the Pasteur Institute. In 1897 she accepted a post as professor of pathology at the Women's Medical College at Northwestern University in Chicago, and when it closed in 1902, she became a professor of pathology at the Memorial Institute for Infectious Diseases, a position which she held until 1909.

Hull House Residency Leads to Industrial Concerns

In Chicago Hamilton became a resident of Hull House, the pioneering settlement designed to give care and advice to the poor of Chicago. Here, under the influence of Jane Addams, the founder of Hull House, Hamilton saw the effects of poverty up close. Investigating a typhoid epidemic in Chicago, she was instrumental in reorganizing the city's health department and in drawing attention to the role flies played in spreading the epidemic. After reading *Dangerous Trades* by Sir Thomas Oliver, Hamilton began her life–long mission to treat the excesses of industrialization. Unlike other countries such as Germany and England, the United States had no industrial safety laws at the time. During her time at Hull House, Hamilton investigated the steel industry and others for occupationally–caused lead poisoning.

In 1910 Hamilton was chosen by the governor of Illinois to head up his Commission on Occupational Diseases, and her research and investigation into the dangers of lead and phosphorous paved the way to the state's first worker's compensation laws. In 1911 she took up similar, non–salaried, duties for the federal government, becoming an investigator of industrial poisons for the fledgling Department of Labor. During World War I, Hamilton investigated the high explosives industry, discovering that nitrous fumes were responsible for a great number of supposedly natural deaths.

In 1919 she became the first female faculty member of Harvard University as assistant professor of industrial medicine, but was denied access to the male bastion of the Harvard Club and to participation in graduation ceremonies. Hamilton kept up her international contacts, serving as the only woman delegate on the League of Nations Health Commission to the U.S.S.R. in 1924, as well as acting as a consultant to the International Labor Office in Geneva, Switzerland. In 1925, she published her *Industrial Poisons in the United States,* the first text on the subject, and became one of the few worldwide authorities in the area of industrial toxins. At this same time, she was also instrumental in influencing the surgeon general to investigate the dangerous effects of tetraethyl lead and radium.

Hamilton retired from Harvard in 1935, but not from active public life. She became a consultant in the U.S. Labor Department's Division of Labor Standards and from 1937–1938 conducted an investigation of the viscose rayon industry. Hamilton demonstrated the toxicity involved in rayon processes, and these findings that led to Pennsylvania's first compensation law for occupational diseases. In her later years, Hamilton, who never married, wrote an autobiography and continued to be active politically, advancing causes of social justice and pacifism. She died of a stroke at her home in Hadlyme, Connecticut, in 1970. Hamilton was 101 at the time of her death, and had been the recipient of honorary degrees from around the world for her work in revealing the dangers of industrial poisons.

SELECTED WRITINGS BY HAMILTON:

Books

Industrial Poisons in the United States. Macmillan, 1925.

Industrial Toxicology. Harper & Brothers, 1934.

Exploring the Dangerous Trades: the Autobiography of Alice Hamilton, M.D. Little, Brown, 1943.

FURTHER READING

Books

American Women Writers. Ungar, 1980, pp. 226–227.

Current Biography: Who's News and Why 1946. H. W. Wilson Company, 1946, pp. 234–236.
Noble, Iris. *Contemporary Women Scientists of America.* Julian Messner, 1988, pp. 13–14.
Notable American Women: the Modern Period. Cambridge: Harvard University Press, 1980, pp. 303–306.
Sicherman, Barbara. *Alice Hamilton, a Life in Letters.* Cambridge: Harvard University Press, 1984.

Sketch by J. Sydney Jones

Anna Jane Harrison
1912–
American chemist

Anna Jane Harrison was the first woman to receive a Ph.D. in chemistry from the University of Missouri. She was also the first woman to chair the Division of Chemical Education for the American Chemical Society (ACS), and the first woman to be elected ACS president in the society's 102–year history. Most of her professional research was in vacuum ultraviolet spectroscopy.

Anna Harrison (Mt. Holyoke College Archive. Reproduced by permission.)

Born two days before Christmas in 1912, Harrison was the only daughter of Albert and Mary Katherine (Jones) Harrison, who also had a son. The family lived in a rural farming community near Benton City, Missouri, and when Harrison's father died when she was merely seven years old, her mother continued to operate the family farm until 1960. Harrison and her brother were raised with a spirit of independence and responsibility, qualities she was known for all her life.

Harrison received two bachelor's degrees from the University of Missouri, one in chemistry and two years later, one in education. Although not inclined toward the sciences as a child, she later became impressed with her math and science studies in high school, an interest she later attributed to her excellent teachers. In college, she pursued chemistry and physics classes, but was discouraged by the department head because she was a woman.

After teaching in a one-room schoolhouse in rural Missouri for a few years, Harrison returned to her alma mater for graduate work, getting both master's and doctorate degrees in physical chemistry. In the 1940s, except for a few exceptions, the only viable career for women in chemistry was education. Harrison accepted an instructor position at Sophie Newcomb College for women at Tulane University. Two years later, she was promoted to assistant professor, and following a brief wartime position with the National Defense Research Council (in toxic smoke collection and detection), she accepted an assistant professorship at Mount Holyoke College in Massachusetts when the war ended in 1945. Harrison was eager to join other like–minded female scientists at Mt. Holyoke whom she had met at ACS meetings, and indeed, she spent the remainder of her teaching career there. Of her almost 40 years in education, 34 of them were completed as a faculty member at Mt. Holyoke. Flanked by numerous awards and honors, Harrison retired as professor emeritus in 1979.

While at Mt. Holyoke, Harrison experienced an unusually short advancement from assistant professor to associate professor, to full professor in just seven years (at that time, the average tenure at each of these levels was ten years for women). She was well-liked by both colleagues and students, instructing chemistry in a manner that made the subject matter fascinating and inviting. During this time she also engaged in technical research, establishing the structure of many organic molecules through the use of spectroscopy, and studying the manner by which organic compounds were absorbed in vacuum ultraviolet. Harrison was also the recipient of an American Association of University Women (AAUW) fellowship, under which she was able to conduct research into flash photolysis at Cambridge University in England (1952–1953). She took a short sabbatical from 1959 to 1960, during which Harrison furthered her work on photolysis by high frequency ultraviolet light for the National Research Council in Canada (under another fellowship). Upon return to Mt. Holyoke, she was promoted to department chair, serving in that capacity from 1960 to 1966.

Harrison was also named the William R. Kenan, Jr. professor in 1976, an honor which she continued to hold until her retirement as professor emeritus in 1979. During this period, she also was the recipient of the James Flack Norris award in chemistry education from the ACS (1977), where she became president in 1978 and recipient of the ACS Award in chemical education (1982). Upon her "retirement" in 1979, Harrison became more active in her membership with the American Association for the Advancement of Science (AAAS), serving as a director (1979–1985), president (1983), and chairman of the board (1984–1985). Harrison also served as Distinguished Visiting professor to the U.S. Naval Academy in 1980. From 1988–1991, she served on the board of directors for Sigma Xi, and on the board of directors for Volunteers in Technical Assistance from 1990–1994.

Harrison is known for her lively sense of humor. An enthusiastic traveler, she particularly enjoyed travels to the Oregon wilderness, South America, and anywhere less frequented by others. She resides in South Hadley, Massachusetts.

SELECTED WRITINGS BY HARRISON:

Books

(Textbook with Edwin S. Weaver) *Chemistry: A Search to Understand,* 1989.

FURTHER READING

Books

American Men & Women of Science. 17th ed. New York: R.R. Bowker, 1989–1990, p. 535.

Bailey, Martha J. *American Women in Science.* Denver: ABC–CLIO, 153.

Shearer, Benjamin F. and Barbara S. Shearer, eds. *Notable Women in the Physical Sciences.* Westport, CT: Greenwood Press, 1997, 172–175.

Who's Who of American Women. 21st ed. New Providence: Marquis, 1999–2000.

Sketch by Lauri R. Harding

Ethel Browne Harvey

1885–1965

American marine biologist and embryologist

Ethel Browne Harvey was responsible for discovering many of the mechanisms of cell division, some of which generated interest in the popular press. In 1937, Harvey announced that she had was able to stimulate fragments of sea urchin eggs—which contained no cell nucleus—to divide. This caused a public furor because it was seen as reproduction without parental inheritance. This was a radical notion and affected the whole theory of cell division and genetics. Harvey spent most of her career researching cell division and development, using sea urchin eggs as her primary subject model.

Ethel Browne Harvey was born in Baltimore, Maryland, on December 14, 1885, the youngest child of Bennet Browne, and obstetrician/gynecologist and professor, and Jennie (Nicholson) Browne. Ethel had two brothers and two sisters. Her parents were progressive and believed in education for girls, so the young Browne girls attended Baltimore's Bryn Mawr School, the first American all–girls prep school.

With her parents' support, Harvey received a full college education. She graduated from what was then known as Women's College of Baltimore (later Goucher College) in 1906. After graduation, Harvey had her first experience at the Marine Biological Lab at Woods Hole, Massachusetts, a relationship that would span nearly 60 years. She earned her MA at Columbia University on a Goucher Fellowship a year later, studying zoology. In 1909, she was elected to Corporation Membership at the Marine Biological Lab. At Columbia, Harvey earned her Ph.D. in 1913, again studying zoology. While a graduate student, Harvey published six papers. She had already expressed an interest in the basic forms of life, researching embryology and cytology.

Between 1913 and 1931, Harvey bounced between positions and research, with yearly excursions to the lab at Woods Hole. For example, she spent a year on fellowship at the University of California (1914–15), teaching for several years at New York University (1928–32). Her research during the 1920s focused on sea urchin embryology, and she did much experimental work on the subject. In this period, Harvey married Princeton professor Edmund Newton Harvey in 1916. He was also a marine biologist, but they did not work together. They had two sons together, Edmund Jr. and Richard.

In 1931, she joined the biology department at Princeton as an Investigator. It was here that she announced her most important work on sea urchin eggs. Her 1937 announcement illustrated that the eggs could be divided without a nucleus when redistributed by centrifugal force. At the time, the popular press picked up on her discovery emphasizing that, as the headline in the September 13, 1937, issue of *Life* proclaimed, "New Life is Created without Sex," while the December 6, 1937, *Newsweek* stated that, "Birth without Parents: Woman's Findings Add to Doubt on Accepted Genetics Theory."

Harvey did other work on the sea urchin. She was the first to devise a way to determine the sex of a sea urchin. She published a book in 1956 which laid out all her work on the sea urchin and its embryology, entitled *The American* Arbacia *and Other Sea Urchins.* It is still used as a reference book. Though her work received wide attention, Harvey was never a faculty member at Princeton. Indeed, she only had a corner of her husband's lab at both Princeton and Woods Hole. The only support she received for her sea urchin work was a 1937 grant from the American Philosophical Society.

Before her retirement in 1959, Harvey received numerous accolades from her peers, including membership in many biological societies around the world. The Marine Biological Laboratory elected her a trustee from 1950–56, after a lifelong relationship. She was the first woman in 50 years to be elected to the board. Harvey died of peritonitis on September 2, 1965, in Falmouth, Massachusetts.

SELECTED WRITINGS BY HARVEY:

Books

The American Arbacia and Other Sea Urchins. Princeton: Princeton University Press, 1956.

FURTHER READING

Books

Bailey, Martha J. "Harvey, Ethel Browne." *American Women in Science: A Biographical Dictionary.* Denver: ABC–CLIO, 1994, pp. 154–55.

Haraway, Donna J. "Harvey, Ethel Browne." *Notable American Women, The Modern Period: A Biographical Dictionary.* Edited by Barbara Sicherman and Carol Hurd Green. Cambridge, MA: Belknap Press, 1980, pp. 319–21.

Kass–Simon, G. and Patricia Farnes, eds. "Ethel Browne Harvey: Induction and Merogony." *Women of Science: Righting the Record.* Bloomington: Indiana University Press, 1990, pp. 217–20.

Siegel, Patricia Joan and Kay Thomas Finley. "Ethel Browne Harvey." *Women in the Scientific Search: An American Bio–bibliography, 1724–1979.* Metuchen, NJ: The Scarecrow Press, Inc., 1985, pp. 364–67.

Periodicals

Butler, E. G. "Memorials—Ethel Browne Harvey." *The Biological Bulletin* (August 1967): 9–11.

"Dr. Ethel Harvey, Biologist, Was 79." *The New York Times* (September 3, 1965): 27.

"New Life Is Created Without Sex." *Life* (September 13, 1937): 70–72.

"Science. Birth Without Parents: Woman's Findings Add to Doubt on Accepted Genetics Theory." *Newsweek* (December 6, 1937): 36–37.

Sketch by Annette Petrusso

Margaret Harwood
1885–1979

American astronomer

For nearly 50 years Margaret Harwood was associated with the **Maria Mitchell** Observatory in Nantucket, Massachusetts, most of that time as its director. During those years she conducted importance research, particularly on "variable stars." These stars, called "variable" because their brightness level changes, can be extremely difficult to find and measure, but Harwood rose to the challenge and did important work on them even after her retirement from Mitchell.

Harwood was born in Littleton, Massachusetts on March 19, 1885 to Herbert Joseph and Emelie Augusta Green Harwood. She received her bachelor of arts degree from Radcliffe College in 1907 and went on to the University of California-Berkeley, where she was awarded her master's degree in 1916. Although she got her degree at Berkeley, she spend much of her time on the East Coast. In 1907, shortly after graduating from Radcliffe, she became a computer assistant at the Harvard College Observatory. ("Computer" at that time was defined as "an individual who does computations.") In 1912, she became an astronomical fellow at the Maria Mitchell Observatory.

After receiving her degree from Berkeley, Harwood returned to the Mitchell Observatory as its director, a post she held until her retirement in 1957. (From 1944 to 1946, she also worked n the staff of the Massachusetts Institute of Technology's Radiation Laboratory.) While there, she not only worked on he own research, but also encouraged other women to pursue careers in astronomy. Among them was **Henrietta Hill Swope**, daughter of the president of General Electric and originally a business administration student. She met Harwood at the Mitchell Observatory, and it was Harwood who suggested that Swope pursue astronomy as a career at the Harvard Observatory. Swope followed Harwood's advice and went on to an important career at Harvard and later at the Mount Wilson and Palomar Observatory in California.

Like many other women in the sciences, Harwood was hampered by a widespread belief that women were not suited to scientific careers. One incident in her career points up these difficulties: In 1917, she discovered an asteroid, which was also sighted by astronomer George H. Peters four days later. Despite the fact that Harwood had seen the asteroid first, it was Peters who received the credit. One of the perks that went along with discovering an asteroid was being given the chance to name it. Peters named the asteroid, known as Asteroid No. 886, "Washingtonia." Perhaps Harwood would have given it a different name, perhaps not. What mattered was that she was denied the credit she deserved.

Harwood did receive recognition for her work in later years, however. She received the **Annie J. Cannon** Prize in

Astronomy, an award jointly given my the American Astronomical Society and the American Association of University Women. She also received a distinguished achieve medal from her alma mater, Radcliffe, in 1957.

Among the professional association in which Harwood was active were the American Association for the Advancement of Science, the American Association of Variable Star Observers, the Royal Astronomical Society, and the International Astronomical Union. Not surprisingly, given her longtime association with the Mitchell Observatory, she was also an active member of the Maria Mitchell Association.

After retiring from her post at the Maria Mitchell Observatory, Harwood remained active in astronomical research. Part of the Annie J. Cannon Prize, in fact, is a research grant, and Harwood used this grant to further her own studies of variable stars. She settled in Cambridge, Massachusetts, where she died in February 1979, a month before her 94th birthday.

FURTHER READING

Books

Bailey, Martha J. *American Women in Science: A Biographical Dictionary.* Denver: ABC–CLIO, 1994.

Shearer, Benjamin F. and Barbara S, Shearer, eds. *Notable Women in the Physical Sciences: A Biographical Dictionary.* Greenwood Press, 1997.

Sketch by George A. Milite

Harriet Ann (Boyd) Hawes
1871–1945
American archaeologist

Harriet Hawes was the first woman archaeologist to head an excavation. A classicist and a scientist, she worked on the Greek island of Crete, discovering the ancient town of Gournia, one of Crete's "ninety cities" of Homer's *Odyssey*. Despite her international acclaim as an archaeologist, Hawes devoted much of her free time to social activism, becoming involved with the political issues of the day.

Harriet Ann Boyd Hawes was born in Boston, Massachusetts, on October 11, 1871, to Alexander and Harriet Fay (Wheeler) Boyd. The fifth child and the only girl, Hawes grew up in a family of men when her mother died suddenly during Hawes's infancy. She was close to her father, a leather–merchant, and to her brothers, especially Alexander, Jr., who shared his fascination with ancient history with her.

Hawes graduated from Prospect Hill School in 1888 before going on to Smith College, from which she graduated with a B.A. in 1892 and an M. A. in 1901. In between her years of schooling, Hawes taught classics—ancient and modern languages—in North Carolina and Delaware. From 1900–1906 she also taught modern Greek, epigraphy, and Greek archaeology at Smith.

Undaunted by Discrimination

In 1896, Hawes attended the American School of Classical Studies (ASCS) in Athens, Greece. However, as a woman, she was not permitted to take part in excavations sponsored by ASCS. She had been awarded the Agnes Hoppin fellowship in 1900, and she used the money to finance her own excavation. Hawes wanted to follow up on recent archaeological work in Crete, and the fellowship allowed her to go.

Once in Crete, Hawes was advised by Arthur J. Evans, a British archaeologist excavating Knossos, to try the Kavousi region. In 1901, after securing funding from the American Exploration Society of Philadelphia, Hawes focused on the part of the region known as Gournia, in which she discovered an Early Bronze Age Minoan town site. The first woman to direct an excavation, she was also the first archaeologist to make such a discovery. Gournia was notable in part for its residents, artisans, and the part it played in the larger tapestry of Cretan society. The excavation, continued in 1903 and 1904, offered a significant amount of archaeological information to current studies. In fact, Hawes' discovery is still the only town from the Minoan age to be found well-preserved. In 1902, the Archaeological Institute of America sponsored her national lecture tour to describe her findings, which were later published in 1908.

Hawes met her husband, Charles Henry Hawes, a British anthropologist, in Crete, and they married on March 3, 1906. In December of that year, their son, Alexander, was born, followed by their daughter, Mary, in August of 1910. Hawes and her husband co-wrote a book on Crete during this time. After teaching appointments in Wisconsin and New Hampshire, Charles Hawes took a position as assistant director of the Boston Museum of Fine Arts in 1919. The following year, Hawes returned to teaching, this time at Wellesley College, where she lectured on pre-Christian art. She remained there until her retirement in 1936.

Political and Social Activism

A lifelong activist, Hawes devoted much of her life to political and social causes. She was a volunteer war nurse in Thessaly (1897), Florida (1898), and Corfu (1916), and in 1917 she organized the Smith College Relief Unit to aid French civilians. Later, in 1933, she aided union shoe workers on strike, and was subsequently sued for $100,000 by the company.

Hawes and her husband retired to a farm in Alexandria, Virginia. After Charles' death in 1943, Hawes moved to a Washington, D.C. rest home, where she died of peritonitis on March 31, 1945. Smith College loved its archaeologist, awarding Hawes the honorary L.H.D. degree in 1910, creating a scholarship in her name in 1922, and holding a memorial symposium in Crete in 1967.

SELCTED WRITINGS BY HAWES:

Books

Gournia, Vasiliki and Other Prehistoric Sites on the Isthmus of Hierapetra, Crete. Philadelphia: American Exploration Society, 1908.

FURTHER READING

Books

Bailey, Martha J. *American Women in Science*. Denver: ABC–CLIO, 1994.

James, Edward T., ed. *Dictionary of American Biography*. Supplement three. NY: Charles Scribner's Sons, 1973.

James, Edward T., et al, eds. *Notable American Women 1607–1950*. Cambridge: Belknap Press, 1971.

McHenry, Robert, ed. *Liberty's Women*. Springfield: G & C Merriam Company, 1980.

Ogilvie, Marilyn Bailey. *Women in Science: Antiquity Through the Nineteeth Century*. Cambridge: MIT Press, 1986.

Sketch by Helene Barker Kiser

Ellen Amanda Hayes
1851–1930
American mathematics educator

Ellen Amanda Hayes was born on September 23, 1851. Her maternal grandparents, originally from Granville, Massachusetts, founded the small town of Granville, Ohio, in 1805 and it was in their home that Hayes was born. Hayes's grandparents, as well as her parents, would set the stage for her love of learning, career, and political interests.

Hayes's father, Charles Coleman Hayes, made his living as a tanner after serving as an officer in the Civil War. Her mother, Ruth Rebecca (Wolcott), taught all six of her children to read, gave them a smattering of astronomy, and instructed them in botany, supplying them with the names plants in Latin. Both generations, parents and grandparents, believed in education without regard to gender. Hayes's mother had been trained as a teacher and graduated from the Granville Female Academy, a school that enjoyed the support of, and accepted as a trustee, Hayes's grandfather, Horace Wolcott. Although Hayes's father was uneducated, he too encouraged the education of his children.

Hayes left the home instruction supplied by her mother when she was seven and went to the Centerville school. That school had only one room for all levels of instruction and kept no grades. At age 16, Hayes was herself a teacher at a country school, saving the money she earned to attend college. After entering Oberlin College in 1872 as a preparatory student, Hayes began her college career as a freshman in 1875. Her endeavors mainly centered on the fields of mathematics and science, but she also became well versed in English literature, Greek, Latin, and history. Her mother's introduction to astronomy must have left a lasting impression because Hayes spent time at the Leander McCormick Observatory at the University of Virginia in 1887–1888, where she studied the Minor Planet 267, confirming its definite orbit, and producing other important papers on Comet *a* and planetary conic curves.

After graduating from Oberlin with a bachelor of arts degree, Hayes spent a year as the principal of the women's department at Adrian College in Michigan. In 1879, she became a teacher of mathematics at Wellesley College. By 1888, she was a full professor and had assumed the role of chair of the department. In 1897, a department of applied mathematics was created at Wellesley and Hayes took the helm. Her responsibilities included giving instruction in seven levels of applied mathematics.

A Controversial Woman

Although Hayes spent 37 years at Wellesley, the association was often far from congenial because of Hayes's view on education and politics. She was never silent or restrained about either subject. Hayes was adamant about females taking mathematics and science courses and highly critical of the school for allowing students to choose electives that would make it possible for them to evade these studies. Reforms concerning working conditions, politics, and the education of women was something Hayes worked toward all her life. Her views on and support of the union movement and workers rights caused her to receive threats and to be arrested. She closely studied the Russian Revolution of 1917 as it unfolded, writing and speaking openly about the situation. Although Hayes never affiliated herself with the Communist party and disagreed with many of its doctrines, her association with socialist causes did much to brand her a radical and incite serious criticism from Wellesley College. Upon her retirement from Wellesley, Hayes was denied the honorary position of Professor Emeritus usually bestowed on teachers for lengthy and faithful service.

Legacy of a Life Well Spent

At the age of 72, Hayes began her own newspaper. The *Relay* was published monthly and was devoted to giving publicity to facts and movements that Hayes believed were not accurately presented in the mainstream press. Her description of the publication was that "the *Relay*plans to camp in a hut by the side of the road and to keep a lamp or two burning—in the hope of being a friend to wayfarers and especially to the limping Under Dog." Other books written after her retirement include *The Sycamore Trail*, a book which asks readers to question the origin of their beliefs and superstitions, and study the nature of evidence. Most of Hayes' work was self–published.

Upon her death in 1930, Hayes' brain was donated to the Wilder Brain Collection at Cornell University. The epitaph assigned to her by her friends was her favorite quotation: "It is better to travel hopefully, than to arrive."

SELECTED WRITINGS BY HAYES

Books

*Lessons on Higher Algebra,*1891, revised edition 1894.
Elementary Trigonometry, 1896.
Algebra for High Schools and Colleges, 1897.
*Calculus with Applications: An Introduction to the Mathematical Treatment of Science,*1900.

Periodicals

"Comet *a* 1904." *Science* 19 (May 27, 1904): 833–34.

FURTHER READING

Books

Brown, Louise. *Ellen Hayes: Trail–Blazer*. West Park, NY: 1932.
Moskol, Ann. "Ellen Amanda Hayes," in *Women of Mathematics:: A Biobibliographic Sourcebook.* Edited by Louise S. Grinstein and Paul J. Campbell. Westport, CT: Greenwood Press, 1987, pp. 62–66.

Periodicals

Gordon, Geraldine. "Ellen Hayes: 1851–1930." *The Wellesley Magazine* (February 1931): 151–52.
Merrill, Helen A. "Ellen Hayes." *Scrapbook of the History Department of Mathematics* (1944): 41–46. Archives, Wellesley College.

Other

"Ellen Amanda Hayes." *Biographies of Women Mathematicians.* June 1997. http://www.scotlan.edu/lriddle/women/chronol.htm (July 22, 1997).

Sketch by Kelley Reynolds Jacquez

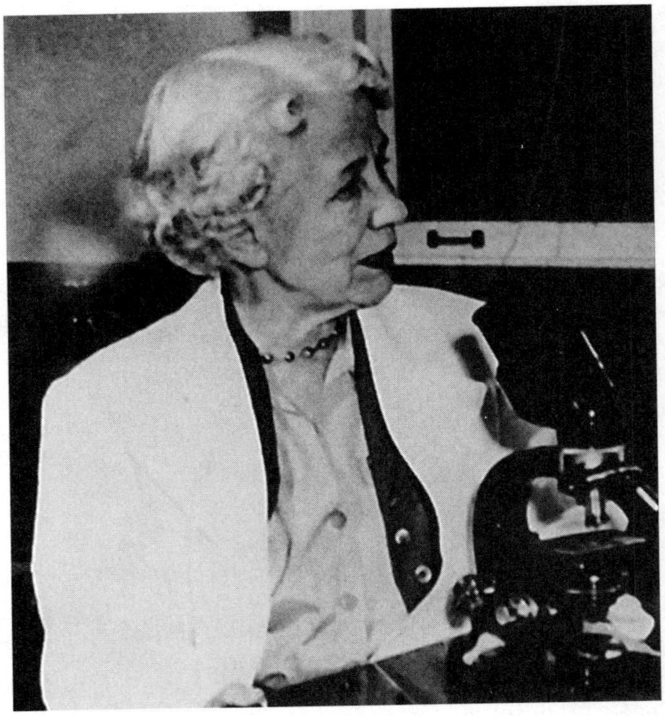

Elizabeth Lee Hazen (The Library of Congress. Reproduced by permission.)

Elizabeth Lee Hazen
1885–1975
American microbiologist and mycologist

Elizabeth Lee Hazen was the codiscoverer, with **Rachel Fuller Brown**, of the antifungal antibiotic named nystatin which proved effective against a wide range of yeast infections of the intestine, skin, and mucous membranes. Having begun life as an orphan on a poor Mississippi farm, she overcame considerable adversity to obtain a Ph.D. from Columbia and work for the New York State Department of Health. For her discovery, she received several major awards, and at the time of her death, she had channeled over 13 million dollars in royalties to support further scientific work.

Hazen was born in Rich, Coahoma County, Mississippi, on August 24, 1885. The middle of three children, she was orphaned before she was four years old. Her cotton farmer father, William Edgar Hazen, and her mother, Maggie Harper Hazen, both died before they were 30. Hazen's younger brother died soon after, and she and her sister, Annis, were eventually taken in by their uncle and aunt, Robert Henry and Laura Hazen. Although Robert Hazen had not been to college, he was determined to obtain the best education for both his daughters and his nieces.

Hazen attended public schools and entered the Mississippi Industrial Institute and College at Columbus, where she received her B.S. in 1910.

It was at college that her interest in science flourished, and after teaching high school in Jackson, Mississippi, for six years and taking summer classes at the University of Tennessee and the University of Virginia, she eventually began graduate study in the Department of Biology at New York's Columbia University. In 1917 she received her M.S., but further education was delayed when she volunteered to work in the U.S. Army laboratories during World War I. After the war, she took a job in the laboratory of a West Virginia hospital and did not return to Columbia until 1923. In 1927 she received her Ph.D. in microbiology at the age of forty–two; she was one of only a handful of women to obtain such an advanced degree in the medical sciences.

During the next four years, Hazen was an instructor at Columbia's College of Physicians and Surgeons, and in 1931 she joined the New York State Department of Health, Division of Laboratories and Research. Until the early 1940s, she concentrated on infectious diseases and demonstrated a keen scientific detective ability, having tracked down the sources of an outbreak of anthrax as well as the cause of the first case in the United States of *Clostridium botulinum,* a type of food poisoning found in improperly preserved foods. Her work during World War II led her to concentrate on fungal (called mycotic) infections that afflict humans, and she returned to Columbia University's Mycology Laboratory, having been encouraged by the recent discovery by Alexander Fleming of the antibacterial antibiotic called penicillin.

Hazen began to look systematically for an antifungal agent that might exist in nature, and collaborated at the New York State Department of Health's Division of Laboratories with the organic chemist, Rachel Fuller Brown, who worked at the State's Central Laboratory. Hazen collected and assayed soil samples and sent them to Brown for testing. In 1948 they discovered in the soil of a Virginia farm belonging to Hazen's friends a new antibiotic they first called fungicidin. By 1950 it had been renamed nystatin and was announced by the National Academy of Science.

Once the patent rights were settled and commercial production of this new drug had begun, the two scientists decided to have the funds from its sale distributed equally between two funds that would support related scientific research. In 1958 Hazen accepted an associate professorship at Albany Medical College. Two years later she retired and became a full–time guest investigator in the Columbia University Mycology Laboratory. In 1973 she moved to a Seattle nursing home where her ill sister was living, since her own health was failing, and she died there of acute cardiac arrhythmia on June 24, 1975. She had never married.

Among the many awards she received during her lifetime, one was especially noteworthy; a month before she died, she and Brown became the first women to receive the Chemical Pioneer Award given by the American Institute of Chemists. The Institute changed its bylaws to recognize Hazen who was a microbiologist and not a chemist. Hazen also shared the 1955 Squibb Award in Chemotherapy with Brown and received the Distinguished Service Award from the New York State Department of Health in 1968. Hazen's friends knew her as a warm, out–going person who shunned the spotlight. She always let Brown present their joint papers, and regularly avoided the press. Her friends knew well that the passion of her life was her work.

SELECTED WRITINGS BY HAZEN:

Books

Laboratory Identification of Pathogenic Fungi Simplified, Thomas, 1955.

FURTHER READING

Books

Baldwin, Richard S., *The Fungus Fighters: Two Women Scientists and Their Discovery.* Cornell University Press, 1981.

Periodicals

Bacon, W. Stevenson. "Elizabeth Lee Hazen: 1885–1975." *Mycologia* (September–October, 1976): 961–969.

Sketch by Leonard C. Bruno

Olive Clio Hazlett
1890–1974
American mathematician

Olive Clio Hazlett was one of the most active women working in mathematics prior to 1940. She is best known for her work in the area of linear algebra. The majority of her research was conducted in linear algebra and also in modular invariants, making important contributions in both areas.

Hazlett received her undergraduate degree from Radcliffe College in 1912. She began work on her Ph.D. at the University of Chicago in 1913, receiving her doctorate there in 1915. She conducted additional study and research work at Harvard University and in Rome, Zurich, and Göttingen as a Guggenheim fellow. Hazlett taught mathematics for more than 40 years. She began her career in 1916 at Bryn Mawr College in Pennsylvania, remaining there for two years before accepting a position as assistant professor at Mount Holyoke College in Massachusetts. Hazlett taught at

Mount Holyoke for eight years, attaining the position of associate professor in 1924. In 1925, she took a position at the University of Illinois, enticed there by the excellent library facilities and the assurance of sufficient research time to develop her mathematical theories. She completed her career at the University of Illinois, retiring as emeritus associate professor in 1959.

Career Advancement Denied

Although recognized for her outstanding and prolific accomplishments, Hazlett's career did not reflect her mathematical brilliance. As was common with many gifted women mathematicians of her era, she was denied advancement in her profession. She attained the level of associate professor, and remained at that level throughout her career. This meant Hazlett often was relegated to teaching introductory courses and undergraduates, long after her male peers had advanced to full professorships and graduate students. In spite of this, her name appeared in seven editions of *American Men and Women of Science*. Hazlett also took an active role in the professional associations of her profession, including the American Mathematical Society, and served as associate editor of the *Transactions of the American Mathematical Society* for 12 years, from 1923 to 1935. She was also a member of the Society's council from 1926 to 1928, and a member of the New York Academy of Sciences. The award of a Guggenheim Fellowship in 1928 allowed her to study in Europe for one year.

While at the University of Illinois, Hazlett suffered a series of mental breakdowns during the 1930s and 1940s. Margaret Rossiter, in her book *Women Scientists in America*, states that Hazlett never fully recovered from her illness. "Isolated and moderately successful but with aspirations of full equality, [she] denied the potential psychological dangers in [her] situation."

Hazlett died on March 11, 1974, in a Keene, New Hampshire, nursing home at age 83. She had never married, and lived out her life on what Rossiter termed a "pitiable pension," resulting from the low pay she had received throughout her career.

FURTHER READING

Books

Bailey, Martha J. *American Women in Science: A Biographical Dictionary*. Santa Barbara: ABC–CLIO, Inc., 1994, p. 159.

Rossiter, Margaret W. *Women Scientists in America: Struggles and Strategies to 1940*. Baltimore: Johns Hopkins University Press, 1982.

Periodicals

Obituary. *New York Times* (March 12, 1974): 40:4.

Other

Riddle, Larry. "Olive Clio Hazlett." *Biographies of Women Mathematicians*. June 1997. http:www/scott-lan.edu./lriddle/women/chronol.htm (July 21, 1997).

Sketch by Jane Stewart Cook

Beulah Louise Henry
1887–?
American inventor

Beulah Louise Henry, a prolific inventor, was nicknamed "Lady Edison" by the popular press during the 1930s. Although she lacked technical or mechanical training, her inventions were both complex and intricate, running the gamut from toys and dolls to a bobbinless sewing machine and football inflator. Henry received her first patent in 1912 at the age of 25 for an ice cream freezer with a vacuum seal, but many of her ideas and inventions were instead sold or licensed to various corporations. As early as 1930, 40 of her ideas had already been sold.

Henry was born in 1887 in Raleigh, North Carolina, to Col. Walter R. Henry and Beulah Williamson Henry. She came from a creative family—her father was an art connoisseur and lecturer, her mother an artist , and her only brother (Peyton), a songwriter. Beulah was a direct descendant of Patrick Henry and granddaughter of Governor W.W. Holden of North Carolina. Her creative abilities emerged at an early age, when she began to draw machines and inventions while still a child. She also had an artistic bent and enjoyed painting watercolors, though she will always be known as an inventor. Between 1909 and 1912 Henry attended Presbyterian (now Queens) College and Elizabeth College both in Charlotte, North Carolina. In 1913, she patented a handbag and a parasol. Henry then moved to New York City with her parents in 1919, Henry continued her invention and patent activity.

From Toys to Typewriters

Several more patents for a spring-limb doll and another parasol were granted in the mid-1920s. A manufacturer of her original umbrella one with detachable, snap-on covers of various colors to fit a single frame claimed to have sold 40,000 umbrellas in 60 days. By 1924 at the age of 37, Henry claimed she was president of two new companies to commercialize her inventions and had patents granted in four different countries.

With no technical training, Henry attributed her success to intuition or her "inner vision" though not all of

Beulah Louise Henry (Corbis/Bettmann-UPI. Reproduced by permission.)

her inventions were so instantaneous. Her intuition may have been aided by a rare condition called synthesia or color-hearing—the ability to perceive sound as color. Henry, however, did not leave her inventions to intuition alone. She relied on a large laboratory staffed with mechanics and pattern makers who made models of each gadget. She also took ideas from seemingly unrelated devices. She realized that the pins that made sound in a music box could also be used to hold layers of paper together in a typewriter. As she was quoted later, "If necessity is the mother of invention, then resourcefulness is the father."

By 1927 Henry had 47 successful inventions to her credit, 16 of them patented. She was an inventor for the Nicholas Machine Works of New York City. She also served as a consultant to various companies manufacturing products invented by her, such as Merganthaler Linotype Co., Klinert Rubber Co., several doll manufacturers, her own Henry Umbrella Co., Display Mannequin Co., and Ideal Toy Corporation. She also became interested in other areas of science, joining the New York Microscope Society, the Museum of Natural History, the National Audubon Society, and the New York Women's League for Animals.

Henry continued inventing through most of her life. By 1970, when she received her last patent, she had over 100 inventions to her credit. About half of these were patented, most of them mechanical in nature. Her toys included a "Miss Illusion" doll with interchangeable wigs and eyes that changed colors; an eating toy animal, a movable lip for toy figures, and a toy cow that gave milk. Henry received 11 patents related to typewriters, including a supplemental ribbon attachment, several duplicating attachments, and two feeding and aligning devices. She also invented the Protograph, an attachment that makes an original and four copies of a letter or record without carbon paper.

Henry invented labor-saving gadgets for the home as well, including a can opener with an attachment for opening cans with tear strips, a Baster oven, a double chain-stitch sewing machine, and a bobbinless sewing machine. Even some of her simpler inventions, such as the Latho soap holder, a sponge with a piece of soap held inside, were more complex than they seemed. Henry invented not only the product, but also a machine that cut to specifications.

Unlike many inventors, Henry profited from her inventions. Though she no longer has the most patents for an American woman (in her own name), the few who have surpassed her have patents concentrated in only one specific area. The wide variety of "Lady Edison's" patents and their ingenuity make her an inventor who deserves special recognition.

FURTHER READING

Books

MacDonald, Anne L. *Feminine Ingenuity: Women and Invention in America.* New York: Ballantine Books, 1992.

Stanley, Autumn. *Mothers and Daughters of Invention: Notes for a Revised History of Technology.* Metuchen: Scarecrow Press, Inc., 1993.

Other

http://web.mit.edu/invent/www/inventorsR–Z/whm2.html.

Sketch by Laurel M. Sheppard

Herrad of Landsberg
1130(?)–1195
German natural philosopher

Herrad of Landsberg was a German abbess who wrote an important work of science, *Hortus Deliciarum*, or *Garden of Delights*, which provided a vivid picture of twelfth–century convent life, as well as an overview of the scientific knowledge of the day.

Born into the Landsberg family, members of the gentry, at about 1130, Herrad was sent as a child to study at the convent of Hohenberg, on Mount St. Odile, in Alsace. In

1167, she succeeded Relind as abbess there and assumed responsibility for the large community of 47 nuns and 13 novices. The nuns were Augustinian canonesses and they enjoyed many freedoms, perhaps far more than they would have as women in the secular world. In 1187, Herrad built a large hospital on the convent grounds and served as the hospital's chief physician until her death in 1195.

Herrad wrote most of *Hortus Deliciarum* in the years between 1160 and 1170, although she continued to add to it until 1190. In 324 folio–size parchment pages, it was an encyclopedia of astronomy, philosophy, natural history, geography, and medicinal botany, as well as religion and history, agriculture, astrology, and meteorology. The technical terms were given in both German and Latin, and it was used as a text for teaching Latin to the nuns. *Hortus Deliciarum* was based primarily on Biblical sources and on Herrad's own experience and knowledge; however she also quoted liberally from secular writers.

Like her contemporary, **Hildegard of Bingen**, Herrad was interested in the relationship between the universe or macrocosm and the human body, the microcosm. The influence of the heavenly bodies on each component of the human body was a central tenant of medieval science. Herrad also explained the inversion of climates in the northern and southern hemispheres, dividing the world into two frigid, two temperate, and two tropical zones. "Computus" tables, which were used to determine the dates of religious festivals, were very important in the middle ages, and Herrad's was considered one of the best. She calculated the dates for Easter and the day of the week for Christmas for 532 years, from 1175 to 1706.

Herrad drew the illustrations for *Hortus Deliciarum* herself, although assistants may have done the coloring. The work was considered to be of great artistic value. Although the only manuscript copy was destroyed in the Franco–Prussian War in 1870, an early nineteenth–century scholar had copied large portions of it and traced the illustrations.

Herrad was one of the last of the powerful, scholarly, medieval abbesses, as increasingly, convents came under the control of male abbots.

SELECTED WRITINGS BY HERRAD:

Books

(Rosalie Green, ed.) *Hortus Deliciarum*. London: Warburg Institute, University of London, 1979.

FURTHER READING

Books

Alic, Margaret. *Hypatia's Heritage: A History of Women in Science from Antiquity through the Nineteenth Century*. Boston: Beacon Press,1986.

Eckenstein, Lina. *Women under Monasticism*. 1896. Reprint, New York: Russell and Russell, 1963.

Singer, Charles. *From Magic to Science: Essays on the Scientific Twilight*. New York: Dover, 1958.

Sketch by Margaret Alic

Caroline Lucretia Herschel
1750–1848
German-born English astronomer

Although mostly known for assisting her famous brother William Herschel, Caroline Herschel was a skilled astronomer in her own right who made significant astronomical discoveries. As her brother's assistant, she was the first woman in England honored with a government position. Herschel discovered the Andromeda and Cetus nebulae and was also the first woman to discover a comet. Along with **Mary Somerville**, she was the first woman to be awarded an honorary membership in the Royal Society.

Caroline Lucretia Herschel was born in Hanover, Germany in 1750. Her early life was marked by a lack of love and encouragement from her mother whose main focus was housekeeping duties. Her father, Isaac Herschel, a musician in the Hanoverian Guard, wanted all of his six children educated, but his wife refused to allow it for their two daughters. However, her father did include her in intellectual conversations with her brothers, as well as music instruction. Her father also introduced her to astronomy, showing her comets and teaching her the constellations. At age 17, her father died as did her hopes for an education. Under the control of her mother and her brother Jacob, she was nothing more than a servant.

Leaves Home to Live With William

Herschel led a harsh life until her brother William, who was 11 years her senior, heard about her plight from another brother and invited her to live with him in Bath, England, where he was an orchestra leader. Their mother refused to let her go until William promised to provide funds for her mother to retain a maid. In August 1772, Herschel left for England. Over the next five years, her horizons expanded. A neighbor taught her cooking, marketing, and English. William encouraged his sister to be independent and enroll in voice lessons and the harpsichord. She soon became an integral part of William's musical performances at small gatherings. He also used their meal times to teach Herschel mathematics.

Herschel longed to be self–supporting and by the age 27 was in demand as a soloist for oratorios. But William was becoming increasingly interested in astronomy and often asked for her help. Herschel did everything from

Caroline Herschel (The Library of Congress. Reproduced by permission.)

grinding and polishing mirrors to copying his astronomy catalogs, tables, and papers. Herschel was not happy to be taken away from her music to perform these tasks, but would do anything to help her brother.

Makes Celestial Discoveries

In 1781, William discovered Uranus, which he called "Georgium Sidus," after King George III. This discovery assured him recognition in British scientific circles as well as the court. He was appointed to the position of court astronomer and was knighted. The appointment gave William a modest stipend that allowed him to give up music and devote himself to astronomy. This also meant Caroline had to give up singing and move with her brother to another house that would accommodate his telescopes.

Herschel was a reluctant scientist, but eventually grew to love astronomy. Without music she focused on providing her brother with the support he needed. She systematically collected data and trained herself in geometry, learned formulas and logarithmic tables, and gained an understanding of the relationship of sidereal time (time measured by means of the stars) to solar time. Her record–keeping was meticulous and systematic. The numerical calculations and reductions, which saved her brother precious time, were all done without error, and the volume of her work was enormous.

When Herschel was not engaged in tasks for her brother, she too searched the night skies using a small Newtonian reflector telescope. But it was only when William was away that Herschel was able to do her own work. To her credit, in early 1783, Herschel discovered the Andromeda and Cetus nebulae, and by year's end, had discovered an additional 14 nebulae to those already catalogued. As a reward, William presented her with a new Newtonian sweeper of 27 inches, with a focal length of 30. Herschel was also the first woman to discover a comet, and between 1789 and 1797 she had discovered another seven comets. Her discoveries made her famous in the astronomical community and brought her the attention of the King, who gave her a salary of 50 pounds per year to officially recognize her as William's assistant. Herschel's appointment by the Court made her the first female in England honored with a government position and was the first money she ever earned on her own.

Calculations and Cataloguing

Herschel calculated and catalogued nearly 2,500 nebulae. She also undertook the task of reorganizing John Flamsteed's *British Catalogue*, which listed nearly 3,000 stars. Herschel's listings were divided into one–degree zones in order for William to use a more systematic method of searching the skies.

Her brother married in 1788, causing her concern about having to share his attention and move to her own quarters. But her concerns were without merit, as she was warmly and graciously accepted by her new sister–in–law. The two women became friends and Lady Herschel was a great support to her. The marriage turned out to be productive for Herschel, who was free from domestic duties to pursue astronomy on her own.

On August 25, 1822, William died, leaving Herschel without support. She decided to returned to Hanover after his death, thinking she would not want to be in England without him. She regretted this decision, since Germany was no longer her home and there was less interest in astronomy there. However, she continued with her work and in 1825, at the age of 75, she finished the extensive *A Catologue of the Nebulae which have been observed by William Herschel in a Series of Sweeps*, which recorded the position of about 2,500 nebulae. For this work the Royal Astronomical Society awarded Herschel a gold medal. At age 85, she was made an honorary member of the Royal Astronomical Society and was similarly honored by the Royal Irish Academy. On her 96th birthday, she was awarded the Gold Medal of Science by the King of Prussia. Although she was finally being given her long overdue recognition, a lifetime of undervaluing her skills and complete devotion to her brother did not allow her to enjoy these awards. Herschel died on January 9, 1848. Her work helped to open the field of astronomy to other women in the nineteenth century and beyond.

FURTHER READING

Books

Alic, Margaret. *Hypatia's Heritage: A History of Women in Science from Antiquity through the Nineteenth Century.* Boston: Beacon Press, 1986.

Hoskin, Michael A. "Caroline Herschel," in *Dictionary of Scientific Biography.* Volume VI. Edited by Charles Coulston Gillispie. New York: Charles Scribners' Sons, 1981, pp. 322–23.

Osen, Lynn M. "Caroline Herschel." *Women in Mathematics.* Cambridge: MIT Press, 1974.

Schweighauser, Charles A., ed. *Astronomy from A to Z: A Dictionary of Celestial Objects and Ideas.* Springfield, IL: Sangamon State University, 1991.

Other

Nysewander, Melissa. "Caroline Herschel." *Biographies of Women Mathematicians.* June 1997. http://www/scottlan.edu/lriddle/women/chronol.htm (July 21, 1997).

Sketch by Corrine Johnson

Elisabetha Koopman Hevelius
1647–1693
Polish astronomer

Elisabetha Hevelius, the wife of the famous Polish astronomer Johannes Hevelius, collaborated with her husband on astronomical observations for many years, and wrote up and published their results after his death.

Elisabetha Koopman (or Korpmann) Hevelius was born in 1647, the daughter of a wealthy merchant. Little is known about her background, other than that she was well educated and always had been very interested in astronomy. At age 16, she married Johannes Hevelius, a 52–year old–widower. He was a wealthy brewer and a well–known amateur astronomer in Danzig. Around this time, there was a great deal of public interest in astronomy, and a surprising number of women were becoming observational astronomers.

At the time of their marriage, Hevelius's husband was compiling a new star catalogue. He also was revising the Rudolphine Tables of planetary motion, based on the work of Johannes Kepler, by making new observations from the observatory he had built in 1640, across the roofs of three adjacent houses. However his first three assistants had died and his household servants had proved unsatisfactory as observational astronomers; so he enlisted the help of his new wife. She proved to be an accurate and steadfast observer. She also helped to run the family brewery, as well as raise their three daughters. In 1679, the English astronomer Edmond Halley, who predicted the return of Halley's comet, observed with Hevelius when he visited her in Danzig.

The Heveliuses worked together for over 20 years, and it is impossible to separate their individual contributions to astronomy. In 1679, a great fire swept through Danzig, destroying the observatory, all of their data, and most of the printed copies of her husband's *Machinae Coelestis.* Two engravings in that work showed Hevelius and her husband observing with a large brass sextant and a third showed her observing with a telescope.

After her husband's death in 1687, Hevelius carried on their work alone, publishing his *Firmamentum Sobieskanum sive Uranographie.* She wrote a preface for this work, and she dedicated it to John Sobieski, King of Poland. She also named a constellation after the king. In 1690, Elisabetha Hevelius edited and published the Heveliuses' joint work, *Prodromus Astronomiae,* a catalogue of the positions of 1,888 stars, under her husband's name. It was the largest and the last star catalogue ever compiled without the use of a telescope. Hevelius died three years later, in 1693.

SELECTED WRITINGS BY HEVELIUS:

Books

(Editor) *Firmamentum Sobiescianum sive Uranographie,* by Johannes Hevelius. Danzig, 1687.

(With Johannes Hevelius) *Prodromus Astronomiae.* Danzig, 1690.

FURTHER READING

Books

Schiebinger, Londa. *The Mind Has No Sex? Women in the Origins of Modern Science.* Cambridge: Harvard University Press, 1989.

Periodicals

Davis, Herman S. "Women Astronomers (400 A.D.–1750)." *Popular Astronomy* 6 (1898): 129–38.

Sketch by Margaret Alic

Jacqueline N. Hewitt
1958–
American astrophysicist

Jacqueline Hewitt, a professor of physics at Massachusetts Institute of Technology (MIT), has made historic contributions to the study of gravitational lensing. Hewitt was the first to discover what Einstein predicted in 1936—

ring–shaped objects produced by distant galaxies. Einstein rings are an example of gravitational lensing, in which electromagnetic radiation (including light) is affected by its passage through a gravitational field, similar to the way light is lensed as it passes through glass. In an Einstein ring, the way the radiation is distributed is very symmetrical, producing a striking ring image. Einstein rings are beneficial as a means of measuring the size of galaxies and the volume and apportionment of dark matter in the universe. Hewitt's discovery of the Einstein rings may provide a key to understanding the universe.

Hewitt was born on September 4, 1958, in Washington, D.C. Her father, Warren E. Hewitt, retired from the State Department, where he was employed as an international lawyer. Her mother, Trudy G. (Graedel) Hewitt was a homemaker through Jacqueline's childhood. Math was Hewitt's favorite subject as a child, but she did not decide to become a scientist until later in life. She majored in economics at Bryn Mawr and graduated magna cum laude in 1980. An astronomy course her sophomore year sparked her interest in science, and she decided to continue her education at the Massachusetts Institute of Technology in Cambridge, Massachusetts. She earned a Ph.D. in physics in 1986. "Astronomy is mostly physics, so that made me want to study physics, which I thoroughly enjoyed," Hewitt explained in a November 11, 1997, letter to contributor Pamela Proffitt. While completing her Ph.D., Hewitt worked as a research assistant in the Department of Physics at MIT. That same year Hewitt married Robert P. Redwine, a nuclear physicist. They have two children, Keith, born in 1988, and Jonathan, born in 1993.

Hewitt's postdoctoral appointment was with the Very Long Baseline Interferometry (VLBI) at MIT from 1986 to 1988. After her postdoctoral appointment, until 1989, Hewitt was a research staff member in the Department of Astrophysical Sciences at Princeton, New Jersey. In 1989 she returned to MIT as an assistant professor to teach physics and was promoted to associate professor of physics at MIT in 1994. Hewitt believes there is a close interaction between teaching and research. "I often use examples of my research in my teaching," she explained in her 1997 letter, "and the teaching often will give me ideas for research and keeps me from forgetting the underlying physics!" In addition to her teaching duties, Hewitt is a principal investigator for the Radio Astronomy Group of the Research Laboratory of Electronics at MIT.

Discovers Einstein Rings

Hewitt began studying the stars while attending MIT. Frank Ockenfels, writing for *Esquire* magazine, quoted Hewitt as saying that, "To discover something there, she felt, would be like coming upon a new continent on earth." With MIT professor, Bernard F. Burke, Hewitt began gathering data using the Very Large Array radio telescope near Socorro, New Mexico. She decided to use a radio telescope instead of an optical one because optical images of gravitational lenses are very faint. The gravitational lenses emit large amounts of energy at radio wave lengths and are easier to detect. Hewitt recorded about four thousand radio images and hoped these would provide her with a database of information that might contain gravitational lenses.

In the fall of 1986, while at her postdoctoral appointment with the Very Long Baseline Interferometry group at MIT's Haystack Observatory, Hewitt was looking at the data she had collected at the VLA in New Mexico when saw a ring on her computer screen. *Discover* magazine, in the July 1988 issue, described the object as "a faint, glowing, elliptical ring about [two] arc seconds across at its widest (the full moon spans about 1,800 arc seconds), accompanied by two bright spots." The objects were found in the constellation Leo.

In her 1997 letter Hewitt said that she was " . . . doing a deliberate search for gravitational lenses with the VLA, but wasn't expecting to find the Einstein ring because we expected them to be very rare. In fact, it is not quite as rare as we thought it would be. It is actually quite reasonable to expect that several Einstein rings would be found with the VLA, as they have been now." The discovery of the Einstein ring could answer questions regarding the size of the universe and the ultimate fate of the universe, whether it will keep on expanding or whether it will collapse in on itself.

Award–winning Physicist

Hewitt has found her many awards an important source of encouragement when her career, combined with raising two children, was at times overwhelming. Of all her awards, Hewitt cites the David and Lucile Packard Fellowship in 1990 as the one that gave her the confidence and financial support to begin her work. In addition to several other awards, Hewitt was elected by faculty colleagues from MIT to receive the 1995–1996 Harold E. Edgerton Award for her contributions to the study of gravitational lenses. In 1995, Hewitt was awarded the Maria Goeppert–Mayer Award for her contribution in radio astronomy.

On the subject of being a woman in physics, Hewitt is happy to report that her colleagues have been supportive and nondiscriminating. However, she has found it particularly difficult to balance her scientific career and raising children within the structure of the traditional university academic system. Hewitt hopes there will be substantial societal changes that will make it easier for women who want a family as well as a career in science.

SELECTED WRITINGS BY HEWITT:

Books

(With J.M. Moran) *Gravitational Lenses: Proceedings of a Conference Held at the Massachusetts Institute of Technology, Cambridge, Massachusetts, in Honour of Bernard F. Burke's 60th Birthday, June 20, 1988.* Springer–Verlag, 1989.

Periodicals

(With C. B. Moore) "15 GHz Monitoring of the Gravitational Lens MG 0410+0534." *The Astrophysical Journal* (November 1997).

(With C.A. Katz and C.B. Moore) "Multifrequency Radio Observations of the Gravitional Lens System MG 0414+0534." *The Astrophysical Journal* (February 1, 1997).

(With D.B. Haarsma, J. Lehár, and B. F. Burke) "The 6 cm Light Curves of B0957+561, 1979–1994: New Features and Implications for the Time Delay." *The Astrophysical Journal* (April 10, 1997).

(With E.L. Turner, D.P. Schnieder, B. F. Burke, G. I. Langston, and C. R. Lawrence) "Unusual Radio Source MG1131+0456: a Possible Einstein Ring." *Nature* (June 9, 1988).

FURTHER READING

Books

Kayser, R., T. and L. Nieser Schramm, eds. *Gravitational Lenses, Proceedings of a Conference Held in Hamburg, Germany 9–13 September 1991.* Berlin; New York: Springer–Verlag, 1992.

Quasars and Gravitational Lenses: Proceedings of the 24th Liege International Astrophysical Colloquium, June 21–24, 1983. Liege, Belgium: Universitåe de Liáege, Institut d'Astrophysique, 1983.

Mellier, Y., B. Fort, and G. Soucail, eds. *Gravitational Lensing (Lecture Notes in Physics, Vol. 360).* Berlin; New York: Springer–Verlag, 1990.

Periodicals

Einstein, Albert. "Lens–like Action of a Star by the Deviation of Light in the Gravitational Field." *Science* 84 (1936): 506.

"Finding Einstein's Ring." *Discover* 9 (July 1988): 15.

Ockenfels, Frank. "Jacqueline Hewitt." *Esquire* (December 1988): 102.

Verschuur, Gerrit L. "A New 'Yardstick' for the Universe." *Astronomy.* 16 (November 1988): 60–3.

Waldrop, M. Mitchell. "Einstein's Impossible Ring: Found." *Science* 240 (June 24, 1988): 1733.

Other

"Hewitt wins 1995 Edgerton award." http://rleweb.mit.edu/fiscal/news/hewitt.html. October 6, 1997.

"Maria Goeppert–Mayer Award." http://hq.aps.org/praw/mgm/descrip.html. October 11, 1997.

"MIT Radio Astronomy Group Publications." http://space.mit.edu/RADIO/papers.html. October 6, 1997.

Proffitt, Pamela, letter from Jacqueline Hewitt, October 1997.

"1995 MGM Prize Recipient." http://www.aps.org/praw/mgm/95winner.html. October 10, 1997.

Web site of The Radio Astronomy Group of the Research Laboratory of Electronics: http://rleweb.mit.edu

Sketch by Monica Stevens and Pamela Proffitt

Hope Hibbard
1893–1988
American zoologist

As a scientist, Hope Hibbard focused on cell biology (cytology), specifically studying cytoplasmic inclusions and cell structures. Her other primary interests where marine biology and invertebrate animals. Though Hibbard was recognized by her peers for her research, she was also respected for her writing and teaching, especially at the school where she spent the bulk of her career, Oberlin College in Ohio.

Hibbard was born in Altoona, Pennsylvania, on December 18, 1893, the daughter of Herbert Wade Hibbard, a professor of mechanical engineering, and his wife Mary Scofield. She earned her A.B. from the University of Missouri in 1916. Hibbard did her graduate work in zoology at Bryn Mawr College, where she earned her A.M. in 1918, and her Ph.D. in 1921. While earning her Ph.D., Hibbard worked as a demonstrator in the biology department for a year, 1919–20. Her dissertation, "Cytoplasmic Inclusions in the Egg of Echinarachnuius Parma," concerned sea urchin eggs and their fertilization.

After completing her graduate work, Hibbard worked as an associate professor at Elmira College for four years from 1921–25. In 1925 Hibbard went to the University of Paris (the Sorbonne) where she did post–graduate work on the Sarah Berliner fellowship of the American Association of University Women. After the year–long fellowship ended, she stayed on in Paris, working at the Sorbonne as a preparateur in a comparative anatomy techniques laboratory. In 1927 Hibbard earned another year–long fellowship through the International Education Board. The following year, 1928, she was awarded her D.es.Sc. in zoology from the Sorbonne.

Hibbard began teaching zoology at Oberlin College in 1928, and through the next 30 or so years, she worked through the ranks: assistant professor, 1928–30; associate professor, 1930–33; and full professor in 1933. In 1952 she was named the Adelia A. Field Johnston Professor of Biology. She was appointed chair of zoology department the following year, 1953, and held the post for four years, until 1957. Hibbard retired in 1961, earning an emeritus professorship.

Hibbard belonged to several scientific societies, including the American Society of Zoologists, American

Association for the Advancement of Science, and the American Society of Naturalists. She was especially active in the American Association of University Women, which had awarded her the fellowship that allowed her to go to Paris. She was named an honorary life member of this organization in 1987. Hibbard died a year later, in 1988.

FURTHER READING

Books

Bailey, Martha J. "Hibbard, Hope." *American Women in Science: A Biographical Dictionary*. Denver: ABC–CLIO, 1994, p. 161.

Sketch by Annette Petrusso

Beatrice Hicks (The Library of Congress. Reproduced by permission.)

Beatrice Hicks
1919–1979
American engineer

Beatrice Hicks built a distinguished career in the field of engineering at a time when women engineers were a rarity. She co–founded and served as the first president of the Society of Women Engineers (SWE), and held the presidency of the Newark Controls Co. from 1955 until her death in 1979. Hicks received the SWE's Achievement Award, its highest honor, in 1963, and was the first woman awarded an honorary doctorate of engineering by the Rensselaer Polytechnic Institute.

Hicks was born January 2, 1919, in Orange, New Jersey, to William and Florence (Neben) Hicks. She decided to become an engineer at age 13 when her father, an engineer and founder of the Newark Controls Company in Bloomfield, New Jersey, took her to the Empire State Building and the George Washington Bridge and explained that the structures had been designed by engineers. She received a bachelor of science degree in chemical engineering from Newark College of Engineering in 1939 and studied electrical engineering from 1939 to 1943.

Despite her engineering degree, when Hicks joined the staff of Western Electric in 1942, she was hired as a technician. However, her supervisor successfully lobbied for a salary increase and the title of engineer for her; she remained at Western Electric for three years.

Named Vice President of Engineering Firm

In 1945, Hicks joined her father's firm, Newark Controls Co., as chief engineer, and a year later added the role of vice president to her responsibilities. She also decided to further her education, earning a master of science degree in physics from Stevens Institute of Technology in 1949, the year after her marriage to engineer Rodney Chipp. In 1955, Hicks became president of Newark Controls. Hicks' work at Newark Controls focused on the effects of the environment on pressure switches, and she invented the gas density switch, an integral part of systems using artificial atmospheres.

Hicks co–founded the Society of Women Engineers (SWE) and was elected its first president in 1950. She remained active in the SWE throughout her career, serving as a board member from 1952 to 1953 and as a trustee from 1960 to 1964. She also served as director of the First International Conference of Women Engineers and Scientists, organized by the SWE and held in New York in 1964. *Mademoiselle* magazine named Hicks its 1952 "Woman of the Year in Business." She was a U.S. delegate to the Tenth International Management Congress in Sao Paulo, Brazil, in 1954, and to the Eleventh International Management Congress in Paris three years later, and was selected with her husband to participate in Project Ambassador, a goodwill and fact–finding tour of South America sponsored by the National Society of Professional Engineers in 1959. Hicks received the SWE's highest honor, the Achievement Award, in 1963, "in recognition of her significant contributions to the theoretical study and analysis of sensing devises under extreme environmental conditions, and her substantial achievements in international technical understanding, professional guidance, and engineering education." In 1965

Hicks became the first woman named an honorary doctor of engineering by Rensselaer Polytechnic Institute.

FURTHER READING

Periodicals

"Beatrice Hicks, Society's First President, Dies." *Society of Women Engineers Newsletter* (November/December, 1979): 5.

Sketch by Karen Withem

Hildegard of Bingen
1098–1179
German natural philosopher

Hildegard of Bingen, a scholarly and influential abbess, was one of the most important scientists of the twelfth century. She was the earliest woman scientist whose major works have survived intact. Her writings helped to spread the natural philosophy of the ancient Greeks, at a time when Europe was just emerging from the Dark Ages, and she also was responsible for a number of original scientific ideas. She wrote important treatises on natural history and medicine, as well as religious and mystical works which included her cosmology, her theory of the natural order of the universe. In addition, she was a prolific composer of religious music. Many of her poems and hymns have been translated and recorded and are considered to be among the finest of medieval music, as well as the earliest surviving music known to be composed by a woman.

Hildegard was born in 1098 at her family's estate on the Nahe River, the tenth child of wealthy gentry, Hildebert and Matilda. As was common for younger daughters from noble families, at the age of eight Hildegard was sent to live in her relative Jutta's small cloistered community of women within the Benedictine monastery of Disibodenberg. Her early education, under Jutta's direction, focused on Latin, the Scriptures, and music. As a teenager, she formally became a Benedictine nun. Eventually, her fields of study broadened to include natural history, German folk medicine, and ancient Greek cosmologies that had been translated into Latin and reached the convents and monasteries of Germany.

From childhood on, Hildegard endured periods of serious illness. Beginning at the age of 15, she also apparently experienced intense hallucinatory visions. Scholars have attributed these visions to epilepsy, migraine headaches, or similar disorders. Alternatively, she may have attained altered states of consciousness via the meditative chanting of the Benedictine liturgy. Despite her infirmities, Hildegard became abbess of the Disibodenberg convent in 1136, following Jutta's death.

Hildegard of Bingen (The Granger Collection, New York. Reproduced by permission.)

Records Visions

Most twelfth-century scholars, both women and men, were monastics and therefore twelfth–century science was inseparable from theology. Thus, spiritual visions were a common device for the presentation of scientific as well as theological ideas. Women, in particular, found that their writings were better received if they were presented as visions sent by God. In 1141, Hildegard began to write her first and most influential book of visions, *Liber Scivias*. Although Hildegard proclaimed herself to be an uneducated woman who was simply recording God's words, *Scivias* included her initial scientific cosmology. Using spiritual allegory, Hildegard attempted to present coherent explanations of the physical universe. Following the Greeks, she portrayed the earth as a sphere made up of the four elements and surrounded by layers of atmosphere and water. But the details of her cosmology were unique. For example, the outer shells of her universe were egg–shaped. The *purus aether* contained the fixed stars, moon and inner planets; the inner fire was the source of lightening and hail; and the outer fire encompassed the sun and the outer planets. Hildegard proposed that the winds of each shell were responsible for the movements of the heavenly bodies and for seasonal changes on earth. In addition to her cosmology, *Scivias* included interesting biological concepts. Hildegard believed that humans developed from a seed and inherited various qualities as well as physical form from their parents. *Scivias* also included fourteen liturgical songs and a new type of morality play designed to be sung. *Scivias* was first printed in Paris in 1513.

Establishes Independent Convent

At the Council of Trier in 1147, the Archbishop of Mainz presented the first two sections of *Scivias* to Pope Eugenius III and they were declared to be authentic prophecies. Hildegard was officially encouraged to continue her writing. This pronouncement brought Hildegard her first fame and a measure of influence. Eventually she was to earn the epithet "Sibil of the Rhine." Since the rapid growth of her convent, the increase in pilgrims, and her many responsibilities interfered with her scholarly work, Hildegard had a vision instructing her to establish a new independent convent. The monks of Disibodenberg opposed the move, but after a protracted struggle, Hildegard's political influence prevailed. In 1150, she established a new convent on Mount St. Rupert near the major medieval town of Bingen, taking with her about 18 young nuns and the monk Volmar, her secretary and scribe.

As Hildegard's fame and prestige increased, the new convent also expanded rapidly. She became famous as a healer with miraculous powers. She also carried on a voluminous correspondence, advising and prophesying for heads of state and high church officials. Hildegard traveled widely after about 1155, teaching medicine and theology, inciting religious fervor and encouraging the persecution of sects she considered heretical.

Writes Natural History and Medical Encyclopedias

Over the next ten years, Hildegard worked on her natural history encyclopedia, *Liber Simplicis Medicinae* or *Liber Subtilitatum Diversarum Naturarum Creaturarum*. It was renamed *Physica* when it was edited for publication in 1533. This was a straightforward work, written in the style of other medieval natural history texts, and was the most scientific of her writings. It included descriptions of a large number of plants and animals, as well as stones and metals, with German as well as Latin terms, and medical applications. Hildegard always suggested small dosages of medicines—simple remedies for the poor and expensive compound medicines for the wealthy. A very popular work, *Physica* became a medical school text and Hildegard was considered to be the first important German medical writer.

Hildegard's second book of visions, *Liber Vitae Meritorum*, was begun in 1158 and finished in 1162. She then began work on her mature cosmology, *Liber Divinorum Operum Simplicis Hominis*. In this work, completed in 1170, she attempted to bring her cosmology into line with the accepted scientific theories of the time, abandoning her egg–shaped universe for a universe made up of concentric spheres, with the outer spheres of water, air and fire being of equal width. Once again, however, Hildegard's scheme was unique in its details. She was particularly interested in the relationship between the universe or macrocosm and the human body, the microcosm. This was a central paradigm, a theoretical and philisophical framework, of medieval science and Hildegard investigated the ways in which the heavenly bodies influenced each component of the human body. As in *Scivias*, Hildegard included detailed explanatory illustrations, probably produced by assistants working under her supervision. Hildegard herself often was pictured in the corner of the illustrations, recording the visions as they came from God.

The last of Hildegard's scientific works, *Liber Compositae Medicinae* or *Causea et Curae*, was written in the didactic, or instructional, style of *Physica*. In it, she describes the relationships between the macrocosm and specific diseases of the microcosm, the human body, and prescribed medicinal remedies. She was the first medical writer to stress the importance of boiling drinking water. Although she practiced a kind of horoscope, predicting people's nature based on which day of the lunar month they were conceived, since she used the day of conception rather than the day of birth, she could not be accused of promoting astrology; nor could she be proved wrong.

Hildegard died in 1179 at the age of 81. She was added to the Roman Martyrology and investigated for sainthood. Although the Church never canonized her, she often is referred to as St. Hildegard. Two of her assistants, the Benedictine monks Godefrid and Theodor, wrote her biography between 1180 and 1191.

Hildegard's writings were well known during her lifetime and later were printed and widely distributed. Her scientific work was influential well into the Renaissance. In the late twentieth century, both her scholarly treatises and her music have been rediscovered and are enjoying a renewed popularity.

SELECTED WRITINGS BY HILDEGARD OF BINGEN:

Books

Illuminations of Hildegard of Bingen. Edited by Michael Fox. Sante Fe: Bear and Co., 1985.

Hildegard von Bingen's Mystical Visions: Translated from Scivias. Translated by Bruce Hozeski. Santa Fe: Bear and Co., 1995.

The Book of the Rewards of Life (Liber Vitae Meritorum). Translated by Bruce W. Hozeski. New York: Oxford University Press, 1997.

The Letters of Hildegard of Bingen. 2 vols. Edited and translated by Joseph L. Baird and Radd K. Ehrman. New York: Oxford University Press, 1998.

Symphonia: A Critical Edition of the "Symphonia Armonie Celestium Revelationum" (Symphony of the Harmony of the Celestial Revelations). 2nd ed. Translated and commentary by Barbara Newman. Ithaca: Cornell University Press, 1998.

FURTHER READING

Books

Alic, Margaret. *Hypatia's Heritage: A History of Women in Science from Antiquity through the Nineteenth Century*. Boston: Beacon Press,1986.

Flanagan, Sabina. *Hildegard of Bingen, 1098–1179: A Visionary Life*. New York: Routledge, 1998.

Lachman, Barbara. *The Journal of Hildegard of Bingen: Inspired by a Year in the Life of the Twelfth–Century Mystic*. New York: Bell Tower, 1995.

Pagel, Walter. "Hildegard of Bingen." In *Dictionary of Scientific Biography*. Vol. 6. Edited by Charles C. Gillespie. New York: Scribner, 1972.

Singer, Charles. *From Magic to Science: Essays on the Scientific Twilight*. New York: Dover, 1958.

Steele, Francesca Maria. *The Life and Visions of St. Hildegarde*. London: Heath, Cranton and Ousely, 1914.

Thorndike, Lynn. *A History of Magic and Experimental Science*. Vol. 2. New York: Columbia University Press, 1923.

Sketch by Margaret Alic

Gladys Lounsbury Hobby (The Library of Congress. Reproduced by permission.)

Gladys Lounsbury Hobby
1910–1993
American microbiologist and bacteriologist

Gladys Lounsbury Hobby was one of less than a handful of women who were part of the extensive network which brought penicillin from the laboratory to the clinic. Discovered by Sir Alexander Fleming in 1928, penicillin was one of the first antibiotics, medicines that could combat infections. In her book *Penicillin: Meeting the Challenge,* Hobby detailed the efforts in the early 1940s to discover a way to manufacture large amounts of penicillin, which would greatly aid in the treating of war wounded. In addition to her work as a microbiologist, Hobby wrote many articles and was also a teacher.

Hobby was born November 19, 1910, in New York City. She received her bachelor of arts degree from Vassar College in 1931; she then attended Columbia University, receiving her master's degree in 1932 and her doctorate in bacteriology three years later. From 1934 to 1943, she worked on perfecting penicillin specifically for several infectious diseases as part of a research team at the Columbia Medical School, while also being professionally involved at Presbyterian Hospital in New York City. In 1944, Hobby went to work for Pfizer Pharmaceuticals in New York, where she researched streptomycin and other antibiotics, discovering how antimicrobial drugs worked. In 1959, Hobby became chief of research at the Veteran's Administration Hospital in East Orange, New Jersey, where she worked on chronic infectious diseases. Before retiring in 1977, she was assistant research clinical professor in public health at Cornell Medical College.

Retirement for Hobby meant continuing her work. Hobby became a freelance science writer and a consultant. It was during this time that she penned her book, *Penicillin: Meeting the Challenge,* about the drug's odyssey from the laboratory to the hands of the clinician. Hobby, having taken meticulous notes, detailed each researcher's contribution to producing a safe penicillin on a large scale basis. She also authored more than 200 articles and was the founder and editor of the journal *Antimicrobial Agents and Chemotherapy.*

Hobby was a member of several professional organizations, including the American Association for the Advancement of Science, the American Academy of Microbiology, and the American Society of Microbiology. Hobby died suddenly of a heart attack on July 4, 1993, at her home in a retirement community in Pennsylvania.

SELECTED WRITINGS BY HOBBY:

Books

Penicillin: Meeting the Challenge. Yale University Press, 1985.

FURTHER READING

Periodicals

Saxon, Wolfgang. "Gladys Hobby, 82, Pioneer in Bringing Penicillin to Public." *New York Times* (July 9, 1993)

Sketch by Denise Adams Arnold

Dorothy Crowfoot Hodgkin
1910–
Egyptian-born English chemist and crystallographer

Dorothy Crowfoot Hodgkin employed the technique of x–ray crystallography to determine the molecular structures of several large biochemical molecules. When she received the 1964 Nobel Prize in chemistry for her accomplishments, the committee cited her contribution to the determination of the structure of both penicillin and vitamin B_{12}.

Dorothy Crowfoot Hodgkin (Source unknown.)

Hodgkin was born in Egypt on May 12, 1910 to John and Grace (Hood) Crowfoot. She was the first of four daughters. Her mother, although not formally educated beyond finishing school, was an expert on Coptic textiles, and an excellent amateur botanist and nature artist. Hodgkin's father, a British archaeologist and scholar, worked for the Ministry of Education in Cairo at the time of her birth, and her family life was always characterized by world travel. When World War I broke out, Hodgkin and two younger sisters were sent to England for safety, where they were raised for a few years by a nanny and their paternal grandmother. Because of the war, their mother was unable to return to them until 1918, and at that time brought their new baby sister with her. Hodgkin's parents moved around the globe as her father's government career unfolded, and she saw them when they returned to Britain for only a few months every year. Occasionally during her youth she traveled to visit them in such far–flung places as Khartoum in the Sudan, and Palestine.

Hodgkin's interest in chemistry and crystals began early in her youth, and she was encouraged both by her parents as well as by their scientific acquaintances. While still a child, Hodgkin was influenced by a book that described how to grow crystals of alum and copper sulfate and on x rays and crystals. Her parents then introduced her to the soil chemist A. F. Joseph and his colleagues, who gave her a tour of their laboratory and showed her how to pan for gold. Joseph later gave her a box of reagents and minerals which allowed her to set up a home laboratory. Hodgkin was initially educated at home and in a succession of small private schools, but at age eleven began attending the Sir John Leman School in Beccles, England, from which she graduated in 1928. After a period of intensive tutoring to prepare her for the entrance examinations, Hodgkin entered Somerville College for women at Oxford University. Her aunt, Dorothy Hood, paid the tuition to Oxford, and helped to support her financially. For a time, Hodgkin considered specializing in archaeology, but eventually settled on chemistry and crystallography.

Crystallography was a fledgling science at the time Hodgkin began, a combination of mathematics, physics, and chemistry. Max von Laue, William Henry Bragg, and William Lawrence Bragg had essentially invented it in the early decades of the century (they had won Nobel Prizes in 1914 and 1915, respectively) when they discovered that the atoms in a crystal deflected x rays. The deflected x rays interacted or interfered with each other. If they *constructively* interfered with each other, a bright spot could be captured on photographic film. If they *destructively* interfered with each other, the brightness was cancelled. The pattern of the x–ray spots—*diffraction pattern* —bore a mathematical relationship to the positions of individual atoms in the crystal. Thus, by shining X rays through a crystal, capturing the pattern on film, and doing mathematical calculations on the distances and relative positions of the spots, the molecular structure of almost any crystalline material could theoretically be worked out. The more complicated the structure, however, the more elaborate and arduous the calculations. Techniques for the practical application of crystallography were few, and organic chemists accustomed to chemical methods of determining structure regarded it as a black art.

After she graduated from Oxford in 1932, Hodgkin's old friend A. F. Joseph steered her toward Cambridge University and the crystallographic work of J. D. Bernal. Bernal already had a reputation in the field, and researchers from many countries sent him crystals for analysis. Hodgkin's first job was as Bernal's assistant. Under his guidance, with the wealth of materials in his laboratory, the young student began demonstrating her particular talent for x–ray studies of large molecules such as sterols and vitamins. In 1934, Bernal took the first x–ray photograph of a protein crystal, pepsin, and Hodgkin did the subsequent analysis to obtain information about its molecular weight and structure. Proteins are much larger and more complicated than other biological molecules because they are polymers—long chains of repeating units—and they exercise their biochemical functions by folding over on themselves and assuming specific three–dimensional shapes. This was not well understood at the time, however, so Hodgkin's results began a new era; crystallography could establish not only the structural layout of atoms in a molecule, even a huge one, but also the overall molecular shape which contributed to biological activity.

Research and Recognition at Oxford

In 1934, Hodgkin returned to Oxford as a teacher at Somerville College, continuing her doctoral work on sterols at the same time. (She obtained her doctorate in 1937). It was a difficult decision to move from Cambridge, but she needed the income and jobs were scarce. Somerville's crystallography and laboratory facilities were extremely primitive; one of the features of her lab at Oxford was a rickety circular staircase that she needed to climb several times a day to reach the only window with sufficient light for her polarizing microscope. This was made all the more difficult because Hodgkin suffered most of her adult life from a severe case of rheumatoid arthritis, which didn't respond well to treatment and badly crippled her hands and feet. Additionally, Oxford officially barred her from research meetings of the faculty chemistry club because she was a woman, a far cry from the intellectual comradery and support she had encountered in Bernal's laboratory. Fortunately, her talent and quiet perseverance quickly won over first the students and then the faculty members at Oxford. Sir Robert Robinson helped her get the money to buy better equipment, and the Rockefeller Foundation awarded her a series of small grants. She was asked to speak at the students' chemistry club meetings, which faculty members also began to attend. Graduate students began to sign on to do research with her as their advisor.

An early success for Hodgkin at Oxford was the elucidation of cholesterol iodide's molecular structure, which no less a luminary than W.H. Bragg singled out for praise. During World War II, Hodgkin and her graduate student Barbara Low worked out the structure of penicillin, from some of the first crystals ever made of the vital new drug. Penicillin is not a particularly large molecule, but it has an unusual ring structure, at least four different forms, and crystallizes in different ways, making it a difficult crystallographic problem. Fortunately they were able to use one of the first IBM analog computers to help with the calculations.

In 1948, Hodgkin began work on the structure of vitamin B–12 the deficiency of which causes pernicious anemia. She obtained crystals of the material from Dr. Lester Smith of the Glaxo drug company, and worked with a graduate student, Jenny Glusker, an American team of crystallographers led by Kenneth Trueblood, and later with John White of Princeton University. Trueblood had access to state of the art computer equipment at the University of California at Los Angeles, and they sent results back and forth by mail and telegraph. Hodgkin and White were theoretically affiliated with competing pharmaceutical firms, but they ended up jointly publishing the structure of B–12 in 1957; it turned out to be a porphyrin, a type of molecule related to chlorophyll, but with a single atom of cobalt at the center.

Increasing Recognition Culminates in Nobel Prize and Order of Merit

After the war, Hodgkin helped form the International Union of Crystallography, causing Western governments some consternation in the process because she insisted on including crystallographers from behind the Iron Curtain. Always interested in the cause of world peace, Hodgkin signed on with several organizations that admitted Communist party members. Recognition of Hodgkin's work began to increase markedly, however, and whenever she had trouble getting an entry visa to the U.S. because of her affiliation with peace organizations, plenty of scientist friends were available to write letters on her behalf. A restriction on her U.S. visa was finally lifted in 1990 after the Soviet Union disbanded.

In 1947, she was inducted into the Royal Society, Britain's premiere scientific organization. Professor Hinshelwood assisted her efforts to get a dual university/college appointment with a better salary, and her chronic money problems were alleviated. Hodgkin still had to wait until 1957 for a full professorship, however, and it was not until 1958 that she was assigned an actual chemistry laboratory at Oxford. In 1960 she obtained the Wolfson Research Professorship, an endowed chair financed by the Royal Society, and in 1964 received the Nobel Prize in chemistry. One year later, she was awarded Britain's Order of Merit, only the second woman since Florence Nightingale to achieve that honor.

Hodgkin still wasn't done with her research, however. In 1969, after decades of work and waiting for computer technology to catch up with the complexity of the problem, she solved the structure of insulin. She employed some sophisticated techniques in the process, such as substituting atoms in the insulin molecule, and then comparing the altered crystal structure to the original. Protein crystallography was still an evolving field; in 1977 she said, in an interview with Peter Farago in the *Journal of Chemical Education,* "In the larger molecular structure, such as that of insulin, the way the peptide chains are folded within the molecule and interact with one another in the crystal is very suggestive in relation to the reactions of the molecules. We can often see that individual side chains have more than one conformation in the crystal, interacting with different positions of solvent molecules around them. We can begin to trace the movements of the atoms within the crystals."

In 1937, Dorothy Crowfoot married Thomas Hodgkin, the cousin of an old friend and teacher, Margery Fry, at Somerville College. He was an African Studies scholar and teacher, and, because of his travels and jobs in different parts of the world, they maintained separate residences until 1945 when he finally obtained a position teaching at Oxford. Despite this unusual arrangement, their marriage was a happy and successful one. Although initially worried that her work with x rays might jeopardize their ability to have children, the Hodgkins produced three: Luke, born in 1938, Elizabeth, born in 1941, and Toby, born in 1946. The children all took up their parents scholarly, nomadic habits, and at the time of the Nobel Ceremony traveled to Stockholm from as far away as New Delhi and Zambia. Although Hodgkin officially retired in 1977, she continued to travel widely and expanded her lifelong activities on behalf of world peace, working with the Pugwash Conferences on Science and World Affairs.

SELECTED WRITINGS BY HODGKIN:

Periodicals

"The X–Ray Analysis of Complicated Molecules." *Science* 150 (November 19, 1965): 979–88.

FURTHER READING

Books

McGrayne, Sharon B. *Nobel Prize Women in Science.* Carol Publishing Group, 1993.

Opfell, Olga S. *The Lady Laureates.* Scarecrow Press, 1986.

Periodicals

Journal of Chemical Education. 54 (1977): 214.

Nature (May 24): 1984, p.309.

New Scientist (May 23, 1992): 36.

Sketch by Gail B. C. Marsella

Ellen Dorrit Hoffleit
1907–
American astronomer

Ellen Dorrit Hoffleit has had a long and distinguished career in astronomy, with a special interest in the study of variable stars. She is credited with the discovery of 1,000 variable stars and has observed and documented their properties. Hoffleit was the director of the **Maria Mitchell** Observatory from 1957 to 1978 and has worked at both the Harvard Observatory and the Yale Observatory. An asteroid was named in her honor in 1987. Her enthusiasm for astronomy has made her a role model for several generations of women who were encouraged to enter the field by her example. She continues to work at the Yale Observatory, where she holds the title of senior research astronomer.

Hoffleit was born on March 12, 1907, in Florence, Alabama, to Fred and Kate (Samo) Hoffleit and grew up in Western Pennsylvania, where her father worked for the Pennsylvania Railroad. She had one brother named Herbert. Although Hoffleit's first name is Ellen, she is known as Dorrit by her friends and colleagues. She has never married.

As a child, Hoffleit thought she would become an artist, but a childhood interest in stars was to lead her on a different path. When she was nine, her father and mother separated. Her father wanted to return to the family farm in Alabama to conduct experiments in plant biology. Her mother, who had been educated in Germany, felt the rural Alabama schools did not offer the education she wanted for her two children and did not move. Hoffleit's brother was a child prodigy, who graduated from high school at age 14 and was accepted at Harvard University. Hoffleit moved with her mother and brother to Cambridge, Massachusetts, and attended high school there while her mother supported the family by working as a nurse. Upon graduation Hoffleit was accepted at Radcliffe College. After she graduated with an A.B. degree in mathematics in 1928, she was offered a high–paying job as a statistician, but turned it down in favor of a position as an assistant in the Harvard Observatory. "It was terribly exciting," she recalled in an interview in 1997. "Exploration and discovery, that's what the job was. It's much better to pick the jobyou like than the one that pays more." She worked on the staff at the observatory while earning an M.A. from Radcliffe in 1932 and a PhD in astronomy in 1938. She did her doctoral work under the direction of the noted Harvard astronomer Harlow Shapley, whose studies of the properties of stars was to influence her later work.

After she earned her PhD degree, she continued to work at the Harvard Observatory as a research associate until 1943, when she joined the staff at the Aberdeen Proving Ground in Maryland as a mathematician at the Ballistic Research Laboratories. During her stay there, she protested the discriminatory practice that prevented women from earning professional salaries. In 1948, she returned to the Harvard Observatory as an astronomer, although she continued to consult as a technical expert for the Ballistics Research Lab until 1961. In 1956 her old doctoral professor and associate, Harlow Shapley, retired from Harvard, and Hoffleit left the Harvard Observatory to work at the Yale Observatory.

Studies and Catalogs Special Stars

One of Hoffleit's areas of study has been bright stars, whose intensity is bright enough to be seen by the human eye without the aid of a telescope. One of the first books she wrote at Yale is entitled *Bright Star Catalogue*, which was first published in 1964. When she updated the book in 1982, it contained a list of the names and locations of over 9,000 bright stars visible from Earth. It has become a standard guide to the stars for professional and amateur astronomers alike.

Another of her areas of study has been variable stars, whose brightness varies over time. She is credited with the discovery of 1,000 new variable stars and has observed and documented their properties. These studies provided information on a variety of phenomena related to stars. Her work in this field led to her election as president of the American Association of Variable Star Observers from 1961 to 1963.

Hoffleit has also done research in the areas of meteors, galactic structure, and stellar spectra, which involves the analysis of light coming from stars.

Helps Other Women Become Astronomers

Shortly after she started working at Yale, Hoffleit had the opportunity to become the director of the Maria Mitchell Observatory at Nantucket, Massachusetts, in addition to her work at Yale. She took the position in 1957 and held it until 1978. The observatory is named after America's first woman astronomer, who was also the first woman elected as a fellow of the American Academy of Arts and Sciences. One of the programs Hoffleit instituted was a summer study course for women undergraduates to encourage them to pursue a career in astronomy. Over a period of 21 summers at Nantucket, she taught 102 women students, of whom more than 20 now have doctorates in astronomy and many others are active in the field. For some of the women, it was the first time they realized they could have a career in astronomy and they credit Hoffleit for giving them the confidence to continue their studies.

Continues to Work After Retirement

Although she retired from Yale in 1975, Hoffleit still has the title of senior research astronomer at the Yale Observatory. It is a title she has held since 1969. In 1987 an asteroid was named Dorrit in her honor. She was awarded the George van Biesbroeck Award in 1988, the Annenberg Award in 1993, and the Glover Award in 1995. In 1998 Hoffleit was inducted into the Connecticut Womens' Hall of Fame. She has written biographical sketches of several women astronomers, and in 1992 she finished a history book entitled *Astronomy at Yale*, 1701–1968. In 1995, Hoffleit and two of her colleagues finished an 18–year project when they published the fourth edition of *The General Catalogue* of *Trigonometric Stellar Parallaxes*. This comprehensive reference book provides the precise distances to 8,112 stars and is a valuable tool used by astrophysicists in their investigations of the size and age of the universe.

In April 1999, at age 92, Hoffleit was still going into work every day as a volunteer. Her eyesight, which had been badly dimmed by cataracts, was improved after she had surgery in late 1998. She spent much of her time writing about the history of astronomy and astronomers she has known. She also occasionally did some work on variable stars. Hoffleit's enthusiasm for astronomy was still evident in her conversation. "I think everyone should pick a job that they love," she told Chris Cavette in an interview.

SELECTED WRITINGS BY HOFFLEIT:

Books

Astronomy at Yale, 1701–1968. New Haven: Connecticut Academy of Arts and Sciences, 1992.

Women in the History of Variable Star Astronomy. Cambridge, MA: American Association of Variable Star Observers, 1993.

The Education of American Women Astronomers Before 1950. Cambridge, MA: American Association of Variable Star Observers, 1994.

(With William F. van Altena, and John T. Lee). *The General Catalogue of Trigonometric Stellar Parallaxes, 4th Edition.* New Haven: Yale Department of Astronomy, 1995.

FURTHER READING

Books

Bailey, Martha J. *American Women in Science.* Santa Barbara: ABC–CLIO, Inc., 1994, pp. 163–64.

Shearer, Benjamin F. and Barbara S. Shearer, eds. *Notable Women in the Physical Sciences.* Westport, CT: Greenwood Press, 1997.

Who's Who of American Women 1997–1998. New Providence, NJ: Marquis Who's Who, 1996.

Other

Cavette, Christopher J., interview with Dorrit Hoffleit conducted April 1, 1999.

DeCotis, Mark, ed. "Astronomer Finds Eyesight Dimmed at 90, but Not Enthusiasm." *FLORIDA TODAY Space Online.* 10 Apr 1997. http://www.flatoday.com/space/explore/stories/1997/041097a.htm (28 Mar 1999)

Sketch by Chris Cavette

Helen Sawyer Hogg (Mt. Holyoke College Archive. Reproduced by permission.)

Helen Sawyer Hogg
1905–1993
American–born Canadian astronomer

Helen Sawyer Hogg was the foremost person in Canada in the twentieth century to popularize astronomy. In addition to writing an astronomy column in the *Toronto Star* for thirty years, she located variable stars in globular clusters and cataloged them, using her data to determine the stars' distance. Hogg was the first to use the seventy–two–inch telescope at the Dominion Astrophysical Observatory in British Columbia to take extensive photographs; previously the telescope had been used only for obtaining stellar spectra. She taught science at the University of Toronto for four decades, and was the first woman to become president of the Royal Canadian Institute. In 1989, the observatory at the National Museum of Science and Technology in Ottawa was dedicated in her name.

Born in Lowell, Massachusetts, on August 1, 1905, to Edward Everett Sawyer, a former vice president of the Union National Bank in Lowell, and Carrie Myra (Sprague) Sawyer, Helen (Battles) Sawyer attended the Charles W. Morey School in Lowell and Lowell High School. In 1925, after witnessing a total eclipse of the sun, she decided on a career in astronomy. Sawyer received her bachelor's degree from Mount Holyoke College in 1926, and a master's degree from Radcliffe College in 1928. She continued at Radcliffe for her Ph.D. under the supervision of Harlow Shapley, and was the first of his students at Harvard to work on variable stars in globular clusters. Globular clusters are huge conglomerations of densely concentrated stars that exist in the outer halo of the Milky Way galaxy.

Began Independent Study of Stars

On September 6, 1930, Sawyer married Frank Scott Hogg, Harvard's first astronomy Ph.D., in Cambridge. The following year she moved with Hogg to Victoria, British Columbia, where he had accepted a post at the Dominion Astrophysical Observatory. Barred from holding a position in the observatory herself, ostensibly because Frank Hogg already had an appointment there, Helen instead began to assist her husband, initially at no salary. In 1929, Edwin Powell Hubble proposed the theory of the expanding universe and set off a flurry of efforts to measure the distance of galaxies beyond the Milky Way using spectrographic images of stars, which is the process of dispersing radiation into a spectrum and then photographing or mapping the spectrum. Hogg's approach was innovative but complementary; she used the observatory's seventy–two–inch telescope to take actual photographs of variable stars, or stars which change brightness in generally regular intervals. She concentrated on stars in globular clusters within our own galaxy, cataloging the cyclical changes in their brightness as an aid to determining their distance and evolution. The process was a tedious one, requiring hours of careful focusing and a makeshift arrangement for exchanging photographic plates. So determined was Helen to continue with her career that she brought her first child to the observatory with her in a basket.

In 1935 the Hoggs moved to Ontario, where Helen was able to obtain an assistantship at the David Dunlap Observatory of the University of Toronto. She was a research associate at the observatory from 1936 until her death, and held a concurrent position at the university in the department of astronomy, moving gradually up through the academic ranks. She was promoted to professor in 1957, and become professor emeritus in 1976. At the Dunlap Observatory, Hogg continued her work with variable stars, and she gained a reputation as a world authority on the subject of the night sky. A longtime co–worker, Christine Clement, told the *Toronto Star,* "The sky could be almost completely overcast, but Helen could look at a hole in the clouds and know what we could observe through it." Hogg took several brief sabbaticals (for the academic year 1940–41 she was professor and acting chair of the department of astronomy at Mount Holyoke College, and in 1955–56 she was program director for astronomy for the National Science Foundation in the United States), but she made her professional life in Toronto.

Wrote for Academics and Laypeople

Hogg contributed over a hundred articles to scientific journals, and was the author of *The Stars Belong to*

Everyone, published in 1976. From 1951 to 1981 she contributed the weekly column "The Stars" to the *Toronto Star* and delighted her readers with explanations of phenomena such as the blue moon. She was the recipient of numerous awards and honors, including honorary degrees from Mount Holyoke College, the Universities of Waterloo and Toronto, McMaster University, and St. Mary's University. In 1950 she won the Cannon Prize of the American Astronomical Society, and in 1967 the Centennial Medal of Canada and the Rittenhouse Medal. In 1976 she was named a Companion of the Order of Canada, a privilege shared by few. Asteroid number 2917, which orbits between Jupiter and Mars, bears her name.

Hogg was a member of the International Astronomical Society and a fellow of the Royal Society of Canada. She was president of the American Association of Variable Star Observers from 1939 to 1941. She also had to her credit a list of firsts: she was the first woman president of the physical sciences section of the Royal Society of Canada, a post she held in 1960 and 1961; the first female president of the Royal Canadian Institute, from 1964 to 1965; one of the first two women to serve on the board of directors of the Bell Telephone Company of Canada, from 1968 to 1978; and the founding president of the Canadian Astronomical Society, 1971 to 1972.

Frank Hogg died in 1951, leaving Helen and their three children, Sarah Longley, David Edward, and James Scott. On November 28, 1985, at the age of eighty, Hogg married Francis E. L. Priestley; he died in 1988. In 1989, the Helen Sawyer Hogg Observatory of the National Museum of Science and Technology in Ottawa was dedicated, and in June of 1992, the University of Toronto named its telescope in the Andes Mountains in Chile after her. Hogg enjoyed stamp collecting, knitting, gardening, and photography. She was active late into her life, and only days before her death had been interviewed for an educational video aimed at encouraging young women to seek careers in science. Hogg died of a heart attack on January 28, 1993.

SELECTED WRITINGS BY HOGG:

Books

Man and His World: The Noranda Lectures. University of Toronto Press, 1968.

Out of Old Books (collection of journal articles), David Dunlap Observatory, 1974.

The Stars Belong to Everyone: How to Enjoy Astronomy. Doubleday, 1976.

Periodicals

(With Christine M. Clement and Andrew Yee) "The Long–Term Behavior of the Population II Cepheid V1 in the Globular Cluster Messier 12." *Astronomical Journal* (November 1, 1988): 1642.

"Memories of the Plaskett Era of the Dominion Astrophysical Observatory, 1931–1934." *Journal of the Royal Astronomical Society of Canada* (December 1, 1988): 328.

(With Steve Butterworth and Amelia Wehlau) "Observations of Variable Stars in the Globular Cluster M80" *The Astronomical Journal* (April 1, 1990): 1159.

FURTHER READING

Books

Jarrell, Richard A. *The Cold Light of Dawn: A History of Canadian Astronomy.* University of Toronto Press, p. 120.

Farnes, Patricia, G. Kass–Simon, and Deborah Nash, eds. *Women of Science.* Bloomington: Indiana University Press, 1990, pp. 105–106.

Periodicals

Barnes, Alan. "Helen Hogg, 87, Was Pioneering Woman Astronomer." *Toronto Star* (January 29, 1993): A25.

Dickinson, Terence. "Canada's Best–Known Astronomer Was at the Forefront of Discovery." *Toronto Star* (February 7, 1993): B7.

Pearce, Joseph. "Some Recollections of the Observatory." *Journal of the Royal Astronomical Society of Canada* 62: 296.

Sketch by Sebastian Thaler

Mary Jane Hogue
1883–1962
American biologist

Mary Jane Hogue was an internationally recognized biologist best known for her tissue culture work on human nerve cells. Her studies of the effects of the poliomyelitis virus on humans, rabbits and guinea pigs led to significant advances in the understanding and treatment of polio.

Hogue was born on October 12, 1883, in West Chester, Pennsylvania to Mr. and Mrs. Thomas C. Hogue. She grew up with her sister, Helena, and attended West Chester Public High School, graduating in 1901. She did exceptionally well in all her studies, but science particularly fascinated her. By 1905, she held a degree in zoology from Goucher College, then known as Woman's College of Baltimore City.

A Founders Scholarship award initiated Hogue's graduate education at Bryn Mawr College. For two years she was immersed in embryology, experimental morphology, cytology, and the structure and function of the central nervous system. Always applying for more opportunity to learn, she put in a request for overseas graduate study in Germany. In a letter of recommendation, a professor heading up a laboratory where Hogue performed experiments on starfish eggs, wrote "I am delighted with what she has done . . . she has shown splendid independence of thought and action. I shall be very sorry to have her go".

Studied with Noted Biologist Theodor Boveri

She received the Goucher College Van Meter Fellowship to study with the noted German biologist, Theodor Boveri at the University of Wurzburg in Germany. An exemplary worker, Hogue won entry to many academic opportunities. During the second year, she continued her analysis and cytological study to complete her dissertation entitled "The Influence of Centrifugal Force on the Eggs of *Asearis megalocaphala.*" She occupied the American Woman's Table at the Zoological Station in Naples on break, and in the spring of 1909, Hogue was awarded a PhD in zoology from the University of Wurzburg, a remarkable accomplishment for a woman at that time.

Hogue moved to New York City upon her return to America, working part–time as an instructor at Miss Chapin's School, and furthering her protozoology studies at Columbia University. Her dedication and scientific skill and her affable manner secured her steady work during the lean economic times to follow. For 14 years beginning in 1910 with her next teaching appointment at the Pennsylvania College for Women, she traveled to many institutions. From 1911–1914, she instructed at Mount Holyoke, moving to Wellesley from 1914–1918, and again to the Base Hospital laboratory at Fort Sill, Oklahoma during World War One.

Named Emeritus Professor of Anatomy

After the war, a tissue culture collaboration in the Department of Embryology at the Carnegie Institution of Washington sparked a keen interest in bacteriology. In 1919, Hogue was awarded a two–year fellowship at the school of Hygiene and Public Health at Johns Hopkins. While a professor of bacteriology at the North Carolina College for Women for two years beginning in 1922, Hogue consulted at the Wesley Long Hospital in Greensboro. In 1924, she accepted a position as professor of anatomy at the University of Pennsylvania Medical School, returning to her home–town of West Chester where she lived for the rest of her life. In 1952, the University of Pennsylvania named her Emeritus Associate Professor of Anatomy in honor of her 28 years of extraordinary service and dedication.

The Marine Biological Laboratories in Wood Holes on the Cape in Massachusetts was a favorite sojourn, beginning her affiliation in the summer of 1905 with a Life Histories course on a scholarship from Goucher College. In 1912, she concentrated on the protozoan population of oyster beds. She was named an Independent Investigator in 1935, and became a member of the MBL Corporation. Hogue was also a member in the American Association for the Advancement of Science, the American Association of Anatomists, the American Society for Tropical Medicine, the American Society of Parasitologists, the American Society of Zoologists, the American Association of University Women, the American Heart Association, and the Pennsylvania Academy of Science.

Her work encompassed a broad area, including research in the fields of oncology, bacteriology, and embryology. An author of more than 80 papers, Hogue attracted the attention and admiration of scientists all over the world. Her investigations revealed that after the death of an organism, nerve cells can live for over a week. The analysis of the poliomyeletis virus, a focus of much of Hogue's work, was significant in the treatment of polio. She holds the distinction of being one of the first scientists to successfully photograph the attack of a polio virus on nerve cells.

Hogue worked tirelessly and energetically, often using words like "thrilling" and "exciting" to described her projects. She taught herself to paint as a way to enhance the learning of her students, and became an accomplished amateur water colorist and valued member of the West Chester Art Association. She took yearly excursions with her sister to paint on site, finding time for another beloved activity, bird watching. After her formal retirement in 1952, Hogue continued to work in her laboratory until a few weeks before her death on September 11, 1962.

SELECTED WRITINGS BY HOGUE:

Periodicals

"The Effects of Poliomyelitis Virus on Human Brain Cells in Tissue Culture."*Journal of Experimental Medicine*, (July 1, 1955).

"A Method for Preventing Moisture Condensation During Photography of Tissue Cultures in Hanging Drops."*Science*, (August 1949).

"Studies on the Development of the Starfish Egg."*Journal of Experimental Zoology*, (December 1, 1919).

FURTHER READING

Other

New York Times, "Dr. Mary Hogue, Anatomist, Was 78". (September 13, 1962), p 37:4.

Hogue, May Jane. Records. Goucher College Archives. Julia Rogers Library, Baltmore, Maryland.

"Mary Jane Hogue (1883–1962)." *MBL.* http://www.mbl.edu/html/WOMEN/hogue.html (February 18, 1999).

Sketch by Kyra Anderson

Mary Emilee Holmes
1849–1906
American geologist

Distinguished as the first woman to become a member of the Geological Society of America, Mary Emilee Holmes was also one of two women who were the first in the nation to earn a doctorate degree in the earth sciences field. In addition to having a respected career as educator and researcher, Holmes was also a social activist, being editor and proprietor of the "Freedmen's Bulletin" starting in 1885, and founder of the Mary Holmes Seminary in West Point, Mississippi.

Holmes was born in 1849 and in 1868, at the age of 19, received her bachelor's degree from Rockford College in Illinois. She taught school in the area for a few years, and was then offered a faculty position at Rockford College in 1871. For the next eleven years, she remained an inspiring professor, combining her interest and knowledge in paleontology and zoology with geology and other earth sciences subjects, to give students a comprehensive understanding of natural history. However, she eventually resigned to pursue a doctorate degree from the University of Michigan, which she obtained in 1888. Within months of this, on May 20, 1889, she was elected a fellow member of the Geological Society of America, newly established in 1888. Her name is listed under "Officers and Fellows" in Volume I (1890) of the *Bulletin,* published by the Society. (Holmes remained the only female member for five years, until 1894, when Florence Bascom, –the other woman who had earned a doctorate degree in earth sciences, was elected into membership. Bascom was actually the first woman in America to receive a doctorate in "geology" *per se.* It is interesting to note that only a fourth of the male members of the Geological Society at that time had doctorate degrees.) In August, 1893, Holmes was distinguished by presenting a paper at the women's 5–day section of the World Congress of Geology held in Chicago.

During these years, Holmes became increasingly involved with social causes, and in 1883 began work in Presbyterian ministries and mission societies. She became president of the Presbyterian Home Mission Society, a position she retained for the next 23 years. During the same years, Holmes also served as secretary of the Synodical Home Mission Society. She focused her energies on social issues during the Civil War, and was active in the abolitionist movement. At the time of her death in 1906, Holmes was still serving as president and secretary of the Presbyterian Home and Synodical Home mission societies.

FURTHER READING

Books

Bailey, Martha J. *American Women in Science.* Denver: ABC–CLIO, p. 167.

Elliot, Clark, ed. *Biographical Index to American Scientists – 17th Century to 1920.* New York: Greenwood Press, 1990.

Herzenberg, Caroline L. *American Men and Women of Science.* 1st and 2nd eds.

Rossiter, Margaret W. *Womrn Scientists in America.* Baltimore: Johns Hopkins University Press, pp. 83, 98.

Other

Arnold, Lois Barber. "American Women in Geology: A historical perspective." *Geology* 5 (1977): 493–504, provided by the Geological Society of America.

Sketch by Lauri R. Harding

Erna Schneider Hoover
1926–
American computer scientist

Erna Hoover is recognized for being one of the first women pioneers in computer technology. She designed a switching system for phone traffic, and was awarded one of the earliest software patents for her work.

Born June 19, 1926, in Irvington, New Jersey, Erna Schneider and her younger siblings, a brother who died from polio at age five, and a sister, were raised by their dentist father and former teacher mother in South Orange, where Hoover attended public school. An active child, Hoover enjoyed swimming, sailing, and canoeing in the Adirondacks, and was always welcome in the boys' softball games. Interested in science at an early age, Hoover read **Marie Curie's** biography, which taught her that women could succeed despite the odds.

Graduating from Wellesley College in 1948 as a Phi Beta Kappa and Durant Scholar, Hoover earned her B.A. in classical and medieval philosophy and history, with honors. She went on to Yale University for her Ph.D. in philosophy and foundations of mathematics, and her 1951 dissertation was titled "An Analysis of Contrary to Fact Conditional Sentences."

Hoover went on to teach philosophy and logic at Swarthmore College until 1954, when she joined Bell Laboratories as a senior technical associate. Promoted in 1956, Hoover entered into Bell Labs' internal training program the following year, which was the equivalent of a master's degree in computer science. The existing switching systems were electronic, and the company realized the importance of the then new computer technology.

After completing her training, Hoover was assigned to work on the switching project, which would replace the unreliable electronic relay circuitry in thousands of offices with special computers. Because even in the space of only one hour an office can process over 200,000 traffic requests, the switching systems would often become overwhelmed if a larger number of requests were made simultaneously, causing the system to freeze up. Hoover's background proved invaluable, since symbolic logic has applications in switching circuit design. Using her knowledge of feedback theory and analyzing traffic and pattern statistics, she designed the stored program control—the brains—which senses amount of traffic and imposes an order of call. Hoover's switching system was the first reliable device to use computer techniques, including transistor circuits and memory-stored control programs. Technological communication became revolutionized.

For her Feedback Control Monitor for Stored Program Data Processing System, Hoover was awarded patent #3,623,007 in November of 1971, one of the first software patents ever issued. The application was made in 1967, while Hoover was on maternity leave, and the patent lawyers had to bring the papers to her home for a signature.

Hoover was promoted to supervisor and was able to research radar control programs of the Safeguard Anti-Ballistic Missile System, which, designed to intercept intercontinental ballistic missile warheads, helped contribute to the ending of the cold war. In 1978, Hoover was the first woman to ever be promoted to Technical Department Head, a position she would retain until her retirement in 1987. Her department applied artificial intelligence techniques, large databases, and transaction systems in order to support telephone operations through the use of software.

Hoover's accomplishments are all the more notable when the prevailing wisdom of the 1950s is considered—chiefly, that women belong in the home. In fact, Hoover had been unable to find tenure-track college teaching due to her gender and marital status, which is what prompted her to join Bell Laboratories. Hoover's husband, Charles Wilson Hoover, Jr., whom she married in 1953, was supportive of her work and pleased that his wife had career interests. The couple both worked at Bell Labs, while care was found for their three daughters, born in 1956, 1959, and 1967. Despite the fact that many suggested her children would turn out badly, Hoover proudly states that "in fact, all have gone to good colleges and pursued graduate work."

Hoover is committed to education and research, and has served on the boards of many higher education organizations in New Jersey. In addition, she is a member of the New Jersey Council for the Humanities, the American Association of University Women, and several community groups. Hoover was also the recipient of the Wellesley College Alumni Achievement Award. In her free time, the Hoovers enjoy their four grandchildren, and are active hikers, skiers, travelers, and tennis players.

FURTHER READING

Periodicals

"Wellesley to Honor Jersey Scientist." *The Star–Ledger.* (February 14, 1990).

Other

"Inventors–Erna Schneider Hoover." http://web.mit.edu/afs/athena.mit.edu/org/i/invent/www/inventorsA–H/hoover.html

Kiser, Helene Barker, interview with Erna Hoover conducted July 23, 1999.

Sketch by Helene Barker Kiser

Lou Henry Hoover
1874–1944
American geologist

Lou Henry Hoover, wife of Herbert Hoover, the thirty–first president of the United States, was a notable geologist in her own right. On her extensive travels, she worked to make geological surveys of the areas. She also translated an important Latin manuscript on mineralogy, one that had long eluded other scholars.

Lou Henry was born on March 29, 1874, in Waterloo, Iowa. Her father, Charles Delano Henry, a banker, and her mother, Florence Weed Henry, raised Lou and her younger sister there until 1884, when Florence's health prompted the family to move to California. While growing up Hoover was somewhat of a tomboy, camping and horseback riding often with her father, which gave Hoover a lifelong affinity for the outdoors.

After high school, Hoover began studying at a teacher's school. While there, she attended a lecture series on geology. Her interest in the subject was so great that in 1894 she enrolled in the geology department of Stanford University. Hoover graduated in 1898 with an A.B. degree in geology.

Because of her love for the outdoors, she wanted to find a husband who shared her interests. Her geology professor introduced her to a fellow student, Herbert "Bert" Hoover, and the two were married on February 10, 1899 in a civil ceremony in Monterey, California. The very next day, the couple traveled to China where Herbert would be working as a mining engineer. They remained in China for two years, and it proved to be only the first of many countries in which they lived abroad for a time.

The birth of her two children, Herbert Jr. in 1903, and Allan Henry in 1907, did not slow Hoover's travels down. Herbert's business engagements drew them to many parts of the world, where Hoover would aid her husband at mining sites by creating geological surveys. At each of their homes, Hoover took over the gardening, planting traditional California foliage and tending the grounds.

Lou Henry Hoover (Corbis/Bettmann. Reproduced by permission.)

By 1912, Hoover had finished a translation of a mineralogy manuscript from 1556, *De Re Metallica*, by Georgius Agricola. The manuscript had long baffled translators, due to slang that had lost its meaning over time and to the fact that Agricola actually made up his own words and descriptions on occasion. But Hoover's background in geology and fluency in Latin, French, and German enabled her to complete the translation, and its importance has held for almost a century.

When her husband was elected president, Hoover took on the task of decorating the White House. She was also involved with the Girl Scouts, acting as the organization's president for a time. In 1931, during the Great Depression, Hoover gave radio addresses aimed at American women, asking them to remember the needy with clothing and food donations. She was known as a worldly, educated, and sophisticated lady, but according the *New York Times*, she was not a haughty person, and even insisted on continuing to drive herself. Her last act as First Lady was to invite Mrs. Roosevelt in socially, and this gesture is now commonplace among the wives of each succeeding president.

In 1933, after Roosevelt took over the presidency, the Hoovers made their home in both Palo Alto, California, and New York City. She continued her charity concerns by serving as honorary chairman of the American Women's division of the Commission for Relief in Belgium in 1940. During World War II, she managed England's American Women's Hospital. Hoover died suddenly of a heart attack in New York City on January 7, 1944.

SELECTED WRITINGS BY HOOVER:

Books

1912 translation, *De Re Metallica, Georgius Agricola,* 1556.

FURTHER READING

Books

James, Edward T., et al, eds. *Notable American Women 1607–1950.* Cambridge: Belknap Press, 1971.
Mayo, Edith P., ed. *The Smithsonian Book of First Ladies.* NY: Henry Holt, 1996.

Periodicals

Obituary. *The New York Times* (January 8, 1944).

Sketch by Helene Barker Kiser

Grace Murray Hopper
1906–1992
American computer scientist

Grace Hopper, who rose through Navy ranks to become a rear admiral at age eighty–two, is best known for her contribution to the design and development of the COBOL programming language for business applications. Her professional life spanned the growth of modern computer science, from her work as a young Navy lieutenant programming an early calculating machine to her creation of sophisticated software for microcomputers. She was an influential force and a legendary figure in the development of programming languages. In 1991, President George Bush presented her with the National Medal of Technology "for her pioneering accomplishments" in the field of data processing.

Admiral Hopper was born Grace Brewster Murray on December 9, 1906, in New York City. She was the first child of Marry Campbell Van Horne Murray and Walter Fletcher Murray. Encouraged by her parents to develop her natural mechanical abilities, she disassembled and examined gadgets around the home, and she excelled at mathematics in school. Her grandfather had been a senior civil engineer for New York City who inspired her strong interest in geometry and mathematics.

At Vassar College, Hopper indulged her mathematical interests, and also took courses in physics and engineering. She graduated in 1928, then attended Yale, where she

Grace M. Hopper (The Library of Congress.)

received a master's degree in 1930 and a doctorate in 1934. These were rare achievements, especially for a woman. As Robert Slater points out in *Portraits in Silicon,* U.S. doctorates in mathematics numbered only 1,279 between 1862 and 1934. Despite bleak prospects for female mathematicians in teaching beyond the high school level, Vassar College hired her first as an instructor, then as a professor of mathematics. Hopper taught at Vassar until the beginning of World War II. She lived with her husband, Vincent Foster Hopper, whom she had married in 1930. They were divorced in 1945 and had no children.

Begins Computer Work in Navy

In 1943, Hopper joined the U.S. Naval Reserve, attending midshipman's school and obtaining a commission as a lieutenant in 1944. She was immediately assigned to the Bureau of Ships Computation Project at Harvard. The project, directed by Howard Aiken, was her first introduction to Aiken's task, which was to devise a machine that would assist the Navy in making rapid, difficult computations for such projects as laying a mine field. In other words, Aiken was in the process of building and programming America's first programmable digital computer—the Mark I.

For Hopper, the experience was both disconcerting and instructive. Without any background in computing, she was handed a code book and asked to begin computations. With the help of two ensigns assigned to the project and a sudden plunge into the works of computer pioneer Charles Babbage, Hopper began a crash course on the current state of computation by way of what Aiken called "a computing engine."

The Mark I was the first digital computer to be programmed sequentially. Thus, Hopper experienced first–hand the complexities and frustration that have always been the hallmark of the programming field. The exacting code of machine language could be easily misread or incorrectly written. To reduce the number of programming errors, Hopper and her colleagues collected programs that were free of error andgenerated a catalogue of subroutines that could be used to develop new programs. By this time, the Mark II had been built. Aiken's team used the two computers side by side, effectively achieving an early instance of multiprocessing.

By the end of the war, Hopper had become enamored of Navy life, but her age —a mere forty years—precluded a transfer from the WAVES into the regular Navy. She remained in the Navy Reserves and stayed on at the Harvard Computational Laboratory as a research fellow, where she continued her work on the Mark computer series. The problem of computer errors continued to plague the Mark team. One day, noticing that the computer had failed, Hopper and her colleagues discovered a moth in a faulty relay. The insect was removed and fixed to the page of a logbook as the "first actual bug found." The words "bug" and "debugging," now familiar terms in computer vocabulary, are attributed to Hopper. In 1949, she left Harvard to take up the position of senior mathematician in a start–up company, the Eckert–Mauchly Computer Corporation. Begun in 1946 by J. Presper Eckert and John Mauchly, the company had by 1949 developed the Binary Automatic Computer, or BINAC, and was in the process of introducing the first Universal Automatic Computer, or UNIVAC. The Eckert–Mauchly UNIVAC, which recorded information on high–speed magnetic tape rather than on punched cards, was an immediate success. The company was later bought by Sperry Corporation. Hopper stayed with the organization and in 1952 became the systems engineer and director of automatic programming for the UNIVAC Division of Sperry, a post she held until 1964.

Hopper's association with UNIVAC resulted in several important advances in the field of programming. Still aware of the constant problems caused by programming errors, Hopper developed an innovative program that would translate the programmer's language into machine language. This first compiler, called "A–O," allowed the programmer to write in a higher–level symbolic language, without having to worry about the tedious binary language of endless numbers that were needed to communicate with the machine itself.

One of the challenges Hopper had to meet in her work on the compiler was that of how to achieve "forward jumps" in a program that had yet to be written. In *Grace Hopper, Navy Admiral and Computer Pioneer,* Charlene Billings explains that Hopper used a strategy from her schooldays—the forward pass in basketball. Forbidden under the rules for women's basketball to dribble more than once, one teammate would routinely pass the basketball down the court to another, then run down the court herself and be in a position to receive the ball and make the basket. Hopper defined what she called a "neutral corner" as a little segment at the end of the computer memory which allowed her a safe space in which to "jump forward" from a given routine, and flag the operation with a message. As each routine was run, it scouted for messages and jumped back and forth, essentially running in a single pass.

During the early 1950s, Hopper began to write articles and deliver papers on her programming innovations. Her first publication, "A Manual of Operation for the Automatic Sequence Controlled Calculator," detailed her initial work on Mark I. "The Education of a Computer," offered in 1952 at a conference of the Association of Computing Machinery, outlined many ideas on software. An article appearing in a 1953 issue of *Computers and Automation,* "Compiling Routines," laid out principles of compiling. In addition to numerous articles and papers, Hopper published a book on computing entitled *Understanding Computers,* with Steven Mandrell.

The Development of COBOL

Having demonstrated that computers are programmable and capable not only of doing arithmetic, but manipulating symbols as well, Hopper worked steadily to improve the design and effectiveness of programming languages. In 1957, she and her staff at UNIVAC created Flow–matic, the first program using English language words. Flow–matic was later incorporated into COBOL, and, according to Jean E. Sammet, constituted Hopper's most direct and vital contribution to COBOL.

The story of COBOL's development illustrated Hopper's wide–reaching influence in the field of programming. IBM had developed FORTRAN, the densely mathematical programming language best suited to scientists. But no comparable language existed for business, despite the clear advantages that computers offered in the area of information processing.

By 1959, it was obvious that a standard programming language was necessary for the business community. Flow–matic was an obvious prototype for a business programming language. At that time, however, IBM and Honeywell were developing their own competing programs. Without cooperative effort, the possibility of a standard language to be used throughout the business world was slim. Hopper, who campaigned for standardization of computers and programming throughout her life, arguing that the lack of standardization created vast inefficiency and waste, was disturbed by this prospect.

The problem was how to achieve a common business language without running afoul of anti–trust laws. In April 1959, a small group of academics and representatives of the computer industry, Hopper among them, met to discuss a standard programming language specifically tailored for the business community. They proposed contacting the Defense Department, which contracted heavily with the business industry, to coordinate a plan, and in May a larger group met with Charles Phillips. The result was the formation of several committees charged with overseeing the design and development of the language that would eventually be known as COBOL—an acronym for "Common Business Oriented Lan–guage." Hopper served as a technical advisor to the Executive Committee.

The unique and far–ranging aspects of COBOL included its readability and its portability. Whereas IBM's FORTRAN used a highly condensed, mathematical code, COBOL used common English language words. COBOL was written for use on different computers and intended to be independent of any one computer company. Hopper championed the use of COBOL in her own work at Sperry, bringing to fruition a COBOL compiler concurrently with RCA in what was dubbed the "Computer Translating Race." Both companies successfully demonstrated their compilers in late 1960.

Hopper was elected a fellow of the Institute of Electrical and Electronics Engineers (IEEE) in 1962 and of the American Association for the Advancement of Science (AAAS) in 1963. She was awarded the Society of Women Engineers Achievement Award in 1964. She continued her work with Sperry, and in 1964 was appointed staff scientist of systems programming, in the UNIVAC Division.

Returns to Navy Life

While at Sperry, Hopper remained active in the Navy Reserves, retiring with great reluctance in 1966. But only seven months later, she was asked to direct the standardization of high level languages in the Navy. She returned to active duty in 1967 and was exempted from mandatory retirement at age of sixty–two. She served in the Navy until age seventy–one.

Although she continued to work at Sperry Corporation until 1971, her activities with the Navy brought her increasing recognition as a spokesperson for the usefulness of computers. In 1969, she was named "Man of the Year" by the Data Processing Management Association. In the next two decades, she would garner numerous awards and honorary degrees, including election as a fellow of the Association of Computer Programmers and Analysts (1972), election to membership in the National Academy of Engineering (1973), election as a distinguished fellow of the British Computer Society (1973), the Navy Meritorious Service Medal (1980), induction into the Engineering and Science Hall of Fame (1984) and the Navy Distinguished Service Medal (1986). She lectured widely and took on vested interests in the computer industry, pushing for greater standardization and compatibility in programming and hardware.

Hopper's years with the Navy brought steady promotions. She became captain on the retired list of the Naval Reserve in 1973 and commodore in 1983. In 1985 she earned the rank of rear admiral before retiring in 1986. But her professional life did not end there. She became a senior consultant for the Digital Equipment Corporation immediately after leaving the Navy and worked there until her death, on January 1, 1992. In its obituary, the *New York Times* noted that "[l]ike another Navy figure, Admiral Rickover, Admiral Hopper was known for her combative personality and her unorthodox approach." Unlike many of her colleagues in the early days of computers, Hopper believed in making computers and programming languages increasingly available and accessible to nonspecialists.

SELECTED WRITINGS BY HOPPER:

Books

"A Manual of Operation for the Automatic Sequence Controlled Calculator." In *Annals of the Harvard Computation Laboratory.* Vol. 1. Cambridge: Harvard University Press, 1946.

(With Steven Mandrell) *Understanding Computers.* West Publishing, 1984.

Periodicals

(With John W. Mauchly) "Influence of Programming Techniques on the Design of Computers." *Proc. IRE* 41 (October, 1953).

"The Education of a Computer." *Annals of the History of Computing* 9 (1988).

FURTHER READING

Books

Billings, Charlene W. *Grace Hopper, Navy Admiral and Computer Pioneer,* Enslow, 1989.

Slater, Robert. *Portraits in Silicon.* Cambridge: MIT Press, 1987.

Periodicals

New York Times (January 3, 1992).

Sammet, Jean E. "Farewell to Grace Hopper—End of an Era!" *Communications of the AMC* (April, 1992).

Sketch by Katherine Williams

Dorothy Millicent Horstmann
1911–
American virologist

Dorothy Millicent Horstmann played a significant yet often unacknowledged role in the development of the polio vaccine. In the late 1940s and early 1950s, before polio immunizations were considered feasible, she conducted groundbreaking animal studies which proved that the polio virus reaches the nervous system through the bloodstream. In 1952, while working at the Yale School of Medicine, she set up an experiment to determine whether polio first appeared in the blood before moving on to the brain. She fed monkeys and chimpanzees small quantities of polio virus, then examined the blood for traces of the it. The animals did not immediately develop symptoms of polio, yet small traces of virus were observable in their blood. Many of the animals later developed paralysis, one of polio's debilitating symptoms.

Horstmann was born July 2, 1911, in Spokane, Washington, to Henry and Anna (Humold) Horstmann. She received her B.A. in 1936 and her M.D. in 1940 from the University of California. After holding an internship at the San Francisco City and County Hospital from 1939 to 1940, she did her medical residency at Vanderbilt University. In 1942, she began her long affiliation with the Yale University School of Medicine. In 1945, Horstmann was appointed associate professor of medicine at Yale; from 1947 to 1948, she held a National Institutes of Health postdoctoral research fellowship there. In 1961, Horstmann rose to professor of epidemiology and pediatrics, and in 1969 she was named John Rodman Paul Professor of Epidemiology and Pediatrics. Since 1982, she has held the titles of emeritus professor and senior research scientist at Yale. Horstmann was led to her experiments by the work of William McDowell Hammon, who showed that injections of gamma globulin, an antibody–rich serum extracted from plasma, could produce temporary immunity to polio. From this lead, Horstmann hypothesized that the polio virus first traveled through the bloodstream before finally settling in the nervous system. The discoveries she made during her experiments with monkeys and chimpanzees were initially dismissed by some virologists as inconclusive, because in most patients who had developed polio, no virus had been found in their blood. It was subsequently established, however, that by the time the symptoms of polio became clinically evident, the virus had already left the bloodstream and established itself in the nervous system. Horstmann's work and the parallel studies of David Bodian at Johns Hopkins University proved that polio is an intestinal infection which can enter the nervous system through the bloodstream.

Throughout the 1950s and 1960s, Horstmann participated in field trials to establish the effectiveness and safety of polio vaccines. During her distinguished career, Horstmann also studied maternal rubella and the rubella syndrome in infants. She holds four honorary doctorates and has received numerous honors and awards, including the James D. Bruce Award of the American College of Physicians, 1975, Denmark's Thorvold Madsen Award, 1977, and the Maxwell Finland Award of the Infectious Diseases Society of America, 1978. She is a member of the National Academy of Sciences, the American Society of Clinical Investigations, the American College of Physicians, and the Royal Society of Medicine.

SELECTED WRITINGS BY HORSTMANN:

Books

Report on a Visit to the U.S.S.R., Poland, and Czechoslovakia to View Work on Live Poliovirus Vaccine, Yale University Press, 1960.

Periodicals

"Controlling Rubella: Problems and Perspectives." *Annals of Internal Medicine* 83 (September 1975).

FURTHER READING

Books

Klein, Aaron E. *Trial by Fury: The Polio Vaccine Controversy.* Scribner, 1972.

Smith, Jane S. *Patenting the Sun: Polio and the Salk Vaccine.* Morrow, 1990.

Other

"Leaders in American Medicine: Dorothy M. Horstmann, M.D." (videocassette), The National Audiovisual Center, 1979.

Sketch by Tom Crawford

Ruth Hubbard
1924–
Austrian–born American biologist

Ruth Hubbard is a biologist who has made important contributions to our understanding of the biochemistry of vision. She has also researched and written on the sociology and history of science, and on issues of women and science, women's health and biology, women in academia, and the ethics of genetic testing and gene therapy.

Ruth Hubbard was born in 1924 in Vienna, Austria, the daughter of Jewish physicians, Helene (Ehrlich) and Frank Hoffmann. The family emigrated from Austria to the United States in 1938, shortly after the Nazi invasion of Austria. They settled in Boston where Frank Hoffmann reestablished his medical practice. Hubbard became a United States citizen in 1943 and attended Radcliffe College, planning to become a physician. Graduating in 1944, in the midst of the second world war, Hubbard began working on infrared vision at Harvard University with George Wald. However her husband, Frank Hubbard, whom she had married in 1942, was in the army, stationed in Chattanooga. Hubbard joined him there and worked as a technician at the Tennessee Public Health Service.

Partners with Nobel Prize Winner George Wald

In 1946, Hubbard returned to Radcliffe to work toward her doctorate. She also rejoined George Wald in his laboratory where she studied the visual pigments, including rhodopsin, a molecule that responds to light. Hubbard demonstrated how light changes the shape of these molecules, initiating the events that lead to the electrical charges resulting in vision. She spent the 1948 academic year in London, England, as a U.S. Public Health Service Fellow at the University College Hospital Medical School. She earned her Ph.D. in biology from Radcliffe in 1950. In 1952, she was awarded a John Simon Guggenheim Fellowship to work at the Carlsberg Laboratory at the University of Copenhagen.

In 1958 Hubbard, who had been divorced from Frank Hubbard since 1951, married George Wald, with who she had been working closely for many years. They had two children, Elijah and Deborah Hannah Wald. Hubbard remained at Harvard as a research fellow in biology until 1959 when she was promoted to research associate. Hubbard and Wald coauthored countless publications, and were corecipients of the Paul Karrer Medal of the University of Zurich in 1967, the same year Wald won the Nobel Prize in Medicine for his research on vision. Hubbard had her own research funding and worked independently for many years, making important studies on the biological synthesis and mechanisms of the pigments involved in vision.

Becomes First Woman to be Tenured at Harvard

During the 1960s, Hubbard had become interested in the sociology of science as well as women's status in the scientific community. In particular, she came to realize that very few women scientists held tenure–track faculty positions, regardless of their scientific achievements and recognition. Although she continued to teach photochemistry, she added courses on health, women's issues, and science and society. Hubbard began to raise questions of bias in her books, arguing that social, political, and personal agendas of the scientists conducting research leads to choices about which questions scientists ask, and affects the way answers are interpreted. "Scientists do not just hold up a mirror to nature. They use something more like a coarse sieve through which fall all the things they don't notice or take to be irrelevant. [. . .] Our scientific reality, like all reality, is a social construct," she said in her book, *The Politics of Women's Biology.*

Scheduled by the American Association for the Advancement of Science to present a talk on being a woman and a scientist, Hubbard interviewed her female peers and stumbled on a startling inequity. None of them were tenured. "I don't know whether any of us, until that moment realize that we were all accomplished and were all recognized in our fields but that none of us had real jobs," she claimed in an article in *Scientific American* in June 1995. She joined a group petitioning the administration to address the discrepancy and in 1973, became the first woman to receive tenure at Harvard.

Hubbard has been an outspoken critic of genetic reductionism—the tendency to attribute all human characteristics to heredity without considering environmental influences. She also has been concerned with possible abuses of the new genetic technologies, particularly in the areas of health care and reproduction. Her controversial book *Exploding the Gene Myth*, coauthored with her son, Elijah Wald, addresses this concern with "genomania." She aims to dismantle the myth that everything we are and do comes out of our genes. Hubbard's political concerns were shared by her husband, who died in 1997.

Hubbard has written over 150 articles on science and on women's issues, for both scientific and popular publications. In 1985 she won the Peace and Freedom award of the Women's International League for Peace and Freedom. Hubbard holds honorary degrees from Macalester College in St. Paul, Minnesota, from Southern Illinois University at Edwardsville, and from the University of Toronto. She has been an emeritus professor at Harvard since 1990. In 1992, she was awarded the AIBS Distinguished Service Award, cited by one nominator as "a role model as an exemplary scientist and as a leader in working for women's rights."

SELECTED WRITINGS BY HUBBARD:

Books

"Have Only Men Evolved?" In *Biological Woman: The Convenient Myth.* Edited by Ruth Hubbard, Mary Sue Henifen, and Barbara Fried. Cambridge, MA: Schenkman, 1982.

(With Marian Lowe, editors) *Genes and Gender II: Pitfalls in Research on Sex and Gender.* New York: Gordian, 1979.

The Politics of Women's Biology. New Brunswick, NJ: Rutgers University Press, 1990.

Profitable Promises: Essays on Women, Science, and Health. Monroe, ME: Common Courage Press, 1995.

(With Margaret Randall) *The Shape of Red: Insider/Outsider Reflections.* San Francisco: Cleis, 1988.

(With Elijah Wald) *Exploding the Gene Myth: How Genetic Information is Produced and Manipulated by Scientists, Physicians, Employers, Insurance Companies, Educators, and Law Enforcers.* Boston: Beacon Press, 1993.

Periodicals

(With D. Bownds and T. Yoshizawa) "The Chemistry of Visual Photoreception." *Cold Spring Harbor Symposia on Quantitative Biology* 30 (1965): 301–15.

"100 Years of Rhodopsin." *Trends in Biochemical Science* 1 (1976): 154–58.

"Absorption Spectrum of Rhodopsin: 280 nm Absorption Band." *Nature* (1969) 221: 435–37.

"Molecular Isomers in Vision." *Scientific American* 216 (June 1967): 64–70.

"Sexism in Science." *Radcliffe Quarterly* 62 (March 1976): 8–11.

"The Stereoisomerization of 11–cis–Retinal." *Journal of Biological Chemistry*241 (1966): 1814–18.

FURTHER READING

Books

American Men and Women of Science 20th ed. New Brunswick, NJ: R.R. Bowker, 1998, p 1040.

O'Neill, Lois Decker, ed. *The Women's Book of World Records and Achievements.* Garden City, NY: Doubleday, 1979.

Who's Who in America. Vol. 1. 52d ed. New Providence, NJ: Marquis Who's Who, 1998.

Periodicals

Holloway, Marguerite. "Profile: Ruth Hubbard: Turning the Inside Out." *Scientific American* 272 (June 1995): 49–50.

"Hubbard Named 1992 AIBS Distinguished Service Award Winner." *BioScience* (April 1992): 323.

Other

Aqueno, F. "Exploding the Gene Myth, A Conversation with Ruth Hubbard" 1997. Http://eng.hss.cmu.edu/gender/exploding–the–gene–myth.html (March 13, 1999).

"Ruth Hubbard." *Contemporary Authors Online.* The Gale Group, 1999. http://www.galenet.com.

Sketch by Margaret Alic

Marie Aimee (Lullin) Huber
fl. 1800s
Swiss entomologist

Marie Aimee Huber was the wife of Francois Huber, the blind naturalist and expert on honeybees. Marie Huber helped her husband conduct research on bees and kept detailed observations about their experiments. In addition, she was his reader and correspondent, keeping Francois in touch with other scientists and researchers.

Francois Huber was born to a wealthy Swiss family. His father exposed him to the natural sciences, and he showed an early interest in the honeybee, due in part to his reading of Reamure and the influence of Charles Bonnett. In fact, Francois was such a devoted scholar that he caused his own blindness at the age of 17 due to his constant studying. About this time, he met Marie Aimee Lullin at a dancing school, and fell in love with this Swiss Republic magistrate's daughter. Marie was devoted to Francois, so much so that when family and friends opposed the marriage due to his blindness, she became even more committed to him.

But Marie's parents would not allow the marriage. Marie brushed off all other suitors, waiting until the age of 25 when she did not need the consent of her parents to marry. Even then her father did not attend the ceremony. Many years later, her parents accepted the marriage, which was blessed and happy, producing a daughter, a son, and a wealth of scientific information over the next 40 years until Marie's death.

Although honeybees had been of interest for many years, no one had ever studied their lives and habits in detail until the Hubers. Their book, *Nouvelles Observations sur les Abeilles*, published under Francois's name, made an impact in the scientific world, full as it was of ground–breaking discoveries and pioneering research.

With Francois as director and Marie as bench scientist, the pair studied beeswax, honey, combs, oxygen use, pollen, brood rearing, antennae, memory, mutation of workers into queens, queen behavior and mating, swarm origination and behavior, and drones. They also studied the honeybees' natural enemies, the wax moths. Tireless in their experiments, accurate in their observations, and precise in their writing, the Hubers contributed a world of information to the study of honeybees and other insects, paving the way for later scientists and research.

Without the help of his wife, who became his "eyes," Francois could not have learned so much about the life and behavior of honeybees as he did. Marie died in her sixties, and Francois went to live with his daughter and her family in Lausanne, Switzerland, where he remained until his death in 1831.

FURTHER READING

Books

Mozans, H. J. *Woman in Science*. Notre Dame: University of Notre Dame Press, 1991.

Sanders, Lloyd C. *Celebrities of the Century*. Ann Arbor: Gryphon Books, 1971.

Periodicals

"Impossible Career: A Life of Francois Huber." *Gleanings in Bee Culture* 8 (October 1957): 593–96.

Sketch by Helene Barker Kiser

Margaret Lindsay (Murray) Huggins
1854–1915
Irish-English astronomer

Lady Margaret Huggins, a well-known observational astronomer in her own day, is best known for her collaboration with her husband William Huggins. Together, they helped to prove that the earth and stars are composed of the same elements. Because of her collaboration with her more famous husband, Margaret Huggins's contributions to astronomy often have gone unrecognized.

Margaret Lindsay Murray was born in Dublin, Ireland, in 1854. Her father, John Murray, was a lawyer. Her mother died when she was very young and following her father's remarriage, she spent a great deal of time alone. One bright spot in Huggins' lonely life was her grandfather. He was an amateur astronomer and he spent his evenings introducing her to the constellations. Her interest stimulated, she began to study the heavens on her own, constructing her own instruments. She used a dark lantern and a star atlas to study the heavens at night. By the age of 10, Huggins had undertaken a systematic study of sunspots. After reading a magazine article, she managed to build her own spectroscope to study the unique bands and lines, or spectra, formed by the light emitted from stars. She also taught herself photography.

Huggins' interest in spectroscopy led her to ask a Dublin telescope maker to arrange a meeting with Sir William Huggins. Twenty–six years her senior, William Huggins was an established astronomer who had first built an observatory in his home on Upper Tulse Hill in London in 1856. His early spectroscopic observations had established that, although some types of nebulae, clouds of dust or gas in interstellar spaces, could resolve into individual stars with a powerful telescope, others were made up of gases, which could eventually form into stars. He also had developed a method for determining the motions of stars and the rotations of the sun and planets. At the time of their marriage in 1875, Margaret Huggins had realized that photography could be used to study solar spectra and her photographic expertise became an important component of their collaboration. As Marcia Bartusiak quoted from Huggins's descriptions of her methods: "Our exposures on each star had to be very long. I have, I think, worked on one for about three hours. . . I can go and stand well at good heights on ladders and twist well. (Astronomers need universal joints and vertebrae of india rubber.)" In 1899, the Hugginses published *An Atlas of Representative Stellar Spectra* that included their original spectrographic plates.

In the early years of their collaboration, William Huggins authored the publications, while crediting his wife as his assistant. Later, the publications included both names and it is difficult to determine individual contributions. Their joint publications included papers on chemical spectra, the planets, and the spectra of the stars Sirius and Nova Aurigae and the Andromeda and Orion nebulae. Most of these works were published in the *Proceedings of the Royal Society*. In addition, they published two volumes on the observations made at their Tulse Hill Observatory. Margaret Huggins' artistic skill was evident in the pencil drawings that accompanied these works.

Margaret Huggins was a very intelligent and talented woman with many interests besides astronomy. She was a fine painter who also collected and restored antiques. She accompanied her husband on the piano and organ, when he played his Stradivarius violin, and she published a book on the life and work of the Italian violin maker Giovanni Paolo Maggini. Childless, the Hugginses shared their life with their dog Kepler, named for the astronomer who first computed the elliptical orbits of the planets. Kepler was said to have the ability to bark out the answers to arithmetic problems, as long as the solution was either three or four.

Although women were not awarded regular fellowships in the Royal Astronomical Society, Huggins received an honorary membership in 1903. Margaret Huggins died in 1915, five years after her husband. She was a close friend of the American astronomer **Sarah Whiting**, director of the Wellesley College Observatory in Massachusetts, and she donated a number of personal items to Wellesley. These included many antiques, books, a collection of her drawings, a collection of astronomical instruments, including spectroscopes, and the manuscript notebooks of William Huggins.

SELECTED WRITINGS BY HUGGINS:

Books

Kepler. A Biography. London: Hazell Watson and Viney, n.d.

Gio: Paolo Maggini, His Life and Work. London: W. E. Hill and Sons, 1892.

(with William Huggins) *An Atlas of Representative Stellar Spectra. From 4870 to 3300. Together with a Discussion of the Evolutional Order of the Stars, and the Interpretations of Their Spectra. Preceded by a Short History of the Observatory and Its Work*. London, 1899.

(with William Huggins, editors) *The Scientific Papers of Sir William Huggins, K.C.B., O.M.* London: William Wesley and Son, 1909.

FURTHER READING

Books

Bartusiak, Marcia. *Through a Universe Darkly: A Cosmic Tale of Ancient Ethers, Dark Matter, and the Fate of the Universe*. New York: HarperCollins, 1993.

Clerke, Agnes M. *A Popular History of Astronomy during the Nineteenth Century*. 1885. Reprint. London: Adam and Charles Black, 1908.

Ogilvie, Marilyn Bailey. "Marital Collaboration: An Approach to Science." In *Uneasy Careers and Intimate Lives: Women in Science 1789–1979*. Edited by Pnina G. Abir–Am and Dorinda Outram. New Brunswick: Rutgers University Press, 1987.

Sketch by Margaret Alic

Ellen Hutchins
1785–1815
Irish botanist

Ellen Hutchins was born in Ballylickey, west Cork, Ireland, in 1785 and educated in Dublin. As a teenager, she developed a chronic illness that required regular medical attention. She was placed under the care of Dr. Whitley Stokes, one of the foremost naturalists of his time, and Hutchins developed an interest in botany through him. Hutchins began by studying what were then called cryptograms, an archaic term for the lower plants, in the Bantry Bay area. She was primarily interested in seaweeds and lichens and became a pioneer in the study of algae. Stokes introduced her to many prominent naturalists throughout the course of her career, including Dawson Turner, J.E. Smith, and James Townsend Mackay, a curator of the Trinity College Botanic Gardens, established in 1806. Hutchins provided important research support to these and other scientists, all the while tending to her elderly mother and invalid brother, in addition to battling her own illness.

Hutchins was a painter as well as a scientist and was able to meld her two interests by providing drawings and paintings for scientific publications, including *Flora Hibernica, English Botany, and Historia Fuci*. Her promising career was cut short by an early death on February 10, 1815. She died at Ardnagashel House, Bantry, County Cork.

Hutchins's contributions to the fields of botany and painting have both been memorialized. Several plants are named after her, including *Hutchinsia alpina*, an Alpine cress, and *Jungermannia hutchinsiae*, a native liverwort. In addition, her watercolors are displayed in museums throughout Great Britain, including the Royal Botanic Gardens in Kew, England.

FURTHER READING

O'Ceirin, Kit, and Cyril O'Ceirin. *Women of Ireland: A Biographic Dictionary*. Minneapolis: Irish Books and Media, 1996.

Sketch by Kristin Palm

Ida Henrietta Hyde
1857–1945
American physiologist

The opportunities of generations of women scientists and academics have been enlarged and enhanced by the pioneering work of Ida H. Hyde, a physiologist of respected stature and the first woman to win a doctorate at Germany's Heidelberg University. Hyde's research in vertebrate and invertebrate circulatory, respiratory, and nervous systems was only outdone by her untiring efforts at securing scholarships and placement for worthy women scientists.

Ida Henrietta Hyde personally knew the difficulties a woman faced in the late–nineteenth century. She was born in Davenport, Iowa, on September 8, 1857, one of four children of German immigrant parents. Her father, Meyer Heidenheimer, was a merchant, and her mother was Babette Loewenthal Heidenheimer. Upon their arrival in the United States, they adopted the name Hyde. Education at the time was something reserved for men, and at age sixteen Hyde was apprenticed to a millinery establishment, where she remained for the next seven years. But she always retained a dream of studying and attended evening classes at the Chicago Athenaeum. Finally Hyde quit her job and entered the University of Illinois in 1881, but she had only enough money for one year of study. Already she was leaning toward natural history, the study of plants and animals.

There followed another seven–year stint of work, this time teaching in the Chicago public schools, before she could return to college. She enrolled at Cornell University in 1888, earning her B.S. in pre–medicine in 1891. From there she went on to two years of graduate study at Bryn Mawr, studying with the well known physiologist Jacques Loeb. During the summers she studied and worked at the marine laboratory at Woods Hole in Massachusetts. Hyde's research project toward a graduate degree was on development, and she was invited to Germany's University of Strassburg to continue her work. She won a fellowship from the Association of Collegiate Alumnae—the American Association of University Women, as it was later known—enabling her to accept the invitation.

Takes Degree from Heidelberg

More hurdles faced Hyde in Germany, however, for Strassburg would not let a woman earn a doctorate, even though research she submitted was considered sufficient for the degree by her professor. She had to transfer to the University of Heidelberg, where, still facing prejudice against women in academia, she finally received her Ph.D. in physiology. Before returning to the United States in 1896, Hyde visited two other European research facilities. She spent some time at the Naples Zoological Station, a European equivalent of Woods Hole, where she researched the physiology of salivary glands. Briefly, she also conducted research at the University of Berne, Switzerland.

Once back in America she was instrumental in setting up a visiting research position for women at the Naples laboratory. From 1896 to 1897, while a research fellow at Radcliffe College, Hyde became the first woman to do research at the Harvard Medical School, and in 1898 she accepted a position at the University of Kansas as an assistant professor in physiology. She became a noted educator as well as researcher, writing both a basic text in physiology (*Outlines of Experimental Physiology,* 1905) and a laboratory manual (*Laboratory Outlines of Physiology,* 1910). She contributed scores of articles to journals on topics from embryonic development to the microtechniques for individual cell study. Her achievements were honored in 1902 by her election to the American Physiological Society as the first woman member. In 1905 she became a full professor of physiology in the newly–created physiology department at the University of Kansas, researched marine physiology at Woods Hole for several summers, and completed most of the requirements for a medical degree through summer study from 1908 to 1912 at Rush Medical College in Chicago.

Hyde retired from the University of Kansas in 1920, but not from active involvement in both scientific and social pursuits. During 1922 and 1923, she worked once again at Heidelberg, researching the effects of radium, and she donated $25,000 to fund the Ida H. Hyde Woman's International Fellowship through the American Association of University Women. Always a champion of women's rights, Hyde set an example by her life and works for others to follow. On August 22, 1945, at the age of 88, she died of a cerebral hemorrhage in Berkeley, California, where she had spent the final years of her life.

SELECTED WRITINGS BY HYDE:

Books

Outlines of Experimental Physiology, University of Kansas, 1905.

Laboratory Outlines of Physiology, University of Kansas, 1914.

Periodicals

"The Effect of Distention of the Ventricle on the Flow of Blood Through the Walls of the Heart." *American Journal of Physiology* 1 (1898): 215–224.

"A Study of the Respiratory and Cardiac Activities and Blood Pressure in the Skate Following Intravenous Injection of Salt Solutions." *University of Kansas Science Bulletin* 5, no. 4 (1911): 27–63.

"The Development of a Tunicate without Nerves." *University of Kansas Science Bulletin* 9, no. 15 (1915): 175–179.

"Before Women Were Human Beings." *Journal of the American Association of University Women* (June 1938): 226–236.

FURTHER READING

Books

American Women 1935–1940: A Composite Biographical Dictionary. Vol. 1. Detroit: Gale, 1981, p. 444.
Notable American Women 1607–1950. Vol. 2. Cambridge: Harvard University Press, 1971, pp. 247–249.
Ogilvie, Marilyn Bailey. *Women in Science, Antiquity through the Nineteenth Century.* Cambridge: MIT Press, 1986, pp. 103–104.
Read, Phyllis J., and Bernard L. Witlieb. *The Book of Women's Firsts.* Random House, 1992, p. 224.
Women in the Scientific Search: An American Bio–Bibliography. Scarecrow Press, 1985, pp. 268–270.

Periodicals

"Ida H. Hyde, Pioneer." *Journal of the American Association of University Women* (fall 1945): 42.
Sloan, Jan Butin. "The Founding of the Naples Table Association for Promoting Scientific Research by Women, 1897." *Signs: Journal of Women in Culture and Society* (autumn 1978): 208–216.

Sketch by J. Sydney Jones

Libbie Henrietta Hyman
1888–1969
American zoologist

Libbie Hyman (Corbis/Bettmann-UPI. Reproduced by permission.)

Libbie Hyman, a world-renowned authority on invertebrates (animals without backbones), was one of the most important American zoologists of the mid-twentieth century. Following years of research in developmental biology, she authored the standard English language reference book on the taxonomy, or classification, and physiology of the hundreds of thousands of species of lower invertebrates.

Born in 1888 in Des Moines, Iowa, Hyman was the third of four children of Jewish immigrants, Joseph and Sabina (Neumann) Hyman. Her father had escaped from Russian-controlled Poland, and her mother had emigrated from Germany. Growing up in Fort Dodge, Iowa, where her father, a tailor, ran an unsuccessful clothing store, Hyman's home life was not a happy one. From an early age, Hyman occupied herself with collecting and identifying moths, butterflies, and plants. Graduating from the public high school as valedictorian in 1905, she took additional high school courses in science and German, but was only able to get a factory job pasting labels on boxes of rolled oats. When her English and German teacher, Mary Crawford, discovered what Hyman was doing, she helped her obtain a tuition scholarship to the University of Chicago for the following year. Working at various jobs to support herself while attending college, Hyman lived with an aunt and uncle until her father's death in 1907, when her mother and three bachelor brothers moved to Chicago. Although her family never approved of her career, she continued to live with them until her mother's death in 1929.

Hyman first majored in botany, switched to chemistry due to anti-Semitism in the botany department, and then changed again to zoology in her third year. Encouraged by zoology graduate student Mary Blount, Hyman took an invertebrate zoology course with the controversial scientist Charles Manning Child. After receiving her bachelor's degree in zoology in 1910, she became Child's first graduate student. Hyman succeeded Blount as the laboratory assistant for the elementary zoology and comparative vertebrate anatomy courses. Eventually, she was asked to write laboratory manuals for these courses. These became standard texts, and she continued to revise them until 1960.

After earning her Ph.D. in 1915, Hyman remained at Chicago as Child's research assistant. For the next 16 years, she studied the embryological development of flatworms and other invertebrates, and the ability of these organisms to regenerate body parts. Although her research was directed at demonstrating Child's hypothesis of metabolic gradients, or patterns of development, in organisms, most of her publications represented independent experimental work, and her background in chemistry enabled her to bring a new dimension to Child's research. Hyman preferred taxonomy to experimental science, and her first taxonomic paper appeared in 1925. She was considered an expert on the identification and classification of free-living (nonparasitic) flatworms, receiving specimens for identification from all over the world.

The royalties from Hyman's laboratory manuals provided her with financial independence and, with Child on the verge of retirement, Hyman decided to work on her own. According to some sources, as a Jewish female with a reportedly abrasive personality, not even the University of Chicago was willing to offer her a regular faculty position. In 1931 she resigned her laboratory post and traveled to Europe for 15 months. She then settled in New York City and began work on the first volume of *The Invertebrates.* At the time, there was no comprehensive reference work on the invertebrates in English. Hyman began to synthesize and integrate the anatomy, embryology, physiology, and ecology of each class of these animals. After several years of working at home, the American Museum of Natural History offered her an office and laboratory space, without a salary. She had a photographic memory and a facility with languages that enabled her to do her own translations. She spent her summers at Woods Hole Marine Biological Laboratory, in Massachusetts, and other marine laboratories, where she prepared her own biological specimens and did the all of the drawings for her books. As they appeared, each volume of *The Invertebrates* was acclaimed for its comprehensiveness, clarity, and critical scholarship. When the University of Chicago granted 20 honorary doctorates in science, to celebrate the university's fiftieth anniversary, Hyman was one of two women so honored, based on the first published volume of *The Invertebrates.*

Hyman continued her laboratory studies throughout her life and published some 145 scientific papers. She was involved with various scientific societies, serving as vice–president of the American Society of Zoologists and as president of the Society of Systematic Zoology. She also edited the journal *Systematic Zoology.* Hyman held honorary doctorates from Goucher, Coe, and Upsala Colleges, as well as from the University of Chicago. She was an elected member of the National Academy of Sciences and the American Academy of Arts and Sciences, and she received gold medals from the Linnean Society of London and the American Museum of Natural History.

Hyman finished only the first six of ten projected volumes of *The Invertebrates.* However these remain primary references in invertebrate zoology. Suffering from Parkinson's disease during the last 10 years of her life, Hyman continued to work at the Museum of Natural History until her death in 1969. A rare species of planarian from Lake Tahoe, *Dendrocoelopsis hymanae*, was named in her honor.

SELECTED WRITINGS BY HYMAN:

Books

A Laboratory Manual for Elementary Zoology. Chicago: University of Chicago Press, 1919.

A Laboratory Manual for Comparative Vertebrate Zoology. Chicago: University of Chicago Press, 1922.

The Invertebrates. New York: McGraw–Hill, 1940–1967.

Comparative Vertebrate Anatomy. Chicago: University of Chicago Press, 1942.

Periodicals

"The Effect of Oxygen Tension on Oxygen Consumption in Planaria and Echinoderms." *Physiological Zoology* 2 (1930): 505–34.

"Taxonomic Studies on the Hydras of North America. I, II, III." *Transactions of the American Microscopical Society* 48 (1929): 406–15; 49 (1930): 322–33; 50 (1931): 20–29.

FURTHER READING

Books

Kass–Simon, G. "Biology is Destiny." In *Women of Science: Righting the Record.* Edited by G. Kass–Simon and Patricia Farnes. Bloomington: Indiana University Press, 1990.

Kelly, Diane A. "Libbie Henrietta Hyman." In *Notable Women in the Life Sciences: A Biographical Dictionary.* Edited by Benjamin F. Shearer and Barbara S. Shearer. Westport, CT: Greenwood Press, 1996.

Rossiter, Margaret W. *Women Scientists in America: Struggles and Strategies to 1940.* Baltimore: Johns Hopkins University Press, 1982.

Winsor, Mary P. "Libbie Henrietta Hyman." In *Notable American Women: The Modern Period: A Biographical Dictionary.* Edited by Barbara Sicherman, Carol Hurd Green, Ilene Kantrov, and Harriette Walker. Cambridge: Harvard University Press, 1980.

Yost, Edna. *American Women of Science.* Philadelphia: J. B. Lippincott, 1955.

Sketch by Margaret Alic

Hypatia of Alexandria (Corbis-Bettmann. Reproduced by permission.)

Hypatia of Alexandria
370(?)–415
Greek mathematician, astronomer, and philosopher

Hypatia was the earliest known woman scientist who whose life has been recorded in some detail. The daughter of a mathematician, she was trained in mathematics and philosophy and became head of the Neoplatonic school at Alexandria, where she taught philosophical doctrines dating back to Plato's Academy. Hypatia was a respected teacher and influential citizen of Alexandria, greatly admired for her knowledge. Although Hypatia's original work has not survived, she is known from the letters of her student Synesius of Cyrene. She is also mentioned in the fifth–century *Ecclesiastical History* of Socrates Scholasticus, and in the tenth–century *Lexicon* of Suda (or Suidas). Information about Hypatia is fragmentary and oblique, fact and fiction have mingled, and her life has become the stuff of legend, inconsistencies, and conflicting opinions.

Hypatia was born in Alexandria, Egypt; the year is generally thought to be 370, although some scholars argue for an earlier date, 355. Founded on the Nile River by Alexander the Great in 332 B.C., Alexandria had been the center of scholarly attainment in science, and during Hypatia's time was the third largest city in the Roman Empire. Hypatia's father, Theon, was a member of the Museum, a place of residence, study, and teaching similar to a modern university. A mathematician and astronomer, Theon had predicted eclipses of the sun and the moon which were observed in Alexandria, and his scholarship included commentaries on Euclid and Ptolemy. Hypatia was taught by Theon, collaborated with him, and did independent work. Whereas Theon also produced poetic work and a treatise on the interpretation of omens, Hypatia's works seem to have been strictly mathematical.

Becomes Head of Neoplatonic School

Hypatia was recognized as a gifted scholar and eloquent teacher, and by 390 her circle of influence was well–established. By 400, she was head of the Neoplatonic school, for which she received a salary. Socrates Scholasticus, the Byzantine church historian, wrote that Hypatia was so learned in literature and science that she exceeded all contemporary philosophers. Philostorgius, another historian, noted that she surpassed her father in mathematics, and especially in astronomy. From Synesius' letters to and about her, it is clear Hypatia had extensive knowledge of Greek literature. Her students were aristocratic young men, both pagan and Christian, who rose to occupy influential civil and ecclesiastical positions. They came from elsewhere in Egypt, and from as far away as Cyrene, Syria, and Constantinople to study privately with Hypatia in her home. They were united through intellectual pursuits and considered Hypatia their "divine guide" into the realm of philosophical and cosmic mysteries, which included science.

By wearing a tribon, the characteristic rough white robe of the philosopher, Hypatia indicated that she did not wish to be treated as a woman. She traveled freely about the city in her chariot, instructed her students in Platonic and Aristotelian philosophy, visited and lectured at public and scientific institutions. She had exerted political influence and may have held a political position. In one of his letters to her, Synesius asks Hypatia to intervene with her powerful friends to restore the property of two young men. Throughout his life Synesius remained devoted to Hypatia, praised her erudition, and asked for advice on his own writings. He must have visited her the several times he visited Alexandria, including in 410, when he was consecrated as Bishop of Ptolemais by Theophilus, the patriarch of Alexandria.

Works on Commentaries and Scientific Instruments

Although several of Theon's mathematical and astronomical works have survived, Hypatia's have not. It is known that Hypatia wrote a treatise titled *Astronomical Canon*, presumably on the movements of the planets, and a commentary on the algebraic work of Diophantus of Alexandria, which contains the beginnings of number theory. Diophantus, who lived in the third century A.D., is quoted by Theon, and some scholars believe that the survival of most of Diophantus' original 13 books of the *Arithmetica* is due to the quality of Hypatia's work. The surviving texts, including six in Greek and four translated into Arabic, contain notes, remarks, and interpolations that may come from Hypatia's commentary. Hypatia also wrote *On the Conics of Apollonius*, in which she elaborated on Apollonius' third–century B.C.theory of conic sections.

In collaboration with Theon, Hypatia also worked on Ptolemy's *Almagest*, the second–century work which brought together disparate works of early Greeks in 13 volumes and served as the standard reference on astronomy for more than 1,000 years. In the *Almagest*, Ptolemy introduced a method of classifying stars, and used Apollonius' mathematics to construct a masterful (though incorrect) theory of epicycles to explain the movement of the sun, moon and planets in a geocentric system. Hypatia may have corrected not only her father's commentary but also the text of *Almagest* itself, and may also have prepared a new edition of Ptolemy's *Handy Tables*, which appears in the work of Hesychius under the title *The Astronomical Canon.*

Synesius' letters reveal Hypatia's interest in scientific instruments. In one instance he asks her to have a hydroscope (an instrument for measuring the specific gravity of a liquid) made for him. In another, he consults her about the construction of an astrolabe, an instrument used to measure the position of the stars and planets.

Meets a Violent Death

In Hypatia's time, Christianity became the official religion of the Roman empire, and Greek temples were converted to Christian churches. In 411, Cyril succeeded Theophilus as bishop of Alexandria. One of his actions, following Jewish–Christian riots, was to expel Jews from the city. Orestes, the civil governor, disapproved of Cyril's actions and the growing encroachment of the Christian church on civil authority. Cyril roused negative sentiment toward Orestes, and Orestes was attacked by five hundred Nitrian monks, who lived in monasteries outside the city. The monk Ammonius threw a stone that wounded Orestes. Intervention by the populace saved Orestes, who then ordered Ammonius tortured to the extent that he died. Cyril applauded Ammonius' actions as admirable.

Hypatia fell victim to these political hostilities. She was a close associate of Orestes, and undoubtedly was defamed by Cyril. Admiration for her turned to resentment, and she was perceived as an obstacle to the conciliation of Orestes and Cyril. In March of 415, during Lent, as Hypatia rode in her chariot through the streets of Alexandria, she was attacked upon by a fanatical mob of antipagan Christians. The mob dragged Hypatia into the Caesareum, then a Christian church, where she was stripped naked and murdered. According to ancient accounts, Hypatia's flesh was stripped from her bones, her body mutilated and scattered throughout the streets, then burned piecemeal at a place called Cinaron.

Following Hypatia's murder many of her students migrated to Athens, where they contributed to the Athenian school, which in 420 acquired a considerable reputation in mathematics. The Neoplatonic school at Alexandria continued until the Arab invasion of 642. The books in the library at Alexandria were subsequently used as fuel for the city's baths, where they lasted six months. Hypatia's works were probably among them.

FURTHER READING

Books

Bregman, Jay. *Synesius of Cyrene: Philosopher–Bishop.* Berkeley: University of California Press, 1982.

Dzielska, Maria. *Hypatia of Alexandria.* Translated by F. Lyra. Cambridge: Harvard University Press, 1995.

Fitzgerald, Augustine. *The Letters of Synesius of Cyrene.* London: Oxford University Press, 1926.

Lefkowitz, Mary R. *Women in Greek Myth.* Baltimore: Johns Hopkins University Press, 1986.

Snyder, Jane McIntosh. *The Woman and the Lyre: Women Writers in Classical Greece and Rome.* Carbondale: Southern Illinois University Press, 1989, pp. 113–121.

Socrates (Scholasticus). *Ecclesiastical History.* London: Samuel Bagster and Sons, 1844, pp. 480–483.

Waithe, Mary Ellen. "Finding Bits and Pieces of Hypatia." In *Hypatia's Daughters: Fifteen Hundred Years of Women Philosophers.* Edited by Linda Lopez McAlister. Bloomington: Indiana Univ. Press, 1996, pp. 4–15.

Periodicals

Rist, J. M. "Hypatia." *Phoenix* (autumn 1965): 214–225.

Other

Adair, Ginny. "Hypatia." *Biographies of Women Mathematicians.* June 1997. http://www.scottlan.edu/lriddle/women/chronol.htm (July 22, 1997).

Sketch by Jill Carpenter

I

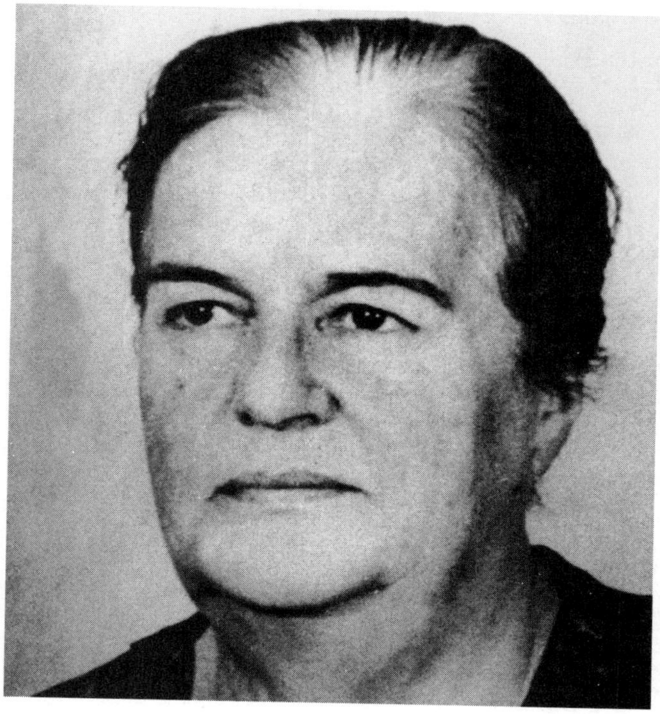

Valentina Ivanovna Iveronova

Valentina Ivanovna Iveronova
1908–1983
Russian crystallographer and physicist

Valentina Ivanovna Iveronova was an internationally renowned crystallographer in Russia and a professor at the Departments of Physics and Solid-State Physics of Moscow University. Under Iveronova's guidance, the department conducted research into the short range order of solid solutions, dynamics of lattice, crystal defects' influence on x-ray scattering patterns, and dynamics of x-ray scattering in ideal and real crystals, thus significantly advancing the knowledge in these areas.

Iveronova also took part in the development of the dynamic theory of x-ray scatteriing, and her book with G. P. Revkevich on this subject became a standard reference around the world. Another textbook Iveronova edited, *General Physics Practical Course,* became the major reference for physics faculties in Russia. Iveronova was awarded the Order "Band of Honor" in 1957 and the Order of Lenin in 1961. These orders were Russia's highest awards at that time.

In 1979 Iveronova and her colleague, A.A. Katsnelson, received the Fedorov prize for their outstanding achievements in the field of short–range order of solid solutions. For the first time they proved that short–range order in such systems is heterogeneous and also determined its effects on many physical properties. The results of these investigations were summarized in the monograph "Short-range Order in Solid Solutions."

Shows Early Interest in Math

Iveronova was born on September 17, 1908 in Moscow, the youngest of two sisters and a brother, to Ivan Aleksandrovich Iveronov and Olga Ivanovna Iveronova. Her father was the professor and rector of the Peter the Great Agricultural Academy (now The Timiryazev of Agricultural Sciences) until his death in 1915. Her mother had a diploma in teaching and after the Revolution worked as a teacher at a secondary school. Iveronova was greatly affected by her father's death. Iveronova was interested in mathematics since childhood and both her parents encouraged her to pursue a career in science.

She entered Moscow State University (MSU) in 1925 and graduated in 1930 with a specialization in x-ray diffraction and its application. After graduation from MSU she worked for a short time at several Moscow research institutes. She received her Ph.D. from MSU in 1936, after completing research into recrystallization of metals and their alloys.

In 1938 she returned to MSU, where she remained until her death. She obtained a degree of Dr. of Science in 1947, after additional work involving recrystallization and metal solid solutions. The following year she became a professor at MSU in the Department of Physics. In 1951 Iveronova was promoted to chief of the General Physics Department and remained in this position until 1968. In 1953, when the physics department moved to new facilities in the Lenin Hills, Iveronova upgraded the curriculum to double the number of students and improve the quality of teaching. During her tenure as department head, she also taught general physics courses.

Distinguishes Herself in Research

From 1969 until her death, Iveronova was a professor-consultant and chair of the Solid State Physics Department.

In this position she taught many courses, including cinematic and dynamics theory of x-ray scattering. Under her guidance, research for 30 Ph.Ds was completed. In addition, Iveronova made time to be involved with several scientific organizations, including the "Znaniye (Knowledge) Society." For several years, Iveronova was also Vice President of the Council on Physics at the Ministry for High and Middle Education of USSR.

Iveronova was married to German Stepanovich Zhdanov, a famous physician and professor of MSU, who died in 1991 in Moscow. They had one daughter, Natalja Zhdanova, who was born in 1933. She followed in her mother's footsteps and received a Dr. of Science in physics.

Iveronova died on July 27, 1983 from heart failure. During her career she took part in numerous international congresses on crystallography, authored over 130 papers, and wrote or edited four major books in her field. Her paper, "The Role of General Physics Courses for Training Physics in the Universities of USSR," was published in 1966 in the British publication *The Education of Physicists.*

SELECTED WRITINGS BY IVERONOVA:

Books

(Editor) *Physical Laboratories General Course.* 1st ed. Moscow: GTTI, 1951.

ibid. Second Edition. Moscow: Fizmatgiz, 1962.

ibid. Third Edition. Moscow: Nauka, 1967–1968.

(With A. A. Katsnelson) *Short Range Order in Solid Solutions.* Moscow: Nauka, 1977.

(With G.P. Revkevich) *Theory of X-Ray Diffraction.* Moscow State University. First Edition, 1972. Second Edition, 1978.

Periodicals

(With T.P. Kostetskaya) "X-ray Investigation of Tiredness by Bending of Different Sign." *Journal of Technical Physics* 19, no. 4 (1940): 304–08.

(With A.A. Katsnelson) "The Problem of Crystal Mosaics in Polycrystal Metals." *Journal of Technical Physics* 25, no. 4 (1955): 696–99.

(With N.S. Andreeva) "The Problem of Structure Peculiarities of Fibrillar Proteins." *Doclady of Science Academy of USSR* 191, no. 1 (1955): 111–14.

(With A.P. Zvyagina) "Spectrum of Thermal Oscillations and Characteristic Debay–Temperature of CsCl Type Crystal Lattice." *Izvestiya of Science Academy of USSR* 26, no. 3 (1962): 340–44.

(With A.A. Katsnelson, M.D. Kondrat'eva, and G.P. Revkevich) "Direct Evidence of Concentration Nonhomogeneousness in Cu–Pt Alloy on Initial Stage of Ordering." *Fiz. Met. and Metalloved* 31, no. 3 (1971): 661–63.

(With A.V. Kuznetsov) "Calculation of X–Ray Absorption Interference Coefficient Dependence on Dislocation Density." *Solid State Physics (S–P)* 15, no. 9 (1973): 2689–94.

(With A.A. Katsnelson) "Modern Problems of Short–Range Order." *Reine und Angewandte Metallkunde in Einzerdarstellung* 24 (1974): 306–19

FURTHER READING

Books

Kass–Simon, G. and Patricia Farnes, ed. *Women of Science: Righting the Record.* Bloomington: Indiana University Press, 1990.

Periodicals

J. Crystallog. (Rus.) 29, no. 1 (1984): 189.

J. Uspekhi Phys. Nauk (Rus.) 143, no. 1 (1984): 131–32.

J. Vestnik MSU (Rus.) ser.3 (1984): 92.

Other

Sheppard, Laurel M. Correspondence with A.A. Katsnelson, Moscow State University, June and July 1999.

Sketch by Laurel M. Sheppard

J

Shirley Ann Jackson (AP/Wide World Photos. Reproduced by permission.

Shirley Ann Jackson
1946–
American physicist

Shirley Ann Jackson is a theoretical physicist who has spent her career researching and teaching about particle physics—the branch of physics which uses theories and mathematics to predict the existence of subatomic particles and the forces that bind them together. She was the first African American woman to receive a Ph.D. from the Massachusetts Institute of Technology (MIT), and she spent many years conducting research at AT & T Bell Laboratories. She was named professor of physics at Rutgers University in 1991 and is the recipient of many honors, scholarships, and grants.

Jackson was born on August 5, 1946, in Washington, DC. Her parents, Beatrice and George Jackson, strongly valued education and encouraged her in school. Her father spurred on her interest in science by helping her with projects for her science classes. At Roosevelt High School, Jackson attended accelerated programs in both math and science, and she graduated in 1964 as valedictorian. Jackson began classes at MIT that same year, one of fewer than twenty African American students and the only one studying theoretical physics. While a student she did volunteer work at Boston City Hospital and tutored students at the Roxbury YMCA. She earned her bachelors degree in 1968, writing her thesis on solid–state physics, a subject then in the forefront of theoretical physics.

Although accepted at Brown, Harvard, and the University of Chicago, Jackson decided to stay at MIT for her doctoral work, because she wanted to encourage more African American students to attend the institution. She worked on elementary particle theory for her Ph.D., which she completed in 1973. Her research was directed by James Young, the first African American tenured full professor in MIT's physics department. Jackson's thesis, "The Study of a Multiperipheral Model with Continued Cross–Channel Unitarity," was subsequently published in the *Annals of Physics* in 1975.

Jackson's area of interest in physics is the study of the subatomic particles found within atoms, the tiny units of which all matter is made. Subatomic particles, which are usually very unstable and short–lived, can be studied in several ways. One method is using a particle accelerator, a device in which nuclei are accelerated to high speeds and then collided with a target to separate them into subatomic particles. Another way of studying them is by detecting their movements using certain kinds of nonconducting solids. When some solids are exposed to high–energy particles, the crystal lattice structure of the atoms is distorted, and this phenomenon leaves marks or tracks that can be seen with an electron microscope. Photographs of the tracks are then enhanced, and by examining these photographs physicists like Jackson can make predictions about what kinds of particles have caused the marks.

As a postdoctoral student of subatomic particles during the 1970s, Jackson studied and conducted research at a number of prestigious physics laboratories in both the United States and Europe. Her first position was as research associate at the Fermi National Accelerator Laboratory in Batavia, Illinois (known as Fermilab) where she studied hadrons—medium to large subatomic particles which include baryons and mesons. In 1974 she became visiting scientist at the accelerator lab at the European Center for Nuclear Research (CERN) in Switzerland. There she explored theories of strongly interacting elementary particles. In 1976 and 1977, she both lectured in physics at the

Stanford Linear Accelerator Center and became a visiting scientist at the Aspen Center for Physics.

Jackson joined the Theoretical Physics Research Department at AT & T Bell Laboratories in 1976. The research projects at this facility are designed to examine the properties of various materials in an effort to discover useful applications. In 1978, Jackson became part of the Scattering and Low Energy Physics Research Department, then in 1988 she moved to the Solid State and Quantum Physics Research Department. At Bell Labs, Jackson explored theories of charge density waves and the reactions of neutrinos, one type of subatomic particle. In her research, Jackson has made contributions to the knowledge of such areas as charged density waves in layered compounds, polaronic aspects of electrons in the surface of liquid helium films, and optical and electronic properties of semiconductor strained–layer superlattices. On these topics and others she has prepared or collaborated on over 100 scientific articles.

Jackson has received many scholarships, including the Martin Marietta Aircraft Company Scholarship and Fellowship, the Prince Hall Masons Scholarship, the National Science Foundation Traineeship, and a Ford Foundation Advanced Study Fellowship. She has been elected to the American Physical Society and selected a CIBA–GEIGY Exceptional Black Scientist. In 1985, Governor Thomas Kean appointed her to the New Jersey Commission on Science and Technology. Then in the early 1990s, Governor James Florio awarded her the Thomas Alva Edison Science Award for her contributions to physics and for the promotion of science. Jackson is an active voice in numerous committees of the National Academy of Sciences, the American Association for the Advancement of Science, and the National Science Foundation, where her aim has been to actively promote women in science.

Jackson is very involved in university life at Rutgers University, where in addition to being professor of physics she is also on the board of trustees. She is a lifetime member of the MIT Board of Trustees and was formerly a trustee of Lincoln University. She is also involved in civic organizations that promote community resources and developing enterprises. She is married and has one son.

SELECTED WRITINGS BY JACKSON:

Books

(With R. People) "Structurally Induced States from Strain and Confinement." In *Semiconductors and Semimetals.* Academic Press, 1990.

Periodicals

(With P. A. Lee and T. M. Rice) "Amplitude Modulation of Discommensurations in Charge Density Wave Structures." *Bulletin of the American Physical Society* 22 (1977): 280.

(With P. M. Platzman) "The Polaronic State of Two Dimensional Electrons on the Surface of Liquid Helium." *Surface Science* 142 (1984): 125.

(With F. M. Peeters) "Frequency Dependent Response of an Electron on a Liquid Helium Film." *Physical Review* B31 (1985): 7098.

FURTHER READING

Books

Carwell, Hattie. *Blacks in Science: Astrophysicist to Zoologist.* Exposition Press, 1977, p. 60.

Notable Black American Women. Detroit: Gale, 1992, pp. 565–566.

Blacks in Science and Medicine. Hemisphere, 1990, p. 130.

Sketch by Barbara A. Branca

Mary Corinna (Putnam) Jacobi
1842–1906
American physician

Mary Putnam Jacobi was a prominent woman physician who worked for the improvement of educational and professional standards for doctors and for increased opportunities for women. A scientist as well as practicing physician, she wrote over 100 papers on medicine.

Mary Putnam Jacobi was born in London, the oldest of eleven children of American parents, Victorine (Haven) and George Palmer Putnam. Her father was the founder of G. P. Putnam's Sons publishers. In 1848, the family returned to the United States, settling first in Staten Island, New York, and later moving to the semirural suburbs of Yonkers and Morrisania, New York. Jacobi was educated primarily at home by her mother, although she attended a private school in Yonkers for one year and commuted to a public school in Manhattan during the years of 1857 –1859. She also studied Greek with a private tutor.

Jacobi was a precocious child with scientific interests and literary talent. Her first publication was an essay in the *Atlantic Monthly* when she was 17. Although her parents were wary of her scientific aspirations, they did not stand in her way. However for years, Jacobi remained undecided about whether to pursue medicine or scientific research. She graduated from the New York College of Pharmacy in 1863 and earned her M.D. degree from the Female (later Woman's) Medical College of Pennsylvania in 1864. She then spent several months at the New England Hospital for Women and Children, founded in Boston by the physician

Maria Zakrzewska. Throughout the Civil War years, Jacobi volunteered in New York army hospitals and traveled, first to an army camp in Louisiana to tend her brother who had contracted malaria, and then to South Carolina where her sister, a teacher of freed slaves, had become ill with typhoid. Anxious to learn more science, Jacobi also studied chemistry with Ferdinand Mayer, to whom she was briefly engaged, while her younger brother acted as her chaperone in the laboratory.

Jacobi was not satisfied with either her formal education or her hospital training and, having finally decided to become a practicing physician, she moved to Paris, hoping to enter the École de Médicine, which had never admitted a woman. She attended lectures, clinics and laboratories, while persisting in her efforts. Finally, the minister of public education admitted her to the École, over the objections of the faculty. As Jacobi wrote in 1873: "It is astonishing how many invincible objections on the score of feasibility, modesty, propriety, and prejudice will melt away before the charmed touch of a few thousand dollars." She graduated in 1871 with high honors and won a bronze medal for her thesis. Throughout this period, Jacobi supported herself by writing articles, essays, and news reports for American magazines and journals, on medicine, French politics, and the outbreak of the Franco–Prussian War. She even wrote a romantic novel.

Breaking off an engagement to a French soldier, Jacobi returned to New York in 1871 as one of the best–trained and best–known physicians in the United States. She began a successful private medical practice and involved herself with educational and professional activities. She served as a physician at the New York Infirmary for Women and Children, founded by **Elizabeth Blackwell**, at Mount Sinai Hospital, and later at St. Mark's Hospital. She was a professor of pharmacy and therapeutics at the Woman's Medical College of the New York Infirmary for 25 years, and she introduced the first laboratory courses there. She also lectured on pediatrics at the New York Post–Graduate Medical School. Jacobi's primary concern was improving the medical education and professional standards of women physicians. In 1872, she founded the Association for the Advancement of the Medical Education of Women, which later became the Women's Medical Association of New York City, and she served as its president until 1903.

Jacobi met her future husband when she applied for membership in the Medical Society of the County of New York. Abraham Jacobi was the Society's president and a leading pediatrician who had escaped from Germany in the 1840s, following his imprisonment for political activities. They married in 1873. Of the Jacobis' three children, only Marjorie, born in 1878, survived childhood.

Jacobi, like her husband, was concerned with social issues, particularly environmental conditions that caused illness. She helped to establish the Working Women's Society, that became the New York Consumers' League in 1890, and she was committed to women's suffrage. Together, the Jacobis wrote a book on infant nutrition.

When the Harvard Medical School announced the topic for its annual Boylston Medical Prize, "Do women require mental and bodily rest during menstruation and to what extent?," Jacobi was encouraged to enter the competition anonymously. She sent out 1000 questionnaires to young women and conducted scientific measurements on women at the New York Infirmary. Her answer was a resounding "No." Jacobi's essay won the prize and she later revised it into a book. During her lifetime, Jacobi published papers on physiology, pathology, neurology, pediatrics, and medical education. Several of her works on gynecology were the result of original research and she also wrote books on women's suffrage and educational theory.

In 1896, while vacationing in Greece, Jacobi recognized the first symptoms of a brain tumor. Within a few years she had become an invalid, unable to speak; but true to her intellectual spirit, she wrote a detailed account of the progress of the disease which caused her death in 1906.

SELECTED WRITINGS BY JACOBI:

Books

"Social Aspects of the Readmission of Women into the Medical Profession." In *Papers and Letters Presented at the First Women's Congress of the Association for the Advancement of Women, October, 1873*. New York: Association for the Advancement of Women, 1874.

The Question of Rest for Women During Menstruation. New York: Putnam, 1877.

(Ruth Putnam, ed.) *Life and Letters of Mary Putnam Jacobi*. New York: Putnam, 1925.

(with Women's Medical Association of New York) *Mary Putnam Jacobi, M.D., A Pathfinder in Medicine, With Selections from her Writings and a Complete Bibliography*. New York: Putnam, 1925.

FURTHER READING

Books

Hume, Ruth Fox. *Great Women of Medicine*. New York: Random House, 1964.

Lubove, Roy. "Mary Corinna Putnam Jacobi." In *Notable American Women 1607–1950: A Biographical Dictionary*. Edited by Edward T. James, Janet Wilson James, and Paul W. Boyer. Cambridge: Harvard University Press, 1971.

Truax, Rhoda. *The Doctors Jacobi.* Boston: Little, Brown, 1952.

Walsh, Mary Roth. "The Quirls of a Woman's Brain." In *Women Look at Biology Looking at Women: A Collection of Feminist Critiques*, edited by Ruth Hubbard, Mary Sue Henifin, and Barbara Fried. Cambridge, MA: Schenkman, 1979.

Sketch by Margaret Alic

Aletta Henriette Jacobs
1854–1929
Dutch physician

Aletta Jacobs was the first woman in Holland to attend university and her efforts led to the opening of all Dutch universities to women. She also became the first Dutch woman medical doctor and opened the world's first birth control clinic. An ardent feminist and social reformer, she worked hard for the cause of women's suffrage.

The eighth of eleven children of progressive Jewish parents, Anna de Jongh and Abraham Jacobs, Aletta Jacobs was born in 1854, in Sappemeer, in the province of Groningen, the Netherlands. From early childhood, she wanted to become a physician like her father and older brother. Educated at home and at local schools, her father arranged for her to study Latin and Greek, and he allowed her to assist him in preparing medicines. Jacobs stayed only two weeks at a finishing school; subsequently obtaining permission to sit in on classes at the local boys' high school. At 16, she passed the required examination for becoming an assistant pharmacist and apprenticed with one of her brothers. Her sister, Charlotte Jacobs, later became the first woman pharmacist in the Netherlands.

Having researched her options, Jacobs found that there were no laws prohibiting a woman from attending university. In 1871, she wrote to the liberal prime minister of Holland, requesting permission to attend medical lectures for one year at the University of Groningen and then take the exams. As a result, Jacobs entered the university that spring, becoming the first woman in the Netherlands to attend university classes. After she was forced to reapply the following year, all universities in the country were opened to women students, and her youngest sister, Frederika Jacobs, became the first Dutch woman to earn a teaching certificate in mathematics. Nevertheless, until 1874, Jacobs was the only female student at the University of Groningen. Although many of the students were supportive of her, her brother Johan announced that he would rather see her dead than in medical school.

Jacobs's progress through school was slow, due to frequent bouts of malaria. After finally finishing her course work at the University of Amsterdam, she was unable to take the state examination until 1878, due to an attack of typhus. The three–week examination was grueling, with two of the professors aggressively opposed to a woman becoming a physician; but in the end, Jacobs became the first woman in the Netherlands to receive a license to practice medicine. She defended her thesis, "Localization of Physiological and Pathological Phenomena in the Brain," before the medical faculty at Groningen a year later and was awarded her doctorate in medicine.

Jacobs took over her father's medical practice in Amsterdam, despite tremendous opposition from male physicians, who advised her to confine her practice to midwifery. Soon she was limiting her practice to women and children, conducting a free clinic for the poor two mornings per week, and teaching courses on hygiene and child care. This experience increased her awareness of social problems and she began campaigning for shorter working hours and workplace safety. When the medical community ridiculed her efforts, she took her campaign to the women of Holland and eventually the laws were changed.

In 1881, Jacobs undertook the first systematic study of contraception. Many of her patients were worn down from too many pregnancies, and in 1882 she began prescribing diaphragms as birth control, effectively opening the first birth control clinic in the world. Despite intense opposition from medical and religious sectors, her patients were grateful. Prompted by the of large number of women who came to her with venereal diseases, Jacobs began campaigning against state–run and regulated prostitution, again unleashing a storm of opposition.

Jacobs's political activities led to her acquaintance with Carel Victor Gerritsen, a radical journalist and politician. Although their opposition to the marriage laws prompted them to carry on a "free union" for several years, they finally married in 1892. Jacobs became one of the first professional women to retain her maiden name after marriage. Although they very much wanted a family, the couple's only child lived for just one day. They raised the Jacobs's nephew as their foster son.

Noting that there were no laws prohibiting women from voting, Jacobs first tried to register to vote in 1883. The voting laws were promptly changed to prohibit women. As president of the Dutch chapter of the Association for Women's Suffrage, Jacobs faced a long struggle. It was not until 1919 that women achieved the right to vote. Jacobs retired from medicine in 1904 and her husband died the following year. She then became a full–time social reformer, crusading for women's suffrage, women's rights, sex education, and prison reform. In 1900, Jacobs translated the feminist classic, *Women and Economics* by Charlotte Perkins Gilman, into Dutch, and in 1910 she translated *Women and Labor* by Olive Schreiner. A pacifist, during World War I Jacobs worked for peace with Jane Addams. Later she worked with the International Alliance of Women.

Jacobs moved to The Hague in her later years, to be close to her adopted family, the Broese van Groenous. She died at Baarn in 1929, having outlived all of her siblings. Her memoirs were published in the Netherlands in 1924 and her library, of about 4,000 titles on the history of women, is located at the University of Kansas.

SELECTED WRITINGS BY JACOBS:

Books

(Harriet Feinberg, ed, Annie Wright, trans.) *Memories: My Life as an International Leader in Health, Suffrage, and Peace*. New York: The Feminist Press at the City University of New York, 1996.

Periodicals

"Holland's Pioneer Woman Doctor." *Medical Woman's Journal* 35 (September 1928): 257–59.

FURTHER READING

Books

Hensley, Kelly. "Aletta Henriette Jacobs." In *Notable Women in the Life Sciences: A Biographical Dictionary.* Edited by Benjamin F. Shearer and Barbara S. Shearer. Westport, CT: Greenwood Press, 1996.

Periodicals

"Facts and Figures about Dutch Women in Medicine."*Journal of the American Medical Women's Association* 13 (June 1958): 251–53.

Sketch by Margaret Alic

Sof'ja Aleksandrovna Janovskaja (also transliterated as Sofia Yanovskaya)

1896–1966

Russian mathematician

Sof'ja Aleksandrovna Janovskaja made her mark in the mathematical community not for what she discovered but what she promoted: the legitimacy of mathematical logic as an independent and worthy discipline. A Bolshevik during Russia's civil war (1918–1921), Janovskaja believed mathematical logic was a science with real–world applications, distinctly different from the philosophical idealism that she considered an exclusively bourgeoisie concept.

Janovskaja was born on January 31, 1896, in Pruzhany, Poland (now part of Belarus). Although scholars know little about Janovskaja's early life, some evidence suggests that the Janovskajas were native Poles, perhaps belonging to the local gentry. When Janovskaja was just a few years old, the family moved to Odessa, where she was educated in the classics and mathematics. In 1915, Janovskaja enrolled in the Higher School for Women in Odessa, where she studied until the 1917 Revolution disrupted life throughout Russia.

Janovskaja began aiding anti–royalist political prisoners in 1917 as a member of the underground Red Cross, and in November of 1918 she joined the Bolshevik faction of the Russian Communist Party—a risky move, as the party remained illegal in Odessa until late the following year. In 1919 she served as a political commissar in the Red Army and edited the *Kommunist*, Odessa's daily political newspaper that was printed out of the city's catacombs. Janovskaja was a worker in the Odessa Regional Party until 1923, when she decided her duty as a party member would be better served by using the sciences to support the tenets of the revolution.

Pursues Career in Mathematics

In the early years of the Soviet Union, the principles of the revolution gave way for the advancement of women in professional—especially scientific—fields. Talented and dedicated, Janovskaja quickly established herself in the Soviet mathematical community. From 1924 to 1929, she studied at the Institute of Red Professors in Moscow and took seminars at Moscow State University. She began directing a seminar on mathematical methodology at Moscow State University in 1925, and she officially joined the faculty a year later. By 1931, she was a professor, and she earned her doctorate from the Mechanical–Mathematical Faculty of Moscow State University in 1935.

With the breakout of World War II, Janovskaja was evacuated to Perm, where she taught at Perm University from 1941 to 1943. She returned to Moscow in 1943 to take the post as director of Moscow State University's seminar on mathematical logic, and three years later she became the first faculty member to teach mathematical logic in the philosophy department.

Joins the Debate on Mathematical Logic

For years, Western dialectical philosophers dismissed mathematical logic as being idealist—that is, based on preconceived (or *a priori*), abstract notions of number. Such a logic, these philosophers charged, lacked any material applications, and therefore the pursuit of mathematical logic would not further the proletarian cause. Because the concepts used in mathematical logic were said to be predetermined in an ideal realm removed from the material world, mathematical logic appeared to lack the Marxist–Leninist worldview derived from historical experience.

Janovskaja disagreed with these dialecticians about the nature of mathematical logic. The notion of numbers, Janovskaja contended, came from observing groups of things in the material world, and from those many experiences arriving at the general idea of numbers. Other concepts and rules used in mathematical logic were similarly induced from the collective human experience in the material world. Janovskaja saw parallels between the laws governing logic and the Communist Party's monistic philosophy; her writings frequently include the statement by Lenin that all laws are the result of billions of experiences. Janovskaja not only promoted mathematical logic as a pure science, she became a mathematical historian, studying how mathematical methods had evolved throughout time. Janovskaja believed the value of both pursuits would be in their applicability to real–world problems.

Contributions as Educator

Janovskaja produced no original works, but her translations and commentaries made the works of René Descartes, Georg Hegel, and Karl Marx accessible to Russian students. She wrote several lucid articles for the *Great Soviet Encyclopedia*, explaining formalism, logistics, and mathematical paradoxes in simple language accessible to most readers. Still, scholars consider Janovskaja's greatest contributions to be her two journal articles on the history of mathematical logic in the Soviet Union: "The Foundations of Mathematics and Mathematical Logic" (1948) and "Mathematical Logic and Foundations of Mathematics" (1959).

In the classroom Janovskaja did not prove abstract theorems. She preferred to explore actual problems such as the hangman's paradox, in which a man sentenced to death must use his final request to put the hangman in a logical bind. Janovskaja taught at least two courses each school year, incorporating new ideas and material in such a way that she never taught the same course twice. According to Boris A. Kushner, a student who knew Janovskaja at Moscow State University during the 1960s, students found Janovskaja's style engaging and the faculty were not incensed by her lack of original work. "Her whole personality, kind, open and deep, the tremendous and dangerous war she conducted against demagogic dialecticians—all that commanded respect," Kushner wrote in his remembrance of the teacher in *Modern Logic*.

Janovskaja was recognized for her years of contribution to the field in 1951, when she received the prestigious Order of Lenin award. Her efforts to create a department of mathematical logic at Moscow State University were successful, and she was named the department's first chair on March 31, 1959. She died on October 24, 1966.

In many ways, Janovskaja is considered more of a philosopher than a mathematician. Her work is more concerned with the nature of problems and the methods to be used than with the answers themselves. In her 1963 paper, "On Philosophical Questions of Mathematical Logic>," Janovskaja listed logical concepts and problems and described how they were philosophical in nature. "These questions have not been listed in order to offer any answers at all. I do not know sufficiently the questions to allow myself to do so."

SELECTED WRITINGS BY JANOVSKAJA:

"Foundations of mathematics and mathematical logic" *Matematika v SSSR za tridcat let 1917–1947* (1948): 11–45.

"Mathematical logic and foundations of mathematics" *Matematika v SSSR za sorok let 1917–1957* (1959): 13–120.

FURTHER READING

Books

Anellis, Irving H. "Sof'ja Janovskaja." In *Women in Mathematics*. Edited by Louise S.Grinstein and Paul J. Campbell. New York: Greenwood Press, 1987, pp. 80–85.

Periodicals

Anellis, Irving H. "The Heritage of S.A. Janovskaja." *History and Philosophy of Logic* 8 (1987), 45–56.

Bashmakova, I.G., et. al. "Sofia Aleksandrovna Yanovskaya." *Russian Mathematical Surveys* 21 (May–June 1966), 213–221.

Bochenski, J.M. "S.A. Janovskaja." *Studies in Soviet Thought* 13 (1973): 1–10.

Kushner, Boris A. "Sof'ja Aleksandrovna Janovskaja: A Few Reminiscences." *Modern Logic* 6 (January 1996): 67–72.

Other

"Sof'ja Janovskaja." *Biographies of Women Mathematicians*. Http://www.scottlan.edu/lriddle/women/chronol.htm (July 22, 1997).

Sketch by Bridget K. Hall

Mae Carol Jemison
1956–
American physician and astronaut

Mae Carol Jemison received two undergraduate degrees and a medical degree, served two years as a Peace Corps medical officer in West Africa, and was selected to join the National Aeronautics and Space Administration's astronaut training program before her thirtieth birthday. Her eight–day space flight aboard the space shuttle *Endeavour* in 1992 established Jemison as the United States' first female African–American space traveler.

Mae Carol Jemison was born on October 17, 1956, in Decatur, Alabama, the youngest child of Charlie Jemison, a roofer and carpenter, and Dorothy (Green) Jemison, an elementary school teacher. Her sister, Ada Jemison Bullock, became a child psychiatrist, and her brother, Charles Jemison, is a real estate broker. The family moved to Chicago, Illinois, when Jemison was three to take advantage of better educational opportunities there, and it is that city that she calls her hometown. Throughout her early school years, her parents were supportive and encouraging of her talents and abilities, and Jemison spent considerable time in

Mae Jemison (National Aeronautics and Space Administration.)

her school library reading about all aspects of science, especially astronomy. During her time at Morgan Park High School, she became convinced she wanted to pursue a career in biomedical engineering, and when she graduated in 1973 as a consistent honor student, she entered Stanford University on a National Achievement Scholarship.

At Stanford, Jemison pursued a dual major and in 1977 received a B.S. in chemical engineering and a B.A. in African and Afro–American Studies. As she had been in high school, Jemison was very involved in extracurricular activities including dance and theater productions, and served as head of the Black Student Union. Upon graduation, she entered Cornell University Medical College to work toward a medical degree. During her years there, she found time to xpand her horizons by visiting and studying in Cuba and Kenya and working at a Cambodian rfugee camp in Thailand. When she obtained her M.D. in 1981, she interned at Los Angeles County/University of Southern California Medical Center and later worked as a general pactitioner. For the next two and a half years, she was the area Peace Corps medical officer for Sierra Leone and Liberia where she also taught and did medical research. Following her return to the United States in 1985, she made a career change and decided to follow a dream she had nurtured for a long time. In October of that year she applied for admission to NASA's astronaut training program. The *Challenger* disaster of January 1986 delayed the selection process, but when she reapplied a year later, Jemison was one of the 15 candidates chosen from a field of about 2,000.

Joins Eight-Day Endeavour Mission

When Jemison was chosen on June 4, 1987, she became the first African American woman ever admitted into the astronaut training program. After more than a year of training, she became an astronaut with the title of science–mission specialist, a job which would make her responsible for conducting crew–related scientific experiments on the space shuttle. On September 12, 1992, Jemison finally flew into space with six other astronauts aboard the *Endeavour* on mission STS–47. During her eight days in space, she conducted experiments on weightlessness and motion sickness on the crew and herself. Altogether, she spent slightly over 190 hours in space before returning to Earth on September 20. Following her historic flight, Jemison noted that society should recognize how much both women and members of other minority groups can contribute if given the opportunity.

In recognition of her accomplishments, Jemison received several honorary doctorates, the 1988 *Essence* Science and Technology Award, the *Ebony* Black Achievement Award in 1992, and a Montgomery Fellowship from Dartmouth College in 1993, and was named Gamma Sigma Gamma Woman of the Year in 1990. Also in 1992, an alternative public school in Detroit, Michigan—the Mae C. Jemison Academy—was named after her. Jemison is a member of the American Medical Association, the American Chemical Society, the American Association for the Advancement of Science, and served on the Board of Directors of the World Sickle Cell Foundation from 1990 to 1992. She is also an advisory committee member of the American Express Geography Competition and an honorary board member of the Center for the Prevention of Childhood Malnutrition. After leaving the astronaut corps in March 1993, she accepted a teaching fellowship at Dartmouth and also established the Jemison Group, a company that seeks to research, develop, and market advanced technologies.

FURTHER READING

Books

Hawthorne, Douglas B. *Men and Women of Space.* Univelt, 1992, pp. 357–359.

Smith, Jessie Carney, ed. *Notable Black American Women.* Detroit: Gale Research, 1992, pp. 571–573.

Sketch by Leonard C. Bruno

Sophia Jex-Blake (Photo Researchers, Inc. Reproduced by permission.)

Sophia Jex-Blake
1840–1912
English physician

Perhaps more than any other woman, Sophia Jex-Blake was responsible for opening up the medical profession to women in Great Britain. Flamboyant and aggressive, she led her troops of women and supporters into the "Battle of Edinburgh" and her writings were major contributions to the history of women in medicine.

Jex-Blake was the youngest of three children in the wealthy and prominent English family of Maria (Cubitt) and Thomas Jex-Blake. Her father had retired by the time of her birth in 1840, and her parents, conservative and religious, were determined to give their children excellent educations. Jex-Blake's early education came from governesses and boarding schools. In 1858 she entered Queen's College in London where she studied and worked as a tutor in mathematics until 1861. However her tutoring was as a volunteer, since her father objected to her earning a salary. She continued her studies in Edinburgh and then accepted a teaching position at a girls' school in Germany.

Jex-Blake's original ambition was to start her own school and she traveled to America in 1865 to visit schools and colleges. Her account of her trip was published in 1867. However in Boston, Jex-Blake became a patient of Dr. Lucy Sewall and her group of young women physicians at the New England Hospital for Women and Children. She began volunteering there and decided n a new career. After being turned down by Harvard Medical School, in 1868 she became the first student at Dr. **Elizabeth Blackwell**'s Women's Medical College of the New York Infirmary for Women and Children. However the following year, her father's illness and death forced her to return to England.

"Battle of Edinburgh" Begins

Hoping to complete her medical education in England, Jex-Blake applied to the University of London, but was told that the university's charter had been worded so as to exclude all possibility of women studying for medical degrees. Next, she turned to the University of Edinburgh and what was to become a protracted struggle for the admission of women. In 1862 she had tried, without success, to help her friend Elizabeth Garrett Anderson study there; but she had been led to believe that their policy on women might change in the future. In 1869, Jex-Blake and four other women received provisional admittance to the preliminary exams required for entering medical students and were told that they could study medicine in special, female-only classes, for extra tuition. Two other women joined them and they all did well in their courses—too well. When one of them won a prestigious Hope Scholarship, it was taken from her and given to the next man on the list. The situation quickly deteriorated. Soon, no instructors could be found for their separate classes. Finally an adjunct anatomy teacher agreed that they could attend his regular classes. Next the women were refused permission to study at the Royal Infirmary, which was required for the medical degree. The animosity of male students and faculty towards the women eventually became so intense that they formed a mob, blocking the women's entrance to the Surgeon's Hall, and a riot erupted. These events served to turn public opinion in favor of the women. Nevertheless, when Jex-Blake brought a libel action against a university staff member whom she accused of instigating the riot, she was awarded a pittance in damages and forced to pay a thousand pounds in legal fees.

Public opinion was changing, but the "Battle of Edinburgh" was far from over. The lecturers who had previously admitted the women, now barred them from their classes. In 1872, the university decided that they would not allow the women to earn degrees, but would award them certificates of proficiency if they dropped their cause. Jex-Blake and the others sued the university for breach of contract and lost in 1873. So they took their case to Parliament which, after years of fighting, passed the Russell Gurney Enabling Act of 1876, allowing women to be tested by the medical examining boards.

Founds Women's Medical Schools

While the political maneuverings continued, Jex-Blake founded the London School of Medicine for Women in

1874 and staffed it with a respected faculty that included Elizabeth Blackwell. In 1877, at the age of 36, Jex-Blake completed her medical studies at the University of Berne in Switzerland, with a thesis on puerperal (childbed) fever. The Irish College of Physicians granted her the legal right to practice medicine in Great Britain. After clashing with Elizabeth Garrett Anderson at the London School, Jex-Blake returned to Edinburgh in 1878, where she operated a private clinic which evolved into the Edinburgh Hospital and Dispensary for Women. From 1886 until 1898, she also ran the Edinburgh School of Medicine for Women.

Jex-Blake retired in 1899, settling in Rotherfield, Sussex, where she continued to welcome students and physicians from around the world, until her death in 1912.

SELECTED WRITINGS BY JEX-BLAKE:

Books

A Visit to Some American Schools and Colleges. London: Macmillan, 1867.

"Medicine as a Profession for Women." In *Woman's Work and Woman's Culture*. Edited by Josephine Butler. London: Macmillan, 1869.

Medical Women: A Thesis and a History. Edinburgh, 1886. Reprint, New York: Source Book Press, 1970.

FURTHER READING

Books

Norris, Carol Brooks. "Sophia Jex-Blake." In *Notable Women in the Life Sciences: A Biographical Dictionary*. Edited by Benjamin F. Shearer and Barbara S. Shearer. Westport, CT: Greenwood Press, 1996.

Ogilvie, Marilyn Bailey. *Women in Science: Antiquity through the Nineteenth Century: A Biographical Dictionary with Annotated Bibliography*. Cambridge: MIT Press, 1991.

Roberts, Shirley. *Sophia Jex-Blake, A Woman Pioneer in Nineteenth-Century Medical Reform*. New York: Routledge, 1993.

Todd, Margaret, M.D. *The Life of Sophia Jex-Blake*. London: Macmillan, 1918.

Sketch by Margaret Alic

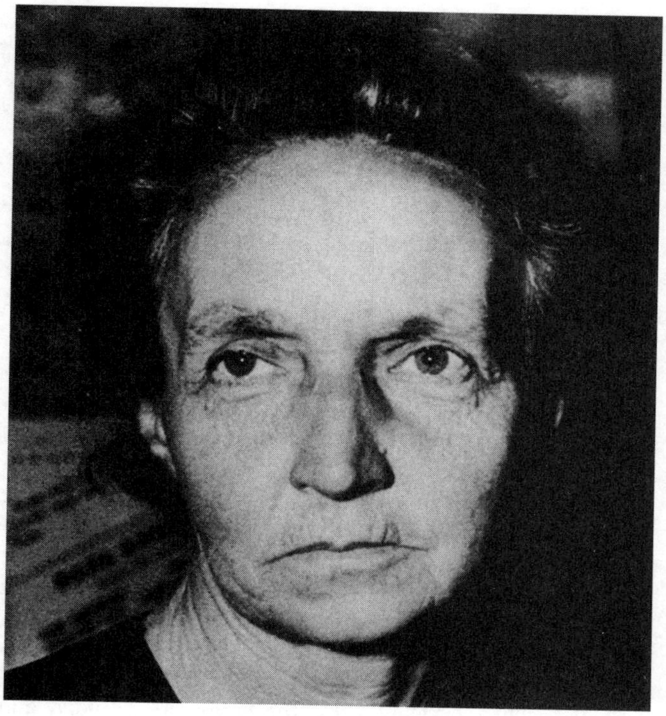

Irène Joliot-Curie (The Library of Congress. Reproduced by permission.)

Irène Joliot-Curie
1897–1956
French chemist and physicist

Irène Joliot-Curie, elder daughter of famed scientists Pierre and **Marie Curie**, won a Nobel Prize in chemistry in 1935 for the discovery, with her husband Frédéric Joliot-Curie, of artificial radioactivity. She began her scientific career as a research assistant at the Radium Institute in Paris, an institute founded by her parents, and soon succeeded her mother as its research director. It was at the Institute where she met her husband and lifelong collaborator, Frédéric Joliot. They usually published their findings under the combined form of their last names, Joliot-Curie.

Born on September 12, 1897, in Paris to Nobel laureates Marie and Pierre Curie, Irène Curie had a rather extraordinary childhood, growing up in the company of brilliant scientists. Her mother, the former Marie Sklodowska and her father, Pierre Curie, had been married in 1895 and had become dedicated physicists, experimenting with radioactivity in their laboratory. Marie Curie was on the threshold of discovering radium when little Irène, or "my little Queen" as her mother called her, was only a few months old. As Irène grew into a precocious, yet shy child, she was very possessive of her mother who was often preoccupied with her experiments. If, after a long day at the laboratory, the little Queen greeted her exhausted mother with demands for fruit, Marie Curie would turn right around and walk to the market to get her daughter fruit. Upon her father Pierre Curie's untimely accidental death in 1908, Irène was then more influenced by her paternal grandfather, Eugene Curie. It was her grandfather who taught young Irène botany and natural history as they spent summers in the country. The elder Curie was also somewhat of a political radical and atheist, and it was he who helped shape Irène's leftist sentiment and disdain for organized religion.

Curie's education was quite remarkable. Marie Curie made sure Irène and her younger sister, Eve Denise (born in 1904), did their physical as well as mental exercises each day. The girls had a governess for a time, but because Madame Curie was not satisfied with the available schools, she organized a teaching cooperative in which children of the professors from Paris' famed Sorbonne came to the laboratory for their lessons. Madame Curie taught physics, and other of her famous colleagues taught math, chemistry, language and sculpture. Soon Irène became the star pupil as she excelled in physics and chemistry. After only two years, however, when Irène was 14, the cooperative folded and Irène enrolled in a private school, the College Sevigne, and soon earned her degree. Summers were spent at the beach or in the mountains, sometimes in the company of such notables as Albert Einstein and his son. Irène then enrolled at the Sorbonne to study for a diploma in nursing.

During World War I, Madame Curie went to the front where she used new x-ray equipment to treat soldiers. Irène soon trained to use the same equipment and worked with her mother and later on her own. Irène, who was shy and rather antisocial in nature, grew to be calm and steadfast in the face of danger. At age 21, she became her mother's assistant at the Radium Institute. She also became quite adept at using the Wilson cloud chamber, a device which makes otherwise invisible atomic particles visible by the trails of water droplets left in their wake.

Work on Artificial Radioactivity Leads to a Nobel Prize

In the early 1920s, after a jubilant tour of the United States with her mother and sister, Irène Curie began to make her mark in the laboratory. Working with Fernand Holweck, chief of staff at the Institute, she performed several experiments on radium resulting in her first paper in 1921. By 1925 she completed her doctoral thesis on the emission of alpha rays from polonium, an element that her parents had discovered. Many colleagues in the lab, including her future husband, thought her to be much like her father in her almost instinctive ability to use laboratory instruments. Frédéric was several years younger than Irène and untrained in the use of the equipment. When she was called upon to teach him about radioactivity, Irène started out in a rather brusque manner, but soon the two began taking long country walks. They married in 1926 and decided to use the combined name Joliot-Curie to honor her notable scientific heritage.

After their marriage, Irène and Frédéric Joliot-Curie began doing their research together, signing all their scientific papers jointly even after Irène was named chief of the laboratory in 1932. After reading about the experiments of German scientists Walther Bothe and Hans Becker, their attention focused on nuclear physics, a field yet in its infancy. Only at the turn of the century had scientists discovered that atoms contain a central core or nucleus made up of positively charged particles called protons. Outside the nucleus are negatively charged particles called electrons. Irène's parents had done their work on radioactivity, a phenomenon which occurs when the nuclei of certain elements release particles or emit energy. Some emissions are called alpha particles which are relatively large particles resembling the nucleus of a helium atom and thus contain two positive charges. In their Nobel Prize-winning work, the elder Curies had discovered that some elements, the radioactive elements, emit particles on a regular, predictable basis.

Irène Joliot-Curie had in her laboratory one of the largest supplies of radioactive materials in the world, namely polonium, a radioactive element discovered by her parents. The polonium emitted alpha particles which Irène and Frédéric used to bombard different elements. In 1933 they used alpha particles to bombard aluminum nuclei. What they produced was radioactive phosphorus. Aluminum usually has 13 protons in its nuclei, but when bombarded with alpha particles which contain two positive charges each, the protons were added to the nucleus, forming a nucleus of phosphorus, the element with 15 protons. The phosphorus produced is different from naturally–occurring phosphorus because it is radioactive and is known as a radioactive isotope.

The two researchers used their alpha bombardment technique on other elements, finding that when a nucleus of a particular element combined with an alpha particle, it would transform that element into another, radioactive element with a higher number of protons in its nucleus. What Irène and Frédéric Joliot-Curie had done was to create artificial radioactivity. They announced this breakthrough to the Academy of Sciences in January of 1934.

The Joliot-Curies' discovery was of great significance not only for its pure science, but for its many applications. Since the 1930s many more radioactive isotopes have been produced and used as radioactive trace elements in medical diagnoses as well as in countless experiments. The success of the technique encouraged other scientists to experiment with the releasing the power of the nucleus.

It was a bittersweet time for Irène Joliot-Curie. An overjoyed but ailing Marie Curie knew that her daughter was headed for great recognition but died in July of that year from leukemia caused by the many years of radiation exposure. Several months later the Joliot-Curies were informed of the Nobel Prize. Although they were nuclear physicists, the pair received an award in chemistry because of their discovery's impact in that area.

From Popular Nobel Laureate to Unpopular Political Activist

After winning the Nobel Prize, Irène and Frédéric were the recipients of many honorary degrees and named officers of the Legion of Honor. But all these accolades made little impact on Irène who preferred spending her free time reading poetry or swimming, sailing, skiing or hiking. As her children Helene and Pierre grew, she became more interested in social movements and politics. An atheist and political leftist, Irène also took up the cause of woman's suffrage. She served as undersecretary of state in Leon Blum's Popular Front government in 1936 and then was elected professor at the Sorbonne in 1937.

Continuing her work in physics during the late 1930s, Irène Joliot-Curie experimented with bombarding uranium nuclei with neutrons. With her collaborator Pavle Savitch, she showed that uranium could be broken down into other radioactive elements. Her seminal experiment paved the way for another physicist, Otto Hahn, to prove that uranium bombarded with neutrons can be made to split into two atoms of comparable mass. This phenomenon, named fission, is the foundation for the practical applications of nuclear energy—the generation of nuclear power and the atom bomb.

During the early part of World War II, Irène continued her research in Paris although her husband Frédéric had gone underground. They were both part of the French Resistance movement and by 1944, Irène and her children fled France for Switzerland. After the war she was appointed director of the Radium Institute and was also a commissioner for the French atomic energy project. She put in long days in the laboratory and continued to lecture and present papers on radioactivity although her health was slowly deteriorating. Her husband Frédéric, a member of the Communist Party since 1942, was removed from his post as head of the French Atomic Energy Commission in 1950. After that time, the two became outspoken on the use of nuclear energy for the cause of peace. Irène was a member of the World Peace Council and made several trips to the Soviet Union. It was the height of the Cold War and because of her politics, Irène was shunned by the American Chemical Society when she applied for membership in 1954. Her final contribution to physics came as she helped plan a large particle accelerator and laboratory at Orsay, south of Paris in 1955. Her health worsened and on March 17, 1956, Irène Joliot-Curie died as her mother had before her, of leukemia resulting from a lifetime of exposure to radiation.

SELECTED WRITINGS BY JOLIOT-CURIE:

Books

(With Frédéric Joliot-Curie) *Oeuvres Scientifiques Completes,* Paris, 1961.

Periodicals

(With P. Savic) "Sur les radioelements formes par l'uranium irradie par les neutrons." *Journal de physique et le radium* 8 (1937): 385.

FURTHER READING

Books

Opfell, Olga S. *The Lady Laureates: Women Who Have Won the Nobel Prize.* Scarecrow, 1978.

Pflaum, Rosalynd. *Grand Obsession: Madame Curie and Her World.* Doubleday, 1989.

Sketch by Barbara A. Branca

Mary Ellen Jones
1922–

American biochemist

Mary Ellen Jones, a prominent biochemist and enzymologist, is known for isolating carbamyl phosphate, one of a number of molecules that are the building blocks of biosynthesis. By synthesizing this substance, Jones helped lay the groundwork for major advances in biochemistry, particularly in research on deoxyribonucleic acid (DNA) and ribonucleic acid (RNA). She has explored enzyme action, how the products of metabolism (metabolites) control enzyme activity, and metabolic pathways. The metabolic pathway is essential for cell division and differentiation, and studies of it are crucial to the understanding of the developing fetus and child, of cancer, and of some mutations in humans. Jones was recognized for her work by being named the first woman Kenan Professor at the University of North Carolina at Chapel Hill in 1980.

Mary Ellen Jones was born on December 25, 1922, in La Grange, Illinois, to Elmer Enold and Laura Anna (Klein) Jones. She earned her bachelor of science degree from the University of Chicago in 1944. She then went on to receive her Ph.D. in biochemistry at Yale University, where she was a U.S. Public Health Service Fellow in the department of physiological chemistry from 1950 to 1951.

Jones solidly established herself as an enzymologist during her postdoctoral studies with Fritz Lipmann, a 1953 Nobel Prize winner for physiology or medicine, who was then director of the Chemical Research Laboratory at Massachusetts General Hospital. In the 1950s he and a team of researchers discovered a group of molecules that were considered the building blocks of biosynthesis. It was during this time that Jones isolated cabamyl phosphate, one of the most important of these essential molecules. The synthesis of this molecule made important advances in biochemistry possible. Carbamyl phosphate is present in all life. Knowledge of it led to scientific understanding of two universally essential pathways of biosynthesis, the production of a chemical compound by a living organism.

Jones and Lipmann noticed that during certain biosynthetic reactions, the energy–releasing reaction was a splitting of adenosine triphosphate (ATP) that yielded a mononucleotide and inorganic pyrophosphate. The discovery suggested that DNA and RNA synthesis might occur with the liberation of inorganic pyrophosphate from ATP and other trinucleotides—a suggestion that was later proven true by the biochemist Arthur Kornberg. Jones remained in the Biochemical Research Laboratory at Massachusetts General Hospital until 1957 and served as a faculty member in the Department of Biochemistry at Brandeis University until 1966.

In 1966, Dr. Jones joined the University of North Carolina as an associate professor of biochemistry, was promoted to professor two years later, and in 1968 was appointed professor in the department of zoology. She left Chapel Hill in 1971 for the University of Southern California and was a professor of biochemistry there until 1978. She returned to the University of North Carolina as a professor and chair of the biochemistry department and was named a Kenan Professor in 1980.

Dr. Jones is the author of over ninety papers related to biochemistry and has received international recognition for her creative scientific research. She has been a member of the Institute of Medicine since 1981, was inducted into the National Academy of Sciences in 1984, and in 1986 served as president of the American Society of Biological Chemists and was named the North Carolina American Chemical Society distinguished chemist. She was awarded the Wilbur Lucius Cross Medal in 1982 by the graduate school at Yale University for her work as a "gifted investigator of the chemistry of life."

SELECTED WRITINGS BY JONES:

Books

(Editor, with Patricia A. Hoffee) *Purine and Pyrimidine Nucleotide Metabolism.* Academic Press, 1978.

Structural and Organization Aspects of Metabolic Regulation. John Wiley and Sons, 1990.

FURTHER READING

Jones, Mary Ellen, correspondence with Janet Kieffer Kelley, March 6, 1994.

Sketch by Janet Kieffer Kelley

Lynda Jordan
1956–
American biochemist

Lynda Jordan is a world–renowned scientist who has investigated an enzyme called phospholipase A2 or PLA2, which helps cause diseases such as asthma, diabetes, and arthritis when the enzyme's cells mutate. Her findings may one day show us how to treat these illnesses more effectively.

Jordon was born in Roxbury, Massachusetts to Charlene and Veasley Smith on September 20, 1956. After her father's death, Jordan's mother remarried Charles Jordan, and Lynda took his name. Jordon lived in one of the toughest housing projects in Boston, but was able to work her way out with the help of several mentors. She attended Dorchester High School in Dorchester, Massachusetts and then North Carolina A& T University, where she got her BA in 1974. Jordan then went on to graduate school at Atlanta University and the Massachusetts Institute of Technology (MIT), where she got her Ph.D. in 1985.

Jordan also attended the prestigious Institut Pasteur in Paris, France, where she researched projects in the area of pharmacology and thrombosis from 1985–1987. From 1987–1997, she was a professor at North Carolina A&T University, a primarily African–American university, in an effort to serve as a role model and continue her research. There Jordan researched the enzyme phospholipase, also called A2 or PLA2. PLA2 is a substance found in every cell in our bodies. Jordan has set herself the task of cracking its genetic code, and therefore making the treatment of such diseases as asthma, diabetes, and arthritis easier. She was able to isolate calcium–independent high–molecular weight phospholipase A2 during the late 1980s at North Carolina A&T. "It was one of the greatest accomplishments we've made in our research," Jordan said in an article in *Black Issues in Education* in 1994.

The enzyme Jordan is studying actually comes from the human placenta, the mass of membranes, blood and tissues that protects a developing fetus in a mother's body. In her latest research Jordan is studying the physiological role PLA2 plays in our bodies as well as its structural characteristics. Those discoveries, she hopes, will contribute to our knowledge about PLA2 cells that go awry, causing disease.

In 1993 Jordan's work became even more important to her when she was diagnosed with a disease caused by PLA2 diabetes. Coming to terms with diabetes has been an emotionally draining process, she says, but has steered her in a new direction researching PLA2's role in her disease.

At MIT, where from August, 1997 to July, 1999 she was a visiting professor, Jordan revamped the biochemistry laboratory course for undergraduates, as well a participated in research on phospholipase. In July, 1999 she'll return to North Carolina A&T.

During her career Jordan has worked to be a mentor for African–American undergraduate and graduate students. AT MIT she served as an in–house consultant to the administration, providing advice about the recruitment and matriculation of African–American students. She also conducted workshops for minority and female students on successful matriculation.

Jordan has won more than 40 awards, including the Giants in Science Award from the Quality Education for Minorities in February, 1999; The Science Medal Award from Harvard College in March 1998; and the MIT/Wellesley Upward Bound Alumna Award in February 1998.

FURTHER READING

Periodicals

Hawkins, B. Denise. "Sister, Scientist, Mentor: Lynda Jordan." *Black Issues in Higher Education* (December 1994): 14–17.

Sketch by Barbara Boughton

Madeleine M. Joullié
1927–
American chemist

Madeleine Joullié has distinguished herself not only as a talented chemist but also as an outstanding teacher. In 1999 she was the holder of the University of Pennsylvania's Class of 1970 Chair in Chemistry, Joullié is a recipient of the university's Lindback Award for Distinguished Teaching.

Born in Paris on March 29, 1927, Joullié was the daughter of a businessman who traveled extensively. When she was a child, the family moved to Rio de Janeiro, and she received her early schooling there. When it came time for her to attend college, her father suggested that she go to the United States, where he felt she would receive a more well–rounded education than she would in Brazil.

Joullié went to Simmons College in Boston, where she majored in chemistry. Moving from Rio to Boston was something of a culture shock, so she spent much of her time studying. In addition to chemistry, she made a point of taking as many language courses as she could fit into her schedule. She received her bachelor's degree in 1949 and from there went on to the University of Pennsylvania in Philadelphia for her graduate work. She has remained there since.

She received her master's degree from Penn in 1950 and her Ph.D. in 1953. She began her career teaching undergraduate organic chemistry; in 1957 she became a research associate. Two years later, in 1959, she became an assistant professor of chemistry. She also married Richard Prange that year. Prange, a physicist, later took a job at the University of Maryland, so the two became an early "commuter couple." Both avid cyclists, they took the opportunity to explore both Washington and Philadelphia by bicycle.

Joullié and her research group made a major discovery in 1976, when they synthesized the interferon inducer tilorone. Interferons are proteins that inhibit certain viral infections, and they have implications for a variety of diseases. More recently, she has made noteworthy progress in the synthesis of molecules known as cyclopeptide alkaloids and cyclodepsipeptides. What this means is that she has been able to create substances that can be used for purposes such as drug production. By conducting synthesis experiments, she has also been able to better understand the structure of molecules, which ultimately leads to the improved production of useful substances.

Over the course of her career, Joullié has received numerous awards for her scientific work, including the American Chemical Society's Garvan Medal in 1978. But her skills and contributions as a teacher have been equally impressive. In June 1999, Penn's Graduate Student Associations Council made Joullié the first recipient of its new Distinguished Achievement Award in recognition of her "deep and abiding interest in the training, development, and careers of both undergraduate and graduate students."

FURTHER READING

Books

Shearer, Benjamin F. and Barbara S, Shearer, eds. *Notable Women in the Physical Sciences: A Biographical Dictionary.* Westport, CT.: Greenwood Press, 1997.

Periodicals

"Garvan Medal."*Chemical and Engineering News* (August 29, 1977): 50–1.

Other

"GSAC Award to Dr. Joullié." Almanac Honors and Other Things. 1999. http://www.upenn.edu/almanac/v45/n33/honors.html (July 5, 1999).

Sketch by George A. Milite

K

Isabella Lugoski Karle (AP/Wide World Photos. Reproduced by permission.)

Isabella Lugoski Karle
1921–
American chemist, crystallographer, and physicist

Isabella Karle is a renowned chemist and physicist who has worked at the Naval Research Laboratory in Washington, D.C., since 1946 and heads the X-Ray Diffraction Group of that facility. In her research, she applied electron and x–ray diffraction to molecular structure problems in chemistry and biology. Along with her husband Jerome Karle, she developed procedures for gathering information about the structure of molecules from diffraction data. For her work, she has received numerous awards such as the Annual Achievement Award of the Society of Women Engineers in 1968, the Federal Woman's Award in 1973, and the Lifetime Achievement Award from Women in Science and Engineering in 1986. Her work has been described in the book *Women and Success.*

Isabella Lugoski Karle was born on December 2, 1921, in Detroit, Michigan. Her parents were Zygmunt A. Lugoski, a housepainter, and Elizabeth Graczyk, who was a seamstress. Both her parents were immigrants from Poland, and Karle spoke no English until she went to school. While still in high school, she decided upon a career in chemistry, even though her mother wanted her to be a lawyer or a teacher. She received her B.S. and M.S. degrees in physical chemistry from the University of Michigan in 1941 and 1942. Determined to continue her studies, Karle ran into serious financial problems since teaching assistant positions at the University of Michigan were reserved exclusively for male doctoral students. She managed to stay in school on an American Association of University Women fellowship, however, and in 1943 also became a Rackham fellow. She received her Ph.D. in physical chemistry from the University of Michigan in 1944, at the age of twenty–two.

After receiving her doctorate, Karle worked at the University of Chicago on the Manhattan Project (the code name for the construction of the atomic bomb), synthesizing plutonium compounds. She then returned to the University of Michigan as a chemistry instructor for two years. In 1942 she had married Jerome Karle, then a chemistry student. In 1946 she and her husband joined the Naval Research Laboratory, where she worked as a physicist from 1946 to 1959. In 1959 she became head of the x–ray analysis section, a position she maintained through the 1990s.

Investigates Structure of Crystals

When Karle began her work at the Naval Research Laboratory, information about the structure of crystals was limited. Scientists had determined that crystals were solid units, in which atoms, ions, or molecules are arranged sometimes in repeating, sometimes in random patterns. These patterns or networks of fixed points in space have measurable distances between them. Although chemists had been able to investigate the structure of gas molecules by studying the diffraction of electron or x–ray beams by the gas molecules, it was believed that information about the occurrences of the patterns—or phases—was lost when crystalline substances scattered an x–ray beam. The Karles, working as a team, gathered phase information using a heavy–atom or salt derivative. The position of a heavy atom in the crystal could be located by scattered x–ray reflections, even though light atoms posed more serious problems. When a heavy atom could not be introduced into a crystal, its structure remained a mystery. In 1950 Jerome Karle, in collaboration with the chemist Herbert A. Hauptman, formulated a set of mathematical equations that would theoretically solve the problem of phases in light–atom crystals. It was Isabella Karle who solved the practical problems and designed and built the diffraction machine that photographed the diffracted images of crystalline structures.

While investigating structural formulas and the make–up of crystal structures using electron and x–ray diffraction, Karle made an important discovery. She found that only a few of the phase values—no more than three to five—are sufficient to evaluate the remaining values. She could then use symbols to represent these initial values and also numerical evaluations. This process for determining the location of atoms in a crystal was amenable to processing in high–speed computers. Eventually, it became possible to analyze complex biological molecules in a day or two that previously would have taken years to analyze. The rapid and direct method for solving crystal structure resounded through chemistry, biochemistry, biology, and medicine, and Karle herself has been active in resolving applications in a range of fields.

In addition to describing the structure of crystals and molecules, Karle also investigated the conformation of natural products and biologically active materials. After a crystallographer determines the chemical composition of rare and expensive chemicals, scientists can synthesize inexpensive substitutes that serve the same purpose. Karle headed a team that determined the structure of a chemical that repels worms, termites, and other pests and occurs naturally in a rare Panamanian wood. The team was then able to produce a synthetic chemical that mimics the natural chemical and is equally effective as a pest repellent. In another application, Karle studied frog venom. Using extremely minute quantities of purified potent toxins from tropical American frogs, the team headed by Karle established three–dimensional models, called stereoconfigurations, of many of the toxins and showed the chemical linkages of each of these poisons. The inexpensive substitutes of the toxins were of great importance in medicine. The venom has the effect of blocking nerve impulses and is useful to medical scientists studying nerve transmissions. Karle has also researched the effect of radiation on deoxyribonucleic acid (DNA), the carrier of genetic information. She demonstrated how the structural formulas of the configurations of amino acids and nucleic acids in DNA may be changed when exposed to radiation. Her research into structural analysis also established the arrangement of peptide bonds, or combinations of amino acids.

Karle has held several concurrent positions, such as member of the National Committee on Crystallography of the National Academy of Science and the National Research Council (1974–1977). She has long been a member of the American Crystallographic Society and served as its president in 1976. She was elected to the National Academy of Sciences in 1978. From 1982 to 1990 she worked with the Massachusetts Institute of Technology, and she has been a civilian consultant to the Atomic Energy Commission.

Karle has received numerous awards including the Superior Civilian Service Award of the Navy Department in 1965, the Hildebrand Award in 1970, and the Garvan Award of the American Chemical Society in 1976. She has received several honorary doctorates. Her most recent awards have been the Gregori Aminoff Prize from the Swedish Academy of Sciences in 1988 and the Bijvoet Medal from the University of Utrecht, the Netherlands, in 1990. She has written over 250 scientific articles.

Isabella and Jerome Karle have three daughters, Louise Isabella, Jean Marianne, and Madeline Diane. All three have become scientists like their parents. Jerome Karle, who is chief scientist at the Laboratory for Structure and Matter of the U.S. Naval Laboratory, received the Nobel Prize in chemistry in 1985 for developing a mathematical method for determining the three–dimensional structure of molecules.

SELECTED WRITINGS BY KARLE:

Periodicals

"Modular Design of Synthetic Protein Mimics." *Journal of the American Chemical Society* 112 (December 5, 1990): 9350–56.

FURTHER READING

Books

Kundsin, Ruth. *Women and Success.* Morrow, 1974.

McGraw–Hill Modern Scientists and Engineers. McGraw–Hill (New York), 1980, pp. 147–48.

Noble, Iris. *Contemporary Women Scientists of America.* Meissner, 1979.

Sketch by Evelyn B. Kelly

Joyce Jacobson Kaufman
1929–
American chemist

Joyce Kaufman is one of the most distinguished American chemists. Her research, both experimental and theoretical, has spanned the fields of chemistry and physics, with important applications in biomedicine and supercomputers. She has developed new methods for designing pharmaceutical drugs and predicting their potential toxicity and has studied the biological mechanisms of narcotics and their antagonists.

Kaufman was born into the Jewish family of Robert and Sara (Seldin) Jacobson, in New York City, in 1929.

After her parents' separation in 1935, Kaufman and her mother went to live with her mother's parents, Jacob and Mary Seldin, in Baltimore. In 1940, her mother married Abraham Deutch, a successful businessman, who supported Kaufman through college.

Kaufman began reading before the age of two, and by the time she was six, she had exhausted the children's section of the local library. She began reading biographies of scientists and, at the age of eight, the biography of **Marie Curie** sparked her interest in chemistry. That same year, Kaufman attended a summer course at Johns Hopkins University for mathematically and scientifically gifted children. She attended a public high school for exceptional students, completing the three–year course in two years. Kaufman's family was supportive of her scientific aspirations, and several of her relatives were scientists and mathematicians. She married Stanley Kaufman, an engineer, in 1948.

Kaufman graduated with a B. S. degree with honors, from Johns Hopkins University in 1949. During her freshman year there, she did research in quantitative chemical analysis with Professor Clark Bricker. Following graduation, Kaufman went to work at the U. S. Army Chemical Center in Maryland, initially as a technical librarian establishing a scientific indexing system for technical reports. After one year, she became a research chemist, developing new methods of chemical analysis. In 1952, one of her professors from Johns Hopkins, the physical chemist Walter S. Koski, invited her to return to his laboratory on a research contract, to study boron compounds. Kaufman completed her masters degree in 1959 and her doctorate in chemistry and chemical physics in 1960 in Koski's laboratory, with her thesis, "Ionization Potentials of Some Boron Compounds." In the summer of 1960, Kaufman attended the Summer Institute of the Quantum Chemistry Group at the University of Uppsala in Sweden. In 1962 she was a visiting scientist at the Centre de Méchanique Ondulatoire Appliquée in Paris, where she lived with her mother and her six–year–old daughter, Jan Caryl. The following year, Kaufman received a second doctoral degree in theoretical physics from the Sorbonne in Paris.

In 1960, Kaufman began theoretical research, applying quantum mechanics to chemical problems, at the Martin Company Research Institute for Advanced Studies. She became head of the quantum chemistry group there in 1962. In 1969, Kaufman returned to Johns Hopkins, where she held a joint appointment in the Department of Chemistry and the Department of Anesthesiology and Clinical Care Medicine of the School of Medicine. In 1977, she became an associate professor in the Department of Surgery.

Kaufman continued her close collaboration with Koski, working in experimental physical chemistry, chemical physics, and theoretical quantum chemistry, a field of physical chemistry that uses the laws of quantum mechanics to explain chemical phenomena. She has researched the chemical physics of explosives, rocket fuels, and other high energy compounds. She has also made important contributions to biomedical research, including animal studies on the mechanisms of drugs and anesthetics, the design of drugs, molecular modeling of pharmaceuticals, and the toxicology of drugs. She has been involved in the development and analysis of tranquilizers and narcotics and has studied the structure of carcinogens. Kaufman also has developed new computer methods for predicting the effectiveness and toxicity of drugs. Using her theoretical quantum chemical methods, Kaufman has predicted types of drugs that subsequently have been developed and proven effective for treating human disease. Kaufman has trained more than 160 undergraduates in her laboratory, as well as numerous postdoctoral fellows and medical interns and residents. She has collaborated extensively with visiting senior scientists.

Kaufman has received numerous awards, including the Maryland Chemist Award in 1974. She was elected a fellow of the American Institute of Chemists in 1965 and the American Physical Society in 1966. Her most prestigious honor was the Garvan Medal of the American Chemical Society, awarded in 1974 for her quantum studies on drug action. The Garvan Medal is awarded annually to an outstanding American woman chemist. Kaufman has been active in several scientific societies and various government scientific advisory boards, as well as serving on a number of editorial boards for journals and other publications. Kaufman remains a Principal Research Scientist in the Department of Chemistry at Johns Hopkins University.

SELECTED WRITINGS BY KAUFMAN:

Books

"Theoretical Insights into Pharmacology." In *Biomolecular Structure, Conformation, Function, and Evolution.* Edited by R. Srinivasan, E. Subramanian, and N. Yathindra. Oxford: Pergamon Press, 1981.

"Quantum Chemical and Theoretical Predictions of Toxicity." In *Structure-Activity Correlation as a Predictive Tool in Toxicology: Fundamentals, Methods, and Applications.* Edited by Leon Golberg. Washington, D.C.: Hemisphere Publishing, 1983.

(With W. A. Sokalski) "Library of Atomic Multipole Moments for Biopolymer Building Blocks." In *Theoretical Biochemistry and Molecular Biophysics.* Edited by David L. Beveridge and Richard Lavery. Schenectady, NY: Adenine Press, 1991.

Periodicals

(With W. S. Koski) "Infrared Study of the Exchange of Deuterium between Decaborane and Diborane." *Journal of the American Chemical Society* 78 (1956): 5774–75.

"Semi–rigorous LCAO–MO–SCF Methods for Three–Dimensional Molecular Calculations." *Journal of Chemical Physics* 43 (1965): S152–56.

(With E. Kerman) "Quantum Chemical Calculations on Antipsychotic Drugs and Narcotic Agents." *International Journal of Quantum Chemistry* 6S (1972): 319–35.

(With W. S. Koski and K. M. Wilson) "Physicochemical Aspects of the Action of General Anesthetics." *Nature* 242 (1973) 65–66.

FURTHER READING

Books

Bailey, Martha J. *American Women in Science 1950 to the Present: A Biographical Dictionary.* Santa Barbara CA: ABC-CLIO, 1998.

Koski, Walter S. "Joyce Jacobson Kaufman (1929–)." In *Women in Chemistry and Physics: A Biobibliographic Sourcebook.* Edited by Louise S. Grinstein, Rose K. Rose, and Miriam H. Rafailovich. Westport, CT: Greenwood Press, 1993.

Sketch by Margaret Alic

Elizabeth Waterbury Keller
1918–1997
American biochemist

Biochemist Elizabeth Keller is best known for her studies of the mechanisms that trigger the formation of proteins, the basis of all biochemical processes within cells, in DNA. She developed a "cloverleaf" model that shows how transfer RNA (tRNA) transcribes genetic information within DNA so that proteins can be formed; the model is still used in textbooks. In her *New York Times* obituary, her colleague, Cornell biochemist Joseph Calvo, said, "Anybody in the field would know that [cloverleaf] design today but would not know Betty . . . [she] figured out a way to make proteins outside the cell so they could be studied."

She was born Elizabeth Waturbury Beach on December 28, 1918, in the Fujian Province of China, of missionary parents. She was educated in the United States, receiving a bachelor of science degree from Chicago in 1940, and a master of science degree from George Washington University in 1945, and a Ph.D. from Cornell University Medical College in 1948. In 1941 she married Geoffrey Keller, but the couple later divorced. She married Dr. Leonard Spector in 1984.

After earning her doctorate, Keller spent more than 20 years in research and teaching at various institutions, including Huntington Memorial Laboratory of Massachusetts General Hospital, Harvard University, the United States Public Health Service, and the Massachusetts Institute of Technology. In 1962, she was invited by Dr. Richard Holley to join his biochemical research team at Cornell University.

At Cornell, Keller helped build on the continuum of research into the biochemistry of genetics. She studied nucleic acid structures and how they influence the formation of proteins. She developed her now–famous cloverleaf model of transfer RNA by using such simple materials as paper, pipe cleaners, and Velcro o represent over 70 subunits of the genetic material. An apocryphal tale says that she sent a sketch of her discovery in a Christmas card to her colleague Dr. Robert Holley, who won the Nobel Prize in 1968 for his discovery of RNA's genetic code, based in part on Keller's contribution to his achievement by sharing some of his prize money with her and other members of their team.

Dr. Keller's contributions were an important part of the tremendous effort to unlock the secrets of the genetic code, providing information on which other scientists could build. She was named emeritus professor of biochemistry, molecular and cell biology in 1988, and remained at the university doing research in molecular biology until shortly before her death from acute leukemia at age 79.

SELECTED WRITINGS BY KELLER:

(With W. A. Noon). *Proceedings of the National Academy of Science, U.S.A.* 81 (1984): 7417–7420.

FURTHER READING

Books

American Men and Women of Science. 20th ed. New Providence, NJ: R.R. Bowker, 1998.

Periodicals

Obituary, *New York Times.* (December 28, 1997): I, 28.3

Other

Biography, Robert W. Holley. http://www.nobel.se/laureates/medicine–1968–l–bio.html

Reichard, P. Nobel Prize presentation speech. "Nobel Prize in Physiology or Medicine 1968." http://www.nobel.se/laureates/medicine–1968–press.html

Thomas, Nigel J. T. "The Life and Scientific Work of Marshall W. Nirenberg." http://www.calstatela.edu/faculty/nthomas/nirember.htm

Lecture. "BIOL100 Concepts of Biology." http://umbcf.umbc.edu/˜farabaug/lecture1.2html

Sketch by Jane Stewart Cook

Evelyn Fox Keller
1936–
American biologist and physicist

A scientist who has openly addressed the issue of discrimination against women in the scientific community, Evelyn Keller is known for her work in designing mathematical models of biological processes. Over the last ten years, however, she has focused on the historical and philosophical issues of developmental genetics.

Evelyn Fox was born March 20, 1936, in New York City. Her parents, Albert and Rachel, were working–class Russian Jewish immigrants. During her childhood, Keller, the youngest of three children, was not interested in science. But when she learned about the "unconscious" from her older sister Frances, her interest was fired. She decided to become a psychoanalyst.

Discovering Science

After graduating from high school, Keller enrolled at Queens College in Brooklyn, with the goal of going to medical school. Her calculus professor, impressed by his brightest student, asked why she wasn't majoring in mathematics. She replied that she didn't want to be an accountant. "Well then," he said, "why don't you major in physics?" To which she replied, "What's that?"

At the end of the term, she was ready to transfer out–preferably to Antioch College or Reed College. However, as a transfer student, she was ineligible for most forms of financial aid, and because of her family's economic status, the plan was impossible. "This was a big blow. I felt I had shot myself in the foot," she says. "It was infuriating." Nevertheless, she was determined to leave—just as much as her parents were determined that she stay. Her brother Maurice came up with a compromise, Brandeis University in Massachusetts.

Keller thrived at Brandeis. "She simply devoured the math," recalls physics professor Sam Schweber, with whom she worked independently during her senior year. "She had no difficulty at all with the technical material, which is unusual." During her studies, she "fell in love" with theoretical physics, and applied for and won a National Science Foundation Fellowship, which would allow her to attend Harvard graduate school. She received her bachelor's degree in physics magna cum laude in 1957.

A Shock to the System

For Keller, the years at Harvard would be filled with "almost unmitigated provocation, insult, and denial." Students and professors told her that she couldn't possibly understand physics, and that her lack of fear was proof of her ignorance. Keller reported that she was told not to concern herself "with the foundations of quantum mechanics (the only thing that did concern me) because, very simply, I was not, could not be, good enough."

Despite the criticism, she did well in her courses. When she turned in especially good work, professors suspected her of plagiarism. "On one such occasion, I had written a paper the thesis of which had provoked much argument and contention in the department. This I learned, by chance, several weeks after the debate was well underway. In an effort to resolve the paradox created by my results, I went to see the professor for whom I had written the paper. After an interesting discussion, which incidentally resolved the difficulty, I was asked, innocently and kindly, from what article(s) I had copied my argument."

She passed her orals and decided to forego physics and return to her original plan to be a psychoanalyst. However, in the interim, she spent the summer with her brother and his family at Cold Spring Harbor, New York, where Maurice worked for the Long Island Biological Laboratories. The biologists welcomed her. She worked beside them in the labs, and discovered an idea for her physics thesismolecular biology. She went back to Harvard and found a physics professor who himself was switching to molecular biology. Walter Gilbert, a 1980 Nobel laureate, agreed to be her advisor. Keller earned her Ph.D. in theoretical physics in 1963.

In the fall of 1962, she went to work as an assistant research scientist for Joseph Bishop Keller, in the Courant Institute of Mathematical Sciences at New York University. They married in 1963, had a son, Jeffrey, in 1964 and a daughter, Sarah, in 1966.

From New York University, Keller joined a new department of mathematical biology at Cornell Medical College. She left there in 1969 to become an associate professor in mathematics at New York University, where she remained until 1972, when she joined the Division of Natural Science at the State University of New York at Purchase. From 1972 to 1974, she served as chair of the division's mathematics board of study. She became a professor of mathematics and humanities at Northeastern University in 1982, remaining at that position until 1988, when she went to the University of California at Berkeley. Since 1992, she has been a professor of the history and philosophy of science at the Massachusetts Institute of Technology.

Creates Mathematical Model of a Biological Process

During the early 1960s and much of the 1970s, Keller's early work with Lee Segel in mathematical biology reflected the renaissance of the subject at that time. Together, they created mathematical models of chemotaxis, the movement of cells toward or away from chemicals, and of slime mold aggregation.

According to Keller, it was not so much an inspiration that led her to apply mathematics to these questions, but rather her training as a theoretical mathematician. Her work drew deeply on parallels between biology and physics. In her "Mathematical Aspects of Bacterial Chemotaxis," she writes, "The individual cells may execute a random motion, which, when averaged over a large population, gives rise to a macroscopic flux in the direction of the gradient. Physics provides us with a well known analogy in Brownian motion."

During the 1980s, she devoted much of her time to gender issues in science. Her book on Barbara McClintock, *A Feeling for the Organism*, was called "a welcome and useful addition to the growing literature on the recent history of . . . women's achievement in science." She considers her highest achievement to be *Reflections on Gender and Science*, which was published in 1985, reissued in 1995 as the tenth anniversary edition, and was translated into more than seven languages.

In the 1990s, she turned her attention to contemporary issues in developmental biology. Some of her new work appeared in *Refiguring Life: Metaphors of 20th Century Biology*, which Columbia University Press published in 1995. "It's really exciting," Keller says. "Molecular biology is subverting its own paradigm." As of 1997, she was at work on a book about explanations in developmental biology, which has the working title, "Making Sense of Life: Explanations in Developmental Biology."

Keller received a MacArthur Foundation grant in 1992. She has also received honorary degrees from Technical University of Luleá, in 1996; Rensselaer Polytechnic Institute, in 1995; Simmons College, in 1995; the University of Amsterdam, in 1993; and Mount Holyoke College, in 1991. Her numerous awards include include the 1991 Alumni Achievement Award from Brandeis, the 1990 AAUW Achievement Award, the 1985 Radcliffe Graduate Society Medal, and the 1981–82 Mina Shaughnessy Award.

SELECTED WRITINGS BY KELLER:

Books

"The Anomaly of a Woman in Physics." In *Working it Out*. Edited by S. Rudick and P. Daniels. New York: Pantheon, 1977.

A Feeling for the Organism: The Life and Work of Barbara McClintock. 2d ed. New York: W. H. Freeman, 1993.

"Mathematical Aspects of Chemotaxis." In *Chemotaxis*. Edited by S. Sorkin. Farmington, CT: S. Karger, 1974, pp. 79–93.

Reflections on Gender and Science. New Haven: Yale University Press, 1985

Secrets of Life, Secrets of Death. New York: Routledge, 1992.

Periodicals

"Assessing the Keller–Segel Model: How Has it Fared?" *Lecture Notes in Biomathematics* 38 (1980): 379–87.

"The Force of the 'Pacemaker' Concept in Theories of Aggregation in Cellular Slime Mold." *Perspectives in Biology and Medicine* 26, no. 4 (1983); 515–2.

"A Mathematical Description of Biological Clocks." *Currents of Modern Biology* 1 (1968): 279–84

(With Lee A. Segel) "A Model for Chemotaxis." *Journal of Theoretical Biology* 30 (1971): 225–234.

(With Lee A. Segel) "Slime Mold Aggregation Viewed as an Instability." *Journal of Theoretical Biology* 26 (1970): 399–415.

(With M. Meselson) "Unequal Photosensitivity of the Two Strands of DNA in Bacteriophage Lambda." *Journal of Molecular Biology* 7 (1963): 583–89..

"Women in Science: An Analysis of a Social Problem." *Harvard Magazine* (October 1974): 14–19.

FURTHER READING

Periodicals

Horning, Beth. "The Controversial Career of Evelyn Fox Keller." *Technology Review* (January 1993).

Sketch by Fran Hodgkins

Frances Oldham Kelsey
1914–
Canadian-born American pharmacologist and physician

Frances Oldham Kelsey became nationally famous in 1962 when she prevented the sedative drug thalidomide from entering the United States. Thalidomide was found to have caused birth defects in 10,000 European children in the late 1950s and early 1960s. For preventing an American thalidomide tragedy, Kelsey was awarded the government's highest civilian award, the President's Distinguished Federal Civilian Service Award. Kelsey's vigilance led to the strengthening of investigational drug regulations, greater attention to the safety of drugs in pregnancy, and increased interest in research on teratology, the biological study of congenital deformities and abnormal development.

Kelsey was born in Cobble Hill, British Columbia, on July 24, 1914. In 1934, she received a bachelor's degree in science from McGill University in Montreal and attained a master's degree in science there in 1935. Kelsey received her professional degrees, a doctorate in pharmacology in 1938 and an M.D. in 1950, from the University of Chicago. She completed an internship at Sacred Heart Hospital in Yankton, South Dakota, in 1954 and was associate professor of pharmacology at the University of South Dakota from

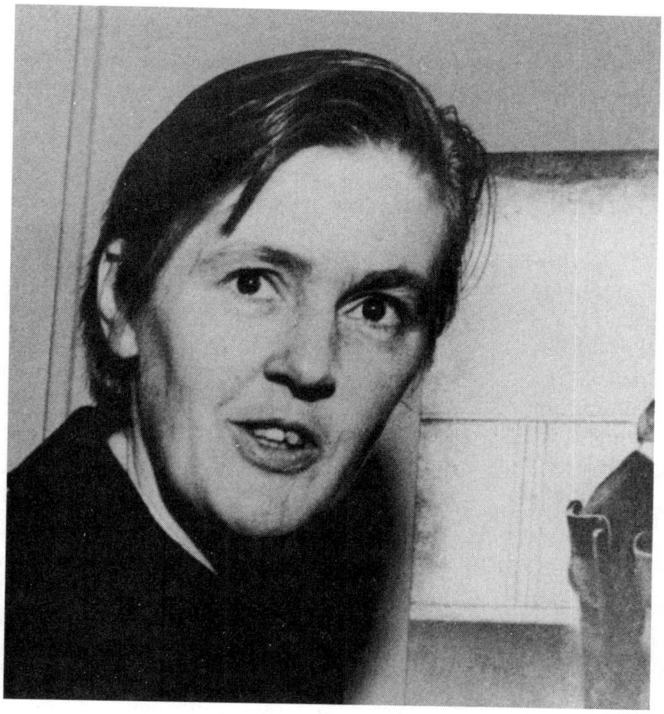

Frances Oldham Kelsey (The Library of Congress. Reproduced by permission.)

1954 to 1957. She remained in South Dakota until 1960, and was in private practice there between 1957 and 1960. In 1955, Kelsey became a naturalized U.S. citizen. She had married F. Ellis Kelsey in 1943, and they had two children.

Studies Side Effects of Drugs on Children

Early in her career, Kelsey investigated the cause of 107 deaths, most of them in children, from a new sulfa drug. In the 1940s, she coauthored several papers with her husband on the metabolism of antimalarial drugs. In 1943, they published a study in the *Journal of Pharmacy and Experimental Therapy* about the effects of antimalarial drugs on the embryo. They found that the drug could be broken down by the liver of adult rabbits, but fetal livers could not break it down, and the drug could have deleterious effects. This research laid the groundwork for Kelsey's continuing interest in the safety of drugs during pregnancy.

Attains Pharmaceutical Regulatory Position

Kelsey's civil service career began in August, 1960, when she became a medical officer for the Food and Drug Administration (FDA). After one month on the job, Kelsey was asked to review what was expected to be a simple and routine marketing application for thalidomide. Thalidomide, a sleep inducer, had been developed in West Germany in the 1950s, and was widely marketed in Europe; belief in its safety was so widespread that the drug was available without prescription.

Kelsey soon became suspicious of the safety of thalidomide. In February, 1961, she read a letter from a doctor in the *British Medical Journal* suggesting an association between thalidomide and peripheral neuritis, a tingling sensation in the arms and legs of adult users. Kelsey promptly asked Richardson–Merrill, distributor of thalidomide, for additional animal study data and reports of all clinical trials of thalidomide to supplement the company's application for American approval. She later notified the company that she suspected thalidomide might have some effect on unborn children, although she did not yet suspect it as a cause of deformity. Throughout her review, Kelsey remained concerned that the company had failed to provide adequate data to demonstrate the safety of thalidomide.

In November, 1961, a German scientist alleged a strong association between use of the drug by pregnant women and an increase in deformed babies born in Germany. Finally, in December, 1961, the company acknowledged the German reports and requested that women of childbearing age discontinue its use. More than 10,000 cases of phocomelia, a condition causing underdevelopment or absence of arms and legs, in European children were eventually attributed to use of thalidomide. Seventeen cases of thalidomide embryopathy resulting from a then–legal experimental distribution of the drug were later documented in the United States.

Receives Congressional Gold Medal

On July 15, 1962, the *Washington Post* ran an article about Kelsey that began, "This is the story of how the skepticism and stubbornness of a government physician prevented what could have been an appalling American tragedy. . . ." A wave of publicity and acclaim swept the world. Only a month later, Congress voted to award a gold medal to Kelsey "in recognition of the distinguished service to mankind . . . by withholding, despite the great pressures brought to bear upon her, approval of the horror–drug thalidomide which has caused thousands of babies to be deformed." In October, 1962, with Kelsey present at the ceremony, President Kennedy signed a landmark drug law, the Kefauver–Harris Amendments. The law required drug manufacturers to register with the Food and Drug Administration proof that new drugs were both effective and safe, and provided for more rapid recall of new drugs deemed hazardous. In 1963, Kelsey became chief of the Investigational Drug Branch of the FDA, and in 1968 was appointed director of the Office of Scientific Investigations.

SELECTED WRITINGS BY KELSEY:

Books

(With F. E. Kelsey and E. M. K. Geiling) *Essentials of Pharmacology.* Lippincott, 1947, 4th edition, 1960.

Periodicals

"Drug Embryopathy—the Thalidomide Story." *Maryland State Medical Journal* (December 1963).

"Problems Raised for the FDA by the Occurrence of Thalidomide Embryopathy in Germany 1960–1961." *South Dakota Journal of Medicine and Pharmacy* (January 1964).

"Drugs in Pregnancy." *Minnesota State Medical Association Journal* (February 1965): 175–180.

"Events After Thalidomide." *Journal of Dental Research* 46 (1967): 1201–1205.

"Thalidomide Update: Regulatory Aspects." *Clinical Pharmacology and Therapeutics* 3 (1988): 3.

"Good Clinical Practice in the U.S.: Impact of European Guidelines." *Drug Information Journal* 26 (1992): 125–132.

FURTHER READING

Books

Sjostrom, H., and R. Nilsson. *Thalidomide and the Power of the Drug Companies.* Penguin, 1972.

Periodicals

"Dr. Kelsey Will Receive a High Presidential Award." *New York Times* (August 12, 1962): 1.

"Drug Reform Bill is Signed at White House, With Dr. Kelsey Present." *New York Times* (October 11, 1962): 31.

Grigg, W. "The Thalidomide Tragedy—25 Years Ago." *FDA Consumer* (February 1987): 14–17.

Hunter, M. "Stiffer Drug Law Urged by Kennedy." *New York Times* (August 12, 1962): 1.

Sketch by Laura Newman

Helen Dean King
1869–1955
American geneticist and zoologist

Helen Dean King bred 150 generations of rats for laboratory experiments. This breeding operation gave scientists the ability to breed pure strains of animals, and it expanded King's research in such areas as sex, regeneration, inbreeding, and heredity. In the process, King also discovered several new types of rat, including the waltzing rat, and worked to domesticate the Norway rat. Her findings in inbreeding were applicable to other fields, including the breeding of race horses.

King was born on September 27, 1869, in Owego, New York, to George Alonzo King and Leonora Louise Dean King. The Kings were a locally prominent family. Her father was president of a leather company, the King Harness Company. As a youth, King attended the Owego Free Academy. King earned her undergraduate degree from Vassar College in 1892. She did her graduate work at Bryn Mawr College, earning her Ph.D. in 1899, majoring in morphology and minoring in paleontology and physiology.

While a graduate student, King worked as a fellow in the biology department for one year, 1896–97. After earning her Ph.D., King taught science at the Baldwin School in Bryn Mawr, Pennsylvania, from 1899 until 1907. Simultaneously, King worked as an assistant in biology at Bryn Mawr, until 1906. While associated with Bryn Mawr, King's research focused on embryological issues such as regeneration and developmental anatomy, mostly involving amphibians.

In 1909, King joined the staff at the Wistar Institute of Anatomy and Biology in Philadelphia. She moved through the ranks from an assistant in anatomy and biology in 1909 to an assistant professor of embryology by 1913. King spent the rest of her career at Wistar, though she was never promoted to a full professorship. (This was not uncommon for female professors in this era.) Still, she was a key member of the staff, as well as a member of the Wistar Advisory board for 24 years.

King's most fruitful work was done at Wistar. In her first year, King began her inbreeding experiments to ensure a uniform stock of laboratory rats. Among other subjects, she spent time analyzing the effects of close inbreeding, and concluded that, if the stock has certain characteristics (among them strong health), inbreeding has certain advantages over outbreeding. Her findings became a source of popular debate in newspapers throughout the United States in the late 1910s and 1920s, as the implications of incest was exploited.

While conducting her inbreeding and generation breeding experiments on rats in 1919, King also worked on the domestication of the wild Norway rat. She focused on their life processes, carefully studying and isolating their mutations. Because of her work in this area, subsequent researchers knew how to breed pure strains of animals for their studies.

In 1932, King was awarded the Ellen Richards Prize from the Association to Aid Scientific Research of Women for her research accomplishments. Sixteen years later, she retired from Wistar. King died on March 7, 1955, in Philadelphia.

SELECTED WRITINGS BY KING:

Periodicals

"Studies on Inbreeding I. The Effects of Inbreeding on the Growth and Variability in the Body Weight of the Albino Rat." *Journal of Experimental Zoology* (July 1918): 335–78.

"Studies on Inbreeding III. The Effects of Inbreeding with Selection, on the Sex Ratio of the Albino Rat." *Journal of Experimental Zoology* (October 1918): 1–35.

FURTHER READING

Books

Bailey, Martha J. "King, Helen Dean." *American Women in Science*. Denver: ABC–CLIO, 1994, pp. 192–93.

Bogin, Mary. "King, Helen Dean." *Dictionary of Scientific Biography*. Vol 17, Sup. II. Edited by Frederic L. Holmes. New York: Charles Scribner's Sons, 1990, pp. 474–77.

Ogilvie, Marilyn Bailey. "King, Helen Dean." *Women in Science: Antiquity through the Nineteenth Century*. Cambridge: MIT Press, 1986, pp. 108–110.

Siegel, Patricia Joan, and Kay Thomas Finley. "Helen Dean King." *Women in the Scientific Search: An American Bio–Bibliography, 1724–1979*. Metuchen, NJ: Scarecrow Press, Inc., 1985, p. 358.

Sketch by Annette Petrusso

Mary Henrietta Kingsley (The Granger Collection, New York. Reproduced by permission.)

Mary Henrietta Kingsley
1862–1900
British naturalist

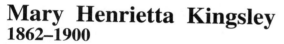

Mary Kingsley is remembered as an explorer who traveled to remote and dangerous areas of the world and described them in best-selling books. Her contribution to science is in the many natural specimens she brought back, which are still housed in museums. Her ethnological and natural studies of the West African region are still the most in depth today.

Mary Kingsley, the older of two children born to George Kingsley, a physician, and his wife, was given almost no formal education. Because her mother was an invalid and her younger brother was quite sickly, it was expected that Mary should devote herself entirely to their care because of her father's frequent and extensive travels. Kingsley also managed "handyman" work around the house. When she got older, her father allowed her to learn German in order to translate articles for him.

But in 1892, her parents died within weeks of each other and her brother moved elsewhere. Although she continued to nurse her brother when he was in town, Kingsley was able to pursue her own interests. Her father had been doing studies in anthropology, including natural history and religion, and Kingsley decided to carry on his work.

She first went to the Canary Islands, but soon traveled to West Africa among the bush tribes, becoming an adept sailor in the process. Because she was among cannibals and violent people, it was important to be trusted, and Kingsley worked as a trader of cloth and tobacco during her travels. Clothed in the period's elaborate dresses and in danger from death by the people and animals around her, Kingsley's studies were remarkable. She conducted anthropological studies of the African tribes; explored the Ogoive and Calabar rivers by canoe; studied fish, native plants and vines, insects, reptiles, and wild animals; and collected specimens. Kingsley also became the second person to climb to the top of West Africa's highest point, Mount Cameroon (Mungo Mah Lobeh). She managed to survive the dangers surrounding her, including being covered in swamp leeches and falling into a pit of spikes meant for catching game.

Kingsley's travels gained her instant fame and reputation. She became politically active on the side of West Africans, speaking out against missionaries and others who tried to intervene in the tribal way of life, and wrote two best-selling books on her travels. In addition, the specimens she collected in pickling jars became housed by her generous gift in the British Museum. Among her discoveries were six new species and a new genus of fish, three of which were named in her honor, an extremely rare lizard, and a snake which had never been seen before.

Kingsley volunteered to serve as an army nurse in South Africa during the Boer War. After a short time of service, she died there of enteric fever and, according to her wish, she was buried at sea. In her memory, England established The Mary Kingsley Society of West Africa to continue her good work on behalf of the tribes people.

SELECTED WRITINGS BY KINGSLEY:

Books

Travels in West Africa. London: Macmillan, 1897.
West African Studies. London: Macmillan, 1899.

FURTHER READING

Books

Mozans, H. J. *Woman in Science*. Notre Dame: University of Notre Dame Press, 1991.
Robinson, Jane. *Wayward Women: A Guide to Women Travellers*. Oxford: Oxford University Press, 1990.
Uglow, Jennifer S., ed. *The Continuum Dictionary of Women's Biography*. NY: Continuum, 1989.

Sketch by Helene Barker Kiser

Maria Margaretha (Winkelmann) Kirch
1670–1720
German astronomer

Maria Winkelmann Kirch, one of the first famous women astronomers, discovered a comet in 1702. Although she collaborated with her husband and children, she also had several independent publications. She was actively involved in the establishment of the Berlin Academy of Sciences, but lost her position there after her husband's death.

Kirch was born in 1670 at Panitzsch, near Leipzig, Germany. Her father was a Lutheran clergyman who educated his daughter himself. After his death, her uncle took over her education. Kirch received training in astronomy from Christoph Arnold, who was known as the "astronomical peasant." He was a self–taught amateur astronomer and farmer who lived in a neighboring village. At Arnold's house, she met Gottfried Kirch, the most prominent astronomer in Germany at the time. In 1692 she married the widower, who was 30 years her senior. Although her uncle would have preferred that she marry a young Lutheran minister, her marriage to Kirch enabled her to pursue her career as an astronomer. Gottfried Kirch had been training his three sisters in astronomy, and he also took over the further education of his new wife.

Kirch collaborated with her husband on astronomical observations and calculations. The Kirch family was in the business of producing Christian, Jewish, and Turkish calendars, as well as other books of computations and observations. The astronomically–accurate calendars were similar to almanacs and included the positions of the sun, moon, and planets; the phases of the moon; solar and lunar eclipses; accurate times for sunrises and sunsets; and astrology.

Joins Berlin Academy of Sciences

In 1700, Gottfried Kirch was appointed astronomer at the newly founded Berlin Academy of Sciences. Maria was his recognized, but unofficial, assistant. Kirch and her husband took an active role in developing the academy's observatory. Often the two observed together, one looking to the north and the other to the south; other times, they observed on alternate nights. The government had ruled that German territories must have calendars similar to the Gregorian calendar of the Roman Catholic Church, and the Kirchs' production of these calendars became a major source of income for the academy. Maria Kirch also was the acting meteorologist at the academy, keeping records of the weather and making predictions.

Discovers Comet

Maria Kirch discovered a new comet in 1702. As Londa Schiebinger, in *The Mind has no Sex?*, quoted from Gottfried Kirch's notes: "Early in the morning (about 2:00 A.M.) the sky was clear and starry. Some nights before, I had observed a variable star, and my wife (as I slept) wanted to find and see it for herself. In so doing, she found a comet in the sky. . . I was surprised that I had not seen it the night before." Together, the Kirchs observed the comet for the next two weeks, and Maria Kirch wrote up the report. Comets were major discoveries at the time, and this was the first such discovery at the new academy. News of the new comet was sent immediately to the king. However this news, as well as the published reports, bore the name of Gottfried, not Maria, Kirch. Apparently Gottfried Kirch at first was hesitant to acknowledge his wife's work. Later, he was assured that it was appropriate for him to do so, and when the report of the comet was reprinted after eight years, in the first volume of the journal of the Berlin Academy, Maria Kirch was credited. Nevertheless, the comet was not named after Maria Kirch and she never received recognition for her discovery.

In 1707 Kirch wrote to her friend, the scientific philosopher Gottfried Wilhelm von Leibniz, of her observations on the aurora borealis. She hoped that, as president of the academy, Leibniz would be able provide the Kirch family with housing that was more convenient to the observatory. Kirch published three pamphlets in German, under her own name, between 1709 and 1711. However, her lack of proficiency in Latin prevented her from publishing in Germany's only scientific journal. In 1709, the orbits of Saturn and Venus placed them in a straight line, or conjunction, with the sun. Kirch's writings on this event, and the upcoming conjunction of Jupiter and Saturn in 1712, were her most important published works. She also published a pamphlet in 1711 predicting the appearance of a new comet. All of these writings included astrological predications, which were not unusual in scientific publications of the time.

Maria Kirch was quite famous in her own day. Leibniz presented her at the royal court of Frederick I of Prussia, so she could inform them of her observations of sunspots. As Schiebinger quoted in her book, from Leibniz's letter of introduction to the court: "I do not believe that this woman easily finds her equal in the science in which she excells . . . She favors the Copernican system (the idea that the sun is at rest) like all the learned astronomers of our time. And it is a pleasure to hear her defend that system through the Holy Scripture in which she is also very learned. She observes with the best observers, she knows how to handle marvelously the quadrant and the telescope."

Petitions to Become Academy Astronomer

When Gottfried Kirch died in 1710, his position needed to be filled immediately. Since there were no other qualified candidates, Kirch petitioned the Berlin Academy of Sciences to appoint herself and her son, Christfried, as assistant astronomers, in charge of the calendars. At this time, astronomy still was considered something of a craft, and it was traditional in the crafts professions for a widow to be allowed to carry on the family business after her husband's death. Kirch needed the position, and the accompanying house, to support her family. Although Leibniz promoted her candidacy, the academy had already come under criticism for employing a woman, and they were afraid of setting a precedent. They allowed her to stay in the house for a time, but refused to grant her a salary; although later that year, they presented her with a medal. Kirch took her case to the king, but Leibniz, her only supporter, had left Berlin by then. She continued to petition the academy for the next year and a half, but to no avail. Kirch was devastated. As Schiebinger quoted in her book, from a preface that Kirch wrote at the time, the "female sex as well as the male possesses talents of mind and spirit . . . [a woman can be] as skilled as a man at observing and understanding the skies." In Kirch's place, an incompetent man was appointed astronomer. He took advantage of her expertise, but refused to allow her to use the observatory.

In 1712, Kirch moved to the well–equipped private Berlin observatory of Baron Bernhard Frederick von Krosigk, where the Kirchs had worked previously, while the academy observatory was being built. With her son studying at the university in Leipzig, Kirch continued her observing and had two students to assist her. The published reports from that time bore her name. She further supported herself and her daughters by doing the calendars for Breslau and Nuremberg. When Krosigk died in 1714, Kirch briefly became an assistant to a mathematics professor in Danzig, until the family of Johannes Hevelius, the teacher of Gottfried Kirch, offered Maria and her son the use of Hevelius's observatory.

In 1716, the Kirchs received an invitation from Peter the Great of Russia to come to work in Moscow. Instead, they returned to Berlin where Christfried became the academy astronomer. Christfried was not qualified for the position, but with his mother as his "assistant," was able to carry out his duties. Kirch continued to calculate the calendars. However in 1717, she was criticized by the academy council for talking to visitors at the observatory, rather than leaving the public functions to her son. Shortly thereafter, the council evicted her from her house and the observatory. Kirch was forced to abandon astronomy. She died of a fever in 1720.

Her daughters, Christine and Margaretha, had been trained in astronomy since the age of ten, and they remained at the academy as assistants to Christfried. In addition to calendars, they calculated almanacs and ephemerides (tables of the positions and motions of the heavenly bodies). However, having witnessed their mother's persecution at the hands of the academy council, they kept a low profile. After Christfried died in 1740, the sisters were forced to continue their observations from their home, with inadequate instruments. Christine (c. 1696–1782), the elder daughter, never married, and she continued to support herself by preparing the academy's calendars until her death. It was the twentieth century before another woman scientist worked at the Berlin Academy.

SELECTED WRITINGS BY KIRCH:

Books

(Winkelmann) *Vorstellung des Himmels bey der Zusammenkunfft dreyer Grossmächtigsten Könige*. Potsdam, 1709.

(Winkelmann) *Vorbereitung, zur grossen Opposition, oder merckwürdige Himmels–Gestalt im 1712*. Cölln an der Spree, 1711.

FURTHER READING

Books

Schiebinger, Londa. *The Mind Has No Sex? Women in the Origins of Modern Science*. Cambridge: Harvard University Press, 1989.

Periodicals

Schiebinger, Londa. "Maria Winkelmann at the Berlin Academy: A Turning Point for Women in Science." *Isis* 78 (1987): 305–32.

Sketch by Margaret Alic

Vera Kistiakowsky
1928–
American physicist

Vera Kistiakowsky is a professor of physics at the Massachusetts Institute of Technology (MIT) who has worked to advance the interests of women in the sciences. Kistiakowsky gained international recognition in the scientific community following her "backward charge exchange" experiment in high-energy particle physics while at MIT. A prolific author of more than 100 technical research papers, Kistiakowsky has also written and spoken extensively on matters such as the military budget and the escalating global arms race.

Born in Princeton, New Jersey in 1928, Kistiakowsky was the only child of George Bogdan and Hildegard (Moebius) Kistiakowsky. Kistiakowsky's father was a prominent research chemist who served as science and technology advisor to President Dwight D. Eisenhower. In an interview with Harding, Kistiakowsky related that she had "enormous respect and love" for her father, who encouraged her to pursue her interests and focus her energy on them. Both father and daughter were tall and athletically–inclined, and they often skied and hiked together. Young Kistiakowsky was particularly thrilled when her father presented her with her very own horse during one summer spent with him. They shared many hours during the summers horseback-riding and talking.

Kistiakowsky was an excellent student who skipped several grades and entered Mt. Holyoke College at the age of 15. She had intended to pursue a career in medicine, but became inspired by Mt. Holyoke's well-established and staffed chemistry department. She graduated with her bachelor's degree in 1948, then went on to obtain her Ph.D. in nuclear chemistry from the University of California at Berkeley in 1952.

Kistiakowsky discovered that finding a job was difficult, and she was limited by the fact that her husband, Gerhard Emil Fischer, whom she had married in 1951, was not finished with his Ph.D. (The marriage would end in divorce in 1970.) Kistiakowsky took a job as a staff scientist at the U.S. Naval Research Defense Laboratory in Berkeley and then spent a year as a Berliner Fellow at the University of California's Radiation Laboratory. When her husband completed his Ph.D., Kistiakowsky sent out 100 letters to universities and colleges and only got one answer—a rejection from an all-male college in Boston. Her husband, however, was immediately offered a job as an instructor at Columbia University. Since they were hiring her husband, Kistiakowsky was hired as a research associate, although the couple had the same degree. At Columbia Kistiakowsky worked with **Chien-Shiung Wu**, the most well-respected woman physicist in the country. Kistiakowsky became a physics instructor at Columbia in 1957, and in 1959 her husband got a job in Boston. She accepted a teaching position at Brandeis University, where she continued as an adjunct associate professor until 1963. At that time she was offered a position with MIT and remained there for the next 30 years. There she changed her focus from nuclear to particle physics. During this time Kistiakowsky and her husband had two children, Marc and Karen.

Forms Organization to Advance Women Scientists

At MIT Kistiakowsky became increasingly concerned for the plight of many fellow women scientists who had reached an impasse in their careers and professions. Although there were more women students, there were few women faculty members. In 1969, Kistiakowsky and some friends formed a group called Women in Science and Engineering (WISE) and began what was to become a lifetime commitment to making science professions more accessible for women. The following year, Kistiakowsky, joined by 19 of her female colleagues, wrote a letter to the American Physical Society, asking that it establish a committee (which she ultimately chaired) to assess the status of women in physics.

A distinguished speaker with an authoritative voice, Kistiakowsky has remained proactive in other matters for which she has developed convictions, often to the chagrin of the MIT administration. Early on, she made public her concern for the efficacy of the Strategic Defense Initiative (SDI) (dubbed the "Star Wars" program), despite its political popularity, and pledged not to request or accept SDI money for MIT research. In 1986, Kistiakowsky was honored as the Outstanding Woman Military Expert by the Center for Defense Information. Kistiakowsky, in her interview with Harding, also articulated her strong beliefs that undergraduate educational curricula should not be affected or influenced by Defense Department research funding, which she believes should be confined to graduate research off-campus. However, she does credit MIT with making research funds available to students. Her scholarly treatment of the subject, "Military Funding of University Research," was published in *The Annals of the American Academy of Political and Social Science*. Kistiakowsky has also advised, chaired, or directed various committees for such organizations as the American Association for the Advancement of Science (AAAS), the Association for Women in Science, the senate of Phi Beta Kappa, and as Director for the Council for a Liveable World.

In later years Kistiakowsky shifted her research focus from nuclear and high-energy particle physics to optical astrophysics. Kistiakowsky believes there is order in the universe, explaining to Harding in an interview that ". . .it is just one outcome of chaos." Kistiakowsky enjoys gardening and spending time with her son and daughter, both of whom are scientists.

SELECTED WRITINGS BY KISTIAKOWSKY:

Periodicals

"Keep the Pentagon Out of Civilian Economy." *Bulletin of Atomic Scientists* 45 (April, 1989): 5.

"Military Funding of University Research." *Annals of the American Academy of Political and Social Science* 502 (March 1989): 141.

(With D.J. Helfand) "Observations of [SIII] Emission from Galactic Radio Sources: The Detection of Distant Planetary Nebulae and a Search for Supernova Remnant Emission." *Journal of Astronomy* 105 (1993): 2199.

"Women in Engineering, Medicine and Science." *Report from the Conference on Women in Science and Technology.* Washington, D. C.: National Research Council, June 1973.

"Women in Physics: Unnecessary, Injurious, and Out of Place?" In *History of Physics.* Edited by Spencer R. Weart and Melba Phillips. New York: American Institute of Physics, 1985.

FURTHER READING

Books

American Men and Women of Science. 17th ed. New Providence: R.R. Bowker, 1989-1990.

McMurray, Emily J., ed. *Notable Twentieth-Century Scientists.* Detroit: Gale Research Inc.

Notable Women in the Physical Sciences: A Biographical Dictionary. Westport, CT: Greenwood Press, 1997.

O'Neill, Lois Decker, ed. *The Women's Book of World Records and Achievements.* Garden City, NJ: Anchor Press, 1979.

Rossiter, Margaret W.*Women Scientists in America.* Baltimore: Johns Hopkins University Press.

Who's Who of American Women.. 21st ed. New Providence: Marquis, 1999–2000.

Other

Harding, Lauri R., interview with Vera Kistiakowsky conducted on July 22, 1999.

Kaufman, Ron. "Women Astronomers Press Manifesto For Equal Rights." *The Scientist.* http://www.the-scientist.library.upenn.edu/yr1993/sep/kaufman3930906.html

Mehta, Prabhat. "Area scientists speak out against war." *The Tech* 110, no. 59 (January 1991): http://www-tech.mit.edu/V110/N59/war5.59n.html

"Documentation Preserved: Report from the International Catalog of Sources for History of Physics and Allied Sciences." http://www.aip.org/history/spr95/docpres.html

Sketch by Lauri R. Harding

Flemmie Pansy Kittrell
1904–1980
American nutritionist and educator

Flemmie Pansy Kittrell was an internationally-known nutritionist whose emphasis on child development and family welfare drew much-needed attention to the importance of the early home environment. During her more than forty years as an educator, she traveled abroad extensively, helping to improve home-life conditions in many developing nations. She was a founder of Howard University's school of human ecology and the recipient of several major awards which acknowledged her unique accomplishments. As the first African American woman to earn a Ph.D. in nutrition, she strove constantly to focus attention on the important role that women could play in the world and to push for their higher education.

Kittrell was born in Henderson, North Carolina, on Christmas Day, 1904. She was the youngest daughter of Alice (Mills) and James Lee Kittrell, both of whom were descended from African American and Cherokee forebears. Learning was of central importance to Kittrell's parents, and her father often read stories and poetry to her and her eight brothers and sisters. Her parents knew the importance of encouragement and the children frequently received praise for their perseverance and achievements.

After graduating from high school in North Carolina, Kittrell attended Hampton Institute in Virginia, receiving her Bachelor of Science degree in 1928. With the encouragement of her professors she enrolled at Cornell University, although there were not many black women during that era who became graduate students. In 1930 Kittrell received her M.A. from Cornell and in 1938, from the same institution, she accepted her Ph.D. in nutrition with honors.

Kittrell was offered her first job teaching home economics in 1928 by Bennett College in Greensboro, North Carolina, and it was to Bennett she returned after obtaining her Ph.D. She then became dean of women and the head of the home economics department at Hampton Institute in 1940, where she remained until 1944. In that year Kittrell accepted the personal offer of Howard University president Mordecai Johnson to preside over the home economics department at Howard University in Washington, D.C. At Howard, Kittrell developed a curriculum that broadened the common perception of home economics so that it included such fields as child development research.

In 1947 Kittrell embarked upon a lifetime of international activism, carrying out a nutritional survey of Liberia sponsored by the United States government. Her findings concerning "hidden hunger," a type of malnutrition which occurred in ninety percent of the African nation's population, led to important changes in Liberian agricultural and fishing industries. Kittrell then received a 1950 Fulbright award which led to her work with Baroda University in India, where she developed an educational plan for nutritional research. In 1953, Kittrell went back to India as a teacher of home economics classes and nutritional seminars. Then, in 1957, Kittrell headed a team which traveled to Japan and Hawaii to research activities in those countries related to the science of home economics. Between 1957 and 1961, Kittrell was the leader of three more tours, to West Africa, Central Africa, and Guinea.

During this period Kittrell remained at Howard University. In 1963, her fifteen–year struggle to obtain a building for the school of human ecology resulted in the dedication of a new facility. This innovative building attracted national attention as it provided a working example for the nation's Head Start program, which was just getting off the ground. Retiring from Howard University in 1972, Kittrell was named Emeritus Professor of Nutrition.

Kittrell's achievements were regularly recognized by awards and honors. For instance, she was chosen by Hampton University as its outstanding alumna for 1955. In 1961 she received the Scroll of Honor by the National Council of Negro Women in recognition of her special services. Cornell University gave her an achievement award in 1968 and the University of North Carolina at Greensboro conferred on her an honorary degree in 1974. Also, a scholarship fund was founded in honor of Kittrell's career by the American Home Economics Association.

Kittrell continued to work despite her retirement from teaching in 1972. From 1974 to 1976 she was a Cornell Visiting Senior Fellow, and she served as a Moton Center Senior Research Fellow in 1977 and a Fulbright lecturer in India in 1978. Kittrell died unexpectedly of cardiac arrest on October 3, 1980, in Washington, D.C. During her life she had credited much of her success not only to her education, but also to the strength, love, and family unity she enjoyed in her parents' home, where learning was a very important aspect of family life.

FURTHER READING

Books

Sammons, Vivian O. *Blacks in Science and Medicine.* Hemisphere Publishing, 1990, pp. 143–144.

Smith, Jesse Carney, ed. *Notable Black American Women.* Gale, 1992, pp. 636–638.

Sketch by Leonard C. Bruno

Margaret Knight
1838–1914
American Inventor

Despite her lack of formal education, inventor Margaret Knight owned the rights to 27 patents, many for heavy machinery, and created a total of 90 inventions. These facts make her very unusual in the history of women in science. Knight's best known invention is a machine that produced flat–bottomed paper bags, versions of which are still used today.

Knight was born on February 14, 1838, in York, Maine, the daughter of Hannah (Teal) and James Knight. Called Mattie by her family and friends, Knight grew up in Manchester, New Hampshire. Though she attended public schools for a period of time in that city, her schooling was incomplete and she never learned any scientific theory. Instead, she worked in mills as a child. Considered a tomboy, Knight was very interested in mechanical devices as a child, preferring woodworking tools such as a jackknife over dolls and other toys intended for girls.

Produces First Invention

When Knight was about 12 years old, she devised her first invention. One of her brothers worked in a cotton textile mill, and when she visited him there one day, she witnessed an industrial accident. A steel–tipped shuttle (a device that holds the thread during weaving) became dislodged from its loom and stabbed a worker. Inspired, Knight came up with a device that stopped the motion of the loom when the shuttle came loose. Knight's invention was soon put to use in the factory. She did not patent this invention.

As an adult, Knight, moved to Springfield, Massachusetts, where she worked for the Columbia Paper Bag Company. While working there, she invented a machine to fold square–bottomed paper bags.

Fights for First Patent

In 1869, Knight went to Boston to supervise the making of the prototype of her machine. Another inventor, Charles F. Annan, saw her invention and quickly patented his own version. Knight contested in court, and ultimately won the right to the patent, her first, in 1870. She was offered $50,000 for the rights to the device, but Knight refused, and went into business for herself and formed the Eastern Paper Bag Company.

Knight continued to patent new inventions for the next three decades. In the 1880s, after a move to Ashland, Massachusetts, her inventions focused on domestic concerns. In 1883, she invented a shield for dresses and skirts. The next year she patented robe claps, and in 1885, a spit. In 1890, Knight moved again, to South Framingham, MA, and began work on a machine that cut shoes. She refined this invention several times through 1894 and received about six patents. The same year, she also patented two other items: a window frame and sash and a numbering machine.

After the turn of the century, Knight's attentions turned to larger machines and automobiles. She invented items for rotary motors and engines, including valves. One of her best known inventions in this area is the sleeve–valve engine. The unmarried Knight died on October 12, 1914, in Framingham of pulmonary congestion and gallstones, and was buried in Newton, Massachusetts. An obituary published in a local paper gave tribute to Knight by comparing her to Thomas Alva Edison.

FURTHER READING

Books

James, Edward T., et al. *Notable American Women 1607–1950: A Biographical Dictionary, Volume II.* Cambridge: Belknap Press, 1971, pp. 339–40.

McDonald, Anne L. *Feminine Ingenuity: Women and Invention in America.* New York: Ballantine Books, 1992, pp. 50–57, 232, 254–55.

McHenry, Robert. *Famous American Women: A Biographical Dictionary from Colonial Time to the Present.* New York: Dover Publications, 1980, p. 228.

Mozans, H.J. *Woman in Science.* New York: D. Appleton and Company, 1913, pp. 350–51.

Ogilvie, Marilyn Bailey. *Women in Science: Antiquity through the Nineteenth Century: A Biographical Dictionary with Annotated Bibliography.* Cambridge: MIT Press, 1986, pp. 110–11.

Uglow, Jennifer, ed. *The Macmillan Dictionary of Women's Biography.* New York: Macmillan, 1989, p. 301.

Vare, Ethlie Ann and Greg Ptacek. *Mothers of Invention: From the Bra to the Bomb: Forgotten Women and Their Unforgettable Ideas.* New York: William Morrow and Company, 1988, pp. 49–50.

Other

"Margaret Knight, Inventor." http://reality.sgi.com/rcu/women/knight.html (March 11, 1999).

"Prolific Female Inventors of the Industrial Era." http://web.mit.edu/invent/www/inventorsR–Z/whm2.html (March 11, 1999).

Sketch by Annette Petrusso

Eleanora Bliss Knopf
1883–1974
American geologist

Eleanora Bliss Knopf was a geologist with the United States Geological Survey. She helped interpret the complex geological history of mountainous regions in Pennsylvania and New England. To help analyze the folding and structural changes in rock due to high temperatures and pressures, she sought the latest tools and techniques from scientists abroad, translating their works into English and introducing new approaches in the United States.

Knopf was born Eleanora Frances Bliss on July 15, 1883, in Rosemont, Pennsylvania. Her mother, Mary Anderson Bliss, studied languages and wrote poetry. Her father, General Tasker Howard Bliss, served as Chief of Staff of the United States Army during World War I. Bliss attended the Florence Baldwin School and entered Bryn Mawr College in 1900. She graduated in 1904 with an A.B. in chemistry and an A.M. in geology. Her mentor in geology was **Florence Bascom**, the first American woman to earn a Ph.D. in geology.

After graduating from Bryn Mawr, Bliss worked as an assistant curator in the geological museum there and as a demonstrator in the geology laboratory until 1909. Under Bascom's direction, Bliss and classmate Anna Isabel Jonas undertook a challenging dissertation on the geology of the Doe Run–Avondale district, just west of Bryn Mawr. Bliss was awarded her doctorate in 1912. That year, the United States Geological Survey (USGS) hired Bliss to continue working on the areas near the site where she had done the research for her dissertation. At the USGS she met geologist Adolph Knopf, a widower with three children; they married in 1920. The family moved to New Haven, Connecticut, where Adolph Knopf had been offered a teaching position at Yale University.

At that time, the faculty at Yale University did not hire women, and Knopf worked out of her husband's office and taught private courses. One of her former students, John Rodgers, described her in a memorial as a petite woman with a great deal of intellectual fortitude: "She never tolerated slipshod work or reasoning, and her criticisms were often the more devastating for being calmly and politely expressed." In addition to her teaching, Knopf continued to take USGS assignments, a practice she would continue until 1955. She actively sought new techniques to help her interpret the geologic faults and folds in the mountains along the border between New York and New England known as the Taconic region. She was one of the first geologists to use stereotypically viewed airplane photographs for field mapping. She also delved into the international geological literature, translating works from German. She introduced European techniques and approaches to the United States, including the use of laboratory work to study the deformation of rocks.

In 1951, Adolph Knopf took a new post at Stanford University in California. Eleanora Knopf worked as a research associate there, helping her husband to study a geological formation in the Rocky Mountains known as the Boulder batholith. She continued the work after his death in 1966; she herself died of arteriosclerosis in Menlo Park, California, on January 21, 1974.

SELECTED WRITINGS BY KNOPF:

Periodicals

(With Anna I. Jonas) "Stratigraphy of the Crystaline Schists of Pennsylvania and Maryland." *American Journal of Science* 5 (1923): 40–62.

(With Louis M. Prindle) "Geology of the Taconic Quadrangle." *American Journal of Science* 24 (1932): 257–302.

FURTHER READING

Books

Sicherman, Barbara, and Carol Hurd Green, eds. *Notable American Women: The Modern Period.* Vol. 6. Cambridge, MA: Belknap Press, 1980, pp. 401–403.

Periodicals

Rodgers, John. "Memorial to Eleanora Bliss Knopf, 1883–1974." *The Geological Society of America Memorials* 6 (1977): 1–4.

Sketch by Miyoko Chu

Mimi A. R. Koehl
1948–
American biologist

Mimi Koehl combines research principles of engineering and biology in an effort to broaden the understanding of how mechanics—such as the movement of air and water—affect the way living organisms develop and change. An artist's eye for form, a scientist's drive to understand function, and a researcher's determination to solve puzzles frequently combine to land Mimi Koehl in unlikely places with unique laboratory materials. In her efforts to understand how the mechanics of fluids and solids have shaped biological evolution, Koehl has dropped plastic frogs from her home's deck, crafted wings from construction paper and aluminum foil, and baked balsa wood models under a heat lamp.

Born in 1948 to a mother who was an artist and a father who was a physicist, Koehl grew up in an atmosphere that blended science and art. She originally enrolled at Gettysburg College as an art student, but switched to a biology major when a required class introduced her to the multitude of fascinating and perplexing shapes of living creatures. Koehl graduated from Gettysburg College with a bachelor's degree in biology in 1970. She then entered the graduate program of zoology at Duke University. Stephen Wainwright, her graduate adviser, encouraged her to move beyond the type of thinking that narrowly defines research questions in specialized fields. Wainwright encouraged student researchers to think outside the box by working backwards. He urged students to take nature's answers—for example, wings—and try to determine the basic problems that such an engineering response would solve. This emphasis on "why" instead of "what" helped hone Koehl's thinking and shaped her creative approach to scientific research.

Koehl completed her doctorate at Duke in 1976. She was named a postdoctoral fellow at the University of Washington in 1976 and accepted another postdoctoral fellowship at the University of York, England in 1977. An assistant professor of biology at Brown University from 1978 to 1979, Koehl also taught at Oxford University and the Zoologisches Institut der Universitat Basel as a visiting professor. In 1979, she joined the Department of Zoology at the University of California, Berkeley, as an assistant professor; in 1987, she was appointed a professor in the renamed Department of Integrative Biology at Berkeley.

Koehl simultaneously established herself as an educator and earned recognition as a researcher. Among her fellowships and grants are the North Atlantic Treaty Organization (NATO) Postdoctoral Fellowship in Science, the Presidential Young Investigator Award, the John Simon Guggenheim Memorial Foundation fellowship, and several National Science Foundation grants. She was assured international recognition in 1990 when she was selected to receive a MacArthur Foundation fellowship grant, often referred to as a MacArthur "genius award."

Model Solves Mystery of Flying Frogs

The plummeting plastic frog experiment is typical of Koehl's ingenious approach to research. When a colleague—Sharon Emerson, an evolutionary biologist—asked Koehl to help her unravel the mystery of Borneo's flying frogs, Koehl tackled the puzzle from her "how" perspective. The scientists knew the "what:" this subset of frogs flew. The researchers wanted to know how the frogs flew and how flying solved some problem for the creatures.

Koehl and Emerson made molds from the bodies of Borneo frogs, then used plastic dental gel, wire, and thread to make models. They rigged up a cardboard wind tunnel to simulate the force of air rushing past a frog as it launches itself and tossed the models off Koehl's deck to watch how the frog models turned and twisted in flight. What Emerson and Koehl discovered was that the flying frog's large webbed hands and feet, rubbery skin flaps, and spread–eagle flight launch actually made the frogs poor fliers. But those special features helped flying frogs turn in mid–air, float rather than plummet to the ground, and land on their feet. Flying frogs are not built for flying but for falling safely—an evolution of structure in response to environment, Koehl noted. The frogs live in forests and must maneuver from the safety of the trees, around branches and tree–trunk hugging–predators, to the forest floor in order to breed. The ability to dodge tree limbs and hungry enemies and land unhurt increases the frogs' chances of survival.

Biomechanics Called into Question

Biomechanics is a relatively new scientific specialty that focuses on solving medical problems with engineering techniques. Most research in this area is conducted with a view to solving a specific health problem—designing a better artificial hip joint, a more comfortable prosthetic leg, or a smaller, more efficient artificial heart. But Koehl uses the principles of biomechanics to identify how a particular physical trait solves an organism's problems. "I love surprises—when people think they understand something and it actually works another way," Koehl was quoted as saying in *Notable Women in the Life Sciences.* "At one point I was studying appendages on zooplankton that looked like combs, and were thought to be used for filter feeding. During my study, I found that water wouldn't go through the gaps because they were so tiny and the water was too sticky. So these appendages were not filters at all, as had been previously assumed." Such research is more than an academic exercise. Copepods are a vital link in the ocean food chain, so understanding how they feed may help maintain the delicate ecological balance that sustains life both in the sea and on land and may help shape the politics of environmental protection. How marine organisms survive constant pummeling in the ocean may provide clues on how to build structures and vessels for the sea. Understanding how living structures function, evolve, and develop physical traits to cope with environmental challenges will add new insight to fields ranging from genetic engineering of farm animals to man's ability to adapt to conditions in space.

Koehl focuses her research efforts on ocean life. A believer in field as well as laboratory work, she spent the latter part of 1997 conducting research in the waters around Hawaii. She is continuing her study of copepods and investigating how the mechanics of sea anemones affect and are affected by fluid flow.

SELECTED WRITINGS BY KOEHL:

Periodicals

"The Interaction of Moving Water and Sessile Organisms." *Scientific American* 247 (1982): 124–134.

"Aerodynamics, Thermoregulation, and the Evolution of Insect Wings: Differential Scaling and Evolutionary Change." *Evolution* 39 (1985): 488–504.

"The Interaction of Behavior and Morphology in the Evolution of a Novel Locomotor Type: Flying Frogs." *Evolution* 44 (1990): 1931–1946.

(With J. G. Kingsolver) "Selective Factors in the Evolution of Insect Wings." *Annual Review of Entomology* 39 (1994): 425–451.

"When Does Morphology Matter?" *Annual Review of Ecological Systems* 27 (1996): 501–542.

"Mechanisms of Particle Selection by Tentaculate Suspension Feeders During Encounter, Retention and Handling." *Journal of Experimental Marine Biology and Ecology* 209 (1997): 47–73.

FURTHER READING

Books

Shearer, B. F., and B. S. Shearer, eds. *Notable Women in the Life Sciences.* Westport, CT: Greenwood Publishing, 1996, pp. 239–243.

Periodicals

Franklin, Deborah. "The Shape of Life." *Discover* (December 1991): 10–16.

Smith, A. D. "Bay Area Brain Trust: 101 Achievers Who Make This the Smartest Place on Earth." *San Francisco Focus Magazine* 42 (1995): 30–47.

Other

Koehl. "Mimi A. R. Koehl." 10/27/97. http://ib.berkeley.edu/faculty.Koehl, MAR.html (29 Oct. 1997).

Sketch by A. Mullig

Marian Elliot Koshland
1921–1997
American immunologist and educator

Marian Elliott Koshland was an internationally recognized immunologist who spent her life studying the way antibodies fight illness. She is best known for her discovery that the differences in amino acid composition of antibodies accounts for their efficiency and effectiveness in fighting a seemingly infinite number of foreign invaders.

Koshland was born in New Haven, Connecticut on October 25, 1921, to Waller Watkins and Margaret Ann (Smith) Elliot. Her formal education was postponed during the year–long quarantine imposed during her brother's recovery at home from typhoid fever. The tutoring Koshland received from her father nurtured an intellectual drive that propelled her through high school graduation with great success.

In her sophmore year at Vassar, when Koshland was introduced to antibodies and the new science of immunology, she knew she had found a lifelong career. She graduated with a BA in 1942, and headed to the University of Chicago, the farthest west her finances would allow, unwittingly landing at a national center for wartime research. Finances dictated she work through graduate school, a situation that provided opportunity on projects such as the atomic bomb, the development of an Asiatic cholera vaccine, and assisting the Commission of Air Borne Diseases in combatting transmission of airborne pathogens in army barracks.

On May 25, 1945, Koshland married biochemist Daniel Edward Koshland, Jr. and soon began a family. With MS and PhD degrees in bacteriology earned in 1943 and 1949, she accepted a two–year fellowship in the Department of Bacteriology at Harvard Medical School. By the end of her post, Koshland gave birth to twins and doubled the size of her family. The task of devoting time to both childcare and work was accomplished by taking on part–time, risky research projects that appealed to her creative mind. For the next twenty years Koshland researched and lectured while raising her five children: Ellen, Phyllis, James, Gail, and Douglas.

Koshland worked as a bacteriologist until 1965 when she made her final move, to Berkeley spending her first year as an associate research immunologist, and the next four years as a lecturer in the Department of Molecular Biology. She was named professor of Microbiology and Immunology in 1970, acting as head of that department and of the graduate affairs division from 1982 to 1989.

After her appointment as professor, Koshland discovered a B cell antibody subunit called the J chain. From this point on, her research focused on B cells and the role they play in the immune response. In 1991, she and colleagues identified a specialized intracellular pathway that transports antibodies into blood circulation, allowing for the multiplication of B cells essential in fighting infection.

Throughout her tenure at Berkeley as a researcher, lecturer, and educator, Koshland published numerous articles in her field, contributing significantly to the understanding of immunology. At the 1997 national meeting of the American Association of Immunologists, Koshland gave a talk that "was a marvel, and put together complex biochemical phenomena in an understandable context of biolgical function. It was a testament not only to the quality and timeliness of her own work, but also to how far the field has come," according to Jim Allison in his profile of her in the July 15, 1998*Journal of Immunology*.

Koshland was a member of the National Academy of Science, the American Society of Biological Chemists, American Academy of Microbiologists, and the American Association of Immunologist, serving as president from 1982–1983. She served on the council of the National Academy of Science, the National Institute of Allergy & Infectious Disease, the National Institute of Health, and the National Science Board. Koshland, affectionately known as Bunny, worked in her laboratory until a short time before her death of lung cancer on October 28, 1997.

SELECTED WRITINGS BY KOSHLAND:

Periodicals

Science (March 6, 1981): 1027.

"Sheer Luck Made Me An Immunologist." *Annual Review of Immunology* (1996): ix–xv.

Other

Koshland, Marian E. Papers. Bancroft Library, University of California Berkeley.

FURTHER READING

Books

American Men and Women of Science. 20th ed. New Providence, NJ: Bowker, 1998, p. 548.

Periodicals

Allison, Jim. "In Memoriam Marian Koshland 1921–1997." *Journal of Immunology* (July 15, 1998).

Sketch by Kyra Anderson

Sonya Vasilievna Kovalevskaya (Also transliterated as Sofia Vasilevna Kovalevskaia) 1850–1891

Russian mathematician and educator

Sonya Vasilievna Kovalevskaya has been applauded by some as the most astounding mathematical genius to surface among women in the last two centuries, and one of the first women to make contributions of high quality to the field.

The middle of three children, Kovalevskaya was born on January 15, 1850, in Moscow. Her father, Vasilli Korvin–Krukovski, was an Artillery General in the Russian army. He was a educated and disciplined man who was fluent in English and French, and was a stern but benevolent parent. Her mother, Elizaveta Fyodorovna Schubert, came from a family of German scholars who had emigrated to Russia in the mid–1700s. Kovalevskaya's grandfather, Fyodor Fyodorovich Schubert, and great–grandfather, Fyodor Ivanovich Schubert, were noted mathematicians.

A singular incident in Kovalevskaya's childhood seems to have been a portent of her devotion to the study of mathematics. While living at the family estate, she came upon a room where the wallpaper consisted of sheets of Mikhail Ostrogradsky's lithographed lectures on the differential and the integral calculus. The child spent hours trying to decipher the formulae. Years later, at the age of 15, she astonished her tutor with how quickly she grasped and assimilated the conceptions of differential calculus. Kovalevskaya wrote in her memoirs that she "vividly remembered the pages of Ostrogradsky . . . and the conception of space seemed to have been familiar to me for a long time."

It was also rather exceptional that her father allowed Kovalevskaya to study with a tutor at all. She described her father as one who "harbored a strong prejudice against learned women." It has been suggested that the best explanation is that Kovalevskaya's own fierce determination was the catalyst for changing her father's mind. Once the tutelage was over, however, she faced an uncertain future for obtaining advanced education. She knew her father would never agree to sending her to a university. During that time, women were not allowed to attend the universities in Russia and most fathers, including Kovalevskaya's, were unwilling to give consent to daughters to study abroad. Again, Kovalevskaya's determination was stronger than her father's will.

The device she used to get her way was a popular one at the time; she began searching for a husband. The type of husband she was looking for had to agree to sign papers allowing Kovalevskaya to travel, live apart from him, and pursue an education. The agreement also came with the understanding that the marriage was a platonic one, without the marital rights usually afforded a husband. She found such a man in Vladimir Kovalensky, who made his living translating and publishing books while pursuing a degree in paleontology. Along with his high intellect, Kovalensky also distinguished himself by supporting liberal causes.

The resistance by Kovalevskaya's family to the marriage was anticipated and overcome by using the same sort of guile that had created the situation. She sent notes to a number of distinguished family friends happily announcing her impending marriage, thereby forcing her father to either give public approval or publicly admit that his daughter was rebellious. To make certain her father would not renege on the announcement, Kovalevskaya ensconced herself in Kovalensky's apartment, refusing to leave, until she felt secure that the marriage would indeed take place. The couple was married in September 1868.

Studies with the Masters

In early 1869 the newlyweds left Russia and settled in Heidelberg, Germany. This was where Kovalevskaya was to fulfill her dream of a higher education. Because she was a woman, the officials at the University of Heidelberg demanded that she secure the written permission of each of her professors before full admittance was granted. She undertook a class schedule of 22 hours per week, 16 of which were spent studying mathematics with Paul Du Bois–Reymond and Leo Köenigsberger, both of whom were students of the renowned mathematician Karl Weierstrass. After three successful semesters of study at the university, Kovalevskaya left for Berlin, seeking out Weierstrass. Their initial meeting marked a personal as well as professional relationship that lasted a lifetime.

Kovelevskaya did not arrive in Berlin unannounced, however. The praises of her professors at Heidelberg preceded her, and this did much to persuade Weisertrass' decision to become Kovelevskaya's mentor. In addition, Weierstrass had written a paper where he gave credit to Kovalevskaya's grandfather, Fyodor Schubert, for a mathematical maxim eight years before meeting Kovelevskaya. Unfortunately, winning Weierstrass' acceptance was not the only obstacle to the continuation of her studies—the university forbade women from attending Weierstrass' formal lectures. The obstacle was removed when Weierstrass agreed to teach Kovalevskaya privately twice a week, giving her the same courses as his regular university students.

In the beginning, Weierstrass never imagined that Kovalevskaya would want a formal degree in mathematics, believing that a married woman would have no use for one. In the fall of 1872 however, Kovalevskaya confided the truth about her marriage and he began to steer her toward work on a dissertation. By the spring of 1874, Kovalevskaya had written three doctoral dissertations, each of them in Weierstrass' opinion worthy of a degree, and one so outstanding that both were confident of forthcoming recognition. They were not disappointed. Weierstrass submitted Kovalevskaya's work to the University of Göttingen and she was awarded her doctoral *summa cum laude* in the fall of 1874, becoming the first woman to earn a doctorate in mathematics.

Confronted Detours Along the Way

Elated but exhausted by her labors, Kovalevskaya and her husband returned to Russia to relax with friends and family. Both were also hoping to secure positions in the academic world, but for a combination of reasons neither was welcomed to university posts. Kovalevskaya found herself discriminated against because of her gender, and Kovalensky's liberal activities spawned suspicion among Russian academics. Kovalevskaya and her husband decided to consummate their relationship, and Kovalevskaya's only child, Sofia, was born in 1878. For the next five years, Kovalevskaya and her husband put aside their respective fields of study and concentrated on trying to make a living at various commercial endeavors.

During this time it became apparent that Kovalevskaya was as gifted at writing as she was at mathematics and for a time her heart was torn between the two pursuits. The fiction she produced, including the novella *Vera Barantzova*, were met with acclaim and translated into several foreign languages. Meanwhile, Kovalensky was involved in questionable financial dealings. Faced with prosecution from charges of mishandling stock, Kovalensky committed suicide in April of 1883.

Recognition at Last

Kovalevskaya returned to her study of mathematics and through the efforts of a friend and fellow student of

Weierstrass, Gosta Mittag–Leffler, Kovalevskaya was offered a position at Stockholm University as a *privatdozent* (a licensed lecturer who could receive payment from students but not from the university) in 1884. Five years later, Kovalevskaya became the first female mathematician to hold a chair at a European university. This appointment was accompanied by the editorship of the journal *Acta Mathematica*, where she came in contact with the leading European mathematicians of the day. In 1888, Kovalevskaya's paper on the study of the motion of a rigid body received the Prix Bordin, given by the French Académie Royale des Sciences.

Kovalevskaya died in 1891 of influenza when she was only 41 years old, at the height of her mathematical career. Although she published only ten papers during her lifetime, Kovalevskaya's work has withstood the test of time. The research that won her the Prix Bordin is now known as the Kovelevskaya top, and her doctoral dissertation on partial differential equations lives on as the Cauchy–Kovelevskaya Theorem.

SELECTED WRITINGS BY KOVELEVSKAYA:

Scientific Works, 1948

FURTHER READING

Books

Bell, Eric Temple. "Master and Pupil: Weierstrass and Sonya Kovalevskaya." *Men of Mathematics*. New York: Simon and Schuster 1937, pp. 423–429.

Cooke, Roger. *The Mathematics of Sonya Kovalevskaya.* New York: Springer–Verlag, 1984.

Kennedy, Don H. *Little Sparrow*. Athens: Ohio University Press, 1983.

Koblitz, A.H. *A Convergence of Lives: Sophia Kovaleskaia, Scientist, Writer, Revolutionary*. Boston: Birkhäuser, 1983.

Koblitz, Ann Hibner. "Sonya Kovalevskaya." In *Women for Mathematics: A Biobibliographic Sourcebook.* Edited by Louise S. Grinstein and Paul J. Campbell. Westport, CT: Greenwood Press, 1987, pp. 103–113.

Osen, Lynn M. "Sonya Corvin–Krukovsky Kovalevsky." In *Women in Mathematics*. Cambridge: MIT Press, 1979, pp. 117–140.

Periodicals

Tabor, Michael. "Modern Dynamics and Classical Analysis." *Nature* 310 (July 26, 1984): 277–282.

Other

Wilson, Becky. "Sonya Kovalesvskya." *Biographies of Women Mathematicians*. June 1977. http://www.scottlan.edu/lriddle/women/chronol.htm (July 22, 1997).

Sketch by Kelley Reynolds–Jacquez

Mathilde Krim
1926–
Italian-born American geneticist and philanthropist

Geneticist Mathilde Krim is best known as a cofounder of the American Foundation for AIDS Research (AmFAR). Krim first learned of acquired immunodeficiency syndrome (AIDS) while researching interferon at New York's Sloan–Kettering Cancer Center in 1980, when she heard about an unusual and fatal immune system breakdown of some of her colleagues' patients. In 1983 she founded the AIDS Medical Foundation, which was dedicated to providing funds for AIDS research and escalating public awareness of the disease. Her organization merged with a California–based group to form AmFAR in 1985, and in October, 1993, Krim received the prestigious John W. Gardner Leadership Award for her directorship of AmFAR. In acceptance she summarized her role in the fight against AIDS: "When the first cases of AIDS were reported, studied and first understood to be due to a transmissible infectious agent, there was a total vacuum of leadership committed to interpreting these facts for the public. I could see the real impending threat to the public health, which was obvious to any biologist. I was struck by the totally misguided stigma—obviously due to age–old prejudice and to ignorance of biological facts—that was being attached to the disease. I became, therefore, easily convinced that, both as a product of Judeo–Christian culture and as a biologist, I needed to call on widely shared values to foster human solidarity in the face of AIDS and that I had to explain the simple biological and historical facts necessary for the nature of the epidemic and its pattern of spread to be understood correctly."

Early Career in Genetics and Interferon Research

Krim was born Mathilde Galland in Como, Italy, on July 9, 1926. Her father was a Swiss zoologist; her mother was Czechoslovakian. Because of her international upbringing, Galland became fluent in several languages, including French, German, Italian, and later English and Hebrew. As a child her interest in science was inspired by her maternal grandfather, a school teacher. In 1932 her family moved to Switzerland to escape economic depression in Italy. She earned a B.S. in genetics from the University of Geneva in 1948 and completed her Ph.D. in 1953. While in graduate school, Galland was fascinated by the technology of the newly invented electron microscope. When asked to deter-

Mathilde Krim (Photograph by T. Gates. Archive Photos, Inc. Reproduced by permission.)

mine if the microscope was capable of viewing a gene, she examined the chromosomes of frogs' eggs in great detail. She eventually saw some "beautiful double threads," making her possibly the first person ever to view DNA.

Galland became involved in the Zionist movement at the conclusion of World War II, after viewing dramatic news footage of the liberation of Jewish prisoners from a Nazi concentration camp. She joined a local branch of the Irgun—a Zionist underground organization in southern France—and began cleaning guns and smuggling weapons. While engrossed in these pursuits she fell in love with a Bulgarian medical student, also a member of the Irgun. Against the wishes of her parents, she converted to Judaism, married, and moved to Israel. At the Weitzmann Institute of Science in Rehovot, Israel, she took a position as a junior scientist and later became a research associate. While she was there, her team pioneered a way to determine the sex of an unborn child through amniocentesis, a procedure that involves analyzing the fetal chromosomes found in the amniotic fluid surrounding a fetus.

In the 1950s Galland's personal life changed dramatically. She divorced her husband and gained custody of their only daughter, Daphne. In 1958 she remarried, this time to Arthur B. Krim, a New York attorney who was chairman of United Artists, former finance director of the Democratic party, and later founder of Orion Pictures. The Krims moved to New York City, where they moved in important social circles as a result of Arthur Krim's entertainment industry connections and political associations. However, after a while the glamour wore thin, and Krim joined a cancer research team in the virus research division at Cornell Medical College. At Cornell, Krim studied the protein interferon, an antiviral agent which she believed would gain widespread notice as useful in curing cancer. She continued working with interferon when she moved to New York's premiere clinic for cancer treatment, the Memorial Sloan–Kettering Cancer Center, and pushed for an interferon laboratory at Sloan–Kettering. Krim lobbied for the support of the National Institutes of Health as well as the National Cancer Institute for research into its effectiveness as a treatment for cancer. However, the cost of interferon treatment was considered prohibitive until the 1980s, when cloning techniques made it possible to produce greater amounts.

In the Laboratory and in the Public Eye Fighting AIDS

From 1981 to 1985 Krim worked on ways of treating leukemia with interferon. It was during this period that she became involved in AIDS research. AIDS is caused by the human immunodeficiency virus (HIV, which attacks the human immune system's defensive army of cells and inhibits their ability to eliminate foreign matter such as infectious bacteria from the body. Without such cells, the body is in a weakened state and is more likely to succumb to such opportunistic diseases as pneumonia, tuberculosis, and cancer. Krim initially worked on using interferon to treat Karposi's sarcoma, a type of cancer found in many persons with AIDS, but by 1983, it had become obvious that her role in the fight against AIDS would grow beyond the laboratory. Perceiving that public prejudice would be increased once it became widely known that AIDS was primarily affecting homosexual men, she felt that she should speak out and explain that infection was not a result of sexual orientation—that AIDS was caused by a virus.

While supporting AIDS research, Krim's personal crusade has been for AIDS prevention and treatment. She has strongly supported community testing of experimental drugs and has objected to the restriction of such drugs to control groups. Under Krim's direction, AmFAR has promoted the idea of community–based clinical research by offering financial support and technical assistance to groups of primary–care physicians practicing medicine in areas with a high population of persons with AIDS. By forming local, nonprofit clinical research centers, more clinical trials of experimental drugs could be conducted, upgrading the level of care to thousands of HIV patients.

Krim has also been a champion for AIDS education. She has promoted the use of condoms and of safe sexual practices to people worldwide. AmFAR has funded programs for AIDS education and prevention as well as needle exchanges to decrease the spread of AIDS and other infectious diseases among drug users. AmFAR has also lobbied the federal government for support and helped pass the Disabilities Act of 1990, which protects people with AIDS from discrimination. Krim's efforts have brought government officials, drug company executives, drug treatment experts, gay activists, and minority leaders together in the battle against AIDS. Through speaking engagements she is also alerting the country to another new health threat, multi–drug resistant tuberculosis (MDRTB), which is a serious problem in many cities along the Atlantic seaboard, especially among those who are HIV positive as well as the homeless, those in prison, and the poor. Under Krim's stewardship, AmFAR has provided over $65 million to more than 1,300 research teams. Most of the endowments are for small start–up or "seed" grants of $50,000 per year. Some of these have been grants in genetic research that may lead to the future use of gene therapy to treat AIDS.

Krim once told an interviewer for *The Advocate* that she views herself as "a hybrid"—part scientist and part activist. She has not been involved in laboratory research since the early 1980s but stays abreast of scientific developments so that she can make informed recommendations about how research money can best be spent. Known for her compassion and vision, Krim fears that AIDS not only kills people but harms our culture in that it suppresses our ability to "feel fulfillment and freedom." Although the government and other social and religious institutions have not responded quickly enough in her view, she believes that great strides have been made in managing the disease medically. Life expectancy for persons with AIDS has improved significantly from the mid–1980s into the 1990s, and she is optimistic that sufficient medical technology exists to allow people to live full and normal lives with the AIDS virus.

During her career, Krim has written or collaborated on over seventy scientific papers. A naturalized U.S. citizen, she has served on the boards of various philanthropic organizations and is the founding co–chairperson of AmFAR and current chairman of the board as well as a member of the organization's scientific advisory committee. In 1986 Krim became an associate research scientist at both St. Luke's Roosevelt Hospital Center and the College of Physicians and Surgeons at Columbia University in New York. For her extraordinary work against AIDS, Krim has received numerous awards, most notably the John W. Gardner Leadership Award and seven honorary doctorates.

SELECTED WRITINGS BY KRIM:

Books

Partners for the Cure, Reflection and Rededication: AIDS Research in the Second Decade, American Foundation for AIDS Research, 1993.

Periodicals

(With C. E. Metroka, S. Cunningham–Rundles, et. al.) "Generalized Lymphadenopathy in Homosexual Men: An Update of the New York Experience." *Annals of the New York Academy of Sciences: Acquired Immune Deficiency Syndrome* 437 (1984): 400–11.

(With S. E. Krown, F. X. Real, et. al.) "Recombinant Leukocyte A Interferon in Karposi's Sarcoma." *Annals of the New York Academy of Sciences: Acquired Immune Deficiency Syndrome* 437 (1984): 431–38.

FURTHER READING

Books

Moritz, Charles, ed. *Current Biography Yearbook 1987.* H. W. Wilson, 1987, pp. 325–28.

Periodicals

Kraft, Ronald Mark. "Hetero Heroes: Mathilde Krim." *The Advocate* (November, 1993): 68–70.

Robertson, Nan. "On the Front Lines." *Modern Maturity* (April–May, 1990): 72.

van Dam, Laura. "Fighting the Plague: An Interview with Mathilde Krim." *Technology Review* (July, 1992): 21.

Sketch by Barbara A. Branca

Stephanie Louise Kwolek
1923–
American chemist

Stephanie Louise Kwolek is best known for her contributions to the development of Kevlar™, the lightweight, incredibly strong polymer used in bulletproof vests, and other products. Over the course of a 40-year career as a researcher with E.I. DuPont de Nemours and Co. in Buffalo, New York, and Wilmington, Delaware, Kwolek obtained 16 patents for a variety of groundbreaking materials and devised new processes in polymer chemistry.

Kwolek was born on July 31, 1923, in New Kensington, Pennsylvania. She was the oldest daughter of John and Nellie (Zajdel) Kwolek. Her early interest in science was stimulated by her father's love of the natural world. Another early interest of Kwolek's was fashion design. Although she never pursued this field, much of her scientific research centered on fibers. Maintaining her interest in science throughout adolescence, Kwolek enrolled at the Carnegie Institute of Technology (now Carnegie–Mellon University) in Pittsburgh, Pennsylvania, and graduated with a B.S. in chemistry in 1946. She accepted a position as a chemist in the rayon department at DuPont in Buffalo, New York, planning to save money for medical school. Four years later, she moved to Wilmington, Delaware, to conduct polymer research in the company's textile fibers pioneering research laboratory. New ground was steadily being broken in the field of polymer research when Kwolek came to DuPont and she became so engrossed in her research there that she ended up foregoing medical school and working for the company for her entire professional career. "I became so interested in the work I was doing that I stayed on," Kwolek told Kristin Palm in an interview. "It was very challenging. It differed from day to day. It was very exciting because you never knew what you might come up with. It was a constant learning process."

One of Kwolek's first jobs was to "scout" for new polymers, which entailed researching low–temperature processes for the preparation of polymers, which are strings of large, chain–like molecules. The low–temperature process made possible the preparation of unmeltable polymers. From this research, Kwolek, along with her colleagues, authored as series of patents and publications on the preparation of polyamides, polyurethanes, polysulfonamides, polyester, and polyureas. While investigating low–temperature process, Kwolek and her colleagues also made possible the preparation of polymers that formed Lycra™ spandex fibers, the stretchy material used in athletic wear.

In an interview with Palm, Kwolek emphasized that she and her colleagues did not discover new products but, rather, devised the processes by which new products could be developed. One of the most notable products to result from her and her colleagues' work was a fabric known by the trade name Nomex. Nomex is fire–resistant and is now commonly used in protective gear for firefighters. Kwolek and her colleagues also searched for low temperature methods to make nylon, which is usually prepared in a molten state. As a result of this work, Kwolek and her colleague Paul W. Morgan authored a publication on "The Nylon Rope Trick," which describes a procedure that has been used as a demonstration in classrooms nationwide. This experiment involves dissolving the two polymers that nylon is made of in two solvents, one of which is water. These solutions are poured, one on top of the other, into a beaker and the resulting film which forms at the interface is pulled out from the center as a rope, reembling scarves pulled from a magician's hat. While this is not the way nylon is made in the laboratory, it is a simple way to explain chemical processes to students. Kwolek and Morgan published an account of their experiment in the *Journal of Chemical Education* in 1959.

Makes Lifesaving Discover

In 1964 Kwolek began searching for a new strong, but light–weight, fiber that could be used to reinforce radial tires. In the course of her research, she unexpectedly discovered that polyamides that have rod–like molecules form liquid crystalline solutions under very specific conditions. In most polymers, the molecules flow in unordered chains, but in liquid crystals they line up all in one direction, which is why the resulting fiber is so strong. The polymer creation process involves "spinning" a solution in a machine known as a spinneret. Kwolek devised a viscous solution that was much different from typical liquid crystal solutions, which are clear. At first, the person running the spinneret refused to put Kwolek's solution in the machine for fear of clogging it. He eventually acquiesced, however, and the result was a product so strong Kwolek hesitated to report her findings, believing she must have made a mistake. There was no mistake, however, and the resulting product was Kevlar™. This light, super–strong product is used in such lifesaving gear as bulletproof vests and military wear, including helmets. Kevlar is also used in mooring ropes, fiber–optic cables, aircraft parts, brake linings, and canoes, among other products. Kevlar™ is five times stronger than the same weight of steel.

Kwolek retired from DuPont in 1986, and in 1995 she was inducted into the National Inventors Hall of Fame in Akron, Ohio. While she thoroughly enjoyed her career, Kwolek told Palm in an interview that she faced many challenges as a woman in a predominantly male field. "It certainly was difficult at times because the opportunities were not open to women from the 1940s through probably the 1970s," she explained. "Things finally got better in the 1980s for women but the opportunities for advancement were limited."

Kwolek served as a consultant to DuPont for several years following her retirement and continues to give talks, acts as a mentor for professional women's and serve as a model for students. She regularly receives letters from students interested in her work and tries to personally answer all of them. She also enjoys gardening, music, traveling, and reading.

SELECTED WRITINGS BY KWOLEK:

Periodicals

(With Paul Morgan) "Amine Acid–Aceptors for the Preparation of Piperazine Polyamides by Low Temperature Solution Polycondensation." *Journal of Polymer Science: Part A* 2 (1964): 209–217.

(With Paul Morgan) "Low Temperature Solution Polycondensation of Piperazine Polyamides." *Journal of Polymer Science: Part A* 2 (1964): 181–201.

(With Paul Morgan) "The Nylon Rope Trick: Demonstration of Condensation Polymerization." *Journal of Chemical Education* 36, no. 4 (1951): 182–184.

(With Paul Morgan) "Preparation of Polyamides, Polyurethanes, Polysulfonamides and Polyesters by Low Temperature Solution Polycondensation." *Journal of Polymer Science: Part A* 2 (1964): 2693–2703.

"Study of the Preparation of a Piperazine Polyurea and Polyamide by Low Temperature Solution Polymerization." *Journal of Polymer Science: Part A* 2 (1964): 5149–5160.

FURTHER READING

Other

Chemical Heritage Foundation, http://www.chemheritage.org/perkin/Kwolek/kwolek.html

DuPont Lavoisier Academy, http://www.dupont.com/corp/r–and–d/lavoisier/kwolek.html

Lemelson–MIT Awards Program, http;//web.mit.edu/invent/www/inventorsI–Q/kwolek.html

National Inventors Hall of Fame, http://www.invent.org/book/book–text/64.html

Palm, Kristin, interview with Stephanie Louise Kwolek conducted May 15, 1999.

Sketch by Kristin Palm

L

Elise L'Esperance (UPI/Corbis-Betmann. Reproduced by permission.)

Elise Depew (Strang) L'Esperance
1879–1959
American pathologist

Elise Depew Strang L'Esperance was one of the first crusaders against cancer to emphasize detection and prevention. She established the first cancer prevention clinic at the New York Infirmary for Women and Children, which later became the model for similar clinics in New York and other large American cities. She also was the first women to achieve the rank of full professor in preventive medicine.

L'Esperance was born in 1879 in Westchester, New York, the second daughter of physician Albert Strang and Kate Depew Strang. Kate Depew Strang was the sister of Chauncey Depew, a famed financier and United States Senator. L'Esperance attended St. Agnes Episcopal School in Albany and upon graduation decided to follow in her father's footsteps and study for the M.D. degree. At age 16, she entered the Women's Medical College of the New York Infirmary for Women and Children. It was 1896. Within three years she had achieved her degree; she also married David L'Esperance, a lawyer, while she was still a student.

L'Esperance wanted to be a pediatrician, so after interning at New York Babies Hospital she opened her own practice in Manhattan, where she continued until 1908. During this time, she became interested in research on tuberculosis, and as a member of the Tuberculosis Research Commission, became increasing drawn to pathology.

After deciding to specialize in that field in 1910, she took a job as assistant to Dr. James Ewing, a cancer specialist at Cornell University Medical School, who had previously refused to employ a woman. Apparently L'Esperance changed his mind about women doctors; after two years she was promoted to instructor of pathology. "It was only a technician's job," she said of her assistant's job with Ewing to a reporter at the New York *World–Telegram.* "But I knew I could pick up a tremendous amount of information from one of the greatest pathologists in the world." After becoming an instructor, she achieved the rank of assistant professor in 1920, the first woman to hold that position on the Cornell faculty. In April of 1950 she became a full professor in the department of preventive medicine.

In 1932, L'Esperance and her sister, May Strang, used an inheritance from their uncle, Chauncey Depew, to establish the first of three clinics in New York City devoted to detecting cancer. The clinic, the Kate Depew Strang Tumor Clinic at the New York Infirmary for Women and Children, was named for the L'Esperance's mother, who had died of cancer. L'Esperance filled the clinic with a staff made up entirely of women physicians who were dedicated to treating women and children. "We thought they (the cancer clinics) made more sense than a stained glass window," she told Margaret Follin Eicks, a reporter at the New York *World–Telegram* about the decision to open the clinics. After establishing the New York infirmaries, Strang embarked on an extensive campaign to educate the public about cancer prevention. Largely through her work, the value of early cancer detection became accepted by both physicians and the public.

L'Esperance believed cancer could be defeated if it was caught early—even in seemingly healthy people. Her first clinic proved so popular that a second was opened in 1940. Several others were then opened around the country and expanded to care for men and adolescents. The clinics developed and used new techniques for detecting cancer, including the Pap smear. By 1950, the clinics had treated

35,000 healthy patients, and cancerous conditions had been found in about one percent. L'Esperance believed that if doctors only knew how to look for premalignant cancers, it would be possible to prevent fully malignant tumors.

The distinguished pathologist published more than 30 peer–reviewed papers in medical journals during her career and was editor of the *Medical Women's Journal* and the *Journal of the American Medical Women's Association.* She received many awards, including the Elizabeth Blackwell Citation in 1950 and the Albert Lasker Award of the American Public Health Association in 1951, an extremely prestigious honor.

L'Esperance also bred show horses, owned her own stable, and drove her harness ponies in the National Horse Show at Madison Square Garden in New York yearly. During her elderly years she resided with her sister in Westchester, New York. She was often described as "a tall, fast–moving, strongly built woman" who liked to wear unusual hats even while seeing patients in her office. "There never was any place to hang the thing (in the x–ray room)," she once said. "So I kept it on. Got in the habit. Now I'd feel headless without it." L'Esperance died on January 21, 1959. She was 80 years old.

SELECTED WRITINGS BY L'ESPERANCE:

Periodicals

"The Strang Cancer Prevention Clinics: A Symposium." *Journal of the American Medical Women's Association* (April, 1948): 131–146.

FURTHER READING

Books

Notable Women in the Life Sciences. Greenwood Press, 1996.

Periodicals

"Dr. L'Esperance, Specialist, Dead." *New York Times* (January 22, 1959):31

"Medicine. Prevention Is Her Aim." *Time* 55 (April 3, 1950): 78–79

Sketch by Barbara Boughton

Marie-Louise Lachapelle (The Granger Collection, New York. Reproduced by permission.)

Marie-Louise (Dugès) Lachapelle
1769–1821
French midwife

Marie-Louise Lachapelle was one of the most important medical women in nineteenth-century France. Her school established new professional standards for midwifery and she wrote a three-volume work that became a standard obstetrics text.

Marie-Louise Lachapelle was born in 1769. Her father, Louis Dugès, was a health official, and her mother, Marie Jonet Dugès, was the head midwife at the Hôtel Dieu in Paris. Lachapelle's maternal grandmother also had been a prominent midwife. From an early age, Lachapelle studied midwifery and assisted her mother. By the age of 15, she was competent to attend difficult childbirths. In 1792, Lachapelle married a surgeon at the Hôtel St. Louis. However her husband died three years later and she went back to work as a midwife to support herself and her young daughter.

Originally established as a hospital for the poor, associated with the Cathedral of Notre Dame, by the eighteenth century the Hôtel Dieu was considered to be the best maternity hospital in Europe and it encompassed the most important school of midwifery in France. A number of well-known midwives and obstetricians had studied and taught at the school, since its founding in the sixteenth century. Lachapelle's mother had reorganized the maternity department at the Hôtel Dieu and Lachapelle joined her there as associate head midwife. She became head midwife after her mother's death in 1797. Two years later, she helped to organize a new maternity department, connected with the Hôtel Dieu, but located at Port Royal de Paris. The Hospice de la Maternité, or Maison d'Accouchements, was established as a teaching hospital, for the training of midwives in both medical theory and practice. The midwives who trained there were expected to form a teaching corps for training midwives in rural areas.

Lachapelle travelled to Germany, to study with the famous obstetrician Franz Carl Naegele at the University of Heidelberg. She then returned to the Maison d'Accouchements, as director and instructor. It was the most rigorous school of midwifery in Europe, and included lectures at the École de Médecine, as well as daily instruction from Lachapelle. After one year of study and examinations, the midwifes received diplomas from the Ecole de Médecine. Women came from all over Europe to attend the school and it served as a model for subsequent midwifery schools. Lachapelle's methods were very advanced for the time. For example, childbed fever was epidemic in maternity wards. Although the method of transmission of this often-fatal disease was unknown, Lachapelle's methods kept the incidence of the disease very low in her hospital. Lachapelle was responsible for training a number of important professional midwives, the most famous of whom was **Marie Boivin**.

Lachapelle wrote several medical works. Five of her case histories were published in the first volume of the new journal, *L'Annaire Médico-Chirugical*, in 1819. From her approximately 40,000 case studies, Lachapelle compiled valuable statistical tables that were incorporated into her book, *Practice of Obstetrics*. In addition to her original observations and expertise, she documented her work with the medical literature. It was a detailed and scientific treatment of midwifery, arguing against intervention by the obstetrician or the use of forceps or other instruments, except in extreme cases. Lachapelle completed only the first volume of this work before her death from stomach cancer in 1821. Her nephew, Antoine Dugès, a professor of medicine at the University of Montpellier, edited her notes and published the three volumes between 1821 and 1825. The work was widely used as an obstetrics text. It went through many editions over the years and was translated into German.

SELECTED WRITINGS BY LACHAPELLE:

Books

Pratique des Accouchements; ou Mémoires et Observations Choisies, sur les Points les Plus Importants de l'Art. Paris: J. B. Baillière, 1821–1825.

FURTHER READING

Books

Hurd-Mead, Kate Campbell. *A History of Women in Medicine, from the Earliest Times to the Beginning of the Nineteenth Century.* Haddam: Haddam Press, 1938. Reprint, Boston: Milford House, 1973.

Wolfe, Irmgard. "Marie-Louise Lachapelle." In *Notable Women in the Life Sciences: A Biographical Dictionary.* Edited by Benjamin F. Shearer and Barbara S. Shearer. Westport: Greenwood Press, 1996.

Sketch by Margaret Alic

Christine Ladd-Franklin
1847–1930
American logician and psychologist

Christine Ladd–Franklin made fundamental contributions to the scientific understanding of color vision and to syllogistic reasoning (deductive reasoning) and symbolic notation in logic. Although official policies of her era excluded women from advanced studies and academic positions at major universities, Ladd–Franklin studied logic and mathematics at Johns Hopkins University, researched color vision at universities in Göttingen and Berlin, and went on to lecture in psychology and logic at Johns Hopkins and Columbia University. Throughout her career she was an outspoken and effective campaigner for opening graduate programs and academic employment to women.

Christine Ladd was born in Windsor, Connecticut, on December 1, 1847. Her parents were Eliphalet Ladd, a New York merchant, and Augusta (Niles) Ladd. Her relatives included William Ladd, who founded the American Peace Society, and John Milton Niles, a former postmaster–general of the United States. Ladd–Franklin grew up in Connecticut and New York. At the age of twelve, after the death of her mother, Ladd–Franklin went to stay with her father's family in Portsmouth, New Hampshire. She graduated as valedictorian of her class from Wesleyan Academy in Wilbraham, Massachusetts, in 1865 and attended Vassar College, where she studied mathematics. Ladd–Franklin received her A.B. from Vassar in 1869 and spent the next nine years teaching secondary school. During this period, she wrote articles on mathematics for the *Educational Times,* an English publication.

When Ladd–Franklin sought to attend lectures in mathematics at the recently established Johns Hopkins University, she was admitted by the English mathematician J. J. Sylvester, who knew of her work. She also attended the lectures of logician Charles Sanders Peirce and of mathematics professor William Story. Ladd–Franklin studied at

Christine Ladd-Franklin (Archives of the History of American Psychology. Reproduced by permission.)

Johns Hopkins from 1878 to 1882. Sylvester persuaded the mathematics department to grant Ladd a $500 annual fellowship, which was renewed for three years. Her Ph.D. thesis, entitled "The Algebra of Logic," was published in 1883 in Peirce's *Studies in Logic by Members of the Johns Hopkins University.* In this work, Ladd proposed that logical statements could be analyzed more easily for validity when presented in the form of "inconsistent triads," which she later called "antilogisms," than when expressed as classical syllogisms. An antilogism comprises "three statements that are together incompatible." One example given by Ladd–Franklin in "The Antilogism," *Mind,* 1928, is "It is impossible that any of these measures should be idiotic, for none of them is unnecessary, and nothing that is necessary is idiotic." Her work was praised in its time, and Eugene Shen wrote in *Mind,* 1927, "No scheme in logic is more beautiful than that based on the eight propositions of Dr. Ladd–Franklin."

An Authority on Color Vision

Ladd–Franklin turned to investigations of vision in the 1880s and began publishing articles on this subject in 1887. During a visit to Europe in 1891 and 1892, she studied Ewald Herwig's theory of color perception with G. E. Müller in Göttingen and did experiments in Müller's laboratory. She also attended lectures by the mathematician Felix Klein. Ladd–Franklin went on to visit Berlin, where she worked in the laboratory of Hermann von Helmholtz and attended lectures by Arthur König on Helmholtz's theory of color vision. Herwig believed that color perception arises from three opposing pairs of basic colors, while Helmholtz maintained that all the colors the eye sees can be generated from three basic colors–red, green, and blue. Ladd–Franklin synthesized these ideas, proposing her own color theory, which she presented to the International Congress of Psychology in London in 1892. She claimed that color vision had evolved from light (white) sensitivity by the addition of differentiation between yellow and blue light, followed by the separation of the yellow sensitivity into the perception of red and green. Consequently, yellow and white as well as blue, red and green, are perceived as basic colors. After a period of controversy, Ladd–Franklin's ideas were accepted by psychologists for many years.

An associate editor of *Baldwin's Dictionary of Philosophy and Psychology* in 1901 and 1902, Ladd–Franklin resumed lecturing in logic and psychology at Johns Hopkins from 1904 to 1909. In 1914 she became a lecturer at Columbia, where she continued teaching until 1927, when she was nearly eighty years old. In the late twenties, she investigated the visual phenomenon of "blue arcs," which she believed showed that active nerve fibers emit a faint light. A collection of her major works on vision was published as *Colour and Colour Theories* in 1929.

Opening Closed Doors

Ladd–Franklin's professional career was shaped by the restrictions placed on women scientists and scholars in the late nineteenth and early twentieth centuries. She studied mathematics instead of physics because university laboratories did not admit women, and mathematics did not require laboratory work. Like other women, Ladd–Franklin was a "special student" at Johns Hopkins, a status outside normal admissions. When she completed her graduate work in 1882, the university would not grant her a degree. The situation was similar during her visit to Germany, where Ladd–Franklin was only allowed auditor status, and Müller delivered lectures to her privately. Even Ladd–Franklin's teaching positions at Johns Hopkins and Columbia were temporary, not permanent, appointments. One of the greatest disappointments of her career was suffered in 1914 when a leading group of experimental psychologists refused her request to attend their meeting on color vision at Columbia. Ladd–Franklin, a leading authority on the subject, gained admittance only by having one of the members take her as his guest. Johns Hopkins awarded its first doctorate to a woman in 1893, and officially began to admit women in 1907. In 1926, the school awarded Ladd–Franklin the Ph.D. in mathematics that she had earned in 1882.

Ladd–Franklin and other women in academic fields devised strategies to open American doctoral programs to women. The Association of Collegiate Alumnae, predecessor of the American Organization of University Women, was formed in 1881. Ladd–Franklin proposed that the ACA start a fellowship for study overseas. The $500 fellowship that was established in 1890 helped American women gain entrance to lectures and later to earn doctoral degrees at German universities. Once women had been admitted abroad, it became easier to persuade American graduate schools to accept them also. From 1900 to 1917, Ladd–Franklin administered the Sarah Berliner fellowship, which supported new women doctorates in research. She hoped to persuade graduate schools to take the fellows into their faculty, since there was no cost to the school. This program did help women establish academic careers, but most worked at women's colleges. The scholarship did not fulfill Ladd–Franklin's goal of placing women in academic positions at coeducational schools.

Christine Ladd married Fabian Franklin, a member of the mathematics faculty at Johns Hopkins, on August 24, 1882. The couple had two children, of whom only one, Margaret, survived into adulthood. In 1895 Franklin became a journalist, and the family later moved to New York when he became an associate editor of the *New York Evening Post.* In addition to her scholarly work and articles about women's education, Ladd–Franklin published opinions on many subjects. In letters to the editors of the *New York Times* during World War I, she objected to tight collars for soldiers and advocated calling citizens of the United States "Usonians." Ladd–Franklin died of pneumonia in New York City on March 5, 1930.

SELECTED WRITINGS BY LADD–FRANKLIN:

Books

"On the Algebra of Logic." *Studies in Logic by Members of the Johns Hopkins University.* Edited by C. S. Peirce. Little Brown, 1883, pp. 17–71.

Colour and Colour Theories. Harcourt, Brace, 1929.

Periodicals

"Some Proposed Reforms in Common Logic." *Mind* 15 (1890): 75–88.

"Women and Letters." *New York Times* (December 13, 1921): 18.

"Women and Economics." *New York Times* (May 28, 1924): 22.

"The Antilogism." *Mind* 37 (1928): 532–34.

FURTHER READING

Books

Ogilvie, Marilyn Bailey. "Christine Ladd–Franklin." *Women in Science.* Cambridge: MIT, 1986, pp.116–17.

Rossiter, Margaret W. *Women Scientists in America.* Baltimore: Johns Hopkins University Press, 1982.

Periodicals

Church, Alonzo, "A Bibliography of Symbolic Logic." *Journal of Symbolic Logic* (December, 1936): 138.

"Dr. Ladd–Franklin, Educator, 82, Dies." *New York Times* (March 6, 1930): 23.

Shen, Eugene. "The Ladd–Franklin Formula in Logic: The Antilogism." *Mind* 37 (1927): 54–60.

"To Restore Ideal at Johns Hopkins." *New York Times* (February 23, 1926): 12.

Venn, J. "Studies in Logic." *Mind* 8 (1883): 594–603.

Sketch by Sally M. Moite

Elizabeth Rebecca Laird
1874–1969
Canadian-American physicist

Elizabeth Laird is well known for her work in electron physics and soft x rays. She almost single–handedly transformed Mount Holyoke's physics department into a well–respected organization, with research rooms, laboratories, and reading rooms.

Elizabeth Laird was born on December 6, 1874, the daughter of Methodist clergy, in Owen Sound, Ontario. After graduating from South Collegiate, she attended the University of Toronto, graduating as valedictorian in 1896 with high honors in physics and math. While at Toronto, she was awarded both the Mulock Scholarship in Mathematics and Physics and the American Association for the Advancement of Science scholarship. Despite her achievements, Laird was unable to attend graduate school right away. The scholarship which would have made her studies possible was open only to men, so she became a mathematics teacher at Ontario Ladies' College in Whitby.

In 1898 she was able to commence studies at Bryn Mawr College. That year she was awarded the President's European physics fellowship, which enabled her to work at the University of Berlin with Max Planck. She earned her Ph.D. in 1901. After completion of her doctorate, Laird joined the faculty of Mount Holyoke College, where she would remain until her retirement in 1940, rising through the ranks to full professor and head of the physics department.

During her years at Mount Holyoke, Laird was offered several other research opportunities. In 1909 she worked at Cavendish Laboratory at Cambridge University. In 1913, she was awarded the Sarah Berliner Research fellowship from the American Association of University Women, which allowed her to study discharge rays at the University of Wurzburg. In 1919 she was invited to the University of

Elizabeth Laird (Mt. Holyoke College Archive. Reproduced by permission.)

Chicago to work in the physics laboratory. And in 1925, she was appointed honorary research fellow at Yale University.

Laird was known as an enthusiastic teacher who took interest in her students. In addition to her inspirational teaching, Laird was a diligent researcher. Among her many research topics were soft x rays, ultraviolet light, the Raman effect, spectroscopy, magnetism, spectral analysis, solid vibration, radioactivity, thermal conductivity, cathode rays, humidity, microwave electronics, and radar. She published dozens of papers in many scientific journals.

Laird retired in 1940, intending to travel with her sister, Annie. However, Annie's unexpected death cut short those plans. Laird was then asked to work as a physicist on radar development at the University of Western Ontario, a position she accepted. In addition to her research on microwave electronics and radar, she taught a course on radio and navy techniques for the Royal Canadian Air Force. After the war, she continued her research until her second retirement in 1953 as honorary professor of physics.

In recognition of her achievements, Laird was awarded the honorary D.Sc. from the University of Toronto and L.L.D. from the University of Western Ontario. She was a fellow of the American Association for the Advancement of Science, the American Physical Society, and a member of the History of Science Society, the Optical Society of America, the American Association of University Professors, and the American Association of Physics Teachers.

At the end of her life, Laird was involved in many community groups. She willed money to Memorial University to fund a lecture series on science by Canadians. In 1970, the Elizabeth Laird Memorial Lecture was established in her honor at the University of Western Ontario. Laird died on March 26, 1969.

SELECTED WRITINGS BY LAIRD:

Periodicals

"Entladungsstrahel at atmospheric pressure and at diminished pressures." *Physics Review* (1911).

"Transmission by thin films in the extreme ultraviolet." *Physics Review* (1920).

"Absorption in the region of soft x–rays." *Physics Review* (1927).

FURTHER READING

Books

Bailey, Martha J. *American Women in Science*. Denver: ABC–CLIO, 1994.

Siegel, Patricia Joan, and Kay Thomas Finley. *Women in the Scientific Search*. New Jersey: The Scarecrow Press, 1985.

Other

Special Collections Archives. Mt. Holyoke College.

Sketch by Helene Barker Kiser

Marie-Jeanne Lalande
1768–1832
French astronomer

Related by marriage to the famous French astronomer Joseph Jerome Lafrancais de Lalande ("Jerome Lalande," 1732–1807), Marie–Jeanne Amelie Harlay Lafrancaise de Lalande was in her own right an accomplished and respected astronomer and navigational calculator extraordinaire. It was she who constructed and prepared three hundred pages of horary tables for the senior Lalande's famous work, *Abrege de navigation* (1793). Independently, Lalande also calculated tables for finding the time of day while at sea, by assessing the altitude of the sun and stars. Her observations were printed in 1791 by order of France's National Assembly. She also reduced observations and calculated ten thousand stars, which were published in a catalogue in 1799. Others of her astronomical calculations were published as part of Jerome Lalande's astronomical almanac, *Connaissance des temps*. While many of her accomplishments are difficult to enumerate because they merge with those of her astronomer husband and famous astronomer "uncle," the mere fact that the senior Lalande regarded her with such professional esteem and respect, incorporating her work into many of his own, speaks well enough for her competence.

Born in France in 1768, Lalande later married Michel Jean Jerome Lefrancais de Lalande (1776–1839), with whom she had two children. Both she and her husband were instructed in astronomy by their renowned relative, Jerome Lalande. Although Jerome most often referred to Lalande and her husband as his "niece and nephew," their true blood relation was more complicated than that: Lalande's husband Michel was actually the grandson of Jerome's uncle. Michel became one of Jerome's more known proteges, but Jerome often employed Lalande to do his calculation tables for his published works.

While little is known of Lalande's personal avocations and interests, it is known that her entire family was devoted to astronomy. A contemporary student of astronomy will find several planetary designations in the Lalande name, e.g. the lunar crater Lalande (a major impact crater 25 km in diameter) which was photographed by Apollo 16's mapping camera, and the Lalande 21185, a dim M–class star which is eight light–years from the sun and located in the southern region of the Ursa Major constellation. While to some, the surname of Lalande may by synonymous with astronomy, even the family members' first names were affected. Lalande's daughter was born on January 20, 1790, which coincided with the date that a comet had first been seen from Paris by astronomer **Caroline Herschel**; thus, Lalande named her daughter Caroline. Their son Isaac was named after Sir Isaac Newton.

FURTHER READING

Books

Asimov, Isaac. *Asimov's Biographical Encyclopedia of Science and Technology.* Garden City: Doubleday and Company, 1982, p. 203.

Gillispie, Charles Coulston. *Dictionary of Scientific Biography.* Vol VII. New York: Charles Scribner's Sons.

Mozans, H.J. *Women in Science.* Notre Dame: University of Notre Dame Press, 182.

Ogilvie, Marilyn Bailey. *Women in Science: Antiquity through the Nineteenth Century.* Cambridge: MIT Press, 118.

Other

"Frame AS16–0849." http://www.vgl/org/webfiles/lan/llnd0849.htm.

"Lalande 21185." http://garber.simplenet.com/121185.htm.

Sketch by Lauri R. Harding

Bertha Aranelle Lamme
1869–1943
American engineer

Bertha Lamme, the first woman to graduate in the United States with an engineering degree other than civil engineering, was considered an expert in motor design. The only female student and the first woman to graduate from the College of Engineering at Ohio State University, she received the degree of "mechanical engineer in electrical engineering" in1893. When she received her diploma at the graduation ceremony, "a spontaneous ripple of applause broke over the crowd," reported *The Ohio State Lantern* in June 13, 1893.

At that time, Ohio State designated a mechanical engineer graduate as one who completed either mechanical or electrical engineering, as electrical engineers were also required to take mechanical engineering courses. These courses included mechanics, strength of materials, thermodynamics, and machinery. Electrical engineering courses included electrical machinery, technical drawing, and telephony/telegraphy.

Lamme was born to James Given Lamme and Sarah Anna Garver on December 16, 1869, on a farm near Springfield, Ohio. She was a middle child with an older brother, Benjamin, and a younger sister, Florence. Her brother, also a mechanical engineer with a degree from Ohio State (1888), most likely played a major influence in her future career since they were close growing up. She attended high school in Bethel Township, Clark County at a school named Olive Branch.

According to Benjamin in his autobiography, his sister decided to pursue engineering, "more for the pleasure of it than anything else," and after graduation she joined her brother at Westinghouse Electric and Manufacturing Company in Pittsburgh. An engineering department had been formed in 1895 with Albert Schmid as head, who had encouraged her to come work for them. Lamme remained at Westinghouse until 1905, when she married her supervisor, Russell S. Feicht, who had also graduated in mechanical engineering from Ohio State in 1890.

Designs Electrical Machines

Like her brother, Lamme was involved in the design of motors and generators. She was also quite skilled in mathematics and worked on machine design calculations. Her achievements are somewhat overshadowed by those of both her brother and husband, who later became famous for their accomplishments. Benjamin eventually became chief engineer and was put in charge of the design of the first turbogenerators at Niagara Falls. He also authored numerous technical publications and held approximately 150 patents. Feicht became director of engineering and designed the 2,000–horsepower motor, said to be the largest in the world at the time, displayed at the 1904 World's Fair.

It is not clear what Lamme's specific achievements were, since she worked as part of a team and records are scarce. In addition, she may not have been given proper credit for her designs, since she was not allowed access to the shop floor or the field where her designs were tested and implemented. Lamme may have made major contributions to her brother's achievements (and later her husband's), but this can only be assumed since there is little documentation.

However, she was still recognized for her skills in several ways. A 1907 edition of the *Pittsburgh Dispatch* stated, "She is accounted a master of the slide rule and can untangle the most intricate problems in ohms and amperes as easily and quickly as any man expert in the shop." In her brother's autobiography he stated that she "worked with him while achieving marked success of her own in the same art.".

Lamme may have continued to play an important role in her brother's and husband's engineering efforts. She continued to work at home for some time after she left Westinghouse, and her brother lived with them the remainder of his life. On April 19, 1910, Lamme gave birth to her only child, Florence Lamme Feicht, who at an early age also displayed mathematical ability. Florence followed in her mother's footsteps and later worked as a physicist at the U.S. Bureau of Mines in Pittsburgh. Bertha Lamme Feicht died on November 20, 1943 of natural causes, shortly before her 74th birthday.

Though it may never be known exactly how Lamme contributed to the advancement of electrical motors, it is clear she was a pioneer in her own right. She was one of the first woman engineers in the country, as well as one of the first woman engineers at Westinghouse. Her name continues to be remembered in several ways. In 1971, Ohio State established the Lamme Power Systems Laboratory to memorialize both Lamme and her brother. Two years later, the Society of Women Engineers established an annual scholarship fund in her name, which is supported by the Westinghouse Educational Foundation.

FURTHER READING

Books

Lamme, Benjamin. *Benjamin Garver Lamme, Electrical Engineer, An Autobiography.* New York: G.P. Putnam's Sons. 1926

Farnes, Patricia and G. Kass–Simon. *Women of Science: Righting the Record.* Bloomington: Indiana University Press, 1990, pp. 168–173.

Periodicals

"The Woman Behind." *News in Engineering* (September 1987) The Ohio State University:18.

Collins, Timothy. "1893 OSU Graduate 1st Woman Engineer" *The Ohio State Lantern* (March 27, 1973): 10.

Other

Ohio State University Archives, Biographical Files, Bertha Lamme.

Ohio State University Archives, Biographical Files, Benjamin Lamme.

Ohio Statue University Annual Report, 1892–1893.

Sketch by Laurel M. Sheppard

Rebecca Craighill Lancefield
1895–1981
American bacteriologist

Rebecca Craighill Lancefield is known throughout the world for the system she developed to classify the bacterium streptococcus. Her colleagues called her laboratory at the Rockefeller Institute for Medical Research (now Rockefeller University) "the Scotland Yard of streptococcal mysteries." During a research career that spanned six decades, she meticulously identified over fifty types of this bacteria. She used her knowledge of this large, diverse bacterial family to learn about pathogenesis and immunity of its afflictions, ranging from sore throats, rheumatic fever and scarlet fever to heart and kidney disease. The Lancefield system remains a key to the medical understanding of streptococcal diseases.

Born Rebecca Craighill on January 5, 1895, in Fort Wadsworth on Staten Island in New York on January 5, 1895, she was the third of six daughters. Her mother, Mary Montague Byram, married William Edward Craighill, a career army officer in the Army Corps of Engineers who had graduated from West Point. Lancefield received a bachelor's degree in 1916 from Wellesley College, after changing her major from English to zoology. Two years later, she earned a master's degree from Columbia University, where she pursued bacteriology in the laboratory of Hans Zinsser. Immediately on graduating from Columbia, she formed two lifelong partnerships. She married Donald Lancefield, who had been a classmate of hers in a genetics class. And she was hired by the Rockefeller Institute to help bacteriologists Oswald Avery and Alphonse Dochez, whose expertise on pneumococcus was then being applied to a different bacterium. This was during World War I, and the project at Rockefeller was to discover whether distinct types of streptococci could be isolated from soldiers in a Texas epidemic so that a serum might be produced to prevent infection. The scientists employed the same serological techniques that Avery had used to distinguish types of pneumococci. Within a year, Avery, Dochez, and Lancefield had published a major report which described four types of streptococci. This was Lancefield's first paper.

Lancefield and her husband took a short hiatus to teach in his home state at the University of Oregon, then returned to New York. Lancefield worked simultaneously on a Ph.D. at Columbia and on rheumatic fever studies at the Rockefeller Institute in the laboratory of Homer Swift, and her husband joined the Columbia University faculty in biology. Before World War I, physicians had suspected that a streptococcus caused rheumatic fever. But scientists, including Swift, had not been able to recover a specific organism from patients. Nor could they reproduce the disease in animals using patient cultures. Lancefield's first project with Swift, which was also her doctoral work, showed that the alpha–hemolytic class of streptococcus, also called green or viridans, was not the cause of rheumatic fever.

Develops Classification of Streptococci

As a result of her work with Swift, Lancefield decided that a more basic approach to rheumatic fever was needed. So she began sorting out types among the disease–causing class, the beta–hemolytic streptococci. She used serological techniques while continuing to benefit from Avery's advice. Her major tool for classifying the bacteria was the precipitin test. This involved mixing soluble type–specific antigens, or substances used to stimulate immune responses, with antisera (types of serum containing antibodies) to give visible precipitates. Precipitates are the separations of a substance, in this case bacteria, from liquid in a solution—the serum—in order to make it possible to study the bacteria on its own.

Lancefield soon recovered two surface antigens from these streptococci. One was a polysaccharide, or carbohydrate, called the C substance. This complex sugar molecule is a major component of the cell wall in all streptococci. She could further subdivide its dissimilar compositions into groups and she designated the groups by the letters A through O. The most common species causing human disease, *Streptococcus pyogenes,* were placed in group A. Among the group A streptococci, Lancefield found another antigen and determined it was a protein, called M for its matt appearance in colony formations. Because of differences in M protein composition, Lancefield was able to subdivide group A streptococci into types. During her career, she identified over fifty types, and since her death in 1981 bacteriologists have identified thirty more.

Lancefield's classification converged with another typing system devised by Frederick Griffith in England. His typing was based on a slide agglutination method, in which the bacteria in the serum collects into clumps when an antibody is introduced. For five years the two scientists exchanged samples and information across the Atlantic Ocean, verifying each other's types, until Griffith's tragic death during the bombing of London in 1940. Ultimately, Lancefield's system, based on the M types, was chosen as the standard for classifying group A streptococci.

In further studies on the M protein, Lancefield revealed this antigen is responsible for the bacteria's virulence because it inhibits phagocytosis, thus keeping the white blood cells from engulfing the streptococci. This finding came as a surprise, because Avery had discovered that virulence in the pneumococcus was due to a polysaccharide, not a protein. Lancefield went on to show the M antigen is also the one that elicits protective immune reactions.

Researches Pathogenesis and Immunity of Streptococci

Lancefield continued to group and type strep organisms sent from laboratories around the world. Until the end of her life, her painstaking investigations helped unravel the complexity and diversity of these bacteria. Lancefield's colleague Maclyn McCarty, told contributor Carol L. Moberg that Lancefield was "never satisfied with quick answers," and her success came from a determination to stick with scientific problems for a long time. Her thoroughness, he added, was a significant factor in her small but substantial bibliography of nearly 60 papers.

Once her system of classification was in place, however, Lancefield returned to her original quest to elucidate connections between the bacteria's constituents and the baffling nature of streptococcal diseases. She found that a single serotype of group A can cause a variety of streptococcal diseases. This evidence reversed a long–standing belief that every disease must be caused by a specific microbe. Also, because the M protein is type–specific, she found that acquired immunity to one group A serotype could not protect against infections caused by others in group A.

From her laboratory at Rockefeller Hospital, Lancefield could follow patient records for very long periods. She conducted a study which determined that once immunity is acquired to a serotype, it can last up to thirty years. This particular study revealed the unusual finding that high titers, or concentrations, of antibody persist in the absence of antigen. In the case of rheumatic fever, Lancefield illustrated how someone can suffer recurrent attacks, because each one is caused by a different serotype.

In other studies, Lancefield focused on antigens. She and Gertrude Perlmann purified the M protein in the 1950s. Twenty years later she developed a more conservative test for typing it and continued characterizing other group A protein antigens designated T and R. Ten years after her official retirement, she made a vital contribution on the group B streptococci. She clarified the role of their polysaccharides in virulence and showed how protein antigens on their surface also played a protective role. During the 1970s, an increasingly high–rate of infants were being born with group B meningitis, and her work laid the basis for the medical response to this problem.

During World War II, Lancefield had performed special duties on the Streptococcal Diseases Commission of the Armed Forces Epidemiological Board. Her task involved identifying strains and providing antisera for epidemics of scarlet and rheumatic fever among soldiers in military camps. After the commission dissolved, her colleagues in the "Strep Club" created the Lancefield Society in 1977, which continues to hold regular international meetings on advances in streptococcal research.

An associate member at Rockefeller when Maclyn McCarty took over Swift's laboratory in 1946, Lancefield became a full member and professor in 1958 and emeritus professor in 1965. While her career and achievements took place in a field dominated by men, Lewis Wannamaker in *American Society for Microbiology News* quotes Lancefield as being "annoyed by any special feeling about women in science." In *Profiles of Pioneer Women Scientists,* Elizabeth O'Hern cites Lancefield as saying that women "sometimes expect too much." Nevertheless, most recognition for Lancefield came near her retirement. In 1961, she was the first woman elected president of the American Association of Immunologists, and in 1970 she was one of few women elected to the National Academy of Sciences. Other honors included the T. Duckett Jones Memorial Award in 1960, the American Heart Association Achievement Award in 1964, the New York Academy of Medicine Medal in 1973, and honorary degrees from Rockefeller University in 1973 and Wellesley College in 1976.

In addition to her career as a scientist, Lancefield had one daughter. Lancefield was devoted to research and preferred not to go on lecture tours or attend scientific meetings. Rockefeller's laboratories were not air–conditioned and her main diversion was leaving them during the summer and spending the entire season in Woods Hole, Massachusetts. There she enjoyed tennis and swimming with her family, which eventually included two grandsons. Official retirement did not change her lifestyle. She drove to her Rockefeller laboratory from her home in Douglaston, Long Island, every working day until she broke her hip in November 1980. She died of complications from this injury on March 3, 1981, at the age of eighty–six. Her husband Donald died the following August.

The pathogenesis of rheumatic fever still eludes scientists, and antibiotics have not eliminated streptococcal diseases. Yet the legacy of Lancefield's system and its fundamental links to disease remain and a vaccine against several group A streptococci is being developed in her former laboratory at Rockefeller University by Vincent A. Fischetti.

SELECTED WRITINGS BY LANCEFIELD:

Periodicals

(With O. T. Avery and A. R. Dochez) "Studies on the Biology of Streptococcus. I. Antigenic Relationships between Strains of *Streptococcus haemolyticus.*" *Journal of Experimental Medicine* 30 (1919): 179–213.

"The Antigenic Complex of *Streptococcus haemolyticus.*" *Journal of Experimental Medicine,* a series of five reports, 47 (1928): 91–103, 469–480, 481–491, 843–855, 857–875.

"The Serological Differentiation of Human and Other Groups of Hemolytic Streptococci." *Journal of Experimental Medicine* 57 (1933): 571–595.

"Specific Relationship of Cell Composition to Biological Activity of Hemolytic Streptococci." *The Harvey Lectures, 1940–1941* series 36 (1941): 251–290.

(With M. McCarty and W. N. Everly) "Multiple Mouse–protective Antibodies Directed Against Group B Streptococci. Special Reference to Antibodies Effective Against Protein Antigens." *Journal of Experimental Medicine* 142 (1975): 165–179.

FURTHER READING

Books

O'Hern, E. M. *Profiles of Pioneer Women Scientists.* Acropolis Books, 1985, pp. 69–78.

Periodicals

McCarty, M. "Rebecca Craighill Lancefield." *Biographical Memoirs, National Academy of Sciences* 57 (1987): 226–246.

Schwartz, J. N. "Mrs. L." *Research Profiles* (summer 1990): 1–6.

Wannamaker, L. "Rebecca Craighill Lancefield." *American Society for Microbiology News* 47 (1981): 555–558.

Other

McCarty, Maclyn, interview with Carol L. Moberg conducted on February 9, 1994.

Sketch by Carol L. Moberg

Marie Lavoisier
1758–1836
French chemist

Marie Lavoisier, together with her husband Antoine Lavoisier, established chemistry as a modern scientific discipline. Their many discoveries included the identification of oxygen and the nature of combustion, oxidation, and respiration. They established the law of conservation of matter as a principle for experimental design. Although it is impossible to separate Marie Lavoisier's contributions from those of her more famous husband, she is known to have assisted with experiments and kept all of the laboratory notes and records. She translated and wrote commentaries

Marie Lavoisier (Painting by Jacques-Louis David. Corbis-Bettmann. Reproduced by permission.)

on important scientific papers and edited and illustrated her husband's ground-breaking treatises on chemistry.

Marie Anne Pierrette Paulze was born in 1758, the daughter of Jacques Paulze, a scholarly aristocrat. When she was 14, her father quickly arranged for her to marry his friend and colleague, the 28 year old Antoine Lavoisier, to protect her from a proposed match with an elderly, penniless suitor who was bringing extreme pressure to bear on Paulze in hopes of acquiring his daughter's prospective fortune. Antoine Lavoisier was already an established chemist and he immediately began to direct the education of his gifted young wife. In order to translate the newest works on chemistry, he taught her Latin, German, and English. She also studied with the French painter Louis David and soon was using her talents to illustrate her husband's publications.

Discovers the Nature of Fire

At the time of the Lavoisiers' marriage, one of the most pressing scientific questions involved the nature of heat and fire. The prevailing theory described combustion as the decomposition of complex compounds into simpler components and required the presence of a substance called phlogiston as the essential element of combustion. According to this theory, heat liberated the phlogiston, leaving behind a fine powder. Reduction of this powder required that the phlogiston be replaced. However, the Lavoisiers noted that, taking into account the gas produced, the products of combustion weighed more than the reactants, rather than less as predicted by the phlogiston theory. The Lavoisiers set out to prove or disprove the existence of phlogiston. In 1774, Joseph Priestly visited the Lavoisiers in Paris and told them of his discovery of "dephlogisticated air." They repeated Priestly's experiments and identified "oxygen" as the elemental gas in the atmosphere that supported combustion and was also a component of many acids. Their important new theory was announced in 1783: both combustion and oxidation were due to the chemical combination of oxygen and a flammable substance, rather than the release of phlogiston. In a dramatic ceremony, Marie Lavoisier burned the writings of the German chemist Georg Ernst Stahl and others who had promoted the theory of phlogiston.

Hosts Scientific Salon

In addition to conducting all of their scientific correspondence, Marie Lavoisier turned her and her husband's home into a scientific salon. Arthur Young visited there and left this account in his *Travels in France and Italy During the years 1787, 1788 and 1789*: "Madame Lavoisier, a lively, sensible, scientific lady, had prepared a *déjeuné Anglois* of tea and coffee, but her conversation on Mr. Kirwan's "Essay on Phlogiston," which she is translating from the English, and on other subjects, which a woman of understanding that works with her husband in his laboratory knows how to adorn, was the best repast." Lavoisier's translation of "Essay on Phlogiston" was published in 1788. Her translation of Richard Kirwan's other crucial paper, "Strength of Acids and the Proportion of Ingredients in Neutral Salts," including her original scientific commentary, appeared in *Annales de Chimie* in 1792. Her other major translations included the works of the English chemists Joseph Priestly and Henry Cavendish.

In 1789 Antoine Lavoisier published *Traité Élémentaire de Chimie*, the first modern chemistry textbook. It featured a new chemical nomenclature, a redefinition of "element," and a listing of the 23 known elements as the basis of all chemical reactions. It also included the most famous of Marie Lavoisier's work: her original watercolors and drawings, and 13 copperplate illustrations depicting, with great accuracy and precision, the design of their experiments.

In other important experiments, carried out in their laboratory at the Paris Arsenal, the Lavoisiers demonstrated that the weight of the products of a chemical reaction always equaled the weight of the reactants, thus establishing the law of conservation of matter. Their studies on metabolism demonstrated that animal respiration and inorganic combustion were analogous chemical processes. Thus, physiological processes obeyed the laws of chemistry.

Husband Guillotined in French Revolution

Although his political views were progressive, Antoine Lavoisier had become extremely wealthy as a member of the *Ferme-Générale*, the company of aristocrats who collected taxes and shared the revenues with the French king. In 1794, the French revolutionaries beheaded Marie Lavoisier's husband and her father, who had held an executive position in the *Ferme*. Initially, Lavoisier herself became a fugitive and was briefly imprisoned. With the Lavoisier estate confiscated by the Republic, she was cared for by an old family servant until her property was restored the following year.

Of his projected eight-volume work, *Mémoires de Chimie*, Antoine Lavoisier had completed much of the first volume, all of the second and fragments of the fourth volume at the time of his death. Marie Lavoisier began editing it as a two-volume work in 1796 with the help of a collaborator. After the two quarreled, she completed it herself, with her own introduction. She published it under her late husband's name in 1805 and distributed it for free among members of the scientific community.

Marries Count Rumford

In 1805, the childless widow Marie married Count Rumford, who was an applied scientist, an American-born Tory, and founder of the Royal Institution of Great Britain. After their marriage, Lavoisier kept her slain husband's name. Rumford had first attended Lavoisier's salon in 1801 and over the next four years they became very close friends, traveling through Europe together and eventually marrying. However within a few months of the marriage, their relationship turned sour. Rumford expected Lavoisier to be completely subservient and he demanded control of her fortune. They separated after four years. Lavoisier continued to conduct her scientific salon and carried on relationships with many of the greatest scientists of the day. Although she was unable to conduct further scientific investigations, her business and philanthropic activities continued until her death in 1836.

SELECTED WRITINGS, TRANSLATIONS, AND ILLUSTRATIONS BY LAVOISIER:

Books

Traité Élémentaire de Chimie, by Antoine Lavoisier. Paris: Couchet, 1789.

Mémoires de Chimie, by Antoine Lavoisier. Paris, 1805.

Periodicals

"Essai sur le phlogistique," by Richard Kirwan. Paris, 1788.

"De la force des Acides, & de la proportion des Substances qui composens les Sels neutres," by Richard Kirwan. *Annales de Chimie* 14 (1792): 152, 211, 238–286.

FURTHER READING

Books

Young, Arthur. *Travels in France and Italy During the years 1787, 1788 and 1789*. London: J. M. Dent, 1927.

Periodicals

Duveen, Denis I. "Madame Lavoisier 1758–1836." *Chymia* 4 (1953): 13–29.

Houlihan, Sherida and John H. Wotiz. "Women in Chemistry Before 1900." *Journal of Chemical Education* 52 (1975): 362–4.

Sketch by Margaret Alic

Mary Leakey
1913–1996
English paleontologist and anthropologist

For many years Mary Leakey lived in the shadow of her husband, Louis Leakey, whose reputation, coupled with the prejudices of the time, led him to be credited with some of his wife's discoveries in the field of early human archaeology. Yet she has established a substantial reputation in her own right and has come to be recognized as one of the most important paleoanthropologists of the twentieth century. It was Mary Leakey who was responsible for some of the most important discoveries made by Louis Leakey's team. Although her close association with Louis Leakey's work on Paleolithic sites at Olduvai Gorge—a 350–mile ravine in Tanzania—has led to her being considered a specialist in that particular area and period, she has in fact worked on excavations dating from as early as the Miocene Age (an era dating to approximately 18 million years ago) to those as recent as the Iron Age of a few thousand years ago.

Develops an Interest in Archaeology

Mary Leakey was born Mary Douglas Nicol on February 6, 1913, in London. Her mother was Cecilia Frere, the great–granddaughter of John Frere, who had discovered prehistoric stone tools at Hoxne, Suffolk, England, in 1797. Her father was Erskine Nicol, a painter who himself was the son of an artist, and who had a deep interest in Egyptian archaeology. When Mary was a child, her family made frequent trips to southwestern France, where her father took her to see the Upper Paleolithic cave paintings. She and her father became friends with Elie Peyrony, the curator of the local museum, and there she was exposed to the vast collection of flint tools dating from that period of human

Mary Leakey (AP/Wide World Photos. Reproduced by permission.)

prehistory. She was also allowed to accompany Peyrony on his excavations, though the archaeological work was not conducted in what would now be considered a scientific way—artifacts were removed from the site without careful study of the place in the earth where each had been found, obscuring valuable data that could be used in dating the artifact and analyzing its context. On a later trip, in 1925, she was taken to Paleolithic caves by the Abbé Lémozi of France, parish priest of Cabrerets, who had written papers on cave art. After her father's death in 1926, Mary Nicol was taken to Stonehenge and Avebury in England, where she began to learn about the archaeological activity in that country and, after meeting the archaeologist Dorothy Liddell, to realize the possibility of archaeology as a career for a woman.

By 1930 Mary Nicol had undertaken coursework in geology and archaeology at the University of London and had participated in a few excavations in order to obtain field experience. One of her lecturers, R. E. M. Wheeler, offered her the opportunity to join his party excavating St. Albans, England, the ancient Roman site of Verulamium; although she only remained at that site for a few days, finding the work there poorly organized, she began her career in earnest shortly thereafter, excavating Neolithic (early Stone Age) sites in Henbury, Devon, where she worked between 1930 and 1934. Her main area of expertise was stone tools, and she was exceptionally skilled at making drawings of them. During the 1930s Mary met Louis Leakey, who was to become her husband. Leakey was by this time well known because of his finds of early human remains in East Africa; it was at Mary and Louis's first meeting that he asked her to help him with the illustrations for his 1934 book, *Adam's Ancestors: An Up-to-Date Outline of What Is Known about the Origin of Man*

In 1934 Mary Nicol and Louis Leakey worked at an excavation in Clacton, England, where the skull of a hominid—a family of erect primate mammals that use only two feet for locomotion—had recently been found and where Louis was investigating Paleolithic geology as well as fauna and human remains. The excavation led to Mary Leakey's first publication, a 1937 report in the *Proceedings of the Prehistoric Society.*

Excavates at Olduvai Gorge

By this time, Louis Leakey had decided that Mary should join him on his next expedition to Olduvai Gorge in Tanganyika (now Tanzania), which he believed to be the most promising site for discovering early Paleolithic human remains. On the journey to Olduvai, Mary stopped briefly in South Africa, where she spent a few weeks with an archaeological team and learned more about the scientific approach to excavation, studying each find *in situ*— paying close attention to the details of the geological and faunal material surrounding each artifact. This knowledge was to assist her in her later work at Olduvai and elsewhere.

At Olduvai, among her earliest discoveries were fragments of a human skull; these were some of the first such remains found at the site, and it would be 20 years before any others would be found there. Mary Nicol and Louis Leakey returned to England. Leakey's divorce from his first wife was made final in the mid–1930s, and he and Mary Nicol were then married; the couple returned to Kenya in January of 1937. Over the next few years, the Leakeys excavated Neolithic and Iron Age sites at Hyrax Hill, Njoro River Cave, and the Naivasha Railway Rock Shelter, which yielded a large number of human remains and artifacts.

During World War II, the Leakeys began to excavate at Olorgasailie, southwest of Nairobi, but because of the complicated geology of that site, the dating of material found there was difficult. It did prove to be a rich source of material, however; in 1942 Mary Leakey uncovered hundreds, possibly thousands, of hand axes there. Her first major discovery in the field of prehuman fossils was that of most of the skull of a *Proconsul africanus* on Rusinga Island, in Lake Victoria, Kenya, in 1948. *Proconsul* was believed by some paleontologists to be a common ancestor of apes and humans, an animal whose descendants developed into two branches on the evolutionary tree: the *Pongidae* (great apes) and the *Hominidae* (who eventually evolved into true humans). *Proconsul* lived during the Miocene Age, approximately 18 million years ago. This was the first time a fossil ape skull had ever been found—only a small number have been found since—and the Leakeys hoped that this would be the ancestral hominid that paleontologists had sought for decades. The absence of a "simian shelf," a reinforcement of the jaw found in modern apes, is one of the features of *Proconsul* that led the Leakeys to infer that this was a direct ancestor of modern humans. *Proconsul* is now generally believed to be a species of *Dryopithecus,* closer to apes than to humans.

Discovers Zinjanthropus, or "Dear Boy"

Many of the finds at Olduvai were primitive stone hand axes, evidence of human habitation; it was not known, however, who had made them. Mary's concentration had been on the discovery of such tools, while Louis's goal had been to learn who had made them, in the hope that the date for the appearance of toolmaking hominids could be moved back to an earlier point. In 1959 Mary unearthed part of the jaw of an early hominid she designated *Zinjanthropus* (meaning "East African Man") and whom she referred to as "Dear Boy'; the early hominid is now considered to be a species of *Australopithecus*— apparently related to the two kinds of australopithecine found in South Africa, *Australopithecus africanus* and *Australopithecus robustus*— and given the species designation *boisei* in honor of Louis Leakey's sponsor Charles Boise. By means of potassium–argon dating, recently developed, it was determined that the fragment was 1.75 million years old, and this realization pushed back the date for the appearance of hominids in Africa. Despite the importance of this find, however, Louis Leakey was slightly disappointed, as he had hoped that the excavations would unearth not another australopithecine, but an example of *Homo* living at that early date. He was seeking evidence for his theory that more than one hominid form lived at Olduvai at the same time; these forms were the australopithecines, who eventually died out, and some early form of *Homo,* which survived—owing to toolmaking ability and larger cranial capacity—to evolve into *Homo erectus* and, eventually, the modern human. Leakey hoped that Mary Leakey's find would prove that *Homo* existed at that early level of Olduvai. The discovery he awaited did not come until the early 1960s, with the identification of a skull found by their son Jonathan Leakey that Louis designated as *Homo habilis* ('man with ability"). He believed this to be the true early human responsible for making the tools found at the site.

Working on Her Own

In her autobiography, *Disclosing the Past,* released in 1984, Mary Leakey reveals that her professional and personal relationship with Louis Leakey had begun to deteriorate by 1968. As she increasingly began to lead the Olduvai research on her own, and as she developed a reputation in her own right through her numerous publications of research results, she believes that her husband began to feel threatened. Louis Leakey had been spending a vast amount of his time in fundraising and administrative matters, while Mary was able to concentrate on field work. As Louis began to seek recognition in new areas, most notably in excavations seeking evidence of early humans in California, Mary stepped up her work at Olduvai, and the breach between them widened. She became critical of his interpretations of his California finds, viewing them as evidence of a decline in his scientific rigor. During these years at Olduvai, Mary made numerous new discoveries, including the first *Homo erectus* pelvis to be found. Mary Leakey continued her work after Louis Leakey's death in 1972. From 1975 she concentrated on Laetoli, Tanzania, which was a site earlier than the oldest beds at Olduvai. She knew that the lava above the Laetoli beds was dated to 2.4 million years ago, and the beds themselves were therefore even older; in contrast, the oldest beds at Olduvai were two million years old. Potassium–argon dating has since shown the upper beds at Laetoli to be approximately 3.5 million years old. In 1978 members of her team found two trails of hominid footprints in volcanic ash dated to approximately 3.5 million years ago; the form of the footprints gave evidence that these hominids walked upright, thus moving the date for the development of an upright posture back significantly earlier than previously believed. Mary Leakey considers these footprints to be among the most significant finds with which she has been associated.

In the late 1960s Mary Leakey received an honorary doctorate from the University of the Witwatersrand in South Africa, an honor she accepted only after university officials had spoken out against apartheid. Among her other honorary degrees are a D.S.Sc. from Yale University and a D.Sc. from the University of Chicago. She received an honorary D.Litt. from Oxford University in 1981. She has also received the Gold Medal of the Society of Women Geographers.

Louis Leakey was sometimes faulted for being too quick to interpret the finds of his team and for his propensity for developing sensationalistic, publicity–attracting theories. In recent years Mary Leakey has been critical of the conclusions reached by her husband—as well as by some others—but she has not added her own interpretations to the mix. Instead, she has always been more concerned with the act of discovery itself; she has written that it is more important for her to continue the task of uncovering early human remains to provide the pieces of the puzzle than it is to speculate and develop her own interpretations.

Leakey spent some time in the last years of her life lecturing and fund raising. However, she continued to excavate sites in Kenya and at Olduvai Gorge until just before her death. In August of 1996 she was able to travel to Laetoli to look at the footprints once more before they were covered with materials that will preserve them. Leakey died on December 9, 1996 in Nairobi, Kenya. Her legacy lies in the vast amount of material she and her team unearthed; she left it to future scholars to deduce its meaning.

SELECTED WRITINGS BY LEAKEY:

Books

(Illustrator) Louis Leakey. *Stone Age Africa: An Outline of Prehistory in Africa.* Oxford University Press, 1936. Reprint, Negro Universities Press, 1970.

(With Louis Leakey) *Some String Figures from North East Angola* (booklet), [Lisboa, Portugal], 1949.
(With L. Leakey) *Excavations at the Njoro River Cave: Stone Age Cremated Burials in Kenya Colony.* Clarendon Press, 1950.
Olduvai Gorge. Volume III: *Excavation in Beds I and II, 1960–63,* foreword by J. D. Clark. Cambridge University Press, 1971.
Olduvai Gorge: My Search for Early Man. Collins, 1979.
Africa's Vanishing Art: The Rock Paintings of Tanzania. Doubleday, 1983.
Disclosing the Past: An Autobiography. Doubleday, 1984.

FURTHER READING

Books

Cole, Sonia. *Leakey's Luck: The Life of Louis Seymour Bazett Leakey, 1903–1972.* Harcourt, 1975.
Isaac, Glynn, and Elizabeth R. McCown, eds. *Human Origins: Louis Leakey and the East African Evidence,* Benjamin–Cummings, 1976.
Johanson, Donald C., and Maitland A. Edey. *Lucy: The Beginnings of Humankind.* Simon & Schuster, 1981.
Leakey, Louis. *By the Evidence: Memoirs, 1932–1951.* Harcourt, 1974.
Leakey, Richard. *One Life: An Autobiography.* Salem House, 1984.
Malatesta, Anne, and Ronald Friedland. *The White Kikuyu: Louis S. B. Leakey.* McGraw–Hill, 1978.
Moore, Ruth E. *Man, Time, and Fossils: The Story of Evolution.* Knopf, 1961.
Reader, John. *Missing Links.* Little Brown, 1981.

Periodicals

Linnee, Susan. *Mary Leakey: Curiosity led her to discovery of man's origin.* Associated Press, 1996.
Payne, Melvin M. "The Leakeys of Africa: Family in Search of Prehistoric Man." *National Geographic* (February 1965): 194–231.

Sketch by Michael Sims

Henrietta Swan Leavitt
1868–1921
American astronomer

Henrietta Swan Leavitt (The Granger Collection, New York. Reproduced by permission.)

Henrietta Leavitt's most famous discovery was the "period–luminosity" relation for variable stars (those changing in brightness), an important method of obtaining distances to far–off galaxies. She also identified 2,400 new variable stars and established brightness scales that helped other astronomers with their own observations.

Henrietta Swan Leavitt was born in Lancaster, Massachusetts, on July 4, 1868, to Henrietta Swan Kendrick and George Roswell Leavitt, a Congregationalist minister who had a parish in Cambridge. After attending public school in Cambridge, Leavitt moved with her family to Cleveland, Ohio, where she attended Oberlin College from 1885 to 1888. She switched, however, to the Society for the Collegiate Instruction of Women (now Radcliffe College) in 1892. During her senior year, she took an astronomy course, which fired her interest in the subject. After receiving an A.B. from Radcliffe in 1892, Leavitt took another astronomy course, then spent a number of years home because of an illness that left her severely deaf. After some traveling, Leavitt volunteered as a research assistant at Harvard College Observatory in 1895, and was appointed to the permanent staff in 1902 by the astronomer Edward Pickering at a salary of thirty cents an hour. Leavitt worked at Harvard from 1902 until her death. While Pickering gave Leavitt little chance to do theoretical work, she became chief of the photographic photometry department at the observatory.

Establishes Scale of Star Brightnesses

In 1907 Pickering asked Leavitt to establish a "north polar sequence" of star brightnesses to serve as a standard for the entire sky. This standard was desirable because the photographic process in astronomy was complex—the brightness of star images on film was not proportional to their actual brightness, and each telescope gave different results for different color stars. Once determined, brightnesses could be estimated by comparing one star with another, rather than referring to photographic images. Leavitt used 299 plates from thirteen telescopes, and compared stars ranging from the fourth to the twenty–first magnitude in brightness (each increasing unit of magnitude corresponds to a reduction in brightness by a factor of 2.512 on a logarithmic scale). The results were published in the *Annals of Harvard College Observatory.* In 1913 Leavitt's system was adopted by the International Committee on Photographic Magnitudes. She made this work a lifelong project, and established brightness sequences for 108 areas in the sky. When Pickering developed forty–eight "Harvard standard regions" in the sky, Leavitt derived secondary brightness standards for them. These were used as international standards until superseded by improved methods.

Discovers Period-Luminosity Relation

Leavitt discovered 2400 new variable stars, about half those known at the time. Most notably, she studied photographs of the Magellanic Clouds (the Milky Way's two companion galaxies) taken at Harvard's observatory in Arequipo, Peru. Of the 1800 variable stars Leavitt detected on the Magellanic Cloud pictures, some were Cepheid variables, whose change in brightness is extremely regular. (Cepheids were named after the first star of this type to be discovered, Delta Cephei.) In 1908 Leavitt found that the brighter the Cepheid was overall, the longer it took to change its magnitude. Leavitt reasoned that since the Cepheids in the Magellanic Clouds were nearly all the same distance from Earth, their periods were related to their light output: the longer the period of pulsation, the brighter the star. By 1912 Leavitt had proven that Cepheids' apparent brightness increased linearly with the logarithm of their periods. That year, she published a table of the length of twenty–five Cepheid periods—ranging from 1.253 days to 127 days, with an average of 5 days—and their apparent brightness.

Before this period–luminosity relation had been established, cosmic distances could only be determined out to about 100 light–years. With it, however, distances of out to ten million light–years could be calculated. The intrinsic brightness of a Cepheid could now be gotten directly from a measure of its period, and this allowed the distance to be calculated. Astronomer Ejnar Hertzsprung adapted the period–luminosity relation so it could determine the actual distance of stars from Earth. Hertzsprung and astronomer Harlow Shapley found that the Magellanic Clouds were in the range of 100,000 light–years from Earth—an astonishing and unexpectedly high value. Leavitt was not aware as she worked that the Magellanic Clouds lay outside our own Galaxy.

Leavitt died of cancer December 21, 1921, in Cambridge. During her lifetime she had little opportunity to give free rein to her intellect, but her talents did not go unnoticed. According to *Women of Science,* her colleague **Margaret Harwood** described her as possessing the best mind at the observatory, and contemporary astronomer **Cecilia Payne-Gaposchkin** said Leavitt was the most brilliant woman at Harvard.

SELECTED WRITINGS BY LEAVITT:

Periodicals

"1,777 Variables in the Magellanic Clouds." *Annals of Harvard College Observatory* 60, no. 4 (1908): 87–108.

"Ten Variable Stars of the Algol Type." *Annals of Harvard College Observatory* 60, no. 5 (1908): 109–146.

FURTHER READING

Books

Kass–Simon, G., and P. Farnes, eds. *Women of Science.* Bloomington: Indiana University Press, 1990.

Ogilvie, M. B. *Women in Science.* Cambridge: MIT Press, 1986.

Sketch by Sebastian Thaler

Esther Miriam (Zimmer) Lederberg
1922–
American geneticist

Esther Lederberg was a major contributor to the revolution in the science of bacterial genetics. Her work led directly to our modern understanding of hereditary mechanisms as well as the birth of the field of molecular biology. With her husband, Joshua Lederberg, she discovered transduction, which is the transfer of bacterial genes from one organism to another via bacteriophages (viruses that infect bacteria). Although most of his work was in collaboration with his wife, Joshua Lederberg alone received the Nobel Prize for his work in the field of bacterial genetics in 1958.

Esther Lederberg was born in 1922 in New York City, the daughter of David and Pauline (Geller) Zimmer. She received her bachelor's degree in genetics from Hunter College in New York City in 1942 and her master's degree from Stanford University in 1946. That same year, she

Esther Lederberg (UPI-Corbis-Bettmann. Reproduced by permission.)

married fellow geneticist Joshua Lederberg, a professor at the University of Wisconsin. From 1946 to 1949, Lederberg was a National Cancer Institute predoctoral fellow at the University of Wisconsin where she earned her Ph.D. in 1950 for her research on mutant strains of bacteria.

As an associate in genetics at the University of Wisconsin, Lederberg continued to collaborate with her husband. It was a very exciting time in the field of bacterial genetics, with the discovery of DNA as the basis of heredity and with rapid advances in our understanding of how this genetic material is transmitted. The Lederbergs and others demonstrated that a fertility factor was required for bacteria to undergo sexual conjugation and the exchange of genetic material. This was the first example of a bacterial plasmid, or extrachromosomal DNA, that could be transmitted to another bacterium. In 1951, Esther Lederberg discovered that a strain of the common bacterium *Escherichia coli*, or *E. coli*, contained a virus that she named lambda phage. Lederberg isolated the phage and proved that it could be transmitted to other bacterial cells, via sexual conjugation and recombination, as if it were another gene. This led, in 1956, to the Lederbergs' discovery of transduction, the transfer of bacterial genes from one organism to another via phage.

In 1952, the Lederbergs invented a simple method of "replica plating," or exactly transferring bacterial colonies from one agar plate to another. Since then, this technique has enabled researchers to isolate countless bacteria that contain specific mutations or changes in their DNA. Furthermore, it enabled the Lederbergs to demonstrate that mutations occur spontaneously in bacteria and are not the result of environmental factors or inducers.

In 1956, the Lederbergs were jointly awarded the Pasteur Award of the Illinois Society for Microbiology, and the following year, Esther Lederberg was awarded a Fullbright Fellowship in bacteriology to work at Melbourne University in Australia. In 1958, Joshua Lederberg received the Nobel Prize for his work in the field of bacterial genetics, much of which had been carried out in collaboration with his wife.

The Lederbergs returned to the Stanford University Medical School in 1959—, Joshua Lederberg as head of the Department of Genetics and Esther Lederberg as a research geneticist in the department. They were divorced in 1968. Esther Lederberg became a research associate in the Department of Medical Microbiology, where she held an American Cancer Society Senior Dernham Fellowship. She was promoted to senior scientist in 1971 and research professor in 1974. From 1976 to 1986, Lederberg was director of the Plasmid Reference Center, which oversaw the collection collection and cataloguing of bacterial plasmids, or extrachromosomal DNA, which had become crucial research tools in molecular biology. During her later career, Lederberg's research interests focused on bacterial plasmids, genetic recombination and transformation, the introduction of foreign DNA into bacteria, and DNA repair mechanisms.

Lederberg is a fellow of the American Association for the Advancement of Science and a member of several other scientific organizations. In 1985, she became an Emeritus Professor in Microbiology and Immunology at Stanford University.

SELECTED WRITINGS BY LEDERBERG:

Periodicals

"The Mutability of Several Lac–Mutants of *Escherichia coli*." *Genetics* 33 (1948): 617.

Lysogenicity in *E. coli* K–12." *Genetics* 36 (1951): 560.

(With J. Lederberg, N. D. Zinder, and E. R. Lively) "Recombination Analysis of BacterialHeredity." *Cold Spring Harbor Symposia on Quantitative Biology* 16 (1951): 413–43.

"Allelic Relationships and Reverse Mutation in *Escherichia coli*." *Genetics* 37 (1952): 469–83.

(With J. Lederberg) "Replica Plating and Indirect Selection of Bacterial Mutants." *Journal of Bacteriology* 63 (1952): 399–406.

(With J. Lederberg and L. L. Cavalli) "Sex Compatibility in *Escherichia coli*." *Genetics* 37 (1952): 720–30.

(With J. Lederberg) "Genetic Studies of Lysogenicity in *Escherichia coli*." *Genetics* 38 (1953): 51–64.

(With M. L. Morse and J. Lederberg) "Transduction in *Escherichia coli* K–12." *Genetics* 41 (1956): 142–56.

(With S. N. Cohen) "Transformation of *Salmonella typhimurium* by plasmid deoxyribonucleic acid." *Journal of Bacteriology* 119 (1974): 1072–74.

FURTHER READING

Books

American Men & Women of Science. Vol. 4. 19th ed. New Providence, NJ: R. R. Bowker, 1995–96.

Brock, Thomas D. *The Emergence of Bacterial Genetics*. Plainview, NY: Cold Spring Harbor Laboratory Press, 1990.

Stent, Gunther S. and Richard Calendar. *Molecular Genetics: An Introductory Narrative*. 2d ed. San Francisco: W. H. Freeman and Company, 1978.

Who's Who of American Women: A Biographical Dictionary of Notable Living American Women. 3rd. ed. Chicago: A. N. Marquis Co., 1964–1965.

Sketch by Margaret Alic

Inge Lehmann
1888–1993
Danish geophysicist

Trained as a mathematician and an actuary, Danish geophysicist Inge Lehmann used painstaking analyses, measurements and observations of shock waves generated by earthquakes to propose in 1936 that the earth had a solid inner core. Throughout her long career which extended far beyond her official retirement in 1953, Lehmann conducted research in Europe and North America and was active in international scientific organizations including serving as the first president and a founder of the European Seismological Federation.

Lehmann was one of two daughters born to Alfred Georg Ludvig Lehmann, a University of Copenhagen professor of psychology, and Ida Sophie Torsleff. She was born on May 13, 1888. As a child, she attended and graduated from the first coeducational school in Denmark, an institution founded and run by Hanna Adler, the aunt of future Nobel Prize–winning physicist Niels Bohr . She began her university education by studying mathematics at the University of Copenhagen from 1907 to 1910. She continued her mathematical studies the following year at Cambridge University in England before returning to Denmark, where she worked as an actuary from 1912 to 1918. She also continued her formal education. In 1920 she earned her masters degree in mathematics from the University of Copenhagen and later studied mathematics at the University of Hamburg. In 1925 she began her career in seismology as a member of the Royal Danish Geodetic Institute and helped install the first seismographs at her Copenhagen office. "I was thrilled by the idea that these instruments could help us to explore the interior of the earth, and I began to read about it," she was quoted in a 1982 article published in the *Journal of Geological Education*. Lehmann later helped establish seismograph stations in Denmark and Greenland.

After further study with seismologists in France, Germany, Belgium and the Netherlands and after earning a master of science degree in geodesy from the University of Copenhagen in 1928, Lehmann was named chief of the Royal Danish Geodetic Institute. In that position, which she held until her retirement in 1953, she was Denmark's only seismologist for more than two decades. She was responsible for supervising the Denmark's seismology program, overseeing the operation of the seismograph stations in Denmark and Greenland and preparing the institute's bulletins.

Discovers Inner Core of the Earth

Despite this heavy work load, Lehmann still found time to explore scientific research. In 1936 she published her most significant finding, the discovery of the earth's inner core, under the simple title of "P'." The letter P stood for three types of waves generated by Pacific earthquakes that Lehmann had been carefully observing through the planet for ten years. By studying the shock waves generated by earthquakes, recorded on seismographs as travel–time curves, she theorized that the earth has a smaller solid inner core. Within a few years, work by other scientists, including Harold Jeffreys and, substantiated her findings.

Lehmann continued her research well after her retirement in 1953, exploring the nature of the planet's interior in Denmark, in Canada at the Dominion Observatory in Ottawa and in the United States at the University of California at Berkeley, the California Institute of Technology, and the Lamont Doherty Earth Observatory at Columbia University. She was a named a fellow of both the Royal Society of London and Edinburgh and was named to the Royal Danish Academy of Science and Letters and the Deutsche Geophysikalische Gesellschaft. In 1971 she was awarded the William Bowie Medal of the American Geophysical Union in recognition of her "outstanding contributions to fundamental geophysics and unselfish cooperation in research." She was also awarded honorary doctorates by the University of Copenhagen and Columbia University.

Lehmann remained single throughout her long and productive life. Her interests were not restricted to science. She was concerned with the poor in her native Denmark and the plight of European refugees. Travel in conjunction with her work also afforded her frequent opportunities to pursue two of her hobbies—visiting art galleries throughout Europe and the United States and the outdoors. Lehmann enjoyed hiking, mountain climbing and skiing. She died in 1993 at the age of 105.

SELECTED WRITINGS BY LEHMANN:

Periodicals

"P'." *Travaux Scientifiques,* Volume 14, 1936.

FURTHER READING

Books

Bolt, Bruce A. *Inside the Earth.* W. H. Freeman, 1982, pp. 18–21.

Current Biography Yearbook, 1962. H. W. Wilson, 1962, pp. 250–252.

Periodicals

Rossbacher, Lisa A. "The Geologic Column." *Geotimes* (August 1993): 36.

EOS Transactions American Geophysical Union, (July 1971): 537–38.

Journal of Geological Education 30 (1982): 291–92.

Sketch by Joel Schwarz

Nicole-Reine Étable de la Brière LePaute
1723–1788
French astronomer

Nicole-Reine Étable de la Brière Lepaute was at the forefront of eighteenth-century astronomy and she was considered to be one of the best astronomical mathematicians of her day. Her famous accomplishments included her calculation for the return of Halley's comet and her charts of solar eclipses.

Lepaute, sometimes referred to as Hortense Lepaute, was born in 1723 at Luxembourg Palace in Paris, where her father was a member of the court of Elisabeth d'Orléans, the queen of Spain. As a child, Lepaute was known for her intelligence and high spirits and she educated herself by reading and attending lectures. In 1748, she married Jean-André Lepaute, the royal clockmaker of France. Her interests in mathematics and astronomy were encouraged by her husband and his colleagues. Although she had no children of her own, Lepaute helped to educate two of the young men in her husband's family.

She collaborated with her husband, doing astronomical observations and calculations. Her first major investigation involved the movements of pendulums of various lengths. Her findings were published in her husband's 1755 treatise, *Traité d'horlogerie.*

Halley's comet had been observed in 1531, 1607, and 1682, and in 1757 astronomers were again expecting its return. Jérôme Lalande, the director of the Paris Observatory, asked Lepaute and the mathematician, Alexis Clairaut, to solve the orbit of the comet, so as to predict accurately when it would be visible. It was a huge problem. Never before had scientists been able to predict the return of a perturbed comet (one whose orbit is affected by planets) to the perihelion (the point of its orbit that is closest to the sun.) As P. V. Rizzo quoted from Lalande's *Bibliographie Astronomique* of 1803: "During six months we calculated from morning to night, sometimes even at meals. . . The assistance rendered by Mme. Lepaute was such that, without her I should never have been able to undertake the enormous labour, in which it was necessary to calculate the distance of each of the two planets Jupiter and Saturn from the comet, separately for each successive degree for 150 years." On November 14, 1758, Lepaute, Clairaut, and Lalande reported the correct dates to the Academy of Sciences. Halley's comet was first sighted on December 25 of that year and reached perihelion on March 13. In his book *Comets*, Clairaut gave Lepaute due credit for their accomplishment, but he subsequently withdrew the acknowledgment, reportedly at the request of someone who was jealous of Lepaute. Consequently, Clairaut alone usually receives credit for the prediction.

Lepaute published several astronomical treatises, including calculations based on all of the observations made of the 1761 transit of Venus, when the orbits of Earth and Venus lined up in such a way that Venus appeared to cross the sun. Lepaute then began calculating the upcoming eclipses of 1762 and 1764. The annular, or ringed, eclipse of 1764 had never before been observed in France. She published a chart showing the path and extent of the eclipse at every quarter-hour, for all of Europe. She made a separate chart for Paris, illustrating the phases of the eclipse. In order to carry out these calculations, Lepaute had to make a table of parallactic angles, the angle of displacement of an object caused by changes in the position of the observer. She later expanded this table for publication by the French government.

Between 1759 and 1774, Lepaute and Lalande collaborated on the annual *Connaissance des Temps*, the Academy of Science's astronomical and navigational almanac. Lepaute also did calculations for Lalande's *Connoissance des mouvemens célestes.* In 1774, Lepaute took over the production of the *Epheméris*, the tables of the positions and motions of the celestial bodies. She published the seventh volume, which covered the decade to 1784, and in 1783, she published the eighth volume, which covered the decade to 1792. For the latter volume, Lepaute herself made all of the computations of the positions of the sun, moon, and planets, an immense undertaking. With this final work, Lepaute's eyesight weakened, and she was forced to abandon her career. In 1788, the year of her death from a malignant fever, Lepaute was awarded membership in the Académie des Sciences of Béziers. A crater on the moon was named in her honor.

SELECTED WRITINGS BY LEPAUTE:

Books

(with J. A. Lepaute) "La Table des longueurs des pendules." In *Traité d'horlogerie*. Paris, 1755.

Explications de la carte qui représente le passage de l'ombre de la lune au travers de l'Europe dans l'eclipse du soleil centrale et annulaire du I Avril 1764. Paris, 1762.

(with J. Lalande) "Tables du soleil, de la lune et des autres planètes." In *Ephémérides du mouvement céleste*. Vol. 7. Paris, 1774.

FURTHER READING

Books

Alic, Margaret. *Hypatia's Heritage: A History of Women in Science from Antiquity through the Nineteenth Century*. Boston: Beacon Press,1986.

Ogilvie, Marilyn Bailey. *Women in Science, Antiquity through the Nineteenth Century: A Biographical Dictionary with Annotated Bibliography*. Cambridge: MIT Press, 1991.

Schiebinger, Londa. *The Mind Has No Sex? Women in the Origins of Modern Science*. Cambridge: Harvard University Press, 1989.

Periodicals

Rizzo, P. V. "Early Daughters of Urania." *Sky & Telescope* 14 (1954): 7–10.

Sketch by Margaret Alic

Iulya Isevolodovna Lermontova
1846–1919
Russian chemist

Iulya Lermontova was the first Russian woman to earn a doctorate in chemistry. Although she made several important contributions to organic chemistry, the study of compounds containing carbon, she is known primarily for her life–long friendship with the great Russian mathematician **Sofia Kovalevskaia**.

Iulya Lermontova was born in 1846 into a wealthy family with an estate near Moscow. Her father was Director of the Moscow Cadet Corps, and he hired their best instructors to tutor his children. Lermontova showed an early interest in chemistry, and her parents encouraged her unsuccessful attempts to study at Moscow University and at the St. Petersburg Agricultural Academy. The University of St. Petersburg had opened its doors to women students in 1861; but the government closed the schools because of political agitation by the students. When they were reopened, women were barred from attending. Many educated aristocratic Russian women were determined to go abroad to study. Since an unmarried woman could not obtain a passport without her parents' consent, it was common in radical student circles for women to enter into "marriages of convenience" in order to study abroad. Sometimes, these women managed to take their friends along as well.

Begins Study with R.W. Bunsen

Sofia Kovalevskaia had arranged such a marriage for herself and was studying in Heidelberg, Germany. Lermontova's parents were opposed to their daughter studying abroad, but Kovalevskaia convinced them to allow Lermontova to join her in Heidelberg. There, the two women formed the core of a "women's commune." Kovalevskaia had received a special dispensation to attend mathematics and physics lectures at the university, and Lermontova also obtained permission to attend chemistry courses. However R. W. Bunsen, the discoverer of cesium and the inventer of the Bunsen gas burner, had sworn that no woman would ever enter his laboratory. To his chagrin, Kovalevskaia charmed him into accepting both herself and Lermontova as students. For the next two years, Lermontova studied qualitative and quantitative chemical analysis in Bunsen's laboratory and, on the recommendation of D. I. Mendeleev, carried out research on the separation of platinum metals.

In 1870, the young women moved to Berlin, where Kovalevskaia studied mathematics with Karl Weierstrass, who, along with his two unmarried sisters, treated Kovalevskaia and Lermontova as their adopted daughters. Lermontova attended the lectures of A. W. von Hofmann and worked in his laboratory. She published her research on the compound diphenene, and Hofmann reported on it at a meeting of the German Chemical Society. Eventually Weierstrass convinced Göttingen University to award Kovalevskaia a doctorate degree without taking exams; however, Lermontova had to pass both written and oral examinations, in addition to presenting her thesis, *The Study of Methylene Compounds*. It was a horrible ordeal for Lermontova, who had never before taken an exam, and Weierstrass later learned that several of the examiners had intended to fail her. Nevertheless, Lermontova received her doctorate in chemistry *magna cum laude* from Göttingen in 1874. One of her examiners, Friedrich Wöhler, presented her with a piece of the mineral in which he had discovered the element titanium.

Works on Petroleum Distillation

Returning to Russia, Lermontova worked at Moscow University for one year, in the laboratory of the eminent chemist V. V. Markovnikov. There, she synthesized organic compounds, including the first synthesis of glutaric acid. After an attack of typhus interrupted her work for a year, she moved to St. Petersburg to A. M. Bulterov's organic chemistry laboratory. There she carried out several important studies and synthesized a number of new compounds. When she was recalled to Moscow because of family affairs, Butlerov and M. D. L'vov completed and published her work under her name. Although Butlerov had obtained her a teaching position in the new "Higher Courses for Women ," Lermontova was unable to return to St. Petersburg. Instead, she worked on petroleum distillation in Markovnikov's laboratory and designed an apparatus for continuously treating petroleum. With this last work, Lermontova achieved substantial recognition as a chemist and she was active in the Russian Chemical Society and the Russian Technical Society. She reviewed articles and wrote notices for the Chemical Society's journal.

Kovalevskaia returned to Moscow with her husband, a paleontologist, and daughter Sofia (Fufa), Lermontova's goddaughter. They moved into the small apartment that Lermontova shared with her sister, and the three scientists set out to perfect an electric light bulb, unaware of Thomas Edison's recent success. Fufa would continue to live with Lermontova for much of her childhood, and again while she was a medical student in Moscow. In addition, Lermontova probably provided Kovalevskaia with financial assistance. Lermontova wrote "Recollections of Sóphia Kovalévsky" at the request of Kovalevskaia's Swedish friend, Anna Carlotta Leffler.

Following her parents' deaths, Lermontova took over management of the family estate in 1886. There she applied her scientific expertise to the latest agricultural methods and to developing large scale cheese production, until her death in 1919.

SELECTED WRITINGS BY LERMONTOVA:

Periodicals

"The Composition of Diphenene." *Berichte* 5 (1872): 231.

FURTHER READING

Books

Alic, Margaret. *Hypatia's Heritage: A History of Women in Science from Antiquitythrough the Nineteenth Century.* Boston: Beacon Press,1986.

Koblitz, Ann Hibner. "Career and Home Life in the 1880s: The Choices of Mathematician Sofia Kovalevskaia." In *Uneasy Careers and Intimate Lives: Women in Science 1789–1979.* Edited by Pnina G. Abir–Am and Dorinda Outram. New Brunswick: Rutgers University Press, 1987.

Leffler, Anna Carlotta. "Biography of Sonya Kovalévsky." In *Her Recollections of Childhood,* by Sonya Kovalévsky. Translated by Isabel F. Hapgood. New York: Century,1895.

Periodicals

Steinberg, Charlene. "Yulya Vsevolodovna Lermontova (1846–1919)." *Journal of Chemical Education* 60 (1983): 757–58.

Sketch by Margaret Alic

Rita Levi-Montalcini
1909–
Italian-born American neurobiologist

Rita Levi–Montalcini is recognized for her pioneering research on nerve cell growth. During the 1950's she discovered a protein in the nervous system, which she named the nerve growth factor (NGF). Her subsequent collaboration with biochemist Stanley Cohen at Washington University in St. Louis, Missouri, led to the isolation of that substance. Later applications of their work have proven useful in the study of several disorders, including Alzheimer's disease, cancer, and birth defects. Levi–Montalcini's and Cohen's work was recognized in 1986 when they were jointly awarded the Nobel Prize for physiology or medicine. Levi–Montalcini became the fourth woman to receive the Nobel in that field.

Levi–Montalcini, the third of four children of Adamo Levi and Adele Montalcini, was born into an upper–middle–class Jewish family in Turin, Italy, in 1909. She grew up in a traditional family and was steered by her father to pursue an education at an all–girls' high school that prepared young women for marriage. She graduated from high school when she was 18, having demonstrated exceptional intellectual ability, but was unable to enter a university because of the limited education that had been offered to her. Levi–Montalcini was uncertain what she wanted to do with her life (though she was certain she did not want to marry and have children), and it wasn't until three years later, when her beloved governess was stricken with cancer, that she decided to become a doctor.

After having convinced her father she wanted to enter medical school, Levi–Montalcini passed the entrance exams with distinction. She enrolled in the Turin School of Medicine in 1930, where she studied under Dr. Giuseppe

Rita Levi-Montalcini (AP/Wide World Photos. Reproduced by permission.)

Levi, a well–known histologist and embryologist who introduced Levi–Montalcini to research on the nervous system. She graduated from medical school in 1936 and became Levi's research assistant. With the rise of Fascism in the late 1930's, Jews were restricted from academic positions as well as the medical profession, and Levi–Montalcini was forced to resign from her academic and clinical posts in 1938. The following year, she accepted a position at the Neurological Institute in Brussels, where she worked until the Nazi invasion in 1939 precipitated her return to Italy.

Conducts Research in Hiding

Upon returning to Italy, she took up residence in Turin with her family. Restrictions imposed upon Jews had increased during her absence, and Levi–Montalcini was forced to set up a private laboratory in her bedroom. Again working with Levi, who had also been banned from his academic post, Levi–Montalcini began researching the nervous system of chicken embryos. In a memoir published in *Women Scientists: The Road to Liberation,* Levi–Montalcini recalls, "Looking back to that period I wonder how I could have found so much interest in, and devoted myself with such enthusiasm to, the study of a small neuroembryological problem, when all the values I cherished were being crushed, and the triumphant advance of the Germans all over Europe seemed to herald the end of Western civilization. The answer may be found in the well–known refusal of human beings to accept reality at its face value, whether this be the fate of the individual, of a country, or of the human race." Her research at the time, in fact, laid the groundwork for her discovery of NGF.

By 1942 the Allied bombing of Turin forced Levi–Montalcini and her family to move to the countryside, where she continued experimentation on chicken embryos to study the mechanisms of nerve cell differentiation, or the specialization of nerve cells. Contrary to previous studies conducted by the respected neuroembryologist Viktor Hamburger, who theorized that nerve cells reached their destinations because they were directed by the organs to which they grew, Levi–Montalcini hypothesized that a specific nutrient was essential for nerve growth. When Nazi troops invaded northern Italy in 1943, Levi–Montalcini was again forced to relocate, this time to Florence, where she remained for the duration of the war under an assumed name. Following the liberation of Florence in 1944, Levi–Montalcini worked as a doctor in a refugee camp, and, when northern Italy was liberated the following year, she resumed her post as research assistant to Levi in Turin. Hamburger, who was interested in a paper Levi–Montalcini had published on her wartime experiments, contacted her in 1946, inviting her to fill a visiting research position at Washington University in St. Louis. This temporary position ultimately lasted over three decades.

Fortuitous Collaborations Yield Results

Levi–Montalcini's early work at Washington University concerned further experimentation on the growth processes of chicken embryos in which she observed a migratory sequence of nerve cells. Her observations validated her theory on the existence of a "trophic factor," which provided the essential nutrients for nerve cell differentiation. In 1950 she began studying mouse tumors that had been grafted onto chicken embryos, and which Elmer Bueker had earlier demonstrated were capable of eliciting a proliferation of nerve cells. After repeating Bueker's results, Levi–Montalcini reached a different conclusion. Instead of maintaining that the nerve cells proliferated in response to the presence of the tumor, she deduced that the nerve cells grew out of the tumor and that, thus, the tumor released a substance that elicited the growth. Traveling to Rio de Janeiro in 1952, Levi–Montalcini further tested her hypothesis using tissue cell cultures. Her tissue culture experiments regarding the presence of a substance in the tumor proved highly successful. However, there remained the important step of isolating this substance, which she called "the nerve–growth promoting agent" and later labeled nerve growth factor. Upon returning to Washington University, Levi–Montalcini began working with American biochemist Stanley Cohen between 1953 and 1959. During that time, they extracted NGF from snake venom and the salivary glands of male mice. Through these experiments, Cohen was able to determine the chemical structure of NGF, as well as produce NGF antibodies. Levi–Montalcini maintained her interest in the research of NGF; and, when she returned to italy in 1961, she established a laboratory at the Higher Institute of Health in Rome to perform joint NGF research with colleagues at Washington University.

A Lifetime of Accomplishments Is Recognized

By 1969 Levi–Montalcini established and served as director of the Institute of Cell Biology of the Italian National Research Council in Rome. Working six months out of the year at the Institute of Cell Biology and the other six months at Washington University, Levi–Montalcini maintained labs in Rome and St. Louis until 1977, at which time she resumed full–time residence in Italy. During this time she received numerous awards for her work, including becoming the tenth woman to be elected to the National Academy of Sciences in 1968. Despite her success, Levi–Montalcini was the only director of a laboratory conducting NGF research for many years. Later researchers, realizing the significance of understanding the growth of nerve fibers in treating degenerative diseases, have continued the work that Levi–Montalcini began in the late 1930s.

Levi–Montalcini remains active in the scientific community, upholding status as professor emeritus at Washington University since 1977, as well as contributing greatly to scientic studies and programs in her native country. Since winning the Nobel Prize in 1986, she was appointed president of the Italian Multiple Sclerosis Association and also became the first woman to attain membership to the Pontifical Academy of Sciences in Rome. In 1987 she was awarded the National Medal of Science, the highest honor among American scientists.

Keeping abreast with current scientific trends, Levi–Montalcini conducts further research at the Institute of Cell Biology in Rome, focusing on the importance of NGF in the immune and endocrine systems. Additionally, with her twin sister, who is an artist, Levi–Montalcini has established educational youth programs that provide counseling and grants for teenagers interested in the arts or sciences. Recognized not only for her astute intuitive mind and her dedication to fully understanding the mechanisms of NGF, Levi–Montalcini, frequently described by her congenial manner and wit, has influenced three generations of scientists during her own lifetime.

SELECTED WRITINGS BY LEVI–MONTALCINI:

Books

"Reflections on a Scientific Adventure." In Women Scientists: The Road to Liberation. Edited by Derek Richter. Macmillan Press, 1982, pp. 99–117.

(Editor with Pietro Calissano) *Molecular Aspects of Neurobioloay.* Springer–Verlag, 1986.

In Praise of Imperfection: My Life and Work. Basic Books, 1988.

Periodicals

"The Nerve Growth Factor." *Scientific American* (June, 1979): 68–77.

"The Nerve Growth Factor 35 Years Later." *Science* 237 (1987): 1154–61.

FURTHER READING

Periodicals

Holloway, Marguerite. "Finding the Good in the Bad." *Scientific American* (January, 1993): 32, 36.

Levine, Joe. "Lives of Spirit and Dedication." *Time* (October 27, 1986): 66–8.

Marx, Jean L. "The 1986 Nobel Prize for Physiology or Medicine." *Science* (October 31, 1986): 543–44.

Randall, Frederika. "The Heart and Mind of a Geniu." *Vogue* (March, 1987): 480, 536.

Schmeck, Harold M., Jr. "Two Pioneers in Growth of Cells Win Nobel Prize." *New York Times* (October 14, 1986): Al, C3.

Suro, Roberto. "Unraveler of Mysteries." *New York Times* (October 14, 1986): C3.

Sketch by Elizabeth Henry

Graceanna (or Grace Anna) Lewis
1821–1912
American naturalist

The name of Graceanna Lewis would have historical significance even if she had never engaged in scientific scholarship. A Quaker, she was a staunch abolitionist whose family home in Pennsylvania was part of the Underground Railroad for runaway slaves. Later, she was involved in the women's suffrage movement. But her interest in the world around her, coupled with unusually keep powers of observation, led her to a distinguished career as a naturalist and teacher.

Graceanna (some sources list her as Grace Anna) Lewis was born on the family farm in Chester County, Pennsylvania on August 3, 1821. She was the third of five children of John and Esther Fussell Lewis, whose Quaker families had come to America in the seventeenth century. John Lewis died in 1824 when Graceanna was only three. Esther Lewis, who had been a teacher before she married, now ran the farm, but made sure her children received a broad liberal education.

Early Life

Young Graceanna and her sisters (a brother had died in infancy) were educated first at home by their mother. When they were old enough, they were sent to the nearby Quaker–run Kimberton Boarding School. The curriculum included a number of science classes, including botany, chemistry, and astronomy. Graceanna was influenced by Abigail Kimber, daughter of the school's owners, who would herself become a botanist. Although she was not yet sure whether she wanted to pursue a career in science, she was impressed by how the study of science fit in with her own outlook as a Quaker the importance of finding a natural order to the universe.

In 1842 Lewis traveled to York, Pennsylvania to teach at a girls' boarding school begun by her uncle, Bartholomew Fussell. She taught a number of subjects, including astronomy and botany. Often visiting lecturers would pass through town, including a number of scientists. There is some evidence that the normally level–headed Lewis had more than a passing interest in the "science" known as phrenology, whose practitioners believed that different personality traits resided in different areas of the skull. They also believed that people's head could be "read" to determine their true personality. There is no evidence that this was any more than a case of a still impressionable young woman being caught up in what was a hugely popular scientific movement in antebellum America. In fact, her writings indicate that any interest she had was soon replaced with healthy skepticism.

Fussell closed his school in 1844, and Lewis moved back to the family farm, where she taught briefly at nearby schools. Over the next few years she would begin to think about science as more than a subject that provoked intriguing ideas. A close friend of hers, Mary Townsend, wrote a book on insects in the mid–1840s. While not strictly a scientific text, the book was a well–ordered depiction of the insect world, and it impressed Lewis greatly. Mary Townsend, always frail, died a young woman in 1851. Lewis was shaken at the loss but she also got the notion around this time that she would like to create "a study kindred to (Townsend's)."

Turning Toward Science

Esther Lewis had died in 1848, and her three unmarried daughters were left to run the farm. By the mid–1860s, two of the three had also died, leaving Graceanna Lewis alone on the farm. Moreover, with the Civil war now having been fought and finished, the cause of abolition (which had taken up much of the Lewis family's time and energy) was no longer a cause.

Gradually, Lewis turned back to her earlier idea of creating a "study" the question was, what would her study be about. For many years, she had observed the local birds and their habits, and she decided at last to create an ornithological study. The beauty that birds possessed, she felt, fit perfectly with her desire to put together a work that could "discover God in nature."

Of course, since she had no scientific training, or access to the training that could prepare her to embark on a scientific project. Undaunted, she turned first to neighbors who were scientists, either by profession or avocation. These men provided Lewis with science texts and advice. Pennsylvania ornithologist, Spencer Baird, told Lewis about the Academy of Natural Sciences in Philadelphia, which housed a collection of nearly 25,000 bird specimens (the largest in the world). Lewis decided to move to Philadelphia, where she became active both in her new project and in the local Quaker community.

In 1862 Lewis had made the acquaintance of John Cassin, the Academy's curator and then considered the nation's leading expert on birds. Cassin allowed her to explore the collections and gave her free rein. He also served as a mentor to her. By 1869, Deborah Warner writes in her biography, *Graceanna Lewis: Scientist and Humanitarian,* Lewis was "truly the best educated woman naturalist in the United States."

Cassin died that year, and Lewis had already begun the first phase of her work. She published her *Natural History of Birds* in 1868. Originally written to be the first of a ten–part series, the work was, as Warner notes, the first one "about birds as living animals" instead of merely as specimens. Lewis described bird songs, behavior, migration, and physical attributes of the birds.

Unfortunately, the book was not as well receive as Lewis had hoped it would be, and lack of financial resources kept her from publishing the other nine sections. There was no doubt about her scholarship, however, and she continued to conduct her own research. Having obtained a microscope, she examined bird plumage and made careful drawings of the crystalline forms she saw. She wrote and illustrated a number of articles that made their way into such respected publications as *The American Naturalist.*

The contribution to science that Lewis thought was her most important was her Chart of the Animal Kingdom. She made several such charts, in fact, outlining species of birds, plants, and fish, as well as different races of humankind. One of her charts, along with a wax model, was exhibited in Philadelphia at the Centennial Exhibition of 1876; the chart was quite well received by scientists and naturalists who saw it, and it attracted attention overseas as well as in the U.S.

One of the most difficult obstacles Lewis faced during her lifetime was lack of funds. With no real job, and no independent wealth. She had to struggle to make a living. She advertised as a lecturer and made some money giving lessons in ornithology, zoology, and botany. In 1874 she traveled to Poughkeepsie, New York, where she lectured at Vassar College for a week. She had tried to secure a position at Vassar some years earlier, but she was passed over. Until 1884, she taught in girls' schools, giving occasional lectures and still trying to conduct research. In the early 1870s she had plans to convert her family farm into a model community, but this plan never materialized, and she simply sold the land in 1878. This gave her some money, but still left her unable to pursue her research the way she wanted to.

Nonetheless, she remained active even after she officially stopped teaching in 1885. She corresponded with scientists from different universities and museums, and contributed to scholarly publications until 1896. She continued to conduct research until she was well into her 80s. Later, she was also taken up in the cause of women's suffrage, a logical direction for the woman who had been so active in the abolition movement years before.

Lewis was the ninth woman to be elected to the Academy of Natural Sciences, but her election was not effortless. When her name was first proposed in 1870 it was rejected. Past elections (both of men and women) seemed to be based on who had contributed not necessarily to science, but to the Academy through donations. The forthrightly honest Lewis voiced her displeasure to the Academy at being turned down; eventually, the Academy reversed itself and accepted her. Lewis was not what one would call a campaigner for women's rights rather, she was a believer in fairness and justice. Those were her guiding principles, whether she was engaged in science, teaching, or social reform.

Lewis spent her last years living with her sister in Media, Pennsylvania. Among the last things she worked on was a family history. She died on February 25, 1912 at the age of 90. Three years later, on Memorial Day, 1915, suffragists gathered at her grave to pay tribute to her, not just as a supporter of suffrage, but as a supporter of science and of women's rights to pursue whatever career they might choose.

FURTHER READING

Books

Oglivie, Marilyn Bailey. *Women in Science: Antiquity through the Nineteenth Century.* Cambridge: MIT Press, 1986.

Bailey, Martha J. *American Women in Science: A Biographical Dictionary.* Denver: ABC–CLIO, 1994.

Warner, Deborah Jane. *Graceanna Lewis: Scientist and Humanitarian.* Smithsonian Institution Press, 1979.

Sketch by George A. Milite

Margaret Adaline (Reed) Lewis
1881–1970
American anatomist and physiologist

Margaret Lewis was a pioneer in several scientific fields. Her work in embryology, bacteriology, anatomy, cytology, and physiology paved the way for the work of many later scientists. She was an expert in tissue culture and was one of the very first cancer researchers with an expertise in tumor studies.

Born on November 9, 1881, in Kittaning, Pennsylvania, Margaret Reed was the daughter of Joseph Cable Reed and Martha Adaline (Walker) Reed. After studying at Woods Hole Marine Biological Laboratory for a time, Lewis graduated from Goucher College in 1901 with an A.B. degree. Among her early positions, Lewis was an assistant in zoology at Bryn Mawr College, a preparator in zoology and biology instructor at Columbia University, a physiology lecturer at the New York Medical College for Women, a zoology and biology lecturer at Barnard College, and an anatomy and physiology instructor at the Johns Hopkins Hospital training school for nurses. Lewis also conducted research at the University of Zurich, the University of Paris, and the University of Berlin.

Lewis's earliest interests focused on amphibian embryology and crayfish regeneration. She also conducted experiments with ultramicroscopic viruses and cell cytology. While in Germany, Lewis was the first scientist to conduct experiments in in vitro mammalian tissue culture.

Lewis married Warren Harmon Lewis in 1910, and for the rest of her life collaborated with him on pioneering research. The couple also had three children, Margaret, Warren, and Jessica. Continuing the work Lewis had begun in Berlin, the Lewises researched mammalian tissue culture, experimenting to identify cells that could be cultured. They also developed what became known as the Locke–Lewis solution and the Lewis culture. The solution, clear and nutritive, aided studies of cell structure. The culture involved suspension of cells on custom slides which facilitated growth and observation. The couple was able to further define and describe the cells' organelles, in addition to determining what cells could be grown and under what conditions. Many living cells were described morphologically using Lewis's method.

In 1915, Lewis joined the Carnegie Institute of Washington as a collaborator and, later, researcher in the Department of Embryology, where she would remain until the 1940s. Here, Lewis began cell experiments to determine acid effects and cell physiology. pH values were just starting to be understood as important factors in cell growth and development, and Lewis used this knowledge to expand the amount of time cultured cells could be kept alive.

This new research provided a breakthrough in the understanding of cancer cells and other "scavenging cells." It was believed that the "good" cells and the "bad" cells were of different types. But Lewis determined that there were certain conditions under which monocytes (white blood cells) would transform into macrophages ("scavenging cells"). The resulting scavengers would then feed off of other cells. This research, which included dye chemotherapy, was a major breakthrough in the early years of cancer research. Because of Lewis's work, many more experiments followed, further educating scientists in the development and treatment of tumors.

Because the Lewises were rapidly known around the world as foremost authorities in the field, they were asked to co–author the chapter on tissue culture for a widely used textbook on cytology. The Lewises were invited to be guest researchers at several institutions, including Stanford University, Woods Hole, the Mt. Desert Island Biological Laboratory, and the Harpswell Laboratory.

Following many years at Carnegie, Lewis moved to the Wistar Institute of Anatomy and Biology in Philadelphia, where she would remain until her retirement as emeritus member in 1964. During her lifetime, Lewis published nearly 200 papers and pioneered many research techniques. She was a member of the Tissue Culture Society, Sigma Xi, the American Association of Anatomists, and Phi Beta Kappa. Lewis was awarded an honorary LL.D. from Goucher College in 1938, and she and her husband were awarded the William Wood Gerhard Medal of the Pathological Society of Philadelphia. In her spare time, Lewis enjoyed mountain climbing and music. She died on July 20, 1970.

SELECTED WRITINGS BY LEWIS:

Periodicals

"Development of connective–tissue fibers in tissue cultures of chick embryos #h microform." *Contributions to Embyology* 6, no. 17 (1917).

FURTHER READING

Books

Bailey, Martha J. *American Women in Science*. Denver: ABC–CLIO, 1994.

Shearer, Benjamin F. and Barbara S. Shearer, eds. *Notable Women in the Life Sciences*. Westport, CT: Greenwood Press, 1996.

Siegel, Patricia Joan, and Kay Thomas Finley. *Women in the Scientific Search*. Metuchen, NJ: Scarecrow Press, Inc., 1985.

Sketch by Helene Barker Kiser

Leona Woods (Marshall) Libby
1919–1986
American physicist

Leona Libby, a founder of high–energy physics, was a pioneer in nuclear energy technology, working on the atom bomb among other projects. She discovered cold neutrons, researched isotope ratios, and was involved in other firsts in nuclear technology.

Leona Woods was born on August 9, 1919, in La Grange, Illinois. Her father, Wreightstill Woods, was a lawyer, and her mother, Mary Holderness Woods, raised her five children on the family farm. Libby's early studies were in chemistry, and at age nineteen she graduated from the University of Chicago with a B.S. degree in 1938. She went on to get her PhD, which she received in 1943, while working with Nobel laureate Robert Mulliken on quantum chemistry and diatomic molecular spectroscopy.

Building the Bomb

While still a student, Libby became the youngest member and the only female working with Nobel laureate Enrico Fermi at the Chicago Metallurgical Laboratory in Chicago's Manhattan District, on a secret project later known as the Manhattan Project. Here, the scientists built the first nuclear fission reactor in the world, the CP–1, and six later reactors, and developed the atomic bomb used against Japan in World War II. Libby was responsible for constructing the neutron detectors, and in the process, received a state-of-the-art education in nuclear physics.

The work was grueling but exciting. The team members were constantly covered in black graphite dust. Here, Libby met and married her first husband, John Marshall, Jr., and the couple had two children. Libby continued working throughout both pregnancies, a fact she proclaimed as evidence that the technology was not dangerous or harmful. In 1944, Libby worked as a consulting physicist at the Hanford plutonium production reactor in Washington state.

Nuclear Research Continues

In 1946, Libby returned to the University of Chicago, first as a fellow at the Institute for Nuclear Studies, then as a research associate for Nuclear Studies, and finally as assistant professor of Nuclear Studies. The research had moved toward fundamental particle physics, with a concentration on the nucleus. Libby discovered cold neutrons and built the first rotating neutron spectrometer. She also researched nuclear explosions and neutron diffusion. In 1958, Libby joined the staff of Brookhaven National Laboratory in New York as a visiting scientist. Two years later, she joined the faculty of New York University as an associate professor, teaching atomic and nuclear physics. In 1964, Libby moved to Colorado to join the faculty of the university at Boulder as physics professor, where she also consulted for several research organizations.

In 1966, Libby divorced John Marshall and married Willard Frank Libby, a chemist and Nobel laureate. Her interests began to broaden to include aspects of cosmology. She discovered that tree ring isotope ratios could measure ancient historical climates. In 1970, while still at Boulder, Libby joined the faculty of UCLA's School of Engineering as a visiting professor, and two years later became adjunct professor after leaving Boulder. Her research on ancient wood and climates continued during this time in addition to her work in particle physics, and she also retained her staff position at R & D Associates.

Her husband died in 1980, and Libby worked to edit his collected papers for publication. Popular backlash against nuclear energy had begun, and Libby was an active spokesperson for nuclear power. Before her death in Santa Monica, California, on November 10, 1986, Libby was researching superheavy quasar fission products. She had a long publishing career, including books and hundreds of scientific articles. She was a fellow of the American Physical Society, a fellow of the Royal Geographical Society, a member of the National Science Foundation Postdoctoral Fellowship Evaluation Board, and a bicentennial lecturer at the University of Utah. In 1992, the fiftieth anniversary of the CP–1, Libby was posthumously honored as one of the Women Pioneers in Nuclear Science.

SELECTED WRITINGS BY LIBBY:

Books

Past Climates: Tree Thermometers, Commodities, and People. Austin: University of Texas Press, 1983.

The Uranium People. New York: Crane, Russack, 1979.

FURTHER READING

Books

Grinstein, Louise S., et. al, eds. *Women in Chemistry and Physics: A Bibliographic Sourcebook*. Westport, CT: Greenwood Press, 1993.

O'Neill, Lois Decker, ed. *The Women's Book of World Records and Achievements*. New York: Anchor Press, 1979.

Shearer, Benjamin F. and Barbara S. Shearer, eds. *Notable Women in the Physical Sciences*. Westport, CT: Greenwood Press, 1996.

Periodicals

"Dr. Leonea Libby, 67; Worked on Atom Bomb." *New York Times* (November 12, 1986): 1027.

Sketch by Helene Barker Kiser

Ruth Smith Lloyd
1917–
American anatomist

Ruth Smith Lloyd was the first African American woman to earn a Ph.D. in anatomy. Lloyd, who spent a large portion of her teaching career at Howard University, specialized in issues surrounding fertility as well as research on the female sex cycle and the relation of sex hormones to growth.

Ruth Smith Lloyd was born in Washington, DC, on January 25, 1917. The youngest of three girls born to Mary Elizabeth Smith and Bradley Donald Smith, Lloyd graduated from Dunbar High School in Washington and went on to receive her A.B. from Mt. Holyoke College in 1937. At this point, Lloyd planned to study zoology and then begin teaching at the high school level. However, after she attained her master's degree at Howard University, her professors encouraged her to work towards an advanced degree in anatomy. Her mentor at Howard recommended specifically that she study at Western Reserve University, and it was there that she began her serious studies in anatomy. In 1941 Lloyd earned her Ph.D. in anatomy, thus becoming the first African American woman to achieve that goal.

While studying at Western Reserve, Lloyd worked in the school's fertility laboratories, which kept colonies of monkeys. Lloyd would eventually concentrate her research and teaching efforts in the field of endocrinology and medical genetics. In 1941 she took a position at the Howard University college of medicine as an assistant in physiology. After a brief period, during which she taught zoology at Hampton Institute, Lloyd took time to begin raising her family. In 1939 she married a physician, Sterling M. Lloyd, with whom she would have three children.

In 1942, Lloyd returned to Howard University, where she remained for the rest of her professional career. That same year she was promoted to an instructor, and by 1958 she was an assistant professor of anatomy. Soon afterward, she became an associate professor at Howard's graduate school, where she remained until her retirement. Lloyd, who now lives in her native Washington, DC, said in an interview with Leonard C. Bruno that even upon reflection, she is unimpressed with her unique accomplishments. She sees little that is unusual or remarkable about her story, and described herself to Bruno as an average person with a normal life.

FURTHER READING

Lloyd, Ruth S., interview with Leonard C. Bruno conducted January 6, 1994.

Sketch by Leonard C. Bruno

Martha Daniell Logan
1704–1779
American horticulturist

Martha Logan was a prominent horticulturist in colonial America. She was quite knowledgeable about plants of all kinds, including vegetable crops, and was well-known to readers of her printed features as well as to those who patronized her nursery.

Martha Daniell Logan was born on December 29, 1704, in St. Thomas Parish, South Carolina. Her father, Robert Daniell, and her mother, Martha (Wainwright) Daniell, Robert's second wife, had four children, and Logan was the second. Robert Daniell was both wealthy and well–known, the state's deputy-governor, and owned a significant amount of property, including ships, land, and slaves.

Logan's childhood was typical of the time and her privilege. She learned reading and writing, and was also taught needle craft. In addition, gardening was a skill and hobby in which Logan became experienced. Shortly after her father's death, 14–year-old Logan married George Logan, Jr. on July 30, 1719, at about the same time as her mother's remarriage to George's father. The younger Logans lived on the plantation Martha's father had willed to her, not far from Charleston, South Carolina. Over the years, six of their eight children survived.

In 1742, the Logans opened a kind of boarding school, where children were taught reading, writing, needlework, and sewing. A few years later, in 1751, Logan began publishing her column on horticulture, "Gardener's Kalendar," which appeared for nearly 40 years in various newspapers and almanacs. In it, Logan explained herb culture, horticulture, and vegetable culture, based on traditions, personal experience, and folklore.

Two years after the first appearance of her column, Logan's son, Robert, began advertising a nursery business, which Martha later took over. Because gardening was "in style" among the wealthy landowners of the time, the nursery's trade in imported and rare seeds, flowers, shrubs, plants, and fruits made a name for Logan as a master horticulturist. In addition to her nursery business and her public writing, Logan corresponded with John Bartram, the noted expert in botany, for many years, and they traded knowledge, plants, and seeds.

On June 28, 1779, Logan died in Charleston. She was buried in the family vault in the churchyard of St. Phillip's with her husband, who died in 1764, and the children who predeceased her. Unfortunately, the vault is no longer in existence.

SELECTED WRITINGS BY LOGAN:

Books

A Gardener's Calendar Done by a Colonial Lady. Edited by Alica Logan White. Charleston: National Society of the Colonial Dames of America in the State of South Carolina, 1976.

FURTHER READING

Books

James, Edward T., et al, eds. *Notable American Women 1607–1950*. Cambridge: Belknap Press, 1971.

Shearer, Benjamin F. and Barbara S. Shearer, eds. *Notable Women in the Life Sciences*. Westport, CT: Greenwood Press, 1996.

Spruill, Julia C. *Women's Life and Work in the Southern Colonies*. New York: W. W. Norton, 1972.

Sketch by Helene Barker Kiser

Cynthia Evelyn Longfield
1896–1991
Irish entomologist and explorer

Dubbed the doyenne of British *Odonata*, Cynthia Longfield was a self–educated expert on the dragonfly, penning the classic, *The Dragonflies of the British Isles,* as well as a host of articles on various examples of the species from around the world. An indomitable traveler, Longfield conducted field work and gathered specimens of dragonflies from all corners of the globe in her native Ireland and England, in Africa, the Pacific, South America, and Southeast Asia. The first woman president of the London Natural History Society, she was also the first woman member of the Council of the Entomological Society.

Born Cynthia Evelyn Longfield in 1896 in London's fashionable Belgravia district, Longfield was one of three daughters of Mountifort and Alice Mason Longfield. Heir to a substantial estate in Ireland, Castle Mary in County Cork, Mountifort watched the family fortune slowly slip away. Still, during Longfield's youth, growing up in Ireland and in England, the family led a privileged life. She formed an early love for the outdoors and nature, sporting a butterfly net on her Irish outings. In London, she was only a short walk away from the Natural History Museum, where, in 1913, a separate Department of Entomology was established, reflecting the era's interest in the study of the class *Insecta.*

Travel Leads to a Life in Science

Longfield soon embarked on an independent study of insects, her abiding passion. The death of an early suitor in the First World War led her to choose a profession over having a family, an uncommon life during a time when women were expected to put home and family first. Travel and study became the focus of her life.

Longfield first traveled to Egypt in 1921 and 1922; returning, she found that Castle Mary had been ruined in the Irish Civil War. Longfield, without any definable occupation, soon became a member of the *St. George* expedition to the Pacific. During this time she met Cyril Collenette, another self–taught researcher, who for a time became a second suitor. Ultimately, though the two remained friends for life, they decided against marriage. On this voyage, Longfield also began the meticulous collection of specimens that would become her hallmark. At this juncture her collecting was confined to mosquitoes, beetles, butterflies, and moths. Later during the same expedition she began collecting dragonflies as well.

A Fully Trained Field Entomologist

By the time she returned to England in 1925, Longfield was well trained in entomology, both from her hands–on experience in the field and her extensive readings. Her insect collections were sent to the British Museum of Natural History, where Longfield began to be accepted as an independent researcher. She traveled further, collecting *Odonata* in South America, Southeast Asia, and Canada. Eventually, she became an associate member at the museum, and responsibility for the *Odonata* collection was gradually turned over to her. After that time, her research began to concentrate on specimens from Africa and the British Isles. Longfield also served as president of the London Natural History Society in 1932, and vice president from 1934 to 1936. These were demanding positions that took up much of her time. With publication of *The Dragonflies of the British Isles* in 1937, she was recognized as one of the foremost experts on *Odonata* in the world.

Longfield continued as curator of the museum's *Odonata* collection and pursued her studies through the turbulence of the Second World War. In 1956, at the age of 60, Longfield retired from the museum, leaving London for Park House, a small cottage on the edge of the Castle Mary estate. She continued to travel and to write, however, collaborating on the 1960 book, *Dragonflies,* and attending conferences. Cynthia Longfield died in 1991.

SELECTED WRITINGS BY LONGFIELD:

Books

The Dragonflies of the British Isles. London: Warne, 1937

(With Philip Corbet and Norman Moore) *Dragonflies.* London: Collins, 1960.

Periodicals

"A List of the Odonata of the State of Matto Grosso, Brazil." *Transactions of the Entomological Society of London* 77 (1929): 125–39.

"Two New Species of the Genus *Umma.*" *Stylops* 2 (1933): 139–40.

"Studies on African Odonata, with Synonmy and Descriptions of New Species and Subspecies." *Transactions of the Entomological Society of London* 85 (1936): 467–98.

"The British Dragonflies (Odonata) in 1952 and 1953." *Entomologist* 87 (1954): 87–91.

FURTHER READING

Books

Hayter–Hames, Jane. *Madam Dragonfly: The Life and Times of Cynthia Longfield.* Edinburgh: Pentland Press, 1991.

"Cynthia Longfield." *Stars, Shells and Bluebells: Women Scientists and Pioneers.* Dublin: Women in Technology and Industry, 1997.

Sketch by J. Sydney Jones

Kathleen Lonsdale
1903–1971
English crystallographer

Kathleen Lonsdale was an early pioneer of x–ray crystallography, a field primarily concerned with studying the shapes of organic and inorganic molecules. In 1929, she was the first to prove experimentally that the hexamethylbenzene crystal, an unusual form of the aromatic compound, was both hexagonal and flat in shape. In 1931, she was the first to use Fourier analysis to illustrate the structure of hexachlorobenzene, an even more difficult organic structure to analyze.

In 1945, Lonsdale was the first woman, along with microbiologist Marjory Stephenson, admitted as a fellow to the Royal Society. She was the first female professor at University College, London, the first woman named president of the International Union of Crystallography, and the first woman to hold the post of president of the British Association for the Advancement of Science. She accepted her achievements as a pioneering woman scientist with characteristic humility. In 1966, the "lonsdaleite," a rare form of meteoric diamond, was named for her. According to the *Journal of Chemical Education,* upon learning that

Kathleen Lonsdale (AP/Wide World Photos. Reproduced by permission.)

Clifford Frondel at Harvard University had suggested the name, she wrote to him: "It makes me feel both proud and rather humble that it shall be called lonsdaleite. Certainly the name seems appropriate since the mineral only occurs in very small quantities (perhaps rare would be too flattering) and is generally rather mixed up!"

Lonsdale was born January 28, 1903 in Newbridge, Ireland, a small town south of Dublin. She was the youngest of ten children born to Jessie Cameron Yardley and Harry Frederick Yardley, who was postmaster for the British garrison stationed there. Her father was a heavy drinker, and in 1908, when Kathleen was five years old, her parents were separated. Her mother moved the family moved to Seven Kings, England, a small town east of London. Growing up in England, Kathleen won a scholarship to attend County High School for Girls in Ilford. At the age of 16, she enrolled in Bedford College for Women in London, where in 1922 she received a B.S. in mathematics and physics. She graduated at the head of her class, receiving the highest marks in ten years, and among her oral examiners was William Henry Bragg, the 1915 Nobel Laureate in Physics. He was so impressed with her academic performance that he invited her to work with him and a team of scientists using X–ray technology to explore the crystal structure of organic compounds.

Lonsdale worked with Bragg from 1922 to 1927, first at University College, London, and then at the Royal Institution. During these years she also completed her research for a master's thesis on the structure of succinic acid and related compounds; she published it in 1924, with collaborator William Thomas Astbury, as a theory of space groups that included tables for 230 such groups and mathematical descriptions of crystal symmetries.

Continues Work on the Structure of Crystals

On August 27, 1927, she married Thomas Lonsdale, who was a fellow student of hers. They moved from London to Leeds, where her husband worked for the British Silk Research Association by day and completed his doctoral dissertation on the torsional strengths of metals by night. Lonsdale worked at the University of Leeds, studying the structure of hexamethylbenzene, and in 1929 she produced the first proof of its hexagonal, planar shape. Her discovery was made independently of her colleagues' work in London, and it was supported by Bragg even though it contradicted his own theory that the compound had a "puckered" shape.

In 1930, the Lonsdales returned to London, where her husband had found a permanent post at the Testing Station of the Experimental Roads Department in the Ministry of Transport at Harmondsworth. Between 1929 and 1934, Lonsdale gave birth to their three children; she worked at home during this period, developing formulae for the structure factor tables. These formulas were published in 1936 as "Simplified Structure Factor and Electron Density Formulae for the 230 Space–Groups of Mathematical Crystallography." For the study of ethane derivatives contained in this book, Lonsdale received her doctorate of science.

In 1934, Lonsdale returned to the Royal Institution, where she would work with Bragg until his death in 1942. Upon her return, however, she found that no X–ray equipment was available. Forced to make do with a large electromagnet, Lonsdale undertook experimental work that eventually proved the difference between sigma and pi electronic orbitals, thus establishing the existence of molecular orbitals. She then turned her attentions to the field of thermal vibrations, finding that divergent X–ray beams could be used to measure the distance between carbon atoms.

Lonsdale was made a fellow of the Royal Society in 1945, and in 1946 she founded her own crystallography department at University College, London. In 1949, Lonsdale was named professor of chemistry at the college, her first permanent academic post following years of living from one grant to the next. During these years, she wrote a popular textbook, *Crystals and X–Rays* (1948), and served as editor–in–chief of the first three volumes of the *International X–Ray Tables* (1952, 1959, and 1962). In 1949, Lonsdale began working with South African scientist Judith Grenville–Wells (later Milledge), eventually collaborating with her on a study of diamonds, as well as on studies of minerals at high temperatures and high pressures, and how solid state reactions work. Milledge later became executor of Lonsdale's literary estate. In the 1960s, Lonsdale became fascinated with body stones (in lectures, she was fond of exhibiting an x ray of a bladder stone from Napoleon III), and she undertook extensive chemical and demographic studies of the subject. She retired from University College in 1968.

Lonsdale and her husband were committed pacifists. They became Quakers in 1936 and together worked toward world peace, as well as prison reform. During World War II, she and her husband gave shelter to refugees, and in 1943 Lonsdale spent a month in jail for refusing to register for war duties and then refusing to pay a fine of two pounds. In 1956, she wrote a book in reaction to extensive nuclear testing by the United States, the Soviet Union, and Great Britain. Entitled *Is Peace Possible?,* the book explored the relationship between world peace and world population needs, as viewed through her own experience as the youngest of ten children. Lonsdale was against nuclear weapons of any kind, and she worked tirelessly for world peace.

In 1956, just a day after the first of her ten grandchildren was born, Lonsdale was named a Dame Commander of the Order of the British Empire, and in 1957 she received the Davy Medal of the Royal Society. In 1966, she became the first female president of the International Union of Crystallography, and in 1968 the first woman to hold the post of president of the British Association for the Advancement of Science. Following her husband's retirement from the Ministry of Transport, the Lonsdales moved to Bexhill–on–Sea. On April 1, 1971, she died of cancer in London.

SELECTED WRITINGS BY LONSDALE:

Books

Simplified Structure Factor and Electron Density Formulae for the 230 Space–Groups of Mathematical Crystallography. G. Bell and Sons, 1936.

Crystals and X–Rays. G. Bell and Sons, 1948.

(With N. F. M. Henry) *International Tables for X–Ray Crystallography.* Kynoch Press, Volume 1, 1952, Volume 2, 1959, Volume 3, 1962.

Removing the Causes of War (Swarthmore Lectures), Allen & Unwin, 1953.

Is Peace Possible?, Penguin Books, 1957. (With J. Kasper) *International Tables for X–Ray Crystallography,* Volume 2, Kynoch Press, 1959.

(With C. H. MacGillavry and G. D. Reich) *International Tables for X–Ray Crystallography,* Volume 3, Kynoch Press, 1962.

I Believe (Arthur Stanley Eddington Memorial Lecture), Cambridge University Press, 1964.

(With others) *The University, Technology, and Society,* Heriot–Watt University, 1968.

Periodicals

(With William Thomas Astbury) "Tabulated Data for the Examination of the 230 Space–groups by Homogenous X–Rays." *Philosophical Transactions of the Royal Society* 224A (1924): 221–257.

"The Structure of the Benzene Ring in C6(CH3)6." *Proceedings of the Royal Society* 123A (1929): 494–515.

"Diamonds, Natural and Artificial." *Nature London* 153 (1944): 669–672.

"Human Stones" *Scientific American* 219 (1968): 104–111.

FURTHER READING

Books

Biographical Memoirs of Fellows of the Royal Society. Volume 21, Royal Society (London), 1975, pp. 447–489.

Kass–Simon, G. and P. Farnes, editors, *Women of Science* Indiana University Press, 1990, pp. 355–359.

Periodicals

Julian, Maureen M., "Profiles in Chemistry: Dame Kathleen Lonsdale (1903–1971)." *Journal of Chemical Education* 59 (November, 1982): 965–966.

Mason, Joan, "The Admission of the First Women to the Royal Society of London." *Notes and Records of the Royal Society of London* 46 (1992): 279–300.

Sketch by Mindi Dickstein

Jane Lubchenco
1947–
American marine ecologist

Jane Lubchenco has been active in research and public policy related the environment. Specifically, she studies evolutionary population and community ecology, focusing on experimental marine ecology. The depth and breadth of her scientific work has lead to numerous grants, including the MacArthur Foundation's "genius" grant in 1993. Lubchenco is interested in biodiversity, conservation biology, evolutionary population, and community ecology. In terms of more specific organisms, Lubchenco studies marine and algal ecology, the life histories of algal, plant–herbivore interactions, predator–prey interactions, and the related area of competition.

However, Lubchenco is not only interested in ecology solely for pure scientific study. She is concerned with real-world implementation—the very survival of the earth despite human pollution—and her work has affected research policy. Lubchenco is also concerned with supporting women's ambitions in science, and has published a personal account of how she and her husband, Bruce Menge, have successfully balanced career and family.

Lubchenco was born on December 4, 1947, in Denver, Colorado. Her mother worked as a part–time pediatrician while Lubchenco and her five sisters were young. Watching her mother try to juggle career and family influenced Lubchenco's later decisions about her own career. She earned her undergraduate degree in 1969 from Colorado College.

Lubchenco began her graduate work at the University of Washington, where she earned her M.S. in 1971. That same year she married another ecologist, Bruce Menge. Lubchenco continued her graduate work at Harvard University, where she earned her Ph.D. in ecology in 1975. After graduation, Lubchenco continued to work at Harvard as an assistant professor. In 1976, she began an association with the National Science Foundation working as a Principal Investigator.

Applies for Unique Position

While Lubchenco was at Harvard, she and her husband, who was also a professor in the Boston area, made an important decision about their future. They were thinking about having children and decided they wanted to balance this future family with their jobs. They applied jointly for one, full–time position that they could split, a unique request at the time. In the April 1993 of *BioScience* the couple wrote, "We wanted to have it all but not go crazy in the process. We sought not what later came to be called 'the mommy track,' in which career goals would be sacrificed, nor the so–called 'fast track,' which we were already on and for us would have precluded having sufficient time with our children, but rather what we intended as a 'sane track.' The ideal arrangement seemed to be one in which we could each work part–time but do so in mainstream positions."

Oregon State University was willing to try the experiment, and they were both hired as half–time assistant professors in 1978. They eventually had two sons, Alexei, born in 1979, and Duncan, born in 1982. Throughout the '80s, Lubchenco continued to be active in her field. Concurrently from 1978 on, she was affiliated with the Smithsonian Institution as a research associate. In 1978, she began a relationship with the Ocean Trust Foundation, serving as a science advisor there until 1984. In 1988 she became an associate professor, then a full professor in the Zoology Department. She held a full–time position on her own beginning in 1989. From 1989 until 1992, she served as Chair of the department. While working at Oregon State, Lubchenco continued field research in Panama that she began in 1977, and continued through 1983.

She held many different visiting positions and advisorships. From 1981–88, she was the science advisor in West Quoddy Marine Station. In 1985, she was a visiting professor at Chile's Universidad de Antofagasta; in 1987, she held a similar position at China's Institute of Oceanography. This varied research earned Lubchenco several grants from the Andrew W. Mellon Foundation, from 1989–91, and again in 1993.

Wins "Genius" Grant

In 1991, Lubchenco was a key figure in the Ecological Society of America's Biosphere Initiative. Lubchenco and other scholars published an agenda for future research, emphasizing global change and biological diversity. From 1992–93, she was president of the Ecological Society, after having served as its vice president from 1988–89. This is but one of many honors Lubchenco earned in the '90s. She also earned a fellowship in 1992, when she was named a Pew Scholar in Conservation and the Environment. In 1993, Lubchenco worked as a section coordinator for the United Nations Environmental Program's Global Biodiversity Assessment, and she received an honorary doctorate of science from her alma mater, Colorado College. She also was awarded a John D. & Catherine T. MacArthur fellowship, the so–called "genius" grant, in 1993. In 1995, Lubchenco was elected president of the American Association for the Advancement of Science.

In July 1997 Lubchenco published what could be called a manifesto in *USA Today* magazine. In this article, Lubchenco links science, especially ecology, to the everyday world, and challenges her fellow scientists to reprioritize their "social contract." She also sums up the scope of her own work when she writes, "It no longer is sufficient to talk just about sustainable agriculture, sustainable forestry, or sustainable fisheries. It is the sustainability of the biosphere that is the proper concern. This is an entirely new world."

SELECTED WRITINGS BY LUBCHENCO:

Periodicals

(With Bruce A. Menge) "Split Positions can Provide a Sane Career Track–Personal Account." *BioScience* (April 1993).

"Needed: a New Social Contract with Science." *USA Today Magazine* (July 1997).

"The Role of Science in Formulating a Biodiversity Strategy." *BioScience* (June 1995).

FURTHER READING

Books

Holman, Jill. "Jane Lubchenco." *Notable Women in the Life Sciences: A Biographical Dictionary.* Benjamin F. Shearer and Barbara S. Shearer, eds. Westport, CT: Greenwood Press, 1996, pp. 267–70.

Sketch by Annette Petrusso

Shannon Lucid (Photograph by Joe Skipper. Archive Photos. Reproduced by permission.)

Shannon Ann Lucid
1943–
American astronaut and biochemist

Shannon Lucid made aeronautic history in 1996 when she set the record for the most flight hours in orbit by a woman as well as the international record for the most flight hours in orbit by a non–Russian. During six months that year she flew 75.2 million miles in 188 days, four hours and 14 seconds while orbiting on the Russian Space Station Mir. (The previous female record, 170 days, was set by a Russian cosmonaut.) Lucid has logged a total of 5,354 hours (223 days) in space. For her achievements, Dr. Lucid was awarded the Congressional Space Medal of Honor by President Clinton at the end of 1996, the first and only woman to have earned this prestigious award. Lucid was also awarded the Order of Friendship Medal by Russian President Boris Yeltsin in 1997, one of the highest Russian civilian awards and the highest award that can be presented to a noncitizen.

Lucid was born on January 14, 1943, in Shanghai, to Baptist missionaries Joseph and Myrtle Wells. Most of her first year was spent in a Japanese prison camp, where she would not have survived had not her parents saved their rations to feed her. The family moved back to the United States as part of a prisoner exchange program, then returned to China after the war. When Lucid was six, the family moved to Bethany, Oklahoma, after being forced out of China by the Communists. Her father became an evangelist preacher, giving sermons around the country.

Pursues a Science Career

The family remained in Bethany, where Lucid attended public school, excelling in math and science. After reading about the early pioneers, she decided she wanted to be one, until she realized space was about the only place left to explore. *Biography Today* quotes her as saying, ". . . People thought I was crazy because that was long before America had a space program." In junior high, Lucid discovered a book on Robert Goddard, the father of rocketry, that solidified her future. She decided to follow in his footsteps even though one teacher told her girls were not allowed to be rocket scientists. In eighth grade, Lucid even worked on a science experiment to make her own rocket fuel. During high school, her science teacher, Blanche Moon, did encourage her to pursue a science career. Lucid also became interested in flying at this time, finally earning her private pilot's license at age 20. Later, she earned her commercial, instrument, and multi-engine licenses.

Lucid graduated from Bethany High School in 1960, the second in her class. She received a bachelor of science degree in chemistry from the University of Oklahoma in 1963, the first woman to do so. She remained at the university for a year as a teaching assistant, then became a senior lab technician at the Oklahoma Medical Research Foundation in 1964. She left the foundation in 1966 to work as a chemist for Kerr–Mcgee, where she met her husband, Michael Lucid. They married in 1968 and their first daughter was born about a year later.

Lucid returned to the University of Oklahoma in 1969 to work for the Health Science Center's Department of Biochemistry and Molecular Biology as a graduate assistant. She earned her master of science and doctor of philosophy degrees in biochemistry in 1970 and 1973, respectively. Not even the birth of her second child the day before an important exam could stop Lucid from completing her requirements. Much to her professor's surprise she showed up to take the test. Lucid returned to the Oklahoma Medical Research Foundation in 1974 as a research associate, where she investigated the effect of cancer–causing agents on rats. She remained here until she was selected to join the astronaut candidate training program. Her third child Michael was born in 1976.

From Scientist to Astronaut

In 1978 Lucid was among the first group of women to be selected by NASA for astronaut training. Thirteen women had qualified as Mercury astronauts in the 1960s, but they were not allowed to enter the training program because they were not military pilots. In *Biography Today*, Lucid remarked that after the seven men were selected, "It was incredible, the feeling of anger, because there were no females included in the selection." She along with surgeon Margaret Rhea Seddon, geophysicist Kathryn D. Sullivan, electrical engineer Judtih A. Resnick, physicist **Sally K. Ride**, and physician Anna Fisher were chosen from among 8,000 applicants, 1,500 of them women. A year later, all six women achieved the full rank of astronaut.

Lucid is qualified for assignment as a mission specialist on Space Shuttle flight crews. Some of her technical assignments have included: the Shuttle Avionics Integration Laboratory (SAIL); the Flight Software Laboratory, in Downey, California, working with the rendezvous and proximity operations group; astronaut office interface at Kennedy Space Center, Florida, payload testing, shuttle testing, and launch countdowns; spacecraft communicator (CAPCOM) in the JSC Mission Control Center during numerous Space Shuttle missions; Chief of Mission Support; and Chief of Astronaut Appearances.

On June 17, 1985, Lucid made her first trip into space aboard the space shuttle *Discovery*. During this seven–day mission the crew deployed communications satellites for Mexico (Morelos), the Arab League (Arabsat), and the United States (AT&T Telstar). They used the Remote Manipulator System (RMS) to deploy and later retrieve the SPARTAN satellite, which performed 17 hours of x–ray astronomy experiments while separated from the space shuttle. In addition, the crew activated the Automated Directional Solidification Furnace (ADSF), six Getaway Specials, and participated in biomedical experiments.

Lucid's next space flight occurred on *Atlantis* in October 1989. In this five–day mission during the crew deployed the Galileo spacecraft on its journey to explore Jupiter, operated the shuttle solar backscatter ultraviolet instrument (SSBUV) to map atmospheric ozone, and performed numerous secondary experiments. In August 1991 Lucid returned in *Atlantis* for a nine–day mission during which the crew deployed the fifth tracking and data relay satellite (TDRS–E). The crew also conducted 32 physical, material, and life science experiments, mostly relating to the extended duration orbiter and space station Freedom.

Two years later in November, Lucid spent 14 days in space aboard the space shuttle *Columbia*. She and the crew tested the effects of space flight on the neurological, cardiovascular, metabolic, and musculoskeletal systems of humans and rats. Engineering tests were also conducted. The flight, one of the most successful in NASA's history, also made Lucid the American woman with the most hours in space, 838 total. On this flight, the shuttle orbited the Earth 225 times, traveling 5.8 million miles in 336 hours.

Setting a Space Record

Lucid's involvement with the Mir program began in 1994, when Robert "Hoot" Gibson, then the head of NASA's astronaut office, asked if she were interested in starting full–time Russian–language instruction with the possibility of going to Russia to train for a Mir mission. Lucid said yes even though this did not necessarily mean she would be going to Russia, much less flying on Mir. As she explained in *Scientific American*, "From a personal standpoint, I viewed the Mir mission as a perfect opportunity to combine two of my passions: flying airplanes and working in laboratories . . . For a scientist who loves flying, what could be more exciting than working in a laboratory that hurtles around the earth at 17,000 miles per hour?"

Fortunately, Lucid was eventually selected. After three months of intensive language study, she began training at Star City, the cosmonaut instruction center outside Moscow in January 1995. Every morning she woke at five o'clock to begin studying. Most of the day was spent in classrooms listening to Mir and Soyuz system lectures—all in Russian. In the evenings Lucid continued to study the language and struggled with workbooks written in technical Russian. "I worked harder during that year than at any other time in my life. Going to graduate school while raising toddlers was child's play in comparison," Lucid said in *Scientific American*.

In February 1996, after she had passed all the required medical and technical exams, the Russian spaceflight commission certified Lucid as a Mir crew member. She then traveled to Baikonur, Kazakhstan, to watch the launch of the Soyuz carrying her crewmates—Commander Yuri Onufriyenko, a Russian air force officer, and flight engineer and Yuri Usachev, a Russian civilian—to Mir. Lucid went back to the United States for three weeks of training with the crew of shuttle mission STS–76. On March 22, 1996, she lifted off from the Kennedy Space Center on the shuttle *Atlantis*. Three days later the shuttle docked with Mir, making Lucid the second American astronaut to live aboard the Russian space station as part of a program to study how long–term travel in space affects the human body.

Lucid returned on September 26, 1996, aboard STS–79. Her return was delayed for six weeks while NASA replaced the shuttle's twin booster rockets and bad weather interfered. Assigned as a board engineer 2, she performed 35 life science and physical science experiments, including how protein crystals grow in space and how quail embryos develop in zero gravity. Many of the experiments also provided useful data for the engineers designing the international space station. The results from investigations in fluid physics, for example, help the space station's planners build better ventilation and life–support systems. Research on combustion in microgravity may also lead to improved procedures for fighting fires on the station.

During her stay on Mir, Lucid also spent two hours every day running on a treadmill to counteract the effects of weightlessness, attaching herself to the machine with a bungee cord. This regimen prevented significant weight and muscle loss normally encountered by other astronauts, leaving Lucid in such good physical shape that she was able to walk off the shuttle without assistance.

Though Lucid realized her dream of being a space explorer and will probably be best remembered for her space endurance record, she should also be acknowledged for her other accomplishments. She became a scientist in a time when it was frowned upon, and completed her education while parenting young children. Her research on Mir and other shuttle flights will help future astronauts find space an easier environment to live in. All of these accomplishments earned Lucid the Freedom Forum's highest award, the Free Spirit Award, which she received in 1997 in recognition of her work and accomplishments in the space program.

SELECTED WRITINGS BY LUCID:

Periodicals

"Six Months on Mir." *Scientific American* (May 1998).

FURTHER READING

Books

Biography Today, Scientists and Inventors Series. Edited by Laurie Harris and Cherie Abbey. Vol. 2. Omnigraphics, Inc., 1998, pp 86–97

Periodicals

Lane, Earl. "115 Days on Mir and Still Lucid/Astronaut breaks U.S. spaceflight record." *Newsday* (July 16, 1996): A08

"Astronaut Shannon Lucid to Receive Freedom Forum 'Free Spirit' Award," *U.S. Newswire* (February 13, 1997).

Other

"Biography of Shannon Lucid." www.jsc.nasa.gov/bios/htmlbios/lucid.html

Sketch by Laurel M. Sheppard

Mary Elizabeth (Horner) Lyell

1808–1873

British geologist

The wife of the famous nineteenth–century geologist, Charles Lyell, Mary Horner Lyell was herself an accomplished geologist and conchologist, an expert on the shells of mollusks. Although she collaborated closely with her husband, who was the founder of modern geological science, she has not necessarily received credit for her own contributions to geology.

The eldest of six daughters of geologist Leonard Horner, Mary Lyell was born in London in 1808. She received an excellent education. Her father was a fellow of the Geological Society and later, warden of London University. Her interest in science developed with her marriage to Lyell in 1832, in Bonn, Germany. Charles Lyell had studied with her father, and the first edition of his influential book, *Principles of Geology*, was just being published. This work, which established the antiquity of geological formations, was an essential component for the development of the evolutionary theories of Charles Darwin and Alfred Russel Wallace.

After a honeymoon traveling up the Rhine Valley and through Switzerland and France, the Lyells settled in London. There is scant information about Mary Lyell's specific contributions to her husband's work. She traveled with him throughout Europe and North America, accompanying him on almost all of his geological expeditions. She became an expert in conchology, and her proficiency in French and German enabled her to translate scientific papers. In addition to her assistance in the geological field work, Lyell read scientific works to her husband, whose eyesight was poor, and she handled his voluminous correspondence.

The Lyells' intellectual circle included, in addition to Charles Darwin and his family, many women who were interested in science, particularly natural history. Among these women were Mary Somerville, Charles Lyell's sisters Marianne and Caroline, and Mary Lyell's sister, Lady Frances Bunbury. Charles Lyell's lectures at King's College were so popular among women that the Bishop of London banned women from the lecture halls. Lyell resigned his King's College professorship in protest and moved his lectures to the Royal Institution, which had a more liberal policy toward women. A similar controversy erupted over the presence of women at Lyell's lectures to the Geological Society.

In recognition of his scientific accomplishments, Charles Lyell was knighted in 1848 and made a baronet by Queen Victoria in 1864. In 1872, the Lyells traveled to the Aurignac Cave in the south of France, where human skeletons had been discovered, buried with extinct mammals, including cave–bear, mammoth, and woolly rhinoceros, a discovery which Lyell included in the new edition of his *Antiquity of Man*. The following year, after a short illness, Mary Lyell died, apparently from pneumonia.

FURTHER READING

Books

Lyell, Charles. *Life, Letters and Journals of Sir Charles Lyell Bart.*. Edited by Katherine M. Lyell. 2 vols. London: John Murray, 1881.

Ogilvie, Marilyn Bailey. *Women in Science, Antiquity through the Nineteenth Century: A Biographical Dictionary with Annotated Bibliography*. Cambridge: MIT Press, 1991.

Wilson, Leonard G. "Lyell, Charles." In *Dictionary of Scientific Biography.* Edited by Charles Coulston Gillispie. Vol. 8. New York: Charles Scribner's Sons, 1973.

Sketch by Margaret Alic

Mary Mason Lyon
1797–1849
American educator

Mary Mason Lyon was the founder of Mount Holyoke College, formerly Mount Holyoke Female Seminary, one of the oldest women's colleges in the country. Although not a scientist, Mary Lyon is important to the history of women in science, since she insisted on incorporating a science curriculum that involved laboratory and field work. In establishing Mount Holyoke, Lyon created a real academic environment for women at a time when women's education was considered unimportant. In emphasizing science education for women, Lyon created unprecedented opportunities for women scientists.

Lyon was born in Buckland, Massachusetts, on February 28, 1797, to Aaron and Jemima Lyon. She and her six brothers and sisters lived on the family's 100-acre farm. Aaron Lyon died in 1803, and his widow was left to run the farm on her own with the help of her children. Lyon spent most of her time on the farm doing chores typical of a young girl of the time—everything from baking bread to spinning wool to churning butter. Luckily, her mother also sent her to school, where she proved to be a bright and capable student.

Teaches in One-Room Schoolhouse

Jemima Lyon remarried when Mary was 13 and moved to her new husband's home, leaving her children in charge of the family farm. Mary left school to help out, and her older brother paid her one silver dollar a week for her work. She did this for three years until she was offered a position to teach at a summer school in Shelburne Falls, which bordered Buckland. She was chosen because she was known in the community for her intelligence. She had no formal training as a teacher, but learned quickly on the job. Teaching in a one–room schoolhouse with children of varying ages was not easy work, but Mary found it rewarding enough to want to continue her own education.

This task was easier said than done. Secondary schools for young women were expensive; moreover, they focused mainly on home economics and decorative arts. However, Mary Lyon was determined to succeed. Using a small inheritance and other money she had saved, she began traveling to different schools in the region, where she served as both teacher and student. She earned her room and board by weaving coverlets and blankets. Her interest in science began in 1817 when she was a student at the Sanderson Academy in Ashfield, Massachusetts, where she took courses in geography, geology, and astronomy.

By 1834 she was the assistant principal at the Ipswich Female Seminary. Here she learned to manage a school and began to develop a plan to open up educational opportunities for women. Her idea was to establish an institution of higher learning for women where they could obtain a true academic education. Over the next two years she put together her plan, developing a curriculum, writing circulars to publicize the school, and gaining the support of people who shared her goals and who could secure financial backing. One of her most influential benefactors was the geologist Edward Hitchcock, with whom Lyon had studied some years earlier.

Founds Mount Holyoke Female Seminary

The school was chartered in 1836, and on November 6, 1837 the Mount Holyoke Female Seminary officially opened its doors in South Hadley, Massachusetts. Lyon, who served as the school's first principal, set a rigorous program, including entrance examinations, a three–year course of study, a list of required courses, and the expectation that students would perform the school's domestic work as a cost–saving measure. In return, Lyon made sure that the school was independent (she secured donations of funds and equipment, and refused to affiliate Holyoke with any particular religious or civic group), affordable (tuition was $60 per year, which even families of modest means could afford), and comparable in curriculum to men's schools.

To that end, Lyon required all Holyoke students to take a minimum of seven courses in science and mathematics to graduate, which was unusual for a women's seminary. By now Lyon's particular area of interest was chemistry, she made time to teach chemistry classes despite her administrative responsibilities. Science courses at Holyoke included lab and field work, and Lyon invited important scientists of the day to give lectures. Her emphasis on science inspired many women to continue careers in science, not only as teachers, but researchers as well.

Lyon remained active at Holyoke until her death there on March 5, 1849, just days after her 52nd birthday. But her inspiration survived her for generations; Holyoke trustees and alumna were instrumental in the founding of Wellesley, Mills, and Smith Colleges. Mount Holyoke became a four–year college in 1861, and was chartered by Massachusetts as a college in 1888. It officially became Mount Holyoke College in 1893, and today is considered one of the preeminent colleges in the United States.

FURTHER READING

Books

Green, Elizabeth Alden. *Mary Lyon and Mount Holyoke: Opening the Gates*. Hanover, NH: University Press of New England, 1979.

Rosen, Dorothy Schack. *A Fire in Her Bones, the Story of Mary Lyon*. Minneapolis, MN: Carolrhoda Books, 1994.

Other

"Mary (Mason) Lyon." *Britannica Online.* http.www.eb.com:195 (July 14, 1999).

"Mary Lyon." *Mary Lyon on the Web.* http://www.mtholyoke.edu/marylyon/intro.html (July 14, 1999).

Sketch by George A. Milite

M

Madge Thurlow Macklin
1893–1962
American geneticist

Madge Thurlow Macklin pioneered the field of genetics. Based on her thorough data, Macklin emphasized how important family history of disease—especially for several cancers—was in the diagnosis of patients, and she crusaded to have genetics added to the curriculum of all North American medical schools. Despite these important contributions and perhaps because of her support of eugenics (a medical movement advocating improvement of the species through controlled breeding practices), Macklin was largely unrecognized for her work.

Madge Macklin was born in Philadelphia, Pennsylvania, on February 6, 1893, to William Harrison Thurlow, an engineer, and his wife Margaret De Grofft Thurlow. She had three sisters and one brother. While still young, the family moved to Baltimore, Maryland, where she also received her undergraduate education at Goucher College. She graduated in 1914 with an A.B. Macklin won a fellowship to attend Johns Hopkins medical school. She studied physiology and then went on to the medical school proper at the same institution. While in medical school, she married Charles Macklin in 1918. She was awarded her M.D., with honors, in 1919. She and her husband had three daughters, Carol (born 1919), Sylva (born 1921), and Margaret (born 1927).

After graduation, she and her husband moved to London, Ontario, Canada, where he had an appointment in histology and embryology at Western Ontario University. While her husband was a full professor, she received only part–time, one–year appointments at Western Ontario beginning in 1921, to teach embryology. She also helped teach his histology classes. Though her controversial support of eugenics may have been a factor in her lack of support by the University, it was also nearly unheard of for husband–wife teams to hold academic appointments together.

At Western Ontario, Macklin began her quest to have genetics added to medical school curricula. She supported her point with her carefully conducted research. As a scientist, she valued experiments that were controlled and used sound statistical techniques. Because of her disciplined approach to scientific research, Macklin laid important early groundwork in human genetics and related statistical methodology.

As a genetics researcher, Macklin's most significant studies showed that some cancers—stomach and breast, for example—are affected by both heredity and the environment. This knowledge was an important consideration in cancer prevention. Though her undergraduate alma mater bestowed an honorary degree on her in 1938 for her work, she never taught genetics while at Western.

During her time at Western Ontario, Macklin was also an outspoken supporter of eugenics. She believed eugenics to be another method of preventive medicine. Though eugenics was debunked and considered racist by most scientists by the 1930s, Macklin continued to support it for many years. In 1930, she helped found the Canadian Eugenics Society.

After years of short appointments, Macklin's appointment was not renewed at Western Ontario in 1945. She was immediately hired as a National Research Council Associate at Ohio State University. While her husband continued his work at Western Ontario, Macklin moved to Columbus where she worked as a research associate and lectured on medical genetics. She returned for holidays and vacations to their London home during her appointment. In 1957, she was awarded the American Medical Women's Association's **Elizabeth Blackwell** Medal.

Macklin retired in 1959, and returned to London to care for her ailing husband, who died shortly thereafter. During that same year, she was elected president of the American Society for Human Genetics. She held this post until her death, caused by a heart attack, on March 17, 1962.

SELECTED WRITINGS BY MACKLIN:

Books

The Role of Inheritance in Disease. Baltimore: Williams & Wilkins, Co., 1935.

Periodicals

"The Value of Accurate Statistics in the Study of Cancer." *Canadian Public Health Journal* (1934): 369–73.

FURTHER READING

Books

Bailey, Martha J. "Macklin, Madge Thurlow." *American Women in Science: A Biographical Dictionary.* Denver, Colorado: ABC–CLIO, 1994, p. 228.

Mehler, Barry. "Macklin, Madge Thurlow." *Notable American Women: The Modern Period, A Biographical Dictionary.* Barbara Sicherman & Carol Hurd Green, eds. Cambridge, MA: Belknap Press, 1980, pp. 451–52.

Siegel, Patricia Joan, and Kay Thomas Finley. "Madge Thurlow Macklin." *Women in the Scientific Search: An American Bio–bibliography, 1724–1979.* Metuchen, NJ: The Scarecrow Press, Inc., pp. 242–44.

Periodicals

Soltan, Hubert C. "Madge Macklin–Pioneer in Medical Genetics." *The University of Western Ontario Medical Journal* (October 1962): 6–11.

Sketch by Annette Petrusso

Grace MacLeod
1878–1962
Scottish-American nutritionist

Grace MacLeod is an important American nutritionist, significant in the development of her field. She helped Columbia University become, at least for a time, into one of the premiere institutions for nutrition studies. Her research focused largely on energy metabolism, but also included studies of calcium utilization, protein efficiency, and iron availability. She also was responsible for the education of many nutrition teachers.

MacLeod was born on August 6, 1878, in Rothsay, Scotland, the daughter of Joseph and Jessie (MacGregor) MacLeod. The family emigrated to the United States in 1882 and settled in Cambridge, Massachusetts, where MacLeod attended public schools. While attending Cambridge English High School, one of her teachers, Miss Stickney, awakened MacLeod's interest in chemistry. She took her student to meet Ellen H. Richards, a professor and her future mentor at the Massachusetts Institute of Technology (MIT), which MacLeod entered upon graduation.

At MIT MacLeod won the Marion Hovey Scholarship in her sophomore year, earning the prize in her junior and senior years as well. With Richards's support, she also developed and taught a class in applied chemistry at Boston in her junior year. After earning her bachelor's degree in 1901, MacLeod began a two–year stint teaching college preparatory chemistry, physics, and German at Mt. Hermon School for Boys. From 1903 to 1910 she taught at the Springfield, Massachusetts, Technical High School.

MacLeod moved to New York City in 1910, when she was hired by Pratt Institute's School of Household Sciences and Arts in Brooklyn. She taught chemistry and physics, and developed a reputation as a good teacher. During this period, MacLeod earned her master's degree from Columbia University in 1914, studying under nutrition pioneer Dr. **Mary Swartz Rose**. Her father's death at a young age forced MacLeod to shoulder many responsibilities, such as helping her mother raise her two younger sisters, which delayed her doctorate for another year.

In 1917, MacLeod left Pratt to become the assistant editor for the journal *Industrial and Engineering Chemistry*. Two years later she was hired by the Teachers' College at Columbia University to fill a nutrition instructor position that had been established. MacLeod finally completed her Ph.D. at Columbia in 1924. Her doctoral thesis, "Studies of the Normal Basal Energy Requirements," focused on energy metabolism, a subject she continued to study throughout her career.

After earning her Ph.D. MacLeod was put on the tenure track at Columbia and moved from assistant professor to associate professor, and finally to full professor of nutrition. Though MacLeod often labored in the shadow of her mentor Mary Swartz Rose at Columbia, they were close friends and colleagues whose work complemented the other's. They coauthored articles on such topics as calcium and protein utilization, availability of iron, and the supplementary value of foods, publishing them in such prestigious publications as *Journal of Biological Chemistry*, *Journal of Nutrition*, and *Journal of American Home Economics Association*.

MacLeod's work at Columbia helped establish nutrition as a professional field. The study of nutrition, which was based on biochemistry (unlike home economics, which focused on economics, children, housing, and textiles), nutrition gave women a forum for scientific research when other fields were closed to them. At Columbia MacLeod trained teachers—including those who eventually taught in land–grant university home economics programs, dieticians, and so–called home demonstrators. MacLeod made sure her students met her high scholarly ideals, and refused to accept mediocrity. She was respected by pupils and faculty for her keen judgement and warm personality.

While working at Columbia in the mid–1920s MacLeod was also the cooperating investigator in the nutrition laboratory at the Carnegie Institution in Boston, where she set up a respiration chamber (used to measure metabolism). She was the associate editor of the *Journal of Nutrition* from 1936–39 and served on that publication's editorial board from 1940–45. MacLeod also served on the editorial board of the *Journal of the American Dietetic Association* from 1940–44. She was active in many local organizations as well, and often spoke to community groups. During World War II she chaired the Food and Nutrition Council of Greater New York.

MacLeod retired from Columbia in 1944, and the title of Professor Emeritus of Nutrition was bestowed upon her. In that year, she and Clara Mae Taylor revised the fourth edition of *Foundations of Nutrition*, first published by Mary Swartz Rose. In 1956, MacLeod and Taylor also co–wrote a fifth edition, entitled Foundations of Nutrition. After

MacLeod left, the nutrition program at Columbia was restructured, and within a decade or so the field lost much of the status MacLeod had helped it to gain.

In 1958, MacLeod left New York City and moved to Knoxville, Tennessee where her sister Florence lived. She died on November 16, 1962, after a short illness and was buried in her family's plot at the Cambridge Cemetery, Cambridge, Massachusetts.

SELECTED WRITINGS BY MACLEOD:

Books

(Revised with Clara Mae Taylor) *Rose's Foundations of Nutrition.* 4th ed. New York: MacMillan Company, 1944.

(With Clara Mae Taylor and Mary Swartz Rose) *Foundations of Nutrition,* 5th ed. New York: MacMillan Company, 1956.

Periodicals

"Reminiscences of Ellen H. Richards." *Journal of Home Economics* (December 1942): 705–09.

FURTHER READING

Books

Bailey, Martha J. *American Women in Science.* Denver: ABC–CLIO, 1994, p. 229.

Cattell, Jaques, et al, eds. *American Men of Science: A Biographical Directory.* 10th ed. Vol. L–R. Tempe: The Jacques Cattell Press, Inc., 1961, p. 2601.

Rossiter, Margaret W. *Women Scientists in America: Before Affirmative Action, 1940–72.* Baltimore: Johns Hopkins University Press, 1995, p. 170.

Rossiter, Margaret W. *Women Scientists in America: Struggles and Strategies to 1940.* Baltimore: The Johns Hopkins University Press, 1982, p. 200.

Periodicals

Taylor, Clara Mae. "Grace MacLeod A Biographical Sketch (August 6, 1878–November 16, 1962)." *The Journal of Nutrition* (May 1968): 3–7.

Sketch by Annette Petrusso

Icie Gertrude (Macy) Hoobler
1892–1984
American biochemist

A pioneering American biochemist, Icie Macy Hoobler was one of the first women to head a major research laboratory. She made important contributions in the field of nutrition, particularly the nutrition of pregnant and nursing mothers, infants, and children. Macy's research helped to establish vitamin and mineral requirements for children and adults. She was an early advocate of proper dietary practices and wrote an important book, *Hidden Hunger*, on malnutrition.

Icie Gertrude Macy was born in 1892 on her family's farm near Gallatin, Missouri. She was the third of four children, and the second daughter of Perry and Ollevia Elvaree Critten Macy. Although her parents had received little formal education, they were determined that their children would be well educated. Macy rode her horse to a one–room school until the sixth grade, when she joined her older sister at boarding school. There, Macy was inspired by her biology teacher. However her father was determined that she become a musician and, to please him, she earned an A. B. degree in English and music teacher certification from Central College for Women in Lexington, Missouri, in 1914.

Macy continued her studies at the University of Chicago. There she met Mary L. Sherrill, who was completing her doctorate in chemistry at Chicago in the summers while teaching at Randolph–Macon College. Sherrill, who later became head of the chemistry department at Mount Holyoke College, became Macy's mentor. Despite her limited background in science, Macy earned her B.S. degree in chemistry in 1916 and studied physics with Robert A. Millikan, who won the Nobel Prize in 1923.

Becomes a Biochemist

After graduation, Macy became the first woman graduate teaching assistant in the chemistry department at the University of Colorado in Boulder. Her first year there, she taught inorganic chemistry and worked with Harry A. Curtis. The following year, she taught physiological chemistry at the medical school and studied biochemistry with Robert C. Lewis. Lewis had earned his doctorate at the Sheffield Scientific School of Yale University with Lafayette B. Mendel, a pioneer of biochemistry, or physiological chemistry, as it was then known. Believing that there would be more opportunities for women in biochemistry, Lewis urged Macy to continue her studies with Mendel. After earning her master's degree from Colorado in 1918, Macy arrived at Yale, where she discovered that there were no suitable living arrangements for the few women graduate students.

Although Mendel was primarily interested in proteins and vitamins, Macy's thesis work focused on the nutritional value and toxicity of cotton seed and its products, since cotton seed flour was being substituted for wheat flour due to shortages caused by the first world war. Macy demonstrated that "cotton seed meal injury," which occurred in animals fed cotton seed, was due to a poison, gossypol, present in the plant. In 1920, Macy became the fourth woman to earn a doctorate in physiological chemistry from Yale.

At Mendel's urging, Macy took a position as the staff biochemist at Western Pennsylvania Hospital in Pittsburgh. There, she found that there were no restroom facilities for women and that, as a woman doctor, she was barred from both the doctors' and the nurses' dining rooms. However, in addition to performing clinical laboratory tests and teaching interns, Macy continued to pursue her research interests. She had been inspired by a lecture by Mendel, in which he talked about the unknown composition of mother's milk and stressed that women could make important contributions to nutritional research and studies of childhood malnutrition. Macy began studying the calcium and magnesium levels of human fetuses.

In 1921, Macy presented her first scientific paper, at a Chicago meeting of the Federation of American Societies for Experimental Biology. At that meeting, Agnes F. Morgan, chair of the Department of Household Science at the University of California at Berkeley, offered Macy, who had been ill with measles and kidney disease, a part–time teaching position in food chemistry. However, Macy's teaching load turned out to be very demanding. The following year, Mendel and E. V. McCollum, of Johns Hopkins University, recommended her for the directorship of a new research program, the Nutrition Research Laboratory at the Merrill–Palmer School for Motherhood and Child Development and the Children's Hospital of Michigan in Detroit. Macy would remain there from 1923 until 1954; although in 1931 her laboratory became the Research Laboratory of the Children's Fund of Michigan.

Studies Nutrition and Child Development

The Children's Fund Laboratory produced over 300 research papers and several books during Macy's tenure, and she directed the research efforts of as many as 60 scientists at a time. Graduate students in biological chemistry at the University of Chicago worked in her laboratory, and she directed the doctoral research of a number of women students from Chicago.

The laboratory was involved in a number of long–term studies. Macy's research on female metabolism established the nutritional requirements of pregnant and nursing women and documented the effects of maternal nutrition on children's health, growth, and development. At a time when breast feeding was being superseded by the use of infant formulas, Macy's group studied the vitamin content and immune factors in mothers' milk and the effects of smoking on breast milk. They compared the composition of milk from humans, goats, and cows. Macy's work helped to establish the minimum daily requirements for vitamins B, C, and D, as well as other dietary standards for children, and led to the supplementation of cow's milk. The addition of vitamin D to milk was a major factor in the eradication of rickets, a disease caused by a lack of this vitamin in the diet. The laboratory also carried out studies on the storage of minerals in children's bodies and the effects of diet on recovery from malnutrition.

Macy became an advocate for good nutrition, through her work with the Food and Nutrition Board of the National Research Council, and her laboratory investigated nutrition in Michigan child–care facilities. With Thomas J. Cooley of Children's Hospital, Macy conducted studies on anemia. She carried out other investigations of blood composition and collaborated in studies on the effects of iodine–supplemented salt, demonstrating that iodine stimulated the utilization of calcium in children.

Once Macy was settled in her permanent position at Merrill–Palmer, and had achieved financial security, her two nieces, Helen and Christine, came to live with her. They were the daughters of Macy's older sister, who had died in 1917. In 1938, Macy married a widower, B. Raymond Hoobler, a pediatrician, a professor at Wayne State University, and the former director of the Children's Hospital. Raymond Hoobler died five years later, at the age of 71.

Experiences Discrimination

Macy's salary never approached that of her male counterparts and, as one of the few women in a male–dominated profession, she often experienced discrimination. In 1942, for example, she was invited to speak at a meeting of the Chicago Club; however, when she arrived and the officials realized that she was a woman, they denied her admittance. Only after a great deal of negotiation by her husband, and a vote by the board of trustees, was she allowed to speak at the meeting.

Despite frequent professional slights, Macy won 22 awards over the course of her career, including the 1946 Garvan Medal of the American Chemical Association, an annual award given to an outstanding American woman chemist. Earlier, she had been the first woman to be elected chair of both a division (biochemistry) and a local section of the Chemical Society. She received honorary doctorates from Wayne State University in 1945 and from Grand Valley State College in 1971. Macy was active in at least 20 professional societies. She was a fellow of the American Association for the Advancement of Science and the American Institute of Chemists. A charter member of the American Institute of Nutrition, she served as its president in 1944. She was on the editorial board of the *Journal of the American Dietetic Association*, and she was the first woman member of the Detroit Engineering Society. Macy also was active in Iota Sigma Pi, a national honor society for women chemists, helping to establish early chapters at the University of Colorado and at Yale, and later, running a job placement service for women chemists.

When the Children's Fund ended after 25 years, Macy received funding to return to the Merrill–Palmer Institute, where she remained until her retirement in 1959. She continued to serve as a consultant there until 1974, although she built a home in Ann Arbor, Michigan. Macy returned to Gallatin, Missouri in 1982, where she died two years later.

SELECTED WRITINGS BY MACY HOOBLER:

Books

Nutrition and Chemical Growth in Childhood. 3 vols. Springfield, IL: Charles C. Thomas, 1942–51.

(With H. H. Williams) *Hidden Hunger.* Lancaster, PA: Jaques Cattell Press, 1945.

(With H. J. Kelly and R. E. Sloan) *The Compositions of Milks.* National Research Council – National Academy of Sciences, publication no. 254. Washington, D.C.: National Academy of Sciences, 1953.

(With H. J. Kelly) *Chemical Anthropology: A New Approach to Growth in Children.* Chicago: University of Chicago Press, 1957.

(With H. H. Williams and A. G. Williams) *Boundless Horizons: Portrait of a Woman Scientist.* Smithtown, NY: Exposition Press, 1982.

Periodicals

(With J. B. Eckley) "Sensitiveness of Some Cyanide Reactions." *Proceedings of the Colorado Scientific Society* 11 (1918): 269.

"Nutrition During Pregnancy and Lactation." *Modern Medicine* (April 1955): 79–84.

"Metabolic and Biochemical Changes in Normal Pregnancy." *Journal of the American Medical Association* 168 (1958): 2265–71.

FURTHER READING

Books

Cavanaugh, Margaret A. "Icie Gertrude Macy (1892–1984)." In *Women in Chemistry and Physics: A Biobibliographic Sourcebook*, edited by Louise S. Grinstein, Rose K. Rose, and Miriam H. Rafailovich. Westport, CT: Greenwood Press, 1993.

Stimson, Nancy F. "Icie Gertrude Macy Hoobler." In *Notable Women in the Physical Sciences: A Biographical Dictionary*, edited by Benjamin F. Shearer and Barbara S. Shearer. Westport, CT: Greenwood Press, 1997.

Periodicals

Koppert, S. J. "Icie Macy Hoobler: Pioneer Woman Biochemist." *Journal of Chemical Education* 65 (1988): 97–98.

Williams, H. H. "Icie Macy Hoobler." *Journal of Nutrition* 114 (1984): 1351–62.

Sketch by Margaret Alic

Ada Isabel Maddison

1869–1950

English mathematician

In spite of her accomplishments and education, Ada Isabel Maddison remained a shy woman throughout her life. In fact, while serving as an assistant at Bryn Mawr to President M. Carey Thomas in 1913, she received a note from Thomas invoking her to "[Speak] distinctly. When you get embarrassed, your voice gets lower and lower. I am sure the Faculty thinks it is shyness, as it is. You must conquer it."

Maddison was born on April 13, 1869, in Cumberland, England. Her parents were John and Mary Maddison. She took college preparatory courses at Miss Tallies School in Cardiff, South Wales, then entered the University of South Wales where she studied from 1885 to 1889. After leaving the University of South Wales she attended Girton College, Cambridge, for another three years. While at Girton she met and befriended Grace Chisholm Young, the first woman to receive a doctorate in Germany.

During their first year at Girton, both women attended a lecture given by Arthur Cayley, a mathematician who played a central role in founding the modern British school of pure mathematics and author of more than 900 published articles addressing almost every aspect of modern mathematics. Later, while at Bryn Mawr attending graduate lectures, Maddison studied Cayley's papers on modern algebra.

Maddison succeeded at passing the examinations of the Honour School at Oxford in 1892, and in the same year passed the Cambridge Mathematical Tripos Examination, first class. The examination was equivalent to the highest class of honors at Cambridge, 27th Wrangler, but the accomplishment did little to secure a degree since Maddison was not allowed to receive one.

Between 1892 and 1893 Maddison attended lectures given by Dr. **Charlotte Angas Scott** at Bryn Mawr. During the same time, she began her investigation into the singular solutions of differential equations, which was later published in 1896 in the *Quarterly Journal of Pure and Applied Mathematics* in 1896. Scott was sufficiently impressed by Maddison to write: "[She] has a powerful mind and excellent training." In acknowledgment of Scott's teaching skill, Maddison wrote an article on her for the *Bryn Mawr Alumnae Bulletin* in January 1932 entitled "Charlotte Angas Scott: An Appreciation."

In 1893, Maddison received her Bachelor of Science degree with Honours from the University of London. She was also given a resident mathematics fellowship at Bryn Mawr for the 1893–1894 school year. In 1895, she became the first person awarded the Mary E. Garrett Fellowship by Bryn Mawr to be used for study abroad. Maddison chose to attend the University of Göttingen, where she renewed her acquaintance with Grace Chisholm Young and met Annie Louis MacKinnon, who in 1894 had received her Ph.D. in mathematics from Cornell University. Both Maddison and MacKinnon were elected to the American Mathematical Society in 1897. Maddison concentrated on the lectures of Felix Klein, author of the *Erlanger Programm*, and David Hilbert, considered the greatest influence on geometry since Euclid. These lectures must have had an impact on Maddison because her field of specialization became algebraic geometry. In 1896, she published a translation of Felix Klein's work, "The Arithemitizing of Mathematics," in the *Bulletin of the American Mathematical Society*.

Mathematician Turned Administrator

Maddison completed the work for her Ph.D. at Bryn Mawr and received the degree in 1896. Her dissertation was entitled "On Singular Solutions of Differential Equations of the First Order in Two Variables, and the Geometric Properties of Certain Invariants and Covariants of Their Complete Primitives." Concurrent with her studies, Maddison acted as assistant secretary to the president of Bryn Mawr. She then stepped into the dual role of reader in mathematics and secretary to the president, serving both positions for more than seven years. In 1904, she again accepted the tasks associated with two positions, becoming an associate professor and assistant to the president.

Although Maddison had never studied in Dublin, she was awarded a B.A. degree by the University of Dublin in 1905. That university was the first to award degrees to women in the British Isles. The degree was conferred on Maddison based on her work at Girton College.

Between 1910 and 1926, when she retired from teaching, Maddison remained the assistant to the president and jointly held the administrative position of Recording Dean. These duties left her little time for mathematics or research, which must have given her some cause for regret because in 1937 she wrote, "I confess to feeling ashamed of having deserted mathematics for a less rarified atmosphere of work among people and things." She always considered mathematics "the most perfect of the sciences" and felt that her loyalty remained steadfast with the discipline.

In 1897 Maddison became a member of the Daughters of the British Empire and in the same year she was elected to the American Mathematical Association. Maddison also joined the London Mathematical Society and remained a member throughout her lifetime. In spite of her considerable responsibilities as an administrator, Maddison found time to aid in the compilation of a study on women who had graduated from college. The study dealt with such issues as marriage, children, and occupations.

After her retirement from Bryn Mawr, Maddison returned to England. After a time she came back to Pennsylvania, and it was there that she died in 1950. Upon her death, Bryn Mawr was bequeathed ten thousand dollars, with instructions that the gift is used for nonfaculty members as a pension fund in honor of the woman with whom she had such a long working relationship, President M. Carey Thomas.

SELECTED WRITINGS BY MADDISON:

"On Certain Factors of C– and P–Discriminants and Their Relation to Fixed Points on the Family of Curves." In *Quarterly Journal of Pure and Applied Mathematics* 26 (1893): 307–21.

"Note on the History of the Map Coloring Problem." In *Bulletin of the American Mathematical Society* 3 (1897): 257.

Handbook of Courses Open to Women in British, Continental, and Canadian Universities 1896; supplement 1897; Second edition 1899; supplement 1901.

FURTHER READING

Books

Whitman, Betsy S. "Ada Isabel Maddison." In *Women of Mathematics*. Edited by Louise S. Grinstein and Paul J. Campbell. Westport, CT: Greenwood Press, 1987, pp. 144–46.

Periodicals

Whitman, Betsy S. "Women in the American Mathematical Society before 1900." *Association for Women in Mathematics Newsletter* 13, no. 5 (September–October 1893): 7–9.

Williams, Mary. "Ada Isabel Maddison." (Handwritten manuscript, 5 pp. n.d.) The Mary Williams Collection, Schlesinger Library, Radcliffe College, Cambridge, Massachusetts.

Other

"Ada Isabel Maddison." *Biographies of Women Mathematicians*. http://www.scottlan.edu/lriddle/women/chronol.htm (August 1997).

Sketch by Kelley Reynolds Jacquez

Michelle Ann Mahowald (Photograph by Joan Mahowald. Reproduced by permission.)

Michelle Anne Mahowald
1963–1996
American neuromorphic engineer

Dr. Michelle "Misha" Mahowald was an internationally recognized expert in the emerging field of neuromorphic engineering, which uses analog very large scale integrated (VLSI) circuit technology and silicon models to make devices that mimic the functioning of biological neural systems. In 1992, she became the first woman at the California Institute of Technology (Caltech) to receive the Clauser Prize, for her Ph.D. thesis in computational neuroscience awarded for work that demonstrates the potential of opening new avenues of human thought and endeavor. Only two years later, she was one of six women scientists to be featured in thea PBS documentary, "Discovering Women." Mahowald was inducted into the Women in Technology International (WITI) Hall of Fame in 1996, six months before her untimely death.

Mahowald was born on September 12, 1963, in Minneapolis, and at the age of two weeks was adopted by Joan Fischer Mahowald and Alfred Mahowald. She also has an adopted sister Sheila Marie who was adopted two years later; Sheila's daughter, Emily Michelle, is Misha's godchild. Mahowald showed an early aptitude for math, which was encouraged by her teachers at St. Helena Elementary School in Minneapolis. In junior high, Mahowald was sent to Holy Angels High School to take advanced math classes. During her childhood, she loved watching *Star Trek* with her family, because she dreamed of becoming an astronaut.

Mahowald attended a girl's Catholic high school, Derham Hall, in Highland Park near St. Paul, Minnesota and graduated from there in 1981. At Derham, she was also encouraged to take evening math classes at the University of Minnesota. During high school she was elected to the National Honor Society and received several awards for her achievements in science including a Recognition of Creativity Certificate from the Science Encouragement Committee of 3M and the Bausch and Lomb Honorary Science Award. She scored in the upper 3% of the SAT test. In addition to math, Mahowald showed talent in art and writing and loved gymnastics and dance. She admired Russian dancer Mikhail Baryshnikov, led her to adopt Misha as her nickname.

During high school, a close friend's father—who was a professor at a local university—recommended she attend Caltech or the Massachusetts Institute of Technology (MIT). Because MIT misplaced her early admission papers, she enrolled at Caltech. Mahowald first majored in astrophysics but decided to switch to biology. She excelled in this subject under the direction of her research mentor, Professor Carver Mead. She received a B.S. degree in biology in 1985, with a specific interest in the physics of nervous systems.

While doing her graduate work at Caltech under Mead, Mahowald became interested in electronics and helped develop the silicon retina a set of neuromorphic chips that could compute the depth of an object from a binocular image. Mahowald also earned four patents for the silicon retina work and later published a book based on this work. In 1991, in conjunction with researcher Rodney Douglas at Oxford University, she developed a silicon neuron with electrical properties very similar to biological neurons that could be used for building large, biologically realistic neural networks. A prototype chip containing five-silicon neurons was eventually developed. This work was featured in the prestigious science journal *Nature*, which said the silicon neuron could emerge as the technology of choice for modeling the nervous system. The neuron research formed the basis of subsequent research for which she earned her the doctorate in 1992.

In June of 1992, Mahowald joined the MRC Anatomical Neuropharmacology Unit at Oxford to work with scientists Kevin Martin and Rodney Douglas on analog VLSI models of microcircuits of the visual cortex. The three scientists later moved to the University of Zurich to establish the Institute für Neuroinformatick. While there, Mahowald and another colleague developed a neuromorphic sensory–motor integrated circuit that could be used to control an autonomous vehicle. In 1996 Mahowald attended a National Science Foundation workshop on the synergistic neuroscience and mathematics/physics/engineering approaches for understanding information processing in biological and artificial intelligent systems in Arlington, Virginia.

Mahowald was killed in a train accident on December 26, 1996, in Zurich. Though her life may have ended suddenly, her work continues to inspire scientists around the world. The Institute für Neuroinformaticks, under the direction of Dr. Martin, Dr. Douglas, and a team of 20 scientists, continues her research. Mahowald believed this is what science is all about. Her mother recalls in a letter that "Michelle once told me she loved science because scientists learned from others and built upon their work. She hoped not so much to concentrate on commercial products but more on discoveries that could build knowledge in the scientific world."

SELECTED WRITINGS BY MAHOWALD:

Books

An Analog VLSI System for Stereoscopic Vision. Kluwer Academic Publishing, 1994

Scientific Papers

(With Marinus Maris) "Neuromorphic Sensory–Motor Mobile Robot Controller with Attention Mechanism." AI Lab, Department of Computer Science, University of Zurich, Winterthurstr 190, CH–8057. Zurich, Switzerland

FURTHER READING

Periodicals

Hopper, Laurence. "Scientists Produce Electronic Device to Mimic Brain." *Wall Street Journal* (December 19, 1991).

Wilder, Clinton. "Recreating the Human Brain Cell." *Computer World* (January 27, 1992).

Other

Letter from Joan Mahowald to Laurel Sheppard, July 1999.

Sketch by Laurel M. Sheppard

Maud Worcester Makemson
1891–1977
American astronomer

Maud Makemson (Photograph by Margaret Brown. Vassar College Libraries. Reproduced by permission.)

Maud Makemson was known for her research on astrodynamics and celestial mechanics. The author of publications on Polynesian astronomy, navigation, and the Mayan calendar, she also coauthored a textbook on astrodynamics and was a consultant for General Dynamics, researching how astronauts could orient themselves on the moon without radar or radio.

Maud Lavon Worcester was born on September 16, 1891, in Center Harbor, New Hampshire, to Ira Eugene Worcester and Fannie Malvina (Davisson) Worcester. The men of her family were seamen, and Makemson always loved the water. She graduated from the Girls' Latin School in Boston, where she was first introduced to astronomy. After high school, she attended Radcliffe College for a year as a classics major before teaching school for a year and then moving with her family to Pasadena, California in 1911. There she met and married Thomas Emmet Makemson in 1912, becoming a mother of three before divorcing seven years later.

To support her children, Makemson worked at a variety of jobs. She became a newspaper reporter as well as a public school teacher. During this time she published a couple of stories and had two original plays produced. But in May of 1921, the course of her life changed forever. She was able to view the aurora borealis just outside of Phoenix, and was so dazzled that she matriculated to the University of California, Berkeley, to pursue her A.B. degree in astronomy, which she received in 1925, following a year as the Phoebe Hearst scholar and assistant in astronomy. Makemson received her A.M. degree in 1927 and her Ph.D. in 1930. While a student she was a research assistant and an instructor.

After completing her degrees, Makemson joined the faculty of Rollins College as assistant professor of astronomy and math, but in 1932 she joined Vassar College, where she remained until 1957, when she retired at the rank of professor, chairman of the astronomy department, and director of the college observatory. She was known to welcome and encourage scouts and schoolchildren from the area who wanted to visit the observatory.

While at Vassar, Makemson wrote a voluminous number of scientific papers, and became a consultant to many individuals and groups. She also wrote two important books in the field. *The Morning Star Rises*, published in 1941, explained Polynesian astronomy and navigation. In the course of her research on the book, she traveled to Hawaii to research an ancient star map. This made headlines at the time because a bicentennial celebration planned for King Kamehameha's birth would have to be postponed several years, due to her discoveries during the research. Makemson also gave navigation courses at Vassar and attended conferences.

Her next book publication, the 1951's *The Book of the Jaguar Priest*, was written with the help of a Guggenheim fellowship. Her research involved the translation of the ancient "Book of the Chilam Balam of Tizimin." This manuscript was one of the few surviving texts of the Maya Indian tribes of Yucatan. Makemson discovered in her study of this sacred text a correlation between the Mayan, Julian, and Gregorian (Christian) calendars, which had been a mystery for hundreds of years. Her work solved the riddle and further added to her fame and respect.

Due to her success and scholarship, she was awarded a Fulbright fellowship to teach astronomy at Ochanomizu Women's University in Tokyo, Japan, during 1953 and 1954. Makemson became in demand as a lecturer and speaker at astronomical conferences in many regions. She was a member of Phi Beta Kappa, Sigma Xi, the American Astronomical Society, the American Institute of Aeronautics and Astronautics, and a fellow of the Association of Variable Star Observers and the American Association for the Advancement of Science. In addition to her other research and academic responsibilities, Makemson studied the orbits of planets, including one named for Vassar and another named for the first observatory director, **Maria Mitchell**. In her free time, Makemson enjoyed exploring, once participating in excavation of an Apache Indian site in Arizona.

After retirement from Vassar, Makemson went to UCLA as a research astronomer and lecturer, where she coauthored a textbook on astrodynamics. During this time she also consulted for Consolidated-Lockheed. But in 1964, Makemson moved to Ft. Worth, Texas, to be near her only surviving child, Donald. In Texas, she consulted for the Applied Research Laboratories of General Dynamics, researching how astronauts could orient themselves on the moon without radar or radio. She also began work on a translation of a 1645 Latin astronomy system, which she continued until her death on December 25, 1977 in Weatherford, Texas. Vassar College now sponsors the Maud Makemson Memorial Fund.

SELECTED WRITINGS BY MAKEMSON:

Books

The Morning Star Rises. New Haven: Yale University Press, 1941.

The Book of the Jaguar Priest. Henry Schuman, Incorporated, 1951.

FURTHER READING

Books

Block, Maxine, ed. *Current Biography*. New York: H. W. Wilson, 1941.

Other

Makemson, Maud. Biographical File. Vassar College Archives. Poughkeepsie, NY.

Sketch by Helene Barker Kiser

Harriet Florence (Mylander) Maling
1919–1987
American pharmacologist

Harriet Maling is recognized for her work in pharmacology, particularly cardiovascular and autonomic drugs. She was head of the physiology section in the chemical pharmacology laboratory at the National Heart and Lung Institute of the National Institutes of Health.

Harriet Mylander was born on October 2, 1919, in Baltimore, Maryland, where she spent all of her childhood and teenage years. While a college student at Goucher College, she owned rental property in the Baltimore area, which provided for her education. When Maling graduated in 1940 with her A.B. degree, she stated, "I am planning on a career which requires an unusual number of different fields — biology, medical sciences, chemistry, physics, mathematics, and psychology. I am anxious to lay a firm foundation for research work in biophysics."

Begins Work in Pharmacology

The following year, she attended Radcliffe College, intending to study biophysics. She soon switched her

Harriet Mylander Maling (Radcliffe College Archives. Reproduced by permission.)

interest to medical science and physiology and applied to Johns Hopkins Medical School. During the last year of her schooling there, her interest now firmly in pharmacology, Maling received a fellowship from the American Association of University Women. In 1944, she graduated from Radcliffe with her Ph.D. Her dissertation was entitled "The Inhibition of Spinal and Bulbar Reflexes in Mammals."

On September 1, 1943, Maling married Henry Forbes Maling, a member of the Naval Academy staff. They had four children—Joan, Walter, Anne, and Charles—within five years. While raising children, Maling continued her research work.

In 1944, Maling took a position as an assistant pharmacologist and, later, as an instructor at Harvard Medical School. From 1951 to 1954 she worked for George Washington University as assistant professor and as assistant research professor for the medical school. In 1954 she accepted a position at the National Institutes of Health as a pharmacologist in the National Heart and Lung Institute. Here she began her research in cardiovascular and autonomic drugs. Her work was so successful that she was appointed head of the section on physiology in the Laboratory of Chemical Pharmacology.

Maling wrote dozens of scientific papers and was a member of many professional organizations. She was a member of Phi Beta Kappa, the American Association for the Advancement of Science, the American Society for Pharmacology and Experimental Therapeutics, the Society of Experimental Biology, the New York Academy of Science, and the American Association of University Women. She was also a member of the editorial board for a technical professional journal. Maling died on March 15, 1987, in Peabody, Massachusetts.

SELECTED WRITINGS BY MALING:

Periodicals

"Fatigue of the depressor reflex." *American Journal of Physiology* 142 (1944).

(With Otto Krayer). "The action of the erythrophleum alkaloids upon the isolated mammalian heart." *Journal of Pharmacology and Experimental Therapy* 86 (1946).

(With P.A. Shore, V.H. Cohn, and B. Highman). "Distribution of norepinephrine in the heart." *Nature* 181 (1958).

(With W.M. Butler, M.G. Horning, and B.B. Brodie) "The direct determination of liver triglycerides." *Journal of Lipid Research* 2 (1961).

FURTHER READING

Books

Bailey, Martha J. *American Women in Science.* Denver: ABC–CLIO, 1994.

Other

Special Collections Archives. Radcliffe College.

Sketch by Helene Barker Kiser

Vivienne Malone-Mayes
1932–1995
American mathematics educator

Vivienne Lucille Malone–Mayes was a prominent mathematics educator who taught at Baylor University in Waco, Texas, for nearly three decades. As a black woman who grew up in a segregated society, she was a pioneer in her field and an inspiration for younger students. Malone–Mayes was the fifth African American woman to receive a doctorate in pure mathematics in the United States, and she was the first black full–time professor at Baylor.

Malone–Mayes was born on February 10, 1932, in Waco, Texas. Her father, Pizarro Ray Malone, was a visiting teacher in the Waco public schools for many years and also worked for the Urban Renewal Agency. Her mother, Vera Estelle Allen Malone, was a junior high school teacher. It is little wonder, then, that education was stressed in their home. Malone–Mayes later recalled that the only lie her parents ever encouraged her to tell was about her age when she started school. She was only five years old, but her parents told her to say she was six so that she would beadmitted. Always an excellent student, Malone–Mayes graduated from her racially segregated high school in 1948 at age 16.

Leaving her home in Waco, Malone–Mayes traveled to Nashville, Tennessee, where she became a student at Fisk University. Her first ambition was to be a physician. However, she changed that goal after meeting her future husband, James Jeffries Mayes, a dental student. He convinced her that two doctors in the same family would never see each other, so Malone–Mayes switched her major from pre–med to mathematics. She received a B.A. degree in 1952. On September 1 of that year, she and Mayes were married.

Two years later, Malone–Mayes received an M.A. degree in mathematics, also from Fisk University. She promptly moved back to Waco, where she became chairperson of the math department at Paul Quinn College and her husband opened a dental practice. Malone–Mayes eventually spent seven years at Paul Quinn. She later chaired the math department at Bishop College in Dallas for a year. She and her husband had one daughter, Patsyanne. The couple divorced in 1985.

A Career Filled with Firsts

By 1961, Malone–Mayes was eager to refresh her education and she applied to Baylor University. Her application was rejected on grounds of race. She turned instead to the University of Texas at Austin, which had already been required by federal law to desegregate. Malone–Mayes endured much emotional stress and social ostracism as a black female graduate student. She later recalled that many classmates liked to gather at a cafe that would not serve blacks; the closest she came to joining them was marching in picket lines protesting the cafe's policy. For her thesis topic, Malone–Mayes chose "A Structure Problem in Asymptotic Analysis." In 1966, she received a Ph.D. from the University of Texas, making her the second black, and the first black woman, to earn a doctorate in math from that institution.

Malone–Mayes was immediately hired as a professor by Baylor, the same university that had rejected her as a student just five years before. She remained in that position until 1994, when she was forced to retire due to ill health. During her years as a professor, Malone–Mayes continued to break racial barriers, becoming the first African American elected to the executive committee of the Association for Women in Mathematics. She also served on the board of directors of the National Association of Mathematicians, a group oriented toward the black community. In 1988, she participated in a panel featuring prominent female mathematicians that was part of the American Mathematics Society's Centennial Celebration in Providence, Rhode Island.

Malone–Mayes had an active life outside of academia. For many years she served as youth choir director and organist at her local Baptist church. She also volunteered for a number of charitable organizations, and she served as advisor for a traditionally black sorority at Baylor. Her last years were marred by health problems, however. She was plagued by lupus, a chronic inflammatory disease that can damage multiple systems of the body. On June 9, 1995, Malone–Mayes died of a heart attack in Temple, Texas. In an obituary in the *Association for Women in Mathematics Newsletter*, **Etta Falconer** and Lee Lorch wrote of their friend and colleague: "With skill, integrity, steadfastness and love she fought racism and sexism her entire life, never yielding to the pressures or problems which beset her path. She leaves a lasting influence."

SELECTED WRITINGS BY MALONE-MAYES:

Books

(With Howard Rolf) *Pre-calculus,* 1977.

FURTHER READING

Periodicals

Falconer, Etta and Lee Lorch. "Vivienne Malone–Mayes: In Memoriam." *Association for Women in Mathematics Newsletter* (November–December 1995).

Simpson, Elizabeth. "'You Had to Make It All Alone': Black Baylor Teacher Recalls Road to Success." *Waco Tribune–Herald* (August 22, 1988): 1A, 3A.

Other

Falconer, Etta, Dr., and Dr. Lee Lorch. "Vivienne Malone–Mayes: In Memoriam." *Biographies of Women Mathematicians.* June 1997. http://www.scottlan.edu/lriddle/women/chronol.htm (July 22, 1997).

Miscellaneous newspaper clippings and press releases. The Texas Collection, Baylor University Library, Waco, TX.

Sketch by Linda Wasmer Smith

Margaret Eliza Maltby
1860–1944
American physicist

Margaret Maltby was one of the first professional women physicists and one of the first women to earn a Ph.D. in physics. During her almost 30 years at Barnard College, Maltby influenced a generation of American women scientists. As chair of the fellowship committee of the American Association of University Women (AAUW), she promoted the scientific careers of many women.

Born on her family's farm in Bristolville, Ohio, Maltby was the youngest child of Lydia Jane (Brockway) and Edmund Maltby. Her sisters, 15 and 11 at the time of her birth, called her Minnie, a name she hated and, as an adult, Maltby changed her name to Margaret. Interested in both art and science, Maltby spent a year in preparatory school at Oberlin College in Ohio, before entering college there. She graduated from Oberlin in 1882 and moved to New York City to study at the Art Students' League. A year later she returned to Ohio to teach high school. In 1887 Maltby moved to Boston, where she taught physics at Wellesley College, while earning her second bachelor's degree in chemistry and physics at the Massachusetts Institute of Technology (MIT). In 1891, she earned her master's degree from Oberlin and began graduate studies at MIT.

In 1893, Maltby was awarded a research fellowship for study at Göttingen University in Germany. She arrived there at about the same time as two other women who also held fellowships from the Association of Collegiate Alumnae, the mathematicians Grace Chisholm Young and Mary Winston Newson. The three women found rooms at a boarding house and applied to the Minister of Education for permission to attend lectures. Although they received permission they requested, they were advised that, as women, they would not be allowed to work for degrees. Nevertheless, in 1895 Maltby became the first American woman to receive a Ph.D. from Göttingen, for her dissertation on the physical chemistry of conductivity. Maltby remained at Göttingen for another year on a postdoctoral fellowship, before returning to Wellesley where she headed the physics department for one year. She spent another year teaching mathematics and physics at Lake Erie College in Painesville, Ohio.

Maltby returned to Germany to work as a research assistant with her postdoctoral advisor, Friedrich Kohlrausch, who had become president of the Physikalisch–Technische Reichsanstalt in Charlottenburg. Her work there, measuring electrical conduction in basic solutions of chlorides and nitrates, appeared in *Wissenschaftliche Abhandlungen*, the Reichsanstalt's publication, in 1899 and 1900.

Back in the United States in 1899, Maltby spent a year as a researcher in theoretical physics with A. G. Webster at Clark University, before beginning her long career at Barnard College in New York City, first as a chemistry instructor, and after 1903, as professor of physics. Although from 1913 until her retirement, Maltby was chair of the physics department, her promotions came slowly and without salary increases. She was 52 before she became an associate professor. Margaret Rossiter quoted from Maltby's chapter in a book on careers for women: "There seems to be no prejudice against a woman, if she can do the work as well as or better than a man. It is difficult to be specific, for such opportunities have been open to women so few years . . . Perhaps the conservative academic world is more imbued with the idea of women's limitations in this direction than the industries, for it has been difficult for women to get full professorships in the department of physics." However at the time, there were no employment opportunities for women physicists outside of teaching positions at women's colleges.

Although her career as a teacher and administrator left little time for research, Maltby was a dedicated instructor and her reputation as a physicist already was firmly established. In 1906 she was one of 150 physicists, and the only woman physicist, to be starred in the first edition of *American Men of Science*, indicating that her colleagues judged her to be one of the most important American scientists in her field. Maltby actively sought graduate and postdoctoral fellowships for her women students. For many years, she served as chair of the fellowship committee of the AAUW, and in 1929 she published a history of their fellowships with biographies of the awardees. In 1926, the AAUW established the Margaret E. Maltby Fellowship in her honor. Shortly before her retirement in 1931, Maltby introduced what is thought to have been the first course in the physics of music.

Maltby never married. In fact, Barnard College barred married women from its faculty. In 1906 Maltby had intervened, unsuccessfully, on behalf of **Harriet Brooks,** a physics instructor who was told that she would lose her position when she married. In 1901, Maltby adopted Philip Randolph Meyer, the orphaned son of a close friend. In her later years, Maltby suffered from debilitating arthritis and she died in 1944.

SELECTED WRITINGS BY MALTBY:

Books

"Methode zur Bestimmung grosser elektroylytischer Widerstände." *Zeitschrift für Physikalische Chemie.* Göttingen, 1895.

"The Physicist." In *Careers for Women.* Edited by Catherine Filene. Boston: Houghton–Miflin, 1920.

(American Association of University Women, Committee on Fellowships) *History of the Fellowships Awarded by the American Association of University Women, 1888–1929.* New York: Columbia University Press, 1929.

FURTHER READING

Books

Ogilvie, Marilyn Bailey. *Women in Science, Antiquity through the Nineteenth Century: A Biographical Dictionary with Annotated Bibliography.* Cambridge: MIT Press, 1991.

Rossiter, Margaret W. *Women Scientists in America: Struggles and Strategies to 1940.* Baltimore: The Johns Hopkins University Press, 1982.

Wiebusch, Agnes Townsend. "Margaret Eliza Maltby." In *Notable American Women 1607–1950: A Biographical Dictionary.* Edited by Edward T. James, Janet Wilson James, and Paul W. Boyer. Cambridge: Harvard University Press, 1971.

Sketch by Margaret Alic

Ines Mandl
1917–
Austrian-American biochemist

Ines Mandl's research in enzymes and elastic tissue provided important insights into the progress of diseases such as emphysema. She spent most of her career at Columbia University, where she was a professor in the College of Physicians and Surgeons. Her contributions to science were recognized with numerous awards, including the American Chemical Society's Garvan Medal in 1982.

An only child, Mandl was born in Vienna, Austria on April 19, 1917, to Ernst and Ida Bassan Hochmuth. Ernst Hochmuth was an industrialist, and the family was well known in Viennese society. Young Ines went through public school until she was 14 (Austria did not offer public schooling for girls past that age), but she went on to a private school. She was married at 19 to Hans Alexander Mandl.

The rise of the Nazis meant severe changes and losses of freedom for Jewish families in Vienna; when Austria was taken over in the summer of 1938, Ines and Hans Mandl left their home and moved to England. (Ines's parents went to the United States) When the Second World War began in 1939, the Mandls went to Ireland, where Ines attended the National University of Ireland as a chemistry student. She received a diploma in chemistry from the university in 1944.

After the war ended in 1945, Ines and Hans Mandl left Ireland for the United States. There, Ines found a position in New York with the International Chemical Corporation. Luckily for her, she had a chance to work with Carl Neuberg, who had some years earlier coined the term *biochemistry*. Like Ines Mandl, Neuberg had left Europe as the Nazis took over; he was now a consultant at International Chemical and a professor at New York University.

It was at Neuberg's urging that Mandl enrolled in college to continue her education. While she worked for International, she also attended the Polytechnic Institute of Brooklyn, where she got her master's degree in 1947 and her Ph.D. in 1949 (the first woman at Polytechnic to achieve this). During these years she collaborated with Neuberg on his research and coauthored a number of articles and papers on fructose and other sugars.

Researches Enzymes and Collagens

After receiving her doctorate, Mandl became a research associate at Columbia University's College of Physicians and Surgeons, where she would remain until her retirement in 1986. Her particular area of specialization was the protein collagen, which is a major component of connective tissue. Over the years she studied various enzymes that could break down collagen. By understanding how connective tissue could be broken down, she hoped to find out how to keep the process from occurring. Her work yielded important results in pulmonary disease, particularly in infants. Her research also showed smoking's effects on lung tissue, and her studies of enzymes opened the door to possible therapies for certain types of emphysema.

Her training in biochemistry was extremely useful in her research, and her ability to develop biochemical approaches to medical questions gained her a reputation as a key player in her field. She served as director of the obstetrics and gynecology laboratories at Delafield Hospital (affiliated with Columbia) beginning in 1959, and she created the first interdisciplinary symposium on collgenease (the enzymes that can break down collagen). In 1972, she started up the journal *Connective Tissue*, which she edited for the rest of her tenure at Columbia. The following year she was named associate professor of biochemistry, and she attained full professor status three years later.

Mandl was awarded the Carl Neuberg Medal (named after her mentor) by the American Society of European Chemists and Pharmacists in 1977. Five years later, she won the American Chemical Society's Garvan Medal. The University of Bordeaux in France awarded her an honorary doctorate in 1983, and in 1992, six years after her retirement, she was awarded the Austrian Honor Cross, First Class Golden Honor Emblem of Vienna.

SELECTED WRITINGS BY MANDL:

Books

Collagenase: First Interdisciplinary Symposium. New York: Gordon and Breach, 1972.

Periodicals

"Collagenase." *Science* 169 (1970): 1234–38.

FURTHER READING

Books

Shearer, Benjamin F. and Barbara S. Shearer, eds. *Notable Women in the Physical Sciences: A Biographical Dictionary.* Westport, CT.: Greenwood Press, 1997.

Periodicals

"Garvan Medal." *Chemical and Engineering News* 60 (September, 1982): 54–55.

Sketch by George A. Milite

Hilde Proescholdt Mangold

1898–1924

German embryologist

German embryologist Hilde Mangold identified cells or "organizer regions" that directed the development of tissues and organs. Her groundbreaking experiments had a major impact on the science of experimental embryology. Her thesis advisor, Hans Spemann, won the Nobel Prize in Physiology or Medicine for this discovery of organizer regions 11 years after Mangold's death.

Hilde Proescholdt Mangold was born into a well–to–do merchant family in the small town of Gotha, in Thuringia, Germany, in 1898. Little is known about her background or childhood, other than she was very interested in literature and art, as well as in science. Growing up in a small town, she loved the outdoors and was well acquainted with natural history.

Mangold attended the University of Frankfurt, where she first heard a lecture by the embryologist Hans Spemann. In 1920, she arrived at the University of Freiburg–im–Breisgau to become a graduate student–research assistant with Spemann. Mangold threw herself into the exciting and intellectual student life of Freiburg. As predoctoral students, Mangold and her friends could take whatever courses interested them, including art and philosophy, as long as they performed well in their laboratory work. Mangold also arranged to take a special laboratory course on cytology to study the chromosomes of insects, since chromosomes had recently been recognized as the basis of heredity. She spent her free time hiking and skiing in the surrounding mountains of the Black Forest and studying wildflowers in the Rhine Valley.

Spemann was interested in how cells in embryos develop into different types of cells, tissues, and organs, and the differentiation and specialization of cells during embryonic development. The experiments in his laboratory involved operating on and transplanting parts of amphibian embryos. The fragility of the embryos and the constant problem of bacterial contamination made these experiments extremely difficult. It usually took a student two years to complete a single experiment, since the embryos were only available during the breeding season in the spring. Mangold, like the other students, had to make her own delicate glass instruments for the operations, which were carried out under a microscope. Hers were among the most difficult of the experiments because they involved transplanting embryos from one species to another.

Discovers "Organizer Regions"

In 1921 and 1922, while transplanting sections of salamander embryos, Mangold discovered "organizer regions" that induced undifferentiated tissues to develop into specific types of organs. Thus, she demonstrated that the patterns of development of cells are influenced by their interaction with other cells. She received her Ph.D. for this work in 1922, and she and Spemann published their results in 1924, in what was, at the time, the most prestigious journal of experimental embryology. Although Spemann allowed his other students to publish their work as sole authors, in this case he recognized the immense significance of Mangold's work, and therefore insisted that he be first author on the publication of Mangold's dissertation research. It was one of the very few Ph.D. dissertations in history that would lead directly to the Nobel Prize.

In 1921, Mangold married Otto Mangold, an embryologist and the most senior of Spemann's students. When he was appointed head of the division of experimental embryology at the Kaiser Wilhelm (now the Max Planck) Institute for Biology, in the spring of 1924, the couple and their infant son moved to Berlin–Dahlem. Shortly after their move, in September of 1924, the gas heater in their kitchen exploded and Mangold died of severe burns, just as her landmark paper was being published. Mangold's son died in his early twenties, a victim of the Nazis.

In 1929, in the "Feitschrift" or tribute to Hans Spemann, Otto Mangold published, under his late wife's name, an account of her experiments completed in the spring of 1923. In this work, Mangold had repeated her organizer experiment with other combinations of salamander species. As her friend and fellow student Viktor Hamburger wrote in his article about her: "She was an unusually gifted, vivacious, and charming young woman. Her considerable scientific talents would undoubtedly have borne fruit, had her life not been cut short by a tragic accident."

SELECTED WRITINGS BY MANGOLD:

Periodicals

(With Hans Spemann) "On the Induction of Embryonic Anlagen by Implantation of Organizers from Different Species." *Wilhelm Roux' Archiv für Entwicklungsmechanik der Organismen* 100 (1924): 599–638.

"Organisatortransplantationen in verschiedenen Kombinationen bei Urodelen." *Wilhelm Roux' Archiv für Entwicklungsmechanik der Organismen* 117 (1929): 697–710.

FURTHER READING

Books

Hamburger, Viktor. *The Heritage of Experimental Embryology: Hans Spemann and the Organizer.* New York: Oxford University Press, 1988.

Periodicals

Hamburger, Viktor. "Hilde Mangold, Co–discoverer of the Organizer." *Journal of the History of Biology* 17 (1984): 1–11.

Sketch by Margaret Alic

Anna Morandi Manzolini
1716–1774
Italian anatomist

Anna Morandi Manzolini's chosen work, the study of human anatomy, was a relatively new science in the first half of the eighteenth century. The great Italian medical schools of Salerno are credited with fostering its beginnings. Later, the University of Bologna, where Manzolini was a professor, made numerous advancements in the study of anatomy, many of which can be attributed to Manzolini.

Manzolini first began to learn about the anatomy of the human body from her husband, Giovanni Manzolini, an anatomy professor at the University of Bologna, whom she married when she was 20. Although she had six children to care for, she still found time to help her husband in his work by sculpting intricate and accurate wax models of the human body and its structure, which he used to illustrate his lectures.

So great was her skill that, when her husband became too ill with tuberculosis to teach, she was invited to lecture in his place. When he died in 1760, she was made a professor of anatomy in her own right, with the added title of *modellatrice*. Her fame as a sculptor of anatomical models spread throughout Europe, and she sold many of her models for others to use. Joseph II, Emperor of Austria, is said to have bought some of them. She was invited to lecture in London and in St. Petersburg, and was made a member of both the British Royal Society and the Russian Royal Scientific Society. She was offered the chair of anatomy at Milan. It is said that authorities there were willing to have her come to Milan at any price, but she preferred to remain in her beloved Bologna.

Dissection Discoveries Turned Into Models

In this new science of human anatomy, knowledge of the living human body was gained through dissection of the dead. Manzolini was said to have abhorred dead bodies, but she overcame the disgust she felt and went on to sculpt the anatomically correct models that later became the prized possession of the university's museum. One of her models showed how the fetus is nourished in the womb. She also discovered, through dissection, the oblique muscle structure of the eye. The knowledge that she gained about the organs and structure of the body was brought to her students and other professors. She was visited in Bologna by many doctors and professors from other cities and countries eager to see her great model collection. Her models were later copied and used by other anatomists throughout the world.

Morandi died in 1774 at the age of 58. She spent her entire life in Bologna. She held the chair of anatomy at the University of Bologna at her death and, in her honor, a bust of her was placed in the Pantheon in Rome and at the university museum. Her skill as a teacher and model sculptor greatly contributed to many advances in the science of anatomy.

FURTHER READING

Books

Alic, Margaret. *Hypatia's Heritage, A History of Women in Science from Antiquity through the Nineteenth Century.* Boston: Beacon Press, 1986.
Dakin, Theodora P. *A History of Women's Contribution To World Health.* Lewiston: The Edwin Mellen Press, 1991.
Mozans, H. J. *Women in Science.* New York: D. Appleton and Co., 1913.
Ogilvie, Marilyn Bailey. *Women in Science, Antiquity Through the Nineteenth Century.* Cambridge: MIT Press, 1986, p. 125.
Schiebinger, Londa. *The Mind Has No Sex?* Cambridge: Harvard University Press, 1989.

Sketch by Jane Stewart Cook

Jane Haldimand Marcet
1769–1858
English science writer

Jane Haldimand Marcet helped to popularize the study of science in the early nineteenth century. Her books on chemistry, botany, and natural philosophy, which were among the first basic science texts, were best–sellers and had a profound influence on the development of science. Her use of experimental demonstrations was a major innovation in science education. Because her books were published anonymously, under one of several pseudonyms, or wrongly attributed, Marcet has not always received proper credit for her work.

Marcet was born in London of Swiss parents in 1769. Her father, Anthony Francis Haldimand, was a wealthy merchant who eventually left Marcet a large fortune. Her childhood was spent in London and with relatives in Geneva, Switzerland. When Marcet was 15, her mother died and she took over the management of the large family and household. As hostess to her father's friends, Marcet met and eventually studied painting with the artists, Sir Joshua Reynolds and Thomas Lawrence.

In 1799, she married Alexander Marcet, a Swiss physician, who eventually devoted most of his time to experimental chemistry and became a chemistry lecturer. The Marcets had two children. With her husband's encouragement, Marcet began to educate herself in science, attending the chemistry lectures of Sir Humphry Davy at the Royal Institution. These lectures so impressed Marcet, that she became Davy's student. The Marcets were at the center of London intellectual circles, and Marcet had easy access to expertise in various sciences. Among her close friends were the feminist novelist Maria Edgeworth, the novelist and political economist Harriet Martineau, and the scientific writer **Mary Somerville**.

Although scientific knowledge was growing at a phenomenal rate at the start of the nineteenth century, basic science books were almost unknown. With the encouragement of her husband and friends, Marcet began writing. She published the first edition of *Conversations on Chemistry, intended more especially for the Female Sex*, in two volumes, in 1805. Although Marcet published the book anonymously, she identified herself as a woman in the preface. Nevertheless, it was widely believed that the author was a man and finally, with the 13th edition in 1837, Marcet identified herself.

Conversations on Chemistry was written in a form that was typical of the time: a dialogue between a fictional teacher, Mrs. Bryan, and her students Caroline and Emily. Caroline, who loved explosions and other spectacular experiments, provided a contrast with the serious scientific approach of Mrs. B. and Emily, and enabled Marcet to describe the latest discoveries in chemistry in an understandable and lively fashion. Marcet's original drawings and woodcuts illustrated the experiments and the apparatus. As a young apprentice bookbinder, Michael Faraday read *Conversations on Chemistry* while binding it and became inspired to become a chemist. Eventually, he and Marcet became good friends. As one of the first textbooks, at a time when chemistry courses and lecture series were proliferating, *Conversations on Chemistry* had a profound influence on the development of the science.

Marcet eventually published 16 English editions of *Conversations on Chemistry*, each one carefully updated. She always included the latest discoveries by Faraday, Davy, and others, which aroused interest in each new edition. There were at least 15 American editions, usually entitled *Mrs. Bryan's Conversations*, and by 1853 160,000 copies had been sold in the United States. However many of these American editions were blatant plagiarisms. One admirer of Marcet, quoted in Edgar Smith's book, wrote: "We are informed by one of the American editors of this work that his reason for not placing the name of Jane Marcet on the title–page, was because scientific men believed it fictitious!" In some American versions, the characters were changed to two boys and a male tutor. The book also was attributed to **Margaret Bryan**, a London schoolteacher who had published recent texts on astronomy and natural philosophy. Occasionally, Marcet's books were attributed to her husband, who handled her correspondence.

In 1817 and again in 1820, Marcet wrote *Conversations on Botany* for young people and published it anonymously. This book was often attributed to sisters Elizabeth and Sarah Mary Fitton, who were well–known English naturalists at the time. This work featured conversations between "Mother" and "Edward" and included 20 of Marcet's colored plates. In it, Marcet introduced her readers to the system of plant classification invented by Carl Linnaeus.

Marcet's earliest writing, *Conversations on Natural Philosophy*, was not published until 1819. The 14th edition was revised and edited by her son, Francis Marcet, a fellow of the Royal Society and a professor in Geneva, Switzerland. Marcet's close friendship with the naturalist August de Candolle was the inspiration for her *Conversations on Vegetable Physiology, Comprehending the Elements of Botany*, published in 1829. Like her other books, these were very popular and went through many editions. All of Marcet's books were translated into French and pirated in the United States, often with only the American editor's name on the cover and title page.

A prolific writer with many interests, Marcet's most successful book was not on science: *Conversations on Political Economy* was first published in 1816 and often reprinted. Later in her life, Marcet wrote many popular children's books on various subjects. Marcet died in London, at the home of her son–in–law Edward Romilly, in 1858, at the age of 89.

SELECTED WRITINGS BY MARCET:

Books

(Thomas Cooper, reviser) *Conversations on Chemistry; in which the Elements of that Science are Familiarly Explained and Illustrated by Experiments.* Philadelphia: M. Carey & Son, 1818.

Conversations on Natural Philosophy in which the Elements of that Science are Familiarly Explained. Edited by Thomas P. Jones. Philadelphia: Grigg and Elliot, 1836.

Conversations on Botany. London: Longman, Orme, Brown, Green & Longmans, 1840.

FURTHER READING

Books

Alic, Margaret. *Hypatia's Heritage: A History of Women in Science from Antiquity through the Nineteenth Century*. Boston: Beacon Press,1986.

Myers, Greg. "Fictionality, Demonstration, and a Forum for Popular Science: Jane Marcet's *Conversations on Chemistry*." In *Natural Eloquence: Women Reinscribe Science*. Edited by Barbara T. Gates and Ann B. Shteir. Madison: University of Wisconsin Press, 1997.

Ogilvie, Marilyn Bailey. *Women in Science: Antiquity through the Nineteenth Century*. Cambridge: MIT Press, 1991.

Smith, Edgar Fahs. *Old Chemistries*. New York: McGraw Hill, 1927.

Periodicals

Armstrong, Eva V. "Jane Marcet and Her 'Conversations on Chemistry." *Journal of Chemical Education* 15 (1938): 53–57.

Sketch by Margaret Alic

Lynn Margulis
1938–
American biologist

Lynn Margulis is a renowned theoretical biologist and professor of botany at the University of Massachusetts at Amherst. Her research on the evolutionary links between cells containing nuclei (eukaryotes) and cells without nuclei (prokaryotes) led her to formulate a symbiotic theory of evolution that was initially spurned in the scientific community but has become more widely accepted.

Margulis, the eldest of four daughters, was born in Chicago on March 5, 1938. Her father, Morris Alexander, was a lawyer who owned a company that developed and marketed a long–lasting thermoplastic material used to mark streets and highways. He also served as an assistant state's attorney for the state of Illinois. Her mother, Leone, operated a travel agency. When Margulis was fifteen, she completed her second year at Hyde Park High School and was accepted into an early entrant program at the University of Chicago.

Education and Early Career

Margulis was particularly inspired by her science courses, in large part because reading assignments consisted not of textbooks but of the original works of the world's great scientists. A course in natural science made an immediate impression and would influence her life, raising questions that she has pursued throughout her career: What is heredity? How do genetic components influence the development of offspring? What are the common bonds between generations? While at the University of Chicago she met Carl Sagan, then a graduate student in physics. At the age of nineteen, she married Sagan, received a B.A. in liberal arts, and moved to Madison, Wisconsin, to pursue a joint master's degree in zoology and genetics at the University of Wisconsin under the guidance of noted cell biologist Hans Ris. In 1960 she and Sagan moved to the University of California at Berkeley, where she conducted genetic research for her doctoral dissertation.

The marriage to Sagan ended before she received her doctorate. She moved to Waltham, Massachusetts, with her two sons, Dorion and Jeremy, to accept a position as lecturer in the department of biology at Brandeis University. She was awarded her Ph.D. in 1965. The following year, she became an adjunct assistant of biology at Boston University, leaving twenty–two years later as full professor. During her tenure at Boston University she taught two or three courses per semester and directed a $100,000–a–year research lab. In 1967 she married crystallographer Thomas N. Margulis. The couple had two children before they divorced in 1980. Since 1988, Margulis has been a distinguished university professor with the Department of Botany at the University of Massachusetts at Amherst.

Her interest in genetics and the development of cells can be traced to her earliest days as a University of Chicago undergraduate. She always questioned the commonly accepted theories of genetics, however, challenging the traditionalists by presenting hypotheses that contradicted current beliefs. She has been called the most gifted theoretical biologist of her generation by numerous colleagues. A profile of Margulis by Jeanne McDermott in the *Smithsonian* quotes Peter Raven, director of the Missouri Botanical Garden and a MacArthur fellow: "Her mind keeps shooting off sparks. Some critics say she's off in left field. To me she's one of the most exciting, original thinkers in the whole field of biology." Although few know more about cellular biology, Margulis considers herself a "microbial evolutionist," mapping out a field of study that doesn't in fact exist.

Evolutionary Theory

As a graduate student, Margulis became interested in cases of non–Mendelian inheritance, occurring when the genetic make–up of a cell's descendants cannot be traced solely to the genes in a cell's nucleus. For several years, she concentrated her research on a search for genes in the cytoplasm of cells, the area outside of the cell's nucleus. In the early 1960s, Margulis presented evidence for the existence of extranuclear genes. She and other researchers had found DNA in the cytoplasm of plant cells, indicating that heredity in higher organisms is not solely determined by genetic information carried in the cell nucleus. Her continued work in this field led her to formulate the serial endosymbiotic theory, or SET, which offered a new approach to evolution as well as an account of the origin of cells with nuclei.

Prokaryotes—bacteria and blue–green algae, now commonly referred to as cyanobacteria—are single–celled organisms that carry genetic material in the cytoplasm. Margulis proposes that eukaryotes (cells with nuclei) evolved when different kinds of prokaryotes formed symbiotic systems to enhance their chances for survival. The first such symbiotic fusion would have taken place between fermenting bacteria and oxygen–using bacteria. All cells with nuclei, Margulis contends, are derived from bacteria that formed symbiotic relationships with other primordial bacteria some two billion years ago. It has now become widely accepted that mitochondria—those components of eukaryotic cells that process oxygen—are remnants of oxygen–using bacteria. Margulis' hypothesis that cell hairs, found in a vast array of eukaryotic cells, descend from another group of primordial bacteria much like the modern spirochaete still encounters resistance, however.

The resistance to Margulis' work in microbiology may perhaps be explained by its implications for the more theoretical aspects of evolutionary theory. Evolutionary theorists, particularly in the English–speaking countries, have always put a particular emphasis on the notion that competition for scarce resources leads to the survival of the most well–adapted representatives of a species by natural selection, favoring adaptive genetic mutations. According to Margulis, natural selection as traditionally defined cannot account for the "creative novelty" to be found in evolutionary history. She argues instead that the primary mechanism driving biological change is symbiosis, while competition plays a secondary role.

Gaia Hypothesis

Margulis doesn't limit her concept of symbiosis to the origin of plant and animal cells. She subscribes to the "Gaia" hypothesis first formulated by James E. Lovelock, British inventor and chemist. The "Gaia theory" (named for the Greek goddess of the earth) essentially states that all life, as well as the oceans, the atmosphere, and the earth itself are parts of a single, all–encompassing symbiosis and may fruitfully be considered as elements of a single organism.

Margulis has authored more than one hundred and thirty scientific articles and ten books, several of which are written with her son Dorion. She has also served on more than two dozen committees, including the American Association for the Advancement of Science, the MacArthur Foundation Fellowship Nominating Committee, and the editorial boards of several scientific journals. Margulis is co–director of NASA's Planetary Biology Internship Program and, in 1983, was elected to the National Academy of Sciences.

SELECTED WRITINGS BY MARGULIS:

Books

Origins of Life. 2 vols. Gordon and Breach, 1970-71.

(With Dorion Sagan) *Microcosmos: Four Billion Years of Microbial Evolution.* Summit Books, 1986.

(With Karlene Volume Schwartz) *Five Kingdoms: An Illustrated Guide to the Phyla of Life on Earth.* W. H. Freeman, 1987.

(With Dorion Sagan) *Garden of Microbial Delights.* Harcourt, 1988.

FURTHER READING

Periodicals

"The Creativity of Symbiosis." *Scientific American* 266, no. 1 (1992,): 131.

McCoy, Dan. "The Wizard of Ooze." *Omni* 7, no. 49 (1985): 49–78.

McDermott, Jeanne. "A Biologist Whose Heresy Redraws Earth's Tree of Life." *Smithsonian* 20, no. 72 (1989): 72–80.

"The Microbes' Mardi Gras." *Economist* 314, no. 7643 (1990): 85–86.

Sketch by Benedict A. Leerburger

Maria the Jewess
fl. First century (?)
Alexandrian alchemist

Maria the Jewess is credited with establishing the theoretical and practical foundations of alchemy, the forerunner of modern chemistry in the western world. She was one of the first chemists to combine the theories of alchemical science with the practical chemistry of the craft traditions. Although her theoretical contributions remained influential into the Middle Ages and beyond, Maria was more famous for her designs of laboratory apparatus.

Although nothing is known of her life, there are many references to Maria in ancient texts, and she is believed to have lived during the first century in Alexandria, Egypt. Founded by Alexander the Great in 332 B.C., under the ruler Ptolemy, Alexandria became the center of Greek science, featuring a higher learning institution called the Museum, the Great Library, a zoo, botanical gardens, and an astronomical observatory. However, by the first century the Greco–Roman world had entered an intellectual decline. Alchemy was the only remaining science that continued to develop during a time when most scientists believed there was nothing new to discover and that all important knowledge could be found in the works of the ancient Greeks.

The Egyptian goddess Isis was traditionally known as the founder of alchemy, but the science probably originated with women who used the chemical processes of distillation, extraction, and sublimation to formulate perfumes and cosmetics in ancient Mesopotamia. Likewise, Babylonian women chemists used recipes and equipment derived from the kitchen. Thus, ancient alchemy was identified with women, and the work of the early alchemists occasionally was referred to as *opus mulierum*, or "women's work." Artists working with dyes and theories of color were also important sources for the practical aspects of Egyptian alchemy; but alchemical theory was steeped in the Gnostic tradition, which was centered in Alexandria. Gnosticism was a mixture of Jewish, Chaldean, and Egyptian mysticism, neo–platonism, and Christianity. In alchemy, as in Gnosticism, the male and female elements were considered to be of equal importance.

Maria's Many Names

Alchemy was a secretive science—perhaps to protect its practitioners from persecution. However, both the mystical cults and the crafts also had traditions of secrecy. In any case, it was common for alchemists to write under the name of a deity or famous person. Thus, Maria wrote under the name of Miriam the Prophetess, sister of Moses. In addition, she is referred to in alchemical literature as Maria the Jewess, Miriam, Mary, Maria Prophetissa, and Maria the Sage. Maria's many alchemical treatises have been expanded, corrupted, and confused with other writings over the ages. However, fragments of her work, including one called the *Maria Practica*, are extant in ancient alchemical collections. She was quoted often by other early alchemists, particularly the Egyptian encyclopedist Zosimus (c. 300). Maria the Jewess also may have been the author of "The Letter of the Crown and the Nature of the Creation by Mary the Copt of Egypt" which was found in a volume of Arabic alchemical manuscripts, translated from Greek. This work summarized the major theories of Alexandrian alchemy and described the manufacture of colored glass, as well as other chemical processes.

Although the ultimate goal of the alchemist was to transmute common metals into silver and gold, the ancient alchemists were scientists who examined the nature of life and chemical processes. Although their science was based in Aristotelian theory, they were the first true experimenters. Maria believed that metals were living males and females and that the products of her laboratory experiments were the result of sexual generation. The early alchemists believed that the base metals were evolving toward the perfect metal—gold. They clearly distinguished between gilding or forming alloys of base metals to simulate gold and silver, and true transmutation. By transferring the "spirit" or vapor of gold to a base metal, as measured by the transfer of color, alchemists saw themselves as encouraging a natural process.

Designs Water Bath and Still

Maria invented and improved techniques and tools that remain basic to modern laboratory science, and her writings described her designs for laboratory apparatus in great detail. Her water bath, the *balneum mariae* or "Maria's bath," was similar to a double-boiler and was used to maintain a constant temperature or to slowly heat a substance. Two thousand years later, the water bath remains an essential instrument in the laboratory. In modern French, the double-boiler is called a *bain-marie*.

Distillation was essential to experimental alchemy, and Maria invented a still or *alembic* and another, three-armed, still called the *tribikos*. The liquid to be distilled was heated in an earthenware vessel on a furnace. The vapor condensed in the *ambix*, which was cooled with sponges, and a rim on the inside of the *ambix* collected the distillate and carried it to three copper delivery spouts fitted with receiving vessels. Maria described how to make the copper tubing from sheet metal that was the thickness of a pastry pan. Flour paste was used to seal the joints.

Invents Reflux Apparatus

Maria studied the effects of arsenic, mercury, and sulfur vapors on metals. Her work included softening the metals and impregnating them with colors. For these experiments she invented the *kerotakis* process, her most important contribution to alchemical science. Her apparatus also came to be known as the *kerotakis*, a cylinder or sphere with a hemispherical cover set on a fire. Suspended from the cover at the top of the cylinder was a triangular palette, used by artists to heat their mixtures of pigment and wax, and containing a copper–lead alloy or some other metal. Solutions of sulfur, mercury, or arsenic sulfide were heated in a pan near the bottom of the cylinder. The sulfur or mercury vapors condensed in the cover, and the liquid condensate flowed back down, attacking the metal to yield a black sulfide called "Mary's Black." This was believed to be the first step of transmutation. A sieve separated impurities from the black sulfide and continuous refluxing produced a gold–like alloy. Plant oils, such as attar of roses, also were extracted using the *kerotakis*.

Maria has been credited with inventing or improving the hot–ash bath and the dung–bed as laboratory heat sources, as well as perfecting processes for producing phosphorescent gems. Maria's theoretical work included the concept of the macrocosm, or universe, and the microcosm, or individual body, and she applied this concept to the processes of distillation and reflux.

By the third century, the alchemists of Alexandria were being persecuted, and their texts were destroyed. Much of this work was rescued by the Arabs, who venerated Maria and adopted her alchemical theories. However, when alchemy was rediscovered in medieval Europe, it was primarily in the form of quackery. Laboratory chemistry advanced very little from the time of Maria to the mid–seventeenth century.

SELECTED WRITINGS BY MARIA:

Other

Fragment in *Collection des anciens alchimisits Grecs*, vol. 3, edited by M. Berthelot. Paris, 1888.

FURTHER READING

Books

Alic, Margaret. *Hypatia's Heritage: A History of Women in Science from Antiquity through the Nineteenth Century*. Boston: Beacon Press,1986.
Lindsay, Jack. *The Origins of Alchemy in Graeco–Roman Egypt*. New York: Barnes & Noble, 1970.
Read, John. *Prelude to Chemistry*. New York: Macmillan, 1937.
Taylor, F. Sherwood. *The Alchemists: Founders of Modern Chemistry*. New York: Henry Shuman, 1949.

Periodicals

Alic, Margaret. "Women and Technology in Ancient Alexandria: Maria and Hypatia." *Women's Studies International Quarterly* 4 (1981): 305–12.
Holmyard, E. J. "An Alchemical Tract Ascribed to Mary the Copt. The Letter of the Crown and the Nature of the Creation by Mary the Copt of Egypt." *Archivio di Storia della Scienza* 8 (1927): 161–7.
Hopkins, Arthur John. " A Study of the Kerotakis Process as Given by Zosimus and Later Alchemical Writers." *Isis* 29 (1938): 326–54.

Sketch by Margaret Alic

Sagrario Martinez-Carrera
1925–
Spanish crystallographer

Dr. Sagrario Martinez-Carrera is internationally recognized for her pioneering work on high resolution and low temperature crystallography of the imidazole structure at -150°C. She also was one of the first researchers to recognize the importance of computing to the crystallography field, which eventually helped the Instituto de Quimica Fisica in Madrid become the country's leading institute in that field. Martinez-Carrera has published over 80 papers in this field, and has been a member of the American Crystallographic Association since 1962.

Sagrario Martinez-Carrera (Reproduced by permission of Saerario Martinez-Carrera.)

Martinez-Carrera was born on May 10, 1925 in Barcelona, Spain to Leandro Martinez Lopez, a judge, and Pilar Carrera Labarra. The family (including two brothers and a sister) remained in Barcelona until she was five years old, sending her to the nuns of Saint Vincent Paul to learn reading and writing. For the next three years, the family resided in Sevilla, where a private tutor continued Martinez-Carrera's education. When she was eight years old, her family moved to Madrid, where she attended the school of Madres Concepcionistas and became interested in chemistry in discussions with friends. In 1944, she entered the Universidad Complutense (now part of the University of Madrid system), earning her a bachelor's in chemistry in 1949.

Martinez-Carrera earned her Ph.D. in 1955, conducting research into the crystal structure of sodium ditionate dihydrate for her thesis, which was published in *Acta Crystallographica* in 1956. That same year, she helped organize the first international symposium on crystallography to be held in Spain. In 1957 she became a research associate at Spain's High National Research Council (Consejo Superior de Investigaciones Cientificas [CSIC]) at the Instituto de Quimica Fisica, studying inorganic compounds of high symmetry. Funds were so scarce that students had to use tables to calculate electron density and autocorrelation functions by hand.

Studyies Computing Methods

From 1958 to 1960, Martinez-Carrera studied high resolution crystallography under a postdoctoral fellowship at the Holland's Antwerp University with Dr. Caroline MacGillavry, a well–known crystallographer and the first woman to be elected to the Royal Netherlands Academy of Science. While at Antwerp, Martinez-Carrera learned computing and how to work with three–dimensional data, becoming one of the first crystallographers to apply computing to crystallography. During this time, she did her important research involving the crystal structure of imidazole at -150°C.

Martinez-Carrera returned to Madrid, but soon realized that computers were the key to future advancements. Hence, from 1961 to 1963, she did more postdoctoral work, learning how to use the IBM 7070 computer at the University of Pittsburgh in the United States. She became an expert about programming methods, which allowed her to apply them to her work and teach them to others when she returned to Madrid in 1965. In a letter to Maureen Julian quoted in *Women in Science*, she commented, " I would like one day to do the structure of a big molecule like a protein but Spain is a poor country and there is little money for research."

Advancing the Science of Crystallography

Martinez-Carrera took a position as a research fellow at the CSIC until 1971 when she was promoted to full professor. She focused her research on simple organic compounds, implementing the then primitive direct methods, and continued promoting crystallography among Spanish scientists as a research field, for solving problems and for developing people. She played a major role in increasing the number of students pursuing a Ph.D. in this obscure field and, in 1974, organized the International Congress on Anomalous Scattering held in Madrid. From 1974 until 1982, she acted as advisor to the president of the CSIC, helping to prioritize projects, choose staff, and purchase equipment.

Martinez-Carrera retired in 1990, remaining in Madrid and doing charitable work for several private organizations. Her dedication to becoming an expert in the field of crystallography and teaching it to others about crystallography and led to the CSIC becoming a renowned school in crystallography, and helped increase collaboration in this type of research around the country.

SELECTED WRITINGS BY MARTINEZ-CARRERA:

Periodicals

"The Crystal Structure of Imidazole at –150°C." *Acta Crystallographica*, 20, (1966): 783–789.

(With Rogers, D., J.M. Franco, and S. Garcia–Blanco) "The Crystal Structures and Absolute Stereochemistries of Monobromoisodehydrobispulegone and Dibromodehydrobispulegone." *Acta Cryst.* B31 (1975): 2742–2742.

(With Martinez–Ripoll, M., F.H. Cano, S. Garcia–Blanco, and W.H. Gundel) "The Crystal and Molecular Structure of BNA, a Cyclotetracondensate from Quaternary Salts of Nicotinamide," *Acta Cryst.* B33 (1977): 494–500.

(With Perez–Salazar, A., F.H. Cano, J. Fayos, and S. Garcia–Blanco) "The Alkaloid Otosenine. Evidence of a Weak –N:.C–O Intra–Annular Bond." *Acta Cryst.* B33 (1977): 3525–3527.

(With Fonseca, I., and S. Garcia–Blanco) "Structure of Oxodipine: a New Calcium Antagonist." *Acta Cryst.* C42 (1986): 1792–1794.

(With Fajardo, M., M.P. Gomez–Sal, P. Royo, and S. Garcia–Blanco) "Synthesis and Structural Characterisation of the Mixed–Metal Cluster Cation [Nb(n5–C5H4R)2¢AuP(C6H5)32]+ with R=H or Si(CH3)3," *J. Organomet. Chem.*. 312 (1986): C44–C46.

(With Sanz–Aparicio, J., C. Pico, M. Gaitan, A. Jerez, and M.L. Veiga) "Mixed Oxides of the System M(V)–Te(IV)–O2 (M= Nb, Ta, Sb); II. Crystal Structure of Ta2Te2O9," *Mat. Res. Bull.* 22 (1987): 1405–1412.

(With Fandos, R., M. Gomez, P. Royo, S. Garcia–Blanco, and J. Sanz–Aparicio) "New Tantalum Ylide Complexes: Crystal and Molecular Structure of (n5–C5Me5)Cl4Ta(CH2=PMePh2) Containing a Neutral Phosphorus Ylide." *Organometallics* 6 (1987): 581–1583.

(With Sanz–Aparicio, J., and S. Garcia–Blanco) "Lattice–Energy Calculations on Organometallic Compounds," *Acta Cryst.*, B44 (1988): 259–262.

(With Iglesias, M., and C. Pino) "Decontaminant Agents in the Catalytic Cracking of Petroleum. X–ray Crystal Structure of Bismuth–tri–diethyl Phosphoro Dithioate, Bi[(C2H5O)2PS2]3," *Polyhedron* 8, (1989): 483–489.

FURTHER READING

Books

Farnes, Patricia, and G. Dass–Simon, eds. *Women of Science: Righting the Record.* Bloomington: Indiana University Press, 1990, pp. 335–377

Sketch by Laurel M. Sheppard

Ursula Bailey Marvin
1921–
American planetary geologist

In the time between her master's and doctoral degrees from Harvard, Ursula Bailey Marvin had achieved more recognition in the field of geology than many scientists do in a lifetime. In addition to concurrently holding university teaching positions as well as positions in private industry, Marvin is also notable for becoming a first achiever in many areas. While a graduate student at Harvard, she became the first female research assistant and teaching assistant in its Department of Geology (now the Department of Earth and Planetary Sciences). She ultimately became the first woman on the faculty in that department. Marvin was also the first female geologist to be employed by the Union Carbide Corporation.

In 1991, Marvin was immortalized in the skies when an asteroid was named in her honor ("Asteroid Marvin") by the Minor Planet Bureau of the International Astronomy Union. She again was honored when a mountain peak rising through the Antarctic ice sheet was named after her in 1992 ("Marvin Nunatak") by the U.S. Board on Geographic Names.

Marvin was born in Bradford, Vermont on August 20, 1921, daughter of Harold Leslie and Alice Miranda (Bartlett) Bailey. She graduated from Tufts University in 1943 and went on to receive her master's degree in science from Harvard/Radcliffe in 1946. Her career moved so rapidly that, despite having completed most of the academic requirements for her doctoral degree, she did not pause to complete the candidacy until 1969, when she officially received her Ph.D. from Harvard. In 1947 she was granted an assistantship in research on silicate minerals with the geology department at the University of Chicago. She married geologist Thomas Crockett Marvin in 1952 and then joined him as a mineralogist at Union Carbide for the next six years. Together, they traveled to South America and Africa searching for ore deposits for the company. When they returned, Marvin divided her time between research in mineralogy at Harvard, and teaching mineralogy at her alma mater, Tufts University, where she continued in that capacity for the next three years.

Marvin's lengthiest professional tenure was as geologist for the Smithsonian Astrophysical Observatory in Cambridge, Massachusetts (1961–1998), where she ultimately achieved the distinction of senior geologist emeritus. However, throughout her career, Marvin has held numerous concurrent posts and appointments. She was a geology lecturer at Harvard from 1974–1992 and the federal women's program coordinator for the Smithsonian Astrophysical Observatory from 1974–1977. She was a member of NASA's Lunar Sample Analysis Planning Team from1976–1978 and a member of two polar expeditions for the National Science Foundation's (NSF) Antarctic Search Meteorites Team (1978–1979 and 1981–1982), and again in 1985 for NSF's Seymour Island Antarctic expedition. She served as trustee at Tufts University from 1975–1985, where she remains trustee emeritus (1988–). She was also a trustee for the Universities Space Research Association (USRA) from1979–1984 where she also served as chairperson from 1982–1983. She was secretary–general of the International Commission on History and Geological Sciences from 1989–1996 and vice–president for North America in 1996. She was a member of the Lunar & Planetary Science Council of the USRA from 1987–1991. From 1993–1999, Marvin chaired the NSF–NASA–Smithsonian Institute's Antarctic Meteorite Working Group and serves as a member of NASA's Advisory Committee on Astromaterials (1998–).

In an interview with Harding, Marvin said that she loves to do archival as well as field research. She has published more than 80 technical papers on meteorites and analyses of lunar samples and in later publications, has focused on the history of geology and meteoritics. For this work Marvin was the honored recipient of the History of Geology Award in 1986 from the Geological Society of America, an award which Marvin says was particularly meaningful to her

In 1991, Marvin was immortalized in the skies when an asteroid was named in her honor ("Asteroid Marvin") by the Minor Planet Bureau of the International Astronomy Union. She was honored again when a mountain peak rising through the Antarctic ice sheet was named after her in 1992 ("Marvin Nunatak") by the U.S. Board on Geographic Names. In 1997 Marvin received Lifetime Achievement Awards from Women in Science and Engineering and the Harvard-Smithsonian Center for Astrophysics.

While Marvin's professional research has focused on the analysis of meteorites and lunar samples, she also took part in the geological mapping of images of the Galilean satellites of Jupiter. In her personal time, she and her husband particularly enjoy worldwide birding, and important aspect of their travel and outdoor activities.

SELECTED WRITINGS BY MARVIN:

Books

Continental Drift, 1973.
(contributing author) *Astronomy from Space,* 1983.
(contributing author) *The Planets,* 1985.

FURTHER READING

Books

American Men & Women of Science. 17th ed. New York: R.R. Bowker, 1989–1990.
Bailey, Martha J. *American Women in Science.* Denver: ABC–CLIO.

O'Neill, Lois Decker, ed. *The Women's Book of World Records and Achievements.* Garden City, NY: Anchor Press, 1979.

Who's Who of American Women. 21st. ed. New Providence, RI: Marquis, 1999–2000.

Other

Harding, Lauri R., interview with Ursula Marvin conducted on July 27, 1999.

Sketch by Lauri R. Harding

Anne L. Massy
1867–1931
Irish zoologist

Anne L. "Annie" Massy contributed greatly to the understanding of two distinct areas of zoology through her research on birds and on mollusks and other marine invertebrates. She published 22 papers during her career.

Creatures of the Sea

Focusing mainly on the mollusks of Ireland, Massy received many of her specimens for study through her work with the fisheries branch of the Department of Agriculture and Technical Instruction (later known as the Department of Lands and Fisheries). Through the 30 years she was associated with this organization, she had access to its collection of specimens brought up by dredging and trawling, including specimens from the little–known Atlantic slope off the western coast of Ireland. She published papers on the cephalopods (the group of mollusks that includes squid, cuttlefish and octopi), including describing a new species. She also related the number of rings on an oyster's shell to its age.

Massy also devoted much time and effort to the study of pteropods, small mollusks (subclass *Ophisobranchia*) in the same class as gastropods, which includes snails and slugs. Pteropods have winglike lobes on their feet, which earn them their common name, sea butterflies. (Pteropod means wing–foot.)

Massy's advice and opinions were widely sought, by museums and expeditionary committees alike. The *Terra Nova* Antarctic expedition brought her pteropods and cephalopods, on which she produced valuable research reports around 1916. At the time of her death, she was working on the pteropods brought back by another Antarctic expedition. She also examined the collections of the museums of India, Natal, and South Africa.

Why did these distinguished scientific organizations come to her for her opinions? The reason is best summed by G.P. Farrah, of the Department of Lands and Fisheries, in the tribute he wrote to her in *The Irish Naturalists' Journal*: "In all her researches Miss Massy was a careful, critical, and accurate worker and was never satisfied on doubtful points until she had got the opinion of the best authority available." Her work was so respected that a cephalopod species was named after her, *Cirrotenthia massyi.*

Creatures of the Air

Annie Massy's interests were not limited to marine invertebrates. "A marked feature in Miss Massy's character, and one that will long be remembered, was her great devotion to the study of bird life," wrote C.B. Moffat in her obituary in *The Irish Naturalists' Journal.* Moffat recalls that Massy told young birding enthusiasts that "the pursuit (which she took part in even in her most busy times), more than doubled the pleasures of life."

In 1904, Annie Massy was one of the founders of the Irish Bird Protection Society. Her work with the society resulted in the 1930 passage of the Wild Birds Protection Act in Ireland. She resigned as secretary of the organization (a post she had taken on in 1924 to revive the dying group) just three days before her death.

Annie Massy died April 10, 1931, at Howth County, Ireland. Farrah wrote of her passing: "Her death in the midst of her activities has left a gap in the ranks of our Irish zoologists which it will be hard to fill."

SELECTED WRITINGS BY MASSY:

Periodicals

"Preliminary Notice of New and Remarkable Cephalopods from the South West Coast of Ireland." *Ann. Mag. Nat. Hist.* 7th ser., no. XX. (1097).

"The Pteropoda and Heteropoda of the Coasts of Ireland." *Fisheries Ireland Sci., Invest.* (1909).

FURTHER READING

Periodicals

Obituary *The Irish Naturalists Journal* (July 1931).

Sketch by Fran Hodgkins

Sybilla Masters
?–1720
American inventor

Sybilla Masters is also considered to be the first woman inventor in the United States. She was the first woman to receive a patent in the United States, as well as the first American to receive a British patent. Although the patents were granted in her husband's name, Masters received credit in the official documents. Masters patented an innovative method of cleaning and curing corn and an original system of working and staining palmetto leaf and straw for use in hats and chairs.

Masters was born Sybilla Righton, the second daughter of two Quakers, William and Sarah Righton. She was the second of seven children. Her birth date and place of birth are not known, but historians speculate it was probably Bermuda. Her father was a merchant seaman who probably moved from Bermuda to West New Jersey around 1687. By 1690, there is evidence that he owned an estate, called Bermuda, on the Delaware River, and Masters was probably raised there. She moved to Philadelphia sometime in the mid–1690s, when she married a prosperous merchant and landowner, Thomas Masters, a Quaker who served as the mayor of Philadelphia from 1707–1708 and provincial councilor from 1720–1723. The Masters had four children, Sarah, Mary, Thomas, and William, who lived and most likely three or four children who died as infants.

Two Successful Patents

Masters was interested in inventing and, although her husband was wealthy, aimed at accumulating a personal fortune from her ideas. To that end, she traveled to London around 1712 to patent her inventions and sell them abroad. While in London, she patented her two primary inventions, the corn cleaning and curing instrument and the palmetto straw and leaf worker/stainer. The patents were actually granted in her husband's name, but Masters received credit in the official documents.

Masters' corn cleaning and curing device was patented on November 25, 1715 and given patent number 401 in England. Until this time, corn was processed using a grinding method that pulverized the corn. Masters devised a machine in which the corn was stamped twice through two series of mechanisms that included wooden cogwheels, mortars, and drying trays. The resultant cornmeal was marketed as "Tuscarora Rice"—Masters' name for her product—and promoted as a consumption cure. Despite the fact that her husband bought her Governor's Mill in Philadelphia to manufacture her product in 1714, Masters failed to profit from Tuscarora Rice, because it never became popular in Europe or the United States.

Masters was granted her second patent (number 403 in England) on February 18, 1716. She developed a new process for working and staining palmetto leaves, straw, and chips used in bonnets and hats, baskets, chairs, and stools. Palmetto leaves were native to the Americas, and Masters held a monopoly on their importation into England. She purchased a shop in London and called it the "West India Hat and Bonnet" to sell the headgear, as well as "dressing and child-bed baskets, and matting . . . and other beautiful furniture for the apartments of persons of quality." (*London Gazette*, March 18, 1716)

Masters and her husband returned to Philadelphia in 1716. A year later, on July 15, 1717, she received patents in Pennsylvania for the same inventions, making her the first American woman to receive a patent. Her Tuscarora Rice was arguably one of the first patent medicines on the market in the United States. Masters died on August 23, 1720, probably in Philadelphia.

FURTHER READING

Books

Bowman, John, ed. *The Cambridge Dictionary of American Biography.* New York: Cambridge University Press, 1995, p. 478.

Earle, Alice Morse. *Two Centuries of Costume in America.* Vol. II. New York: The Macmillan Company, 1903, p. 570.

James, Edward T., ed. *Notable American Women, 1607–1950: A Biographical Dictionary.* Vol. II. Cambridge: Belknap Press, 1971, pp. 508–09.

Macdonald, Anne L. *Feminine Ingenuity: Women and Invention in America.* New York: Ballantine Books, 1992, p. 3.

Read, Phyllis J. and Bernard L. Witlieb. *The Book of Women's Firsts: Breakthrough Achievements of Almost 1,000 American Women.* New York: Random House, 1992, p. 272.

Stanley, Autumn. *Mothers and Daughters of Invention: Notes for a Revised History of Technology.* Metuchen, NJ: The Scarecrow Press, Inc., 1993, pp. 44, 521.

Vare, Ethlie Ann, and Greg Ptacek. *Mothers of Invention: From the Bra to the Bomb: Forgotten Women and Their Unforgettable Ideas.* New York: William Morrow and Company, Inc., 1988, pp. 30–34.

Williams, Selma R. *Demeter's Daughters: The Women Who Founded America, 1587–1787.* New York: Atheneum, 1976.

Periodicals

Needles, Samuel H. "The Governor's Mill, and the Globe Mills, Philadelphia." *The Pennsylvania Magazine of History and Biography.* (1884): 279–93.

Sketch by Annette Petrusso

Mildred Esther Mathias
1906–1995
American botanist

Mildred Mathias was a prominent botanist with an expertise in umbellifers, plants of the carrot family. She devoted her life to taxonomy and botany education. Because of her contributions to science, several plant species and one genus were named in her honor.

Mildred Esther Mathias was born on September 19, 1906, in Sappington, Missouri. Her father, Oliver John Mathias, a teacher, and her mother instilled in Mathias an early love for learning and the outdoors.

Begins Work in Botany

An excellent student and diligent worker, Mathias attended the Junior College of Flat River in the afternoons while still attending Desloge High School. She graduated from high school in 1923. She went on briefly to the States Teachers College in Cape Girardeau before transferring to Washington University in St. Louis. Her parents also moved to St. Louis so that Mathias could continue to live at home. She began her studies in mathematics, but in her junior year, no mathematics courses were available to women. Mathias switched to botany, and received her A.B. in 1926 and her M.S. the following year.

Mathias stayed on at Washington for her doctoral studies in systemic botany, and conducted research at the Missouri Botanical Garden as an assistant. Her studies focused on Umbelliferae, or the carrot family, of which she would remain a foremost expert throughout her life. She was the first person to define the umbellifer genera and species accurately. Eventually, she would publish more than 60 papers on Umbelliferae, including descriptions of 100 new species, new combinations, and several new genera. She graduated in 1929, and embarked on a road trip across the western United States to further her knowledge.

Mathias married Gerald L. Hassler, a thermodynamic engineer, on August 30, 1930. Unusual for the time, Mathias kept her maiden name professionally because she had already published several papers. Mathias continued her research after marriage and after giving birth to four children. Her field expertise was so recognized that an umbellifer genus was named *Mathiasella* in her honor. Several plant species are also named after her..

In 1932, Mathias became a research associate at the New York Botanical Garden, and in 1936 she took the same position at the University of California, Berkeley, where she remained until 1942. In 1947, Mathias joined the University of California Los Angeles as an herbarium botanist, but soon rose through the ranks to full professor and vice chair of the department until her retirement in 1974. Known as an outstanding professor, Mathias was dedicated to her students and to excellence in research. She often lectured about the importance of identification and taxonomy as well as the nomenclature of botany.

Influence Extends beyond Botany

Mathias's influence extended beyond the botany department at UCLA. She worked with the department of pharmacology to collect possible medicinal specimens from Africa and South America. In the early 1950s, Mathias began to educate the public on California horticulture. UCLA's campus was planted with trees on her recommendation. The university's eight–acre botanical garden was later named after her. In 1956, Mathias was appointed director of the Los Angeles Botanical Garden, and she remained in that capacity for almost 20 years. Mathias also became co–host of a weekly television gardening show and a writer for popular magazines. Her garden show exhibits won numerous awards.

Mathias was dedicated to conservation efforts as well. In San Gabriel, Mathias was directly responsible for the declaration of Rancho Los Tunas as a protected state park. She was founder and president of the Organization for Tropical Studies, which protected field sites from development. Through her efforts, Costa Rica was incorporated as part of the protected area, and the Los Cruces Biological Station was created. She also helped establish the United States Natural Reserve System, which acquired over 30 pieces of land for preservation and research.

Mathias was extremely active in the field, holding memberships in dozens of professional organizations. She was executive director of the Association of American Botanical Gardens and Arboreta, president of the Botanical Society of America and the American Society of Plant Taxonomists, and member of the Society for the Study of Evolution, the American Association for the Advancement of Science, and the American Society of Naturalists.

Named Woman of the Year

Mathias's numerous awards included the Charles Lawrence Hutchinson Medal, the Nature Conservancy National Award, the California Conservation Council Merit Award, the UCLA Medical Auxiliary Woman of Science Award, the American Horticultural Society Scientific Citation, the Liberty Hyde Bailey Medal, and the Medal of Honor from the American Garden Club. The Los Angeles Times named her Woman of the Year in 1964.

Mathias hardly slowed down after her retirement. She became known as "the Jungle Queen" in reference to her physical stamina and new occupation of leading guided tours to the gardens and natural areas of over thirty countries. UCLA honored her with 1990's Emeritus of the Year Award, the first time the award had been given for work done after retirement. Mathias was loved by everyone who came into contact with her, and is remembered as a truly wonderful and giving person. She died on February 16, 1995, after suffering a stroke brought on by the work she loved, working in her garden.

SELECTED WRITINGS BY MATHIAS:

Books

Color for the Landscape: Flowering Plants for Subtropical Climates. Arcadia, CA: California Arboretum Foundation, 1973.

FURTHER READING

Books

Bailey, Martha J. *American Women in Science.* Denver: ABC–CLIO, 1994.

Other

"Mildred Esther Mathias Hassler (1906–1995)." http://www.lifesci.ucla.edu/botgard/html/bg–am.html. May 10, 1999

"The NRS bids fond adieu to its 'founding mother'". http://nrs.ucop.edu/pubs/transv13/MMobit.html. May 10, 1999.

Sketch by Helene Barker Kiser

Annie Russell Maunder
1868–1947
Irish astronomer

Annie Russell Maunder specialized in sunspot research with her husband, Edward Walter Maunder, detecting dark spots appearing on the sun's surface. In 1898, she obtained a photograph of a solar prominence (a cloud of gas arising from the atmosphere of the sun) six solar radii in length—the largest captured on film up to that time. Maunder was also active in the British Astronomical Association, serving as vice–president of the association several times up to 1942, and planning the general form of their official journal (*Journal of the British Astronomical Association*) and serving as editor from 1894 to 1896 and from 1917 to 1930. She also held a paid position at the Greenwich Observatory, at the time a distinction most unusual for a woman.

Annie Russell was born on April 14, 1868, in County Tyrone, Ireland. The daughter of Rev. W. A. Russell, she was educated at Victoria College in Belfast and Girton College in Cambridge. In 1889 she received the highest mathematical honor available to women at Girton, a Senior Optime in the Mathematical Tripos. In 1891 Russell was hired as a "computer" to assist Edward Maunder, head of the solar photography department at the Royal Observatory in Greenwich and founder of the British Astronomical Association. Her job was to examine and measure daily sunspot photographs. Russell and Maunder became friends and were married in 1895. In 1897 and 1898 Annie Russell Maunder was a Pfeiffer student for research at Girton College. Throughout her career she worked in close collaboration with her husband on a variety of astronomical subjects, though her own favorite was the sun; among her contributions were eclipse observations and photographs made during expeditions to Lapland in 1896, India in 1898, Algiers in 1900, Mauritius in 1901, and Labrador in 1905. The Maunders were prolific writers, and contributed frequently as coauthors to *Monthly Notices of the Royal Astronomical Society* and the *Journal of the British Astronomical Association.*

Obtains Longest Coronal Streamer on Film

While in India for the 1898 eclipse, Maunder obtained on film the longest coronal extension (or solar prominence) then known. She equipped a camera to photograph the greatest possible extension of coronal streamers (or solar extensions), and she did in fact photograph one with a length of six solar radii. In related work Maunder proposed that the Earth influenced the number and areas of sunspots, and that sunspots frequency decreased from the eastern to the western edge of the Sun's disk as viewed from the Earth. She also proposed that changes in the Sun caused changes in the Earth's climate, and contributed (with support from a research grant from Girton College) to a photographic survey of the Milky Way.

In 1892 she failed to obtain membership in the Royal Astronomical Society, but she did become a member of the British Astronomical Association, which welcomed female members. On several occasions, she was asked to be president of the association, but refused on account of her soft–spokenness. She was a representative at the Womens' International Congress in London in 1899.

Maunder was interested in the history of astronomy, especially in the origin of the forty–eight ancient constellations, noting that the southern limit of those constellations gave clues to the latitude of their observers. She shared with her husband a fascination for the astronomy of the early Hindus and Persians, and wrote many articles on the subject. Maunder survived Edward, who died in 1928, by nineteen years; she died on September 15, 1947.

SELECTED WRITINGS BY MAUNDER:

Books

(With Edward Maunder) *The Heavens and Their Story.* R. Culley, 1908.

Catalogue of Recurrent Groups of Sun Spots for the Year 1874 to 1906. Neill, 1909.

FURTHER READING

Books

Ogilvie, Marilyn Bailey. *Women in Science: Antiquity Through the Nineteenth Century.* Cambridge: MIT Press, 1986, pp. 129–230.

Periodicals

Journal of the British Astronomical Association (December 1947): 238.

Sketch by Sebastian Thaler

Antonia Caetana de Paiva Pereira Maury
1866–1952
American astronomer

Antonia Maury (Science Photo Library. Photo Researchers, Inc. Reproduced by permission.)

Antonia Maury's long career included 25 years at the Harvard College Observatory. While there, she used her expertise in spectroscopy (the study of light wavelengths) to create a classification system of spectral lines that later proved to correspond to the appearance of particular stars. Maury's system in fact improved on the system developed by **Annie Jump Cannon**, the famed "census taker of the skies" who also worked out of Harvard. The Maury classification system is considered an integral element of the development of theoretical astrophysics.

Antonia Caetana de Paiva Pereira Maury was born in Cold Spring, NewYork, on March 21, 1866. Her family had long been involved in science. Her mother, Virginia Draper Maury, was a sister of the astronomer Henry Draper and daughter of the chemist John Draper. Her father, Mytton Maury, was a cousin of the oceanographer Matthew Fontaine Maury; although a minister himself, he was an amateur naturalist and editor of a geography magazine. Maury's younger sister, **Carlotta Joaquina Maury**, was a noted paleontologist.

Maury was educated at home and attended Vassar College, from which she obtained a bachelor of arts degree in 1887. Because of her interest in astronomy, her father wrote to the Harvard astronomer Edward Pickering asking him to hire the young Antonia. Pickering had doubts about hiring a Vassar graduate for a mere assistant's position (for which he could pay no more than 25 cents an hour), but he decided to give her a chance.

Devises Stellar Classification System

Her first task at Harvard was the classification of northern stars according to spectra. She assisted Pickering in identifying binary stars, groups of two stars that revolve around each other under mutual gravitation. She quickly mastered spectroscopy and set to work on revising the classification system then in place, which she found inadequate. Light which passes through chemical elements is absorbed at specific wavelengths characteristic to the elements. These chemical signatures show up as absorption lines in light spectra, making it possible to study both the chemical constitution of stars and the light they emit by means of spectroscopy. Maury realized that classifications could be made on the basis of the lines themselves—their intensity, width, and distance from one another. By 1891, she had mapped out her classification scheme.

During this time, however, Pickering's fear had become reality; Maury had grown bored with the Harvard routine. Moreover, she feltstifled by Pickering's supervision. Maury was an innovator—something Pickering did not admire, although he recognized her talents. Maury left the Observatory in 1891 to become a teacher, but returned periodically to continue her work on the classification system. She published her system in 1897, and left the Harvard Observatory, to which she would not return for more than 20 years.

Maury served as a visiting teacher and lecturer; she also tutored students privately. In 1918, she returned to Harvard as a research associate and continued her work on binary stars, in particular spectroscopic binaries. In 1920, Harlow Shapley became director of the Observatory, and

Maury's working relationship with him was far more amiable than her experience with Pickering had been.

She retired from Harvard in 1935 and moved to Westchester County, New York, where she became curator of the Draper Observatory and Museum in Hastings–on–Hudson; the museum had formerly been part of the Draper family estate. She retired from that position in 1938 and spent the rest of her life pursuing, in addition to astronomy, such other interests as ornithology and conservation. In 1943, Maury was awarded the Annie J. Cannon Prize by the American Astronomical Society. She died in Dobbs Ferry, New York, on January 8, 1952.

SELECTED WRITINGS BY MAURY:

Periodicals

"Spectra of Bright Stars Photographed with the 11–inch Draper Telescope as a Part of the Henry Draper Memorial and Discussed by Antonia C. Maury under the direction of Edward C. Pickering." *Annals of the Astronomical Observatory of Harvard College* 28, part 1 (1897).

"The Spectral Changes of Beta Lyrae." *Annals of the Astronomical Observatory of Harvard College* 84, no. 8 (1933).

FURTHER READING

Books

Abbott, D., ed, *Biographical Dictionary of Scientists:Astronomers.* Bedrick Books, 1984.

Ogilvie, Marilyn Bailey. *Women In Science: Antiquity through the Nineteenth Century.* Cambridge: MIT Press, 1986.

Sketch by George A. Milite

Carlotta Joaquina Maury
1874–1938
American paleontologist

Carlotta Joaquina Maury was a specialist in the stratigraphy and fossil fauna of Brazil, Venezuela, and the West Indies, contributing a number of scientific reports on these regions and describing several new fossil genera and species. In 1916, she headed up her own paleontological expedition to the Dominican Republic. Maury taught, traveled and consulted widely, acting for many years as an advisor to the Venezuelan division of the Royal Dutch Shell Petroleum Company, and as the official paleontologist to the government of Brazil.

Maury was born January 6, 1874, at Hastings–on–Hudson, New York, one of three children of Mytton Maury, who was an Episcopal minister, and Virginia (Draper) Maury. The Maury family line dated back to Matthew Maury, who left England and arrived in Virginia in 1718. Maury's great–grandfather, James Maury, was appointed by George Washington to be the first U.S. consul to Liverpool, a post he held for 40 years. Many of the other Maury family members had scientific backgrounds. The hydrographer and meteorologist Commodore Matthew Fontaine Maury was a cousin, and Carlotta's father edited many revisions of his treatises. Maury's elder sister, **Antonia Maury**, had a distinguished career as a research astronomer at the Harvard Observatory, classifying the spectra of stars. Carlotta's grandfather on her mother's side was the physicist John William Draper.

Maury displayed an early interest in zoology and geology. She attended Radcliffe College for a year, then spent three years at Cornell University, graduating in 1896 with a bachelor of philosophy degree. She received the Schuyler Fellowship for graduate research from Cornell, studied at the University of Paris for two years, then received a Ph.D. degree from Cornell in 1902, with a thesis titled "A Comparison of the Oligocene of Western Europe and the Southern United States."

Maury also studied at Columbia University and from 1904 through 1906 was an assistant in the department of paleontology there. From 1907 through 1909 she was a geologist for the Louisiana state geological survey, preparing reports on the region's petroleum and rock salt deposits. From 1909 through 1912 she lectured in geology at Barnard College, accepting only a token salary for her services. From 1912 through 1915 she was professor of geology and zoology at Huguenot College of the University of the Cape of Good Hope, South Africa.

Maury was a paleontologist for the Venezuelan geological expedition headed by Arthur Clifford Veatch conducted from 1910 to 1911. In 1916, as a Sarah Berliner Fellow, she organized and conducted the Maury expedition to the Dominican Republic. In addition to her paleontological work for the Royal Dutch Petroleum Company and the Brazilian government, Maury provided reports to New York City's American Museum of Natural History. Her specialty was the study of South American and West Indian stratigraphy and fossil fauna. Maury was known to have a sparkling personality, to enjoy philosophical discussions, and to sprinkle her prolific writings with humor and poetic charm.

Maury was a fellow of the American Association for the Advancement of Science, the Geological Society of America, and the American Geographical Society, and a corresponding member of the Brazilian Academy of Sciences. She never married. In 1936 she moved from Hastings–on–Hudson to Yonkers, New York, and she died January 3, 1938, at her home in Yonkers.

SELECTED WRITINGS BY MAURY:

Periodicals

"The Soldado Rock Section." *Science* 82 (1935): 192–193.

FURTHER READING

Books

The National Cyclopedia of American Biography. Vol. 28. White, 1940, pp. 25–26.

Periodicals

"Miss C. J. Maury, Paleontologist." *New York Times* (January 4, 1938): 23.

Sketch by Jill Carpenter

Martha Dartt Maxwell
1831–1881
American naturalist and taxidermist

Known as the Colorado huntress and naturalist, Martha Dartt Maxwell was one of the first American women field naturalists and among the first American women to collect and display her own animal specimens. Maxwell is credited as the first taxidermist to pose specimens in a natural position, thus ensuring that natural history displays in museums had authenticity. She also advocated her belief that in such museums, animals should be grouped together by the habitats in which they are found.

Martha was born in Dartt's Settlement, Pennsylvania, on July 21, 1831. She was the only child of Spencer and Amy (Wooster) Dartt. When Martha was two, her father died. Her mother eventually remarried her husband's first cousin, Josiah Dartt, when Martha was 10. Because Amy Dartt was quite ill for most of Martha's childhood, her early education took place at home under the tutelage of her maternal grandmother, Abigail Wooster. Her grandmother shared her love of nature with her granddaughter, introducing her to local wildlife and natural phenomenon.

When Martha was 11, her family began a missionary trip to Oregon. Illness decimated the ranks of their group, taking the life of her grandmother, among others. The family stopped and settled in Baraboo, Wisconsin, in 1845. Because her mother was still ill, and she had two younger half sisters to take care of, Martha took charge of the household. She was still determined to get an education, which her stepfather supported, although the family lived in poverty.

Martha managed to attend Oberlin College, in Oberlin, Ohio, for a year and a half from 1851–52. She worked to support herself, but could not make enough to survive. Upon her return to Baraboo, she taught school for a year, then returned to college at Lawrence University, in Appleton, WI, attending from 1853–54. Through her roommate at Lawrence University, Martha met a wealthy local businessman, James Maxwell. Twenty years older than her, James Maxwell was a widower with six children. They married in 1854, and had one child together, Mabel, in 1858.

James Maxwell lost his fortune in the Panic of 1857, a period of great economic depression, and the family relocated to Colorado in 1860. He found work in the local sawmill industry and as a cattle driver. Martha co–owned boarding houses, and used the money she saved to buy a ranch. One day when she was absent from her claim, a German taxidermist jumped her claim. When she returned, she became fascinated by his specimens and asked him to teach her the art. He refused, and eventually the court awarded her back her claim on the land.

This experience determined the course of Martha Maxwell's life. She had already been interested in the nature of the west, and decided to become a taxidermist. She returned to Baraboo and spent the next four years learning the craft. After a brief stay in Vineland, New Jersey, where Maxwell had bought land, she returned to Colorado with her daughter and husband in 1868.

That year, she began taking camping trips to hunt and collect specimens of all kinds of birds and animals. Though she was a strict vegetarian and did not enjoy killing animals, Maxwell believed that taxidermy was her way of preserving nature. She became a skilled taxidermist by trial and error, and began posing her specimens in life–like positions reflective of the animal's habitat. This artistic skill of Maxwell's led to some local attention. She began to sell some mounted pieces and built up her own collection. This collection was displayed at nearby fairs.

In 1870, Maxwell sold her first collection of specimens to St. Louis's Shaw's Garden. This sale led to more work, collecting for and selling specimens to the Smithsonian Institution. Maxwell's skill as a collector of specimens paid off when she discovered a new subspecies of owl, what came to be known as the Rocky Mountain Screech Owl. In 1877, a Smithsonian ornithologist named this animal Scops asio maxwelliae for her, the first woman to be so honored.

Maxwell's collection was so large that she opened up a museum in Colorado in the mid–1870s. Her first Rocky Mountain Museum opened in Boulder in 1874. She moved it to Denver in 1875. Of her collection, Helen Hunt of the Boulder Colorado News in 1875, wrote, "That a pioneer woman could shoot wild cats and grizzlies seemed not unnatural or improbable but that the same woman could also stuff an animal skillfully and with artistic effort seemed unlikely. I found Mrs. Maxwell to be a sculptor of animals with a rare gift."

In 1876, Maxwell's work became internationally lauded. She represented Colorado at the Centennial Exhibition of 1876, in Philadelphia, PA. With the help of the Colorado legislature her collection of 47 mammals and 224 birds, most every animal found in Colorado, was displayed. Maxwell made no money off the project. When the Exhibition was over, the Colorado legislature backed out of its promise to pay to transport the collection back. Maxwell was forced to stay on the East Coast, where she exhibited the collection.

Maxwell found it hard to make a living, working odd jobs to make ends meet. During this time, she furthered her education by attending the Women's Laboratory at the Massachusetts Institute of Technology. She studied zoology and chemistry and learned to use a microscope for the first time. With her half–sister Mary Dartt, Maxwell wrote and published a book in 1879 about herself entitled *On the Plains, and Among the Peaks; or, How Mrs. Maxwell Made her Natural History Collection*. Unfortunately, it did not sell well.

Maxell spent the last years of her life in Far Rockaway, New York, where she owned and ran a bath house/museum from 1880–81. This venture also proved unsuccessful. She died on May 31, 1881, in Brooklyn, New York, of a blood poisoning caused by an ovarian tumor. Her collection fell into uncaring hands and eventually was lost.

SELECTED WRITINGS BY MAXWELL:

Books

(With Mary Dartt) *On the Plains, and Among the Peaks; or, How Mrs. Maxwell Made her Natural History Collection.* Philadelphia: Claxton, Remsen, and Haffelfinger, 1879.

FURTHER READING

Books

Abir–Am, Pnina and Dorinda Outram, eds. *Uneasy Careers and Intimate Lives: Women in Science, 1789–1979.* New Brunswick: Rutgers University Press, 1987, pp. 73–75.

Bailey, Martha J. *American Women in Science: A Biographical Dictionary.* Denver: ABC–CLIO, 1994.

Benson, Maxine. *Martha Maxwell: Rocky Mountain Naturalist.* Lincoln: University of Nebraska Press, 1986.

Bonta, Marcia Myers. *Women in the Field: America's Pioneer Women Naturalists.* College Station: Texas A&M Press, 1991.

Ewan, Joseph and Nesta Dunn Ewan. *Biographical Dictionary of Rocky Mountain Naturalists: A Guide to the Writings and Collections of Botanists, Zoologists, Geologists, Artists, and Photographers, 1682–1932.* Utrecht: Bohn, Scheltema & Holkema, 1981.

Sterling, Keir B., et al, eds. *Biographical Dictionary of American and Canadian Naturalists and Environmentalists.* Westport: Greenwood Press, 1997.

Periodicals

De Lapp, Mary. "Pioneer Women Naturalist." *The Colorado Quarterly* (Summer 1964): 91–96.

Ewan, Joseph. Review of *Martha Maxwell: Rocky Mountain Naturalist*, by Maxine Benson. *Isis* (June 1987): 320–21.

Sketch by Annette Petrusso

Barbara McClintock
1902–1992
American geneticist

Barbara McClintock was a pioneering American geneticist whose discovery of transposable or "jumping genes" in the 1940s baffled most of her contemporaries for nearly three decades. A recluse by nature, McClintock spent nearly fifty years working apart from the mainstream of the scientific community. Yet her colleagues had such a high regard for her as an adherent to rigid scientific principles that they accepted her discovery of transposable genes decades before others could confirm her observations. McClintock was eventually awarded the Nobel Prize in medicine or physiology in 1983 for this prescient discovery.

McClintock's childhood years shaped her to be a woman who lived outside of the conventional expectations of both the scientific and secular worlds. The third of four children, she was born on June 16, 1902, in Hartford, Connecticut. Her parents, Thomas Henry McClintock and Sara Handy, were married in 1898. Her father graduated with a medical degree from Boston University shortly after their marriage, but it took him several years to establish a solid and profitable practice. After the birth of the fourth child, her mother began to show emotional strain. McClintock had an adversarial relationship with her mother, and so to relieve some of the tension she was sent off to live with an aunt and uncle in rural Massachusetts. This was an arrangement that continued off and on throughout the early years of her life, and McClintock, characteristically, insisted that she was never homesick while away from her parents. She was happy to roam the outdoors, where she developed a love of nature that was to last a lifetime.

McClintock's differences with her mother continued when she returned home, and she grew to be solitary and independent. Her family moved to Brooklyn, New York in 1908, where her father had obtained a position as a company

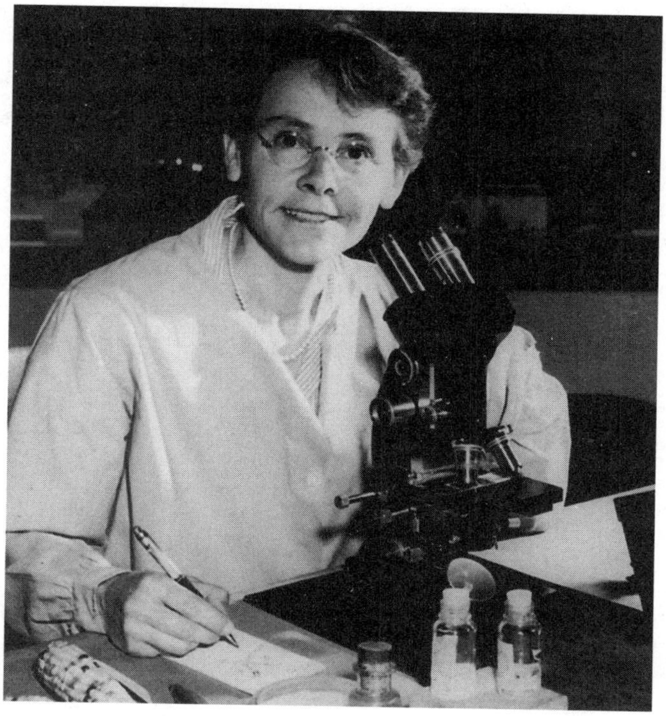

Barbara McClintock (AP/Wide World Photos. Reproduced by permission.)

physician with Standard Oil. Interestingly, this future scientist's father forbade any of his children's teachers to give them homework, regarding six hours a day in school as ample education, and as a result McClintock had plenty of time to pursue outside interests, such as playing the piano and ice skating. An inveterate tomboy, she asked to wear boys' clothes at a young age, a wish her parents granted. Once, a neighbor who saw her playing sports with boys chided McClintock to do girl things. Despite her own conventional views of a woman's role in society, Sara quickly called the neighbor and told her never to reprimand her daughter again.

Begins Investigations in Cytology

After graduating from Erasmus High School in Brooklyn, McClintock enrolled at Cornell University in 1919. During her freshman and sophomore years she had a normal college social life, including dating and even playing tenor banjo in a jazz band. Elected president of the freshman class, she was popular among her fellow students and was asked to join a sorority. But when McClintock learned that the sorority would not accept Jewish students, she refused the invitation. This kind of reaction was to be characteristic of McClintock throughout her life. She never hesitated to snub the social conventions of her time, especially those concerning women's role in society. She decided early on to remain an independent, single woman devoted to her work; she had little inclination to marry or start a family.

McClintock became interested in the study of the cells, known as cytology, under the tutelage of Lester Sharp, a professor who gave her private lessons on Saturdays. She exhibited a keen intellect as an undergraduate and was invited to take graduate–level genetics courses while still in her junior year. She received her B.S. in 1923 and entered graduate school, where she majored in cytology and minored in genetics and zoology. At that time, geneticists favored studies of the fruit fly *Drosophila*, which produces a new offspring every ten days. This rapid production of successive generations offered geneticists the opportunity to see quickly the results of genetic traits passed on through crossbreeding. It was studies of *Drosophila* that produced much of the early evidence of the relationship between genes and chromosomes. Chromosomes are the strands of biological material seen at the time of cell division, and studies confirmed that they carried the genes that passed hereditary traits from one generation to the next. At Cornell, the main focus of genetic research was corn, or maize, whose varicolored kernels, relatively long life spans, and larger chromosomes (which could be more easily viewed under the microscope) offered geneticists the opportunity to identify specific genetic processes.

While still in graduate school, McClintock had refined and simplified a technique originally developed by John Belling to prepare slides for the study of chromosome structures under a microscope. McClintock made modifications to this technique that enabled her to apply it to detailed chromosomal studies of maize. She obtained her M.A. degree in 1925 and her Ph.D. two years later and then was appointed an instructor in Cornell's botany department. McClintock's research at that time focused on linkage groups, the inherited sets or groups of genes that appear on a chromosome. Geneticists had already discovered these linkage groups in *Drosophila,* and McClintock set out to relate specific linkage groups to specific chromosomes in maize.

Robert A. Emerson, a pioneer in the genetics of maize, was a professor at Cornell at this time, and he was drawing promising young geneticists to the university. Marcus Rhoades, who would become a renowned geneticist in his own right, came to do his graduate work at Cornell and formed an immediate friendship with McClintock that was to last throughout their lives. Years later, in an interview with McClintock's biographer, Evelyn Fox Keller, Rhoades said: "I've known a lot of famous scientists. But the only one I thought was really a genius was McClintock." Other young graduate students migrating to Cornell included George Beadle, who went on to win a Nobel Prize for his work in molecular genetics, and Harriet Creighton, who was a student of McClintock's. Together, these young scientists formed the core of a supportive and enthusiastic group of geneticists at Cornell studying the sequences of genes on chromosomes.

In 1931, McClintock and Creighton published a landmark study proving a theory geneticists had previously believed without proof: that a correlation existed between genetic and chromosomal crossover. Their study revealed that genetic information was exchanged during the early stages of meiosis, the process of cell division. They found that this exchange occurred when parts of homologous chromosomes (chromosomes on which particular genes are identically located) were exchanged in the same division that produced sex cells. These experiments were to become recognized as the cornerstone of modern genetic research; Horace Freeland Judson has called them "one of the truly great experiments of modern biology." This groundbreaking work and McClintock's successive studies further establishing this relationship eventually led to her election to the National Academy of Sciences in 1944 and presidency of the Genetics Society of America in 1945.

Works for Many Years without a Permanent Appointment

Despite having achieved worldwide recognition among her colleagues, the 1930s were difficult years for McClintock. The Great Depression had impacted university funding and she found herself in the precarious position of having no stipend from Cornell University and no large grants to support her research. She received a Guggenheim Fellowship in 1933 that enabled her to go to the Kaiser Wilhelm Institute in Berlin, but she left after only a short stay because of her concerns over Hitler's rise to power and his anti–Semitic beliefs. Fortunately, by this time funding had been garnered from the Rockefeller Foundation to help support her efforts. In 1936, she received an appointment to the University of Missouri as an assistant professor of botany, her first faculty appointment. During this time, she performed further experiments delineating the cellular processes of chromosomal interactions, especially their effects on large–scale mutations. Although this appointment provided a secure base for McClintock to continue her work, her relationship with the University of Missouri did not develop. After five years, the university decided that McClintock did not fit into its future plans.

Embarks on Nobel Prize-winning Research

In the following decade, as war dominated much of the world, McClintock had perhaps her most productive years as a geneticist. In the summer before the bombing of Pearl Harbor, Marcus Rhoades obtained an invitation for his out–of–work friend and colleague to spend the summer at the Cold Spring Harbor Laboratory in New York. Run by the Carnegie Institute of Washington, the laboratory was a self–contained facility that had its own summer houses for researchers. On the first of December, 1941, McClintock was offered a one–year position at Cold Spring, where she would spend the remainder of her career. By the summer of 1944, McClintock had initiated the studies that would lead to her discovery of genetic transposition. She had noticed different–colored spots that did not belong on the green or yellow leaves of a particular plant. She surmised that the larger the discoloration patch, the earlier the mutation had occurred, believing that many large patches on the leaves meant the mutation had occurred early in the plant's development. From this observation, McClintock determined that mutations occurred at a constant rate that did not change within a plant's life cycle, which led her to the concept of regulation and control in the passing on of genetic information. Investigating how this passing on of genetic information could be regulated, McClintock next noticed that in addition to these regular mutations there also occurred exceptions, in which there were different types of mutations not normally associated with the plant. Convinced that something must occur at the early stages of meiosis to cause these irregular mutations, McClintock put the full forces of her intellect into identifying what it might be, again working with maize.

McClintock discovered kernels on a self–pollinated ear of corn that had distinctive pigmentation but should have been clear, suggesting a loss of some genetic information that normally would have been passed on to inhibit color. Finally, after two years, she found what she called a controlled breakage in the chromosome, and in 1948 she coined the term "transposition" to describe how an element is released from its original position on the chromosome and inserted into a new position. As a result of this "jumping gene," plant offspring could have an unexpected pattern of heredity due to a specific genetic code that other offspring did not have. In fact, two transposable genes were involved in the process: one, which she called a "dissociator" gene, allowed the release of the "activator" gene, which could then be transposed to a different site.

In 1950, McClintock published her research on transposition, but her work was not well received. Her discovery went against the genetic theory then current that genes were stable components of chromosomes; also, very few of her contemporaries could actually understand her work. It wasn't until the 1970s—when technology had been developed that enabled geneticists to study genes on the molecular, rather than cellular, level—that McClintock's ideas were truly understood by the scientific community. Her discovery presaged many later discoveries, such as genetic imprinting or the "presetting" of genetic activity. Her work also would eventually be used to explain inheritance patterns that seemed to lie outside the strict Mendelian law based on simple ratios of dominant and recessive genes. In 1983, McClintock was awarded the Nobel Prize for physiology or medicine for her discovery of mobile genetic systems.

One of the most intriguing aspects of McClintock's discovery is how she deduced the theory of transposition and proved it while other pioneering geneticists remained in the dark. Some have called her a "prophet" of genetics, and her discovery may have owed much to her ability to have "a feeling for the organism," as she told Evelyn Fox Keller. Forming an intense identification with the plants she studied, McClintock was able to notice the slightest differences, even on a cellular level. Although McClintock adhered strictly to the scientific method in proving her theories, she told Keller that as scientists she and her colleagues were also "limiting ourselves" by using this method. Interested in Eastern thought and religion, she practiced methods to control her own body temperature and blood flow, and she seemed to some to have the ability to see what was going on in her own mind long before she could prove it.

McClintock spent the remainder of her life at Cold Spring Harbor, studying transposition. Although very private, McClintock could be sociable and she loved to talk about science, philosophy, and art. She was known, at times, to accompany the local children home from the school bus, describing to them the intricacies of nature as they walked. She often complained in her later years that scientists no longer stayed over the summer at Cold Spring Harbor, and she rarely became well acquainted with them. She died on September 2, 1992, shortly after friends had celebrated her ninetieth birthday. She was acknowledged as a true pioneer in every sense of the word, and many of her fellow scientists believe that her accomplishments came from an intense desire for knowledge and the commitment to keep working on a problem. In an obituary in *Nature,* Gerald R. Fink aptly notes that her "burning curiosity, enthusiasm, and uncompromising honesty serve as a constant reminder of what drew us all to science in the first place."

SELECTED WRITINGS BY MCCLINTOCK:

Books

The Control of Gene Action in Maize. Brookhaven Symposia in Biology, 1965.

FURTHER READING

Books

Batstein, David, and Nina Federoff, eds. *The Dynamic Genome: Barbara McClintock's Ideas in the Century of Genetics.* Cold Spring Harbor Laboratory Press, 1991.

Judson, Horace Freeland. *The Eighth Day of Creation: Makers of the Revolution in Biology.* New York: Simon and Schuster, 1979, p. 216.

Keller, Evelyn Fox. *A Feeling for the Organism: The Life and Work of Barbara McClintock.* W. H. Freeman, 1983.

Periodicals

Fincham, J. R. S. "Moving with the Times." *Nature* (August 20, 1992): 631–632.

Fink, Gerald R. "Barbara McClintock (1902–1992)." *Nature,* (September 24, 1992): 272.

Sketch by David Petechuk

Margaret Sumwalt McCouch
1901–1998

American marine biologist

Margaret Sumwalt McCouch spent many years as a teacher and researcher, mostly in her home state of Pennsylvania. Despite her strong interest in science and what the Marine Biological Laboratory Archives describes as an "active and productive scientific career," she almost lost her chance to become a scientist.

McCouch was born Margaret Sumwalt on April 21, 1901 in Pennsylvania. After completing her bachelor's degree she spent time at the Marine Biological Laboratory (located in Woods Hole, Massachusetts) as a botany student. From there she went to Philadelphia to do graduate work at the University of Pennsylvania. She served there as an instructor in the physiology department and in 1929 was awarded a Ph.D. in physiology.

It was thanks to Merkel H. Jacobs, director of the Marine Biological Laboratory from 1926 to 1937, that McCouch was able to obtain her degree. Jacobs was also a professor of physiology at the University of Pennsylvania, and he arranged for the young student to get a paying position as a lab assistant. He also arranged for Penn to let her complete her course of study tuition–free. At first the school refused, but Jacobs was persistent and ultimately succeeded.

McCouch maintained ties with the Marine Biological Laboratory, where she served as a summer instructor from 1931 to 1933. Later, she did research in Baltimore and served as assistant professor at the Women's Medical College of Pennsylvania, as well as assistant professor of pharmacology at the University of Michigan. One of her primary areas of interest was the structure of trematodes (for example, flukes and flatworms). She also studied electrophysiology, the study of how electrical phenomena affect the function of different organisms. Other areas of study included permeability and water balance, as well as the pharmacology of certain derivatives of morphine. During this varied career, she was a member of the National Institute of Health and the U. S. Public Health Service.

She was married to Grayson McCouch, who predeceased her. After she retired, she settled in Chadds Ford, Pennsylvania, where she died on May 7, 1998, shortly after her 97th birthday.

SELECTED WRITINGS BY MCCOUCH:

"Permeability of the Fundulus egg to ions: chorion versus skin." *Proceedings of the Society of Experimental Biological Medicine* 25 (1928).

(With William R. Amberson and Eva M. Michaelis) "Factors concerned in the origin of concentration potentials across the skin of the frog." *Journal of Cell & Comparative Physiology* 4, no. 1 (1933).

(With Eugene M. Landis) "An automatic recording apparatus for measurement of colloid osmotic pressure." *Journal of Laboratory and Clinical Medicine* 22 (1937).

FURTHER READING

Other

"Margaret Sumwalt McCouch." *Marine Biological Laboratory Library Archives.* http://www.mbl.edu/html/WOMEN/sum.html (July 13, 1999).

Sketch by George A. Milite

Elizabeth McCoy
1903–1978
American microbiologist

Elizabeth McCoy was known for her varied research interests, in industrial microbiology, the taxonomy or classification of bacteria, bacterial pollution of fresh water lakes, and bacteria that colonize the roots of plants. She received patents on bacterial fermentation and on a research antibiotic. An inspired teacher, McCoy spent her entire academic career at the University of Wisconsin in Madison, where she promoted the careers of many young microbiologists.

McCoy's grandparents had come to Wisconsin as pioneers and her parents, Esther Williamson and Cassius James McCoy, grew up on neighboring farms. Although both her parents began their careers as school teachers, McCoy's father later became a builder in Madison and her mother became a nurse. Elizabeth McCoy was born in Madison in 1903. Summers were spent on the family farm and, since her brother had other interests, McCoy was taught to farm by her father. In later years, she took over management of the farm.

Attending progressive public schools, McCoy excelled in Latin, mathematics, and chemistry. From childhood, she was interested in bacteria that caused disease in humans and farm animals. When it came time to choose her college major, McCoy's dual interests in farming and bacteriology led her to study general bacteriology in the College of Agriculture at the University of Wisconsin. As an undergraduate she studied with an old family friend, the bacteriologist Dr. William Dodge Frost. During her senior year, she was offered a graduate research associate position in the department with Edwin B. Fred, who supervised both her master's degree and her Ph.D.

Research Takes Her All Over the World

As a graduate student, McCoy began her research into *Clostridium*, anaerobic bacteria that live in the absence of oxygen and produce acetone and butyl alcohol by fermentation. Over the next 12 years McCoy coauthored a large number of papers on this research and wrote the section on *Clostridium* for Bergey's *Manual of Determinative Bacteriology*. In 1940, the University of Wisconsin sent her to Arroy, Puerto Rico, to help with a government butyl alcohol fermentation plant. McCoy was able to stem an outbreak of bacteriophages (organisms that kill bacteria) that was ruining the fermentation with a culture she developed. She would eventually patent the method used in the plant.

McCoy's other research project as a graduate student involved bacteria that inhabit the root nodules of plants. After receiving her Ph.D. in 1929, McCoy continued this research as a National Research Council Postdoctoral Fellow at the Rothamsted Experimental Station in England, and at the Botanical Institute of Karlova University in Prague, Czechoslovakia. The following year she returned to Wisconsin where she was appointed assistant professor of bacteriology. In 1943, McCoy was made full professor, only the second woman at the University of Wisconsin, outside of the home economics and nursing departments, to attain that rank. In 1936 McCoy spent a year as an associate in medicine at the George Williams Hooper Foundation of the University of California in San Francisco. Her work there developed into a long–lasting research interest in various types of food poisoning.

Discovers Antibiotic

During the second world war, McCoy worked for the United States Office of Scientific Research and Development, studying the recently–discovered antibiotic, penicillin. McCoy isolated a strain of fungi that produced enough antibiotic that it could be made available to the general public. McCoy also developed screening methods to search for new antibiotics and, in the process, discovered oligomycin, an antibiotic which proved to be important for research biochemists. She carried out genetic studies on antibiotic resistance, nutritional studies on chickens treated with antibiotics, and studies on staphylococcal bacteria that cause food poisoning. From 1940 on, McCoy was interested in bacteriophages, the viruses that infect bacteria. She and her coworkers produced some of the earliest pictures of bacteriophage, taken with an electron microscope.

Works for Clean Water

McCoy began spending her summers at the Trout Lake Station in the lake district of northern Wisconsin and eventually she became director of the bacteriological laboratory there. Her research examined the roles of various microorganisms in lakes. In 1969, she was awarded a Sea Grant to study the bacterial populations of Lake Michigan, with regard to fish spawning. She also was chairperson of the graduate school committee that oversaw research projects on Lake Mendota in Madison and worked to protect and improve water quality there.

McCoy spent more than 40 years in the Department of Bacteriology at the University of Wisconsin in Madison. She published three books and 103 research papers and was a popular teacher who supervised 47 Ph.D. students and at least 110 master's degree students. She was the only woman on the regional research review committee. McCoy served as an editor of *Biological Abstracts* and the *Journal of Bacteriology*. Although she retired in 1973, McCoy continued working until her death in 1978. From 1971 on, McCoy was editor of the *Transactions* of the Wisconsin Academy of Sciences, Arts and Letters and in 1976 became president of the academy. During those years, she also was involved in a cooperative effort with the State of Wisconsin and the Environmental Protection Agency on waste management. McCoy was a member of a number of scientific societies and the recipient of several awards, including a posthumous honorary doctorate from the University of Wisconsin at Milwaukee.

McCoy, who never married, donated her family farms to the Wisconsin Alumni Research Foundation. Her patents on oligomycin and bacterial fermentation were assigned to the Wisconsin Alumni Research Foundation.

SELECTED WRITINGS BY MCCOY:

Books

(With E. B. Fred and I. L. Baldwin) *Root Nodule Bacteria and Leguminous Plants*. University of Wisconsin Studies in Science. Number 5, supplement. Madison: University of Wisconsin Press, 1939.

Periodicals

(With A. F. Langlykke and W. H. Peterson) "Products from the Fermentation of Glucose and Arabinose by Butyric Anaerobes." *Journal of Bacteriology* 29 (1935): 333–47.

(With A. T. Henrici) "The Distribution of Heterotrophic Bacteria in the Bottom Deposits of Some Lakes." *Transactions of the Wisconsin Academy of Sciences, Arts and Letters* 31 (1938): 323–61.

(With L. S. McClung) "Serological Relations Among Spore–Forming Anaerobic Bacteria." *Bacteriological Reviews* 2 (1938): 47–97.

"Changes in the Host Flora Induced by Chemotherapeutic Agents." *Annual Review of Microbiology* 8 (1954): 257–72.

(With J. I. Frea and F. M. Strong) "Purification of Type B Staphylococcal enterotoxin." *Journal of Bacteriology* 86 (1963): 1308–13.

(With E. B. Roslycky and O. N. Allen) "Physiochemical Properties of Phages of *Agrobacterium radiobacter*." *Canadian Journal of Microbiology* 9 (1963): 119–209.

FURTHER READING

Books

O'Hern, Elizabeth Moot. *Profiles of Pioneer Women Scientists*. Washington, D.C.: Acropolis Books, 1985.

Periodicals

Sarles, W. B. "Obituary: Elizabeth McCoy." *American Society for Microbiology News* 44 (1978): 266–67.

Sketch by Margaret Alic

Marcia Kemper McNutt
1952–
American marine geophysicist

Marcia McNutt is a marine geophysicist whose principal research involves the use of marine geophysical data collected by remote sensors that measured acoustic energy, variations in the gravity field, and variations in the magnetic field. McNutt uses this data to study the physical properties of the earth beneath the oceans. Some of her most notable work involves French Polynesia and its volcanic history. McNutt is a veteran of at least two dozen oceanographic expeditions.

McNutt was born on February 19, 1952, in Minneapolis, Minnesota. She is the daughter of Patricia Suzanne (McClain) and Richard Charles McNutt. Her father owned a family plate glass business. McNutt was interested in science as a child, and especially enjoyed the outdoors. She visited the California oceans with her grandmother throughout her childhood. McNutt graduated as valedictorian of her class at the Northrop Collegiate School in Minneapolis.

After graduation, McNutt entered Colorado College, where a mentor encouraged her to pursue science. She also took a month-long trip with a geology class in Colorado's mountains, an experience that made science real and exciting to her. McNutt graduated summa cum laude from Colorado College in 1973 with a B.A. in physics and went on to graduate school at the Scripps Institute of Oceanography. Her graduate education was paid for in part by a National Science Foundation Graduate Fellowship.

The year 1978 was significant for McNutt. She earned her Ph.D. in Earth sciences from Scripps and on July 1, 1978, married Marcel Edward Hoffmann. They eventually had three daughters: Meredith, Ashley, and Dana. McNutt also held her first real position, working as an visiting assistant professor at the University of Minnesota from 1978–1979. In this time period, she became affiliated with the National Aeronautic and Space Administration's

(NASA) Science Steering Group Geopotential Research Mission.

After leaving Minnesota in 1979, McNutt was hired by the United States Geological Survey, in Menlo Park, California. She worked as a geophysicist researcher, focusing on earthquake predication. McNutt also expanded her professional horizons in another way. She was a member of the John Muir Geophysical Society, and served as that group's secretary from 1979–1983. She was also an associate editor at the *Journal of Geophysical Research* from 1980–1983.

In 1982, McNutt left the United States Geological Survey when she was hired by the Massachusetts Institute for Technology (MIT). She began her academic career as an assistant professor in geophysics in the Department of Earth, Atmospheric and Planetary Sciences. She rose through the ranks, becoming an associate professor in 1986, then a full professor in 1989. McNutt's abilities as a teacher were recognized and appreciated by her students. In 1985, she received the Graduate Student Council Award for teaching.

McNutt's life changed drastically August 3, 1988, when she became a widow with three young children. However, she continued to persevere in her career. She became a member of the American Geophysical Union, a professional organization which bestowed her with the Macelevane Award in 1988 for outstanding research by a young scientist. Three years later she became the Earl A. Griswold Professor of Geophysics at MIT and, in 1995, the director of the Joint Program in Oceanography and Applied Ocean Science and Engineering, a cooperative graduate educational program between MIT and Woods Hold Oceanographic Institution.

By this time, McNutt had done numerous oceanic explorations aboard ships affiliated with Woods Hold, Scripps, Lamont-Doherty Earth Observatory, and Oregon State University. She served as the chief scientist on five of these explorations, mostly in French Polynesia, where she made her most significant scientific contributions. She discovered that French Polynesia has been a locus for abnormally high amounts of volcanic activity for well over 100 million years. McNutt argued that French Polynesia was, in a sense, Earth's "stovepipe," in that large updrafts of heat from the deep mantle keep the inner layer of the Earth's crust in the underlying region in a perpetually partial molten stage, allowing many volcanic islands to form. She also discovered that the Earth's crust under the region is only about two-thirds its normal thickness. McNutt published these findings in *Science,* one of the most prestigious science journals in the world.

McNutt left MIT in 1997, when she was hired as director for the Monterey Bay Aquarium Research Institute, in Moss Landing, California. She also served as the Institute's president and CEO. This provided a new challenge for McNutt, who described the research as high-risk and high-tech. Two years later, she reached another career high when she was elected to a two-year term as president of the American Geophysical Union, having been the president of the tectonphysics section from 1994–1999. In 1999, McNutt also remarried, to Ian Wallace Young, a sea captain.

Of her life as a scientist, McNutt told Charles H. Ball of *MIT Tech Talk* that, "What's nice about geophysics is that it's not always apparent what needs to be done next, and you often find that taking a circuitous route is the quickest way to get from A to B."

SELECTED WRITINGS BY MCNUTT:

Periodicals

"Deep Causes of Hotspots." *Nature* (August 23, 1990): 701–03.

"Flexure Reveals Great Depth." *Nature* (February 15, 1990): 596–98.

(with Mikhail G. Kogan) "Gravity Field over Northern Eurasia and Variations in the Strength of the Upper Mantle." *Science* (January 22, 1993): 473–80.

(with Anne V. Judge) "The Superswell and Mantle Dynamics Beneath the South Pacific." *Science* (May 25, 1990): 969–976.

FURTHER READING

Periodicals

Ball, Charles H. "Faculty Member, Alumna Among WGBH's 'Discovering Women'." *MIT Tech Talk* (March 22, 1995).

Crabb, Charlene. "Sounding Out a Rumbling Earth: Marcia McNutt is Exploring the Planet's Deep Interior." *U.S. News & World Report* (December 30, 1991): 78.

"McNutt to be WHOI director." *MIT Tech Talk* (May 22, 1995).

"McNutt Will be Next AGU President–Elect." *Physics Today* (April 1998): 59–60.

Other

Petrusso, Annette, correspondence with Marcia McNutt, April 22, 1999.

Sketch by Annette Petrusso

Mary Alice McWhinnie
1922–1980
American marine biologist

Mary Alice McWhinnie will be remembered as the person who opened up the previously men–only research opportunities of Antarctica to American women scientists. In addition, she was the first person who recognized the importance of krill to the ecosystem of the world's oceans, and to fight to protect these crustaceans, which form the basis of the Antarctic's food chain.

Mary Alice McWhinnie was born in Elmhurst, Illinois, on August 10, 1922, one of five children of David Anthony McWhinnie and Ruth Margaret (Brann) McWhinnie. Her father was a draftsman who worked at Webcor during World War II, while her mother was executive assistant to a vice president at DePaul University.

As a girl, Mary Alice was always interested in the outdoors and nature. She spent hours with her father in the garden, where she plucked worms off the garden plants. During family summer vacations in Wisconsin, Mary Alice went along with her father when he fished, learning to maneuver their rowboat and asking questions about the fish they caught.

After graduating from high school, McWhinnie attended DePaul University, where she received her bachelor's degree in biology in 1944. Upon graduation she became an assistant in biological sciences until 1950. She received her master's degree in biology in 1946, also from DePaul, and in 1952 earned her Ph.D. from Northwestern University.

Dr. McWhinnie remained at DePaul her entire career, starting out as a biology instructor in 1950. She became an assistant professor of biology in 1952, an associate in 1955, and finally a full professor in 1960. She served as department chair from 1966–1968.

Curiosity leads her to Antarctica

Dr. McWhinnie had not intended to become a polar researcher. Her interest in life around the polar regions, in krill in particular, was sparked by a experiment in her Chicago laboratory in winter, 1958. At the time, she was studying crayfish and was particularly interested in how often they molted, or shed their shells, and how they developed. However, she was unable to duplicate the experiments she had completed the summer before. Suddenly, she realized what was wrong: the tanks the crayfish were in were being filled with tap water from Chicago's winter–cold water system. Dr. McWhinnie measured the water temperature and realized that the cold–blooded crayfish couldn't function in water that was about two degrees above freezing. When she put the crayfish in room–temperature water, they exhibited the same behavior they had the summer before.

Dr. McWhinnie knew crayfish have cold–water cousins, small animals called krill that live in the icy waters around Antarctica. "I wanted to know why they could live in icy water and my crayfish couldn't," Dr. McWhinnie was quoted in Barbara Land's *The New Explorers: Women in Antartica.* "Suddenly, I wanted to go to the Antarctic to study krill, to see what kind of biochemical tricks they had to play around with."

In 1959, she prepared a proposal to the National Science Foundation (NSF), which sponsored Antarctic research. The NSF was impressed with her proposal. However, when McWhinnie read in the letter they sent that the lodging arrangements at McMurdo, the NSF's Antarctic research station, were barracks that accommodated thirty men, she realized that the NSF had not understood that she was a woman. So, she decided not to pursue the idea. Six months later the NSF wanted to know why she hadn't followed up on her proposal. Although there were no women working in Antarctica, the NSF was willing to change and discuss her work. They offered her the chance to cruise to Antarctica aboard the *Elatnin*, which she eagerly accepted. Using the ship's onboard research laboratories, she was able to study krill immediately after capturing them. Several other research cruises followed, and in 1972, she was the ship's chief scientist. That year she set foot on Antarctic soil for the first time.

In 1974, Dr. McWhinnie became the scientific leader at McMurdo. She invited a former student, Sister Mary Odile Cahoon, who was teaching at St. Scholastica College, to be her research assistant. One of her assistants had to be a women and according to Sister Mary Odile Cahoon, quoted in *The New Explorers: Women in Antartica*, "It wasn't surprising that Mary Alice would look for a mature assistant . . . I'm sure they felt more comfortable having a couple of maiden aunts test the situation." Sister Cahoon and Dr. McWhinnie were the first women to winter at McMurdo. They knew it would be difficult, but it was an important opportunity to study the winter biology of krill.

The World's Expert on Krill

Dr. McWhinnie's research revealed much about krill that was previously unknown. She discovered that krill have an average life span of over two years, and that they grow new exoskeletons regularly, even if they have not outgrown the old. She became the world's leading authority on krill and their biology. In 1977, Dr. McWhinnie addressed scientists in London concerning the need to preserve and protect krill. Because it forms the basis of the Antarctic food web, overfishing by humans could do unimaginable damage to the Antarctic ecosystem.

As she was preparing for another trip to Antarctica, for the 1979–80 research season, Dr. McWhinnie fell seriously ill. Unbeknownst to her or to anyone else, she had developed oat cell cancer of the lungs, which had spread to her brain. She died March 17, 1980, at Hinsdale Hospital in Hinsdale, Illinois.

During her accomplished career, Dr. McWhinnie was a member of the National Academy of Science's Panel on Biological and Medical Sciences and of the National Science Foundation's Committee on Polar Research and the Advisory Committee on Research. Through her efforts to understand this small but vitally important animal, Dr. Mary Alice McWhinnie did much to protect Antarctica—not just for generations of human researchers, but also for generations of wildlife.

FURTHER READING

Books

Jaques Cattell Press, ed.*American Men and Women of Science* 13th Edition, New York: R.R. Bowker, 1976.

Bailey, Martha J. *American Women in Science: A Biographical Dictionary.* Santa Barbara: ABC–CLIO, 1994.

Land, Barbara. *The New Explorers: Women in Antarctica,* New York: Dodd, Mead & Co. (Date), Chapter 4.

Periodicals

Obituary *The Chicago Tribune*, March 20, 1980, section 3, page 19.

Other

Hodgkins, Fran, interview with Dr. Dolores McWhinnie, De Paul University, conducted February, 1999.

Sketch by Fran Hodgkins

Margaret Mead (Archive Photos. Reproduced my permission.)

Margaret Mead
1901–1978
American anthropologist

One of the most fascinating women of the twentieth century, Margaret Mead redefined and expanded the field of anthropology, the science of human culture. In fact, she turned anthropology into a household word. Ambitious and always controversial, Mead popularized the idea that human differences arose from the imperatives of individual cultures at least as much as from biological determinants.

The oldest child in a family of intellectuals, Mead was born on December 16, 1901, in Philadelphia. Eventually she had a younger brother and three younger sisters, one of whom died in infancy. While raising her family, Mead's mother, Emily Fogg Mead, had a fellowship in sociology which she used to study Italian immigrant families. Mead's father, Edward Sherwood Mead, taught at the Wharton School of Commerce at the University of Pennsylvania. The family moved frequently, to farms and towns in Pennsylvania and New Jersey. A precocious child, Mead's early education was in the hands of her parents, her paternal grandmother and various tutors and craftspeople. When she did attend school, it was often only part–time. Although her parents were agnostics, Mead decided at age eleven to be baptized an Episcopalian, the beginnings of her lifelong involvement with the church.

Mead met the 20 year-old theology student, Luther Sheeleigh Cressman, in 1917, and they became engaged during her senior year at Doylestown High School in Pennsylvania. She liked the idea of being a minister's wife and her engaged status meant that she could embark on her college career without the usual social distractions. Mead first attended her father's alma mater, DePauw University in Indiana, but she felt out of place in the Midwestern milieu of fraternities and sororities. She transferred to Barnard College in New York City, where she lived communally with a group of women who called themselves the "Ash Can Cats" and who would remain Mead's lifelong friends.

Discovers Anthropology

It was at Barnard that Mead established what was perhaps the most important relationship of her life. Ruth Benedict, fifteen years older than Mead, was an instructor in the Anthropology Department under Franz Boas, whose radical new ideas on anthropology would influence and inspire Mead throughout her career. Benedict was Boas' protégée and Mead became Benedict's. In addition to anthropology, the two women shared a love for writing poetry.

In 1923 Mead married Cressman. At the time she was completing her master's degree in psychology with research based on her mother's studies on Italian immigrants and working as an assistant to William Fielding Ogburn, helping him to edit the *Journal of the American Statistical Association*. But Mead had determined that her doctoral

studies would be in anthropology. The only question was where she would do her field work. Anthropologists were worried that opportunities to study untouched indigenous cultures in remote parts of the world would soon disappear. Mead decided to do field work in Polynesia and Boas instructed her to focus on adolescents, rather than on the ethnography, or description, of an entire culture. Her father, who had previously offered her a trip around the world if she didn't marry Cressman, now agreed to pay Mead's fare to Samoa. A fellowship from the National Research Council covered her stipend.

Studies Adolescence in the South Pacific

Mead, a very small and extremely energetic young woman, who was never very adept at learning new languages, set off alone for Samoa in 1925 to carry out the first study ever made of adolescent girls in an indigenous society. Her record of that trip, *Coming of Age in Samoa*, became a best-seller and made her reputation, both as an anthropologist and as a writer. Furthermore, Mead believed that she had proved her thesis: the intensity and stress that westerners associate with adolescence were the products of western society, not inherent in human societies.

Leaving Samoa, Mead sailed for Europe and her reunion with Cressman. But on the voyage she met Reo Franklin Fortune, a New Zealander on his way to Cambridge to study psychology. Mead and Cressman returned New York and Mead became a curator of ethnology at the American Museum of Natural History, a position she would hold for the rest of her life. She divorced Cressman in 1928: Cressman went on to become a famous archeologist and Mead headed for New Zealand to marry Fortune.

Mead and Fortune set off to do field work together in Melanesia. This time Mead studied infants and children and together she and Fortune developed new methodologies for field studies in anthropology. Returning to New York the following year, they each published three major books and spent the summer of 1930 doing field work with the Omaha Indians of Nebraska. Then they headed back to New Guinea, where Mead had a grant to compare sex roles in different cultures, attempting to separate biological from cultural determinants. There, over Christmas of 1932, Mead met the ethnographer Gregory Bateson, son of the great geneticist William Bateson. After emerging from the jungles of New Guinea, Mead divorced Fortune and in 1936 she and Bateson were married in Singapore.

As in many of her later writings, Mead's popular account of her field work in New Guinea, *Sex and Temperament in Three Primitive Societies*, included controversial conclusions about American society. Increasingly, Mead was incorporating aspects of psychology and psychoanalytic theory into her anthropology and when she and Bateson began their field work in Bali in 1936, one of their innovations was a heavy reliance on photography and cinematography to document cultures.

Mead was devoting her life to studying infants and children, but she thought she would never have a child of her own. Finally in 1939, after a number of miscarriages, she gave birth to her only daughter, Mary Catherine Bateson. Prior to the birth, Mead insisted that the obstetrician and nurses view the Bateson-Mead film "First Days in the Life of a New Guinea Baby." Also present at the birth were a cinematographer, a child development psychologist, and the pediatrician Benjamin Spock. Although both Mead and Bateson spent much of the second world war traveling on various anthropological missions for the U.S. government, their daughter was well–cared for, growing up in communal households made up of Mead's professional colleagues and closest friends. Mead and Bateson divorced in 1950. From 1955 on, Mead shared a home with her collaborator Rhoda Métraux.

Redefines Anthropology

After the war, Mead turned her attention to issues of women, marriage and family, in the United States and other cultures, culminating with the publication of *Male and Female* in 1949. Mead and Benedict also began building a multidisciplinary team of researchers to study postwar ´migŕs, comparing contemporary cultures "at a distance" and attempting to describe national characteristics. This eventually led to Mead's involvement, in the 1960s, with both the World Council of Churches and the United Nations.

An adjunct professor at Columbia University for most of her career, Mead also was a visiting professor at a number of prestigious universities. From 1959 on, she was a regular visitor at the Menninger Foundation in Topeka, Kansas, where she continued to integrate anthropology with psychology. A dedicated and inspiring teacher, Mead trained a generation of anthropologists, guiding the early careers of numerous men and women. As Jane Howard described it, "Electricity lingered in rooms where her classes had met . . . for an hour after the class was over." She used the income from her books to support her research and she often contributed her speaking fees to the museum or to her Institute for Intercultural Studies which funded young anthropologists.

By the 1960s, Mead had become a legend. A long forked stick, her "cudgel", first acquired while recovering from a broken ankle, became her symbol. She appeared frequently on television talk shows and wrote for the popular media and film crews accompanied her later field visits. In all, Mead made 15 field trips during her career. She authored, edited, or collaborated on 39 books and 1,397 other publications, as well as some 43 tapes and films. She received 28 honorary degrees and countless other awards. Mead was elected to the National Academy of Sciences in 1975 and she was president, and later chairman, of the American Association for the Advancement of Science.

Margaret Mead died of pancreatic cancer on November 15, 1978. Numerous services were held in her memory, including two at the United Nations. A section of the park outside the Natural History Museum was dedicated as

"Margaret Mead Green." On January 20, 1979, at the largest of the memorial services, Ambassador to the United Nations Andrew Young, on behalf of Mead's friend President Jimmy Carter, presented Mary Catherine Bateson with her mother's Presidential Medal of Freedom.

SELECTED WRITINGS BY MARGARET MEAD:

Books

Coming of Age in Samoa: A Psychological Study of Primitive Youth for Western Civilization. 1928. Reprint, New York: William Morrow, 1961.

Growing up in New Guinea: A Comparative Study of Primitive Education. 1930. Reprint, New York: William Morrow, 1975.

Sex and Temperament in Three Primitive Societies. 1935. Reprint, New York: William Morrow, 1963.

Male and Female: A Study of the Sexes in a Changing World. 1949. Reprint, New York: William Morrow, 1975.

An Anthropologist at Work: Writings of Ruth Benedict. Boston: Houghton Mifflin, 1959.

Anthropologists and What They Do. New York: Watts, 1965.

Blackberry Winter: My Earlier Years. New York: William Morrow, 1972.

Letters from the Field 1925–1965. New York: Harper and Row, 1977.

Periodicals

"What I Owe to Other Women." *Redbook* (April 1964): 18.

"My First Marriage." *Redbook* (November, 1972): 50–52, 54.

"Of Mothers and Mothering." *The Lactation Review* 4: 1, 4–19.

FURTHER READING

Books

Bateson, Mary Catherine. *With a Daughter's Eye: A Memoir of Margaret Mead and Gregory Bateson*. New York: William Morrow, 1984.

Howard, Jane. *Margaret Mead: A Life*. New York: Simon and Schuster, 1984.

Sketch by Margaret Alic

Lise Meitner
1878–1968
Austrian physicist

In 1938, along with her nephew Otto Robert Frisch, Meitner developed the theory behind nuclear fission that would eventually make possible the creation of the atomic bomb. She and lifelong collaborator Otto Hahn made several other key contributions to the field of nuclear physics. Although Hahn received the Nobel in 1944, Meitner was not recognized for her contribution.

Elise Meitner was born November 7, 1878 to an affluent Vienna family. Her father Philipp was a lawyer and her mother Hedwig travelled in the same Vienna intellectual circles as Sigmund Freud. From the early years of her life, Meitner gained experience that would later be invaluable in combatting—or overlooking—the slights she received as a woman in a field dominated by men. The third of eight children, she expressed interest in pursuing a scientific career, but her practical father made her attend the Elevated High School for Girls in Vienna to earn a diploma that would enable her to teach French—a much more sensible career for a woman. After completing this program, Meitner's desire to become a scientist was greater than ever. In 1899, she began studying with a local tutor who prepped students for the difficult university entrance exam. She worked so hard that she successfully prepared for the test in two years rather than the average four. Shortly before she turned 23, Meitner became one of the few women students at the University of Vienna.

At the beginning of her university career in 1901, Meitner could not decide between physics or mathematics; later, inspired by her physics teacher Ludwig Boltzmann, she opted for the latter. In 1906, after becoming the second woman ever to earn a Ph.D. in physics from the University of Vienna, she decided to stay on in Boltzmann's laboratory as an assistant to his assistant. This was hardly a typical career path for a recent doctorate, but Meitner had no other offers, as universities at the time did not hire women faculty. Less than a year after Meitner entered the professor's lab, Boltzmann committed suicide, leaving the future of the research team uncertain. In an effort to recruit the noted physicist Max Planck to take Boltzmann's place, the university invited him to come visit the lab. Although Planck refused the offer, he met Meitner during the visit and talked with her about quantum physics and radiation research. Inspired by this conversation, Meitner left Vienna in the winter of 1907 to go to the Institute for Experimental Physics in Berlin to study with Planck.

Soon after her arrival in Berlin, Meitner met a young chemist named Otto Hahn at one of the weekly symposia. Hahn worked at Berlin's Chemical Institute under the supervision of Emil Fischer, surrounded by organic chemists—none of whom shared his research interests in radiochemistry. Four months older than Hahn, Meitner was not only intrigued by the same research problems but had

Lise Meitner (The Library of Congress. Reproduced by permission.)

the training in physics that Hahn lacked. Unfortunately, Hahn's supervisor balked at the idea of allowing a woman researcher to enter the all–male Chemical Institute. Finally, Fischer allowed Meitner and Hahn to set up a laboratory in a converted woodworking shop in the Institute's basement, as long as Meitner agreed never to enter the higher floors of the building.

This incident was neither the first nor the last experience of sexism that Meitner encountered in her career. According to one famous anecdote, she was solicited to write an article by an encyclopedia editor who had read an article she wrote on the physical aspects of radioactivity. When she answered the letter addressed to Herr Meitner and explained she was a woman, the editor wrote back to retract his request, saying he would never publish the work of a woman. Even in her collaboration with Hahn, Meitner at times conformed to gender roles. When British physicist Sir Ernest Rutherford visited their Berlin laboratory on his way back from the Nobel ceremonies in 1908, Meitner spent the day shopping with his wife Mary while the two men talked about their work.

Becomes First Woman Professor in Germany

Within her first year at the Institute, the school opened its classes to women, and Meitner was allowed to roam the building. For the most part, however, the early days of the collaboration between Hahn and Meitner were filled with their investigations into the behavior of beta rays as they passed through aluminum. By today's standards, the laboratory in which they worked would be appalling. Hahn and Meitner frequently suffered from headaches brought on by their adverse working conditions. In 1912 when the Kaiser–Wilhelm Institute was built in the nearby suburb of Dahlem, Hahn received an appointment in the small radioactivity department there and invited Meitner to join him in his laboratory. Soon thereafter, Planck asked Meitner to lecture as an assistant professor at the Institute for Theoretical Physics. The first woman in Germany to hold such a position, Meitner drew several members of the news media to her opening lecture.

When World War I started in 1914, Meitner interrupted her laboratory work to volunteer as an x–ray technician in the Austrian army. Hahn entered the German military. The two scientists arranged their leaves to coincide and throughout the war returned periodically to Dahlem where they continued trying to discover the precursor of the element actinium. By the end of the war, they announced that they had found this elusive element and named it protactinium, the missing link on the periodic table between thorium (previously number 90) and uranium (number 91). A few years later Meitner received the Leibniz Medal from the Berlin Academic of Science and the Leibniz Prize from the Austrian Academy of Science for this work. Shortly after she helped discover protactinium in 1917, Meitner accepted the job of establishing a radioactive physics department at the Kaiser Wilhelm Institute. Hahn remained in the chemistry department, and the two ceased working together to concentrate on research more suited to their individual training. For Meitner, this constituted a return to beta radiation studies.

Throughout the 1920s, Meitner continued her work in beta radiation, winning several prizes. In 1928, the Association to Aid Women in Science upgraded its Ellen Richards Prize—billing it as a Nobel Prize for women—and named Meitner and chemist Pauline Ramart–Lucas of the University of Paris its first recipients. In addition to the awards she received, Meitner acquired a reputation in physics circles for some of her personal quirks as well. Years later, her nephew Otto Frisch, also a physicist, would recall that she drank large quantities of strong coffee, embarked on ten mile walks whenever she had free time, and would sometimes indulge in piano duets with him. By middle age, Meitner had also adopted some of the mannerisms stereotypically associated with her male colleagues. Not the least of these, Hahn later recalled, was absent–mindedness. On one occasion, a student approached her at a lecture, saying they had met earlier. Knowing she had never met the student, Meitner responded earnestly, "You probably mistake me for Professor Hahn."

Begins Work on Uranium

Meitner and Hahn resumed their collaboration in 1934, after Enrico Fermi published his seminal article on "transuranic" uranium. The Italian physicist announced that when he bombarded uranium with neutrons, he produced two new elements—number 93 and 94, in a mixture of lighter elements. Meitner and Hahn joined with a young German chemist named Fritz Strassmann to draw up a list of all the substances the heaviest natural elements produced when bombarded with neutrons. In three years, the three confirmed Fermi's result and expanded the list to include about ten additional substances that resulted from bombarding these elements with neutrons. Meanwhile, physicists **Irène Joliot–Curie** and Pavle Savitch announced that they had created a new radioactive substance by bombarding uranium by neutrons. The French team speculated that this new mysterious substance might be thorium, but Meitner, Hahn, and Strassmann could not confirm this finding. No matter how many times they bombarded uranium with neutrons, no thorium resulted. Hahn and Meitner sent a private letter to the French physicists suggesting that perhaps they had erred. Although Joliet–Curie did not reply directly, a few months later she published a paper retracting her earlier assertions and said the substance she had noted was not thorium.

Current events soon took Meitner's mind off these professional squabbles. Although her father, a proponent of cultural assimilation, had all his children baptized, Meitner was Jewish by birth. Because she continued to maintain her Austrian citizenship, she was at first relatively impervious to the political turmoil in Weimar Germany. In the mid–1930s she had been asked to stop lecturing at the university but she continued her research. When Germany annexed Austria in 1938, Meitner became a German citizen and began to look for a research position in an environment hospitable to Jews. Her tentative plans grew urgent in the spring of 1938, when Germany announced that academics could no longer leave the country. Colleagues devised an elaborate scheme to smuggle her out of Germany to Stockholm where she had made temporary arrangements to work at the Institute of the Academy of Sciences under the sponsorship of a Nobel grant. By late fall, however, Meitner's position in Sweden looked dubious: her grant provided no money for equipment and assistance, and the administration at the Stockholm Institute would offer her no help. Christmas found her depressed and vacationing in a town in the west of Sweden.

Posits Theory of Nuclear Fission

Back in Germany, Hahn and Strassmann had not let their colleague's departure slow their research efforts. The two read and reread the paper Joliet–Curie had published detailing her research techniques. Looking it over, they thought they had found an explanation for Joliet–Curie's confusion: perhaps instead of finding one new substance after bombarding uranium, as she had thought, she had actually found two new substances! They repeated her experiments and indeed found two substances in the final mixture, one of which was barium. This result seemed to suggest that bombarding uranium with neutrons led it to split up into a number of smaller elements. Hahn immediately wrote to Meitner to share this perplexing development with her. Meitner received his letter on her vacation in the village of Kungalv, as she awaited the arrival of her nephew, Frisch, who was currently working in Copenhagen under the direction of physicist Niels Bohr. Frisch hoped to discuss a problem in his own work with Meitner, but it was clear soon after they met that the only thing on her mind was Hahn and Strassmann's observation. Meitner and Frisch set off for a walk in the snowy woods—Frisch on skis, with his aunt trotting along—continuing to puzzle out how uranium could possibly yield barium. When they paused for a rest on a log, Meitner began to posit a theory, sketching diagrams in the snow.

If, as Bohr had previously suggested, the nucleus behaved like a liquid drop, Meitner reasoned that when this drop of a nucleus was bombarded by neutrons, it might elongate and divide itself into two smaller droplets. The forces of electrical repulsion would act to prevent it from maintaining its circular shape by forming the nucleus into a dumbbell shape that would—as the bombarding forces grew stronger—sever at the middle to yield two droplets—two completely different nuclei. But one problem still remained. When Meitner added together the weights of the resultant products, she found that the sum did not equal the weight of the original uranium. The only place the missing mass could be lost was in energy expended during the reaction.

Frisch rushed back to Copenhagen, eager to test the revelations from their walk in the woods on his mentor and boss, Bohr. He caught Bohr just as the scientist was leaving for an American tour, but as Bohr listened to what Frisch was urgently telling him, he responded: "Oh, what idiots we have been. We could have foreseen it all! This is just as it must be!" Buoyed by Bohr's obvious admiration, Frisch and Meitner spent hours on a long–distance telephone writing the paper that would publicize their theory. At the suggestion of a biologist friend, Frisch coined the word "fission" to describe the splitting of the nucleus in a process that seemed to him analogous to cell division.

Theory Makes Atom Bomb Possible

The paper "On the Products of the Fission of Uranium and Thorium" appeared in *Nature* on February 11, 1939. Although it would be another five and a half years before the American military would successfully explode an atom bomb over Hiroshima, many physicists consider Meitner and Frisch's paper akin to opening a Pandora's box of atomic weapons. Physicists were not the only ones to view Meitner as an important participant in the harnessing of nuclear energy. After the bomb was dropped in 1944, a radio station asked First Lady Eleanor Roosevelt to conduct a transatlantic interview with Meitner. In this interview, the two women talked extensively about the implications and future of nuclear energy. After the war, Hahn found himself in one of the more enviable positions for a scientist—the winner of the 1944 Nobel prize in chemistry—although, because of the war, Hahn did not accept his prize until two years later. Although she attended the ceremony, Meitner did not share in the honor.

But Meitner's life after the war was not without its plaudits and pleasures. In the early part of 1946, she travelled to America to visit her sister—working in the U.S. as a chemist—for the first time in decades. While there, Meitner delivered a lecture series at Catholic University in Washington, D.C. In the following years, she won the Max Planck Medal and was awarded numerous honorary degrees from both American and European universities. In 1966 she, Hahn, and Strassmann split the $50,000 Enrico Fermi Award given by the Atomic Energy Commission. Unfortunately, by this time Meitner had become too ill to travel, so the chairman of the A. E. C. delivered it to her in Cambridge, England, where she had retired a few years earlier. Meitner died just a few weeks before her 90th birthday on October 27, 1968.

SELECTED WRITINGS BY MEITNER:

Periodicals

(With Otto R. Frisch) "On the Products of the Fission of Uranium and Thorium" *Nature* 143 (March 1939): 239.

"Looking Back." *Bulletin of the Atomic Scientists* (November, 1964).

FURTHER READING

Books

Crawford, Deborah. *Lise Meitner, Atomic Pioneer.* Crown, 1969.

Irving, David. *The German Atomic Bomb: The History of Nuclear Research in Nazi Germany.* Simon and Schuster, 1967.

Rhodes, Richard. *The Making of the Atom Bomb.* Simon and Schuster, 1988.

Periodicals

Watkins, Sallie. "Lise Meitner and the Beta–ray Energy Controversy: An Historical Perspective." *American Journal of Physics* 51 (1983): 551–553.

Watkins, Sallie. "Lise Meitner: The Making of a Physicist." *Physics Teacher* (January, 1984): 12–15.

Sketch by Shari Rudavsky

Dorothy Reed Mendenhall
1874–1964

American obstetrician and medical researcher

Dorothy Reed Mendenhall was a well–respected researcher, obstetrician, and pioneer in methods of childbirth. She was the first to discover that Hodgkin's disease was not a form of tuberculosis, as had been thought. This finding received international acclaim. As a result of her work, the cell type characteristic of Hodgkin's disease bears her name. The loss of her first child due to poor obstetrics changed her research career to a lifelong effort to reduce infant mortality rates. Mendenhall's efforts paid off with standards being set for weight and height for children ages birth to six, and also in programs that stressed the health of both the mother and child in the birthing process.

Dorothy Reed Mendenhall, the last of three children, was born September 22, 1874, in Columbus, Ohio, to William Pratt Reed, a shoe manufacturer, and Grace Kimball Reed, both of whom had descended from English settlers who came to America in the seventeenth century. Mendenhall attended Smith College and obtained a baccalaureate degree. Although she initially contemplated a career in journalism, Mendenhall's interest in medicine was inspired by a biology course she attended.

When they opened the school up to women, Mendenhall applied to Johns Hopkins Medical School in Baltimore, Maryland. In 1900, she was one of the first women to graduate from this school with a doctorate of medicine degree. The next year she received a fellowship in pathology at Johns Hopkins. While there, she taught bacteriology and performed research on Hodgkin's disease, which physicians then believed was a form of tuberculosis. She disproved this theory when she discovered a common link between diagnosed patients. She found that the blood of these patients carried a specific type of cell. The presence of these giant cells, now known as the Reed cell, distinctly identifies the disease. Mendenhall's work produced the first thorough descriptions, both verbal and illustrated, of the tissue changes that occur with Hodgkin's. She was the first to describe the disease's growth through several progressive states. Mendenhall determined that a patient's prognosis worsened with each successive stage. She incorrectly speculated, however, that the disease was a chronic inflammatory process. Her finding of the distinctive cell had world–wide importance and was a significant step forward in the understanding and treatment of Hodgkin's disease. Today, researchers know that Hodgkin's is a type of cancer characterized by a progressive enlargement of the lymph nodes.

Pioneering Efforts Lower Infant Mortality Rates

Because she felt that there were few opportunities for advancement at Johns Hopkins, Mendenhall transferred her work to Babies Hospital of New York, becoming the first resident physician there. In 1906, she married Charles Elwood Mendenhall and began to raise a family. She had four children, one who died a few hours after birth. This loss was to shape the rest of her career. Mendenhall undertook a study of infant mortality, that, when released, brought government attention to the problems of maternal and child health. To determine the extent of infant mortality in the United States, she obtained epidemiological data for the Wisconsin State Board of Health. A major problem she identified was the prevalence of malnutrition among children. In her efforts to remedy the problems of childbearing and childrearing, Mendenhall developed correspondence courses for new and prospective mothers. She also lectured to groups across Wisconsin and wrote bulletins on nutrition for the United States Department of Agriculture. Mendenhall's efforts helped create some of Wisconsin's first infant welfare clinics, particularly in Madison. In 1937, she was gratified when Madison had the lowest infant mortality rate in the United States.

While employed as a field lecturer for the Department of Home Economics at the University of Wisconsin, in 1918, Mendenhall initiated a nationwide effort in which all children under six years of age were weighed and measured. This project helped establish standards for that normal, healthy children of these ages should weigh and how tall they should be. In 1926, Mendenhall undertook a study of birthing methods in Denmark, which had one of the lowest rates of childbirth complications. She later travelled to the country to gain firsthand information on their techniques, which included the utilization of specialized midwives and a reduced role of medical procedures. Through this, Mendenhall determined that there was too much medical intervention in normal childbirth, and that this intervention is often the source of health problems for the mother and child. She helped institute natural childbirth in the U.S. and also suggested that obstetrics become a specialty profession. From 1917 to 1936, Mendenhall also worked intermittently as a medical officer for the United States Children's Bureau. After her husband's death, she withdrew from public life. In her spare time she loved to read Marcus Aurelius. As a tribute to her dedication as a researcher, teacher, and physician, Smith College dedicated Sabin–Reed Hall in 1965. The hall honors Mendenhall and Florence Sabin, a fellow student at both Smith and Johns Hopkins. Mendenhall died July 31, 1964, in Chester, Connecticut, from heart disease.

SELECTED WRITINGS BY MENDENHALL:

Periodicals

"On the Pathological Changes in Hodgkin's Disease with Especial Reference to Its Relation to Tuberculosis." *Johns Hopkins Hospital Reports* 10 (1902): 133–96.

"Prenatal and Natal Conditions in Wisconsin." *Wisconsin Medical Journal* (March 1917): 353–69.

FURTHER READING

Books

Sicherman, Barbara, Carol Hurd Green, Ilene Kantrov, and Harriette Walker, eds. *Notable American Women: The Modern Period* Cambridge, MA: Belknap Press, 1980, pp. 468–70.

Sketch by Barbara Proujan

Maud Leonora Menten
1879–1960
Canadian pathologist

Although Maud Menten's career was in medical pathology, her contributions to science spans several different fields. With Leonor Michaelis, she developed a general theory of enzyme reactions, known as Michaelis–Menten kinetics, a cornerstone of biochemistry. As a histochemist, she developed the "azo–dye technique" that researchers use to identify chemical properties of biological tissues. In addition, she may have been the first to separate different proteins using a technique called electrophoresis.

Menten was born in 1879 in Port Lambton, Ontario. There is no information available concerning her background or childhood. She was educated at the University of Toronto, where she received her bachelor of arts degree in 1904 and her bachelor of medicine degree in 1907. In the years 1904 through 1907 she was a demonstrator in physiology in the laboratory of A. B. Macallum, where she studied potassium in cells.

Since there were few opportunities for women researchers in Canada at the time, Menten moved to the Rockefeller Institute for Medical Research in New York City in 1907, as a research fellow. There, with Simon Flexner and J. W. Jobling, she authored the Institute's first monograph, on radioactive bromide and cancer. In the years 1910–1912, and again in 1913 and 1914, she worked as a research fellow at Western Reserve University in Cleveland with Dr. George Crile. She was one of the first women in Canada to earn a medical degree when she received her doctor of medicine degree in 1911 from the University of Toronto.

Develops Theory of Enzyme Reaction

Working in the laboratory of the Berlin Municipal Hospital in Germany, in 1913, Menten and Michaelis developed the Michaelis–Menten equation that defined the relationship between an enzyme, a protein that causes a biological reaction, and its substrate, the molecule that the enzyme acts upon. This is one of the fundamental equations of biochemistry. This equation enabled Menten and Michaelis to develop a mathematical expression for the rate, or speed, at which the enzyme reaction occurs. It was not until 1949 that the validity of their equation could be demonstrated experimentally.

In 1915 and 1916, Menten conducted cancer research at the Barnard Skin and Cancer Hospital in St. Louis, Missouri. She earned her Ph.D. in biochemistry in 1916, at the University of Chicago, where she worked with A. P. Matthews. That year, she became a demonstrator in pathology at the University of Pittsburgh School of Medicine, where she remained until her retirement in 1950, not becoming a full professor until 1949. In addition to her full–time teaching duties, Menten was a practicing pathologist, first at the E. S. Magee Hospital, and from 1926 on, at the Children's Hospital of Pittsburgh.

Separates Adult Hemoglobin from Fetal Hemoglobin

Menten continued her research throughout her career. In 1924, Menten and Helen Manning discovered that toxin from the Salmonella bacterium causes abnormally high blood glucose levels. In 1944, Menten and her collaborators may have been the first to use an important new technique, electrophoresis, to separate different proteins. This technique involves placing a mixture of proteins in an electric field. The different proteins separate because they move at different speeds depending on their size and electric charge. Menten and her coworkers succeeded in separating adult hemoglobin, the protein that carries oxygen in red blood cells, from fetal hemoglobin, so that the different properties of the two hemoglobins could be studied. A few years later, Linus Pauling used the same method to separate normal hemoglobin from the hemoglobin that results in sickle–cell anemia, thus demonstrating the molecular basis of a disease for the first time.

Also in 1944, Menten and her coworkers published their azo–dye technique for detecting the enzyme known as alkaline phosphatase. In later work, she used this technique to demonstrate that decreases in the amount of this enzyme correlated directly with the amount of kidney damage due to disease. This research opened up the new field of enzyme histochemistry. The azo–dye method has become a major tool that is used routinely, both in various types of biochemical and biological research and in diagnostic medicine.

Menten published some 70 scientific papers over the course of her career. These publications were in the fields of physiology, hematology, or the study of blood, pathology, and cancer therapy, in addition to biochemistry. Her studies on the toxins produced by a variety of different bacteria and on the oxidative enzymes and nucleic acids produced by tumor cells were of particular significance.

Following her retirement, Menten continued her cancer research at the Medical Research Institute of British Columbia in Vancouver. Poor health forced her into full retirement in 1955. Menten was a member of numerous scientific societies. She was fluent in several languages, and she was an accomplished musician and artist, whose paintings were included in several exhibitions. Menten died in 1960 in Leamington, Ontario.

SELECTED WRITINGS BY MENTEN:

Periodicals

(With L. Michaelis) "Die Kinetik der Invertinwerkung." *Biochemische Zeitschrift* 49 (1913): 333.

(With M. A. Aadersch and D. A. Wilson) "Sedimentation Constants and Electrophoretic Mobilization of Adult and Fetal Carbonylhemoglobin." *Journal of Biological Chemistry*151 (1944): 301.

(With J. Junge and M. H. Green) "A Coupling Histochemical Azo–dye Test for Alkaline Phosphatase in the Kidney." *Journal of Biological Chemistry* 153 (1944): 471.

(With J. Janouch) "Changes in Alkaline Phosphatase in Kidney Following Renal Damage with Alloxan." *Proceedings of the Society of Experimental Biology and Medicine* 63 (1946): 33.

FURTHER READING

Books

Cattell, Jaques, ed. *American Men of Science: A Biographical Dictionary, vol. 2: Biological Sciences.* 9th ed. Lancaster, PA: Science Press, 1955.

Miller, Jane A. "Women in Chemistry." In *Women of Science: Righting the Record.* Edited by G. Kass–Simon and Patricia Farnes. Bloomington: Indiana University Press, 1990.

Periodicals

Stock, Aaron H. and Anna–Mary Carpenter. "Obituary: Prof. Maud Menten." *Nature* 189 (1961): 965.

Sketch by Margaret Alic

Maria Sibylla Merian
1647–1717
German-born Dutch naturalist

A naturalist who specialized in insects, Maria Merian also was one of the finest scientific artists of her day. As one of the first entomologists to capture and observe live specimens, Merian discovered the complex life cycles of a number of insects. Her books were fundamental references on entomology for a century and Carl Linnaeus relied

Maria Sibylla Merian (The Granger Collection, New York. Reproduced by permission.)

heavily on Merian's work as he developed his system of biological classification.

Merian, who was born in Frankfurt am Maim, Germany, in 1647, was the youngest of three children in a home of naturalists and artists. Her father, Matthaüs Merian the Elder, who died when she was three, was a well-known Swiss botanical artist and engraver. Her mother remarried the flower painter Jacob Marell. Her older brother, Matthaüs Merian, was a famous portrait painter. Merian's parents encouraged her early interest in biological illustration. Consequently, she studied first with her stepfather and his apprentice Abraham Mignon, and then with Marell's student, Johann Graff, whom she married in 1665. Merian received training in sketching and oil and watercolor painting, not just of flowers, but also of birds and insects. As a child, she studied silkworms, moths, and butterflies and painted them accurately on parchment. Her journals dating from 1660 indicate that she was the first to describe the metamorphosis of the silk moth. At a time when accurate illustrations were essential for learning about the natural world, artists such as Merian easily moved into the realm of science.

First Scientific Publication

In 1670, Merian and her family moved to Nuremberg, Germany. Instead of working with her husband as a painter, Merian established her own business selling fine silks, satins, and linens, that were painted with her flower patterns. She lead a group of women students of assistants and apprentices. Merian also sold paints and she began experimenting with techniques and developed a washable watercolor for fabrics. She also developed a new printing technique where the prints of engravings were hand-painted. She this technique used for her color catalogue, *Neues Blumenbuch*, of garden flower patterns for embroidery and painting.

Merian began studying caterpillars, hoping to find one that could be used for manufacturing fine thread similar to that of like the silkworm. Her five-year search resulted in her first scientific publication, *Wonderful Metamorphosis and Special Nourishment of Caterpillars*. Its 50 copperplate illustrations depicted the life stages of each species. The first two volumes of her work on European insects were published in 1679 and 1683. Merian's engravings for these books pictured the developmental stages of the insects and the plants on which they fed at each stage.

In 1682, Merian returned to Frankfurt to care for her widowed mother. A few years later she left Graff and reclaimed her maiden name. She converted to Labadism, a strict Protestant sect founded by Jean de Labadie, and went with her two daughters to live at Labadie's commune in a castle in the Dutch province of Friesland. When she refused to return to Nuremberg with her husband, she was publicly censured and later divorced by him. Labadie's community, where her half-brother also lived, provided her protection from her husband and was supportive of independent and intellectual women. Merian learned Latin during the ten years she spent there and was fascinated by the exotic tropical plants and insects sent back from the Labadist community in the Dutch colony of Surinam in South America.

Sails to Surinam

Because the commune dissolved, Merian moved to Amsterdam in 1691, where she supported herself and her daughters by selling colored fabrics and paints and doing scientific illustrations for natural history books. Amsterdam was full of superb natural history collections which inspired Merian and her daughters to sail for Surinam in 1699 to further Merian's research into the life cycles of insects. For the next two years, they collected and painted tropical plants and animals. Malaria, however, forced her early return to Amsterdam. Merian's exotic specimens and her illustrations, were displayed and sold in Amsterdam to finance her research and travel.

Merian's most successful and important scientific work, *Metamorphosis Insectorum Surinamensium*, including 60 of her illustrations, was published in Dutch and Latin, and later translated into French. *Metamorphosis* was unique in a number of ways, including its use of native American names for plants and the descriptions of their uses. It was designed for art lovers, but for scientists as well. Merian sold it in advance in order to finance its costly printing.

Merian's works were reviewed in the major European journals and remained popular well into the nineteenth century, going through numerous editions. Following Merian's death of unknown causes in 1717, her daughter Dorothea illustrated the third volume on European insects and published a Latin edition of her mother's work on the life cycle of the silkworm. Several species of plants, butterflies, and beetles were named Merian's honor.

SELECTED WRITINGS BY MERIAN:

Books

(As Maria S. Gräffin) *Der Raupen wunderbare Verwandlung und sonderbare Blumennahrung*. Nuremberg, 1679.

(As Maria S. Gräffin) *Neues Blumenbuch*. Nuremberg, 1680.

Metamorphosis Insectorum Surinamensium. Edited by Helmut S. Gräffin. 1705. Reprint, Leipzig, 1975.

De Europische Insecten. Amsterdam, 1730.

Flowers, Butterflies, and Insects: All 154 Engravings from 'Erucarum Ortus'. New York: Dover, 1991.

FURTHER READING

Books

Calabrese, Diane M. "Maria Sibylla Merian." In *Notable Women in the Life Sciences: A Biographical Dictionary*. Edited by Benjamin F. Shearer and Barbara S. Shearer. Westport, CT: Greenwood Press, 1996.

Schiebinger, Londa. *The Mind Has No Sex? Women in the Origins of Modern Science*. Cambridge: Harvard University Press, 1989.

Sketch by Margaret Alic

Helen Abbot Merrill
1864–1949
American mathematician

Helen Abbot Merrill took up mathematics as a vocation and avocation at a time when women were rarely visible in the field. She was most active as an instructor, co–writing textbooks as well as publishing articles on pedagogy. Merrill also wrote a "mathematical amusement" book, a populist work for young readers entitled *Mathematical Excursions*. Even in her spare time she was devoted to broader aspects of her profession, joining many mathematical, academic, and scientific organizations, and serving as vice–president of both the Mathematical Association of America and the American Mathematical Society.

Merrill was born March 30, 1864 in Orange, New Jersey, near Thomas Edison's facilities at Llewellyn Park. Her family traced its ancestry back to 1633, when Nathaniel Merrill settled in Massachusetts. Her father, George Dodge Merrill, had many business concerns, including being an inventor. Her siblings included a sister, Emily, and two brothers, Robert and William, who both grew up to become Presbyterian ministers.

An Experimental Situation

Merrill began high school in 1876 at Newburyport, and entered Wellesley College six years later in one of the first graduating classes in the history of the college. Originally, her major was classical languages, an interest she would keep up throughout her life. However, as a freshman she committed to mathematics. At that time, Wellesley was still considered something of an experiment, but Merrill responded to the close–knit atmosphere and wrote a history of her graduating class as a commemorative booklet. Merrill graduated with a B.A. after four years and began her career as a teacher. Working at the Classical School for Girls in New York, Merrill was allotted courses in Latin and history as well as mathematics. She was assigned to a variety of students, including "mill girls" from New Brunswick, New Jersey, and immigrant children in the Germantown section of Philadelphia.

In 1893, Merrill was asked to return to Wellesley, this time as an instructor, in exchange for a stipend and housing. Helen Shafer, who had hired Merrill, allowed her time off intermittently for graduate studies at the universities of Chicago, Göttingen, and eventually Yale. Merrill earned a Ph.D. from Yale in 1903 and her thesis on "Sturmian differential equations was published the same year. Merrill moved up from instructor to associate professor status at Wellesley. The college benefitted directly from Merrill's excursions, as she introduced courses in functions and descriptive geometry for her undergraduate students based on her graduate work.

"Flowery," Not Thorny Paths

Merrill dedicated herself to providing a "flowery path" for her young charges to follow into the normally thorny subject of mathematics. She did not lower her standards for undergraduates; in fact, the courses Merrill taught were often in subjects generally offered only at the graduate level. However, she was quick to offer tailored assistance to any young woman she considered a diamond in the rough.

After being promoted to full professor in 1916, Merrill was appointed head of the mathematics department the next year. She was particularly active as associate editor of the Mathematical Association of American's monthly newsletter, member of the executive council, and later vice president in 1920. With a fellow MAA member, Clara E. Smith, who would also serve as vice president of the group,

Merrill authored two textbooks. Merrill remained at Wellesley until her retirement, when she was named a Lewis Atterbury Stimson professor.

Merrill was also an amateur historian, fulfilling archival duties at Wellesley. She was elected as an executive committee member of the National Historical Society. Her interest in music and language led her to become as student again, taking summer courses at the University of California at Berkeley. She also traveled across Europe and the Americas. Merrill retired as professor emerita in 1932, and died at her home in Wellesley on May 1, 1949.

SELECTED WRITINGS BY MERRILL:

Books

(With Clara E. Smith) *Selected Topics in College Algebra*, 1914.

(With Clara E. Smith) *A First Course in Higher Algebra,* 1917.

Mathematical Excursions: Side Trips along Paths Not Generally Traveled in Elementary Courses in Mathematics, 1933.

Periodicals

"On Solutions of Differential Equations Which Possess an Ooscillatoin [*sic*] Theorem," in *Transactions of the American Mathematical Society* 4 (1903): 423–33.

"Why Students Fail in Mathematics," in *Mathematics Teacher* 11 (1918): 45–56.

"Three Mathematical Songs," in *Mathematics Teacher* 25 (1932): 36–37.

FURTHER READING

Books

Green, Judy and Jeanne LaDuke. "Women in American Mathematics: A Century of Contributions." *A Century of Mathematics in America*, Volume 2. Edited by Peter Duren. Providence, RI: American Mathematical Society, 1989, pp. 384, 386.

Henrion, Claudia. "Helen Abbot Merrill." *Women of Mathematics.* Edited by Louise S. Grinstein and Paul J.Campbell. Westport, CT: Greenwood Press, 1987, pp. 147–151.

The National Cyclopedia of American Biography. Volume 42. Reprint. Ann Arbor, MI: University Microfilms, 1967–71, pp. 171–72.

Siegel and Finley. *Women in the Scientific Search:: An American Bio–bibliography, 1724–1979.* Metuchen, NJ: The Scarecrow Press, Inc., 1985, pp. 214–15.

Periodicals

"Helen A. Merrill of Wellesley, 85." *The New York Times* (May 3, 1949): p. 25.

"Helen Abbot Merrill." *Yale University Obituary Record* (July 1, 1949): 142.

Other

"Helen Abbot Merrill." *Biographies of Women Mathematicians.* June 1997. http://www.scottlan.edu/lriddle/women/chronol.htm (July 22, 1997).

Sketch by Jennifer Kramer

Marie Meurdrac
fl. seventeeth century
French chemist

Marie Meurdrac wrote the first major treatise on chemistry since **Maria** and **Cleopatra**, the Alexandrian alchemists of the first century. Meurdrac's work formed a bridge between the ancient science of alchemy and the new chemistry of the seventeenth–century scientific revolution.

There is no biographical information about Meurdrac, a seventeenth–century French woman who presumably was self–educated. During the seventeenth century, upper–class women throughout Europe were beginning to teach themselves about science, conducting experiments, and writing scientific works. According to Meurdrac's preface to her book, she originally began writing in order to retain the knowledge that she had learned through long study and repeated experimentation. For two years after completing the book, she debated whether to publish it. As Lloyd Bishop and Will DeLoach quoted from her preface: "it was not the profession of a lady to teach; that she should remain silent, listen and learn, without displaying her own knowledge; that it is above her station to offer a work to the public and that a reputation gained thereby is not ordinarily to her advantage since men always scorn and blame the products of a woman's wit. . . On the other hand. . . that minds have no sex and that if the minds of women were cultivated like those of men, and if as much time and energy were used to instruct the minds of the former, they would equal those of the latter." Meurdrac first published her work in 1666. Later editions appeared in 1674 and 1711, and an Italian translation appeared in 1682.

Meurdrac believed herself to be the first woman to write a treatise on chemistry. To Meurdrac, chemistry consisted of distillation and the mixing of various substances. In the seventeenth century, the science of chemistry was still based on ancient Greek and Arab alchemy and like her predecessors, Meurdrac believed that substances were formed of three principles or elements: salt, sulfur, and mercury. The first section of Meurdrac's six–part work dealt with laboratory principles, techniques, and apparatus, including vessels, furnaces, and fires. Other sections covered the properties of the three basic elements, animals, the chemical uses of minerals and metals, and the preparation and properties of medicines, both simple and complex. In the latter section, she recommended the herb rosemary as a universal panacea. Her book included a table of weights and a table of 106 alchemical symbols. Like many treatises that discussed medicinal remedies, the final section consisted of recipes for cosmetic. Meurdrac referred to the latter as "rare secrets" for ladies. She included a recipe for, as quoted by Londa Schiebinger, the "water of the queen of Hungary," which Meurdrac claimed to have copied from a recipe written by the queen, who remained youthful at the age of 72. Meurdrac stated that she personally tested all of the remedies listed in her book.

SELECTED WRITINGS BY MEURDRAC:

Books

La Chymie Charitable et Facile, en Faveur des Dames. Paris, 1666.

FURTHER READING

Books

Alic, Margaret. *Hypatia's Heritage: A History of Women in Science from Antiquity through the Nineteenth Century.* Boston: Beacon Press,1986.

Miller, Jane A. "Women in Chemistry." In *Women of Science: Righting the Record.* Edited by G. Kass–Simon and Patricia Farnes. Bloomington: Indiana University Press, 1990.

Schiebinger, Londa. *The Mind Has No Sex? Women in the Origins of Modern Science.* Cambridge: Harvard University Press, 1989.

Periodicals

Bishop, Lloyd O. and Will S. De Loach. "Marie Meurdrac – First Lady of Chemistry?" *Journal of Chemical Education* 47 (1970): 448–49.

Houlihan, Sherida and John H. Wotiz. "Women in Chemistry before 1900." *Journal of Chemical Education* 52 (1975): 362–64.

Sketch by Margaret Alic

Ynes Mexia
1870–1938
American botanist

Although Ynes Mexia came to botany late in life, she made many important contributions to botanical science and herbariums via numerous collecting expeditions. In her trips to Alaska, and more importantly, Central and South America, Mexia collected about 150,000 specimens which were eventually housed in some of the finest botanical collections in the world, including the Field Museum in Chicago and Harvard University's herbarium. She discovered a new genus of Compositae (the largest family of flowering plants which includes common weeds, chrysanthemums, and sunflowers), which was named *Mexianthus mexicanus* in her honor, as well as hundreds of other previously unknown plant species.

Ynes Enriquetta Julietta Mexia was born on May 24, 1870, in Washington, D.C. Her grandfather was José Antonio Mexia, a general under Santa Anna. Her father, Enrique Antonio Mexia, was probably representing Mexico in Washington when his daughter was born to him and the former Sarah Wilmer. The Mexia family lived primarily in Texas where they owned land near what is now the town of Mexia. Mexia attended schools in Texas, Philadelphia, Mexico City, Ontario, Canada, and Maryland, including private Quaker schools in Philadelphia and Maryland. In 1897, Mexia married Herman de Laue, who died in 1904. She married Augustin A. de Reygados in 1907, but divorced him a year later. She had no children. After her divorce, she moved to San Francisco and was employed as a social worker.

In 1921, Mexia was admitted to the University of California in Berkeley as a special student. Focusing on the natural sciences, Mexia took several classes in botany. These classes led Mexia to devote her remaining years to botany and collecting botanical specimens. Though Mexia never finished her degree, she continued to attend classes throughout her life.

Beginning in 1925 with a trip to Mexico, Mexia collected botanical specimens in remote locations in South America, including Brazil, Peru, Ecuador, Bolivia, Argentina, and Chile. With the help of her agent and curator Nina Floy Bracelin, Mexia paid for her expeditions by selling specimens to herbariums and other institutions. Her Mexican–American background aided her in understanding the language and culture of the people living in the remote areas where she collected. Her knowledge of South American culture also helped future researchers when they traveled to these areas. A keen observer, Mexia studied more than plants; she also studied the local animals, especially birds.

In her brief, ten–year career as a botanical collector, Mexia accomplished more than any woman before her in terms of numbers of plants collected and range of travel. Her work was important to completing many a botanical collection. She was also proud to claim that she had never lost a specimen. She was praised by scientific contemporaries for her many discoveries and her meticulous collection of rare specimens. Mexia's 1928 expedition to Mt. McKinley National Park in Alaska was the first general collecting trip in this area. Mexia was happiest in the field and she stayed active late into her life. She survived many accidents, including a fall off a cliff, but illness finally stopped her during her last collecting trip to Mexico in 1937–38. She became ill with a stomach problem and had to return home early. She died of lung cancer a few months later, on July 12, 1938, in Berkeley, California.

SELECTED WRITINGS BY MEXIA:

Books

(With Edwin Bingham Copeland) *Brazilian Ferns Collected by Ynes Mexia.* Berkeley: The University of California Press, 1932.

Periodicals

"Botanical Trails in Old Mexico." *Madroño* (September 1929).

FURTHER READING

Books

Bailey, Martha J. *American Women in Science: A Biographical Dictionary.* Denver: ABC–CLIO, 1994, pp. 248–49.

Ewan, Joseph. *Notable American Women, 1607–1950: A Biographical Dictionary.* Ed. E.T. James. Cambridge, MA: Belknap Press, 1971, pp. 533–34.

Siegel, Patricia Joan and Kay Thomas Finley. *Women in the Scientific Search: An American Bio–bibliography, 1724–1979.* Metuchen, NJ: The Scarecrow Press, Inc., 1985, pp. 101–04.

Periodicals

"Biographical Notes. Mexia, Ynes." *Leaflets of Western Botany* (January 1957): 95–96.

Sketch by Annette Petrusso

Helen Abbott Michael
1857–1904
American chemist and botanist

Helen Cecilia De Silver Abbott Michael was a writer and a pioneering plant chemist whose work in chemotaxonomy has had lasting effects in the twentieth century. Raised and educated at a time when professional opportunities in the sciences for women were very limited, Michael managed to carve out an independent career for herself. Her work in the chemical make–up of plants led her to two major theories. Firstly, she postulated that evolution might in fact be traced in the chemistry of plant compounds. She also theorized that plant chemistry might reflect morphology and thus form a basis for the chemical classification of plants. This latter theory came to fruition some 70 years later. A woman of great learning and greater curiosity, Michael also wrote poetry and published on the arts and philosophy. Towards the end of her life she became a medical doctor, opening a clinic for the poor in Boston. It was while working at this clinic that Michael became ill and died at age 46.

Begins Studying Medicine

Michael was born two days before Christmas in 1857, in Philadelphia, Pennsylvania, the youngest child of James Abbott and Caroline Montelius. A well–to–do family, the Abbotts had their daughter educated at home. Around the mid–1870s, Michael began piano studies at home; this was followed up by studies in Europe where she worked with major musicians and was encouraged to undertake a professional career in music. But by 1881, she had found another course for her life.

Influenced by the writings of Helmhotz on optics, she decided to study science. Back in Philadelphia, she studied physics, and then decided to move on to zoology and the dissection of animals. This study led her logically to medicine, which she pursued for almost two years at Philadelphia's Women's Medical College. Poor health, however, forced her to drop out of her medical studies in 1883. A newspaper account from that year about children dying from the poisonous effects of the roots of wild parsnips inspired Michael to turn from medicine to studying the chemical make–up and processes of plants.

Advances Plant Evolution Theory

Michael studied organic chemistry with leading scientists of the day in Philadelphia, but took no advanced degrees. Unaffiliated with a research institute, she brought her family wealth to bear in conducting her own private research projects, as well as working with Professor Henry Trimble of the Philadelphia College of Pharmacy. From 1884 to 1887, Michael prepared nine papers in plant chemistry for lecturers and publication. In one of her best known studies, that on the *Yucca angustifolia,* Michael was able—despite somewhat rudimentary laboratory conditions and equipment that prevented the isolation of pure compounds—to find various oils and resins, as well as saponin in the roots. She also analyzed the bark of *Sacara indica* and *Fouqueria splendens.* So well received was Michael's work that the trustees of the College of Pharmacy invited her to lecture, and also established new laboratories with space for women researchers. One of her most advanced theories was that plant evolution can be traced via various chemical markers. In promoting her theory, she gave public lectures in New York and Washington, D.C., at the U.S. National Museum. Much the same theory was put forward by Holger Erdtmann some 70 years later.

Touring Europe in 1887, Michael met with many of the important chemists of the day. Returning to America, Michael studied at Tufts College with Professor Arthur Michael, a noted American organic chemist. The two were married in 1888 and set up house in the Beacon Hill area of Boston. In 1891 the couple moved to the Isle of Wight, equipped a private laboratory, and continued cooperative research projects for the next four years. In 1895, they returned to Boston, where Arthur Michael once again took up his position at Tufts and Helen Michael continued her studies in chemistry, a discipline for which she was becoming increasingly well known. Elected a member of the American Philosophical Society in 1887, she also became a member of the Franklin Society in 1895, a fellow of the American Association for the Advancement of Science, and a member of the Academy of Natural Sciences.

Increasingly, however, Michael began to be involved in other, non–scientific pursuits. She was drawn into philosophical and social questions, and wrote poetry as well as reviews of the arts. A growing social awareness brought her to new concerns about the plight of the poor. She entered medical school once again, this time at Tufts College, and in 1903, after three years of study, earned her medical degree. She thereafter set up a free hospital for the poor in Boston, where she practiced. However, only a year after opening the clinic, she contracted influenza from one of her patients. Helen Abbot Michael died on November 29, 1904.

SELECTED WRITINGS BY MICHAEL:

Books

Studies in Plant and Organic Chemistry and Literary Papers. Cambridge, Massachusetts: Riverside Press, 1907.

Periodicals

"Evolution Used in the Sense of Progression." *Botanical Gazette* 11 (1886).

"A Chemical Study of Yucca angustifolia." *Transactions of the American Philosophical Society* 16 (1888).

FURTHER READING

Books

Bailey, Martha J.*American Women in Science: A Biographical Dictionary.* Denver: ABC CLIO, 1994, pp 249–50.

Creese, Mary R. S. "Helen Abbot Michael." *American Chemists and Chemical Engineers.* Volume 2. Edited by Wyndham D. Miles and Robert F. Gould. Guilford, Connecticut: Gould Books, 1994, pp. 187–88.

Finley, K. Thomas and Patricia J. Siegel. "Helen Cecilia De Silver Abbott Michael." *Women in Chemistry and Physics: A Biobibliographic Sourcebook.* Edited by Louise S. Grinstein and Rose K. Rose. Westport, Connecticut: Greenwood Press, 1993, pp. 405–09.

Periodicals

Tarbell, Ann Tracy and D. Stanley Tarbell. "Helen Abbot Michael: Pioneer in Plant Chemistry." *Journal of Chemical Education* 59/7 (1982): 548–49.

Sketch by J. Sydney Jones

Cynthia Dominka Millis
1958–1998
American toxicologist

Cynthia Dominka Millis helped expand scientific understanding of the toxic effects of polybromated biphenyls (PBBs), chemical compounds related to the better–known PCBs, which caused widespread poisoning in Michigan during the early 1970s.

Cynthia Millis, or Cindy, was born March 27, 1958, in Lynn, Massachusetts. She was the youngest of the four children of Andrew Millis, a machinist, and Helen (Jernelavitch) Millis. A bright student who was always interested in science, she graduated with honors from Lynn Classical High School in 1976.

After graduation, she attended Michigan State University, originally intending to become a veterinarian. However, after witnessing the abortion of a foal, she was dissuaded from veterinary medicine and instead pursued her degree in agricultural biochemistry. She received her bachelor's degree in that field, while simultaneously fulfilling the requirements for a B.A. in chemistry, in 1980. She then obtained her master's degree in biochemistry from Michigan State, where she studied with Steven D. Aust, Ph.D. He recalls her as "very remarkable." She published several papers with Aust during 1985 as she researched the toxic effects of PBBs on the liver.

After receiving her master's, she took a position as a research associate at Repligen Corporation in Cambridge, Massachussetts. There, she researched the use of hydroxylated indoles as dye precursors, and secured patents on the process in both the United States and Canada. The patents were held jointly with her colleagues W.C. Herlihy and J. Carroll.

After 11 months in the doctoral program at the Department of Chemistry at the University of British Columbia, Millis returned to the United States to take her degree at Pennsylvania State University. After receiving her Ph.D., she worked as a postdoctoral fellow at the University of Maryland Department of Chemistry.

While a postdoctoral fellow, she fell ill, and returned to her family's cabin in Contocook, New Hampshire, to recuperate. While there, she died in a fire on November 16, 1998. She was 40 years old. She had been due to start a new position with New Hampshire Bureau of Radiological Health December 4, 1998.

Although her career was all too brief, Cynthia Millis added much to our understanding of the actions of PBBs and how their photosynthetic products behave and effect living tissues.

FURTHER READING

Other

Hodgkins, Fran, personal interview with Millis' sister, Kathryn Millis, April 1999.

Sketch by Fran Hodgkins

Beatrice Mintz
1921–
American embryologist

Beatrice Mintz is an embryologist who has been responsible for a number of advances in the understanding of cancer while working in the laboratories at the Institute for Cancer Research in Philadelphia. She has published over 150 papers on a wide range of experimental approaches in the field of developmental biology, helping to establish the role of genes in differentiation and disease. She developed new strains of mice with a genetic predisposition to melanoma, thus offering the first experimental opportunity to analyze the progression of this disease, which is the fastest growing cancer among young people in the United States. In one experiment, she successfully accomplished the hereditary transmission of human skin melanoma cells to transgenic mice. In another experimental approach, she injected the human betaglobulin gene into fertilized mouse eggs, and this gene was then transmitted by that generation of mice to their offspring in a Mendelian ratio.

Mintz was born in New York City on January 24, 1921 to Samuel and Janie Stein Mintz. She attended Hunter College and received her A.B. in 1941; she graduated *magna cum laude,* and a member of Phi Beta Kappa. In the following year she did graduate work at New York University and then transferred to the University of Iowa where she received an M.S. in 1944 and a Ph.D in 1946. She served as a professor of biological science at the University of Chicago from 1946 to 1960. Since then, she has devoted her efforts to investigations at the Institute for Cancer Research.

Of Mice and Men

Mintz has made her most important contributions to cancer research with her experiments on the embryos of mice. The techniques she has developed to manipulate the embryos have made it possible to establish the genetic transmission of certain kinds of cancer, such as melanoma, a dangerous skin cancer. She has utilized a number of delicate laboratory techniques, such as injecting a few individual cells into the blastocysts—or early embryos—of mice in vitro, and then surgically transferring these early embryos into surrogate mothers, who then gave birth to mice whose traits were traceable. She has managed to inject the liver cells of fetal mice into the placental circulation of other mouse fetuses, thus ultimately developing a new pool of donor–strain stem cells for red and white blood cells. She has also developed techniques for in–vitro freezing of cells in liquid nitrogen before culturing them. She concluded from her investigations that human DNA could be assimilated into the germ line of mice for in–vivo research into the regulation of genetic diseases.

In the early 1960s, Mintz pioneered techniques for producing mammalian chimeras using mouse embryos. Chimera is a word from Greek mythology which describes an animal with a goat's head, a lion's body, and a serpent's tail. The mammalian chimeras Mintz produced were also composites, though they were merely the composites of genetic strains from different mice. She invented methods to develop them from more than one fertilized egg; she would take as many as fifteen embryos of different strains of mice and push them together until the cells aggregated into a single large blastocyst, which was then implanted into a foster mother. The offspring of these mice often reveal differing patterns of pigmentation and skin graft reactions.

In another experiment, Mintz succeeded in producing individuals with four, rather than two, parents. Early embryos consisting of only a few cells were removed from pregnant mice and placed in close contact with similar cells of genetically unrelated embryos to form a composite, unified embryo; this was then surgically implanted in the uterus of a mouse, which gave birth to a mouse that was a cellular mosaic—its tissues comprising genetically different kinds of cells. This technique is particularly valuable for tracing the tissue site of specific genetic diseases. In addition, Mintz established that when mouse embryo cells from a malignant tumor known as tetracarcinoma were combined with normal mouse embryo cells, the cancer cells developed into normal cells.

Named Outstanding Woman in Science

Mintz was awarded a Fulbright research fellowship at the universities of Paris and Strasbourg in 1951, and she has continued to receive many honors and awards, including the Papanicolaou Award for Scientific Achievement in 1979, and an Outstanding Woman in Science citation from the New York Academy of Sciences in 1993. She was also the recipient of two other honors, the Genetics Society of America Medal in 1981, and the Ernst Jung Gold Medal for Medicine in 1990. Five colleges, including her alma mater, have awarded her honorary doctorate degrees. She has been invited to deliver over twenty–five special lectureships, including the Ninetieth Anniversary Lecture at the Woods Hole Marine Biological Laboratory in 1978, and the first Frontiers in Biomedical Sciences Lecture at the New York Academy of Sciences in 1980. She is a member of the National Academy of Sciences and serves on the editorial boards of various scientific journals.

SELECTED WRITINGS BY MINTZ:

Books

"Experimental embryology," *McGraw-Hill Yearbook of Science and Technology.* McGraw–Hill, 1978, pp. 160–162.

"Gene Therapy: Production of Four-Parent Individuals." *Encyclopedia of Bioethics.* Edited by W. T. Reich. Macmillan, 1978, pp. 519–520.

Periodicals

"Changing the Mammalian Genome." *Proceedings of the Pontifical Academy of Science* 73 (1980): 216–223.

(With T. A. Stewart and E. F. Wagner) "Human Beta-globulin Gene Sequences Injected into Mouse Eggs, Retained in Adults and Transmitted to Progeny." *Science* 217 (1982): 1046–1048.

(With W. K. Silvers) "Transgenic Mouse Models of Malignant Skin Melanoma." *Proceedings of the National Academy of Sciences* 90 (1993): 8817–8821.

FURTHER READING

Books

McGraw–Hill Encyclopedia of Science and Technology. Vol. 3. McGraw–Hill, 1992, p. 5593.

Periodicals

Hawkes, Nigel. "A Weapon to Change the World." *Times* (London) March 2, 1993, p. 16.

Runkle, Guy, and Arlene J. Zaloznik. "Malignant Melanoma." *American Family Physician.* 49 (January 1994): 91.

Sketch by Maurice Bleifeld

Maria Mitchell
1818–1889
American astronomer

Maria Mitchell was the first famous American woman scientist. Although her only major contribution to astronomy was her discovery of a comet in 1847, as a founding faculty member of Vassar Female College and director of the college observatory, Mitchell inspired a generation of women astronomers. As the most prominent American woman scientist, she dedicated herself to opening up the scientific professions to women. She was the progenitor of a long and branched lineage of American women scientists.

Born in 1818 on Nantucket Island in Massachusetts, Maria Mitchell was the third of ten children in the middle–class Quaker family of William and Lydia (Coleman) Mitchell. Her mother was a librarian and her father was a school teacher, bank officer, and amateur astronomer. Her parents valued education for their daughters, as well as their sons, and Mitchell attended private elementary schools from the age of her four. From 1827 until 1833, she attended her father's school and she then spent a year at Cyrus Peirce's school for young ladies. Peirce encouraged her to pursue mathematics and her father taught her to use telescopes and navigational instruments. By the age of 12 she was assisting her father with astronomical observations and he taught her to calculate the positions and orbits of celestial bodies. Mitchell helped her father to time an annular solar eclipse and used the data to determine the longitude of their home.

Since American observatories at the time did not hire women, Mitchell never imagined that her childhood avocation eventually would put her into the spotlight as one of the first professional women scientists. Having completed her schooling at 16 and faced with earning a living, Mitchell opened her own school. The following year she became librarian of the Nantucket Atheneum, where she continued to educate herself by reading advanced texts. At night she used her small telescope to sweep the sky for comets, nebulae and double stars. Through her father's connections, she met and formed close relationships with astronomers at the Harvard College Observatory.

Discovers Comet

In 1831 the King of Denmark had offered a gold medal to the first person to discover a new comet that was visible only with a telescope. On October 1, 1847, Mitchell sighted a new telescopic comet and calculated its exact position. Over the next few days, observers in Europe sighted the same comet and it was almost a year before Mitchell's priority was announced and she was awarded the prize.

The medal brought Mitchell both widespread acclaim and a part–time position computing the positions of Venus

Maria Mitchell (Archive Photos. Reproduced my permission.)

for the *Nautical Almanac*, a government publication of celestial navigation. More significantly, Mitchell became a popular symbol for the professional advancement of women scientists. The famous biologist and educator Louis Agassiz nominated her for membership in the new American Association for the Advancement of Science (AAAS) in 1850 and she was elected unanimously. In 1874 she would be elected a fellow of the AAAS. Traveling to Europe in 1857, as the chaperone for the daughter of a Chicago banker, Mitchell met with various European scientists including the Herschel family of astronomers, including **Caroline Herschel**, the astronomer and popular science writer **Mary Somerville**, and Alexander von Humboldt, a geographer and champion of women scientists.

Joins Vassar College Faculty

In Mitchell's youth, astronomy had been a practical subject of use to navigators and surveyors. By the mid–nineteenth century, improved telescopes and new techniques had transformed astronomy into a rapidly–developing professional science and one that might afford opportunities for women. When William Vassar decided to establish a college that would offer women an education comparable to the best of the men's colleges, he determined that Vassar College would have an excellent observatory under the direction of Maria Mitchell. When the school opened in 1865, Mitchell and her father moved to Poughkeepsie, New York, and she became one of the first faculty members, directing the observatory and introducing young women to the science of observational astronomy. The Women's Educational Association of Boston raised the money to purchase Mitchell one of the best telescopes in the country. Mitchell proved to be a demanding and charismatic teacher who was devoted to her astronomy students. Furthermore, she was determined to create graduate educational and professional opportunities for them. A number of these young women went on to teach and work in various college observatories, with the result that astronomy became one of the few scientific professions that was open to American women in the nineteenth century. Among the students who were inspired by Mitchell were the astronomers **Mary Whitney** and **Antonia Maury**, the chemist **Ellen Swallow Richards**, and the psychologist **Christine Ladd–Franklin**.

In 1868, Mitchell made the first daily photographic series of sun spots and she recognized that these spots were not clouds above the surface of the sun, as many astronomers thought. She also studied binary or double stars and published her observations of Jupiter and Saturn and their satellites. However she was not an ambitious scientist. Most of her publications were popular science articles, including profiles of the Herschels and Mary Somerville, and she edited the astronomy section of *Scientific American*.

Advances Women's Education

Increasingly, Mitchell turned her concerns to expanding educational opportunities for women. She argued that not only was science a good profession for women, but that science needed woman professionals. As Sally Kohlstedt quoted from a note that Mitchell wrote in 1868, she had decided "In case of my outliving father & being in good health, to give my effort to the intellectual culture of women without regard to salary." Mitchell revisited Europe in 1873, meeting with astronomers, visiting observatories, and studying the status of women's education there. Returning to New York, she helped establish the Association for the Advancement of Women, serving as president for two years, and chairing their Committee on Science until her death.

Mitchell directed the Vassar Observatory until shortly before her death in Lynn, Massachusetts, in 1889. In 1848 she became the first woman ever elected to the American Academy of Arts and Sciences, over the violent objections of botanist Asa Gray. In the end, he erased "Fellow" from her certificate and wrote in "Honorary member ." No other woman was elected to the Academy until the twentieth century. In 1869 Mitchell was elected to the American Philosophical Society and the following year she received an honorary Ph.D. from Rutgers Female College. She also was awarded two honorary LL.D. degrees, from Hanover College in Indiana and from Columbia University. A crater on the moon was named after her. The Maria Mitchell Association on Nantucket, founded by her cousins and supported by a variety of sources including Vassar College, worked to improve education on Nantucket and to encourage women astronomers, providing them fellowships for study at the Harvard College Observatory.

SELECTED WRITINGS BY MITCHELL:

Books

Maria Mitchell: Life, Letters, and Journals. Phebe Mitchell Kendall, ed. Boston: Lee and Shepard, 1896. Reprint, Freeport, New York: Books for Libraries Press, 1971.

Periodicals

"Mary Somerville." *The Atlantic Monthly* 5 (1860): 568–71.

"Reminiscences of the Herschels." *Century Magazine* 38 (1889): 903–9.

"The Astronomical Science of Milton as Shown in *Paradise Lost.*" Edited by Phebe Mitchell Kendall. *Poet–Lore* 6 (June1894): 313.

FURTHER READING

Books

Kohlstedt, Sally Gregory. "Maria Mitchell and the Advancement of Women in Science." In *Uneasy Careers and Intimate Lives: Women in Science 1789–1979.* Edited by Pnina G. Abir–Am and Dorinda Outram. New Brunswick, NJ: Rutgers University Press, 1987.

Ogilvie, Marilyn Bailey. *Women in Science: Antiquity through the Nineteenth Century: A Biographical Dictionary with Annotated Bibliography.* Cambridge: MIT Press, 1991.

Wright, Helen. *Sweeper in the Sky: The Life of Maria Mitchell, First Woman Astronomer in America.* New York: Macmillan, 1949.

Periodicals

Kidwell, Peggy Aldrich. "Three Women of American Astronomy." *American Scientist* 78 (1990): 244–51.

Sketch by Margaret Alic

Helen Swift Mitchell
1921–1984
American nutritionist

Helen Swift Mitchell was an eminent nutritionist who helped define the role of vitamins in nutrition. She was coauthor of the standard textbook *Nutrition in Health and Disease*, which has been published for 71 years and has sold more than a million copies.

Born in Bridgeport, Connecticut, Mitchell received her B.A. in 1917 from Mount Holyoke College and her Ph.D. in physiological chemistry from Yale University in 1921. Like many women in the early twentieth century she taught high school students for several years before getting her doctorate.

After receiving her Ph.D. Mitchell went on to accept the position of research director of Battle Creek Sanitarium in Battle Creek College in 1921. Then she was offered a post on the staff of Battle Creek College. She taught physiology and nutrition at the college from 1924–1935 and then became a researcher at Massachusetts State College in1935. She concentrated her research on the cause and prevention of nutritional anemia and cataracts.

During World War II Mitchell took a leave of absence and became the principal nutritionist for the Office of Defense, Health, and Welfare. Later during the war, she was chief nutritionist for the Department of State. It was during this period that Mitchell made her most important contribution.

Helps Develop RDA

As part of the President's National Defense Advisory Counsel, Mitchell and other top nutritionists, biochemists, and physicians were asked to define nutrition standards for men in the army. The scientists also wanted to prepare the country for rationing, if that should ever occur.

Despite the growth of the nutrition field after World War I, knowledge about the elements of a good diet was sparse. Though the vitamins necessary for human survival were known, there was still ignorance about how to apply these facts to the life of the average American. Most Americans, and even many physicians, did not know how much vitamins they or their patients needed in their daily diets. And not only were there no standards of vitamins for the average fighting man, there were none for pregnant women or children either.

Though the committee had a great task in front of them, they dove in. As night fell, the men decided to go out on the town, while the four women on the committee met in a hotel room, according to **Lydia Jane Roberts** of the University of Chicago, another nutritionist on the committee.

Mitchell, Roberts, and two other professors, worked out tentative drafts for vitamin standards for different groups in the American population that night. The next day, all regrouped to discuss the plan. After many more meetings, and correspondence among many experts, the committee came up with what's now known as the RDA—the "recommended daily or dietary allowances" for different groups in the United States. After the War, Mitchell returned to the life of a university professor. She was selected in 1946 for the post of dean of home economics at the University of Massachusetts. She retired in 1960, when she was presented with an honorary degree from the university. She also took on the post of professor emeritus.

She wasn't idle during her retirement, however. She served as an exchange professor at Hokaido University in Japan from 1960–1962, and later worked as a consultant to the Harvard School of Public Health and the Head Start program.

Mitchell published more than 70 articles. She was also elected to the American Public Health Association as a fellow. She served as a member of the American Dietetic Association, the American Institute of Nutrition, the Institute of Food Technologists, and the American Home Economics Association. Mitchell died from a stroke on Dec. 13, 1984 at the age of 89. She spent her last days in Pleasant Hill, Tennessee.

SELECTED WRITINGS BY MITCHELL:

Books

Nutrition in Health and Disease. Philadelphia: Lippincott, 1976.

FURTHER READING

Books

Bailey, Martha J. *American Women in Science: A Biographical Dictionary*. Denver: ABC–CLIO, 1994, pp. 252–253.

Roffiter, Margaret W. *Women Scientists in America*. Baltimore: John Hopkins University Press, pp. 2–3

Periodicals

"Helen S. Mitchell Dies; Nutritionist and Writer." *New York Times* (Dec. 13, 1984): D–30

Sketch by Barbara Boughton

Mary Wortley Montagu
1689–1762
English writer and scientist

Lady Mary Wortley Montagu was a "scientific lady," a scholar, and an important feminist writer. Montagu introduced an inoculation against smallpox to England, signifying her most important contribution to science. In addition, her letters and diaries are considered to be among the most significant literary works of eighteenth–century England.

Lady Mary Wortley Montagu (Archive Photos. Reproduced by permission.)

Lady Mary was born in 1689, the daughter of Evelyn Pierrepoint, the fifth Earl and first Duke of Kingston, and Lady Mary Fielding. She was the great–granddaughter of Sir John Evelyn, the famous diarist, and the niece of the novelist Henry Fielding. Although her mother died when she was four years old and her father had little interest in his family, the gifted child made good use of her father's extensive library to educate herself. One of her mentors was the Bishop Burnet of Salisbury. At age 20, Lady Mary sent him her English translation of the first–century Greek philosopher Epictetus, along with a letter in which she wrote: "My sex is usually forbid studies of this nature. . . We are permitted no books but such as tend to the weakening and effeminating of the mind."

Lady Mary's flaunting of convention revealed itself in 1712 when, to avoid an arranged marriage, she eloped with Edward Wortley Montagu, a Whig member of parliament. Her son Edward was born the next year, followed by their daughter while in Constantinople. It was not long before she realized that her husband had been a poor choice; yet throughout her life, her beauty, wit, and intelligence guaranteed that she would always be at the center of intellectual society.

Introduces Smallpox Inoculation

In 1716, Edward Wortley Montagu was appointed British Ambassador to Constantinople and the couple made the long journey to Turkey. Mary Montagu's collection of letters about Turkish life and culture was published the year after her death. While in Turkey, Montagu first witnessed the procedure of variolation, a method of smallpox immunization which was common in the Middle East, as well as in China, India, and many parts of Africa. Montagu was particularly interested in the method, since her brother had died of smallpox and she herself had suffered a mild attack. On April 1, 1717, she described the procedure in a letter to her friend Sarah Chiswell: "The small–pox, so fatal, and so general amongst us, is here entirely harmless by the invention of *ingrafting*. . . the old woman comes with a nut–shell full of the matter of the best sort of small–pox [pus from a victim of a mild attack] . . . and puts into the vein as much venom as can lie upon the head of her needle . . . There is no example of any one that has died in it; and you may believe I am very well satisfied of the safety of the experiment, since I intend to try it on my dear little son. . ." Montagu went on to say that she would write to doctors in England about the method, if she knew of any who were honest enough to favor the eradication of smallpox and thereby lose such a large part of their medical practice. She did have her son inoculated and later, when he was in the habit of running away from his school, his mother, in advertising a reward for his return, mentioned his variolation scars as his identifying trait.

After her return to England, Montagu had her daughter inoculated against smallpox and, as a frequent visitor to the court of King George I, she was able to interest Caroline, the Princess of Wales, in the procedure. Montagu then directed experiments in which inoculations were given first to several condemned prisoners in exchange for their freedom, and then to six orphans. The subjects survived and appeared to be immune to smallpox. After Princess Caroline had her children inoculated, many English people followed this practice and, consequently, it spread rapidly throughout England, continental Europe, and North America. Despite the immunization's success, Montagu's prediction proved correct: the medical profession, as well as the Church, vigorously attacked the procedure. In response to this opposition, Montagu anonymously published "Plain Account of the Inoculating of the Small–Pox by a Turkey Merchant." Variolation was not perfect, and perhaps two or three percent of the inoculations resulted in fatalities. Still, this was a small number in comparison with the 45,000 people who were dying annually of smallpox in the British Isles. Variolation continued to be practiced until the introduction of Edward Jenner's cowpox vaccine at the end of the century.

Montagu's work marked the first step toward the public acceptance of immunization against disease, as well as the beginnings of a germ theory of disease. Although Montagu was not a trained scientist, her contribution has been summed up by Robert Reid in *Microbes and Men*: "She had applied certain scientific principles to her observation. She had, like others before her, thought up a theory to link inoculation of mild smallpox with immunity from smallpox, and had devised experiments, immoral as they undoubtedly were, to test her theory. Finally she had published her results: broadcast with a fanfare would perhaps be a better description. Her flair for personal publicity was an important ingredient in her successful impact on eighteenth–century scientific thinking. . . In the tradition of the English amateur natural philosopher, the tradition of Bacon and of Boyle, she had made her contribution to science well."

In addition to her scientific work, Montagu surrounded herself with the intellectual company of literary and scientific individuals at her salon at Twickenham. Her salon included scientists, the poets Alexander Pope and John Gay, and numerous other intellectuals. Montagu herself wrote poems, as well as one play. She also was a member of the Bluestocking Society, a salon of scientists and intellectuals, whose name derived from the clothing worn by male member and botanist Benjamin Stillingfleet. Only later did "bluestocking" become a derogatory label aimed at intellectual women.

Follows Algarotti to Italy

In 1736, at the age of 47, Montagu fell passionately in love with a 24 year old Italian, Francesco Algarotti, the author of a popular book for women on Newtonian science. Three years later, she left her husband and moved to Italy to be with him. Although Algarotti had moved on to the court of Frederick the Great in Berlin, Montagu decided to make her home in Italy, eventually settling in Venice and reestablishing her salon on the Grand Canal. Like many English women before and after her, Montagu found that Italian culture was much more accepting of women scholars, writers, and scientists. Some of her most enduring writings are her letters from this period that concern the education of her oldest granddaughter Mary Bute.

Following her husband's death, Montagu did return to England, dying of breast cancer shortly thereafter in 1762. Her lasting fame was due, however, more to her brilliant writings, her unconventional lifestyle, and her uncompromising feminism, than to her important work on immunization.

SELECTED WRITINGS BY MONTAGU:

Books

Essays and Poems and Simplicity, a Comedy. Edited by Robert Halsband and Isobel Grundy. Oxford: Clarendon, 1993.

The Letters and Works. Edited by Lord Wharncliffe and W. Moy Thomas. 2 vols. 3d ed. 1861. Reprint, London: George Bell, 1886–1908.

FURTHER READING

Books

Reid, Robert. *Microbes and Men*. New York: Saturday Review Press, 1975.

Periodicals

Strohl, E. Lee. "The Fascinating Lady Mary Wortley Montagu 1689–1762." *Archives of Surgery* 89 (1964): 554–8.

Sketch by Margaret Alic

Agnes Mary (Claypole) Moody
1870–1954
British-American zoologist

Agnes Moody was known as one of the top 1,000 scientists in America during her time. An animal histologist, Moody was also one of the very few women working within that specialty. Her contributions include studies in histology, embryology, and sociology.

Born on the first day of the year in 1870 in Bristol, England, Agnes Mary Claypole and her identical twin sister, **Edith Jane Claypole**, who also became a scientist, grew up with relatives because their mother, Jane (Trotter) Claypole, died shortly after the twins' birth, An older brother also died before their birth. Edward Waller Claypole, their father, was a teacher, geologist, and paleontologist who believed in the theory of evolution, which went against the prevailing wisdom of the day. His difficulty in finding work led him to move to the United States, alone, in 1872 to teach in various American schools. In 1879, Edward married Katherine Trotter, a relative of Jane's, took a job at Buchtel College in Akron, Ohio, and sent for the twins to join them.

The sisters were taught at home by their parents. Science and scientific research were common topics of discussion in the Claypole home during their childhood and teenage years. The girls went to Buchtel College, where Moody received her Ph.B. in 1892. From Buchtel, Moody went on to Cornell University, where she received her Master of Science degree in 1894. At Cornell, her research involved the Cayuga Lake lamprey, an eel–like fish, and its digestive tract. This became her thesis work and also her first publication, as her thesis was reprinted in the Proceedings of the Animal Microscopical Society as an animal histology prize report.

Upon the completion of her degree, Moody went on to the University of Chicago, where she received her doctorate in 1896. Her dissertation focused on Anurida maritima, an order of small insects, and their development and egg production. This work was also published, once in the Journal of Morphology and later as a monograph.

Begins Teaching Career

After graduation, Moody accepted a position at Wellesley College as a zoology instructor, where she remained for two years. In 1898, Moody returned to Cornell University, this time as an assistant in histology and embryology. Although Moody had a Ph.D. and an exemplary reputation, as well as membership in the American Association for the Advancement of Science, a woman could not hold a higher rank than assistant at the university. But in deference to her knowledge and skill, Moody did become a teacher in the required laboratory courses, the first woman at Cornell to be allowed such an opportunity. Moody remained at Cornell until 1900, and during her time there, she was a frequent and active participant at Marine Biological Laboratory at Woods Hole in Massachusetts.

Moody relocated to California in 1900 to be near her father and ailing stepmother, and when her father died suddenly shortly after she arrived, Moody took over his teaching position at Throop Polytechnic Institute (now known as California Institute of Technology). She remained at Throop until her marriage to Robert Orton Moody, son of scientist Mary Blair Moody, in 1903. Robert was a professor of anatomy at the University of California, Berkeley, which became Moody's adopted home, even after she began teaching in Oakland some years later. Moody was on the Berkeley City Council, the Berkeley Commission of Public Charities, and the Berkeley School Board.

Moody did not teach again until 1918, when she joined the faculty of Mills College as a lecturer in sociology. She remained at Mills until 1923. After a brief period in London, Moody continued her research on her own, not affiliated with any university or research organization. Moody died in Berkeley in 1954.

SELECTED WRITINGS BY MOODY:

Books

The Embryology and Oogenesis of Anurida maritima (Guer). Boston: Ginn and Company, 1898.

Periodicals

"The Enteron of the Cayuga Lake Lamprey." *Proceedings of the American Microscopical Society* 16, 1895.

FURTHER READING

Books

Bailey, Martha J. *American Women in Science.* Denver: ABC–CLIO, 1994.

Ogilvie, Marilyn Bailey. *Women in Science: Antiquity through the Nineteenth Century.* Cambridge: MIT Press, 1986.

Shearer, Benjamin S. and Barbara S. Shearer, eds. *Notable Women in the Life Sciences.* Westport, CT: Greenwood Press, 1996.

Sketch by Helene Barker Kiser

Ruth Ella Moore
1903–
American bacteriologist

Ruth Moore achieved distinction when she became the first African American woman to earn a Ph.D. in bacteriology from Ohio State in 1933. Her entire teaching career was spent at Howard University in Washington, D.C., where she remained an associate professor emeritus of microbiology until 1990.

Ruth Ella Moore was born in Columbus, Ohio, on May 19, 1903. After receiving her B.S. from Ohio State in 1926, she continued at that university and received her M.A. the following year. In 1933 she earned her Ph.D. in bacteriology from Ohio State, becoming the first African American woman to do so. Her achievement was doubly significant considering that her minority status was combined with that era's prejudices against women in professional fields. During her graduate school years (1927–1930), Moore was an instructor of both hygiene and English at Tennessee State College. Upon completing her dissertation at Ohio State—where she focused on the bacteriological aspects of tuberculosis (a major national health problem in the 1930's)—she received her Ph.D. in 1933.

That same year she took a position at the Howard University College of Medicine as an instructor of bacteriology. In 1939 she became an assistant professor of bacteriology, and in 1948 she was named acting head of the university's department of bacteriology, preventive medicine, and public health. In 1955 she became head of the department of bacteriology and remained in that position until 1960 when she became an associate professor of microbiology at Howard. She remained in that department until her retirement in 1973, whereupon she became an associate professor emeritus of microbiology. Throughout her career, Moore has been concerned with public health issues, and as such is a member of the American Public Health Association and the American Society of Microbiologists.

FURTHER READING

Books

Sammons, Vivian O. *Blacks in Science and Medicine.* Hemisphere, 1990, p. 176.

Sketch by Leonard C. Bruno

Emmeline Moore
1872–1963
American aquatic biologist and conservationist

While many scientists who study fish turn their attention to the sea, Emmeline Moore focused on the importance of freshwater lakes and rivers. She also blazed a new path for women in the field of biology as one of the first women to be in charge of a state fisheries department.

Emmeline Moore was born April 29, 1872, in Batavia, New York. As a girl she watched the polliwogs in a wetland near her family's farm, and as a result became interested in biology. She attended and graduated from Genesco Normal School in 1895. She taught in public schools from 1985 to1903, then went on to earn her bachelor's degree from Cornell University in 1905. She then went to Massachusetts to attend Wellesley College, where she earned her master's degree in 1906. After getting her master's, she returned to teaching, this time as a biology instructor at a normal school, until 1910. She then left the United States for South Africa, taking a one–year post as a substitute professor of botany at Huguenot College in 1911. She returned to Cornell for her doctoral studies and earned her Ph.D. in 1914. For the next five years, Moore once again returned to teaching, this time as an instructor and assistant professor at Vassar College.

However, a new opportunity was about to present itself to her. In 1919, she left academia to join the staff of the New York State Conservation Department. At that time, the only opportunity for women scientists was teaching. However, New York State was willing to hire not only more scientists than other states were, but also more women scientists. The reason was probably a combination of factors, according to Margaret Rossiter in her book *Women Scientists in America: Struggles and Strategies to 1940.* Rossiter suggests that the state's civil service rules were more open than those of other states, its pay scales more attractive, and its male bosses more liberal.

Whatever the reason, Emmeline Moore left Vassar for New York in 1919 to join the New York Conservation Department as a research biologist. She became New York's first investigator-biologist in the field of fish culture, pioneering studies of fish diseases and pollution, and rose quickly through the ranks to become chief aquatic biologist.

In her work, Moore was one of the first to recognize the importance of studying state freshwater resources to determine what existed as far as fish populations and the challenges to those populations, such as fishing and disease. In her monograph *Problems in Fresh Water Fisheries,* published in 1926 as part of the Conservation Commission's 15th annual report, she proposed a program of fisheries research for the state. Moore wrote that it was no longer feasible simply to stock ponds, lakes and rivers with hatchlings and that eggs of certain species were becoming difficult to obtain for hatcheries.

Throughout her career at the commission, she surveyed and studied the state's many waterways, including the Erie-Niagara system, the Lake Champlain watershed, and the St. Lawrence watershed. Her work was not restricted to New York, however. Research projects took her all over the United States and Canada, to Alaska, and to Europe and Africa. The importance of her work was recognized in 1928, when she became the president of the American Fisheries Society, the first women president in that organization's history. She was also honored by Boston Society of Natural History, and in1951 she was recognized at an international conservation conference held in Rochester, N.Y. And in 1958, she received the singular honor of having a state marine research ship named after her, the *Emmeline M.*

Moore remained with the Commission for the remainder of her professional career, eventually becoming the director of the State Biological Survey. She retired from the post in 1944. After retirement, she served as an honorary fellow at the University of Wisconsin, and also at the Yale University oceanography lab as a research assistant. Emmeline Moore died on September 12, 1963, in a nursing home after a long illness. She was 91.

SELECTED WRITINGS BY EMMELINE MOORE:

Other

Some plants of importance in pond fish culture. Appendix IV to the Report of the U.S. Commissioner of Fisheries for 1919. Washington, DC: U.S. Government Printing Office, 1920.

Problems in Fresh Water Fisheries. Annual Report, New York Conservation Commission 1925. Albany, NY, 1926.

(And others.) *A biological Survey of the Oswego River System..* A supplement to the 17th Annual Report, New York Conservation Commission 1927 Albany, NY, 1928.

(And others.) *A biological survey of the Erie-;Niagara System.* A supplement to the 18th Annual Report, New York Conservation Commission 1928 Albany, NY, 1929.

(And others.) *A biological survey of the Champlain Watershed.* A supplement to the 19th Annual Report, New York Conservation Commission 1929 Albany, NY, 1930.

FURTHER READING

Books

American Men and Women of Science 9th Edition, New York: R.R. Bowker, 1976.

Bailey, Martha J. *American Women in Science: A Biographical Dictionary.* Santa Barbara, Calif.: ABC-CLIO, 1994.

Clepper, Henry, Ed. *Leaders of American Conservation.* New York: The Roland Press Co., 1971.

Stroud, Richard H. *Nationaal Leaders of American Conservation.* Washington, DC: Smithsonian Institution Press, 1985.

Periodicals

Obituary. *The New York Times,* September 14, 1963, p. 25.

Sketch by Fran Hodgkins

Cathleen Synge Morawetz
1923–
American mathematician

In 1984 Cathleen Synge Morawetz became the first woman in the United States to head a mathematical institute, the Courant Institute of Mathematical Sciences at New York University. Since receiving her Ph.D. from the university in 1951, her research on fluid dynamics and transonic flow has been influential in the fields of aerodynamics, acoustics, and optics. In 1993 she was elected president of the American Mathematical Society.

Born on May 5, 1923, to mathematician John Synge and Eleanor Mabel Allen Synge, Morawetz grew up in Toronto, Canada, and won a scholarship in mathematics to the University of Toronto. She served in a wartime post in 1943–44 before earning her B.A. in 1945. That same year she married chemist Herbert Morawetz (with whom she eventually had four children) and began graduate studies at the Massachusetts Institute of Technology (MIT), from which she received her master's degree in 1946. At a time when few scientific fields were open to women, Morawetz briefly considered working for Bell Laboratories in New Jersey but decided to pursue a Ph.D. instead.

While editing the book *Supersonic Flow and Shock Waves,* written by New York University mathematicians Richard Courant and Kurt Friedrichs, she became interested in the phenomenon of transonic flow, or the behavior of air at speeds approximating that of sound. Spurred by the urgency of this research (in the late years of World War II, the new jet engine enabled aircraft to approach supersonic flight) she decided to pursue a Ph.D. in the subject. Working under Friedrichs at New York University (NYU), she wrote her doctoral thesis on imploding shock waves and received her degree in 1951. After a brief stint as a research associate at MIT, she joined NYU's mathematics faculty as a research assistant in 1952, publishing scores of scientific articles during her upward climb to full professor in 1965. Morawetz also rose within NYU's Courant Institute of Mathematical Sciences, where she received the ultimate honor of being named the institute's director in 1984—the first woman ever to head a mathematical institution of that stature in the United States. She has also served as the editor of several scientific journals, including the *Journal of Mathematical Analysis and Applications* and *Communication in Pure and Applied Mathematics.*

Morawetz continued research in the field of fluid dynamics, the study of forces exerted upon liquids and gases and the effects of those forces on motion. She conclusively demonstrated that all airplane wings produce shock waves if they are moving fast enough. Her findings have contributed to important advances in aerodynamics, acoustics, and optics. Similarly, her work on transonic flow has been applied in two widely different areas: the use of seismic waves (movement caused by vibrations within the earth) in prospecting for oil and the development of medical imaging techniques.

A member of the American Academy of Arts and Sciences, Morawetz has received several major awards, including two Guggenheim Fellowships, the Gibbs Lectureship of the American Mathematical Society, and the Lester R. Ford Award from the Mathematical Association of America. She also holds honorary degrees from Smith College, Brown University, Princeton University, and Duke University. In 1994, in addition to being the only woman member of the Applied Mathematics Section of the National Academy of Sciences, Morawetz was elected the second woman president to head the American Mathematical Society. In a university press release, NYU President L. Jay Oliva summarized the esteem in which she is held by her peers: "Morawetz is an outstanding mathematician, and has long been one of the leading lights at our prestigious Courant Institute. I know that the American Mathematical Society will benefit greatly by her considerable acumen and compelling leadership."

SELECTED WRITINGS BY MORAWETZ:

Periodicals

(With I. Kolodner) "On the Non–existence of Limiting Lines in Transonic Flows." *Communication in Pure and Applied Mathematics* (February 1953): 97–102.

"Energy Flow: Wave Motion and Geometrical Optics." *Bulletin of the American Mathematical Society* (July 1970): 661–74.

"The Mathematical Approach to the Sonic Barrier." *Bulletin of the American Mathematical Society* (March 1982):127–45.

"Giants." *American Mathematical Monthly* (November 1992): 819–28.

FURTHER READING

Books

Grinstein, Louise S., and Paul J. Campbell, eds. *Women of Mathematics* Greenwood Press, 1987, pp. 152–55.

Periodicals

"Cathleen Morawetz, First Woman to Head a Mathematics Institute," *Series in Applied Mathematics News* 17, no. 4 (1984): 5.

Kolata, Gina Bari. "Cathleen Morawetz: The Mathematics of Waves." *Science* 206 (1979): 206–07.

Other

"NYU Mathematician Cathleen Morawetz Elected Next President of 30,000–Member American Mathematical Society." New York University press release, December 20, 1993.

Sketch by Nicholas Pease

Ann Haven Morgan
1882–1966
American zoologist and ecologist

Ann Haven Morgan was known to her students as "Mayfly Morgan" because of her passion for the mayflies that were the subject of her Ph.D. dissertation. Her passions extended much further, however. A promoter of conservation, or applied ecology, she wrote about animal adaptations and noted the impact of human populations on wilderness and natural habitats. Morgan's long career at Mount Holyoke College was coupled with a lifelong commitment to conservation education. In addition to scientific papers, she produced a textbook and two popular field guides notable for their clarity and grace of language.

Morgan was born May 6, 1882, in Waterford, Connecticut, to Stanley Griswold and Julia Alice Douglass Morgan. The eldest of three children, she took pleasure in exploring the woods and streams near her home, and throughout life professed her fondness for "oozy mudholes." In 1902, after graduation from Williams Memorial Institute at New London, she entered Wellesley College. Finding it confining, in 1904 she transferred to Cornell University, where in 1906 she received an A.B. degree. She spent the subsequent three years at Mount Holyoke College in South Hadley, Massachusetts, as a biology assistant and instructor, then returned to Cornell to study for a doctoral degree under the aquatic biologist James George Needham. It was at Cornell that her freshman biology students christened her "Mayfly

Ann Haven Morgan (Mount Holyoke College Archives and Special Collections. Reproduced by permission.)

Morgan." At about the same time she received the Ph.D. in 1912, she changed her name from "Anna" to "Ann."

Upon graduation Morgan returned to Mount Holyoke, where her promotions were rapid. She was named associate professor in 1914, chairman of the zoology department in 1916, and full professor in 1918. Morgan's career at Mount Holyoke was punctuated by postgraduate work at the University of Chicago and summer research and teaching at Cornell and the Marine Biological Laboratory at Woods Hole, Massachusetts. In 1920 Morgan was a visiting fellow at Harvard and, in 1921, at Yale. She spent the summer of 1926 at William Beebe's tropical laboratory in Kartabo, British Guiana. Her studies of aquatic life focused primarily on the American Northeast, ranging from land–locked salmon in New Hampshire to water bugs in a pond near Northampton.

Field Book on Ponds and Streams Becomes Popular Favorite

Morgan's *Field Book of Ponds and Streams: An Introduction to the Life of Fresh Water*, published in 1930 with her own drawings and photographs and a foreword by Needham, described the "lively populations" of freshwater habitats as well as methods of collection and preservation. It was an instant success and became a longtime favorite of fishermen and amateur naturalists as well as professional biologists. In 1935 she published Field Book of Animals in Winter; it was based on a course she had taught, and it inspired an educational film produced by Encyclopedia Brittannica Films.

The pioneering zoologist **Cornelia Clapp** considered Morgan her successor at Mount Holyoke. Morgan was an outstanding teacher, inspiring many students to enter biological fields. In the 1930s, she and her colleague, A. Elizabeth Adams, won funding from the National Academy of Sciences, the National Research Council, Sigma Xi, the American Association for the Advancement of Science, and the Rockefeller Foundation. In 1933, when Morgan was 50, she was one of three American women "starred" in recognition of their excellence, in James McKeen Cattell's *American Men of Science*. *Time* magazine, reporting on the honor, noted that her recent publications dealt with spotted newts, although mayflies remained her favorite subjects. The diminutive Morgan was portrayed as moving briskly about her laboratories in her physician's coat, and lecturing her classes "in clear, crisp tones."

After retirement from Mount Holyoke in 1947, Morgan continued her energetic pace, conducting workshops for teachers and promoting conservation education—appreciation and intelligent care of living things and the environment—as integral to science programs. As members of the National Commission on Policies in Conservation Education, Morgan and Adams traveled to the western United States and Canada to study conservation programs, and Morgan returned to apply what she had learned to the Connecticut River Valley. In 1955 Morgan published *Kinships of Animals and Man*, a textbook that treats zoological structure and function, animal behavior, evolution, and ecology. It is a comprehensive work, a culmination of her teaching career, and is considered a classic text.

Morgan died of stomach cancer on June 5, 1966, at her home in South Hadley. She was buried at Cedar Grove Cemetery in New London.

SELECTED WRITINGS BY MORGAN:

Books

Field Book of Ponds and Streams: An Introduction to the Life of Fresh Water. New York: G. P. Putnam's Sons, 1930.

Field Book of Animals in Winter. New York: G. P. Putnam's Sons, 1939.

Kinships of Animals and Man: A Textbook of Animal Biology. New York: McGraw–Hill, 1955.

FURTHER READING

Books

Bonta, Marcia Myers. *Women in the Field: America's Pioneering Women Naturalists*. College Station, TX: Texas A&M University Press, 1991, pp. 245–249.

Rossiter, Margaret W. *Women Scientists in America: Struggles and Strategies to 1940.* Baltimore: Johns Hopkins University Press, 1982, pp. 19, 145, 174, 294.

Shearer, Benjamin F., and Barbara S. Shearer, eds. *Notable Women in the Life Sciences: A Biographical Dictionary.* Westport, CT: Greenwood Press, 1996, pp. 293–297.

Sicherman, Barbara, and Carol Hurd Green, eds. *Notable American Women: The Modern Period, A Biographical Dictionary.* Cambridge: Belknap Press, 1980, pp. 497–498.

Periodicals

"Best Women." *Time* (March 20, 1933): 38.

Sketch by Jill Carpenter

Margaretta Hare Morris
1797–1867
American entomologist

Margaretta Hare Morris was one of the first American women field entomologists. She made important contributions to agricultural science with studies on the 17–year locust and the Hessian fly, which are devastating to farmer's crops. Morris was the first practicing woman naturalist and only the second woman elected to the Philadelphia Academy of Natural Sciences. She is also recognized for her illustrations of botanical papers.

Morris was born on December 3, 1797, probably in Philadelphia, Pennsylvania. She was the daughter of Luke and Ann (Willing) Morris. Her father died sometime before 1812. After that date, Morris, her mother, and her sister, Elizabeth Carrington Morris, moved to Germantown, Pennsylvania, where they spent the rest of their lives. Like her botanist sister Elizabeth, Morris never married. There is also no evidence that she had a formal education or ever held a job. She and her mother did attend scientific lectures given in Germantown, and Morris was apparently acquainted with scientists.

Morris's primary research covered two areas: Hessian flies and 17–year locusts. She raised her own Hessian fly specimens to observ their life cycles. She discovered that Hessian fly larvae were of two separate species, not one as previously believed. The larvae of one species were laid not on the stalk but on the grain and became trapped in the wheat stalk as it grew. This helped to spread the insect, which was transported from one country to another in straw. Morris also discovered the main predator of the Hessian fly, which was of vital interest to agriculturists. In December 1840, Morris published her first paper on the subject, which appeared in *Transactions of the American Philosophical Society*. She published further papers on the subject in 1840 and 1849.

Morris made a similar discovery with 17–year locusts, a subject that she first published on in 1846 in *Proceedings of the Boston Society of Natural History.* She observed that their eggs penetrated fruit trees' roots. After several growing seasons, this made the trees weaker, and finally, unable to produce fruit. She published again on the subject in 1850. In order to get papers published by the leading scientific publications of the day, a woman had to find a male member of a scientific society to read it before the membership. Because Morris's work was well-respected, she had little difficulty finding men willing to do so.

Morris's scientific peers also recognized her importance in another way. In 1850, she was elected to the American Association for the Advancement of Science. By the late 1850s, she was made an honorary member of the Philadelphia Academy of Natural Sciences. Morris died on May 29, 1867 in Germantown, Pennsylvania.

SELECTED WRITINGS BY MORRIS:

Periodicals

"On the Cecidomyia destructor, or Hessian Fly." *Transactions of the American Philosophical Society* (1843): 49–52.

"On the Seventeen Year Locusts." *Proceedings of the Boston Society of Natural History* (1851): 110.

FURTHER READING

Books

Bailey, Martha J. *American Women in Science: A Biographical Dictionary.* Denver: ABC–CLIO, 1994, p. 261.

Bonta, Marcia Myers. *Women in the Field: America's Pioneering Women Naturalists.* College Station: Texas A&M University Press, 1991, pp. 145– 47.

Elliott, Clark A. *Biographical Dictionary of American Science: The Seventeenth Though the Nineteenth Centuries.* Westport: Greenwood Press, 1979, pp. 185–86.

Graustein, Jeannette E. *Thomas Nuttall, Naturalist: Explorations in America, 1808–1841.* Cambridge: Harvard University Press, 1967, p. 374.

Kass–Simon, G., and Patricia Farnes, eds. *Women of Science: Righting the Record.* Bloomington: Indiana University Press, 1990, p. 255.

Rossiter, Margaret W. *Women Scientists in America: Struggles and Strategies to 1940.* Baltimore: Johns Hopkins University Press, 1982, p. 76.

Siegel, Patricia Joan and Kay Thomas Finley. *Women in the Scientific Search: An American*

Bio–bibliography, 1724–1979. Metuchen, NJ: Scarecrow Press, 1985, pp. 159–160.

Sketch by Annette Petrusso

Maria Eimmart Müller
1676–1707
German astronomer and illustrator

Maria Eimmart Müller was one of the first astronomical artists. She was trained in astronomy at her father's observatory in Nuremberg, Germany. Müller used the telescope to make faithful drawings of the Sun, Moon (including its mountains), eclipses, sunspots, and comets. Her early death ended a promising career.

Müller was born in Germany in 1676. She was the daughter of Georg Christoph Eimmart, who, in 1678, built an observatory on the Nuremberg city wall. Georg Eimmart was also a painter and engraver who served as director of the Nuremberg Academy of Art from 1699–1704. Müller learned about astronomy from her father. Her education also included studying French, Latin, drawing, and mathematics which was essential to understanding astronomy.

The education Müller received was helpful in making sketches of astronomical phenomenon. For six years, from 1693–1698, Müller made 250 sketches of phases of the Moon. which were used to draw a new lunar map. These illustrations were probably used in a book published by her father, entitled *Micrographia Stellarum Phases Lunae Ultra 300*. There is also speculation that Müller wrote a book about the Sun under her father's name, entitled *Ichnographia nova contemplationum de sole* in 1701. Scholars are divided on the authenticity of this claim. What is known more concretely is that Müller made several sketches of the total eclipse of 1706. Müller's body of artistic work also include many drawings of ancient statues, birds, and flowers.

In 1706, Müller married Johann Heinrich Müller, an astronomer in his own right. He worked as director of Georg Eimmart's observatory as well as a physics teacher in a Nuremberg school. Later, he was an astronomy professor at Altorf. Through Germany's inheritance laws, Johann Müller acquired Georg Eimmart's observatory upon his death. It appears Müüller continued her interest in astronomy with her husband. She died in 1707 while giving birth.

FURTHER READING

Books

Alic, Margaret. *Hypatia's Heritage: A History of Women in Science from Antiquity to the late Nineteenth Century.* London: The Women's Press, 1986, pp. 120–21.

Schiebinger, Londa. *The Mind Has No Sex? Women in the Origins of Modern Science.* Cambridge: Harvard University Press, 1989, pp. 40–45, 66–67, 78–82.

Periodicals

"Some Notable Women of Science." *Nature* (1931): 976–77.

Sketch by Annette Petrusso

Sandra Murray
1947–
American cell biologist

As a high school student, Sandra Murray was told by a guidance counselor that science was no career for someone who was black and female. Rather than becoming discouraged, she continued to pursue her interest in biology and attained success as a researcher and educator.

Sandra Murray was born on October 7, 1947 in Chicago, as the second of three children. Her parents, Charles and Muggy Wise Murray, owned a moving company. Often, families would leave odds and ends behind when they moved; Charles Murray would take these odds and ends and fashion toys for his children. This sparked an interest in Sandra as to how things worked. When she was older, her interest extended to how the human body functioned. Forced to spend three months in a hospital while recovering from corrective surgery on her shoulder, she asked the doctors countless questions about her condition and insisted on seeing her x rays.

Murray did well enough in high school that she was chosen for a special biomedical research program that allowed high school students to take special weekend classes at the University of Chicago. It was during this time that Sandra's counselor admonished her for aiming too high in her career aspirations. For a while, Sandra's confidence was shaken; what if she *did* try to pursue a science career but failed? Fortunately, she decided not to give up. She worked after school in the anatomy laboratory of the University of Illinois School of Medicine, and in 1964 she enrolled there as a student.

Murray was still not completely sure she could succeed at science, and she put off choosing a major. She also had to work her way through school, and it took her six years to get her degree. After she took her first biology course in college during her sophomore year, though, she knew that biology was what she wanted to study.

After graduating from Illinois in 1970, she went on to the graduate biology program at Texas Southern University in Houston. She completed her master's in 1973 and went to the University of Iowa for her doctorate. A Ford Foundation Fellowship allowed her to devote most of her time to her research, which focused on how glandular hormones affected the growth of cancer cells. She was awarded her Ph.D. in 1980.

Shortly thereafter, Murray took a postdoctoral position at the University of California at Riverside. There, she continued her research on hormones, primarily the effects of deoxyribonucleic acid (DNA) and ribonucleic acid (RNA) on the glands that produce the various hormones. Eventually, Murray was offered a position on the medical school faculty at the University of Pittsburgh. During her career, her research has taken her to the Marine Biological Laboratory at Woods Hole, Massachusetts, and the Scripps Research Institute on Molecular Biology at La Jolla, California. Mindful of the difficulties in recruiting minorities for the sciences, she has also made time to visit a number of colleges with high minority enrollments, such as Morgan State University in Baltimore and Spelman College in Atlanta, to offer both instruction and encouragement.

FURTHER READING

Books

Kessler, James H., et al. *Distinguished African–American Scientists of the Twentieth Century.* Oryx Press, 1996.

Sketch by George A. Milite

Mary Esther Murtfeldt
1848–1913
American entomologist and botanist

Mary Murtfeldt was one of the first female professional entomologists in the United States and was acting state entomologist of Missouri for eight years. Murtfeldt did significant work on the relationship of insects to the pollination of plants, including the pollination of yucca in which she showed that this plant is only pollinated by the yucca moth. Murtfeldt was a fellow of the American Association for the Advancement of Science and also belonged to the Entomological Society of America, as well as the American Association of Economic Entomologists.

Murtfeldt was born in New York City in 1848 to Charles and Esther Murtfeldt. She came from a large family, which included three sisters, Louise, Augusta, and Josephine, and two brothers, George and William. Murtfeldt's parents had a strong appreciation of education, which led to Murtfeldt's later attendance at college.

As a child Murtfeldt developed a crippling illness, which put her on crutches for the rest of her life. This illness prevented Murtfeldt from completing her college education at Rockford College in Illinois, which she attended from 1858 to 1860. It is also probably the reason Murtfeldt lived at home most of her life, after the family moved to Kirkwood, Missouri, near St. Louis.

Collects New Specimens of Insects

The family lived in a house on three acres, making it possible for Murtfeldt to collect new specimens of insects without leaving the family's property. This resulted in Murtfeldt assembling a collection of mounted insects that became so large it could no longer be kept in the house. Consequently, the collection was donated to the United States Department of Agriculture.

In 1868 Murtfeldt became interested in entomology through her father's appointment as editor of *Colman's Rural World* (an agricultural periodical) and as Corresponding Secretary of the Missouri Board of Agriculture. Through these appointments she met Charles V. Riley, the then state entomologist of Missouri. Until 1877 Murtfeldt was his assistant and during this period did her important work on the relationship of insects to pollination of plants.

Murtfeldt remained under the guidance of Riley from the beginning of her professional career in 1868 until his death in 1895. Even though Riley left St. Louis in 1878 for service in Washington with the U.S. Department of Agriculture's Bureau of Entomology, Murtfeldt was appointed field agent and remained under his supervision. Riley had the reputation of being a stern taskmaster, and his work often overshadowed those of his assistants, probably including those of Murtfeldt.

Becomes Acting State Entomologist

In 1888 Murtfeldt was appointed the acting state entomologist and remained in this position until 1896. She was most likely the first woman to be in this position. Around the same time she was a field agent in the Division of Entomology for the U.S. Department of Agriculture, from 1880–1893. In this position she attended scientific meetings and presented numerous papers, perhaps one of the first women to do so.

Murtfeldt left the state agency in 1896 to become a staff contributor on entomology and botany for the city paper, the *St. Louis Republic.* Several years later she wrote *Stories of Insect Life.* Murtfeldt remained at the paper until her death on February 23, 1913 from heart disease.

Since Murtfeldt's specialty was moths, she had gathered an outstanding collection. In addition, she was a prolific author, publishing numerous articles on Tortricidae (an important family of moths within the order Lepidoptora) and several books on insects. Though her books were compilations of others' work, her papers were original, as they were published in peer–reviewed journals. Perhaps

Murtfeldt's most important contribution to entomology, however, is not her research, but her role as a female scientist at a time when women in the sciences were quite a rarity.

SELECTED WRITINGS BY MURTFELDT:

Books

(Contributor) Tracy, S. M. *Flora of Missouri.* Missouri State Horticultural Society Report, 1885.

Outlines of Entomology: Prepared for the Use of Farmers and Horticulturists at the Request of the Secretary of the State Board of Agriculture and the State Horticultural Society of Missouri. Jefferson City, MO, 1891.

(With Clarence M. Weed) *Stories of Insect Life.* Boston: The Athenaeum Press, 1899.

FURTHER READING

Books

Howard, L.O. *A History of Applied Entomology.* Smithsonian Miscellaneous Collections, Vol. 84, Pl. 5 (1930): 25, 92, 102.

Ogilvie, Marilyn B. *Women in Science, Antiquity Through the Nineteenth Century. A Biographical Dictionary with Annoted Bibliography.* Cambridge: MIT Press, 1986, pp. 139–40.

Osborn, Herbert. *Fragments of Entomological History.* Columbus, OH. Pl 7 (1937): 153–54, 165, 240.

Periodicals

Obituary. *Entomolgical News* XXIV, no. 6 (1913): 241–42.

Obituary. *Journal of Economic Entomology* 6 (1913): 288–89.

Other

Sheppard, Laurel M. Personal communication with Edward H. Smith, Professor of Entomology Emeritus, Cornell University, June 1999.

Sketch by Laurel M. Sheppard

N

Prudence Hero (Rutherford) Napier
1916–1997
English primatologist

Prudence Hero Rutherford Napier collaborated throughout her distinguished career with her husband, John R. Napier, who founded the first research center for the study of lemurs, monkeys, and apes in London at the Royal Free Hospital. Originally an amateur zoologist, she became an expert in her own right and was consulted by zoologists from all over the world.

Napier was born in Liverpool to a member of British Parliament. Little is known about her childhood. She received her schooling at Roedean College, but showed no real aptitude for scholarship. Her interest in the active life led her to become a skilled lacrosse player, skier, and mountain climber. She met John Napier in 1936, when he was a medical student. They married and had two children. When the children were young, she served as her husband's secretary and laboratory assistant Her obituary in the *London Times* says her children remembered "returning home to find the house smelling of boiling monkey bones."

Becomes an Expert on Primate Anatomy and Taxology

Napier's growing interest in primate morphology (the study of their structure and forms) included both Old World and New World primates. Her research focused on the comparative anatomy and taxonomy (classification) of primates. She coauthored with her husband *A Handbook of the Living Primates*, *Old World Monkeys*, and *The Natural History of the Primates*. She also wrote an introductory book on primates titled *Monkeys and Apes*, and two upper–level books titled *Chimpanzees* and *Lorises, Lemurs and Bushbabies*.

During the 1970s, the couple lived for a time in Washington, D. C., where John Napier set up the Department of Primatology at the Smithsonian Museum. When Prudence returned to England, she began taxonomy and cataloging work on primates at the British Museum of Natural History. Out of this work grew a series of three books on Old and New World monkeys. In addition to their research, Napier and her husband served as advisors to many zoos, the most prominent being Twycross Zoo in Leicestershire, known for its excellent collection of primates. After her husband's death, she succeeded him as the zoo's president. The last book that the couple coauthored, *The Natural History of the Primates* in 1985, is considered a classic and is still being used to teach college students.

The books written singly by her and jointly with her husband sought to catalogue and distribute what they called "the bricks and mortar" of the science—the basic facts about the physical structure of primates, their habitats, and their behaviors. They saw their research as being important to human biologists, zoologists, and those in the medical research field, saying that they saw a need for these scientists to have "up–to–date, factual information on primate biology" on which to base further studies of their own. As the field of primatology grew and as more laboratory work and field work was being conducted, they dedicated themselves to "making primate biology as comprehensible to as wide a selection of scientists as possible."

Napier was conscious of the gaps that existed in the knowledge of primates at all levels. Her concern that some species would be lost before they could be studied is apparent throughout her writings. She was quick to credit fellow scientists for any new insight that furthered primate research. Both of the Napiers considered primatology the "basic science of biology," and they encouraged research and medical organizations to make grant monies available to enable students, allowing them to undertake field research.

In 1982 the Napiers retired to the Isle of Mull, where they wrote *The Natural History of the Primates*. After John's death, Pru Napier continued their work by revising and updating the vast body of primate knowledge they had amassed together. She died on June 6, 1997, at the age of 81.

SELECTED WRITINGS BY NAPIER:

Books

(With John R. Napier) *A Handbook of Living Primates*. London: Academic Press, 1967.

(Editor, with John R. Napier) *Old World Monkeys. Evolution, Systematics, and Behavior*. London: Academic Press, 1970.

Catalogue of primates in the British Museum (Natural History). Part I: Families Callitrichidae and Cebidae. London: British Museum (Natural History), 1976.

Catalogue of primates in the British Museum (Natural History) and elsewhere in the British Isles. Part II: Family Cercopithecidae, subfamily Cercopithecinae.. London: British Museum (Natural History), 1981.

Catalogue of primates in the British Museum (Natural History) and elsewhere in the British Isles. Part III: Family Cercopithecidae, subfamily Colobinae.. London: British Museum (Natural History), 1985.

(With John H. Napier). *The Natural History of the Primates*. Cambridge, MA: The MIT Presss, 1985.

FURTHER READING

Periodicals

Obituary, *London Times* (July 3, 1997): 27a.

Sketch by Jane Stewart Cook

Elizabeth F. Neufeld
1928–
French–born American biochemist

Elizabeth Neufeld (AP/Wide World Photos. Reproduced by permission.)

Elizabeth F. Neufeld is best known as an authority on human genetic diseases. Her research at the National Institutes of Health (NIH) and at University of California, Los Angeles (UCLA), provided new insights into mucopolysaccharide storage disorders (the absence of certain enzymes preventing the body from properly storing certain substances). Neufeld's research opened the way for prenatal diagnosis of such life–threatening fetal disorders as Hurler syndrome. Because of this research, she was awarded the Lasker Award in 1982 and the Wolf Prize in Medicine in 1988.

She was born Elizabeth Fondal in Paris, on September 27, 1928. Her parents, Jacques and Elvire Fondal, were Russian refugees who had settled in France after the Russian revolution. The impending occupation of France by the Germans brought the Fondal family to New York in June 1940. Her parents' experience led them to instill in Neufeld a strong commitment to the importance of education "They believed that education was the one thing no one could take from you," she told George Milite in a 1993 interview.

Neufeld first became interested in science while a high school student, her interest sparked by her biology teacher. She attended Queens College in New York, receiving her bachelor of science degree in 1948. She worked briefly as a research assistant to Elizabeth Russell at the Jackson Memorial Laboratory in Bar Harbor, Maine. From 1949 to 1950 she studied at the University of Rochester's department of physiology. In 1951 she moved to Maryland, where she served as a research assistant to Nathan Kaplan and Sidney Colowick at the McCollum–Pratt Institute at Johns Hopkins University. In 1952 Neufeld moved again, this time to the West Coast. From 1952 to 1956 she studied under W. Z. Hassid at the University of California, Berkeley. She received her Ph.D. in comparative biochemistry from Berkeley in 1956 and remained there for her postdoctoral training. She first studied cell division in sea urchins. Later, as a junior research biochemist (working again with Hassid) she studied the biosynthesis of plant cell wall polymers—which would prove significant when she began studying Hurler syndrome and related diseases.

Neufeld began her scientific studies at a time when few women chose science as a career. The historical bias against women in science, compounded with an influx of men coming back from the Second World War and going to college, made positions for women rare; few women could be found in the science faculties of colleges and universities. Despite the "overt discrimination" Neufeld often witnessed, she decided nonetheless to pursue her interests. "Some people looked at women who wanted a career in science as a little eccentric," she told Milite, "but I enjoyed what I was doing and I decided I would persevere."

Begins Research on Hurler Syndrome

After spending several years at Berkeley, Neufeld moved on to NIH in 1963, where she began as research biochemist at the National Institute of Arthritis Metabolism and Digestive Diseases. It was during her time at NIH that Neufeld began her research on mucopolysaccharidoses (MPS), disorders in which a complex series of sugars known as mucopolysaccharides cannot be stored or metabolized properly. Hurler syndrome is a form of MPS. Other forms of MPS include Hunter's Syndrome, Scheie Syndrome, Sanfillipo, and Morquio. These are all inherited disorders. Defectively metabolized sugars accumulate in fetal cells of victims. The disorders can cause stunted physical and mental growth, vision and hearing problems, and a short life span.

Because some plant cell wall polymers contain uronic acids (a component of mucopolysaccharides), Neufeld, from her work with plants, could surmise how the complex sugars worked in humans. When she first began working on Hurler syndrome in 1967, she initially thought the problem might stem from faulty regulation of the sugars, but experiments showed the problem was in fact the abnormally slow rate at which the sugars were broken down.

Working with fellow scientist Joseph Fratantoni, Neufeld attempted to isolate the problem by tagging mucopolysaccharides with radioactive sulfate, as well as mixing normal cells with MPS patient cells. Fratantoni inadvertently mixed cells from a Hurler patient and a Hunter patient—and the result was a nearly normal cell culture. The two cultures had essentially "cured" each other. Additional work showed that the cells could cross–correct by transferring a corrective factor through the culture medium. The goal now was to determine the makeup of the corrective factor or factors.

Identifies Enzyme Deficiency

Through a combination of biological and molecular techniques, Neufeld was able to identify the corrective factors as a series of enzymes. Normally, the enzymes would serve as catalysts for the reactions needed for cells to metabolize the sugars. In Hurler and other MPS patients, enzyme deficiency makes this difficult. A further complication is that often the enzymes that do exist lack the proper chemical markers needed to enter cells and do their work. Neufeld's subsequent research with diseases similar to MPS, including I–Cell disease, showed how enzymes needed markers to match with cell receptors to team with the right cells.

This research paved the way for successful prenatal diagnosis of the MPS and related disorders, as well as genetic counseling. Although no cure has been found, researchers are experimenting with such techniques as gene replacement therapy and bone marrow transplants.

In 1973 Neufeld was named chief of NIH's Section of Human Biochemical Genetics, and in 1979 she was named chief of the Genetics and Biochemistry Branch of the National Institute of Arthritis, Diabetes, and Digestive and Kidney Diseases (NIADDK). She served as deputy director in NIADDK's Division of Intramural Research from 1981 to 1983.

In 1984 Neufeld went back to the University of California, this time the Los Angeles campus, as chair of the biological chemistry department, where she continues her research. In addition to MPS, she has done research on similar disorders such as Tay–Sachs disease. But her concerns go beyond research. She strongly believes that young scientists just starting out need support and encouragement from the scientific community, because these scientists can bring new and innovative perspectives to difficult questions and issues. At the same time, young scientists can learn much from the experience of established scientists. In her capacity as department chair, Neufeld encourages interaction among established scientists, young scientists, and students.

Neufeld has chaired the Scientific Advisory Board of the National MPS Society since 1988 and was president of the American Society for Biochemistry and Molecular Biology from 1992 to 1993. She was elected to both the National Academy of Sciences (USA) and the American Academy of Arts and Sciences in 1977 and named a fellow of the American Association for Advancement in Science in 1988. In 1990 she was named California Scientist of the Year.

Married to Benjamin Neufeld (a former official with the U.S. Public Health Service) since 1951, she is the mother of two children. Although her work takes up a great deal of her time, she enjoys hiking when she gets the chance, and travel "when it's for pleasure and not business."

SELECTED WRITINGS BY NEUFIELD:

Books

(Editor with V. Ginsburg) *Methods in Enzymology,* Volume 8, Academic Press, 1966.

(Contributor) *NIH: An Account of Research in its Laboratories and Clinics,* edited by DeW. Stetten and W. T. Carrigan, Academic Press, 1984, pp. 330–336.

FURTHER READING

Books

O'Neill, Lois Decker, editor, *The Women's Book of World Records and Achievements,* Anchor Press, 1979.

Other

Neufeld, Elizabeth F., interview with George Milite conducted December 17, 1993.

Sketch by George A. Milite

Hanna Neumann (Mathematisches Forschungs-institut Oberwolfach. Reproduced by permission.)

Hanna Neumann
1914–1971
German mathematician and educator

Hanna Neumann was a well-traveled mathematician who was known for her work in group theory, which is a branch of mathematics concerned with identifying mathematical groups and determining their properties. Neumann was also known as an inspired and dedicated teacher.

Born in Berlin on February 12, 1914, Neumann was the youngest of three children of Hermann and Katharina von Caemmerer. Her father was a historian who was killed in World War I, leaving only a war pension to support the family. To earn extra money, Neumann coached younger children in academics and developed into an organized and studious pupil as a result. She entered the University of Berlin in 1932 and became inspired by her mathematics professor, Ludwig Bieberbach. He influenced her studies toward geometry, but it would be professors Erhard Schmidt and Issai Schur that would introduce her to analysis and algebra. Her future husband, Bernhard H. Neumann, was also a mathematics student at the university. They became secretly engaged in 1934, but due to the rise of the Nazis in Germany, Bernhard (who was Jewish) moved to England and their plans were put on hold. Neumann remained in Germany and lost her job at the Mathematical Institute as a result of her activities to protect other Jewish lecturers. Neumann was advised that because of her political stance, she should avoid the oral exam on "political knowledge," which was required for a doctorate, and switch to the *Staatsexamen* final. This exam was a written essay and she chose as her topic the epistemological basis of numbers in Plato's later dialogues. She graduated with distinctions in mathematics and physics.

Teaches in England

To escape the Nazis, Neumann moved to England and began working in Bristol. Her natural talent for learning new languages benefitted her career by being able to read journals and books in a number of different languages. She experimented with finite plane geometries, wrote several papers, and presented them at lecture courses. Neumann also contributed an explanation of the two types of quadrangles found in finite planes: those whose diagonal points are collinear, and those that are not (the Fano configuration).

In 1938, Neumann moved to Cardiff, England, and married Bernhard in secret to protect his parents, who were still living in Germany, from any reprisals. In 1939, their first child, Irene, was born. The family was soon uprooted because of their classification as "least restricted" aliens, whom are barred from living along the coast. Moving to Oxford, Neumann resumed her doctoral studies while pregnant with her second child, Peter. The acute housing shortage grew as European refugees swamped England, forcing Neumann and her children to move into a rented van in 1942. It would be here, by candlelight, that she would write her doctoral thesis, submitting it in 1943. Her third child, Barbara, was born shortly after, and when the war ended the entire family were able to move back to Cardiff. Bernhard was decommissioned from the army and returned to his job at the University College in Hull, where Neumann began her teaching career as a temporary assistant lecturer of applied mathematics. Their fourth and fifth children, Walter and Daniel, were born in 1946 and 1951, respectively. She continued to work at Hull for the next 12 years, changing the curriculum toward the more pure mathematics that she herself had been trained in.

In 1955, Neumann received a D.Sc. from Oxford based on her research and papers, two of which were published in the *American Journal of Mathematics*. A highly motivated individual, she chose to work as the secretary of a local United Nations Association in her spare time. Her husband had moved to Manchester to lecture in 1948. As she continued to search for a job that would bring her and her husband closer together, the faculty of Technology of the University of Manchester finally added an honors program that would enable her wish to come true.

Breaks New Ground

Neumann was hired as senior lecturer at the University of Manchester in 1958 and set about making very abstract ideas more accessible for her students. She worked with a model building group, lectured on prime numbers and the dissection of rectangles into incongruent squares, and advised several graduate students. Neumann went beyond the confines of a teacher/student relationship and regularly invited staff and students over to her home for coffee and discussions. She mentored many individuals who would themselves go on to become successful mathematicians, including John Bowers, Jim Wiegold, and Chris Houghton.

In the following summer, Neumann toured the universities in Hungary, lecturing on her research on groups and analysis. She also attended the 12th British Mathematical Colloquium, held in 1960, and was asked to speak about wreath products (a group construction). A group theory, such as the wreath products, consists of a set of elements subject to one binary operation and meeting a set of mathematical requirements.

Upon her return to England, Neumann began preparing for a joint study leave with her husband to the Courant Institute of Mathematical Sciences in New York. Her three sons accompanied them and the oldest, Peter, began to study under Gilbert Baumslag, one of the professors at Courant. During the course of the year, Peter and his parents solved the problem of the structure of the semigroup of varieties of groups, demonstrating that it is free. Neumann also presented a number of lectures and taught a graduate course on varieties of groups. During this time, Bernhard Neumann was invited to organize a research department of mathematics at the Australian National University and Hanna was offered a post as a reader.

The Next Frontier

Neumann began her new job in Australia in 1964. She overhauled the department and trained its teachers on subject matter covered in the new syllabuses. The material reflected the changes in mathematics worldwide, including more emphasis on pure mathematics and take–home assignments that promoted the use of ideas and theorems firsthand. Due to the difficulty of the subject matter, Bernhard's research students helped part–time with tutoring.

A conference on the theory of groups was organized by Neumann in 1965. The next year, she finished a monograph about group varieties. With the royalties, she was finally able to buy a good camera and revive her hobby of photography, collecting shots of flowers and trees. She also enjoyed extensive bike rides, later taking to four wheel drives with her husband in the outback.

In January of 1966, the Australian Association of Mathematics Teachers was formed and Neumann was elected to the position of vice–president. She took on the responsibility of bringing together math teachers representing all areas of Australia. In 1967, she became president of the Canberra Mathematical Association and helped prepare pamphlets for teachers; her most famous one was on probability. During a sabbatical leave in 1969, Neumann wrote letters to publicize the inadequacy of Australian mathematics programs compared to the rest of the world and the need for reorganization of the content in many courses. She also visited the United States on a National Science Foundation Senior Foreign Scientist Fellowship. During her stay at Vanderbilt University in Nashville, Tennessee, Neumann and Ian Dey solved the problem on the free product of finitely many finitely–generated Hopf groups.

Neumann's return to Australia was short lived, for she accepted a lecture tour of Canada in 1971, speaking at the universities of British Columbia, Calgary, Alberta, Saskatchewan, and Manitoba. All of this travel and intense lecturing exhausted her and she fell ill on November 12, checking into a hospital only to lapse immediately into a coma. Neumann did not regain consciousness and died two days later at age 57. After her death, a memorial fund was created from supporters all over the world to further Neumann's courageous and inspiring teaching.

FURTHER READING

Newman, M. F. "Hanna Neumann." In *Women of Mathematics: A Biobibliographic Sourcebook.* Edited by Louise S. Grinstein and Paul J. Campbell. Westport, CT: Greenwood Press, 1987, pp. 156–160.

Newman, M.F. and G. E. Wall. "Hanna Neumann." *Journal of the Australian Mathematical Society* 17 (1974): 1–28.

Records of the Australian Academy of Science 3, no. 2. (1975).

Other

"Hanna Neumann 1914-1971." Published by the Australian Science Archives Project on ASAPWeb, 1995. Australian Academy of Science. http://www.asap.unimelb.edu.au/bsparcs/aasmemoirs/neumann.htm (July 22, 1997).

Sketch by Nicole Beatty

Mary Frances (Winston) Newson
1869–1959
American mathematician

Mary Newson was the second American woman to complete a Ph.D. at Germany's University of Gottingen, and the first American woman to earn the degree in mathematics from a European university, an achievement for which she was later honored by the Women's Centennial Congress. She studied and researched differential equations.

The fourth child of Thomas and Caroline (Mumford) Winston, Mary Frances Winston Newson, called May, was born August 7, 1869, in Forreston, Illinois. Her father, a country doctor, and her mother taught the children at home except for occasional times when they went to public school. The public school often did not live up to the Winstons' standards, and the children never remained for long.

At the age of 15, Newson enrolled at the University of Wisconsin. She graduated with an A.B. in mathematics in 1889 and became an alumna of the university's Phi Beta Kappa chapter. Newson taught high school mathematics for a time, and then went to teach at Downer College. She applied to Bryn Mawr for a mathematics fellowship to study with **Charlotte Scott** in 1891. At the college, Newson studied differential equations, Chrystal's algebra, modern analytical geometry, theory of functions, and theory of substitutions. She was asked to remain at Bryn Mawr for another year, but decided to return home and continue her studies at the University of Chicago.

In 1893, while at the University of Chicago, Newson attended the International Mathematical Congress at the World's Columbian Exposition, held in nearby Evanston. At the congress she met the University of Gottingen's Felix Klein, who suggested she come abroad to study. Although she applied for an Association of Collegiate Alumnae fellowship, she was turned down. But **Christine Ladd-Franklin**, who often spent her own money to support female mathematicians in their research, offered her $500 for travel and living expenses, which Newson readily accepted.

While at the University of Gottingen, Newson studied differential equations, which were also the subject of her dissertation. Her free time was spent hiking the forests and mountains of the area. She was at Gottingen for three years, and in 1895, Newson received the European fellowship from the Association of Collegiate Alumnae, the same organization that had earlier turned her down. She finished her dissertation in 1896, although it was not published until a year later because she could not find an American publisher capable of printing the German symbols, and she graduated with a Ph.D. magna cum laude. While waiting for her dissertation's publication, Newson taught high school in Missouri, and became one of only 22 women members of the American Mathematical Society.

Embarks on Teaching Career

In 1897, Newson was offered a position as head of the mathematics department at Kansas State Agricultural College, a position she accepted and held until her 1900 marriage to Henry Byron Newson, a fellow mathematician at the University of Kansas. She did not teach while raising their children, Caroline, born in 1901, Josephine, born in 1903, and Henry Winston, born in 1909, but she did publish a translation of David Hilbert's famous lecture delivered in 1900 in Paris to the International Congress of Mathematicians. The lecture was comprised of 23 mathematical problems for the new century.

Newson's husband died of a heart attack in 1910, leaving no pension or life insurance. Newson was unable to find a job until 1913, when she accepted a position at Washburn College. During her time at Washburn, a political science professor was dismissed for discussing his views with students, and Newson was one of eight other professors who resigned in protest of his dismissal, a case that became one of the first academic freedom investigations. In 1921, Newson accepted a position at Eureka College, heading the science and mathematics department until her retirement in 1942.

At Eureka, Newson was chairperson of the international relations roundtable of the American Association of University Women. She was honored by the Women's Centennial Congress in 1940. Newson died on December 5, 1959. In her memory, her three children started a fund to support the Mary Winston Newson Memorial Lecture on International Relations, held annually at Eureka College since 1970.

SELECTED WRITINGS BY NEWSON:

Other

"Uber den Hermite'schen Fall der Lame'schen Differentialgleichungen." Ph.D. dissertation. Hanover, Germany: Göttingen University, 1897.

FURTHER READING

Books

Bailey, Martha J. *American Women in Science.* Denver: ABC–CLIO, 1994.

Grinstein, Louise S. and Campbell, Paul J., eds. *Women of Mathematics.* New York: Greenwood Press, 1987.

Sketch by Helene Barker Kiser

Margaret Morse Nice
1883–1974
American ornithologist

Margaret Morse Nice became one of America's leading ornithologists due to her insistence on the importance of studying the behavior of individual birds to better understand the nature of each species as a whole. Her

Margaret Morse Nice (AP/Wide World Photos. Reproduced by permission.)

detailed observations provided a major contribution to the study of birds and have had a lasting effect on the field of ornithology, despite the fact that she never held a faculty appointment or received university funding. Most of her contributions were made by investigating birds in her own backyard.

Nice was born Margaret Morse on December 6, 1883, in Amherst, Massachusetts, to Anson and Margaret (Ely) Morse. Her father was a professor of history at Amherst College; he was also a dedicated gardener and had a deep love of the wilderness. Her mother had studied botany at Mount Holyoke and helped inspire in her daughter a love of nature, teaching her the name of wild flowers as they walked in the woods. In her autobiography, *Research Is a Passion with Me,* Nice would later describe how in her family's two–acre orchard and garden, "we learned of nature at first hand, planting and weeding in our own small gardens." Her interest in ornithology began early: she was recording her observations of birds by the age of twelve.

Nice attended a private elementary school and the public high school in Amherst, and then in 1901 she enrolled in Mount Holyoke College, as had her mother. At first she concentrated on languages, but later switched to the natural sciences. She graduated in 1906 and the following year received a fellowship to study biology for two years at Clark University in Worcester, Massachusetts. In August of 1909, she married Leonard Blaine Nice, whom she had met there. That same year, the couple moved to Cambridge, where Leonard Nice entered Harvard Medical School. In 1913, he was appointed the head of the physiology department at the University of Oklahoma and Nice moved with him to Norman, Oklahoma.

Nice's first paper, which dealt with bobwhites, was published after more than two years of research. Mostly confined to her house during the years her four daughters were born, Nice would not publish any more ornithological research until 1920. Frustrated by her inability to pursue her studies in this field, Nice began studying how her daughters acquired language. This work later earned her a master's degree in psychology from Clark University in 1915, and she published 18 articles on child psychology.

Researches Territorial Behavior of Birds

In the 1920s, Nice was influenced to return to the study of birds by an older friend, Althea Sherman, an amateur ornithologist. In 1920, Nice published a description of Oklahoma bird life. Thirty–five more articles about Oklahoma birds followed, and in 1924 she published a book on the subject, *The Birds of Oklahoma.* In 1927, her husband accepted a teaching position in Columbus, Ohio, and the family moved to a house on the bank of a river which attracted a number of nesting and migratory birds, including sparrows. There, Nice studied the territorial behavior of birds by placing colored bands on them and following them for years in a way no one had before. Her studies resulted in several publications, the most important of which was her two–part *Studies in the Life History of the Song Sparrow,* published in 1937 and 1943. With the publication of these volumes, she became one of the world's leading ornithologists. *Notable American Women* quoted German evolutionary biologist Ernst Mayr as saying that Nice had "almost singlehandedly, initiated a new era in American ornithology."

Nice and her family moved to Chicago in 1936, where her husband had accepted an appointment at the University of Chicago Medical School. She was not able to do nearly as many field observations there, but she continued to write and study. Her knowledge of languages enabled her to expose Americans to European ornithology through translations and reviews of articles in German and other languages. During this period she became increasingly active as a conservationist, advocating the preservation of wildlife and restrictions on the use of pesticides.

Nice was president of the Wilson Ornithological Society in 1938 and 1939, the first woman to be elected president of a major American ornithological society. She was also associate editor of the journal *Bird–Banding* from 1935 to 1942 and 1946 to 1974. Mount Holyoke awarded her an honorary doctorate in 1955. In 1969, the Wilson Ornithological Society inaugurated a grant in her name to be given to self–trained amateur researchers. Nice died in Chicago on June 26, 1974, at the age of ninety.

SELECTED WRITINGS BY NICE:

Books

(With Leonard Blaine Nice) *The Birds of Oklahoma,* University of Oklahoma, 1924, revised edition, 1931.

Studies in the Life History of the Song Sparrow. 2 vols. [New York], 1937 and 1943, Dover, 1964.

The Watcher at the Nest. Macmillan, 1939.

Research Is a Passion with Me. Consolidated Amethyst, 1979.

FURTHER READING

Books

Conway, Jill K., ed. *Written by Herself.* Vintage Books, 1991.

Sicherman, Barbara, and Carol Hurd Green, eds. *Notable American Women: The Modern Period.* Cambridge: Belknap Press, 1980.

Periodicals

Trautman, Milton B. "In Memoriam: Margaret Morse Nice." *The Auk* (July, 1977).

Sketch by Margo Nash

Dorothy Virginia Nightingale
1902–?
American chemist

Dorothy Nightingale, a pioneer in the field of physical chemistry, was known for her work on organic synthetic reactions in chemistry. She studied the Freidel-Crafts reaction, which produces such products as high-octane gasoline, synthetic rubber, cleaning products, and plastics. She received the American Chemical Society's Garvan Medal for distinguished service in chemistry in 1959.

Dorothy Virginia Nightingale, an only child, was born on February 21, 1902, in Fort Collins, Colorado. Her father, William David Nightingale, and her mother, Jennie Beem Nightingale, a former teacher and secretary, were homesteaders until 1919 when the family moved to Columbia, Missouri. Nightingale became interested in chemistry at a young age. Her mother was working in a rooming house where some students from the Colorado Agricultural and Mechanical College lived, and Nightingale often went with the students to be entertained by their chemistry experiments.

After graduating from high school, Nightingale entered the University of Missouri. Her original plan was to study history and foreign languages, and worked as a grader for the German department. But her first chemistry class inspired her and her professor, Herman Schlundt, encouraged her in her interest. She soon switched her major, expecting to teach high school chemistry, and graduated with her A.B. degree in 1922.

Nightingale stayed on at the university to complete her A.M. degree in organic chemistry, studying luminescent compounds and determining organomagnesium halide spectra. After graduating in 1923, Nightingale was invited to stay on at the university as a chemistry instructor, and she accepted. She was only the second woman in the department at that time. Nightingale remained at the University of Missouri until her retirement in 1972, moving from assistant professor to associate professor to full professor and director of graduate studies. During this time, she continued her own studies, focusing on the merexide and alloxantine series. She completed her Ph.D. in organic chemistry from the University of Chicago in 1928.

A diligent researcher, Nightingale's interests were focused on organic synthetic reactions. Much of her study was devoted to Freidel-Crafts reactions, which produced ethylbenzene, cumene, high-octane gasoline, synthetic rubber, elastomers, cleaning products, and plastics. One of her important discoveries was that the reaction result, i.e. the resulting products, were affected by the temperature at the time of the reaction. What is most significant about Nightingale's research is that unlike other researchers, she did not settle for merely creating the new products from the reactions. Rather, she devoted her research to understanding how the processes themselves actually happened. She wanted to figure out under what precise circumstances the reactions would occur.

In 1938, Nightingale took a leave of absence to accept an honors fellowship at the University of Minnesota. Her research focused on the way aluminum chloride affected aromatic hydrocarbons. After her return to the University of Missouri, she devoted more detailed study to ketones. Because of her knowledge and understanding of the varied Freidel-Crafts reactions, Nightingale was appointed to the Committee on Medical Research for the Office of Scientific Research and Development during the World War II years of 1942 to 1945. Because the reaction was instrumental in the compound synthesis of a substance similar to quinine, a natural drug, Nightingale's work was important to research on antimalarial drugs. After completing her civilian service, Nightingale took a year at UCLA as a research associate before returning to the University of Missouri.

Nightingale was known as an inspirational teacher. Over 50 graduate students on both the Master's and Ph.D. levels asked her to direct their research. A prolific writer, Nightingale published nearly half of all of the university's organic chemistry publications during her tenure. She received the American Chemical Society's Garvan Medal for distinguished service in chemistry in 1959, and was a member of Sigma Delta Epsilon, Sigma Xi, Phi Beta Kappa, the American Chemical Society, and the American Association of University Women.

In her free time, Nightingale enjoyed music, photography, horseback riding, motoring, and climbing with the Colorado Mountain Club, of which she was an active member. Upon her retirement as Emeritus Professor in 1972, Nightingale moved to Boulder, Colorado.

SELECTED WRITINGS BY NIGHTINGALE:

Periodicals

"Studies in the Alloxantine Series." *Journal of the American Chemical Society* (1937).

"Alkylation and the Action of Aluminum Halides on Alkylbenzenes." *Chemical Review* (1939).

"Anomalous Nitration Reactions." *Chemical Review* (1947).

FURTHER READING

Books

Bailey, Martha J. *American Women in Science*. Denver: ABC–CLIO, 1994.

Grinstein, Louise S., et. al, eds. *Women in Chemistry and Physics: A Bibliographic Sourcebook*. Westport, CT: Greenwood Press, 1993.

Shearer, Benjamin F. and Barbara S. Shearer, eds. *Notable Women in the Physical Sciences*. Westport, CT: Greenwood Press, 1996.

Sketch by Helene Barker Kiser

Ida Tacke Noddack
1896–1979
German chemist

Working with fellow chemist Walter Noddack (her future husband) and x–ray specialist Otto Berg, Ida Tacke discovered element 75, rhenium, in 1925, thus solving one of the mysteries of the periodic table of elements introduced by Russian chemist Dmitri Ivanovich Mendeleev in 1869. Ida Tacke Noddack's continuing study of the periodic table also led her to be the first to suggest in 1934 that physicist Enrico Fermi had not made a new element in an experiment with uranium as he thought, but instead had discovered nuclear fission. Her prediction was not verified until 1939.

Ida Tacke was born in Germany on February 25, 1896 and studied at the Technical University in Berlin, where she received the first prize for chemistry and metallurgy in 1919. In 1921, soon after receiving her doctorate, she set out to isolate two of the elements that Mendeleev had predicted when he proposed the Periodic System and displayed all known elements in a format now called the periodic table. Mendeleev had left blank spaces on his table for several elements that he expected to exist but that had not been identified. Two of these, elements 43 and 75, were located in Group VII under manganese.

Assuming that these elements would be similar in their properties to manganese, scientists had been searching for them in manganese ores. Tacke and Walter Noddack, who headed the chemical laboratory at the Physico–Technical Research Agency in Berlin, focused instead on the lateral neighbors of the missing elements, molybdenum, tungsten, osmium, and ruthenium. With the assistance of Otto Berg of the Werner–Siemens Laboratory, who provided expertise in analyzing the X–ray spectra of substances, Tacke and Noddack isolated element 75 in 1925 and named it rhenium, from *Rhenus,* Latin for the Rhine, an important river in their native Germany. It took them another year to isolate a single gram of the element from 660 kilograms of molybdenite ore. They also believed they had discovered traces of element 43, which they dubbed masurium. Later research, however, did not confirm their results. Now known as technetium, element 43 has never been found in nature, although it has been produced artificially.

In 1926, Ida Tacke married Walter Noddack. They would work together in their research until Walter Noddack's death in 1960, and together would publish some one hundred scientific papers. The Noddacks were awarded the Leibig Medal of the German Chemical Society in 1934 for their discovery of rhenium.

In 1934 Ida Noddack challenged the conclusions of Enrico Fermi and his group that they had produced transuranium elements, artificial elements heavier than uranium, when they bombarded uranium atoms with subatomic particles called neutrons. Although other scientists agreed with Fermi, Noddack suggested he had split uranium atoms into isotopes of known elements rather than added to uranium atoms to produce heavier, unknown elements. She had no research to support her theory, however, and for five years her hypothesis that atomic nuclei had been split was virtually ignored. "Her suggestion was so out of line with the then–accepted ideas about the atomic nucleus that it was never seriously discussed," fellow chemist Otto Hahn would later comment in his autobiography. In 1939, after much research had been done by many scientists, Hahn, Fritz Strassmann and **Lise Meitner** discovered that Noddack had been right. They named the process nuclear fission.

The Noddacks moved from Berlin to the University of Freiburg in 1935, to the University of Strasbourg in 1943, and to the State Research Institute for Geochemistry in Bamberg in 1956. In 1960, Walter Noddack died. Ida Noddack received the High Service Cross of the German Federal Republic in 1966. During her life she received honorary membership in the Spanish Society of Physics and

Chemistry and the International Society of Nutrition Research, as well as an honorary doctorate of science from the University of Hamburg. Ida Noddack retired in 1968 and moved to Bad Neuenahr, a small town on the Rhine. She died in 1979.

FURTHER READING

Books

Hahn, Otto. *A Scientific Autobiography.* Scribner, 1966.

Weeks, Mary E. *The Discovery of the Elements.* Mack, 1954, pp. 321–322.

Periodicals

Habashi, Fathi. "Ida Noddack, 75 & Element 75." Reprint from *Chemistry* (February 1971). In *Element Profiles,* American Chemical Society, 1972, pp. 81–82.

Starke, Kurt. "The Detours Leading to the Discovery of Nuclear Fission." *Journal of Chemical Education* (December 1979): 771–775.

Sketch by M. C. Nagel

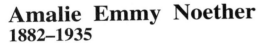

Amalie Emmy Noether
1882–1935
German-born American mathematician

Emmy Noether (Mathematisches Forschungsinstitut Oberwolfach. Reproduced by permission.)

Amalie Emmy Noether was a world–renowned mathematician whose innovative approach to modern abstract algebra inspired colleagues and students who emulated her technique. Dismissed from her university position at the beginning of the Nazi era in Germany—for she was both Jewish and female—Noether emigrated to the United States, where she taught in several universities and colleges. When she died, Albert Einstein eulogized her in a letter to *New York Times* as "the most significant creative mathematical genius thus far produced since the higher education of women began."

Noether was born on March 23, 1882, in the small university town of Erlangen in southern Germany. Her first name was Amalie, but she was known by her middle name of Emmy. Her mother, Ida Amalia Kaufmann Noether, came from a wealthy family in Cologne. Her father, Max Noether, a professor at the University of Erlangen, was an accomplished mathematician who worked on the theory of algebraic functions. Two of her three younger brothers became scientists—Fritz was a mathematician and Alfred earned a doctorate in chemistry.

Noether's childhood was unexceptional, going to school, learning domestic skills, and taking piano lessons. Since girls were not eligible to enroll in the gymnasium (college preparatory school), she attended the Städtischen Höheren Töchterschule, where she studied arithmetic and languages. In 1900 she passed the Bavarian state examinations with evaluations of "very good" in French and English (she received only a "satisfactory" evaluation in practical classroom conduct); this certified her to teach foreign languages at female educational institutions.

Begins a Teaching Career

Instead of looking for a language teaching position, Noether decided to undertake university studies. However, since she had not graduated from a gymnasium, she first had to pass an entrance examination for which she obtained permission from her instructors. She audited courses at the University of Erlangen from 1900 to 1902. In 1903 she passed the matriculation exam, and entered the University of Göttingen for a semester, where she encountered such notable mathematicians as Hermann Minkowski, Felix Klein, and David Hilbert. She enrolled at the University of Erlangen where women were accepted in 1904. At Erlangen, Noether studied with Paul Gordan, a mathematics professor who was also a family friend. She completed her dissertation entitled "On Complete Systems of Invariants for Ternary Biquadratic Forms," receiving her Ph.D., summa cum laude, on July 2, 1908.

Noether worked without pay at the Mathematical Institute of Erlangen from 1908 until 1915, where her university duties included research, serving as a dissertation adviser for two students, and occasionally delivering lectures for her ailing father. In addition, Noether began to work with Ernst Otto Fischer, an algebraist who directed her toward the broader theoretical style characteristic of Hilbert. Noether not only published her thesis on ternary biquadratics, but she was also elected to membership in the Circolo Matematico di Palermo in 1908. The following year, Noether was invited to join the German Mathematical Society (Deutsche Mathematiker Vereinigung); she addressed the Society's 1909 meeting in Salzburg and its 1913 meeting in Vienna.

Formulates the Mathematics of Relativity

In 1915, Klein and Hilbert invited Noether to join them at the Mathematical Institute in Göttingen. They were working on the mathematics of the newly announced general theory of relativity, and they believed Noether's expertise would be helpful. Einstein later wrote an article for the 1955 Grolier Encyclopedia, characterizing the theory of relativity by the basic question, "how must the laws of nature be constituted so that they are valid in the same form relative to arbitrary systems of co–ordinates (postulate of the invariance of the laws of nature relative to an arbitrary transformation of space and time)?" It was precisely this type of invariance under transformation on which Noether focused her mathematical research.

In 1918, Noether proved two theorems that formed a cornerstone for general relativity. These theorems validated certain relationships suspected by physicists of the time. One, now known as Noether's Theorem, established the equivalence between an invariance property and a conservation law. The other involved the relationship between an invariance and the existence of certain integrals of the equations of motion. The eminent German mathematician Hermann Weyl described Noether's contribution in the July 1935 *Scripta Mathematica* following her death: "For two of the most significant sides of the general theory of relativity theory she gave at that time the genuine and universal mathematical formulation."

While Noether was proving these profound and useful results, she was working without pay at Göttingen University, where women were not admitted to the faculty. Hilbert, in particular, tried to obtain a position for her but could not persuade the historians and philosophers on the faculty to vote in a woman's favor. He was able to arrange for her to teach, however, by announcing a class in mathematical physics under his name and letting her lecture in his place. By 1919, regulations were eased somewhat, and she was designated a Privatdozent (a licensed lecturer who could receive fees from students but not from the university). In 1922, Noether was given the unofficial title of associate professor, and was hired as an adjunct teacher and paid a modest salary without fringe benefits or tenure.

Noether's enthusiasm for mathematics made her an effective teacher, often conducting classroom discussions in which she and her students would jointly explore some topic. In *Emmy Noether at Bryn Mawr*, Noether's only doctoral student at Bryn Mawr, Ruth McKee, recalls, "Miss Noether urged us on, challenging us to get our nails dirty, to really dig into the underlying relationships, to consider the problems from all possible angles."

Lays the Foundations of Abstract Algebra

Brilliant mathematicians often make their greatest contributions early in their careers; Noether was one of the notable exceptions to that rule. She began producing her most powerful and creative work about the age of 40. Her change in style started with a 1920 paper on noncommutative fields (systems in which an operation such as multiplication yields a different answer for a x b than for b x a). During the years that followed, she developed a very abstract and generalized approach to the axiomatic development of algebra. As Weyl attested, "she originated above all a new and epoch–making style of thinking in algebra."

Noether's 1921 paper on the theory of ideals in rings is considered to contain her most important results. It extended the work of Dedekind on solutions of polynomials—algebraic expressions consisting of a constant multiplied by variables raised to a positive power—and laid the foundations for modern abstract algebra. Rather than working with specific operations on sets of numbers, this branch of mathematics looks at general properties of operations. Because of its generality, abstract algebra represents a unifying thread connecting such theoretical fields as logic and number theory with applied mathematics useful in chemistry and physics.

During the winter of 1928–29, Noether was a visiting professor at the University of Moscow and the Communist Academy, and in the summer of 1930, she taught at the University of Frankfurt. Recognized for her continuing contributions in the science of mathematics, the International Mathematical Congress of 1928 chose her to be its principle speaker at one of its section meetings in Bologna. In 1932 she was chosen to address the Congress's general session in Zurich.

Noether was a part of the mathematics faculty of Göttingen University in the 1920s when its reputation for mathematical research and teaching was considered the best in the world. Still, even with the help of the esteemed mathematician Hermann Weyl, Noether was unable to secure a proper teaching position there, which was equivalent to her male counterparts. Weyl once commented: "I was ashamed to occupy such a preferred position beside her whom I knew to be my superior as a mathematician in many respects." Nevertheless, in 1932, on Noether's fiftieth birthday, the university's algebraists held a celebration, and her colleague Helmut Hasse dedicated a paper in her honor, which validated one of her ideas on noncommutative algebra. In that same year, she again was honored by those outside her own university, when she was named cowinner of the Alfred Ackermann–Teubner Memorial Prize for the Advancement of Mathematical Knowledge.

Teaches in Exile

The successful and congenial environment of the University of Göttingen ended in 1933, with the advent of the Nazis in Germany. Within months, anti–Semitic policies spread through the country. On April 7, 1933, Noether was formally notified that she could no longer teach at the university. She was a dedicated pacifist, and Weyl later recalled, "her courage, her frankness, her unconcern about her own fate, her conciliatory spirit were, in the midst of all the hatred and meanness, despair and sorrow surrounding us, a moral solace."

For a while, Noether continued to meet informally with students and colleagues, inviting groups to her apartment. But by summer, the Emergency Committee to Aid Displaced German Scholars was entering into an agreement with Bryn Mawr, a women's college in Pennsylvania, which offered Noether a professorship. Her first year's salary was funded by the Emergency Committee and the Rockefeller Foundation.

In the fall of 1933, Noether was supervising four graduate students at Bryn Mawr. Starting in February 1934, she also delivered weekly lectures at the Institute for Advanced Study at Princeton. She bore no malice toward Germany, and maintained friendly ties with her former colleagues. With her characteristic curiosity and good nature, she settled into her new home in America, acquiring enough English to adequately converse and teach, although she occasionally lapsed into German when concentrating on technical material.

During the summer of 1934, Noether visited Göttingen to arrange shipment of her possessions to the United States. When she returned to Bryn Mawr in the early fall, she had received a two–year renewal on her teaching grant. In the spring of 1935, Noether underwent surgery to remove a uterine tumor. The operation was a success, but four days later, she suddenly developed a very high fever and lost consciousness. She died on April 14th, apparently from a post–operative infection. Her ashes were buried near the library on the Bryn Mawr campus.

Over the course of her career, Noether supervised a dozen graduate students, wrote forty–five technical publications, and inspired countless other research results through her habit of suggesting topics of investigation to students and colleagues. After World War II, the University of Erlangen attempted to show her the honor she had deserved during her lifetime. A conference in 1958 commemorated the fiftieth anniversary of her doctorate; in 1982 the university dedicated a memorial plaque to her in its Mathematics Institute. During the same year, the 100th anniversary year of Noether's birth, the Emmy Noether Gymnasium, a coeducational school emphasizing mathematics, the natural sciences, and modern languages, opened in Erlangen.

SELECTED WRITINGS BY NOETHER:

Books

Collected Papers. Springer–Verlag, 1983.

FURTHER READING

Books

Brewer, James W. *Emmy Noether: A Tribute to Her Life and Work.* Edited by Martha K. Smith. Marcel Dekker, 1981.

Kramer, Edna E. *The Nature and Growth of Modern Mathematics* Princeton University, 1981, pp. 656–672.

Magill, Frank N., ed. *Great Events from History II.* Books International, 1991, pp. 650–654, 716–719.

Osen, Lynn M. *Women in Mathematics.* Cambridge: MIT Press, 1979, pp. 141–152.

Perl, Teri *Math Equals: Biographies of Women Mathematicians.* Addison–Wesley, 1978, pp. 172–178.

Srinivasan, Bhama and Judith D. Sally. *Emmy Noether in Bryn Mawr: Proceedings of a Symposium.* Springer–Verlag, 1983.

Periodicals

Kimberling, Clark H. "Emmy Noether" *The American Mathematical Monthly* (February 1972): 136–149.

Sketch by Loretta Hall

Marianne North
1830–1890
English naturalist and artist

Marianne North was perhaps the best-known of the nineteenth-century botanical illustrators. At a time when few women traveled alone, North made numerous long journeys to the far corners of the earth, exploring, painting, and identifying new species of plants.

North was born in Hastings, England, in 1830, the elder daughter of Frederick North, a member of parliament. Although she received little formal education, her family was wealthy and cultured and close family friends included some of the best-known artists and botanists of the day. As a child, North traveled through Europe with her parents, studying flower painting and developing her interests in music and botany. After her mother's death in 1855, she continued to live with her father until his death in 1869, managing their households in Hastings and London, and

Marianne North (The Granger Collection, New York. Reproduced by permission.)

traveling with him through Austria, Turkey, Syria, and Egypt.

During the nineteenth century, travelers were returning to Europe with large collections of exotic plants from around the world. With the new system of biological classification developed by Carl Linnaeus, thousands of plants were being identified and classified for the first time and accurate drawings of these species were necessary. Both the taxonomists, who were classifying organisms, and the horticulturalists, who were breeding new garden varieties, required the assistance of botanical artists such as North.

Following her father's death, North was free to travel the world. In 1871 and 1872, North collected and painted flowers in the United States, Canada, Jamaica, and Brazil. In the United States, she visited the famous American naturalists Louis and **Elizabeth Agassiz**. She visited Emily and **Elizabeth Blackwell**'s pioneering hospital, the New York Infirmary for Women and Children, and had dinner with President and Mrs. Ulysses S. Grant. Soon after her return to England, she left again for the Canary Islands. In 1875, in the company of friends, she traveled to Japan, Singapore, Java, and Ceylon, via the United States. While crossing America, she explored Yosemite and the redwood forests on her own. After visiting Japan, while recovering from an attack of rheumatism at the British colony of Sarawak on the island of Borneo, North discovered the largest known carnivorous pitcher plant. Sir Joseph Hooke, Director of the Royal Botanical Gardens, later named the species *Nepenthes northiana* in her honor. In 1877, North journeyed to Ceylon, India, and the Himalayas.

One of North's closest friends was the scientist Sir Francis Galton, a cousin of Charles Darwin, the originator of the theory of natural selection. Like Darwin, North was interested in the geographical distribution of plants. She also was interested in zoology, particularly insects, fish, and birds. On a subsequent voyage in 1880, at Darwin's suggestion, North traveled to Australia, as well as New Zealand and Hawaii, for additional botanical collecting. In 1882 she went to South Africa and then to the Seychelles in the Indian Ocean, where she discovered a new capucin tree which was later named *Northea seychellana*. North identified a number of new plant species, including *Crinum northianum* of Borneo, *Areca northiana*, and *Kniphofia northiana from South Africa*.

In 1879, North staged an exhibition of 500 of her flower paintings at the Kensington Museum in London and created a botanical catalogue to accompany the exhibit. Three years later she built and opened the North Gallery at the Royal Botanical Gardens at Kew, outside London, to hold her permanent collection of over 800 oil paintings of plants in their natural settings.

Despite deafness and other health problems, North made a last voyage to Chile to search for a monkey puzzle tree. She then retired to Alderley in Gloucestershire, where she gardened and worked on her memoirs, until her death in 1890. North's sister, Catherine Addington Symonds, who also was a botanical illustrator, edited and published North's two-volume autobiography in 1892. It was so successful that Symonds published a supplementary volume in 1893, chronicling North's first European travels and her journeys to Egypt and Syria with her father.

SELECTED WRITINGS BY NORTH:

Books

(Catherine Symonds, editor) *Recollections of a Happy Life, being the Autobiography of Marianne North.* 2 vols. London: Macmillan, 1892.

(Catherine Symonds, editor) *Some Further Recollections of a Happy Life, Selected from the Journals of Marianne North, chiefly between the years of 1859 and 1869.* London: Macmillan, 1893.

A Vision of Eden: The Life and Work of Marianne North. New York: Hart, Rinehart and Winston, 1980.

FURTHER READING

Books

Alic, Margaret. *Hypatia's Heritage: A History of Women in Science from Antiquity through the Nineteenth Century.* Boston: Beacon Press, 1986.

Periodicals

Moon, Brenda E. "Marianne North's *Recollections of a Happy Life*: How they Came to be Written and Published." *Journal of the Society for the Bibliography of Natural History* 8 (1978): 497-505.

Sketch by Margaret Alic

Antonia Coello Novello
1944–
American physician

Antonia Coello Novello was the first woman and the first Hispanic to be appointed Surgeon General of the United States. Noted for her philosophy of "good science, good sense" and for her approachability, Novello was dedicated to the prevention of AIDS, substance abuse, and smoking, as well as to the education of the American public. Her special concerns were for women, children, and Hispanics—populations often overlooked by public health services.

The Makings of a Doctor

Antonia Coello was born in Fajardo, Puerto Rico, on August 23, 1944, the oldest of three children. At eight years old, she suffered two blows that she would carry all of her life. Her father, Antonio Coello, died, leaving her mother, Ana Delia Flores Coello, to raise her children alone until she later remarried Ramon Flores, an electrician. Novello was also diagnosed with a chronic condition called congenital megacolon, an illness in which her colon was overly large and not functioning properly, which required regular hospitalization. Although an operation would have helped Novello, it was not performed until she was 18 years old, and even after the surgery, complications followed her for years.

Because of her childhood illness, Novello grew up wanting to be a doctor. During her career, she would carry her experiences with her: empathy with and respect for the patient, dedication to the patient's welfare, and a determination to never let another patient "fall through the cracks."

Novello's mother, principal of the local school, pushed her daughter to live up to her potential. She never treated her as a "sick kid" by coddling her; rather, Novello was constantly pushed and challenged, especially in her school work. Her hard work paid off, and Novello graduated high school at age fifteen. She went on to the at University of Puerto Rico at Rio Piedras, where she received her B.S. in 1965, and then to medical school the University of Puerto Rico at San Juan where she received her M.D. in 1970.

That same year, Novello married Joseph Novello, then a navy flight surgeon and later a psychiatrist and host of a radio talk show. The Novellos moved to Michigan, where Novello began an internship at the University of Michigan Medical Center. The following year, the Intern of the Year Award was bestowed on Novello for her dedication and performance in the Department of Pediatrics. But during her residency, two more blows struck. Her favorite aunt died as a result of kidney failure. Then, Novello herself developed kidney problems and was hospitalized. So in 1973, Novello chose pediatric nephrology as her subspecialty, first at the University of Michigan, and later at Georgetown University Hospital in Washington, D.C. Her residency completed, Novello began in private practice in 1976 in Springfield, Virginia.

But in 1978, Novello felt herself becoming too emotionally involved with her young patients and their families, and gave up her private practice. First she thought of joining the navy, but was told the navy was "looking for a few good *men*, so she applied to the United States Public Health Services. Novello accepted a position in the artificial kidney and chronic uremia program at the National Institutes of Health (NIH) in Bethesda, Maryland. She was soon promoted to staff physician and then to executive secretary for the Division of Research Grants, a position she held until 1986. During this time, she attended Johns Hopkins University, graduating in 1982 with Master's in Public Health. Upon graduation in 1982, Novello was appointed as a congressional fellow and worked on the National Transplant Act of 1984 in addition to drafting cigarette labels that warn the smoker of health risks.

In 1986, the NIH promoted Novello again, this time to deputy director of the National Institute of Child Health and Human Development, one of the few top positions at the NIH. But only a few years later, Novello was tapped for what would become her most public position—United States Surgeon General.

West Side Story Comes to the West Wing

During her interview with the Secretary of Health, Novello related in an interview with the Achievement Organization, she asked "Are you calling me to be the Surgeon General because I'm Puerto Rican and I'm female? I will not be your quota. Where did you find me, now, after twelve years of doing my same job? Why?" She was assured that she had been selected because of her qualifications, and said in the interview that "the time was right for a woman and the time was right for a minority. But I also believe that they needed someone who knew AIDS. . .the time was right for someone who was kind of conservative, but with common sense."

On October 17, 1989, President George Bush officially nominated Novello for the post, and she was embraced by Congress. Unlike President Ronald Reagan's nomination of C. Everett Koop in 1981, Novello was a popular choice, experienced and knowledgeable in the field. The fourteenth United States Surgeon General, Novello was sworn in on

March 9, 1990. Novello remarked that "the American dream is well and alive. . .today the West Side Story comes to the West Wing."

As Surgeon General, Novello targeted health issues particular to children, women, and minorities, in addition to issues such as smoking, substance abuse, and AIDS. Particular to children, Novello's concerns were immunizations, prenatal care, accidents, drug abuse, and harmful chemicals. She also attacked the R. J. Reynolds Company for their cartoon "spokesperson," Joe Camel, who appealed to children. Despite her schedule, Novello was often found in hospital children's wards visiting and encouraging the young patients. Novello told the Achievement Organization "how can we make the kids be better when we forget that the statistic is a face? Give them options. Give them hope." Particular to women, Novello's concerns were domestic violence, heterosexual AIDS, and breast cancer. Particular to minorities, especially Hispanics, Novello's concerns were the general lack of health care and education among these populations, as well as the fact that minorities suffer from serious diseases at a higher percentage than the majority population.

Her tenure as Surgeon General ended in 1993, when she returned to the position she had held since 1986 at Georgetown University School of Medicine. Among her many awards, Novello received a Public Health Service Commendation Medal in 1983, an NIH Certificate of Recognition in 1985, a John F. Kennedy School of Government certificate in 1987, and the Surgeon General's Exemplary Service Medal in 1989. Novello's spare time is spent reading and collecting antiques. She continues to be outspoken on public health issues, especially those of children, to whom she says to have a goal, work hard, and give service.

SELECTED WRITINGS BY NOVELLO:

Periodicals

"Healthy Children Ready to Learn: the Surgeon General's Initiative for Children." *Journal of School Health* 61, no. 8 (1991): 359–60.

"The HIV/Aids Epidemic: A Current Picture." *Journal of Acquired Immune Deficiency Syndromes* , 1993.

"Surgeon General's Report on the Health Benefits of Smoking Cessation." *Public Health Reports* 105, no. 6 (1990): 545–48.

FURTHER READING

Books

Graham, Judith, ed. *Current Biography Yearbook.* NY: H. W. Wilson Company, 1992.

Novas, Himilce. *The Hispanic 100.* NY: Carol Publishing Group, 1995.

Saari, Peggy, ed. *Prominent Women of the 20th Century.* NY: UXL, 1996.

Periodicals

Cohn, Victor. *The Washington Post,* May 8, 1990.

Krucoff, Carol. "Antonia Novello: A Dream Come True." *The Saturday Evening Post* 263, no. 4 (1991).

Other

Achievement Organization. "An Interview with Antonia Novello, M.D." 1994. http://www.achievement.org/autodoc/page/novOint–1 (24 March 1999)

Sketch by Helene Barker Kiser

Christiane Nüsslein-Volhard
1942–
German geneticist

Christiane Nüsslein–Volhard, winner of the 1995 Nobel Prize in Physiology or Medicine, is the first German woman to win in this category. She is most noted for her contribution to research in identifying genes that control the early stages of embryonic development in fruit flies. Nüsslein–Volhard and two other scientists, Edward B. Lewis and Eric F. Wieschaus, paved the way for the study of the human counterparts to genes that influence human development, including ones responsible for birth defects.

Nüsslein–Volhard was born on October 20, 1942, in Magdeburg, Germany. The daughter of Rolf Volhard, an architect, and Brigitte (Hass) Volhard, a musician and painter, Christiane decided at a young age that she wanted to be a scientist. She stood out in a family of artists and architects—two of her four siblings are architects, and all of the children are amateur painters and musicians (Nüsslein–Volhard herself plays the flute and sings). If her family had any doubts about her chosen career, the earliness of her decision helped them to grow accustomed to the idea. Teachers also adjusted to her determination, and she moved easily through school.

Embarks on Scientific Career

Even though few women of her generation chose scientific careers, Nüsslein–Volhard found that being female in a male–dominated field presented little in the way of an obstacle to her studies. She received degrees in biology, physics, and chemistry from Johann-Wolfgang-Goethe-University in 1964 and a diploma in biochemistry from

Christiane Nüsslein-Volhard (AP/Wide World Photos, Inc. Reproduced by permission.)

Eberhard–Karls University in 1968. In 1973 she earned a Ph.D. in biology and genetics from the University of Tübingen. Nüsslein–Volhard was married for a short time as a young woman and never had any children. She decided to keep her husband's last name because it was already associated with her developing scientific career.

In the late 1970s Nüsslein–Volhard finished post–doctoral fellowships in Basel, Switzerland, and Freiburg, Germany, and accepted her first independent research position at the European Molecular Biology Laboratory (EMBL) in Heidelberg, Germany. She was joined there by Eric F. Wieschaus who was also finishing his training. Because of their common interest in *Drosophila*, or fruit flies, Nüsslein–Volhard and Wieschaus decided to work together to find out how a newly fertilized fruit fly egg develops into a fully segmented embryo.

Nüsslein–Volhard and Wieschaus chose the fruit fly because of its incredibly fast embryonic development. They began to pursue a strategy for isolating genes responsible for the embryos' initial growth. This was a bold decision by two scientists just beginning their scientific careers. No one had done anything like this before, and it wasn't certain whether they would be able to actually isolate specific genes.

Unique Strategy Creates Useful Mutants

Their experiments involved feeding male fruit flies sugar water laced with deoxyribonucleic acid (DNA)–damaging chemicals. When the male fruit flies mated with females, the females often produced dead or mutated embryos. Nüsslein–Volhard and Wieschaus studied these embryos for over a year under a microscope which had two viewers, allowing them to examine an embryo at the same time. They were able to identify specific genes that basically told cells what they were going to be—part of the head or the tail, for example. Some of these genes, when mutated, resulted in damage to the formation of the embryo's body plan. Nüsslein–Volhard became known for her ability to spot the slightest deviation from the norm and know whether it was significant to the way the embryo would develop.

Nüsslein–Volhard and Wieschaus published the results of their research in the English scientific journal *Nature* in 1980. They received a great deal of attention because their studies showed that there were a limited number of genes that control development and that they could be identified. This was significant because similar genes existed in higher organisms and humans and, importantly, these genes performed similar functions during development. Nüsslein–Volhard and Wieschaus's breakthrough research could help other scientists find genes that could explain birth defects in humans. Their research could also help improve in–vitro fertilization and lead to an understanding of what causes miscarriages. With this important work recognized by the scientific community, Nüsslein–Volhard began lecturing at universities in Germany and the United States. She was the Silliman Lecturer at Yale University and the Brooks Lecturer at Harvard.

Launches Controversial New Research

In 1991 she and Wieschaus received the Albert Lasker Medical Research Award, which is considered second only to the Nobel. During this time Nüsslein–Volhard had begun new research at the Max Planck Institute in Tübingen, Germany, similar to the work she did on the fruit flies. This time she wanted to understand the basic patterns of development of the zebra fish. She chose zebra fish as her subject because most of the developmental research on vertebrates in the past was on mice, frogs, or chickens, which have many technical difficulties, one of which was that one couldn't see the embryos developing. Zebra fish seemed like the perfect organism to study because they are small, they breed quickly, and the embryos develop outside of the mother's body. The most important consideration, however, was the fact that zebra fish embryos are transparent, which would allow Nüsslein–Volhard a clear view of development as it was happening.

Despite her prize–winning research on fruit flies, she received skeptical feedback on her zebra fish work. Other scientists claimed it was risky and foolish. When she submitted papers about her laboratory's work for publication, one reviewer even asked her why she was bothering. Nüsslein–Volhard was not one to be stopped by criticism or to rest on her laurels. Even though her reputation was built on her fruit fly research, her love of new challenges pushed her to take on this risky new project and set her sights to the future.

Unique Research Wins Nobel

Then on October 9, 1995, in the midst of criticism about her new research, Nüsslein–Volhard, Wieschaus, and Edward B. Lewis of the California Institute of Technology won the Nobel Prize in Physiology or Medicine for their work on genetic development in *Drosophila*. Lewis had been analyzing genetic mutations in fruit flies since the forties and had published his results independently from Nüsslein–Volhard and Wieschaus.

It has yet to be proven if zebra fish will actually provide any answers to the complex genetic questions Nüsslein–Volhard has raised. But her love of genetics compels her to continue. Her home country of Germany recognizes her as a national treasure, despite her controversial research. Nüsslein–Volhard herself dismisses public fear about gene research on embryos. "No one has in their grasp the genes that make humans wiser, more beautiful, or that make blue eyes," she said when she accepted the Nobel Prize. Her research, she says, has helped people "become wiser, understand biology better, understand how life functions."

SELECTED WRITINGS BY NÜSSLEIN-VOLHARD:

Periodicals

"Embryology Goes Fishing." *Nature* (May 22, 1986): 380–1

"Determination of Anteroposterior Polarity in Drosophila." *Science* (December 18, 1987): 1675–81

"From Egg to Organism: Studies on Embryonic Pattern Formation." *The Journal of the American Medical Association* (October 2, 1991): 1848

"Large–Scale Mutagenesis in the Zebrafish—In Search of Gene–Controlling Development in a Vertebrate." *Current Biology* (March 1, 1994): 189–202

"Of Flies and Fishes." *Science* (October 28, 1994): 572

Sketch by Pamela Proffitt

Zelia Maria Magdalena Nuttall
1857–1933
American archaeologist

Zelia Nuttall had no formal training in archaeology, but she made several important contributions to the field, specifically the discovery of two pictographic work of ancient Mexico. Nuttall was born on September 6, 1857, in San Francisco, California. She was the second of six children born to Magdalena Parrott and Robert Kennedy Nuttall, a second–generation Irishman and physician. Parrott was the daughter of a Mexican mother and an American father who had been United States consul at Mazatlan and, after that, a wealthy San Francisco banker. Nuttall spent much of her childhood traveling throughout Europe with her family and, while she learned several European languages, received little formal schooling. The family returned to San Francisco in 1876. In 1880, Nuttall married Alphonse Louis Pinart, a French ethnologist working in San Francisco. Nuttall accompanied Pinart on work projects in the West Indies, France, and Spain. Their daughter Nadine was born in 1882. The couple separated in 1884 and were formally divorced in 1888.

Rekindles Interest in Mexico

Nuttall had been interested in Mexico since childhood and her fascination was revived after her family visited there in 1884. Skilled in the fundamentals of anthropology through her travels with Pinart, she studied terra cotta heads at Teotihuacan, near Mexico City, hypothesizing that they were used for funeral ceremonies. She published a paper on her research in the *American Journal of Archaeology* in June 1886. The paper was favorably received and anthropologist Frederic W. Putnam invited Nuttall to serve as director of the Central American section of the Peabody Museum at Harvard. Nuttall declined so that she could continue her research, but did accept his invitation to serve as honorary special assistant in Mexican archaeology at the museum. Putnam served as her mentor as well.

In 1886, Nuttall traveled to Europe again with her brother, George Henry Falkiner Nuttall, who later became an esteemed biologist. She then settled in Dresden, Germany, but continued her travels and research. In 1901, she published *The Fundamental Principles of Old and New World Civilizations*, a book detailing the parallels between the cultures of ancient Mexico, Egypt, and the Middle East. The book was well received at the time, although its broad theories are less accepted today. During this time, Nuttall also discovered two ancient pictographic representation of Mexican military and religious life. This discovery is generally regarded as her most important. These pictographic records are known as the Codex Magliabecchiano and the Codex Nuttall.

Unearths Ancient Culture

In 1902 Nuttall relocated to Mexico, where she purchased a famous mansion, Casa Alvarado, in the Mexico City suburb of Coyoacan. In the garden there, she pursued her interest in Mexican botany. She continued her archaeological research as well and made further critical discoveries. Studying figurines found near her home, she concluded that Mexican culture was older than previously believed. Archaeological finds from the Isla de Sacrificios, near Veracruz, led her to conclude that the island may have served as a settlement for worshippers of Quetzalcoatl, a feathered serpent of Mexican lore.

In 1911, Nuttall again traveled to Europe, where she continued research begun in Mexico on English explorer Sir Francis Drake. She conducted research for this project in Alaska and Hawaii as well. In 1914 she published the results of her endeavor in New Light on Drake . She returned to Casa Alvarado in 1917 and began to research the religious significance for the Aztecs of the "shadowless moment," a semi–annual event during which the sun does not cast a shadow. She read a paper on the topic to academic societies in Oxford, England, Rome, Washington, D.C., and Mexico City in 1926 and 1927. She also propelled Mexican schools to institute an Aztec New Year's Day in honor of the newfound religious holiday.

Following this discovery, Nuttall focused less on her research and became well known as a hostess at Casa Alvarado. She entertained many distinguished visitors to Mexico, including the writer D.H. Lawrence, who based the character of Mrs. Norris in his The Plumed Serpent on Nuttall. Nuttall died from an intestinal tumor at Casa Alvarado on April 12, 1933.

SELECTED WRITINGS BY NUTTALL:

Monographs

Standard or Head–Dress? An Historical Essay on a Relic of Ancient Mexico. Cambridge, MA: Peabody Museum of American Archaeology and Ethnology, 1888.

The Atlatl or Spear–Thrower of the Ancient Mexicans, A Penitential Rite of the Ancient Mexicans. Cambridge, MA: Peabody Museum of American Archaeology and Ethnology, 1891.

The Fundamental Principles of Old and New World Civilizations: A Comparative Research Based on a Study of the Ancient Mexican Religious, Sociological and Calendrical Systems. Cambridge, MA: Peabody Museum of American Archaeology and Ethnology,1901.

A Penitential Rite of the Ancient Mexicans. Cambridge, MA: Peabody Museum of American Archaeology and Ethnology, 1904.

The Codex Nuttall: A Picture Manuscript from Ancient Mexico. The Peabody Museum Facsimile. New York: Dover Publications, 1975.

FURTHER READING

Books

Bailey, Martha J. *American Women in Science: A Biographical Dictionary*. Denver: ABC–CLIO, 1994.

Hart, James D. *A Companion to California*. New York: Oxford University Press, 1978.

James, Edward T. *Notable American Women 1607–1950: A Biographical Dictionary*. Vol. 2. Cambridge, MA: Belknap Press, 1971.

Library–Anthropology Resource Group. *International Dictionary of Anthropologists*. New York: Garland Publishing, 1991.

Sketch by Kristin Palm

O

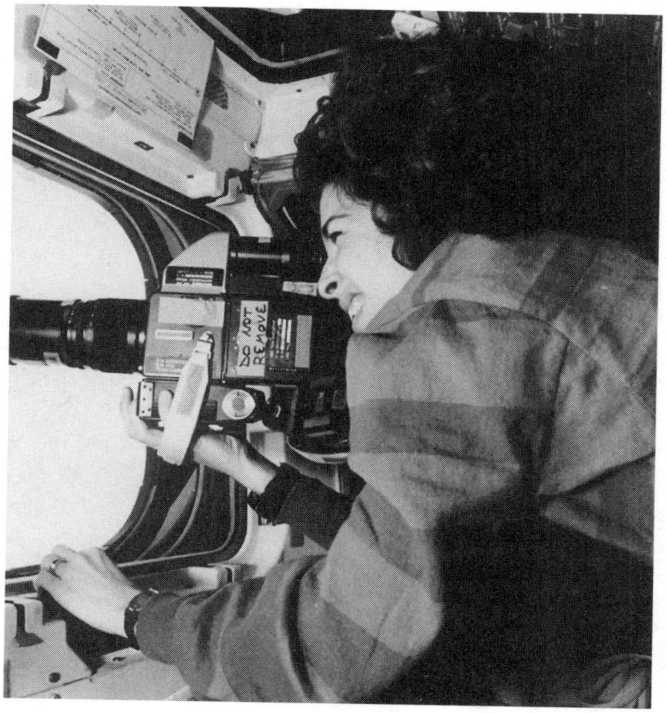

Ellen Ochoa (U.S. National Aeronautics and Space Administration (NASA). Reproduced by permission.)

Ellen Ochoa
1958–
American electrical engineer and astronaut

A specialist in optics and optical recognition in robotics, Ellen Ochoa is noted both for her distinguished work in inventions and patents and for her role in American space exploration. Among her optical systems innovations are a device that detects flaws and image recognition apparatus. In the late 1980s she began working with the National Aeronautics and Space Administration (NASA) as an optical specialist. After leading a project team, Ochoa was selected for NASA's space flight program. She made her first flight on the space shuttle Discovery in April 1993, becoming the first Hispanic woman astronaut.

The third of five children of Rosanne (Deardorff) and Joseph Ochoa, she was born May 10, 1958, in Los Angeles, California. She grew up in La Mesa, California; her father was a manager of a retail store and her mother a homemaker. Ochoa attended Grossmont High School in La Mesa and then studied physics at San Diego State University. She completed her bachelor's degree in 1980 and was named valedictorian of her graduating class; she then moved to the department of electrical engineering at Stanford University. She received her master's degree in 1981 and her doctorate in 1985, working with Joseph W. Goodman and Lambertus Hesselink. The topic of her dissertation was real–time intensity inversion using four–wave mixing in photorefractive crystals. While completing her doctoral research she developed and patented a real–time optical inspection technique for defect detection. In an interview with Marianne Fedunkiw, Ochoa said that she considers this her most important scientific achievement so far.

In 1985 she joined Sandia National Laboratories in Livermore, California, where she became a member of the technical staff in the Imaging Technology Division. Her research centered on developing optical filters for noise removal and optical methods for distortion–invariant object recognition. She was coauthor of two more patents based on her work at Sandia, one for an optical system for nonlinear median filtering of images and another for a distortion–invariant optical pattern recognition system.

Becomes Astronaut

It was during her graduate studies that Ochoa began considering a career as an astronaut. She told Fedunkiw that friends were applying who encouraged her to join them; ironically, she was the only one from her group of friends to make it into space. Her career at NASA began in 1988 as a group leader in the Photonic Processing group of the Intelligent Systems Technology Branch, located at the NASA Ames Research Center in Moffett Field, California. She worked as the technical lead for a group of eight people researching optical-image and data-processing techniques for space-based robotics. Six months later she moved on to become chief of the Intelligent Systems Technology Branch. Then in January 1990 she was chosen for the astronaut class, becoming an astronaut in July of 1991.

Her first flight began April 8, 1993, on the orbiter *Discovery*. She was mission specialist on the STS-56 Atmospheric Research flight, which was carrying the Atmospheric Laboratory for Applications and Science, known as ATLAS-2. She was responsible for their primary payload, the Spartan 201 Satellite, and she operated the robotic arm, known as the RPM to deploy and retrieve it. The satellite was designed to make independent solar observations to measure solar output and determine how the solar wind is produced. Ochoa was the lone female member of the five-person team which made 148 orbits of the earth.

Ochoa's technical assignments have also included flight–software verification in the Shuttle Avionics Integration Laboratory (SAIL), where she was crew representative for robotics development, testing and training, as well as crew representative for flight-software and computer-hardware development. Ochoa was the Payload Commander on the Space Shuttle's Atmospheric Laboratory for Applications and Science-3 mission (ATLAS-3), November 3–14, 1994. The ATLAS-3 mission's purpose was to continue studying the energy of the Sun and to learn how changes in the sun's irradiance affect the Earth's climate and environment. Ochoa used the RMS to retrieve a research satellite.

From May 27 to June 6, 1999, Ochoa was part of the historic *Discovery* shuttle mission that docked with the International Space Station. Ochoa coordinated the transfer of supplies and also operated the RMS during an eight hour space walk. The *Discovery* crew delivered four tons of materials and supplies for the first crew that will live on the station in early 2000.

Ochoa is a member of the Optical Society of America and the American Institute of Aeronautics and Astronautics. She has received a number of awards from NASA including the NASA Group Achievement Award for Photonics Technology in 1991 and the NASA Space Flight Medal in 1993. In 1994, she received the Women in Science and Engineering (WISE) Engineering Achievement Award. She has also been recognized many times by the Hispanic community. Ochoa was the 1990 recipient of the National Hispanic Quincentennial Commission Pride Award. She was also given *Hispanic* magazine's 1991 Hispanic Achievement Science Award, and in 1993 she won the Congressional Hispanic Caucus Medallion of Excellence Role Model Award.

Ochoa is married to Coe Fulmer Miles, a computer research engineer. They have no children. Outside of her space research, Ochoa counts music and sports as hobbies. She is an accomplished classical flautist—in 1983 she was the Student Soloist Award Winner in the Stanford Symphony Orchestra. She also has her private pilot's license and in training for space missions flies "back seat" in T–38 aircraft.

SELECTED WRITINGS BY OCHOA:

Periodicals

(With George F. Schils and Donald W. Sweeney) "Detection of Multiple Views of an Object in the Presence of Clutter." *Optical Engineering* 27 (1988): 266.

(With Joseph W. Goodman and Lambertus Hesselink) "Real–time Enhancement of Defects in a Periodic Mask Using Photorefractive BSO." *Optics Letters* 10 (1985): 430.

(With Goodman and Hesselink) "Real–time Intensity Inversion Using Two–Wave and Four–Wave Mixing in Photorefractive BGO." *Applied Optics* 24 (1985): 1826.

FURTHER READING

NASA Johnson Space Center, "Missions Highlights STS–56." (May 1993).

NASA Johnson Space Center, "Biographical Data—Ellen Ochoa." (June 1999).

Fedunkiw, Marianne, interview with Ellen Ochoa, conducted March 18, 1994.

Sketch by Marianne Fedunkiw

Ida Helen Ogilvie
1874–1963
American geologist

Ida Ogilvie was instrumental in making careers in geology accessible to women. The founder and first chair of Barnard College's geology department, she was also a renowned field researcher, conducting explorations in Maine, New Mexico, Mexico, California, and her home state of New York. Her areas of specialization included glacial geography and petrology.

Born on February 12, 1874, in New York City, Ida Helen Ogilvie was the daughter of Clinton Ogilvie, who traced his ancestry to the Earl of Airlie in Scotland, and of Helen Slade Ogilvie, a Mayflower descendant who was related to many of the colonial founders of America. The wealthy family expected their daughter to follow the usual debutante–wife–matron progression of the Gilded Age. But Ogilvie had different plans. She received her early education at home, being taught to speak French before English and learning how to draw expertly, before going to the Brearley School. She also attended schools in Europe before entering Bryn Mawr, and it was at that women's college that she found an abiding interest in geology, studying under Florence Bascom who had just founded Bryn Mawr's program in geology. She earned an A.B. from Bryn Mawr in 1900 and then studied at the University of Chicago for two years, where she began to focus on both petrology, or the origin of rocks, and glacial geology. She published her first paper in petrology in 1902 and then went to Columbia University, where she earned her doctorate in 1903.

Founds the Geology Department at Barnard

That same year she became the first lecturer in geology at Columbia University's Barnard College. She did not want to give up teaching graduate courses at Columbia, however, so she focused on the one field in geology where a lecturer was needed, glacial geology, even though her real love was petrology. From 1903 until her retirement in 1941, Ogilvie was the chair of Barnard's geology department, responsible not only for administration, but also for instruction and research. She was honored for her work in geology by being the second woman elected to the Geological Society of America.

Additionally, she took on the responsibilities of a farm she purchased at Bedford, New York, where she raised registered Jersey cattle, as well as horses, dogs, and ponies. During World War I she turned this into a model farm, recruiting young women from across the United States into agriculture during the manpower shortage created by the hostilities. After the war, some of her recruits stayed on, and Ogilvie bought a larger farm of 660 acres in Germantown, New York, the Hermitage, where she continued to breed her prize–winning herd.

With all of these responsibilities, Ogilvie was still able, until 1920, to do distinguished research, investigating glaciation in Canada, conducting field mapping in Maine and New York, and studying volcanic activities. Thereafter, she concentrated on instruction, becoming a noted lecturer who fretted over each presentation and who encouraged and nurtured her students. She also helped endow scholarships for young women in the sciences at Barnard, Columbia, and Bryn Mawr. After retiring from teaching in 1941, she devoted herself full time to her farm and to her hobby of knitting afghans in geologic designs. She died at the age of eighty–nine on October 13, 1963, at her farm in Germantown, having, as Elizabeth Wood reported in the *Bulletin of the Geological Society of America,* "lived a long and mostly happy life, doing the things she wanted to do."

SELECTED WRITINGS BY OGILVIE:

Periodicals

"Glacial Phenomena in the Adirondacks and Champlain Valley." *Journal of Geology* 10 (1902): 397–412.

"An Analcite–Bearing Camptonite from New Mexico." *Journal of Geology* 10 (1902): 500–507.

"Geological Notes on the Vicinity of Banff, Alberta." *Journal of Geology* 12 (1904): 408–414.

"The Effect of Superglacial Debris on the Advance and Retreat of Some Canadian Glaciers." *Journal of Geology* 12 (1904): 722–743.

"Geology of the Paradox Lake Quadrangle, N.Y." *New York State Museum Bulletin* no. 96 (1905): 461–509.

"The High–Altitude Conoplain; A Topographic Form Illustrated in the Ortiz Mountains." *American Geologist* 36 (1905): 27–34.

"A Contribution to the Geology of Southern Maine." *New York Academy of Sciences Annals* 17 (1907): 519–558.

"Some Igneous Rocks from the Ortiz Mountains, New Mexico." *Journal of Geology* 16 (1908): 230–238.

"The Interrelation of the Sciences in College Courses" *Columbia University Quarterly* 17, no. 3 (1915): 241–252.

"Field Observations on the Iowan Problem." *New York Academy of Sciences Annals* 26 (1916): 432–433.

FURTHER READING

Books

Arnold, Lois Barber. *Four Lives in Science.* Schocken Books, 1984, pp. 117–119.

Periodicals

"Dr. Ida Ogilvie of Barnard Dies; First Geology Chairman Was 89." *New York Times* (October 15, 1963): 39.

"Geology Attracts Feminine Workers." *New York Times* (November 27, 1938): 4.

"38–Year Career at Barnard Ends." *New York Times* (May 26, 1941): 17.

Wood, Elizabeth A. "Memorial to Ida Helen Ogilvie." *Bulletin of the Geological Society of America* (February 1964): 35–39.

Sketch by J. Sydney Jones

Jane Marion Oppenheimer
1911–1996
American embryologist

Jane Oppenheimer is known for her wide-ranging areas of expertise. From embryology to science history and biography, Oppenheimer became an expert in each discipline she undertook, influencing scientists in disciplines from biology to psychology. She is perhaps most remembered for her work on the Apollo-Soyuz Test Project, in which she studied weightlessness and its physiological effects.

Born September 19, 1911, in Philadelphia, Pennsylvania, Jane Marion Oppenheimer was the daughter of James H. Oppenheimer and Sylvia (Stern) Oppenheimer. She graduated with a degree in zoology from Bryn Mawr College, and went on to Yale University, from which she received her doctorate in zoology in 1935.

While at Yale, Oppenheimer began work on experimental biology and embryology, which would remain her chief research interest for the rest of her life. She worked with John Spangler Nicholas on the embryos of *Fundulus heteroclitus*—the common minnow. Nicholas had created a dechorionation method which enabled the researcher to manipulate the embryos, and Oppenheimer soon took charge of the experimental research. Recognizing her talent, Nicholas happily turned the *Fundulus* work over to her capable hands.

After graduation Oppenheimer began teaching biology at Bryn Mawr College, where she continued her work in experimental embryology. Her particular areas of interest were embryological history, especially as related to the theory of evolution, and central nervous system growth and development in fish. Her experiments included fate-mapping and the studies of induction, regulation, gastrulation, and differentiation.

Her publications on *Fundulus* were pioneering and her discoveries added greatly to scientific understanding of teleost embryology. One particularly noteworthy discovery, made through grafting experiments, was that the dorsal lips of fish and amphibians exhibit the same organizers (An organizer is part of the embryo that causes a part, or parts, near it to grow or change.). Through her research, much became known about the development of fish embryos.

But Oppenheimer's most public work in experimental embryology occurred in 1975 with the Apollo-Soyuz Test Project, in which *Fundulus* was used to assess the physiological effects of weightlessness. During this, the first joint Soviet-American space exploration, Oppenheimer's was one of four American experiments on board a satellite. *Fundulus* embryos were studied during five stages of development while in space, in order to determine the effect of weightlessness on embryo development. For her work on Apollo-Soyuz, Oppenheimer was awarded both the Soviet Kosmos Award and the Achievement Award from NASA.

A science historian, Oppenheimer spent considerable time and effort researching scientific biographies and timelines, with particular interest in British medicine of the 1700s. Oppenheimer felt strongly about the use in knowing how modern scientific ideas had gradually developed over time. Understanding the past shed greater light on current studies and scientific research. Current scientists, who have not studied foreign languages in depth, still benefit from her numerous publications. Disciplined, detail-oriented, and precise, Oppenheimer also loved dramatically recreating scientific personalities and discoveries.

A prolific reader and writer, Oppenheimer published dozens of scientific articles and books on embryology and scientific biography in addition to her over four hundred book reviews. Among her professional ties were the American Society of Zoologists, the American Philosophical Society, the Academy of Arts and Letters, and the American Academy of Arts and Sciences. She was the recipient of many awards during her lifetime, including Yale's Wilbur Lucius Cross Medal, the Christian R. and Mary F. Lindback Award, the American Association of the History of Medicine and Medical Library Association's Otto H. Hafner Award, the Distinguished Daughter of Pennsylvania Award, and the Estonian Academy of Sciences' Karl Ernst von Baer Medal.

Oppenheimer was the William R. Kenan, Jr. Professor when she retired in 1980 from Bryn Mawr, but she continued her research and writing until her death in Philadelphia on March 19, 1996. At the time of her death, interest in and research on *Fundulus* had been rekindled among the scientific community, and Oppenheimer once again enjoyed recognition for her painstaking work and contribution to science.

SELECTED WRITINGS BY OPPENHEIMER:

Books

Essays in the History of Embryology. Cambridge: MIT Press, 1967.

Foundations in Experimental Embryology. New York: Hafner Press, 1974.

FURTHER READING

Other

Obituary. *Pittsburgh Post-Gazette.* March 23, 1996, p C–3.

Hollyday, Margaret. "Jane Marion Oppenheimer." *Society for Developmental Biology.* http://sdb.bio.purdue.edu/SDBNews/Oppenheimer.html

Sketch by Helene Barker Kiser

Eleanor Anne Ormerod
1828–1901
English entomologist

Eleanor Ormerod was the first economic entomologist, studying insects that were important for agriculture, either as pests or as beneficial organisms. She transformed the subject into an important specialized subdivision of both biology and agricultural science. Ormerod published several books on economic entomology, as well as a large number of reports which she produced and distributed for free.

Ormerod was born in 1828 at Sedbury Park, her family's large estate in West Gloucestershire, England. Ormerod was the youngest of the ten children who were educated at home by their mother, Sarah (Latham) Ormerod, a botanical artist. Her father, George Ormerod, a strict and distant parent, was an archeologist and historian, specializing in early England. Ormerod also taught herself Latin and modern languages. While helping her brother William, who later became a well–known surgeon and anatomist, prepare for his examinations in biology, Ormerod first learned to use a microscope. In 1852, she began learning entomology by dissecting beetles and matching them with descriptions in J. F. Stephens's *Manual of British Beetles*.

Ormerod gradually took over management of the estate from her father, gaining experience in agriculture. Since the Ormerod estate was composed of forest, park, and cultivated fields, it was excellent for collecting a large variety of insects. Soon, Ormerod had become a self–taught expert on insects that attacked crops, forests, and domestic animals. She also studied snails, slugs, worms, spiders, and fungi, and the interactions of these organisms with insect pests. In 1868, Ormerod offered to make a collection of agriculturally–important insects for the Royal Horticultural Society. Her collection, made with the help of farm laborers, earned her the Flora Medal of the Society in 1870. Two years later, she sent her award–winning models of insect pests to the International Polytechnic Exhibit in Moscow.

Following her father's death in 1873, Ormerod's oldest brother inherited the estate and she moved with her sister Georgiana, first to Torquay, and then to Isleworth, near the Royal Botanical Gardens at Kew. The director of the gardens, Sir Joseph Hooker, and his wife became her close friends and her work aided the gardens in numerous ways. Ormerod's inheritance enabled her to live comfortably and produce scientific reports which she distributed without charge. She often worked in collaboration with her sister, who was a fellow of the Entomological Society of London.

Ormerod's first scientific paper was published in the *Journal of the Linnaean Society* in 1873. Four years later she wrote a seven–page pamphlet entitled "Notes for Observations of Injurious Insects." She distributed it to her colleagues and to public agencies in England and abroad. Ormerod's world–wide correspondence with entomologists soon reached some 1,500 letters per year. From 1888 on, her friend Anne Hartwell served as her private secretary, assisting with the replies. She utilized the papers, reports, notes, and observations that she received in her *Annual Reports of Observations of Injurious Insects*, which she published between 1877 and 1900. However, much of Ormerod's writing was based on her own original observations and anatomical discoveries. In 1881, Ormerod published her *Manual of Injurious Insects, with Methods of Prevention and Remedy*. A second enlarged edition was published in 1890. Ormerod's pamphlets and other publications included her original drawings and diagrams. Her writings were of such impact that 170,000 copies were printed of one her leaflets on the warble fly.

Ormerod began her public career in 1882, when she was pressed into serving as the consulting entomologist for the Royal Agricultural Society of England, a position similar to that of the salaried entomologists employed by governments of other countries. She held that position for ten years, until forced to resign by poor health. Ormerod also became a popular lecturer and gave a series of talks at the Royal Agricultural College in Cirencester. Her lectures at the South Kensington Museum were collected in her *Guide to the Methods of Insect Life*, published in 1884. She served on numerous committees dealing with economic entomology, appeared frequently as an expert witness in court cases, and was an examiner in agricultural entomology at the University of Edinburgh. She was also recommended for a lecturer position at the University of Edinburgh, but although she had invented the field of economic entomology, the university would not hire a woman professor.

Although Ormerod was interested in the inherent biological balances of nature, her usual recommendations for pest control were mineral oil, soap, kerosene or chemicals, as well as pruning and burning. She introduced a controversial arsenic–based pesticide called "Paris–green" and lobbied hard for its use in orchards.

Ormerod was a fellow of the Royal Meteorological Society and was awarded numerous scientific medals and honorary memberships and fellowships in scientific societies that did not admit women. She was the first woman to receive an honorary doctorate in law from the University of Edinburgh. Ormerod, both of her sisters, and four of her seven brothers, remained unmarried. She died in 1901 in St. Albans, England, where she and her sister had settled in 1887.

SELECTED WRITINGS BY ORMEROD:

Books

The Hessian Fly, Cecidomyia destructor, in Great Britain: Being Observations and Illustrations from Life. With Means of Prevention and Remedy from the Reports of the Department of Agriculture, U.S.A. London: Simpkin, Marshall, and Co., 1886.

Handbook of Insects Injurious to Orchard and Bush Fruits, with Means of Prevention and Remedy. London: Simpkin, Marshall, Hamilton, Kent, 1898.

(Robert Wallace, editor) *Eleanor Ormerod, L.L.D., Economic Entomologist. Autobiography and Correspondence.* New York: E. P. Dutton, 1904.

FURTHER READING

Books

Alic, Margaret. *Hypatia's Heritage: A History of Women in Science from Antiquity through the Nineteenth Century.* Boston: Beacon Press,1986.

Mozans, H. J. [John Augustine Zahm]. *Women in Science.* 1913. Reprint, Cambridge: MIT Press, 1974.

Ogilvie, Marilyn Bailey. *Women in Science, Antiquity through the Nineteenth Century: A Biographical Dictionary with Annotated Bibliography.* Cambridge: MIT Press, 1991.

Sketch by Margaret Alic

P

Katherine Evangeline Hilton (Van Winkle) Palmer
1895–1982

American paleontologist

Katherine Evangeline Hilton Van Winkle Palmer was an internationally recognized tertiary paleontologist and director of the Paleontological Research Institution for over 26 years. Her primary interest was in the study of mollusk fossils, which she compared with present-day species

She was born Katherine Evangeline Hilton Van Winkle on February 4, 1895 in Oakville, Washington. Her parents were M. Edith (Hilton) and Jacob Outwater Van Winkle. She grew up in the Pacific Northwest, an area rich in undeveloped land and fossilized animals and attended the University of Washington in Seattle, graduating in 1918. From there, she took a position as an assistant geologist at the University of Oregon and stayed there until 1922 when she returned to the University of Washington as an assistant professor of paleontology and historic geology.

On Christmas Eve 1921, she married Ephraim Palmer, a professor of nature study at Cornell. The couple would have two sons, Laurence and Robin. It is likely that she decided to finish her Ph.D. at Cornell University to be with her husband. She was awarded her Ph.D. in paleontology in 1925. In 1929 she was curator of paleontology at Oberlin College in Ohio.

In 1945, Palmer was named technical expert on zoology at the New York State Museum. She spent almost two years in Canada as a zoology specialist at McGill University's Redpath Museum from 1950–1951, and worked briefly in 1951 at the Provence Museum in Quebec. In 1952 she was named director of the Paleontological Research Institute in Ithaca, a position she held until her retirement in 1978, when she became director emeritus. During these years she was also active in a number of professional organizations and societies. From 1954–1971 she was secretary–treasurer of the Cushman Foundation for Mineral Research in Ithaca, and she was president of the American Malacological Union in 1960 (malacology is the branch of zoology that deals specifically with mollusks). She was a fellow of the Paleontology Society, the Geological Society of America, and the American Association for the Advancement of Science. Among her awards was an honorary degree from Tulane University in New Orleans.

Palmer's husband died in 1970. By then she was 75, but she showed no signs of slowing down. Palmer managed to continue her research and other activities despite the fact that her oldest son was an invalid for many years. When she finally retired from the Paleontological Research Institute she was 83 years old. She was actively engaged in research on Cenozoic paleontology until the very end and left uncompleted studies on Florida and Alabama Eocene mollusks. She died in Ithaca at the age of 87 in September, 1982.

SELECTED WRITINGS BY PALMER:

Paleontological Research Institution, Fifty Years, 1932–1982. Paleontological Research Institution, 1982.

Periodicals

"Paleontology of the Oligocene of the Chehalis Valley," *Geology* 1, no. 2, (1918): 69–97.

(with G. D. Harris) "New or Otherwise Interesting Tertiary Molluscan Species from the East Coast of America." *Bulletin of American Paleontology* 8, no. 33 (1919): 32.

"A New Fauna from the Cook Mountain Eocene near Smithville, Bastrop County, Texas." *Journal of Paleontology* 2, no. 1 (1928): 20–31.

"Gastropoda of the Clabornian mid–Eocene of the Southern United States." *Bulletin of American Paleontology* VII, no. 32 (1937): 730.

"Fossil Fresh–water Mollusca from the State of Monagas," *Bulletin of American Paleontology* 31, no. 118 (1945): 34.

"Fun with Fossils," *Science Monthly*, Vol. 64, No. 5, 1947, pp 385–388.

"A New Nautiloid Eutrephoceras Everdami, New Species from the Cowlitz Formation, Upper Eocene of Washington." *Journal of Paleontology* 35, no. 3 (1961): 532–534.

FURTHER READING

Books

Bailey, Martha J. *American Women In Science: A Biographical Dictionary.* Denver: ABC-CLIO, 1994.

World Who's Who in Science. New Providence, NJ: Reed Elsevier, 1964.

Periodicals

Caster, Kenneth E. "Memorial to Katherine Van Winkle Palmer, 1895–1982." *Journal of Paleontology* 57, no. 5 (1983): 1141–1144.

Sketch by Laurel M. Sheppard

Barbara Frances Palser
1916–
American botanist

Barbara Palser distinguished herself in the field of botany during a career that lasted well over half a century. Her work as a researcher, teacher, editor, and administrator has taken her from New Brunswick, New Jersey to Melbourne, Australia.

She was born Barbara Frances Palser in Worcester, Massachusetts on June 2, 1916 to George Norman and Cora Munson Palser. She went to Mount Holyoke College in western Massachusetts, where she received her bachelor's degree in 1938 and her master's degree in 1940. From there, she went to the University of Chicago, where she was awarded a Ph.D. in botany in 1942.

Palser stayed on at Chicago for the next 23 years, beginning as an instructor, then becoming assistant professor in 1945, associate professor in 1951,and full professor in 1960. During those years she conducted research, focusing on plant anatomy and morphology, as well as experimental anatomy. She also became active in a number of professional associations such as the Botanical Society of America, which she joined in 1943. She was named associate editor of the *Botanical Gazette* (published by the university) in 1952 and editor in 1959 (a position she held until she left Chicago). From 1957 to 1959 she served as botany advisor to the *Encyclopaedia Britannica.*

In 1965, Palser moved to Rutgers University in New Brunswick, New Jersey, where she was associate professor of botany for a year, then professor until 1982. For several years she also served as director of the school's graduate program in botany. After she "retired" in 1982 she remained quite active. She served as visiting research fellow in Australia at the University of Melbourne from 1984 to 1985. In 1991 she became adjunct professor of botany at the University of Massachusetts–Amherst.

Palser served as secretary of the Botanical Society of America from 1970 to 1974, then as vice president, and finally in 1976 as president. Among the other organizations in which she has been active are the International Society for Plant Morphology, the American Institute of Biological Sciences, and the Council of Biology Editors. She was awarded an honorary doctorate from Mount Holyoke in 1978, and received the Botanical Society of America's Merit Award in 1985.

FURTHER READING

Books

American Men and Women of Science 1998–99. 20th ed. New Providence: R. R. Bowker, 1998.

Bailey, Martha J. *American Women in Science: A Biographical Dictionary.* Denver: ABC–Clio, 1994.

World Who's Who in Science. Marquis Who's Who, 1969.

Sketch by George A. Milite

Ivy May Parker
1907–1985
American petroleum engineer

Ivy May Parker was an internationally recognized expert on pipeline corrosion. She was named First Lady of Petroleum by the Desk and Derrick Club in 1966 at the International Petroleum Exposition, the highest tribute paid to women in that industry and the third to receive it. She was the first woman to receive a Ph.D. in chemistry from the University of Texas. Her many contributions included the development of water- and oil-soluble inhibitors, internal coatings for tankage, filtration methods for large volumes of refined petroleum, and products quality control.

Parker was born on a ranch in Quay County, New Mexico, on September 11, 1907 to Sanders E. and Myrtle E. (Peggram) Parker. Her early education took place in a one room schoolhouse for grades 1–8, a two and a half mile walk from the ranch. For the last year of grammar school, Parker and her sister were sent to Hereford, a town 130 miles from home, to stay with an aunt so they could attend a better school. It was there that she had her first experience with chemistry. The Parker children attended high school in Tucumcari, New Mexico, while her father remained at the ranch. At times they were left alone for a few days so their mother could go home to help.

Hired by Shell Oil

At her mother's insistence, Parker began her freshman year as a home economics major with a specialty in textiles at Teacher's College (now West Texas State University) in Canyon, Texas. However, she soon switched her major to chemistry since she found it far more interesting. Her sophomore year she won an essay contest sponsored by the

Ivy Parker (Corbis/Bettmann-UPI. Reproduced by permission.)

American Chemical Society with an essay titled "Relation of Chemistry to Health." She finished her bachelor's degree in 1928, and because there were no teaching positions available at the time, accepted a teaching fellowship at the University of Texas at Austin. There she earned her master's in 1931 and her Ph.D. in chemistry four years later.

Though Parker's graduate work had been sponsored by the petroleum industry, major oil companies refused to hire a female chemist since they claimed there were no facilities for women in their plants. As a result Parker was forced to take a teaching job near Lubbock, Texas, at Mary Hardin Baylor College for a year. She was finally hired by Shell Oil in Deer Park, Texas (a suburb of Houston) to work in the research laboratory in 1936. Here she was assigned to boiler water and cooling problems, including corrosion. One of her major contributions was the development of an electrolytic titration method for the determination of chloride in crude oil. Titration is a way of determining the concentration of a dissolved substance. By the time she left Shell, Parker had been promoted to supervisor of the analytical laboratory.

From 1943–1945 she served as a senior research chemist at the U.S. Abercrombie Refinery at Old Ocean, Texas, where she also set up a program to assure water potability for the housing development there. When this plant closed after the war, Parker obtained a corrosion engineer position at Plantation Pipeline Company in Atlanta. She was responsible for a 3,200 mile pipeline that ran from Texas to Washington, D.C., handling 14 million gallons of oil products every day. Parker traveled 15,000 miles per year inspecting the line for corrosion and devising corrective measures, earning the nickname of "Doc."

She also served as editor of NACE's journal *Materials Protection* from 1962–1968. She remained at Plantation until she retired in the 1970s. In 1974, NACE recognized her with two awards: a certificate of appreciation for chairing NACE's committee on internal corrosion and the R.A. Brannon Award for Outstanding Contributions to the Advancement of NACE.

Helps Women Engineers

In addition to her involvement in other technical associations such as the American Chemical Society and the American Institute of Chemists, Parker found time to counsel engineering students, judge science fairs, and help recruit women into engineering. She joined the Society of Women Engineers in 1957 and served on several of its national committees. She chaired the SWE's Board of Trustees the society her by making her a fellow in 1982. A year later she received a certificate of recognition for her board service, only the fourth person to receive such recognition in SWE's 33–year history.

After she retired, Parker moved back to Austin, Texas to live with her younger sister Bertha. They later moved to Canyon, Texas, where Parker had gone to college. Ivy Parker died on September 7, 1985, several days before her 78th birthday. To commemorate her achievements the NACE Southeast Region established the Ivy Parker Award for Outstanding Contributions in 1969 (of which she was the first recipient). Parker received the title of First Lady of Corrosion from the National Association of Corrosion Engineers (NACE) in 1983. SWE established a scholarship in her name in 1986. Parker joins the small but select ranks of women who managed to establish remarkable engineering careers when women were still virtually unknown.

SELECTED WRITINGS BY PARKER:

Periodicals

"Use of Common Inhibitors in Products Pipelines: A Survey of Practices." *Corrosion* 3, no. 4 (April 1947): 157–168.

FURTHER READING

Books

Who's Who of American Women 6th ed. Chicago: A.N. Marquis Co., 1970–1971, pp 168.

Kass–Simon, G. and Farnes, Patricia, eds. *Women of Science: Righting the Record.* Bloomington: Indiana University Press, 1990.

Periodicals

Barr, Laneda. "Ivy M. Parker First Lady of Petroleum." *U.S. Woman Engineer* (November/December 1985): 4–19.

"Personality Ivy M. Parker." *Materials Performance* (June 1982): 72–75.

"Dr. Ivy Parker, Atlanta SWEM, Named First Lady of Petroleum" *SWE Newsletter* (July-August 1966): 8.

Sketch by Laurel M. Sheppard

Edith Marion Patch

1876–1954

American entomologist

Edith Patch was known worldwide as the foremost authority on aphids. She studied the insects from both economic and ecological perspectives. Her research on the characteristic of aphids, including food, habits, and variations, was far-reaching.

Edith Marion Patch was born on July 27, 1876 to William Patch and Salome Jenks Patch. She and her five older brothers and sisters lived in Worcester, Massachusetts, until Patch was eight, when the family moved to Minneapolis, Minnesota. A couple of years later, the Patches moved again, this time to a ten-acre farm, where Patch was able to explore the nearby woodlands, swamp, and lake. She showed an early interest in the natural surroundings, and spent most of her time exploring the land and studying the wildlife and insects. She wrote of her particular interest in the monarch butterfly, which served as her subject of a prize-winning essay, written while attending South High School. She used her prize money to buy a book on the study of insects.

Patch studied English at the University of Minnesota, and graduated with a B.S. degree in 1901. While in college, she also became interested in the study of aphids, which would become her lifelong work and passion. After graduation, she taught high school while applying for agricultural positions in entomology. But many believed that the study of insects was particularly unladylike, and Patch was met with many rejections.

But in 1903, she was offered an instructorship in entomology at the University of Maine, where she also taught agricultural English. The following year, Patch created and became head of the Department of Entomology at the Maine Agricultural Experiment Station, affiliated with the University of Maine. She was only the second woman on the university faculty. Patch was also able to conduct research in Hertfordshire, England's Rothampsted Experimental Station for a time. She remained in the university position until 1937, receiving her M.S. degree from the University of Maine in 1910 and her Ph.D. from Cornell University in 1911. Upon her retirement, the University of Maine granted her an honorary D.Sc.

Dr. Edith M. Patch (Corbis/Bettmann-UPI. Reproduced by permission.)

Becomes Internationally Known Entomologist

Patch quickly became known world wide as an expert on aphids (Aphidae), and as an exceptional entomologist in general. Her aphid research included characteristics, life histories, habits, food preferences, ecology, and variations of the insect group from ecological and economic standpoints. In addition to this work, Patch studied many farm pests, including the potato plant louse, the strawberry crown borer, the wooly apple aphid, and the brown-tail moth. Her research was so expansive that many insect species and one new genus were named for her.

Patch's research work allowed her to author almost 15 books, the majority of which explained her studies from an ecological or economic standpoint. In addition to her extensive publications, Patch also kept up a large volume of correspondence with entomologists across the country and abroad. She offered to aid the government and other institutions in the study of aphids, for which she received no payment. Patch was president of the American Nature Study Society, and the first female president of the Entomological Association of America. She was a member of Phi Beta Kappa, the American Society of Naturalists, the American

Association for the Advancement of Science, and the American Association of Economic Entomologists.

After her retirement, Patch continued to write on science, nature and natural history. Her articles were published in popular magazines and juvenile magazines, and she also published over two dozen books for children and young adults. Described by those who knew her as ambitious, persistent, particular, careful, helpful, and generous, Patch was well loved by colleagues and students alike. She died on September 27, 1954, in Orono, Maine.

SELECTED WRITINGS BY PATCH:

Books

Food–Plant Catalogue of the Aphids of the World, Including the Phylloxeridae. Orono: Maine Agricultural Experiment Station Annual Report, 1955.

Aphid Pests of Maine, Food Plants of the Aphids, Psyllid Notes. Orono: Maine Agricultural Experimental Station, bulletin 202, 1912.

FURTHER READING

Books

Bailey, Martha J. *American Women in Science.* Denver: ABC–CLIO, 1994.

Mallis, Arnold. *American Entomologists.* New Brunswick, NJ: Rutgers University Press, 1971.

Mozans, H. J. *Woman in Science.* Notre Dame: University of Notre Dame Press, 1991.

Ogilvie, Marilyn Bailey. *Women in Science: Antiquity Through the Nineteenth Century.* Cambridge: MIT Press, 1986.

Sketch by Helene Barker Kiser

Jennie R. Patrick
1949–
American chemical engineer

Jennie R. Patrick is the first African American woman to earn a doctorate degree in chemical engineering. A successful chemical engineer, manager, and educator who has applied her skills with a number of different companies and universities, she has also been honored with the Outstanding Women in Science and Engineering Award in 1980, and by CIBA-GEIGY Corporation in its Exceptional Black Scientist poster series in 1983.

Jennie R. Patrick (Reproduced by permission of Jennie R. Patrick.)

Patrick was born January 1, 1949, in Gadsden, Alabama, one of five children of James and Elizabeth Patrick, working-class parents who emphasized knowledge as an escape from poverty. Patrick was both nurtured and challenged in a segregated elementary school and junior high, but in high school she was one of the first participants in a controversial and sometimes explosive program of racial integration, where she successfully overcame violence and unsupportive white teachers to graduate with an A-minus average in 1969.

Patrick was accepted at several prestigious universities, but chose to begin her pursuit of engineering at Tuskegee Institute, which she attended until 1970 when the chemical engineering program was eliminated. She then transferred to the University of California at Berkeley to finish her degree, receiving her B.S. in 1973 and meanwhile working as an assistant engineer for the Dow Chemical Company in 1972 and for the Stauffer Chemical Company in 1973. She continued her education at the Massachusetts Institute of Technology (MIT), receiving a Gilliland Fellowship in 1973, a DuPont Fellowship in 1974, and a Graduate Student Assistant Service award in 1977. She was also awarded a fellowship in 1975 from the American Association of University Women, and a National Fellowship Foundation Scholarship in 1976.

Conducts Research on Superheated Liquids

Her research at MIT involved the concept of superheating, where a liquid is raised above its boiling temperature but does not become a vapor. She investigated the temperature to which pure liquids and mixtures of two liquids could be superheated. Patrick finished her research and completed her doctorate in 1979. While pursuing her graduate studies, Patrick worked as an engineer with Chevron Research in 1974 and with Arthur D. Little in 1975.

After completing her doctorate, Patrick joined the Research and Development Center at General Electric (GE) in Schenectady, New York, where she held the position of research engineer. Her work there involved research on energy–efficient processes for chemical separation and purification, particularly the use of supercritical extraction. In supercritical processes, the temperature and pressure are varied so that a substance is not a liquid or a gas, but a fluid. Unique properties make these fluids useful in both separations and purification processes. She has published several papers on this work, and has received patents for some of her advancements.

Patrick remained at GE until 1983, when she accepted a position at Philip Morris as a project manager in charge of the development of a program to improve several of the company's products. Patrick transferred to the Rhom and Haas Company in 1985, as manager of fundamental chemical engineering research. In this position she interacted with all aspects of the chemical business, from engineering to marketing to manufacturing. By being exposed to the overall business she was able to direct development of new research technology within her division and promote its implementation throughout the company. In 1990, Patrick became assistant to the executive vice president of Southern Company Services, a position that emphasized her management skills in both the business and technical aspects of the company. Having earlier held adjunct professorships at Rensselaer Polytechnic Institute from 1982 to 1985 and the Georgia Institute of Technology from 1983 to 1987, Patrick decided to make teaching a bigger part of the her life. In January 1993, she left Southern Company Services and returned to Tuskegee University, as the 3M Eminent Scholar and Professor of Chemical Engineering. In addition to her teaching duties, Patrick is developing research projects in material sciences, is actively involved in leadership roles at Tuskegee, and remains firmly committed to helping minority students find success, particularly in the fields of science and engineering.

SELECTED WRITINGS BY PATRICK:

Books

(With F. Palmer) "Supercritical Extraction of Dixylenol Sulfone." In *Supercritical Fluid Technology.* Edited by J. M. L. Penninger, et. al. Elsevier, 1985, pp. 379–384.

Periodicals

(With R. C. Reid) "Superheat–Limit Temperature of Polar Liquids," *Industrial and Engineering Chemistry Fundamentals.* (November, 1981): 315–317.

(With R. D'Souza and A. S. Teja) "High Pressure Phase Equilibria in the Carbon Dioxide–n–Hexadecane and Carbon Dioxide–Water Systems." *Canadian Journal of Chemical Engineering* (February, 1988): 319–325.

"Let Others' Experience Be Your Roadway to Success." *The Black Collegian* (September/October 1992): 39.

FURTHER READING

Books

Outstanding Young Women of America, Junior Chamber of Commerce, 1979, p. 981.

Sammons, V. O., editor, *Blacks in Science and Medicine,* Hemisphere Publishing Co., 1990, p. 185.

Periodicals

Bradby, Marie, "Professional Profile: Dr. Jennie R. Patrick." *US Black Engineer* (Fall 1988): 30–33.

"Engineering Their Way to the Top." *Ebony* (December 1984): , pp. 33–36.

Kazi–Ferrouillet, Kuumba, "Jennie R. Patrick: Engineer Extraordinaire." *NSBE Journal* (February, 1986): 32–35.

Sketch by Jerome P. Ferrance

Ruth Patrick
1907–
American limnologist

Ruth Patrick has pioneered techniques for studying the biodiversity of freshwater ecosystems over a career that spans 60 years. Her studies of microscopic species of algae, called diatoms, in rivers around the world have provided methods for monitoring water pollution and understanding its effects. Federal programs to monitor the status of freshwater rely on Patrick's method of growing diatoms on glass slides. Her studies of the impact of trace elements and heavy metals on freshwater ecosystems have demonstrated how to maintain a desired balance of different forms of algae. For example, she showed that addition of small amounts of manganese prevents the overgrowth of blue–green algae and permits diatoms to proliferate.

Patrick received the prestigious Tyler Ecology Award in 1975, and serves on numerous governmental advisory committees. She advanced the field of limnology, the study of freshwater biology, and in the late 1940s established the

Ruth Patrick (AP/Wide World Photos. Reproduced by permission.)

Department of Limnology at the Academy of Natural Sciences in Philadelphia. She remained its director for more than four decades. Headquarters for her research are in Philadelphia, with a field site in West Chester, Pennsylvania. An estuary field site at Benedict, Maryland, on the Patuxent River near Chesapeake Bay, serves for studies of pollution caused by power plants.

Patrick was born in Topeka, Kansas, on November 26, 1907. Her undergraduate education was completed at Coker College, where she received a B.S. degree in 1929. She obtained both her M.S. degree in 1931 and her Ph.D. in botany in 1934 from the University of Virginia. The roots of Patrick's long and influential career in limnology can be traced to the encouragement of her father, Frank Patrick. He gave his daughter a microscope when she was seven years old and told her, "Don't cook, don't sew; you can hire people to do that. Read and improve your mind." Patrick's doctoral thesis, which she wrote at the University of Virginia in Charlottesville, was on diatoms, whose utility derives from their preference for different water chemistries. The species of diatoms found in a particular body of water says a lot about the character of the water.

Confronted with Bias against Women Scientists

When Patrick joined the Academy of Natural Sciences in 1933, it was as a volunteer in microscopy to work with one of the best collections of diatoms in the world; she was told at the time that women scientists were not paid. For income she taught at the Pennsylvania School of Horticulture and made chick embryo slides at Temple University. In 1937 persistence paid off, and she was appointed curator of the Leidy Microscopical Society with the Academy of Natural Sciences, a post she held until 1947. She also became associate curator of the academy's microscopy department in 1937, and continued in that capacity until 1947, when she accepted the position of curator and chairman of the limnology department at the academy. Continuing as curator, in 1973 she was offered the Francis Boyer Research Chair at the academy.

Conducts Pioneering Studies of Freshwater Ecosystems

In the late 1940s Patrick gave a paper at a scientific meeting on the diatoms of the Poconos. In the audience was William B. Hart, an oil company executive, who was so impressed with the possibilities of diatoms for monitoring pollution that he provided funds to support Patrick's research. Freed from financial constraints, Patrick undertook a comprehensive survey of the severely polluted Conestoga Creek, near Lancaster, Pennsylvania. It was the first study of its kind, and launched Patrick's career. She matched types and numbers of diatoms in the water to the type and extent of pollution, an extremely efficient procedure now used universally.

By her own account Patrick has waded into 850 different rivers around the globe in the course of her research. She participated in the American Philosophical Society's limnological expedition to Mexico in 1947 and led the Catherwood Foundation's expedition to Peru and Brazil in 1955. Patrick was an advisor to several presidential administrations and has given testimony at many hearings on environmental problems and before congressional committees on the subject of environmental legislation. She was an active participant in drafting the federal Clean Water Act.

Pens Book on Groundwater Concerns

In 1987 Patrick coauthored a book, *Groundwater Contamination in the United States,* which provides an overview of groundwater as a natural resource, and a state–by–state description of policies designed to manage growing problems of contamination and depletion. Another of her concerns is global warming, the rise in the earth's temperature attributed to the buildup of carbon dioxide and other pollutants in the atmosphere. In an interview reported in the *Philadelphia Inquirer* in 1989, Patrick said, "We're going to have to stop burning gasoline. And we're going to have to conserve more energy, develop ways to create electricity from the sun and plants, and make nuclear power both safe and acceptable."

Patrick has received many awards in addition to the Tyler prize, including the Gimbel Philadelphia Award for 1969, the Pennsylvania Award for Excellence in Science and Technology in 1970, the Eminent Ecologist Award of the Ecological Society of America in 1972, and the

Governor's Medal for Excellence in Science and Technology in 1988. She holds many honorary degrees from United States colleges and universities. Patrick has authored over 130 papers, and continues to influence thinking on limnology and ecosystems. Her contributions to both science and public policy have been vast.

SELECTED WRITINGS BY PATRICK:

Books

(With E. Ford and J. Quarles) *Groundwater Contamination in the United States.* University of Pennsylvania Press, 1987.

Periodicals

"Managing the Risks of Hazardous Waste." *Environment* (April, 1991): 13–35.

FURTHER READING

Periodicals

Detjen, Jim. "In Tiny Plants, She Discerns Nature's Warning on Pollution." *Philadelphia Inquirer* (February 19, 1989).

Other

"The Wonderful World of Dr. Ruth Patrick." Unpublished paper by Geraldine J. Gates, Wharton School, University of Pennsylvania, February 16, 1987.

Sketch by Karen Withem

Flora Wambaugh Patterson
1847–1928
American mycologist and vegetable pathologist

The second woman scientist to be employed by the United States Department of Agriculture (USDA), Flora Wambaugh Patterson specialized in the taxonomy of fungi. She also studied plants' fungal diseases, systemic mycology, and insects.

Patterson was born on September 15, 1847, in Columbus, Ohio. She was the daughter of A.B. and Sarah (Sells) Wambaugh, and had at least one brother named Eugene. Patterson's father was a Methodist minister. She received her primary and secondary education through private tutors and attended Antioch College, graduating in 1860 with her A.B. She went on to earn an M.L.A. at Cincinnati Weslyan College in 1865.

On August 12, 1869, in Cincinnati, Patterson was married to Captain Edwin Patterson, and and they would have two sons. Within ten years of their marriage, Edwin suffered a debilitating accident when the steamboat he was aboard blew up. He was bedridden for the rest of his short life, and Patterson was forced to pursue a career to support herself and her family. She finished her A.M. degree from Cincinnati Weselyan in 1883. Edwin died on September 7, 1889.

Turns Tragedy into Triumph

After her husband's death, Patterson moved her sons to Iowa, where her brother Eugene was a law professor. She attended graduate school there, at the State University of Iowa, from 1891–1892. Here she became interested in botany and related subjects. When her brother was hired at Harvard, she planned to follow him. She applied to and was accepted by Yale, but the institution ultimately revoked her admittance. Instead, Patterson attended Radcliffe from 1892–1895, again studying botany and plant pathology. She also learned how to run a herbarium and care for a mycological collection while employed as an assistant at the Gray Herbarium at Harvard. From 1894 until 1895, Patterson was also employed as an assistant editor of *Economic Fungi.*

The State University of Iowa granted Patterson her second A.M. in 1895. After graduation, she found employment in a private school in Boston as a biology instructor. She also took the civil service exam, and, on January 15, 1895, she went to work for the USDA as an assistant pathologist. She was only the second woman to be employed by this federal department. Patterson was in charge of the division of vegetable physiology and pathology's herbarium. In 1901, she was promoted to the mycologist in charge of pathology collections, the herbarium, taxonomy of fungi, and mycology exchange for the newly created Bureau of Plant Industry. She also did inspection work. In Patterson's obituary in *Phytopathology*, Beverly Galloway writes, "Mrs. Patterson's heart and soul were in the work of making our collections really worthwhile."

While working for the Department of Agriculture, Patterson was known as a loyal employee and a conscientious scientist who was focused on her work. She also continued to do her own research, especially on *Exoscaceae,* a fungus family, despite her demanding duties. Patterson's articles were published in professional journals concerned with botany and horticulture. Most of her publications were through the Department of Agriculture. Patterson also shared her career with others. She worked in the People's Gardens of Washington, D.C., and contributed to a book called *Careers for Women* by Catherine Filene.

Patterson retired from the Department of Agriculture in April 1923. She died on February 5, 1928, in Brooklyn, New York in the home of her son, Henry. In her obituary in *Mycologia*, Vera K. Charles wrote, "Though born in the early half of the last century she had been able to bridge the early period of conservatism or intolerance of too advanced scientific thought and action and present an open mind to the examination of the modern interpretation of science. . ."

SELECTED WRITINGS BY PATTERSON:

(With Vera Charles) *Mushrooms and Other Common Fungi.* Washington: U.S. Government Printing Office, 1915.

FURTHER READING

Books

Bailey, Martha J. *American Women in Science: A Biographical Dictionary.* Denver: ABC–CLIO, 1994, pp. 294–95.

Cattell, J. McKeen and Jaques Cattell. *American Men of Science: A Biographical Dictionary.* New York: The Science Press, 1927, p. 755.

Leonard, John William, ed. *Woman's Who's Who of America: A Biographical Dictionary of Contemporary Women in the United States and Canada, 1914–15.* New York: American Commonwealth Company, 1915, pp. 626–27.

Ogilvie, Marilyn Bailey. *Women in Science Antiquity through the Nineteenth Century: A Biographical Dictionary with Annotated Bibliography.* Cambridge: MIT Press, 1986, p. 184.

Siegel, Patricia Joan and Kay Thomas Finley. *Women in the Scientific Search: An American Bio–bibliography, 1724–1979.* Metuchen: Scarecrow Press, Inc., 1985, p. 84.

Periodicals

Charles, Vera K. "Mrs. Flora Wambaugh Patterson." (January–February 1929): 1–4.

Galloway, Beverly T. "Flora W. Patterson." *Phytopathology* (November 1928): 877–879.

Sketch by Annette Petrusso

Cecilia Payne-Gaposchkin
1900–1979
English-born American astronomer

Cecilia Payne-Gaposhkin (AP/Wide World Photos. Reproduced by permission.)

Cecilia Payne–Gaposchkin was a pioneer in the field of astronomy and one of the most eminent female astronomers of the twentieth century. She was the first to apply the laws of atomic physics to the study of the temperature and density of stellar bodies and to conclude that hydrogen and helium, the two lightest elements, were also the two most common elements in the universe. Her revelation that hydrogen, the simplest of the known elements, was the most abundant substance in the universe has since become the basis for analysis of the cosmos. Yet she is not officially credited with the discovery, made when she was a 25–year–old doctoral candidate at Harvard, because her conservative male superiors convinced her to retract her findings on stellar hydrogen and publish a far less definitive statement. While she is perhaps best known for her later work in identifying and measuring variable stars with her husband, Sergei I. Gaposchkin, Payne–Gaposchkin helped forge a path for other women in the sciences through her staunch fight against sexual discrimination at Harvard College Observatory, where she eventually became the first woman appointed to full professor and the first woman named chairman of a department that was not specifically designated for a woman.

Cecilia Helena Payne was born on May 10, 1900, in Wendover, England, the eldest of three children born to Edward John and Emma Leonora Helena (Pertz) Payne of Coblenz, Prussia. Her father, a London barrister, died when she was four years old. Her mother, a painter and musician, introduced her to the classics, of which she remained fond throughout her life. Payne–Gaposchkin recalled that Homer's *Odyssey* was the first book her mother read to her as a child. She knew Latin by the time she was 12 years old, became fluent in French and German, and showed an early interest in botany and algebra. As a schoolgirl in London she was influenced by the works of Isaac Newton, Thomas Huxley, and Emmanuel Swedenborg.

In 1919 she won a scholarship to Newnham College at Cambridge University, where she studied botany, chemistry, and physics. During her studies there, she became fascinated with astronomy after attending a lecture on Albert Einstein's theory of relativity given by Sir Arthur Eddington, the university's foremost astronomer. Upon completion of her studies in 1923 (at that time women were not granted degrees at Cambridge), Payne–Gaposchkin sought and obtained a Pickering Fellowship (an award for female students) from Harvard to study under Harlow Shapley, the newly appointed director of the Harvard Observatory. Thus, Payne–Gaposchkin embarked for the United States, hoping to find better opportunities as a woman in astronomy. Harvard Observatory in Boston, Massachusetts, became her home for the rest of her career—a "stony–hearted stepmother," she was said to have called it.

Harvard: A Stony–Hearted Stepmother

Payne–Gaposchkin's career at Harvard began in 1925, when she was given an ambiguous staff position at the Harvard Observatory. By that time she had already published six papers on her research in the field of stellar atmospheres. That same year, she was awarded the first–ever Ph.D. in astronomy at Radcliffe. Her doctoral dissertation, *Stellar Atmospheres,* was published as Monograph No. 1 of the Harvard Observatory. A pioneering work in the field, it was the first paper written on the subject and was the first research to apply Indian physicist Meghnad Saha's recent theory of ionization (the process by which particles become electrically charged by gaining or losing electrons) to the science of measuring the temperature and chemical density of stars. However, she was discouraged in her views and was convinced to alter them by Henry Norris Russell, a renowned astronomer at Princeton who several years later reached her same conclusions and published them, thereby receiving credit for their origin. Despite this, Payne–Gaposchkin's research remains highly regarded today; Otto Struve, a notable astronomer of the period, was quoted in *Mercury* magazine as saying that *Stellar Atmospheres* was "undoubtedly the most brilliant Ph.D. thesis ever written in astronomy."

In 1926 when she was 26 years old, she became the youngest scientist to be listed in *American Men of Science.* But her position at Harvard Observatory remained unacknowledged and unofficial. It was not until 1938 that her work as a lecturer and researcher was recognized and she was granted the title of astronomer, which she later requested to be changed to Phillips Astronomer. From 1925 until 1938 she was considered a technical assistant to Shapley, and none of the courses she taught were listed in the Harvard catalogue until 1945. Finally, in 1956 when her colleague Donald Menzel replaced Shapley as director of the Harvard Observatory, Payne–Gaposchkin was "promoted" to professor, given an appropriate salary, and named chairman of the Department of Astronomy—the first woman to hold a position at Harvard University that was not expressly designated for a woman.

Payne–Gaposchkin's years at Harvard remained productive despite her scant recognition. She was a tireless researcher with a prodigious memory and an encyclopedic knowledge of science. She devoted a large part of her research to the study of stellar magnitudes and distances. Following her 1934 marriage to Gaposchkin, a Russian emigre astronomer, the couple pioneered research into variable stars (stars whose luminosity fluctuates), including research on the structure of the Milky Way and the nearby galaxies known as the Magellanic Clouds. Through their studies they made over two million magnitude estimates of the variable stars in the Magellanic Clouds.

From the 1920s until Payne–Gaposchkin's death on December 7, 1979, she published over 150 papers and several monographs, including "The Stars of High Luminosity" (1930), a virtual encyclopedia of astrophysics, and *Variable Stars* (1938), a standard reference book of astronomy written with her husband. She also published four books in the 1950s on the subject of stars and stellar evolution. Moreover, though she retired from her academic post at Harvard in 1966, becoming Emeritus Professor of Harvard University the following year, she continued to write and conduct research until her death. Her autobiography, writings collected after her death by her daughter, Katherine Haramundanis, was entitled *Cecilia Payne-Gaposchkin: An Autobiography and Other Recollections* and was published in 1984.

Payne–Gaposchkin was elected to the Royal Astronomical Society while she was a student at Cambridge in 1923, and the following year she was granted membership in the American Astronomical Society. She became a citizen of the United States in 1931. She and her husband had three children: Edward, born in 1935, Katherine, born in 1937, and Peter, born in 1940—a noted programmer analyst and physicist in his own right. In 1934 Payne–Gaposchkin received the Annie J. Cannon Prize for significant contributions to astronomy from the American Astronomical Society. In 1936 she was elected to membership in the American Philosophical Society. Among her honorary degrees and medals, awarded in recognition of her contributions to science, are honorary doctorates of science from Wilson College (1942), Smith College (1943), Western College (1951), Colby College (1958), and Women's Medical College of Philadelphia (1961), as well as an honorary master of arts and doctorate of science from Cambridge University, England (1952). She won the Award of Merit from Radcliffe College in 1952, the Rittenhouse Medal of the Franklin Institute in 1961, and was the first woman to receive the Henry Norris Russell Prize of the American Astronomical Society in 1976. In 1977 the minor planet 1974 CA was named Payne–Gaposchkin in her honor.

Payne–Gaposchkin is remembered as a woman of boundless enthusiasm who refused to give up her career at a time when married women with children were expected to do so; she once shocked her superiors by giving a lecture when she was five months pregnant. Jesse Greenstein, astronomer at the California Institute of Technology and friend of Payne–Gaposchkin, recalled in *The Sciences* magazine that "she was charming and humorous," a person given to quoting Shakespeare, T.S. Eliot, and Gilbert and Sullivan. Her daughter remembers her in the autobiography *Cecilia Payne–Gaposchkin* as a "world traveler,. . .an inspired seamstress, an inventive knitter and a voracious reader." Quoted in *Sky and Telescope,* Payne–Gaposchkin revealed that nothing compares to "the emotional thrill of being the first person in the history of the world to see something or to understand something."

SELECTED WRITINGS BY PAYNE-GAPOSCHKIN:

Books

Stellar Atmospheres. W. Heffer and Sons, 1925.

The Stars of High Luminosity. McGraw–Hill, 1930.

(With S. Gaposchkin) *Variable Stars.* Harvard Observatory Monograph No. 5, 1938.

Stars in the Making. Harvard University Press, 1952.

Introduction to Astronomy. Prentice–Hall, 1954; second edition, 1970.

The Galactic Novae. Interscience, 1957.

Stars and Clusters. Harvard University Press, 1979.

Cecilia Payne–Gaposchkin: An Autobiography and Other Recollections. Edited by Katherine Haramundanis. Cambridge University Press, 1984.

Periodicals

"Stellar Evolution." *Science Monthly* (May 1926): 419.

(With H.N. Russell and D.H. Menzel) "The Classification of Stellar Spectra." *Astrophysical Journal* (1935): 107–108.

"New Stars." *Telescope* no. 4 (1937): 100–106.

"The Topography of the Universe." *Telescope* no. 8 (1941): 112–114.

"Interesting Variable Stars." *Popular Astronomy* no. 49 (1941): 311–319.

"Problems of Stellar Evolution." *Sky and Telescope* 2, no. 9 (1943): 5–7.

"Variable Stars and Galactic Structure." *Nature* no. 170 (1952): 223–5.

"Myth and Science." *Journal for the History of Science* 3 (1972): 206–211.

"Fifty Years of Novae." *Astronomical Journal* no. 82 (1977): 665–673.

"The Development of Our Knowledge of Variable Stars." *Annual Review of Astronomy and Astrophysics* no. 16 (1978): 1–13.

FURTHER READING

Books

Abir–Am, P. and D. Outram, eds *Uneasy Careers and Intimate Lives: Women in Science 1789–1979.* Rutgers University Press, 1987.

Kass–Simon, G. and Patricia Farnes, eds. *Women of Science: Righting the Record.* Bloomington: Indiana University Press, 1990.

Periodicals

Bartusiak, Marcia. "The Stuff of Stars." *The Sciences* (September/October 1993): 34–39.

Dobson, Andrea K. and Katherine Bracher. "A Historical Introduction to Women in Astronomy." *Mercury* (January/February 1992): 4–15.

Lankford, John. "Explicating an Autobiography." *Isis* (March 1985): 80–83.

Lankford, John and Ricky L. Slavings. "Gender and Science: Women in American Astronomy, 1859–1940." *Physics Today* (March 1990): 58–65.

Smith, E. "Cecilia Payne–Gaposchkin." *Physics Today* (June 1980): 64–66.

Whitney, C. "Cecilia Payne–Gaposchkin: An Astronomer's Astronomer." *Sky and Telescope* (March 1980): 212–214.

Sketch by Mindi Dickstein

Louise Pearce
1885–1959
American medical researcher

Louise Pearce was an eminent medical researcher in the early twentieth century who helped find a cure for African sleeping sickness, a disease spread by the tsetse fly. She also advanced the world's knowledge of the treatment of infectious diseases, including syphilis. After she successfully tested a new drug called *tryparsamide* on people infected with sleeping sickness in the Belgian Congo, she received the Order of the Crown of Belgium in 1921.

Louise Pearce was born to Susan Elizabeth and Charles Ellis Pearce in Winchester, Massachusetts, on March 5, 1885. Her father was a tobacco dealer She had one younger brother, Robert Pearce, who went on to become a lawyer in New York, New York. The family moved to a California ranch sometime after 1889. Pearce went to the Girls' Collegiate School in Los Angeles, graduating in 1903. She then attended Stanford University, where she studied physiology and histology (a science that studies the exact characteristics of organs and tissues in the body), and graduated with a B.A. in 1907.

Because of her interest in the human body, Pearce attended Johns Hopkins University School of Medicine, graduating third in her class in 1912. Though she was asked to serve a year later at the prestigious Phipps Psychiatric Clinic at Johns Hopkins, she declined, and went instead to the Rockefeller Institute for Medical Research in New York

City, because she wanted to do laboratory research. At the Rockefeller Institute she was a fellow under Simon Flexner, who was director of the Institute.

In 1919, Pearce and Wade Hampton Brown, a pathologist at the Rockefeller Institute, announced that they had found a new compound, partly derived from arsenic, that was effective against sleeping sickness in laboratory animals. The two scientists' paper about their research was published in the *Journal of Experimental Medicine*.

Sleeping sickness, also known as *trypanosomiasis*, develops in tropical areas from a microscopic parasite called *Trypanosoma gambiense*, which is then spread by the tsetse fly. During the early twentieth century it had spread through Africa like a plague. Because Brown had a family, Pearce was selected to try out the drug, alone, in the city of Leopoldville in the Belgian Congo. While in the Congo, she treated 77 patients in all stages of the disease. The result was that within days parasites were driven from the patients' blood streams. Within weeks the parasites were killed off. Most patients, even the severest cases, were returned to good health. The next year Pearce was awarded the Belgian Order of the Crown. In 1953 Belgium's leaders also awarded her the King Leopold II Prize and the Royal Order of the Lion.

After she returned from the Congo, Pearce continued to work with Brown intensively on the biology of syphilis and cancer. She and Brown painstakingly documented the physiological effects of syphilis in rabbits, which they found acted quite like human syphilis. They hoped that the same drug they used for African sleeping sickness, tryparsamide, would kill the syphilis infection, even after the disease had penetrated to the spinal cord and brain. And indeed the drug did prove to be effective. It remained the treatment of choice for syphilis until the discovery of penicillin. The two researchers also made the discovery that some syphilitic animals were prone to cancer.

In 1929 Pearce and Brown began to breed their rabbits in order to observe the workings of more than a dozen infectious diseases and congenital deformities. In 1935, after the laboratory was moved to Princeton, New Jersey, Pearce bought a house with British novelist Ida A. R. Wiley and Sara Josephine Baker, who would later become Chief of the Department of Child Hygiene in the New York City's health department. In 1942, after Brown died, Pearce was asked by the Rockefeller Institute to discontinue the research and write up the results. For the rest of her life, she devoted herself to writing up their voluminous findings, including discoveries about achondroplasia, a form of dwarfism, and osteopetrosis, a rare bone disease that causes usually dense bones to be vulnerable to fractures.

Pearce, who was a suffragette, served as president of the Woman's Medical College of Pennsylvania in 1946 until her retirement in 1951. She served with the aim of keeping the position open for women. Pearce received honorary doctorates from Beaver College, Bucknell College, Wilson College, Skidmore College, and the Medical College of Pennsylvania. In 1951 she received the **Elizabeth Blackwell** Award from the New York Infirmary. Pearce died on August 9, 1959, after becoming sick while returning home from Europe. In memory of her friend Pearce, Ida Wiley left most of her estate to the Women's Medical College of Pennsylvania.

FURTHER READING

Books

Biermaan, Carol A., Louise S. Grinstein, and Rose K Rose. *Women in the Biological Sciences.* Westport, CT: Greenwood Press, 1997.

Green, Carol Hurd and Barbara Sicherman. *Notable American Women: The Modern Period.* Cambridge, MA: Belknap Press, 1980.

Sketch by Barbara Boughton

Annie Smith Peck
1850–1935
American archaeologist and explorer

Annie Smith Peck, archaeologist and explorer, was a pioneer mountain climber. She was the first woman to climb many of the mountains in the Americas. Known for her physical stamina and bravery, Peck also measured the mountains she climbed, adding scientific data to the prevailing knowledge of the peaks.

Annie Peck was born on October 19, 1850, in Providence, Rhode Island, to George Bachelor Ann Power (Smith) Peck. The youngest child and only living daughter, Peck grew up in the shadow of her older brothers. Because they would not allow her to play with them, Peck determined to become more physically adept than any boy, and this willpower gave her the physical strength and confidence to tackle obstacles later in life.

Peck attended Dr. Stockbridge's School for Young Ladies, Providence High School, and the Rhode Island State Normal School. She received her bachelor's and master's degrees in Greek from the University of Michigan. In 1884, she traveled to Hanover, Germany, where she studied German and music. The following year, she was the first woman to study at the American School of Classical Studies in Athens, Greece.

Discovers Her Lifelong Passion

Like many women of the time, Peck's first employment was as a teacher, first in Providence, then in Michigan, Ohio, and New Jersey. In 1881, Peck taught Latin and

Annie Smith Peck (UPI/Corbis-Bettmann. Reproduced by permission.)

elocution at Purdue University, and in 1886 she taught Latin, classic art, and archaeology at Smith College. In 1885, Peck became interested in mountain climbing. While traveling from Germany to Athens, she was able to view the Matterhorn, and became the third woman to climb it, which sparked what would become her lifelong passion. Peck wanted to continue her travels, and began giving lectures on Roman and Greek archaeology, and, later, mountain climbing. The lectures became her primary source of income, financing her many climbing trips.

Peck's successful career as a mountain climber is all the more notable because of her gender, lack of funds and proper equipment, and the inexperience of her climbing assistants. She completed most of her climbs without oxygen supplements. Her climbing costume was a donated outfit of knickerbockers and a tunic, which was considered shocking at the time. Peck was demanding and relentless, more admired than liked, according to many accounts.

Among the mountains she conquered and measured in the Americas were Popocatepetl, Mount Orizaba, Mount Sorata, the Fuffingerspitze, the Jungfrau, Mount Shasta, Monte Cristallo, Mount Coropuna (on which she put a pennant that read "Votes for Women"), and Mount Huascaran. The last mountain couldn't be measured by triangulation due to strong winds, so Peck estimated the altitude at 24,000 ft (7,315 m), which set a world record. Peck's arch rival, climber Fanny Bullock Workman, challenged the findings, and because she had significant funding at her disposal, hired an engineering team to measure the altitude, which they subsequently determined to be 21,812 ft (6,648 m). Regardless, the Huascaran climb proved to be a western hemisphere record, and Peck was honored with a gold medal and a silver slipper from the Peruvian government and the Lima Geographical Society. The Society also named the north peak Ana Peck in her honor.

In addition to her mountain expeditions, Peck wrote guidebooks and handbooks. She also toured South America by airplane, which was unusual for the time. She was a member of the Society for Women Geographers, founder of the American Alpine Club, and fellow of the Royal Geographic Society. In 1935, she began a worldwide trip, but had to stop at Athens due to fatigue. She died on July 18 of that year from bronchial pneumonia in New York.

SELECTED WRITINGS BY PECK:

Books

A Search for the Apex of America: High Mountain Climbing in Peru and Bolivia. New York: Dodd, Mead, 1911.

FURTHER READING

Books

Bailey, Martha J. *American Women in Science.* Denver: ABC–CLIO, 1994.

Baker, Daniel B., ed. *Explorers and Discoverers of the World.* Detroit: Gale Research Inc., 1993.

James, Edward T., et al, eds. *Notable American Women 1607–1950.* Cambridge, MA: Belknap Press, 1971.

Robinson, Jane. *Wayward Women.* New York: Oxford University Press, 1990.

Sketch by Helene Barker Kiser

Elizabeth Gifford Peckham
1854–1940
American entomologist

Elizabeth Gifford Peckham was a specialist in the entomology and behavior of spiders and wasps, as well as the taxonomy of a specific group of spiders, *attidae.* She collaborated with her husband Dr. George Williams Peckham and together the couple published numerous publications, including several well-regarded pieces on the social habits of wasps. Peckham was cited in the first three editions of *American Men and Women of Science.*

Peckham was born on December 19, 1854. She attended Vassar, graduating with her A.B. degree in 1876. As a student, she studied entomology. After graduation, Peckham worked in a library. In 1880, she moved west to Wisconsin when she married Dr. George W. Peckham, a fellow entomologist interested in spiders. He taught high school biology in Milwaukee, Wisconsin, and held both medical and law degrees. The couple had three children. They shared an interest in entomology, especially spiders. In George Peckham's obituary published in the *Entomological News,* R.A. Muttkowski wrote, "From the time of their marriage, these two are inseparably linked in all phases of their work, in their researches, in their travels, in their very thoughts."

The couple managed to publish regularly on the taxonomy of spiders within a few years of their marriage, despite the fact that George held down increasingly demanding positions in the public schools in Milwaukee, and later as director of Milwaukee Public Library. The Peckhams published their work through the Natural History Society of Wisconsin, Geological and Natural History Survey of Wisconsin, and Wisconsin Academy of Sciences, Arts, and Letters.

After Peckham earned her A.M. from Vassar in 1889, the Peckhams' work turned to wasps. In 1898, they published their definitive piece on wasps, "On the Instincts and Habits of Social Wasps," in *Wisconsin Geological Survey No. 2.* Unusual for the time, Peckham was given individual credit for her work. For the most part, women scientists who worked with their husbands did not receive individual acknowledgment for their work. Indeed, she was given first authorship for their 1905 book, *Wasps Social and Solitary.* This popular book explained the couple's interests in the species and made astute observations about animal life. They observed that wasps were localized and had a routine of constant action. As Eileen Crist wrote in Social Studies of Science, "The Peckhams put themselves into the writing, they describe their presence as a feature of the scenes or episodes they observe. They express their 'admiration and delight,' disclosing unembarrassed exhilaration about the wasps they describe."

Both the Peckhams were outstanding writers, but their research seems to have ended in 1910 when George retired from his post at the library. After he died on January 10, 1914, Peckham went back to school. She attended Cornell, earning her Ph.D. in 1916. At the time, Cornell was recognized as having one of the best entomology programs in the United States. Peckham died on January 3, 1940.

SELECTED WRITINGS BY PECKHAM:

Books

(With George W. Peckham) *Wasps Social and Solitary,* 1905.

Periodicals

(With George W. Peckham) "On the Instincts and Habits of Social Wasps." *Wisconsin Geological Survey No. 2* (1898).

FURTHER READING

Books

Bailey, Martha J. *American Women in Science: A Biographical Dictionary.* Denver: ABC–CLIO, 1994, p. 299.

Bonta, Marcia Myers. *Women in the Field: America's Pioneering Women Naturalists.* College Station: Texas A&M, 1991, pp. 150–151.

Ogilive, Marilyn Bailey. *Women in Science: Antiquity through the Nineteenth Century: A Biographical Dictionary with Annotated Bibliography.* Cambridge: MIT Press, 1986, p. 185.

Siegel, Patricia Joan and Kay Thomas Finley. *Women in the Scientific Search, 1724–1979.* Metuchen: The Scarecrow Press, 1985, p. 165.

Periodicals

Crist, Eileen, "Naturalists' Portrayals of Animal Life: Engaging the Verstehen Approach." *Social Studies of Science* (1996): 799–838.

Muttkowski, R.A. "George Williams Peckham, M.D., LL.D." *Entomological News and Proceedings of the Entomological Section* (April 1914): 145–48.

Sketch by Annette Petrusso

Florence Peebles
1874–1956
American biologist and zoologist

Possessing both multiple educational degrees and multiple talents, Florence Peebles is best known for the important research she performed on tissue regeneration, both in plant and animal species. Although her working hypotheses and experiments are known to only a few scientists, her theories have remained applicable to the study of living tissue regeneration, rejuvenation, and reproduction. Peebles was skilled in both zoology and biology, and was well known not only as a competent researcher, but also as an outstanding educator and sensitive humanitarian.

Peebles was born in Pewee Valley, Kentucky, to Elizabeth (Cummins) and Thomas Peebles in 1874. After attending the private Girls' Latin School in Baltimore, she went on to Woman's College of Baltimore (Goucher College), graduating with a B.A. degree in 1895. She completed graduate studies at Bryn Mawr College (where she ultimately received her Ph.D. in 1900), University of Halle (1899), University of Munich (1899), University of Bonn (1905), University of Wurzburg (1911), and the University of Freiburg (1913). She also received an honorary LL.D. degree from her alma mater, Goucher College (1954).

While at Bryn Mawr, Peebles had studied under the famous Thomas Hunt Morgan, and her studies reflected his interest in tissue regeneration, especially involving marine specimens. Accordingly, she spent a great deal of research time over the next thirty years at the marine biology laboratory in Wood Holes, Massachusetts, where her zoological expertise became such that she held the American Women's Table at the Naples Zoological Station in Italy for five separate years. Developing her basic theories from research at Wood Holes, Peebles' most recurring thematic premise was the effect that external influences in the environment could have upon the development of living tissue. Her suggested theory was that an animal's or cell's characteristics could be modified by external factors, and that a cell's response to a regenerative stimulus was determined by prior exposure during its early development to a set of distinct conditions. Though her work was technically non–published, she made important contributions to scientific literature, and received fellowship support for much of her research.

Most of Peebles' professional life was spent teaching, first as a demonstrator in biology at Bryn Mawr, then as full–time instructor and professor, serving briefly as acting head of the biology department in 1913. She also headed the biology department at Sophie Newcomb College, Tulane University for a few years before returning to a professorship at Bryn Mawr. For several years (1928–1942), Peebles also was professor of biological sciences at California Christian (now Chapman) College, where she established a bacteriology department in 1928 and biology department in 1935. Although she attempted retirement a few times, new horizons beckoned, and she eventually founded a biology laboratory at Lewis and Clark College in Portland, Oregon, which is named in her honor.

In her later years (at the age of 80), Peebles developed a strong interest in gerontology, and when she officially retired in 1946, she moved to Pasadena, California, where she engaged in community service as a counselor for the aged. She also sponsored a young Japanese student from Tokyo, putting her through Pasadena City College, and tutoring her in the sciences. Prior to her protegee's graduation, Peebles suffered a stroke in 1956 and died at home in December 1956, at the age of 83.

FURTHER READING

Books

Bailey, Martha J. *American Women in Science.* Denver: ABC–CLIO, 299.

Kass–Simon, G., and Patricia Farnes, eds. *Women of Science: Righting the Record.* Bloomington: Indiana University Press, 220–221.

Ogilvie, Marilyn Bailey. *Women in Science: Antiquity through the Nineteenth Century.* Cambridge: MIT Press, 145.

Other

"Florence Peebles." *SJSU Virtual Museum.* htpp://www.sjsu.edu/depts/Museum/pee.html (28 June 1999)

Sketch by Lauri R. Harding

Mary Engle Pennington
1872–1952
American chemist

Mary Engle Pennington was a bacteriological chemist who revolutionized methods of storing and transporting perishable foods. Denied a B.S. degree in 1895 because she was a woman, Pennington went on to head the U.S. Department of Agriculture's food research lab. As persuasive as she was resourceful, Pennington was able to convince farmers, manufacturers, and vendors to adopt her techniques. She developed methods of slaughtering poultry that kept them fresh longer, discovered ways to keep milk products from spoiling, and determined how best to freeze fruits and vegetables. Pennington was the first female member of the American Society of Refrigerating Engineers. She eventually went into business for herself as a consultant and investigator in the area of perishable foods.

Pennington was born October 8, 1872, in Nashville, Tennessee. She was the first of two daughters born to Henry and Sarah B. Molony Pennington. Pennington spent most of her early life in Philadelphia, where her family moved to be closer to their Quaker relatives. With her father, a successful label manufacturer, she shared a love of gardening.

Pennington found her way to the field of chemistry through a library book on that subject. Her interest prompted her to enter the Towne Scientific School of the University of Pennsylvania, an uncommon occurrence for a woman at that time. In 1895 she received a certificate of proficiency, having been denied a B.S. because of her gender. Not to be deterred, Pennington continued academic work, earning her Ph.D. at age twenty–two from the University of Pennsylvania with a major in chemistry and minors in zoology and botany. This degree was conferred under an old statute that made exceptions for female students in "extraordinary cases." Pennington then accepted a two–year fellowship at the university in chemical botany,

Mary E. Pennington (Corbis/Bettmann-UPI. Reproduced by permission.)

followed by a one–year fellowship in physical chemistry at Yale.

From 1898 to 1906 Pennington served as instructor in physiological chemistry at Women's Medical College. During this same period, she started and operated a clinical laboratory performing analyses for physicians, and was a consultant to Philadelphia regarding the storage of perishable foods during the marketing process. Her reputation for quality work led to an appointment as head of the Philadelphia Department of Health and Charities Bacteriological Laboratory. One of her first goals here was the improvement of the quality of milk and milk products. Her natural gift of persuasion aided her in convincing ice–cream manufacturers and vendors to adopt simple steps to help avoid bacterial contamination of their foods.

The Pure Food and Drug Act was passed in 1906, and the U.S. Department of Agriculture planned to establish a research laboratory to help provide scientific information for prosecutions under the act. Specifically, this lab would be concerned with the quality of eggs, dressed poultry, and fish. With the encouragement of Harvey W. Wiley, chief of the chemistry section of the USDA and a longtime family friend, Pennington took and passed the civil service exam in 1907 under the name M. E. Pennington. Unaware that Pennington was a woman, the government gave her a post as bacteriological chemist. Wiley promoted her to head the food research lab in 1908. That same year she delivered an address for Wiley to a startled all–male audience at the First International Congress of Refrigeration.

During Pennington's tenure the laboratory effected alterations in the warehousing of food, its packaging, and use of refrigeration in transport. Pennington eventually developed techniques that were commonly used for the slaughter of poultry, ensuring safe transport and high quality long after the butchering occurred. In the area of eggs, a highly perishable item especially in warm weather, she again used her powers of persuasion. She worked to convince farmers to collect and transport eggs more frequently during warmer weather. She is also credited with developing the egg cartons that prevent excessive breakage during transport.

During World War I, Pennington consulted with the War Shipping Administration. The United States had forty thousand refrigerated cars available for food transport at the start of the war. Pennington determined only three thousand of these were truly fit for use, with proper air circulation. Following the war she was recognized for her efforts with a Notable Service Award given by Herbert Hoover.

Pennington made another career change in 1919 when she accepted a position as manager of research and development for New York's American Balsa Company, a manufacturer of insulating material. In 1922 she made her final career move, starting her own business in New York as a consultant and investigator in the area of perishable foods. She was particularly interested in frozen foods, helping to determine the best strains of fruits and vegetables for freezing, and the best method for freezing them.

Pennington was the author of books, articles, pamphlets, and several government bulletins. She gave many addresses and was the recipient of several awards, including the American Chemical Society's 1940 Garvan Medal to honor a woman chemist of distinction. Pennington, in fact, was one of the first dozen female members of the society. She was the first female member of the American Society of Refrigerating Engineers, and the first woman elected to the Poultry Historical Society's Hall of Fame. She served as director of the Household Refrigeration Bureau of the National Association of Ice Industries from 1923 to 1931.

Pennington earned herself the reputation for always producing quality work. She was accepted in industry even while she was working for the government in enforcing the Pure Food and Drug Act. She maintained her interest in gardening and botany, growing flowers in her apartment. She was a lifelong member of the Quaker Society of Friends. Pennington, who never married, was still working as a consultant and as vice president of the American Institute of Refrigeration when she died on December 27, 1952, in New York City.

SELECTED WRITINGS BY PENNINGTON:

Books

(With H. M. P. Betts) *How to Kill and Bleed Market Poultry.* Government Printing Office, 1915.

(With Paul Mandeville) *Eggs.* Progress Publications, 1933.

FURTHER READING

Books

American Chemists and Chemical Engineers. Edited by Wyndham Miles. American Chemical Society, 1976.
Notable American Women: The Modern Period. Edited by Barbara Sicherman and Carol Green. Belknap Press, 1980.

Periodicals

"Mary E. Pennington." *Chemical and Engineering News* (January 5, 1953).

Sketch by Kimberlyn McGrail

Marguerite Catherine Perey
1909–1975
French physicist

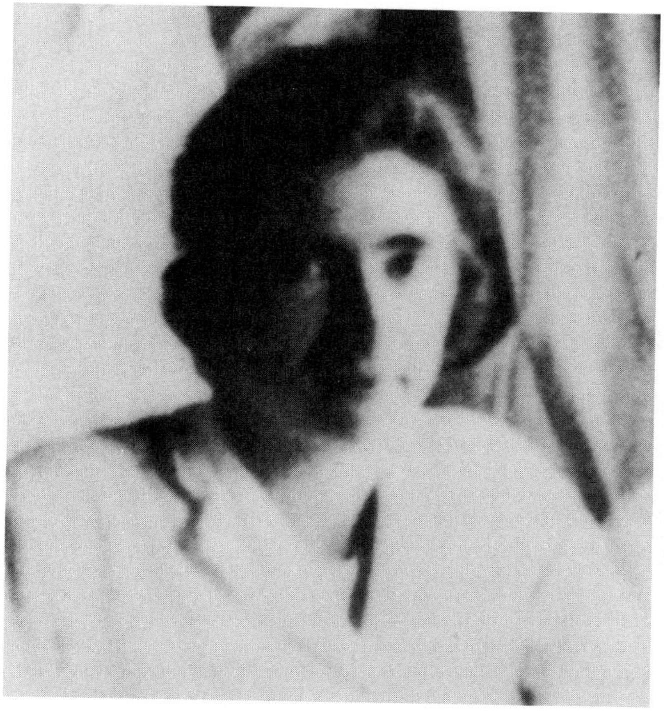

Marguerite Catherine Perey (Photo Researchers, Inc. Reproduced by permission.)

Marguerite Perey is best known for her discovery of francium, the 87th element in the Periodic Table. Francium, a rare, highly unstable, radioactive element, is the heaviest chemical of the alkali metal group. Perey's work on francium and on such scientific occurrences as the actinium radioactive decay series led to her admission to the French Academy of Sciences. Perey was the first woman to be admitted to the 200 year–old Academy—even **Marie Curie** had been unable to break the sex barrier.

Marguerite Perey was born in Villemomble, France, in 1909. As a child, she showed an interest in science and wanted to become a doctor. Her father's early death, however, left her family without the resources for such an education. Nonetheless, Perey was able to study physics and showed a talent for scientific endeavors. Because of her technical prowess, she was able to secure a position as a lab assistant (initially for a three–month stint) in Marie Curie's laboratory at the Radium Institute in Paris. Curie, for all her influence, made an unpretentious first impression, so much so that Perey, upon first meeting her at the Institute, thought she was the lab's secretary. This incident, combined with Curie's tendency to be aloof with strangers, might have portended a short career at the Curie lab for Perey. In fact, after the initial meeting, Perey thought she would only stay at the Radium Institute for her three months and leave. But Curie saw that Perey was both talented and dedicated, and she encouraged the younger woman, thus building a working relationship that extended beyond Perey's initial intentions.

Discovers Francium

Perey worked with Curie until the latter's death in 1934; thereafter she continued her mentor's research. Perey discovered the sequence of events that lead to the process known as the actinium radioactive decay series. This research inadvertently led to her most important discovery. She was aware of the existence of actinouranium, actinium–B, actinium–C, and actinium–D as part of the decay series she was trying to interpret. During this time, scientists were still trying to discover what they then believed to be the only three elements missing in the Periodic Table (which at the time contained 92 elements). One of these was Element 87. As Perey attempted to confirm her results of actinium radioactive decay, she found that other elements kept cropping up, disrupting the procedure. One of the elements was Element 87, with an atomic weight of 223. The element was highly charged—in fact, the most electropositive of all the elements. Because of this property, she considered naming it catium (from cation, which is a term for positively charged ions). But the word sounded too much like "cat" to her colleagues. As a result, she decided on francium, in honor of her homeland (and the place where the element had been discovered).

The following year, Perey took a position at France's National Center for Scientific Research. She remained there until 1949, when she became a professor of nuclear physics at the University of Strassbourg. She later became director of Strassbourg's Nuclear Research Center, holding that post for the rest of her life. By the time of her admission into the French Academy, Perey had already been diagnosed with the cancer that would slowly kill her. (She was undergoing treatment at the time of her appointment and was unable to attend the ceremonies.) She remained at the Nuclear Research Center and continued to conduct research. Eventually, the battle against the cancer grew more fierce, and, after a fifteen–year struggle, she succumbed in Louveciennes, France, on May 14, 1975.

FURTHER READING

Books

Brock, William H. *The Norton History of Chemistry.* Norton, 1992.

Heiserman, David L. *Exploring Chemical Elements and Their Compounds.* TAB Books, 1992.

Reid, Robert. *Marie Curie.* Saturday Review Press/Dutton, 1974.

Vare, Ethlie Ann and Greg Ptacek. *Mothers of Invention: From the Bra to the Bomb: Forgotten Women and Their Unforgettable Ideas.* New York: Morrow, 1988.

Periodicals

Times, London (May 15, 1975): 20.

Sketch by George A. Milite

Candace Dorinda Bebe Pert
1946–
American neuroscientist and biochemist

Candace B. Pert is a leading researcher in the field of chemical receptors, places in the body where molecules of a drug or natural chemical fit like a key into a lock, thus stimulating or inhibiting various physiological or emotional effects. As a graduate student, Pert codiscovered the brain's opiate receptors, areas that fit painkilling substances such as morphine. Her work led to the discovery of endorphins, the naturally occurring substances manufactured in the brain that relieve pain and produce sensations of pleasure.

Candace Dorinda Bebe Pert was born in New York City on June 26, 1946, to Mildred and Robert Pert. She went to General Douglas MacArthur High School in Levittown, New York. She attended Hofstra University but dropped out in 1966. That year she married Agu Pert and the couple moved to Philadelphia so that her husband could get a doctorate at Bryn Mawr College. In 1966, Candace Pert gave birth to the first of the couple's three children.

In 1967, to help support the family, Pert took a job as a cocktail waitress. On one occasion she chatted with a customer who turned out be an assistant dean at Bryn Mawr. The dean encouraged Pert to finish her B.A. at Bryn Mawr, and helped her through the admissions process. In 1970, Pert got her B.A. in biology and that year entered the doctoral pharmacology program at Johns Hopkins University in Baltimore.

Her first research assignment, working under Dr. Solomon Snyder, was to explore the mechanisms that regulate the production of acetylcholine, the body's most important neurotransmitter. Neurotransmitters are chemicals that stimulate or inhibit other neurons throughout the body, which in turn regulate the heart and other organs. Then in the summer of 1972, again working with Dr. Snyder, she embarked on her next project, the search for an opiate receptor. Opiate receptors were believed to exist, but finding them was another matter. Although techniques for locating receptors of hormones had been put into practice, many scientists thought it would be difficult, if not impossible, to transfer the technique to an opiate receptor.

Makes Surprising Discovery of Opiate Receptors

Receptors evolve from a chain of amino–acid molecules; these molecules are shaped by electrical forces into a three–dimensional shape with an electrically active indentation which recognizes correspondingly shaped molecules. These indentations are the points at which a receptor binds with a chemical substance or neurotransmitter. Using technology borrowed from identifying insulin receptors, Pert used radioactive drugs to identify receptor molecules that bonded with morphine and other opiate drugs in animal brain cells. The first report on her finding was published in *Science* in March 1973. Pert went on to investigate whether opiate receptors developed before birth. She used pregnant rats to evaluate the brains of the fetuses and found that during fetal development opiate receptors were present.

Pert and her colleagues mulled over why opiate receptors existed. It was certainly not that animals had evolved opiate receptors to interact with poppy plants, the natural source of opium. The scientist speculated that there might be an unknown neurotransmitter, naturally produced in the body, that fulfilled a similar function. Other experiments had already shown that stimulating the brainstem of rats caused pain relief, and that the best pain relief was obtained when a specific part of the brain was stimulated. After initial investigations proved inconclusive, Pert turned to other areas of research. Eventually two Scottish scientists, John Hughes and Hans Kosterlitz, found the transmitters, which they called endorphins.

The discovery of endorphins led to the discovery of other types of receptors and corresponding chemicals in the brain. Uncovering the intricate system of chemicals changed the scientific conception of the brain as an organ that signals the rest of the body using just a few chemicals. Now it is understood that the nervous system uses many substances to signal pain, pleasure and emotions as well as sensory data. Many had mistakenly hoped that the discoveries would immediately result in a cure for drug addictions or a nonaddicting pain killer for cancer patients, especially since the media had sensationalized these possibilities. Although these hopes proved over optimistic, in 1978 Snyder, Hughes and Kosterlitz received the prestigious Lasker Award for their discoveries; Pert did not. The fact that the biochemist, who had received her Ph.D. in 1974, had not been recognized for her part in the discovery caused a controversy that even erupted on the editorial pages of the prominent journal *Science.*

Pert refused to become involved in any controversy, however, and continued on at Hopkins as a National Institutes of Health fellow from 1974–1975, as a staff fellow from 1975–1977, a senior staff fellow from 1977–1978, and then as research pharmacologist from 1978–1982. In 1982, she became chief of the section on brain chemistry at the National Institutes of Mental Health (NIMH). There, the neuroscientist turned her attention to Valium receptors in the brain and the receptors where the street drug PCP, or "angel dust," takes hold. In 1986, Pert led the NIMH team that discovered peptide T. Peptides are substances that are synthesized from amino acids and are intermediate in molecular weight and chemical properties between amino acids and proteins, and have been linked to the manifestation of emotions.

Pert left NIMH in 1987 and worked for laboratories in the private sector. She also started her own company, Peptide Design, to encourage research on peptides. The company was in existence from 1987–1990. Since then, Pert has become an adjunct professor in the department of physiology at Georgetown University. Among her other areas of research have been investigations into the immune system and the nature of the human immunodeficiency virus (HIV) that causes AIDS. Pert won the Arthur S. Fleming Award in 1979. She is a member of the American Society of Pharmacologists and Experimental Therapeutics; the American Society of Biological Chemists; the Society of Neuroscientists; and the International Narcotics Research Conference.

Since her first discovery of an opiate receptor, Pert has located endorphin receptors throughout the body, even in the pituitary gland. She suspects that the location of receptors in sites where there is no clear connection with conscious pain serves the function of signaling the central nervous system when there is a problem with an organ. She believes, as she told an *Omni* interviewer, that scientists will eventually be able to chart the various receptors of the brain and the reactions they produce. "There's no doubt in my mind that one day—and I don't think that day is all that far away—we'll be able to make a color-coded map of the brain. A color–coded wiring diagram, with blue for one neurochemical, red for another, and so on—that's the neuroscientist's ambition."

SELECTED WRITINGS BY PERT:

Periodicals

(With Solomon Snyder) "The Opiate Receptor: Demonstration in Nervous Tissue." *Science* (March 2, 1973).

(With others) "Octapeptides Deduced From the Neuropeptide Receptor-like Pattern of Antigen T4 in Brain Potently Inhibit Human Immuno-deficiency Virus Receptor Binding and T-Cell Infectivity." *Academy of Science USA* 83 (1986): 9254–9258.

FURTHER READING:

Books

Snyder, Solomon. *Brainstorming: The Science and Politics of Opiate Research.* Cambridge: Harvard University Press, 1989.

Weintraub, Pamela, ed. *The Omni Interviews*, Omni Press, 1984, pp. 118–31.

Periodicals

"The Body Telling the Mind." *Fortune* (September 8, 1980): 97.

Sketch by Margo Nash

Mary Locke Petermann
1908–1975
American biochemist

Mary Locke Petermann isolated and identified the structure of animal ribosomes, organelles that are now known as the sites of protein synthesis in cells. She began her original investigation of the particles (for a time they were known as "Petermann's particles") because they were interfering with her studies of DNA and RNA. This pioneering work and her continued research established the importance of ions in stabilizing ribosomes and elucidated ribosomal transformations.

Peterman was born in Laurium, Michigan, on February 25, 1908, one of three children and the only daughter of Albert Edward and Anna Mae (Grierson) Petermann. Her mother was a graduate of Ypsilanti State Teachers' College. Her father, a graduate of Cornell University, became a lawyer for Calumet and Hecla Consolidated Copper Company in Calumet, Michigan, after World War I; he later was president and general manager. The Petermann family lived

Mary Locke Petermann (The Library of Congress. Reproduced by permission.)

in a large company house and enjoyed high status in the community.

Petermann was interested in science at an early age and decided in high school that she wanted to pursue a career in science. Her counselor advised against it, telling her that her only option with a science degree would be teaching at a woman's college. Mary was undeterred and after graduating from Calumet High School in 1924, entered Smith College as a chemistry major. But she credited Smith's strong liberal arts standing as a particularly important element of her education. Most of her friends at Smith, in fact, were humanities majors, and Petermann said later that their influence gave her a more well–rounded background than she would have gotten if she spent all her time with other science students.

In 1929, she graduated from Smith with high honors in chemistry and membership in Phi Beta Kappa. After a year at Yale University as a technician, she spent four years working at the Boston Psychopathic Hospital, investigating the acid–base balance of mental patients. In 1936 she entered the University of Wisconsin; she received a Ph.D. degree in physiological chemistry in 1939, with a thesis project on the role of the adrenal cortex in ion regulation.

Discovers "Petermann's Particles"

In 1939 Petermann became the first woman chemist on the staff of the Department of Physical Chemistry at the University of Wisconsin. She remained at Wisconsin as a postdoctoral researcher until 1945. During these six years she and Alwin M. Pappenheimer began to investigate the physical chemistry of proteins. Petermann discovered what were at first called "Petermann's particles," but were named ribosomes at a meeting of the Biophysical Society in 1958. While Petermann was doing her research at Sloan–Kettering, George Palade was doing similar research at the Rockefeller Institute. The ribosomes were alternately known as "Palade's particles." When they were named ribosomes in 1958, Palade was hailed as the "father of the particles." He pointed out that in that case, Petermann deserved credit as the "mother of the particles." Ribosomes are structures where protein synthesis occurs in a cell. Petermann's research isolated several types of ribosomes and clarified their properties. She also pioneered the study of antibodies. This research later led to Rodney Porter winning a Nobel Prize in 1972 for his work on the structure of immunoglobulins.

After leaving the University of Wisconsin in 1945, Petermann accepted the position of research chemist at Memorial Hospital in New York City to explore the role of plasma proteins in cancer. (According to Mary L. Moller, Petermann had been recommended to the director, Cornelius Rhoads, as "the girl out in Wisconsin.") In 1946 she was appointed Finney–Howell Foundation fellow at the newly founded Sloan–Kettering Institute, where she explored the role of nucleoproteins in cancer. She became an associate member of the institute in 1960, the first woman member in 1963, and member emeritus in 1973 when she retired. Concurrent with her work at Sloan–Kettering, she also taught biochemistry in the Sloan–Kettering Division, Graduate School of Medical Sciences, Cornell University. In 1966, she became the first woman appointed a full professor at Cornell. She authored or coauthored almost 100 scientific papers.

As the Sloan Award recipient in 1963, Petermann was honored for what the accompanying citation explained was her "many basic and distinguished contributions to the knowledge of the relevance of proteins and nucleoproteins in abnormal growth. An even greater contribution has been her fundamental work on the nature of the cell ribosome." Petermann used her award money to work for a year in the Swedish laboratory of Nobel laureate Arne Tiselius. She also lectured in several European countries, including England and France. In 1966 she received the Garvan Medal of the American Chemical Society, which honors contributions made by women scientists, an honorary doctorate from Smith College, and the Distinguished Service Award from the American Academy of Achievement.

Petermann never married. In 1974, the year before her death, she organized the Memorial Sloan–Kettering Cancer Center Association for Professional Women and served as its first president. She died in Philadelphia on December 13, 1975, of intestinal cancer, which had been misdiagnosed as a "nervous stomach" earlier that year. In 1976 the Educational Foundation of the Association for Women in Science named one of its graduate scholarships in her honor.

SELECTED WRITINGS BY PETERMANN:

Books

The Physical and Chemical Properties of Ribosomes. Oxford: Elsevier Publishing Company, 1964.

Periodicals

"How Does a Ribosome Translate Linear Genetic Information?" *Subcellular Chemistry* 1 (1971): 73.

FURTHER READING

Books

Moller, Mary L. "Mary Locke Petermann (1908–1975)." In *Women in Chemistry and Physics.* Grinstein, Louise S., Rose K. Rose, and Miriam H. Rafailovich, eds. Wesport, CT: Greenwood Press, 1993.

O'Neill, Lois Decker, ed. *The Women's Book of World Records and Achievements.* New York: Doubleday, 1979.

Sketch by Jill Carpenter

Rózsa Péter
1905–1977
Hungarian mathematician

Rózsa Péter was one of the early investigators in the field of recursive functions, a branch of mathematical logic. Recursive functions are those mathematical functions whose values can be established at every point, for whole numbers one and above. These functions are used to study the structure of number classes or functions in terms of the complexity of the calculations required to determine them, and have useful applications to computers and other automatic systems. Péter wrote two books and numerous papers on recursive functions, which are related to Alan Turing's theory of algorithms and machines and to Kurt Gödel's undecidability theorem of self-referential equations. Péter also wrote a popular treatment of mathematics, *Playing with Infinity*, which was translated into 14 languages. A teacher and teacher-training instructor before her appointment to a university post, Péter won national awards for her contributions to mathematics education and to mathematics.

Péter was born in Budapest on February 17, 1905. She received her high school diploma from Mária Terézia Girls' School in 1922, then entered the university in Budapest to study chemistry. Although her father, an attorney, wanted her to stay in that field, Péter changed to the study of mathematics. One of her classmates was László Kalmár, her future teacher and colleague. Péter graduated from the university in 1927, and for two years after graduation she had no permanent job, but tutored privately and took temporary teaching assignments.

In 1932, Péter attended the International Mathematics Conference in Zurich, where she presented a lecture on mathematical logic. She published papers on recursive functions in the period 1934–1936, and received her Ph.D. summa cum laude in 1935. In 1937, Péter became a contributing editor of the *Journal of Symbolic Logic*. Péter lost her teaching position in 1939 due to the Fascist laws of that year; Hungary was an ally of Nazi Germany and held similar purges of academics. Nevertheless, she published papers in Hungarian journals in 1940 and 1941.

In 1943, Péter published her book, *Playing with Infinity*, which described ideas in number theory, geometry, calculus and logic, including Güdel's undecidability theory, for the layman. The book, many copies of which were destroyed by bombing during World War II, could not be distributed until 1945. The war claimed the life of Péter's brother, Dr. Nicholas Politzer, in 1945, as well as the lives of her friend and fellow mathematician, Pál Csillag, and her young pupil, Káto Fuchs, who had assisted Péter with *Playing with Infinity*.

In the late 1940s, Péter taught high school and then became head of the mathematics department of the Pedological College in Budapest. She also wrote textbooks for high school mathematics. In the 1950s, Péter published further studies of recursive functions; her 1951 book, *Recursive Functions*, was the first treatment of the subject in book form and reinforced her status as "the leading contributor to the special theory of recursive functions," as S. C. Kleene observed in the *Bulletin of the American Mathematical Society*.

Péter was appointed professor of mathematics at Eötvös Loránd University in Budapest in 1955, where she taught mathematical logic and set theory. The official publication of *Playing with Infinity* occurred in 1957. In this version, she wrote in the preface, she tried "to present concepts with complete clarity and purity so that some new light may have been thrown on the subject even for mathematicians and certainly for teachers."

In the 1960s and 1970s, Péter studied the relationship between recursive functions and computer programming, in particular, the relationship of recursive functions to the programming languages Algol and Lisp. Péter retired in 1975. She continued her research, however, publishing *Recursive Functions in Computer Theory* in 1976.

Péter's awards included the Kossuth Prize in 1951 for her scientific and pedagogical work, and the State Award, Silver Degree in 1970 and Gold Degree in 1973. Péter was a member of the Hungarian Academy of Sciences and was made honorary President of the János Bolyai Mathematical Association in 1975. Interested in literature, film and art as well as mathematics, Péter translated poetry from German and corresponded with the literary critic Marcel Benedek.

She noted in *Playing with Infinity* that her mathematical studies were not so different from the arts: "I love mathematics not only for its technical applications, but principally because it is beautiful; because man has breathed his spirit of play into it, and because it has given him his greatest game—the encompassing of the infinite." Péter died on February 17, 1977.

SELECTED WRITINGS BY PÉTER:

Playing with Infinity: Mathematics for Everyman. Translated by Z. P. Dienes, 1962

Recursive Functions. Third revised edition, translated by István Földes, 1967

Recursive Functions in Computer Theory. Translated by I. Juhász, 1981

FURTHER READING

Books

"Algorithms and Recursive Functions." In *Mathematics at a Glance.* 2d ed. New York: Van Nostrand Reinhold, 1989, pp. 340–

Periodicals

Császár, Akos. "Rózsa Péter: February 17, 1905–February 16, 1977." *Matematikai Lapok* (published in Hungarian), 25 (1974): 257–258.

Dömölki, Bálint, et al. "The Scientific Work of Rózsa Péter." *Matematikai Lapok* (published in Hungarian), 16 (1965): 171–184.

Kleene, S.C. "Rekursive Funktionen." *Bulletin of the American Mathematical Society* (March 1952): 270–272.

Nelson, D. "Rózsa Péter, Rekursive Funktionen." *Mathematical Reviews* (1952): 421–422.

"Playing with Infinity: Telegraphic Reviews." *American Mathematical Monthly* 84, (February 1977): 147.

Robinson, Raphael M. "Rózsa Péter. Rekursive Funktionen." *Journal of Symbolic Logic* 16 (1951): 280–282.

Ruzsa, Imre Z. and János Urbán, "In Memoriam Rózsa Péter." *Matematikai Lapok* (published in Hungarian), 26 (1975): 125–137.

Sudborough, I. Hal. "Rózsa Péter, Rekursive Funktionen in der Komputer–Theorie." *Mathematical Reviews* 55, no. 6926.

Turán, Pál. "To the Memory of Mathematician Victims of Fascism." *Matematikai Lapok* (published in Hungarian), 26 (1975): 259–263.

Other

Kocsor, Klára, notes on articles in Hungarian, January, 1994.

Sketch by Sally M. Moite

Almira (Hart) Lincoln Phelps
1793–1884
American science writer and educator

Almira Hart Lincoln Phelps was an educator and the author of science textbooks. She had a major influence on the development of science education in nineteenth–century America, and on the development of secondary education for young women. Her teaching innovations included experimental methods in botany and chemistry.

Born in Berlin, Connecticut in 1793, Phelps was the youngest of 17 children of Samuel Hart and the tenth child with his second wife Lydia Hinsdale Hart. Growing up on the family farm, Phelps was influenced by the religious, but politically progressive views, of her parents. Her sister Emma was her first teacher, and their intellectual family life supplemented her education in the local schools. Phelps studied at the Berlin Academy, and in 1809 she began teaching at a rural school near Hartford, Connecticut. The following year, she went to live with her sister, Emma Willard, and her husband, physician John Willard. Emma Willard was the head of a female academy in Middlebury, Vermont, and Phelps studied mathematics and philosophy with Emma and Willard's nephew, who was a student at Middlebury College.

In 1812 Phelps attended her cousin Nancy Hinsdale's school for girls in Pittsfield, Massachusetts, in order to obtain her teaching credentials for secondary school, and the following year she returned to teach at the Berlin Academy. In 1814, Phelps opened a small boarding school for girls in her home. Two years later, she became headmistress of an academy in Sandy Hill, New York. There, using methods developed by Emma Willard, she introduced several new subjects to the curriculum.

Becomes Botanist

Phelps left teaching to marry Simeon Lincoln, a conservative newspaper editor in Hartford, in 1817. Their first child, a son born in 1820, lived less than a year. Lincoln died of yellow fever in 1823, leaving Phelps with two baby daughters to support, and the debts from both her husband's and her father–in–law's estates. She returned to teaching at a public school in New Britain, Connecticut. Shortly thereafter, Phelps joined the staff of Emma Willard's Troy Female Seminary in New York, a model boarding school for girls. While teaching and sharing administrative duties with her sister, Phelps was influenced by the famous educator Amos Eaton, a botanist and naturalist at the Troy Lyceum and later, founder of Rensselaer Polytechnic Institute. A believer in the education of women, Eaton's science lectures at the Lyceum attracted students from the Female Seminary and included experiments and demonstrations. For the first time, Phelps began to study science. Eaton became her mentor in both botany and chemistry, and Phelps developed a botany course for her students that included many field trips. Since no suitable science textbooks were available at the time, Eaton encouraged Phelps to write one.

Phelps's *Familiar Lectures on Botany*, published in 1829, was the first of her popular textbooks. It went through nine editions in ten years and had sold 375,000 copies before the end of the century. It also was popular in Europe. The text stressed field observations and collections, as well as botanical nomenclature and taxonomy or classification. Phelps followed this with other texts covering chemistry, geology, and natural philosophy. Her science texts included poetry, history, and imaginative ideas, as well as religion and morality. These books helped to establish a standard science curriculum in the public schools. Their success eventually made Phelps both wealthy and famous. Her sister Emma Willard also became a successful author of books on science and history.

Works to Educate Young Women

In 1831, she married John Phelps, a widower with six children, including a daughter who was a student at the Troy Seminary. Phelps moved with her two daughters to Vermont, where her new husband was a lawyer and state senator. The Phelpses had another son in 1833 and a daughter in 1836. Over the next eight years, although devoted to her large family and her church and social responsibilities, Phelps continued to write texts, including *Lectures to Young Ladies* in 1833. She also revised her botany book, wrote magazine articles, and gave lectures on education.

With her husband's support, Phelps accepted a position as principal of a new female seminary in 1838, and the family moved to West Chester, Pennsylvania. However, the school failed, and the following year Phelps became superintendent of a new school in New Jersey, the Rahway Female Institute. In 1841, she became principal of Patapsco Female Institute at Ellicott's Mills, Maryland. Her husband was the school's business manager until his death. Patapsco provided Phelps with the opportunity to develop a school that, like the Troy Female Seminary, offered girls a college–level curriculum, particularly in the sciences. The school trained young women as teachers and embodied Phelps's educational ideals.

Phelps retired to Baltimore in 1856, after her daughter Jane died in a railroad accident. She continued writing, completing more than 20 books and numerous articles during her lifetime. In 1859, Phelps was elected to the American Association for the Advancement of Science, and she presented several papers at their meetings. Although she worked for educational opportunities for women, Phelps was an active member of the Woman's Anti–Suffrage Association. She died in Baltimore in 1884, on her 91st birthday. Her herbarium of plants collected throughout her life was presented to the Maryland Academy of Sciences, of which she was the first woman member.

SELECTED WRITINGS BY PHELPS:

Books

Familiar Lectures on Botany. Including Practical and Elementary Botany, with General and Specific Descriptions of the most Common Native and Foreign Plants, and a Vocabulary of Botanical Terms. For the Use of Higher Schools and Academies. Hartford: H. and F. J. Huntington, 1829.

Lectures to Young Ladies, Comprising Outlines and Applications of the Different Branches of Female Education, for the use of Female schools, and Private Libraries. Delivered to the Pupils of Troy Female Seminary. Boston: Carter, Hendee and Co., 1833.

Botany for Beginners: An Introduction to Mrs. Lincoln's Lectures on Botany. For the Use of Common Schools and the Younger Pupils of Higher Schools and Academies. New York: Huntington & Savage, 1849.

FURTHER READING

Books

Arnold, Lois Barber. *Four Lives in Science: Women's Education in the Nineteenth Century*. New York: Schocken, 1984.

Bolzau, Emma L. *Almira Hart Lincoln Phelps: Her Life and Work*. Philadelphia: University of Pennsylvania Press, 1936.

Ogilvie, Marilyn Bailey. *Women in Science, Antiquity through the Nineteenth Century: A Biographical Dictionary with Annotated Bibliography*. Cambridge: MIT Press, 1991.

Rudolph, Frederick. "Almira Hart Lincoln Phelps." In *Notable American Women 1607–1950: A Biographical Dictionary*. Edited by Edward T. James, Janet Wilson James, and Paul W. Boyer. Cambridge: Harvard University Press, 1971.

Slack, Nancy G. "Nineteenth–Century American Women Botanists: Wives, Widows, and Work." In *Uneasy Careers and Intimate Lives: Women in Science 1789–1979*. Edited by Pnina G. Abir–Am and Dorinda Outram. New Brunswick: Rutgers University Press, 1987.

Periodicals

Kohlstedt, Sally Gregory. "In from the Periphery: American Women in Science, 1830–1880." *Signs* (Autumn 1978): 81–96.

Sketch by Margaret Alic

Lucy Weston Pickett
1904–1997
American chemist

A pioneer in the use of spectroscopy for the study of molecules, Lucy Weston Pickett is remembered not only for her achievements in chemistry research, but also for her role in educating hundreds of future chemists and scientists in the 38 years she taught with distinction at Mt. Holyoke College in Massachusetts.

Pickett was born in Beverly, Massachusetts in 1904, the daughter descendant of a long line of New England sea captains. Her mother, Lucy Weston, was an elementary school principal. Pickett had one brother, Thomas, whose professional life paralleled hers in later years, and they remained close throughout their lives. Young Pickett had intended to study Latin, but changed her mind during her first college semester, thanks to an inspiring freshman course in chemistry. By her junior year, she was carrying a double major in chemistry and mathematics. She graduated *summa cum laude* in 1925 from Mt. Holyoke.

Like many female science graduates of her time, Pickett believed that she needed to sacrifice either professional ambition or marriage, considered to be mutually–exclusive interests for many women professionals. Despite an early romance in college, Pickett decided to defer marriage and pursue chemistry professionally, and she returned to Mt. Holyoke for her master's in chemistry, obtained in 1927. While completing her doctoral degree at the University of Chicago, Pickett was offered a teaching position at her alma mater, Mt. Holyoke, and she remained there from 1930 until her retirement in 1968. When she joined the department faculty, she was the youngest member, now among a group of her former professors and mentors.

Pickett's years as an educator were enhanced by her many fellowship awards, under which she completed significant research in the areas of x–ray crystallography, molecular structure and analysis (through spectroscopy), and the vacuum ultraviolet spectra of select organic compounds. Her early fellowships enabled her to continue with graduate school (Mary E. Woolley Fellowship, 1928–1929, and Robert Carr Fellowship, 1929–1930). Another was under the auspices of the American Association of University Women (AAUW), under which she traveled to the Royal Institution in London to work with the renowned x–ray crystallographer, Sir William Bragg (1932–1933). In 1938, Pickett continued molecular spectroscopic research at Harvard under a Labor Fellowship, during which time she was introduced to infrared techniques. She continued this work at the University of Liege in Belgium under an Educational Foundation fellowship (1939). From these collaborative efforts with eminent scientists of the time came two of her first, and important, published research papers (Pickett and Corin, 1939; Pickett and Henri, 1939). During the next two decades, Pickett continued to teach and further her research under numerous grants from various sources, and she also published several technical papers in professional journals. The routine use of spectroscopy in contemporary science is, to a large degree, a result of Pickett's and her colleagues' fundamental research and expansive application of that methodology during those years.

Pickett, when at Mt. Holyoke, lived off campus with three other professors, all sharing a housekeeper. The arrangement allowed her to be free of domestic concerns and to focus on her research and teaching, for which she is remembered. Her father passed away during this time, in 1935, and a few years later, her mother came to live with her. Pickett, meanwhile, rose through her tenured ranks quite rapidly, being promoted from instructor to assistant professor in 1934, to associate in 1940, and to full professor in 1945, half the average time for such advancement. She was named the Camille and Henry Dreyfus Professor in 1954, and she was the first Mary Lyon Professor in 1958 (both Mt. Holyoke distinctions). Pickett also chaired the chemistry department at the college from 1954–1962.

In 1957, Pickett was the honored recipient of the American Chemical Society's prestigious Garvan Award, recognizing women for their achievement in the sciences, in this case, for Pickett's valuable research in molecular spectroscopy. The following year, she received an honorary doctorate degree from Ripon College in Wisconsin. She retired from Mt. Holyoke in 1968, at which time she was honored with the establishment of the Lucy W. Pickett Lectureship, which funds a lecture series at the college, presented by distinguished world scientists. She was also awarded an honorary Doctor of Science degree from Mt. Holyoke.

Pickett moved to Bradenton, Florida after retirement, but that was hardly the end of her service to others. She began to tutor disadvantaged students and became a volunteer in a local retirement home, a library, a hospital, and a residential facility for handicapped persons. She also traveled to Peru (where she became quite fascinated with Mayan cultures), Africa, Russia, and Greece. She died back home in Bradenton in 1997, at the age of 93. A memorial fund in her name has been set up at Mt. Holyoke College to help support faculty research projects.

SELECTED WRITINGS BY PICKETT:

Periodicals

"Some new experiments on the chemical effects of X–rays and the energy relations involved." *JACS* 52 (1930): 465–479.

(With G.L. Clark and E.D. Johnson) "New studies on the chemical effects of X–rays." *Radiology* 50 (1930): 245–261

(With E.P. Carr and H. Strucken) "The absorption spectra of a series of dienes." *RMP* 14 (1942):260–264.

"Developments in the teaching of analytical chemistry." *JCE* 20 (1943): 102.

(with B.B. Loeffler and E. Eberlin) "Far ultraviolet absorption spectra of small–ring hydrocarbons." *JCP* 28 (1958): 345–347.

FURTHER READING

Books

Grinstein, Louis S., Rose K. Rose, and Miriam H. Rafailovich, eds. "Women in Chemistry and Physics." Westport, CT: Greenwood Press, 1997, 495–501.

Kass–Simon, G. and Patricia Farnes, eds. "Women of Science: Righting the Record." Bloomington: Indiana University Press, 1993, 312–313.

Shearer, Benjamin F. and Barbara S. Shearer, eds. "Notable Women in the Physical Sciences." Westport, CT: Greenwood Press, 1997, 311–315.

Other

"New & Notable," under *The College Street Journal* (See 'In Memoriam') http://www.mtholyoke.edu/offices/comm/csj/971205/notable.html, 3.

"'Women Studying Together': Science Education for American Women in the Nineteenth Century." http://www.cs.brown.edu/people/plm/wis/scied.html

Sketch by Lauri R. Harding

Susan LaFlesche Picotte
18651915
Native American physician

Susan LaFlesche Picotte (The Granger Collection, New York. Reproduced by permission.)

Susan LaFlesche Picotte was the first Native American women physician in the United States. She practiced preventive medicine, and urged adoption of modern hygienic practices and public sanitation. She lobbied to have a hospital established on the Omaha reservation and won, serving as its attending physician for the last two years of her life. The hospital was renamed in her honor after her death.

Susan LaFlesche was born on June 17, 1865, on the Omaha reservation in northeastern Nebraska. She was the daughter of Chief Joseph LaFlesche (Iron Eye) and his wife Mary Gale (One Woman). Her father was of French and Ponca ancestry; her mother was British and Omaha. A progressive leader of his people, Chief LaFlesche saw to it that his five children received a good education to prepare them for the larger world beyond the reservation.

LaFlesche began her education at mission schools on the reservation. In 1879, following the footsteps of her eldest sister, Susette, she and another sister, Marguerite, were enrolled in a woman's seminary, the Elizabeth Institute for Young Ladies in New Jersey. This prepared LaFlesche to teach at the Presbyterian mission school on the Omaha reservation, which she did for two years. In 1884, she again left the reservation for the east, where she became a student at the Hampton Normal and Agricultural Institute in Virginia. This school began as an industrial school for freed slaves, and eventually admitted Native Americans. She graduated from Hampton with honors in 1886.

Becomes First Native American Physician

LaFlesche had dreamed of becoming a doctor from an early age. She confided her ambition to Alice Cunningham Fletcher, an anthropologist and champion of Native American rights, who was living and working on the Omaha reservation. In 1886, through Fletcher's assistance, LaFlesche was sponsored by the Connecticut branch of the Women's National Indian Association for enrollment at the Women's Medical College in Philadelphia, Pennsylvania. She was an excellent student, graduating at the head of her class in 1889 as the nation's first Native American woman physician. She was not yet 24 years old.

After completing a short internship in Philadelphia, LaFlesche returned home. She was appointed by the United States government as physician for the Omaha agency school. She also accepted the post of medical missionary for Women's National Indian Association, her medical school benefactor.

In these dual roles, she ministered to her people's physical and spiritual needs, treating as many as 100 patients a month, in addition to assisting them with financial and personal difficulties. Through her network of government and missionary contacts, she fought to ease reservation restrictions and boost tribal autonomy. At the same time, she battled the twin scourges of poverty and alcoholism within the 1,300–member tribe. She was a firm believer in preventive medicine, and urged adoption of modern hygienic practices and public sanitation. Her determined attempts to abate the alcohol addiction that caused so much misery and death on the reservation helped bring about the passage of laws against the sale of liquor and prohibition stipulations in property leases.

The difficult task of serving as doctor, teacher, interpreter, and advocate took its toll. She traveled, most often on horseback, in all kinds of weather to see her far-flung patients. As a result, she suffered from poor health throughout her life. In 1893, she stepped down from her post as school physician because the work had become too physically demanding.

Shortly thereafter, she married Henry Picotte, a farmer of French and Sioux ancestry. He was the brother-in-law of her sister, Marguerite. They established a home in Bancroft, Nebraska, where she continued to practice medicine. They had two sons, Caryl and Pierre. Henry died in 1905 after a long illness.

After her husband's death, LaFlesche Picotte became active as a missionary for the Presbyterian Board of Home Missions. At this time, she also became involved in efforts against government restrictions on reservation lands, helping to win tribal control over land allotments. In 1913, a lifelong dream and 30 years of committed effort came to fruition when the Presbyterian Board established a hospital at Walthill, a town on the Omaha reservation. LaFlesche Picotte served as its attending physician for the last two years of her life. She died at Walthill on September 18, 1915, from a cancerous bone infection. The hospital was renamed in her honor.

FURTHER READING

Books

Bataille, Gretchen, ed. *Native American Women.* New York & London: Garland Publishing, 1993, pp. 147–149.

Garrity, John A. and Mark C. Cannes, eds. *American National Biography.* Vol. 17. New York: Oxford University Press, 1999, pp. 487–488.

Green, Norma Kidd. *Iron Eye's Family: The Children of Joseph LaFlesche.* Lincoln: Johnson Publishing, 1969.

James, Edward T., ed. *Notable American Women, 1607–1950.* Vol. III. Cambridge, MA: Belknap Press, 1971, pp. 65–66.

Mathes, Valerie Sherer. "Dr. Susan LaFlesche Picotte: The Reformed and the Reformer." *Indian Lives: Essays on Nineteenth and Twentieth–Century Native Americans.* Albuquerque: University of New Mexico Press, 1985, pp. 61–90.

Periodicals

Hauptman, Laurence. "Medicine Woman: Susan LaFlesche, 1865–1915." *New York State Journal of Medicine* (September 1967): 1783–88.

Mathes, Valerie Sherer. "Susan LaFlesche Picotte: Nebraska's Indian Physician, 1865–1915." *Nebraska History* 63 (Winter 1982): 502–31.

Other

LaFlesche Family Papers. Nebraska State Historical Society, Lincoln.

Sketch by Jane Stewart Cook

Elizabeth Lucas Pinckney
1722(?)–1793
American agricultural scientist

Elizabeth Lucas Pinckney, usually referred to as Eliza Pinckney, was a plantation manager who successfully experimented with the cultivation and extraction of indigo for dyes. She also left one of the largest surviving collections of letters written by an American colonial woman.

Born in the West Indies, probably in 1722, Pinckney was the eldest of four children of George Lucas, a lieutenant colonel in the British army, who later became lieutenant governor of the British colony of Antiqua. Pinckney was educated in England and became an intellectual and accomplished young woman. When her mother became ill in 1738, her father moved the family to his plantation on Wappoo Creek in South Carolina, not far from Charleston. However the following year, with the outbreak of the War of Jenkins' Ear, a sea–based conflict between England and Spain, Lucas was forced to return to the army in Antigua. Pinckney took over the management of all three of her father's plantations in the South Carolina.

At Wappoo, Pinckney had a fine library for her studies, and she tutored her sister Polly. She also taught two black girls to read, hoping to make them the teachers of the other black children on the plantation. Pinckney had always been interested in science, and in 1741 she sighted a comet whose return had been predicted by Sir Isaac Newton.

Experiments with Indigo

At her father's urging, Pinckney began to experiment with different types of plantation crops, including indigo, ginger, cotton, and alfalfa. Indigo, grown from West Indian seeds, was the most successful. At the time, British textile manufacturers were forced to buy indigo blue dyes from French colonies. Furthermore, rice was South Carolina's only staple export, and war in Europe had nearly eliminated the demand. Although earlier attempts at growing indigo in South Carolina had failed, Pinckney undertook a long series of experiments to determine the best time for sowing the seeds and the proper soil. In 1741, Lucas sent his daughter an experienced indigo maker, Nicholas Cromwell, from the French island of Montserrat, to teach her the complex process of producing dye from the freshly cut plants. However, Cromwell destroyed the first products with lime water, fearing that the fledgling South Carolina industry would out–compete that of his home island. Pinckney continued to experiment and finally, in 1744, with the help of Cromwell's brother Patrick, produced a successful crop and dye. Seed from the crop was widely distributed among local planters and, by 1747, almost 100,000 pounds of indigo were being exported from Carolina. Indigo remained the mainstay of the Carolina economy until the American Revolution.

Marries Charles Pinckney

Among Eliza Pinckney's close friends were Charles Pinckney and his wife, an educated couple from whom she often borrowed books. In 1744, following his first wife's death, she married Charles Pinckney, a lawyer and political figure 20 years her senior. They lived on the waterfront in Charleston, and Eliza Pinckney began cultivating silkworms and producing silk on his plantation on the Cooper River. She also experimented with the cultivation of flax and hemp. Within five years, the couple had four children, one of whom died in infancy. In 1753, the family moved to London, planning to stay until the children had completed their education. However when war broke out between England and France in 1758, Pinckney and her husband returned to Carolina. That year, Charles Pinckney died of malaria and Eliza Pinckney took over the operation of his seven plantations.

Pinckney's sons returned from England to fight in the American Revolution. Her son Charles became George Washington's aide, represented South Carolina at the Constitutional Convention, and ran for president of the United States in 1804 and 1808. Her son Thomas became governor of South Carolina.

In her later years, Pinckney lived with her widowed daughter, Harriott Horry, and helped to raise three of her son's motherless children. Pinckney died of cancer in 1793, while under medical care in Philadelphia. President George Washington was one of her pallbearers.

SELECTED WRITINGS BY PINCKNEY:

Books

(Elise Pinckney and Marvin R. Zahniser, eds.) *The Letterbook of Eliza Lucas Pinckney, 1739–1762*. Chapel Hill: University of North Carolina Press, 1997.

FURTHER READING

Books

Pinckney, Elise. "Elizabeth Lucas Pinckney." In *Notable American Women 1607–1950: A Biographical Dictionary*. Edited by Edward T. James, Janet Wilson James, and Paul W. Boyer. Cambridge: Harvard University Press, 1971.

Ravenel, Harriott Horry Rutledge. *Eliza Pinckney*. New York: Charles Scribner's Sons, 1902.

Sketch by Margaret Alic

Elena Lucrezia Cornaro Piscopia
1646–1684
Italian mathematician

Elena Cornaro Piscopia may have been the first woman to receive a doctoral degree. She earned her doctorate of philosophy from the University of Padua and became a lecturer in mathematics.

Born in 1646, into the wealthy, noble family of the Venetian House of Cornaro, Piscopia's family traced its lineage to the Roman family of Cornelii. Her ancestors included statesmen, cardinals, and popes. The husband of Queen Caterina Cornaro of Cyprus had conferred a castle named "Piscopia" on this branch of the family. Piscopia's mother was Zaneta Giovanna Boni, of Val di Sabia, near the city of Novara in the Piedmont Mountains. Her father, Gianbattista Cornaro Piscopia, a public official, devoted himself to his children's education. Piscopia had two older brothers, an older sister who died at an early age, and a younger sister.

Recognized as Child Prodigy

It was the parish priest at St. Luke's in Venice who first recognized the seven–year–old Piscopia as a prodigy. At the urging of Monsignor Gianbattista Fabris, she received tutoring in grammar, Latin, Greek, and music, by John Valier, Doctor Bartolotti, Alexander Anderson, and Luigi Ambrosio Grandenigo. Later she was taught mathematics by a Jesuit. By the age of 17, Piscopia was an excellent musician. She sang, composed music, and played the harpsichord, clavichord, harp, and violin. Piscopia also learned French, English, and Spanish, as well as philosophy, dialectics, and astronomy. But her first love was theology, and she studied Hebrew with the rabbi of the Venetian Synagogue, as well as the Arabic and Chaldaic languages. By the time she was 19, Piscopia was venerated as the most learned young woman in Italy. Scientists, clergy, and royalty from all over Europe came to the Palazzo Cornaro in Venice, and later to the smaller Palazzo Cornaro in Padua, to meet Piscopia. She participated in popular academic debates.

Enters the University of Padua

Piscopia, having promised herself to the Benedictine Order, refused several offers of marriage and secretly observed the monastic rules. Quietly, she devoted herself to the poor and sick. However, her father was anxious to show off her learning and wanted her to undergo the examinations and defend a thesis for a doctorate in theology. So in 1667, Piscopia petitioned the rector of the University of Padua, one of the most important seventeenth–century universities. Italian universities, unlike those in the rest of Europe, had never been completely closed to women, and the seventeenth century saw a resurgence in Italian women mathematicians and scientists. However, no woman had ever received a doctorate in theology. Although the rector approved her petition, various authorities objected. Finally a compromise was reached: Piscopia could work for her doctorate in philosophy. She attended classes at the University of Padua between 1672 and 1678. Her father provided her with servants, tutors, and female companions at his palace in Padua. As Nicola Fusco quoted from a letter that Piscopia wrote to her father from Padua, about 1672: "With the joy of my studies, the salubrity of the air, and the diligent care of the physicians, I feel much stronger; therefore, I hope that in the future I may resume my studies and thus rescue the name of our House from extinction and oblivion."

Piscopia underwent the usual examinations, although the university officials were determined that this would not set a precedent for other women. Piscopia was awarded her master's and doctorate of philosophy in 1678, in a ceremony at the cathedral of Padua, since the University Hall proved to be too small for the crowds who came to watch. Piscopia became a lecturer in mathematics at the university that same year. She died in 1684, at the age of 38. Although a few of Piscopia's literary writings, poetry, and letters, written in several languages, have survived, most of her manuscripts have been lost.

Piscopia was famous throughout Europe. The university had a medal coined in her honor and a marble statue of Piscopia stands in the old University Building of Padua. A large stained–glass window in the Gothic Library of Vassar College, in Poughkeepsie, New York, portrays Piscopia at her commencement. She also is depicted in a mural in the Italian Classroom of the Cathedral of Learning at the University of Pittsburgh. In the eighteenth century, Dorothea Erxleben cited Piscopia as a precedent for her own attempts to study for her medical degree in Germany. However it would be almost 300 years before another woman earned a doctorate at the University of Padua.

FURTHER READING

Books

Fusco, Nicola. *Elena Lucrezia Cornaro Piscopia 1646–1684.* Pittsburgh: The United States Committee for the Elena Lucrezia Cornaro Piscopia Tercentenary, 1975.

Mozans, H. J. [John Augustine Zahm]. *Women in Science.* 1913. Reprint, Cambridge: MIT Press, 1974.

Weiser, Marjorie P. K. and Jean S. Arbeiter. *Womanlist.* New York: Atheneum, 1981.

Sketch by Margaret Alic

Dorothy Riggs Pitelka
1920–1994
American zoologist

Dorothy Pitelka was known as an expert on protozoa, the single–celled animals that are among the most primitive forms of life. By understanding the structure of these tiny animals, she was able to better understand the workings of organisms such as viruses that cause certain types of cancer.

Her parents, Theodore Dalzell and Winifred Clark Riggs, were American citizens working in Marsovan, Turkey when Dorothy was born on September 13, 1920. She received her bachelor's degree from the University of Colorado in 1941 and from there went to the University of California–Berkeley, where she would get her Ph.D. in 1948 and pursue her work for the next 40 years. While at Berkeley, she met Frank Alois Pitelka, who like her was working toward a Ph.D. in zoology (and who also earned a reputation as an outstanding scientist); the two were married on February 5, 1943 and had three children. (One of those children, Louis, has also made a name for himself as a plant ecologist, studying the effects of pollutants on plant life.)

Beginning her Berkeley career as a lecturer in the zoology department, she was named assistant research zoologist in 1952 and research zoologist in 1953. She was named adjunct professor of zoology in 1971. Pitelka held these titles until her retirement in 1984, when she was given emerita status. In 1957–58, she was named a fellow of the U.S. Public Health Service's National Cancer Institute and conducted research in Paris.

Pitelka's research focused primarily on the structure and development of protozoa, which she examined under an electron microscope. She wrote a book on the subject, called, appropriately enough, *Electron–Microscopic Structure of Protozoa,* in 1963. She took her protozoan research a step further when she examined different tumors cells and viruses to find answers about their development and behavior particularly their interactions with other cellular structures.

Pitelka's achievements led to her election as president of the Society of Protozoologists in 1964 (she served until 1967). She was on the editorial boards of several zoology journals, and was a member of such organizations as the American Society of Cell Biology and the American Association of Cancer Research. Pitelka and her husband (who remained active at Berkeley as well) remained in Berkeley after her retirement, and it was there that she died on February 6, 1994.

SELECTED WRITINGS BY PITELKA:

Books

Pitelka, Dorothy Riggs. *Electron–Microscopic Structure of Protozoa.* Macmillan, 1963.

FURTHER READING

Books

American Men and Women of Science. 17th ed. (1989–90). R. R. Bowker, 1989.

Bailey, Martha J. *American Women in Science: A Biographical Dictionary.* Denver: ABC–CLIO, 1994.

World Who's Who in Science, Marquis Who's Who, 1969.

Sketch by George A. Milite

Margaret Pittman
1901–1995
American bacteriologist

Margaret Pittman identified the bacteria that are responsible for several diseases. She developed new methods for standardizing and testing vaccines against infectious diseases and contributed to our understanding of how vaccines work.

One of three children of Virginia Alice (McCormick) and James Pittman, Margaret Pittman was born in 1901 in Prairie Grove, Arkansas. At about 1908, the family moved to Cincinnati, Arkansas, formerly an Indian trading center, where Pittman and her older sister Helen often assisted their father, a country doctor, in his practice. Pittman attended a rural two–room school and then finished high school in three years while living with her grandparents in Prairie Grove. She spent two years at an academy in Silasm Springs, near her home, and then entered Hendrix College, a Methodist school in Conway, Arkansas. One of the few women at the college, Pittman majored in mathematics and biology, won the medal in mathematics, and graduated magna cum laude in 1923. Pittman and her brother and sister returned home from college each summer to help their widowed mother raise and can vegetables and fruit.

Pittman became a teacher of science and Spanish at the Girl's Academy of Galloway College, in Searcy, Arkansas. After one year, she became the principal of the school. Although she had hoped to attend medical school, she had saved only enough money in two years of teaching to pay for one year of graduate school in bacteriology at the University of Chicago. She received her master's degree in 1926 and was encouraged by her advisor, I. S. Falk, to study for her doctorate. Pittman received a research fellowship from the Influenza Commission of the Metropolitan Life Insurance Company, and she augmented this income with babysitting. She received her Ph.D. from the University of Chicago in 1929. Her thesis dealt with the virulence of the bacterium that causes pneumonia and the pathology of that disease in mice.

By the time she received her Ph.D., Pittman already was working as a research scientist with Rufus Cole at the Rockefeller Institute for Medical Research in New York City, studying the bacterium *Hemophilus influenzae*. By 1931, Pittman had isolated and identified six distinct types of this organism, including the type responsible for most childhood meningitis, and had developed an antiserum for treating this fatal disease. This work earned her an international reputation as a bacteriologist.

Identifies Bacterium Responsible for Meningitis

In 1934, with the country in the midst of the Depression, Pittman was forced to accept a lower–paying job at the New York Department of Health Laboratories, where she carried out diagnostic tests and prepared compounds. In 1936, she moved to the National Institutes of Health (NIH) in Washington, D. C. Initially, Pittman worked with Sara E. Branham, who had been her professor at the University of Chicago. One of their first discoveries was that the degree of the reaction between an antibody, or immune serum, and a bacterium was a measure of the potency of the antiserum. Although they published this work, it is usually credited to Orjan Ouchterlony, who rediscovered the phenomenon in 1949. Pittman and Branham were developing an antiserum against the meningococcus bacterium that causes a form of meningitis, and they introduced the use of statistical methods in this type of research, as well as a new method of standardizing the potency of the antiserum..

Pittman is thought to have been the first woman laboratory chief at the NIH. In 1941, when the NIH moved to Bethesda, Maryland, she was given her own laboratory. Because of the emergency medical needs created by the Second World War, Pittman began studying the problem of bacterial contamination in blood and blood products, such as antisera and vaccines, and brought about improvements in the preparation and testing of these products. Eventually, she became chief of the Laboratory of Bacterial Products in the Division of Biologics Standards.

Sets Standards for Whopping Cough Vaccine

In 1944, Pittman was asked to work on developing standards for the pertussis or whooping cough vaccine. Again, she introduced an improved statistical method for standardizing the vaccine. In the United States between 1945 and 1954, there was a 10–fold drop in mortality from whooping cough, as a result of her improvements. She was considered to be the world's expert on the taxonomy, or classification, of the organism that caused whooping cough, as well as on Hemophilus bacteria, and she identified the Hemophilus species that causes epidemic conjunctivitis, or "pinkeye."

Pittman was the NIH project director for the Cholera Research Laboratory in Dacca, East Pakistan, now Bangladesh, and she studied the relationship between laboratory tests and field trials of the cholera vaccine. She worked with the World Health Organization on cholera, tetanus, and typhoid vaccines, studied the mechanism of immunization against typhoid, and worked for the international standardization of vaccines. Following her retirement in 1971, Pittman continued to work at the NIH and as a consultant to various laboratories and government agencies. She published more than 92 scientific papers over the course of her career.

Pittman received a number of awards, including the Federal Woman's Award in 1970 and an honorary LL.D. in 1954 from Hendrix College. The NIH established a lecture series in her honor in 1994. PIttman was involved with numerous professional societies and served as the first woman president of the Washington Academy of Science, where she was active in promoting science education. She died in 1995.

SELECTED WRITINGS BY PITTMAN:

Books

"*Bordetella Pertussis*—Bacterial and Host Factors in the Pathogenesis and Prevention of Whooping Cough." In *Infectious Agents and Host Reactions*. Edited by S. Mudd. Philadelphia: W. B. Saunders Co., 1970.

Periodicals

(With I. S. Falk) "Studies on Respiratory Diseases. XXXIV. Some Relations Between Extracts, Filtrates and Virulence of Pneumococci." *Journal of Bacteriology* 19 (1930): 327–61.

"Variation and Type Specificity in the Bacterial Species *Hemophilus influenzae*." *Journal of Experimental Medicine* 53 (1931): 471–92.

(With S. E. Branham and M. E. Sockrider) "A Comparison of the Precipitation Reaction in Immune Serum Agar Plates with the Protection of Mice by Antimeningococcus Serum." *Public Health Report* 58 (1938): 1400–8.

(With H. J. Bohner) "Laboratory Assays of Different Types of Field Trial Typhoid Vaccines and Relationship to Efficacy in Man." *Journal of Bacteriology* 91 (1966): 1713–23.

"Pertussis Toxin: the Cause of the Harmful Effects and Prolonged Immunity of Whooping Cough: a Hypothesis." *Reviews of Infectious Diseases* 1 (1979): 401–12.

FURTHER READING

Books

American Men & Women of Science. 18th ed. New Providence, NJ: R. R. Bowker, 1992–93.

O'Hern, Elizabeth Moot. *Profiles of Pioneer Women Scientists*. Washington, D.C.: Acropolis Books, 1985.

Other

Harden, Victoria A, NIH Historian, information provided to Margaret Alic on June 2, 1999.

Sketch by Margaret Alic

Julia Barlow Platt
1857–1935
American embryologist and neuroscientist

Julia Barlow Platt is best remembered for her investigation of the aquatic salamander *Necturus* embryo, which led her to derive groundbreaking conclusions about the head structure of amphibian embryos.

Platt was born in San Francisco, California, on September 14, 1857 to Ellen Loomis (Barlow) and George King Platt, a Vermont lawyer who was state attorney from 1840–1842. George Platt died nine days after his daughter's birth. It is believed that Julia Platt spent at least a portion of her childhood in Burlington, Vermont. She received her

Ph.B. with an emphasis on literature and science from the University of Vermont in 1882. The following year, Platt's mother died, but she was left with enough money to continue her education, however.

Pursues Scientific Education

In 1887, Platt pursued further study at Radcliffe College and Harvard Annex in Boston, where she conducted laboratory work at the Museum of Comparative Zoology under anatomist Howard Ayres. Ayres specialized in the morphology of the vertebrate, head and this became Platt's primary area of study as well. While working with Ayers, Platt advanced a controversial theory regarding the order in which anterior-end segments form in chick embryos. Because her findings contradicted those of earlier researchers, her work was initially contested but eventually accepted.

Platt then went on to study at Bryn Mawr, where she studied with zoologist E.B. Wilson, at Woods Hole Laboratory in Massachussetts, where she furthered her research on embryonic head formation, and at the University of Freiburg, where she worked in the laboratory of Robert Ernst Wiedersheim, a prominent comparative zoologist. Under Wiedersheim's supervision, Platt made important discoveries regarding the segmentation anterior to the ear.

In the summer of 1891, Platt traveled to Faro in Sicily to gather the species *Amphioxus*, which she studied in Wiedersheim's laboratory. In 1892, she published her findings on this organism's central nervous system and again found her work embroiled in controversy. Some of the questions raised by Platt in these studies remain unanswered, but many of her observations have been verified.

Posits Most Controversial Theory

During the winter of 1892–1893, Platt went to the newly established University of Chicago, where she worked with Whitman in his laboratory. Here, she laid out the most controversial theory of her career, and the one for which she is best known. During embryo formation, the cells form three layers the ectoderm, or outer layer; the mesoderm, or middle layer; and the endoderm, or inner layer. Prior to Platt's research, it was commonly believed that each layer played a particular role in the embryo's further development; this was known as the "germ–layer theory." This theory was widely accepted, largely because it was laid out so neatly. Platt's research, however, led her to challenge this theory. In 1893 and 1894 she published her findings, which stated that cartilage in amphibian embryo heads form from ectodermal, not mesodermal, cells. This theory contradicted the orderliness of the germ-layer theory, and many prominent scientists spoke out against Platt's findings. Beginning in about 1895, however, additional research by others in the field began to confirm Platt's findings.

After further research at the University of Munich, Radcliffe, and the University of Frieburg, Platt applied for and received her doctorate in zoology from the University of Frieburg in 1898 at the age of 41. She was unable to secure a professorship, however, perhaps due to the controversy her work generated, along with her tenacious personality. She then gave up scientific research and in 1899 moved to Pacific Grove, California, where she became deeply involved in community affairs. In the 1920s she adopted a teenage boy, Harold. At the age of 74, she was elected first woman mayor of Pacific Grove. Platt died on May 28, 1935 and was buried at sea in Monterey Bay.

SELECTED WRITINGS BY PLATT:

Periodicals

"Studies on the Primitive Axial Segmentation of the Chick." *Bulletin of Mus. Comp. Zoology* 17 (1889): 171–190.

"The Anterior Head–Cavities of Acanthias." *Zoological Anz.* 13 (1890): 239.

"A Contribution to the Morphology of the Vertebrate Head, Based on a Study of Acanthias Vulgaris." *Journal of Morphology* 5 (1891): 79–112.

"Further Contribution to the Morphology of the Vertebrate Head." *Anatomy Anz.* 6 (1891): 251–265.

"Ectodermic Origin of the Cartileges of the Head." *Anatomy Anz.* 7 (1893): 506–509.

FURTHER READING

Books

Creese, Mary R.S. *Ladies in the Laboratory? American and British Women in Science, 1800–1900: A Survey of Their Contributions to Research.* Lanham, MD: Scarecrow Press, 1998.

Other

Marine Biological Laboratory, www.mbl.edu/html/WOMEN/platt.html

Sketch by Kristin Palm

Agnes Pockels
1862–1935
German physicist

Agnes Pockels was a self–taught physicist who conducted her experiments at home, publishing her findings in numerous papers over a 40–year period. Her pioneering work on surface films laid the foundation for future work in this field. The techniques she developed are still used by surface chemists.

Pockels was born in Venice, Italy, which was part of the Austrian empire at that time, in 1862 to Theodor and Alwine (Becker) Pockels. Her father was a captain in the Royal Austrian army, which required the family to move many times during Agnes's childhood. An unfortunate post in a part of northern Italy with a high malaria infestation caused serious health problems for the whole family that persisted for the rest of their lives. When Theodor Pockels's illness forced his early discharge from the army, he moved the family to Brunswick, Lower Saxony, now part of Germany, in 1891.

Pockels excelled in all her classes at Municipal High School for Girls in Brunswick. She shared a love of the natural sciences, especially physics, with her younger brother Friedrich who went on to become a professor of physics. After graduation, Pockels remained at home since women were not admitted into universities in Germany at that time. When women were admitted later, her parents requested that she not apply, most likely because she was the only one to care for them. Struggling with her own frail health, she managed the household, assumed the care of her younger brother Friedrich until his marriage in 1900, and nursed both her father and mother until their deaths in 1906 and 1914. Despite these responsibilities, she managed to pursue her education independently. She read whatever textbooks she could find, most supplied by her brother Friedrich, and launched a series of landmark experiments.

Without laboratory equipment, Pockels' education could only go so far. However, she was able to create her own sort of laboratory in the kitchen. Washing dishes, she became fascinated with the effect films had on water. This lead to a series of experiments, performed mainly in the kitchen, to study the surface tension of water. She invented a slide trough and recorded her observations in her diary. "This is really true and no joke or poetic license. . ." Pockels sister–in–law later wrote, "what millions of women see every day without pleasure and are anxious to clean away, i.e. the greasy washing–up water, encouraged this girl to make observations and eventually to . . . scientific investigation."

Letter Published in *Nature*

For the next 10 years, Pockels researched surfactants—substances that reduce surface tension when dissolved in an aqueous solution. She added salts to a solution, noted the resulting stream of currents, and measured the changes in the surface tension with a float attached to a balance placed on the liquid surface. Pockels didn't know whether her findings were important or if they had already been studied by physicists. The professor of physics at Göttingen University where her brother attended was uninterested in her experiments.

In a move that would change her life, Pockels started a subscription to a new German science journal in 1890 and read about British physicist Lord Rayleigh. Rayleigh had been studying oil films on water and had published his results in three papers. Curious to know whether her work had any value, Pockels decided to write to Lord Rayleigh. In 1891 she sent her now famous letter describing her experiments and their results. Instead of ignoring the letter from the untrained 29–year old woman, Lord Rayleigh was so impressed with the quality and findings of her work, he had the translation from German to English published in the journal *Nature* in 1891. The publication established Pockels as a genuine scientist and inspired her to continue her work.

Pockels received wide recognition for her contributions to the understanding of surface layers and surface films. The techniques she developed were used by physical chemists to define the physical properties of organic molecules before the advent of x–ray diffraction. Her methods of certifying a clean surface, essential in this type of work, were universally adopted as standard practice in this branch of physics. In her second paper she observed what is now known as "Pockel's point"—the point at which layers of molecules on a given surface layer will begin to stack when compressed.

In 1931 Pockels was awarded the Laura Leonard Prize for "Quantitative Investigation of the Properties of Surface Layers and Surface Films." In 1932 she received an honorary doctorate from Carolina–Wilhelmina University in Brunswick, Germany. That same year, the Nobel prize–winning physical chemist Friedrich W. Ostwald published a review of her remarkable work, stating that Pockels had established the foundations for quantitative methods in surface layer or film research. Although Pockels published her work until 1933, her care taking demands and her own failing health prevented her from keeping current in the field later in life. Pockels died in 1935 at the age of 73.

SELECTED WRITINGS BY POCKELS:

"Kolloid Z." *Chemistry Abstracts* 27 (1933): 1798.
Letter to Lord Raleigh. *Nature* 46 (1892): 418.
"Surface Tension." *Nature* 43 (1891): 437.

FURTHER READING

Books

Rayner–Canham, Marelene and Geoffrey. *Women in Chemistry: Their Changing Roles From Alchemical Times to the Mid–Twentieth Century.* American Chemical Society and Chemical Heritage Foundation, 1998.

Periodicals

Giles, C. H., and Forrester, S. D., "The Origins of the Surface Film Balance." *Chemistry and Industry* (January 9, 1971): 43–53.

Other

"Pockels, Agnes." *CWP.* http://www.physics.ucla.edu/~cwp (February 1999).

Sketch by Kyra Anderson

Pelageya Yakovlevna Polubarinova-Kochina
1899–
Russian mathematician and hydrologist

In a remarkable career that spanned over seventy years, Pelageya Yakovlevna Polubarinova–Kochina played a major role in the worldwide development of the theory of hydrodynamics. "Kochina's research activity is characterized by a deep and well–organized link with practice, a subtle attention to the physical essence of the phenomena being considered, an exact mathematical formulation of the relevant physical problems, and by a brilliant mastery of the mathematical apparatus," once wrote the respected mathematician P. S. Aleksandrov, in an article later printed in the *Association for Women in Mathematics Newsletter.*

Kochina was born in the Russian city of Astrakhan on May 13, 1899. Her mother was Anisiya Panteleimonovna, and her father, an accountant named Yakov Stepanovich Polubarinov. Kochina had an older brother and a younger sister and brother. During her school years, Polubarinov moved the family to St. Petersburg to get the best possible education for his children. After Kochina graduated from the Pokrovskii Women's Gymnasium in 1916, she began taking courses in the Bestudzevskii women's program, which was incorporated into the University of Petrograd following the October Revolution of 1917.

After her father died in 1918, Kochina began working at the main physics laboratory to support her mother and younger siblings while also pursuing her education. Her sister, however, contracted tuberculosis and died; and though Kochina also developed the disease, she managed to graduate in 1921 with a degree in pure mathematics from Petrograd University. She continued to work in the main physics laboratory (now known as the geophysics laboratory) in the division of theoretical meteorology under the direction of A. A. Fridman, whose interest in hydrodynamics greatly influenced Kochina's later work.

Russia's experience in World War I had exposed the country's deficiencies in industrial capacity, and the new Soviet government expanded research efforts in order to apply mathematics to technological and industrial problems. Kochina excelled in this endeavor, as did Nikolai Evgrafovich Kochin, a colleague who attended night classes at Petrograd University. The two young people shared more than a professional interest; after three years of working together, they married in 1925. The couple embraced their country's post–revolutionary attitudes completely, and their wedding was a simple affair at a Leningrad office, followed by tea at a restaurant for their witnesses.

Begins Research on Filteration and Hydrodynamics

Although Kochina remained professionally active, she quit her job at the laboratory to raise her daughters, Ira and Nina. During these years, she taught at a worker's high school and at the Institute of Transportation and the Institute of Civil Aviation. She also served as a deputy in the Leningrad city soviet (legislature). In 1934 Kochina was appointed a professor at Leningrad University. However, the following year, her husband became head of the mechanics division of the Steklov Mathematics Institute, and the family moved to Moscow. Kochina now turned her attention from teaching to research, becoming a senior researcher in Kochin's division; she also served in the Moscow soviet, eventually becoming a deputy in the Supreme Soviet of the Russian Republic. While working at the institute, Kochina began to concentrate on problems in filtration, and in 1940, after completing her dissertation on theoretical aspects of filtration, she was awarded a Ph.D. in physical and mathematical sciences. When her husband died in 1944, Kochina finished delivering his course of lectures on the theory of interrupted currents.

In addition to working at the Academy of Sciences, Kochina lectured on her research activities, teaching at the Hydrometeorological and Aircraft Building Institute and at the University of Moscow's Aviation Industry Academy. In 1946 she was named a corresponding member of the Academy of Sciences and awarded the State Prize of the Soviet Union. Two years later, she became director of the Institute of Mechanics' division of hydromechanics, which focused on filtration problems. In 1958, Kochina was named an academician of the Academy of Sciences, the highest ranking in that organization, and was asked to help create a Siberian branch of that institution. The following year, at age sixty, she left Moscow for a decade of work in Siberia. During this time she was a department director at the Hydrodynamics Institute as well as head of the department of theoretical mechanics at the University of Novosibirsk. She returned to Moscow in 1970 to direct the section for mathematical methods of mechanics at the Academy of Sciences' Institute for Problems in Mechanics.

Although Kochina's training was in pure mathematics, her professional life was dedicated to finding solutions for practical problems in hydrodynamics. In 1952, relatively early in her career, she wrote *Theory of Ground Water Movement;* J. M. Roger De Wiest's English translation of that work notes that "In this book, reference is made to over thirty of her original and significant contributions on the hydromechanics of porous media (groundwater and oil flow)." One of Kochina's major accomplishments was the development of a general method for solving two–dimensional problems of the steady seepage of subsurface water in homogeneous subsoils. This process has important applications in the design of dam foundations. She obtained significant results in the theory of tides and free–flowing currents, and she resolved problems relating to soil drainage and salt accumulation during her work on irrigation and hydroelectric projects. Her solution to the problem of describing the location of the boundary between an oil–bearing domain and surrounding water as the oil is removed by wells was a well–received innovation. Since

Kochina's pioneering work, the topic has been widely researched by others.

In addition to technical topics in mathematics and hydrology, Kochina was also fascinated with the history of mathematics and mechanics. She wrote the first extensive studies of mathematician Sofia Kovalevskaia's life and work, published descriptions of the scientific legacy of Karl Weierstrass and A. A. Fridman, and wrote two biographies of her husband, one during the Stalin era and one in the post–Stalinist period beginning in 1970. On her seventieth birthday, Kochina was named a Hero of Socialist Labor. She has actively participated in women's movements for peace, and on her eightieth birthday she was awarded the order of the Friendship of Nations.

SELECTED WRITINGS BY POLUBARINOVA-KOCHINA:

Books

Theory of Ground Water Movement, translated by J. M. De Wiest. Princeton University Press, 1962.

FURTHER READING

Books

Grinstein, Louise S., and Paul J. Campbell, eds. *Women of Mathematics.* Greenwood Press, 1987, pp. 95–102.

Periodicals

Aleksandrov, P. S., G. I. Barenblum, A. I. Ishlinskii, and O. A. Oleinik. "Pelageya Yakovlevna Kochina: On Her 80th Birthday." *Association for Women in Mathematics Newsletter* (January–February 1982): 9–12.

Sketch by Loretta Hall

Judith Graham Pool
1919–1975
American physiologist

Judith Graham Pool is responsible for the development of the process of cryoprecipitation, an important discovery that revolutionized the treatment of hemophilia. In cryoprecipitation, a concentrated amount of antihemophiliac factor (AHF) (a blood clotting agent) is isolated from blood plasma and frozen for storage. It can then be administered to the hemophiliac to prevent uncontrollable bleeding. In addition to other blood–related research, Pool also was a forgotten though key player in the rediscovery of a microelectrode, known as the Ling–Gerard electrode.

Pool was born on June 1, 1919, in Queens, New York, the oldest of three children born to Leon Wilfred and Nellie (Baron) Graham. Leon worked as a stockbroker while his wife taught school. Pool became interested in science while in high school, and studied biochemistry while a student at the University of Chicago. Robert and Susan Massie quote Pool in their book, *Journey*, as saying, "My parents didn't take the idea of such a career seriously. My mother doubted that anyone would want to marry me." She earned her B.S. in 1934, graduating Phi Beta Kappa, and, while still a student at Chicago, married Ithiel de Sola Pool in 1938, a political science student. The couple had two sons, Jonathon and Jeremy and divorced in 1958.

After graduation, Pool worked as an assistant in physiology at the University of Chicago from 1940–1942, until her husband got a job as a political science professor at Hobart and William Smith Colleges in Geneva, New York. Pool herself began teaching physics at the same institution in 1943. After Ithiel developed tuberculosis in 1945, the couple returned to Chicago, and her husband entered the hospital. Pool finished work on her Ph.D. in physiology at the University of Chicago in 1946, and worked as an assistant in physiology and pharmacology in the toxicity lab at the University of Chicago.

While a graduate student, Pool did research on the electrical potential of a muscle fiber. As early as 1942, Pool published an article with two other people about this subject. She worked in the lab of one of her coauthors, Ralph Waldo Gerard who was nominated for a Nobel Prize in 1950 for this work. However, while writing her dissertation, Pool had been the first (since **Ida Hyde** who originally made this discovery) to use a microelectrode to determine a muscle fiber's potential. Both Pool and Hyde's contributions to this area have been overlooked. Despite such discoveries, Pool also worked in Chicago area in various jobs as a secretary, teacher at a school for the mentally challenged, and an English and physics instructor, as well as a researcher.

Astute Observation Leads to the Development of Cryoprecipitation

After his recovery, Ithiel was hired by Stanford University in 1949. Pool found work at the Stanford Research Institute in 1950. In 1953, Pool was hired as a research fellow at Stanford's School of Medicine. Her work was supported by a grant of the Bank of America-Giannini Foundation, which supported hemophilia research. She knew nothing about the subject but had solid research credentials. The foundation wanted a researcher and Pool wanted a Ph.D. She quickly rose through the ranks, from research associate 1957–60), to senior research associate (1960–70), then senior scientist (1970–72), and finally full professor of medicine from 1972–75. Pool was also awarded a Fulbright scholarship to do research in Norway from 1958–59.

At Stanford, Pool's research necessarily switched from muscle physiology to blood physiology. In the mid–1960s, Pool made her most important discovery, which led to the development of cryoprecipitation. Hemophiliacs have less AHF in their blood than other people, which causes them to bleed uncontrollably. They require transfusions to raise the AHF level in their blood. Pool observed differences in AHF levels in plasma from the beginning of a transfusion to the end. She also noticed that the residue left in the bag of plasma after the transfusion was high in AHF. From this observation, Pool developed a way of separating and storing cryoprecipitate, a cold-insoluble protein that contains AHF. Her procedure allowed hemophiliacs to infuse themselves at home and avoid constant hospitalization. Still used today, cryoprecipitate is inexpensive to make and can be stored in a freezer for a year. Pool downplayed her discovery to the Massies in *Journey*. She told them, "I had no greater insight than anyone else. I just happened to be there at the right moment." However, her keen observation skills and inquiring mind allowed her to discover what no one else had.

Pool's discovery changed the way hemophiliacs are treated, and she was lauded by many professional organizations. In 1968, the National Hemophilia Foundation awarded her its Murray Thelin Award; in 1973, the Hobart and William Smith Colleges gave her their **Elizabeth Blackwell** Award; and in 1975, the University of Chicago awarded her the Professional Achievement Award. She was a member of the national advisory committees for the National Institutes of Health and the American Red Cross Program, was the first chair of the Professional Women of Stanford University Medical Center, and worked diligently to advance the place of women in science.

Pool gave birth to a daughter, Lorna, in 1964. She was remarried in 1972 to Maurice D. Sokolow. They divorced in 1975. Pool died on July 13, 1975, of a brain tumor. Posthumously, The National Hemophilia Foundation changed the name of its grants to honor Pool and her contributions to hemophilia research. They became known as the Judith Graham Pool Research Fellowships.

FURTHER READING

Books

American Men and Women of Science: The Physical and Biological Sciences. Vol. 5. New York: R.R. Bowker Company/Jaques Cattell Press, 1972, p. 4973.

Bailey, Martha J. *American Women in Science: A Biographical Dictionary.* Denver: ABC–CLIO, 1994, p. 308.

Kass–Simon, G. and Patricia Farnes, eds. *Women of Science: Righting the Record..* Bloomington: Indiana University Press, 1990, pp. 244–46.

Massie, Robert, and Suzanne Massie. *Journey.* New York: Warner Books, 1973, pp. 298–300.

Sicherman, Barbara, and Carol Hurd Green, eds. *Notable American Women: The Modern Period: A Biographical Dictionary.* Cambridge: Belknap Press, 1980, pp. 553–54.

Siegel, Patricia Joan, and Kay Thomas Finley. *Women in the Scientific Search: An American Bio–bibliography, 1724–1979.* Metuchen: The Scarecrow Press, 1985, pp. 271–72.

Periodicals

"Dr. Judith G. Pool, Hemophilia Expert." *The New York Times* (July 15, 1975): 36.

Sketch by Annette Petrusso

Helen Beatrix Potter
1866–1943
British mycologist, artist, and writer

Although best known as the author and illustrator of *The Tale of Peter Rabbit* and other classic children's stories, Beatrix Potter began a career in biology, specifically mycology, which is the study of fungi. It was only after repeated rebuffs by the male scientific establishment that she turned to writing children's books as her career.

Helen Beatrix Potter was born in Bolton Gardens, Kensington, England, in 1866, the elder of two children of Helen (Leech) and Rupert Potter. Beatrix Potter had a lonely childhood. Both of her parents had inherited fortunes from the cotton industry in Lancashire, and her father, a nonpracticing lawyer, was an amateur painter and photographer. Left in the care of servants and governesses, Potter was educated at home by tutors, even after her younger brother was sent to boarding school. She developed her interest in natural history during summer vacations in Scotland and the Lake District of England. Potter collected and painted plants, birds, and other animals, and prepared animal skeletons. She also studied astronomy, geology, and fossils. However it was her talent for drawing that was encouraged by her parents, and she eventually earned an art student's certificate via private instruction. Potter also kept a diary, from ages 14 to 31, that was written in a secret code she invented. It wasn't until 1966 that it was finally decoded and translated.

Becomes Expert on Fungal Taxonomy

Potter's scientific endeavors were encouraged by her uncle, Sir Henry Roscoe, a chemist. She also was assisted by Charles McIntosh, a Scottish postman and well–known expert on mosses, fungi, and algae. Potter collected many

Beatrix Potter (AP/Wide World Photos, Inc. Reproduced by permission.)

species of fungi and studied them with a microscope. She also spent long hours at the British Museum of Natural History, near her home in London, studying and drawing fungi. She became an expert on fungal taxonomy, or classification, a very difficult field since it depended on identifying sexual structures that were seldom or never observed. Despite Potter's expertise, she was ignored or rebuffed by the scientists she approached at the British Museum.

In her late twenties, Potter made hundreds of scientifically accurate drawings of fungi for a book she planned to write. Roscoe introduced her to the director of the Royal Botanical Gardens, but he was not interested in her drawings. However the assistant director, George Massee, became interested in Potter's work, despite the fact that some of her observations and conclusions contradicted his own. Potter had succeeded in germinating the spores of more than 40 species of fungi, a remarkable achievement, and had made accurate drawings at magnifications of 600X. In 1897, her original study, "The Germination of the Spores of *Agaricineae*," a group of fungi that included the common cultivated variety, was presented to the Linnaean Society of London by Massee. Potter was not present, since women were barred from the society's meetings. Potter withdrew the work before publication in order to complete additional experiments and, although she made many more microscopic slides of spore development, the paper was never published.

Abandons Science as Career

Potter also studied lichens. In 1867 a Swiss botanist, Simon Schwendener, had observed that lichens were composed of an alga and a fungus living interdependently, or symbiotically. However, most Swiss and German botanists believed that the fungus was a parasite, and English botanists ridiculed the idea that there was a fungus present at all. In 1896, Potter demonstrated that the alga, but not the fungus, contained chlorophyll for photosynthesis and that the fungus could absorb large amounts of water which triggered photosynthesis by the alga. Although Potter made accurate drawings to illustrate her results, she was once again rebuffed and ridiculed by the scientific community. With these discouraging experiences, Potter abandoned her scientific studies, as well as her coded journal. Instead, she decided to become an illustrator.

Potter's first two children's books were privately printed, but soon Frederick Warne & Co. began publishing these enormously popular stories. In all, Potter wrote and illustrated some two dozen children's books. She oversaw the design and production of her books and the merchandising of her characters. Over her parents' objections, she also became engaged to Norman Warne, her publisher's son, in 1905. However her fiancé died of leukemia a month later. That year, with the royalties from *Peter Rabbit*, Potter bought a farm near the village of Sawrey in the Lake District. In 1913, she married a country lawyer, William Heelis. Eventually she gave up writing and illustrating for sheep farming and land conservation activities.

Potter died of uterine cancer in 1943 in Sawrey. Her land was left to the National Trust and her former home became a museum. In 1967, her paintings of fungi were used as technical illustrations for a guide to the fungi of England. The Linnaean Society of London honored her in 1997.

SELECTED WRITINGS BY POTTER:

Books

The Tale of Peter Rabbit. London: Frederick Warne and Co., 1902.

The Journal of Beatrix Potter from 1881 to 1897, transcribed from her code writing by Leslie Linder. New York: Frederick Warne and Co., 1966.

Beatrix Potter's Letters, selected and introduced by Judy Taylor. London: Frederick Warne, 1989.

FURTHER READING

Books

Lane, Margaret. *The Tale of Beatrix Potter*. Rev. ed. London: Frederick Warne and Co., 1968.

Linder, Leslie. *A History of the Writings of Beatrix Potter including Unpublished Work.* London: Frederick Warne and Co., 1971.

Periodicals

Gilpatrick, Naomi. "The Secret Life of Beatrix Potter." *Natural History* (October 1972): 38–41, 88–97.

Lurie, Alison. "Beatrix Potter: More than just Peter Rabbit." *Ms. Magazine* 6 (September 1977): 42–45.

Sketch by Margaret Alic

Helen Walter (Dodson) Prince
1905–
American astronomer

Helen Dodson Prince is an eminent astronomer who has done extensive studies of solar activity, particularly solar flares. She has published over 100 papers in astronomy journals. Her research helped make the McMath–Hulbert Observatory of the University of Michigan into an international center of solar studies.

The daughter of Henry Clay and Helen Falls (Walter) Dodson, Prince was born in Baltimore in 1905. She received her bachelor's degree in mathematics in 1927 from Goucher College in Baltimore. Following graduation, she went to work as a statistician for the Maryland Department of Education. Deciding to become an astronomer, Prince entered graduate school at the University of Michigan in 1931. She earned her master's degree the following year, and received a research assistantship to pursue her doctorate in astronomy, which she completed in 1934 with her thesis, "A Study of the Spectrum of 25 Orionis."

From 1933 until 1945, Prince was first an instructor and then an assistant professor of astronomy at Wellesley College. During the summers, she pursued her research. At the Maria Mitchell Observatory on Nantucket Island, she continued her spectral studies of the star 25 Orionis, studying the patterns of bands and lines that are observed when a star's light is dispersed through a prism. Later, she spent summers at the Observatoire de Paris, Section d'Astrophysique, at Meudon, France. There she developed her interest in the activities of the Sun.

During the war years of 1943 to 1945, Prince worked at the Radiation Laboratory of the Massachusetts Institute of Technology, on the mathematical development of radar. She then returned to Goucher College as an assistant professor of mathematics and astronomy. In 1947 she began teaching part–time at Goucher and accepted a shared appointment at the McMath–Hulbert Observatory of the University of Michigan, on Lake Angelus near Pontiac, Michigan. There she continued her research on solar activity, taking motion pictures of single spectral lines. In 1950 she became an associate professor of astronomy at the University of Michigan, working full–time at the observatory. She married Edmond Lafayette Prince in 1956 and was promoted to full professor the following year. She became associate director of the observatory in 1962 and she continued to train students throughout her career.

In 1951, Prince began a collaboration with pioneering Canadian radio astronomer Arthur Covington, which lasted for more than 20 years. Together, they combined optical and radio studies to better classify and understand solar flares. Prince's work focused on the occurrence of the flares and their effects on space and on the earth's magnetic field.

She received an honorary doctorate of science from Goucher College in 1952. In 1955 she was awarded the **Annie Jump Cannon** Prize given by the American Astronomical Society to outstanding women astronomers. Prince retired from the University of Michigan in 1976 and became a professor emeritus. In 1979, she became a consultant to the Applied Physics Laboratory at Johns Hopkins University, from her home in Alexandria, Virginia.

SELECTED WRITINGS BY PRINCE:

Books

(With E. Ruth Hedeman) *Experimental Comprehensive Solar Flare Indices for "Major" and Certain Lesser Flares, 1975–1979.* Boulder, CO: World Data Center A for Solar–Terrestrial Physics, National Oceanographic and Atmospheric Administration, National Geophysical and Solar–Terrestrial Data Center, 1981.

(With E. Ruth Hedeman and Edmond C. Roelof) *Evolutionary Charts of Solar Activity (Calcium Plages) as Functions of Heliographic Longitude and Time, 1964–1979.* Boulder, CO: World Data Center A for Solar–Terrestrial Physics, National Oceanographic and Atmospheric Administration, 1981.

Periodicals

"The Spectrum of 25 Orionis, 1933–1939." *Astrophysical Journal* 91 (1940): 126.

(With E. Ruth Hedeman) "The Frequency and Position of Flares within a Spot Group." *Astrophysical Journal* 110 (1949): 242.

(With E. R. Hedeman and R. R. McMath) "Photometry of Solar Flares." *Astrophysical Journal* supp. 20 (1956): 241–70.

(With E. R. Hedeman) "Solar Minimum and the International Years of the Quiet Sun." *Science* 143 (1964): 237.

(With O. C. Mohler) "McMath–Hulbert Observatory of the University of Michigan." *Solar Physics* 5 (1968): 417–22.

FURTHER READING

Books

O'Neill, Lois Decker, ed. *The Women's Book of World Records and Achievements.* Garden City, NY: Doubleday, 1979.

Roberts, Rebecca L. "Helen W. Dodson Prince." In *Notable Women in the Physical Sciences: A Biographical Dictionary.* Edited by Benjamin F. Shearer and Barbara S. Shearer. Westport, CT: Greenwood Press, 1997.

Who's Who in the World. 7th ed. Chicago: Marquis Who's Who, 1984–85.

Sketch by Margaret Alic

Mary Proctor
1862–?
Irish-born English-American astronomy writer and educator

Mary Proctor made astronomy accessible to many people in the early twentieth century, especially children. Proctor accomplished this via books and articles as well as lectures.

Proctor was born in 1862 in Dublin, Ireland, and raised in England. She was the daughter of Richard A. and Mary (Mills) Proctor. Richard A. Proctor was a well–known astronomer, lecturer and writer. In 1881, he was founded the journal *Knowledge*, which he also edited. Richard Proctor passed his passions on to his daughter, with whom he was extremely close. While still a teenager, Proctor took care of his papers and wanted to emulate his accomplishments. She attended school in London, where she graduated from the College of Preceptors. The Proctor family moved to the United States around 1886. Proctor attended Columbia University, where she began writing in earnest.

Proctor's first articles were on the topic of comparative mythology, and written with her father's encouragement and help. She also wrote numerous articles as well as some books on astronomy. Proctor's take on astronomy was not scholarly, but popular. One such book, *Evenings with the Stars*, published in 1924. Proctor's articles appeared in such prestigious publications as *Popular Astronomy* (where she served an editorship), *Scientific American* and *Popular Science News.*

Many of her publications were targeted specifically at a juvenile audience. To that end, she published in publications such as *Youth's Companion* and *School Journal.* In 1898, Proctor also wrote a text for children on astronomy entitled *Stories of Starland*, which was used in public schools in New York City and elsewhere. Other children's titles included *Giant Sun and His Family, Legend of the Stars*, and *The Children's Book of Heavens.*

In 1893, Proctor began a secondary career as a lecturer on astronomy. Her first appearance in this capacity was at the Chicago World's Fair. Assuming she would be talking to children, Proctor devised an age–appropriate presentation. She was forced to make last–minute changes when she discovered her audience was mostly adults, but the lectures were very successful. The audience and Chicago papers both gave her positive reviews. Subsequently, Proctor lectured in many countries (including England and Canada) to audiences of both adults and children more than 400 times. She was affiliated with the New York City Board of Education as a lecturer, giving annual lectures open to everyone. Proctor also taught astronomy in private schools in New York City.

Proctor's contributions to the field were recognized by her peers. In 1898, the American Association for the Advancement of Science elected her as a fellow. She also belonged to other professional organizations including the British Astronomical Society and was an honorary member of the Toronto Astronomical Society. The date of her death is unknown and sources imply she never married.

SELECTED WRITINGS BY PROCTOR:

Books

Evenings with the Stars. New York: Harper & Brothers, 1925.

FURTHER READING

Books

Bailey, Martha J. *American Women in Science: A Biographical Dictionary.* Denver: ABC–CLIO, 1994, pp. 309–10.

Cattell, J. McKeen, ed. *American Men of Science: A Biographical Dictionary.* 2nd ed. New York: The Science Press, 1910, p. 380.

Johnson, Rossiter, ed. *The Twentieth Century Biographical Dictionary of Notable Americans.* Volume VIII. Boston: The Biographical Society, 1904.

The National Cyclopedia of American Biography. Volume IX. Ann Arbor: University Microfilms, 1967, pp. 282–83.

Siegel, Patricia Joan and Kay Thomas Finley. *Women in the Scientific Search: An American Bio–bibliography, 1724–1979.* Metuchen: The Scarecrow Press, Inc., 1985, p. 53.

Sketch by Annette Petrusso

Margie Profet
1958–
American biomedical researcher

As a self–made scientist, Margie Profet's approach to scientific the discipline is relatively unique. She told Terry McDermott in the *Seattle Times*, "I'm very opportunistic and if I think of a neat idea, I work on it." Profet conducts biomedical research from a Darwinian perspective, one that believes that the human body is an adaptation to its environment. In this evolutionary medical theory, bodily defense mechanisms happen for a reason, there are few accidents, and there is a balance between costs and benefits. Her theories concern everyday questions and bodily functions such as menstruation, allergies, and morning sickness in pregnancy. Because Profet lacks advanced degrees, her theories are controversial with scientists and physicians. However, Profet has been lauded for her work, and in 1993 she was awarded a MacArthur Foundation "genius" grant.

Profet was born August 7, 1958, in Berkeley, California, to Bob (a physicist) and Karen (an engineer) Profet. With her three siblings, Profet grew up in Manhattan Beach, California, where her parents worked in the aerospace industry. Profet received her first undergraduate degree from Harvard University in 1980. She majored in political philosophy, and it was while writing her senior thesis that she decided she wanted to devote her intellectual life to original thought. After graduation, Profet went to Europe, where she worked for a year as a computer programmer in Munich, Germany, from 1980 to 1981. After returning to the United States, Profet decided to pursue her lifelong interest in biology. She entered the University of California, Berkeley, and earned another B.A. in 1985, this time in physics. Profet was unhappy with the structures, limitations, and regimentations of academia, and decided to pursue her interests on her own time. She has never taken a college–level biology class.

Living in San Francisco, Profet supported herself with a series of part–time jobs while she pursued her own research. Beginning in 1986, Profet derived what became her first published theory, which concerned morning sickness and pregnancy. It was inspired by conversations she had with pregnant friends and relatives. Profet concluded, after much research and reflection, that morning sickness happens for a reason. She believes that certain foods contain toxins that could harm a developing embryo in the first trimester, when the fetus is most vulnerable and when most significant birth defects can develop.

Profet believes that the nausea caused by certain foods and scents is a defense mechanism to protect the vulnerable embryo when it needs it the most. After the first trimester, when the embryo is less susceptible because it has begun to develop its own defenses, there is usually little to no morning sickness. In 1995, Profet published a book, *Protecting Your Baby–to–Be*, explaining this idea for women in their first trimester of pregnancy. In it, she outlines specific foods to avoid.

While working through her morning sickness theory for publication, Profet had her second insight, inspired by her own experiences with allergies. Beginning with the observation that certain allergic reactions are often immediate—scratching, sneezing, vomiting, etc.—Profet formulated a hypothesis that argues allergies are reactions to toxins. She believes that the human body's immune system battles these environmental toxins—plant–borne compounds—that are potentially harmful to cells. The toxins themselves can cause allergies, or a toxin and allergen can be linked. The toxins must be immediately expelled by the body, hence the immediacy of a sneeze or a scratch. Additionally, Profet theorizes that allergic reactions do not happen to everybody because they are a last ditch defense method against toxins. Because other, first–line defenses work in some people, they do not need to have allergic reactions. Profet published these findings in 1991 in the *Quarterly Review of Biology*.

During this period, Profet was hired by Professor Bruce Ames, a toxologist at the University of California at Berkeley, to be a biology research associate in his laboratory. In June 1993, she was awarded a five–year $225,000 grant by the John D. & Katherine T. MacArthur Foundation. Soon after receiving the grant, Profet moved to Seattle, Washington, and became affiliated with the University of Washington and its molecular biotechnology department.

In the fall of 1993, Profet published her seminal theory on why women menstruate in the September issue of the *Quarterly Review of Biology*. This was a subject that had intrigued her since the age of seven when she first learned what it was. Profet wondered why women's bodies cast off so much blood and tissue, including the nutrients therein, and concluded that it is an evolutionary adaptation. She believes the process of menstruation defends the uterus, fallopian tubes, and related organs from pathogens and other potentially damaging microbes that append themselves to sperm. By menstruating, the body sheds the uterus's outer lining where these pathogens persist. The blood that douses the area is full of immune cells that can neutralize any remaining microbes.

Profet's approach to science has been called visionary, because she questions phenomenons for which there are already accepted answers. Still, Profet has many critics to her ideas, methodology, and lack of graduate education. She explained to Terry McDermott that her view is "No matter what aspect of physiology you look at the core question is: What's it there for? Maybe it is just a fluke or a by–product. But maybe it has a function. You have to know that. Otherwise, you're doing blind medical intervention."

SELECTED WRITINGS BY PROFET:

Book

Protecting Your Baby–to–Be. New York: Addison–Wesley Publishing, 1995.

Periodicals

"The Function of Allergy: Immunological Defense Against Toxins." *Quarterly Review of Biology* (March 1991): 23.

"Menstruation as a Defense against Pathogens Transported by Sperm." *Quarterly Review of Biology* (September 1993): 335.

FURTHER READING

Periodicals

Angier, Natalie. "Biologists Advise Doctors to Think like Darwin." *The New York Times* (December 24, 1991): C1.

"Radical New View of Role of Menstruation." *The New York Times* (September 21, 1993): C1.

Bloch, Hannah. "School Isn't My Kind of Thing." *Time* (October 4, 1993): 72.

McDermott, Terry. "Darwinian Medicine—It's a War Out There and Margie Profet, A Leading Theorist in a New Science, Thinks the Human Body Does Some Pretty Weird Things to Survive." *The Seattle Times* (July 31, 1994): 10.

McNichol, Tom. "Bleach Blanket Biologist." *USA Weekend* (October 8, 1995): 14.

Oliwenstein, Lori. "Dr. Darwin: Darwinian Medicine Studies the Evolutionary Purpose of Disease." *Discover* (October 1995): 110.

Rudavsky, Shari. "Margie Profet. (Researcher of Evolutionary Physiology)." *Omni* (May 1994): 69.

Williams, Emily. "Allergies First Attracted Notice in Modern Times." *The Dallas Morning News* (October 11, 1993): 6F.

Sketch by Annette Petrusso

Q

Edith H. Quimby (The Library of Congress. Reproduced by permission.)

Edith H. Quimby
1891–1982
American biophysicist

A pioneer in the field of radiology, Edith H. Quimby helped develop diagnostic and therapeutic applications for x rays, radium, and radioactive isotopes when the science of radiology was still in its infancy. Her research in measuring the penetration of radiation enabled physicians to determine the exact dose needed with the fewest side effects. Quimby also worked to protect those handling radioactive material from its harmful effects. While a radiology professor at Columbia University, she established a research laboratory to study the medical uses of radioactive isotopes, including their application in cancer diagnosis and treatments. In recognition of her contributions to the field, the Radiological Society of North America awarded her a gold medal for work which "placed every radiologist in her debt."

Quimby was born on July 10, 1891, in Rockford, Illinois, to Arthur S. Hinkley, an architect and farmer, and Harriet Hinkley (whose maiden name was also Hinkley). The family—Quimby was one of three children—moved to several different states during Quimby's childhood. She graduated from high school in Boise, Idaho, and went on a full tuition scholarship to Whitman College in Walla Walla, Washington, where she majored in physics and mathematics. Two of her teachers at Whitman, B. H. Brown and Walter Bratton, were major influences in directing her toward a career in scientific research. After graduating in 1912, Quimby taught high school science in Nyssa, Oregon, and then went to the University of California in 1914 to accept a fellowship in physics. While in the graduate program there, she married fellow physics student Shirley L. Quimby. She earned her M.A. in 1915 and returned to teaching high school science, this time in Antioch, California. In 1919, when her husband moved to New York to teach physics at Columbia University, she went with him. The move to New York was a pivotal point in Quimby's career, as she began working under Dr. Gioacchino Failla, chief physicist at the newly created New York City Memorial Hospital for Cancer and Allied Diseases. This began a scientific association that was to last forty years.

Quimby began studying the medical uses of x rays and radium, especially in treating tumors. At that time, physicians and researchers knew extremely little about this area; before Quimby's research, each doctor had to determine on a case–by–case basis how much radiation each patient needed for treatment. Quimby focused her attention on measuring the penetration of radiation so that radiotherapy doses could be more exact and side effects minimized. After several years of research, she successfully determined the number of roentgens (a now obsolete unit of radiation dosage) per minute emitted in the air, on the skin, and in the body. Her research on the effects of radiation on the skin was especially noteworthy to the scientific community, and her study was frequently quoted in the professional literature for many years.

From 1920 to 1940, Quimby conducted numerous experiments to examine various properties of radium and x rays. During this period she wrote dozens of articles for scientific journals, describing the results of her research and listing standards of measurement. In 1940 Quimby was the first woman to receive the Janeway Medal of the American Radium Society in recognition of her achievements in the field.

Becomes Professor and Establishes Isotope Laboratory

From 1941 to 1942, Quimby taught radiology courses at Cornell University Medical College. The following year she became associate professor of radiology at Columbia University College of Physicians and Surgeons, where she taught radiologic physics. While at Columbia, she and Failla founded the Radiological Research Laboratory. There they studied the medical uses of radioactive isotopes in cooperation with members of Columbia's medical departments. They focused their research on the application of radioactive isotopes (different forms of the same element whose unstable nuclei emit alpha, beta, or gamma rays) in treating thyroid disease, and for circulation studies and diagnosis of brain tumors. These inquiries made Quimby a pioneer in the field of nuclear medicine.

Quimby participated in other aspects of radiology research as well. She researched the use of synthetically produced radioactive sodium in medical research, and devoted considerable efforts to investigating ways to protect those handling radioactive substances from the harmful effects of exposure. Very early on, Quimby foresaw the potential for increased diagnostic and therapeutic use of atomic energy in medicine through radioactive isotopes.

In addition to her research and lecturing, Quimby worked on the Manhattan Project (which developed the atom bomb). She also worked for the Atomic Energy Commission, acted as a consultant on radiation therapy to the United States Veterans Administration, served as an examiner for the American Board of Radiology, and headed a scientific committee of the National Council on Radiation Protection and Measurements. A prolific writer, Quimby published a considerable amount of literature on various aspects of the medical uses of x rays, radium, and radioactive isotopes. She also coauthored a widely respected book entitled *Physical Foundations of Radiology.*

After her official retirement in 1960 as professor emeritus of radiology, Quimby continued to write, lecture, and consult well into the 1970s. She was a member of several radiology societies, including the American Radium Society, for which she served as vice president. In her nonprofessional life, Quimby was a member of the League of Women Voters.

On Quimby's death on October 11, 1962, at the age of ninety–one, Harald Rossi of Columbia University wrote in *Physics Today* that "all too often the creative achievements of scientific pioneers are overshadowed by further developments made by others or simply become anonymous components of accepted practice. Fortunately, Quimby's exceptional service to radiological physics was widely recognized."

SELECTED WRITINGS BY QUIMBY:

Books

(With Sergei Feitelberg and Solomon Silver) *Radioactive Isotopes in Clinical Practice.* Lea and Febiger, 1958.

Safe Handling of Radioactive Isotopes in Medical Practice. Macmillan, 1960.

(With Paul N. Goodwin) *Physical Foundations of Radiology.* Harper, 1970.

FURTHER READING

Books

Current Biography. H. W. Wilson, 1949, pp. 492–493.

Periodicals

New York Times (October 13, 1982): 28.

Physics Today (December, 1982): 71–72.

Sketch by Donna Olshansky

R

Estelle R. Ramey (The Library of Congress. Reproduced by permission.

Estelle R. Ramey
1917–
American physiologist and educator

Estelle Ramey is known for her research in the endocrine aspects of stress, including the relationship between sex hormones and longevity, as well as for her activism in the feminist movement. In 1989 she was named by *Newsweek* magazine as "one of twenty–five Americans who have made a difference."

Ramey was born in Detroit, Michigan, on August 23, 1917, to Henry, a businessman, and Sarah L. White. She graduated from Brooklyn College at the age of nineteen and took a job as a teaching fellow in the department of chemistry at Queens College, New York City. "Dr. Whittaker, my old teacher, was appointed chairman of the department at Queens College," Ramey recalled in correspondence with Jill Carpenter, "and he was a unique man for his times. He did not equate gender with ability."

Ramey completed her M.S. degree in chemistry at Columbia University in 1940 and was working toward a Ph.D. degree when she married law student James T. Ramey (they have two children, James and Drucilla). When her husband's career took them to Knoxville, Tennessee, Ramey applied for a job in the department of chemistry at the University of Tennessee. Ramey told Carpenter: "I was brusquely informed by the chairman that he had never hired a woman, would never hire a woman, and I ought to go home and take care of my husband. A few months later, Pearl Harbor was bombed and the war started. The chemistry department began to lose its male faculty and a chastened chairman called to offer me a job teaching thermodynamics to Air Cadets and biochemistry to Nurse Cadets." Ramey taught at the University of Tennessee from 1942 through 1947.

When her husband joined the newly created Atomic Energy Commission in Chicago, Ramey entered the University of Chicago. She was a Mergler Scholar in 1949, and earned a Ph.D. from the university's School of Medicine in 1950. Also in 1950, she received a U. S. Public Health Service postdoctoral fellowship in endocrinology and became an assistant professor of physiology at the medical school, the first woman faculty member in that department. In 1956 she joined the faculty of Georgetown University Medical School in Washington, D.C. Her tenure at Georgetown was punctuated by stints as visiting professor at Stanford University, Harvard University, and Yale University. In 1977 she was awarded an honorary doctorate by Georgetown, and in 1987 the university named her professor emerita of biophysics.

Advisory boards, boards of directors, and committees on which Ramey has served include Educational Telecommunications, Planned Parenthood, Big Sisters of Washington, the National Institutes of Health, the National Academy of Science, the Veteran's Administration for Women Veterans, the Chief of Naval Operations, the Admiral H. G. Rickover Foundation, the MacDonald Hospital for Women, and President Carter's Committee on the Status of Women. She is a member of the nominating committee of the MacArthur Foundation, and her honors include the Outstanding Alumna Award from the University of Chicago, 1973; the Public Broadcasting Company Woman of Achievement Award, 1984; and the National Women's Democratic Club Woman of Achievement Award, 1993. Ramey is a past president of the Association for Women in Science (AWIS) and founder of the AWIS Educational Foundation. She holds 17 honorary doctorates, has lectured at dozens of colleges and government agencies, and has published more than 150 articles in the scientific and popular press.

SELECTED WRITINGS BY RAMEY:

Periodicals

"Boredom: The Most Prevalent American Disease." *Harper's* (November, 1974): 12–22.

FURTHER READING

Ramey, Estelle R., correspondence with Jill Carpenter, January, 1994.

Sketch by Jill Carpenter

Kamal Jayasing Ranadive
1917–
Indian biologist and cancer researcher

Kamal Jayasing Ranadive introduced tissue culture technology into India and helped to found the first Indian cancer research center. Additionally, she developed a new method of growing in vitro animal cells. For her 30 years of work in cancer and leprosy research, Ranadive received the Padmabhushan Award in 1982, the highest award given by the Indian government.

Born on November 8, 1917, Ranadive earned her B.S. in biology from the University of Bombay in 1939 and went on to receive a M.S. in cytology at the same institution two years later. While working at Tata Memorial Hospital in Bombay, Ranadive continued her studies in cytology and in cancer research, earning her Ph.D. in microbiology in 1949, again from the University of Bombay. Her dissertation, "Experimental Studies in Breast Cancer," pointed to an early interest in cancer research, which has continued to be the focus of Ranadive's career.

In 1949 Ranadive accepted a fellowship for postdoctoral research at the Rockefeller Foundation in the U.S. During her two–year stay, she did tissue culture research at Johns Hopkins and at Columbia University Medical Center. Returning to India, she began her cancer research as a scientist at the Indian Cancer Research Center in Bombay in 1952.

Performs Dual Career as Researcher and Administrator

The same year Ranadive started work for the Indian Cancer Research Center, she also opened the Experimental Biology Laboratory and Tissue Culture Laboratory in Bombay, and in 1966 she was named the acting director of the Indian Cancer Research Center. Both as a researcher and as administrator, Ranadive broke new ground for Indian women in the sciences.

When the wealthy Tata family provided cancer research funding in 1970, an enlarged cancer research institute was formed, the Tata Memorial Hospital and Cancer Research Institute, with Ranadive as the head of the Biology Division. She held this position until her retirement in 1978. Ranadive's cancer research has included studies on breast cancer, the etiology of cancer problems specific to India, and the mechanisms of cell carcinogenesis. In fact, she developed the first human liposarcoma and myxofibrosarcoma cell strains. In leprosy research, Ranadive conducted the first successful isolation of an acid–fast microorganism from lepromatous leprosy.

Since her retirement and new title of emeritus scientist, Ranadive has continued to conduct research in cancer and leprosy, as well as in the medical health of tribal groups in India. This latter research has contributed two noteworthy projects: "Immunohematology of Tribal Blood," a study of infant deaths and nutritional characteristics of western Indian tribal cultures, and "Analysis of Cytokines and Oncogene Expression in Tribal Blood Samples." Additionally, Ranadive has also advised students in master's and doctoral programs, as well as introducing the discipline of applied biology to medical research at the University of Bombay.

A Much-Honored Scientist

For her researches, involving over 200 publications in cancer and leprosy, as well as for her career in administration and in academia, Ranadive has received many awards and honors. In addition to the "Padmabhushan," she is the recipient of the Dr. Basantidevi Amirchand Award in 1958, and the Jubilee Research Award from the Medical Council of India in 1964, both for her cancer research. She has also received the International Watumull Award in 1964 for her work in leprosy, specifically for her isolation of the ICRC bacillus, and the Sandoz Award and Gold Medal Award for research in cancer–producing bodies specific to India. Thirteen years after retirement, in 1991, Ranadive received both the Distinguished Woman Award from Benaras University and the Tata Memorial Hospital Award for outstanding work in cancer control and prevention.

In addition to her Rockefeller Foundation fellowship, Ranadive has also won a fellowship from the World Health Organization. A member of the American and Japanese Tissue Culture Associations, the Cell Research Organization of UNESCO, and the Indian Council of Medical Research, among other affiliations, Ranadive has also served on the editorial boards of many journals, including *International Journal of Cancer, Proceedings of Cell Biology,* and *Year Book of Cancer,* among others. She continues to be an inspiration for young female scientists in India, demonstrating that there is room for all in the sciences. She helped found the Indian Women Scientist Association and was its president in 1973.

SELECTED WRITINGS BY RANADIVE:

Periodicals

"Experimental Studies on Carcinogenesis." *Indian Journal of Cancer* (March 1965): 26–35.

(With C.V. Bapat) "Studies on the Pathogenicity of the ICRC Bacillus." *International Journal of Leprosy and Other Mycobacterial Diseases* (January–March 1966): 7–16.

(With S. V. Bhide) "Effect of Urethan on Nucleic Acids." *Nature* (July 2, 1966): 82–3.

(With S. V. Gothoskar) "Experimental Studies on the Aetiology of 'Kangri Cancer'." *British Journal of Cancer* (December 1966): 751–55.

(With N. A. Sheth and S. V. Bhide) "Incorporation of 32P into Nucleic Acids in Mammary Tissue of Mice Susceptible and Resistant to Breast Cancer." *Journal of the National Cancer Institute* (April 1971): 731–34.

(With K. A. Karande) "Influence of Hormones and Chemical Carcinogen on Murine Leukaemia." *British Journal of Cancer* (October 1973): 299– 309.

(With N.A. Sheth and A. R. Sheth) "In Vitro Binding of Radioiodinated Human Placental Lactogen to Murine Mammary Gland." *European Journal of Cancer.* (October 1974): 566–70.

FURTHER READING

Books

Directory of Indian Women Today. Edited by Ajit Cour and Arpana Cour. New Delhi: International Publications, 1978.

Lotlikar, Sarojini. "Kamal J. Ranadive." *Notable Women in the Physical Sciences.* Edited by Benjamin F. Shearer and Barbara S. Shearer. Westport, Connecticut: Greenwood Press, 1997, pp. 319–22.

Who's Who in Science: A Biographical Dictionary of Notable Scientists from Antiquity to the Present. New York: Marquis' Who's Who, 1968.

Sketch by J. Sydney Jones

Marie Gertrude Rand
1886–1970
American experimental psychologist

Gertrude Rand was a psychologist best known for her work in collaboration with her husband, Clarence Ferree, in the field of physiological optics. The Ferree–Rand perimeter, a map of the retina for perceptual abilities which aids greatly in ophthalmologic diagnoses, was the fruit of their combined research efforts. Rand also contributed in the areas of the diagnosis of color blindness and in the development of lighting technology. Together, Ferree and Rand also were consultants for the illumination of the Holland Tunnel in New York.

Rand was born on October 29, 1886 in Brooklyn, New York, the third child of Mary Catherine (Moench) and Lyman Fisk Rand, who later became the president of a manufacturing company. Graduating from Brooklyn's Girls High School in 1904, Rand went on to earn a B.A. at Cornell University with a major in experimental psychology, a field then coming into vogue. From Cornell, she went on to Bryn Mawr College and studied under Clarence Errol Ferree, who also directed her dissertation work on the sensitivity of the retina to color. Earning her Ph.D. in 1911, Rand stayed on at Bryn Mawr, first as a doctoral fellow working with Ferree, then, in 1912 and 1913, as a Sarah Berliner Research Fellow, and from 1913 to 1927, as an associate in experimental psychology. Rand married Ferree in 1918, but continued to use her own name professionally.

Conducts Research in Illumination and Color Perception

Working in the general area of illumination and color perception, Rand and Ferree developed their mapping system, the Ferree–Rand perimeter. Rand was also co–inventor of many other optical and ophthalmologic devices, including a light–sense tester, an acuity projector, a multiple–exposure tachistoscope, and a variable illuminator. She also invented, on her own, the Ran Anomalscope. She was considered a pioneer in the study of indoor lighting systems, serving on the National Research Council from 1924 to 1927, and teaming up with her husband on developing industrial lighting systems.

In 1928, the couple moved to the Wilmer Ophthalmological Institute of the Johns Hopkins University Medical School, where Rand taught in research ophthalmology. She stayed there until 1935, when she became the associate director of the Research Laboratory of Physiological Optics in Baltimore, leaving that position only after her husband's death in 1942. Throughout this same period, Ferree and Rand served as research consultants for industry; it was during their years at Johns Hopkins that the couple developed a glare–controlled lighting system for New York's Holland Tunnel. During World War II, Rand and her husband also consulted with the United States Navy on night–vision studies.

Helps Develop Color-Blindness Test

After the death of her husband, Rand returned to her earlier research on the effects of color on the retina. Moving to the Knapp Foundation at Columbia University College of Physicians and Surgeons, Rand collaborated with Legrand Hardy and M. Catherine Ritter on the detection and measurement of color blindness. By the early 1950s, the trio had developed the system of color plates bearing their names to test for the type and degree of color blindness in a patient.

Rand was widely acknowledged as a pioneer in the field of physiological optics, and was the first woman elected a fellow of the Illuminating Engineering Society in 1952, receiving that society's Gold Medal in 1963. She was also the first woman to receive the Edgar D. Tillyer Medal of the Optical Society of America, in 1959. Rand retired from academia in 1957, though she remained a consultant to the Knapp Laboratories until her death in 1970. It is to her credit as a teacher that one of her students, Louise Sloan, became the second woman to win the Tillyer Medal in the year following Rand's death.

SELECTED WRITINGS BY RAND:

Books

The Factors That Influence the Sensitivity of the Retina to Color. Princeton, NJ: Psychological Review, 1913.

(With Clarence Errol Ferree) *Radiometric Apparatus for Use in Psychological and Physiological Optics.* Princeton, NJ: Psychological Review, 1917.

(With C. E. Ferree) *Studies in Physiological Optics.* 2 Volumes. Baltimore, MD: Wilmer Institute, 1934.

FURTHER READING

Books

Bailey, Martha J. *American Women in Science: A Biographical Dictionary.* Denver: ABC–CLIO, 1994, p. 318.

Garber, Elizabeth. "Rand, Marie Gertrude." *Notable American Women, the Modern Period: A Biographical Dictionary.* Edited by Barbara Sicherman and Carol Hurd Green. Cambridge, MA: Belknap Press, 1980, p. 565.

Rossiter, Margaret W. *Women Scientists in America: Before Affirmative Action, 1940–1972.* Baltimore: Johns Hopkins University Press, 1995, p. 308.

Who Was Who in American History: Science and Technology. Chicago, Illinois: Marquis Who's Who, 1976, p. 496.

Periodicals

Ogle, Kenneth N. "Gertrude Rand: Edgar D. Tillyer Medalist for 1959." *Journal of the Optical Society of America* 49 (1959): 937–41.

"Dr. Gertrude Rand, 84, Dead; Researcher on Human Vision." *New York Times* (2 July 1970): 35.

Sketch by J. Sydney Jones

Mary Jane Rathbun
1860–1943
American marine zoologist

Mary Jane Rathbun was a self–educated marine zoologist who described numerous species of crustaceans and developed the nomenclature and classification of that group of animals. She was the first woman scientist to work at the Smithsonian Institution in Washington, D. C. Her research papers, as well as the records, notes, and files that she compiled in her more than 53 years at the United States National Museum, provided the basis for the next generation of research on marine invertebrates, general zoology, and ecology.

The second daughter and youngest of five children of Jane Furey and Charles Howland Rathbun, Mary Jane Rathbun was born in 1860 and grew up in Buffalo, New York, where she attended public schools. Her mother died when she was still an infant, and she was raised by an elderly nurse. She and her brother Richard developed their interest in zoology by studying the fossils they found in the rock quarries that their father owned and operated. Rathbun's graduation from Buffalo Central School in 1878 marked the end of her formal education.

In 1873, Richard Rathbun had become an assistant to Spencer F. Baird, the head of the United States Fish Commission. In 1880, he also became curator of marine invertebrates at the National Museum of the Smithsonian Institution. In 1881, Rathbun began working with her brother during the summers, as a volunteer at the Marine Biological Station at Woods Hole, Massachusetts, cataloguing specimens of marine animals brought in by the Fish Commission survey ships. In 1884, Baird hired Rathbun at the Fish Commission, to organize and catalogue the National Museum's collections. Two years later she joined the museum staff, officially as a clerk and copyist, but in reality, carrying out her brother's duties as curator of marine invertebrates, while he was occupied at the Fish Commission. It was a new department within the museum, and although her brother was the official head, Rathbun built up the department and handled most of the administrative responsibilities, a situation that her brother officially acknowledged as early as 1889. Although Rathbun remained at the National Museum until her retirement in 1939, her highest official position was that of assistant curator from 1907 to 1914. She resigned in 1914, so that her salary could be used to hire a younger assistant with a large family to support. Rathbun remained an honorary associate, without a salary, and devoted herself to her research. Eventually, her brother became assistant secretary of the Smithsonian Institution and director of the National Museum.

Despite all of her duties at the Museum, Rathbun continued her course of self–education in marine biology, and in 1891 she started publishing her research. Her primary interest was taxonomy, or classification, of decapod crustaceans, both fossil animals and modern specimens, which include lobsters, crabs, crayfish, and shrimp. She was an expert in carcinology, or the study of crabs. She published 158 scientific papers and comprehensive treatises over the course of her career, dealing with crustaceans from around the world. Her work standardized the classification of the class Crustacea and established the nomenclature or naming of this group of organisms. She named the Chesapeake Bay blue crab, *Callinectes sapidus*, Latin for "beautiful swimmer."

Rathbun received an honorary masters degree from the University of Pittsburgh in 1916, and she was awarded a Ph.D. by George Washington University in 1917 for her study, "The Grapsoid Crabs of America." She died in Washington D. C., in 1943, of a fractured hip.

SELECTED WRITINGS BY RATHBUN:

Books

The Brachyura. Cambridge: U. S. National Museum, 1907.

Periodicals

"The Grapsoid Crabs of America." *U. S. National Museum Bulletin* 97 (1918).

"The Fossil Stalk–eyed Crustacea of the Pacific Slope of North America." *U. S. National Museum Bulletin* 138 (1926).

"The Fossil Crustacea of the Atlantic and Gulf Coastal Plain." *Geological Society of America Special Paper* 2 (1935).

FURTHER READING

Books

Ogilvie, Marilyn Bailey. *Women in Science, Antiquity through the Nineteenth Century: A Biographical Dictionary with Annotated Bibliography*. Cambridge: MIT Press, 1991.

Schmitt, Waldo L. "Mary Jane Rathbun." In *Notable American Women 1607–1950: A Biographical Dictionary*. Edited by Edward T. James, Janet Wilson James, and Paul W. Boyer. Cambridge: Harvard University Press, 1971.

Sketch by Margaret Alic

Sarah Ratner
1903–
American biochemist

Sarah Ratner is a biochemist whose research has focused on amino acids, the subunits of protein molecules. Her use of nitrogen isotopes to study metabolism—the chemical processes by which energy is provided for the body—resulted in the discovery of argininosuccinic acid, a substance formed by a sequence of reactions that take place in the liver. Ratner's awards for her work include the Carl Neuberg Medal from the American Society of European Chemists in 1959.

Ratner was born in New York City on June 9, 1903, the daughter of Aaron and Hannah (Selzer) Ratner. She received her bachelor of arts degree from Cornell University before proceeding to Columbia University for graduate studies, where she received an M.A. in 1927. Ratner worked as an assistant in biochemistry in the College of Physicians and Surgeons of Columbia University until she received her Ph.D. in biochemistry from the university in 1937. Following her graduation she was appointed a resident fellow at the College of Physicians and Surgeons and rose to the position of assistant professor. In 1946 she became an assistant professor of pharmacology at the New York University College of Medicine in New York City. Later, she became associated with the New York City Public Health Research Institute as an associate member of the division of nutrition and physiology and became a member of the department of biochemistry in 1957.

In her research Ratner used an isotope of nitrogen to study chemical reactions involving amino acids, particularly arginine. Isotopes are atoms of an element that have a different atomic mass than other atoms of the same element. Through her studies she discovered an intermediate molecule, called argininosuccinic acid, which forms when the amino acid citrulline is converted to arginine. Ratner determined that argininosuccinic acid plays an important role in the series of chemical reactions that occurs in the liver and leads to the formation of urine. This sequence of reactions is known as the urea cycle. Urea, a product of protein metabolism, has a high nitrogen content and is excreted by mammals.

The American Chemical Society honored Ratner with the Garvan Medal in 1961, and in 1974 she was elected to the National Academy of Sciences. In addition, she received research grants from the National Institutes of Health (NIH) for over twenty years, and from 1978 to 1979 she was the institutes' Fogarty Scholar–in–Residence and served as a member of the advisory council. She has received honorary doctorates from the University of North Carolina–Chapel Hill, Northwestern University, and State University of New York at Stony Brook.

Sketch by M. C. Nagel

Dr. Dixie Lee Ray (AP/Wide World Photos, Inc. Reproduced by permission.)

Dixy Lee Ray
1914–1994
American marine biologist and government official

Through her career as a marine biologist, Dixy Lee Ray developed a concern about both threats to the environment and the need for greater public understanding of science. Her increasing scientific activities in the public sphere brought her to national attention with her appointment by President Richard Nixon to the Atomic Energy Commission (AEC) in 1972. Within a year she was designated to head the AEC as its first woman chair. Later, in 1977, putting into practice her conviction that scientists need to be more active in public affairs, she was elected governor of her home state of Washington.

Ray was born to Alvis Marion Ray, a commercial printer and Frances (Adams) Ray on September 3, 1914, and was one of five girls. Early on, she developed a love of the outdoors and a fascination with marine biology, when the Ray family spent their summers on Fox Island in Puget Sound. She went on to major in zoology at Mills College and graduated Phi Beta Kappa in 1937. One year later, she received her M.A. there and proceeded to teach science in the public schools of Oakland, California, until 1942. She then left to do graduate work on a John Switzer fellowship at Stanford University. Continuing there as a Van Sicklen fellow, she received her Ph.D. degree in biological science in 1945. That year, she started a twenty–seven–year career at the University of Washington, first as an instructor in zoology, then rising to the rank of assistant professor in 1947, and finally to associate professor in 1957. While affiliated with the university, from 1952 to 1953, she was awarded a Guggenheim fellowship.

Conducted Research in Marine Biology

Ray's particular field of marine biology research dealt largely with invertebrates, especially crustacea. She studied the effects of the isopod Limnoria and fungi in damaging submerged wood, and, as an executive committee member of the Friday Harbor Laboratories in Washington in 1957, she was director of a symposium on the damage caused by marine organisms to boats, drydocks, and wharf filings. She also found time to serve as a special consultant in biological oceanography to the National Science Foundation from 1960 to 1962. Ray sailed with the crew of the Stanford University research ship, *Te Vega,* in 1964, as chief scientist and visiting professor in the International Indian Ocean Expedition, which was a multinational exploration of the little–studied environment of the Indian Ocean.

A year earlier, she had accepted the position of director of the Pacific Science Center in Seattle and converted a collection of six imposing buildings left over from the 1962 World's Fair in that city into an active science center. The complex featured a science museum and a meeting place for scientific symposia. The Pacific Science Center also began to sponsor the prestigious Arches of Science Award, which honors scientists for contributing to the understanding of the discipline by the general public.

When she was first appointed to the Atomic Energy Commission, she admitted that she had to learn a great deal more about the potential and problems of atomic energy. Because of the long–term limitations of the fossil fuel supply, she was convinced that atomic power plants could serve as an invaluable source of energy. She proposed a multibillion–dollar program to develop new sources of nuclear power and to generate new ways of converting coal to gaseous and liquid fuels. She also campaigned to eliminate defects in atomic power plants. Her own interest in protecting the environment often led her into disagreement with environmental groups, which she considered "too strident." She expressed outspoken views on the subject in two books, *Trashing the Planet* (1990), and *Environmental Overkill* (1993), as well as in magazine articles and television interviews.

Ray received honorary degrees from her alma mater, Mills College, as well as from a number of other colleges and universities. Among the many other honors she received was the Clapp Award in Marine Biology in 1958, the Seattle Maritime Award in 1967, the Frances K. Hutchinson Medal for Service in Conservation in 1973, the United Nations Peace Medal in 1973, the Francis Boyer Science Award in

1974, and the American Exemplar Medal of the Freedom Foundation at Valley Forge in 1978. She was a member of many scientific societies and was elected a foreign member of the Swedish Academy of Science and the Danish Royal Society for Natural History. Among her hobbies was the study of American Indians, which resulted in a collection of artifacts from the Kwikseutanik tribe. The tribe welcomed her as an honorary member with the name Oo'ma, signifying Great Lady. On the occasion of her death from bronchial complications at the age of seventy–nine, the *New York Times* obituary of January 3, 1994, which ran the day after her death, acknowledged that she showed her mettle early at the age of twelve, when she became the youngest girl to climb Washington's highest peak, Mount Rainier.

SELECTED WRITINGS BY RAY:

Books

(Editor) *Marine Boring and Fouling Organisms.* University of Washington Press, 1959.

(With Louis R. Guzzo) *Trashing the Planet.* Regnery Gateway (Washington, D.C.), 1990.

(With Guzzo) *Environmental Overkill.* Regnery Gateway (Washington, D.C.), 1993.

Periodicals

(With Daniel E. Stunts) "Possible Relation between Marine Fungi and Limnoria Attack on Submerged Wood." *Science*(January 9, 1959).

"An Integrated Approach to Some Problems of Marine Biological Deterioration and Destruction of Wood in Sea Water." *Marine Biology* Oregon State College Biology Colloquium (1959).

FURTHER READING

Books

Current Biography. H. W. Wilson (New York), 1973, pp. 345–348.

Periodicals

Gillette, Robert. "Ray Nominated to AEC." *Science* (July 21, 1972): 246.

Sketch by Maurice Bleifeld

Mina S. Rees (The Library of Congress. Reproduced by permission.)

Mina S. Rees
1902–1997
American mathematician

Mina S. Rees was the founding president of the Graduate Center of the City University of New York, and the first woman elected to the presidency of the American Association for the Advancement of Science. She was recognized by both the United States and Great Britain for organizing mathematicians to work on problems of interest to the military during World War II. After the war she headed the mathematics branch of the Office of Naval Research, where she built a program of government support for mathematical research and for the development of computers.

Rees was born in Cleveland, Ohio, on August 2, 1902, to Moses and Alice Louise (Stackhouse) Rees. Educated in New York public schools, Rees received her A.B. *summa cum laude* from Hunter College in New York City in 1923, and taught at Hunter College High School from 1923 to 1926. She completed an M.A. at the Teacher's College of Columbia University in 1925, and became an instructor at the Mathematics Department of Hunter College the following year. She continued her training in mathematics at the University of Chicago, where she received a fellowship for

1931 to 1932, and earned a Ph.D. in mathematics in 1931 with a dissertation on abstract algebra. Returning to Hunter, Rees was promoted to assistant professor in 1932 and associate professor in 1940.

In 1943, in the midst of World War II, Rees joined the government as a civil servant, working as executive assistant and a technical aide to Warren Weaver, the chief of the Applied Mathematics Panel (AMP) of the National Research Committee in the Office of Scientific Research and Development. The AMP, located in New York City, established contracts with mathematics departments at New York University, Brown, Harvard, Columbia, and other universities. Under these contracts, mathematicians and statisticians studied military applications such as shock waves, jet engine design, underwater ballistics, air-to-;air gunnery, the probability of damage under anti-aircraft fire, supply and munitions inspection methods, and computers. In 1948, in recognition for her wartime service, Rees received a Certificate of Merit from President Truman, as well as the Medal for Service in the Cause of Freedom from King George VI.

Joins Office of Naval Research

From 1946 to 1953, Rees worked for the Office of Naval Research (ONR), first as head of the mathematics branch and then, from 1950, as director of the mathematics division. Under Rees, the ONR supported programs for research on hydrofoils, logistics, computers, and numerical methods. Rees emphasized the study and development of mathematical algorithms for computing. The ONR supported the development of linear programming and the establishment in 1947 of an Institute for Numerical Analysis at the University of California at Los Angeles, and also worked with other military and civilian government agencies on the acquisition of early computers. In addition, the ONR funded university research programs to build computers, such as Project Whirlwind at MIT, lead by Jay Forrester, and the Institute for Advanced Study project under John Neumann. The ONR also awarded grants to support applied and basic mathematical research.

In 1953, Rees returned to Hunter College as Dean of Faculty and Professor of Mathematics. She was married in 1955, to Dr. Leopold Brahdy, a physician. In 1961, she was appointed dean of graduate studies for the City University of New York (CUNY), which established graduate programs by pooling distinguished faculty from the City Colleges, including Hunter. The following year, Rees became the first recipient of the Award for Distinguished Service to Mathematics established by the Mathematical Association of America. Rees was appointed provost of the Graduate Division in 1968 and the first president of the Graduate School and University Center in 1969. By the time Rees retired as emeritus president in 1972, CUNY's graduate school had created 26 doctoral programs and enrolled over two thousand students. During her post-war years at Hunter and CUNY, Rees served on government, scientific, and educational advisory boards and held offices in mathematical, scientific, and educational organizations. She became the first female president of the American Association for the Advancement of Science in 1971. In 1983 Rees received the Public Welfare Medal of the National Academy of Sciences, an award that confers honorary membership in that organization. She died on October 25, 1997, at the Mary Manning Walsh Home in Manhattan.

SELECTED WRITINGS BY REES:

Periodicals

"The Nature of Mathematics." *Science* (5 October 1962): 9–12.

"The Mathematical Sciences and World War II." *American Mathematical Monthly* (October 1980): 607–21.

"The Computing Program of the Office of Naval Research, 1946–1953." *Annals of the History of Computing* 4, no. 2 (April 1982): 102–20.

FURTHER READING

Books

Dana, Rosamond, and Peter J. H. Hilton. "Interview with Mina Rees." In *Mathematical People,* edited by Donald J. Albers and G. L. Alexanderson. Cambridge, MA: Birkhauser, 1985, pp. 256–65.

Periodicals

———. "Award for Distinguished Service to Mathematics." *American Mathematical Monthly* (February 1962): 185–87.

Saxon, Wolfgang. "Mina S. Rees, Mathematician and CUNY Leader, Dies at 95" (obituary). *New York Times* (28 October 1997): B10.

Sketch by Sally M. Moite

Maria Reiche
1903–1998
German archaeologist and mathematician

Known as the "Lady of the Lines," Maria Reiche devoted her life to the study and preservation of the Nazca Lines, huge etchings made by ancient inhabitants of the Peruvian desert. These lines constitute the largest concentration of petroglyphs or "geoglyphs" in the world.

Maria Reiche (Photograph by Alejandro Balaguer. AP/Wide World Photos. Reproduced by permission.)

Reiche's research led to a new appreciation of the scientific achievements of pre–Incan civilizations.

Reiche was born in Dresden, Germany in 1903. Her father was a lawyer and military officer who died in the first world war. Her mother, a theologian, struggled to feed her family in an impoverished Germany, during and after World War I. Although it was not easy to attend high school at that time in Germany, Reiche graduated from the Staedtische BildungsanstaltIt, then the most prestigious girls' school in Dresden. Always drawn to mathematics, Reich continued her studies in mathematics, physics, philosophy, geography, and education in Dresden and Hamburg, completing her master's degree in Dresden in 1928. However Reiche was unwilling to live in Nazi Germany and, in 1932, she left for Peru.

In Cusco, Peru, in the Andes Mountains, Reiche taught languages and gymnastics and tutored the sons of the German consul. It was here that Reiche became fascinated with the culture of the Incas, who had built observatories to study the stars and construct calendars. She began examining the mathematical concepts of the Incan astronomers.

Sees the Nazca Lines

After completing her teaching contract in 1934, Reiche went to Lima, Peru, and offered her services as a translator to Julio Tello, an archaeologist at the University of San Marcos. Tello took her on an archaeological dig at Paracas, on the coast of Peru. There she overheard a local talking about giant figures carved into the ground in the Pampa Colorada near Nazca. Tello was not interested, but Reiche decided to examine them herself. The Nazca Lines were located in a high desert valley near the Peruvian coast, about 250 miles south of Lima, in a rocky area that contained ferrous oxide, so that the ground was grayish white. In a plain that was about five miles wide and 60 miles long, early inhabitants, between 900 B.C. and 600 A.D., had cleared rocks and made shallow etchings which had survived the centuries.

An American anthropologist at the Museum for Archaeology, Paul Kosok, had photographed the lines and began discussing them with Reiche in 1939. Eventually, camping out or living in a small house, Reiche began to study them full–time. Using a rake and a broom, she cleaned them of small rocks and debris. There were thousands of lines, straight, spiraled or zigzagging, extending as far as five miles up into the surrounding hills. Eventually, Reiche realized that they formed some three hundred huge pictures, including a spider, a monkey, a hummingbird, a whale, a 900–feet–long heron, a flower, a dog, a tree, a cat with a fish's tail, a condor, a lizard, and various abstract designs. Following the lines and reproducing them on paper, Reiche decided that they constituted a giant calendar, tracing the movements of the sun, moon, and constellations. Reiche theorized that the Indians had used them to determine when to plant and irrigate crops. She began to examine the mathematical relationships between the figures and the constellations. Her results have not been widely–accepted because of the very large number of lines and many possible correlations. Shortly before her death, Reiche began a new mathematical study, to determine whether the lines were used to predict cyclical weather phenomena such as El Niño, which periodically caused major flooding along the coast of Peru.

Preserves the Nazca Lines

Reiche's book, *Mystery on the Desert*, first published in 1949, brought worldwide attention to the Nazca Lines. Other archaeologists began to study them and develop their own theories about their significance. To Reiche's dismay, the lines also attracted the attention of UFO enthusiasts and other paranormal theorists.

Reiche built a small museum near the lines, financed through visitor's contributions and overseas institutions. She became their protector, paying guards with the royalties earned from her books to keep vehicles away. In addition to curbing vandalism, she successfully fought a government plan to "reconstruct" the lines and a plan to flood the plains for agriculture. Acid rain from mining operations in the nearby mountains also threatened the lines. Eventually, the Nazca Lines became one of Peru's major tourist attractions and Reiche became a heroine to the residents of Nazca, for having brought in tourist dollars to the poverty–stricken region. Every year, her birthday was celebrated with street dances and ceremonies. In 1993, the Peruvian government gave Reiche its highest award, the Order of the Sun, and she was awarded four honorary doctorates from Peruvian universities. She also received the highest German decoration, the Bundesverdienstkreuz First Class in 1983.

Reiche became nearly blind and deaf during the last years of her life. In 1993 her family tried to take her back to Germany, but she refused to leave her work. She died in Lima in 1998, one month after being diagnosed with ovarian cancer. Several schools in Nazca bear her name and the United Nations Educational, Scientific and Cultural Organization declared the Nazca Lines to be a World Cultural Heritage Site.

SELECTED WRITINGS BY REICHE:

Books

Mystery on the Desert. Stuttgart: Heinrich Fink GmbH, 1968.

Peruvian Ground Drawings. Munich: Kunstraum München, 1974.

(With Marilyn Bridges) *Markings: Aerial Views of Sacred Landscapes.* New York: Aperture, 1986.

Conversaciones con Maria Reiche. Lima: Editorial Horizonte, 1992.

Contribuciones a la Geometría y Astronomía en el Antiguo Perú . Lima: Asociación María Reiche para las Líneas de Nasca, Epígrafe Editores S.A., 1993.

Other

(With Peter Spry–Leverton and Christopher B. Donnan) *Mysteries of Peru.* Central Independent Television, Great Britain: Atlas Video, 1993. Videorecording.

FURTHER READING

Other

Associated Press. "Guardian Angel of Peru's Nazca Lines dead at 95." *Cable News Network Interactive.* 1998. http://www.qtm.net/~geibdan/a1998/jun/gua.html (5 July 1999).

Dornieden, Michael. "Zum Tode von Frau Dr. Maria Reiche." http://www.hightek.com/~mdornieden/reiche.html (10 July 1999).

Evangelisch–Lutherischen Christuskirche in Lima/Peru. "TRAUERFEIER FÜR MARIA REICHE AM 10. Juni 1998 im Nationalmuseum Lima." (Memorial Service for Maria Reiche, in German/Spanish). http://www.geocities.com/athens/parthenon/1046/mariareiche.html (10 July 1999).

Lama, Abraham. "SCIENCE–PERU: Maria Reiche to Rest With the Enigmas She Unraveled." *Inter Press Service.* 11 June 1998. http://www.oneworld.org/ips2/june98/1910075.html (5 July 1999).

Sketch by Margaret Alic

Ellen Swallow Richards
1842–1911
American chemist

Ellen Swallow Richards was an applied scientist, sanitary chemist, and the founder of home economics. For twenty–seven years she was employed by the Massachusetts Institute of Technology (MIT), where she taught chemistry and developed methods for the analysis of air, water, and consumer products. Her work as a scientist and educator led to improvements in the home and opened the door to scientific professions for women.

Swallow was born on December 3, 1842, in Dunstable, Massachusetts. She was the only child of Peter Swallow, a teacher, farmer, and store keeper, and Fanny Gould Taylor, a teacher. She was educated at home by her parents until the family moved to Westford, Massachusetts, in 1859. There she attended Westford Massachusetts Academy, where she enrolled in mathematics, French, and Latin. In 1863 she graduated from the academy, and the family relocated to Littleton, Massachusetts.

Swallow worked at an assortment of jobs—storekeeping, tutoring, housecleaning, cooking, and nursing—to earn enough money to continue her education. Because of her mother's ill health, she struggled with exhaustion and mental depression for a period of several years.

By 1868 Swallow had saved enough money to attend Vassar college, where she excelled in astronomy and chemistry. Her chemistry professor, convinced that science should be applied to practical problems, contributed to Swallow's developing interest in consumer and environmental science. Receiving a bachelor of arts degree in 1870, Swallow decided to apply to MIT to further her study of chemistry and became one of the first women students at that institution. She received a bachelor of science degree from MIT in 1873. In that same year, after submitting a thesis on the estimation of vanadium in iron ore, she received her masters of arts degree from Vassar. Although she continued her studies at MIT an additional two years, she was never awarded a doctorate.

Swallow married Robert Hallowell Richards, a professor of mining engineering, on June 4, 1875. The couple had no children and were able to devote their full support to each other's professional career. In her leisure time Richards enjoyed gardening, entertaining, and traveling. She also took an active interest in improving her own home. At one time she boasted of having year–round hot water and a telephone.

A Successful Career at MIT

Richards helped establish a laboratory at MIT for women. While still an undergraduate, she had taught chemistry at the girls high school in Boston through a project funded by the Woman's Education Association. With the help of this association, Richards convinced MIT of the need for a women's lab, and in 1876, armed with the title of assistant, she began teaching chemical analysis, industrial chemistry, mineralogy, and biology to a handful of women students. In addition to their traditional studies, the students assisted in testing a variety of consumer products for composition and adulterations. After seven years, in which four students graduated and the rest were accepted as regular MIT students, the laboratory closed.

In 1884 MIT opened a new laboratory for the study of sanitation, and Richards was appointed assistant and instructor in sanitary chemistry. Her teaching duties included instruction in air, water, and sewage analysis. In addition, she was responsible for completing a two–year survey of Massachusetts inland waters (begun in 1887 for the state board of health). Her success in analyzing nearly forty thousand water samples was attributed to her knowledge of methodology, apparatus, and her excellent supervisory and record–keeping skills. The water survey work and her involvement with environmental chemistry were significant contributions to the new science of ecology.

Founder of Home Economics

Richards was a pioneer in the effort to increase educational opportunities for women. She was one of the founders of the Association of Collegiate Alumnae, which later changed its title to the American Association of University Women. She organized the science section for the Society to Encourage Studies at Home, a correspondence school founded in 1887 by Anna Tickenor. Her correspondence with students provided insight into the daily life and problems faced by women in the home. Richards learned that women were seeking help with a wide range of problems, not all of which were scientific in nature, including manners of dress, food preparation, and exercise.

In 1890 Richards opened the New England Kitchen in Boston as a means of demonstrating how wholesome foods could be selected and prepared. In 1899 she organized and chaired a summer conference at Lake Placid, New York, that established the profession of home economics. Conference participants explored new ways of applying sociology and economics to the home and developed courses of study for schools and colleges. Later she helped found the American Home Economics Association and provided financial support for its publication, the *Journal of Home Economics.*

In addition to her work at the sanitation laboratory, Richards consulted, lectured, authored ten books, and published numerous papers, including bulletins on nutrition for the United States Department of Agriculture. In 1910, in recognition of her commitment to education, she was appointed to supervise the teaching of home economics in public schools by the council of the National Education Association. In that same year she was awarded an honorary doctorate from Smith College. Richards died of heart disease in 1911 at the age of sixty–eight.

SELECTED WRITINGS BY RICHARDS:

Books

The Chemistry of Cooking and Cleaning: A Manual for House–keepers. Estes and Lauriat, 1882.

FURTHER READING

Books

Ogilvie, Marilyn. *Women in Science.* Cambridge: MIT Press, 1986, pp. 149–52.

Sketch by Mike McClure

Sally Ride
1951–
American astronaut and physicist

Sally Ride is best known as the first American woman sent into outer space. She also served the National Aeronautics and Space Administration (NASA) in an advisory capacity, being the only astronaut chosen for President Ronald Reagan's Rogers Commission investigating the mid–launch explosion of the space shuttle *Challenger* in January, 1986, writing official recommendation reports, and creating NASA's Office of Exploration. Both scientist and professor, she has served as a fellow at the Stanford University Center for International Security and Arms Control, a member of the board of directors at Apple Computer Inc., and a space institute director and physics professor at the University of California at San Diego. Ride has chosen to write primarily for children about space travel and exploration. Her commitment to educating the young earned her the Jefferson Award for Public Service from the American Institute for Public Service in 1984, in addition to her National Spaceflight Medals recognizing her two groundbreaking shuttle missions in 1983 and 1984. Newly elected president Bill Clinton chose her as a member of his transition team during the fall of 1992.

Sally Ride (U.S. National Aeronautics and Space Administration.)

Sally Kristen Ride is the older daughter of Dale Burdell and Carol Joyce (Anderson) Ride of Encino, California, and was born May 26, 1951. As author Karen O'Connor describes tomboy Ride in her young reader's book, *Sally Ride and the New Astronauts,* Sally would race her dad for the sports section of the newspaper when she was only five years old. An active, adventurous, yet also scholarly family, the Rides traveled throughout Europe for a year when Sally was nine and her sister Karen was seven, after Dale took a sabbatical from his political science professorship at Santa Monica Community College. While Karen was inspired to become a minister, in the spirit of her parents, who were elders in their Presbyterian church, Ride's own developing taste for exploration would eventually lead her to apply to the space program almost on a whim. "I don't know why I wanted to do it," she confessed to *Newsweek* prior to embarking on her first spaceflight.

The opportunity was serendipitous, since the year she began job–hunting marked the first time NASA had opened its space program to applicants since the late 1960s, and the very first time women would not be excluded from consideration. NASA needed to cast a wider net than ever before, as *Current Biography* disclosed in 1983. The program paid less than private sector counterparts and offered no particular research specialties, unlike most job opportunities in academia. All it took was a return reply postcard, and Ride was in the mood to take those risks. This was, after all, a young lady who could patch up a disabled Toyota with Scotch tape without breaking stride, as one of her friends once discovered. Besides, she had always forged her own way before with the full support of her open–minded family.

Student Sets Own Agenda

From her earliest years in school, Ride was so proficient and efficient at once, she proved to be an outright annoyance to some of her teachers. Though she was a straight–A student, she was easily bored, and her brilliance only came to the fore in high school, when she was introduced to the world of science by her physiology teacher. The impact of this mentor, Dr. Elizabeth Mommaerts, was so profound that Ride would later dedicate her first book primarily to her, as well as the fallen crew of the *Challenger.* While she was adaptable to all forms of sport, playing tennis was Ride's most outstanding talent, which she had developed since the age of ten. Under the tutelage of a four–time U.S. Open champion, Ride eventually ranked eighteenth nationally on the junior circuit. Her ability won her a partial scholarship to Westlake School for Girls, a prep school in Los Angeles. After graduating from there in 1968, Ride preferred to work on her game full time instead of the physics program at Swarthmore College, Pennsylvania, where she had originally enrolled. It was only after Ride had fully tested her dedication to the game that she decided against a professional career, even though tennis pro Billie Jean King had once told her it was within her grasp. Back in California as an undergraduate student at Stanford University, Ride followed her burgeoning love for Shakespeare to a double major, receiving B.S. and B.A. degrees in tandem by 1973. She narrowed her focus to physics for her masters, also from Stanford, awarded in 1975. Work toward her dissertation continued at Stanford; she submitted "The Interaction of X–Rays with the Interstellar Medium" in 1978.

Ride was just finishing her Ph.D. candidacy in physics, astronomy, and astrophysics at Stanford, working as a research assistant, when she got the call from NASA. She became one of thirty–five chosen from an original field of applicants numbering eight thousand for the spaceflight training of 1978. "Why I was selected remains a complete mystery," she later admitted to John Grossmann in a 1985 interview in *Health.* "None of us has ever been told." Even after three years of studying x–ray astrophysics, Ride had to go back to the classroom to gain skills to be part of a team of astronauts. The program included basic science and math, meteorology, guidance, navigation, and computers as well as flight training on a T–38 jet trainer and other operational simulations. Ride was selected as part of the ground–support crew for the second (November, 1981) and third (March, 1982) shuttle flights, her duties including the role of "capcom," or capsule communicator, relaying commands from the ground to the shuttle crew. These experiences prepared her to be an astronaut.

A Series of NASA Firsts

Ride would subsequently become, at thirty–one, the youngest person sent into orbit as well as the first American woman in space, the first American woman to make two spaceflights, and, coincidentally, the first astronaut to marry another astronaut in active duty. She and Steven Alan Hawley were married at the groom's family home in Kansas on July 26, 1982. Hawley, a Ph.D. from the University of California, had joined NASA with a background in astronomy and astrophysics. When asked during a hearing by Congressman Larry Winn, Jr., of the House Committee on Science and Technology, how she would feel when Hawley was in space while she remained earthbound, Ride replied, "I am going to be a very interested observer." The pair were eventually divorced.

Ride points to her fellow female astronauts Anna Fisher, **Shannon Lucid**, Judith Resnik, Margaret Seddon, and Kathryn Sullivan with pride. Since these women were chosen for training, Ride's own experience could not be dismissed as tokenism, which had been the unfortunate fate of the first woman in orbit, the Soviet Union's **Valentina Tereshkova**, a textile worker. Ride expressed her concern to *Newsweek* reporter Pamela Abramson in the week before her initial shuttle trip. "It's important to me that people don't think I was picked for the flight because I am a woman and it's time for NASA to send one."

From June 18 to June 24, 1983, flight STS–7 of the space shuttle *Challenger* launched from Kennedy Space Center in Florida, orbited the Earth for six days, returned to Earth, and landed at Edwards Air Force Base in California. Among the shuttle team's missions were the deployment of international satellites and numerous research experiments supplied by a range of groups, from a naval research lab to various high school students. With Ride operating the shuttle's robot arm in cooperation with Colonel John M. Fabian of the U.S. Air Force, the first satellite deployment and retrieval using such an arm was successfully performed in space during the flight.

Ride was also chosen for *Challenger* flight STS–41G, which transpired between October 5 and October 13, 1984. This time, the robot arm was put to some unusual applications, including "ice–busting" on the shuttle's exterior and readjusting a radar antenna. According to Henry S. F. Cooper, Jr., in his book *Before Lift–off,* fellow team member Ted Browder felt that because Ride was so resourceful and willing to take the initiative, less experienced astronauts on the flight might come to depend upon her rather than develop their own skills, but this mission also met with great success. Objectives during this longer period in orbit covered scientific observations of the Earth, demonstrations of potential satellite refueling techniques, and deployment of a satellite. As STS–7 had been, STS–41G was led by Captain Robert L. Crippen of the U.S. Navy to a smooth landing, this time in Florida.

Ride had been chosen for a third scheduled flight, but training was cut short in January, 1986, when the space shuttle *Challenger* exploded in midair shortly after takeoff. The twelve–foot rubber O–rings that serve as washers between steel segments of the rocket boosters, already considered problematic, failed under stress, killing the entire crew. Judy Resnik, one of the victims, had flown as a rookie astronaut on STS–41G. Ride remembered her in *Ms.* magazine as empathetic, sharing "the same feelings that there was good news and bad news in being accepted to be the first one." As revealed a few months later in the *Chicago Tribune,* program members at NASA began to feel that their safety had been willfully compromised without their knowledge. "I think that we may have been misleading people into thinking that this is a routine operation," Ride was quoted as saying.

Responds to Challenger Tragedy

Ride herself tried to remedy that misconception with her subsequent work on the Rogers Commission and as special assistant for long–range and strategic planning to NASA Administrator James C. Fletcher in Washington, D.C., during 1986 and 1987. In keeping with the Rogers Commission recommendations, which Ride helped to shape, especially regarding the inclusion of astronauts at management levels, Robert Crippen was eventually made Deputy Director for Space Shuttle Operations in Washington, D.C., as well.

As leader of a task force on the future of the space program, Ride wrote *Leadership and America's Future in Space.* According to *Aviation Week and Space Technology,* this status report initiated a proposal to redefine NASA goals as a means to prevent the "space race" mentality that might pressure management and personnel into taking untoward risks. "A single goal is not a panacea," the work stated in its preface. "The problems facing the space program must be met head–on, not oversimplified." The overall thrust of NASA's agenda, Ride suggested, should take environmental and international research goals into consideration. A pledge to inform the public and capture the interest of youngsters should be taken as a given. Ride cited a 1986 work decrying the lack of math and science proficiency among American high school graduates, a mere six percent of whom are fluent in these fields, compared to up to ninety percent in other nations.

Top Priority: Educating Children

While with NASA, Ride traveled with fellow corps members to speak to high school and college students on a monthly basis. As former English tutor Joyce Ride once told a *Boston Globe* reporter, her daughter had developed scientific interests she herself harbored in younger days, before encountering a wall of silence in a college physics class as a coed at the University of California in Los Angeles. As Joyce remarked, she and the only other young woman in the class were "nonpersons." Speaking at Smith College in 1985, Sally Ride announced that encouraging women to enter math and science disciplines was her "personal crusade." Ride noted in *Publishers Weekly* the next year that her ambition to write children's books had been met with some dismay by publishing houses more in the mood to read an autobiography targeted for an adult audience. Her youth–oriented books were both written with childhood friends. Susan Okie, coauthor of *To Space and Back,* eventually became a journalist with the *Washington Post. Voyager* coauthor Tam O'Shaughnessy, once a fellow competition tennis player, grew up to develop workshops on scientific teaching skills.

Ride left NASA in 1987 for Stanford's Center for International Security and Arms Control, and two years later she became director of the California Space Institute and physics professor at the University of California at San Diego. She has flown Grumman Tiger aircraft in her spare time since getting her pilot's license. The former astronaut keeps in shape, when not teaching or fulfilling the duties of her various professional posts, by running and engaging in other sports, although she once told *Health* magazine she winds up eating junk food a lot. Ride admitted not liking to run but added, "I like being in shape."

SELECTED WRITINGS BY RIDE:

Books

(With Susan Okie) *To Space and Back.* Lothrop, 1986.

Leadership and America's Future in Space: A Report to the Administrator by Dr. Sally K. Ride, August 1987. NASA, August, 1987.

(With Tam O'Shaughnessy) *Voyager: An Adventure to the Edge of the Solar System.* Crown, 1992.

FURTHER READING

Books

Astronauts and Cosmonauts Biographical and Statistical Data. U.S. Government Printing Office, 1989.

Cooper, Henry S. F., Jr. *Before Lift–off.* Johns Hopkins University Press, 1987.

Current Biography. H. W. Wilson, 1983, pp. 318–21.

Hearing before the Committee on Science and Technology, U.S. House of Representatives, Ninety–eighth Congress, First Session, July 19, 1983. U.S. Government Printing Office, 1983.

O'Connor, Karen. *Sally Ride and the New Astronauts: Scientists in Space.* F. Watts, 1983.

Periodicals

Adler, Jerry, and Pamela Abramson. "Sally Ride: Ready for Liftoff." *Newsweek* (June 13, 1983): 36–40, 45, 49, 51.

Caldwell, Jean. "Astronaut Ride Urges Women to Study Math." *Boston Globe* (June 30, 1985): B90, B92.

Covault, Craig. "Ride Panel Calls for Aggressive Action to Assert U.S. Leadership in Space." *Aviation Week and Space Technology* (August 24, 1987): 26–27.

Goodwin, Irwin. "Sally Ride to Leave NASA Orbit; Exodus at NSF." *Physics Today* (July, 1987): 45.

Grossmann, John. "Sally Ride, Ph.D." *Health* (August 1985): 73–74, 76.

Ingwerson, Marshall. "Clinton Transition Team Takes on Pragmatic Cast." *Christian Science Monitor* (November 30, 1992): 3.

Lowther, William. "A High Ride through the Sex Barrier." *Maclean's* (June 27, 1983): 40–41.

Peterson, Sarah. "Just Another Astronaut." *U.S. News and World Report* (November 29, 1982): 50–51.

Roback, Diane. "Sally Ride: Astronaut and Now Author." *Publishers Weekly* (November 28, 1986): 42, 44.

Rowley, Storer, and Michael Tackett. "Internal Memo Charges NASA Compromised Safety." *Chicago Tribune* (March 9, 1986): 8.

Sherr, Lynn. "Remembering Judy: The Five Women Astronauts Who Trained with Judy Resnik Remember Her . . . and That Day." *Ms.* (June 1986): 57.

Sherr. "A Mission to Planet Earth: Astronaut Sally Ride Talks to Lynn Sherr about Peaceful Uses of Space." *Ms.* (July/August 1987): 180–81.

Sketch by Jennifer Kramer

Dorothea Klumpke Roberts
1861–1942
American astronomer

Although American, Dorothea Klumpke Roberts spent most of her life in Paris where she was the first woman to work and study at the Paris Observatory. She was also the first woman to receive a doctorate in mathematics from the Sorbonne. Roberts was a well-known observational astronomer in her day, as a well as a respected mathematician.

Roberts was born in San Francisco in 1861, the daughter of Dorothea Matilda (Tolle) and John Gerard Klumpke. Her early education was in public and private schools in San Francisco, until her mother decided to take her daughters to Europe to be further educated. Roberts studied languages, mathematics, and astronomy in Germany, Switzerland, and France. Her oldest sister Anna became an artist and the biographer of her close friend, the artist Rosa Bonheur; her youngest sister Julia became a professional violinist; and her sister Augusta became a physician and was the first female intern at a Paris hospital.

Roberts received her bachelor of science degree from the Sorbonne in Paris, in 1886. In 1893, she became the first woman to be awarded a doctorate in mathematics from the Sorbonne. Her thesis, a theoretical study of the rings of Saturn, completed the work of great Russian woman mathematician, **Sonia Kovalevskaya**. In 1887 she went to work at the Paris Observatory and was an assistant there until 1901. The first woman to work and study there, she examined the pattern of bands and lines that form when a star's light is dispersed through a prism, known as a star's spectra. She also studied meteorites and comets. In 1891, she was appointed director of the Bureau of Measurements within the observatory, where she supervised the charting and cataloguing of stars from photographic plates. At the international astrophotographic conferences held at the observatory, Roberts was in charge of translating the foreign scientific papers into French. She lectured frequently on astronomy and in 1899 she made two ascents in balloons to observe the Leonid meteor shower and a partial solar eclipse.

In 1893, Roberts presented a paper on charting stars and other celestial bodies to the Congress of Astronomy and Physics during the World's Columbian Exposition in Chicago. This work won her a $300 award from the French Académie des Sciences. In 1897 she won the Prix des Dames from the Société Astronomique de France.

Her marriage to Isaac Roberts, a Welsh astronomer, interrupted her independent career. Her work was confined to her husband's private observatory in Crowborough, Sussex, England, until his death in 1904. After her husband's death, Roberts returned to France, where she lived with her mother and sister, at the Château Rosa Bonheur at By, and resumed her career in astronomer. Her primary interest was in the measurements of nebulae, the clouds of dust and gas from which new stars are formed.

Roberts authored numerous scientific papers. In 1928, she published her *Celestial Atlas*, in memory of her husband. She published a supplement to *Celestial Atlas* in 1932, the same year that she won Helene-Paul Helbronner prize for this work from the Académie des Sciences.

Roberts was a member of a number of astronomical societies in Britain, the United States, and France, and she was the first woman elected to the Astronomical Society of France. In 1934, she received the Cross of the Legion of Honor from the French government. Roberts died in San Francisco in 1942.

SELECTED WRITINGS BY ROBERTS:

Books

Contributions à l'étude des anneaux de Saturne. Paris: Gauthier–Villars et Fils, 1893.

Periodicals

"The Bureau of Measurements of the Paris Observatory." *Astronomy and Astrophysics* 12 (1893): 783–88.

"La Femme dans l'Astronomie." *Astronomie* 13 (1899): 162–70, 206–15.

FURTHER READING

Books

Mozans, H. J. [John Augustine Zahm]. *Women in Science*. 1913. Reprint, Cambridge: MIT Press, 1974.

Ogilvie, Marilyn Bailey. *Women in Science, Antiquity through the Nineteenth Century: A Biographical Dictionary with Annotated Bibliography*. Cambridge: MIT Press, 1991.

Sketch by Margaret Alic

Edith Adelaide Roberts
1881–1977
American botanist

Edith Adelaide Roberts was known for her significant contributions to the study of plant ecology, particularly in Dutchess County, New York. She studied native plant propagation, established the first outdoor ecological laboratory in the country, and researched plant physiology.

Edith Roberts was born on April 28, 1881, in Dover, New Hampshire. She grew up in Rollinsford with her parents Joseph, a farmer, and Addie (Littleford) Roberts. She graduated from Smith College in 1905 with an A.B. degree and from the University of Chicago in 1911 with her M.S. degree. During these years, she also studied at Woods Hole, Massachusetts, taught at several high schools, and served as associate professor of botany at Mount Holyoke College. She continued her studies at the University of Chicago as a fellow in the botany department, completing her doctorate in 1916.

For three years, Roberts did extension work for the United States Department of Agriculture. In 1919, she joined the faculty of Vassar College as an associate professor of botany. In 1922 she was promoted to full professor, a position she retained until her retirement as professor emeritus in 1948.

Establishes Outdoor Lab

During her second year at Vassar, Roberts founded the Dutchess County Outdoor Ecological Laboratory, the first one in the United States. The Lab was created on a parcel of land originally overrun with poison ivy and other weeds. When completed, with the aid of funds donated by Roberts through additional lectures, the land contained almost all 2,000 plant species native to the county. Roberts intended to prove that native plants could be propagated in order to reclaim parcels of land.

Continuing her studies of ecology, Roberts co–authored a book on how plants are associated in groups, and how those groups cycle into other plant groups. The book also explained how plants flourish in relation to environmental factors of location, soil quality, light, and moisture. In 1935, she became an honorary landscape consultant for Dutchess County.

Three years later, Roberts co–authored a book on plant life in Dutchess County, one of the first books to focus on a specific area for botanical study. It was also the first book that identified and mapped a county's vegetation in its entirety. The book, which took fifteen years of study, was intended to help farmers, estate owners, and country–dwellers develop their land both aesthetically and for economic benefit through the understanding and use of native plants.

During the last few years at Vassar, Roberts studied chloroplast structure and conducted research using powerful electron microscopes. After retirement, she contributed to scholarly publications, in addition to her work in the food technology department of the Massachusetts Institute of Technology. In 1948, she and Mildred Southwick discovered that plants, not fish livers, are the original source for vitamin A.

Known as a workaholic, as well as a private person, Roberts was also remembered for her sense of humor. She was a member of Phi Beta Kappa, Sigma Xi, the Botanical Society of America, the American Forestry Association, and the American Association for the Advancement of Science. Roberts died in Massachusetts in early March of 1977.

SELECTED WRITINGS BY ROBERTS:

Books

(With Elsa Rehman). *American Plants for American Gardens: Plant Ecology—the Study of Plants in Relation to Their Environment.* New York: Macmillan Company, 1929.

(With Helen Wilkinson Reynolds). *The Role of Plant Life in the History of Dutchess County.* Privately Printed. 1938.

FURTHER READING

Books

Bailey, Martha J. *American Women in Science.* Denver: ABC-CLIO, 1994.

Other

Special Collections Archives. Vassar College.

Sketch by Helene Barker Kiser

Lydia Jane Roberts
1879–1965
American nutritionist

Lydia Roberts was a pioneer researcher in nutrition who was largely responsible for determining the minimum daily requirements for vitamins and minerals.

Roberts was born in 1879 in Hope Township in Barry County, Michigan. The third of four children, she was the youngest of three daughters of Warren and Mary (McKibbin) Roberts. Shortly after her birth, her family moved to the farming community of Martin, Michigan, where her father worked as a carpenter. Roberts attended elementary and high schools in Martin and, in 1899, completed a one–year program at the Mt. Pleasant Normal School (later Central Michigan University).

After teaching school for several years in Michigan, Roberts taught in Miles City and Great Falls, Montana, and then in Virginia. In 1909 her teaching credentials were upgraded to a Life Certificate by the Mt. Pleasant Normal School. Subsequently, she taught third grade in Dillon, Montana and worked at Western Montana College. During a summer spent working at the Montana Children's Institute, Roberts became interested in diet and health. In 1915 she entered the University of Chicago to further her education.

Majoring in home economics, Roberts was encouraged by the department chairperson, biochemist Katharine Blunt, to continue her studies after earning her B.S. in 1917. Home economics at Chicago was a rapidly growing and scientifically oriented department that was becoming the center of applied nutritional research. Roberts earned her master's degree in 1919 with her thesis, "A Malnutrition Clinic as a University Problem in Applied Nutrition," published in the *Journal of Home Economics*. It was based on her work at a child nutrition clinic set up by Blunt and Rush Medical College. That year, Roberts became an assistant professor in the department. With the aid of her students, she compiled the book *Nutrition Work with Children*, which became a classic in the field and went through a number of editions over the years. In 1928, Roberts was awarded her Ph.D. and promoted to associate professor. The following year, Blunt resigned as chair, and Roberts headed a three–person committee that ran the department while a nationwide search was conducted for Blunt's successor. In 1930, the position was offered to Roberts, and she remained at Chicago as a full professor and department chair until her retirement in 1944.

In addition to administration and teaching, Roberts continued her research on children's nutritional requirements. Her work focused on requirements for calories, proteins, vitamins, and minerals, as well as practical methods for achieving these requirements. She was a member of the Council of Foods and Nutrition of the American Medical Association and the Food and Nutrition Board of the National Research Council where, during the second world war, she headed the committee that set the recommended daily allowances for vitamins and minerals and the recommendations for vitamin and mineral supplementation of flour and bread.

In Chicago, Roberts lived with her elder sister Lillian. However, after her mandatory retirement from the university, she became chair of the home economics department of the University of Puerto Rico in 1946. In 1943, she had made a survey of nutrition on the island for the U. S. Department of Agriculture, and her study with Rosa Stefani, *Patterns of Living in Puerto Rican Families*, was published in 1949. After her second retirement in 1952, she continued working on a nutritional improvement program in a rural Puerto Rican community, which was tied to economic development and which became the model for an island–wide program. Roberts died in 1965, after collapsing at her desk of a ruptured abdominal aneurysm.

SELECTED WRITINGS BY ROBERTS:

Books

Nutrition Work with Children. Chicago: University of Chicago Press, 1927.

(With Rosa Luisa Stefani) *Patterns of Living in Puerto Rican Families*. 1949. Reprint, New York: Arno Press, 1975.

"Beginnings of the Recommended Dietary Allowances." In *Essays on the History of Nutrition and Dietetics*, compiled by Adelia M. Beeuwkes, E. Neige Todhunter, and Emma Seifrit Weigley. Chicago: American Dietetic Association, 1967.

Periodicals

(With N. A. Fernandez, J. C. Burgos, I. C. Plough, and C. F. Asenjo) "Nutritional Status of People in Isolated Areas of Puerto Rico. Survey of Barrio Mavilla, Vega Alta, Puerto Rico." *American Journal of Clinical Nutrition*. 17 (November 1965): 305–16.

FURTHER READING

Books

Doyle, Margaret D. and Eva D. Wilson. *Lydia Jane Roberts: Nutrition Scientist, Educator, and Humanitarian*. Chicago: American Dietetic Association, 1989.

Ihde, Aaron J. "Roberts, Lydia Jane." In *Notable American Women: The Modern Period: A Biographical Dictionary*. Edited by Barbara Sicherman, Carol Hurd Green, Ilene Kantrov, and Harriette Walker. Cambridge: Harvard University Press, 1980.

Periodicals

Bing, Franklin C. "Lydia Jane Roberts – A Biographical Sketch." *Journal of Nutrition* 93 (September 1967): 1–13.

Martin, Ethel Austin. "Lydia Jane Roberts, June 30, 1879 – May 28, 1965." *Journal of the American Dietetic Association* 47 (August 1965): 127–28.

Martin, Ethel Austin. " The Life Works of Lydia J. Roberts." *Journal of the American Dietetic Association* 49 (October 1966): 299–302.

Sketch by Margaret Alic

Julia Robinson
1919–1985
American mathematician

Excelling in the field of mathematics, Julia Robinson was instrumental in solving Hilbert's tenth problem—to find an effective method for determining whether a given diophantine equation is solvable with integers. Over a period of two decades, she developed the framework on which the solution was constructed. In recognition of her accomplishments, she became the first woman mathematician elected to the National Academy of Sciences, the first female president of the American Mathematical Society, and the first woman mathematician to receive a MacArthur Foundation Fellowship.

Robinson was born Julia Bowman on December 8, 1919, in St. Louis, Missouri. Her mother, Helen Hall Bowman, died two years later; Robinson and her older sister went to live with their grandmother near Phoenix, Arizona. The following year their father, Ralph Bowman, retired and joined them in Arizona after becoming disinterested in his machine tool and equipment business. He expected to support his children and his new wife, Edenia Kridelbaugh Bowman, with his savings. In 1925, her family moved to San Diego; three years later a third daughter was born.

At the age of nine, Robinson contracted scarlet fever, and the family was quarantined for a month. They celebrated the end of isolation by viewing their first talking motion picture. The celebration was premature, however, as Robinson soon developed rheumatic fever and was bedridden for a year. When she was well enough, she worked with a tutor for a year, covering the required curriculum for the fifth through eighth grades. She was fascinated by the tutor's claim that it had been proven that the square root of two could not be calculated to a point where the decimal began to repeat. Her interest in mathematics continued at San Diego High School; when she graduated with honors in mathematics and science, her parents gave her a slide rule that she treasured and named "Slippy."

Julia Robinson (Mathematisches Forschungs-institut Oberwolfach. Reproduced by permission.)

At the age of 16, Robinson entered San Diego State College. She majored in mathematics and prepared for a teaching career, being aware of no other mathematics career choices. At the beginning of Robinson's sophomore year, her father found his savings depleted by the Depression and committed suicide. With help from her older sister and an aunt, Robinson remained in school. She transferred to the University of California, Berkeley, for her senior year and graduated in 1940.

At Berkeley, she found teachers and fellow students who shared her excitement about mathematics. In December of 1941, she married an assistant professor named Raphael Robinson. At that time she was a teaching assistant at Berkeley, having completed her master's degree in 1941. The following year, however, the school's nepotism rule prevented her from teaching in the mathematics department. Instead, she worked in the Berkeley Statistical Laboratory on military projects. She became pregnant but lost her baby; because of damage to Robinson's heart caused by the rheumatic fever, her doctor warned against future pregnancies. Her hopes of motherhood crushed, Robinson endured a period of depression that lasted until her husband rekindled her interest in mathematics.

In 1947 she embarked on a doctoral program under the direction of Alfred Tarski. In her dissertation, she proved the algorithmic unsolvability of the theory of the rational number field. Her Ph.D. was conferred in 1948. That same year, Tarski discussed an idea about diophantine equations (polynomial equations of several variables, with integer coefficients, whose solutions are to be integers) with Raphael Robinson, who shared it with his wife. By the time she realized it was directly related to the tenth problem on Hilbert's list, she was too involved in the topic to be intimidated by its stature. For the next twenty–two years she attacked various aspects of the problem, building a foundation on which Yuri Matijasevic proved in 1970 that the desired general method for determining solvability does not exist. While working at the RAND Corporation in 1949 and 1950, Robinson developed an iterative solution for the value of a finite two–person zero–sum game. Her only contribution to game theory is still considered a fundamental theorem in the field.

Robinson's heart damage was surgically repaired in 1961, but her health remained impaired. Her fame from the Hilbert problem solution resulted in her appointment as a full professor at Berkeley in 1976, although she was expected to carry only one–fourth of the normal teaching load. Eight years later she developed leukemia and died on July 30, 1985.

SELECTED WRITINGS BY ROBINSON:

Books

(With Martin Davis and Yuri Matijasevic) "Hilbert's Tenth Problem. Diophantine Equations: Positive Aspects of a Negative Solution." In *Mathematical Developments Arising from Hilbert's Problems.* Edited by F. E. Browder, American Mathematical Society, 1976.

Periodicals

"Definability and Decision Problems in Arithmetic." *Journal of Symbolic Logic* 14 (1949): 98–114.

"Existential Definability in Arithmetic." *Transactions of the American Mathematical Society* 72, no. 3 (1952): 437–449.

(With Martin Davis and Hilary Putnam) "The Decision Problem for Exponential Diophantine Equations." *Annals of Mathematics* 74, no. 3 (1961): 425–436.

FURTHER READING

Periodicals

"Julia Bowman Robinson, 1919–1985." *Notices of the American Mathematical Society* (November 1985): 738–742.

Reid, Constance. "The Autobiography of Julia Robinson." *The College Mathematics Journal* (January 1986): 2–21.

Smorynski, C. "Julia Robinson, In Memoriam" *The Mathematical Intelligencer* (Spring 1986): 77–79.

Sketch by Loretta Hall

Daisy Maude (Orleman) Robinson
1869–1942
American biologist and physician

Daisy Robinson (Corbis/Bettmann-UPI. Reproduced by permission.)

Daisy Maude Orleman Robinson served as a physician in the French army at the beginning of World War I. When the United States entered the war, she transferred to the United States Army as a surgeon and was given the commission of major. In recognition for her medical services, she received commendations from both the United States and France. When the war was over, Robinson returned to New York to work for the State Department of Health. Later in her career, she served as a regional consultant for the United States Public Health Service as Acting Surgeon–General for a short period of time. Her varied medical career also included a private practice in dermatology. She conducted research on the hazardous effects of x rays and the use of x ray in the treatment of leprosy; and on the identification and treatment of shingles, cancer, and venereal diseases.

Robinson was born in Fort Riley, Kansas. She was the daughter of Colonel Louis Orleman, a soldier and engineer who served under William Tecumseh Sherman in the Civil War. She received her medical education from George Washington University (1890; 1894) and the University of Zurich (1892–1894). She married Andrew Rose Robinson, who, along with others, established the Polyclinic Hospital in New York City.

Wins Awards for Service During War

In her early years (1885–1887), Robinson taught in a public school. After graduating from George Washington University, she worked as a physician for the U. S. Pension Bureau until 1893. A stint as surgeon and associate principal at a private school followed from 1895 to 1904. Prior to the United States entering the war, women doctors and dentists were disqualified from U.S. military service because of their gender. So, when World War I began, she left her private practice in the United States to serve as a military doctor in France. When the United States entered the war, she served her country for the duration of the war. (Women doctors in France cared for civilians as well as soldiers, setting up and running clinics in cooperation with the French Army.) In 1917, the Medical Women's National Association, later the American Medical Women's Association, sponsored the American Women's Hospitals. This group raised $200,000, and established its first hospital in Neufmoutiers, France. It later moved to Luzancy-sur-Marne. More than 1,000 women doctors registered with the AWH to serve overseas. In recognition of their exemplary service to its country, France awarded medals of honor—the Croix de Guerre; the French Legion of Honor; and the Medaille de la Reconnaissance Francaise—to some of these women doctors, including Robinson.

After the war, Robinson left the military to work for the New York State Department of Health and the U. S. Public Health Service. She also became vice president of the North West Dispensary in New York City, and served as president of the women's auxiliary board of her husband's hospital, where she was a lecturer. She also was a lecturer and diagnostician for the New York State Department of Health Division of Social Hygiene. In connection with her work in public health, she was awarded a fellowship to the American Public Health Association. She was also a member of the American Medical Association.

Robinson retired in 1938. At the time of her death, she lived in Washington, D.C. She died while on vacation in Jacksonville, Florida, on March 12, 1942. Her active private medical career was unusual enough for its day, and, to successfully combine it with both military and public medicine was an extraordinary accomplishment for a woman of her time.

FURTHER READING

Books

Bailey, Martha J. *American Women in Science, A Biographical Dictionary.* Santa Barbara: ABC—CLIO., 1994, p. 330.

Periodicals

Obituary, *New York Times* (March 14, 1942): 15:3.

Other

GG American Women and the Military. http://www.gendergap.com,/military/USmil5.htm

Sketch by Jane Stewart Cook

Emily Warren Roebling
1843–1903
American engineer

Emily Warren Roebling was the wife of Washington A. Roebling, the chief engineer for the construction of the Brooklyn Bridge—the longest suspension bridge in the world—from 1869 to 1883. When her husband became gravely ill, Roebling assumed the position of his assistant and took over the management of the huge project. She visited the construction site daily to carry instructions between her husband and the construction supervisors and to inspect the work in progress. In time, she learned enough about bridge construction to prepare engineering sketches and make design decisions on her own. When the bridge opened, she was publicly given credit for her role. Bronze plaques on the towers at each end of the bridge acknowledge her outstanding contribution.

Emily Warren was born in 1843 in the town of Cold Spring on the upper portion of the Hudson River in New York. Her father was Sylvanus Warren, who had wisely invested in the nearby West Point Foundry, which made cannons and other large guns for the military. Her mother's maiden name was Phebe Lickley. While the Warrens were not considered rich, they were well off and were important members of society in the local area. Emily was the second youngest of 12 children, of whom only six lived to become adults. Her oldest brother, G.K. Warren, graduated with distinction from West Point Academy and embarked on a career as both a soldier and an engineer in the army. In 1859, he returned to Cold Spring to teach mathematics at West Point. That same year, their father died, and G.K. took charge of raising his younger brothers and sisters. Emily showed a natural skill for mathematics, as well as an interest in science, and her brother encouraged her in her studies.

Marries Into a Bridge-Building Family

During the Civil War, G.K. Warren rose to the rank of general. In 1863 he was assigned a new aide named Washington A. Roebling, whose father, John A. Roebling was a noted bridge engineer. Emily met young Roebling in 1864 during a grand ball held for the officers of her brother's unit. They fell in love immediately, corresponded constantly, and were married in Cold Spring on January 18, 1865. The war ended a few months later.

After the war, Washington joined his father in Cincinnati, Ohio to help in the construction of a bridge across the Ohio River. Emily and Washington lived there until 1867, when they left for a belated honeymoon tour of Europe. As part of the trip, they visited and inspected several modern steel bridges. Of special interest to Washington was the use of caissons, large chambers lowered into a river and pressurized with air to allow the manual excavation of the riverbed in order to form a solid footing for bridge piers. Washington's father was at that time involved in the design of the Brooklyn Bridge across the East River between Manhattan and Brooklyn, and caissons would be necessary in the construction. It was a new, and somewhat dangerous technique, and Washington and his father wanted to learn all they could.

By this time, Roebling was pregnant. Their son, John A. Roebling, II, was born in Germany. Shortly before giving birth, she had a serious fall and suffered from internal bleeding for nearly a month. The injury was so severe that she knew she could not have any more children. When they returned to the United States, Washington began working with his father on the Brooklyn Bridge project, while Roebling took care of the baby.

On June 21, 1869, the final bridge plans were approved. A few days later, Washington's father was involved in an accident when an incoming ferry boat crushed his foot while he was inspecting one of the bridge towers. Doctors amputated his toes, but the senior Roebling insisted on binding the wound and taking the matter in his own hands. Within a week, he began to show signs of tetnus infection, also known as lockjaw. He died on July 22, 1869.

Husband's Illness Forces Her to Take Charge

With his father's death, Washington assumed the position of chief engineer for the project. Work progressed steadily until late 1870, when a fire was discovered inside the timbers of one of the caissons beneath the river. All efforts by the workmen failed to extinguish it, and Washington himself entered the smoky, pressurized chamber to direct the firefighting. When he emerged several hours later, he was stricken with a case of the "bends" caused by too rapid decompression upon returning to normal atmospheric pressure. This was not an unusual occurrence for workmen in the caissons, many of whom suffered from a variety of medical problems. At the time the reasons were not well known, nor were the means of prevention. Although Washington recovered quickly from his first attack, he suffered a second, more serious, case of the bends in 1872. This attack left him weak and nauseous, with pain in his limbs, sharp mood swings, and an inability to concentrate. The stress of managing the enormous project began to affect him. After battling his illness for months, he and his wife left for a health spa in Germany, leaving his subordinates to carry on the work.

The trip to Germany failed to restore Washington's health, and they returned to the United States early in 1874. They took up residence in Trenton, New Jersey, while Washington supervised work on the bridge through correspondence and meetings. By 1877, his condition had improved slightly, and they moved to a house on Columbia Heights in Brooklyn near the bridge construction, where he could watch the work through binoculars from a window in his bedroom. He was still seriously ill, and Roebling shielded him from visitors.

Washington's prolonged absence from the job site caused speculation that he was totally incapacitated and was no longer fit to be chief engineer. To head off these rumors, Roebling passionately addressed the American Society of Civil Engineers, defending her husband's role. She was the first woman ever to formally speak to the organization. She also began taking a more active role in the project. She had been involved since they had moved to Trenton, writing his correspondence and managing his affairs, and in the process she had learned a great deal about bridge-building and project management. Now she personally attended the job site daily and discussed engineering details with construction supervisors. After their initial shock, the supervisors found Roebling to be extremely knowledgeable and began to tell her about their daily problems and progress. On one occasion, a contractor had a question about how a part should be formed, and Emily made a sketch and explained each step in the process. When an important decision needed to be made, a delegation of officials would troop up to the Roebling house and present the facts to her. Whatever decision she made, it would be accepted as if it had come directly from the chief engineer himself.

Roebling's daily visits to the construction site earned her the admiration and respect of everyone involved with the project. In December 1881, they paid her the ultimate compliment when she was invited to join a group of officials in a walk across the partially completed bridge. In a way, it was as much a test of her courage as it was an honor because the walkway consisted of nothing more than a few planks laid side–by–side on an otherwise open bridge structure. With a light breeze blowing, she led the party, chatting and remarking on the views. When they reached the New York side, almost 1,600 feet away, everyone toasted her with champagne.

When the bridge officially opened on May 24, 1883, Congressman Abram S. Hewitt publicly praised Roebling for her role, and her husband told her "I want the world to know that you, too, are one of the Builders of the Bridge." Later, the Roeblings moved to Troy, New York, to be near their son, who was attending Rensselaer Polytechnic Institute as his father had done. In 1888, they moved back to Trenton, where they had a large house built. Although Washington continued to live a quiet, secluded life, Roebling entertained often. She became vice president of the Daughters of America, and was active in many other organizations. She also attended New York University, where she studied law and got her degree, and became an activist for women's suffrage.

Roebling's health began to fail about 1900. She collapsed in 1902 while her husband was in a hospital in recuperating from intestinal surgery. The doctors diagnosed her as having stomach ulcers. Washington returned home to be with his wife, who died of stomach cancer on February 28, 1903.

FURTHER READING

Books

Kass–Simon, G. and Patricia Farnes, eds. *Women of Science.* Bloomington: Indiana University Press, 1990, pp. 172–73.

McCullough, David. *The Great Bridge.* New York: Simon and Schuster, 1972, pp. 452–478, 516–518, 553–556.

Periodicals

Weigold, M.E. "Bridge Builder Extraordinaire: Emily Roebling." *Ms.* (May 1983).

Others

Dixon, S. "Emily Warren Roebling." Penn State College of Engineering. http://www.engr.psu.edu/wep/EngCompSp98/SDixon/body.html (23 Mar 1999).

Sketch by Chris Cavette

Elizabeth Roemer
1929–
American astronomer

Elizabeth Roemer made a career of studying comets, in particular "lost comets." These are comets whose orbits are calculated based on their previous returns or "rediscovery." Most people are familiar with Halley's Comet, which appears once every 76 years. What they often fail to realize is that the orbits of comets give us important information about planets, orbits and gravitational pull. Roemer not only made a name for herself through discovering lost comets, but also thanks to her remarkably accurate photographic records of comets.

Roemer was born on September 4, 1929 in Oakland, California. By the time she entered college she knew she was interested in astronomy. She received her bachelor's degree from the University of California–Berkeley in 1950, for the next two years she took graduate courses at Berkeley while teaching adult classes for the Oakland school system. Later she became an assistant researcher and a lab technician at the Lick Observatory. She received her Ph.D. form Berkeley in 1955.

Roemer spent the next year on the Berkeley faculty as research astronomer; she then spent a year at the Yerkes Observatory at the University of Chicago as a research associate. In 1957, she took a position as an astronomer with the U.S. Naval Observatory. She was stationed in Flagstaff, Arizona, and spent the next nine years there.

It was during her years at the Naval Observatory that she began to establish herself as an authority on lost comets. Using a powerful 40–inch reflecting telescope, she was able to track the size and orbital paths of numerous comets and asteroids (which essentially are small planets). One, originally known as asteroid 1657, was renamed Roemera in her honor by one of her colleagues.

In 1966, Roemer accepted a position as associate professor of astronomy at the University of Arizona in Tucson. Three years later she was named full professor in the school's Lunar and Planetary Laboratory. In 1980 she was also named senior astronomer at the Stewart Observatory. She was named professor emerita in 1998 and continues her research on comets and asteroids. Roemer's research interests focus on comets, but not just their orbits. She has studied and written on the astrophysical properties of comets, and also on the measurements of comets and other celestial bodies. She has also done research on minor planets and satellites. Because all the planets, stars, comets, and other celestial bodies are affected by the orbits of other bodies, understanding the orbital patterns of one type of object opens the door to a more thorough understanding of other objects' orbital patterns

Not surprisingly, Roemer has won the praise of other scientists for her dedication, hard work, and successes. The awards she has won over the years include the Dorothea Klumpke Roberts Prize from Berkeley in 1950, the national Academy of Sciences' Benjamin Apthorp Gould Prize in 1971, and the NASA Special Award in 1986. Here memberships include the International Astronomical Union, the British Astronomical Association, and the Royal Astronomical Society of London. She has also authored numerous articles on the properties of comets. Fred Whipple, writing in *The Mystery of Comets* (1985) notes that Roemer's "innumerable precise photographic observations of comets have been the basis for a great many cometary orbits of importance, and her notes on the physical characteristics have been invaluable."

SELECTED WRITINGS BY ROEMER:

Periodicals

Roemer, Elizabeth. "Activity of Comets at Large Heliocentric Distance." *Publications of the Astronomical Society of the Pacific* 74: October 1962, pp. 351–65.

Roemer, Elizabeth. "Astronomic Observations and Orbits of Comets." *Astronomical Journal* 66: October 1961, pp. 368–71.

Roemer, Elizabeth. "Comet Notes." *Publications of the Astronomical Society of the Pacific* 83: June 1971, pp. 370–71.

FURTHER READING

Books

Shearer, Benjamin F. and Barbara S, Shearer, eds. *Notable Women in the Physical Sciences: A Biographical Dictionary.* Greenwood Press, 1997.

Whipple, Fred. *The Mystery of Comets.* Smithsonian Institution Press, 1985.

Sketch by George A. Milite

Nancy Grace Roman
1925–
American astronomer

Nancy Grace Roman is famous for developing satellite observatories to explore the universe from a vantage point that is free from atmospheric interference. She also pioneered using satellites for gamma, x-ray, and radio observations. In addition, she has conducted observational astronomical research using traditional earth–based telescopes, studying topics such as stellar motions, photoelectric photometry and spectroscopy.

Roman was born in Nashville, Tennessee on May 16, 1925 to a U.S. Geological Survey geophysicist, Irwin Roman, and his wife, Georgia Frances (Smith) Roman. Educated at Western High School in Baltimore, Maryland, Roman graduated in 1943. She then earned a B.A. in astronomy at Pennsylvania's Swarthmore College, where she was named a Joshua Lippincott Memorial Fellow and worked in the Sproul Observatory. From 1946 to 1948 Roman attended graduate courses at the University of Chicago, assisting at the Yerkes Observatory in Williams Bay, Wisconsin. She earned her Ph.D. in astronomy in 1949; her doctoral research investigated the radial veloci-

Nancy Grace Roman (The Library of Congress. Reproduced by permission.)

ties, spectra, and convergent point of the Ursa Major group of stars. Her dissertation appeared in the September 1949 *Astrophysical Journal.*

Also in 1949, Roman worked as a summer research associate at the Case Institute of Technology's Warner and Swasey Observatory, cataloguing high luminosity objects and classifying objective spectra. That fall, she returned to Yerkes, where she served as a research associate between 1949 and 1952, and then as an astronomy instructor from 1952 to 1955. She also made a brief visit in 1953 to Toronto's David Dunlap Observatory to study the radial velocities of certain high–speed faint stars. At Yerkes she researched stellar astronomy and galactic structure, specializing in radial velocity measurements, photoelectric photometry, and spectral classification. She was particularly interested in stellar clusters.

In 1955, Roman moved to the United States Naval Research Observatory (NRO) in Washington, D.C., where she first worked in radio astronomy, soon becoming the head of the microwave spectroscopy lab. Using a 50–foot cast aluminum mirror, Roman researched radio star spectra and the galactic distribution of radio emitters. In addition, she used radar to find the distance between the earth and the moon. During this time she attended a 1957 Soviet Academy of Sciences Symposium to dedicate their new Bjuraken Astrophysical Observatory, and the following year she edited the fifth International Astronomical Union Symposium on large scale galactic structure. In 1958 and 1959 she worked as an NRO consulting astronomer, educating others about radio astronomy and planning the institution's research programs. Roman dramatically expanded her work when in March of 1959 she became the head of the observational astronomy program head at the National Aeronautics and Space Administration (NASA). At NASA Roman developed an ambitious plan to observe objects in space by using rockets and satellite observatories. Charged with developing these efforts, in February, 1960, she was named chief of astronomy and astrophysics at NASA's office of satellites and sounding rockets.

Throughout the 1960s Roman designed instrumentation and made substantial measurements from gamma ray, radio, and visible light satellites, such as the Orbiting Solar Observatories. Her programs gave astronomers the planetary surface knowledge that ultimately led to the successful 1976 *Viking* probes that were designed to collect data from Mars. She became the astronomy program head in 1964 and the chief of the astronomy and relativity program in 1972, remaining in this position until 1979. Her published work from this period generally deals with new satellite data, but she still did earth–based observation, such as her 1967 Kitt Peak Observatory radial velocity and spectral research. She received a NASA award for Exceptional Scientific Research in 1969, and a medal for Outstanding Leadership in 1978. Roman was also granted honorary doctorates from Russell Sage, Hood, Bates, and Swarthmore Colleges between 1966 and 1976.

Roman improved her orbiting observatories throughout the 1970s and 1980s. She measured X ray and ultraviolet readings from the enormously successful OAO–3 or *Copernicus* satellite, launched in 1972, and recorded stellar spectra from the U.S. space station *Skylab*, which circled the earth between 1973 and 1979. During 1979 and 1980 she was also NASA program scientist for a projected space telescope; unfortunately, a decade of cost overruns and delays postponed the launch of NASA's Hubble space telescope until April 25, 1990. Meanwhile, as a NASA consulting astronomer, beginning in 1980, and a senior scientist for the Astronomical Data Center from 1981 onwards, Roman worked to prepare computer–readable versions of astronomical catalogues, databases, and other bibliographic tools.

SELECTED WRITINGS BY ROMAN:

Books

(Editor) *Comparison of the Large Scale Structure of the Galactic System with That of Other Systems.* Cambridge University Press, 1958.

Periodicals

"The Ursa Major Group." *Astrophysical Journal* 110 (1949): 205–241.

FURTHER READING

Books

The Women's Book of World Records and Achievements. Edited by Lois Decker O'Neill. Anchor Books, 1979, pp. 88, 153.

Periodicals

Blackburn, Harriet B., interview with Roman, *Christian Science Monitor* (June 13, 1957).
"Scientist Accepts Soviet Bid." *New York Times* (September 7, 1956): 21.
"6 Women Hailed for U.S. Service." *New York Times* (February 6, 1962): 39.

Sketch by Julian A. Smith

Mary Swartz Rose
1874–1941
American nutritionist

Mary Swartz Rose was a noted authority on nutrition who made important contributions in both academia and government. At the time of her death, she was professor of nutrition at Columbia University's Teachers College.

She was born Mary Davies Swartz in Newark, Ohio on October 31, 1874, the daughter of a judge. She graduated from the local high school and taught there for three years. (One of her pupils, Karl T. Compton, would later serve as president of MIT.) She decided that she wanted to continue with her own education and went to Denison University in Granville, Ohio. She received a Bachelor of Arts degree in 1901 and studied for a year at Mechanics Institute in Rochester, New York. From there she went on to Teachers College, where she received a Bachelor of Science degree in 1906. She then went on to Yale University, where she was awarded a Ph.D. in physiological chemistry in 1909.

After getting her doctorate, she returned to Teachers College, this time as an instructor in nutrition. She became an assistant professor in 1910 and occupied her time teaching and writing. She authored several books on nutrition over the next several years, including *Laboratory Handbook for Dietetics, Feeding the Family,* and *Everyday Foods in War Time*. During the First World War, Rose took an active role in government programs. She served as director of both the Bureau of Conservation of the Federal Food Board and the New York State Food Commission.

Today, many of us take the study of nutrition for granted. In the early part of the twentieth century, however, nutrition as a science was only just coming into its own. The work of scientists like Rose gave people a more thorough understanding of how different foods affected people's health, as well as how to choose foods according to their nutritional value.

After the war, Teachers College made Rose an associate professor, and in 1921 she became a full professor. She stayed at Teachers for the rest of her life, continuing to write textbooks and serve on numerous committees. She was a member of the League of Nations' nutrition commission and the American Medical Association's Council on Foods. She served as president of the American Institute of Nutrition from 1937 to 1938.

Her husband, Anton Richard Rose, was also a scientist; he served as a chemist with the Prudential Insurance Company. The couple had one son, Richard Collin Rose. Late in 1940 Mary Rose took ill, and she died at her home six weeks later on February 1, 1941.

SELECTED WRITINGS BY ROSE:

Books

Everyday Foods in Wartime. Macmillan, 1918.
Feeding the Family. Macmillan, 1940.
Laboratory Handbook for Dietetics. Macmillan, 1939.
*Teaching Nutrition to Boys and Girls.*Macmillan, 1932.

FURTHER READING

Books

Current Biography 1941 (obituary). H. W. Wilson Company, 1941.

Periodicals

Obituary, *New York Times* (February 2, 1941): 46.

Sketch by George A. Milite

Clemence Augustine Royer
1830–1902
French scholar

Clemence Augustine Royer was a self–taught scholar, best known for her translations of Darwin's *On the Origin of Species* that included her introductions. A woman ahead of her time, Royer was an independent thinker and self–described rebel who wrote on feminism, economics, philosophy, science, pacifism, and politics.

Augustine–Clémence Audouard was born in Nantes, France on April 21, 1830 to Joséphine Gabrielle Audouard, a young seamstress who developed her skills in order to gain and maintain financial independence. Legitimized seven years later when her parents married, she took the name of her father, army captain Augustin–René Royer.

Captain Royer, an engineer by trade, had joined the army when he was 19. In 1832, nearly 25 years later, he was part of the failed rebellion of 1832 attempting to crown Henri V as King of France. During her father's subsequent exile from France, Royer and her mother sojourned in Lake Lucerne, Switzerland, a place to which Royer had a strong and vivid connection. The family was reunited in Paris a few years later. Tired of a life in hiding, Captain Royer gave himself up to the French government in 1835. He was acquitted after a trial and awarded a pension from the army, which he used along with a some inheritance to support the family for the next seven years.

Leaves Paris For Schooling in Convent

When she was 10, the family moved to the more affordable outskirts of Paris and enrolled Royer at a convent school. She entered enthusiastically, initially winning prizes and honors, but after 18 months grew depressed in reaction to the strict Catholic training she received. Shocked to discover she could be sinning unknowingly, she tried in vain to achieve an ecstatic religious experience. Writing in the third person in her unpublished autobiography excerpted in Joy Harvey's *Uneasy Careers and Intimate Lives*, she tells that she concluded "she was an unworthy being and tortured herself about this." Her parents removed her after 18 months, but Royer refused to abandon her extreme religious rituals.

Back in Paris, both parents took over her schooling in math, literature, music, and theater. By 1843, Captain Royer's financial struggles and mounting jealousy of his much younger wife strained her parents' marriage and there was much fighting. They separated when Royer was 18, and the following year her father died. No longer under the influence of his dictatorial patriarchy, she felt liberated. With little interest in marriage, Royer took her inheritance and pursued the only course of study offered to a woman at the time, preparation to become a secondary school teacher.

Royer passed her courses in three years with honors, and in 1854, accepted a position in Wales requiring her to learn English. While in Britain, she was exposed to Unitarian beliefs and began to read Rousseau and Voltaire, experiences that threw her Catholic tenets into question. Finding no satisfactory answers within the church, she quit teaching and moved to Switzerland in 1856. Royer later wrote of her outrage quoted in Joy Harvey's *Almost a Man of Genius* " . . . she was seized with an ardent rancor against the teachers who had betrayed her childhood and failed to shake her reason."

Meets Pascal Duprat, Publisher and Politician

This began a period of reeducation for Royer. She lived simply and read steadily on all subjects. In 1858 she met politician and editor, Pascal Duprat, the man who became her lover and the father of her only child. They never married, indeed, Duprat already had a wife and daughter. But their union was one of commitment, passion, and a shared life vision.

Royer wrote her only work of fiction, the novel *Les Jumeaux D'Hellas* at Duprat's suggestion. She assisted Duprat in running *Le Nouvel économiste*, a social science publication, and contributed many articles. This was a time of intellectual and creative stimulation for Royer, surrounded by Duprat and his circle of Republican, independent thinkers. Her politics now greatly diverged from those of her Catholic mother and Legitimist Royalist father.

In 1859 Royer began her successful lectures on science, and encouraged women who had been in attendance at her previous lectures on philosophy to overcome their apprehension and learn this new subject. She believed as quoted in *Uneasy Careers* that the "difference of language, ideas and opinions between the two sexes renders them in some degree, strangers to each, dividing and disuniting them not only in society but in the family."

The publication in 1862 of her award–winning essay on taxation theory helped establish Royer as a prominent author. But it was her brilliant 1862 translation of Darwin's *Origins of Species*, including her controversial and inspirational preface, that had a profound affect on her readership and garnered her wide recognition. According to *Uneasy Careers*, Darwin called her the "oddest and cleverest woman in France." In 1866, Royer wrote the introduction for the 2nd Edition, and was hired once more for the 3rd edition, but a dispute with Darwin over her critical treatment of pangenesis ended the relationship.

By the mid–1860s, Royer's articles, books, and lectures earned her a living. Duprat lived secretly with her in Paris, hiding from both the French government and his wife. In 1866, Royer and Duprat made a home together in Florence, Italy, where Royer gave birth to their son, Rene. It was in Florence that Royer wrote her book on social evolution, *L'origine de l'homme et des sociétés*, released in 1870. By this time, the Empire had ended, and Duprat lived openly with Royer and Rene back in Paris.

Becomes First Women Accepted To The Société d'Anthropologie

In 1870, The Société d'Anthropologie accepted Royer as a full member. She was the first women to be elected to a French scientific society, and remained the only woman in that organization for 15 years. Very active in the Société, Royer's work was recorded on all butone occasion. The manuscript, "Sur la natalité" submitted in 1875, was suppressed by the Société.

Royer wrote of her concern with France's declining birth rate. She believed a large population was a healthy part of social evolution, imperative for what she called vital competition. Royer saw motherhood as an obligation, a woman's necessary contribution to society, and asserted that laws therefore should grants rights to women who bear children, in or out of wedlock. She argued for women's rights to education, to earn their own money, own property, and to ensure the inheritance rights of illegitimate children.

In the 1880s, Royer became associated with International Congress on Women's Rights. She served jointly with Leon Richer as an honorary president of the 2nd meeting in 1889, held in France. Her involvement in feminism intensified when she joined a coed Masonic lodge. Here she met Maria Deraismes, the founder of the French feminist newspaper *La fronde*, who hired Royer as a journalist from 1893 to 1902.

Royer believed passionately in the concept of the female genius, that women have a unique point of view unrepresented in the rigidly male realm of science. She imagined a matriarchal society, where sex roles were reversed. She saw grandparents as an essential component of a family's child–care system, enabling both the mother and father to pursue professional endeavors. Part of the household until her death in 1876, Royer's own mother helped raise her grandson, Rene.

Spends Last Years in Poverty

Duprat died in 1885. Royer applied for and received a portion of Duprat's pension for three years. She moved into a retirement home in 1885. The last 17 years of her life were spent in poverty. She subsisted on her journalism, and on annual grants from the Minister of Education that increased after she was awarded the Legion of Honor in 1890. That year, her final work *La Constitution du monde:Natura rerum* was published.

Although she took some courses in 1876 at Laboratory of Anthropology, Royer was not a formally trained scientist. She was an astonishing thinker with an innately logical and lively mind capable of addressing any subject. The French critic and linguist, Ernest Renan called her "almost a man of genius." A pacifist, she supported the International League of Peace and Freedom founded in 1867 in Geneva. Royer died at home on February 6, 1902. Soon after, her efforts for peace were acknowledged in Monaco, at the International Peace Congress.

SELECTED WRITINGS BY ROYER:

Books

La Constitution du monde: Natura rerum. Paris: Schleicher Freres, 1900

Les Jumeaux d'Hellas. Brussels: Lacroix, Verbroecken, 1864.

Periodicals

"La Nation dans l'humanité et a dans la série organique." *Journal des Economistes* (November 1875): 234–249.

Other

"Origine de l'homme et des sociétés." Paris, 1869.

"Préfaces" and "Avant–propos" to Royer's translation of *De l'origine des espèces,* by Charles Darwin. First Edition, 1862.

FURTHER READING

Books

Abir–Am, P.G., and Outram, D., eds. *Uneasy Careers and Intimate Lives, Women in Science, 1789–1979.* New Brunswick: Rutgers University Press, 1987.

Harvey, Joy. *Almost a Man of Genius*. New Brunswick: Rutgers University Press, 1997.

Josephson, H. *Biographical Dictionary of Modern Peace Leaders*. Westport, CT: Greenwood Press, 1962.

Uglow, J. S., *The Continuum Dictionary of Women's Biography*. New York: Continuum Publishing Co., 1989.

Wilson, Katharina M. *An Encyclopedia of Continental Women Writers*. New York: Garland Pub., 1991.

Sketch by Kyra Anderson

Vera Cooper Rubin
1928–
American astronomer

Vera Cooper Rubin, one of America's foremost women astronomers, has spent her life observing galactic structure, rotation and dynamics. Her pioneering spectroscopic research of the 1970s demonstrated the possible existence of a large percentage of dark matter in the universe, matter that is invisible to the naked eye. Scientists now speculate that up to 90 percent of the universe may be composed of dark matter.

Rubin was born on July 23, 1928, in Philadelphia, the daughter of electrical engineer Philip Cooper and Rose Applebaum, and was educated at Vassar College, receiving her B.A. in 1948. Rubin earned her M.A. at Cornell in 1951; her thesis studied the evidence for bulk rotation in the universe, and later influenced Gérard de Vaucouleurs' work on the "local supercluster" of galaxies. She received her Ph.D. in astronomy under Russian–American physicist George Gamow (1904–1968) three years later at Georgetown University. Rubin's pioneering dissertation studied galactic distribution, and demonstrated a "clumpiness" in

Vera Rubin (© 1993 R.T. Nowitz. Photo Researchers, Inc. Reproduced by permission.)

the spread of galaxies; virtually ignored in 1954, this effect was not seriously studied until the 1970s.

Rubin spent a year as an instructor in math and physics at Montgomery County Junior College before moving back to Georgetown University as research associate (1955–65), lecturer (1959–62), and then assistant professor (1962–65). She also did observational work at Kitt Peak Observatory in Arizona, and became the first official female observer at Palomar Observatory in California in 1965 (astrophysicist **Margaret Burbidge** had previously observed there unofficially). Also in 1965, Rubin joined the Department of Terrestrial Magnetism (DTM) at Washington's Carnegie Institute. For the rest of the 1960s, Rubin studied spectroscopy and galactic rotations, structure and dynamics.

Discovers Dark Matter

In particular, Rubin studied the rotation of spiral galaxies. She and DTM physicist W. Kent Ford used a spectrograph to study the rate of rotation within galaxies. They found that the stars closest to the center of a galaxy and those farthest out were traveling at the same rate of speed. Mathematical research had suggested the stars farthest from a galaxy's center would travel at a slower pace. In addition, the amount of mass in both the darker and brighter parts of a galaxy was constant, suggesting that some form of unseen matter was present. Earlier astronomers, including Fritz Zwicky, had speculated that a previously unknown "dark matter" might exist. Rubin and Ford's observations of galactic rotation speed seemed to verify that hypothesis. Continuing investigation of dark matter has been a major research effort among astronomers since the 1980s.

Rubin has contributed numerous papers to *Astrophysical Journal, Astronomical Journal,* and *Bulletin of the American Astronomical Society.* She also served as associate editor of the *Astronomical Journal* from 1972 to 1977, of *Astrophysical Journal Letters* from 1977 to 1982, and joined the editorial board of *Science Magazine* from 1979 to 1987. Rubin has sat on numerous astronomical committees, including those of Harvard University, the National Academy of Sciences (to which she was elected in 1981), and the American Astronomical Society. She has also received honorary degrees from Creighton University in 1978, Harvard University in 1988, and Yale University in 1990.

To promote women in astronomy, Rubin joined the council of American Women in Science in 1984, and in 1987 became a president's distinguished visitor at Vassar College. In 1988 she became the Beatrice Tinsley visiting professor at the University of Texas. Meanwhile, to encourage young girls to study science, she wrote a children's book on astronomy. In recent years Rubin has sat on the board of directors of the Astronomical Society of the Pacific, and has been a member of several other scientific societies. She was also on the visiting committee of the Space Telescope Scientific Institute between 1990 and 1992. In 1948 Rubin married physicist Robert J. Rubin. The couple have four children: David, Allan, Judith, and Karl. All four have become scientists as well.

"Observing is spectacularly lovely," Rubin said in *Mercury.* "I enjoy analyzing the observations, trying to see what you have, trying to understand what you're learning. It's a challenge, but a great deal of fun. It's not only fun, but a lot of it is just plain curiosity—this incredible hope that somehow we can learn how the universe works. What keeps me going is this hope and curiosity."

SELECTED WRITINGS BY RUBIN:

Books

(Editor with George V. Coyne) *Large Scale Motions in the Universe.* Princeton University Press, 1988.

Periodicals

"Rotation of the Andromeda Nebula from a Spectroscopic Survey of Emission Regions." *Astrophysical Journal* no. 159 (1970): 379.

(With W. K. Ford, Jr., N. Thonnard, M. S. Roberts, and J. A. Graham) "Motion of the Galaxy and the Local Group Determined from the Velocity Anisotropy of Distant Sc I Galaxies. I. The Data. II. The Analysis for the Motion." *Astrophysical Journal* no. 81 (1976): 681, 719.

"Women's Work." *Science '86* (July–August 1986): 58–65.

FURTHER READING

Books

A Hand Up: Mentoring Women in Science. American Women in Science, 1993, pp. 75–78.

Lightman, Alan, and Roberta Brawer. "Vera Rubin." In *Origins: The Lives and Worlds of Modern Cosmologists.* Cambridge: Harvard University Press, 1990, pp. 285–305.

Tufty, Barbara. "First Woman Permitted to Observe the Universe at Palomar." In *The Women's Book of World Records and Achievements.* Edited by O'Neill, Lois Decker. Anchor, 1979, p. 151.

Periodicals

Bartusiak, Marcia. "The Woman Who Spins the Stars." *Discover* (October 1990): 88–94.

Stephens, Sally. "Vera Rubin: An Unconventional Career." *Mercury: The Journal of the Astronomical Society of the Pacific.* (January–February 1992): 38–45.

Sketch by Julian A. Smith

Augusta Rucker
1873–?
American zoologist and physician

A zoologist whose specialty was the study of the Texas *Koenenia* and its position among the Arachnida, Augusta Rucker changed career in middle age, becoming a physician at an infirmary in New York in 1911.

From Zoology to Medicine

Little is known of Rucker's personal life. She was born on May 24, 1873, and grew up in Paris, Texas, where she graduated from high school. She earned a bachelor's degree in zoology in 1896 and a master's degree in the same discipline in 1899 at the University of Texas. During her graduate studies, she worked as a tutor in biology. After receiving her M.A., she taught at the same university for one year. As a working zoologist, she became a fellow of the Texas Academy and focused her studies on the *Koenenia,* an arachnid.

Rucker left zoology work in 1909 to attend Johns Hopkins University, where she earned her medical degree in 1911. Thereafter she worked as an attending physician at the New York Infirmary for Women and Children, where she distinguished herself for many years in her service to mothers and babies. She is also listed as practicing at the Ruptured and Crippled Hospital in New York. Such a career change is indicative of the popularity of the medical profession for women in turn–of–the–century America.

Listed in the first edition of *American Men and Women of Science,* Rucker was a prominent physician in her day, noted more for her medical work than for her zoological research.

FURTHER READING

Books

American Men of Science: A Biographical Directory. 2d ed. Edited by J. McKeen Cattell. New York: Science Press, 1910, p. 403.

Bailey, Martha J. *American Women in Science: A Biographical Dictionary.* Denver: ABC–CLIO, 1994, pp. 335–36.

Siegel, Patricia Joan. *Women in the Scientific Search: An American Bio–bibliography, 1724–1979.* Metuchen, NJ: Scarecrow Press, 1985, pp. 360–61.

Sketch by J. Sydney Jones

Mary Ellen Rudin
1924–
American mathematician

Mary Ellen Rudin's mathematical specialty is set theoretic topology, a modern, abstract geometry that deals with the construction, classification, and description of the properties of mathematical spaces. Rudin's approach is often to construct examples to disprove a conjecture. As an incoming freshman at the University of Texas, Rudin was chosen by the topologist R. L. Moore and trained almost exclusively by the unorthodox "Moore method" of active and competitive mathematical problem–solving. Rudin credits Moore with building her confidence that given the axioms, she should be able to solve any problem, even if it involves building a complicated structure.

Rudin was born December 7, 1924, in Hillsboro, Texas, to Irene Shook and Joe Jefferson Estill. Her father was a civil engineer and her mother, before she married, was a teacher. Rudin's parents were from Winchester, Tennessee, and both of her grandmothers were graduates of Mary Sharp College in Winchester. Advanced education was valued in both families, and her parents expected that she would go to the university to "do something interesting."

Rudin grew up in Leakey, Texas, a small isolated town in the hills of southwest Texas, where her father worked on road building projects. Her childhood surroundings were simple and primitive, and as a child she had lots of time to think and to play elaborate, complicated, and imaginative games, something she says contributed to her later success as a mathematician. Rudin'sperformance was generally in the middle of her class of five students, and she expected she would make Cs at the university; she made As.

Trained by the R. L. Moore "Method"

Rudin had no special course of study in mind when she went to the University of Texas at Austin. On her first day, Moore helped her register for classes, asked about her mathematical background, and enrolled her in his mathematics class. Although she took courses in other fields and was good at them, she continued to study with Moore through her B.S. degree in 1944 and her Ph.D. degree in 1949, and had a class from him every single semester. Rudin has said, "I am a mathematician because Moore caught me and demanded that I become a mathematician."

Moore, known for his unorthodox Socratic teaching style, preferred his students to be naive; he required that they be unspoiled by mathematical terminology, notation, methods, results, or ideas of others. He also required his students to actively think, rather than passively read. Moore forbade them to read the work of others and sometimes removed books from the library so that his students would not see them. He never referred to the work of others; rather, he gave definitions and required his students to prove theorems, some that had been solved, some that had not. Students were required to think about problems just as research mathematicians do. In the classroom, Moore called on the weakest students first, then proceeded through the class to the top students. Rudin was generally at the top of the class.

Rudin solved one of the unsolved problems as her thesis research, finding a counterexample to a well–known conjecture. At the time she wrote her thesis, she had never seen a mathematics paper. While the Moore method produced students who were independent, confident and creative, there were lacunae in their knowledge of mathematics and deficient in their mathematical language. Rudin has used a more traditional approach in her own teaching, requiring her students to learn as much as possible about what has been done by others, but she acknowledges that her students are not always as confident as she was.

Research at Duke, Rochester, and Wisconsin

After Rudin received her Ph.D. in 1949, Moore told her she would be going to Duke University. At Duke, she worked on a problem related to Souslin's conjecture and began to be known for her work. She also met mathematician Walter Rudin at the university and married him in 1953. Together, they went to the University of Rochester where Walter had a position, and Rudin taught part–time and researched mostly as she pleased until 1958, when they moved to Madison, Wisconsin. Rudin held a similar position at the University of Wisconsin; she was a lecturer from 1959 to 1971, when she was appointed full professor.

Rudin has likened facility in research in mathematics to a career in music. "It must be done every day," she says. "If you don't play for three years, you're not likely to be of concert pianist quality when you start playing again, if ever again." She also notes that mathematical research requires a high tolerance for failure; successes are much less frequent than failures; she may have three exciting breakthroughs in a year. Rudin prefers to work on topological problems while lying on the couch in her Frank Lloyd Wright–designed home, surrounded by the activities of her family. Rudin's productivity has been strong and consistent; she has almost 90 scientific papers and book chapters to her credit.

Rudin's counterexamples, she says, are "very messy" topological spaces that show that some ideas you thought were true, are not. She compares her many–dimensional examples, which are difficult for some people to imagine, to a business problem that has 20 aspects. The aspects are the dimensions of the problem, the number of factors taken into account.

Rudin has been at the University of Wisconsin since 1959, where she assembled a strong research group in topology. She is the first to hold the **Grace Chisholm Young** Professorship, which she assumed in 1981. Her visiting professorships include stints in New Zealand, Mexico, and China. Moore imbued Rudin with a sense of responsibility for publication and responsibility to the mathematical community, and she has held offices and worked on numerous committees of the American Mathematical Society, the Mathematical Association of America, the Association for Women in Mathematics, and the Association for Symbolic Logic. Over the years she has received several research grants from the National Science Foundation, and has served on mathematical advisory boards for the National Academy of Sciences, the National Science Foundation, and the United Nations.

Rudin and her husband have four children, and she notes that they are all skilled in pattern recognition. Now professor emerita, Rudin continues to lecture widely, produce vital papers in her field, and to promote and speak about women in mathematics. She is a Fellow of the American Academy of Arts and Sciences, has received the Prize of Niewe Archief voor Wiskunk from the Mathematical Society of the Netherlands, and has been awarded four honorary doctorates. In 1995 Rudin was elected to the Hungarian Academy of Sciences.

FURTHER READING

Books

Albers, Donald J., Gerald L. Alexanderson and Constance Reid. *More Mathematical People: Contemporary Conversations.* Boston: Harcourt Brace Jovanovich, 1990, pp. 282–303.

Periodicals

Ford, Jeff. "Geometry with a Twist." *Research Sampler* (Spring 1987): 20–23.

Other

Carr, Shannon. "Mary Ellen Rudin." *Biographies of Women Mathematicians.* June 1997. http://www.scottlan.edu/lriddle/women/chronol.htm (July 21, 1997).

Sketch by Jill Carpenter

Dorothea Rudnick
1907–1990
American embryologist

Dorothea Rudnick was an celebrated embryologist who studied the process of differentiation. This independent thinker made a dramatic turn toward the end of her undergraduate career, and went on to perfect a transplantation technique used to probe the mysteries of embryonic development.

On January 17, 1907, in Oconomowoc Wisconsin, Dorothea Rudnick was born to Paul Rudnick, a chemist, and Rose (Ulrich) Rudnick. She was the middle child between two brothers, both of whom went on to become physicists. Her quick and capable mind was especially suited for science, in fact, she said of her childhood in Edna Yost's *Women of Modern Science* that she "grew up in a home where we breathed in an analytical atmosphere." But mainly, she eschewed these subjects, selecting languages and humanities, and graduated from Parker High in 1922. She enrolled at the University of Chicago, majoring in French, Italian, and German. She excelled in all her studies, but longed for foreign travel. Not yet 16 years old and with no money of her own, she knew she would have to wait.

Career Changes Course

Two years later, she had waited long enough. She left school and took an accounting job in downtown Chicago in order to save enough to finance a long trip to Europe. A year and a half later, she returned to the University with the conviction that whatever her vocation, it would have to include firsthand experience. She discovered her calling in a zoology class, and remained at the University of Chicago after completing her undergraduate degree in 1928 in languages, intent on developing her scientific and analytical gifts. She took a course in embryology and became fascinated with the tools available for analyze history through studying developmental and structural patterns in the animal kingdom.

Rudnick studied differentiation in chick embryos, successfully tracing the origin of the thyroid gland to two sites in the protoplasm. Her research was reported in *Procedure for the Society for Experimental Biology and Medicine* in her second year of graduate school. Rudnick applied for and received fellowships for the last two years of school, graduating Phi Beta Kappa with a Ph.D. in zoology in 1931.

The Osborne Zoological Laboratory at Yale University awarded Rudnick a Sessell Fellowship her first year out of school. This was followed by a National Research Fellow appointment at the University of Rochester until 1937, and a three–year post as an assistant at Storrs Experimental Agriculture Station. She taught at Wellesley College for a year before transferring to Albertus Magnus College in New Haven, Connecticut to accept an assistant professorship in zoology in 1940. She stayed at Albertus for 37 years, becoming a full professor in biology in 1948. Concurrently, Rudnick resumed her association with Yale, making the short drive to the nearby Osborne laboratory to conduct her ongoing research in embryology and developmental genetics on evenings and weekends.

Conducted Transplantation Studies on Chick Embryo

In her investigations, Rudnick employed the delicate transplantation techniques for which she became famous. Rudnick examined the eggs of White Leghorn chickens and a breed of short-legged chickens called Creepers. In one famous experiment, the limb–forming segments of Creepers "donor" embryos were excised and transplanted to the body cavity of White Leghorn donor embryos. The donor segments were shown to "grow" the expected body part in the host embryo. In these transplantation studies she went on to demonstrate that observed leg abnormalities in one–fourth of the offspring of Creeper intercrosses were due to factors within the limb–forming area itself, and not to the internal environment, such as, for example, the circulatory system.

Pioneering Work on Enzyme Systems Wins Guggenheim

Rudnick applied the same drive, expertise and enthusiasm for all her studies, including her trailblazing work on chromosomes. In earlier years at Yale, her tissue culture work demonstrated that rat embryos would grow and develop up to a certain point in vitro. Rudnick extensively analyzed the enzymatic development in the chick, primarily investigating tissues of the brain, retina, and liver. She often collaborated with colleagues, most notably with Drs. Mela and Waelsh, in outlining the developmental pathway of a protein associated with liver function in chick embryos. Her work on enzyme systems in protein synthesis won the Guggenheim award in 1952 and took her to Europe again, this time to collaborate in foreign embryology laboratories and speak at international conferences.

In addition to teaching and research responsibilities, Rudnick found time to serve on the committee for the revision of scientific nomenclature, and as secretary and general editor at the Connecticut Academy of Arts and Sciences from 1948 to 1986. She was a Member of the American Association for the Advancement of Science, the American Society of Zoologists, the International Institute of Embryology, the American Association of Anatomists, the Society of the Study of Development and Growth, and the Connecticut Academy of Arts and Science.

Rudnick was considered an expert in her field. She authored numerous articles for journals, encyclopedias, symposia, and textbooks. A proficient linguist, Rudnick translated the work *Theodor Boveri: Life and Work of a Great Biologist* from German, and reviewed books in English, French and German. In 1977 Albertus Magnus College named Rudnick Emeritus Professor. During the award ceremony, she was recognized for her remarkable achievements and devoted service and loyalty. Rudnick died in Los Alamos, New Mexico on January 10, 1990.

SELECTED WRITINGS BY RUDNICK:

Books

(Translator) *Theodor Boveri, Life and Work of a Great Biologist, 1862–1915.* by Fritz Baltzer. Berkeley: University of California Press, 1967.

Periodicals

"Bilateral Localization of Prospective Thyroid in the Early Chick Blastoderm." *Procedures of the Society of Experimental Biology and Medicine* (1930): 132–134.

"The Development of Embryonic Rat Embryos in Tissue Culture."*Procedure of the National Academy of Sciences* (1934): 656–58.

"Differentiation of Prospective Limb Material from Creeper Chick Embryos in Coelomic Grafts."*Journal of Experimental Zoology* (1945): 1–17.

Other

(Book review), "'Principles of Embryology' by C.H. Waddington, 1956." *Science* (1956): 1085

"Reproduction." *Encyclopedia Britannica*, 1959.

FURTHER READING

Books

Who's Who of American Women. 6th ed. New Providence, NJ: Marquis, 1969, p. 1066.

Yost, Edna. *Women of Modern Science* New York: Dodd, Mead and Co., 1959.

Periodicals

"Albertus Plans Service for Dorothea Rudnick." *The New Haven Register* (February 15, 1990).

Other

Voss, Julianne. "Biographical Essay." http://web.mit.edu/afs/athena.mit . . . –studies/www/dev–bio/rudnick.3.html (February 18, 1999).

Sketch by Kyra Anderson

Anna Worsley Russell
1807–1876
British naturalist

Anna Worsley Russell was the most accomplished field botanist of her day, as well as a famous botanical artist. She contributed to scientific journals on various subjects and was an early member of the Botanical Society of London.

Anna Worsley Russell was born in 1807, the daughter of Philip John Worsley, who owned a sugar refinery in Bristol, England. She was one of four sisters in a intellectual Unitarian family. Russell's early interest was in entomology, the study of insects, later extended to botany. Her brother was a geologist and one of her sisters married the botanist, the Reverend Thomas Butler. Many other members of the extended family also were botanists, although Russell was the most distinguished of them. She was godmother to her nephew, the novelist Samuel Butler.

In 1835, Russell contributed a list of flowering plants of the area surrounding Bristol to the *New Botanist's Guide*, which won her the respect of other prominent botanists. Two years later, she was largely responsible for a plant catalogue of the Newbury area, published by her cousin. When the Botanical Society of London was founded in 1836, it became the first scientific society to actively encourage participation by women. In the 20 years of its existence, about ten percent of the society's members were women. This was not surprising for several reason: the society was outside of the scientific establishment, membership fees were relatively low, and their meetings dealt with a variety of social problems such as food adulteration and sewage treatment. Furthermore, it was a time when a large number of British women were studying botany; in fact, botany was being promoted as the most suitable science for women. Russell was elected to the society in 1839 and was one of its active members, at least as far as exchanging collections. She also donated some of her collection of mosses to the society. In 1844, she married Frederick Russell from Brislington, near Bristol. They continued to live in Bristol for some years before moving to Kenilworth. The Russells had no children.

In 1843, Russell published her observations of bats. She also contributed to the *Phytologist*, a botany journal, and in 1857, she published a rare botanical discovery made by her nephew, Tom Butler, an undergraduate at Cambridge. Despite her varied interests, Russell is remembered primarily as a botanical artist. More than 700 of her drawings of fungi are in the Department of Botany at the British Museum of Natural History. She died in 1876.

SELECTED WRITINGS BY RUSSELL:

Periodicals

(As A. Worsley) "Anecdotes of Bats Flying by Day-Light." *Zoologist* 1 (1843): 212.
"*Sonchus palustris*." *Phytologist* 2 (1857): 279.

FURTHER READING

Periodicals

Allen, D. E. "The Botanical Family of Samuel Butler." *Journal of the Society for the Bibliography of Natural History* 9 (1979): 133–36.
Allen, D. E. "The Women Members of the Botanical Society of London, 1836–1856." *British Journal for the History of Science* 13 (1980): 240–54.

Sketch by Margaret Alic

Elizabeth Shull Russell
1913–
American geneticist

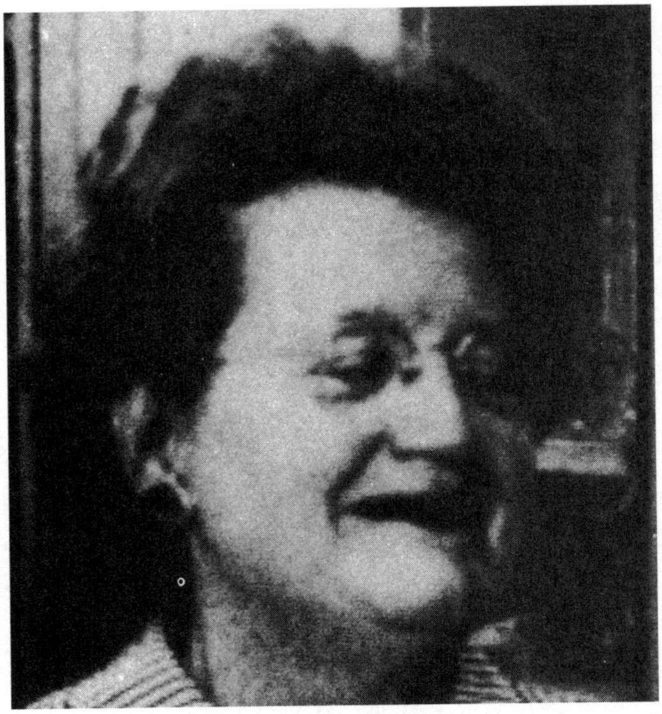

Elizabeth S. Russell (AP/Wide World Photos, Inc. Reproduced by permission.)

The Roscoe B. Jackson Laboratory in Bar Harbor, Maine, has been the professional home of geneticist Elizabeth Shull Russell since the late 1930s. For the last five decades it has also been the birthplace of millions of laboratory mice which have been meticulously bred and characterized by Russell and the center's staff. Through her efforts, laboratory mice populations—which include dozens of strains exhibiting particular characteristics that make them desirable for research—are available to scientists worldwide. Russell has also used the mice for her own ongoing research in mammalian genetics and the study of such conditions as hereditary anemias, muscular dystrophy, cancer and aging.

Russell was born on May 1, 1913, in Ann Arbor, Michigan. Her mother, Margaret Jeffrey Buckley, held a master's degree in zoology and was a teacher at Grinnell College in Iowa during an era when few women even attended college. Her father, Aaron Franklin Shull, was a zoologist and geneticist who taught at the University of Michigan. Both the Buckleys and the Shulls had scientists in their families. Elizabeth's uncle on her mother's side was a physicist, and on her father's side there was a geneticist, a plant physiologist and a botanical artist. Her parents met in 1908 when both attended a summer course at the laboratory in Cold Spring Harbor on Long Island, New York. It seemed quite natural that Russell became interested in the plants and animals in her surroundings; as a girl she carefully catalogued every flowering plant near their summer home.

Russel entered the University of Michigan at the age of 16 and graduated in 1933 with a degree in zoology. This was during the midst of the Great Depression, however, and few jobs were available teaching science. Upon hearing of a scholarship program at Columbia University, her father convinced her to participate in it. Russell's coursework at Columbia included genetics, which was to prove her greatest interest. She became influenced by a paper written by Sewall Wright of the University of Chicago, entitled "Physiological and Evolutionary Theories of Dominance." He proposed that the specific way in which characteristics are inherited must be from either the nucleic acids or proteins on the chromosomes (geneticists now know that inheritance is controlled by the nucleic acid DNA). Upon receiving her master's degree, Russell went to the University of Chicago where she obtained an assistantship and did further graduate work under Wright. Her doctoral thesis explored the effect of genes in the pigmentation of guinea pigs.

Russell received her Ph.D. at Chicago in 1937 and married a fellow graduate student, William L. Russell. They moved to Bar Harbor, Maine, when he was appointed to a position at the Roscoe B. Jackson Memorial Laboratory. As was the general practice of most institutions at the time, only one member of a family could be employed by the laboratory, so Elizabeth Russell was invited to work as an independent investigator, which she did from 1937 to 1946.

Works with Mice at the Jackson Laboratory

While pursuing her research, Russell spent much of her time at the laboratory working with pre-college, college and graduate students that came to Jackson each summer. That first summer of 1937 she had twelve summer students. As several other members of the Jackson family were also named Elizabeth, she soon became known as Tibby, a name that stuck. Over the next several years, the Russells started a family. They would eventually have three sons and a daughter together.

Although Russell had begun her investigations into how a gene controls characteristics by using fruit flies, during the 1940s she helped build up a population of laboratory mice that could be used in researching many more genetic questions. She characterized each strain, whether it be by coat color or the presence of a hereditary disease. With great precision Russell managed the genetically controlled inbred populations, and in 1946 she officially became a member of the research staff. The following year, she and her husband divorced. Russell—with four young children—now pursued her career in earnest even as the lab was starting to appreciate her great potential as a researcher.

In October, 1947, a devastating fire spread across Bar Harbor, destroying the Jackson Laboratory. Almost 10,000 laboratory mice perished—animals which had been carefully bred by Russell and others. In the years following, however, the team helped to once again build up the mouse population.

One day in 1951, while studying the source of mouse skin pigmentation, Russell looked in a cage and observed a most unusual mouse, a female that was dragging its feet in a peculiar way. The mouse was not injured. It appeared that it was born with some kind of muscular defect and Russell named it "Funnyfoot." By breeding Funnyfoot's brothers and sisters, the same trait cropped up in subsequent generations, leading the team to conclude that Funnyfoot and her related offspring had a genetic disease similar in some ways to muscular dystrophy in humans. This particular fact became of great interest to other researchers working on muscular dystrophy. At once, scientists flooded the lab with requests for mice with the funnyfoot trait. There was a big problem, however—the funnyfoot females were unable to reproduce and the mice died young.

Russell devised a plan for breeding more funnyfoot mice, transplanting the ovaries of funnyfoot females into those of normal females without the characteristic. The ovaries contained egg cells (ova) in which the chromosomes carried the faulty gene. When the normal females mated, many funnyfoot offspring were produced, which were then sent to researchers. Alongside the cages of funnyfoot mice were many other strains that were meticulously bred by Russell and her team. Each group of mice and its ancestry were clearly labeled and recorded. Some strains, for instance, had hereditary diseases like anemia, while others had characteristics that made them sterile or prone to tumors. Other mice were to be used for research on blood disease, the immune system, the endocrine system, diabetes, nutrition, or aging.

Assumes the Directorship of the Jackson Laboratory

By 1953, Russell was named staff scientific director at the Jackson Laboratory. The following year she organized a conference at the laboratory where—for the first time—scientists from around the globe were invited to contribute what they were studying about mammalian genetics and its relationship to cancer. The conference was a success and in 1957 Russell became senior staff scientist. The following year Russell was awarded a Guggenheim Fellowship to review what was currently known about mammalian physiological genetics; the grant provided time and money to compile all the current research in one place, resulting in reference material useful to scientists the world over.

During her directorship, Russell's responsibilities were twofold—to provide the research mice that helped support the lab financially and to work on her areas of interest. One very important area of research at the lab under Russell involved studying blood cells of mice, especially the cells which provide the immune response (the ability to fight off invading foreign substances). This research became very important in an era in which there were a growing number of organ transplants. These mice were used in experiments that determined when tissue is accepted or rejected by an organism.

Russell also took an avid interest in blood hemoglobin—a substance which carries oxygen to all parts of a mammal's body—and was especially curious about how the hemoglobins develop. A mammal fetus inside its mother (including humans) has hemoglobin from a very early stage; after birth, however, that hemoglobin changes both its structure and the site of its production. Some of Russell's work concerned the processes of these developmental changes.

Other research topics Russell investigated include different kinds of cancers, blood diseases, and the process of aging. She has written or collaborated on over a hundred scientific papers and several books. Since 1978, Russell has been senior staff scientist emeritus. Throughout her long active career, Russell's role has also been one of mentor to many of the students that have come through the Jackson Laboratory, either as permanent staff working together on biochemistry and microbiology or the many summer graduate students that come from all over the world.

Russell has been made a member of the American Academy of Arts and Sciences and the National Academy of Sciences. During the 1970s she was an active member of the Academy's Council, acting to edit and evaluate scientific papers. She was also a member of the Genetics Society of America, becoming its vice president in 1974 and president from 1975 to 1976. In 1983 she was made a member of the American Philosophical Society. Russell holds an honorary degree from Ricker College and was a trustee of the University of Maine and the College of the Atlantic. Because of her work on the aging of mice she was asked to be a member of the advisory council to the National Institute of Aging. By attending discussion groups at the laboratory, she continues to closely monitor trends in genetics research.

SELECTED WRITINGS BY RUSSELL:

Periodicals

"A Quantitative Study of Genetic Effects on Guinea Pig Coat Colors." *Genetics* 24 (1939): 332–353.

"A Comparison of Benign and Malignant Tumors in Drosophila Melanogaster" *Journal of Experimental Zoology* 34 (1940): 363–385.

(With C. M. Snow, L. M. Murray and J. P. Cormier) "The Bone Marrow in Inherited Macrocytic Anemia in the House Mouse." *Acta Haematologica* 12 (1953): 247–259.

"Symposium of Twenty–Five Years of Progress in Mammalian Genetics and Cancer, Roscoe B. Jackson Memorial Laboratory, June 27–30, 1954." *Journal of the National Cancer Institute* 15 (1954): 551–851.

(With others) "Characterization and Genetic Studies of Microcytic Anemia in House Mouse." *Blood* 35 (1970): 838–850.

(With D. E. Harrison) "Fetal Liver Erythropoiesis and Yolk Sac Cells." *Science* 177 (1972): 187.

(With J. B. Whitney) "Linkage of Genes for Adult Alpha–Globin and Embryonic Alpha–Like Globin Chains." *Proceedings of the National Academy of Sciences USA* 77 (1980): 1087–90.

"A History of Mouse Genetics." *Annual Review of Genetics* 19 (1985): 1–28.

Other

A complete bibliography is on file at the Joan Staats Library at the Roscoe B. Jackson Laboratory in Bar Harbor, Maine.

FURTHER READING

Books

Noble, Iris. *Contemporary Women Scientists of America.* Messner, 1979, pp. 123–137.

Other

Russell, Elizabeth Shull, telephone interview with Barbara A. Branca conducted February 18, 1994.

Sketch by Barbara A. Branca

S

Florence Rena Sabin (The Library of Congress. Reproduced by permission.)

Florence Rena Sabin
1871–1953
American anatomist

Florence Rena Sabin's studies of the central nervous system of newborn infants, the origin of the lymphatic system, and the immune system's responses to infections—especially by the bacterium that causes tuberculosis—carved an important niche for her in the annals of science. In addition to her research at Johns Hopkins School of Medicine and Rockefeller University, she taught new generations of scientists and thus extended her intellectual reach far beyond her own life. In addition, Sabin's later work as a public health administrator left a permanent imprint upon the communities in which she served. Some of the firsts achieved by Sabin include becoming the first woman faculty member at Johns Hopkins School of Medicine, as well as its first female full professor, and the first woman to be elected president of the American Association of Anatomists.

Sabin was born on November 9, 1871, in Central City, Colorado, to George Kimball Sabin, a mining engineer and son of a country doctor, and Serena Miner, a teacher. Her early life, like that of many in that era, was spare: the house where she lived with her parents and older sister Mary had no plumbing, no gas and no electricity. When Sabin was four, the family moved to Denver; three years later her mother died.

After attending Wolfe Hall boarding school for a year, the Sabin daughters moved with their father to Lake Forest, Illinois, where they lived with their father's brother, Albert Sabin. There the girls attended a private school for two years and spent their summer vacations at their grandfather Sabin's farm near Saxtons River, Vermont.

Sabin graduated from Vermont Academy boarding school in Saxtons River and joined her older sister at Smith College in Massachusetts, where they lived in a private house near the school. As a college student, Sabin was particularly interested in mathematics and science, and earned a bachelor of science in 1893. During her college years she tutored other students in mathematics, thus beginning her long career in teaching.

A course in zoology during her junior year at Smith ignited a passion for biology, which she made her specialty. Determined to demonstrate that, despite widespread opinion to the contrary, an educated woman was as competent as an educated man, Sabin proceeded to chose medicine as her career. This decision may have been influenced by events occurring in Baltimore at the time.

The opening of Johns Hopkins Medical School in Baltimore was delayed for lack of funds until a group of prominent local women raised enough money to support the institution. In return for their efforts, they insisted that women be admitted to the school—a radical idea at a time when women who wanted to be physicians generally had to attend women's medical colleges.

Begins Medical Career at Johns Hopkins

In 1893 the Johns Hopkins School of Medicine welcomed its first class of medical students; but Sabin, lacking tuition for four years of medical school, moved to Denver to teach mathematics at Wolfe Hall, her old school. Two years later she became an assistant in the biology department at Smith College, and in the summer of 1896 she worked in the Marine Biological Laboratories at Woods

Hole. In October of 1896 she was finally able to begin her first year at Johns Hopkins.

While at Johns Hopkins, Sabin began a long professional relationship with Dr. Franklin P. Mall, the school's professor of anatomy. During the four years she was a student there and the fifteen years she was on his staff, Mall exerted an enormous influence over her intellectual growth and development into prominent scientist and teacher. Years after Mall's death, Sabin paid tribute to her mentor by writing his biography, *Franklin Paine Mall: The Story of a Mind.*

Sabin thrived under Mall's tutelage, and while still a student she constructed models of the medulla and mid–brain from serial microscopic sections of a newborn baby's nervous system. For many years, several medical schools used reproductions of these models to instruct their students. A year after her graduation from medical school in 1900, Sabin published her first book based on this work, *An Atlas of the Medulla and Midbrain,* which became one of her major contributions to medical literature, according to many of her colleagues.

After medical school, Sabin was accepted as an intern at Johns Hopkins Hospital, a rare occurrence for a woman at that time. Nevertheless, she concluded during her internship that she preferred research and teaching to practicing medicine. However, her teaching ambitions were nearly foiled by the lack of available staff positions for women at Johns Hopkins. Fortunately, with the help of Mall and the women of Baltimore who had raised money to open the school, a fellowship was created in the department of anatomy for her. Thus began a long fruitful period of work in a new field of research, the embryologic development of the human lymphatic system.

Sabin began her studies of the lymphatic system to settle controversy over how it developed. Some researchers believed the vessels that made up the lymphatics formed independently from the vessels of the circulatory system, specifically the veins. However, a minority of scientists believed that the lymphatic vessels arose from the veins themselves, budding outward as continuous channels. The studies that supported this latter view were done on pig embryos that were already so large (about 90mm in length) that many researchers—Sabin included—pointed out that the embryos were already old enough to be considered an adult form, thus the results were inconclusive.

Embryo Research Yields Important Findings

The young Johns Hopkins researcher set out to settle the lymphatic argument by studying pig embryos as small as 23mm in length. Combining the painstaking techniques of injecting the microscopic vessels with dye or ink and reconstructing the three–dimensional system from two–dimensional cross sections, Sabin demonstrated that lymphatics did in fact arise from veins by sprouts of endothelium (the layer of cells lining the vessels). Furthermore, these sprouts connected with each other as they grew outward, so the lymphatic system eventually developed entirely from existing vessels. In addition, she demonstrated that the peripheral ends (those ends furthest away from the center of the body) of the lymphatic vessels were closed and, contrary to the prevailing opinion, were neither open to tissue spaces nor derived from them. Even after her results were confirmed by others they remained controversial. Nevertheless, Sabin firmly defended her work in her book *The Origin and Development of the Lymphatic System.*

Sabin's first papers on the lymphatics won the 1903 prize of the Naples Table Association, an organization that maintained a research position for women at the Zoological Station in Naples, Italy. The prize was awarded to women who produced the best scientific thesis based on independent laboratory research.

Back at Hopkins from her year abroad, she continued her work in anatomy and became an associate professor of anatomy in 1905. Her work on lymphatics led her to studies of the development of blood vessels and blood cells. In 1917 she was appointed professor of histology, the first woman to be awarded full professorship at the medical school. During this period of her life, she enjoyed frequent trips to Europe to conduct research in major German university laboratories.

After returning to the United States from one of her trips abroad, she developed methods of staining living cells, enabling her to differentiate between various cells that had previously been indistinguishable. She also used the newly devised "hanging drop" technique to observe living cells in liquid preparations under the microscope. With these techniques she studied the development of blood vessels and blood cells in developing organisms—once she stayed up all night to watch the "birth" of the bloodstream in a developing chick embryo. Her diligent observation enabled her to witness the formation of blood vessels as well as the formation of stem cells from which all other red and white blood cells arose. During these observations, she also witnessed the heart make its first beat.

Sabin's technical expertise in the laboratory permitted her to distinguish between various blood cell types. She was particularly interested in white blood cells called monocytes, which attacked infectious bacteria, such as *Mycobacterium tuberculosis,* the organism that causes tuberculosis. Although this organism was discovered by the German microbiologist Robert Koch during the previous century, the disease was still a dreaded health menace in the early twentieth century. The National Tuberculosis Association acknowledged the importance of Sabin's research of the body's immune response to the tuberculosis organism by awarding her a grant to support her work in 1924.

In that same year, she was elected president of the American Association of Anatomists, and the following year Sabin became the first woman elected to membership in the National Academy of Sciences. These honors followed her 1921 speech to American women scientists at Carnegie Hall during a reception for Nobel Prize–winning physicist **Marie Curie**, an event that signified Sabin's recognized importance in the world of science.

Although her research garnered many honors, Sabin continued to relish her role as a professor at Johns Hopkins. The classes she taught in the department of anatomy enabled her to influence many first–year students—a significant number of whom participated in her research over the years. She also encouraged close teacher–student relationships and frequently hosted gatherings at her home for them.

One of her most cherished causes was the advancement of equal rights for women in education, employment, and society in general. Sabin considered herself equal to her male colleagues and frequently voiced her support for educational opportunities for women in the speeches she made upon receiving awards and honorary degrees. Her civic–mindedness extended to the political arena where she was an active suffragist and contributor to the Maryland *Suffrage News* in the 1920s.

Immune System Research Continues at Rockefeller Institute

Sabin's career at Johns Hopkins drew to a close in 1925, eight years after the death of her close friend and mentor Franklin Mall. She had been passed over for the position of professor of anatomy and head of the department, which was given to one of her former students. Thus, she stepped down from her position as professor of histology and left Baltimore.

In her next position, Sabin continued her study of the role of monocytes in the body's defense against the tubercle bacterium that causes tuberculosis. In the fall of 1925, Sabin assumed a position as full member of the scientific staff at the Rockefeller Institute for Medical Research (now Rockefeller University) in New York City at the invitation of the institute's director, Simon Flexner. At Rockefeller Sabin continued to study the role of monocytes and other white blood cells in the body's immune response to infections. She became a member of the Research Committee of the National Tuberculosis Association and aspired to popularize tuberculosis research throughout Rockefeller, various pharmaceutical companies, and other universities and research institutes. The discoveries that she and her colleagues made concerning the ways in which the immune system responded to tuberculosis led her to her final research project: the study of antibody formation.

During her years in New York, Sabin participated in the cultural life of the city, devoting her leisure time to the theater, the symphony, and chamber music concerts she sometimes presented in her home. She enjoyed reading nonfiction and philosophy, in which she found intellectual stimulation that complemented her enthusiasm for research. Indeed, one of her co–workers was quoted in *Biographical Memoirs* as saying that Sabin possessed a "great joy and pleasure which she derived from her work . . . like a contagion among those around her so that all were stimulated in much the same manner that she was. . . . She was nearly always the first one at the laboratory, and greeted every one with a *joie de vivre* which started the day pleasantly for all of us."

Meanwhile, she continued to accrue honors. She received fourteen honorary doctorates of science from various universities, as well as a doctor of laws. *Good Housekeeping* magazine announced in 1931 that Sabin had been selected in their nationwide poll as one of the twelve most eminent women in the country. In 1935 she received the M. Carey Thomas prize in science, an award of $5,000 presented at the fiftieth anniversary of Bryn Mawr College. Among her many other awards was the Trudeau Medal of the National Tuberculosis Association (1945), the Lasker Award of the American Public Health Association (1951), and the dedication of the Florence R. Sabin Building for Research in Cellular Biology, at the University of Colorado Medical Center.

Plays Prominent Role in Denver's Public Health

In 1938 Sabin retired from Rockefeller and moved to Denver to live with her older sister, Mary, a retired high school mathematics teacher. She returned to New York at least once a year to fulfill her duties as a member of both the advisory board of the John Simon Guggenheim Memorial Foundation and the advisory committee of United China Relief.

Sabin quickly became active in public health issues in Denver and was appointed to the board of directors of the Children's Hospital in 1942 where she later served as vice president. During this time she became aware of the lack of proper enforcement of Colorado's primitive public health laws and began advocating for improved conditions. Governor John Vivian appointed her to his Post–War Planning Committee in 1945, and she assumed the chair of a subcommittee on public health called the Sabin Committee. In this capacity she fought for improved public health laws and construction of more health care facilities.

Two years later she was appointed manager of the Denver Department of Health and Welfare, donating her salary of $4,000 to the University of Colorado Medical School for Research. She became chair of Denver's newly formed Board of Health and Hospitals in 1951 and served for two years in that position. Her unflagging enthusiasm for public health issues bore significant fruit. A *Rocky Mountain News* reporter stated that "Dr. Sabin . . . was the force and spirit behind the Tri–County chest X–ray campaign" that contributed to cutting the death rate from tuberculosis by 50 percent in Denver in just two years.

But Sabin's enormous reserve of energy flagged under the strain of caring for her ailing sister. While recovering from her own illness, Sabin sat down to watch a World Series game on October 3, 1953, in which her favorite team, the Brooklyn Dodgers, were playing. She died of a heart attack before the game was over.

The state of Colorado gave Sabin a final posthumous honor by installing a bronze statue of her in the National Statuary Hall in the Capitol in Washington, D.C., where each state is permitted to honor two of its most revered citizens. Upon her death, as quoted in *Biographical Memoirs,* the Denver *Post* called her the "First Lady of American Science." Sabin's philosophy of life and work might be best summed up by words attributed to Leonardo da Vinci, with which she chose to represent herself on bookplates: "Thou, O God, dost sell unto us all good things at the price of labour."

SELECTED WRITINGS BY SABIN:

Books

An Atlas of the Medulla and Midbrain: A Laboratory Manual, Friedenwald Company, 1901.
The Origin and Development of the Lymphatic System. Baltimore: Johns Hopkins Press, 1916.
Franklin Paine Mall: The Story of a Mind. Baltimore: Johns Hopkins Press, 1934.

FURTHER READING

Books

Bluemel, Elinor. *Florence Sabin: Colorado Woman of the Century.* University of Colorado Press, 1959.
Kronstadt, Janet. *Florence Sabin.* Chelsea House, 1990.
McMaster, Philip D. and Michael Heidelberger. "Florence Rena Sabin." *Biographical Memoirs.* Columbia University Press, 1960.
Yost, Edna. *American Women of Science.* Frederick A. Stokes, 1943.

Periodicals

Rocky Mountain News March 1, 1951.

Sketch by Marc Kusinitz

Ruth Sager
1918–1997
American biologist and geneticist

Ruth Sager (AP/Wide World Photos, Inc. Reproduced by permission.)

Ruth Sager devoted her career to the study and teaching of genetics. She conducted groundbreaking research in chromosomal theory, disproving nineteenth-century Austrian botanist Gregor Johann Mendel's once-prevalent law of inheritance—a principle stating that chromosomal genes found in a cell's nucleus control the transmission of all inherited characteristics. Through her research beginning in the 1950s, Sager revealed that a second set of genes (nonchrosomomal in nature) also play a role in one's genetic composition. In addition to advancing the science of nonchromosomal genetics, she worked to uncover various genetic mechanisms associated with cancer.

Born on February 7, 1918, in Chicago, Illinois, Ruth Sager was one of three girls in her family. Her father worked as an advertising executive, while her mother maintained an interest in academics and intellectual discourse. As a child, Sager did not display any particular interest in science. At the age of sixteen, she entered the University of Chicago, which required its students to take a diverse schedule of liberal arts classes. Sager happened into an undergraduate survey course on biology, sparking her interest in the field. In 1938, she graduated with a B.S. degree. After a brief vacation from education, Sager enrolled at Rutgers University and studied plant physiology, receiving an M.S. in 1944. Sager then continued her graduate work in genetics at Columbia University and in 1946 was awarded a fellowship to study with botanist Marcus Rhoades. In 1948 she received her Ph.D. from Columbia, and in 1949 she was named a Merck Fellow at the National Research Council.

Two years later, Sager joined the research staff at the Rockefeller Institute's biochemistry division as an assistant, working at first in conjunction with Yoshihiro Tsubo. There she began her work challenging the prevailing scientific idea that only the chromosomal genes played a significant role in genetics. Unlike many of her colleagues of the time, Sager speculated that genes which lay outside the chromosomes behave in a manner akin to that of chromosomal genes. In 1953 Sager uncovered hard data to support this theory. She had been studying heredity in *Chlamydomonas*, an alga found in muddy ponds, when she noted that a gene outside the chromosomes was necessary for the alga to survive in water containing streptomycin, an antimicrobial drug. Although the plant—which Sager nicknamed "Clammy"—normally reproduced asexually, Sager discovered that she could force it to reproduce sexually by withholding nitrogen from its environment. Using this tactic, Sager managed to cross male and females via sexual fertilization. If either of the parents had the streptomycin–resistant gene, Sager showed, the offspring exhibited it as well, providing definitive proof that this nonchromosomal trait was transmitted genetically.

During the time she studied "Clammy," Sager switched institutional affiliations, taking a post as a research associate in Columbia University's zoology department in 1955. The Public Health Service and National Science Foundations supported her work. In 1960 Sager publicized the results of her nonchromosomal genetics research in the first Gilbert Morgan Smith Memorial Lecture at Stanford University and a few months later in Philadelphia at the Society of American Bacteriologists. Toward the end of the year, her observations were published in *Science* magazine. As she continued her studies, she expanded her knowledge of the workings of nonchromosomal genes. Sager's further work showed that when the streptomycin–resistant alga mutated, these mutations occurred only in the non–chromosomal genes. She also theorized that nonchromosomal genes differed greatly from their chromosomal counterparts in the way they imparted hereditary information between generations. Her research has led her to speculate that nonchromosomal genes may evolve before the more common deoxyribonucleic acid (DNA) chromosomes and that they may represent more closely early cellular life.

Sager continued announcing the results of her research at national and international gatherings of scientists. In the early 1960s Columbia University promoted her to the position of senior research associate, and she coauthored, along with Francis J. Ryan, a scientific textbook titled *Cell Heredity*. In 1963 she travelled to the Hague to talk about her work, and the following year she lectured in Edinburgh on nonchromosomal genes. In 1966 she accepted an offer to become a professor at Hunter College of the City University of New York. She remained in New York for nine years, spending the academic year of 1972 to 1973 abroad at the Imperial Cancer Research Fund Laboratory in London. The following year she married Dr. Arthur B. Pardee. Harvard University's Dana Farber Cancer Institute lured her away from Hunter in 1975 with an offer to become professor of cellular genetics and head the Institute's Division of Cancer Genetics.

In the past twenty years, Sager's work has centered on a variety of issues relating to cancer, such as tumor suppressor genes, breast cancer, and the genetic means by which cancer multiplies. Along with her colleagues at the Dana Farber Institute, Sager has been researching the means by which cancer multiplies and grows, in an attempt to understand and halt the mechanism of the deadly disease. She has likened the growth of cancer to Darwinian evolution in that cancer cells lose growth control and display chromosome instability. In 1983 she told reporter Anna Christensen that if researchers discover a way to prevent the chromosomal rearrangements, "we would have a potent weapon against cancer." More recently, she has speculated that tumor suppressor genes may be the secret to halting cancer growth.

Sager continued to publish and serve on numerous scientific panels until her death. In 1992 she offered scientific testimony at hearings of the Breast Cancer Coalition. A member of the Genetics Society of America, the American Society of Bacteriologists, and the New York Academy of Sciences, Sager was appointed to the National Academy of Sciences in 1977. An avid collector of modern art, she was also a member of the American Academy of Arts and Sciences. Sager died of bladder cancer on March 29, 1997, at her home in Brookline, Massachusetts.

SELECTED WRITINGS BY SAGER:

Books

Cell Heredity. New York: Wiley, 1961.

Periodicals

"Tumor Suppressor Genes: The Puzzle and the Promise." *Science.* (15 December 1989): 1406–12.

FURTHER READING

Periodicals

Christensen, Anna. "Potential Weapon in War on Cancer." *United Press International* (7 February 1983).

Pace, Eric. "Dr. Ruth Sager, 79, Researcher on Location of Genetic Material" (obituary). *New York Times* (4 April 1997).

Sketch by Shari Rudavsky

Grace Adelbert Sandhouse
1896–1940
American entomologist

Grace Adelbert Sandhouse was an important entomologist, known for her studies on bees and sawflies, a type of wasp. At the United States Bureau of Entomology and Plant Quarantine, she was in charge of vast collections of insects and published a number of papers on the taxonomy of the insects that interested her the most.

Born in 1896 in Monticello, Iowa, Sandhouse studied zoology and entomology with the naturalist T. D. A. Cockerell at the University of Colorado in Boulder. It was Cockerell who first inspired her interest in bees. Graduating with an A.B. degree in 1920, Sandhouse obtained a graduate fellowship at Colorado. She earned her master's degree in 1923 and published her first scientific papers. Moving to Ithaca, New York, Sandhouse became a teaching fellow at Cornell University and earned her Ph.D. there in 1925.

At a time when professional opportunities for women scientists were limited primarily to the women's colleges, women scientists at the United States Department of Agriculture (USDA), as well as at a few other governmental agencies, were able to pursue their research, publish their results, and obtain promotions. Following graduation, Sandhouse went to work as a senior scientific aide for the Federal Horticulture Board of the USDA. In 1926 she became a junior entomologist with the Division of Insect Identification of the Bureau of Entomology and Plant Quarantine, also within the USDA. She was promoted to assistant entomologist in 1928 and to associate entomologist in 1937.

Sandhouse's research centered on the taxonomy, or identification and classification, of the aculeate Hymenoptera, those bees and wasps which have a stinger or a slender egg–laying tube called an ovipositor. In particular, she studied bees of the genus *Halictus* and the genus *Osmia*. She received large numbers of specimens from around the world, which she identified and classified. Sandhouse's most important publication, in 1939, "The North American Bees of the Genus Osmia (Hymenoptera : Apoidea)" was the first memoir published by the Entomological Society of Washington, of which she was an active member. Sandhouse also published several papers in the *Proceedings* of the U. S. National Museum and other journals. She was a member of the American Association for the Advancement of Science and the Entomological Society of America. Sandhouse died in a hospital in Denver, Colorado, in 1940, at the age of 44, following a long illness. She left several unpublished papers at her death.

SELECTED WRITINGS BY SANDHOUSE:

Books

"The North American Bees of the Genus Osmia (Hymenoptera: Apoidea)." *Memoirs of the Entomological Society of Washington* Washington, D.C., 1939.

Periodicals

(With T. D. A. Cockerell) "Some Eocene Insects of the Family Fulgoridae." *Proceedings of the United States National Museum* 59 (1921): 455–57.

"A Gynandromorphic Bee of the Genus Osmia." *The American Naturalist* 57 (1923): 569–70.

"New North American Species of Bees Belonging to the Genus Halictus (Chloralictus)." *Proceedings of the United States National Museum* 65 (1924): 1–43.

"Notes on Some North American Species of Halictus with the Description of an Apparently New Species." *Proceedings of the Entomological Society of Washington* 35 (1933): 78–83.

"A New North American Species of Crabro (Hymenoptera: Sphecidae)." *Annals of the Entomological Society of America* 31 (1938): 1–4.

"A Review of the Nearctic Wasps of the Genus Trypoxylon (Hymenoptera, Sphecidae)." *The American Midland Naturalist* 24 (1940): 133–76.

FURTHER READING

Books

Bailey, Martha J. *American Women in Science: A Biographical Dictionary*. Denver: ABC–CLIO, 1994.

Bonta, Marcia Myers. *Women in the Field: America's Pioneering Women Naturalists*. College Station: Texas A & M University Press, 1991.

Mallis, Arnold. *American Entomologists*. New Brunswick: Rutgers University Press, 1971.

Periodicals

Cushman, R. A. and Louise M. Russell. "Grace A. Sandhouse." *Proceedings of the Entomological Society of Washington* 42 (1940): 188–9.

Sketch by Margaret Alic

Ethel Sargant
1863–1918
English botanist

Ethel Sargant's work as a botanist centered on research into the anatomy of plants. Early in her career, she studied plant morphology (the study of the form and structure of plants) and plant cytology (the study of the formation, structure, and function of plant cells). She later became interested in the field of phylogenetics, learning how plants originate and develop their unique characteristics. Her research in this area drew important conclusions on how monocotyledons (one–leaved seedlings) originated and evolved. She used the genus *Liliaceae,* particularly the martagon lily, as a research subject throughout her years of study. Sargant was the first woman botanist elected to serve on the board of the famed Linnaean Society (named for Carolus Linnaeus, the father of botanical nomenclature). In 1913, her botanical career reached its peak, when she was named president of the Botanical Section of the British Association. Shortly before her death, she was elected president of the Federation of University Women.

Sargant was born in London, England, to Catherine (Beale) and Henry Sargant, a lawyer. She was educated at North London Collegiate School and Girton College in Cambridge, England. At Girton she studied natural science, graduating in 1884. She supplemented her scientific training with one year at Kew Gardens, gaining invaluable experience in research methods under the tutelage of D. H. Scott. Sargant also traveled to European laboratories, visiting with the foremost botanists of the day. Although she was not known for her classroom lecture prowess, she was an excellent research advisor to her laboratory students.

Lab Work Advances Knowledge of Plant Anatomy

In a laboratory constructed at her home, Sargant began to study plant cells life and plant fertilization processes. She was able to establish the existence of the synaptic stage in cell division, a stage questioned by some botanists of that time. She achieved this scientific advancement by examining the reproductive parts of the Turk's–cap lily, using both stained and unstained slide specimens. She found that synopsis was present with or without specimen staining.

Seeking relief from the visual intensity of constant microscope work, and somewhat disgusted with the state of cell research (she thought some of her peers were more interested in proving their personal theories by "presenting the facts colored beyond recognition"), she began to study of the origin and evolution of monocotyledon seedlings. Her findings were published in "A Theory of the Origin of Monocotyledons Founded on the Structure of Their Seedlings," "The Evolution of Monocotyledons," and "The Reconstruction of a Race of Primitive Angiosperms."

Sargant died at Sidmouth, England, on January 16, 1918, at the age of 54. She had spent most of her botanical career working out of her home laboratory in Girton Village, Cambridge. She left her books and laboratory equipment to Girton College.

SELECTED WRITINGS BY SARGANT:

Periodicals

"The Formation of the Sexual Nuclei in *Lilium martagon*: I. Oogenesis." *Annual of Botany* 10 (1896): 445–477.

"The Formation of the Sexual Nuclei in *Lilium martagon*: II. Spermatogenesis." *Annual of Botany* 11.

FURTHER READING

Books

Ogilvie, Marilyn Bailey. *Women in Science, Antiquity through the Nineteenth Century*. Cambridge: MIT Press, 1986, pp. 156–157.

Periodicals

Obituary, *London Times* (January 23, 1918): 3c.

Wills and Bequests, *London Times* (May 20, 1918): 9f.

Sketch by Jane Stewart Cook

Lucy Way (Sistare) Say
1801–1885
American scientific Illustrator

Lucy Say was the wife of Thomas Say, a famous self–taught naturalist from Philadelphia and a descendant of John Bartram, one of America's earliest naturalists. Thomas Say is also considered the father of American entomology. Lucy Say provided the majority of illustrations for her husband's book, *American Conchology,* and other publications he authored on the subject.

Say became the first woman member of the Academy of Natural Sciences of Philadelphia (her husband and his brother were co–founders and leaders; it was the United States' first science organization) when she was elected as an associate member in 1841. She also may have been the first woman to join an American scientific society.

Say was born on October 14, 1801 in New London, Connecticut to Joseph Sistare and Nancy Way. She grew up in New York City with one brother and one sister.

In the late 1820s Thomas Say accompanied William Maclure, a Scottish geologist and president of the Academy of Natural Sciences of Philadelphia from 1817 to 1840, and other scientists and educators from Philadelphia on the famous "Boatload of Knowledge." The party arrived in New Harmony, Indiana in January 1826, which was on the furthest frontiers of the U. S. at the time. Joining the party was the artist Lucy Way Sistare, whom Say married in 1827. New Harmony, Indiana, a socialist utopian experiment that was also a scientific and cultural center, founded the first kindergarten, first free public school, first free library, and first fully coeducational school in the United States.

In New Harmony, Thomas continued his descriptions of insects and mollusks, culminating in two classics. Say became the illustrator for his books. She also trained school children to assist her in coloring the illustrations by hand.

The Says cared little for money, and they lived very frugally. Thomas's chronic digestive problems worsened in the 1830s, and he died at age 47 in 1834. For the final years of his life, Thomas remained at New Harmony, running the printing press, editing the community newspaper, and eventually managing all of Maclure's affairs there. Shortly after his death Lucy wrote to William Maclure about her husband: "He was the pride of my heart and the recollection of his virtues shall stimulate me to the exercise of the limited talent which I possess to the advancement of that Science for which he sacrificed riches and health." After her husband's death in 1834, Say stayed at New Harmony for several years, publishing the final volumes of his book on mollusks. She also donated her husband's entomological cabinet and library to the Academy of Natural Sciences of Philadelphia.

Say moved back to New York City in 1842 to live with her sister. She returned to New Harmony periodically to visit friends and discuss her husband's work. Say continued collecting specimens throughout her life. Say died in Lexington, Massachusetts on November 15, 1885.

SELECTED WRITINGS BY SAY:

Books

(Illustrator, with Thomas Say) *American Conchology, or Descriptions of the Shells of North America Illustrated From Colored Figures From Original Drawings Executed from Nature.* Parts 1–6, New Harmony, 1830–1834; Part 7, Philadelphia, 1836.

FURTHER READING

Books

Bailey, Martha J. *American Women in Science: A Biographical Dictionary.* Denver: ABC–CLIO, 1994.

Ogilvie, Marilyn Bailey. *Women in Science.* Cambridge: MIT Press, 1986.

Stroud, Patricia Tyson. *Thomas Say: New World Naturalist.* Philadelphia: University of Pennsylvania Press, 1992.

Weiss, Harry B. and Grace M. Ziebler. *Thomas Say: Early American Naturalist.* Springfield, Illinois and Baltimore, Maryland, 1931.

Sketch by Laurel M. Sheppard

Alice T. Schafer
1915–
American mathematician

Alice T. Schafer was born in Richmond, Virginia, on June 18, 1915. Her mother died during childbirth, and Schafer was sent to the countryside area of Scottsburg, Virginia, to live with family friends. She was raised by Pearl Dickerson, a woman Schafer considered her mother and who was supportive of Schafer's ambitions throughout her life.

As a child, Schafer wanted to write novels, but by the third grade she became intrigued with mathematics after a teacher expressed concern that she would not able to master long division. Schafer not only mastered long division, but took math courses throughout her years of primary education. In her senior year of high school Schafer asked the principal to write a letter of recommendation for a scholarship to study mathematics in college. He was only willing to write the letter if she would promise to major in history instead.

After graduating from high school Schafer enrolled at the University of Richmond, where, at the time, the classes for men and women were held on separate sides of the campus. Mathematics classes were not offered on the female side of the campus, however, and as the only woman majoring in math, Schafer had to walk to the men's area of the campus to receive instruction. Women were also not allowed in the main library at the university. Books had to be sent over to the women's section of the campus upon request. In Schafer's junior year she questioned this policy and was finally allowed to sit in the library to read *Cyrano de Bergerac*, a book that was not available for circulation. After reading the book, Schafer was asked not to make any more requests to visit the library. The following summer she was offered a job in the library alphabetizing books. Schafer later quipped that she took the job because she needed the money.

Also in her junior year at Richmond, Schafer won the mathematical prize competition in Real Analysis but received no congratulatory praise from the chairman of the prize committee. Schafer graduated Phi Beta Kappa in 1936 when she was 21 years old with a degree in mathematics.

A Long and Varied Career

Schafer was offered a position at a high school in Glen Allen, Virginia, where she taught for three years. In 1939 she was awarded a fellowship at the University of Chicago and attained her Ph.D. in 1942. (Her dissertation was titled "Projective Differential Geometry.") While at the university, Schafer studied with Ernest P. Lane and Adrian Alberts.

Schafer's first teaching job as a Ph.D. was at Connecticut College, where she taught such classes as linear algebra, calculus, and abstract algebra for two years before accepting a position with Johns Hopkins University in the Applied Physics Laboratory doing research for the war effort. She was the only woman on the five member team of scientists.

Schafer married Richard Schafer, a professor of abstract algebra at MIT, in 1942. They have two children, Richard Stone Schafer, born in 1945, and John Dickerson Schafer, born in 1946. Between the years 1945 and 1961 Schafer taught at such institutions as the University of Michigan, the Drexel Institute of Technology, and Swarthmore College, among others. In 1962, she joined the staff at Wellesley College and stayed there until her forced retirement at the age of 65 in 1980. The retirement proved to be short–lived, however, when in that same year Schafer went to Harvard University as a consultant and teacher of mathematics in the management program. She again became a professor of mathematics, this time at Marymount University, in 1989 and retired in 1996.

A Trailblazer for Women

Schafer has been a visiting professor and lecturer at various colleges, including Brown University and Simmons College. Schafer was the first woman to receive a Honorary Doctor of Science degree from the University of Richmond in 1964 and was presented with the Distinguished Alumna Award, Westhampton College, at the University of Richmond in 1977. During her tenure at Wellesley College, Schafer and two other women professors succeeded at implementing the black studies department there. She is also a cofounder of the Association for Women in Mathematics (AWM), along with Mary W. Gray, and others. The organization was established in 1971 to encourage women to study and seek careers in the mathematical sciences; currently, it boasts a membership of 4,500 from the United States and abroad. More than 300 academic institutions are supporting members of AWM in the United States. The AWM is open to both women and men. Schafer served as its president from 1973 to 1975 and remains active on various committees. A prize was established in her name in 1989 and is given annually to an undergraduate woman for excellence in mathematics.

Schafer is the author of eight articles concerning the progress of women in the field of mathematics and affirmative action. Her other articles include research on space curves and theorems on finite groups. A book published by the American Mathematical Society includes talks given by Schafer at their "100 Years of Annual Meetings Celebration." Her fields of specialization are abstract algebra (group theory). Schafer has three times been the leader of the delegation of women mathematicians to China, the last of which was the U.S.-China Joint Conference on Women's Issues held in Beijing between August 24 and September 2, 1995.

Schafer currently lives in Arlington, Virginia, with her husband.

SELECTED WRITINGS BY SCHAFER:

Books

"Women and Mathematics," in *Mathematics Tomorrow.* Edited by Lynn Arthur Steen. New York: Springer–Verlag, 1981.

Periodicals

"The Neighborhood of an Undulation Point of a Space Curve." *American Journal of Mathematics* 70 (1948): 351–363.

"Mathematics and Women: Perspectives and Progress." *American Mathematical Notices* (September 1991).

(With M.W. Gray) "Guidelines for Equality: A Proposal." *Academe* (December 1981).

"Two Singularities of Space Curves." *Duke Mathematical Journal* (November 1994): 655–670.

Other

"Alice T. Schafer." *Biographies of Women Mathematicians.* June 1997. http://www.scottlan.edu/lriddle/women/chronol.htm (July 22, 1997).

Schafer, Alice T., interview with Kelley Reynolds Jacquez conducted May 8, 1997.

Sketch by Kelley Reynolds Jacquez

Berta Scharrer
1906–
German-born American biologist

Berta Scharrer, together with her husband Ernst Scharrer, pioneered the field of neuroendocrinology—the interaction of the nervous and endocrine systems. Fighting against the then-accepted belief that nerve cells were only electrical conductors, as well as against the prejudice toward women in the sciences, Berta Scharrer established the concept of neurosecretion through her research with insects and other invertebrates. A highly respected educator, she was also among the founding faculty of the department of anatomy at the Albert Einstein College of Medicine in New York.

Berta Vogel Scharrer was born in Munich, Germany on December 1, 1906, the daughter of Karl Phillip and Johanna (Greis) Vogel. She developed an early interest in science, and attended the University of Munich, earning her Ph.D. in 1930 in biology for research into the correlation between sweetness and nutrition in various sugars. Upon graduation, Scharrer took a position as research associate in the Research Institute of Psychiatry in Munich, and in 1934 she was married to Ernst Albert Scharrer, a biologist.

Together they formed an intellectual and domestic partnership that would last until Ernst Scharrer's death in 1965.

In 1928 Ernst Scharrer had discovered what he termed nerve–gland cells in a species of fish and made the rather startling hypothesis that some nerve cells actually were involved in secreting hormonal substances just as cells of the endocrine system do. It was a thesis sure to upset the more conservative members of the scientific community, as the synaptic function between neurons or nerve cells was then thought to be purely electrical. The idea of neurons having a dual function was looked on as something of a heresy: either cells secreted hormones, in which case they were endocrine cells belonging to the endocrine system, or they conducted electrical impulses, making them nerve cells, part of the nervous system. But what Ernst and Berta Scharrer demonstrated was that there existed an entire class of cells which performed both functions. The nerve-gland or neurosecretory cells are actually a channel between the nervous system and the endocrine system—an interface between an organism's environment and its glandular system. Some of the neurohormones secreted by neurosecretory cells actually control the release of other hormones via the anterior pituitary gland. To elucidate such action fully, the Scharrers divided up the animal kingdom between them: Ernst Scharrer took the vertebrates and Berta Scharrer the invertebrates.

Working as a research associate at the Neurological Institute of the University of Frankfurt, where her husband had been named director of the Edinger Institute for Brain Research, Berta Scharrer discovered other nerve–gland cells: in mollusks in 1935, in worms in 1936, and in insects beginning in 1937. But if research into neurosecretion was going well, life in Germany under Hitler was far from positive. The Scharrers decided, in 1937, to immigrate to the United States.

Introduce Neurosecretion to American Neuroscientists

The Scharrers traveled the long way to America, via the Pacific, collecting specimens for research along the way. They joined the Department of Anatomy at the University of Chicago for a year, and then moved on to New York where Ernst Scharrer was visiting investigator at the Rockefeller Institute from 1938 to 1940. Berta Scharrer continued her insect research in New York, and together the Scharrers prepared the results of their research for presentation at the 1940 meeting of the Association for Research in Nervous and Mental Diseases, the first presentation of the concept of neurosecretion in the United States, and one that was warmly received. That same year, Ernst Scharrer took a position as assistant professor in the anatomy department of Western Reserve University School of Medicine in Cleveland, Ohio, a post he would hold until 1946. Berta Scharrer was offered a fellowship assisting in the histology laboratory, which gave her research facilities, but scant professional standing. It was during these years that she accomplished some of her most important research into the localization of neurosecretory cells and their role in animal development, using the South American cockroach, *Leucophaea maderae,* as her research subject.

After the Second World War, Ernst Scharrer accepted a position at the University of Colorado Medical School in Denver, and Berta Scharrer won a Guggenheim Fellowship to continue her research, becoming an assistant professor in Denver in 1947. The next years were some of the Scharrers' most fruitful, as they loved the mountains, skiing, and horseback riding. Professionally these were also important times, for the theory of neurosecretion was beginning to be accepted around the world, especially after a German scientist was able to successfully stain neurosecretory granules—the packaging for neurohormones which some neurons secrete. Thus it became possible to study the fine structure of such granules and follow their course upon secretion. Neurosecretion became an accepted fact, in fact the cornerstone of the emerging field of neuroendocrinology. By 1950 it had also become an accepted fact that a chemical transmission took place at the synapse along with electrical charge. These advancements not only confirmed the Scharrers' work, but also paved the way for advances in their research. Berta Scharrer applied the new findings to her own work on the maturation of the ovarian systems of her South American cockroaches with results that verified earlier findings in the endocrinology of invertebrates.

Wins Full Professorship at Albert Einstein College

In 1955 the Scharrers were offered joint positions at the new Albert Einstein College of Medicine at Yeshiva University in New York: Ernst as department head of anatomy, and Berta as full professor in the same department. This was the first real professional recognition for Berta Scharrer, and the couple left Denver for New York. Here she taught histology—the microscopic structure of tissues—and continued with research into insect glands. Using the electron microscope, she was able to accomplish some of the earliest detailing of the insect nervous system and especially the neurosecretory system. Together with her husband, she published *Neuroendocrinology* in 1963, one of the basic texts in the new discipline. Tragically, her husband died in a swimming accident in Florida in 1965, but Berta Scharrer carried on with their research, acting as chair of the department for two years until a successor could be found. She also went on to elucidate the fine structure of the neurosecretory cell—composed of a cell body, projecting dendrites, the extending long axon, and synaptic contacts at one end, just as in other neurons or nerve cells. Additionally, neurosecretory cells have special fibers allowing for feedback, as well as neurohemal organs—the point at which the neurohormones pass into the blood stream. Neurosecretory cells, it was shown, can affect targets contiguous with them or distant, through the blood stream, as with other hormones. Scharrer also investigated the make–up of the secretory material, discovering that it was a peptide or polypeptide—a combination of amino acids. Scharrer's later research deals with the immunoregulatory property of neuropeptides, or the relationship between the immune and nervous systems in invertebrates.

Continuing with her research and instruction, as well as co–editing *Cell and Tissue Research,* Scharrer became an emeritus professor of anatomy and neuroscience at Albert Einstein College of Medicine in 1978. She was honored with a National Medal of Science in 1983, for her "pioneering contributions in establishing the concept of neurosecretion and neuropeptides in the integration of animal function and development." She has also won the F. C. Koch Award of the Endocrine Society in 1980, the Henry Gray Award of the American Association of Anatomists in 1982, and has been honored by her former country with the Kraepelin Gold Medal from the Max Planck Institute in Munich in 1978 and the Schleiden Medal in 1983. She is a member of the National Academy of Sciences and holds honorary degrees from colleges and universities around the world, including Harvard and Northwestern. Reading and music are among Berta Scharrer's free-time activities, and she has continued scientific research well into her eighties.

SELECTED WRITINGS BY SCHARRER:

Books

(With Ernst A. Scharrer) *Neuroendocrinology.* Columbia University Press, 1963.

An Evolutionary Interpretation of the Phenomenon of Neurosecretion. American Museum of Natural History, 1978.

Periodicals

"Comparative Physiology of Invertebrate Endocrines." *Annual Review of Physiology* 25 (1953): 456–472.

"The Fine Structure of the Neurosecretory System of the Insect Leucophaea Maderae." *Memoirs of the Society of Endocrinology* 12 (1962) 89–97.

"Peptidergic Neurons: Facts and Trends." *General and Comparative Endocrinology* (January 1978): 50–62.

"Neurosecretion: Beginnings and New Directions in Neuropeptide Research." *Annual Review of Neuroscience* 10 (1987): 1–17.

"Insects as Models of Neuroendocrine Research." *Annual Review of Entomology* 32 (1987): 1–16.

"Recent Progress in Comparative Neuroimmunology." *Zoological Science* (December 1992): 1097–1100.

FURTHER READING

Periodicals

"Honorary Degrees Given By Harvard." *New York Times* (October 16, 1982): 9.

"Medal of Science to Berta Scharrer." *Einstein* (Spring 1985): 2.

Other

Palay, Sanford L. "Presentation of the Henry Gray Award to Professor Berta Scharrer at the Ninety-Fifth Meeting of the American Association of Anatomists." (speech) April 5, 1982.

Sketch by J. Sydney Jones

Dorothea Schlözer
1770–?
German mineralogist

In 1787, Dorothea Schlözer became the first woman to earn a Ph.D. degree in Germany. Although well–educated in many subjects, her major interest was in the study of minerals and mines.

Born into a middle–class family in Göttingen, Germany, in 1770, Dorothea Schlözer's father, August Schlözer, was a history professor at the University of Göttingen. He was determined to use his daughter to disprove the theories of Jean–Jacques Rousseau and others, whose arguments for the limited intellectual abilities of women were very much the fashion of the time. In contrast, August Schlözer argued that education was, as quoted by Londa Schiebinger, "the essential destiny of the female sex," as well as a necessity for girls from families that were well–to–do but not members of the landed gentry. Thus from birth, Dorothea Schlözer was raised as part of an educational experiment.

Schlözer's father attempted to demonstrate that a female could be raised to be both an intellectual and an exemplary wife and mother and, throughout her education, the subjects that Schlözer studied were chosen for their acceptability to her future husband. Thus, Schlözer's mother taught her cooking, sewing, and the managing of a wine cellar, while her father supervised her training in mathematics and ancient and modern history. From the time she was six, her father taught her several languages, including German, Latin, Greek, French, English, Italian, Swedish, and Dutch. She learned botany and zoology, optics, and Euclidean geometry, algebra and trigonometry, as well as religion.

Treks Through the Mountains

At the time, the study of minerals was popular among women. Even as a young girl, Schlözer spent months traveling in the Harz Mountains, studying minerals and mines. Sometimes she made these journeys alone. As Schiebinger quoted her father, although these studies ultimately would be of no use to her, "it keeps her busy and, for a seven–year–old girl, that is the best protection against the temptations of the devil."

Receives Degree

It was Johann Michaelis, a family friend and dean of philosophy at Göttingen, who proposed that Schlözer receive a university degree. Forty years earlier, Michaelis had unsuccessfully petitioned the King of Prussia to establish a university for women. As Schiebinger quoted from Schlözer's description of the Michaelis proposal: "He suggested that at the upcoming fifty–year jubilee of the founding of the University of Göttingen I should receive a degree from the university. Unsure whether Michaelis was serious or merely being polite, I returned home and reported the event to my father. Father, fearful that the degree would be merely an honorary one, suggested to Michaelis a full examination by the faculty." Thus, Schlözer was examined for several hours by a faculty committee, in modern languages, mathematics, architecture, logic and metaphysics, classics, geography, and literature. At her father's request, the exam was held privately in Michaelis's home, rather than in public, and was conducted in German, rather than in the customary Latin. According to her father's wishes, Schlözer was dressed as a bride for her examination. The committee was unanimous in their decision to award Schlözer her degree. Schlözer, however, did not attend the public ceremony where her degree was conferred, since her father believed this would be improper. Rather, she watched through a broken window in the neighboring library.

Four years later, in 1791, Schlözer married Matthäus von Rodde, a merchant and a senator from Lübeck. In the years that followed, Schlözer published a series of letters about metal production in Clausthal. She also prepared the tables for her father's *Münz–, Geld–, und Bergwerksgeschichte des russischen Kaiserthums von Jahren 1700–1789*, and published a cookbook.

Schlözer's academic achievements brought her fame, and she was honored at a public session of the Académie des Sciences in Paris in 1801. However in Germany, even among the faculty at the University of Göttingen, there was a serious backlash against education for women, particularly education in the sciences. Schlözer's degree failed to establish a precedent: the University of Göttingen did not award another doctorate to a woman until 1874, when the Russian mathematician, **Sonya Vasilievna Kovalevskaya**, was awarded her degree *in absentia*. Women were not formally admitted to German universities until 1908.

SELECTED WRITINGS BY SCHLÖZER:

Books

Nützliches Buch für die Küche bey Zubereitung der Speisen von dem Koch August Erdmann Lebmann. Dresden, 1818.

FURTHER READING

Books

Schiebinger, Londa. *The Mind Has No Sex? Women in the Origins of Modern Science.* Cambridge: Harvard University Press, 1989.

Sketch by Margaret Alic

Charlotte Angas Scott
1858–1931
English mathematician

Charlotte Angas Scott was the first mathematics department head at Bryn Mawr College and a member of its founding faculty. She developed the curriculum for graduate and undergraduate math majors and upgraded the minimum mathematics requirements for entry and retention at Bryn Mawr. Scott also initiated the formulation of the College Entrance Examination Board in order to standardize such requirements nationwide. At one time, she was the only woman featured in the first printing of *American Men of Science*, and the only mathematician in another venerable reference book, *Notable American Women 1607–1950.* Scott was one of the main organizers of the American Mathematical Society and the only female to leave such an extensive mark on its first 50 years of existence.

Breaking "The Iron Mould"

Scott was born in Lincoln, England, on June 8, 1958, to Caleb and Eliza Exley Scott. As the daughter of the president of Lancashire College, she was provided with mathematics tutors as early as age seven. Her father and grandfather, Walter, were both social reformers as well as educators, and encouraged her to "break the iron mould" and seek a university education. At the age of 18 Scott won a scholarship to Hitchin College, now known as Girton College, the women's division of Cambridge University.

As the 19th century drew to a close, Girton was still an anomaly. Scott and her classmates numbered 11. The young women had to walk three miles to Cambridge to attend classes with those lecturers who allowed them in their classroom, but they had to sit behind a screen where they could not see the blackboard. At that time, a woman caught unescorted on Cambridge campus grounds could be sent to The Spinning House, a prison for prostitutes both active and suspected. A hint of the future could be seen in the changing attitudes of male undergraduates and graduate students, however. Tutors offered to prepare female undergraduates for the "Tripos," a grueling oral examination that lasted over a week's time. The first female student took the mathematics Tripos in 1872, and thereafter more women applied for

Charlotte Scott

permission to take the tests along with their male counterparts. Scott took the examination in January 1880, placing eighth. Although university policy kept her accomplishment a secret, the news spread throughtout the campus. The awards ceremony was disrupted by a crowd of young men shouting "Scott of Girton!" over the name of the man honored in her place. Scott was later "crowned with laurels" in a private ceremony. In February 1881 Cambridge reversed its policy and women were allowed to take examinations with the male students.

Double Duty

Scott remained at Girton as a lecturer for four years while finishing her graduate studies at the University of London. The algebraist Arthur Cayley, a leader in coeducational reform, became Scott's mentor and recommended her for jobs as well as guiding her graduate research. Her doctorate was the first of its kind to be earned by a British female. In the nascent specialty of analysis within algebraic geometry, Scott focused on analyzing singularities in algebraic curves. Both of Scott's degrees at London were of the highest rank.

In 1885 Scott emigrated to the United States, where she joined the faculty of Bryn Mawr College in Pennsylvania. Founded that same year by the Society of Friends, Bryn Mawr was the first women's college to offer graduate degrees. Between 1885 and 1901 Scott successfully lobbied for a series of reforms to the admissions policies and entrance procedures at Bryn Mawr. Once the College Entrance Examination Board was instituted with her help, she served as Chief Examiner from 1902 to 1903. Scott's dedication was finally rewarded in 1909 with Bryn Mawr's first endowed chair and a formal citation.

Helps Organize the AMS

In 1891 Scott was one of the first women to join the New York Mathematical Society, which later evolved into the American Mathematical Society (AMS) in 1895. Scott served on the council that oversaw this transition and received an "acclaimed review" from the group. She would serve on the AMS council again (between 1899 and 1901), and as vice–president in 1905.

Also, in 1899 Scott became the coeditor of the *American Journal of Mathematics*. She would continue to edit and peer review for this publication until two years after her official retirement from Bryn Mawr. Her influence spread internationally with her proof of **Emmy Noether**'s "fundamental theorem," an accomplishment which helped place Bryn Mawr and American mathematics on the world map.

"Auntie Charley"

During her long sojourn in America, Scott was visited regularly by her father and younger brother, Walter, while her sisters remained in England. "Auntie Charley," as Scott was called, would travel to Europe during spring and summer breaks to visit with her expanding circle of relatives and with mathematicians in major European cities. Scott's own personal life was more circumspect, clouded further by the fact that all her personal correspondence was apparently disposed of or lost. She traveled often to Baltimore to visit her close friend Frank Morley, but she never married.

As Scott aged, the deafness that had plagued her since her student days became a stumbling block. However, even rheumatoid arthritis could not dampen her ambitions although it disrupted her publications' schedule for many years. On the advice of a physician Scott took up gardening, only to breed a new species of a chrysanthemum.

Scott retired at age 67, after a 40–year career as one of the many European women who could only find work as scientists and mathematicians in the United States. She stayed on voluntarily at Bryn Mawr until the following year, however, when her last doctoral student graduated. Scott continued mentoring younger mathematicians and inspired another generation of women to follow in her footsteps. She died in November 1931 in Cambridge, England, and was buried next to her cousin Eliza Nevins in St. Giles's Churchyard. Her textbook on analytical geometry, having gone through a second edition in 1924, would be reissued in a third edition 30 years after her death.

SELECTED WRITINGS BY SCOTT:

Books

An Introductory Account of Certain Modern Ideas and Methods in Plane Analytical Geometry. First Edition, 1894 (republished as *Projective Methods in Plane Analytical Geometry* in 1961).

Cartesian Plane Geometry, Part I:: Analytical Conics, 1907.

Periodicals

"A Proof of Noether's Fundamental Theorem." *Mathematische Annalen* 52 (1899): 592–97.

FURTHER READING

Books

Eves, Howard. *An Introduction to the History of Mathematics.* 6th ed. Philadelphia: Saunders College Publishing, 1990.

Green, Judy and Jeanne LaDuke. "Contributors to American Mathematics: An Overview and Selection," in *Women of Science:: Righting the Record.* Edited by G. Kass–Simon and Patricia Farnes. Bloomington and Indianapolis: Indiana University Press, 1990.

———. "Women in American Mathematics: A Century of Contributions," in *A Century of Mathematics in America.*Vol 2. Providence, RI: American Mathematical Society, 1989, pp. 379–389.

Kenschaft, Patricia Clark. "Charlotte Angas Scott." In *Women of Mathematics.* Edited by Louise S. Grinstein and Paul J. Campbell. New York: Greenwood Press, 1987, pp. 193–203.

Lehr, Marguerite. "Charlotte Angas Scott." *Notable American Women, 1607–1950.* Volume 3. Cambridge, MA.: Belknap Press, 1971, pp. 249–250.

Ogilvie, Marilyn Bailey. "Charlotte Angas Scott." *Women in Science.* Cambridge: MIT Press, 1986, pp. 158–59.

Rossiter, Margaret W. *Women Scientists in America: Struggles and Strategies to 1940.* Baltimore: Johns Hopkins University Press, 1982.

Periodicals

Katz, Kaila and Patricia Kenschaft. "Sylvester and Scott." *The Mathematics Teacher* 75 (1982): 490–494.

Kenschaft, Patricia C. "The Students of Charlotte Angas Scott." *Mathematics in College* (Fall 1982): 16–20.

———. "Why Did Charlotte Angas Scott Succeed?" *Association for Women in Mathematics Newsletter* 17, no. 2 (1988): 9–11.

———. "Charlotte Angas Scott 1858–1931." *College Mathematics Journal* 18 (March 1987): 98–110.

Maddison, Isabel and Marquerite Lehr. "Charlotte Angas Scott: An Appreciation." *Bryn Mawr Alumni Bulletin* 12 (1932): 9–12.

Other

Chaplin, Stephanie. "Charlotte Angas Scott." http://www.agnesscott.edu/lriddle/women/chronol.htm (July 1997).

"Charlotte Angas Scott." http://www–groups.dcs.st–and.ac.uk/˜history /Mathematicians/Scott.html (July 1997).

Sketch by Jennifer Kramer

Mary Sears
1905–1997
American marine biologist and oceanographer

Mary Sears was a distinguished biologist and oceanographer whose research at the Woods Hole Oceanographic Institution spanned a period of nearly 50 years. Her research focused on zooplankton and phytoplankton, the small and microscopic animals and plants that are the basis for the food chains of the oceans. She also studied siphonophores, colonial polyps such as the Portuguese man-of-;war. In addition, she was a hydrographer, or oceanographer, with research focusing on the salinity of sea water. However Sears's most important contribution was as an editor of oceanographic literature.

Born in Wayland, Massachusetts in 1905, Sears was one of several children of Edmund Hamilton and Leslie (Buckingham) Sears. She received her A.B. degree from Radcliffe College, in Cambridge, Massachusetts, in 1927, and her master's degree and Ph.D. in zoology and oceanography from Radcliffe in 1929 and 1933, respectively. As a graduate student, she worked at Harvard University with Henry Bigelow, the founder and first director of the Woods Hole Oceanographic Institution in Massachusetts. In 1929 and 1930, Sears worked as an assistant at the United States Bureau of Fisheries.

Becomes a Planktonologist

After receiving her doctorate, Sears went to work as a research assistant at Harvard and, during the summers, as a planktonologist at the Woods Hole Oceanographic Institution, where she was one of the first staff research assistants. She continued as a research assistant at Harvard and a tutor at Radcliffe College until 1940, when she was appointed staff planktonologist at Woods Hole. She was promoted to senior scientist in the newly founded biology department of the Oceanographic Institution in 1963, a position she held until her retirement in 1970. In 1978 she became an emeritus senior scientist.

From 1938 until 1943, Sears was an instructor at Wellesley College, and in 1941–42, as a Wellesley College faculty fellow, she obtained a grant to work in the Guano Islands in Peru. In 1946, she received a Rask-Ørsted Foundation grant to work in Copenhagen, Denmark.

Directs Oceanographic Research for Naval Intelligence

During World War II, many new opportunities opened up for women scientists. From 1943 until 1946, Sears was a lieutenant with Naval Intelligence in Washington, D. C. There, she organized and headed the Oceanographic Unit of the Navy Hydrographic Office, devoted to military oceanography. Prior to the war, this office had been responsible for producing navigational charts. Now, Sears was responsible for preparing reports on enemy waters for Allied submarine operations and amphibious landings. Under Sears's direction, the agency evolved in the Naval Oceanographic Office. She also coordinated naval research at Woods Hole, studying methods for submarines to avoid detection, the behavior of smoke at sea, and the temperature and water density of the ocean layers.

After the war, since women still were not allowed to sail on research vessels, Sears began devoting much of her energy to the editing of oceanographic publications. She was founding editor of the journal *Deep–Sea Research* and served as its editor–in–chief from 1953 until 1974. She also edited important reference works on marine science.

Sears was a corporation member and trustee of the Woods Hole Marine Biological Laboratory for many years and an honorary member and trustee of the Woods Hole Oceanographic Institution. She was chair of the First International Congress on Oceanography, held at the United Nations in 1959. An active member of a number of scientific congresses and societies, Sears was awarded honorary doctorates by Mount Holyoke College in 1962 and by Southeastern Massachusetts University in 1974.

Sears's contributions were summed up by her colleague, Roger Revelle, as quoted in her obituary in the Woods Hole *Labnotes*: she was "the conscience of oceanography who initiated and maintained an uncompromising standard of excellence in scientific publications about the oceans. She played a major role in creating the present world community of oceanographers from numerous countries and almost as many specialties."

Sears died at her home in Woods Hole in 1997 at the age of 92, following a brief illness.

SELECTED WRITINGS BY SEARS:

Books

(Editor) *Oceanography; Invited Lectures Presented at the International Oceanographic Congress held in New York, 31 August–12 September 1959*. American Association for the Advancement of Science Publication no. 67. Washington, D.C: 1961.

(Editor) *Progress in Oceanography*. Oxford: Pergamon Press, 1963.

(Compiler) *Oceanographic Index; Author Cumulation,1946–1970*. Boston: G. K. Hall, 1971.

(Compiler)*Oceanographic Index, Cumulation 1946–1973—Marine Organisms, Chiefly Planktonic*. Boston: G. K. Hall, 1974.

(With Daniel Merriman, editors.) *Oceanography: The Past*. New York: Springer-Verlag, 1980.

FURTHER READING

Books

Press, Jaques Cattell, ed. *American Men and Women of Science: Physical and Biological Sciences*. 14th ed. Vol. 6. New York: R. R. Bowker, 1979.

Rossiter, Margaret W. *Women Scientists in America: Before Affirmative Action 1940–1972*. Baltimore: The Johns Hopkins University Press, 1995.

Who's Who of American Women (and Women of Canada): A Biographical Dictionary of Notable Living Women of the United States of America and Other Countries. 5th ed. Chicago: A. N. Marquis, 1968–69.

Periodicals

Hilchey, Tim. "Mary Sears, 92, Oceanographic Editor and Scientist at Woods Hole." *The New York Times* (September 10 1997): B7.

Other

"In Memorium." *LabNotes* Fall, 1997. http://www.mbl.edu/LABNOTES/7.3/obit.html (10 July 1999).

Sketch by Margaret Alic

Dr. Florence B. Seibert (The Library of Congress.)

Florence Barbara Seibert
1897–1991
American biochemist

A biochemist who received her Ph.D. from Yale University in 1923, Florence B. Seibert is best known for her research in the biochemistry of tuberculosis. She developed the protein substance used for the tuberculosis skin test. The substance was adopted as the standard in 1941 by the United States and a year later by the World Health Organization. In addition, in the early 1920s, Seibert discovered that the sudden fevers that sometimes occurred during intravenous injections were caused by bacteria in the distilled water that was used to make the protein solutions. She invented a distillation apparatus that prevented contamination. This research had great practical significance later when intravenous blood transfusions became widely used in surgery. Seibert authored or coauthored more than a hundred scientific papers. Her later research involved the study of bacteria associated with certain cancers. Her many honors include five honorary degrees, induction into the National Women's Hall of Fame in Seneca Falls, New York (1990), the Garvan Gold Medal of the American Chemical Society (1942), and the John Elliot Memorial Award of the American Association of Blood Banks (1962).

Florence Barbara Seibert was born on October 6, 1897, in Easton, Pennsylvania, the second of three children. She was the daughter of George Peter Seibert, a rug manufacturer and merchant, and Barbara (Memmert) Seibert. At the age of three she contracted polio. Despite her resultant handicaps, she completed high school, with the help of her highly supportive parents, and entered Goucher College in Baltimore, where she studied chemistry and zoology. She graduated in 1918, then worked under the direction of one of her chemistry teachers, Jessie E. Minor, at the Chemistry Laboratory of the Hammersley Paper Mill in Garfield, New Jersey. She and her professor, having responded to the call for women to fill positions vacated by men fighting in World War I, coauthored scientific papers on the chemistry of cellulose and wood pulps.

Although Seibert initially wanted to pursue a career in medicine, she was advised against it as it was "too rigorous" in view of her physical disabilities. She decided on biochemistry instead and began graduate studies at Yale University under Lafayette B. Mendel, one of the discoverers of Vitamin A. Her Ph.D. research involved an inquiry into the causes of "protein fevers"—fevers that developed in patients after they had been injected with protein solutions that contained distilled water. Seibert's assignment was to discover which proteins caused the fevers and why. What she discovered, however, was that the distilled water itself was contaminated—with bacteria. Consequently, Seibert invented a distilling apparatus that prevented the bacterial contamination.

Seibert earned her Ph.D. in 1923, then moved to Chicago to work as a post–graduate fellow under H. Gideon Wells at the University of Chicago. She continued her research on pyrogenic (fever causing) distilled water, and her work in this area acquired practical significance when intravenous blood transfusions became a standard part of many surgical procedures.

After her fellowship ended, she was employed part–time at the Otho S. A. Sprague Memorial Institute in Chicago, where Wells was the director. At the same time, she worked with Esmond R. Long, whom she had met through Wells's seminars at the University of Chicago. Supported by a grant from the National Tuberculosis Association, Long and Seibert would eventually spend thirty–one years collaborating on tuberculosis research. Another of Seibert's long–time associates was her younger sister, Mabel Seibert, who moved to Chicago to be with her in 1927. For the rest of their lives, with the exception of a year in Sweden, the sisters resided together, with Mabel providing assistance both in the research institutes (where she found employment as secretary and later research assistant) and at home. In 1932, when Long moved to the Henry Phipps Institute—a tuberculosis clinic and research facility associated with the University of Pennsylvania in Philadelphia—Seibert (and her sister) transferred as well. There, Seibert rose from assistant professor (1932–1937), to associate professor (1937–1955) to full professor of biochemistry (1955–1959). In 1959 she retired with emeritus status. Between 1937 and 1938 she was a Guggenheim fellow in the laboratory of Theodor Svedberg at the

University of Upsala in Sweden. In 1926 Svedberg had received the Nobel prize for his protein research.

Works on Unknown Aspects of Tuberculosis

Seibert's tuberculosis research involved questions that had emerged from the late–nineteenth–century work of German bacteriologist Robert Koch. In 1882 Koch had discovered that the tubercle bacillus was the primary cause of tuberculosis. He also discovered that if the liquid on which the bacilli grew was injected under the skin, a small bite–like reaction would occur in people who had been infected with the disease. (Calling the liquid "old tuberculin," Kock produced it by cooking a culture and draining off the dead bacilli.) Although he had believed the active substance in the liquid was protein, it had not been proven.

Using precipitation and other methods of separation and testing, Seibert discovered that the active ingredient of the liquid was indeed protein. The next task was to isolate it, so that it could be used in pure form as a diagnostic tool for tuberculosis. Because proteins are highly complex organic molecules that are difficult to purify, this was a daunting task. Seibert finally succeeded by means of crystallization. The tiny amounts of crystal that she obtained, however, made them impractical for use in widespread skin tests. Thus, she changed the direction of her research and began working on larger amounts of active, but less pure protein. Her methods included precipitation through ultrafiltration (a method of filtering molecules). The result, after further purification procedures, was a dry powder called TPT (Tuberculin Protein Trichloracetic acid precipitated). This was the first substance that was able to be produced in sufficient quantities for widespread use as a tuberculosis skin test. For her work, Seibert received the 1938 Trudeau Medal from the National Tuberculosis Association.

At the Henry Phipps Institute in Philadelphia, Seibert continued her study of tuberculin protein molecules and their use in the diagnosis of tuberculosis. Seibert began working on the "old tuberculin" that had been created by Koch and used by doctors for skin testing. As Seibert described it in her autobiography *Pebbles on the Hill of a Scientist,* old tuberculin "was really like a soup made by cooking up the live tubercle bacilli and extracting the protein substance from their bodies while they were being killed." Further purification of the substance led to the creation of PPD (Purified Protein Derivative). Soon large quantities of this substance were being made for tuberculosis testing. Seibert continued to study ways of further purifying and understanding the nature of the protein. Her study in Sweden with Svedberg aided this research. There she learned new techniques for the separation and identification of proteins in solution.

Upon her return from Sweden, Seibert brought the new techniques with her. She began work on the creation of a large batch of PPD to serve as the basis for a standard dosage. The creation of such a standard was critical for measuring the degree of sensitivity of individuals to the skin test. Degree of sensitivity constituted significant diagnostic information if it was based upon individual reaction, rather than upon differences in the testing substance itself. A large amount of substance was necessary to develop a standard that ideally would be used world–wide, so that the tuberculosis test would be comparable wherever it was given. Developing new methods of purification as she proceeded, Seibert and her colleagues created 107 grams of material, known as PPD–S (the S signifying "standard"). A portion was used in 1941 as the government standard for purified tuberculins. Eventually it was used as the standard all over the world.

In 1958 the Phipps Institute was moved to a new building at the University of Pennsylvania. In her memoirs, Seibert wrote that she did not believe that the conditions necessary for her continued work would be available. Consequently, she and Mabel, her long–time assistant and companion, retired to St. Petersburg, Florida. Florence Seibert continued her research, however, using for a time a small laboratory in the nearby Mound Park Hospital and another in her own home. In her retirement years she devoted herself to the study of bacteria that were associated with certain types of cancers. Her declining health in her last two years was attributed to complications from childhood polio. She died in St. Petersburg on August 23, 1991.

In 1968 Seibert published her memoirs, which reveal her many friendships, especially among others engaged in scientific research. She particularly enjoyed international travel as well as driving her car, which was especially equipped to compensate for her handicaps. She loved music and played the violin (privately, she was careful to note).

SELECTED WRITINGS BY SEIBERT:

Books

Pebbles on the Hill of a Scientist. self–published (printed by St. Petersburg Printing Co.), 1968.

FURTHER READING

Periodicals

New York Times (August 31, 1991).

Sketch by Pamela O. Long

Susan Wyber Serjeantson
1946–
Australian geneticist

Susan Serjeantson is a world-renowned expert in genetics and was the first woman to become Deputy Vice-Chancellor of the Australian National University. Her research is in the areas of inherited diseases and transplantation antigens, especially in Pacific peoples. Her studies of how a person's genetic make-up affects his or her susceptibility to disease has led to greatly improved organ transplant tests, making donor matches with recipients more accurate, a process especially critical in bone marrow transplants. These techniques have been adopted in laboratories throughout the world. Serjeantson received both the Clunies Ross Award for Science and Technology and the Ruth Sanger Medal in 1992 for her achievements.

Serjeantson was born on November 14, 1946 in Riverstone, near Sydney, New South Wales to Robert and Nancye Wyber. A year later her brother was born. Her father was a radar technician in the Royal Australian Navy and after being discharged returned to Sydney, where he got married and attended Sydney University, studying mechanical engineering and electrical engineering. Serjeantson's father was a strong advocate of education and encouraged his children to pursue as much education as they could. However, due to tight finances, priority would be given to her brother to pay for his college.

Serjeantson's early years of schooling were spent in England, where her father was working for the British Air Corporation, and then in Adelaide, where he worked for the Weapons Research Establishment for five years. The family returned to Sydney in time for Serjeantson to begin high school at Caringbah High School, a local coeducational school, where she graduated in 1963. Her father sent her there instead of the more conventional girls' school since he believed she would receive a better education in science.

Serjeantson received a B.S. in 1968 from the University of New South Wales on a bond-free scholarship, which did not require her to be bonded into employment. Serjeantson soon became interested in genetics since it combined biology and mathematics, completing an honors project involving the genetics of fruit flies. From this experience, she turned to human population genetics, earning a scholarship to attend the University of Hawaii, which had an excellent program in that area at the time. Her research included field work in Papua New Guinea to study genetic markers, such as blood groups. Serjeantson received her Ph.D. in 1970, the same year the International Biological Program was established to study small indigenous and primitive populations.

A year after she graduated, Serjeantson returned to Papua New Guinea to work as a geneticist at the Institute for Medical Research, where she remained until 1976. Her research involved studying tropical diseases like malaria and leprosy in the western region of Kiunga (where she became engaged to an agricultural officer) and later at a one-person laboratory she set up in Madang, located on the north coast. Serjeantson determined that a common skin disease found there was genetically determined, which was the first demonstration that a person could inherit a susceptibility to an infectious disease. She also proved there was a genetic tendency for leprosy, after visiting 183 villages in remote locations to monitor the disease and take blood samples.

Begins Work on Transplantation Antigens

When she and her husband returned to Australia, Serjeantson accepted a position as a Research Fellow at the John Curtin School of Medical Research, Australian National University. Here she helped set up a laboratory that would test for transplantation antigens. This laboratory was moved to the Colonial War Memorial Hospital at Fiji for six weeks in 1980, the same year Serjeantson became a Fellow. During the early 1980s DNA testing techniques began to emerge, which did not require keeping blood cells alive as with previous methods. Serjeantson and coworkers quickly adapted these techniques, making significant contributions in this area. These techniques provided the means to analyze the genes responsible for encoding transplantation antigens.

Serjeantson became a Senior Fellow in 1986 and was promoted to Head of Human Genetics in 1987, remaining in this position until 1993. She was also named professor in 1988. During her tenure in these various positions, Serjeantson continued working as part of a small team on a project to improve the effectiveness of organ transplantation by developing ways of identifying antigens, the foreign substances present in donor organs which often lead to tissue or organ rejection.

In 1993, Serjeantson became Acting Director of the Institute of Advanced Studies. A year later she was named its Director and also became the first woman Deputy Vice-Chancellor of Australian National University. In 1996, Serjeantson was invited to participate in the Conference of Asia-Pacific Science and Technology Leaders in Beijing, China. That same year she attended the International Symposium on Network and Evolution of Molecular Information in Tokyo, Japan. In 1997, Serjeantson left her position as Vice-Chancellor to return to research, becoming a Visiting Fellow at the John Curtin School of Medical Research. Serjeantson's research has resulted in the publication of 100 research papers and 50 chapters in books. She remains a true role model and mentor for women scientists, not only in Australia but around the world.

SELECTED WRITINGS BY SERJEANTSON:

Books

(With Adrian V. Hill) *Colonization Of The Pacific; A Genetic Trail.* Oxford University Press, 1989.

FURTHER READING

Books

Moyal, Ann. *Portraits in Science.* National Library of Australia, 1994.

Other

Australian Science Archives Project, http://www.asap.unimelb.edu.au/bsparcs/biogs/P002744b.htm, May 31, 1999

Sketch by Laurel M. Sheppard

Kate Olivia Sessions
1857–1940
American horticulturist

Kate Sessions was a horticulturist whose work spanned sixty years. She is recognized for almost single–handedly beautifying the San Diego area with plants she introduced, both to the area and to the field.

Born November 8, 1857, in San Francisco, to Josiah Sessions, a horse breeder, and Harriet Parker Sessions, Kate Olivia Sessions and her younger brother grew up on the family farm in Oakland. She spent her days riding her pony and working in the flower garden. After graduating from the Oakland high school, she traveled to Hawaii, and was amazed at the plant life native to that area.

In 1877, Sessions enrolled in the University of California, Berkeley's science track, from which she received her Ph.B. in chemistry in 1881. She taught at an Oakland primary school for a year and was vice principal of Russ High School for two years, before deciding to strike out on her own with a plant nursery and flower shop in 1885.

In only a few years, Sessions' nursery had grown to thirty acres, leased from the city of San Diego for 300 donated trees and 100 new tree plantings a year. (After her death, this nursery became Balboa Park.) In 1909, Sessions closed the flower shop to concentrate on her growing nursery.

Sessions traveled widely, always on the lookout for new drought–resistant plants which might flourish in the San Diego climate. Of the varieties Sessions introduced, the successful plants include queen palm, flame eucalyptus, bunyabunya tree, silver tree, acacias, hibiscus, mesembryanthemums, silk oak, jasmines, tecomas, Chinese twisted juniper, camphor tree, cork oak, bougainvilleas, Pride of Madeira, and several types of vine, aloe, and other succulents.

Sessions was active in promoting horticulture throughout the San Diego community. In 1909, Sessions helped found the San Francisco Floral Association. She also founded San Diego's Arbor Day holiday. From 1915 to 1918 she acted as supervisor of agriculture in several public schools, and several years later taught adult education gardening classes through the University of California Extension Division.

She was honored with the Kate Olivia Sessions Day in 1935, and in 1939 was the first woman to be awarded the Meyer Medal for her plant introduction. A Pacific Beach school and a park were named after her. Trees were often planted in her honor. Sessions continued to participate in flower shows throughout her lifetime, and her exhibits often won awards. Sought as a public speaker, Sessions also contributed many articles to the popular press, which raised awareness of and interest in horticulture. She died on March 24, 1940, from bronchial pneumonia.

SELECTED WRITINGS BY SESSIONS:

Periodicals

"Color Planting for Pacific Coast Gardens." *Garden Magazine* 32 (December 1920): 205–208.

FURTHER READING

Books

Bailey, Martha J. *American Women in Science.* Denver: ABC–CLIO, 1994.

James, Edward T., et al, eds. *Notable American Women 1607–1950.* Cambridge, MA: Belknap Press, 1971.

Shearer, Benjamin F. and Barbara S., eds. *Notable Women in the Life Sciences.* Westport, CT: Greenwood Press, 1996.

Sketch by Helene Barker Kiser

Lydia White Shattuck
1822–1889
American botanist, chemist, and naturalist

Lydia White Shattuck was considered one of the consummate female authorities of her time in the botanical and natural sciences. Nearly her entire professional tenure was spent as a science educator at her alma mater, Mt. Holyoke College, in Massachusetts, where a science building was later dedicated in her name. While there, she also established an herbarium and botanical garden. Her second love was chemistry, and she was a founding member of the eminent American Chemical Society.

Shattuck was born on June 10, 1822, to Timothy and Betsy (Fletcher) Shattuck of East Landaff (now Easton), New Hampshire. The Shattuck family traces its ancestry back to the early 1600s in New England's history. Her father was a farmer. Shattuck was the fifth-born child, but the first to survive. She was later joined by a younger brother, William, the only other child to survive. Shattuck's father was a deeply religious person, known for his good works in the community. Shattuck learned to love and respect nature from her mother. Hence, at an early age, she developed a precocious interest and knowledge in the natural sciences, exploring the hillsides and streams with her brother, and reveling in the indigenous flora and fauna.

After completing local school at the age of 15, Shattuck began teaching elementary school in several local districts. During the next several years, she took short breaks to attend classes or lectures at institutes of higher

Lydia Shattuck (Mt. Holyoke College Archives. Reproduced by permission.)

learning in Haverhill and Center Harbor, New Hampshire, and in Newbury, Vermont. Paying her own way by earning money as a domestic, at the age of 26 she entered Mt. Holyoke Seminary, a conservative but academically-rigorous college known for producing competent female science educators and scientists. Upon graduation with honors in 1851, Shattuck was offered a faculty position, and she remained on Mt. Holyoke's faculty for the rest of her life.

Shattuck's teaching profession was enhanced with numerous sabbaticals which enabled her to engage in graduate studies and scientific travels. She was one of 15 hand-selected women to be invited to the preeminent Anderson School of Natural History at Penikese Island, near Wood Hole, Massachusetts in 1873, with which she remained associated until 1889. She Also became one of a handful of female chemists who attended the Priestly Centennial in Philadelphia, whose attendees became the founding members of the American Chemical Society. Shattuck was a corresponding member of the famous Torrey Botanical Club of New York City, as well as president of the Connecticut Valley Botanical Association. She engaged in extensive botanical studies in Hawaii, Canada, and Europe, and accentuated her classroom instruction with tales of her travels, in addition to active research in the classification of plants from around the world.

Shattuck developed enduring professional friendships with other prominent scientists of her time. By such association, in combination with her own travels and studies, she became a well-seasoned educator who offered both academic and pragmatic truths to her students. Known as an enthusiastic and inspiring instructor, she brought in several renowned scientists as lecturers in her classes to broaden her students' understanding of the subject. She also taught algebra and geometry, physiology and natural philosophy, physics and astronomy. Her intense interest and excitement in nature encouraged her students to appreciate the beauty of nature along with the intellectual pursuit of the science of nature. She was well regarded by colleagues and pupils alike. While she published no known papers of her own, Shattuck left behind her scientific legacy in countless personal records, correspondences, and lecture notes.

Mt. Holyoke Seminary became a college in 1888 and Shattuck retired as professor emeritus the following year. She was only able to enjoy retirement a few months. She died at Mt. Holyoke later that year, and was buried at Evergreen Cemetery in South Hadley, Massachusetts.

FURTHER READING

Books

Bailey, Martha J. *American Women in Science.* Denver: ABC-CLIO, p. 352.

Elliot, Clark A. *Biographical Dictionary of American Science.* Westport: Greenwood Press, 1979, p. 234.

Grinstein, Louis S. and Carol A. Biermann (with Rose K. Rose), eds. *Women in the Biological Sciences.* Westport: Greenwood Press, 1997, p. 495-500.

James, Edward T., Janet Wilson James, and Paul S. Boyer, eds. *Notable American Women 1607-1950.* Cambridge: The Belknap Press of Harvard University Press, 1971, pp. 273-274.

Rossiter, Margaret W. *Women Scientists in America.* Baltimore: The Johns Hopkins University Press, 1982, pp. 78, 83, 86.

Shearer, Benjamin and Barbara S., eds. *Notable Women in the Life Sciences.* Westport: Greenwood Press, 1996, pp. 354-359.

Other

Lydia W. Shattuck Papers. Holyoke College, Archives and Special Collections, South Hadley, Massachusetts, http://www.mtholyoke.edu/lits/library/arch/col/ms0585r.htm

Sketch by Lauri R. Harding

Jennie Arms Sheldon
1852-1938
American entomologist

Coauthor of the quintessential book on insects for its time, *Insecta,* Jennie Maria Arms Sheldon went on to lead a distinguished and varied career in zoology, geology and entomology, publishing numerous articles of both academic and popular interest.

Sheldon was born in Bellow Falls, Vermont in 1852, daughter of Albert and Eunice Stratton (Moody) Arms. After high school in Greenfield, Massachusetts, she attended the Massachusetts Institute of Technology (MIT) for two years, then became a special laboratory student at the Boston Society of Natural History for another year. Following this, Sheldon taught specialized classes in zoology, biology and geology for the Boston school system for many years, until she married George Sheldon, an historian and writer, in 1897. During summers in the latter 1880s, she also lectured in natural science at Saratoga.

She returned to the Boston Society of Natural History as a staff member in its museum, where she remained for several years, working as an assistant to Alpheus Hyatt for 25 years. Together, they coauthored *Insecta,* (1890) considered by many to be the authoritative "bible" on insects for that time. The 300-page publication was complete with entomological specimen illustrations and fold-out plates. The book was one in a series for the Boston Society of Natural History and was used as a guide for those teaching science classes.

Sheldon later became museum curator for the Pocumtuck Valley Memorial Association, eventually serving as president. She also became quite involved with the Naples Table for Promoting Laboratory Research by Women. Sheldon was also an active member in the American Association for the Advancement of Science (AAAS).

After her marriage, Sheldon continued research work in Deerfield, Massachusetts, studying the concretions of indigenous Champlain clays of the Connecticut Valley (known for their biological, geological and paleontological strata), and publishing several articles (and a book) on her findings. She coauthored one book with her husband, *Newly Exposed Geologic Features Within the '8000-Acre Grant'* (1903). Sheldon also expanded her writings to include popular and general interest books such as *Life of a New England Boy* (1896) and a more technical book on invertebrates, *Guide to the Inverebrata in the Synoptic Collection in the Museum of Boston Society of Natural History* (1905).

Sheldon was also interested in social issues, particularly the sufffragist movement, and was a member of the Equal Suffrage Association for Good Government in Boston. She was also a Free Thinker and a member of the Free Religious Association of America, the George Washington Memorial Association in Washington, and the MIT Association of Women Students. She was listed as a member of the Republican Party in the 1914 version of *Woman's Who's Who of America.*

SELECTED WRITINGS BY SHELDON:

Books

Concretions from the Champlain Clays of the Connecticut Valley. Boston, 1900.

(With Alpheus Hyatt) *Insecta.* Boston: D.C. Heath and Company, (1890).

FURTHER READING

Books

Bailey, Martha J. *American Women in Science.* Denver: ABC-CLIO, 353.

Leonard, J., ed. *Woman's Who's Who in America.* New York: American Commonwealth Co., 1914, 733. Reprint, Detroit: Gale Research, 1976.

Ogilvie, Marilyn Bailey. *Women in Science: Antiquity through the Nineteenth Century.* Cambridge: The MIT Press, 185.

Sketch by Lauri R. Harding

Althea Rosina Sherman
1853–1943
American ornithologist

Althea Sherman was known for her in-depth studies on many species of the birds of Iowa. She conducted most of her research from her country homestead, which she called her "Acre of Birds."

Born October 10, 1853, in National, Iowa, to Mark Bachelor Sherman, a cobbler and mortgage investor, and Sibyl Melissa Clark Sherman, Althea Rosina Sherman grew up with her four sisters and one brother on the family farm, to which she would later return to study birds.

Sherman attended Oberlin College, receiving her A.B. in 1875 and her A.M. in 1882. In between degrees, she taught art in public schools, and from 1882 to 1895, she taught art at both college and high school levels. An artist at heart, Sherman quit teaching to return to art school, first at Chicago's Art Institute and later at New York City's Art Student's League. But the failing health of her parents forced her to return to Iowa to care for them, and when both died soon after her return, her sister, Amelia, moved in.

After the death of her parents, Sherman continued her painting. Soon she began painting the birds she grew to love watching, and this began what would be her life-long scientific study of the many native species. During her almost forty years of bird study, Sherman researched flickers, chimney swifts, screech owls, bats, eastern phoebes, hummingbirds, robins, kestrels, blackbirds, house wrens, catbirds, alder flycatchers, brown thrashers, and sora rails, among dozens of others. Her years of devotion to her birds advanced scientific understanding of many species, replacing previous beliefs on many diverse topics such as feeding schedules, incubation times, and nesting biology.

To conduct her research, Sherman kept close control over her land, allowing it to become as wild as possible in order to attract her beloved birds. She had a fake chimney constructed on her property to attract chimney swifts. She routinely killed predator birds who ate the songbirds she loved. Sherman was emotional, judgmental, and notorious when it came to the birds she studied.

Her considerable productivity is even more remarkable considering the condition of her homestead. Without indoor plumbing and other modernizations, Sherman's home duties were considerable. Relations with her frugal and domineering sister provided further distraction. Even though she outlived Amelia by five years, her age, arthritis, and hearing problems kept her from writing the book she'd always dreamed of. Her chimney swift studies in particular yielded over 400 pages of notes, later organized and published posthumously.

Despite difficulties, Sherman's work remains some of the most in depth research ever conducted in ornithology, since it took place over several decades of careful observation and attention to minute changes and differences in nesting biology. A member of over a dozen professional organizations, including the American Ornithologists' Union, the American Association for the Advancement of Science, and the National Audubon Society, Sherman was also the first woman invited to New York City's Explorer's Club. Along with her detailed scientific studies, Sherman continued her paintings, which were exhibited at ornithological meetings. She died at her homestead in 1943.

SELECTED WRITINGS BY SHERMAN:

Books

Birds of an Iowa Dooryard. Boston: Christopher Publishing House, 1952.

FURTHER READING

Books

Abir–Am, Pnina, and Dorinda Outram, eds. *Uneasy Careers and Intimate Lives.* New Brunswick and London: Rutgers University Press, 1987.

Bailey, Martha J. *American Women in Science.* Denver: ABC–CLIO, 1994.

Bonta, Marcia Myers. *Women in the Field.* College Station: Texas A&M University Press, 1991.

Sketch by Helene Barker Kiser

Patsy O'Connell Sherman
1930–
American chemist

Patsy Sherman is known for inventing Scotchgard™, the well known chemical substance that repels stains and liquids on textiles. As one of the few women employed as a chemist in a major company in the 1950s, Sherman opened the door for other women scientists and inventors. Sherman's close attention to a seemingly insignificant accident led to her important discovery.

Patsy O'Connell was born in Minneapolis, Minnesota, on September 15, 1930. She graduated from Gustavus Adolphus College in Saint Peter, Minnesota in 1952 with a bachelor of arts degree. Upon graduation she joined the staff of the Minnesota Mining and Manufacturing Company, commonly known as 3M, in 1952 as a chemical researcher. Her specific project was the development of a rubber material that would not deteriorate when it came in contact with jet aircraft fuel. She worked with various fluorochemical compounds to create this material, but was not successful.

Accident Leads to a Major Discovery

A fortuitous accident in 1953 took Sherman's research in a very different direction. When a lab assistant spilled some drops of an experimental latex compound on her brand new tennis shoes, not water, soap, nor any other solvent could remove the substance. The lab assistant was annoyed that a new pair of shoes had been destroyed, but Sherman was intrigued. Not only did it not wash off, it would not absorb liquid.

It may not have been what she was looking for, but perhaps, she thought, this substance could be beneficial in ways no one had thought of before. Since it seemed to protect against liquid spills and nothing seemed to penetrate it, maybe it could be made into a protective covering of some sort. Over the next two years, Sherman worked with a colleague Sam Smith to perfect such a substance. In 1955, they were ready to launch their new product an undetectable coating that would protect fabric against spills and dirt. Patented under the name Scotchgard™, it appeared on the market the following year. The concept was revolutionary, and before long Scotchgard™ was being used to protect raincoats, carpets, and upholstered furniture. Over the years,

Scotchgard™ has evolved to the point that it now has many more uses than protecting fabric; one type is actually used to cover and protect photographic film.

Sherman continued at 3M for the rest of her professional career. She became a research specialist, then a research manager in 3M's chemical resources division, and ultimately head of technical development. Education, as well as research, was long a keen interest of hers, and she set up a continuing education program for the company's technical staff. She also found time to serve on the Minnesota State Board of Inventors and was on the board of the National Inventors Hall of Fame.

Although she retired in 1992, Sherman continues her active interest in education, particularly for young people. She frequently travels to visit middle and high school students, where she talks about her own experiences as an inventor and encourages young people to explore the possibilities that science can open up to them. "Anyone can become an inventor," she has said, "as long as they keep an open and inquiring mind and never overlook the possible significance of an accident or apparent failure." The U.S. Patent Museum in Arlington, Virginia, has a special exhibit on Sherman and her Scotchgard™ discovery. Married since 1953 to Hubert T. Sherman, she is also the mother of two daughters.

FURTHER READING

Books

American Men and Women of Science 1998–99. 20th ed. New Providence, N.J.: R. R.Bowker, 1998.

Other

"Invention of the Week."*The Lemelson–MIT Program's Invention Dimension.* http://web.mit.edu/invent/www/sherman.html (July 14, 1999).

"Legacy of Innovation: Patsy Sherman and the Discovery of Scotchgard Fabric Protector." *3M Innovation Chronicles, 1999.* http://www.mmm.com.ru/about 3M/pioneers/sherman.html (July 14, 1999).

Sketch by George A. Milite

Mary Lura Sherrill
1888–1968
American chemist

Mary Sherrill (Mt. Holyoke College Archive. Reproduced by permission.)

Mary Lura Sherrill was a prominent researcher and university teacher who was the first scientist to synthesize anti–malarial drugs. During World War II, she contributed to the Allied effort by developing a gas that prevented soldiers' accidental asphyxiation at the warfront. She also was a renowned teacher and university administrator.

Sherrill was born on July 14, 1888 to a prominent southern family in Salisbury, North Carolina. Her parents were Sarah and Miles Sherrill. Her father had been a soldier in the Confederate Army and later served a member of the state Senate and then state librarian. Sherrill had nine brothers and sisters.

After attending a public high school, she enrolled in Randolph–Macon Women's College, where she received a B.A. in chemistry in 1909. Her interest in chemistry began when she took a class in her freshman year from Professor Fernando Martin. Sherrill then went on to receive an M.A. in physics at Randolph–Macon in 1911. Just after getting her degree, she was offered a job at Randolph–Macon as an instructor, and worked there from 1911–1916.

Sherrill's hard work as a researcher was rewarded in 1916 when she entered the Ph.D. program in chemistry at the University of Chicago. She researched with Julius Stieglitz, who was instrumental in recruiting women chemistry students for the department. Sherrill's research from 1916–1917 concentrated on the synthesis of barbiturates and chemical acids. After 1917 she continued to research at the University of Chicago during the summertime. She also taught at Randolph–Macon and the North Carolina College for Women throughout the rest of those years until 1921.

When World War II began, Sherrill's mentor, Julius Stieglitz, helped direct the research of American chemists working for the war effort. Sherrill became a researcher for the Chemical Warfare Service with Steiglitz from 1920–1921. During that time, she worked on a sneezing gas that could protect soldiers from accidental asphyxiation after being exposed to other more toxic gases. Sherrill held the patent of the gas for its commercial production.

After the war, Sherrill returned to academe and joined the staff of Mount Holyoke College as an assistant professor. During this time she was able to complete her doctoral degree and was awarded her Ph.D. from the University of Chicago in 1923. She was later promoted to associate professor and then professor.

Sherrill's immediate supervisor during her time at Mount Holyoke was **Emma Perry Carr**, who had also been mentored by Steiglitz. In 1946, Sherrill succeeded Carr as department chair in chemistry. The two women eventually became friends as well as coworkers and carried out joint research. They traveled together during the summer and eventually bought a home together.

The two women were nationally known and so successful in pursuing scientific goals that one newspaper of the time remarked: "How they have been able to stand the pace has always been a topic interesting debate. . . Maybe the answer lies in a gorgeous sense of humor and an ability to get rest by jumping from one task to another like lads on the flying trapeze with 'the greatest of ease'."

During her time at Mt. Holyoke, Sherrill focused on the synthesis and purification of organic molecules in order to understand their structure. In 1928 Steiglitz took a break from Mount Holyoke to work in Jacques Errera laboratory in Brussels and that of Johanes van der Waals in Amsterdam. Until 1929 Sherrill endeavored to learn new purification techniques and study the structure of organic compounds more intensively in these laboratories.

Sherrill made another great contribution during World War II, when she developed anti–malarial drugs to replace quinine, which could no longer be obtained. In 1937, Sherrill was awarded the American Chemical Society's Garvan Medal a nationally respected prize awarded to distinguished women chemists that carries a sizeable stipend. Sherrill retired from Mount Holyoke in 1954. In 1961, she moved to High Point, North Carolina because of her failing health. She died on October 27, 1968.

FURTHER READING

Books

Grinstein, L.S., M. Rafailovich, R.K Rose. *Women in Chemistry and Physics: A Bibliographic Sourcebook.* Westport, CT: Greenwood Press, 1993.

Shearer, Benjamin F. and Barbara S. Shearer. *Notable Women in the Physical Sciences.* Westport, CT: Greenwood Press, 1997.

Sketch by Barbara Boughton

Lora Mangum Shields
1912 –?
American biologist

Lora Mangum Shields spent much of her professional life examining the effects of radioactive emissions on the Navajo population in New Mexico. Shields, a Navajo who was the first Native American to receive a doctorate in botany (from the University of Iowa), was also interested in the effects of nuclear testing on the desert vegetation in the New Mexico area. Her research—some of which was conducted using declassified government data that looked at the effects of nuclear testing on humans—was supported in part by grants from the National Science Foundation, the National Institute of Health, and the Atomic Energy Commission. She also received research grants from two major pharmaceutical companies (Squibb and Eli Lily), as well as from foundations such as the March of Dimes and Minority Biomedical Research Support. In recognition of her work, the University of New Mexico honored her with a Scientist of the Year award. Her professional associations included the American Association for the Advancement of Science (AAAS) and the Ecological Society of America.

Shields was born in Choctaw, Oklahoma, on March 13, 1912. She married in 1931 and had one child. Her undergraduate education was obtained from the University of New Mexico, where she received a bachelor of science degree in biology in 1940. She continued her studies at the University of New Mexico, receiving a master of science degree in 1942. In 1947, after completing her Ph.D in botany at the University of Iowa, she returned to New Mexico and became associate professor of biology at New Mexico Highlands University. She became a full professor and head of the department in 1954. In 1971, by virtue of her extensive research into health and environmental issues in New Mexico, she was appointed director of the Environmental Health Division. Shields remained at New Mexico Highlands University until 1978, when she took the position of researcher and visiting professor at Navajo Community College in Shiprock, New Mexico.

Begins Work with Navajo Miners

Beginning in the 1970s, Shields focused the majority of her research on two areas: the deleterious effects of uranium mining on the health of the Navajo population in the Shiprock area and the effects of nuclear testing on plants and other vegetation.

In an article entitled "Navajo Uranium Miners Fight for Compensation," Timothy Benally, Sr., of the Shiprock Navajo Nation, recalls that uranium mining in Shiprock began near the Carrizo Mountain area. During and after World War II, the mining accelerated with the development of atomic and nuclear bombs. In the 1970s, nuclear power plants began using uranium as an energy source. At that time, 100% of federally produced uranium was being mined from Native American lands, much of it in New Mexico. The nuclear fuel chain proceeds as follows: At the front end, uranium ore is mined. Then the ore is milled, converted, and enriched. At that point, it can be used for nuclear weapons or as fuel fabrication for nuclear power reactors. Uranium oxide is the end product of uranium mining, but every ton of this "yellow cake" leaves behind between 1,000 and 40,000 tons of uranium tailings, a potential source of environmental contamination.

Shields' research focused on the effects of decades of uranium exposure by Navajo miners in Shiprock. She examined the amount of lead–210 in Navajo uranium miners' teeth as another avenue of determining levels of radiation exposure. She also studied how plants and other vegetation reacted to radioactive compounds found in air, soil, and water. Shields was able to document the adverse effects radiation exposure had on both human and plant life. Her work has been of vital importance in bringing to light the health and environmental issues surrounding uranium mining and nuclear testing.

FURTHER READING

Books

American Men & Women of Science. Vol. 6. 17th ed. New York: R. R. Bowker, 1989, p. 707.

Bailey, Martha J. *American Women in Science: A Biographical Dictionary.* Santa Barbara: ABC–CLIO, 1994, p. 355.

O'Neill, Lois Decker, ed. *The Women's Book of World Records and Achievements.* Garden City: Anchor Press/Doubleday, 1979, p. 160.

Other

Benally, Timothy Sr. "Navajo Uranium Miners Fight for Compensation." *Native Americans and the Environment.* http://conbiodev.rice.edu/nae/groups/92.html

"Uranium/Nuclear Issues and Native Communities." *NUCLEAR ISSUES.* http://oraibi.alphacdc.com/ien/nuciss.html

Sketch by Jane Stewart Cook

Vandana Shiva
1952–
Indian physicist and environmentalist

Notwithstanding her remote beginnings in the Himalayan forest region of India, Vandana Shiva has become one of the youngest female scientists in the world to receive as much global recognition and prominence in such a short time, as she has. Shiva is as well–known as an environmentalist and feminist as she is a physicist. She has taken up many global causes against social injustices and environmental destruction, for which she has received numerous awards. In 1994, Shiva was honored as one of five women sharing the internationally–prestigious $2 million Right Livelihood Award, considered an alternative Nobel Prize for peaceful environmental and social activism. A prolific author, Shiva's published works promote environmental conservation and biodiversity in tropical forests, especially in her native India.

Born to a Himalayan forester in 1952, young Shiva Garewal went on to receive both bachelor's and master's degrees in physics from Punjab University. She originally intended a career in atomic research at the Atomic Research Institute of India. However, the reality of nuclear hazards (of which she was reminded by her sister), coupled with what she saw as condescending male dominance in the field, resulted in a change of heart and interest. Shiva moved to Canada, where she obtained her doctorate degree from Western Ontario University in 1979. The following year, she returned to India, where she joined the Indian Institute of Management in Bangalore. In 1982, Shiva became a consultant with the United Nations University.

Shiva's world travels and studies, combined with her family's forestry heritage, gave her a palpable appreciation for global natural resources, in particular India's, and the need to protect them from what she saw as Western male–dominated corporate interests. After learning about and witnessing the activities of native Chipko Indian women and their grass–roots movement to save trees (by literally clinging to them when timber industry foresters arrived), Shiva was deeply moved and inspired. She became increasingly more activist and less academically oriented in her research initiatives. Ultimately, she became substantially involved with the Chipko forestry protection initiative in the Himalayas, where, as a result of their combined efforts, commercial logging is no longer permitted above 1,000 meters.

Shiva is also known for her national campaigns to save indigenous seeds and resist the patenting (for intellectual property rights) of life forms. For example, Western corporations struggled for years to obtain a patent to market Indian Neem leaves as natural pesticides, even though such technology has been used locally for many generations. The foreign marketing and patenting of indigenous natural resources is alien to Shiva. She is especially angered by what she views as Western interference with the natural agricultural diversity and social stability of India, by causing farmers to become overly dependent on pesticides and enhanced fertilizers, hormones, and other crop manipulation efforts. Such efforts have often had dire consequences, socially as well as environmentally. She blames them for the conflicts over water irrigation which disrupted the Punjab state in India. Shiva has developed policies to make corporations accountable for the environmental damage they do, warning in a 1992 presentation in Chicago, *Greening of India: Environmental Activism,* that the world must avoid moving into an era of "environmental apartheid."

In 1990, Shiva was appointed Director of the Research Foundation for Science, Technology, and Natural Resource Policy in Dehradun, India. Two years later, she was honored by receiving the United Nations Environmental Program's Global 500 Award. In 1993, Shiva was the honored recipient of the Earth Day International Award. Shiva is also the Science and Environment Advisor of the Third World Network.

SELECTED WRITINGS BY SHIVA:

Books

(With others) *Biodiversity: Social and Ecological Perspectives.* London: Zed Books, 1991.

Monocultures of the Mind: Perspectives on Biodiversity and Biotechnology. London: Zed Books, 1993.

The Violence of the Green Revolution. London: Zed Books, 1991.

Periodicals

"Greening of India: Environmental Activism." *India Currents,* 1991, p. 31.

FURTHER READING

Books

Shearer, Benjamin F. and Barbara S. Shearer, eds. *Notable Women in the Physical Sciences.* Westport: Greenwood Press, 1997, pp. 363–367.

Sketch by Lauri R. Harding

Odette Louise Shotwell
1922–1998
American organic chemist

Well–lettered, titled, and honored in numerous professional circles, Odette Louise Shotwell became as well–known for her outstanding extra–curricular activities and community work, as she was for her important scientific achievements. A research chemist in the environmental sciences, Shotwell conducted extensive research on microbial insecticides and mycotoxins, and was associated with advanced studies of the chemistry of Japanese beetles, as part of a national effort to contain their spread.

Shotwell was born in 1922 to Robert L. and Ruby Mildred (Sammons) Shotwell of Denver, Colorado. Her father was a research entomologist who had graduated from the University of Colorado. Shotwell was the eldest of three children, and she remained close to her sister and brother during her entire life. All three children were stricken with polio in their childhood, but Shotwell endured the worst of it, essentially quadriplegic at the age of 12 and wheelchair–bound for the last 35–40 years of her life. Notwithstanding, she left home to attend Montana State College (now the University of Montana), graduating in 1944 with a bachelor's degree in chemistry. She then became a teaching fellow in the organic chemistry department at the University of Illinois, where she obtained a master's degree in organic chemistry, and ultimately her doctorate degree in 1948. Shotwell's sister, Mrs. Geraldine Mecklenburg, related in a telephone interview with Contributor that when Shotwell graduated from the University of Illinois, all she wanted was "a new car and a mink coat." She did, in fact, reward herself with a new car, but the mink coat was set aside for other priorities. The car was eventually upgraded to a new van, complete with a wheelchair lift.

Shotwell then accepted a position as research chemist with the U.S. Department of Agriculture's Northern Regional Research Laboratory in Peoria, Illinois. In 1961, the city of Bozeman, Montana (where the University of Montana is located) honored her as the Outstanding Woman Alumna of the Year. She was also the recipient of the Outstanding Handicapped Federal Employee Award for 1969, and later promoted into supervision. She remained with the agency (now called the Northern Center for Agricultural Utilization Research) until her retirement in 1989. In 1993, Shotwell was again honored at Montana State College/University of Montana's 100th Anniversary, as one of its 100 outstanding graduates.

In addition to her work in microbial insecticides and mycotoxins, Shotwell also was recognized for her research in developing a cancer–producing toxin (aflatoxin) from molds. In 1982, Shotwell was the honored recipient of the American Oil Chemical Society's Harvey W. Wiley Award. During this time, she also served as consultant for the FDA and the Cancer Health & Welfare Department, as well as active member on the Committee for Protection Against Trichothecene Mycotoxins for the National Academy of Sciences. After her retirement, she continued to work for the USDA as a consultant and collaborator. Shotwell maintained active memberships in several professional organizations, including the American Chemical Society, the American Association for the Advancement of Science, the American Association of Cereal Chemists, and the Association of Official Analytical Chemists.

Shotwell remained proactive in community and civic affairs during her entire professional career. She served on the board of directors and chaired the education committee for the local chapter of the NAACP in Peoria, becoming recipient of the NAACP's Distinguished Service Award in 1972. She also received awards from the J.C. Penney Company and the YMCA. Shotwell served as consultant on an inner–city education program, and was president of the Peoria chapter of the League of Women Voters. She was a board member of a local arts and science center, and also served as chairperson for the Truth Corps of the Mayor's Commission on Human Relations. Shotwell's interest and involvement in these and other community activities continued until her health could no longer accommodate them. Her family moved her from Colorado to Montana in her later years, where she resided in an assisted living center. One of her assistants, Mary Lassner, RN, recalled in a telephonic interview with Contributor, that Shotwell loved to tell stories about her experiences and show people her "molecular ring," given to her as a remembrance for her scientific work. The ring contained clustered molecules set into individual posts. Shotwell died of natural causes in April 1998. She never married, and is survived by her sister.

FURTHER READING

Books

American Men and Women of Science. New York: R.R. Bowker, 17th ed., 1989–1990, 727; 20th ed., 1998–1999, 953.

Bailey, Martha J. *American Women in Science.* Denver: ABC–CLIO, 356.

O'Neill, Lois Decker, ed. *The Women's Book of World Records and Achievements.* Garden City: Anchor Press, 1979, 32.

Who's Who of American Women. New Providence: Marquis, 21st. ed, 1999–2000, 953.

Other

Harding, Lauri R., telephone interview with Mrs. Geraldine Mecklenburg, surviving sister, conducted on July 21, 1999.

Harding, Lauri R., telephone interview with caregiver, Ms. Mary Lassner, RN, conducted on July 21, 1999.

Sketch by Lauri R. Harding

Justine Dittrichin Siegemundin
1650–1705
German midwife and medical writer

Justine Siegemundin was the first scientifically educated midwife in Germany. She is remembered for writing an excellent textbook on obstetrics for midwives and physicians.

Justine Dittrichin Siegemundin was born in 1650. Her father, a pastor in the town of Rohnstock in Silesia, Germany, died when she was four and she was educated by her mother. At the age of 17, Siegemundin married a government official who worked in a small town in Silesia. Four years later, after experiencing medical complications that were misdiagnosed as labor by four midwives, Siegemundin began studying anatomy, physiology, and midwifery on her own and with an experienced physician. Thus, she became the first scientifically knowledgeable midwife in Germany. Although initially she had no intention of practicing midwifery, she soon became a consultant to other midwives. She practiced for 12 years among the poor without pay, and then was appointed midwife for the city of Liegnitz. Siegemundin became midwife to the royal court of Prussia and to the family of the Kurfürst of Brandenburg, traveling to wherever her services were needed, and visiting with various physicians. Finally she was called to Berlin as midwife to Sophia Charlotte, the wife of Frederick I of Prussia.

Siegemundin made clinical notes on all her cases, which she discussed with other midwives and physicians. At the urging of various physicians and members of the royalty, including Queen Mary of England, Siegemundin published her observations in 1689 in Berlin, at her own expense. It was a two-part book. The first part was written as a conversation between two midwives, Justine and Christina. The second part was a quiz, in which Christina was tested on what she had learned.

Although Siegemundin stressed the importance of allowing labor to proceed naturally, if at all possible, her major contributions to obstetrics were her methods for handling difficult labors. She described in detail how to turn the fetus, both internally and externally, in order to prevent a breech, or feet first, birth. The work included 50 copperplate illustrations, detailing fetal positions. The placenta and various membranes also were diagrammed. Siegemundin's treatise concluded with a chapter on medicinal remedies, as well as a section attacking superstitious ideas and practices. The book included an index, a rarity at that time. It was a very popular work and was used in German universities. It went through six editions and was translated into Dutch.

Siegemundin's book included a certificate of approval from the dean and professors of the University of Frankfurt-on-the-Oder. A second preface was written by the assessor of the College of Medicine in Berlin. Nevertheless, Siegemundin's work was attacked as vain speculation by Dr. Andreas Petermann and other male doctors, and later editions included papers dealing with these attacks. Siegemundin, who remained childless, died in 1705.

SELECTED WRITINGS BY SIEGEMUNDIN:

Books

The Midwife of the Royal Family of Prussia, and of the Family of the Kurfürst of Brandenburg. Berlin, 1756.

FURTHER READING

Books

Hurd-Mead, Kate Campbell. *A History of Women in Medicine, from the Earliest Times to the Beginning of the Nineteenth Century.* Haddam, CT: Haddam Press, 1938. Reprint. Boston: Milford House, 1973.

Periodicals

Robb, Hunter. "The Works of Justine Siegemundin, the Midwife." *Johns Hopkins Hospital Bulletin* 5 (1894): 4–13.

Sketch by Margaret Alic

Ellen Kovner Silbergeld
1945–
American toxicologist

Ellen Silbergeld is an American environmental toxicologist and public health policy advocate. She has conducted research and advised policy makers on the toxicological effects of such substances as lead, mercury, dioxin, dibenzofurans, manganese, and Agent Orange.

Ellen Kovner Silbergeld was born on July 29, 1945, in Washington D.C., the first girl and second child of Joseph Kovner, a lawyer, and Mary Gion Kovner, a journalist. Joseph Kovner fell victim to the witch hunts of the House Un-American Activities Committee (HUAC) during the early 1950s and was forced to leave his government job, an event that left a lasting impression on Silbergeld. When she was seven years old, her family moved to Concord, New Hampshire, where her father took up private legal practice. In nearby Boston, one of her father's closest childhood friends, civil liberties lawyer Reuben Goodman, became a mentor to the young Silbergeld. His commitment to civil rights, his rigorous intellect, and his zest for life were, according to Silbergeld, a constant source of stimulation. She was also influenced intellectually by a her mother's friends, who eventually played a role in her decision to attend a women's college. When Silbergeld was in the eighth grade, her family returned to Washington D.C. Although as a young student she enjoyed mathematics and puzzle solving, she avoided the study of science as much as possible and believed she had no talent in the subject.

In 1967, Silbergeld began her undergraduate work in history at Vassar College, in Poughkeepsie, New York. Graduating in 1967, with an A.B. degree in modern history, she accepted a Fulbright Fellowship to England and began a doctoral degree program at the London School of Economics. A year later, disenchanted with the field of economics, she returned to Washington D.C. and took a position as a secretary and program officer for the Committee on Geography at the National Academy of Sciences. It was in this post that Silbergeld first began to develop an interest in science. She remained at the National Academy of Sciences until 1970. By then Silbergeld had begun graduate studies in environmental engineering at Johns Hopkins University in Baltimore. In 1972 she received her Ph.D. and assumed a post-doctoral fellowship in environmental medicine and neurosciences, also at Johns Hopkins University. Her graduate and post-graduate research on the topic of lead neurotoxicity prompted Silbergeld to get involved in public policy regarding lead exposure.

In 1975, Silbergeld became a staff fellow in the Unit on Behavioral Neuropharmacology at the National Institutes of Health (NIH) in Bethesda, Maryland. There, she continued her research on lead and began investigating the toxicology of food dyes. She also conducted research on neurological disorders such as Huntington's disease and Parkinson's disease. In 1979, she became Chief of the Section on Neurotoxicology at NIH, a post she held until 1981. As Section Chief, Silbergeld directed research on the mechanisms of neurotoxic agents such as lead and manganese. She also directed research into the effects of estradiol on the central nervous system.

From 1982 until 1991, she served as the Chief Toxic Scientist and Director of the Toxic Chemicals Program for the Environmental Defense Fund in Washington, D.C. Simultaneously, she maintained research programs at several institutions. As a guest scientist at the National Institute of Child Health Development, from 1982 to 1984, she researched the effects of polycyclic aromatic hydrocarbons (PAHs) on ovarian function.

From 1985 till 1987, as Visiting Professor at the University of Maryland School of Medicine, she studied the effects of tetrachlorodibenzo-p-dioxin (TCDD) on glucocorticoid receptors, and from 1987 to 1989 she investigated lead toxicity and the genetic effects of TCDD as a Visiting Professor in the Program for Toxicology at the University of Maryland. In 1987, as an Associate Faculty member in the Johns Hopkins School of Hygiene and Public Health, she began supervising research into lead toxicity and risk assessment. Her affiliation with Johns Hopkins continued in 1991 as an Adjunct Professor. Ongoing programs of research on the neural and reproductive effects of lead and on the molecular mechanism of TCDD were begun at the University of Maryland School of Medicine in 1989.

Other appointments at the University of Maryland include an affiliate professorship in the School of Law, begun in 1990, a professorship in the Department of Pathology, begun in 1991, and a professorship in the Department of Epidemiology and Preventive Medicine, begun in 1992. Since 1993, Silbergeld has been a Senior Consultant Toxicologist for the Environmental Defense Fund, and since 1996, the Director of the Program in Human Health and the Environment at the University of Maryland.

Silbergeld has published over 200 research and policy articles and is a member of the editorial board for more than half a dozen journals related to environmental health and toxicology. She has served as an advisor and consultant for environmental and health causes throughout her career. She has organized a variety of international symposia and workshops on chemically induced diseases and lead toxicology. Highly commended for both her scientific research and her environmental advocacy, she was designated one of the Four Outstanding Women of Maryland by the Maryland Education Association in 1987. That same year, she received the Warner–Lambert Award for Distinguished Women in Science. In 1990, she received the Governor's Citation for Excellence, in 1991, the Abel Wolman Award, and in 1992, the Barsky Award. The MacArthur Foundation made her a Fellow in 1993, and that year she also received the Earth Month Award of the Maryland Department of the Environment. In 1994, she was an honoree in the Maryland Women's History Project, and, the following year, Chatham College named her one of the Women Who Make a Difference. That year, Silbergerld was awarded a patent for a lead detection procedure.

In 1969, she married Mark Silbergeld, with whom she has two children. Sophia, their daughter, was born in 1981, and their son Nicholas Reuben, named after Reuben Goodman, was born in 1985.

SELECTED WRITINGS BY SILBERGELD:

Books

"Risk assessment and risk management: an uneasy divorce." In *Acceptable Evidence: Science and Values in Risk Management*. Deborah G. Mayo and Rachelle D. Hollander, eds. New York: Oxford University Press, 1991.

FURTHER READING

Books

Shearer, Benjamin F., and Barbara S. Shearer. *Notable Women in the Life Sciences*. Westport, CT: Greenwood Press, 1996.

Sketch by Leslie Reinherz

Dorothy Martin Simon
1919–
American chemist

Dorothy Martin Simon has been responsible for several significant advances in space engineering, particularly in the area of combustion. By relating the fundamental properties of flame to each other through the principles of heat and mass transfer and chemical reaction, she helped establish the present-day theory of flame propagation and quenching. She also contributed to the development of ablative coatings, which protect missiles from heat damage upon reentering the Earth's atmosphere. In recognition of these accomplishments, as well as her success in executive management and public speaking, the Society of Women Engineers presented Simon with their Achievement Award in 1966.

Simon was born Dorothy Martin on September 18, 1919, in Harwood, Missouri. Her parents were Robert William Martin, head of the chemistry department at Southwest Missouri State College, and Laudell Flynn Martin. Simon attended high school at Greenwood Laboratory School in Springfield, where she won the highest sports honor while also earning the highest grade–point average in the school's history. After graduation, she attended the college at which her father taught, where she received a bachelor's degree with honors in 1940. Once again, she was class valedictorian. From there, she went on to the University of Illinois, where her thesis research on active deposits from radon and thoron gas was among the earliest work on radioactive fallout. She obtained a Ph.D. in chemistry in 1945.

Upon completing college, Simon first spent a year as a chemist at the Du Pont Company in Buffalo, New York. During this time, she studied the chemical reactions involved in producing the synthetic fiber now known as Orlon. In 1946, she began working for the Atomic Energy Commission (AEC) at Oak Ridge Laboratory in Tennessee and the Argonne Laboratory in Illinois. Among her accomplishments while with the AEC was the isolation of a new isotope of calcium.

Advances the Understanding of Combustion

In 1949, Simon began six years with the National Advisory Committee for Aeronautics, the agency that evolved into NASA. These proved to be her most fruitful years as a researcher. During this period, her work elucidating the fundamental nature of flames was recognized with a Rockefeller Public Service Award. Simon used the stipend of $10,000 to visit university and technical laboratories in England, France, and the Netherlands. She studied at Cambridge University with Ronald G. W. Norrish, who later won the Nobel Prize in chemistry.

In 1955 she spent a year as group leader at the Magnolia Petroleum Company in Dallas. Then in 1956, Simon began a lengthy association with Avco Corporation, where her early work addressed the design problems of reentry vehicles for intercontinental ballistic missiles. Her research dealt with ablation cooling—a method of protecting the missile body from extreme heat while reentering the Earth's atmosphere by absorbing the heat in a shielding material that is changing phase. This was the topic of a **Marie Curie** Lecture that Simon delivered at Pennsylvania State University in 1962.

Soon Simon's interests turned toward management within the giant conglomerate. She was appointed the first female corporate officer at Avco in 1968. In her capacity as vice president of research, she was responsible for guiding the company's various high–tech divisions. At that time, she was one of the few women to have scaled such heights on the corporate ladder, a fact that was recognized by Worcester Polytechnic Institute when conferring an honorary doctorate upon Simon in 1971. The institute cited her position as "perhaps the most important woman executive in American industry today." Simon later received a second honorary doctorate, this one from Lehigh University. She is a fellow of the American Institute of Chemists, as well as a member of the American Chemical Society and the American Institute of Aeronautics and Astronautics.

Simon is known as an outstanding speaker, who has frequently lectured and written on the challenges of space, research management, and women in science. She served on President Jimmy Carter's Committee for the National Medal of Science, the National Research Council's National Materials Advisory Board, the Department of Defense's Defense Policy Advisory Committee, and the Department of Commerce's Statutory Committee for the National Bureau of Standards. In her free time, she enjoys traveling, cooking, and gardening. Simon was married on December 6, 1946, to Sidney L. Simon—a leading scientist in his own right who became vice president at Sperry Rand. He died in 1975. Simon currently makes her home in Pittsboro, North Carolina.

SELECTED WRITINGS BY SIMON:

Periodicals

(With F.E. Belles and R.C. Weast) "Pressure Limits of Flame Propagation of Propane–Air Mixtures." *Industrial and Engineering Chemistry* 46 (1954): 1010.

"Diffusion Processes as Rate–Controlling Steps in Laminar Flame Propagation." *Selected Combustion Problems: Fundamentals and Aeronautical Applications* Butterworths Scientific Publications, (1954): 59–91.

FURTHER READING

Books

O'Neill, Lois Decker, ed. *The Women's Book of World Records and Achievements.* Doubleday, 1979, pp. 189, 519.

Periodicals

Kelly, Mary. "Earthling Eyes Cast on Space." *Christian Science Monitor* (August 2, 1965): 12.

Other

Burton, David, interview with Linda Wasmer Smith conducted February 9, 1994.

Southwest Missouri State University, material including award nominations, biographical sketches, news clippings, and press release.

University of Illinois Archives, material including award nomination and citation, biographical sketch, news clipping, and résumé.

Sketch by Linda Wasmer Smith

Joanne Malkus Simpson
1923–
American meteorologist

Joanne Malkus Simpson was the first woman to receive a Ph.D. in meteorology. The author of more than 115 papers and contributor to several books, Simpson's research focused on cumulus clouds, weather modification, atmospheric convection, and tropical and satellite meteorology. One of the best in her field, Simpson had to overcome numerous gender barriers to achieve success.

Simpson was born in Boston, Massachusetts, on March 23, 1923 to Russell and Virginia (Vaughan) Gerould. She was the eldest of two children in what she called in an autobiography in *Women and Success*, "an intellectual but unhappy home." She attended a good private school in Boston which encouraged her ever-expanding intellectual interests. Her father's long-time interest in aviation and her mother's interest in women's rights were strong influences. While in school, Simpson worked as an assistant to the Massachusetts State Aeronautics Director and learned to fly. To get her license, she had to study meteorology, a subject which fascinated her.

In 1940, Simpson entered the University of Chicago and studied meteorology. World War II was beginning and Simpson's contribution to the American war effort was related to her burgeoning interest. She completed the University of Chicago's nine-month course that trained women as military weather forecasters and went on to earn her B.S. from the University of Chicago in 1943. After graduation, she taught meteorology at New York University from 1943–44, then at the University of Chicago from 1944–45.

Determination in the Face of Discouragement

Simpson decided to pursue graduate studies in meteorology. Some professors at the University of Chicago were incredulous, even antagonistic. She was told by her advisors that no woman would ever get a doctorate in meteorology and that she should not even try. Simpson earned her M.S.

in 1945; however, no one would serve as her advisor for a Ph.D., and she could not get funding for her studies, despite her strong grades. Eventually, a professor agreed to be her advisor in her work on cumulus clouds. While a Ph.D. candidate, Simpson taught physics and meteorology at the Illinois Institute of Technology from 1946–49 to support herself. She received her Ph.D. in meteorology in 1949, the first woman in the world ever to do so.

Simpson continued to teach at the Illinois Institute of Technology as an assistant professor until 1951, when she was hired by the Woods Hole Oceanographic Institute on Cape Cod, Massachusetts as a meteorologist. She had already spent several summers there while a Ph.D. candidate. Simpson returned to teaching full time in 1961, when she became a full professor of meteorology at University of California at Los Angeles (UCLA). Her then (and second) husband was also hired as a professor, and they became the first couple to have professorships in the same department at that university, helping break down the barrier of nepotism. Because it was deemed unacceptable for married couples to work together, gender bias had, until then, forced the woman out of her job. "I believe I have suffered more grief and loss of potential from this source [nepotism] than from any other sex related restriction," she said in her autobiography.

Before leaving UCLA in 1962, she received the first of many awards, the Meisinger Award from the American Meteorological Association. After her first marriage ended, she wed Robert H. Simpson in 1965. He was also a meteorologist, the founder of the U.S. Weather Bureau's National Hurricane Research Project, and later, director of the National Hurricane Center. Simpson had three children from her first marriage: David, Steven, and Karen Malkus.

In 1965, Simpson was hired by the United States Weather Bureau as a head of the experimental meteorology laboratory in Coral Gables, Florida. Her work included using computers, satellites, and airplanes to study the structure and behavior of potent storm systems. She also conducted experiments with cloud seeding in her own small laboratory, a study she greatly enjoyed.

While in Florida, Simpson also taught at the University of Miami. She returned to teaching full time in 1974 when she was hired by the University of Virginia, Charlotte. In 1975, she was elected to the Council of the American Meteorological Society. A year later, she became W.W. Cocoran professor of environmental sciences at the University of Virginia, the first woman to hold this professorship.

In 1981, Simpson became employed at the Goddard Space Flight Center for the National Aeronautics and Space Administration (NASA). She was the head of the Severe Storms Board until 1988, when she was named chief scientist for meteorology. In this time period, Simpson also worked as a project scientist for a Tropical Rainfall Measuring Mission, a new satellite in Earth Sciences. In 1992, she was named science director on the project, and held this position until 1998. This work focused on short term climate change, global warming, and climate variability.

Over the course of her long career, Simpson received numerous accolades. In 1991, she was honored by the State University of New York at Albany with an honorary D.Sc., and she received the Cleveland Abbe Award from the American Meteorological Association. Yet early in her career, Simpson was not hired for some positions simply because she was a woman, though often she was better qualified than her competitors. Though Simpson more than succeeded in her career, she believed she paid a high price, suffering from health problems and trying to juggle the roles of wife, mother, and scientist. Despite these difficulties, Simpson still enjoyed her meteorological investigations late in life and told Edward F. Taylor of *Weatherwise* in 1984 that "I'm never going to retire, I like the work too much."

SELECTED WRITINGS BY SIMPSON:

Books

"Meteorologist." *Women & Success: The Anatomy of Achievement.* New York: William Morrow and Company, Inc., 1974, pp. 62–67.

Periodicals

(With others) "Tropical Deep Convection and Ozone Formation." *Bulletin of the American Meteorological Society* (June 1997): 1043–55.

FURTHER READING

Books

Bowman, John, ed. *The Cambridge Dictionary of American Biography.* New York: Cambridge University Press, 1995, p. 671.

O'Neill, Lois Decker, ed. *The Women's Book of World Records and Achievements.* Garden City: Anchor Press/Doubleday, 1979, p. 172.

Rossiter, Margaret W. *Women Scientists in America: Before Affirmative Action, 1940–72.* Baltimore: Johns Hopkins University Press, 1995, pp. 80, 140, 243.

Who's Who of American Women, 1999–2000. New Providence: Marquis Who's Who, 1998, p. 961.

Periodicals

Taylor, Edward F. "Joanne Simpson: Pathfinder for a Generation." *Weatherwise* (August 1984): 182–83, 206–07.

Sketch by Annette Petrusso

Charlotte Emma (Moore) Sitterly
1898–1990
American astrophysicist

Charlotte Sitterly was a specialist in astronomy and astrophysics. She was recognized as an expert on the Sun and atomic spectra. During her lifetime, she was the recipient of dozens of awards and honors for her achievements.

Charlotte Emma Moore was born on September 24, 1898, in Ercildoun, Pennsylvania. All six of the Moore children were taught early to be lifelong learners and to value education and knowledge. Their parents, George Winfield and Elizabeth Palmer (Walton) Moore, were both educators by profession.

Sitterly graduated from Swarthmore College in 1920 with an A.B. degree in mathematics. In addition to being an excellent student, she was involved in many extracurricular activities. She tutored other students and assisted faculty members in order to earn money for school. From 1920 to 1925, Sitterly worked in the Princeton Observatory as a computer, measuring and calculating various figures for astronomical study. This tedious measuring and calculating was one of the few jobs in astronomy open to women at that time.

Begins Spectra Study

In 1925, Sitterly went to the Mount Wilson Observatory in California to study the solar spectrum. Several years later, she was offered the Lick Fellowship, which allowed her to complete her doctorate in astronomy in1930 from the University of California, Berkeley. While there, she continued her analysis of solar spectra.

After completing her Ph.D., Sitterly returned to the Princeton Observatory in 1931, this time as a research assistant and, later, as an associate. She would remain at Princeton until 1945. Sitterly's research involved astrophysical problems and atomic spectra, which later opened the door for the study of stellar and solar spectra. In 1933, Sitterly published the first edition of *A Multiple Table of Astrophysical Interest*, which provided new tables of data on atomic spectra. Her work is still recognized as thorough and complete in its explication of spectroscopic, solar spectra, and atomic data.

In 1937, Sitterly was awarded the **Annie Jump Cannon** Prize, an award given only every three years to women astronomers of considerable distinction. Sitterly earned the honor in part because of her proof of the existence of the natural and unstable element technetium, an element that had been found only in artificial conditions. That same year she married Bancroft W. Sitterly, Chair of American University's Physics department.

Sitterly rapidly became known as an authority on atomic spectra, and spectroscopic data was often sent to her for analysis. Scientists in chemistry, astronomy, and physics came to rely on her research. In 1945 she left Princeton to join the National Bureau of Standards as a physicist in the Atomic Physics Division. Here she supervised a research program focusing on the analysis of spectra and preparation of tables. Over a period of nine years, these volumes were published as Atomic Energy Levels. Although she retired in 1968, she continued to work as a consultant to the Office of Standard Reference Data and the United States Naval Research Laboratory.

In 1958, Sitterly was able to travel to Moscow as part of the International Astronomical Union on the Joint Commission on Spectroscopy. In fact, she believed travel to be an essential duty of a scientist, in part because it facilitated understanding and good will toward other researchers. When not working, Sitterly enjoyed gardening and music, and in the early 1980s she published her mother's genealogy, which she had researched.

Wins Numerous Awards

Among her membership in professional organizations, Sitterly was a fellow of the Optical Society of America and the American Physical Society, and was a member of the Academy of Sciences, the American Association for the Advancement of Science, the Philosophical Society, the American Astronomical Society, Sigma Xi, Phi Beta Kappa, and the Astronomical Society of the Pacific. She was also the first woman to be elected foreign associate by London's Royal Astronomical Society. She was awarded a silver medal from the Department of Commerce in 1951 and a Gold Medal in 1960. In 1961, the United States Civil Service Commission honored her with the Federal Women's Award. Sitterly was given the Annie Jump Cannon Centennial Medal in 1963, and the William F. Meggers Award in 1972. Sitterly was also granted several honorary degrees: a D.Sc. from both Swarthmore College and the University of Michigan, and an honorary doctorate from Germany's Universitat zu Kiel. Sitterly died on March 3, 1990, in Washington, D.C.

SELECTED WRITINGS BY SITTERLY:

Books

(With Henry Norris Russell) *The Masses of the Stars.* Chicago: University of Chicago Press, 1940.

Atomic Energy Levels as Derived from the Analyses of Optical Spectra. Washington, D.C.: National Bureau of Standards, 1945–1958.

FURTHER READING

Books

Bailey, Martha J. *American Women in Science.* Denver: ABC–CLIO, 1994.

Moritz, Charles. *Current Biography Yearbook.* New York: H. H. Wilson, 1962.

Shearer, Benjamin F. and Barbara S. Shearer, eds. *Notable Women in the Physical Sciences.* Westport, CT: Greenwood Press, 1996.

Sketch by Helene Barker Kiser

Maud Slye
1879–1954
American pathologist

Maud Slye devoted her life to cancer research by investigating the inheritability of the disease in mice. Performing extensive breeding studies on the hereditary transmission of cancer, she kept meticulous pedigree records and autopsied thousands of mice during her lifetime. Her work was controversial, however; advocating the archiving of complete medical records for individuals, she believed that human beings could eradicate cancer by choosing mates with the appropriate genotype. Sometimes referred to as "America's **Marie Curie**," Slye received wide publicity for her work and was honored by many organizations.

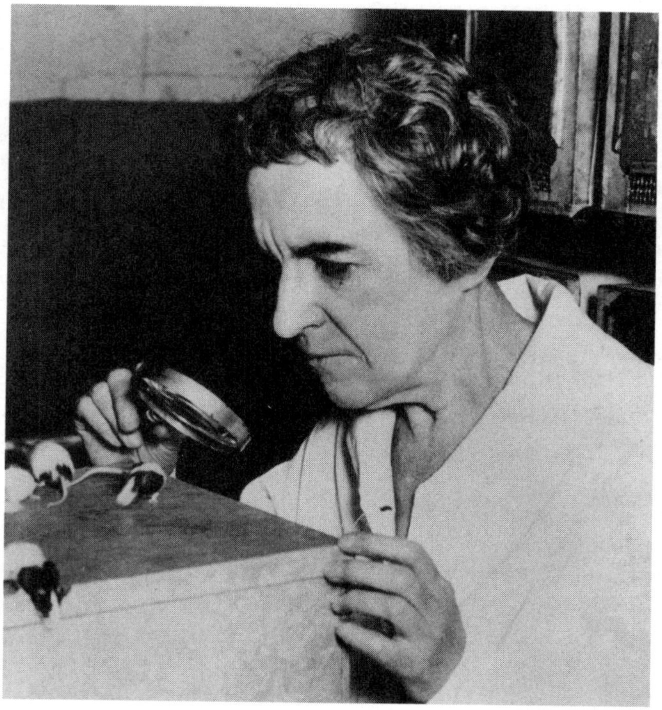

Maud Slye (Corbis-Bettmann-UPI. Reproduced by permission.)

Slye was born in Minneapolis, Minnesota, on February 8, 1879, the daughter of James Alvin and Florence Alden Wheeler Slye. Her family, though poor, traced their ancestry back to John Alden of the Plymouth colony. At age seventeen, Slye entered the University of Chicago with savings of 40 dollars and the desire to become a scientist. Attending the university for three years, she supported herself by working as a secretary for university president William Harper. After a nervous breakdown, Slye convalesced in Woods Hole, Massachusetts, then completed her B.A. degree at Brown University in 1899. Hired as a teacher at the Rhode Island State Normal School, she stayed at the institution until 1905.

In 1908 Slye received a grant to do postgraduate work at the University of Chicago. Interested in the hereditary basis of disease, she began her work with six Japanese "waltzing" mice which were afflicted with a hereditary neurological disorder. Slye became intrigued by the inheritability of cancer when she heard of several heads of cattle at the Chicago stock yards—all with cancer of the eye—that had come from the same ranch. Inspired by this and other data, Slye went forward with her studies, breeding cancerous mice with one another as well as healthy mice with other healthy mice.

In 1911, Slye became a member of the university's newly created Sprague Memorial Institute, and in 1913 she presented her first paper on cancer before the American Society for Cancer Research. Becoming director of the Cancer Laboratory at the University of Chicago in 1919, she was promoted to assistant professor in 1922, then to associate professor in 1926. In 1936, Slye left her mice in the care of an assistant and took her first vacation in 26 years (earlier, when she had visited her ailing mother in California, she rented a boxcar and took her mice with her).

Although Slye discredited a prevailing theory that stated cancer was contagious, it became clear as her work proceeded that the appearance of cancer in an individual was not as simple as the presence of one gene. In later years, Slye posited that two conditions were necessary to produce cancer: inherited susceptibility, and prolonged irritation of the cancer-susceptible tissues. Nonetheless, further studies by other scientists have confirmed that while heredity can be a factor in certain types of cancer, it is much more complex than Slye had perceived.

Slye's work was recognized with several awards and honors, including the gold medal of the American Medical Association in 1914, and the Ricketts Prize in 1915. She also received the gold medal of the American Radiological Society in 1922. A member of the Association for Cancer Research, the American Medical Association, and the American Association for the Advancement of Science, Slye was the author of 42 brochures on cancer and two volumes of poetry, *Songs and Solaces* and *I in the Wind.* At the time of her retirement in 1945 Slye was made professor emeritus of pathology, and she spent her retirement years analyzing data accumulated during her years of research.

She died September 17, 1954, and was buried in Chicago's Oak Woods Cemetery.

FURTHER READING

Books

Current Biography, H. W. Wilson, 1940, pp. 743–745.

Kass–Simon, G., and Patricia Farnes, eds. *Women of Science: Righting the Record.* Bloomingont: Indiana University Press, 1990, pp. 278–279.

O'Neill, Lois Decker, ed. *The Women's Book of World Records and Achievements.* Doubleday, 1979, p. 217.

Periodicals

Reader's Digest (March 1936): 77–80.

Newsweek (April 10, 1937): 26–28.

New York Times (September 18, 1954) 15.

Sketch by Jill Carpenter

Erminnie Adele (Platt) Smith
1836–1886
American geologist and ethnologist

Erminnie Adele Platt Smith was a gifted geologist and ethnologist whose mineralogical studies included monographs on amber and the classification of large collections of specimens for European museums. Such geological contributions, however, were overshadowed by her work in ethnology, which she took up in the last years of her life. She studied the people the Six Nations of the Iroquois federation of upper New York and Canada, and she was the first woman to conduct field research in such anthropological endeavors, tracing Native American myths and compiling a comprehensive dictionary of the Iroquois language. After her death, an award in geology was endowed in her name at Vassar College.

Smith was descended from original settlers in the region of Marcellus, New York, where she was born and grew up. At age two her mother died, and Smith was consequently raised by her father, who imparted to his daughter his love of science, especially geology and botany. She attended the Female Seminary in Troy, New York, graduating in 1853. Two years later she married the wealthy Chicago lumber dealer and merchant Simeon H. Smith. The couple set up home initially in Chicago.

Studies Mineralogy in Germany

With the birth of four sons, Smith devoted the early years of her marriage to raising a family. She still found time, however, to help classify and label mineral specimens for European museums. From Chicago, the family moved to Jersey City, New Jersey, where the husband became the city finance commissioner. When it was decided that the sons should have a European education, Smith accompanied the boys to Germany, where she also renewed her education, studying crystallography and literature at both Strasbourg and Heidelberg, and mineralogy at Freiberg's School of Mines.

Returning to Jersey City, Smith turned her spacious home into one of the largest private mineralogy collections in the United States. She began to give private, at–home lectures on both geological and cultural matters, talks so popular that she founded the Aesthetic Society in 1876, in which a large group of women met monthly to give papers on science and the arts. Upwards of 500 people attended such at–home meetings. Smith was also a member of the New York woman's club Sorosis, whose science programs she directed for several years.

Through a cousin, Smith was introduced to the American Association for the Advancement of Science (AAAS), and in 1879 she read a paper on amber to the membership. It was through the AAAS that Smith thereafter became interested in the fledgling sciences of anthropology and ethnography, concerns which were to dominate the remainder of her life.

Studies the Iroquois

Smith had grown up near the Onondaga reservation, and felt a special affinity to the Native Americans of that region, the Six Nations or tribes of the Iroquois federation. Partially financed by the Smithsonian Institution, she began fieldwork each summer, beginning in 1880, at the Tuscarora reservation near Lewistown, New York, and at other reservations in New York and Canada. She was the first woman to conduct such fieldwork, recording legends and myths of the people, later gathered in *Myths of the Iroquois,* and also compiling an extensive Iroquois–English dictionary of 15,000 words, which is stored at the Smithsonian. Smith introduced a field technique used by many other anthropologists, that of the "native informant." One of Smith's trained informants, John N. B. Hewitt, went on to become a well–known ethnologist.

Noted for her work both in geology and ethnology, Smith became secretary of the anthropology section of AAAS and was also elected the first female fellow of the New York Academy of Sciences, as well as a fellow of the London Scientific Society. Until the end of her relatively short life she continued her work, also, with the Aesthetic Society. She was only 50 when she died, of a cerebral embolism. In 1888 she was remembered by the endowment of an annual award at Vassar College for the best student paper in geology or mineralogy.

SELECTED WRITINGS BY SMITH:

Books

"Myths of the Iroquois." *Second Annual Report of Bureau of American Ethnology.* Washington, D.C.: Bureau of American Ethnology, 1883, pp. 47– 116.

Periodicals

"Concerning Amber." *American Naturalist* 14 (1880): 179–90.

FURTHER READING

Books

Bailey, Martha J. *American Women in Science: A Biographical Dictionary.* Denver: ABC–CLIO, 1994, pp. 363–64.

Elliott, Clark A. *Biographical Dictionary of American Science: The Seventeenth through the Nineteenth Centuries.* Westport: Greenwood Press, 1979, p. 238.

In Memoriam, Mrs. Erminnie A. Smith. Boston, Massachusetts: Lee and Shepard, 1890.

Lurie, Nancy Oestreich. *Notable American Women, 1607–1950: A Biographical Dictionary.* Cambridge, MA: Belknap Press, 1971, pp. 312–13.

Periodicals

Elder, Eleanor S. "Erminnie Adele Platt Smith." *Journal of Geological Education* 30 (1982): 289–90.

Obituary *New York Times* (10 June 1886): 35:5.

Sketch by J. Sydney Jones

Emilie Snethlage
1868–1929
German ornithologist

Emilie Snethlage was born in Kratz, Westphalia, Germany, in 1868 but spent most of her professional career in Brazil. There, the zoologist, ethnologist, and ornithologist worked under rustic conditions to collect birds, traveling by foot, canoe, and horseback. She wrote extensively about her findings, although most of her published material is in Spanish. In 1907, Snethlage became the first female director of the Zoological Museum and Gardens at Porto Belho in Brazil. In 1915, during World War I, she was awarded an honorary membership to the British Ornithologists' Union. In addition, Snethlage was made an honorary member of the Berlin Geographical Society and the Academy of Sciences of Brazil.

FURTHER READING

Chicago, Judy. *The Dinner Party.* New York: Penguin Books, 1996.

Ogilvie, Marilyn Bailey. *Women in Science: Antiquity through the Nineteenth Century.* Cambridge: MIT Press, 1993.

Zilboorg, Caroline, ed. *Women's Firsts.* Detroit: Gale Research, 1997.

Sketch by Kristin Palm

Mary Fairfax Somerville
1780–1872
Scottish-born English mathematics writer

Mary Fairfax Somerville was called the "Queen of nineteenth-century Science" by the London *Morning Post* on her death. She is best known for her work explaining the mathematical and scientific works of others. Somerville was one of the first two women admitted to the Royal Astronomical Society, and a portrait bust of her is on display in the great hall of the Royal Society in London. Somerville College of Oxford University is named after her.

Rebels Against the Norm in Pursuing Education

Somerville was born on December 26, 1780, in Jedburgh, Scotland. Her father was an Englishman, Vice-Admiral Sir William George Fairfax, and her mother was Margaret Charters Fairfax, a Scotswoman. Because girls in Somerville's era were often discouraged from pursuing a formal education, Somerville's earliest schooling consisted of reading the Bible. She disliked playing with dolls, but she loved to roam the Scottish seacoast and countryside. Her father worried about her carefree behavior, and sent her away to boarding school when she was ten. Somerville's experience at the school was a horror. For one assignment, she had to memorize an entire page of a dictionary and recite back the words in their correct order, spelling each properly, citing its meaning, and naming its part of speech. She lasted twelve months. When Somerville returned home, she had learned a little arithmetic, grammar, and French, and also developed an interest in reading.

Most important, however, was Somerville's insatiable curiosity. One day she had noticed some Xs and Ys printed in a fashion magazine and realized the symbols were from a problem in algebra. No one in her immediate circle knew

Mary Somerville (Corbis-Bettmann. Reproduced by permission.)

what algebra was, but Somerville found out herself. She asked a male friend to purchase an algebra text and Euclid of Alexandria's *Elements of Geometry* and began to study them, which upset her parents. Somerville's father forbade her to study mathematics, fearing that she would have to be straitjacketed, because a woman he knew had gone insane trying to understand longitude. Her mother confiscated all of Somerville's candles so she could not read at night. Somerville, however, had a partial victory. She had already read and memorized six of Euclid's books.

In 1804, Somerville married her cousin, Captain Samuel Greig, a Russian naval officer assigned as consul in England, who had little use for science and learning opportunities for women. They had two sons, Woronzow, who lived into middle age, and William George, who died in his youth in 1814. Greig died in 1807, leaving Somerville financially secure.

Somerville returned to Scotland and began to study astronomy and mathematics. She made friends with some scholars at the University of Edinburgh, who recommended her books on mathematics and offered encouragement. Somerville began submitting solutions to problems in a mathematics journal, and in 1811 won a silver medal for solving a mathematical problem.

In 1812, Somerville married another cousin, Dr. William Somerville, who encouraged her in her studies and helped her get published. They had three daughters, Margaret, Martha, and Mary, and one son, Thomas, who died in infancy. Dr. Somerville, a surgeon, was a ranking member of the English medical establishment, and Somerville met many important scientific people in London and Europe. Her friendships with practicing scientists and mathematicians would prove valuable.

Begins Successful Writing Career

Somerville began her publishing career in 1826 with a scientific paper on the magnetic power of sunlight in the *Philosophical Transactions of the Royal Society*. Other scientific articles followed. Her greatest fame, however, came from her explanations of the technical works of other mathematicians and scientists. Her first book, published in 1831, was *The Mechanism of the Heavens*, which explained Pierre Simon Laplace's book on celestial mechanics, and added many of Somerville's own ideas. Celestial mechanics is best understood by people who have a working knowledge of calculus, but Somerville made certain that intelligent laypeople with no training in advanced mathematics could understand her book. She had approached the project of writing the book with some anxiety because she did not have a college education. Somerville was so fearful about the book's success that she insisted that her work be kept secret, and if her editors did not like the manuscript, she wanted it destroyed. The book was a smashing success. It was the first accurate synthesis of celestial mechanics that an educated layperson could understand.

Somerville's next book, *On the Connection of the Physical Sciences*, was published in 1834. It too was a great success and was published in ten editions from 1834 to 1877. The astronomer John Couch Adams, who co–discovered the planet Neptune, said that he got the idea to search for Neptune from an observation he read about the odd orbital movements of Uranus in Somerville's text.

Somerville's husband began to experience health problems in the late 1830s, and the family moved to Italy. She published her most successful book, *Physical Geography*, in 1848. It was the first major work in England to focus on the physical surface of the Earth, including its landforms, soils, climates, and vegetation.

Somerville's husband died in 1860, and her son passed away in 1865. At her husband's death, Somerville was in her mid–eighties, but remained productive. In 1869, she published her last major book, *On Molecular and Microscopic Science*, a two–volume summary of recent advances in physics and chemistry. In that same year, Somerville received a gold medal from the Royal Geographical Society, and was elected to the American Philosophical Society.

Somerville died peacefully in Naples, Italy, on November 29, 1872 at the age of 92. Her father's fears that mathematics would drive her insane proved unfounded. Somerville continued to study algebra for four to five hours a day, and she worked on a mathematical article the day before she died.

SELECTED WRITINGS BY SOMERVILLE:

The Mechanism of the Heavens, 1831.
On the Connection of the Physical Sciences, 1834.
Physical Geography, 1848.
On Molecular and Microscopic Science, 1869.

FURTHER READING

Books

Osen, Lynn M. "Mary Fairfax Somerville." *Women in Mathematics*. Cambridge: MIT Press, 1974, pp. 95–116.

Patterson, Elizabeth C. *Mary Somerville and the Cultivation of Science, 1815–1840*. Boston: Martinus Nijhoff Publishers, 1983.

"Mary Fairfax Somerville." In *Women of Mathematics: A Biobiographic Sourcebook*. Edited by Louise S. Grinstein and Paul J. Campbell. Westport, CT: Greenwood Press, 1987, pp. 208–216.

Perl, Teri. *Math Equals: Biographies of Women Mathematicians*. New York: Addison–Wesley, 1978, pp. 83–99.

Periodicals

Patterson, Elizabeth C. "The Case of Mary Somerville: An Aspect of Nineteenth–Century Science." *Proceedings of the American Philosophical Society* (June 1974): 269–275.

Wood, Shane. "Mary Fairfax Somerville." *Biographies of Women Mathematicians*. June 1997. http://www.scottlan.edu/lriddle/women/chronol.htm (July 21, 1997).

Sketch by Patrick Moore

Queen Sonduk (or Sondok)
fl. Seventh Century
Korean Queen and astronomer

Queen Sonduk ruled the Silla kingdom for approximately 15 years, from A.D. 632(?)–647. The Silla era lasted from approximately A. D. 250 to the end of the seventh century. It was during her reign that the astronomical observatory, Ch'omsongdae—also known as the Tower of the Moon and Stars (or Sun)—was built. This observatory is thought to be the oldest observatory remaining in East Asia and is located in Kyongju, South Korea.

Queen Sonduk succeeded her father, the king, when he chose her as ruler because he had no sons and because she displayed "an unusually quick mind." Many women during this time were able to exert influence on public affairs, as matrilineal heritage co-existed with patrilineal lines of descent. Sonduk ruled during a period of violent political unrest and had to contend with warring factions from the neighboring kingdom of Paekche (Paikche). Even so, she managed to encourage significant scientific and cultural advancements during her reign, and to keep her kingdom intact by strengthening connections with China. She was also revered for her shamanistic qualities, apparently having the ability to predict events.

Observatory Sets Astronomical Standard

Korea looked to China as its main source of scientific knowledge. It then modified and improved on that knowledge to suit its own needs. As a result, new inventions and discoveries were made that caused Korea to excel in astronomy, meteorology, engineering, printing, and ceramics.

Frescoes found in old tombs early in the Three Kingdoms period show movement of the planets and stars—symbols representing heavenly bodies indicate a growing sophistication regarding astronomical concepts. Astronomy, meteorology, and calendar–making assumed importance because they were thought to be tied to the security and well–being of the ruling families and the country as a whole. Improved astronomical devices led to improved observational procedures and better record keeping—vital for continuing the base of scientific knowledge. Numerical records from this time have been studied by modern astronomers, who have concluded that many of these experiments can be accurately reproduced. Records also show that astronomers were working independently from China during the Three Kingdoms period, which includes Queen Sonduk's reign.

The astronomical observatory constructed during Sonduk's reign typifies this kind of development. Standing 30 feet (9.17 meters) high, it was the center of astronomical observation and served as the standard of the meridian. Along with several other antiquities from the Silla era that show strong mathematical and engineering skills, the existence of the Ch'omsongdae Observatory indicates a high degree of scientific advancement over the preceding two kingdoms.

Today, Queen Sonduk's tomb may be visited as one of the major historical sites of the Silla era.

FURTHER READING

Books

A Handbook of Korea. Seoul: Korean Overseas Information Service, 1993, pp. 430–432; 552.

Other

Ahn, Sanghyeon. *A Brief History of the Korean Astronomy*. Shillim-Dong, Seoul: Department of Astronomy, Seoul National University. http://astro.snu.ac.kr/~sha/history.html

History of Scientific Development in Korea. http://www.inworld.net/Korea/text/f230.html

The Queens of the Silla Era. http://www.easc.indiana.edu/

Women in World History Curriculum: Female Heroes of the Regions of the World. 1998. http://home.earthlink.net/~womenwhist/heroine7.html

Sketch by Jane Stewart Cook

Effie Almira (Southworth) Spalding
1860–1947
American botanist

Effie Southworth Spalding was the first woman to be employed by the United States Department of Agriculture (USDA). There, she was an assistant pathologist in the Bureau of Plant Industry. Spalding's area of interests included mycology (a branch of biology dealing with fungi) and the study of cacti.

Effie Almira Southworth was born on October 29, 1860, in North Collins, New York, the first of five children born to Nathaniel Chester and Chloe A. (Rathburn) Southworth. She spent her first year of undergraduate education at Allegheny College before transferring to the University of Michigan, from where she received her Bachelor of Science degree in 1885.

While at the University of Michigan, Spalding's botanical studies included structural botany, elements of biology, algae, fungi, ferns, and cross-fertilization, in addition to her specialized studies of equisetem, perennial plants also known as horsetail. After completing her degree, Spalding went on to Bryn Mawr College as a teaching fellow in biology from 1895 to 1897. At Bryn Mawr, Spalding worked in the botanical laboratory, researching the mechanical system and anatomical structure of the palm, alocasia, and banana plants, among others. She also concentrated on the development of the Asteroma fungus and on the collection and classification of Phanero germs. Her drawings were published in various sources.

First Woman to be Employed by the USDA

In 1888, Spalding was asked to fill a position at the United States Department of Agriculture in the Bureau of Plant Industry. She was asked because of her theoretical and technical abilities in the field. She joined the USDA staff as a plant pathologist, and remained there until 1893. The first woman to be employed by the USDA, Spalding helped open the door for many other women scientists, not merely in plant industry, but in other bureaus of the agriculture department.

After leaving the USDA, Spalding accepted a position as a teaching fellow and assistant in biology at Barnard College, where she remained until 1895. After her time at Barnard, Spalding went on to the University of Hawaii as a laboratory assistant in botany. On January 1, 1896, she married Volney Morgan Spalding. The couple did not have children. Effie Spalding did not work in the field again until 1920, two years after the death of her husband, when she became assistant professor of botany at the University of Southern California in Los Angeles. Spalding remained at the university until 1926. During that time, she completed her Master of Science degree (1923), and held the position of Curator of Herbaria during her final year of 1925 to 1926. She died in 1947.

SELECTED WRITINGS BY SPALDING:

Books

(With D. T. MacDougal). *The Water-Balance of Succulent Plants.* Washington, D.C.: Carnegie Institution of Washington, 1910.

FURTHER READING

Books

Bailey, Martha J. *American Women in Science.* Denver: ABC-CLIO, 1994.

Barnhart, John Hendley. *Biographical Notes Upon Botanists.* Boston: G.K. Hall, 1965.

Harshbarger, John W. *The Botanists of Philadelphia and Their Work.* Philadelphia, 1899.

Other

Special Collections Archives. Bryn Mawr College. http://www.familysearch.org/Search/af/ancestralfilefram

Sketch by Helene Barker Kiser

Dolores Richard Spikes
1936–
American mathematician and university administrator

Dolores Spikes has devoted her career to improving educational opportunities for those who, in her words, "would otherwise be shut out" of higher education. In 1988 she became the first woman in United States history to head a university system (the Southern University System in Louisiana).

Spikes was born Dolores Margaret Richard in Baton Rouge, Louisiana, on August 24, 1936. Her parents, Lawrence and Margaret (Patterson) Richard, had not finished high school, but they instilled a respect for education in their children. Spikes has said that her parents were the most important influence in her life.

She got a scholarship to Southern University in Baton Rouge, where she majored in mathematics and excelled in her studies. She graduated *summa cum laude* in 1957 with a bachelor of science degree. She went on to the University of Illinois at Urbana, where she got her master's degree in 1958. That same year she married Hermon Spikes, whom she had met while a student at Southern.

After her marriage Spikes returned to Louisiana where she taught high school biology and chemistry in the Calcasien Parish system. In 1961, she accepted a position at Southern University as an assistant professor of mathematics. She later became associate professor and then full professor. At around the time she returned to Southern, she also decided to continue her education. She began work on her Ph.D. in pure mathematics at Louisiana State University. It was a busy time, between work, study, and family (she had given birth to a daughter, Rhonda), but Spikes was awarded her doctorate in 1971.

Gradually, Spikes moved into the administrative arena. In 1982 she became assistant to the chancellor and later, executive vice chancellor and chancellor for academic affairs. By 1988 she had become president of the Southern University and A&M system, one of the largest primarily black university systems in the United States.

As president of the Southern system, Spikes worked to improve opportunities for students both at Southern and at other historically black institutions of higher learning. Her work was recognized by President Bill Clinton who, in 1994, named her to the board of advisors of his Historically Black Colleges and Universities committee. She has served on numerous other organizations that deal with the issues faced by land grant colleges, which were created in 1890 to provide quality, affordable education to black students.

In 1997, Spikes left Southern to head the University of Maryland–Eastern Shore (UMES), a land grant college in Princess Anne, Maryland. At UMES, Spikes has continued to work to improve opportunities for students. She has maintained her interest in science, but she has also made it a priority to raise the emphasis at UMES on communication skills and in the arts. Reading is one of her hobbies; she also collects coins and figurines.

FURTHER READING

Books

Hine, Darlene Clark, ed. *Black Women in America. An Historical Encyclopedia*. New York: Carlson Publishing,1993.

Phelps, Shirelle, ed. *Contemporary Black Biography*. Detroit, MI: Gale Research, 1998.

Periodicals

"Thurgood Marshall Black Education Award." *Ebony* (January 1990): 134.

Other

"About President Spikes." University of Maryland–Eastern Shore Administration. 1999. http://www.umes.umd.edu/deps/administration/presidentsoffice/aboutpresident.html (July 8, 1999).

Sketch by George A. Milite

Thressa Campbell Stadtman
1920–
American biochemist

Thressa Campbell Stadtman worked as a biochemist for more than five decades at the National Institute of Health (NIH). Stadtmann's most important contributions to science are her research on vitamin B12–dependent enzymes and selenium biochemistry. She has also studied anaerobic enzyme systems derived from bacteria that cannot grow in the presence of oxygen, amino acid intermediary metabolism, and one-carbon metabolism.

Stadtman was born in Sterling, New York, on February 12, 1920. She was the daughter of John and Bessie (Waldron) Campbell. The Campbells operated a large dairy and fruit farm in Sterling, and Stadtman was educated in local schools. As a youth, Stadtman wanted to become a doctor. Such plans were put aside when Stadtman's father died suddenly of spinal meningitis when she was a teenager. It was the height of the Depression and money was scarce.

Earns Degrees in Bacteriology

However, Stadtman's high school principal, a graduate of Cornell University in Ithaca, New York, helped her get a college education. He arranged for a scholarship so that Stadtman could attend Cornell. She enrolled in the College of Agriculture where she studied bacteriology. Ironically, much of her coursework overlapped with that of medical students. Stadtman graduated from Cornell with a B.S. in 1940. After graduation, she spent a few months as a bacteriologist in a paper mill. Returning to school, Stadtman studied the vitamin requirements of lactic acid bacteria. She earned her M.S. in 1942 in bacteriology and nutrition, then

Thressa Stadtman (Photograph by Greg Pio. (c) 1997 MBARI. Reproduced by permission.)

worked as a research assistant at Cornell's Agricultural Experiment Station during the years 1942–43.

The year 1943 marked two milestones in Stadtman's life. She married Earl Reece Stadtman on October 19, 1943. Like his wife, Earl Stadtman was a biochemist engaged in research. Both were affiliated with the University of California Berkeley, where Stadtman began her Ph.D. work in 1943. When she entered the University of California, Berkeley, she continued to do research in food microbiology, through 1946, as part of the World War II effort. She studied food spoilage problems for the military. Her work also included an investigation of the anaerobic bacteria that produced methane in the terminal steps of sewage digestion. Stadtman earned her Ph.D. in microbiology in 1949. For her thesis, she isolated methane–producing bacteria from the black mud tidal flats of the San Francisco Bay. She also isolated a new methane– producing species that grew on the sodium salt of formic acid. Her thesis described her studies of this organism's fermentation.

After Stadtman earned her Ph.D., she was hired by Harvard Medical School, while her husband worked at Massachusetts General Hospital. She spent a year at Harvard as a research assistant, from 1949–1950, studying microbial oxidation of cholesterol. In 1950, the couple tried to find positions in academia. While her husband was offered jobs at universities, Stadtman had a more difficult time securing a position.

Becomes First Female Staff Member at NIH

In 1950, Stadtman and her husband were hired by the NIH's National Heart Institute (later known as National Heart, Lung, and Blood Institute) as biochemists. She was the first female professional staff member hired there. At the NIH, Stadtman continued to study methane-producing bacteria, focusing on the biochemical roles of vitamin B12. With her fellow scientists, she identified three new B12–dependent enzymes in the late 1950s and 1960s.

By the early 1970s, Stadtman's research at NIH moved to selenium biochemistry. She isolated proteins and nucleic acids from microorganisms that contained selenium as an essential component for catalytic activities. Many of her most important contributions to science have been in this area of research. She was recognized regularly for her work. She won the Hillebrand Award in 1979 from the Chemical Society of Washington. In 1981, Stadtman was elected to the National Academy of Sciences, an honor of the highest magnitude. She was also a member of American Society of Microbiology, American Society of Biochemistry (of which she was secretary from 1978–81), and British Biochemistry Society. Additionally, Stadtman served as the editor-in-chief of *Biofactors* for a time.

Stadtman won the Rose Award from the Chemical Society of Washington in 1987. A year later, in 1988, she was given the Klaus Schwarz Medal by the International Union of Biorganic Chemists. In 1998, at the age of 78, Stadtman was named a corresponding member of the Nordrhein–Westfallische Wisssenschaften, a Northern Germany Academy of Sciences.

FURTHER READING

Books

American Men & Women of Science. 19th ed. New Providence: R.R. Bowker, 1994, p. 1181.

Bailey, Martha J.*American Women in Science: A Biographical Dictionary.* Denver: ABC–CLIO, 1994, p. 368.

Bowman, John S., ed. *The Cambridge Dictionary of American Biography.* New York: Cambridge University Press, 1995, p. 689.

Press, Jaques Cattell, ed.*American Men and Women Scientists.* 12th ed. New York: R.R. Bowker Company, 1973, p. 6047.

Other

Petrusso, Annette, correspondence with Thressa Stadtman, May 21, 1999.

Sketch by Annette Petrusso

Louise Stanley
1883–1954
American chemist

Louise Stanley, the highest ranking woman in the United States Department of Agriculture in her time, was a home economics pioneer. She was responsible for many first studies on nutrition, and wrote about housing, clothing, and housekeeping issues.

Louise Stanley was born June 8, 1883, the first of two children born to Gustavus Stanley and Eliza Winston Stanley. The Stanley family lived in Nashville, Tennessee, and when Louise was three years old, her parents both died. She and her brother were able to live with an aunt, supported by the money her parents had left to them. After attending the Peabody Demonstration School and Ward's Seminary, Stanley entered Peabody College, graduating in 1903 with her A.B. degree.

After Peabody, Stanley went on to the University of Chicago, where she earned a B. Ed. in 1906, and then to Columbia University where she earned her A.M. in 1907. From Columbia, she entered Yale University, graduating in 1911 with a Ph.D. in biochemistry. Stanley was receiving her home economics education at a good time in history, since such studies were offering women professional and scientific employment in growing numbers. She began her formal employment on the faculty of the University of Missouri and soon became professor as well as chair of the home economics department.

While Stanley was at the University of Missouri, the Smith–Hughes Act was passed, offering funding to public schools for home economics education. As part of the American Home Economics Association's legislative committee, Stanley was instrumental in garnering attention to such studies on a federal level. Because of her visibility, passion, and outspokenness, Stanley was soon influential beyond the university environment.

Toward a Better Standard of Living

In 1923, Stanley was appointed to the United States Department of Agriculture as head of the Bureau of Economics, the first woman bureau head in the USDA. She was also the first woman appointed to the American Standards Association, on behalf of the department. During this time, she adopted a daughter, Nancy. While in the Bureau, she headed the first study of consumer purchasing and the first study of rural housing, gaining knowledge of consumption patterns and cost of living. In addition to her studies of housekeeping methods and standardization of manufactured clothing sizes, Stanley emphasized public education on nutrition. To serve families of different needs and incomes, Stanley developed four different diet plans. This angered farmers and others in the agricultural industry, who argued that the government was using public money to ruin the sugar and wheat business. But Stanley persevered in the name of her commitment to good nutrition, and her diet plans were later used both at home and abroad during and after World War II.

During the war, Stanley became special assistant to the administrator of agricultural research, and she took her home economics research abroad, concentrating on Latin America. In addition to doing public education and conducting studies, Stanley became involved with UNESCO and the United Nations Conference for Food and Agriculture. She dedicated much of her work to helping the needy and underpriveleged, and refused to join the Daughters of the American Revolution because of their discrimination against others.

In 1950, Stanley retired from the USDA, and worked for three years in the Office of Foreign Agricultural Relations as a home economics consultant. Just a year later, on July 15, 1954, Stanley died of cancer in Washington, D.C. A lifelong worker for better standards of living and consumer rights, Stanley was awarded an honorary degree from the University of Missouri in 1940, and in 1960 the home economics building was named after her. In 1953, the American Home Economics Association created a scholarship in her honor. A member of the American Chemical Society and the American Home Economics Association, Stanley was instrumental in the rise of home economics as a valid science in American consciousness.

SELCTED WRITINGS BY STANLEY:

Books

Foods, Their Selection and Preparation. New York: Ginn and Company, 1935.

FURTHER READING

Books

Bailey, Martha J. American *Women in Science.* Denver: ABC–CLIO, 1994.

O'Neill, Lois Decker, ed. *The Women's Book of World Records and Achievements.* New York: Anchor Press, 1979.

Sicherman, Barbara, and Green, Carol Hurd, eds. *Notable American Women: The Modern Period.* Cambridge: Belknap Press, 1980.

Siegel, Patricia Joan, and Finley, Kay Thomas. *Women in the Scientific Search.* Lanham, MD: Scarecrow Press, Inc., 1985.

Sketch by Helene Barker Kiser

Genevieve Stearns
1892–1997
American biochemist

Genevieve Stearns was recognized for her work on metabolism and nutrition. The main focus of her research was on infants, children, and pregnant or nursing mothers.

Stearns was born on Christmas Eve, 1892, in Zumbrota, Minnesota, to Clayton H. Stearns and Clara Beierwalter Stearns. Genevieve attended Carleton College and received her bachelor of science degree in 1912. She taught high school for six years before returning to school at the University of Illinois. She worked as a chemistry assistant while she completed her master's degree, and in 1920, Stearns accepted a position as a research associate in nutrition at the University of Iowa's child welfare research station.

After five years at the research station, Stearns again returned to school, this time as a biochemistry assistant at the University of Michigan. She continued her research on metabolism, and her dissertation was titled "Studies on the Intermediary Metabolism of Cystine." She was awarded her doctorate in 1928, and continued her work, begun the previous year, as a research associate in pediatrics at the University of Iowa. Stearns would remain at the University of Iowa for the remainder of her career, advancing to research assistant professor in 1930, research associate professor in 1931, and research professor in 1943. During these years, her work centered on the metabolism of the vitamins A and D as well as minerals during human growth, growth chemistry, and bone and cartilage metabolic disturbance. Stearns also supervised all pediatric blood and chemical work in the department.

Stearns became known internationally as a field scholar. She worked for a very low salary and was not promoted quickly, but the Great Depression was in part responsible, as jobs were scarce and low-paying for everyone. Stearns was recognized with several awards, however, among them the American Home Economics Association's Borden Award in 1942 for her research in metabolism and another Borden in 1946 from the American Institute of Nutrition for her long-term nutritional studies.

In 1950, Stearns was further recognized by the United Nations' World Health Organization, which selected her to join three other American scientists for metabolism seminars in Europe. Stearns' team was the first research group ever sent to a seminar for research rather than teaching purposes.

In 1954, Stearns transferred to University Hospitals in Iowa City as a research professor in orthopedics. She continued her nutrition and metabolism publications, and contributed to a book on the subject. When Stearns retired in 1958 as emeritus research professor, she did not stop working. In 1960, she was a Fulbright professor at the Women's College of Ein Shams University in Cairo, Egypt.

Stearns was a member of several professional societies, including the American Chemical Society, the American Institute of Nutrition, the American Society of Biological Chemists, Sigma Xi, Omicron Nu, and Iota Sigma Pi, for which she served as president. Carleton College presented her with its Alumni Achievement Award, in recognition of her work. She died on April 20, 1997, at Oaknoll Retirement Residence, and her body was donated to the anatomy department at the University, in order to give further aid to science, her life's work.

FURTHER READING

Books

Bailey, Martha J. *American Women in Science.* Denver: ABC-CLIO, 1994.

Other

University of Iowa Libraries Special Collections, archives.

Sketch by Helene Barker Kiser

Joan Steitz Argetsinger
1941–
American biochemist and geneticist

Joan Steitz is an American biochemist and geneticist, best known for her discovery of small nuclear ribonucleoproteins or snRNPs, which play an important role in converting the information encoded in mammalian DNA into instructions for building protein molecules. Her work has led to a deeper understanding of the way in which genetic transcription and translation is controlled.

Joan Argetsinger Steitz was born on January 26, 1941, in Minneapolis, Minnesota. Her father, Glenn Davis Argetsinger, a high school guidance counselor, and her mother, Elaine Magnusson Argetsinger, a speech pathologist, encouraged her to pursue her intellectual interests, and she developed an interest in science at an early age. Steitz attended Antioch College, in Yellow Springs, Ohio, and received a bachelor of science degree in chemistry in 1963. In addition to her college chemistry studies, she had taken classes in molecular genetics, a field that was undergoing rapid development as a result of the 1953 discovery of the double helical structure of the deoxyribonucleic (DNA) molecule. James Watson Francis Crick, and Maurice Wilkins had received the 1962 Nobel Prize in Medicine for this important work. Two of these three laureates were soon to become her mentors.

Under the direction of James Watson at Harvard University, Steitz received a Ph.D. in 1967. Her graduate research centered on the *in vitro* assembly of R17, a ribonucleic acid bacteriophage (a type of virus that attacks bacteria). This research led to a better understanding of how the protein and nucleic-acid components of viruses interact. From 1967 till 1970, Steitz pursued post-doctoral studies under the direction of Francis Crick, at the Medical Research Council Laboratory of Molecular Biology, in Cambridge, England. There, her research focused on the way in which bacterial ribosomes, intracellular organelles that play a role in building proteins within the cell, locate themselves on messenger ribonucleic acid (RNA), the molecule that carries the protein building instructions from a cell's nucleus to its cytoplasm.

In 1970, Steitz returned to the United States, accepting an assistant professorship in the Department of Molecular Biophysics and Biochemistry at Yale University, in New Haven, Connecticut. Her work in molecular genetics yielded, within the decade, a discovery which she considers her most significant, that of small nuclear ribonucleoproteins or snRNPs (pronounced "snurps"). The intricate molecular process by which the double stranded DNA molecule dictates protein synthesis begins with a step known as transcription. During this step, DNA information is transferred to a single stranded heterogeneous nuclear RNA molecule, called hnRNA . Typically, a DNA molecule contains a vast amount of "nonsense," encoded instructions that are not useful during the process of protein synthesis. The snRNPs that Steitz discovered play a significant role in insuring that this nonsense is removed from the hnRNA. They coordinate a process called RNA splicing, in which the hnRNA molecule is snipped into pieces and its useful parts rejoined. The end result of this splicing is that a messenger RNA molecule is formed.

Steitz has identified many different types of snRNPs and helped to determine how they operate within the nucleus. Currently, she is examining snRNPs that are formed when certain herpes viruses infect their host cells. Her research into the structure and function of snRNPs has already seen direct clinical application, especially in the area of diagnosis and treatment of rheumatic disorders.

Steitz was promoted to full professorship at Yale in 1978, and has been a Henry Ford II Professor there since 1988. During the 1976–77 academic year, while on sabbatical as a Josiah Macy Scholar, she conducted research at the Max Planck Institute for Biophysical Chemistry in Göttingen, Germany, and at the Medical Council Center Laboratory of Molecular Biology in Cambridge, England. As a Fairchild Distinguished Fellow she spent the 1984–85 academic year on sabbatical at the California Institute of Technology in Pasadena.

The list of scientific honors that have been bestowed upon Steitz is extensive, beginning in 1975 with the Passano Foundation Young Scientist Award, and followed in 1976 by the Eli Lilly Award in Biological Chemistry. In 1982, Steitz received the U.S. Steel Foundation Award in Molecular Biology, and the following year she shared the Lee Hawley, Sr. Award for Arthritis Research with J. A. Hardin and M. R. Lerner. For her pioneering work on snRNPs, President Ronald Reagan presented her with the National Medal of Science in 1986. She received the Radcliffe Graduate Society Medal for Distinguished Achievement in 1987, and the Dickson Prize for Science, from Carnegie Mellon University, in 1988. Steitz shared the Warren Triennial Prize with Thomas R. Cech in 1989, and in 1992 she received the Christopher Columbus Discovery Award in Biomedical Research. The Antioch College Alumni Association presented her with the Rebecca Rice Award for Distinguished Achievement in 1993. Steitz considers one of her greatest honors to be the Weizman Women and Science Award, which she received in 1994. In 1996, she received the Distinguished Service Award at the Miami Bio-Technology Winter Symposium, as well as the City of Medicine Award.

Steitz has been granted honorary doctoral degrees from various academic institutions, including Lawrence University, the University of Rochester School of Medicine, Mount Sinai School of Medicine, Trinity College, and Harvard University. She has served on the editorial boards of several of the leading journals in the field of genetics and is a member of the National Academy of Sciences, the American Philosophical Society, and the American Academy of Arts and Sciences. She became the director of the Jane Coffin Childs Memorial Fund for Medical Research, a fund that supports post–doctoral fellows, in 1991. Steitz is married to a fellow scientist, with whom she has one son.

FURTHER READING

Books

Shearer, Benjamin F., and Barbara S. Shearer. *Notable Women in the Life Sciences.* Westport: Greenwood Press, 1996.

Sketch by Leslie Reinherz

Nettie Maria Stevens
1861–1912
American biologist and cytogeneticist

Nettie Maria Stevens was a biologist and cytogeneticist and one of the first American women to be recognized for her contributions to scientific research. Although Stevens started her research career when she was

Nettie Maria Stevens (Science Photo Library/Photo Researcher, Inc. Reproduced by permission.)

in her thirties, she successfully expanded the fields of embryology and cytogenetics (the branch of biology which focuses on the study of heredity), particularly in the study of histology (a branch of anatomy dealing with plant and animal tissues) and of regenerative processes in invertebrates such as hydras and flatworms. She is best known for her role in genetics—her research contributed greatly to the understanding of chromosomes and heredity. She theorized that the sex of an organism was determined by the inheritance of a specific chromosome—X or Y—and performed experiments to confirm this hypothesis.

Stevens, the third of four children and the first daughter, was born in Cavendish, Vermont, on July 7, 1861, to Ephraim Stevens, a carpenter of English descent, and Julia Adams Stevens. Historians know little about her family or her early life, except that she was educated in the public schools in Westford, Massachusetts, and displayed exceptional scholastic abilities. Upon graduation, Stevens taught Latin, English, mathematics, physiology and zoology at the high school in Lebanon, New Hampshire. As a teacher she had a great zeal for learning that she tried to impart both to her students and her colleagues. Between 1881 and 1883, Stevens attended the Normal School at Westfield, Massachusetts, consistently achieving the highest scores in her class from the time she started until she graduated. She worked as a school teacher, and then as a librarian for a number of years after she graduated; however, there are gaps in her history that are unaccounted for between this time and when she enrolled at Stanford University in 1896.

Furthers Education at Stanford and Bryn Mawr

In 1896, Stevens was attracted by the reputation of Stanford University for providing innovative opportunities for individuals aspiring to pursue their own scholastic interests. At the age of thirty–five she enrolled, studying physiology under professor Oliver Peebles Jenkins. She spent summers studying at the Hopkins Seaside Laboratory, Pacific Grove, California, and pursuing her love of learning and of biology. During this time, Stevens decided to switch careers to focus on research, instead of teaching. While at Hopkins she performed research on the life cycle of *Boveria,* a protozoan parasite of sea cucumbers. Her findings were published in 1901 in the *Proceedings of the California Academy of Sciences.* After obtaining her masters degree—a highly unusual accomplishment for a woman in that era—Stevens returned to the East to study at Bryn Mawr College, Pennsylvania, as a graduate biology student in 1900. She was such an exceptional student that she was awarded a fellowship enabling her to study at the Zoological Station in Naples, Italy, and then at the Zoological Institute of the University of Würzburg, Germany. Back at Bryn Mawr, she obtained her doctorate in 1903. At this time, she was made a research fellow in biology at Bryn Mawr and then was promoted to a reader in experimental morphology in 1904. From 1903 until 1905, her research was funded by a grant from the Carnegie Institution. In 1905, she was promoted again to associate in experimental morphology, a position she held until her death in 1912.

Contributes to the Understanding of Chromosomal Determination of Sex

While Stevens' early research focused on morphology and taxonomy and then later expanded to cytology, her most important research was with chromosomes and their relation to heredity. Because of the pioneering studies performed by the renowned monk Gregor Mendel (showing how pea plant genetic traits are inherited), scientists of the time knew a lot about how chromosomes acted during cell division and maturation of germ cells. However, no inherited trait had been traced from the parents' chromosomes to those of the offspring. In addition, no scientific studies had yet linked one chromosome with a specific characteristic. Stevens, and the well–known biologist Edmund Beecher Wilson, who worked independently on this type of research, were the first to demonstrate that the sex of an organism was determined by a particular chromosome; moreover, they proved that gender is inherited in accordance with Mendel's laws of genetics. Together, their research confirmed, and therefore established, a chromosomal basis for heredity. Working with the meal worm, *Tenebrio molitor,* Stevens determined that the male produced two kinds of sperm—one with a large X chromosome, and the other with a small Y chromosome. Unfertilized eggs, however, were all alike and had only X chromosomes. Stevens theorized that sex, in some organisms, may result from chromosomal inheritance. She suggested that eggs fertilized by sperm carrying X chromosomes produced females, and those by sperm carrying the Y chromosome resulted in males. She performed further research to prove this phenomenon, expanding her studies to other species. Although this theory was not accepted by all scientists at the time, it was profoundly important in the evolution of the field of genetics and to an understanding of determination of gender.

Stevens was a prolific author, publishing some thirty–eight papers in eleven years. For her paper, "A Study of the Germ Cells of *Aphis rosae* and *Aphis oenotherae,* " Stevens was awarded the Ellen Richards Research Prize in 1905, given to promote scientific research by women. Stevens died of breast cancer on May 4, 1912, before she could occupy the research professorship created for her by the Bryn Mawr trustees. Much later, Thomas Hunt Morgan, a 1933 Nobel Prize recipient for his work in genetics, recognized the importance of Stevens' ground–breaking experiments, as quoted by Ogilvie in the *Proceedings of the American Philosophical Society,* "Stevens had a share in a discovery of importance and her name will be remembered for this, when the minutiae of detailed investigations that she carried out have become incorporated in the general body of the subject."

SELECTED WRITING BY STEVENS:

Periodicals

"Studies in Spermatogenesis with Especial Reference to the 'Accessory Chromosome.'" *Carnegie Institution Publications* (1905).

"A study of the Germ Cells of *Aphis rosae* and *Aphis Oenotherae.*" *Journal of Experimental Zoology* (1905): 313–333.

"Further Studies on Heterochromosomes in Mosquitoes." *Biological Bulletin of the Marine Biological Laboratory* (1911): 109–120.

FURTHER READING

Books

Ogilvie, Marilyn Bailey *Women in Science: Antiquity through the Nineteenth Century.* Cambridge: MIT Press, 1986.

Periodicals

Isis (June 1978): 163–72.

Proceedings of the American Philosophical Society, Held at Philadelphia for Promoting Useful Knowledge 125, American Philosophical Society, (1981): 292–311.

Sketch by Barbara J. Prouian

Sara Yorke Stevenson
1847–1921
French-American archaeologist

Sara Yorke Stevenson was responsible for the establishment of the University Museum in Pennsylvania, as well as for the acquisition of many of its respected Egyptian artifacts. Partly due to her efforts, the museum is still preeminent in its holdings of Egyptian artifacts.

Sara Yorke was born in Paris, France, on February 19, 1847, to banker and cotton broker Edward Yorke, and Sarah (Hanna) Yorke, daughter of a Louisiana cotton plantation owner. Her parents moved to the United States in 1857, but Stevenson remained in Europe to finish her schooling at the Cours Remy and the Institut Descauriet. Her guardians interested her in antiquities, an interest she would keep throughout her life. In 1862, Stevenson joined her parents in Mexico, where they remained for five years until they fled to the United States to escape the political upheaval surrounding the end of Maximilian's power. She later wrote a book about these experiences entitled *Maximilian in Mexico*. When Stevenson's father died in 1868, Stevenson moved to Philadelphia to live with relatives. There she met lawyer Cornelius Stevenson, whom she married on June 30, 1870. Their only child, William, was born eight years later.

Joins Furness-Mitchell Coterie

In Philadelphia, Stevenson became affiliated with the Furness-Mitchell Coterie, a group of wealthy, educated individuals who allowed women opportunities generally not afforded them. Because of this affiliation, Stevenson became involved in many organizations, among them the Equal Franchise Society of Pennsylvania, dedicated to providing women with opportunities, and the Philadelphia Civic Club, for which she served as president, working with Native American children and indigent women. As chairwoman of the French war relief committee, she was honored with the titles of Officier d'Instruction Publique and Chevalier du Legion d'Honneur.

In addition to her civic activities, the intellectual nature of the coterie helped Stevenson attain her various archaeological positions. These included president of the University of Pennsylvania's department of archaeology and paleontology, curator of the American Exploration Society's Egyptian and Mediterranean sections, and trustee and curator of the Philadelphia Museum. Stevenson never actually conducted fieldwork; instead she analyzed data collected by field archaeologists. Her areas of interests centered on cultural evolutionism and cultural diffusion.

Establishes University Museum

Stevenson belonged to many professional organizations, including the Pennsylvania branch of the Archaeological Institute of America, the Oriental Club, the American

Folk-Lore Society, the Numismatic and Antiquarian Society of Philadelphia, the American Philosophical Society, and the American Association for the Advancement of Science. In 1894, Stevenson became the first woman to lecture at the Harvard Peabody Museum. Most notably, Stevenson was a founder of the University Museum. Because of her work, the museum was able to obtain large collections of Egyptian artifacts, collections that were excavated rather than acquired through purchase. Stevenson catalogued, labeled, and displayed these collections, and partly due to her efforts, the museum is still preeminent in its holdings of Egyptian artifacts.

Stevenson was also able to travel in her studies, to Rome in 1897 and to Egypt in 1898. At the World's Columbian Exposition, she was appointed vice president of the jury of awards for ethnology—an extraordinary honor for a woman at that time. The first woman to be granted an honorary degree from the University of Pennsylvania, Stevenson also received an honorary degree from Temple University.

Socially, Stevenson, was known for her sense of humor, outspokenness, and spirited personality. In addition to her scientific and popular publications, Stevenson served as editor of the *Public Ledger* and contributor to "Peggy Shippen's Diary" from 1908 until her death on November 14, 1921.

SELECTED WRITINGS BY STEVENSON:

Books

(With Morris Jastrow, Jr. and Ferdinand Justi). *Egypt and Western Asia in Antiquity.* Philadelphia: Lea Brothers, 1905.

Periodicals

"On the Remains of the Foreignors [sic] Discovered in Egypt by Mr. W. M. Flinders Petrie, 1895, Now in the Museum of the University of Pennsylvania." *Proceedings of the American Philosophical Society* 35 (1896).

"An Ancient Egyptian Rite Illustrating a Phase of Primitive Thought." In *Memoirs of the International Congress of Anthropology* (1893): 298–311. Chicago: Schulte Publishing Co.

FURTHER READING

Books

Bailey, Martha J. *American Women in Science*. Denver: ABC-CLIO, 1994.

Gacs, Ute. *Women Anthropologists.* New York: Greenwood Press, 1988.

Malone, Dumas. *Dictionary of American Biography.* New York: Charles Scribner's Sons, 1935.

Siegel, Patricia Joan and Kay Thomas Finley. *Women in the Scientific Search.* NJ: Scarecrow Press, 1985.

Sketch by Helene Barker Kiser

Susan Smith (McKinney) Steward

1847–1918

American physician

Susan McKinney Steward was the first black female doctor in the state of New York, and only the third in the United States. She had a successful private practice in New York City (Brooklyn and Manhattan), and was regarded as especially knowledgeable about curing the effects of malnutrition in children. Steward was one of the founders of the Women's Hospital and Dispensary in Brooklyn. She was also active in the community, participating in the temperance, suffrage, and civil rights movements.

Steward was born in 1847 to Sylvanus and Anne Eliza (nee Springsteel) Smith, activists who lived among the black elite in Brooklyn, New York. Her father was a prosperous hog farmer in then–rural Brooklyn. As a young person, Steward studied the organ with two of the most prestigious teachers in Brooklyn, John Zundel and Henry Eyre Brown. Steward retained this interest throughout her life, and while she lived in Brooklyn, she played in churches. Before becoming a doctor, Steward taught music in the District of Columbia's public schools for two years.

Steward received her medical education at the New York Medical College and Hospital for Women. The reasons for her career choice are unclear—perhaps related to the deaths of two of her brothers in 1866 from cholera—but it was unusual for a woman at that time. Indeed, women who aspired to be doctors were basically restricted to the study of homeopathic medicine, which is what Steward studied. She proudly paid for her own education, though her father could have provided the funding for her. After three years of dogged study, Steward graduated in 1870, and was valedictorian of her class. After graduation, Steward married the Reverend William G. McKinney, an itinerant preacher. They eventually had two children together, a daughter, Anna, and a son, William.

It took several years for Steward's career to flourish. When it did, her private practice attracted people of all races, ages, and incomes. In 1881, Steward was a founder of the Women's Hospital and Dispensary in Brooklyn, where she served as a staff member until 1896. (The institution later became known as Memorial Hospital for Women and Children.) In 1882, she became associated with the Brooklyn Home for Aged Colored People, where she was a manager and on the attending medical staff. She served on the Home's board of directors from 1892–95. In 1882, Steward also became a staff member at the New York Medical College and Hospital for Women, her alma mater.

Steward retained several memberships in professional associations, including the Kings County Homeopathic Society and the New York State Medical Society. She presented a paper before the former in 1883. It was a case study of one of her patients, a woman exposed to carbolic acid during pregnancy, resulting in her death and that of her baby. Three years later, Steward delivered a paper related to her specialty, childhood diseases, especially related to malnutrition.

While her career prospered, Steward remained active in social causes. She and her sister Sarah were important members of the Equal Suffrage League. Steward herself was one of the founders of the New York Women's Loyal Union. She was active in the temperance movement, and served as president of a local chapter of the Women's Christian Temperance Union. Steward attended the Bridge Street A.M.E. Church, and participated in its missionary activities. Steward also maintained her organ playing and was active in the Brooklyn Literary Union.

In 1887–88, Steward took a year of post–graduate courses at Long Island Medical College, where she was the only woman in the school. Two years later, in 1890, Steward's husband fell ill with a cerebral hemorrhage. He was disabled for the rest of his life, and died on November 25, 1895.

In 1896, Steward was remarried to the Reverend Theophilus Gould Steward, who worked as a chaplain in the United States Army and as a writer. Upon their marriage, Steward left Brooklyn to move with her new husband to Fort Missoula, Montana, where he was stationed. Steward became licensed to practice medicine there. Two years later, Steward moved to Ohio, to become the college doctor and an instructor at Wilberforce University. She remained there until 1902, when her husband returned from his assignments as chaplain in Cuba and the Philippines. Then Steward and her husband moved to his post in Fort Niobrara, Nebraska. In Nebraska, Steward also became licensed to practice medicine and was associated with a chapter of the Women's Christian Temperance Movement.

After a brief stint in Fort McIntosh, Texas, the couple returned to Wilberforce in 1906, after Steward's husband retired from the army. There, Steward resumed her former duties, while her husband became a faculty member in the department of history. Steward remained active in both her professional and social interests. In 1911, she and her husband went to Europe, where she delivered a paper titled *Colored Women in America* to the first Interracial Conference in London. Steward delivered a paper titled *Women in Medicine* to the Colored Women's Club in Wilberforce. This paper was reproduced in pamphlet form and circulated widely, perhaps because it was one of the most complete studies of black women and their contributions to medicine. Steward also served with the Red Cross at the beginning of World War I.

Steward died suddenly at Wilberforce on March 7, 1918. Her body was transferred back to Brooklyn for burial, where W.E.B. DuBois gave the eulogy. After her death, Steward was twice honored. Black female doctors in New York, Connecticut, and New Jersey named their society after her. In 1975, Steward's grandson lobbied to have his grandmother honored by renaming a junior high school in Brooklyn for her, and it became known as the Susan Smith McKinney Junior High.

SELECTED WRITINGS BY STEWARD:

Periodicals

"Colored American Women." *The Crisis III* (November 1911): 33–34.

"Marasmus Intantum." *Transaction of the Homeopathic Medical Society of the State of New York* (1887): 150.

FURTHER READING

Books

Lyons, Maritcha R. "Dr. Susan S. (McKinney) Steward." In *Homespun Heroes and Other Women of Distinction.* Edited by Hallie Quinn Brown. Oxford University Press, 1988, pp. 160–64.

Periodicals

Alexander, Leslie A. "Susan Smith McKinney, M.D., 1846–1918: First Afro–American Physician in New York State." *National Medical Association Journal* (March 1975): 173–75.

Seraile, William. "Susan McKinney Steward: New York State's First African–American Woman Physician." *Afro–Americans in N.Y. Life and History* (July 1985): 27–44. Reprinted in *Black Women in American History: From Colonial Times Through the Nineteenth Century.* Vol. IV. Edited by Darlene Clark Hine. Carlson Publishing, 1990, pp. 1217–34.

Sketch by Annette Petrusso

Alice M. Stewart
1906—
British epidemiologist

Alice M. Stewart is an emeritus fellow of the Leverhulme Trust at the University of Birmingham in England. She has spent her scientific career studying the role of low-level radiation on childhood cancers and the cancer risk to those who have been exposed to low-level radiation from the nuclear industry. Her work in these areas began at Oxford University in the 1950s, when she discovered that x rays given to pregnant women in the first trimester directly affected the fetus and were subsequently a cause of childhood leukemia. (It was a usual practice to administer prenatal x rays to determine abnormalities that could be detrimental to delivery, and to discover if a pregnant woman was carrying more than one child.) Her studies, and those of other scientists, on the effects of low-level radiation on those exposed at such nuclear industries as the Hanford Atomic Works in Hanford, Washington, examined the numbers of cancer deaths from low–dose exposure as compared to high-dose exposure. Her work in these two areas was responsible for changing the thinking on what constitutes "safe" radiation exposure. Her contention that there is no safe level is a controversial one and has elicited emotional debate that continues to the present time.

Stewart began her training as a general physician and later, because of studies and experiments conducted during World War II, became an epidemiologist. She received her medical degree from Cambridge University in 1932, was elected to the British Royal College of Physicians—the youngest woman so honored prior to 1947—and is a founder of the International Epidemiological Society and the Society for Medicine.

Stewart was born on October 4, 1906, in Sheffield, England. Her parents were both physicians, and her mother taught anatomy at the university level. She and her seven brothers and sisters all received a university education—she at St. Leonard's in Scotland, and later at Cambridge and the Royal Free Hospital in London. Stewart credits "pioneer women physicians" and the Royal Free Hospital, which gave preference to women medical students, for her opportunity to receive advanced medical training. When she completed her medical education there, she became medical registrar at the Elizabeth Garrett Anderson Hospital (named for the first woman physician in Britain). When World War II broke out, she was assigned to St. Albans, north of London, to do casualty work. It was at that time she received word about an opening at Oxford University. The shortage of male doctors because of military conscription was a factor in her securing the position. As she stated in an interview with contributor Jane Stewart Cook, "It was there that I was 'roped into' epidemiology, and that turned into the radiation story."

Exposes Low-Dose Radiation Risks

Since 1895, when Professor Wilhelm Konrad Roentgen of Germany discovered the x ray, scientists have wondered about the effects of radiation on human health. Some radiation health risks are readily apparent, such as the immediate results caused by the atom bomb. Others were discovered more slowly, as in the Oxford Survey of Childhood Cancers. Stewart has been involved in making these determinations since the early 1950s and contends that radiation is not less harmful at low doses than high doses. Her main premise is that early methods used to evaluate the effects of radiation have greatly underestimated the risk of cancer from low-level doses. Because exposure to radiation compromises the immune system, and may subsequently lead to the development of a cancer, she thinks deaths that occur from weakened immune systems should also be counted in the radiation risk evaluation, even though cancer is not yet present at the time of death.

The Oxford Survey of Childhood Cancers

Her study of radiation risk began in the early 1950s, when colleague David Hewitt at Oxford University became aware that the number of British children dying from leukemia had increased more than 50 percent. Stewart was then working at Oxford in the Department of Preventive Medicine. Determined to find an answer for the increase in these deaths, she talked local health departments into interviewing the mothers of the 1,694 children who had died within the previous two years. A control group was set up at the same time. Thus began the Oxford Survey of Childhood Cancers. When the information began coming back, it was noticed that twice as many children under the age of 10 whose mothers had been given pelvic x rays during their pregnancies had died. Her findings also indicated that just one rad (unit of radiation) of x ray to a fetus increased its risk of leukemia, shattering the previous idea that ten rads was a safe level.

This news was not what the medical establishment or the nuclear industry wanted to hear. Stewart and Hewitt's work was roundly criticized, and Stewart lost funding for the survey. She continued, however, and her conclusions were far reaching. She determined that a fetus exposed to radiation in the first trimester was at ten times the risk of developing cancer than a fetus not exposed—and the risk mounted with the number of x rays taken, even though one x ray greatly increased the risk. She also found that x rays could harm the eggs stored in the ovaries of women who were not pregnant. This work was done in 1958, and was still hotly rejected by the medical community until 1962, when her findings were confirmed by Dr. Brian MacMahon of the Harvard School of Public Health. MacMahon conducted a study of 700,000 children born between 1947 and 1964 throughout hospitals in the northeastern United States. His study found that children of mothers who had received x rays while pregnant had a cancer mortality 40 percent higher than the group whose mothers were not x-rayed. Stewart's work was validated. The vulnerability to the unborn from x rays was serious and inescapable.

Conducts Radiation Studies Internationally

A study conducted at the Hanford Atomic Works in the state of Washington looked at the effects on nearby general population and Hanford workers exposed to radiation emissions between 1944 and 1992. The conclusion was that low-dose, long-term radiation exposure is more damaging than high-dose, short-term radiation. As a result of this and other similar studies conducted both in the United States and in Britain, it is Stewart's contention that cell mutation from low-level, long-term radiation exposure can cause cancer. The difficulty in reaching this conclusion has been enormous and complex, and explains, in part, the resistance to accepting Stewart's findings.

Three reasons help to explain the difficulty. First, the low-dose effect will be weak, and will not immediately be obvious. Second, the damaging effect will be rare, and only occurs after a long and variable delay—it can occur within a year, or take as long as 80 years. Third, this rare, long–term, variable event is complicated by the fact that background radiation is also present at any given time. Thus, Stewart admits how hard it has been to actually establish a danger, but contends that the risk of adding to population loads of cancer through low-level radiation exposure has been proven through the Oxford Study. As a result of that study, she and other scientists have drawn similar conclusions concerning other low-level exposure, such as that stemming from nuclear industry radiation exposure and fall-out.

Although semi-retired, Stewart continues to write articles about the effects of low-level radiation. Looking back over more than 50 years of study on the subject, she told contributer Jane Stewart Cook that her work "changed the whole radiation story. The safety of low-level radiation isn't what was thought. I proved that low-level doses could be harmful."

SELECTED WRITINGS BY STEWART:

Books

Stewart, A. M., and D. Hewitt. *Current Topics in Radiation Research.* Vol. 1. Amsterdam: North Holland Publishing Company, 1965, pp. 221–253.

Periodicals

Bithell, J. F. and A. M. Stewart. "Pre-Natal Irradiation and Childhood Malignancy: A Review of British Data from the Oxford Survey." *British Journal of Cancer.* (1975): 31; 271–287.

Gilman, E. A., G. W. Kneale, E. G. Knox, and A. M. Stewart. "Pregnancy X–rays and Childhood Cancers: Effects of Exposure Age and Radiation Dose." *Journal of the Society for Radiological Protection.* (1988): 8; 1; 3–8.

Kneale, G. W., A. M. Stewart, and L. M. Kinnier Wilson. "Immunizations Against Infectious Diseases and Childhood Cancers." *Cancer Immunology and Immunotherapy.* (1986) 21; 129–132.

Stewart, Alice. "Delayed Effects of A–Bomb Radiation: A Review of the Recent Mortality Rates and Risk Estimates for Five Year Survivors." *Journal of Epidemiology and Community Health.* (1982): 36; 80–86.

Stewart, Alice. "Detection of Late Effects of Ionizing Radiation: Why Deaths of Survivors are so Misleading." *International Journal of Epidemiology.* (1985): 14; 1; 52–56.

Stewart, Alice. "Low Dose Radiation Cancers in Man." *Advances in Cancer Research.* (1971; 14): 359–390.

Stewart, A. M., G. W. Kneale. "The Immune System and Cancers of Fetal Origin." *Cancer Immunology and Immunotherapy.* (1982; 14): 110–116.

Stewart, A. M., G. W. Kneale. "Radiation Dose Effects in Relation to Obstetrics, X Ray and Childhood Cancer." *The Lancet.* (1970; 1): 1185–1187.

Stewart, Alice, and G. W. Kneale. "Late effects of A-Bomb Radiation: Risk Problems Unrelated to the New Dosimetry." *Health Physics.* (1988): 54; 567–569.

Stewart, A. M., J. Webb, D. Giles, and D. Hewitt. "Malignant Diseases in Childhood and Diagnostic Irradiation In Utero." *The Lancet.* (1956): 2 447.

Stewart A. M., W. Pennybacker, and R. Barber. "Adult Leukaemias and Diagnostic Xrays." *British Medical Journal.* (1962): II 882–890.

FURTHER READING

Books

Elkington, John. *The Poisoned Womb.* Great Britain: Penguin Books, 1985, p. 25; p. 85.

Gofman, John W. *Low-Dose Exposure: An Independent Analysis.* San Francisco: Committee for Nuclear Responsibility, Inc., C.N.R. Book Division, 1990, pp. 21–5.

Gofman, John W. *Radiation and Human Health.* San Francisco: Sierra Club Books, 1981, pp. 126; 329; 338; 387; 411; 687; 740.

Health Effects of Exposure to Low Levels of Ionizing Radiation. Washington: National Academy Press, 1990, pp. 352–370; 371–389.

Lindee, Susan M. *Suffering Made Real, American Science and the Survivors at Hiroshima.* Chicago: University of Chicago Press, 1994, pp. 198; 245

Schubert, Jack and Ralph E. Lapp. *Radiation: What It Is and How It Affects You.* New York: The Viking Press, 1957, p. 13; p. 170; 208–209

Other

Cook, Jane Stewart, interview with Alice Stewart conducted May 14, 1999.

Stewart, Alice M. "Total Risk of Radiation Exposure Underestimated." *Health Risk Viewpoints: Radiation and Cancer* (A publication of the Hanford Health Information Network). http://198.187.0.42/hanford/publications/overview/viewpoints.html

Stewart, Alice. "Low-Level Radiation, The Effects on Human and Non-Human Life." Lecture at the World Uranium Hearing, Salzburg, 1992. http://www.underground-book.com/chapters/uranium/Alice Ste

"X Rays *in Utero*." *Health Risk Viewpoints: Radiation and Cancer* (A publication of the Hanford Health Information Network). http://198.187.0.42/hanford/publications/overview/viewpoints.html

Sketch by Jane Stewart Cook

Grace Anne Stewart
1893–1970
Canadian–American geologist

Grace Anne Stewart was an expert in North American Devonian animals. She researched microfossils and invertebrates, and played a large part in the upkeep of the geological museum at Ohio State University. Well-respected for her sound research, Grace Anne (never merely Grace) was also known as an excellent teacher and a warm personality.

Grace Ann Stewart (Ohio State University Archives. Reproduced by permission.)

Stewart was born on a farm in Minnedosa, Manitoba, Canada on August 4, 1893. Her parents, John and Elizabeth Crerar Stewart, were both Scottish. John was the only boy in his family to continue work as a farmer, and Grace Anne and her four brothers and sisters were also able to observe the careers of their five uncles (three doctors, a lawyer, and a building contractor) as models for the professional life. However, the farm gave Stewart a lifelong love of the outdoors.

Because many men were fighting in World War I at the time, Stewart was able to take advantage of educational opportunities that might not have been available to her otherwise. She was the first woman to graduate from the university with a geology degree, and also became a graduate assistant in the department. Stewart received her B.A. degree in 1918 and her M.A. degree in 1920 from the University of Alberta. During summer breaks from 1918–1920, she worked as an assistant geologist for the Research Council of Alberta. Because her abilities were notable, the University of Chicago offered her a fellowship to work toward her Ph.D. in paleontology, which she completed *cum laude* in 1922. During the summer breaks from 1921–1922, she overcame harsh gender prejudice to work as an assistant paleontologist for Canada's Geological Survey, primarily in the National Museum.

Respected by Students and Scientists Alike

In 1923, Stewart was offered an instructor position at Ohio State University, which she accepted, understanding that the head of the geology department did not share the Geological Survey's attitude toward women. She held the instructorship until 1928, when she was promoted to Assistant Professor. In 1937, she was promoted again to associate professor, and attained the professor rank in 1946, the same year in which she spent part of the time as acting chairman of the department.

Stewart's research focused on Devonian and Silurian invertebrates such as corals, crinoids, ostracodes, and microfossils, primarily from the Ohio area. For her scientific papers, Stewart commissioned illustrations because the department lacked a laboratory. She also worked in the Orton Hall Geological Museum, where she was responsible for effectively ordering displays, identifying and classifying collections, and exchanging material with other universities and museums.

As a teacher, Stewart was liked and respected by colleagues and students alike, attentive to detail, and always motivating students to work independently. In her annual report to the university, she descssribed a class she taught in which the students were asked to recreate Paleozoic periods through drawings and paintings. She particularly enjoyed teaching an introductory class to public school teachers. Stewart was always described in glowing personal terms, supportive of careers and friend to the faculty members in general, particularly the faculty women, for whose group she served as chairman. Stewart also worked hard for the larger university community, serving on committees and writing the geology section for the catalog.

Recognized for her achievements by the scientific community, Stewart was fellow and vice president of the geology section of the Ohio Academy of Science, fellow of the Geological Society of America, fellow of the Paleontological Society, and a member of Sigma Xi. She presented scientific papers for the Ohio Academy of Science, the Paleontological Society, and the American Association for the Advancement of Science, and she also gave lectures as part of a History in the Making series for the Lazarus Society and to the Hard of Hearing League. Summers from 1924–1930 were spent working for the Geological Society of Ohio. She also traveled all over the country to research and exchange information with other scientists. Her abilities were so well known that she was asked to work as a geographer during World War II for the Office of Strategic Services. Stewart's work in the map division garnered her a government commendation.

Stewart retired from Ohio State University in 1954, nine years earlier than required, because of her general discouragement with her career. She repeatedly complained of the lack of equipment, office space, and even a telephone, and expressed displeasure with her slow professional advancement and lack of recognition. She retired to Tucson, Arizona, and shortly thereafter was offered a position studying fossils in Calgary, Alberta. Her stay in Canada was short, however, and she returned to Tucson, preferring the climate and lifestyle.

During her retirement, Stewart continued to write about geology, including an article for the *McGraw-Hill Encyclopedia of Science and Technology* in 1959. Stewart was placed in a nursing home following a stroke in the spring of 1969. She died there on October 15, 1970. Stewart is remembered as a hard worker in all of her endeavors, from the classroom to the field to the museum. Her work served as a prime example to other women in the field.

SELECTED WRITINGS BY STEWART:

Periodicals

"Fauna of the Silica Shale of Lucas County." *Geological Survey of Ohio* 4th ser., no. 32 (1927).

"Middle Devonian Corals of Ohio." *Geological Society of America, Special Papers* no. 8 (1938).

"Ostracodes of the Silica shale, Devonian, of Ohio." *Journal of Paleontology* 10 (1936).

FURTHER READING

Periodicals

"Memorial to Grace Anne Stewart." *The Geological Society of America Memorials* 11 (1973).

Other

The Ohio State University Evaluation Program. *Grace Anne Stewart, Faculty Member's Annual Report.*

The Ohio State University News Bureau information on Grace Ann Stewart. The Ohio State University Library Archives.

Sketch by Helene Barker Kiser

Lucille Farrier Stickel
1915–
American zoologist

Lucille Farrier Stickel was a pioneer in the field of pesticide research, in particular on determining levels of pesticide residue levels in wildlife. Her work in the pharmacotoxicology of environmental pollution, as well as in vertebrate population ecology was elucidated in numerous papers and won her a 1974 Aldo Leopold Award from the Wildlife Society.

Born on January 11, 1915, Stickel earned her B.A. from Eastern Michigan University in 1936 and her M.S. in 1938. Eleven years later she earned a Ph.D. in zoology, doing graduate work also at the University of Michigan. Married in 1941, Stickel worked as a biologist at the Patuxent Wildlife Research Center of the U.S. Fish and Wildlife Service from 1943 to 1947. Following a decade–long hiatus in her career, Stickel again worked at Patuxent Wildlife Research Center from 1961 to 1972 and became its director form 1972 to 1980.

Researches Pesticide Residues

Despite a long break in her career and the early pioneering nature of her work, Stickel managed to compile a body or research that has stood the test of time. When she was doing her initial research into the levels of pesticide residues in the brain tissues of animals, such pesticide research was still in its fledgling stages. Stickel's studies of lethal levels of pesticide absorption in the brains of fish and other wildlife are still in use today to determine permissible levels of pesticide contamination. Her work continues to be important, as such pesticide residues are passed up the food chain and also affect humans when we come into contact with polluted water, through consumption or swimming. Detecting pesticide pollution as well as measuring lethal levels has therefore become a cornerstone of pesticide research. Stickel was honored for her work by a Federal Woman's Award for the Department of the Interior in 1968, by the 1974 Aldo Leopold Award, and by an honorary doctorate of science from her original alma mater, Eastern Michigan University, in 1974.

SELECTED WRITINGS BY STICKEL:

Books

Organochlorine Pesticides in the Environment. Washington, DC: U.S. Dept. of the Interior, Fish and Wildlife Service, [1969].

(With Michael P. Dieter) *Ecological and Physiological Effects of Petroleum on Aquatic Birds: A Summary of Research Activities FY76 through FY78.* Washington, DC: Biological Services Program, Fish and Wildlife Service, U.S. Dept. of the Interior, 1979.

FURTHER READING

Books

American Men and Women of Science. 14th ed. New York: Bowker, 1979, p. 4915.

Bailey, Martha J. *American Women in Science: A Biographical Dictionary.* Denver: ABC–CLIO, 1994, pp.374–75.

Vare, Ethlie Ann and Greg Ptacek. *Mothers of Invention: From the Bra to the Bomb.* New York: William Morrow, 1988, p. 174.

Sketch by J. Sydney Jones

Alice M. Stoll
1917–
American biophysicist

A scientist who worked in the field of medical biophysics, Alice M. Stoll conducted research into the effects of heat and acceleration on the human body, and the rate that heat is given off by burning materials. Her investigations, which permitted evaluation of the thermal protection offered by fire resistant and fire retardant fabrics, led to the development of new fabrics for use in fire hazard protection. Among the honors accorded to Stoll in recognition for her scientific work was the 1969 Society of Women Engineers' Achievement Award.

Stoll, a native of New York City, was born on August 25, 1917. She obtained her undergraduate education at Hunter College, earning a B.A. degree in 1938. Joining the New York Hospital and Medical College at Cornell University, she worked as an assistant in the areas of metabolism, allergies, and spectroscopy. In 1943 Stoll joined the U.S. Navy, remaining in active duty until 1946, then returned to Cornell University where she began research into temperature regulation. She completed a dual M.S. degree in physiology and biophysics in 1948. Remaining at the Medical College until 1953, Stoll worked as a research associate in the area of environmental thermal radiation and as an instructor in the school of nursing. To conduct her research, Stoll had to develop the instrumentation necessary for her work. The instruments she developed—and for which she received patents—measure the heat transfer red to the surroundings from flames and other thermal radiation sources. At this time, Stoll also worked as a consultant for various laboratories, including the Arctic Aerospace Medicine Lab at Ladd Air Force Base in Alaska during 1952 and 1953. Part of her time was also spent on her duties with the Naval Reserve, which she had joined upon completion of her active duty.

Leaving Cornell in 1953, Stoll joined the Naval Air Development Center (NADC) in Warminster, Pennsylvania, as a physiologist in the medical research department. Advancing to special technical assistant in 1956, she became head of the Thermal Laboratory in 1960, and then chief of the Biophysics & Bioastronautics Division in 1964. Stoll retired from the Naval Reserve in 1966 with the rank of commander, but remained at NADC where she was promoted to head of the Biophysics Laboratory in 1970, a position she held until her retirement in 1980.

Stoll conducted research at NADC into the effects of acceleration on the cardiovascular system. Most of her work, however, centered on the transfer of heat from flames and other thermal radiation sources and how this heat transfer affected the human body. Stoll's studies on tissue damage and pain sensation established a relationship between the amount of heat absorbed and the damage which resulted; she established that the source of the heat was not important, as all heat sources could cause the same damage. Models that Stoll designed based on this research were valuable in determining the amount of thermal protection needed to protect the body from different heat sources.

Stoll also investigated the heat transfer properties of various fabrics which could be used to provide thermal protection. Clothing, however, acts not only to protect the skin from heat but can also be a source of heat if it catches on fire; an accidental burning of a test participant during simulated space capsule clothing fires at NADC prompted Stoll to study the burning properties of fabrics under high oxygen concentrations—conditions which could be found in the aerospace environment. This research resulted in the development of methods for measuring the burn protection provided by clothing and fabrics, as well as the invention of "Nomex" (produced by DuPont), a fire–resistant fabric which is now widely used in apparel for fire fighters and race car drivers.

In addition to being recognized by the Society of Women Engineers, Stoll was honored in 1965 with the Federal Civil Service Award and the Paul Bert Award from the Aerospace Medical Association in 1972. A charter member of the Biophysical Society, she has been elected a fellow of the American Association for the Advancement of Science. Stoll has remained active in the American Society of Mechanical Engineers, particularly in the heat transfer and biotechnology sections.

SELECTED WRITINGS BY STOLL:

Periodicals

(With Leon C. Greene) "Relationship Between Pain and Tissue Damage due to Thermal Radiation." *Journal of Applied Physiology* 14 (1959): 373–382.

(With Maria A. Chianta and L. R. Munroe) "Flame Contact Studies." *Journal of Heat Transfer* 86 (1964): 449–456.

(With John A. Weaver) "Mathematical Model of Skin Exposed to Thermal Radiation." *Aerospace Medicine* 40 (1969): 24–30.

(With Chianta) "Method and Rating System for Evaluation of Thermal Protection." *Aerospace Medicine* 40 (1969): 1232–1237.

(With Chianta) "Thermal Analysis of Combustion of Fabric in Oxygen–Enriched Atmospheres." *Journal of Fire & Flammability* 4 (1973): 309–324.

(With Munroe and others) "Facility and a Method for Evaluation of Thermal Protection" *Aviation, Space, and Environmental Medicine* (November 1976): 1177–1181.

FURTHER READING

Books

American Men and Women of Science. 14th ed. New York: R. R. Bowker, 1979, p. 4928.

Engineers of Distinction, 2d ed. Engineers Joint Council 1973, p. 297.

O'Neill, Lois Decker, ed. *The Woman's Book of World Records and Achievements.* Garden City: Anchor Press/Doubleday, 1979, pp. 187–188.

Other

Ferrance, Jerome, correspondence with Alice M. Stoll, January, 1994.

Sketch by Jerome P. Ferrance

Isabelle Stone
1868–?
American physicist and educator

Isabelle Stone devoted her life to furthering education for women. The first woman to receive a Ph.D. from the University of Chicago, she taught physics at several colleges and with her sister founded two girls' schools, one in Rome and one in the United States.

Not much is known about Stone's life. She was born in Chicago on October 18, 1868 to Leander and Harriet Leonard Stone. She attended Wellesley College in Massachusetts, where she received her bachelor's degree in 1890. From there, she returned to her hometown to study at the University of Chicago. She received her Master of Science degree in physics in 1896, and a year later was awarded her Ph.D.

After graduating from Chicago, Stone taught for a year at the Preparatory School of Bryn Mawr University in Pennsylvania; from there, she went to Vassar, where she was an instructor in physics until 1906. It was while she was at Vassar that the American Physical Society was founded; Stone was one of only three women present at the inaugural meeting.

In 1907, Stone and her sister moved to Europe. There they opened the School for American Girls in Rome, which they directed until 1914. They returned to the U.S. and in 1916 Stone accepted a position as head of the physics department of Sweet Briar College in Virginia. She remained there until 1923, when she and her sister again opened a school, this time in Washington, D.C.

In addition to her interest and commitment to teaching, Stone also conducted physical research. Her primary interest was in the electrical properties of thin films, and finding ways of depositing these films in a vacuum. Some of her research was conducted at Columbia University.

Stone's interests went beyond physics. She was active during her lifetime in the American Federation for the Arts, the American Association of University Women, the Institute Français de Washington, and the English–Speaking Union of the U.S. (an organization for Americans interested in British history and literature).

Ironically, this very active woman faded out of the public eye during the 1940s. The last official mention of her was in the eighth edition of *American Men of Science* (now known as *American Men and Women of Science*) in 1944. She also appears in the fifth edition (1968) of *Who Was Who in America*, in keeping with that publication's practice of listing past *Who's Who* entrants who are over 95 years of age and whose entries are no longer being updated.

FURTHER READING

Bailey, Martha J. *American Women in Science: A Biographical Dictionary.* Denver: ABC–Clio, 1994.

Books

Oglivie, Marilyn Bailey. *Women in Science: Antiquity through the Nineteenth Century.* Cambridge: MIT Press, 1986.

Siegel, Patricia Joan and Kay Thomas Finley. *Women in the Scientific Search.* Metuchen, NJ: Scarecrow Press, 1985.

Who Was Who in America. Vol. 5. Marquis Who's Who, 1968.

Sketch by George A. Milite

Alicia Boole Stott
1860–1940
Irish-born English mathematician

Alicia Boole Stott is considered noteworthy for her famous relatives as much for her own discoveries that translate Platonic and Archimedean solids into higher dimensions. She is more likely described when mentioned in other contexts as the daughter of mathematician and Royal Medal recipient George Boole and Mary Everest Boole.

Stott was born on June 8, 1860, in Cork, Ireland, where her father held a professorship at Queen's College. When George Boole died of a fever in 1864, Stott's sisters were dispersed to live with relatives while their mother struggled to support herself in London. Stott was shuttled between her grandmother in England and a great–uncle in Ireland, and was not reunited with her sisters until she was more than 10 years old.

Cardboard Models

Stott was well into her teens by the time she became seriously interested in mathematics. A family friend named Howard Hinton, soon to become her brother–in–law, introduced her to the tesseract, or four–dimensional hypercube. He not only offered Stott intellectual stimulation, he got her a job as secretary to an associate, John Falk. At that time, Hinton was working on a book that would eventually see publication in 1904.

In 1900, Stott (with the encouragement of Walter Stott, an actuarian whom she later married) published an article on three–dimensional sections of hypersolids. They led an ordinary middle–class existence following their marriage and had two children, Mary and Leonard. Walter took note of his wife's interests and introduced her to the work of Pieter Hendrik Schoute of the University of Groningen. The Stotts took a chance and wrote to him describing Stott's work.

Upon viewing photographs of Stott's cardboard models, Schoute elected to relocate to England from the Netherlands in order to collaborate with her. Over their 20–year relationship, Schoute arranged for the publication of Stott's own papers and cowrote others. Stott refined her approach towards deriving the Archimedean solids from the Platonic solids to improve upon Johannes Kepler's. She also coined the term "polytope" as a name for a four–dimensional convex solid form.

Schoute's university colleagues were impressed enough to invite Stott to their tercentenary celebration in 1914, to bestow upon her an honorary doctorate. Unfortunately, the 71–year–old Schoute died before the event. At a loss, Stott resumed her role as homemaker for nearly 20 years.

Stott found another collaborator, H.S.M. Coxeter, a writer who specialized in the geometry of kaleidoscopes, in 1930. She was quite taken with these "magic mirrors" and the challenge they would present to more old–fashioned mathematicians. Stott was inspired to devise a four–dimensional analogue to two of the Archimedean solids, which she called the "snub 24–cell." This construction was not original to her, having been discovered earlier by Thorold Gosset. However, her cardboard models of it in its "golden ratio" relationship with the regular 24–cell are still stored at Cambridge University.

Stott was an animal lover who enjoyed bird watching. She became ill around the time England entered World War II and died on December 17, 1940.

SELECTED WRITINGS BY STOTT:

"On Certain Sections of the Regular Four–Dimensional Hypersolids." In *Verhandelingen der Koninklijke Akademie van Wetenschappen* (1.sectie) 7 (3) (1900): 1–21.

"Geometrical Deduction of Semiregular from Regular Polytopes and Space Fillings." In *Verhandelingen der Koninklijke Akademie van Wetenschappen* (1.sectie) 11 (1) (1910): 1–24.

FURTHER READING

Books

Coxeter, H.S.M. "Alicia Boole Stott." In *Women of Mathematics*. Edited by Louise S. Grinstein and Paul J. Campbell. Westport, CT: Greenwood Press, 1987, pp. 220–24.

Other

Frost, Michelle. "Mary Everest Boole." *Biographies of Women Mathematicians*. http://www.scottlan.edu/lriddle/women/chronol.htm (July 1997).

"Alicia Boole Stott." *MacTutor History of Mathematics Archive*. http://www–groups.dcs.st–and.ac.uk/~history/Mathematicians/Stott.html (July 1997).

Sketch by Jennifer Kramer

Ella Church Strobell
1862–1920(?)
American cytologist

Ella Strobell was a cytologist who studied the structures of cells using a microscope. With **Katherine Foot**, she studied the chromosomes in maturating egg cells. Although their conclusions about chromosomes and heredity were incorrect, Strobell and Foot revolutionized microscopic technology by their use of photography.

The life of young Ella Strobell, who was born in 1862, is even more of a mystery than that of her collaborator Katherine Foot. She was educated in private schools and by tutors. Apparently, like Foot, Strobell carried out her scientific studies without institutional affiliation or outside financial support, a very unusual circumstance in twentieth–century science. Strobell worked, and also may have lived, at 80 Madison Avenue in New York City.

Between 1894 and 1917, Strobell and Foot published at least 23 papers, primarily cytological studies of chromosomes in maturing and fertilized eggs, or oocytes, of the earthworm *Allolobophora foetida.* They developed and utilized the new technology of photomicroscopy, which reproduced the features of cells with a clarity and accuracy that was previously unknown. Until then, researchers had relied on drawing of their microscopic observations. For the first time, the inaccuracies and biases of the human observer and the human hand were eliminated from cytological research. As G. Kass–Simon quoted from one of their papers: "A dozen photographs of a variety of features can be taken in the time required to reproduce any one of them by a careful drawing. The printed photographs can be kept in a form serviceable for frequent reference and the impression first made by a preparation not allowed to fade. . . Of the relative values of these two methods there can be no question, in every case the photographs proving to be the more valuable aid in recalling the preparations." In addition to working out the multiple technical problems of photomicroscopy, Strobell and Foot were among the first to develop methods for using low temperatures to make extremely thin biological preparations for microscopic observations.

Strobell and Foot published hundreds of their photomicrographs. They used these as evidence that the chromosomes were too variable in size and shape to be individual structures that carried the genetic material. The geneticist Thomas Hunt Morgan disagreed with their interpretations; however one of their photomicrographs was the only such photograph in his 1914 book on heredity. Although they were wrong about the function of chromosomes, other prominent scientists at the time also doubted that chromosomes contained the hereditary material. However by 1915, the chromosome theory of heredity was generally accepted. Reprints of Strobell and Foot's cytological studies from 1894 to 1917 were collected and privately printed. There is a copy in the library of the Marine Biological Laboratory at Woods Hole in Massachusetts. Strobell is believed to have died between 1918 and 1920. She may have left Foot an inheritance to continue their research.

SELECTED WRITINGS BY STROBELL:

Periodicals

(With Katherine Foot) "Further Notes on the Egg of *Allolobophora foetida.*" *Zoological Bulletin* 2 (1898): 130–51.

(With Katherine Foot) "Sectioning Paraffine at a Temperature of 25°F." *Biological Bulletin* 9 (1905): 281–86.

FURTHER READING

Books

Cattell, J. McKeen, ed. *American Men of Science: A Biographical Dictionary.* New York: Science Press, 1906.

Kass–Simon, G. "Biology is Destiny." In *Women of Science: Righting the Record.* Edited by G. Kass–Simon and Patricia Farnes. Bloomington: Indiana University Press, 1990.

Sketch by Margaret Alic

Agnes Naranjo Stroud-Lee
1922–

Native American radiation biologist

Nationally recognized for her work in radiobiology, Agnes Naranjo Stroud–Lee has been the recipient of several awards and honors, including the NASA Certificate of Recognition. She was the first Indian woman to hold a position as staff research scientist in a nationally prominent laboratory. She was also the only known Pueblo woman to hold a doctorate degree in biology and zoology at the time.

Born in 1922 into the Native American Tewa tribe of the Santa Clara Indian Pueblos, Stroud–Lee obtained a bachelor's degree from the University of New Mexico in 1945, after which she was offered a position at the prominent Los Alamos Scientific Laboratory as a research technologist in hematology. After one year, she was appointed as an associate cytologist for the Argonne National Laboratory, where she remained until 1969.

Concurrently, Stroud–Lee pursued and obtained her doctorate degree in biology and zoology from the University of Chicago, obtained in 1966. Three years later, in 1969, she accepted a one–year position as director for the Department of Tissue Culture, Pasadena Foundation for Medical Research. This was followed by a five–year position as senior research cytogeneticist at the Data Analysis Section of the Jet Propulsion Laboratory. In 1975, she returned to Los Alamos as a cytogeneticist in the health research division. The position gave her the distinction of being the only Native American woman employed at the level of staff member at a prominent scientific laboratory. She also received the NASA Certificate of Recognition after only one year in that position (1976). She eventually left that post to begin a consulting career in radiobiology and cytogenetics.

Stroud–Lee's more well–known research has been in the analysis of the effects of radiation on animal tumors, the effects of ionizing radiation in vitro and in vivo, and in mammalian radiation biology. She has also done research on the automation of chromosome analysis by computers.

Stroud–Lee has been an active member of the American Society for Cell Biology, the BioPhysical Society, the Radiation Research Society, and the Tissue Culture Association. In 1955, she was the recipient of the A. Cressy Morrison Prize in Natural Sciences from the New York Academy of Sciences. This award acknowledged her important contributions to research at Argonne, ten years prior to her having received her doctorate. Stroud–Lee was also honored as recipient of the Diploma of Honor in Cytology at the First Pan American Cancer Cytology Congress.

Stroud–Lee has been twice married and has one child. She has also been listed in sources under the surname of "Stroud" and "Stroud–Schmink."

FURTHER READING

Books

Bailey, Martha J. *American Women in Science.* Denver: ABC–CLIO, p. 378.

O'Neill, Lois Decker. *The Women's Book of World Records and Achievements.* Garden City: Anchor Press, 1979, 162.

Sketch by Lauri R. Harding

Henrietta Hill Swope
1902–1980
American astronomer

Henrietta Hill Swope is best known for her discovery of 2,000 variable stars, a feat surpassed only by the early twentieth–century astronomer **Henrietta Leavitt**. A variable star is one whose brightness level changes, which makes it difficult both to find and to take accurate measurements. Her work won her numerous honors, including the American Astronomical Society's Annie Jump Cannon Prize.

Henrietta Swope, the daughter of Gerard and Mary Hill Swope, was born in St. Louis, Missouri, on October 26, 1902. Gerard Swope, an electrical engineer by training, was president of General Electric. His daughter attended Barnard College and received her bachelor's degree in 1925; a master's degree from Radcliffe followed three years later. Interestingly, astronomy was not her original career choice. She entered the University of Chicago's School of Commerce and Administration as a graduate student. It took her very little time to decide that a career in business administration was not what she wanted. The astronomer **Margaret Harwood**, then the head of the **Maria Mitchell** Observatory in Nantucket, Massachusetts, suggested that Swope go to the Harvard College Observatory. Swope followed the suggestion and spent the next 14 years at Harvard.

During her years at Harvard, Swope distinguished herself as a gifted astronomer. It was there that she discovered her 2,000 variable stars (Leavitt had discovered 2,400). Working with the astronomer Harlow Shapley, she worked out a formula for determining the distance between other galaxies and our own. Her talents were recognized by both her colleagues and the government. When the U.S. entered World War II, Swope became a mathematician for the U.S. Navy's Hydrographic Office (concurrently, she worked at MIT's Radar Laboratory). In 1947, with the war now over for two years, Swope decided to return to Harvard. Unfortunately, the Observatory's funds were limited, and Harvard offered her only a token salary. Other Harvard astronomers had accepted token salaries in the past; **Annie Jump Cannon** was known for returning her salary to the Observatory. The fact that many of those asked to accept a token salary were women did not escape Swope; despite the fact that she was independently wealthy, she refused the token salary on principle. Her stand was a costly one; apparently even some of her colleagues disagreed with it, and Harvard subsequently refused to take her back.

Swope then returned to her alma mater, Barnard, where she taught astronomy for five years. In 1952, Walter Baade, head of the Mount Wilson and Palomar Observatory in Pasadena, California, offered her a position as his assistant. Baade was familiar with Swope's work and reputation at Harvard, and he felt (correctly, it turned out) that she would be an ideal collaborator. Swope began as a research assistant (she lobbied successfully to have her job title changed to assistant from the older term "computer") and later became a research fellow.

Determines Distance to Andromeda Galaxy

During her years at Mount Wilson, Swope continued to make important discoveries. Using state–of–the–art equipment that she could only have dreamed of at Harvard, Swope was able to determine in 1962 that the Andromeda galaxy is some 2.2 light years away from our own solar system. She also made important discoveries about "dwarf galaxies," whose stars are smaller and thus less luminous.

Swope was recognized and rewarded many times for her groundbreaking work. In addition to the Cannon Prize (which she received in 1968), she was given two awards from Barnard: a Distinguished Alumna Award in 1975 and a Medal of Distinction in 1980. In 1975 the University of Basel in Switzerland awarded Swope an honorary doctorate.

She retired from Mount Wilson in 1977; shortly thereafter she donated funds to the Las Campanas Observatory in Chile for the acquisition of a new telescope (which was named in her honor). Swope spent her remaining years in Pasadena, where she died on November 24, 1980.

FURTHER READING

Books

Payne–Gaposchkin, Cecilia (Katherine Haramundanis, ed.) *Cecilia Payne–Gaposchkin: An Autobiography and Other Recollections.* Cambridge, MA.: Cambridge University Press, 1984.

Shearer, Benjamin F. and Barbara S, Shearer, eds. *Notable Women in the Physical Sciences: A Biographical Dictionary.* Westport.:Greenwood Press, 1997.

Periodicals

Obituaries. *Physics Today* 34 (March 1981): 88.

Sketch by George A. Milite

Paula Szkody
1948–
American astronomer

Paula Szkody is known for her research on variable stars. She was responsible for the discovery of stars with field strengths previously believed to be non–existent, as well as the identification of a system with previously unknown properties.

Born in Detroit, Michigan, on July 17, 1948, Paula was the second of five children born to Julian Szkody, a mechanic and owner of a gas station, and Pauline Wolski Szkody. Szkody was both a tomboy and a bookworm as a child. She attended Dominican High, a private girls' school. She was drawn to science because it was the subject in which she had to work hardest. In high school, she became interested in astronomy after attending a series of science talks on life in the universe.

Szkody won a college scholarship when she placed second in the Detroit Science Fair. This allowed her to go to Michigan State University, where she graduated with a bachelor's in astrophysics in 1970. She was the only woman in her astronomy classes. During her junior year, Szkody spent time at the Observatory of Geneva in Switzerland to study with Edith Mueller. Mueller would later prove to be very influential in Szkody's studies.

Completing her master's in 1972 and her Ph.D. in 1975, Szkody began what would become her lifelong teaching and researching career at the University of Washington. Her doctoral dissertation was entitled "The Emission of Dwarf Novae," in which Szkody studied a system of close binaries. Just after completing her doctorate, Szkody discovered and identified the characteristics of the first system known to have a magnetic dwarf, named AM Her.

Szkody is one of only a handful of scientists in the world with a specialization in cataclysmic variables. In 1996, Szkody discovered a magnetic white dwarf in a cataclysmic binary with a field strength of 250MG, even though no one had believed in the possibility of a field over 100MG prior to her revelation.

Married since 1976 to Donald E. Brownlee, also an astronomer, Szkody is devoted to her husband and her children. When she does have time for herself, she enjoys skiiing, snorkelling, hiking, and traveling. She is involved with Expanding Your Horizons, a program that aids girls in career choices. Szkody is also a member of several professional organizations, such as Phi Beta Kappa, the American Astronomical Society, the International Astronomical Union, the Astronomical Society of the Pacific, the American Association for the Advancement of Science, the American Association of Variable Star Observers, and the American Academy of Arts and Sciences. Of her busy schedule, Szkody said in an interview with the contributer, "I really could use a forty–eight hour day, but it's such an interesting life."

SELECTED WRITINGS BY SZKODY:

Periodicals

"Outburst Spectra of Eleven Dwarf Novae." *Astrophysical Journal Supplement* 73 (1990): 441.

FURTHER READING

Books

Shearer, Benjamin F. and Barbara S. Shearer, eds. *Notable Women in the Physical Sciences.* Westport: Greenwood Press, 1997.

Other

Kiser, Helene Barker, interview with Paula Szkody conducted June 16, 1999.

"Paula's Astronomy Page." www.astro.washington.edu/szkody/

Sketch by Helene Barker Kiser

T

Mignon Talbot (Mount Holyoke College Archives and Special Collections. Reproduced by permission.)

Mignon Talbot
1869–1950
American geologist and educator

Mignon Talbot is known for expanding Mount Holyoke College's geology department during the early 1900s. She was the first woman to be elected to the Paleontological Society. She also discovered a rare dinosaur skeleton, *Podokesaurus holyokensis*, near Mount Holyoke. In John C. Haff's memorial in *Proceedings Volume of the Geological Society of America Annual Report for 1951* he says, "Miss Talbot derived exceedingly great pleasure from the firm friendships developed with students . . . and played a pioneer role in earth science development in this country."

Talbot was born August 16, 1869 in Iowa City, Iowa, to Harriet (Bliss) Talbot and Benjamin Talbot, both originally from New England. She grew up in Iowa City, where her father was superintendent of the Iowa School for the Deaf. She had one sister, Ellen, who eventually became a professor of philosophy at Mount Holyoke, and a brother, Herbert. From 1888–1892, Talbot attended Ohio State University to study geology where Edward Orton, professor of geology and state geologist, supervised her field trips to collect fossils from surrounding areas. His influence, and that of his successor Charles Prosser, is attributed to providing Talbot with her life-long interest in paleontology and stratigraphy.

Talbot received her A.B. degree from Ohio State in 1892 and then went abroad. Upon her return, she taught physical geography in the Columbus public schools from 1896-1902 before returning to Ohio State for five months of graduate work. She also spent several summers at Harvard and Cornell Universities in 1898 and 1901-1902, respectively.

Finds Rare Dinosaur Skeleton

In 1903, Talbot entered Yale University (her father was an alumni) to study with professor Charles Emerson Beecher. She received her doctorate, based on a taxonomic study that resulted in revision of many of the Helderbergian crinoids of New York State, in June 1904. In September of that year, Talbot became an instructor in geology at Mount Holyoke College. In 1905 she became associate professor and chairman and, three years later, was promoted to full professor, remaining as chair.

In 1909 Talbot became the first woman to be elected to the Paleontological Society and a year later she discovered a rare dinosaur skeleton, *Podokesaurus holyokensis*, near Mount Holyoke. This skeleton represented the only nearly complete one found in the northeast at the time. Talbot became a fellow of the Geological Society of America in 1913. In 1917, Williston Hall, where the majority of the early fossil collections Talbot had gathered were stored, was destroyed by fire. The collections had to be rebuilt from scratch through Talbot's efforts and, eight years later, the collections were larger than ever. She was elected vice president of the Paleontological Society in 1926. In 1928, she went on sabbatical leave to Austria, Switzerland, Italy, and the Balkan States. The work she did during this sabbatical was later incorporated as part of her classroom materials. The following year she was promoted to professor of geology and geography, as well as chairman of the combined departments.

Talbot's teaching methods were ahead of their time. In addition to taking students on field trips, she preferred individual instruction and teaching in small groups. She also encouraged students to think independently and work out scientific problems on their own. Because opportunities for women geologists were few, she taught geology as a scientific discipline that also had cultural value. It is no doubt that this physically active, energetic woman was an important role model for her students.

In 1935 Talbot retired from Mount Holyoke, where during her tenure, she made many significant contributions to the department and was a long-term member of various college committees. Among other contributions, she expanded a large collection of Triassic footprints and ripple marks from many different locations, prepared an extensive invertebrate paleontology collection, created a large mineral collection, and enlarged departmental library facilities.

After her retirement Talbot remained active in both college and professional activities despite her poor health. She died on July 18, 1950 at the age of 80 after a long illness. Her life's work can be summed up in remarks made by Kenneth Caster, then secretary of the Paleontological Society, in 1950 in a letter to Talbot's sister: "Both as educator and scientist Miss Talbot was outstanding, and her contribution to geology–paleontology highly significant."

SELECTED WRITINGS BY TALBOT:

Periodicals

"A Contribution to a List of the Faunas of the Stafford Limestone of New York." *American Journal of Science* 16, no. 166, ser. 4 (1903): 148– 150.

"*Podokesaurus holyokensis*, A New Dinosaur from the Triassic of the Connecticut Valley." *American Journal of Science*, 4th ser. 186,469– 479.

"Revision of the New York Helderbergian Crinoids." *American Journal of Science* 20, no. 170 ser. 4 (1905): 17–33.

FURTHER READING

Books

Aldrich, Michelle. "Women in Geology." Edited by Patricia Farnes and G. Kass–Simon. *Women of Science: Righting the Record.* Bloomington: Indiana University Press, 1990, pp 42–67.

Periodicals

Haff, John. "Memorial to Mignon Talbot." *Proceedings Volume of the Geological Society of America, Annual Report for 1951* (July 1952): 157– 158.

Other

Biographical File on Mignon Talbot, Mount Holyoke College Archives and Special Collections

Sketch by Laurel M. Sheppard

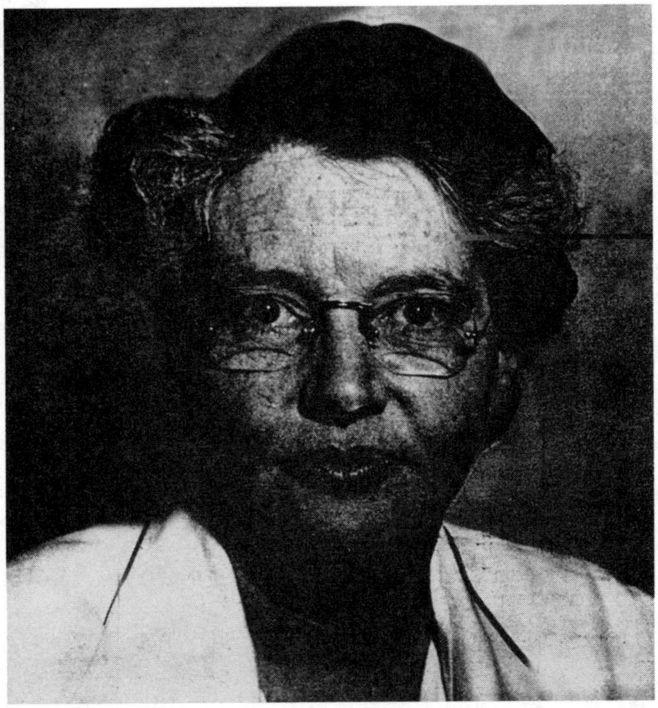

Helen Taussig (The Library of Congress.)

Helen Brooke Taussig
1898–1986
American pediatrician and cardiologist

Physician and cardiologist Helen Brooke Taussig spent her career as the head of the Children's Heart Clinic at Johns Hopkins University. In the course of her work with young children, she discovered that cyanotic infants—known as "blue–babies"—died of insufficient circulation to the lungs, not of cardiac arrest, as had been thought. She and colleague Dr. Alfred Blalock developed a surgical procedure, the Blalock–Taussig shunt, to correct the problem. First used in 1944, the Blalock–Taussig shunt has saved the lives of thousands of children. In 1961, after investigating reports of numerous birth defects in Germany, Taussig determined that the cause was use of the drug Thalidomide, and it was her intervention that prevented Thalidomide from being sold in the United States. She was the recipient of numerous honorary degrees and awards, including the Medal of Freedom in 1964 and the 1977 National Medal of Science.

Taussig was born on May 24, 1898, in Cambridge, Massachusetts, the youngest of four children of well–known Harvard economist Frank William Taussig. Her mother, Edith Guild Taussig, who had attended Radcliffe College and was interested in the natural sciences, died of tuberculosis when Helen was eleven years old. Like her mother, Taussig attended Radcliffe, where she played championship tennis. However, wishing to be further removed from the shadow of her well–known father, she transferred to the University of California at Berkeley, where she earned her B.A. in 1921.

Having decided on a career in medicine, Taussig's educational choices were limited by sex discrimination. Although she began her studies at Harvard University, the medical school did not admit women to its regular curriculum, and would not begin to do so until 1945. Taussig enrolled in Harvard's School of Public Health, where, like other women, she was permitted to take courses but not allowed to work toward obtaining a degree. She also was permitted to study histology as a special student in the medical school. After her studies at Harvard, Taussig took anatomy at nearby Boston University. There, her anatomy professor, Alexander Begg, suggested that she apply herself to the study of the heart, which she did. Also following Begg's advice, Taussig submitted her application to attend the medical school at Johns Hopkins University, where she was accepted.

During her four years of study at Johns Hopkins Medical School, Taussig worked at the Hopkins Heart Station. After receiving her M.D. in 1927, she spent another year there as a fellow, followed by an additional year and a half there as a pediatric intern. During this time, Taussig served as an attending physician at the recently established Pediatric Cardiac Clinic. The new chair of pediatrics, Edwards A. Park, recognized Taussig's abilities and became her mentor. Upon the completion of her pediatric internship in 1930, she was appointed physician–in–charge of the Pediatric Cardiac Clinic in the Harriet Lane Home, the children's division at Johns Hopkins. Taussig would spend her entire career at Johns Hopkins until her retirement in 1963. In 1946 she was appointed associate professor of pediatrics, and was promoted to full professor in 1959, the first woman in the history of the Medical School to hold that title.

Groundbreaking Research on the Child's Heart

Taussig began her studies of congenital heart disease at the Pediatric Cardiac Clinic in 1930. Over the years she examined and treated hundreds of children whose hearts were damaged by rheumatic fever, as well as those with congenital heart disease. She developed new observational methods that led to a new understanding of pediatric heart problems. First Taussig became accomplished in the use of the fluoroscope, a new instrument which passed x–ray beams through the body and projected an image of the heart, lungs, and major arteries onto a florescent screen. Second, she used the electrocardiograph which makes a graphic record of the heart's movements. Third, she became expert at diagnosis through physical examination—made more complex in her case due to the fact that Taussig was somewhat deaf as a result of childhood whooping cough and unable to use a stethoscope, thereby necessitating her reliance on visual examination.

Taussig gradually realized that the blueness of cyanotic children was the result of insufficient oxygen in the blood. In the normal heart, bluish blood from the periphery of the body enters the right atrium (upper receiving chamber) of the heart and then goes to the right ventricle (the lower pumping chamber) to be pumped through a major artery to the lungs. In the lungs, the blood receives a new supply of oxygen that changes its color to bright red. Then it returns to the heart, entering the left atrium and descending to the left ventricle which pumps it to the rest of the body. The two sides of the heart are kept separate by a wall called the septum. Taussig discovered that the insufficient oxygen level of the blood of "blue–babies" was usually the result of either a leaking septum or an overly narrow artery leading from the left ventricle to the lungs. Although at that time surgeons were unable enter the heart to repair the septum surgically, Taussig believed that it might be possible either to repair the artery, or to attach a new vessel that would perform the same function.

She persuaded Dr. Alfred Blalock, the chairman of the Hopkins Department of Surgery, to work on the problem. Blalock was a vascular surgeon who had done experimental research on an artificial artery with the assistance of long–time associate Vivian Thomas. Accepting Taussig's challenge, Blalock set Thomas to work on the technical problems. During the next year and a half, Thomas developed the technical procedures, using about two hundred dogs as experimental animals. In 1944, although earlier than Thomas had planned, the technique was tried on a human infant, a desperately ill patient of Taussig's named Eileen Saxon. With Taussig as an observer and Thomas standing by to give advice concerning the correct suturing of the artery, Blalock performed the surgery successfully. A branch of the aorta that normally went to the infant's arm was connected to the lungs. In the years that followed, the procedure, known as the Blalock–Taussig shunt, saved the lives of thousands of cyanotic children.

The fame of the Pediatric Cardiac Clinic grew rapidly. As they became flooded with patients, Blalock and Taussig developed team methods for dealing with the different phases of treatment. Their management methods became the model for many cardiac centers, as well as other kinds of medical care. Taussig's growing reputation also brought her numerous students. She trained a whole generation of pediatric cardiologists and wrote the standard textbook of the field, *Congenital Malformations of the Heart,* first published in 1947. In addition to her work in congenital heart disease, she carried out research on rheumatic fever, the leading cause of heart problems in children. Taussig is considered the founder of the specialty of pediatric cardiology. Neither her scientific and clinical acumen, nor her enormously demanding schedule, ever prevented Taussig from being a warm, compassionate physician to her many patients and their families. She followed her patients for years, even after her own retirement. She never found it necessary to distance herself from the critically–ill children that she treated, or from their parents. Her warmth and ability to see and treat people as individuals has been recalled by many who knew her.

Influences U.S. Policy on a Dangerous Drug

In the 1950s Taussig served on numerous national and international committees. In 1962, a German graduate of her training program told her of the striking increase in his country of phocomelia, a rare congenital defect in which infants were born with severely deformed limbs. The defect was thought, but not yet proven, to be associated with a popular sedative called Contergan that was sold throughout Germany and other European countries and often taken by women to counteract nausea during early pregnancy. Taussig decided to investigate for herself and spent six weeks in Germany visiting clinics, examining babies with the abnormalities, and interviewing their doctors and mothers. She noted the absence of such birth defect in the infants of American soldiers living at U.S. military installations in Germany where the drug was banned. But there was one exception: a baby whose mother had gone off the post to obtain Contergan was born severely deformed. Taussig's testimony was instrumental in the U.S. Food and Drug Administration's rejection of the application from the William S. Merrell Company to market the drug they renamed Thalidomide in the United States.

Although Taussig formally retired in 1963, she remained deeply involved as a scientist, a clinician, and an activist in causes that affected the health of children. She fought for the right of scientists to use animals in experimental studies and advocated that women in the United States be able to choose to terminate their pregnancies through abortion. She was the author of a hundred major scientific publications, forty–one of which were written after her retirement. She occupied a home in Baltimore, often visited by guests and friends, and owned the cottage in Cape Cod where she had spent many happy childhood summers. Taussig enjoyed fishing, swimming, and gardening, as well as caring for her many pets. In the late 1970s she moved to a retirement community near Philadelphia. She became interested in the embryological causes of congenital heart defects and had begun a study of the hearts of birds when, on May 21, 1986, while driving some of her fellow retirees to vote in a primary election, she was killed in an automobile accident at the age of 87.

SELECTED WRITINGS BY TAUSSIG:

Books

Congenital Malformations of the Heart, Commonwealth Fund, 1947, second edition (two volumes), Commonwealth Fund/Harvard University Press, 1960.

Periodicals

(With Alfred Blalock) "The Surgical Treatment of Malformations of the Heart in which there is Pulmonary Stenosis or Pulmonary Atresia." *Journal of the American Medical Association* 128 (May 19, 1945): 189–202.

"The Thalidomide Syndrome." *Scientific American* 207 (August, 1962): 29–35.

FURTHER READING

Books

Baldwin, Joyce, *To Heal the Heart of A Child: Helen Taussig, M.D.* (juvenile), Walker, 1992.

Nuland, Sherwin B., *Doctors: The Biography of Medicine.* Knopf, 1988, pp. 422–456.

Periodicals

Harvey, W. Proctor, "A Conversation with Helen Taussig." *Medical Times* 106 (November, 1978): 28–44.

Sketch by Pamela O. Long

Olga Taussky-Todd
1906–1995
Austro-Hungarian-born American mathematician

Olga Taussky–Todd is best remembered for her research on matrix theory and algebraic number theory. Matrix theory is the study of sets of elements in a rectangular array that are subject to operations such as multiplication or addition according to specified rules. Number theory is the study of integers and their relationships. During a long, productive career, Taussky–Todd published over 200 research papers and other writings on a wide range of mathematical topics. In 1964 she was named "Woman of the Year" by the *Los Angeles Times*, and in 1970 she received the Ford Prize for an article on sums of squares. Taussky–Todd was also well known for her lectures. In 1981, she gave the **Emmy Noether** Lecture at the annual meeting of the Association for Women in Mathematics, taking as the subject of her talk the many aspects of Pythagorean triangles.

Taussky–Todd was born on August 30, 1906, in Olmütz, Austria–Hungary (now Olomouc, Czechoslovakia). She was the second of three daughters born to Julius David Taussky and Ida Pollach Taussky. Her father was an industrial chemist who also worked as a newspaper journalist. He encouraged his daughters to take their education seriously. Her mother was an intelligent person as well, but had little formal education. In an autobiographical essay published in *Mathematical People: Profiles and Interviews*, Taussky–Todd recalled of her mother: "She was rather bewildered about our studies and compared herself to a mother hen who had been made to hatch duck eggs and then

Olga Taussky-Todd (Reproduced by permission of the Estate of Olga Taussky-Todd.)

felt terrified on seeing her offspring swimming in a pool." However, Taussky–Todd also noted that her mother was more willing than her father to accept the notion of girls actually using their educations later in life to earn a living.

Shortly before Taussky–Todd turned three, her family moved to Vienna. Midway through World War I, the family moved again, this time to Linz in upper Austria. Her father was manager of a vinegar factory there, and he often asked Taussky–Todd to help with such chores as calculating how much water to add to mixtures of various vinegars to achieve the right acidity. Taussky–Todd's best subjects in school were grammar and expository writing. As a girl in Linz, she began a lifelong hobby of writing poems.

First Forays into Number Theory

During Taussky–Todd's last year of high school, her father died, leaving the family without an income. Taussky–Todd took jobs tutoring and working at the vinegar factory. The next year she entered the University of Vienna, determined to prove that her plan to study mathematics was a practical one. Among her professors was noted number theorist Philip Furtwängler. When the time came for Taussky–Todd to decide upon a thesis topic, Furtwängler suggested class field theory. In mathematics, a field is a set that has two operations, addition and multiplication. For each operation, the set is closed, associative, and commutative, and it has an identity element and inverses. As Taussky–Todd wrote in *Mathematical People*, "This decision had an enormous influence on my whole future . . . It helped my career, for there were only a very few people working in this still not fully understood subject. It was definitely a prestige subject."

In 1930, Taussky–Todd received her doctoral degree in mathematics. Based on her thesis, she was promptly offered a temporary post at the University of Göttingen in Germany, where she helped edit David Hilbert's writings on number theory. She also edited Emil Artin's lectures on class field theory. By 1932, the growing political tensions in Germany made it unwise for Jews such as Taussky–Todd to stay there. She returned to Vienna, where she worked as a mathematics assistant. Among those she assisted was Hans Hahn, one of her former professors. Hahn had first introduced Taussky–Todd to functional analysis, the study of a particular type of function.

Travels to United States and England

Taussky–Todd applied for and received a three–year science fellowship from Girton College at Cambridge University in England. It was agreed that she could spend the first year of the fellowship at Bryn Mawr College in Pennsylvania. Taussky–Todd took a few English lessons and embarked for the United States in 1934. At Bryn Mawr, she had the chance to work with Emmy Noether, whom she had earlier met at Göttingen. Noether, who was 24 years older than Taussky–Todd, was already an established figure in modern abstract algebra. Taussky–Todd enjoyed accompanying the older woman on her weekly trips to Princeton University whenever possible. However, she also found that Noether had a critical side. As Taussky–Todd recalled in *Mathematical People*, "She disliked my Austrian accent, my less abstract thinking, and she was almost frightened that I would obtain a [permanent] position before she would."

In 1935, Taussky–Todd traveled to Girton College at Cambridge, where she spent the last two years of her fellowship. The mathematical interests of her colleagues there did not quite match her own. However, she did get some much–needed practice at teaching in English. In 1937 she took a junior–level teaching position at one of the women's colleges at the University of London. The hours were arduous, but she still found time to attend professional seminars. It was at one such seminar that she met fellow mathematician John (Jack) Todd. The two were married in 1938.

Growing Interest in Matrix Theory

Soon thereafter World War II broke out, bringing not only political but also personal upheaval. The newlyweds moved 18 times during the war. For a while, the couple lived in Belfast, Ireland, where Taussky–Todd first began to focus on matrix theory while teaching at Queen's University. A year later Taussky–Todd returned to work at her London college, which had since been relocated to Oxford for safety reasons. In 1943, she took a research job in aerodynamics with the Ministry of Aircraft Production.

There she joined a group that was studying flutter problems in combat aircraft. Flutter refers to the self–excited oscillations of part of an airplane such as the wings. A corresponding problem in mathematics involves the stability of certain matrices. As a result, this job just strengthened Taussky–Todd's growing fascination with matrix theory.

In 1947 Taussky–Todd's husband accepted an invitation to come to the United States for a year and work for the National Bureau of Standards. Taussky–Todd also joined the staff of the bureau field station at the University of California at Los Angeles. After this first year, the couple briefly went back to London. They soon returned to work again for the National Bureau of Standards, however, this time in Washington, D.C. Taussky–Todd's title at the Bureau was mathematical consultant, and as she noted in *Mathematical People*, "this I truly was, because everybody dumped on me all sorts of impossible jobs, from refereeing every paper that was written by a member or visitor to the group, to answering letters from people . . . to helping people on their research."

Ends Personal Odyssey at Caltech

Taussky–Todd and her husband made one last major career move in 1957, accepting positions at the California Institute of Technology. In an autobiographical essay in *Number Theory and Algebra*, Taussky–Todd wrote: "It seemed to me as if an odyssey of 20 years (I left Cambridge, England, in 1937) had ended. I could at last work again with academic freedom and have Ph.D. students." Some of her students went on to play starring roles in the burgeoning of matrix theory that has occurred since the 1960s. In 1977, Taussky–Todd was made a professor emeritus at Caltech.

Taussky–Todd received a number of honors in the course of her prolific career. Upon her retirement, two journals, the *Journal of Linear Algebra* and the *Journal of Linear and Multilinear Algebra*, published issues dedicated to her. Going a step further, the *Journal of Number Theory* published an entire book, *Algebra and Number Theory*, dedicated to Taussky–Todd and two others. Taussky–Todd received the Gold Cross of Honor from the Austrian government in 1978. A decade later she was awarded an honorary D.Sc. degree by the University of Southern California.

Taussky–Todd died on October 7, 1995, at her home in Pasadena, California. An obituary by Myrna Oliver in the *Los Angeles Times* referred to her as "one of the most prominent women mathematicians in the United States." Indeed, a lifetime of contributions to both pure and applied mathematics across several specialty areas had earned her the respect of mathematicians of both genders and many nationalities.

SELECTED WRITINGS BY TAUSSKY-TODD:

"Olga Taussky–Todd: An Autobiographical Essay." *Mathematical People: Profiles and Interviews.* Edited by Donald J. Albers and G.L. Alexanderson, 1985, pp. 310–336.

FURTHER READING

Books

Luchins, Edith H. "Olga Taussky–Todd." *Women of Mathematics:: A Biobibliographic Sourcebook.* Edited by Louise S. Grinstein and Paul J. Campbell. Westport, CT: Greenwood, 1987, pp. 225–235.

"Olga Taussky–Todd." *Number Theory and Algebra: Collected Papers Dedicated to Henry B. Mann, Arnold E. Ross, and Olga Taussky–Todd.* Edited by Hans Zassenhaus. New York: Academic Press, 1977.

Periodicals

Oliver, Myrna. "Olga Taussky–Todd: Noted Mathematician." *Los Angeles Times,* December 3, 1995, p. A44.

Other

Davis, Chandler. "Remembering Olga Taussky Todd." *Biographies of Women Mathematicians.* June 1997. http://www.scottlan.edu/lriddle/women/chronol.htm (July 22, 1997).

Sketch by Linda Wasmer Smith

Charlotte de Bernier (Scarbrough) Taylor
1806–1861
American entomologist

Charlotte de Bernier Taylor was one of the earliest American women field entomologists. She spent years observing and drawing insects. However, since Taylor published in the popular press rather than in scientific journals, her work went largely unrecognized.

The eldest daughter of William and Julia (Bernard) Scarbrough, Taylor was born in 1806 in Savannah, Georgia. Her father was a planter and merchant. He was famous for having sent the first steamship across the Atlantic in 1819. Taylor received her education at Madame Binze's, a fashionable school in New York City, where she became fluent in several languages. Following graduation, Taylor toured Europe. Returning to Savannah in 1829, she married James Taylor, a partner in the mercantile firm of Low, Taylor & Company. The couple had two daughters and a son. Charlotte Taylor's first published writings, in 1853 and 1854, were in a Boston magazine for children, during a period when Taylor was staying in New England.

From an early age, Taylor had been interested in insects, and she read widely, teaching herself entomology and other sciences. In her 30s, as a wealthy woman of leisure, Taylor resumed her entomological studies. She acquainted herself with the current agricultural and zoological literature and, using a powerful magnifying glass and a microscope, she began studying the insects that lived on cotton and wheat crops, the major Georgia plantation products. After 15 years of observing and drawing insects, Taylor began publishing her work in popular journals. "Microscopic Views of the Insect World," appeared in the *American Agriculturist*. About 20 of her articles, including "Insects Belonging to the Cotton Plant" were published in *Harper's New Monthly Magazine*. Taylor's writings were much in demand. They included detailed studies of the anatomy and natural history of silkworms and spiders, and she predicted the revival of the silk–producing industry in the United States. Taylor promoted methods for controlling agricultural pests at a time when most agriculturalists were concerned only with soil conditions and were ignorant of entomology. Her articles, written in a popular, literary style, included drawings, etchings, and paintings that were prepared with the assistance of her daughters, Virginia and Agnes.

With the approach of the Civil War, Taylor moved to the Isle of Man in the Irish Sea. She died there of tuberculosis in 1861, while working on a romance, a portrait of plantation life, and several new entomological articles.

SELECTED WRITINGS BY TAYLOR:

Periodicals

"The Unwelcome Guest of Insects." *Harper's New Monthly Magazine* (September 1858).

"Microscopic Views of the Insect World." *American Agriculturist* (1858–59, 1860).

"Insects Belonging to the Cotton Plant." *Harper's New Monthly Magazine* (June 1860).

FURTHER READING

Books

Bailey, Martha J. *American Women in Science: A Biographical Dictionary*. Denver: ABC–CLIO, 1994.

Malone, Dumas, editor. *Dictionary of American Biography*. Vol. 18. New York: Charles Scribner's Sons, 1936.

The National Cyclopaedia of American Biography. Vol. 2. New York: James T. White & Co., 1899.

Siegel, Patricia Joan and Kay Thomas Finley. *Women in the Scientific Search: An American Bio–bibliography, 1724–1979*. Metuchen, NJ: The Scarecrow Press, 1985.

Sketch by Margaret Alic

Valentina Tereshkova (The Library of Congress. Reproduced by permission.)

Valentina Tereshkova
1937–
Russian cosmonaut

Valentina Tereshkova was the first woman in space. Tereshkova took off from the Tyuratam Space Station in the Vostok VI in 1963, and orbited the Earth for almost three days, showing women had the same resistance to space as men. She then toured the world promoting Soviet science and feminism, and served on the Soviet Women's Committee and the Supreme Soviet Presidium. Valentina Vladimirovna "Valya" Tereshkova was born on March 6, 1937, in the Volga River village of Maslennikovo. Her father, Vladimir Tereshkov, was a tractor driver. A Red Army soldier during World War II, he was killed when Valentina was two. Her mother Elena Fyodorovna Tereshkova, a worker at the Krasny Perekop cotton mill, single-handedly raised Valentina, her brother Vladimir and her sister Ludmilla in economically trying conditions. Assisting her mother, Valentina was not able to begin school until she was ten.

Tereshkova later moved to her grandmother's home in nearby Yaroslavl, where she worked as an apprentice at the tire factory in 1954. In 1955, she joined her mother and sister as a loom operator at the mill; meanwhile, she graduated by correspondence courses from the Light Industry Technical School. An ardent Communist, she joined the mill's Komsomol (Young Communist League), and soon advanced to the Communist Party.

In 1959, Tereshkova joined the Yaroslavl Air Sports Club and became a skilled amateur parachutist. Inspired by the flight of Yuri Gagarin, the first man in space, she volunteered for the Soviet space program. Although she had no experience as a pilot, her 126–jump record gained her a position as a cosmonaut in 1961. Four candidates were chosen for a one–time woman–in–space flight; Tereshkova received an Air Force commission and trained for 18 months before becoming chief pilot of the Vostok VI. Admiring fellow cosmonaut Yuri Gagarin was quoted as saying, "It was hard for her to master rocket techniques, study spaceship designs and equipment, but she tackled the job stubbornly and devoted much of her own time to study, poring over books and notes in the evening."

At 12:30 PM on June 16, 1963, Junior Lieutenant Tereshkova became the first woman to be launched into space. Using her radio callsign Chaika (Seagull), she reported, "I see the horizon. A light blue, a beautiful band. This is the Earth. How beautiful it is! All goes well." She was later seen smiling on Soviet and European TV, pencil and logbook floating weightlessly before her face. Vostok VI made 48 orbits (1,200,000 miles) in 70 hours, 50 minutes, coming within 3.1 miles of the previously launched Vostok V, piloted by cosmonaut Valery Bykovsky. Tereshkova's flight confirmed Soviet test results that women had the same resistance as men to the physical and psychological stresses of space.

Upon her return, she and Bykovsky were hailed in Moscow's Red Square. On June 22, at the Kremlin, she was named a Hero of the Soviet Union and was decorated by Presidium Chairman Leonid Brezhnev with the Order of Lenin and the Gold Star Medal. A symbol of emancipated Soviet feminism, she toured the world as a goodwill ambassador promoting the equality of the sexes in the Soviet Union, receiving a standing ovation at the United Nations. With Gagarin, she traveled to Cuba in October as a guest of the Cuban Women's Federation, and then went to the International Aeronautical Federation Conference in Mexico.

On November 3, 1963, Tereshkova married Soviet cosmonaut Colonel Andrian Nikolayev, who had orbited the earth 64 times in 1962 in the Vostok III. Their daughter Yelena Adrianovna Nikolayeva was born on June 8, 1964, and was carefully studied by doctors fearful of her parents' space exposure, but no ill effects were found. After her flight, Tereshkova continued as an aerospace engineer in the space program; she also worked in Soviet politics, feminism and culture. She was a Deputy to the Supreme Soviet between 1966 and 1989, and a People's Deputy from 1989 to 1991. Meanwhile, she was a member of the Supreme Soviet Presidium from 1974 to 1989. During the years from 1968 to 1987, she also served on the Soviet Women's Committee, becoming its head in 1977. Tereshkova headed the USSR's International Cultural and Friendship Union from 1987 to 1991, and subsequently chaired the Russian Association of International Cooperation.

Tereshkova summarized her views on women and science in her 1970 "Women in Space" article in the American journal *Impact of Science on Society:* "I believe a woman should always remain a woman and nothing feminine should be alien to her. At the same time I strongly feel that no work done by a woman in the field of science or culture or whatever, however vigourous or demanding, can enter into conflict with her ancient 'wonderful mission'——to love, to be loved——and with her craving for the bliss of motherhood. On the contrary, these two aspects of her life can complement each other perfectly."

SELECTED WRITINGS BY TERESHKOVA:

Periodicals

"Women in Space." *Impact of Science on Society* 20, no.1 (January–March, 1970): 5–12.

FURTHER READING

Books

Drexel, John, ed. *Facts on File Encyclopedia of the 20th Century.* Facts on File, 1991, pp. 884–885.

O'Neill, Lois Decker. "Farthest Out of All: The First Woman in Space." In *Women's Book of World Records and Achievements.* Anchor Books, 1979, pp. 739–740.

Sharpe, Mitchell. *'It is I, Sea Gull': Valentina Tereshkova, First Woman in Space.* Crowell, 1975.

Uglow, Jennifer S., ed. *The International Dictionary of Women's Biography.* Continuum, 1982, p. 461.

Periodicals

"Soviets Orbit Woman Cosmonaut." *New York Times* (June 17, 1963): 1, 8.

"2 Russians Land in Central Asia after Space Trip." *New York Times* (June 20, 1963): 1, 3.

Sketch by Julian A. Smith

Giuliana Cavaglieri Tesoro
1921–
Italian-American chemist

Giuliana Cavaglieri Tesoro is famous worldwide for her work on polymers. She is a pioneer in the research on their chemical modification, and has spent many years working with the textile industry and various research organizations. Tesoro has been granted over 100 patents in the field.

Giuliana Cavaglieri was born June 21, 1921, in Venice, Italy, the baby of the family. Both her father, Gino Cavaglieri, a civil engineer, and her mother, Margherita Maroni Cavaglieri, prominent and wealthy Jews, held college degrees. Tesoro was a precocious student, beginning third grade at the age of six.

Tesoro's father died in 1934, and four years later she graduated from Liceo Classico Marco Polo. However, she was unable to go on to an Italian university. At the time, laws prohibited the entrance of Jews. Consequently, she moved to Geneva to study and work at the General Hospital, where she later received an x–ray technician diploma. Shortly after this time, the entire family immigrated to the United States.

Tesoro enrolled at Yale University, and received her Ph.D. in organic chemistry in 1942 when she was 21 years old. The following year, she married Victor Tesoro, a newswriter she had met at Yale. The couple later had two children, Claudia and Andrew. In addition, in 1946 Tesoro became a United States citizen.

After graduation, Tesoro worked as a research chemist for Calco Chemical Company, moving to the same position at Onyx Oil and Chemical Company after one year. At Onyx, she quickly moved up through the ranks, in 1946 becoming head of the organic synthesis department, in 1957 becoming assistant director of research, and in 1955, associate director. In 1958, Tesoro became assistant director of organic research for J. P. Stevens and Company, Incorporated. After 10 years at Stevens, she became a senior chemist for the Textile Research Institute and a year later for Burlington Industries, Incorporated, where she was promoted to director of chemical research in 1971.

During her years as a bench scientist, Tesoro contributed greatly to polymer research. She holds over 100 patents and has written over 100 papers and several books on the field. Her work contributed to the understanding of cross–linking agents, fiber chemical modification, flame retardants and combustion, permanent press properties, and pharmaceutical synthesis.

In 1972, Tesoro joined the faculty of Massachusetts Institute of Technology as a visiting professor, and in 1976 became adjunct professor and senior research scientist. In 1982, Tesoro became a research professor at Polytechnic Institute, where she supervises research in addition to her teaching duties. She was also an editor of *Textile Research Journal*. Despite all of her accomplishments, Tesoro says that nothing is more important to her than her family, and credits them with much of her success as a scientist.

Among her many awards, Tesoro has received the American Dyestuff Reporter Award, the Achievement Award of the Society of Women Engineers, and the Olney Medal, in addition to recognition from Amita and Polymer News. Her memberships include National Research Council committees, the Fiber Society, the American Association for Textile Chemists and Colorists, the American Association for the Advancement of Science, Sigma Xi, the American Institute of Chemists, the American Chemical Society, and a Gordon Research Conference committee. Tesoro lectures frequently on polymers at worldwide conferences.

SELCTED WRITINGS BY TESORO:

Periodicals

"An effective new antistatic finish." *Modern Textiles Magazine* (1957): 47–48.

"Recycling of synthetic polymers for energy conservation." *Plymer News* (1987): 269–268.

"Research on chemical modification of cellulose." *Pure and Applied Chemistry* (1976): 239–245.

FURTHER READING

Books

Bailey, Martha J. *American Women in Science*. Denver: ABC–CLIO, 1994.

Grinstein, Louise S., et. al, eds. *Women in Chemistry and Physics: A Bibliographic Sourcebook*. Westport, CT: Greenwood Press, 1993.

Sketch by Helene Barker Kiser

Marie Tharp
1920–
American oceanographic cartographer and geologist

Marie Tharp is a mapmaker who charted the bottom of the ocean at a time when little was known about undersea geology. Her detailed maps showed features that helped other scientists understand the structure and evolution of the sea floor. In particular, Tharp's discovery of the valley that divides the Mid–Atlantic Ridge convinced other geologists that sea floor was being created at these ridges and spreading outward. The confirmation of "seafloor spreading" led to the eventual acceptance of the theory of continental drift, now called plate tectonics.

Tharp was born in Ypsilanti, Michigan, on July 30, 1920. Her father, William Edgar Tharp, was a soil surveyor for the United States Department of Agriculture's Bureau of Chemistry and Soils; he told his daughter to choose a job simply because she liked doing it. Marie's mother, Bertha Louise (Newton) Tharp, taught German and Latin. The family moved frequently because of William Tharp's mapping assignments across the country. Marie Tharp attended twenty–four different public schools in Iowa, Michigan, Indiana, Alabama (where she almost flunked out of the 5th grade in Selma), Washington, D.C., New York, and Ohio. In 1943 she received her bachelor's degree from Ohio University.

Since most young men were fighting in World War II at the time Tharp graduated, the University of Michigan opened the doors of its geology department to women for the first time. Tharp entered the masters program, which trained students in basic geology and then guaranteed them a job in the petroleum industry. Graduating in 1944, Tharp was hired as a junior geologist with Stanolind Oil & Gas in Tulsa, Oklahoma. Women were not permitted to search for oil in the field, so Tharp found herself organizing the maps and data for the all–male crews. While working for Stanolind, Tharp earned a B.S. in mathematics from the University of Tulsa in 1948.

The year of her second bachelor's degree, Tharp moved to Columbia University, where a group of scientists were about to revolutionize the study of oceanography. Hired as a research assistant by geologist Maurice Ewing, Tharp actually ended up helping graduate students with their data; she never told anyone that she had a graduate degree in geology. One student, Bruce Heezen, asked for help with his ocean profiles so often that after a while Tharp worked with him exclusively. Heezen and Tharp were to work closely together until his death in 1977. In 1950 the geophysical laboratory moved from Columbia University to the Lamont Geological Observatory in Palisades, New York.

Before the early 1950s, scientists knew very little about the structure of the ocean floor. It was much easier and cheaper to study geology on land. But without knowledge of the structure and evolution of the seafloor, scientists could not form a complete idea of how the entire earth worked. In the 1940s, most people believed that the earth was a shrinking globe, cooling and contracting from its initial hot birth. The work of Heezen, Tharp, and other geologists in the next decade—who gathered data on the sea floor using echo sounding equipment—helped replace that idea with the model of plate tectonics, where thin crustal "plates" shift around on the earth's mantle, colliding and grinding into each other to push up mountains and cause earthquakes.

The Mid–Atlantic Ridge, a mountainous bump that runs roughly parallel to and between the coastlines of the Americas and Africa, was one of the first topographical features on the sea floor to be identified. Initial studies were undertaken by those aboard the British ship *H.M.S. Challenger,* who discovered in the 1870s that the rise in the center of the Atlantic acted as a barrier between different water temperatures; and by those aboard the German ship *Meteor* who between 1925 and 1927 revealed the Mid–Atlantic Ridge as rugged and mountainous. The *Meteor* staff also found several "holes" in the center of the Ridge, but did not connect these holes into the continuous rift valley that they were later discovered to be. In the 1930s, the British geologists Seymour Sewell and John Wiseman suspected that a rift valley split the Ridge, but World War II prevented an expedition to confirm this.

By 1950, when Tharp and Heezen moved to Lamont, the time was right for a series of discoveries. In 1952, the pair decided to make a map of the North Atlantic floor that would show how it would look if all the water were drained away. This type of "physiographic" diagram looked very different from the usual method of drawing contour lines for ocean floor of equal depth. Heezen and Tharp chose the physiographic method because it was a more realistic, three–dimensional picture of the ocean floor, and also because contours were classified by the U.S. Navy from 1952 to 1962.

Maps the Ocean Floor

Tharp assembled her first drawing of the North Atlantic ocean floor in 1952, after rearranging Heezen's data into six seafloor profiles that spanned the Atlantic. This initial map showed a deep valley dividing the crest of the Mid–Atlantic Ridge. Tharp pointed out the valley to Heezen. "He groaned and said, 'It cannot be. It looks too much like continental drift,' " Tharp wrote later in *Natural History.* The valley represented the place where newly–formed rocks came up from inside the earth, splitting apart the mid–ocean ridge. At the time, Heezen, like most scientists, thought that continental drift was impossible.

While Tharp was working on detailing and clarifying the first map, Heezen kept another assistant busy plotting the location of the epicenters of North Atlantic earthquakes. Beno Gutenberg and Charles F. Richter had already pointed out that earthquake epicenters followed the Mid–Atlantic Ridge quite closely. But Heezen's group found that the epicenters actually fell within the suspected rift valley. The association of topography with seismicity convinced Tharp that the valley was indeed real.

It took Heezen eight months to agree. By studying rift valleys in eastern Africa, Heezen convinced himself that the land in Africa was simply a terrestrial analogy to what was going on in the middle of the Atlantic: the earth's crust was splitting apart in a huge tensional crack. Heezen then began to wonder whether the earthquake epicenters that had been recorded in the centers of other oceans might also lie in rift valleys. Perhaps, he thought, all the mid–ocean ridges could be connected into a huge 40,000 mile system.

Heezen told Maurice Ewing, director of Lamont, of the valley's discovery. For several years, only Lamont scientists knew of its existence. Heezen presented it to the scientific community in several talks during 1956. In 1959, most of the remaining skeptics were convinced by an underwater movie of the valley, made by French oceanographer Jacques Cousteau towing a camera across it. Today scientists understand how the rift valley represents the pulling apart of the seafloor as the new rock spreads outward from the ridge.

Heezen and Tharp printed their first edition of the North Atlantic map for a second time in 1959. By this time they knew that the Mid–Atlantic Ridge was cut by east–west breaks, now called transform faults. Heezen and Tharp had confirmed only one of these breaks, but they didn't know its exact length or direction. So in its place on the map they put a large legend to cover the space. In the following years, Tharp and Heezen improved their North Atlantic map and expanded their work to cover the globe, including the South Atlantic, Indian, Arctic, Antarctic, and Pacific oceans. In 1977, three weeks before Heezen's death, they published the World Ocean Floor Panorama, based on all available geological and geophysical data, as well as more than five million miles of ocean–floor soundings. In 1978 Tharp and Heezen received the Hubbard Medal of the National Geographic Society.

After about 15 years of work behind the scenes, Tharp finally went on research cruises herself, including trips to Africa, the Caribbean, Hawaii, Japan, New Zealand, and Australia. She retired from Lamont in 1983. Since then she has run a map distributing business in South Nyack, New York, and occasionally consults for various oceanographers. She also keeps Heezen's scientific papers and has written several articles on his life and work. Tharp enjoys gardening in her spare time.

SELECTED WRITINGS BY THARP:

Books

"Mapping the Ocean Floor 1947–1977." *The Ocean Floor.* Edited by R. A. Scrutton and M. Talwani. Wiley, 1982.

Periodicals

"Mappers of the Deep." *Natural History* (October 1986): 49–62.

Other

(With Bruce C. Heezen) "World Ocean Floor" (map), painted by H. C. Berann, Office of Naval Research, 1977.

FURTHER READING

Periodicals

Oceanus (winter 1973–74): 44–48.

Sketch by Alexandra Witze

Theano

fl. 6th Century B.C.

Greek natural philosopher, mathematician, and physician

Theano is one of the earliest women scientists in the historical record. The wife of the famous natural philosopher and mathematician Pythagoras, she wrote treatises and was responsible for helping to spread Pythagorean science throughout the ancient world.

Theano, who lived in the sixth century B.C., may have been a native of Croton in Southern Italy, the daughter of Brontinos or Brotinos. According to other sources, she may have been from Crete, the daughter of Pythonax. Greek science originated with Pythagoras of Samos. He had settled in the Greek colony of Croton between 540 and 520 B.C.There he founded the Pythagorean Community, which was devoted to mathematical and philosophical endeavors. The community included women and men on an equal basis, and there were at least 28 female students and teachers at Pythagoras's school. Theano was Pythagoras's student and later his disciple and a teacher in the school. She apparently married Pythagoras when he was already an old man.

Since all members of the community wrote under the name of Pythagoras, and since the early Pythagoreans took an oath of secrecy, it is not possible to attribute scientific contributions to specific individuals. However, although only a few letters that are attributed to Theano have survived, she was credited with writing treatises on mathematics, physics, and medicine. She also was credited with writings on the Pythagorean concept of the "golden mean," or moderation. Theano, like other Pythagoreans, believed in the macrocosm and the microcosm: that the components of the human body, the microcosm, corresponded to the heavenly bodies, or the universe as a whole, the macrocosm. This was a paradigm, or underlying theory of science, from the time of the ancient Greeks until the Scientific Revolution of the seventeenth and eighteenth centuries.

The Pythagorean Community grew to include some 300 members in Croton. After they gained control of the local government, the democratic populace rebelled. They destroyed the Pythagorean School, and its members were killed or exiled. It is thought that Pythagoras was killed in the uprising and that Theano succeeded him as head of the dispersed Community. With the help of two of her daughters, Theano spread the Pythagorean science and philosophy throughout the Greek world and into Egypt. These daughters of Theano and Pythagoras may have included Damo or Arignote, who were credited with teaching Pythagorean science to other women. Myia, a disciple of Pythagoras, also has been referred to as his daughter, and the offshoots of the Pythagorean School continued to include women. Theano and her daughters had reputations as talented healers. They were said to have won a debate with the physician Euryphon on the question of fetal development, an issue of importance to science throughout all of recorded history. The women argued that the fetus was viable by the seventh month.

As student, disciple, and successor of Pythagoras, the founder of Greek science, Theano must be considered to represent the very beginnings of women's participation in the development of western science.

FURTHER READING

Books

Alic, Margaret. *Hypatia's Heritage: A History of Women in Science from Antiquity through the Nineteenth Century.* Boston: Beacon Press,1986.

Ogilvie, Marilyn Bailey. *Women in Science, Antiquity through the Nineteenth Century: A Biographical Dictionary with Annotated Bibliography.* Cambridge: MIT Press, 1991.

Sketch by Margaret Alic

Marie Thiroux d'Arconville
1720–1805
French anatomist

A prolific writer on a variety of scientific and other subjects, Marie Thiroux d'Arconville also conducted original research and made major contributions to the study of anatomy. However, since she published her works anonymously or under pseudonyms to protect herself and her family from public censure and ridicule, her contributions to science have gone largely unrecognized. Some sources refer to her under the name of Geneviève Charlotte d'Arconville.

Very little is known of Thiroux d'Arconville's background or personal life. She was born in 1720, into an aristocratic Parisian family, at a time when educated Parisian women hosted intellectual and scientific salons. The Jardin Royale des Plantes, the royal botanical gardens in Paris, included a natural history museum, a chemistry laboratory, and an anatomical amphitheater. Courses there were free and open to the public and hundreds of people attended chemistry lessons and human dissections, including Thiroux d'Arconville. Although she never hosted a scientific salon, she did meet with various scientists, including the French philosopher Voltaire and the famous chemist Antoine Lavoisier. At age 14 she became engaged to a parliamentary representative and after their marriage she devoted herself to her husband and children.

At age 23, an attack of smallpox left Thiroux d'Arconville terribly scarred. She responded to this by withdrawing from society, and dressing as an elderly woman. She also retired to her study with her books on physics, chemistry, medicine, and natural history, as well as works of history and morality. The Paris library supplied her with additional books and manuscripts and she also credited a laboratory in her home.

Thiroux d'Arconville's most significant contribution to science was her French translation of Edinburgh anatomist Alexander Monro's *Anatomy*. Monro's 1726 work was one of the first to describe the female skeleton. Thiroux d'Arconville's translation, in two volumes, included her commentary and observations, as well as anatomical illustrations prepared under her direction and based on her dissections. Hers were among the very first drawings of a female skeleton, as distinguished from that of a male. All anatomized drawings of that time were of male skeletons. Nevertheless, her female skeleton was stylized: the bones were thin and delicate; the skull was smaller in proportion to the body than her drawings of a male skull, in accord with the prevalent, but fallacious, belief that men had larger brains than women; and her ribs were very narrow, thereby exaggerating the size of the female pelvis. In the legend to the illustration, Thiroux d'Arconville commented that the female spine was more curved than the male's. She may have been emphasizing those features that she associated with femininity; however, it also is possible that her model may have been disfigured from years of wearing a corset. In any case, it was almost 40 years before another anatomist portrayed the female skeleton. In 1829, when John Barclay published his anatomical work, he chose Thiroux d'Arconville's as the best rendition of the female skeleton. He also used her illustration of a child's skeleton. Thiroux d'Arconville herself believed that hers were the best anatomical renditions created to date.

In 1759, the Paris Académie Royale des Sciences published Thiroux d'Arconville's *Osteology* under the name of Jean–J. Sue, an academy member, professor of anatomy at the royal college of surgery, and the royal censor for surgical books. Apparently even Monro believed it was Sue who had translated his work. However, in the preface published with her collected works, edited by her secretary, Thiroux d'Arconville described how she supervised the drawing of the illustrations and added her own observations to Monro's text. As Londa Schiebinger quoted from this preface: "The figures were drawn under my eyes and there were many that I had redone several times in order to correct a slight fault."

Thiroux d'Arconville's experiments on organic decomposition, or putrefaction, were published in 1766. This was a new field of research, stimulated by concern about food preservation. Over a period of five years, Thiroux d'Arconville experimented with 32 classes of substances which accelerated or delayed decomposition. For example, she studied how beef decomposed in air and in water and how mixtures of acids and mineral waters affected the speed of decomposition. She strongly criticized the famous Dutch physician Hermann Boerhaave, who first isolated urea, for claiming that putrefaction applied only to vegetable matter.

She also introduced bichloride of mercury for use as an antibiotic.

Thiroux d'Arconville's French translations of English works included Peter Shaw's *Chemical Lectures*, which she published in 1759. She also wrote some 16 works on medicine, natural history and philosophy. Her medical works included publications on the action of the heart, surgeries, fractures, plague, and diseases of cattle. In 1744 she published a three-volume biography of Marie de Médicis, former queen and regent of France. She also wrote a biography of King Francis II of France, the husband of Mary, Queen of Scots, and works on morality, one of which was attributed to the French philosopher Denis Diderot. She apparently gave a speech before the Berlin Academy in January of 1770, which was attributed both to her and to Frederick the Great, King of Prussia.

Thiroux d'Arconville believed that women authors should avoid all public notice, since if their work was good, it was ignored, and if it was poor, it was ridiculed. Nevertheless, her anonymous writings included prefaces which were quite personal and openly critical of the works of others. Paradoxically, Thiroux d'Arconville, who died in 1805, did not believe that women should study anatomy or medicine.

SELECTED WRITINGS BY THIROUX D'ARCONVILLE:

Books

(Jean-J. Sue) *Traité d'ostéologie, tranduit de l'Anglois de M. Monro*. Paris, 1759.

Essai pour servir à l'histoire de la putréfaction. Paris, 1766.

(Rossel, editor) *Mêlanges de littérature, de morale et de physique*. Amsterdam, 1775.

FURTHER READING

Books

Hurd-Mead, Kate Campbell. *A History of Women in Medicine, from the Earliest Times to the Beginning of the Nineteenth Century*. Haddam: Haddam Press, 1938. Reprint, Boston: Milford House, 1973.

Schiebinger, Londa. *The Mind Has No Sex? Women in the Origins of Modern Science*. Cambridge: Harvard University Press, 1989.

Sketch by Margaret Alic

Caroline Burling Thompson
1869–1921
American biologist

Caroline Burling Thompson was widely respected for her work as a professor of zoology at Wellesley College and her innovative explorations into the lives of social insects. In particular, her original research and intricately detailed zoological renderings of the common termite broke new ground in the study of the origin of castes among these insects.

Thompson received her Ph.D. in biology from the University of Pennsylvania in 1901. Later in that same year, she took a position at Wellesley College, where she was to remain for more than 20 years. She was a dedicated and encouraging teacher, as well as an inveterate researcher. In the course of her scientific studies, she traveled to the marine laboratories in California, Massachusetts, and Naples, Italy, where she was appointed to the Women's Table of the Marine Biological Laboratory from 1913–1914.

Thompson is chiefly noted for her research on the classification and evolution of the common termite. In 1916, she published her paper, a piece of original research on the brain and frontal gland of a common Eastern United States termite. Accompanied by finely detailed scientific drawings of the organs in question, the study determined that there was little, if any, difference between the brains of the different castes and speculated on the origins of the frontal glands. The latter was important to fellow researchers, as the frontal gland serves as a benchmark for the delineation of different termite subspecies.

Scarcely a year later, Thompson released the results of her research on the origins of the castes of the termite. This would prove to be her most influential study. It had long been believed that much of the complex order in families of termites was the result of a social construct. Thompson's work disproved this theory by determining that the origin of all castes was an inborn trait. This work brought her not only the admiration of fellow researchers around the world, but also, in 1917, an invitation to become a collaborator of the United States Department of Agriculture's Branch of Forest Entomology, a post she held until her death.

Thompson carried out similar studies on another social insect, the honey bee. Though the honey bee had been widely studied, Thompson believed there was still much to learn, and she brought to the undertaking the same sense of open-mindedness which had always characterized her work—both as a teacher and a researcher. Failing health forced her to abandon the project, as well as another termite study, long before completion. She died on December 5, 1921.

FURTHER READING

Other

Waite, Alice. "Caroline Burling Thompson." *The Wellesley Alumnae Quarterly* (February 1922): 102–104.

T.E.S. "Caroline Burling Thompson." *Science* (January 13, 1922).

Sketch by Michael Kiser

Shirley Marie (Caldwell) Tilghman
1946–
Canadian molecular biologist

Shirley Tilghman, a molecular biologist at Princeton University, is well known for her early work on gene cloning and for her discoveries of how genes regulate the development of mammalian embryos. She was one of the designers of the Human Genome Project, whose goal is to sequence all of the DNA in human beings. Tilghman actively promotes science education for the general public and the participation of women in science.

Born in Toronto, Ontario, in 1946, Tilghman was one of four daughters of Shirley (Carre) and Henry Caldwell. The family moved frequently, but Tilghman attended high school in Winnipeg, Manitoba, where she developed her interest in chemistry. Her parents were supportive of her scientific aspirations and she attended Queen's University in Kingston, Ontario. As part of her undergraduate honors curriculum, Tilghman carried out her first original laboratory research. Reading a description of a famous experiment that demonstrated the mechanism by which DNA copied, or replicated, itself Tilghman was struck by the profoundness of the question being asked and the elegance of the experimental demonstration. She decided at that moment to become a molecular biologist. Tilghman received her B.S. with honors in chemistry and biochemistry in 1968. She then spent two years teaching high school in Sierra Leone in West Africa. In 1975, Tilghman earned her Ph.D. in biochemistry at Temple University in Philadelphia, where she worked on hormonal control of glucose metabolism in the liver.

As a Fogarty International Fellow at the National Institutes of Health, working with Philip Leder, Tilghman was involved in the cloning of the first mammalian gene. In 1978, she returned to Temple University for one year, and then worked as an independent investigator at the Fox Chase Cancer Center in Philadelphia, studying the gene that encodes a fetal protein. She also served as an adjunct professor at the University of Pennsylvania. In 1986,

Shirley M. Tilghman (Reproduced by permission of Shirley M. Tilghman.)

Tilghman became Howard A. Prior Professor of the Life Sciences in the Department of Molecular Biology at Princeton University, and two years later she became a Howard Hughes Medical Institute Investigator. She is an adjunct professor in the Department of Biochemistry at the University of Medicine and Dentistry of New Jersey–the Robert Wood Johnson Medical School. Tilghman has two children with her former husband.

Tilghman's major discoveries include the parental imprinting of genes, in which one of the two copies of a gene is not expressed, depending on whether it was inherited from the mother or the father. She is studying the role of these genes in embryonic development and in evolution. Her laboratory also studies the structure, function, evolution, and regulation of several other mice genes.

Tilghman has been a scientific advisor and consultant for many organizations and has served on the editorial boards of several scientific journals. She chaired a National Research Council committee on careers in the life sciences and, since 1993, she has chaired Princeton University's Council on Science and Technology, which promotes science and technical education for non–science majors.

Tilghman is a Fellow of the Royal Society of London and in 1996 she was elected a foreign associate of the National Academy of Sciences of the United States. In 1999, she was appointed director of a new multidisciplinary

Institute for Genomic Analysis at Princeton, which will use physics, chemistry, computer science, mathematics, and engineering to study complex biological systems.

SELECTED WRITINGS BY TILGHMAN:

Periodicals

(With D. C. Tiemeier and P. Leder) "Purification and Cloning of a Mouse Ribosomal Gene Fragment in Coliphage Lambda." *Gene* 2 (1977): 173–91.

(With M. B. Gorin) "Structure of the Alpha–fetoprotein Gene in the Mouse." *Proceedings of the National Academy of Sciences U.S.A.* 77 (1980): 1351–55.

"DNA Methylation: a Phoenix Rises." *Proceedings of the National Academy of Sciences U.S.A.* 90 (1993): 8761–62.

"Science vs. Women – A Radical Solution." *The New York Times* (January 26, 1993): A18–19.

"Why I Became a Scientist." *AWIS Magazine* 24 (January, February 1995): 10–11.

(With A. L. Webber, R. S. Ingram, and J. M. Levorse) "Location of Enhancer is Essential for Imprinting of H19 and Igf2." *Nature* 319 (1998): 711–15.

"The Sins of the Fathers and Mothers: Genomic Imprinting in Mammalian Development." *Cell* 96 (1999): 185–93.

Other

"Regulation of Development in the Mouse." http://www.molbio.princeton.edu/faculty/tilghman.html (4 June 1999).

"The Regulation of Development in the Mouse." *HHMI Research in Progress.* http://www.hhmi.org/science/genetics/tilghman.htm (4 June 1999).

FURTHER READING

Other

Alic, Margaret, interview with Shirley Tilghman conducted June 4, 1999.

Gee, Henry. "Inheritance: She's Got Her Father's Ears." *Nature.* 9 Dec. 1998. http://www.perkin–elmer.co.jp/ab/bionews/bionews–091298b.htm (4 June 1999).

"Genomic Analysis." *Princeton Weekly Bulletin.* 11 Jan. 1999. http://www.princeton.edu/pr/pwb/99/0111/tilghman.htm (4 June 1999).

Hertle, Mark. "Imprinting Differs for Monogamous, Polygamous Species, says Tilghman." *Center News.* 5 Dec. 1996. http://www.fhcrc.org/about/CenterNews/1996/Dec5/Sep.htm (4 June 1999).

"Promiscuity and the Purpose of Imprinting." *Nature Genetics.* Dec. 1998. http://genetics.nature.com/pressrelease/ng1298.html (4 June 1999).

Sketch by Margaret Alic

Beatrice Muriel (Hill) Tinsley
1941–1981
British–born American astronomer

Beatrice Tinsley was one of the major astronomers of the twentieth century. As a result of her work, the evolution of galaxies has become a very active field of research. Her ability to integrate seemingly unrelated data and discoveries into new cosmological models enabled her to make important contributions to our understanding of the universe.

Beatrice Tinsley, born in Chester, England, in 1941, was the second of three daughters of Edward E. O. and Jean (Morton) Hill. Her father was in the army, stationed in Chester, during World War II. Following the war, he became an Anglican minister and, in 1946, the family emigrated to Christchurch, New Zealand, where Tinsley began school. The following year, the family moved to the rural town of Southbridge. They eventually settled in New Plymouth, New Zealand, where Tinsley attended New Plymouth High School, renowned for its academics, music, and sports programs.

The Hills were an exceptional family: Tinsley's father was elected mayor of the city of New Plymouth in 1954; Jean Hill published several books; Tinsley's older sister Rowena Hill became a linguist and a poet; and her younger sister Theodora Hill became a pianist. Tinsley graduated from high school at the age of 16 and, like her sister before her, won top academic honors and a prestigious university scholarship. Tinsley's special talents were in mathematics and science, and she studied mathematics at the boys' high school and with special teachers, since the girls' high school did not offer higher mathematics. However she also was an excellent violinist and poet. In 1958 she joined the National Youth Orchestra of New Zealand.

Studies Cosmology

Tinsley entered Canterbury University in Christchurch in 1957, studying mathematics, physics, and chemistry. She studied higher mathematics and cosmology on her own. Receiving her bachelor of science degree, with highest honors, in 1960, Tinsley continued on at Canterbury, earning her master's degree in physics, with first–class honors, in 1962. Her awards included the Haydon Prize for physics and the Charles Cook Memorial Scholarship. In 1961 she married a physicist, Brian A. Tinsley. After her graduation, Tinsley taught senior science at a girls' school in Christchurch.

In 1962, the Tinsleys moved to Dallas, Texas, where Brian Tinsley took a position as an atmospheric physicist at the Laboratory for Earth and Planetary Sciences at the Southwest Center for Advanced Studies. Since there were no opportunities for Beatrice Tinsley in Dallas, she became a graduate student in astronomy at the University of Texas in Austin in 1963, commuting 200 miles each way. She earned her Ph.D. with Raymond Sachs in 1967. Unable to obtain a position in Dallas, Tinsley abandoned her research for several years and became politically active in the areas of family planning and population control. The Tinsleys adopted their son Alan in 1965, and their daughter Teresa in 1968.

Models the Evolution of Galaxies

Tinsley's doctoral thesis had a profound impact on the world of astronomy. She had studied the effects of star formation and death on the brightness, color, and size of galaxies. In 1971, with funding from the National Science Foundation, and a visiting scientist position at the new University of Texas at Dallas, Tinsley extended her work to the evolution of stars and galaxies and other problems in cosmology. Her computer models of the evolution of stars resulted in much better models for the evolution of galaxies. She developed new methods for studying star formation and for predicting whether stars would become white dwarfs or supernovas at the final stage of their evolution. Tinsley's also made fundamental contributions to question of whether the universe was expanding.

As her work became widely recognized, Tinsley received many invitations for lectures and conferences, and she began publishing between seven and 15 scientific papers every year. At the California Institute of Technology, she collaborated with James E. Gunn. She also worked at the Mount Wilson and Mount Palomar Observatories in 1972, and held a visiting position at the University of Maryland in 1973. However Tinsley's efforts to obtain a position in Dallas, other than as a visiting scientist, were unsuccessful. After designing an astronomy program for the new department at the University of Texas at Dallas, her applications for a position in the program were ignored. Finally, in 1972, she accepted a part–time teaching position at the University of Texas at Austin, resuming her commute from Dallas. The stresses created by this arrangement led the Tinsleys to divorce in 1974. The following year, after six months at the Lick Observatory where she collaborated with Sandra M. Faber, Tinsley became an associate professor in the astronomy department at Yale and was awarded an Alfred P. Sloan Foundation Research Fellowship. She was promoted to full professor in 1978 and was director of graduate studies. Tinsley was known as a fine teacher who promoted the careers of many young astronomers. She was a member of a number of national advisory boards and committees. In 1974, Tinsley won the Annie Jump Cannon award of the American Astronomical Society (AAS).

Tinsley developed melanoma, malignant skin cancer, in 1978 and died of the cancer in 1981, completing her last scientific paper just days before her death. The University of Texas at Austin established the Beatrice Tinsley Centennial Visiting Professorship of Astronomy in her memory, and the AAS established the Beatrice Tinsley Prize for innovative contributions to astronomy.

SELECTED WRITINGS BY TINSLEY:

Books

(With R. B. Larson, editors) *The Evolution of Galaxies and Stellar Populations*. New Haven: Yale University Observatory, 1977.

Periodicals

"Evolution of the Stars and Gas in Galaxies." *Astrophysical Journal* 151 (1968): 547–65.
"Possibility of a Large Evolutionary Correction, the Magnitude–Redshift Relation." *Astrophysics and Space Science* 6 (1970): 344–51.
"Stellar Evolution in Elliptical Galaxies." *Astrophysical Journal* 178 (1972): 319–36.
(With J. Audouze) "Galactic Evolution and the Formation of the Light Elements." *Astrophysical Journal* 192 (1974): 487–500.
(With J. E. Gunn) "An Accelerating Universe." *Nature* 257 (1975): 454–75.
"Evolution of the Stars and Gas in Galaxies." *Fundamentals of Cosmic Physics* 5 (1980): 287–388.

FURTHER READING

Books

Bailey, Martha J. *American Women in Science 1950 to the Present: A Biographical Dictionary*. Santa Barbara: ABC–CLIO, 1998.
Eisberg, Joann. "Beatrice Muriel Hill Tinsley." In *Notable Women in the Physical Sciences: A Biographical Dictionary*. Edited by Benjamin F. Shearer and Barbara S. Shearer. Westport, CT: Greenwood Press, 1997.
Hill, Edward. *My Daughter Beatrice: A Personal Memoir of Dr. Beatrice Tinsley, Astronomer*. New York: The American Physical Society, 1986.
Knapp, Gillian R. "Beatrice Muriel Hill Tinsley (1941–1981)." In *Women in Chemistry and Physics: A Biobibliographic Sourcebook*. Edited by Louise S. Grinstein, Rose K. Rose, and Miriam H. Rafailovich. Westport, CT: Greenwood Press, 1993.

Sketch by Margaret Alic

Mary Lua Adelia (Davis) Treat

1830–1923

American naturalist

Mary Treat was a naturalist who studied the Pine Barrens near her home in southern New Jersey. She wrote popular articles and books about her observations, and discovered a number of new species of plants, insects, and spiders. As an experimentalist, she determined the mechanisms by which a variety of insect–eating, carnivorous plants trap and digest their insect prey.

Treat was born in Trumansville, New York in 1830. Her father was a traveling Methodist minister who moved the family to Ohio when Treat was nine years old. Intermittently, Treat attended a public school and a girls' academy in Ohio. As a young adult, she lived with her sister in New York, until she married Joseph Burrel Treat, a physician from Ohio, in 1863.

Embarks on Nature Study

Although Treat had always been interested in science, particularly nature study, astronomy, and the new science of electricity, it wasn't until after her marriage that she seriously began to study nature. After several years in Iowa, the Treats moved to the small town of May's Landing, New Jersey. Unhappy with the intellectual isolation they found there, in 1868 they resettled in the new community of Vineyard, New Jersey. Charles Landis, who had purchased land for the town, was encouraging fruit growers to keep their orchards free of insect pests, and so the Treats began studying insects and plants. However Joseph Treat soon left Vineyard, moving to New York City where he helped to nominate the women's suffragist, Victoria Woodhull, for the U. S. presidency in 1872. He died a penniless man in New York in 1878. To support herself, Mary Treat began writing about natural history.

Treat began by corresponding and exchanging specimens with the outstanding naturalists of the day, including botanist Asa Gray; entomologist Charles V. Riley; Sir Joseph Hooker, director of the Kew Gardens in London; and Charles Darwin, the father of modern evolutionary theory. After long hours of experimentation and microscopic observation, Treat reported her discoveries to Darwin. Although some of her discoveries about carnivorous plants met with initial skepticism, her observations were eventually corroborated. In his book, *Insectivorous Plants*, Darwin credited Treat with discovering how bladderworts capture insects.

In 1876, Treat became so interested in butterworts that she began spending her winters in Florida, in a cottage on the Saint Johns River near Jacksonville. She demonstrated that the butterworts were annual plants and that they were herbivorous and carnivorous, consuming both pollen and insects. She also discovered a number of new species of bladderworts, as well as a water lily that had been painted by John Jacob Audobon but which botanists had thought was imaginary. She discovered a new amaryllis lily, the Zephyr–lily, which Sereno Watson of Harvard's Gray Herbarium named *Zephranthes treatae* in her honor.

Creates an "Insect Menagerie"

Treat hiked the nearby Pine Barrens of New Jersey, searching for flowers and ferns. She discovered a new root gall on a Virginia oak tree, *Belonocnema treatae* , named by Gustav Mayr of Vienna. In her backyard, surrounded by a large hedge of arbor vitae, she established her insect and spider menagerie, where she made her observations and carried out her experiments. In the woods of her New Jersey home, Treat found two new species of burrowing spiders. In her menagerie at night, she observed their nests and the digger moths that fed on them. One of several ant species discovered by Treat was the widely distributed ant, *Aphaenogaster treatae*, named after her by the Swiss entomologist Auguste Forel.

In the 1870s, Mary Treat wrote ten articles on insects for the *American Entomologist*. Her topics included the tomato worm, oak tree pests, and the life histories of various moths. She wrote 41 articles for *Garden and Forest*, on the flora of the Pine Barrens, and between 1870 and 1896, she published 13 articles on birds. Her most popular book, first published in 1880, was *Home Studies in Nature*. By 1888, Treat's writings were successful enough that she was able to buy a new home. There she planted a garden of indigenous plants of the Pine Barrens and a constructed a new insect menagerie for her studies. In 1893, Treat established a nature study club for young women in her home.

In 1916, following a fall, Treat became an invalid and went live with her sister in Akron, New York, where she died in 1923.

SELECTED WRITINGS BY TREAT:

Books

Injurious Insects of the Farm and Garden. New York: Orange Judd Company, 1882.

Home Studies in Nature. New York: Harper and Brothers, 1885.

My Garden Pets. Boston: D. Lothrop Company, 1887.

FURTHER READING

Books

Bailey, Martha J. *American Women in Science: A Biographical Dictionary*. Denver: ABC–CLIO, 1994.

Bonta, Marcia Myers. *Women in the Field: America's Pioneering Women Naturalists*. College Station: Texas A & M University Press, 1991.

Gershenowitz, Harry. *Essays on the Writings of Mary Treat*. Vineland, NJ: Vineland Historical and Antiquarian Society, 1990.

Sketch by Margaret Alic

Trotula of Salerno
?–1097(?)
Italian medical writer

Trotula was a physician and scholar at the early medical school at Salerno in southern Italy, which was famous for including women students and faculty. She was a major figure in the scientific renaissance that occurred at the end of the dark ages. Throughout medieval times her treatises, particularly her work on obstetrics and gynecology, were considered to be among the most authoritative medical writings. Although she was known as a famous scientist during the middle ages, in more recent times her identity has been questioned.

Very little is known of Trotula's life. She has been identified as a member of an old noble Italian family, di Ruggiero, and as the wife of a physician, Johannes Platearius. Their sons, Matthias and Johannes the Younger, also were medical scholars. After the reorganization of the Salerno school in the mid-eleventh century, all four members of the Platearius family were on the faculty.

The school at Salerno was the first secular medieval medical center and a prototype for other European medical schools and universities. Salerno was a cosmopolitan city, at the crossroads of Europe and the Middle East, and it was here that many of the ancient Greek medical writings were first translated from Arabic into Latin. Although women were midwives, physicians, and healers throughout medieval Europe, it was Italy that had a tradition of educated women dating back to Roman times and, until the nineteenth century, Italy was the only European country with universities that included women students and professors. Thus, it is not surprising that women studied and taught medicine at Salerno. These women were known collectively, throughout the middle ages, as the *Mulieres Salernitanae* or the "Ladies of Salerno." Foremost among them was Trotula.

Writes The Diseases of Women

Trotula's most important medical writing, *Passionibus Mulierum Curandorum* or *The Diseases of Women*, came to be referred to as the *Trotula Major*. In the prologue to this work, Trotula described her decision to study medicine: "Since then women are by nature weaker than men it is reasonable that sicknesses more often abound in them especially around the organs involved in the work of nature. Since these organs happen to be in a retired location, women on account of modesty and the fragility and delicacy of the state of these parts dare not reveal the difficulties of their sicknesses to a male doctor. Wherefore I, pitying their misfortunes and at the instigation of a certain matron, began to study carefully the sicknesses which most frequently trouble the female sex."

Innumerable copies were made of the *Trotula Major* before the advent of the printing press and many additions and interpolations were made by the copyists. Therefore it is difficult to know precisely which sections were written by Trotula. The work included general medicine, as well as obstetrics and gynecology, and a second treatise, *Ornatu Mulierum* or the *Trotula Minor*, dealing with skin diseases and cosmetics, was later incorporated into the *Trotula Major*. However, as Kate Hurd-Mead, in the journal *Isis* , described Trotula's work: "It is full of common sense, practical, up-to-date for its time, in fact far ahead of the eleventh century in its surgery and analgesics as well as in the care of the mother and infant during the post partum period. No book so good of its kind had ever been written, and none followed it for centuries."

Trotula's writings were surprisingly scientific. Although the ancient Greek physician Hippocrates and the Roman physician Galen were her major sources, she went far beyond them. She emphasized cleanliness, balanced diet, exercise and relaxation. Her cures were simple and affordable, without astrological or superstitious elements. The *Trotula Major* discussed normal and abnormal menstruation, birth control, and infertility. She was the first to describe the stitching of a torn perineum (the area between the anus and the posterior part of the external genitalia) following childbirth and she recommended methods for preventing such tears—ancient methods which had been neglected by midwives and physicians for centuries.

Authenticity of Work Disputed

The *Trotula Major* was a very popular work and a standard text in medical schools, and Trotula herself became a figure of folklore. Her writings were even mentioned in Chaucer's *Canterbury Tales*. However, the *Trotula Major* was plagiarized and given different titles, sections were incorporated into other writings, and manuscript copies often omitted her name, or changed it to Trottola, Tortola, or the male form, Trottus. Occasionally, Trotula's husband was named as the author. During the thirteenth century, a woman doctor in Salerno apparently shortened the text and made major revisions, which subsequently were translated into English, French, and German. Although the earliest printed editions of *Passionibus Mulierum Curandorum* ascribed the work to Trotula of Salerno, an edition printed in Basle, Switzerland, in 1566 unaccountably attributed the treatise to a male Greco-Roman physician from the time of Emperor Augustus. Furthermore, twentieth-century medical historians argued that not only was the work much too sophisticated to have been written by a woman, but that a woman would not have written so explicitly about sexuality.

Nevertheless, Italian medical historians always have supported the authenticity of Trotula and the existence of women physicians, students, and faculty at Salerno in the eleventh and twelfth centuries.

With her husband and sons, Trotula also worked on a medical encyclopedia, the *Practica Brevis.* An important twelfth-century Salernitan text, *De Aegritudinum Curatione,* included the work of both Trotula and her husband, among the seven masters of the school of Salerno. Trotula is believed to have died at Salerno about 1097. She was commemorated with a medal in Naples in the nineteenth century. It remains a possibility that the physician and medical scholar, Trotula, may not have authored the treatises ascribed to her. However, the evidence is clear that women scholars were writing treatises and practicing medicine at Salerno at the time that Europe was emerging from the dark ages, and there is no reason to believe that Trotula was not among them.

SELECTED WRITINGS BY TROTULA OF SALERNO:

Books

(Mason-Hohl, Elizabeth translator) *The Diseases of Women.* Los Angeles: Ward Ritchie Press, 1940.

FURTHER READING

Books

Alic, Margaret. *Hypatia's Heritage: A History of Women in Science from Antiquity through the Nineteenth Century.* Boston: Beacon Press,1986.

Hughes, Muriel Joy. *Women Healers in Medieval Life and Literature.* Oxford: Oxford University Press, 1943. Reprint. Freeport, NY: Books for Libraries Press, 1968.

Hurd-Mead, Kate Campbell. *A History of Women in Medicine, from the Earliest Times to the Beginning of the Nineteenth Century.* Haddam, Ct.: Haddam Press, 1938. Reprint. Boston: Milford House, 1973.

Periodicals

Benton, John F. "Trotula, Women's Problems, and the Professionalization of Medicine in the Middle Ages." *Bulletin of the History of Medicine* 59 (1985): 30–53.

Hurd-Mead, Kate Campbell. "Trotula." *Isis* 14 (1930): 349–67.

Mason-Hohl, Elizabeth. "Trotula—Eleventh Century Gynecologist." *Women in Medicine* (October 1940): 8–15.

Stuard, Susan Mosher. "Dame Trot." *Signs* 1 (1975): 537–42.

Sketch by Margaret Alic

Elizabeth Truswell
1941–
Australian palynologist

The day to day affairs of Elizabeth Truswell involve pollens and spores in fossil samples. An Australian scientist, Truswell is involved in the relatively new field of palynology, which uses such fossil samples to determine vegetative history and most recently to help determine the location of petroleum deposits. As Truswell told Ann Moyal in an interview for *Portraits in Science,* "the derivation of palynology is from 'palunos', from the Greek, meaning 'dust'." Early palynologists studied the vegetative history of Europe after the last glaciations. But by the 1940s the field became recognized as a valuable tool in oil exploration, and suddenly palynology was no longer a sideshow to botany or geology. Truswell's work has been in the vegetative history and geology of the Antarctic, of the Australian rainforests, and as a researcher for the Australian Bureau of Mineral Resources and the Australian Geological Survey Organization.

Born in Kalgoorlie, Australia in 1941, Truswell formed an early love for geology, spurred on by the work of her father, a surveyor in the gold mines and later a surveyor for the Public Works Department of Western Australia in Perth. Her mother was a schoolteacher, but Truswell spent much of her youth away from schoolrooms, accompanying her father on his surveys, getting to know and love the bush, or the Australian outback. Attending King Street High School in Perth, she became excited about the possibilities of a career in biology under the tutelage of a dedicated biology teacher. Later, attending college at the University of Western Australia, a lecturer in geology and a pioneer in Australian palynology, introduced the young Truswell to that growing field of study. Truswell's honors thesis was a study of the carboniferous microfloras from the Canning Basin of Western Australia, a descriptive sort of work that necessitated hours at the microscope describing fossil spores. It was fine training for the work that would later come her way.

The recipient of a Commonwealth scholarship, Truswell attended Cambridge University, studying the Cretaceous period, some 100 million years ago, of southern England. Her thesis advisor in England, Norman Hughes, was another pioneer in palynology, and when Truswell entered the field professionally in 1968, working for Western Australian Petroleum in Perth, she was one of the few women in the field. At this initial position, she studied deep borehole material for pollen samples that would indicate possible petroleum reserves. Little fieldwork was involved in this position, so when the opportunity came for a post–doctoral position in palynology at Florida State University in 1973, Truswell jumped at it.

Research in Antarctica

At Florida State, Truswell became part of a research team studying glaciations that had affected the Southern

Hemisphere, specifically that in Gondwanaland, the supposed land mass in the Southern Hemisphere that separated near the end of the Paleozoic to form South America, Africa, and Australia. While at Florida State, Truswell also was offered the chance to study modern glaciation under the auspices of the Deep Sea Drilling Program, later known as the Ocean Drilling Program. Sailing to Antarctica, Truswell studied cores drilled from a mid–ocean ridge halfway between Australia and Antarctica, a ridge where the sea floor is being created. "And it's that ridge that is part of the conveyor belt that's pushing Australia northward," Truswell told Moyal. One of only four women on board this expedition, Truswell also worked on sediments, helping to establish that the Antarctic ice sheet is ten times older than that which covered the Northern Hemisphere in the last glaciation. Scientist had long thought that the two were roughly the same age. She also studied the development of the Antarctic convergence, the point where there is a sudden temperature change in the ocean.

A Working Palynologist

In 1973, after her post–doc at Florida, Truswell joined the Bureau of Mineral Resources (BMR) in Canberra in the paleontology section, preparing and studying spore and pollen samples. "A lot of time is spent looking down a microscope, counting pollen grains," Truswell told Moyal. "It's moments of excitement finding something new or something that's particularly well preserved, something particularly beautiful."

Truswell's researches into the 100–million–year record of the Australian rainforests is part of that "something particularly beautiful." Her recovery and description of fossil flowers has increased the knowledge of those fragile environmental zones so quickly disappearing from this planet. Such studies have also helped to influence scientific and public opinion that such places with ancient lineages are worth preserving.

In 1981, Truswell became Principal Research Scientist at the BMR, and then in 1992 was promoted to Chief Research Scientist. As such she worked as a biostratigrapher, using fossil pollen and spores to build a time frame against which sedimentary basins could be measured. While conducting this rigorous work, she also found time to investigate and continue work on spin–off projects, such as the rainforests and the story of Antarctic vegetation. She also became the Chief Research Scientist at the Environmental Geoscience and Groundwater division of the Australian Geological Survey Organization, a position she held until 1999. Working as an environmental geologist, she helped create the Cape York Land Use Strategy, a multi–use plan for a sensitive wilderness area in Australia.

A member of the Australian Academy of Sciences, Truswell is also a strong proponent of women in science. Concluding her interview with Moyal, she noted that young girls contemplating a career in science should "be themselves as much as possible, to feel that there is freedom out there. They may have to push against any barriers that they come up against, but I think they have to have the confidence in themselves and not be too daunted by what seem to be rather rigid scientific structures."

SELECTED WRITINGS BY TRUSWELL:

Books

"Palynological Observations in the Officer Basin." *Palynological Papers: Australia Bureau of Mineral Resources, Geology and Geophysics*. Canberra: Australian Govt. Pub. Service, 1976.

(With W. K. Harris) *The Palynology of Early Tertiary Sediments, Ninetyeast Ridge, Indian Ocean*. London: Palaeontological Association, 1977.

Palynology of the Permo–Carboniferous in Tasmania: An Interim Report. Hobart, Tasmania: Tasmania Dept. of Mines, 1978.

"Antarctica: A History of Terrestrial Vegetation." *The Geology of Antarctica*. Edited by R. J. Tingey. Oxford: Clarendon Press, 1991, pp. 499–537.

FURTHER READING

Books

Moyal, Ann. *Portraits in Science*. Canberra: National Library of Australia, 1994, pp. 83–97.

Sketch by J. Sydney Jones

Helen Alma (Newton) Turner
1908–1995
Australian statistician and geneticist

Helen Newton Turner was one of the world's first agricultural statisticians and an expert on animal genetics, particularly the breeding of Merino sheep. The author of several textbooks and more than 100 scientific papers, Turner is regarded as one of Australia's greatest geneticists.

Helen Turner was born in Sydney, New South Wales, Australia, in 1908, the daughter of Alphonse and Jessie (Bowmaker) Newton. She earned her bachelor's degree in architecture, with honors, from Sydney University in 1930.

Unable to find a permanent job in architecture, Turner took a secretarial position at the McMaster Animal Health Laboratory at the Commonwealth Scientific and Industrial Research Organisation (CSIRO) of Australia. She would work for CSIRO for more than 40 years. Eventually Turner was promoted to technical officer, and she became increasingly interested in the rapidly developing field of statistics.

Sir Ian Clunies–Ross arranged for her to train in England with two of the world's leading statisticians, R. A. Fisher and Frank Yates. Turner returned to CSIRO in 1939, as a consulting statistician in the Division of Animal Health and Production, although she was employed by the Division of Mathematical Statistics. During the war years of 1942 to 1944, Turner was a statistician with the Department of Home Security and Manpower, in Sydney and Canberra. Upon her return to CSIRO, in 1946, Turner became one of the first agricultural statisticians with the Division of Animal Health and Production. In 1956, she became Senior Principal Research Scientist in the Animal Breeding Section of the Division of Animal Genetics. She was the leader of the sheep genetics research team, a position she held until 1973, when she became an honorary research fellow.

Turner's work was devoted to improving the genetic stock of Australian sheep for wool production, one of Australia's major industries. She was one of the first researchers to introduce quantitative methods to the science of sheep breeding, and her innovations soon became standard practice in the industry, greatly increasing Australian wool production. She also conducted experiments on producing twins in sheep breeding. Turner's responsibilities included convincing farmers to switch from their traditional breeding methods to techniques based on modern genetics. As a result, Turner became a frequent speaker at public forums and on the radio for the Australian Broadcasting Company. Later, she became increasingly involved in Australia's agricultural assistance to developing countries. She traveled extensively around the world, conducting research, lecturing, and consulting. Turner's research had tremendous impacts on research in animal genetics and breeding practices.

Turner earned her doctorate in science from Sydney University in 1970. Among her numerous awards were the Farrer Memorial Medal in 1974, the Ceres Medal of the Food and Agriculture Organization of the United Nations in 1977, and the Rotary Medal for Vocational Excellence in 1985. She was a decorated officer in the Order of the British Empire. Turner was a fellow or member of a number of Australian scientific societies, and she was elected a fellow of the Association for the Advancement of Animal Breeding and Genetics in 1990. In 1991 she was awarded an honorary doctorate of science by Macquarie University.

Turner died in 1995. The Helen Newton Turner Medal Trust, the most prestigious award for Australian livestock genetics, was established in 1993 by an anonymous donation to the Animal Genetics and Breeding Unit of the University of New England.

SELECTED WRITINGS BY TURNER:

Books

(With Sydney S. Y. Young) *Quantitative Genetics in Sheep Breeding*. Ithaca, NY: Cornell University Press, 1969.

"Introduction." In *Prolific Sheep*, edited by Mohamed H. Fahmy. Tucson, AZ: CAB International, 1996.

Periodicals

"Ian Clunies Ross: A Leader of Men." *Australian Veterinary Journal* 44 (1968): 467–80.

FURTHER READING

Books

Moyal, Ann. *Portraits in Science*. Canberra: National Library of Australia, 1994.

O'Neill, Lois Decker, editor. *The Women's Book of World Records and Achievements*. Garden City, NY: Doubleday, 1979.

Who's Who in the World. 6th ed. Chicago: Marquis Who's Who, 1982–83.

Periodicals

Nessy, Allen. "The Contribution of Two Australian Women Scientists to its Wool Industry." *Prometheus* 9 (1991): 81–92.

Nessy, Allen. "Helen Newton Turner and the Wool Industry." *Journal of Australian Studies* 33 (1992): 56–62.

Other

Brash, Lindsay. "Dr Helen Alma Newton Turner (1908–1995)." *The Association for the Advancement of Animal Breeding and Genetics*. 9 Feb. 1998. http://agbu.une.edu.au/~aaabg/hntobit.html (14 July 1999).

Brash, Lindsay. "The Helen Newton Turner Award and Oration." *The Association for the Advancement of Animal Breeding and Genetics*. 12 July 1999. http://agbu.une.edu.au/~aaabg/aaahnt.html (14 July 1999).

Tenkate, Elissa. "Helen Newton Turner." *Australian Science Archives Project*. 26 Aug. 1997. http://www.asap.unimelb.edu.au/bsparcs/other/asfscientists.htm#helen (14 July 1999).

Sketch by Margaret Alic

U

Karen Uhlenbeck (Mathematisches Forschungsinstitut Oberwolfach. Reproduced by permission.)

Karen Keskulla Uhlenbeck
1942–
American mathematician

Karen Uhlenbeck is engaged in mathematical research that has applications in theoretical physics and has contributed to the study of instantons, models for the behavior of surfaces in four dimensions. In recognition of her work in geometry and partial differential equations, she was awarded a prestigious MacArthur Fellowship in 1983.

Karen Keskulla Uhlenbeck was born in Cleveland, Ohio, on August 24, 1942, to Arnold Edward Keskulla, an engineer, and Carolyn Windeler Keskulla, an artist. When Uhlenbeck was in third grade, the family moved to New Jersey. Everything interested her as a child, but she felt that girls were discouraged from exploring many activities. In high school, she read American physicist George Gamow's books on physics and English astronomer Fred Hoyle's books on cosmology, which her father brought home from the public library. When Uhlenbeck entered the University of Michigan, she found mathematics a broad and intellectually stimulating subject. After earning her B.S. degree in 1964, she became a National Science Foundation Graduate Fellow, pursuing graduate study in mathematics at Brandeis University. In 1965, she married Olke Cornelis Uhlenbeck, a biophysicist; they later divorced.

Uhlenbeck received her Ph.D. in mathematics from Brandeis in 1968 with a thesis on the calculus of variations. Her first teaching position was at the Massachusetts Institute of Technology in 1968. The following year she moved to Berkeley, California, where she was a lecturer in mathematics at the University of California. There she studied general relativity and the geometry of space–time, and worked on elliptic regularity in systems of partial differential equations.

In 1971, Uhlenbeck became an assistant professor at the University of Illinois at Urbana–Champaign. In 1974, she was awarded a fellowship from the Sloan Foundation that lasted until 1976, and she then went to Northwestern University as a visiting associate professor. She taught at the University of Illinois in Chicago from 1977 to 1983, first as associate professor and then professor, and in 1979 she was the Chancellor's Distinguished Visiting Professor at the University of California, Berkeley. An Albert Einstein Fellowship enabled her to pursue her research as a member of the Institute for Advanced Studies at Princeton University from 1979 to 1980. She published more than a dozen articles in mathematics journals during the 1970s and was named to the editorial board of the *Journal of Differential Geometry* in 1979 and the *Illinois Journal of Mathematics* in 1980.

In 1983, Uhlenbeck was selected by the John D. and Catherine T. MacArthur Foundation of Chicago to receive one of its five–year fellowship grants. Given annually, the MacArthur fellowships enable scientists, scholars, and artists to pursue research or creative activity. For Uhlenbeck, winning the fellowship inspired her to begin serious studies in physics. She believes that the mathematician's task is to abstract ideas from fields such as physics and streamline them so they can be used in other fields. For instance, physicists studying quantum mechanics had predicted the existence of particle–like elements called instantons. Uhlenbeck and other researchers viewed instantons as somewhat analogous to soap films. Seeking a better understanding of these particles, they studied soap films to learn about the properties of surfaces. As soap films provide a model for the behavior of surfaces in three–dimensions, instantons provide analogous models for the behavior of surfaces in four–dimensional space–time. Uhlenbeck cowrote a book on this subject, *Instantons and 4–Manifold Topology,* which was published in 1984.

After a year spent as a visiting professor at Harvard, Uhlenbeck became a professor at the University of Chicago in 1983. Her mathematical interests at this time included nonlinear partial differential equations, differential geometry, gauge theory, topological quantum field theory, and integrable systems. She gave guest lectures at several universities and served as the vice president of the American Mathematical Society. The Alumni Association of the University of Michigan named her Alumna of the Year in 1984. She was elected to the American Academy of Arts and Sciences in 1985 and to the National Academy of Sciences in 1986. In 1988, she received the Alumni Achievement award from Brandeis University, an honorary doctor of science degree from Knox College, and was named one of America's 100 most important women by *Ladies' Home Journal.*

In 1987, Uhlenbeck went to the University of Texas at Austin, where she broadened her understanding of physics in studies with American physicist Steven Weinberg. In 1988, she accepted the Sid W. Richardson Foundation Regents' Chair in mathematics at the University of Texas. She also gave the plenary address at the International Congress of Mathematics in Japan in 1990.

Concerned that potential scientists were being discouraged unnecessarily because of their sex or race, Uhlenbeck joined a National Research Council planning group to investigate the representation of women in science and engineering. She believes that mathematics is always challenging and never boring, and she has expressed the hope that one of her accomplishments as a teacher has been communicating this to her students. "I sometimes feel the need to apologize for being a mathematician, but no apology is needed," she told *The Alcalde Magazine.* "Whenever I get a free week and start doing mathematics, I can't believe how much fun it is. I'm like a 12–year–old boy with a new train set."

SELECTED WRITINGS BY UHLENBECK:

Books

(With D. Freed) *Instantons and 4–Manifold Topology,* Springer Verlag, 1984.

FURTHER READING

Periodicals

Benningfield, Damond. "Prominent Players." *The Alcalde Magazine* (September/October 1988): 26–30.

Other

Uhlenbeck, Karen, "Some Personal Remarks on My Partly Finished Life," unpublished manuscript.

Sketch by C. D. Lord

V

Dr. Florence W. Van Straten (AP/Wide World Photos. Reproduced by permission.)

Florence Wilhelmina van Straten
1913–
American physicist and meteorologist

Florence W. van Straten worked for many years with the U.S. Navy researching the causes of weather patterns and investigating the possibility of human weather modification. She served as the head of naval tests in cloud seeding to create and dissipate clouds, as well as an educator and writer.

Florence Wilhelmina van Straten was born on November 12, 1913, in Darien, Connecticut, the daughter of Jacques and Rosette (Roozeboom) van Straten, Dutch immigrants. Her father was an executive for Metro–Goldwyn–Mayer, and she thus grew up in various cities in North America and Europe. From an early age, van Straten wanted to be a writer. Influenced by her practical father, she agreed to take chemistry classes in addition to English at New York University, and it was the chemistry that won out. She earned her B.S. in 1933, the M.A. in 1937, and a Ph.D. in chemistry in 1939. From her senior year in college, she had been an instructor of freshman chemistry courses. After graduation, she accepted a teaching fellowship at New York University. With the advent of World War II she joined the Waves, becoming a specialist in meteorology and doing post–graduate work at the Massachusetts Institute of Technology.

Researches Weather Modification

After the war, van Straten continued working for the Navy in a civilian capacity, becoming director of its Technical Requirements Branch of the U.S. Naval Weather Service. During the war she had already begun researching a problem meteorologists had been looking at for generations: how to control and modify the weather so as to stop a hurricane or end rain in flooded areas. In her view, rain was often caused by atmospheric events in tropical areas, for which the standard model involving sub–freezing temperatures in the tops of clouds would not hold. Finally, van Straten developed the theory that rain is dependent upon evaporation rates within a cloud. She concluded that she could create or dissipate clouds by 'seeding' them with some material that could change temperatures by absorbing light. In 1958 van Straten had a chance to test these theories, seeding carbon particles into clouds and successfully dissipating seven clouds, marking the conclusion of fifteen years of theorizing.

In 1962 van Straten left the Naval Weather Service and made her home near Washington, DC, but remained a consultant in atmospheric physics as well as a lieutenant commander in the reserves. She was awarded for her researches in weather modification with the Meritorious Service Award of the U.S. Department of the Navy in 1958 and the Woman of the Year award from the Aerospace Medical Association in 1959. Retirement brought van Straten the time she had always lacked to devote to her first love—writing. She authored a popular study of weather, short stories, and pamphlets on radar and radioactive fallout.

SELECTED WRITINGS BY VAN STRATEN:

Books

Radar as a Meteorological Tool. U.S. Government Printing Office, 1957.

Weather or Not. Dodd, 1966.

FURTHER READING

Periodicals

"Does Something about It: Florence Wilhelmina van Straten." *New York Times* September 24, 1958. p. 52.

Sketch by J. Sydney Jones

Argelia Velez-Rodriguez
1936–
Cuban-born American mathematics educator

Argelia Velez-Rodriguez (Reproduced by permission of Argelia Velez-Rodriguez.)

Since leaving her native Cuba shortly after completing her Ph.D., Argelia Velez-Rodriguez has devoted her career to mathematics and physics education. She has been involved with math education programs of the National Science Foundation (NSF) since 1970 and became director of the Minority Science Improvement Program at the U.S. Department of Education in 1980.

After showing promise in mathematics as a girl, Velez-Rodriguez earned a bachelor's degree in 1955 from the Marianao Institute of Cuba and a Ph.D. in 1960 from the University of Havana. Her doctoral dissertation concerned the use of differential equations in figuring astronomical orbits. Her father, Pedro Velez, had worked in the Cuban Congress under Fulgencio Batista, the leader ousted by Fidel Castro in 1959.

Velez-Rodriguez's first teaching position in the United States was at Texas College, where she began teaching mathematics and physics in 1962. In 1972, she became a professor of math and served as the department's chair at Bishop College in Dallas. Velez-Rodriguez's research at the time focused on differential equations and classical analysis, and it was at Bishop that she first became involved with the NSF programs for improving science education. Velez-Rodriguez has also studied teaching strategies, with a particular focus on helping minorities and disadvantaged students learn mathematics. She directed and coordinated several NSF programs for high school and junior high school mathematics teachers.

Velez–Rodriquez was married to Raul Rodriguez in 1954 in Cuba and they had two young children when the family fled the country in 1962. "I had just finished my Ph.D.," she told contributor Karl Bates in an interview. Her son is now a surgeon, and her daughter is an engineer with a Harvard MBA. She and Rodriguez are divorced, and she is a naturalized citizen of the United States.

FURTHER READING

"Argelia Velez-Rodriguez." *Biographies of Women Mathematicians.* June 1997. http://www.scottlan.edu/lriddle/women/chronol.htm (July 22, 1997).

Other

Velez-Rodriguez, Argelia, interview with Karl Leif Bates, conducted June 17, 1997.

Sketch by Karl Leif Bates

Birgit Vennesland
1913–
Norwegian-born American biochemist

Birgit Vennesland is an internationally recognized scientist in intermediary metabolism, the study of chemical reaction pathways of small organic molecules in cells. Her specific achievements dealt with the enzymology of the dark metabolism of plant tissues. She demonstrated that plants that synthesize carbohydrates during photosynthesis degrade these carbohydrates in the dark by reaction paths that are similar to those occurring in animal tissues. Vennesland's contributions established that the hydrogen transfers were direct and stereospecific (three–dimensional). For her contributions she earned the Stephen Hales Award from the American Society of Plant Physiologists in 1950 and the Garvan Medal of the American Chemical Society in 1964. Vennesland was also awarded an honorary doctorate in 1960 from Mount Holyoke College.

Vennesland was born in Kristiansan, Norway on November 17, 1913, along with her twin sister Kirsten, to Gunnuf Olav and Sigrid Kristine (Bandsborg) Vennesland, a teacher. Though Vennesland's father had already emigrated to the United States after graduating from high school, her mother wanted to give birth in Norway so she returned there from Canada where they were residing at the time. When Vennesland was four years old, her mother brought her back to the United States, to join her father, who was attending dental school in Chicago.

In Chicago, Vennesland and her sister learned English quickly, although Norwegian was still spoken at home. At age 12, Vennesland became a naturalized American citizen. She enjoyed her early schooling and became interested in medicine as a career. Upon graduation from Roosevelt High School, she earned a scholarship to the University of Chicago after passing a physics exam. Since Vennesland could not choose between physics and biology, she selected biochemistry as her course of study since it combined both subjects. Her sister Kirsten also attended the University of Chicago for a medical degree.

Studies Metabolic Pathways

Vennesland earned a B.S. degree in 1934 and went on to earn her Ph.D. in biochemistry in 1938. From this work, Vennesland discovered that the bacteria she was working with would not grow in the absence of carbon dioxide, which led to research showing that the light–catalyzed oxidation–reduction reactions in the green leaf require carbon dioxide. After serving as an assistant at the University of Chicago for one year, she accepted a two–year postdoctoral fellowship in the Department of Biochemistry at the Harvard Medical School. Here she began using radioactive carbon to understand metabolic pathways, one of the first chemists to use this method. This work showed that the carbon of carbon dioxide was converted into the carbon of glycogen in the rat liver.

When this fellowship was completed in 1941, Vennesland returned to the University of Chicago as an instructor in biochemistry, where she remained until 1968. She was promoted to assistant professor in 1944 and during the same year served with the Office of Scientific Research and Development. She was not promoted to full professor until 1957. While at the university she joined a research team to identify the enzyme(s) responsible for the entry of carbon dioxide into metabolic pathways in animal tissues. Vennesland also acted as consultant in molecular biology and physiological chemistry to the National Science Foundation and the U.S. Public Health Service during the years 1954–1963. The following year she was a member of the Wooldridge Commission in Washington D.C.

Through her collaboration with a German scientist, Otto Warburg, Vennesland became a frequent visitor to the Max Planck Institute for Cell Physiology in Berlin, Germany. This led to her election as a member of the Max Planck Society in 1967. In 1968 she moved to Germany to serve as a director of the institute. The following year she and her colleagues began investigating the reduction of nitrate by chlorophyll–containing cells and found that this process is regulated by hydrogen cyanide. In 1970, she was appointed to head the Vennesland Research Institute of the Max Planck Society, where she remained until her retirement in 1981. The same year Vennesland became editor of a journal, *Cyanide in Biology,* and continued to publish scientific papers for a number of years.

In 1987 she moved to Hawaii to live with her sister, who had been the tuberculosis control officer for Hawaii from 1967 to 1978. Vennesland still remained active in her field for several years as Adjunct Professor in biochemistry and biophysics at the University of Hawaii. She is also a fellow of the American Association for the Advancement of Science, the New York Academy of Sciences, and the American Society of Plant Physiologists, as well as a member of the American Society of Biological Chemists.

SELECTED WRITINGS BY VENNESLAND:

Books

(Contributor) "Nitrogen and Carbon Isotopes: Their Application in vivo to the Study of the Animal Organism." In *Advances in Biological and Medical Physics, Volume 1.* J. H. Lawrence and J. G. Hamilton, eds. San Diego, CA: Academic Press, 1948.

(Contributor) "Glutathione Reductase (Plant)." In *Methods in Enzymology, Volume 2.* S. P. Colowick and N. O. Kaplan, eds. San Diego, CA: Academic Press, 1955.

(Contributor) "Decarboxylases in Plants." In *Encyclopedia of Plant Physiology.* W. Ruhland, ed. Berlin: Springer–Verlag, 1960.

Periodicals

(With H. Holt and R.W. Keeton) "The Effect of Gonadectomy on Body Structure and Body Weight in Albino Rats." *American Journal of Physiology* (1936): 515–35.

(With J.B. Conant, R. D. Cramer, et al.) "Metabolism of Lactic Acid Containing Radioactive Carbosyl Carbon." *Journal of Biological Chemistry* no. 137 (1941): 557–66.

"Carbohydrate Metabolism." *Annual Review of Biochemistry* 17 (1948): 2227–2252.

"Some Applications of Deuterium to the Study of Enzyme Mechanisms." *Discussions of the Faraday Society* 20 (1955): 240.
"The Stereospecificity of Glutahione Reductase for Pyridine Nucleotides." *Journal of Biological Chemistry* 235 (1960): 209–212.
"Stereospecificity in Biology." *Forschungsstelle Vennesland der Max–Planck–Gesellschaft, Berlin Dahlem* 48 (1974): 39–65.
"Isotope Time 50 Years Ago." *Federation of American Societies for Experimental Biology and Medicine* 5 (1991): 2868–2869.

FURTHER READING

Books

American Men and Women of Science, 19th ed. New Providence, NJ: R.R. Bowker, 1994.
Bailey, Martha J. *American Women in Science: 1950 to the Present.* Denver: ABC–CLIO, 1986.
Grinstein, Louise, et. al., eds. *Women in the Biological Sciences.* Westport, CT: Greenwood Press, 1997.

Sketch by Laurel Sheppard

Lydia Villa-Komaroff (Reproduced by permission of Lydia Villa-Komaroff.)

Lydia Villa-Komaroff
1947–
American molecular biologist

Lydia Villa-Komaroff is the third Mexican-American to earn a science-related Ph.D. An internationally known molecular biologist, she is most lauded for her work with recombinant DNA and was part of a research team that discovered insulin could be produced from bacteria.

Lydia Villa-Komaroff was born on August 7, 1947, in Las Vegas, New Mexico (not Nevada), the oldest of six children. Her father, John Vias Villa, a violinist for the Santa Fe orchestra and a teacher, and her mother, Drucilla (Jaramillo), a social worker, were both the first in their family to get a college education. Education was highly valued in the family, and all of the Villa children were expected to succeed in school. Villa-Komaroff's interest in science was influenced by an uncle who was a chemist and her mother's love of nature and plants. A story her mother told was another inspiration. Villa-Komaroff's mother contracted rheumatic fever as a child, causing her to miss a year of school. Although she was able to catch up on most of her academic work, she never quite caught up in mathematics, which limited her goal of studying botany. Her mother's inability to succeed in science inspired Villa-Komaroff to succeed herself. Her mother also read to her children, and Villa-Komaroff's grandmother was instrumental in teaching her grandchildren about the natural world. Despite encouragement from her family, Villa-Komaroff still had to overcome cultural messages that as a Mexican-American women she was not expected to pursue a career at all, much less a career in a male-dominated field like science.

After attending the National Science Foundation Summer Science Training Program in Texas during high school,Villa-Komaroff was determined to be a scientist. She went on to the University of Washington in Seattle in 1965, where she developed an interest in cell biology and development. She met her future husband Anthony Komaroff in the university cafeteria when he accidently tripped her. In her sophomore year Villa-Komaroff transferred to Goucher College to be near Komaroff, who had accepted a job with the Public Health Service in Bethesda, Maryland. The couple married in 1970, after Villa-Komaroff graduated from Goucher with an A.B. cum laude in Biology.

While at Goucher, Villa-Komaroff worked for the National Institutes of Health (NIH) during summer breaks. An NIH microbiologist, Dr. Loretta Lieve, sparked her interest in molecular biology and encouraged her to continue her education at Massachusetts Institute of Technology (MIT). Villa-Komaroff regards being a graduate student at MIT as one of the best times of her life.

Begins Ground-Breaking Work With DNA

After graduating with a Ph.D. from MIT in 1975, Villa-Komaroff was a Helen Hay Whitney Postdoctoral Fellow. Her first postdoctoral position was with Dr. Fotis Kafatos in the biology department at Harvard, where she worked on the synthesis of eggshell proteins. As she and Dr. Kafatos did their work, it became apparent that the new technology known as recombinant DNA (techniques used to combine the DNA from one organism to the DNA of bacteria) was the best method to study the regulation and structure of eukaryotic genes. According to Villa-Komaroff in an interview with contributor Helene Barker Kiser, "Eukaryotes are creatures like mice, people, and silkworms that have cells where the genetic material, e.g. DNA, is sequestered in the nucleus. Bacteria are prokaryotes and have no nucleus." The recombinant DNA technique made it possible to study the structure and regulation of genes in detail because the combined DNA reproduced in the bacteria, so there was quite a bit of it to study. This new technology was very exciting and revolutionary, but caused some misplaced concern among people who didn't understand what the researchers were doing. There was a national outcry from people who felt that the use of the recombinant DNA technique might result in the accidental creation of a "monster germ." In 1975 the mayor of Cambridge banned recombinant DNA work in the city and Villa-Komaroff and the other scientists were forced to move the research to a lab in Cold Spring Harbor, New York. There Villa-Komaroff planned to use the recombinant DNA technique to clone the silkworm genome. Although the work didn't produce a lot of tangible results, Villa-Komaroff became very skilled at the technique.

Conducts Ground-Breaking Work on Insulin

Villa-Komaroff was then asked to join Dr. Walter Gilbert's research team at Harvard to use the recombinant DNA technique to clone the rat insulin gene and attempt to produce insulin in bacteria. This proved to be very successful. In about six months, the research team was able to produce insulin from bacteria. The process was patented, and now most diabetics use insulin made by bacteria.

In 1978, Villa-Komaroff returned to Massachusetts as Assistant Professor and later Associate Professor of Molecular Genetics and Microbiology at the University of Massachusetts Medical Center. Although she received tenure, Villa-Komaroff wanted to set up her own lab, so she joined Harvard Medical School in 1986 as Associate Professor in the department of Neuropathology, then Associate Professor in the department of neurology from 1988–1996, chairing the Graduate School Advisory Committee Program in Neuroscience from 1990–1995. During this time, she also served as Acting Head of the Mental Retardation Research Center and the Division of Neuroscience at Boston's Children's Hospital. Her research focused on insulin-related proteins in the human brain, and her work led to greater understanding of the brain's IGF2-insulin-like growth factor—which is involved in regulating cell development and cycles.

In 1996, Villa-Komaroff decided to close her lab in order to accept the positions of Professor in the department of Neurology and Associate Vice President, later Vice President, for Research at Northwestern University. At Northwestern, Villa-Komaroff is involved in many different projects because administrative work allows her to indulge her curiosity. After two short courses in management at MIT, Villa-Komaroff became responsible for administration of all of Northwestern's research units, including policy, and is involved in national policy issues as well. Her husband stayed behind in Boston, but the couple get together as often as they can, usually two weekends a month when "the time is for us and we play. Work doesn't creep in." The couple have no children, but stay close to nieces and nephews, one of whom is in medical school at Northwestern.

Villa-Komaroff views teaching and encouraging students as being just as important as research work, and she frequently makes presentations and has invited students to work in her laboratories, where all of her associates feel part of a team. She urges high school students, particularly girls, to "keep taking math courses so that entire worlds do not become closed to you." Villa-Komaroff remains active in the Society for the Advancement of Chicanos and Native Americans in Science, for which she is a founding member. In her spare time, Villa-Komaroff enjoys photography and reading mystery books.

Among her many awards, Villa-Komaroff has been honored with Goucher's Alumnae Achievement Award, the Hispanic Engineer National Achievement Award in College Education, as well as honorary degrees from St. Thomas University, Goucher College, and Pine Manor College. She has also won the Hispanic Achievement Award in Science and was profiled in a PBS miniseries on women scientists called *Discovering Women*. Villa-Komaroff is a member of the Association for Women in Science, the American Society for Cell Biology, the Society for Neuroscience (Minority Education, Training, and Professional Advancement Committee), and the National Science Federation Advisory Council, among many other organizations. In her own opinion, Villa-Komaroff's favorite honor is as one of the "100 Most Influential Hispanics," for which she was selected in 1997 because of her insulin–cloning research.

SELECTED WRITINGS BY VILLA-KOMAROFF:

Periodicals

(With N. Guttman, D. Baltimore, and H. F. Lodish) "Complete Translation of Poliovirus RNA in a Eukaryotic Cell–Free System." *Proceedings of the National Academy of Science* 72 (1975):4157–4161.

(With W. Gilbert) "Useful Proteins from Recombinant Bacteria." *Scientific American* 4 (1980): 74–94.

"Quantitative Analysis of the Expression of a VIP Transgene." *Molecular Brain Research* (33), 1995.
(With M. F. Lopez, P. Dikkes, and P. Zurakowski) "Insulin–like Growth Factor–II Affects the Appearance and Glycogen Content of Glycogen Cells in the Murine Placenta." *Endocrinology* 137 (1996): 2100–2108.

FURTHER READING

Books

American Men and Women of Science. 17th ed., vol. 1. New York: R.R. Bowker, 1989.
St. John, Betty. *Hispanic Scientists*. Mankato, MN: Capstone Press, 1996.

Other

Kiser, Helene Barker, interview with Lydia Villa-Komaroff conducted April 28, 1999
"ASCB Profile: Lydia Villa-Komaroff." *The American Society for Cell Biology*. http://ns1.faseb.org/ascb/news/vol21no9/profile.html (9 March 1999)
Curriculum Vitae. Lydia Villa-Komaroff. http://www.nsf.gov/bio/bioac/vitaes/komaroff.htm (17 March 1999)
"DNA Detective: Molecular Biologist Lydia Villa-Komaroff." *Discovering Women*. Video produced by WGBH Boston, 1995.

Sketch by Helene Barker Kiser

Marjorie Jean (Young) Vold
1913–1991
Canadian-born American colloid chemist

During the course of a career spanning half a century Marjorie Vold distinguished herself as a researcher, lecturer, and author. She and her husband, Robert D. Vold, were pioneers in the field of colloid science, which studies how particles suspended in molecules affect a substance's molecular properties. Colloid research has relevance to substances ranging from soap and lubricating oil to DNA. Vold managed to maintain enormous energy and output despite a 33–year battle with multiple sclerosis.

Vold was born in Ottawa, Cananda, on October 25, 1913, Marjorie Jean Young was the daughter of Reynold Kenneth and Whilhelmine (Aitken) Young. Her interest in science was sparked at an early age by family members who were scientists. The Youngs moved to the United States in 1918 and Marjorie became a naturalized citizen at the age of eight.

She attended the University of California at Berkeley, receiving her bachelor of science degree in1934. She was class valedictorian and received a University Medal. She remained at Berkeley to complete her studies and received her Ph.D. in 1936. She was only 23 at the time. That same year she married Robert Vold, who had received his Ph.D. in chemistry from Berkeley the year before.The couple had three children—Mary, Robert, and Wylda—over the next few years

Vold's first academic position was as a lecturer at the University of Cincinnati. In 1937 she returned to California, accepting a research position at Stanford University. She remained there until 1941. From 1942–1946 she was an industrial chemist for the Union Oil Company, where she conducted wartime research. In 1947 she and her husband began a 30–year association with the University of Southern California. She began as a research associate and lecturer in chemistry and in 1958 was named adjunct professor of chemistry.

Conducts Colloid Research

Vold's career frequently took her and her husband beyond the halls of USC. From 1953–1954 Marjorie received a Guggenheim Fellowship and Robert a Fulbright Fellowship, which allowed them to conduct colloid research in the laboratories of the University of Utrecht in the Netherlands. In 1955 Marjorie Vold served as honorary reader in physical chemistry at the Indian Institute of Science in Bangalore, India. She served in this position for two years and in 1957 became the first woman to address the Institute.

In addition to her lecturing and research, Vold was also a prolific writer. She wrote or coauthored some 150 scientific papers during her career, and contributed to numerous books. She also coauthored two books. *Colloid Chemistry: The Science of Large Molecules, Small Particles, and Surfaces,* which she coauthored with her husband, was considered one of the most important works on colloid science when it was published in 1964.

Diagnosed with MS in 1958

In 1958, Vold was diagnosed with multiple sclerosis. Although a serious degenerative disease, it affects each person differently. For Vold, it meant confinement to a wheelchair for most of the next three decades. But it had little noticeable effect on her output as a teacher or researcher. She maintained a rigorous schedule and continued to teach and to collaborate with her husband on research. Her hard work was recognized in 1967 when she was awarded the American Chemical Society's Garvan Medal. Her work as a chemist was recognized outside the scientific community as well. In 1966 the *Los Angeles Times* named Vold its "Woman of the Year." In her spare time, Vold did volunteer work for both the Boy and Girl Scouts.

Vold and her husband retired together from USC in 1974. Retirement for Vold, however, did not mean giving up science. In fact, she continued to do research and write papers, even as her health deteriorated. Toward the end of her life, when she was bedridden, she used a computer to design mathematical simulations. Her last paper was submitted to the American Chemical Society in October 1991. A month later, on November 4, Marjorie Vold died at a convalescent hospital in Poway, California. The paper she submitted was published posthumously.

SELECTED WRITINGS BY VOLD:

Books

(With Robert D. Vold) *Colloid Chemistry: The Science of Large Molecules, Small Particles, and Surfaces.* New York: Reinhold Publishing Group, 1964.

(With Robert D. Vold) "A Third of a Century of Colloid Chemistry." In *Colloidal Dispersions and Micellar Behavior.* Edited by K.D. Mittal. Washington, D.C.: American Chemical Society, 1975.

FURTHER READING

Books

Bailey, Martha J. *American Women in Science: A Biographical Dictionary.* Denver: ABC–CLIO, 1994.

Shearer, Benjamin F. and Barbara S. Shearer, eds. *Notable Women in the Physical Sciences: A Biographical Dictionary.* Westport, CT: Greenwood Press, 1997.

Periodicals

"Garvan Medal: Marjorie J. Vold." *Chemical and Engineering News* 45, no. 15 (1967): 87.

Sketch by George A. Milite

Hilda Geiringer von Mises
1893–1973
Austrian-American mathematician

Hilda Geiringer von Mises is best known for the fundamental equation for plane plastic distortions that bears her maiden name. She also made significant contributions to probability theory, both in her studies of the mathematical problems arising from Mendel's biological principles, and in helping to refine and edit her husband's work in the objective study of frequency and statistics. To that end, she published new editions of Richard von Mises's *Probability, Statistics and Truth* and *Mathematical Theory of Probability and Statistics* after his death. Geiringer was also an educator of note, chairing Wheaton College's mathematics department from 1944 to 1959. Ultimately, though, it was research that most sparked Geiringer's interest; she published some 50 articles in the course of her professional life. She was also honored with a special presentation on the 50th anniversary of her graduation from the University of Vienna and was named professor emerita at the University of Berlin.

Geiringer was born on September 28, 1893, in Vienna, Austria. The daughter of a successful textile manufacturer, Ludwig Geiringer, and Martha Wertheimer, she grew up in an assimilated Jewish household. During the time of Geiringer's youth, Vienna was undergoing something of a cultural revolution. The city was home to scientific luminaries such as Sigmund Freud and Ernst Mach; the music of Mahler and Schoenberg filled its concert halls. Geiringer's younger brother, Karl, was influenced by this heady atmosphere and later became a well known musicologist. Hilda also benefited from the climate of the times, attending a well-respected gymnasium, or high school, where she displayed an early acumen in mathematics. After graduation she went on to the University of Vienna, studying pure mathematics under Wilhelm Wirtinger. Despite the dislocations of the First World War, Geiringer earned a doctorate in 1917 with a thesis on double trigonometric series, published in 1918.

Pursues a Career in Mathematics

Because it was extremely difficult for a woman to find a university position in Austria or Germany at the time, Geiringer served as an editor on *Fortschritte der Mathematik* for two years before going to the University of Berlin as assistant to mathematician Richard Martin Edler von Mises at the Institute for Applied Mathematics. In 1921 she married mathematician Felix Pollaczek. The couple was divorced in 1925, leaving Geiringer to raise their daughter, Magda.

In Berlin, Geiringer's interests turned from pure to applied mathematics, partly as a result of the influence of Richard von Mises, the man who would become her second husband. In 1927 she became a lecturer at the University of Berlin, working in probability theory and the development of plasticity theory. In 1930, she developed the fundamental Geiringer equations for plane plastic deformations or distortions.

Years of Dislocation

In 1933 Geiringer became, along with thousands of other Jews and intellectuals, an exile. With Hitler in power, she saw the tenuousness of her position in Germany; well-respected or not, she was a Jew. Taking her daughter first to Belgium and then to Istanbul, Geiringer settled temporarily at the University of Turkey, where she was a professor of mathematics until the outbreak of the Second World War in

1939. At that point, she and Magda fled to the United States, where she found a teaching position at Bryn Mawr. Her former colleague Richard von Mises also emigrated to the United States from Turkey. When their paths crossed this time, however, a different relationship blossomed, and the couple were married in 1943. Geiringer, however, kept her maiden name for all professional purposes.

To live closer to her new husband, who taught at Harvard, Geiringer sought positions at universities and colleges near Boston, but few were willing to consider hiring a female mathematician. Finally, in 1944 she took the position of professor and chairman of the mathematics department at Wheaton College in Norton, Massachusetts, where she remained until her retirement in 1959. During this time, Wheaton's math department expanded greatly, sending several students on to postgraduate courses and careers in mathematics. Geiringer continued her research in statistics on her own time, concentrating on the mathematical basis of Mendelian genetics and plasticity. She considered this research to be the most essential part of her professional life.

Becomes Research Fellow at Harvard

With the death of her husband in 1953, Geiringer felt compelled to complete his unfinished work in probability theory. With a grant from the Office of Naval Research, she became a research fellow at Harvard while keeping her position at Wheaton. She spent much of her time putting von Mises's papers in order. Teaming up with Geoffrey S. Ludford, she completed the manuscript of *Mathematical Theory of Compressible Fluid Flow* and also explored the foundations of probability theory, extending and refining her husband's theories in new editions of his works. After retirement from Wheaton, Geiringer worked full time on her beloved research and lectured widely on probability theory.

Hilda Geiringer von Mises was elected a fellow of the American Academy of Arts and Sciences and was a member of the scientific honorary Sigma Xi. In 1956 the University of Berlin, where she began her career in 1921, elected her professor emerita, with a full salary. Further honors came her way in 1960, when Wheaton College awarded her an honorary degree, and in 1967, when the University of Vienna celebrated the 50th anniversary of her graduation with a special ceremony. Geiringer's life was dedicated largely to mathematics, though she found the time to be not only a caring mother, but an active outdoors person with a penchant for mountain climbing, and an aficionado of literature and classical music. She died in 1973, of pneumonia, while visiting her musicologist brother in Santa Barbara, California.

SELECTED WRITINGS BY GEIRINGER:

Books

Die Gedankenwelt der Mathematik. Berlin: Verlag der Arbeitergemeinschaft, 1922.

"Beitrag zum vollständigen ebenen Plastizitätsproblem." *Verhandlungen des 3. Internationalen Kongresse für Technische Mechanik, Stockholm 24–29 August, 1930.* Vol. 2, 185–190. Stockholm: A. B. Sveriges Litografiska Tryckerier, 1931.

Fondements mathématiques de la théorie des corps plastiques isotropes. Paris: Gauthier–Villars, 1937.

von Mises, Richard. *Probability, Statistics and Truth.* 2d ed. Prepared by Hilda Geiringer. New York, 1957. 4th German edition. Library of Exact Philosophy, volume 7. New York: Springer Verlag, 1973.

von Mises, Richard. *Mathematical Theory of Compressible Fluid Flow.* Completed by Hilda Geiringer and G. S. Ludford. New York: Academic Press, 1957.

von Mises, Richard. *Mathematical Theory of Probability Statistics.* Edited and complemented by Hilda Geiringer. New York: Academic Press, 1964.

(With Alfred Freudenthal) "The Mathematical Theories of the Inelastic Continuum." *Handbuch der Physik (Encyclopedia of Physics).* volume 6, 229–432. New York: Springer Verlag, 1964.

Periodicals

"Trigonometrische Doppelreihen."*Monatshefte für Mathematik und Physik* 29 (1918): 65–144.

"Zur Gleiderungstheorie räumliche Fachwerke." *Zeitschrift für angewandte Mathematik und Mechanik* 12 (1932): 369–76.

FURTHER READING

Books

Bailey, Martha J. *American Women in Science: A Biographical Dictionary.* Denver: ABC–CLIO, 1994, pp. 402–03.

Richards, Joan L. *Notable American Women, the Modern Period: A Biographical Dictionary.* Edited by Barbara Sicherman and Carol Hurd Green. Cambridge, MA: Belknap Press, 1980, pp. 267–68.

Richards, Joan L. *Women of Mathematics: A Biobibliographic Sourcebook.* Edited by Louise S. Grinstein and Paul J. Campbell. Westport, CT: Greenwood Press, 1987, pp. 41–46.

Periodicals

"Dr. Geiringer Retires." *Wheaton College Newsletter.* 47 (1959): 4.

Other

Obituary. *New York Times* (24 March 1973): 36.

Sketch by J. Sydney Jones

W

Priscilla Bell Wakefield
1750–1832
British botanist, author, and philanthropist

Priscilla Bell Wakefield was a philanthropist, an author of children's books, and one of the first women to write and publish on botany and natural science. Her botanical text *Introduction to Botany, in a Series of Familiar Letters* was written as a correspondence between two sisters, and included the Linnean system of classification. By 1841, this classic British work, in its 11th Edition, had received widespread acclaim, and served as the inspiration for many American editions.

Wakefield was born into the Bell family in Tottenham, Middlesex, on January 31, 1750. The Bells were wealthy Quakers. She married London businessman Edward Wakefield in 1771, continuing to uphold the traditions of her Quaker upbringing, though allowing herself occasional freedoms with amusements and manner of dress. Managing the household, Wakefield raised a daughter and two sons, and kept a journal for most of her life.

Begins Writing Career at 40

Toward the end of the eighteenth century, writing popular books and textbooks on botany and natural history had become a novel way women could earn money, and Wakefield was a prominent participant in this new field. She was a vociferous advocate of women's emancipation in work and schooling, and wanted women to be able to achieve economic independence. When she was 40, her husband's business suffered financial misfortune, causing an extended period of economic hardship at home. She began writing, in part to bring in money. She advanced her views on the benefits of botany for women's education and moral improvement. In the space of 20 years, Wakefield published 17 books, adding to her growing bibliography the scientific titles *Domestic Recreation: or Dialogues Illustrative of Natural and Scientific Subjects*, and *An Introduction to the Natural History and Classification of Insects, in a Series of Letters*.

Establishes First Savings Bank in England

A careful observer of nature and people, Wakefield was also a philanthropist, dedicated to social reform. She worked to ameliorate conditions for the disadvantaged, to expand occupational and educational opportunities for women, and to monitor and strengthen moral and intellectual instruction for children. In 1792, she established a lying–in charity for women. Soon thereafter, she founded the Female Benefit Club, and the Penny Bank for Children. In 1798 these merged, creating the Frugality Bank, England's first savings bank.

In addition to her science writing, Wakefield contributed articles to *Variety*, letters to the editors of many journals, and published accounts of her humanitarian efforts in *Reports of the Society of Bettering the Conditions and Increasing the Comforts of the Poor*. But perhaps she is remembered most for her children's books. Intended to enlighten, educate, and entertain, she selected topics with strong moral undertones, stories of people grown wise through encountering and overcoming adversity. In her series recounting the travel adventures of a fictional family, Wakefield inserted warnings against criticism, bigotry, and slavery.

Recognized for her contribution to literature, her obituary in *Gentleman's Magazine* read that "she was eminently successful [in her] efforts to improve the rising generation." The last 15 years of her life were fraught with illness. She died in Ipswich, on September 12, 1832.

SELECTED WRITINGS BY WAKEFIELD:

Books

Instinct Displayed, in a Collection of Well-Authenticated Facts, Exemplifying the Extraordinary Sagacity of Various Species of the Animal Creation. London, 1811.

An Introduction to Botany, in a Series of Familiar Letters. London, 1796 1796.

An Introduction to the Natural History and Classification of Insects. London, 1816.

Mental Improvement, or, The Beauties and Wonders of Nature and Art; in a Series of Instructive Conversations. London, 1794.

Reflections on the Present Condition of the Female Sex; with Suggestions for its Improvement. 1798.

FURTHER READING

Books

Todd, J. *A Dictionary of British and American Women Writers, 1600–1800*. Lanham, MD: Rowman and Allanheld, 1985.

Alic, Margaret. *Hypatia's Heritage: A History of Women in Science from Antiquity to the Late Nineteenth Century*. Milford, CT: The Women's Press, 1986.

Abir-Am, P.G., and Outram, D., eds. *Uneasy Careers and Intimate Lives, Women in Science, 1789–1979*. New Brunswick, NJ: Rutgers University Press, 1987.

Kunitz, Stanley J. *British Authors of the Nineteenth Century*. New York: The H. W. Wilson Company, 1936.

Sketch by Kyra Anderson

Mary Ward
1827–1869
Irish microscopist

Mary Ward is best known for her early innovative work with microscopes, but her scientific activities also included entomology, astronomy, and ornithology. She also wrote and illustrated several texts on science. She managed to accomplish all this despite having no formal training in science.

Ward was born on April 27, 1827 in Ballylin, Ireland, to Henry and Hariette Lloyd King. Her father was a clergyman and her mother was of aristocratic background, and young Mary led a comfortable life. As was common among the nineteenth-century aristocracy, Mary's brother was sent to school, but she and her two sisters were educated at home. From an early age (she began collecting butterflies at the age of three) young Mary showed a strong interest in natural science. When she got a bit older, she would examine her specimens under a magnifying glass and make detailed drawings of them.

Ward was fortunate in that her family was keenly interested in science. In fact, the astronomer William Parsons (third Earl of Rosse) was her cousin. In addition, the Kings counted among their friends scientists such as the Scottish physicist Sir David Brewster. As a result, Ward's interests were encouraged, and she was able to use her knowledge and intelligence to develop her talents.

She soon graduated from magnifying glasses to microscopes, teaching herself how to make slides. Because glass was in relatively short supply in the nineteenth century, Ward's earliest slides were often made of ivory, or sometimes from pieces of window glass. As she grew more proficient in microscopy, she eventually purchased commercially produced slides, but she still made many of her own. She also proved to be an accomplished artist; she made painstakingly accurate drawings of the specimens she examined. Sir David Brewster was so impressed with the young woman's work that he sent her specimens from his own collection, as well as a number of scientific papers. Some of her illustrations appear in his 1855 work, *The Life of Newton.*

In the 1840s, William Parsons was building his "Leviathan of Parsonstown" the 58-foot (17.6 m) reflecting telescope that was the largest of its kind in the world until the early 20th century. His estate, Birr Castle, was only 15 miles (24 km) from the Kings, and his cousin Mary visited often and kept a written account of the telescope's construction. She was also one of the first to use it.

In 1854 Mary King married Captain Henry W. C. Ward, brother of the fourth Viscount Bangor. Over the next dozen years Mary Ward gave birth eight times and had three miscarriages. In 1855, Captain Ward left his regiment, and the couple and their children lived off the dividends of Mary's dowry. Accounts describe Captain Ward as more socialite than family man, and apparently his wife was left with nearly all the responsibility of running the family. Mary Ward managed to accomplish this and still pursue her interest in science. The many scientists she met during her lifetime sent her books and papers on a variety of topics. She also managed to acquire her own collection of science texts, often buying second–hand books when she was able to travel.

Ward became an author herself, writing several books, including *Telescope Teachings* in 1859 and *Microscope Teachings* in 1864. She was the first woman to publish on these topics, and her books (as well as numerous articles) were written in an accessible style to reach a wide audience and to popularize microscopes and telescopes. She was so highly regarded as a scientist that when she visited England in 1862, she was given a personal tour of the Royal Observatory at Greenwich, this despite strict rules barring women from admission.

Mary Ward was killed on August 31, 1869 when she was run over by a steam-powered carriage that had been designed by her cousin William Parsons. (She has been called in some sources the world's first automobile accident victim.) Her husband's ancestral home, Castle Ward in County Down, now houses a display of her microscopes, slides, and illustrations.

SELECTED WRITINGS BY WARD:

Books

Telescope Teachings. London: Groomsbridge, 1859.

Microscope Teachings. London: Groomsbridge, 1864.

FURTHER READING

Books

WITS (Women in Technology and Science), ed. *Stars, Shells, and Bluebells: Women Scientists and Pioneers.* Dublin, WITS, 1997.

Sketch by George A. Milite

Margaret Floy Washburn (Archives of the History of American Psychology. Reproduced by permission.)

Margaret Floy Washburn
1871–1939
American psychologist

Margaret Washburn was a pioneer in the fledgling science of psychology. Her interests, both theoretical and experimental, were wide ranging, and her early studies of animal behavior, vision, and speech introduced a generation of students to a new scientific discipline.

Margaret Washburn was born in New York City in 1871 in a frame house that had been built by her maternal great-grandfather, a successful florist and nurseryman. She was the only child of educated parents, Elizabeth Floy (Davis) and Francis Washburn. Her mother had inherited a considerable fortune, and her father, a former businessman, was an Episcopalian minister. In 1878, he took a parish in Walden, New York, followed by one in the town of Kingston, New York. Washburn could read long before she started primary school at age seven, and she attended the Ulster Academy from 1883 to 1887. At the age of 16, she entered Vassar College, in Poughkeepsie, New York, where she studied biology, chemistry, and philosophy, earning her B.A. in 1891. While there, she also developed a love of poetry.

Enters New Field of Experimental Psychology

Washburn decided to merge her interests in science and philosophy by entering the new field of experimental psychology. She applied to Columbia University to study with James McKeen Cattell, who had just established the first psychology laboratory at Columbia, after training with Wilhelm Wundt in Germany. Columbia admitted Washburn as a "hearer," or auditor, but despite Cattell's support, the trustees refused to admit a woman as a regular graduate student. After one year, Cattell advised Washburn to work with Edward Bradford Titchener, who had just arrived at Cornell University from Wundt's laboratory. At Cornell, women graduate students were not only admitted, they were provided with scholarships. Washburn's dissertation, on how visual images influence motor perceptions of direction and distance, was published in Wundt's German journal, and she was awarded her doctorate in 1894.

Washburn became a professor of psychology, philosophy, and ethics at Wells College. She remained there until 1900, when she returned to Cornell as instructor of social and animal psychology, and the warden, or dean, of Sage College, the women's dormitory. In 1902, Washburn became head of the psychology department at the University of Cincinnati. However the following year, she returned to Vassar College as an associate professor, where she remained until her retirement in 1937. A strong proponent of coeducation, Washburn returned to Vassar, one of the first women's colleges, with some reluctance.

Presents a New Theory in Psychology

Washburn's research focused on social consciousness, emotions, the role of movement in mental life, and animal psychology. In her years at Vassar, she devised experimental studies which were carried out by her students. About 70 of these studies were published, written by Washburn, but coauthored with students. Washburn wrote over 200 publications during the course of her career, and she was the sole author of approximately 60 original research papers. Animal behavior and conscious experience in animals were among Washburn's enduring interests. Her most influential work was *The Animal Mind,* a critical review of the literature of animal psychology. The fourth edition of this book appeared in 1936. Washburn was a theorist as well as an experimentalist, and she believed that consciousness and behavior were separable psychological phenomena. She developed a theory, explained in her book, *Movement and Mental Imagery,* that all mental functions, including thoughts and perceptions, produced physical reactions of some sort. Wundt and Titchener had argued that only consciousness, not physical movement, mattered in psychology, and the American behaviorists believed that only observable behavior mattered. Thus, Washburn's theory linked the two dominant schools of psychology: introspectionism, as the Wundt school was known, and behaviorism.

Washburn became president of the American Psychological Association in 1921. Later, she served as vice–president of the American Association for the Advancement of Science. In 1925, Washburn succeeded Titchener as coeditor of the *American Journal of Psychology*. However because she was at a women's college that offered little support for research or other professional activities, Washburn continued to carry a full teaching load, as well as pay for her research out of her own salary. Due to her heavy schedule, she resigned her editorial position in 1931. In 1929, she became a charter member of the Society of Experimental Psychologists, which was reorganized and opened to women for the first time following Titchener's death. (Titchener had barred women from the society for 25 years.). As Margaret Rossiter quoted from a letter to Washburn from her friend and colleague Karl Dallenbach: "We are counting on your attendance at the meetings of the Experimentalists. There will be no segregation. . . . The inclusion of women marks a great occasion. T's ashes will smolder from the thought of it." Two years later, at Washburn's invitation, the society met at Vassar. The same year, Washburn became only the second woman, after the anatomist **Florence Rena Sabin**, to be elected to the National Academy of Sciences. Washburn never married. In 1937, she suffered a series of debilitating strokes and she died in Poughkeepsie in 1939.

SELECTED WRITINGS BY WASHBURN:

Books

(Translator with E. B. Titchener and Julia Gulliver) *Ethics*, by Wilhelm Wundt. New York, 1897–1901.

The Animal Mind: A Textbook of Comparative Psychology. New York: Macmillan, 1908.

Movement and Mental Imagery: Outlines of a Motor Theory of the Complexer Mental Processes. 1916. Reprint, New York: Arno Press, 1978.

Periodicals

"The Perception of Distance in the Inverted Landscape." *Mind* 3 (1894): 438–40.

"The Genetic Function of Movement and Organic Sensations for Social Consciousness." *American Journal of Psychology* 14 (1903): 337–42.

(With I. Powelson) "The Effect of Verbal Suggestion on Judgments of the Affective Value of Colors." *American Journal of Psychology* 24 (1913): 267–69.

(With S. D. White and S. May) "A Study of Freshmen." *American Journal of Psychology* 28 (1917): 152.

(With E. Hatt and E. B. Holt) "Affective Sensitiveness in Poets and in Scientific Students." *American Journal of Psychology* 34 (1925): 105–6.

(With F. H. Verhoeff) "A New Theory of Binocular Vision." *Archives of Ophthalmology* 15 (1936): 1117–18.

FURTHER READING

Books

Boring, Edwin G. "Margaret Floy Washburn." In *Notable American Women 1607–1950: A Biographical Dictionary*. Edited by Edward T. James, Janet Wilson James, and Paul W. Boyer. Vol. 3. Cambridge: Harvard University Press, 1971.

Ogilvie, Marilyn Bailey. *Women in Science, Antiquity through the Nineteenth Century: A Biographical Dictionary with Annotated Bibliography*. Cambridge: MIT Press, 1991.

Rossiter, Margaret W. *Women Scientists in America: Struggles and Strategies to 1940*. Baltimore: Johns Hopkins University Press, 1982.

Periodicals

Martin, Mabel F. "The Psychological Contributions of Margaret Floy Washburn." *American Journal of Psychology* 53 (1940): 7–20.

Sketch by Margaret Alic

Katharine Way
1903–1995
American physicist

Nuclear physicist Katharine Way worked on the Manhattan Project to develop the first atomic bomb and was one of the first scientists to call attention to the dangers of nuclear weapons. She was the compiler and editor of vast tables of atomic and nuclear data that were used by physicists on a daily basis, prior to the widespread use of computer databases.

Born in 1903, in Sewickley, Pennsylvania, Way was the second child and the first of two daughters of William Addison and Louise (Jones) Way. Way's mother died when she was 12 years old, and her father, a judge, married a physician and moved the family to Southern Pines, North Carolina. There Way's father and stepmother ran an orchid nursery. Way and her younger sister attended Miss Hartridge's boarding school in Plainfield, New Jersey. After two years, Way transferred to Rosemary Hall, a prestigious girls' school in Greenwich, Connecticut.

Although Way attended Vassar College in Poughkeepsie, New York for two years, she became ill, possibly with tuberculosis, and left school, spending two years recuperating at a boarding house at Saranac Lake, New York. She then returned to college at Columbia University in New York City, where Dr. Edward Kasner encouraged her interest in mathematics. She coauthored her first paper with Kasner. After graduating with a B.S. degree from Columbia in 1932, Way became a graduate student in physics at the University of North Carolina in Chapel Hill, obtaining her Ph.D. in 1938. She was the first graduate student of the nuclear physicist John Wheeler. Her initial project, "Spectrographic Determination of Calcium in Plant Ashes," was inspired by her father's orchid–raising venture. Her subsequent research at North Carolina was in nuclear physics and resulted in two additional publications. As a graduate student, Way was an active supporter of striking workers at the North Carolina textile mills.

Joins Manhattan Project

In 1938 Way became a Huff Research Fellow at Bryn Mawr College in Pennsylvania and the following year she was appointed lecturer at the University of Tennessee. Later she became an assistant professor of physics. At the University of Tennessee she was part of a project to construct a source of neutrons for producing an isotope of the element neptunium. However in 1942, in the midst of the second world war, Way went to Washington D.C. to work on mines and minesweeping with John Bardeen, later a Nobel laureate. There she heard rumors about the Manhattan Project to develop an atomic bomb. Soon, John Wheeler had secured her a position in Chicago, working on reactor design and other problems. These included the analysis of Enrico Fermi's sustained nuclear chain reaction, with Alvin Weinberg, and radioactivity data on the products of nuclear fission. Her theoretical work on the latter, conducted with Eugene Wigner, later a Nobel laureate, led to the Way–Wigner formula for the decay of fission products.

Soon, there was a great need for collecting and organizing the vast amounts of data produced by the Manhattan Project. Way took on this task, first as a hobby and later as a vocation. In 1945, she moved to what is now the Oak Ridge National Laboratory (ORNL) in Oak Ridge, Tennessee where she continued analyzing products of nuclear fission and organizing data.

Warns of Nuclear Threat

Way became increasingly concerned about the threat posed by the atomic bomb that she had helped to develop. In 1946 she coedited the book *One World or None*, a project created to increase public awareness of the dangers of the atomic bomb. Contributors for the book included Nobel laureates Niels Bohr, Arthur H. Compton, Hans Bethe, and Albert Einstein. When the Soviet Union successfully tested a nuclear weapon earlier than the United States thought possible, nuclear scientists came under the suspicion of House Un–American Activities Committee (HUAC) a committee formed after World War II to investigate allegations of spying and communist sympathies. Way disagreed with the suspicions of HUAC and protested to the Atomic Energy Commission about investigations of Oak Ridge scientists.

Way then began working for the National Bureau of Standards in Washington, D.C., where she began compiling and editing data full–time. In 1954, in collaboration with Marion Wood, Way developed the Way–Wood systematics for estimating the beta–decay of unmeasured radioactive isotopes and for assigning atomic and isotope numbers to new decay data. In 1953, she established the Nuclear Data Project (NDP) of the National Research Council, organizing a group of physicists to compile "Nuclear Data Sheets." In 1964, the project moved to Oak Ridge, where Way arranged for the publication of a new international journal, *Nuclear Data Sheets*. In 1965 she became editor of a new two–part journal, *Nuclear Data*, consisting of *Nuclear Data Tables* and *Nuclear Data Sheets*. Later, it became *Atomic Data and Nuclear Data Tables* , which she continued to edit until 1982. Way's efforts had a tremendous influence on the organization and presentation of data in basic physics. Way directed the NDP until her retirement in 1968 and it became a model for Information Analysis Centers at ORNL.

In 1974, Way was named a Distinguished Alumnus of the University of North Carolina. Following her retirement, Way returned to North Carolina as an adjunct professor at Duke University, a position she held until 1988. Way was active in the civil rights movement of the 1960s and has been an advocate for the medical needs of the elderly. In 1980, she organized a lecture series on "Health Education for the Elderly." Katharine Way died on December 8, 1995.

SELECTED WRITINGS BY WAY:

Books

(With Dexter Masters, eds.) *One World or None*. Freeport, NY: Books for Libraries Press, 1972.

(With Roswell Clifton Gibbs) *A Directory to Nuclear Data Tabulations*. Washington, D.C.: Nuclear Data Project, National Academy of Sciences, National Research Council, 1958.

(With Lewis Slack) *Radiations from Radioactive Atoms in Frequent Use*. Washington, D.C.: U.S. Atomic Energy Commission, 1959.

Periodicals

(With J. M. Arthur) " Spectrographic Determination of Calcium in Plant Ashes." *Contributions from Boyce Thompson Institute* 7 (1935): 103–12.

"Photoelectric Cross Section of the Deuteron." *Physical Review* 51 (1937): 552–56.

(With M. Wood) "Beta Decay Energy Systematics." *Physical Review* 94 (1954): 119–28.

(With N. B. Gove and R. van Lieshout) "Waiting for Mr. Know–It–All, or Scientific Information Tools We Could Have Now." *Physics Today* 15 (1962): 22–26.

"Free Enterprise in Data Compilation." *Science* 159 (1968): 280–82.

"One World or None—For the Record." *Bulletin of the Atomic Scientists* 38 (2) (1982): 49.

FURTHER READING

Books

Bailey, Martha J. *American Women in Science: A Biographical Dictionary*. Denver: ABC–CLIO, 1994.

Martin, Murray J., Norwood D. Gove, Ruth M. Gove, and Agda Artna–Cohen. "Katharine Way (1903–)." In *Women in Chemistry and Physics: A Bibliographic Sourcebook*, edited by Louise S. Grinstein, Rose K. Rose, and Miriam H. Rafailovich. Westport, CT: Greenwood Press, 1993.

O'Neill, Lois Decker, ed. *The Women's Book of World Records and Achievements*. Garden City, NY: Doubleday, 1979.

Periodicals

Merzbacher, Eugen. Obituary. *Physics Today* 49, no.12 (December 1996): 75.

Sketch by Margaret Alic

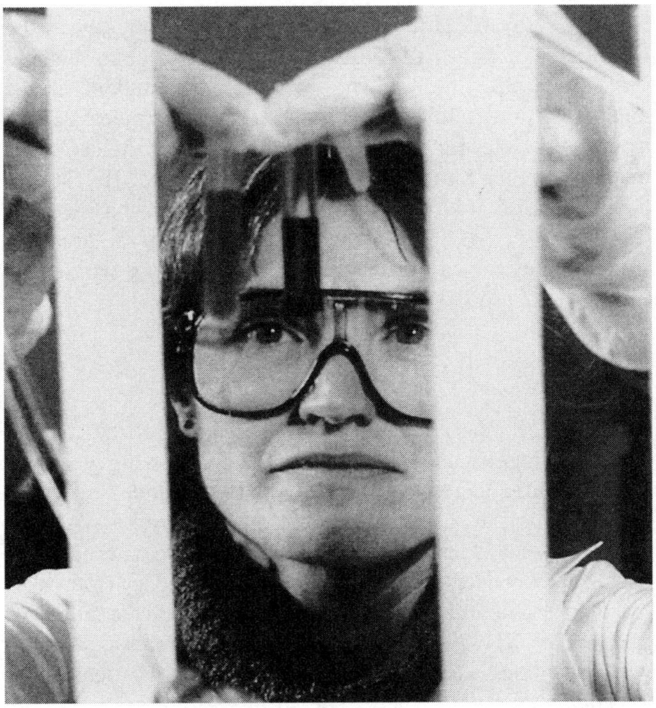

Karen Wetterhahn (AP/Wide World Photos. Reproduced by permission.)

Karen Elizabeth Wetterhahn
1948–1997
American biochemist

Karen Wetterhahn, a physical biochemist, was a well–known cancer researcher who studied the interactions of heavy metals, particularly chromium, with DNA. As a professor at Dartmouth College, she cofounded a mentoring program to encourage women students in science. Her death in 1997, from accidental mercury poisoning, called worldwide attention to deficiencies in laboratory safety.

Karen Wetterhahn was born in Plattsburgh, New York, in 1948, the daughter of Gustave George and Mary Elizabeth (Thibault) Wetterhahn. Her father was a chemist and Wetterhahn developed an early interest in science and mathematics. After attending St. Mary's High School in Champlain, New York, Wetterhahn earned her B.S. degree in math and chemistry, magna cum laude, from St. Lawrence University in 1970. After spending a year as a formulations chemist for the Mearl Corporation in Ossining, New York, Wetterhahn became a research fellow at Columbia University in New York City, earning her Ph.D. in inorganic chemistry and physical biochemistry in 1975 with Stephen Lippard, and winning the Hammett Award in Chemistry. After one year as a National Institutes of Health postdoctoral fellow in biochemistry at the Institute of Cancer Research at the Columbia University College of Physicians and Surgeons, Wetterhahn became the first woman professor in the chemistry department at Dartmouth College in Hanover, New Hampshire. In 1978, she became an assistant professor in the biochemistry program and from 1981 until 1985, she was an Alfred P. Sloan Fellow. Wetterhahn was promoted to associate professor in 1982 and to full professor in 1986. In 1996, she became the Albert Bradley Third Century Professor in the Sciences.

Shows that Chromium Damages DNA

Wetterhahn was the author of more than 85 scientific papers. She studied the mechanisms by which chemicals and metals cause cancer and examined the ways in which these carcinogens are metabolized and interact with DNA. She looked at the effects of the modified DNA. In particular, Wetterhahn determined the mechanism by which chromium damages DNA, possibly causing cancer, a mechanism that became known as the "uptake–reduction model." Wetterhahn was known for her many collaborations and her laboratory included up to 15 researchers, both chemists and biologists.

In the late 1980s, distressed by the attrition rates for women science students at Dartmouth, Wetterhahn helped establish the Women in Science Project (WISP), a mentoring program that provided freshmen women with laboratory experience. The program proved to be a resounding success and became a model for programs across the country. As the dean of graduate studies in 1990, as associate dean of the faculty of sciences from 1990 to 1994, and as acting dean of the faculty of arts and sciences in 1995, Wetterhahn reorganized the life sciences at Dartmouth, emphasizing interdisciplinary connections and collaborations among the biology, chemistry, environmental studies, engineering, and medical school programs. She also created a new major in biophysical chemistry. In 1995, Wetterhahn won a seven–million–dollar grant from the National Institute of Environmental Health Sciences' Superfund Program to study the relationship between heavy metals and human health. It was the largest grant in Dartmouth's history and included studies in biochemistry, epidemiology, toxicology, and the biology of lakes.

Spill Proves Fatal

While on sabbatical, Wetterhahn had begun a collaboration with her former advisor Stephen Lippard and with Jonathan Wilker, a graduate student at the Massachusetts Institute of Technology. They were studying the chemically–active sites of proteins using nuclear magnetic resonance (NMR) spectroscopy. Like other researchers, Wetterhahn was using dimethylmercury as a standard for her NMR experiments. Working in a fume hood, wearing goggles, protective clothing, and latex gloves, and using standard laboratory procedures for handling toxic chemicals, Wetterhahn transferred a small amount of the liquid. Later she remembered spilling a drop on her glove. She removed her gloves and washed her hands. Five months later, in January, Wetterhahn began experiencing symptoms of severe mercury poisoning. She immediately asked her colleagues to inform the scientific community of the dangers of dimethylmercury. Three weeks later, she entered a coma and she died on June 8, 1997, at the age of 48. Wetterhahn was survived by her husband, Leon H. Webb, whom she had married in 1982, and their son and daughter. In the aftermath of this tragedy, it became apparent that not only was dimethylmercury far more toxic than previously thought, but also that standard laboratory gloves offered no protection from the chemical.

SELECTED WRITINGS BY WETTERHAHN:

Periodicals

(With K. M. Borges) "Chromium Cross–Links Glutathione and Cysteine to DNA. *Carcinogenesis* 10 (1989): 2165–68.

(With D. M. Stearns and J. J. Belbruno) "A Prediction of Chromium(III) Accumulation in Humans from Chromium Dietary Supplements." *The Federation of American Societies for Experimental Biology Journal* 9 (1995): 1650–57.

(With A. Barchowsky, E. J. Dudek, and M. D. Treadwell) "Arsenic Induces Oxidant Stress and NF–kB Activation in Cultured Aortic Endothelial Cells." *Free Radicals in Biology and Medicine* 21 (1996): 783–90.

(With J. A. Shumilla and A. Barchowsky) "Inhibition of NF–kB Binding to DNA by Chromium, Cadmium, Mercury, Zinc and Arsenite in Vitro: Evidence of a Thiol Mechanism." *Archives of Biochemistry and Biophysics* 349 (1998): 356–62.

(With J. M. Yuann and K. J. Liu) "In Vivo Effects of Ascorbate and Glutathione on the Uptake of Chromium, Formation of Chromium(V), Chromium–DNA Binding and 8–Hydroxy–2'–Deoxyguanosine in Liver and Kidney of Osteogenic Disorder Shionogi Rats Following Treatment with Chromium(VI)." *Carcinogenesis* 20 (1999): 1267–75.

FURTHER READING

Books

Who's Who in America. 52nd ed. Vol. 2. New Providence, NJ: Marquis Who's Who, 1998.

Other

Endicott, Karen. "Trembling Edge of Science." *Dartmouth Alumni Magazine*. Apr. 1998. http://www.udel.edu/OHS/dartmouth/drtmtharticle.html (16 July 1999).

Lewis, Ricki. "Researchers' Deaths Inspire Actions To Improve Safety." *The Scientist* 11 (no. 21): 1. 21 Oct. 1997. http://www.the– scientist.library.upenn.edu/yr1997/oct/lewisp1971027.html (16 July 1999).

"Publications List for Dr. Karen Wetterhahn Dartmouth College." *NIEHS/EPA Superfund Basic Research Program*. 4 Nov. 1998. http://www.niehs.nih.gov/sbrp/newweb/resprog/publ/drt/wetterha.htm (16 July 1999).

Walhjalt, Bo. "Mail and Comments." 14 June 1997. http://vest.gu.se/~bosse/Mercury/Mail/Msg0005.html (16 July 1999).

Sketch by Margaret Alic

Anna (Johnson) Pell Wheeler
1883–1966
American algebraist

A distinguished mathematics researcher and educator, Anna Johnson Pell Wheeler is best remembered for her interest and research in biorthogonal systems of functions and integral equations. Much of her work was in the area of linear algebra of infinitely many variables—an area which she studied her entire career. Wheeler struggled to gain equality with men in the field of mathematics. In 1910, she was only the second woman at the University of Chicago to receive a doctorate in mathematics. Finding a full–time teaching position was difficult, even though she was often more qualified than the male applicants. Her break came when she substituted for her incapacitated first husband Alexander Pell, at the Armour Institute in Chicago. There, although she did not obtain a permanent position, she convinced her superiors of her competency. She was then hired as an instructor in mathematics at Mount Holyoke College in Hadley, Massachusetts, in 1911, leaving there in 1918 to take a position as associate professor at Bryn Mawr College in Pennsylvania. She remained at Bryn Mawr until her retirement in 1948, becoming head of the mathematics department in 1924. A champion of women in the field of mathematics, she urged her students to persevere toward terminal degrees despite the gender prejudices exhibited by authorities at colleges and universities at that time. It is significant, in her tenure at Bryn Mawr College, that seven of her graduate students received doctorates in mathematics.

During her career, Wheeler was active in many professional associations. She served on the council and the board of the American Mathematical Society, and was also a member of the Mathematical Association of America and the American Association for the Advancement of Science. (In 1927, Wheeler was invited by the American Mathematical Society to deliver their annual Colloquium Lectures—the only woman so honored until 1970.) In 1940, she received recognition from the Women's Centennial Congress as one of the 100 women honored who had succeeded in non–traditional careers. Continuing her support of women mathematicians, Wheeler helped **Noether, Emmy**, the eminent German algebraist, to relocate to Bryn Mawr when she sought political asylum from Nazi Germany in 1933.

Wheeler, of Swedish heritage, was born in Hawarden, Iowa, on May 5, 1883. Her parents were Amelia (Frieberg) and Andrew Johnson. Her father was an undertaker and furniture dealer in the small town of Akron, Iowa. Anna attended the local high school there and received her undergraduate degree from the University of South Dakota in 1903. There, her exceptional ability in mathematics was observed by her professor, Alexander Pell (later to become her first husband). She furthered her education at the University of Iowa and at Radcliffe College, earning master's degrees from both institutions.

Fellowship Allows Study in Europe

In 1906, Wheeler received an Alice Freeman Palmer Fellowship, allowing her to continue her studies at Göttingen University in Germany. There, she was guided in her work in integral equations by such eminent mathematicians as Hermann Minkowski, Felix Klein, and David Hilbert. Her thesis was completed under Hilbert's instruction, but for some reason—speculated to have been a dispute with Hilbert—she did not receive a degree from Göttingen.

Although Wheeler accepted the fellowship with the understanding she could not marry during its term, Pell joined her in Germany at the end of the year, and they were married there in 1907. Her new husband had an interesting past. He was actually a Russian revolutionist named Sergei Degaev, who had fled his country after being implicated in the murder of an officer of the Russian secret police. After emigrating to the United States, Dagaev changed his name to Alexander Pell, and began his new life as a mathematics professor.

The Pells left Germany and returned to the University of South Dakota. Shortly after their return, Pell accepted a position to teach at the Armour Institute of Technology in Chicago. Wheeler completed the work for her Ph. D. at the University of Chicago, and when Pell suffered a stroke in 1911, she assumed his teaching duties. She had hoped for a permanent position with a Midwestern university, but was unsuccessful. Other than taking over her husband's classes, the closest Wheeler came to being employed while in Chicago was when she taught a course at the University the fall semester of 1910. When she did find permanent work, it was out east at Mount Holyoke, and later, at Bryn Mawr. Pell, who was a semi–invalid after his stroke, died in 1921. In 1925, she married Arthur Leslie Wheeler, a classics scholar who had just become professor of Latin at Princeton University in New Jersey. Wheeler continued to teach at Bryn Mawr, even though they lived in Princeton where her husband was teaching. They also enjoyed a summer home in the Adirondack Mountains, to which she often invited her students. When Arthur died suddenly in 1932, she moved back to Bryn Mawr, where she lived and taught for the rest of her life.

Strengthens School's Reputation in Mathematics

Wheeler's work at Bryn Mawr took her beyond the classroom. She was well aware of the need to strengthen the reputation of the school's mathematics department, and set about doing so. She advised reducing teaching loads so that more research could be carried out by the faculty and encouraged professional collaboration and theoretical exchanges with other schools in the Philadelphia area. During this time of increasing administrative responsibilities, Wheeler remained active in publishing the results of her research into integral equations and functional analysis. Her Colloquium Lectures, however, were never published.

Although suffering from arthritis, Wheeler continued to participate in mathematics association meetings after her retirement. She died at age 82 at Bryn Mawr on March 26, 1996, after suffering a stroke. She was eighty–two.

SELECTED WRITINGS BY WHEELER:

Biorthogonal Systems of Functions, 1911.

FURTHER READING

Books

Bailey, Martha J. *American Women in Science: A Biographical Dictionary*. Santa Barbara, CA: ABC–CLIO, Inc., 1994, pp. 414–415.

Ogilvie, Marilyn Bailey. *Women in Science:: Antiquity through the Nineteenth Century*. Cambridge: MIT Press, 1986, pp. 173–174.

Sicherman, Barbara and Carol Hurd Green, eds. *Notable American Women: The Modern Period, A Biographical Dictionary*. Cambridge, MA: Belknap Press, 1980, pp. 725–726.

Periodicals

"Dr. Anna Pell Wheeler" (obituary). *The New York Times* (April 1, 1966): 35: 1.

Other

"Anna Johnson Pell Wheeler." *Biographies of Women Mathematicians.* June 1977. http://www.scottlan.edu/lriddle/women/chronol.htm (July 22, 1997).

Sketch by Jane Stewart Cook

Sarah Frances Whiting
1847–1927
American physicist and astronomer

Sarah Whiting was an innovative professor of physics and astronomer, who trained a generation of women for careers in these emerging fields of science. In her forty years at Wellesley College, she introduced the second laboratory physics course in the country, and the first at a women's college, and built and directed the Wellesley College Observatory.

Sarah Whiting was born in 1847, in Wyoming, New York, the daughter of Joel and Elizabeth Lee (Comstock) Whiting. Her father was a teacher and principal at various academies in New York state. He tutored his daughter in Greek, Latin, and mathematics. Whiting also helped her father prepare the experimental demonstrations for his classes in physics and natural philosophy. She graduated with an A. B. degree from Ingham University for Women in LeRoy, New York, in 1865.

Whiting returned to Ingham University to teach mathematics and classics and then to the Brooklyn Heights Seminary for girls until 1876. While living in New York, she furthered her education, attending scientific lectures, demonstrations and exhibitions, gaining a reputation as an exciting and challenging teacher. Meanwhile, Henry F. Durant was establishing Wellesley College in Massachusetts and searching for a physics teacher to complement his all–female faculty. He arranged for Whiting to attend the new laboratory physics classes at the Massachusetts Institute of Technology (MIT), to prepare her for introducing similar laboratory classes at Wellesley. Whiting was appointed professor of physics at Wellesley in 1876, and for the next two years she attended Edward C. Pickering's physics classes at MIT. She visited various other colleges in New England, to study their teaching methods. She also ordered and installed the equipment for the Wellesley physics laboratory, which opened in 1878.

Builds Astronomical Observatory

While living in Brooklyn, Whiting had attended lectures by the British physicist John Tyndall, on the new developments in optical instruments including the spectroscope, which enabled scientists to observe the unique patterns of lines and bands, or spectra, which form when light passes through a prism. In 1879, Pickering, who had become director of the Harvard College Observatory, invited Whiting to come and observe their use of these instruments for studying the spectra of stars. The following year, Whiting began teaching astronomy, initially called "applied physics," at Wellesley. For the next 20 years, she taught astronomy using only a celestial globe and a 4–inch telescope. Finally, in 1900, her friend and Wellesley trustee, Mrs. John C. Whiting, built an observatory for the college according to Whiting's plans. It was enlarged in 1906 and included sophisticated astronomical instruments, as well as a spectroscopy laboratory. This enabled Whiting and her students to examine and photograph solar and stellar spectra and compare them to laboratory spectra, allowing them to contribute to the rapidly–developing field of astrophysics.

During her sabbatical of 1888–1889, Whiting traveled to England and Germany, visiting scientists and laboratories and studying at the University of Berlin. In 1896, Edinburgh University in Scotland allowed women to study there for the first time. Whiting began her studies there with physicist Peter Guthrie Tait. As Margaret Rossiter quoted from Whiting's unpublished manuscript, "History of the Department of Physics at Wellesley College, 1878–1912:" "For many years I was almost alone in college work in this line [physics,] meeting the somewhat nerve–wearing experiences of constantly being in places where a woman was not expected to be, and doing what women had not to that time conventionally done."

In 1883, Whiting became one of the few women to be elected a fellow of the American Association for the Advancement of Science, and she was awarded an honorary degree from Tufts College in Boston in 1905. She avoided the banquets and "smokers" at meetings of the American Physical Society, viewing them as male–only events. However between 1907 and 1909, the society's president encouraged her to attend. As Rossiter quoted from Whiting's unpublished manuscript: "The introduction of the German Smokers was long a bar to the women being present at the banquets of the Physical Society, but finally a number of the younger women joined and under the presidency of Professor Nichols of Cornell we were present at a banquet. I was not quite sure we were welcome for men had not then as now got over the idea that blue smoke and the presence of ladies at banquets were incompatible."

Whiting was a teacher, rather than a researcher, and her publications dealt primarily with educational methods. Her notable undergraduate students included the Harvard astronomer **Annie Jump Cannon**, who returned to Wellesley as Whiting's postgraduate assistant. Whiting lived in campus dormitories with her unmarried sister until 1906, moving when Mrs. Whitin built her the Observatory House, which was adjacent to the college observatory. Whiting retired from teaching in 1912, but remained director of the observatory until 1916. She and her sister then moved to Wilbraham, Massachusetts, where Whiting died of arteriosclerosis and kidney disease in 1927.

SELECTED WRITINGS BY WHITING:

Books

Daytime and Evening Exercises in Astronomy for Schools and Colleges. Boston: Ginn, 1912.

FURTHER READING

Books

Anslow, Gladys A. "Sarah Frances Whiting." In *Notable American Women 1607–1950: A Biographical Dictionary.* Edited by Edward T. James, Janet Wilson James, and Paul W. Boyer. Cambridge: Harvard University Press, 1971.

Ogilvie, Marilyn Bailey. *Women in Science, Antiquity through the Nineteenth Century: A Biographical Dictionary with Annotated Bibliography.* Cambridge: MIT Press,1991.

Rossiter, Margaret W. *Women Scientists in America: Struggles and Strategies to 1940.* Baltimore: Johns Hopkins University Press, 1982.

Sketch by Margaret Alic

Mary Watson Whitney
1847–1921
American astronomer

Mary Whitney was an astronomer who trained with **Maria Mitchell** and succeeded her as professor and director of the Vassar College Observatory. Her well–trained students were in demand at major American observatories, making astronomy one of the few scientific careers that was available to women at the time. Throughout her career at Vassar, Whitney continued her astronomical research and, like Mitchell, worked for the advancement of women's educational and professional opportunities.

Mary Whitney, the daughter of Mary Watson (Crehore) and Samuel Buttrick Whitney, was born in 1847 in Waltham, Massachusetts. Her father was a successful real estate broker, and Whitney and her four siblings had access to fine educational opportunities. Whitney was an excellent student, particularly in mathematics. She graduated from Waltham High School in 1864 and attended an academy in Waltham for one year, while waiting for Vassar College in Poughkeepsie, New York, to open in 1865. She entered the college with advanced standing and excelled in her studies. She chose to major in astronomy with Maria Mitchell, the preeminent American woman astronomer.

Begins Study with Maria Mitchell

After graduation in 1868, the deaths of her father and older brother caused Whitney to return to Waltham to be with her mother. She taught school for a time in Auburndale, Massachusetts, but spent all of her spare time studying mathematics and astronomy. In August of 1869, she traveled with Maria Mitchell and a group of students to observe a solar eclipse in Iowa. At the urging of Mitchell, the Harvard mathematician Benjamin Peirce invited Whitney to audit his course on vectors. Since Harvard was not open to women, Peirce came to the college gates to escort Whitney to his classroom. Later, she joined the future Harvard professors William Byerly and James Mills Peirce in a graduate–level astronomy course on celestial mechanics. In 1870, Whitney worked with Truman H. Safford at the Dearborn Observatory of the University of Chicago and, in 1872, received her master's degree from Vassar.

The following year, Whitney's sister Adaline, also a Vassar graduate, entered medical school in Zurich, Switzerland. Her family accompanied her and for the next three years, Whitney studied mathematics and celestial mechanics at the University of Zurich. Returning home in 1876 and unable to find a university position, Whitney taught at Waltham High School. Finally, in 1881, she returned to Vassar as Mitchell's private assistant, and succeeded her as professor of astronomy and director of the observatory when Mitchell retired in 1888. Shortly after her arrival at Vassar, Whitney's sister became an invalid, and Whitney cared for her in her home at the observatory.

Whitney was known as an excellent teacher. The astronomy department grew until, by 1906, there were 160 students and eight different astronomy courses, including some of the first courses anywhere on astrophysics and on variable stars. However, following the deaths of her mother and sister, Whitney was determined to conduct with her astronomical research. As a mathematician, she first concentrated on observing and calculating the orbits of comets and minor planets or asteroids. She received encouragement from Benjamin A. Gould, editor of the *Astronomical*

Journal, where she published her results. She also determined the longitude of the new Smith College Observatory and made observations of double stars. Later, she studied variable stars, stars whose brightness changes over a fixed period, and in particular, the Nova Aurigae, whose light dramatically increases and then fades. Following the purchase of a machine for making accurate measurements of stars on photographic plates, Whitney arranged with Columbia University, in 1896, to study and measure their photographic plates of star clusters.

Champions Science Education for Women

In 1894, Whitney used her own funds to hire Caroline Furness as her teaching and research assistant. After the students of Vassar College finished using the telescopes at about 10 p.m., Whitney and Furness would then use them for their research until the early hours of the morning. The scientific output of the Vassar College Observatory far exceeded that of any of the other women's colleges. The staff of the observatory produced 102 publications during Whitney's tenure as director. Many of these were papers on comets, asteroids, and variable stars, published in major American and German astronomical journals.

Whitney was devoted to the cause of women's education. She was the first president of the Vassar Alumnae Association and was active on the science committee of the Association for the Advancement of Women. Although she was refused membership in the international Astronomische Gesellschaft because of her sex, she became a charter member of the American Astronomical Society. In 1907 she became president of the new Maria Mitchell Association of Nantucket, which worked for improved science education. Whitney always had enjoyed nature study, and at Vassar she formed a bird–watching club.

Whitney retired from Vassar in 1910, after she suffered paralysis as the result of a stroke. Furness succeeded her as the Vassar astronomy professor. Whitney died of pneumonia at her home in Waltham in 1921.

SELECTED WRITINGS BY WHITNEY:

Books

"Introduction." In *Catalogue of Stars Within One Degree of the North Pole*, by Caroline E. Furness. Publications of the Vassar College Observatory, no. 1. Poughkeepsie, N.Y., 1900.

(With Caroline Furness) *Observations of Variable Stars Made During the Years 1901–12 Under the Direction of Mary W. Whitney*. Publications of the Vassar College Observatory, no. 3. Poughkeepsie, N.Y., 1913.

Periodicals

"Scientific Study and Work for Women." *Education* 3 (1882): 58– 69.

FURTHER READING

Books

Mack, Pamela E. "Straying from Their Orbits: Women in Astronomy in America." In *Women of Science: Righting the Record*. Edited by G. Kass–Simon and Patricia Farnes. Bloomington: Indiana University Press, 1990.

Ogilvie, Marilyn Bailey. *Women in Science, Antiquity through the Nineteenth Century: A Biographical Dictionary with Annotated Bibliography*. Cambridge: MIT Press, 1991.

Rossiter, Margaret W. *Women Scientists in America: Struggles and Strategies to 1940*. Baltimore: Johns Hopkins University Press, 1982.

Wright, Helen. "Mary Watson Whitney." In *Notable American Women 1607–1950: A Biographical Dictionary*. Edited by Edward T. James, Janet Wilson James, and Paul W. Boyer. Vol. 3. Cambridge: Harvard University Press, 1971.

Periodicals

Furness, Caroline E. "Mary W. Whitney." *Popular Astronomy* 30 (1922): 597–607; 31 (1923): 25–35.

Sketch by Margaret Alic

Sheila Evans Widnall
1938–
American aeronautical engineer

Sheila Widnall is an accomplished researcher, educator, and writer in the field of aerospace engineering. A specialist in fluid dynamics at the Massachusettes Institute of Technology (MIT) for nearly three decades, she has also served in numerous administrative and advisory posts in industry, government, and academia. In August, 1993, Widnall was appointed Secretary of the United States Air Force, the first woman to head one of the country's military branches.

Sheila Evans Widnall was born to Rolland John and Genievieve Alice Evans in Tacoma, Washington, on July 13, 1938. Her father worked as a rodeo cowboy before becoming a production planner for Boeing Aircraft Company and, later, a teacher. Her mother was a juvenile probation officer. Interested in airplanes and aircraft design from her childhood, Widnall decided to pursue a career in science after she won the first prize at her high school science fair. She entered MIT in September, 1956, one of 21 women in a class of 900, and received her Bachelor of Science degree in

Sheila Widnall (AP/Wide World Photos. Reproduced by permission.)

aeronautics and astronautics in 1960. She continued on at MIT to earn a Master of Science degree in 1961 and the Doctor of Science degree in 1964, both in aeronautics and astronautics. Upon graduation, MIT awarded Widnall a faculty post as assistant professor in mathematics and aeronautics. She was the first alumna to serve on the faculty in the school of engineering. In 1970 MIT promoted her to associate professor, and in 1974 to full professor. During her tenure at MIT, Widnall served as head of the Division of Fluid Mechanics from 1975 to 1979, and as director of the Fluid Dynamics Laboratory from 1979 to 1990.

Establishes the Anechoic Wind Tunnel

Widnall specialized in the theories and applications of fluid dynamics, particularly in problems associated with air turbulence created by rotating helicopter blades. Her research focused on the vortices or eddies of air created at the ends and at the trailing edge of helicopter blades as they swirl through the air. These vortices are the source of noise, instability, and vibrations that affect the integrity of the blades and the stability of the aircraft. Widnall pursued similar interests in relation to aircraft that make vertical, short take–offs and landings (that is, V/STOL aircraft) and the noise associated with them. To this end, her studies led her to establish the anechoic wind tunnel at MIT, where researchers study the phenomenon of noise and V/STOL aircraft. During her tenure at MIT, Widnall established a reputation as an expert in her field and lectured widely on her research in vortices and their relation to aerodynamics. Widnall is the author of seventy papers on fluid dynamics as well as other areas of science and engineering; she has also served as associate editor for the scientific publications *Journal of Aircraft, Physics of Fluids,* and the *Journal of Applied Mechanics.*

In addition to writing about aerodynamics, Widnall has also published articles and delivered talks about the changing attitudes and trends in education for prospective engineers and scientists. In 1988, as newly elected president of the American Association for the Advancement of Science (AAAS), Widnall addressed the association on her longstanding interest in seeing more women become scientists and engineers and the problems they face in attaining higher degrees and achieving professional goals. In recognition of Widnall's efforts on behalf of women in science and engineering, in 1986 MIT awarded her the Abby Rockefeller Mauze chair, an endowed professorship awarded to those who promote the advancement of women in industry and in the arts and professions.

Begins a Distinguished Public Career

Along with her technical and scientific interests, Widnall has been active in administration, public policy, and industry consulting. In 1974 she became the first director of university research of the U.S. Department of Transportation. In 1979 MIT nominated Widnall to be the first woman to chair its 936–member faculty; she chaired MIT's Committee on Academic Responsibility for a year beginning in 1991; and she was named associate provost at the university in 1992. In addition to her term as president of the AAAS, Widnall has served on the board of directors for the American Institute of Aeronautics and Astronautics, as a member of the Carnegie Commission on Science, Technology, and Government, and as a consultant to businesses and colleges, including American Can Corporation, Kimberly–Clark, McDonnell Douglas Aircraft, and Princeton University. Her career has been recognized with numerous awards, including the Lawrence Sperry Award from the American Institute of Aeronautics and Astronautics in 1972, the Outstanding Achievement Award from the Society of Women Engineers in 1975, and the Washburn Award from the Boston Museum of Science in 1987. She was elected to the National Academy of Engineering in 1985.

Widnall's association with the Air Force developed through her appointment by President Carter to two three–year terms on the Air Force Academy's board of visitors, which she chaired from 1980–1982. She also served on advisory committees to the Military Airlift Command and to Wright–Patterson Air Force Base in Dayton, Ohio. As Secretary of the Air Force, Widnall is responsible for all administrative, training, recruiting, logistical support, and personnel matters, as well as research and development operations.

She married William Soule Widnall, also an aeronautical engineer, in June, 1960. The couple has two grown children, William and Ann Marie. In her spare time, Widnall enjoys bicycling, wind surfing, and hiking in the Cascade Mountains with her husband in her native Washington.

SELECTED WRITINGS BY WIDNALL:

Periodicals

"Science and the Atari Generation." *Science* (August 12, 1983): 607.

"AAAS Presidential Lecture: Voices from the Pipeline." *Science* (September 30, 1988): 1740–1745.

FURTHER READING

Periodicals

Ewing, Lee. "Panelists Laud Widnall, Approve Her Nomination." *Air Force Times* (August 2, 1993): 4.

Jehl, Douglas. "M.I.T. Professor Is First Woman Chosen as Secretary of Air Force." *New York Times* sec. 1 (July 4, 1993): 20.

Sears, William R. "Sheila E. Widnall: President–Elect of AAAS." *Association Affairs* (June 6, 1986): 1119–1200.

Stone, Steve. "Air Force Secretary Salutes Female Aviators." *Norfolk Virginian–Pilot* (October 10, 1993): B3.

"USAF Head Approved." *Aviation Week & Space Technology* (August 9, 1993): 26.

"Widnall of MIT Is New President–elect Of AAAS." *Physics Today* (February 1986): 69.

Other

Biography, "Dr. Sheila E. Widnall." Office of the Secretary of the Air Force/Public Affairs, November 1993.

Sketch by Karl Preuss

Jane Anne (Russell) Wilhelmi
1911–1967
American endocrinologist

Jane Anne Russell Wilhelmi was known for her work and publications with her husband in metabolism. Metabolism is the process by which an organism gets energy by breaking down foodstuffs into simpler forms. Wilhelmi researched how carbohydrates and proteins are broken down.

Jane Anne Russell was born on February 9, 1911 in Watts, California, to Josiah Howard Russell, a rancher and sheriff, and Mary Ann Phillips Russell. The third girl and last of five children, Russell grew up on the family homestead. Always an excellent student, Russell early showed a particular aptitude for mathematics, and when she graduated in 1928 from Polytechnic High School, she was salutatorian.

Russell went on to the University of California, Berkeley, from which she received her bachelor's degree, graduating as valedictorian in 1932. During these years, she was awarded a Stewart Scholarship, Phi Beta Kappa, the Kraft Prize, and the University Gold Medal. She continued at Berkeley for her Ph.D. in biochemistry, which she completed in 1937. While completing her studies, Russell worked first as a technical assistant in biochemistry and then as an assistant in the institute of experimental biology, both at Berkeley, and she spent a year as a pharmacology research associate at Washington University.

Awarded the California Fellowship in Biochemistry, the Rosenberg Fellowship, and the American Physiological Society's Porter Fellowship, Russell was able to work with Herbert Evans and Carl and **Gerty Cori** on carbohydrate metabolism, focusing on pituitary hormones and the anterior pituitary. During her time as a student, Russell had already amassed a list of scholarly publications on carbohydrate metabolism, and was known internationally as an expert in the field.

In 1938, Russell joined Yale University's School of Medicine as a National Research Council Fellow, continuing in 1939 as a fellow in the department, and in 1941 as an instructor in physiological chemistry, a position she would retain until 1950. While at Yale, Russell did extensive and pioneering research on growth hormones in carbohydrate metabolism, proving that metabolism was controlled by the hormones in the pituitary. For her research and discoveries, Russell was awarded the Ciba Award in 1946. Yet despite her achievements and international recognition, Russell, as a woman, was neither rewarded by nor promoted at Yale. In 1950, she joined the faculty of Emory University as an assistant professor of biochemistry, moving through the ranks to full professor in 1965, a position she retained the rest of her life.

Her closest colleague in the laboratory was Alfred Ellis Wilhelmi, and after their marriage on August 26, 1940, the couple continued to collaborate on metabolism research and publications for nearly three decades. When they went to Emory, Wilhelmi became chairman of the biochemistry department. Together they continued growth hormone research, proving that the hormones were responsible for interfering with structural protein breakdown.

In addition to her research, Russell was known as an inspiring teacher with an extraordinary mind. She was devoted to her family and her home state of California, and enjoyed gardening, knitting, and sewing. Russell was active in organizations working on science policies. Russell died on March 12, 1967, from complications due to breast cancer.

Her publications, many jointly authored with her husband, numbered nearly eighty. Russell was a member of the Endocrine Society, the American Physiological Society, and the National Science Board, in addition to her work with the National Institutes of Health, the National Science Foundation, and the National Research Council. In 1961, Russell and Wilhelmi were awarded the Upjohn Award, and that same year Russell was named Atalanta's Woman of the Year.

SELCTED WRITINGS BY RUSSELL:

Books

Carbohydrate Metabolism in the Hypophysectomized Rat. Berkeley: University of California, Ph.D. dissertation, May 1937.

FURTHER READING

Books

Bailey, Martha J. *American Women in Science.* Denver: ABC–CLIO, 1994.

Sicherman, Barbara, et al, eds. *Notable American Women: The Modern Period.* Cambridge: Belknap, 1980.

Siegel, Patricia Joan, and Kay Thomas Finley. *Women in the Scientific Search.* NJ: Scarecrow Press, 1985.

Sketch by Helene Barker Kiser

Cicely Delphin Williams
1893–1992
Jamaican-English physician

Cicely Delphin Williams devoted her life to improving the health of women and children all over the world. She is known for discovering the causes of the malnutrition illness kwashiorkor, as well as Jamaican vomiting disease. She was the first female physician to be appointed by the British Colonial Medical Service to Ghana and to hold the post of head of Maternity and Child Welfare. She was also noted for her personal heroism as a prisoner of war during World War II.

Williams was born on Dec. 2, 1893, the daughter of a long–established plantation family in Jamaica, originally from Wales. Her father, James Towland Williams, was the director of education in Jamaica. Williams wanted to attend Oxford, where her father had studied, but when it came time to enter college, the family had no money to send her. She was discouraged from becoming a nurse, so Williams resigned herself to an unchallenging existence at home with her family.

William's break came during World War I, when women were admitted to Oxford because of a shortage of doctors. She decided to study tropical medicine and hygiene and was tutored by one of the famed physicians of the time, Sir William Osler. In 1929, she received her B.A. degree from Oxford.

Williams then went on to study for her M.D. degree. However, after she had taken her finals and it came time for her residency, World War I had ended and along with it the doctor shortage. Williams applied to 70 hospitals before being accepted for a gynecological surgery residency at South London Hospital for Women and Children. It was here that Williams discovered that she loved working with children. Although she found the work at South London Hospital challenging, she really wanted to work overseas. Positions for women were still scarce, so Williams decided the best course of action was to work for the overseas British Colonial Office. After two years of petitioning the office, officials finally relented and posted her in the Gold Coast (now Ghana).

In one year, Williams learned the Ghanaian language and started to develop real fondness for her patients. She was struck by how devoted they were to their children and amused at how often they brought them in to see her. Williams began to notice a common illness among toddlers in Ghanaian families. These children had swollen legs and bellies, rashes, and a red tinge to their hair. Williams thought this might be a nutritional disease, but the other doctors told her she was misdiagnosing the illness pellagra, an already identified malnutrition disease that had similar symptoms.

To test her theory, Williams wanted to do autopsies on the children who had died from the disease but was told that local burial customs would not permit it. But in truth, the families were rushing their children home after death because they could not pay the high cost of moving the body. So Williams offered to pay this fee and began to perform postmortems. She found that the Ghanaians called the disease kwashiorkor, or weaning disease, because children developed it when a new baby was born. Williams surmised correctly that the toddlers were not getting enough protein because they were no longer breast–fed and were not yet eating adult food. Convinced she had found a new type of malnutrition, she identified the disease in *Archives of Disease in Children* in 1933. She also wrote an article in the medical journal *Lancet,* which described the differences between kwashiorkor and pellagra.

While performing an autopsy in her investigations of kwashiorkor, Williams contracted blood poisoning. When she recovered she was transferred to the city of Kumasi. She was disappointed, but decided to make the best of it by writing her delayed doctoral thesis "Child Health in the Gold Coast." The thesis was accepted and she received her M.D. degree in 1936.

Williams wanted to return to Africa but was sent to Trengganu, Malaya (now Malaysia) instead. She never achieved the same fondness for Malaya as she did for the Gold Coast, and found health conditions were horrible. The local religious beliefs regarded illness as fate. Infant mortality was high, partly because Western companies were persuading new mothers to buy canned milk that had little nutrition. Williams tried to take on these companies, but was unable to stop them from sending "nurses" to visit new mothers with their products.

When the Japanese invaded Malaya in 1941, Williams escaped to Singapore. Her safety was short–lived when the Allied forces left Singapore in 1942 and the Japanese strafed the city with bombs. Williams moved children in the city's hospitals from makeshift shelter to makeshift shelter until the Japanese troops entered Singapore. Then, to save her young charges, she offered them to any family that would take them. All were placed.

During the Japanese occupation, Williams was held in the Changi prison camp in Singapore. Her life there was filled with hardship and disease. The Japanese Secret Police, the Kempaitai, began to suspect her after she became head of the women's side of the camp and arrested her. She spent her fiftieth birthday in a tiny prison cell with seven men.

In March 1944, suffering from dysentery and the psychological and physical cruelty she had endured, Williams was returned to Changi prison camp. Seven months later the prisoners saw Allied planes. Weak from dysentery and malaria, Williams survived to see the Japanese surrender.

When Williams recovered, she returned to Malaya as head of the Maternity and Child Welfare Services. It was the first powerful post to be held by a woman in the Colonial Service. In 1948, the new World Health Organization named her to be the first director of the Child and Maternal Health section. But Williams was asked to return to Jamaica to direct an investigative team studying Jamaican vomiting sickness. In a year, her team discovered the culprit was a substance in spoiled ackee fruit, and designed the life–saving treatment of glucose therapy.

In 1955, Williams entered the more sedate life of academia when she became a senior lecturer in nutrition in London University. In 1960, she was hired as professor of maternal and child health with the American University in Beirut. After four years, she went back to London to work with the Family Planning Association as an advisor. In 1965 she was awarded the James Spence Memorial Gold Medal by the British Paedeatric Association.

In 1968, she became professor of international family health at Tulane University's School of Public Health. In 1971 the American Public Health Association gave her the Martha May Eliot Award, and a year later she was awarded the Dawson Williams Prize in Paediatrics by the British Medical Association. At her retirement, she remained active and was an honorary Fellow at Somerville and Green Colleges of Oxford. At age 90, she was still making appearances and speeches. In her speeches she often encouraged young doctors to become general practitioners, citing a need for doctors who would look after people and not just diseases. She died on July 13, 1992 at age 98.

SELECTED WRITINGS BY WILLIAMS:

Periodicals

"Kwashiorkor: A Nutritional Disease of Children Associated with a Maize Diet." *Lancet* 16 (November 1935): 1151–52.

"A Nutritional Disease of Childhood Associated with a Maize Diet." *Archives of Disease in Childhood* 8 (1933): 423–33.

FURTHER READING

Books

Craddock, Sally. *Retired Except on Demand: The Life of Cicely Williams.* Oxford: Green College, 1983.

Dally, Ann. *Cicely: The Life of a Doctor.* London: Gollancz, 1968.

Sketch by Barbara Boughton

Emma T. R. Williams
1894–1975
American astronomer

Emma Williams (Vyssotsky) was well–known for her research on stellar spectra, the patterns of bands and lines that are obtained when a star's light is dispersed through a prism. However, since she collaborated with her husband, Alexander Vyssotsky, her career was overshadowed by his.

Born in Media, Pennsylvania in 1894, Williams was the daughter of John J. and Alice (Roberts) Williams. She became interested in mathematics and the physical sciences at an early age and graduated from Swarthmore College in Pennsylvania in 1916, with a bachelor's degree in mathematics. She worked as a demonstrator in mathematics for another year. Unable to find a suitable position in her field, in 1917 Williams went to work for the Fidelity Mutual Life Insurance Company as an actuarial clerk, calculating premiums and dividends. In 1919, she went to Germany as a volunteer with the postwar Child Feeding Program, returning to work at Provident Mutual Life Insurance in 1921.

Four years later, Williams returned to Swarthmore as a mathematics instructor, and the following year she undertook postgraduate studies at the University of Chicago. In

1927, she entered Radcliffe College as a graduate student in astronomy. Although Radcliffe graduate students studied at Harvard University, at that time their degrees were conferred by Radcliffe. At Harvard, Williams met the Russian astronomer Alexander Vyssotsky, whom she married in 1929, just before receiving her Ph.D. in 1930, for her thesis entitled "A Spectrophotometric Study of A Stars." Williams always published under her maiden name. Hers was only the second astronomy Ph.D. awarded by Radcliffe and the third by either Harvard or Radcliffe.

Following her husband to the University of Virginia where he was an assistant professor, Williams became an astronomy instructor there, a position she would hold until 1944. It was a research position, with few teaching obligations. At the Leander McCormick Observatory at the university, Williams and Vyssotsky began working on an ongoing photographic study to determine the distances to stars. Over the years, they discovered a number of relatively nearby dwarf stars, using a special instrument, and determined the parallaxes of the stars, for calculating the stellar distances. Williams was an expert mathematician and statistician, and she and her husband collaborated closely throughout their careers. However, publications often omitted her name.

Emma Williams was awarded the **Annie Jump Cannon** Prize of the American Astronomical Society in 1946, for her studies of star spectra and colors. Two years later, Williams and Vyssotsky published their classic work, *An Investigation of Stellar Motions*. However, in 1944 Emma Williams was forced to leave the university, due to a progressive, debilitating illness. Eventually she was diagnosed with chronic brucellosis, also called undulant or Malta fever, a disease that could be contracted via unpasteurized milk. Although she was finally cured with antibiotics, Williams never fully recovered her health. She died in 1975, at her retirement home in Winter Park, Florida. Williams was survived by her son Victor A. Vyssotsky.

SELECTED WRITINGS BY WILLIAMS:

Periodicals

"Systematic Errors in the Determination of the Contours of the Hydrogen Lines in A–Stars." *Astrophysical Journal* 72 (1930): 127.

"Evidence for Space Reddening from Bright B Stars." *Astrophysical Journal* 75 (1932): 386.

(With A. N. Vyssotsky) "Color Indices and Integrated Magnitudes of 15 Bright Globular Clusters." *Astrophysical Journal* 77 (1933): 301.

(With A. N. Vyssotsky) "Galactic Structure and Kinetic Theory." *Astrophysical Journal* 98 (1943): 187.

(With A. N. Vyssotsky) "The Constants of Galactic Rotation and Precession." *Astronomical Journal* 53 (1948): 27–30.

(With A. N. Vyssotsky) "An Investigation of Stellar Motions; Additions and Corrections." *Astronomical Journal* 56 (1951): 68.

FURTHER READING

Books

Roberts, Rebecca L. "Emma T. R. Williams Vyssotsky." In *Notable Women in the Physical Sciences: A Biographical Dictionary*. Edited by Benjamin F. Shearer and Barbara S. Shearer. Westport, CT: Greenwood Press, 1997.

Who's Who of American Women (and Women of Canada): A Biographical Dictionary of Notable Living Women of the United States of America and Other Countries. 4th ed. Chicago: A. N. Marquis, 1966–67 .

Sketch by Margaret Alic

Heather Williams
1955–
American ornithologist

Heather Williams is a truth seeker. Whether it is as a world class orienteer (long distance running using a map and compass to find specific points and traverse a course) or as an ornithologist/neuroethologist, she challenges herself both mentally and physically in order to give greater meaning and understanding to the world in which she lives. Her tenacious approach to research and discovery has brought Williams substantial success, most notably the MacArthur Foundation award and grant in 1993 as well as recognition as one of the top female orienteers during the 1980s.

Heather Williams was born on July 27, 1955, in Spokane, Washington, to James Edward Williams and Maria Greig Williams. She has three siblings, Greig, Reid, and Alexandra. Because her father was employed by the U.S. foreign service, Williams moved frequently during her childhood. With each move, she was exposed not only to different cultures but also to vastly different flora and fauna. While living in such places as Laos, Turkey, and Bolivia, Williams explored her surroundings and was attracted to the indigenous animal species. The fact that she was exposed to many different animals and enjoyed collecting the smaller of those species further developed her interest in biology.

Williams cultivated her interests through formal study, receiving an A.B. in biology from Bowdoin College in Maine in 1977. Always an achiever, she graduated *summa cum laude* from that institution, and her interests blossomed into a career of scientific inquiry. Williams spent 1977–78 as a Thomas J. Watson Fellow at Hebrew University in Eilat, Israel, before continuing with her masters and then doctoral degrees. While in Israel, she conducted research in marine biology. While she was pursuing her higher degrees, she found her life's work.

Williams chose to continue her studies at Rockefeller University in New York. Her mentor at Rockefeller was Fernando Nottebohm, whose own research pertained to the canary and its behavior. Expanding Nottebohm's research, Williams was award her doctorate in 1985 for her studies of the zebra finch. Her dissertation was entitled "A Motor Theory for Bird Song Perception," and it has been the basis for her scientific endeavors ever since.

Concerned with how a bird hears the sounds or songs of other birds, Williams' research pinpoints both the nerves and parts of the brain that are involved in song recognition, organization, and reconstruction. She has discovered that zebra finches learn songs in three syllable "chunks," which they reorganize to create new songs. The way in which the zebra finch executes the song is also highly stylized and fits into specific behavioral patterns. As with speech, a bird's song is a lateralized function, primarily executed by one half of the brain. The other brain hemisphere does, however, contribute to the song production. This is an interesting fact in that birds do not have a connection (corpus callosum) to coordinate the activity of each of the brain hemispheres. Williams is investigating how brain activity occurring between hemispheres is regulated. She is also interested in sexual dimorphism and its role in song perception, as well as how distinct dialects are maintained within delineated finch groups. Her work not only has insight into zebra finch behavior and biology, but it also implies parallels with other animal species and their communication. Her findings will cross the boundaries of biology to broaden our understanding of neuroscience and psychology.

During the same time period as Williams was pursuing her doctoral degree and conducting postdoctoral research, she also found the time to become the third ranking orienteer in the United States (1980–89) and marry Patrick D. Dunlavey (1986). In 1988, Williams joined the faculty at Williams College in Williamstown, Massachusetts. Still close enough to Rockefeller University in New York, Williams was drawn to the small town atmosphere, knowing she could still confer closely with her Rockefeller colleagues. In 1993, Williams was a member of the course–mapping team for the world championships in orienteering. She and her husband have two children, Maria Greig and Alan Peter Dunlavey.

SELECTED WRITINGS BY WILLIAMS:

Periodicals

(With Jessica McKibben) "Changes in Stereotyped Central Vocal Motor Patterns are Induced by Peripheral Nerve Injury." *Behavioral and Neural Biology* 57 (1992): 67–78.

(With Kirsten Staples) "Syllable Chunking in Zebra Finch (*Taeniopygia guttata*) Song." *Journal of Comparative Psychology* 106 (1992): 278–286.

(With Linda Crane, Timothy Hale, et. al.) "Right–side Dominance for Song Control in the Zebra Finch." *Journal of Neurobiology* 23 (1992): 1006–1020.

Other

(With Franklin Mullins and Jennifer Danforth) "A Comparison of the Effects of Deafening and Vocal Disruption on the Stability of Crystallized Song." *Society for Neuroscience Abstracts* 23. 1997. http://www.williams.edu:803/Biology/ZFinch/nsci97.html (30 October 1997).

FURTHER READING

Books

King, Kathleen Palombo. "Heather Williams." *Notable Women in the Life Sciences: A Biographical Dictionary.* Benjamin F. Shearer and Barbara S. Shearer, eds. Westport, Connecticut: Greenwood Press, 1996.

Other

Williams College faculty information directory. http://www.williams.edu:803/Biology/hwilliams.html (October 30, 1997).

Sketch by Jacqueline L. Longe

Lee Anne (Mordy) Willson
1947–
American astronomer

Lee Anne Willson, University Professor of Astronomy and Astrophysics at Iowa State University, is an observational and theoretical astrophysicist who studies variable stars and stellar atmospheres. She is well–known for her groundbreaking research on the loss of mass by stars, which has influenced ideas about the age of the universe. She has published numerous scientific papers and popular astronomy articles.

Born in Honolulu, Hawaii, in 1947, Lee Anne Willson was the daughter of a scientist. In 1956, the family moved to Saltsjöbaden, Sweden, returning to the United States in 1960. Willson spent her high school years in Reno, Nevada. As a child, she loved reading science fiction and dreamed of becoming an astronaut. Graduating from Harvard University in 1968 with an A.B. in physics, Willson received Fullbright and American Scandinavian Foundation fellowships to study at the University of Stockholm in Sweden for a year. She earned her M.S. degree from the University of Michigan in 1970, while working as a demonstrator at the planetarium, and went on to receive her Ph.D. in astronomy in 1973.

Willson's interest in the evolution of stars began with a seminar she gave in graduate school and led to her doctoral thesis. She studies the spectra, or the patterns of lines and bands of a star's light, that are characteristic of Mira variables. These are red giant stars that get bigger and cooler, and smaller and hotter, over a period of about a year. This stellar pulsation leads to a loss of mass, eventually leaving a small star core, called a white dwarf. Recently, Willson has been studying whether main sequence stars, such as our Sun, also pulsate and lose mass, which would indicate that some stars are younger than previously thought.

After graduating from the University of Michigan, Willson became an instructor in physics and astronomy at Iowa State University in Ames. Willson and her husband, Stephen J. Willson, a mathematician whom she met at Harvard and married in 1969, attended graduate school together at Michigan and subsequently found positions at Iowa. With twice the teaching load of the other professors in the department, Willson was promoted to assistant professor in 1975 and associate professor in 1979. She became a full professor in 1988 and a university professor in 1993. Willson coordinated the astronomy and astrophysics program at Iowa State from 1983 to 1985, and again from 1987 to 1990.

Willson has spent summers as a research associate, visiting scientist, and professor at the University of Washington and has spent her sabbaticals at the Universities of Colorado, Texas, and Toronto, at Uppsala University in Sweden, and at the Kitt Peak National Observatory.

In 1980, Willson was awarded the **Annie Jump Cannon** Prize, a prestigious research grant for young women astronomers. Her extensive involvement in professional organizations has helped to increase the visibility of women astronomers. She has been elected councilor of the American Astronomical Society, council member of the American Association of Variable Star Observers, a director of the Association of Universities for Research in Astronomy (an organization that operates several national observatories), and chair of the Observatories Council. She has chaired the American Astronomical Society's Committee on the Status of Women in Astronomy and served on committees of the American Association for the Advancement of Science and the National Aeronautics and Space Administration.

In addition to her numerous scientific activities, Willson is a dedicated artist and figure skater, and is proficient in several languages. Willson and her husband have a daughter and a son.

SELECTED WRITINGS BY WILLSON:

Books

"Main Sequence Mass Loss and the Age of the Universe." In *Fourteenth Texas Symposium on Relativistic Astrophysics*. Edited by Ervin J. Fenyves. New York: New York Academy of Sciences, 1989.

(With R. Stalio, editors) *Angular Momentum and Mass Loss for Hot Stars, Proceedings of the 1989 Ames/Trieste NATO Advanced Research Workshop*. Boston: Kluwer Academic Publishers, 1990.

Periodicals

"Fluorescent FeI Emission in Long–Period Variables." *Astronomy and Astrophysics* 17 (1972): 354.

"The Dark Sky Paradox and the Origin of the Universe." *Astronomy* 6 (September 1978): 52–57.

(With S. M. Richardson) "Cosmic Contamination: Elemental Clues to the Origin of the Solar System." *Astronomy* 8 (June 1980): 6–22.

"Ancient Monuments and Pre–Historic Astronomy." *Encounters* 5, no. 3 (1982): 7.

(With G. H. Bowen) "Pulsation, Mass Loss, and Stellar Evolution." *Nature* 312 (1984): 429–31.

(With J. Guzik and W. Brunish) "Effects of Main Sequence Mass Loss on Solar Models." *Astrophysical Journal* 319 (1987): 957–65.

"Theoretical Glue: Understanding the Observed Properties of Miras with the Help of Theoretical Models." *Journal of the American Association of Variable Star Observers* 25 (1997): 99–114.

FURTHER READING

Books

American Men and Women of Science. 19th ed. Vol. 7. New Providence, NJ: R. R. Bowker, 1995–96.

Schaber, Joy. "Lee Anne M. Willson." In *Notable Women in the Physical Sciences: A Biographical Dictionary*, edited by Benjamin F. Shearer and Barbara S. Shearer. Westport, CT: Greenwood Press, 1997.

Other

"Lee Anne Willson, University Professor, Iowa State University." http://www.public.iastate.edu/~lwillson/ (19 July 1999).

Sketch by Margaret Alic

Elizabeth Armstrong Wood
1912–
American crystallographer

Elizabeth Armstrong Wood published classic works in the field of crystallography, or the study of crystals, and conducted pioneering work in the electronics field.

Wood was born on October 19, 1912, in New York City to Herbert Ralph and Winona May (Hull) Armstrong. She attended Barnard and received her bachelor's degree in 1933. She went on to earn a master's degree the following year from Bryn Mawr and was then employed by the college as a demonstrator in geology while she continued graduate research. She returned to Barnard as a lecturer in geology and mineralogy in 1938 and the following year earned her doctorate in geology from Bryn Mawr, writing her dissertation on "Mylonization of Hybrid Rocks near Philadelphia, Pa.." In 1941 she was promoted to research assistant at Barnard, but two years later left the college to join the technical staff in crystal research at Bell Telephone Laboratories in Murray Hill, New Jersey. She spent the remainder of her professional career at Bell. In 1947 she married Ira Wood.

While at Bell, Wood was at the forefront of electronics research, as the use of crystals in fine–tuned telecommunications was just beginning. Crystals are used in lasers and other solid–state devices to transmit sound. Wood was primarily known for her research on the physical properties of crystals and on x–ray crystallography. She also studied the geology and petrology of igneous and metamorphic rocks and optical mineralogy. In 1957 she was elected president of the American Crystallographic Association.

Wood also published two classic texts in the field of crystallography: *Crystal Orientation Manual and Crystals and Light: An Introduction to Optical Crystallography*. She retired from Bell in 1967.

SELECTED WRITINGS BY WOOD:

Books

Crystal Orientation Manual. New York: Columbia University Press, 1963.

Crystals and Light. New York: D. VanNostrand Co., 1964.

Science for the Airplane Passenger New York: Ballantine Books, 1968.

Periodicals

"The Question of Phase Transition in Silicon." *Journal of Physical Chemistry* 60 (1956): 508–509.

FURTHER READING

Bailey, Martha J. *American Women in Science: A Biographical Dictionary*. Denver: ABC–CLIO, 1994.

Kass–Simon, G. and Patricia Farnes. *Women of Science: Righting the Record*. Bloomington: Indiana University Press, 1990.

Sketch by Kristin Palm

Geraldine Pittman Woods
1921–
American embryologist

Geraldine Pittman Woods had a rather brief career as a scientist. It is her actions as an administrator, directing the actions of the federal government towards improving the research capabilities of minority institutions and the educational opportunities for minority students, for which she is best known.

Geraldine Pittman was born on January 29, 1921, in West Palm Beach, Florida. Her parents, Susie King Pittman and Oscar Pittman, were comfortably established in the farming and lumber industries of central Florida, and also owned several properties in West Palm Beach.

Jerry began her schooling at a private Episcopal school, but in the fourth grade transferred to Industrial High School. At that time, the school was the only public school in West Palm Beach that allowed African American students. Jerry was not an outstanding student in these early years, and occasionally required tutors to keep her from falling behind her classmates. Despite an early interest in science, she received little encouragement from her teachers or family, who did not consider science a realistic career choice for an African American woman.

Jerry led a comfortable, but busy, life through grade and high school. She participated in church activities, learned to play the piano, and was an avid reader. The relatively care–free life of a Palm Beach teenager was, however, saddened by the death of her father.

After graduating from Industrial High School in 1938, Pittman attended Talladega College in Talladega, Alabama. The college had been established to serve the African American community, and provided an environment not much different from her high school. Uninspired, Pittman made only mediocre progress.

In 1940, her mother became seriously ill, and was admitted to Johns Hopkins Hospital in Baltimore, Maryland. Pittman left Talladega at this time, transferring to Howard University in Washington, D.C., to be closer to her mother. At Howard, she concentrated much harder on her studies, perhaps because of a concern for her mother's health. The faculty at Howard were very impressed with Pittman's performance, and very supportive of her interest in science. One professor in particular, Dr. Louis Hansborough in the Department of Biology/Zoology, was instrumental in her decision to apply to, and her acceptance in, the graduate biology program at Radcliffe College and Harvard University in Cambridge, Massachusetts.

Fortunately, her mother recovered from her illness, and Pittman moved to Cambridge to join top students from throughout the country. It was a great challenge for her to compete with these students, most of whom came from much stronger academic backgrounds. Still, Pittman was totally committed to excelling at Harvard, and became so focused on her work that she earned two graduate degrees in only three years and was elected to Phi Beta Kappa, the national scholastic honor society.

Pittman's doctoral research involved studying the development of nerves in the spinal chord. In the early stages of the development of embryos, the cells that will become nerves are not much different from all the other cells. As the embryo grows, however, the cells become differentiated. Pittman hoped to determine whether this process was controlled by factors within the cell itself or by stimulation from other, adjacent cells. She discovered that both effects are important, and also that the number of nerve cells produced is at least partly dependent on the number of muscle cells present.

Pittman returned to Howard University as an instructor after receiving her doctorate from Harvard in 1945. Shortly thereafter, she married Robert Woods, a student of dentistry at Meharry Medical School in Tennessee. The two commuted between Washington, D.C. and Nashville until Robert graduated. They then moved to California, where, Robert Woods set up a dental practice. Geraldine Pittman Woods temporarily put aside her career to raise a family.

Years later, when all three of her children were teenagers, Woods began the administrative career which was to yield some of her most important accomplishments. At first, she volunteered for local social services and civil rights organizations near Los Angeles, then branched out to statewide activities. Her strong support and advocacy of minority interests earned her an invitation to the White House in 1965, where she helped to launch Project Head Start, a federal program established to help children from low–income families gain preschool experience.

Woods continued her activism through serving on governing boards for many institutes of higher education, philanthropic organizations, and government bodies. Her main goal was to establish programs to get minority students, professors, and institutions involved in research training. In 1969 she was asked to be a special consultant at the National Institute of Health, where she helped develop the Minority Biomedical Research Support (MBRS) program and the Minority Access to Research Careers (MARC) program.

The MBRS program helped minority institutions to better compete for government and philanthropic grants by giving the applicants an understanding of the requirements and organization of grant proposals. Woods herself traveled throughout the country to give seminars at minority institutions on the preparation of grant applications, and gradually, the rate of grant approvals at these institutions improved.

The MARC program was designed to increase the recruitment and retention of minority students in scientific fields. Not only did this program establish scholarships for students at all levels of higher education, but it also provided funding for visiting scholars programs. These programs enabled faculty members from minority institutions to work with colleagues at some of the nation's most prestigious universities, and led to an overall improvement in teaching quality.

Woods is now retired from her position with the National Institute of Health. Her accomplishments have directly led to an increase in the number of professors involved in scientific research training at minority institutions, and an increase in the number of minority students able to enter graduate and professional schools. Her tireless efforts in support of minority interests have helped countless numbers of budding scientists realize their goals.

FURTHER READING

Kessler, James H., J. S. Kidd, Renée A. Kidd, and Katherine A. Morin. "Geraldine Pittman Woods." In *Distinguished African American Scientists of the 20th Century*. Phoenix: Oryx Press, 1996

Smith, Carol Hobson. "Black Female Achievers in Academe," *Journal of Negro Education* 51, no. 3 (1982): 318–341

Sketch by David E. Fontes

Jane Cooke Wright
1919–
American physician

Jane Cooke Wright has carried on the medical legacy of her prominent family through a career in internal medicine, cancer research, and medical education. She has served as director of the Cancer Research Foundation of Harlem Hospital in New York City, faculty member and director of cancer chemotherapy at the New York University Medical Center, and professor of surgery and associate dean at New York Medical College and its affiliate hospitals. Wright has also devoted her efforts to educating fellow practitioners about advances in chemotherapy, a service she performed in her 1983 convention lecture to the National Medical Association entitled "Cancer Chemotherapy: Past, Present, and Future."

Dr. Jane C. Wright (AP/Wide World Photos. Reproduced by permission.)

Wright was born in New York City on November 20, 1919, to Louis Tompkins and Corinne (Cooke) Wright. Her paternal grandfather was one of the first graduates of Tennessee's Meharry Medical College, an institution founded to give former slaves professional training. Another relative, Harold D. West, was Meharry's first black president. Her step–grandfather, William Penn, was the first black person to earn a medical degree from Yale. Her father, Louis Tompkins Wright—one of the first black graduates of Harvard medical college—was the first black physician to be appointed to the staff of a New York City hospital; he was also a pioneer in cancer chemotherapy, and New York City's first black police surgeon. Jane Cooke Wright was the first of two daughters; her sister, Barbara, also became a physician.

Wright was educated in private elementary and secondary schools and won a four–year scholarship to Smith College in Massachusetts, where she set records as a varsity swimmer. Graduating in 1942, Wright entered New York Medical College, again on a four–year scholarship, and received her medical degree with honors in 1945. An internship and assistant residency followed at Bellevue Hospital in New York City. After leaving Bellevue Hospital, she completed her training with a two–year residency in internal medicine at Harlem Hospital.

Wright's first position after residency was as a school and visiting physician at Harlem Hospital in 1949. She became a clinician later that year at the hospital's Cancer Foundation, which was then headed by her father. There she studied the response of tumors and growths to drugs and the application of chemotherapy in the treatment of cancer. She explored the complex relationships and variations between test animal and patient, tissue sample and patient, and individual patient responses to various chemotherapeutic agents. Upon her father's death in 1952, she became the Cancer Foundation's director.

In 1955, Wright joined the New York University Medical Center to direct the cancer chemotherapy research department and teach research surgery. Her continuing research explored animal and human responses to chemotherapeutic agents (such as triethylene thiophosphoromide, CB 1348 and Dihydro E. 73) and isolation perfusion and regional perfusion chemotherapy techniques. In 1961, Wright became adjunct professor of research surgery at the medical center and also served as vice–president of the African Research Foundation, a position which took her on a medical mission to East Africa. In 1964, she was appointed to the President's Commission on Heart Disease, Cancer, and Stroke; the commission's work resulted in a nationwide network of treatment centers for these diseases. The Albert Einstein College of Medicine presented Wright with its Spirit of Achievement Award in 1965.

Wright became associate dean and professor of surgery at New York Medical College in 1967, where she was also responsible for administrating the medical school and developing a program for the study of cancer, heart disease, and stroke. She was awarded the Hadassah Myrtle Wreath in 1967, and the Smith College medal in 1968. In December, 1975, Wright was one of eight scientists saluted by *Cancer Research* in its observation of International Women's Year, and in 1980 was featured on an Exceptional Black Scientists poster by Ciba Geigy. Since 1987, she has been emerita professor of surgery at New York Medical College.

Wright has served on the editorial board of the *Journal of the National Medical Association* and as a trustee of Smith College and of the New York City division of the American Cancer Association. She married David D. Jones, Jr., a graduate of Harvard Law School, on July 27, 1947; the couple have two daughters, Jane and Alison. Her hobbies include sailing, painting, and reading mystery novels.

SELECTED WRITINGS BY WRIGHT:

Periodicals

"Cancer Chemotherapy: Past, Present, and Future." *Journal of the National Medical Association* (August 1984): 773–784; (September 1984): 865–876.

FURTHER READING

Books

Blacks in Medicine and Science. Hemisphere, 1990, p. 258.

Notable Black American Women. Detroit: Gale, 1992, pp. 1283–1285.

Sketch by Jane Stewart Cook

Dorothy Maud Wrinch
1894–1976
British-American mathematician, biologist, and theoretical physicist

Dorothy Wrinch, a mathematical biologist, was at the center of the major transition from classical biology, the study of organisms and their parts, to molecular biology, the molecular basis of biological systems. Her 192 publications, on an astounding array of subjects from pure mathematics and theoretical physics and biology, to philosophy and sociology, attest to her scientific brilliance and versatility.

Dorothy Maud Wrinch, the daughter of British citizens, Hugh Edward Hart and Ada (Souter) Wrinch, was born in 1894, in Rosario, Argentina, where her father was an engineer for a local British water system company. Wrinch grew up in the London suburb of Surbiton. At Surbiton High School, she prepared for the Oxford and Cambridge Joint Board Examination. In 1913, Wrinch received a scholarship to Girton College of Cambridge University. At her father's urging, she studied mathematics and later she would coauthor two mathematical papers with him. Wrinch graduated in 1916, the only Girton woman to obtain the position of Wrangler in the Cambridge Mathematical Tripos, the final examinations.

Studies Philosophy with Bertrand Russell

Instead of beginning graduate studies in mathematics, Wrinch chose to study symbolic logic with the philosopher and social activist Bertrand Russell. She passed the philosophy exams that were required to qualify for a fourth–year scholarship, and received a scholarship from the Surrey Education Committee as well.

Wrinch stayed at Girton as a research scholar and continued working with Russell, even after he was sent to prison in 1918 for his antiwar activities. Wrinch also lectured to mathematics honor students at University College, London. As Russell's emissary to the outside world, Wrinch increasingly found herself in the company of both the major philosophers of the day and the trappings of high society. However Russell's involvement with, and subsequent marriage to her friend Dora Black, left Wrinch on the outskirts.

First Woman to Receive Doctor of Science Degree from Oxford

Wrinch returned to Girton on Yarrow scientific fellowships during the years 1920 through 1923. In 1922, she married John William Nicholson, the director of mathematics and physics at Balliol College in Oxford. Nicholson was well–known for having proposed an early theory of the atom. He recruited students for Wrinch at an Oxford women's college, Lady Margaret Hall, and in 1923 she joined her husband there. After one year, Wrinch was appointed lecturer, a position she held until the late 1930s. In 1927, she became one of the first two women to be elected to the board of the Faculty of Physical Sciences, which opened her lectures to male students, as well as females. Although Wrinch lectured at various Oxford women's colleges, her pay was poor. Additionally, her unusual position as a married woman lecturer with a child (her daughter Pamela was born in 1928) usually left her socially isolated.

In 1929, Wrinch became the first woman to receive a doctor of science degree from Oxford University, on the basis of 15 of her first 42 research publications. She was the sole author on the majority of these papers, only 12 of which were purely on mathematics. Others were on mathematical physics or applied mathematics. Twenty of the papers were on the philosophy of science and the scientific method and, increasingly, Wrinch turned her attention to the philosophy behind scientific theories: first, the theory of the electron, quantum theory, and Albert Einstein's theory of relativity; and later, physiology, genetics, psychology, and sociology. All of her papers, even those coauthored with her husband, were published under her maiden name. During this period, Wrinch also wrote a play about betrayal and a book, *The Retreat from Parenthood*, under the pseudonym Jean Ayling, about the difficulties of women who were combining careers with marriage and family and called for the establishment of "child–rearing institutes."

In 1930, Nicholson experienced an alcohol–induced nervous breakdown and was institutionalized. As Pnina Abir–Am quoted from a letter Wrinch wrote to Bertrand Russell in July, 1930: "At last my miseries are to be, to some extent, at an end!. . . I have gone one step towards being again a free woman. . . It is an awful grief to me to think of a good mathematician going so utterly to pieces." Wrinch subsequently obtained a divorce in 1938.

Proposes Structures for Chromosomes and Proteins

Anxious to leave Oxford and pursue her interest in sociology, Wrinch applied for Rhodes and Rockefeller Fellowships. Despite her impressive credentials and letters of recommendation, she was informed that Rhodes Fellowships were only for men. Furthermore, she had applied for two Rockefeller Fellowships, one in mathematics and one in sociology, and therefore she was judged to not be serious about either subject. However in 1931, Wrinch received two small fellowships, including the Hertha Ayrton Fellowship from Girton, which enabled her to spend a year in Vienna with her daughter. During this period Wrinch was beginning to apply mathematics to biological systems, particularly cell division and chromosome structure. In 1932, she became a founding member of the Biotheoretical Gathering, which also included the science historian Joseph Needham and his wife, the biochemist Dorothy Moyle Needham, and the crystallographer John Desmond Bernal and his student, **Dorothy Crowfoot Hodgkin**, who would later receive the Nobel Prize for chemistry in 1964. Wrinch spent the following year gathering data in various biological laboratories in Paris, Berlin, and England.

Wrinch's first important contribution to biology was to connect the linear sequence of genes on chromosomes, with the linear sequence of amino acids in proteins, and to propose that the specificity of genetic material was encoded by the sequence of the amino acids. This was a major conceptual breakthrough, which might have received more attention had it not been for difficulties with her model of the chromosome.

In 1935, Wrinch received a five–year Rockefeller Foundation grant which enabled her to pursue her cyclol theory, the first proposal for the structure of proteins. The question of how proteins, which all seemed to be similar in molecular structure, could have such diverse biological functions and activities, was a major scientific problem. Furthermore, most scientists then believed that proteins were the genetic material, the basis of heredity. As pointed out by Abir–Am, protein structure was thought to hold the key to the "secret of life." Wrinch's theory, which was influenced by Crowfoot's work, explained many properties of proteins. Although her theory was inaccurate, it had a profound impact on the scientific world and stimulated new approaches to the problem of protein structure. Indeed, Wrinch's cyclol theory may have been the first publication in the new field of molecular biology.

Suddenly, Wrinch was a scientific celebrity with newspapers calling her the "Woman Einstein" for her protein model, which was the center of special interdisciplinary meetings for several years. However, Wrinch's unwavering defense of her theory, in the face of contradictory experimental data, led to strained relationships with many scientists, including Bernal and Crowfoot. Although Wrinch had obtained a five–year research fellowship in 1939 for Somerville College, Oxford, she chose to return to the United States, where she had been a visiting scholar at Johns Hopkins University. There, Wrinch became mired in a controversy with Linus Pauling, who refuted her protein model on physical grounds. Although she had help from Nobel Laureate Irving Langmuir, and although Pauling's arguments against Wrinch were later shown to be wrong as well, ten years later Pauling successfully deduced the correct structure of a protein.

The controversy with Pauling devastated Wrinch's career. She lost her Rockefeller grant and was unable to find a job, even with the help of Albert Einstein. As a single mother in a foreign country at the outbreak of World War II, Wrinch considered abandoning science. However late in 1940, her friend Otto Charles Glaser, a biologist at Amherst College in Massachusetts, secured her a position as visiting research professor at Amherst, Smith, and Mount Holyoke Colleges. Wrinch and Glaser were later married at the Marine Biological Laboratory at Woods Hole in 1941. With Glaser's support, Wrinch produced some of her most solid scientific work during the 1940s; but she never gave up her attachment to the cyclol theory as the basis of protein structure and heredity. Following Glaser's death in 1950, Wrinch moved to the Smith College campus, where she remained as a visiting research professor in the physics department until her retirement in 1971. With financial support from the Office of Naval Research, she studied protein structure with Smith faculty member Galdys Anslow in a former coal bin that they converted into a laboratory. Once again, Wrinch's unconventional results and conclusions caused her to lose funding. However, when new evidence for her structures appeared in 1960, the National Science Foundation granted her a few more years of financial support.

In 1976 Wrinch's daughter Pamela, who was one of the first women to earn a doctorate in international relations from Yale University, was killed in fire. This was a devastating loss for Wrinch, who died three months later at the age of 82 of unknown causes.

SELECTED WRITINGS BY WRINCH:

Books

(As Jean Ayling) *The Retreat from Parenthood*. London: Kegan Paul, Trench, Trubner and Co., 1930.

Fourier Transforms and Structure Factors. Cambridge, MA: American Society for X–Ray and Electron Diffraction, 1946.

Chemical Aspects of the Structure of Small Peptides: An Introduction. New York: Plenum Press, 1960.

Chemical Aspects of Polypeptide Chain Structure and the Cyclol Theory. New York: Plenum Press, 1965.

(Marjorie Senechal, editor) *Structures of Matter and Patterns in Science: Inspired by the Work and Life of Dorothy Wrinch, 1894–1976: The Proceedings of a Symposium Held at Smith College Northampton, Massachusetts, September 28–30, 1977 and Selected Papers of Dorothy Wrinch, from the Sophia Smith Collection*. Cambridge: Schenkman,1980.

Periodicals

(With H. Jeffreys) "The Relation of Geometry to Einstein's Theory of Gravitation." *Nature* 106 (1921): 806–809.

"On Mediate Cardinals." *American Journal of Mathematics* 45 (1923): 87–92.

"The Relations of Science and Philosophy." *Journal of Philosophical Studies* 2 (1927): 153–66.

(With J. W. Nicholson) "A Class of Integral Equations Occurring in Physics." *Philosophical Magazine* 54 (1927): 531–60.
"Aspects of Scientific Method." *Proceedings of the Aristotelian Society* (1928–29): 94–122.
"Chromosome Behavior in Terms of Protein Pattern." *Nature* 134 (1934): 978–79.
"The Cyclol Hypothesis and the 'Globular Proteins.'" *Proceedings of the Royal Society of London, A* 161 (1937): 505–24.

FURTHER READING

Books

Abir–Am, Pnina G. "Synergy or Clash: Disciplinary and Marital Strategies in the Career of Mathematical Biologist Dorothy Wrinch." In *Uneasy Careers and Intimate Lives: Women in Science 1789–1979*, edited by Pnina G. Abir–Am and Dorinda Outram. New Brunswick: Rutgers University Press, 1987.
Julian, Maureen M. "Women in Crystallography." In *Women of Science: Righting the Record.* Edited by G. Kass–Simon and Patricia Farnes. Bloomington: Indiana University Press, 1990.
Olby, Richard. *The Path to the Double Helix.* London: Macmillan, 1974.

Sketch by Margaret Alic

Chien-Shiung Wu
1912(?)–
Chinese-American physicist

Chien-Shiung Wu (AP/ Wide World Photos. Reproduced by permission.)

For more than 30 years, Chien-Shiung Wu was a member of the physics department at Columbia University, where she earned a reputation as one of the world's foremost nuclear physicists. Wu is best known for a classic experiment on beta decay, completed in 1957, which confirmed a prediction made a year earlier by Tsung-Dao Lee and Chen Ning Yang regarding the conservation of parity (the basic symmetry of nature) in reactions involving the weak force. A number of observers have commented on the apparent inequity of the Nobel Prize committee's not having included Wu in the 1957 physics prize, which was awarded to Lee and Yang for this work.

Chien-Shiung Wu was probably born in May of 1912 (some sources say 1915; one source says 1913), in Liu Ho near Shanghai, China. Her father, Wu Zhongyi, was a former engineer who had abandoned his profession in 1911 to take part in the revolution that overthrew the Manchu dynasty. After the war, Wu returned to Liu Ho to open a school for girls. Still filled with revolutionary zeal, he saw it as his mission to make sure that girls as well as boys were able to have an education in the "new China." Chien-Shiung's mother, Fan Fuhua, helped her husband in this effort, providing education to their students' families in their own homes.

Wu attended her father's school until she was nine and then continued her education at the Soochow Girls School, about fifty miles from her home. During her high school years, Wu was active in a number of political causes; her fellow classmates chose her to represent them in some of the causes because, with her stellar scholastic record, she could not readily be dismissed from school on the basis of her involvement in political issues. In 1930 Wu graduated from Soochow as valedictorian of her class and then entered the National Central University in Nanking. By that time she had decided to pursue physics as a career, and in 1934 was awarded a bachelor's degree in that field. After teaching and doing research for two years, Wu left China in 1936, intending to obtain the graduate training in physics that was not then available in her native land. Her original plans to enroll in the University of Michigan changed abruptly when she reached San Francisco and was offered an opportunity to attend the University of California at Berkeley.

Among the factors influencing Wu's decision to remain in California was the presence of Ernest Orlando Lawrence, inventor of the atom–smashing cyclotron (a device that accelerates the speed of nuclear particles), on the Berkeley campus. The chance to study with Lawrence was, Wu decided, too important to pass up. Another factor in her decision was the presence of "Luke" Chia Liu Yuan—a young man she met soon after arriving in San Francisco. Wu and Yuan were married in 1942 and eventually had one son, Vincent Wei–Chen Yuan.

Teaches at Smith, Princeton, and Columbia

Wu received her Ph.D. in 1940, a time of great turmoil in her homeland and in the world at large. The Japanese army had already invaded China, and U.S. involvement in World War II was only a year away. Wu stayed on as a research assistant at Berkeley for two years after receiving her degree, but spent much of that time on war–related work. In 1942 she was offered her first teaching position, at Smith College in Northampton, Massachusetts. She remained at Smith for only one year before accepting an appointment at Princeton University, where she was assigned to teach introductory physics to naval officers. She held this position for only a few months before she was offered a post at Columbia University, where she would join the Manhattan Project—through which the world's first atomic bombs were designed and built. That job, which began in March 1944, was the beginning of a long relationship with Columbia; she eventually became a research associate in 1945, associate professor in 1952, and finally full professor in 1958. She retired from Columbia in 1981.

Tests the Lee-Yang Theory of Parity Nonconservation

The work for which Wu gained fame took place in 1957. It was based on a revolutionary theory proposed by two colleagues, Tsung–Dao Lee, also of Columbia, and Chen Ning Yang, of the Institute for Advanced Study in Princeton, New Jersey. In 1956 Lee and Yang had raised the possibility that a property known as parity may not be conserved in certain types of nuclear reactions. Conservation laws had long been at the heart of physical theories. These laws said that a number of important physical characteristics—mass, energy, momentum, and electrical charge, for instance—were always conserved during physical or chemical changes. As an example, the law of conservation of electrical charge says that the total electrical charge on all particles involved in a physical change would be the same both before and after the event.

Lee and Yang found theoretical reasons to question the conservation of parity in some instances. Parity refers to the theory that the laws of nature are not biased in any particular direction, a concept long held by physicists. When beta particles are emitted by nuclei during radioactive decay, for example, classical theory predicts that they will be emitted without preference to any particular spin orientation. Lee and Yang developed a mathematical argument showing that this might not be the case and outlined experiments through which their theory could be tested.

Lee and Yang presented their ideas to Wu, already recognized as an authority on beta decay (a radioactive nuclear transformation) and the weak force that causes it. Even before her colleagues had published a paper on their theory, Wu had begun to design experiments to test their ideas. Working with colleagues at the National Bureau of Standards's Low Temperature Physics Group, Wu labored almost without rest for six months. In January of 1957, she announced her results: clear evidence for the violation of parity conservation had been observed. Later that same year, Lee and Yang were awarded the Nobel Prize in physics—an award that many observers in the field believe might easily have been shared with Wu.

Although she did not receive a Nobel Prize, Wu has won a host of other awards, including the first Wolf Prize awarded by the state of Israel (1978), the first Research Corporation Award (1959) given to a woman, the Comstock Award of the National Academy of Sciences (1964), and the National Science Medal (1975). She was elected to the National Academy of Sciences in 1958.

SELECTED WRITINGS BY WU:

Books

(With others) *An Experimental Test of Parity Conservation in Beta Decay*. New York, 1957.

(Editor with Luke C. L. Yuan) *Nuclear Physics*. Academic Press, 1961.

FURTHER READING

Books

Kass–Simon, G., and Patricia Farnes, eds. *Women of Science: Righting the Record* Bloomington: Indiana University Press, 1990, pp. 205–208.

McGraw-Hill Modern Men of Science Vol. 2. McGraw–Hill, 1984, pp. 541–542.

McGrayne, Sharon Bertsch. *Nobel Prize Women in Science*. Birchlane Press, 1993, pp. 255–279.

Yost, Edna. *Women of Modern Science*. Dodd, 1959, pp. 80–93.

Sketch by David E. Newton

Y. C. L. Susan Wu
1932–
Chinese-born American aerospace engineer

Aerospace engineer Y. C. L. Susan Wu is a researcher who has excelled in both academics and industry. Her work has earned the respect of leading engineers and scientists and has advanced the potential for cleaner and more efficient methods of coal–fired power generation in the United States.

Ying–Chu Lin Wu was born in Peking, China, on June 23, 1932. Her mother, Kuo–Chun Kung, was a personnel employee for the Taiwanese government; her father, Chi–Yu Lin, was a government accountant. Wu developed an early interest in science, but at that time women were generally discouraged from such pursuits. Her mother's encouragement gave Wu the impetus to continue her studies, and in 1955 she received a bachelor's degree in mechanical engineering from the National Taiwan University.

Engineering jobs were scarce for women in China in the mid–1950s. Because employers viewed jobs as a lifetime commitment for the employee, firms were reluctant to hire women, recognizing the potential pressures of marriage and child–rearing. Wu moved to the United States in 1957 and earned a master's degree from Ohio State University in aeronautical engineering in 1959. After achieving a doctorate from the California Institute of Technology in 1963, Wu found employment at an optics engineering company in Pasadena, California, as a senior engineer. In 1965 Wu accepted a position as an assistant professor at the University of Tennessee Space Institute (UTSI). In 1967 she was promoted to associate professor, and a full professorship in aerospace engineering followed in 1973. She held that position at UTSI for fifteen years.

Focuses on Energy Research

During Wu's tenure at UTSI her research focused on magnetohydrodynamics (MHD) and its application to cleaner coal–fired power generation. Conventional power generators use steam, coal, or oil power to turn an armature on which a continuous wire is wrapped. A magnetic field surrounds the armature and as the wires cut through the magnetic field, a current is induced in the wire, thereby producing electricity. MHD uses conventional power generation theory, but the armature is replaced by plasma, a very hot gas on the order of 5,000°F. When a gas is very hot it becomes an electrical conductor. Sometimes such elements as cesium or potassium ions are introduced into the gas to increase its conductivity. As the electrically conductive plasma cuts through the magnetic field, an electric current is generated. This method of power generation is cleaner and more efficient than traditional coal–fired power plants.

In 1988 Wu left UTSI after twenty–three years to start her own business. She founded ERC, Inc., an aerospace engineering and MHD consulting firm based in Tullahoma, Tennessee. ERC, Inc., works with such agencies as the National Aeronautics and Space Administration (NASA), the Department of Energy, Argonne National Laboratory, Boeing, McDonnell Douglas, and UTSI.

Wu's many honors include the University of Tennessee Chancellor's Research Scholar Award in 1978, Outstanding Educators of America Award in 1973 and 1975, and the Society of Women Engineers Achievement Award in 1985. She was honored by the National Science Foundation in 1987, and she received the Amelia Earhart Fellowship in 1958, 1959, and 1962, the only three–time recipient of the award. A naturalized U.S. citizen, Wu married Jain–Ming (James) Wu in 1959, and they have three children: Ernest, a biologist; Albert, an aerospace engineering consultant; and Karen, a quality control engineer. In her spare time, Wu enjoys classical music, reading, and civic activities.

SELECTED WRITINGS BY WU:

Periodicals

(With D. P. Duclos, R. Denison, and R. W. Ziemer) "Physical Property Distribution in a Low–Pressure Crossed Field Plasma Accelerator." *AIAA Journal* (November 1965).

"The Limiting Circles of One–Dimensional MHD Channel Flows." *AIAA Journal* (August 1968).

(With E. S. Jett and D. L. Denzel) "Eddy Currents in an Infinitely Finely Segmented Hall Generator." *AIAA Journal* (September 1970).

(With G. D. Roy) "Study of Pressure Distribution along Supersonic Magnetohydrodynamic Generator Channels." *AIAA Journal* (September 1975).

(With J. N. Chapman and S. S. Strom) "MHD Steam Power—Promise, Progress, and Problems." *Mechanical Engineering* (September 1981).

(With F. L. Galanga and others) "Experimental Results of the UTSI Coal–Fired MHD Generator." *Journal of Energy* (May–June 1982): 179.

(With J. T. Lineberry and others) "Comparison of Experimental Results from the UTSI Coal–Fired MHD Generator to Theoretical Predictions." *Journal of Energy* (May–June 1982).

(With M. Ishikawa and M. H. Scott) "Power Take–off Analysis and Comparison with Experiments in a Coal–Fired MHD Generator." *Journal of Energy* (September–October 1983).

(With Ishikawa and Scott) "Fault Analysis of Mid Channel Power Takeoff in Diagonal Conducting Wall Magnetohydrodynamic Generators." *Journal of Propulsion and Power* (September–October 1985).

(With R. C. Attig, Chapman, and A. C. Sheth) "Emission Control by Magnetohydrodynamics." *Chemtech* (November 1988).

"SWE Personality Profile: Y. C. L. Susan Wu, 1985 SWE Achievement Award Winner." *U.S. Woman Engineer* (March–April 1990): 31–32.

FURTHER READING

Periodicals

Congressional Record (July 15, 1985): S–9510.

Other

Wu, Y. C. L. Susan, interview with Roger Jaffe conducted January 20, 1994.

Sketch by Roger Jaffe

Hildegarde Howard Wylde
1901–1998
American paleontologist

Hildegarde Howard Wylde was a pioneer in the field of avian paleontology. She was an expert on bird fossils, specifically from the Rancho La Brea tar pits in Los Angeles, California, and was one of the only women ever to become chief science curator at a museum.

Hildegarde Howard was born on April 3, 1901, in Washington, D.C., and grew up in Chevy Chase, Maryland. When she began her scientific studies at the University of California–Los Angeles, she was unable to accompany her male professors and the male students on field trips because women were banned from field work. Nevertheless, Howard persevered in her studies, and during the 1920s, Howard received her bachelor's, master's, and doctoral degrees from the University of California while working as a zoology assistant. During these years, she worked as a research associate with Loye Miller, whom Howard later described as her hero.

Her first assignment was literally on the ground floor, since she worked in the basement with unsorted boxes of saber–toothed tiger bones. Soon, her scientific aptitude became apparent, and as Miller's trusted assistant, Howard collated bird bones and bird fossils that were millions of years old and were taken from the Rancho La Brea tar pits in Hancock Park in Los Angeles.

Her time in the basement was not without reward, however, because it was there that she met Henry Anson Wylde, the future chief of museum exhibits. The couple married in 1930, and were together until Wylde's death in 1984.

After completing her degrees, Wylde joined the staff of the Los Angeles County Natural History Museum as curator of bird fossils and was able to identify well over 100 species. This accomplishment not only promoted Wylde's reputation as an outstanding paleontologist, it also increased the visibility of the museum as a center for paleontological research.

Wylde began to specialize in the research of the Rancho La Brea eagles, eventually studying over 14,000 eagle bones. During the 1920s and 1930s, Wylde's specialty in avian paleontology was an unusual one, and her work was truly pioneering. Some of the bones and fossils she researched dated back over 20 million years, and her scientific papers (numbering over 100 articles) proved her to be a prolific writer and researcher with a keen eye. Her work, in general, was voluminous and well–respected.

Wylde was appointed chief science curator in 1951, the first woman to achieve such distinction, and she would hold that appointment until her retirement a decade later. In 1957, two events occurred that Wylde would remember for the rest of her life. The first was the identification of a bird with a large beak. The bird was neither an albatross nor pelican but part of a new group, which Wylde named *osteodontornus*, meaning "bony–toothed bird." The second event was when Miller gave her what was to become her prized possession, a saber–toothed tiger vertebra, the first fossil found at La Brea.

After her official retirement from the museum, Wylde continued to do fossil research and identification. She also continued her fossil research at the Anza Borrego Desert State Park as a Guggenheim fellow. In 1973, an exhibit of her work was held by the California Academy of Sciences, and in 1977, the Natural History Museum christened the newly opened Hildegarde Howard Cenozoic Hall. Earlier in her career, Wylde was the first woman to be honored with the Brewster Memorial Award for her ornithological research.

Wylde was a member of several professional societies, including the American Association for the Advancement of Science, the Society of Avian Paleontology and Evolution, the American Ornithologists Union, the Society of Vertebrate Paleontology, the California Academy of Science, and the Southern California Academy of Science, for which she served as the first woman president. She was also involved in community groups such as the Leisure World Writers Club and the Leisure World Audubon Society. Hildegarde Wylde loved her work, but in her free time she also enjoyed playing bridge and watching "Jeopardy" and "Casablanca." She died in Aliso Viejo, California, on February 28, 1998.

FURTHER READING

Periodicals

"Up Close: Hildegarde Howard Wylde." *The Orange County Register* (June 8, 1989).
Obituary. *Los Angeles Times* (March 4, 1998): A–18.

Sketch by Helene Barker Kiser

Rosemary Frances Gillian Wyse
1957–
Scottish astrophysicist

Rosemary Wyse is known for her work on how stars are formed and what their chemical composition is, as well as the structure of galaxies. Wyse was awarded the **Annie Jump Cannon** award in 1986 for her innovative work.

Born January 26, 1957, in Dundee, Scotland, Rosemary Frances Gillian Wyse and her two sisters grew up on the coast with their physician father and their art teacher mother. Wyse loved horseback riding, swimming, tennis, and stamp–collecting, and was always filled with curiosity about the world, about how and why things worked as they did. In the Dundee public schools, Wyse became interested in physics, which later led her to a career in astrophysics. Her scientific interests were reaffirmed by her exposure to the television shows "Star Trek" and "Doctor Who," in addition to watching the Apollo moon landings.

Wyse graduated from the University of London's Queen Mary College with a B.Sc. degree in 1977, before going on to Cambridge University, where she would remain until 1983. She completed the equivalent of a master's degree in 1978, and accepted the Bachelor Scholarship from Cambridge's Emmanuel College that same year. Completing her Ph.D. at the Institute of Astronomy in 1983, Wyse was also the recipient of ZONTA International's Amelia Earhart Fellowship and was a Lindemann Fellow of the English Speaking Union of the Commonwealth.

At Cambridge, Wyse and Bernard Jones researched elliptical galaxies, focusing on their formation and structure. Even after Wyse left Cambridge, she continued to work with Gerard Gilmore on star and galaxy formation, discovering that there are actually three layers of metallicity of various thickness in our galaxy, the Milky Way. This work challenged earlier beliefs about which stars belonged to which part of the galaxy. Learning about how metals are distributed in the Milky Way is important in that it can determine things like how old stars are, or how old the galaxy itself is.

After her work at Cambridge, Wyse was the Parisot Postdoctoral Fellow at the University of California, Berkeley, a University of California President's Fellow, a Postdoctoral Research Fellow at the Space Telescope Science Institute, and a Fellow of the Alfred P. Sloan Foundation. Her research on star formation rates (SFRs), involving galaxy structure and chemical composition, was influential in her selection as the 1986 Annie Jump Cannon Award recipient.

Wyse joined the faculty of Johns Hopkins University in 1988. Her work has focused on what is known as the dark, or "missing," matter in the galaxy. Dark matter makes up a large part of the universe, and yet its nature is not yet fully understood. Wyse researches its composition, form, and location in order to "discover" the dark matter. In addition, Wyse continues her research on galaxy formation and evolution.

A member of several professional societies, Wyse is affiliated with the Astronomical Society of the Pacific, the Royal Astronomical Society, the International Astronomical Union, the American Astronomical Society, and the American Association of University Women. In her free time, Wyse enjoys hiking, playing squash, and art.

SELECTED WRITINGS BY WYSE:

Periodicals

"On the Epoch of Elliptical Galaxy Formation." *Astrophysical Journal* 299, no. 2, pt. 1 (December 15, 1985): 593–615.

"Dark Matter in the Galaxy." *International Journal of Modern Physics D3, suppl.* (1994): 53–61.

FURTHER READING

Books

Shearer, Benjamin F. and Barbara J., eds. *Notable Women in the Physical Sciences.* Westport, CT: Greenwood Press, 1997.

Other

Kiser, Helene Barker, interview with Rosemary Wyse conducted June 29, 1999.

Sketch by Helene Barker Kiser

X

Xie Xide (Photograph by Andrew Wong. Reuters/Archive Photos. Reproduced by permission.)

Xie Xide
1921–
Chinese physicist

Xie Xide is the president of Fudan University in Shanghai, China. During the decade of China's Cultural Revolution she was removed from her teaching post and was not allowed to conduct scientific research. Reinstated in 1972, as a university administrator she has been an outspoken advocate for science education in China.

Born in 1921, in South China, she spent her early years in Peking, where her father was a professor of physics at Yenching University, now a part of Peking University. When the Japanese occupied Peking in July of 1937, she fled with her family. Traveling half-way across China, they eventually reached Guiyang, in Guizhou Province. During the journey Xie became ill with tuberculosis, and was hospitalized in Guiyang for close to four years. After recovering, she began her university studies in physics at Amoy University, where her father had found a new teaching post. To escape the Japanese, Amoy University had been evacuated to the remote hill town of Changding in Fukien Province. In 1946 she received her B.Sc.

Shortly after the war ended Xie took a teaching position in physics at the University of Shanghai. A year later, in 1947, she set sail for the United States, part of a wave of young Chinese intellectuals who were seeking higher education abroad. Leaving behind the civil war and political chaos that preceded the emergence of the Communist government in China, she enrolled in a master's degree program at Smith College, in Amherst, Massachusetts. She received her M.A. in 1949, and then began her doctoral studies in the physics department at the Massachusetts Institute of Technology. Her thesis work there concerned the wave function of electrons in highly compressed gases. She was granted her Ph.D. in 1951.

Unable to return directly home because of U.S. government restrictions on travel to China at the time, Xie instead went to England, where she married Cao Tianquin, a biochemist. Together, in 1952, they made their way back to Shanghai on an arduous route via the Suez Canal and Singapore. Back in China, Xie took a post at Fudan University. Her husband joined the Shanghai branch of the Chinese Academy of Science. Xie soon distinguished herself as one of China's top physicists, publishing many professional articles and two texts, *Semi-conductor Physics* (1958) and *Solid Physics* (1962). In 1962 she was promoted in rank to Professor and was appointed the Deputy Director of the Institute of Technical Physics in Shanghai.

In 1966 when the Cultural Revolution began, Xie and her husband were subjected to the anti-intellectual tyranny of Mao Tse-tung's government. Despite her allegiance to the Communist Party, she was kept imprisoned in her own laboratory for a period of nine months. Her husband was incarcerated as well, at his own institute, leaving their then ten-year-;old boy to look after himself alone in the family's apartment. Xie was forced to clean bathrooms at the university, and was eventually sent to the countryside to work in a silicon wafer factory. In 1972 she was allowed to return to her teaching post, where she taught physics to peasants, workers and soldiers, most of them ill-prepared for university classes. The Cultural Revolution came to a close in 1976, when the "Gang of Four" were arrested. Since then Xie has worked hard to regain her footing. She resumed research in surface physics, and in 1977 founded the educational Modern Physics Institute. One year later Xie was appointed vice-president of Fudan University, and in 1982 she became its president. That same year, she was elected to the Central Committee of the Chinese Communist Party, one of the few women and scientists among this elite body of policy-making leaders. Xie has been awarded numerous honorary degrees and is a member of the Chinese Academy of Sciences and the Praesidium. She continues to work to improve the educational opportunities for students in China.

SELECTED WRITINGS BY XIE:

Books

Semi–conductor Physics, 1958.

Solid Physics, 1962.

FURTHER READING

Periodicals

Oka, Takashi. "Xie Xide—The Gentle President of China's Fudan University." *Christian Science Monitor* (March 28, 1984): 21.

Sketch by Leslie Reinherz

Y

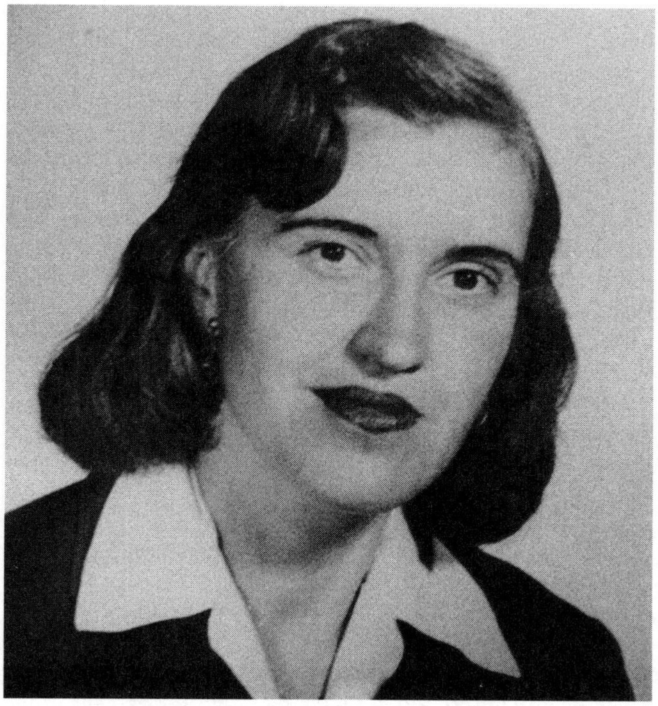

Rosalyn S. Yalow (The Library of Congress. Reproduced by permission.

Rosalyn Sussman Yalow
1921–
American medical physicist

Rosalyn Sussman Yalow was co–developer of radioimmunoassay (RIA), a technique that uses radioactive isotopes to measure small amounts of biological substances. In widespread use, the RIA helps scientists and medical professionals measure the concentrations of hormones, vitamins, viruses, enzymes, and drugs, among other substances. Yalow's work concerning RIA earned her a share of the Nobel Prize in physiology or medicine in the late 1970s. At that time, she was only the second woman to receive the Nobel in medicine. During her career, Yalow also received acclaim for being the first woman to attain a number of other scientific achievements.

Yalow was born on July 19, 1921, in The Bronx, New York, to Simon Sussman and Clara Zipper Sussman. Her father, owner of a small business, had been born on the Lower East Side of New York City to Russian immigrant parents. At the age of four, Yalow's mother had journeyed to the United States from Germany. Although neither parent had attended high school, they instilled a great enthusiasm for and respect of education in their daughter. Yalow also credits her father with helping her find the confidence to succeed in school, teaching her that girls could do just as much as boys. Yalow learned to read before she entered kindergarten, although her family did not own any books. Instead, Yalow and her older brother, Alexander, made frequent visits to the public library.

During her youth, Yalow became interested in mathematics. At Walton High School in the Bronx, her interest turned to science, especially chemistry. After graduation, Yalow attended Hunter College, a women's school in New York that eventually became part of the City University of New York. She credits two physics professors, Dr. Herbert Otis and Dr. Duane Roller, for igniting her penchant for physics. This occurred in the latter part of the 1930s, a time when many new discoveries were made in nuclear physics. It was this field that Yalow ultimately chose for her major. In 1939 she was further inspired after hearing American physicist Enrico Fermi lecture about the discovery of nuclear fission, which had earned him the Nobel Prize the previous year.

Overcomes Sex Bias

As Yalow prepared for her graduation from Hunter College, she found that some practical considerations intruded on her passion for physics. At the time, most of American society expected young women to become secretaries or teachers. In fact, Yalow's parents urged her to pursue a career as an elementary school teacher. Yalow herself also thought it unrealistic to expect any of the top graduate schools in the country to accept her into a doctoral program or offer her the financial support that men received. "However, my physics professors encouraged me and I persisted," she explained in *Les Prix Nobel 1977.*

Yalow made plans to enter graduate school via other means. One of her earlier college physics professors, who had left Hunter to join the faculty at the Massachusetts Institute of Technology, arranged for Yalow to work as secretary to Dr. Rudolf Schoenheimer, a biochemist at Columbia University in New York. According to the plan, this position would give Yalow an opportunity to take some graduate courses in physics, and eventually provide a way for her to enter a graduate a school and pursue a degree. But Yalow never needed her plan. The month after graduating from Hunter College in January, 1941, she was offered a teaching assistantship in the physics department of the University of Illinois at Champaign–Urbana.

Gaining acceptance to the physics graduate program in the College of Engineering at the University of Illinois was one of many hurdles that Yalow had to cross as a woman in the field of science. For example, when she entered the University in September, 1941, she was the only woman in the College of Engineering's faculty, which included four hundred professors and teaching assistants. She was the first woman in more than two decades to attend the engineering college. Yalow realized that she had been given a space at the prestigious graduate school because of the shortage of male candidates, who were being drafted into the armed services in increasing numbers as America prepared to enter World War II.

Yalow's strong work orientation aided her greatly in her first year in graduate school. In addition to her regular course load and teaching duties, she took some extra undergraduate courses to increase her knowledge. Despite a hectic schedule, Yalow earned A's in her classes, except for an A–in an optics laboratory course. While in graduate school she also met Aaron Yalow, a fellow student and the man she would eventually marry. The pair met the first day of school and wed about two years later on June 6, 1943. Yalow received her master's degree in 1942 and her doctorate in 1945. She was the second woman to obtain a Ph.D. in physics at the University.

After graduation the Yalows moved to New York City, where they worked and eventually raised two children, Benjamin and Elanna. Yalow's first job after graduate school was as an assistant electrical engineer at Federal Telecommunications Laboratory, a private research lab. Once again, she found herself the sole woman as there were no other female engineers at the lab. In 1946 she began teaching physics at Hunter College. She remained a physics lecturer from 1946 to 1950, although by 1947 she began her long association with the Veterans Administration by becoming a consultant to Bronx VA Hospital. The VA wanted to establish some research programs to explore medical uses of radioactive substances. By 1950, Yalow had equipped a radioisotope laboratory at the Bronx VA Hospital and decided to leave teaching to devote her attention to full–time research.

That same year Yalow met Solomon A. Berson, a physician who had just finished his residency in internal medicine at the hospital. The two would work together until Berson's death in 1972. According to Yalow, the collaboration was a complementary one. In Olga Opfell's *Lady Laureates* Yalow is quoted as saying, "[Berson] wanted to be a physicist, and I wanted to be a medical doctor." While her partner had accumulated clinical expertise, Yalow maintained strengths in physics, math, and chemistry. Working together, Yalow and Berson discovered new ways to use radioactive isotopes in the measurement of blood volume, the study of iodine metabolism, and the diagnosis of thyroid diseases. Within a few years, the pair began to investigate adult–onset diabetes using radioisotopes. This project eventually led them to develop the groundbreaking radioimmunoassay technique.

Diabetes Mystery Leads to a Discovery

In the 1950s some scientists hypothesized that in adult–onset diabetes, insulin production remained normal, but a liver enzyme rapidly destroyed the peptide hormone, thereby preventing normal glucose metabolism. This contrasted with the situation in juvenile diabetes, where insulin production by the pancreas was too low to allow proper metabolism of glucose. Yalow and Berson wanted to test the hypothesis about adult–onset diabetes. They used insulin "labeled" with iodine–131. (That is, they attached, by a chemical reaction, the radioactive isotope of iodine to otherwise normal insulin molecules.) Yalow and Berson injected labeled insulin into diabetic and non–diabetic individuals and measured the rate at which the insulin disappeared.

To their surprise and in contradiction to the liver enzyme hypothesis, they found that the amount of radioactively labeled insulin in the blood of diabetics was higher than that found in the control subjects who had never received insulin injections before. As Yalow and Berson looked into this finding further, they deduced that diabetics were forming antibodies to the animal insulin used to control their disease. These antibodies were binding to radiolabeled insulin, preventing it from entering cells where it was used in sugar metabolism. Individuals who had never taken insulin before did not have these antibodies and so the radiolabeled insulin was consumed more quickly.

Yalow and Berson's proposal that animal insulin could spur antibody formation was not readily accepted by immunologists in the mid–1950s. At the time, most immunologists did not believe that antibodies would form to molecules as small as the insulin peptide. Also, the amount of insulin antibodies was too low to be detected by conventional immunological techniques. So Yalow and Berson set out to verify these minute levels of insulin antibodies using radiolabeled insulin as their marker. Their original report about insulin antibodies, however, was rejected initially by two journals. Finally, a compromise version was published that omitted "insulin antibody" from the paper's title and included some additional data indicating that an antibody was involved.

The need to detect insulin antibodies at low concentrations led to the development of the radioimmunoassay. The principle behind RIA is that a radiolabeled antigen, such as insulin, will compete with unlabeled antigen for the available binding sites on its specific antibody. As a standard, various mixtures of known amounts of labeled and unlabeled antigen are mixed with antibody. The amounts of radiation detected in each sample correspond to the amount of unlabeled antigen taking up antibody binding sites. In the unknown sample, a known amount of radiolabeled antigen is added and the amount of radioactivity is measured again. The radiation level in the unknown sample is compared to the standard samples; the amount of unlabeled antigen in the unknown sample will be the same as the amount of unlabeled antigen found in the standard sample that yields the same amount of radioactivity. RIA has turned out to be so useful because it can quickly and precisely detect very low concentrations of hormones and other substances in blood or other biological fluids. The principle can also be applied to binding interactions other than that between antigen and antibody, such as between a binding protein or tissue receptor site and an enzyme. In Yalow's Nobel lecture, recorded in *Les Prix Nobel 1977,* she listed more than one hundred biological substances—hormones, drugs, vitamins, enzymes, viruses, non–hormonal proteins, and more—that were being measured using RIA.

In 1968 she became a research professor at the Mt. Sinai School of Medicine, and in 1970, she was made chief of the Nuclear Medicine Service at the VA hospital. Yalow also began to receive a number of prestigious awards in recognition of her role in the development of RIA. In 1976, she was awarded the Albert Lasker Prize for Basic Medical Research. She was the first woman to be honored this laurel—an award that often leads to a Nobel Prize. In Yalow's case, this was true, for the very next year, she shared the Nobel Prize in physiology or medicine with Andrew V. Schally and Roger Guillemin for their work on radioimmunoassay. Schally and Guillemin were recognized for their use of RIA to make important discoveries about brain hormones.

Berson had died in 1972, and so did not share in these awards. Ecstatic to receive such prizes, Yalow was also saddened that her longtime partner had been excluded. According to an essay in *The Lady Laureates,* she remarked that the "tragedy" of winning the Nobel Prize "is that Dr. Berson did not live to share it." Earlier Yalow had paid tribute to her collaborator by asking the VA to name the laboratory, in which the two had worked, the Solomon A. Berson Research Laboratory. She made the request, as quoted in *Les Prix Nobel 1977,* "so that his name will continue to be on my papers as long as I publish and so that his contributions to our Service will be memorialized."

Yalow has received many other awards, honorary degrees, and lectureships, including the Georg Charles de Henesy Nuclear Medicine Pioneer Award in 1986 and the Scientific Achievement Award of the American Medical Society. In 1978, she hosted a five–part dramatic series on the life of French physical chemist **Marie Curie**, aired by the Public Broadcasting Service (PBS). In 1980 she became a distinguished professor at the Albert Einstein College of Medicine at Yeshiva University, leaving to become the Solomon A. Berson Distinguished Professor at Large at Mt. Sinai in 1986. She also chaired the Department of Clinical Science at Montefiore Hospital and Medical Center in the early– to mid–1980s.

By all accounts, Yalow was an industrious researcher, rarely taking time off. For example, some reports claim that she only took a few days off of work following the birth of her two children. In *The Lady Laureates,* Opfell reported that when the VA Hospital put on a party in honor of Yalow's selection for the Lasker Prize, Yalow herself "brought roast turkeys from home and stood in the middle of a meeting peeling potatoes and making potato salad while fellows reported to her."

The fact that Yalow was a trailblazer for women scientists was not lost on her, however. At a lecture before the Association of American Medical Colleges, as quoted in *Lady Laureates,* Yalow opined: "We cannot expect that in the foreseeable future women will achieve status in academic medicine in proportion to their numbers. But if we are to start working towards that goal we must believe in ourselves or no one else will believe in us; we must match our aspirations with the guts and determination to succeed; and for those of us who have had the good fortune to move upward, we must feel a personal responsibility to serve as role models and advisors to ease the path for those who come afterwards."

SELECTED WRITINGS BY YALOW:

Books

Luft, R. and R. S. Yalow, *Radioimmunoassay: Methodology and Applications in Physiology and in Clinical Studies,* Publishing Sciences Group, 1974.

Periodicals

(With Solomon A. Berson, A. Bauman, M. A. Rothschild, and K. Newerly) "Insulin–I131 Metabolism in Human Subjects: Demonstration of Insulin Binding Globulin in the Circulation of Insulin Treated Subjects." *Journal of Clinical Investigation.* 35 (1956): 170–190.

(With Berson) "Assay of Plasma Insulin in Human Subjects by Immunological Methods." *Nature* 184 (1959): 1648–1649.

FURTHER READING

Books

Les Prix Nobel 1977. Almquist & Wiskell International, Stockholm, 1978, pp. 237–264.

Opfell, Olga. *The Lady Laureates: Women Who Have Won the Nobel Prize.* Scarecrow Press, Inc., 1978.

Sketch by Lee Katterman

Anne Sewell Young
1871–1961
American astronomer

Anne Sewell Young was a distinguished astronomer, respected for her research on variable stars and sunspots. Her work, spanning several decades, helped pave the way for later female astronomers and contributed to public interest in astronomy.

Young was born to Reverend Albert and Mary (Sewell) Young in Bloomington, Wisconsin, in 1871. The niece of Charles Young, distinguished professor of astronomy at Princeton University and early researcher on the Sun's corona, Young was well trained in the field. She received her B. L. degree from Carleton College in 1892 and taught mathematics at Whitman College until 1895. She received her M. S. degree from Carleton in 1897 and was a high school principal until her appointment to the astronomy faculty of Mount Holyoke College in 1899. Young rose to the position of professor and was eventually named emeritus professor in 1936, the year of her retirement from the school. During her time at Mount Holyoke, Young also served as director of the John Payne Williston Observatory.

Young continued her studies at the University of Chicago in 1898 and 1902 before receiving her Ph. D. in astronomy from Columbia University in 1906. Her doctoral research and dissertation, based on early photographic measurements, focused on the double cluster of stars within the constellation Perseus.

At the Williston Observatory, Young instituted a program of daily sunspot observations, which later became part of an international research project. She also received recognition for research conducted on asteroid positions, comet orbits, and variable stars. Observing variable stars, which includes any star with a variation in its energy output, was of special interest to her, and she would exchange information on this subject with Edward Pickering, director of the Harvard College Observatory.

As a teacher, Young was widely known as dedicated, encouraging, and inspirational. In order to observe the total eclipse of the sun in 1925, she arranged for the entire student body at Mount Holyoke to travel by train to Central Connecticut. She began educating the public about astronomy by providing a series of open nights at the observatory, helping to promote the field's popularity. Young also wrote a monthly astronomy column for the *Springfield Republican*, a local newspaper, further advancing public interest in the subject.

In addition to her newspaper articles, Young published papers in astronomy journals, reporting her research and observations. Her professional accomplishments include a feature in *Who's Who*, the only early astronomer from Carleton to be so honored, as well as being one of only three astronomers from Carleton ever listed in *American Men of Science*.

In 1923, Young was elected president of the American Association of Variable Star Observers. She was also elected a fellow of the American Astronomical Society and held memberships in the Royal Astronomical Society, the American Association for the Advancement of Science, and the Phi Beta Kappa honorary society. Mount Holyoke appointed Young professor emerita in 1936. Upon her retirement, Young and her sister, Elizabeth, moved to Claremont, California, to live at Pilgrim Place, a home for senior family members of missionaries, where she died in 1961.

SELECTED WRITINGS BY YOUNG:

Books

Rutherford Photographs of the Stellar Clusters h or x Persei. New York: Contributions from the Observatory at Columbia University, no. 24, 1906.

FURTHER READING:

Books

Kass-Simon, G., and Patricia Farnes, eds. *Women of Science: Righting the Record*. Bloomington: Indiana University Press

Ogilvie, Marilyn Bailey. *Women in Science: Antiquity Through the Nineteenth Century*. Cambridge: MIT Press, 1986.

Yost, Edna. *Women of Modern Science.*. New York: Dodd, Mead, and Company, 1959.

Sketch by Helene Barker Kiser

Grace Chisholm Young
1868–1944
English mathematician

A distinguished mathematician, Grace Chisholm Young is recognized as being the first woman to receive a Ph.D. in any field from a German university. Working closely with her husband, mathematician William Henry Young, she produced a large body of published work that made contributions to both pure and applied mathematics.

Grace Emily Chisholm Young was born on March 15, 1868, in Haslemere, Surrey, England, to Anna Louisa Bell and Henry William Chisholm. Her father was a British career civil servant who (following his own father) rose through the ranks to become the chief of Britain's weights

Grace Chisholm Young

and measures. Grace Emily Chisholm was the youngest of three surviving children. Her brother, Hugh Chisholm, enjoyed a distinguished career as editor of the eleventh edition of the *Encyclopaedia Britannica.*

As befitted a girl of her social class, Young received an education at home. Forbidden by her mother to study medicine—which the youngster wanted to do—she entered Girton College, Cambridge (one of two women's colleges there) in 1889. She was twenty–one years of age, and the institution's Sir Francis Goldschmid Scholar of mathematics. In 1892 she graduated with first–class honors, then sat informally for the final mathematics examinations at Oxford; there, she placed first. In 1893 she transferred to Göttingen University in Germany, where she attended lectures and produced a dissertation entitled "The Algebraic Groups of Spherical Trigonometry" under noted mathematician Felix Klein. In 1895 she became the first woman to receive a Göttingen doctorate in any subject. The degree bore the distinction magna cum laude.

She returned to London and married her former Girton tutor, William Henry Young, who had devoted years to coaching Cambridge students. After the birth of their first child, the Youngs moved to Göttingen. There, William Young began a distinguished research career in mathematics, which would be supported in large part by the work of his wife. Grace Chisholm Young studied anatomy at the university and raised their six children, while collaborating with her husband on mathematics in both co–authored papers and those published under his name alone. In 1905 the pair authored a widely regarded textbook on set theory. Grace Chisholm Young's most important work was achieved between 1914 and 1916, during which time she published several papers on derivates of real functions; in this work she contributed to what is known as the Denjoy-Saks-Young theorem.

The Young family lived modestly, and William Young traveled frequently to earn money by teaching. In 1908, with the birth of their sixth child, the Youngs moved from Göttingen to Geneva. William Young continually sought a well–paying professorship in England, but he failed to obtain such a position; in 1913 he obtained a lucrative professorship in Calcutta, which required his residence for only a few months per year, and after World War I he became professor at the University of Wales in Aberystwyth for several years. Switzerland, however, remained the family's permanent home.

With advancing years, Grace Chisholm Young's mathematical productivity slackened; in 1929 she began an ambitious historical novel, which was never published. Writing fiction was but one of her many varied interests, which included music, languages, and medicine. She also wrote children's books, in which she introduced notions of science. Her children followed the path she had pioneered, becoming accomplished scholars of mathematics, chemistry, and medicine. Her son Frank died as a British aviator during the First World War.

Grace Chisholm Young had lived with her husband's extended absences for her entire married life, and the spring of 1940 found them separated again: she in England, and he in Switzerland. From that time onward, neither spouse was able to see the other again—both were prevented from doing so by the downfall of France during the war. William Young died in 1942, and Grace Chisholm Young died of a heart attack in 1944.

SELECTED WRITINGS BY YOUNG:

Books

(With William Henry Young) *The First Book of Geometry.* Dent, 1905. Reprint, 1969.

(With William Henry Young) *The Theory of Sets of Points,* Cambridge University Press, 1906. Reprint, 1972.

Periodicals

"On the Form of a Certain Jordan Curve." *Quarterly Journal of Pure and Applied Mathematics* 37 (1905): 87–91.

(With William Henry Young) "An Additional Note on Derivates and the Theorem of the Mean." *Quarterly Journal of Pure and Applied Mathematics* 40 (1909): 144–145.

"A Note on Derivatives and Differential Coefficients." *Acta Mathematica* 37 (1914): 141–154.

(With William Henry Young) "On the Reduction of Sets of Intervals." *Proceedings of the London Mathematical Society* 14 (1914): 111–130.

"On the Solution of a Pair of Simultaneous Diophantine Equations Connected with the Nuptial Number of Plato." *Proceedings of the London Mathematical Society* 23 (1925): 27–44.

FURTHER READING

Books

Grinstein, Louise S., and Paul J. Campbell, eds. *Women of Mathematics: A Biobibliographic Sourcebook.* Greenwood Press, 1987, pp. 247–254.

Periodicals

Cartwright, M. L. "Grace Chisholm Young." *Journal of the London Mathematical Society* 19 (1944): 185–192.

Grattan–Guinness, Ivor. "A Mathematical Union: William Henry and Grace Chisholm Young." *Annals of Science* 29 (1972): 105–186.

Sketch by Lewis Pyenson

Judith Sharn (Rubin) Young
1952–
American astronomer

A professor at the University of Massachusetts at Amherst, Judith Sharn Young is a well–known astronomer who has made important contributions to our knowledge of star formation, galaxy formation and evolution, and interstellar matter. She has published more than 100 papers and has won several prestigious awards.

Born in Washington, D. C. in 1952, Judith Young is the daughter of Robert J. Rubin, a theoretical physicist at the National Bureau of Standards, and **Vera Cooper Rubin**, an observational astronomer at the Carnegie Institution in Washington. Young's mother is famous for having proved the existence of dark matter. Young was always fascinated by the stars, but did not grow up planning to be an astronomer. Until her senior year in high school, she preferred chemistry and biochemistry. However that year she took an astronomy course that was taught by her mother, and became fascinated with black holes, collapsed stars whose surface gravity is so strong that even light cannot escape from it. Young's three brothers also became scientists.

Young graduated from Harvard University with an honors B. A. in astronomy in 1974. That same year she entered a graduate program in astronomy at the University of Minnesota. In 1975, she married Michael Young, a graduate student in geology at Minnesota. Although she had already passed her qualifying exams, the astronomy faculty advised her not to pursue her Ph.D. because of her marriage; so Young switched to the physics program. Her new advisor, Phyllis Freier, the only woman in the physics department at that time, also was the only physics faculty member who was practicing astronomy. Young earned her M. S. in physics in 1977 and her physics doctorate in 1979. Her thesis was on cosmic rays, and she studied the various isotopes that comprise cosmic rays and enter the galaxy, solar system, and Earth's atmosphere.

In 1979, Young became a postdoctoral assistant at the Five College Radio Astronomy Observatory (FCRAO) at the University of Massachusetts at Amherst. In 1982, she became a visiting assistant professor in the Department of Physics and Astronomy, the first woman on the astronomy faculty at the University of Massachusetts, and only the second woman in the department. In 1984, Young was appointed as a regular assistant professor, and she was promoted to associate professor in 1987 and full professor in 1993.

In 1980, FCRAO was able to significantly improve its radio receivers, enabling Young to begin studying galaxies. In collaboration with the radio astronomer Nick Z. Scoville, Young began examining the amount of carbon monoxide and cold gases in galaxies, since these are the materials that form stars. One of their major discoveries was the demonstration that the more gas present in a galaxy, the more stars are formed. For this discovery of giant molecular clouds in our galaxy and others, Young was awarded the **Annie Jump Cannon** Prize of the American Astronomical Society for 1982–83, an award of research funds given to American women astronomers. In 1986, Young became the first recipient of the **Maria Goeppert–Mayer** Award of the American Physical Society, for young women scientists who have made important contributions to physics. As a condition of accepting this award, Young gave a number of lectures to encourage women's participation in science.

In 1986 Young was awarded a three–year Sloan Research Fellowship. Young and her husband divorced in 1990 and she spent 1991 as a visiting fellow at the University of Hawaii. She is a member of a number of scientific societies, including the Association for Women in Science and the American Astronomical Society, where she has been involved with the Committee on the Status of Women.

Young studies the composition of the interstellar medium to understand how it influences star formation. With her coworkers, she has observed the molecular content and distribution of 300 spiral and irregular galaxies. She has discovered that galaxy collisions seem to have a big effect on formation rate for stars of high mass. In recent years, in addition to studying extragalactic radioastronomy and galactic evolution, Young has ventured into biomedical research.

In addition to teaching undergraduates and graduate students, Young has taught astronomy at her daughter's elementary school. Young's latest project is the construction of a sunwheel at the University of Massachusetts. The sunwheel demonstrates the Sun's position on the horizon throughout the year and is designed to bring greater awareness of astronomy to the university community, to school children, and to the general public.

SELECTED WRITINGS BY YOUNG:

Periodicals

(With N. Z. Scoville) "Extragalactic CO: Gas Distributions Which Follow the Light in IC 342 and NGC 6946." *Astrophysical Journal* 258 (1982): 467.

(With N. Z. Scoville and E. Brady) "The Dependence of CO Content on Morphological Type and Luminosity for Spiral Galaxies in the Virgo Cluster." *Astrophysical Journal* 288 (1985): 487.

(With N. Z. Scoville) "The Molecular Content of Galaxies." *Annual Review of Astronomy and Astrophysics.* 29 (1991): 581–625.

(With J. D. P. Kenney and J. E. Carlstrom) "Molecular Gas Dynamics of the Young Nuclear Starburst in the Barred Galaxy NGC 3504." *Astrophysical Journal* 418 (1993): 687–708.

(With S. Xie and F. P. Schloerb) "A $_{12}$CO, $_{13}$CO and CS Study of NGC 2146 and IC 343." *Astrophysical Journal* 421 (1994): 434–52.

Other

"A Sunwheel for the Campus." http://www.umass.edu/sunwheel/index2.html (20 Jul 1999).

FURTHER READING

Books

Lewandowski, Sue Ann. "Judith Sharn Young." In *Notable Women in the Physical Sciences: A Biographical Dictionary.* Edited by Benjamin F. Shearer and Barbara S. Shearer. Westport, CT: Greenwood Press, 1997.

Periodicals

"Astronomers Honor Seven Theorists and Observers." *Physics Today* (April 1983): 67–70.

"Judith S. Young Receives Maria Goeppert–Mayer Award." *Physics Today* (May 1986): 111.

Other

"Judith Young Graduate Brochure Page." 20 Feb. 1997. http://www– astro.phast.umass.edu/directory/people/young.html (20 July 1999).

Sketch by Margaret Alic

Roger Arliner Young
1899–1964
American zoologist

Roger Arliner Young overcame tremendous obstacles to become the first black woman to receive a doctoral degree in zoology. In spite of gender, race, and educational barriers firmly in place at the time, Young's dedicated commitment to science was unfailing.

Young was born in Clifton Forge, Virginia, in 1899 and grew up in Burgettstown, Pennsylvania. In 1916, she enrolled at Howard University, originally enrolling to study music. It wasn't until 1921 that she took her first science course, general zoology. Her professor was the eminent Ernest Everett Just, the head of the Howard University biology department. Young got a C grade.

Despite Young's average performance, Just apparently saw some promise in her and convinced her to pursue a career in the sciences. She took only two other science courses (vertebrate embryology and invertebrate embryology) and earned a grade of B in both. In 1923, she received her bachelor's degree, seven years after enrolling at Howard.

A Promising Start

After graduation, Young accepted a position as an assistant professor in zoology at Howard and saved enough money from a meager salary to begin studying for her master's degree on a part–time basis at the University of Chicago. There, she excelled in her academic studies. At the same time, she was working with Just as a research assistant, studying the internal structures of the paramecium that allow the creature to regulate salt concentrations. As a result of this significant research, Young published her first scientific paper, "On the Excretory Apparatus in the Paramecium," in the September 12, 1924 issue of *Science.* She was just 25 years old. The paper's appearance made her the first black woman to research and publish professionally in her field. In addition, it appeared two months before a similar paper by the noted Russian cell physiologist Dmitriy Nasonov.

In 1926, Young was elected to Sigma Xi, the national honor society for the biological sciences, a distinction that is usually awarded to doctoral candidates. She earned her master's degree that same year; her future looked bright.

Conducts Summer Research at Woods Hole

The summer of 1927 was the first of many that Young would spend with Just doing research at the Marine Biological Laboratory at Woods Hole, Massachusetts. They worked together well. She had gained his respect for her skill with the technical and theoretical aspects of the research, and he said her work surpassed his own in technical excellence. At Woods Hole's laboratories, Young and Just studied fertilization. Working with a variety of marine organisms, they studied the effects of ultraviolet light on eggs, research that Young would later continue on her own.

During the summer of 1928, Just's wife, Ethel, did not accompany him to Woods Hole, as she had before. Just and Young interacted well with the other researchers, both professionally and socially. They went to dinner with some of the married white couples who were also conducting research at Woods Hole. Young also socialized with the other scientists, going on picnics and day trips around Cape Cod.

The gossip around the Howard campus said Just and Young had a relationship that went beyond a professional interest. Regardless, Just gave Young increasing responsibilities in the Department of Zoology. She stood in for him as acting department head in early 1929 as Just traveled to Europe on a grant. After he returned, Young returned to the University of Chicago to pursue her doctorate in zoology in the fall of 1929. There she studied with Just's own mentor, Frank Lillie, under whose supervision she had worked at the Marine Biological Laboratory during the summer of 1929.

The First Signs of Trouble

In the familiar surroundings of Chicago, Young had no trouble adjusting to the routine of coursework, which occupied her first semester. However, she didn't do as well in her doctorate–level classes as she had in her master's classes. Part of the problem may have been that her eyes were bothering her; it later turned out that she had done them permanent damage during the ultraviolet light experiments at Woods Hole.

The week before the qualifying exam, scheduled for January 10, 1930, Just again left for Europe. Young failed the exam miserably. Simple questions that she had dealt with frequently in her courses, in her teaching, and in her research stumped her.

Young left Chicago, hoping to find some rest and relief from the pressures she had been under—her own studies, the exam, the administrative responsibilities Just had left to her. She wrote to Lillie, who was deeply concerned about her: "The trouble is for two years I've tried to keep going under responsibilities that were not wholly mine but were not shared, and the weight of it has simply worn me out." In her letter, she revealed that she knew as early as August that "unless there was some relief" she would fail the exam.

A Declining Relationship with Just

Young's failure to pass her comprehensives had a negative effect on her increasingly difficult relationship with Just. By 1933 he was gradually giving her less responsibility. By 1935 there was overt conflict between the two. Just called Young's teaching "far below standards" and ultimately said he had "no respect" for her as a person. Young retorted that Just had deliberately distracted her from her scientific work and that where he had once supported her and encouraged her, he now threw up roadblocks that ranged from denying her access to equipment to refusing to read her scientific papers. In spring 1936, she was fired supposedly for missing classes and misusing lab equipment.

Young Rallies to Get Her Doctorate

Despite what had happened at Howard, Young still had allies, chief among them L.V. Heilbrunn, whom she had met through Woods Hole. She joined him at the University of Pennsylvania in 1937 to try again for her doctorate. This time, things went much better. Freed from the administrative duties she'd shouldered at Howard (and possibly, too, of the pressure of Just's presence—or absence—in her life), she received a two–year grant from the General Education Board and borrowed money to pay for the third and final year. She completed her dissertation on "The Indirect Effects of Roentgen Rays on Certain Marine Eggs," which built upon research she had published with Heilbrunn in the *Biological Bulletin* in 1935.

Throughout her ups and downs, Young struggled to make ends meet financially and to support her ailing mother. She had no other relatives to turn to for support. This may explain why she had leaned on Just so much, and why his apparent betrayal of her, both as a scientist and as a woman, seemed to have such a devastating effect.

Post Doctorate Career

After earning her doctorate, Young took a post at the North Carolina College for Negroes (NCCN) in Raleigh, North Carolina, as assistant professor. She soon became head of the biology department at Shaw University, which was also in Raleigh.

Despite her happiness with Shaw's atmosphere, Young remained under tremendous stress due to her financial troubles. She left there in 1947 to return to NCCN as a professor of biology. She then held positions at Paul Quinn College in Texas, Jackson State in Mississippi, and Southern University in Louisiana.

Young's mother died in 1953, and mental problems, which had been developing over the years, began to plague her. She lost the three positions mentioned earlier and was penniless. She resorted to a three-hour-a-day job teaching kindergarten at a poor Catholic parish in Waco, Texas.

She did manage to briefly hold another post at Jackson State, but left there for treatment at the Mississippi State Mental Asylum. She was discharged on December 21, 1962, and took a temporary position as visiting lecturer in biology at Southern University. She died on November 9, 1964 in New Orleans, poor and alone.

SELECTED WRITINGS BY YOUNG:

Periodicals

Heilbrunn, L.V., and R.A. Young. "Indirect Effects of Radiation on Sea Urchin Eggs." *Biological Bulletin*(1935).

Young, R.A. "On the Excretory Apparatus in Paramecium." *Science* (September 12, 1924).

FURTHER READING

Periodicals

Manning, Kenneth R. "Roger Arliner Young: Scientist." *Sage: A Scholarly Journal on Black Women* 6, no. 2 (Fall 1989): 3–7.

Other

Maisel, Merry, and Laura Smart. "Roger Arliner Young: Lifelong Struggle of a Zoologist." In *Women in Science: A Selection of 16 Significant Contributors* March 23, 1998. http://www.sdsc.edu/ ScienceWomen/young (March 12, 1999).

"Roger Arliner Young: Zoologist, Biologist." In *Faces of Science: African Americans in the Sciences.* 9 Novemer 1998. http://www.lib.lsu.edu/lib/chem/display/young.html (March 10, 1999).

Sketch by Fran Hodgkins

A

Abel Wolman Award 537
Aberle, Sophie Bledsoe 1
Ablative coatings 537
Abrege de navigation 310
Académie des Sciences, Helene-Paul Helbronner Prize 489
Academy of Natural Sciences 329, 529
Accelerator systems 147
Acquired immunodeficiency syndrome (AIDS) 300
Actaea, a First Lesson in Natural History 3
Actinium radioactive decay series 449
Actonian Prize 96
Acyclovir 155
Ada (computer language) 72
Adam's Ancestors: An Up-to-Date Outline of What Is Known about the Origin of Man 317
Adams, Elizabeth 404
Adams, John Couch 544
Addams, Jane 224, 270
Adult-onset diabetes 630
Aerospace Medical Association, Paul Bert Award 560
Aerospace Medical Association, Woman of the Year Award 591
Aesthetic Society 542
Aflatoxin 534
African Americans, ethnohistorical sociology of 133
African sleeping sickness 443
Agamede 2
Agassiz, Elizabeth 3, *3*, 91, 421
Agassiz, Louis 3, 421
Aglaonice 4
Agnesi, Maria Gaëtana 5
Agnodice 6
Agricola, Georgius 252
Agricultural statistics 586
Agrostology 86
AIDS Medical Foundation 300
Aircraft, lift distribution of wings of 181
Ajzenberg-Selove, Fay 6
Albert Einstein World Award of Science Medal 70
ALCOA (Aluminum Company of America) 223
Aldo Leopold Award 559
Alembic 361
Alexander, Hattie E. 8
The Alexiad 107
Alfred Ackermann-Teubner Memorial Prize for the Advancement of Mathematical Knowledge 420
Alfred P. Sloan Award for Cancer Research 191
Algae 259
Algebra and Number Theory 572
Algebra, abstract 418
Algebra, linear 231
Algebraic curves 521
Algebraic number theory 570
Allergic reactions 471
Allopurinol 155
Almagest 264
Aluminum, manufacture of 222
Alvariño, Angeles 10, *11*
Amaryllis lily 583
The American Arbacia and Other Sea Urchins 226
American Academy of Arts and Sciences, Newcomb-Cleveland Prize 196
American Academy of Pediatrics, Apgar Award 20
American Academy of Pediatrics, E. Mead Johnson Award 9
American Association of Blood Banks, John Elliot Memorial Award 524
American Association of the History of Medicine, Otto H. Hafner Award 430
American Association for the Advancement of Science 481
American Association of Anatomists 509
American Association of Immunologists 314
American Association of University Women 485
American Astronomical Society 77
American Astronomical Society, Annie Jump Cannon Prize 27, 228, 248, 370, 442, 469, 540, 564, 614, 616, 626, 634
American Astronomical Society, Beatrice M. Tinsley Prize 36
American Astronomical Society, Henry Norris Russell Prize 442
American Astronomical Society, Warner Prize 70
American Botanical Society 59
American Bryological Society 59
American Chemical Society 50, 225, 527, 528
American Chemical Society, Garvan Medal 39, 49, 78, 80, 114, 155, 170, 174, 190, 279, 282, 283, 346, 355, 416, 452, 456, 479, 524, 532, 593
American Chemical Society, James Flack Norris Award 226
American College of Physicians, James D. Bruce Award 255
American Conchology 515
American Concrete Institute 204
American Dyestuff Reporter Award 575
American Fisheries Society 402
American Foundation for AIDS Research 300
American Geophysical Union, William Bowie Medal 322
American Heart Association Achievement Award 314
American Home Economics Association 485
American Home Economics Association, Borden Award 550
American Institute for Public Service, Jefferson Award for Public Service 485
American Institute of Aeronautics and Astronautics, Lawrence Sperry Award 610
American Institute of Chemists, Chemical Pioneer Award 64
American Institute of Electrical Engineers 93
American Lung Association, Edward Livingston Trudeau Medal 20
American Mathematical Society 520
American Mathematical Society, Dannie Heineman Prize 164
American Mathematical Society, Ruth Lyttle Satter Prize 86
American Mathematical Steele Prize for Exposition 127
American Medical Association, Elizabeth Blackwell Medal 343

American Medical Society, Scientific Achievement Award 631
American Meteorological Association, Cleveland Abbe Award 539
American Meteorological Association, Meisinger Award 539
American Oil Chemical Society, Harvey W. Wiley Award 534
American Ornithologists' Union 23
American Ornithologists' Union, Brewster Medal 24
American Pediatric Society 8
American Physical Society, Maria Goeppert-Mayer Award 634
American Public Health Association, Albert Lasker Award 306, 410, 424, 451, 511, 631
American Public Health Association, Martha May Eliot Award 613
American Radium Society, Janeway Medal 473
American Society for Engineering Education 31
American Society for Microbiology, Fisher Award 112
American Society of Bacteriologists 161
American Society of Cell Biology, Wilson Medal 166
American Society of Civil Engineers, Hoover Medal 200
American Society of European Chemists and Pharmacists, Carl Neuberg Medal 355, 479
American Society of Mechanical Engineers 204
American Society of Plant Physiologists, Stephen Hales Award 593
American Society of Refrigerating Engineers 447
American Therapeutic Society, Oscar B. Hunter Award 9
Ames, Bruce 471
Amino acids 157, 479
An Atlas of the Medulla and Midbrain 510
Analytical Institutions 5
Anatomia corporis humanis 201
Anatomical injection 201
Anatomy 578
Ancker-Johnson, Betsy 11
Anderson Natural History School, New England 3
Anderson, Gloria L. 13, *13*
Anderson, John M. 219
Andromeda nebulae 234
Anemia, treatment of 54
Animal genetics 586
Animal histology 400
The Animal Mind 601
Animal Welfare Institute, Schweitzer Medal 215
Annan, Charles F. 294
Annenberg Award 246
Anning, Mary 14
Annual Achievement Award of the Society of Women Engineers 281
Annual Reports of Observations of Injurious Insects 431
Antarctica 379
Anthropology
Anti-malarial drugs 531
Antibiotics 63, 242, 376
Antibodies 297
Antigens 525
Antilogism 308
Antiquity of Man 339
Apgar Score System 16
Apgar, Virginia 15, *16*
Aphaenogaster treatae 583
Aphids 436
Apollo-Soyuz Test Project 429, 430
Applied micropaleontology 17
Applin, Esther Richards 17
Archimedean solids 562
Argininosuccinic acid 479
Arignote 577
Arithmetica 264
Arnold, Christoph 290
Art of Obstetrics 51
Arthur S. Fleming Award 451
Artin, Emil 571
Association for the Advancement of the Medical Education of Women 269
Association for the Advancement of Women 396
Association for Women in Mathematics 353, 517
Association for Women in Mathematics, Louise Hay Award 165
Association to Aid Women in Science, Ellen Richards Prize 288, 383
Astbury, William Thomas 334
Astrodynamics 350
Astronauts 337, 427
  candidates 97
An Astronomical and Geographical Class Book for Schools 66
Astronomical Canon 263, 264
Astronomy at Yale 246
Astronomy, Polynesian 351
Atlantis space shuttle 338
Atlas of Protein Sequence and Structure 128
Atomic bomb 208
Atomic Energy Commission 480
Atomic Energy Commission, Enrico Fermi Award 385
Atomic spectra 540
Atomism 84
Attidae 445
Audobon, John Jacob 583
Auerbach, Charlotte 18
Australian Association of Mathematics Teachers 413
Austrian Academy of Science, Leibniz Prize 383
Austrian Academy of Sciences, Ignaz L. Lieben Prize 46
Austrian Honor Cross 355
Autism Society of America, Tramell Crow Award 217
Autobiography, secular 85
Avery, Mary Ellen 19, *20*
Avery, Oswald 312
Avian paleontology 625
Awards, honors, and prizes
  Abel Wolman Award 537
  Actonian Prize 96
  Albert Einstein World Award of Science Medal 70
  Albert Lasker Award 306, 410, 424, 451, 511, 631
  Aldo Leopold Award 559
  Alfred Ackermann-Teubner Memorial Prize for the Advancement of Mathematical Knowledge 420
  Alfred P. Sloan Award for Cancer Research 191
  American Dyestuff Reporter Award 575
  American Heart Association Achievement Award 314
  American Mathematical Steele Prize for Exposition 127
  Annenberg Award 246
  Annie Jump Cannon Prize 27, 227, 248, 442, 469, 540, 564, 614, 616, 626, 634
  Apgar Award 20
  Arthur S. Fleming Award 451
  Austrian Honor Cross 355
  Award for Distinguished Service to Mathematics 482
  Barsky Award 537
  Basantidevi Amirchand Award 476
  Beatrice M. Tinsley Prize 36
  Benjamin Apthorp Gould Prize 496
  Borden Award 550
  Brewster Medal 24
  Brewster Memorial Award 625
  Bundesverdienstkreuz First Class 484
  Carl Neuberg Medal 355, 479
  Centennial Medal of Canada 248
  Ceres Medal 587
  Charles de Henesy Nuclear Medicine Pioneer Award 631
  Charles Lawrence Hutchinson Medal 367

Chemical Pioneer Award 64
Christian and Mary Lindback Foundation Award for Distinguished Teaching 7
Christopher Columbus Discovery Award in Biomedical Research 551
Ciba Award 611
Clapp Award in Marine Biology 480
Cleveland Abbe Award 539
Clunies Ross Award for Science and Technology 526
Companion of the Order of Canada 248
Comstock Award 623
Congressional Hispanic Caucus Medallion of Excellence Role Mode 428
Congressional Space Medal of Honor 337
Dame Commander of the Order of the British Empire 335
Dannie Heineman Prize 164
Davy Medal 335
Dawson Williams Prize in Paediatrics 613
Diploma of Honor in Cytology 564
Distinguished Federal Civilian Service Award 286
E. Mead Johnson Award 9
Earth Day International Award 534
Ebony Black Achievement Award 273
Edgar D. Tillyer Medal 478
Edward Livingston Trudeau Medal 20
Eli Lilly Award in Biological Chemistry 551
Elizabeth Blackwell Medal 343
Ellen Richards Prize 77, 288, 383, 553
Emily Warren Roebling Award 32
Eminent Ecologist Award 439
Enrico Fermi Award 385
Ernest O. Lawrence Award 147
Ernst Jung Gold Medal for Medicine 395
Essence Science and Technology Award 273
Estonian Academy of Sciences' Karl Ernst von Baer Medal 430
F. C. Koch Award 519
Farrer Memorial Medal 587
Federal Civil Service Award 560
Federal Woman's Award 462
Fedorov prize 265
Fisher Award 112
Flora Medal 431
Ford Prize 570
Frances K. Hutchinson Medal for Service in Conservation 480
Francis Boyer Science Award 480
Free Spirit Award 339
Garvan Medal 39, 49, 78, 80, 114, 155, 170, 174, 190, 279, 282, 283, 346, 355, 416, 452, 456, 479, 524, 532, 593
Genetics Society of America Medal 395
George van Biesbroeck Award 246
Giants in Science Award 165
Glavnauk Prize 25
Global 500 Award 534
Glover Award 246
Gold Cross of Honor 572
Gold Medal Award 112
Gold Medal of Science 235
Gold Medal Prix Extraordinaire 198
Gold Star Medal 574
Great Silver Medal of Galicia 10
Gregori Aminoff Prize 282
Gruenwald Award 32
Guggenheim Award 504
Hammett Award in Chemistry 604
Harold E. Edgerton Award 237
Harvey W. Wiley Award. 534
Helene-Paul Helbronner prize 489
Henry Draper Medal 76
Henry Norris Russell Prize 442
Herschel Medal 36
High Service Cross 417
Hildebrand Award 282
Hispanic Achievement Award in Science 595
Hispanic Engineer National Achievement Award in College Education 595
Hoover Medal 200
Hubbard Medal 577
Hughes Medal 22
Ignaz L. Lieben Prize 46
Industry Innovation Award in the Meat Industry 217
J. Paul Getty Wildlife Conservation Prize 215
J. Robert Oppenheimer Memorial Prize 36
James D. Bruce Award 255
James Flack Norris award 226
James Spence Memorial Gold Medal 613
Janeway Medal 473
Jefferson Award for Public Service 485
John Burroughs Medal 82
John Elliot Memorial Award 524
John W. Gardner Leadership Award 302
Jubilee Research Award 476
Keith Medal, Royal Society of Edinburgh 19
King Leopold II Prize 444
Klaus Schwarz Medal 548
Kossuth Prize 453
Kraepelin Gold Medal 519
Kyoto Prize in Basic Sciences 215
Laura Leonard Prize 464
Lawrence Sperry Award 610
Lee Hawley, Sr. Award for Arthritis Research 551
Leibig Medal 417
Leibniz Medal 383
Lester R. Ford Award 403
Liberty Hyde Bailey Medal 367
Livestock Conservation Institute Award for Meritorious Service 217
Louis Empain Prize 127
Louise Hay Award 165
M. Carey Thomas Prize 511
Maria Goeppert-Mayer Award 237, 634
Martha May Eliot Award 613
Maryland Chemist Award 170, 283
Max Planck Medal 385
Maxwell Finland Award 255
Meisinger Award 539
Meyer Medal 527
Michelson Medal 36
Murray Thelin Award 467
Naples Table Association prize 510
NASA Space Flight Medal 105
National Geographic Society Centennial Award 215
National Hispanic Quincentennial Commission Pride Award 428
National Medal of Science 20, 70, 101, 116, 118, 136, 327, 519, 551, 623
National Medal of Technology 147, 252
Nature Conservancy National Award 367
Newcomb-Cleveland Prize 196
Nobel Prize for Theoretical Physics 208
Nobel Prize in Chemistry 243, 275
Nobel Prize in Physiology or Medicine 112, 153, 155, 325, 372, 423, 629, 631
Olney Medal 575
Order "Band of Honor" 265
Order of Friendship Medal 337
Order of Lenin 265, 574
Order of Merit 244
Order of Merit, Prussia 51
Order of the Sun 484
Ordre National des Grandes Lacs 185
Oscar B. Hunter Memorial Award 9
Otto H. Hafner Award 430
Outstanding Educators of America Award 624
Outstanding Faculty Award, Institute of Electrical and Electronic Engineers 31
Outstanding Professor Award 31
Outstanding Women in Science and Engineering Award 437
Padmabhushan Award 476
Papanicolaou Award for Scientific Achievement 395
Passano Foundation Young Scientist Award 551
Paul Bert Award 560

President's Medal of Freedom 83
Prix Bordin 300
Prix des Dames 489
Public Welfare Medal 482
Research Corporation Award 623
Resnik Challenger Medal 58
Ricketts Prize 541
Right Livelihood Award 533
Rittenhouse Medal 248
Rockefeller Public Service Award 537
Royal Order of the Lion 444
Ruth Lyttle Satter Prize 86, 127
Ruth Sanger Medal 526
Schrödinger prize 47
Schweitzer Medal 215
Scroll of Honor, National Association of Negro Business and Professional Women 13
Sloan Award 452
Society of Women Engineers, Achievement Award 58, 137, 158, 180, 254, 281, 537, 560, 575, 610, 624
Soviet Kosmos Award 430
Squibb Award in Chemotherapy 64
Stephen Hales Award 593
T. Duckett Jones Memorial Award 314
Thorvold Madsen Award 255
Tramell Crow Award 217
Trudeau Medal 511, 525
Tyler Ecology Award 438
United Nations Peace Medal 480
Upjohn Award 612
Upward Mobility Award 32
Warner Prize 70
Warner-Lambert Award for Distinguished Women in Science 537
Warren Triennial Prize 551
White House Initiative Faculty Award for Excellence in Science and Technology 55
William Bowie Medal 322
William F. Meggers Award 540
Wilson Medal 166
Wolf Prize 410, 623
Women in Science and Engineering Achievement Award 428
Ayrton Fan 21, 22
Ayrton, Hertha 21, *21*
Azathioprine 155
Azidothymidine (AZT) 153, 155
Azo-dye technique 386, 387

B

B cells 298
Baade, Walter 564
Babbage, Charles 71
"Backward charge exchange" experiment 292
Bacteria, classification of 376
Bacterial genetics 67, 320
Bactrim 155
Bailey, Florence Augusta Merriam 23, *23*
Baird, Spencer F. 328, 478
Baker, Sara Josephine 444
Barclay, John 578
Bardeen, John 603
Bari, Nina 24
Barnard College 428
Barnes, Eileen 26
Barney, Ida 27
Barry, James Miranda Stuart 27
Barsky Award 537
Bascom, Florence 28, *29*, 250, 295
Basseporte, Madeleine 39
Bassi, Laura Maria Catarina 30, *30*, 125, 158
Bateson, Gregory 381
Baum, Eleanor 31, *31*
Bäumgartel, Elise Jenny 32
Baylor University 352
Beadle, George 373
Becquerel, Antoine-Henri 122
Becquerel, Jean 79
Beebe, William 82
Beecher, Charles Emerson 567
Bees 514
Behn, Aphra 33, *34*
Bell Burnell, Jocelyn Susan 34, *35*
Belles on Their Toes 199
Belling, John 373
Belonocnema treatae 583
Benedict, Ruth Fulton 37, *37*, 380
Benerito, Ruth 38
Berg, Otto 417
Berlin Academy of Sciences 156
Berlin Academy of Sciences, Leibniz Medal 383
Bernal, John Desmond 244, 621
Berson, Solomon A. 630
Beta decay 622
Big bang theory 163
Biheron, Marie Catherine 39
Bile 1
BINAC computer 253
Biology, developmental 394
Biology, theoretical 359
Biomechanics 296
Biometrics Society 115
Biorthogonal systems of functions 605
Biotheoretical Gathering 621
Birch, Thomas 15
Bird, Isabella Lucy 40, *41*
Birds of New Mexico 24
The Birds of Oklahoma 415
Birds of Village and Field 24
Birds Through an Opera Glass 23
Birds, behavior of 414
Black Chronology 133
Black, James 155
Blackburne, Anna 41
Blackwell, Elizabeth (G.B.) 42
Blackwell, Elizabeth (U.S.A.) 43, *43*, 421
Blackwell, Emily 421
Blagg, Mary 44
Blalock, Alfred 568, 569
Blalock-Taussig shunt 568
Blau, Marietta 45, 207
The Blazing World 84
Blodgett, Katharine Burr 47, *48*
Blount, Mary 261
Bluestocking Society 399
Blumenthal, George 163
Blunt, Katharine 490
Boas, Franz 37, 380
Bocchi, Dorotea 49
Bodian, David 255
Bodichon, Barbara 21
Bodley, Rachel 50
Bodtker, Eyvind 206
Boerhaave, Hermann 578
Bohr, Niels 384
Boivin, Marie Anne 51, 301
Boltwood, Bertram 207
Boltzmann, Ludwig 382
The Book of the Jaguar Priest 351
Boole, George 562
Boole, Mary Everest 562
Boring, Alice Middleton 52
Born, Max 209
Boron nuclei 7
Botanical Society of America 172
Botany, cryptogamic 119
Bourgeois, Louyse 53, *53*
Boveri, Theodor 249
Bowers, John 413
Bozeman, Sylvia Trimble 54
Bragg, William Henry 334, 456
Brahe, Sophie 55
Brahe, Tycho 55
Brain, anatomy of 116
Brain, opiate receptors in 450
Bramley, Jenny Rosenthal 56
Brandegree, Katharine 144
Branham, Sara E. 461
Branson, Tom 85
Breit-Rosenthal effect 56
Brewster Memorial Award 625
Brewster, David 600
Bright Star Catalogue 246
Bright stars 246
Brill, Yvonne Claeys 58
British Association for the Advancement of Science 333
British Catalogue 235
British Medical Association, Dawson Williams Prize in Paediatrics 613

British Medical Register 44
British Paedeatric Association, James Spence Memorial Gold Medal 613
Britton, Elizabeth Gertrude Knight 59
Brooklyn Bridge 494
Brooks, Harriet 60, *61*
Browder, Ted 487
Brown, Dorothy Lavinia 61, *62*
Brown, Rachel Fuller 63, *63*, 230
Brown, Wade Hampton 444
Browne, E. T. 130
Browne, Marjorie Lee 64, *65*, 217
Bryan, Margaret 66, 358
Buckland, Mary 66
Buckminster Fullerenes 137
Bulterov, A. M. 325
Bundesverdienstkreuz First Class 484
Bunsen, R. W. 324
Bunting Institute 68
Bunting-Smith, Mary 67, *68*
Burbidge, Eleanor Margaret 69, *69*, 501
Burke, Bernard F. 237
Butenandt, Adolf 157
Bykovsky, Valery 574
Byron, Augusta Ada 71, *71*

C

Cahoon, Mary Odile 379
California Botanical Club 144
Calne, Roy 155
Cambridge University 48
Campbell, George A. 93
Canadian Astronomical Society 248
Canady, Alexa I. 75
Cancer research 138, 190, 305, 329, 394, 513, 541, 555
Cancer therapy index 139
Cannon, Annie Jump 76, *76*, 135, 178, 369, 608
Capacidin 64
Carbamyl phosphate 277
Cardiology, pediatric 569
Cardiovascular drugs 351
Carlock, William 216
Carothers, E. Eleanor 77
Carr, Emma Perry 78, *78*, 221, 532
Carroll, J. 394
Carson, Rachel Louise 81, *81*
Cary, Elizabeth Cabot. <u>See</u> Agassiz, Elizabeth
Cassin, John 328
Cathode ray tubes 57
A Catologue of the Nebulae which have been observed by William Herschel in a Series of Sweeps 235
Cattell, James McKeen 601
Cauchy-Kovelevskaya Theorem 300
Causea et Curae 241
Cavendish, Margaret 83, *83*
Cayley, Arthur 347, 521
Cech, Thomas R. 551
Celestial Atlas 489
Celestial mechanics 350
Cell biology 99
Cell division 226
Cell Heredity 513
Cell structures 238
Celleor, Elizabeth 6
Cells, protein trafficking within 166
Cellular metabolism 153
Cellulose, structure of 166
Centennial Medal of Canada 248
Cetus nebulae 234
Ch'omsongdae Observatory 545
Chang, Sun-Yung Alice 85, *86*
Charles de Henesy Nuclear Medicine Pioneer Award 631
Charles Lawrence Hutchinson Medal 367
Chase, Agnes 86
Châtelet, Gabrielle-Émilie du 88, *88*
Cheaper by the Dozen 199
Chemical Lectures 579
Chemical radioactivity 206
Chemical receptors 450
Chemistry textbooks 358, 390
Chemotaxis 285
Chemotaxonomy 392
Chemotherapeutic agents 619
Child development 293
Child, Charles Manning 261
Childbirth, natural 386
The Children's Book of Heavens 470
Children's Fund Laboratory 346
The Chimpanzee Family Book 215
Chimpanzees, study of 213
Chimpanzees 409
Chinn, May Edward 90
Chladni figures 197
Christopher Columbus Discovery Award in Biomedical Research 551
Chromosomal theory 512
Chromosomes 552, 562
The Chrysanthemum and the Sword: Patterns of Japanese Culture 38
"Chrysopoeia" 95
Ciba Award 611
Cirrotenthia massyi 365
Clairaut, Alexis 323
Clapp, Cornelia Maria 91, *92*, 149, 404
Clark, Jamie Rappaport 92
Clarke, Edith 93
Claypole, Edith Jane 94, 400
Cleopatra the Alchemist 95
Clerke, Agnes Mary 95
Clerke, Ellen Mary 96
Cloverleaf model 284
Clunies Ross Award for Science and Technology 526
Cobb, Geraldyn 97, *97*
Cobb, Jewel Plummer 99, *99*
COBOL programming language 252, 254
Cochran, William G. 115
Codex Magliabecchiano 425
Codex Nuttall 425
Cohen, Stanley 325, 326
Cohn, Mildred 101, *101*
Colborn, Theodore Emily Decker 102
Cold neutrons 330
Colden, Jane 104
Collins, Eileen Marie 105, *105*
Colloid chemistry 596
Colloid Chemistry: The Science of Large Molecules, Small Particles, and Surfaces 596
Colmenares, Margarita 106
Color blindness 477
Color vision 307
Colour and Colour Theories 308
Columbia University 344
Columbia space shuttle 338
Colwell, Rita R. 111
Combustion 192, 314, 315
Comets 290, 495
Coming of Age in Samoa 381
Comnena, Anna 107
Companion of the Order of Canada 248
The Comparative Anatomy of the Nervous System of Vertebrates, Including Man 117
Comparative Correlative Neuroanatomy of the Vertebrate Telencephalon 117
Compilers (computer programs) 253
Complex analysis 217
Computers, programming of 212
Comstock, Anna Botsford 108
Comstock, John Henry 108
Congenital heart disease 569
Congenital Malformations of the Heart 569
Congressional Hispanic Caucus Medallion of Excellence Role Model 428
Congressional Space Medal of Honor 337
Conklin, Edwin 52
Connaissance des temps 311, 323
Connoissance des mouvemens célestes 323
Conservation in Action 82
Conservation of parity 622, 623
Constructive method of proof 24
Contraception 270
Conversations on Botany 358
Conversations on Chemistry 66
Conversations on Natural Philosophy 358
Conversations on Political Economy 358
Conversations on Vegetable Physiology, Comprehending the Elements of Botany 358
Conway, Anne Finch 109, 156
Conybeare, William 67
Cooley, Thomas J. 346

Copernican theory 138
Cori cycle 114
Cori, Carl Ferdinand 102, 112, 611
Cori, Gerty Theresa 102, 112, *113*, 611
Corn, cleaning method for 366
Cornaro Piscopia, Elena. See Piscopia, Elena Cornaro
Cornell University 108, 305
Corporation for Public Broadcasting (CPB) 14
Correlative Anatomy of the Nervous System 117
Correlative Neurosurgery 117
Cortisone 174
Cosmic rays, study of 45
Cotton fibers 38
Council of the Entomological Society 332
Countess of Lovelace. See Byron, Augusta Ada
Courant Institute of Mathematical Sciences 403
Courant, Richard 402
Cousteau, Jacques 576
Covington, Arthur 469
Cox, Gertrude Mary 115
Cox, L. R. 195
Coxeter, H. S. M. 562
Cradle Society 132
Creighton, Harriet 373
Cressman, Luther Sheeleigh 380
Crick, Francis 187, 550, 551
Crippen, Robert L. 487
Cromwell, Nicholas 459
Crosby, Elizabeth Caroline 116, *117*
Crustaceans 478
Cryoprecipitation 466
Cryptogamic botany 119
Crystal Orientation Manual 617
Crystallography 333, 362
Crystals 617
Crystals and Light: An Introduction to Optical Crystallography it 617*
Crystals and X-Rays 334
The Cultures of Prehistoric Egypt 33
Cumming, Elizabeth Bragg 118
Cummings, Clara Eaton 119
Cunitz, Maria 120
Curie, Marie 22, 60, 113, 121, *121*
Curie, Pierre 121
A Curious Herbal 42
Curtis, Harry A. 345
Curtis, Winterton Conway 219
Cyclodepsipeptides 279
Cyclol theory 621
Cyclopeptide alkaloids 279
Cytology 77, 219, 238, 373
Cytoplasmic inclusions 238

D

D'Arconville, Geneviève. See Thiroux d'Arconville, Marie
Dalle Donne, Maria 125
Daly, Marie M. 126
Dame Commander of the Order of the British Empire 335
Damo 577
Dangerous Trades 224
Daraprim 155
Dark matter 163, 500, 626
Darwin, Charles 583
Daubechies, Ingrid 126
Davy, Humphrey 358
Dawes, Elizabeth 108
Dayhoff, Margaret Oakley 128
DDT 81
De Aegritudinum Curatione 585
De atrabile 1
De natura seminis humani 1
De Re Metallica 252
Debierne, André 122
Decades of North American Lichens 119
Decomposition 578
Deep Rover 142
DeLaguna, Frederica Annis 129
Delap, Maude Jane 130
Denjoy-Saks-Young theorem 633
Deraismes, Maria 500
Descartes, René 84, 156
Developmental biology 394
Diabetes 630
"A Dialogue of Cleopatra and the Philosophers" 95
Dichlorodiphenyltrichloroethane (DDT) 81
Dick, George 131
Dick, Gladys Henry 131
Dickson, L. E. 198
Die fossilen Gehirne 145
Dietrich, Amalie 132
Difference Engine 71
Differential equations 85, 347, 414
Differentiation 504
Diggs, Irene 133
Diophantine equations 492
Diophantus of Alexandria 263
Discontinuous and Optimal Control 181
Discontinuous Automatic Control 181
Discoveryspace shuttle 338, 427
The Diseases of Women 584
Diseases, inherited 525
Dissection, techniques of 201
Dissertation sur la nature et la propagation du feu 89
Distinguished Federal Civilian Service Award 286
Djerassi, Carl 170
DNA, structure of 187
Dochez, Alphonse 312
Domestic Recreation: or Dialogues Illustrative of Natural and Scientific Subjects 599
Double stars 609
Douglas, Allie Vibert 134, *134*
Douglas, Rodney 349
Dragonflies 332
The Dragonflies of the British Isles 332
Dragonflies 333
Draper Catalogue of Stellar Spectra 178
Draper, Henry 135
Draper, Mary Anna Palmer 135, 178
Dresselhaus, Mildred Spiewak 136, *136*
Drosophila, embryonic development of 424
Du Bois-Reymond, Paul 299
DuBois, W. E. B. 133
Dugès, Antoine 307
Dumée, Jeanne 138
Duprat, Pascal 499
Durant, Henry F. 607
Dutchess County Outdoor Ecological Laboratory 489
Dwarf galaxies 564
Dyer, Helen M. 138

E

Earle, Sylvia Alice 141, *141*
Earth Day International Award 534
Earth, core of 322
Easley, Annie J. 142
Eastern Paper Bag Company 294
Eastwood, Alice 143, *143*
Eaton, Amos 454
Ebony Black Achievement Award 273
Eckart, Pres 212
Eckert-Mauchly, J. Presper 253
Eclipses, prediction of 4
École Normal Supérieure 122
Ecological Society of America, Eminent Ecologist Award 439
Economic entomology 430
Eddington, Arthur 134
The Edge of the Sea 82
Edgeworth, Maria 358
Edinburgh School of Medicine 28
Edinger, Tilly 144
Edwards, Cecile Hoover 145
Edwards, Helen T. 147
Egyptian society 32
Ehrenfest, Paul 147
Ehrenfest-Afanaseva, Tatiana 147
Eigenmann, Carl H. 149
Eigenmann, Rosa Smith 149, *149*
Eimmart, Georg 406
Einstein rings 237
Einstein, Albert 46, 151
Einstein-Marić, Mileva 150, *150*
Elastic tissue 355
Elders, Minnie Jocelyn 151, *152*

The Electric Arc 21
Electrolytic titration method 435
Electron, discovery of 60
Electron physics 309
Electron-Microscopic Structure of Protozoa 461
Electrophoresis 387
Electrophysiology 375
Elementary Theory of Nuclear Shell Structure 210
Elements of Newton's Philosophy 88
Eli Lilly Award in Biological Chemistry 551
Elion, Gertrude Belle 153, 154
Elizabeth of Bohemia 110, 156
Ellen Richards Research Prize 553
Ellisor, Alva 17
Embryology, experimental 356
Emerson, Gladys Anderson 157, *157*
Emerson, Robert A. 373
Emerson, Sharon 296
Emphysema 355
Emulsion physics 45
Endocrine disruption, theory of 102
Endocrine Society, F. C. Koch Award 519
Endorphins 450
Energy Levels of Light Nuclei 7
Energy metabolism 344
Engineering and Science Hall of Fame 254
ENIAC computer 212
Entomological Association of America 436
Entomology, economic 430
Entretiens sur l'opinion de Copernic touchant la mobilité de la terre 138
Entretiens sur la Pluralité des Mondes 33
Environmental Overkill 480
Environmental toxicology 536
Enzyme reactions, general theory of 386
Enzymes, vitamin B12-dependent 547
Eperimental Designs 115
Epheméris 323
Erdtmann, Holger 393
Ergodic hypothesis 147
Ernst Jung Gold Medal for Medicine 395
Erxleben, Dorothea Christiana Leporin 158
Esau, Katherine 159
Essay on Combustion, with a View to a New Art of Dying and Painting: Wherein the Phlogistic Antiphlogistic
Hypotheses Are Proved Erroneous 192
Essence Science and Technology Award 273
Estonian Academy of Sciences' Karl Ernst von Baer Medal 430
Estrin, Thelma 159
Eternity (symbol) 95
Ethnology 133
Ethnomathematics 202
Euler, Leonhard 89
European Seismological Federation 322
Evans, Alice 160, 160
Evans, Arthur J. 228
Evans, Herbert 611
Evenings with the Stars 470
Everyday Foods in War Time 498
Evolution of the Horse Brain 145
Evolution, branching model of 144
Ewing, James 305
Ewing, Maurice 576
Exploding the Gene Myth 257
Exploring the Deep Frontier: the Adventure of Man in the Sea 142
Extranuclear genes 359

F

Faber, Sandra M. 163, 582
Faber-Jackson relation 163
Fabian, John M. 487
Fabric, fire-resistant 39, 303
Fabulae 6
Falconer, Etta Zuber 55, 164 *165*
Familiar Lectures on Botany 455
Fansidar 155
Faraday, Michael 358
Farlow, William G. 149
Farquhar, Marilyn G. 166
Farr, Wanda Margarite Kirkbride 166, *167*
Farrar, Nettie A. 178
Farrer Memorial Medal 587
Fausto-Sterling, Anne 168
Federal Civil Service Award 560
Federal Woman's Award 462
Fedorov prize 265
A Feeling for the Organism 286
Feicht, Russell S. 311
Felicie, Jacoba 169
The Female Academy 85
Female Benefit Club 599
Fenselau, Catherine Clarke 170
Ferguson, Angella Dorothea 171
Ferguson, Margaret Clay 172
Fermat's Last Theorem 197
Fermi, Enrico 57, 208, 209, 330, 417
Ferree, Clarence 477
Ferree-Rand perimeter 477
Fertility 331
Field Book of Animals in Winter 404
Field Book of Ponds and Streams: An Introduction to the Life of Fresh Water 404
Fielde, Adele Marion 173
Fieser, Louis F. 174
Fieser, Mary Peters 174
Firmamentum Sobieskanum sive Uranographie 236
First 352
- American woman graduate, Göttingen University 354
- anesthesiology professor 16
- birth control clinic 270
- British patent received by an American 366
- computer program 72
- famous American woman scientist 395
- Hispanic engineer, White House Fellowship 107
- Hispanic woman astronaut 427
- president, Society of Women Engineers 239
- scientist to synthesize anti-malarial drugs 531
- winner of two Nobel Prizes 123

First African American
- full-time professor, Baylor University 352
- intern, Harlem Hospital 90

First African American woman
- astronaut 272
- doctor, New York 554
- graduate, Bellevue Hospital Medical College 90
- member, American College of Surgeons 61
- member, board of governors, Mathematical Association of America 202
- member, Tennessee State Legislature 61
- neurosurgeon, United States 75
- Ph.D., astronomy 331
- Ph.D., bacteriology, Ohio State University 402
- Ph.D., chemical engineering 437
- Ph.D., chemistry 126
- Ph.D., curriculum and instruction, Marquette University, School of Education 202
- Ph.D., mathematics 64, 217
- Ph.D., mathematics, University of Texas 353
- Ph.D., nutrition 293
- Ph.D., zoology 635
- student, University of Arkansas Medical School 152
- surgeon in the South 61
- to publish two non-Ph.D. thesis mathematics research articles 202

First American woman
- in space 486
- mathematics degree from a European university 413

First Dutch woman
- certified mathematics teacher 270
- medical doctor 270

First Native American
- Ph.D., botany 532

First Native American woman
staff member, Jet Propulsion Laboratory 563
First Pueblo woman
Ph.D., biology 563
First woman 93, 305
anthropologist, United States 37
archaeologist to head an excavation 228
awarded an honorary membership in the Royal Society 234
board member, Linnaean Society 515
botanist, United States 104
certified, Clinical Engineer 160
chief resident, Meharry Medical College 62
chief scientist, National Oceanic and Atmospheric Administration 142
commander, Space Shuttle mission 105
commencement speaker, University of California 199
Congressional Space Medal of Honor 337
department head, Columbia-Presbyterian Medical Center 16
department head, North Carolina State University 115
Deputy Vice-Chancellor, Australian National University 525
director, Zoological Museum and Gardens (Porto Belho, Brazil) 543
elected foreign associate, Royal Astronomical Society of London 540
elected to a French scientific society 499
engineering degree, University of California at Berkeley 118
engineering degree, United States 118
faculty member, Harvard University 224
faculty member, Johns Hopkins School of Medicine 509
fellow, American Institute of Aeronautics and astronautics 182
fellow, New York Academy of Sciences 542
fellow, Royal Society of London 333
full professor, University of Michigan, Medical School 116
General Electric (GE) scientist 47
graduate, Ohio State University, College of Engineering 311
head of a branch of the military 609
head, Atomic Energy Commission 480
inventor, United States 366
invited to New York City's Explorer's Club 530
invited to visit, Royal Society of London 84
laboratory chief, National Institutes of Health 462
lecturer, Harvard Peabody Museum 554
master's degree, physics, McGill University 60
mayor, Pacific Grove, California 463
medical degree, Germany 158
medical degree, United States 43
member, Academy of Natural Sciences of Philadelphia 515
member, American Academy of Arts and Sciences 396
member, American Concrete Institute 204
member, American Ornithologists' Union 23
member, American Society of Mechanical Engineers 204
member, American Society of Refrigerating Engineers 447
member, Atomic Energy Commission 68
member, Board of Trustees, Aerospace Corporation 160
member, Council of the Entomological Society 332
member, French Academy of Sciences 449
member, Illuminating Engineering Society 478
member, Institution of Electrical Engineers 21
member, Maryland Academy of Sciences 455
member, National Academy of Sciences 510
member, Paleontological Society 567
member, Pontifical Academy of Sciences 327
member, Royal Netherlands Academy of Science 363
member, San Diego Society of Natural History 149
member, Sloan-Kettering Institute 452
member, Société d'Anthropologie 499
member, Torrey Botanical Club 59
member, Verein Deutscher Ingenieure 205
officer, American Astronomical Society 77
Paris Observatory 488
patent holder, United States 366
Ph.D. 459
Ph.D., astrophysics, Canada 134
Ph.D., chemistry, University of Missouri 225
Ph.D., chemistry, University of Texas 434
Ph.D., geology, United States 28, 250
Ph.D., Germany 519, 632
Ph.D., Heidelberg University 260
Ph.D., Johns Hopkins University 28
Ph.D., mathematics 299
Ph.D., mathematics, Sorbonne 488
Ph.D., meteorology 538
Ph.D., physics, Cambridge University 48
Ph.D., physics, United States 56
Ph.D., Polytechnic Institute of Brooklyn 355
pilot, Space Shuttle 105
placed on British Medical Register 44
president, American Association for the Advancement of Science 481
president, American Association of Anatomists 509
president, American Association of Immunologists 314
president, American Chemical Society 225
president, American Fisheries Society 402
president, American Mathematical Society 491
president, American Society for Engineering Education 31
president, American Society of Bacteriologists 161
president, Botanical Society of America 172
president, British Association for the Advancement of Science 333
president, Entomological Association of America 436
president, International Union of Crystallography 333
president, London Natural History Society 332
president, major medical ornithological society 415
president, national medical association 8
president, New York Academy of Sciences 191
president, Paleontological Society 211
president, Society of Hispanic Professional Engineers 106
professor, Cornell University 108
professor, Newark College of Engineering 200
professor, physics, University of Bologna 30
professor, preventive medicine 305
professor, Stanford University 181
professor, University College, London 333
recipient, Henry Norris Russell Prize 442
recipient, doctor of science degree from Oxford University 620
Secretary of the United States Air Force 609
spaceflight 573

staff member, National Institutes of Health 548
staff member, U.S. Department of Agriculture 546
student, Moscow State University 25
Surgeon General, United States 422
teacher, École Normal Supérieure 122
tenured physics professor, Harvard University 186
tenured professor, Harvard University 257
to discover a comet 234
to hold a chair at a European university 300
university student in the Netherlands 270
vice president, American automotive industry 11
winner, Nobel Prize for Theoretical Physics 208
winner, Nobel Prize 121
writer, major secular autobiography 85
Fisher, Anna 338, 487
Fisher, Elizabeth F. 176
Fisher, Ronald A. 115, 587
Fission, nuclear 417
Fitton, Elizabeth 358
Fitton, Sarah Mary 358
Flammel, Perrenelle Lethas 177
Flamsteed, John 235
Fleming, Alexander 242
Fleming, Williamina Paton 76, 135, 177
Fletcher, Alice Cunningham 179, 457
Flexner, Simon 386, 444
Flora Hibernica, English Botany, and Historia Fuci 259
The Flora of County Kerry 130
Flügge, William 181
Flügge-Lotz, Irmgard 181
Fluid dynamics 402, 609
Fluorine-19 chemistry 13
Foods, perishable 447
Foot, Katherine A. 182, 562
Ford Prize 570
Ford, W. Kent 163, 501
Forel, Auguste 583
Forster, Johann Reinhold 41
Fortune, Reo Franklin 381
Fossey, Dian 183, *184*
Fossil fauna 370
Fossils, mollusk 433
Foundations of Nutrition 344
Fourier, Jean-Baptiste 127
Fowler, William A. 70
Frances K. Hutchinson Medal for Service in Conservation 480
Francis Boyer Science Award 480
Francium 449
Franklin Paine Mall: The Story of a Mind 510
Franklin, Melissa 186
Franklin, Rosalind Elsie 187, *187*
Fratantoni, Joseph 411
Fred, Edwin B. 376
Free, Helen M. 189
Freedom Forum, Free Spirit Award Free 339
Freidel-Crafts reactions 416
Freier, Phyllis 634
French Academy of Sciences 449
Frend, William 71
Freshwater ecosystems 438
Fridman, A. A. 465
Friedrichs, Kurt 402
Friend, Charlotte 191, *191*
Frisch, Otto Robert 382
Frugality Bank 599
Fulhame, Elizabeth 192
Fuller, A. Oveta 193
Fuller, Charles G. 182
Function theory 24
The Fundamental Principles of Old and New World Civilizations 425
Fundamental theorem 521
Fungal disease, antibiotics for 63
Fungal infections 231
Furness, Caroline 609
Furness-Mitchell Coterie 553
Furth, Jacob 191
Furtwängler, Philip 571

G

Gaia theory 360
Galactic masses, estimates of 69
"Galaxies, "Great Wall" of 196
Galaxies, dwarf 564
Galaxies, evolution of 581
Galaxies, formation of 634
Galaxies, rotation of 70
Galaxies, structure of 500, 626
Gallagher, John 163
Galton, Francis 421
Gamma globulin 255
Gaposchkin, Sergei I. 441
Garden of Delights 233
Gardner, Julia Anna 195
Gassendi, Pierre 84
Gauss, Carl 197
Geller, Margaret Joan 196
Gene cloning 580
The General Catalogue of Trigonometric Stellar Parallaxes 246
General Motors 12
General Physics Practical Course 265
General theory of relativity 419
General Zoology 219
Genes, extranuclear 359
Genes, sequence of 621
Genes, transposable 372
Genetic diseases, human 410
Genetics Society of America Medal 395
Genetics, bacterial 320
Genetics, developmental 168
Genetics, nonchromosomal 512
Geology, planetary 364
George van Biesbroeck Award 246
Geotrupes blackburnii 42
Gerard, Ralph Waldo 466
Germ-layer theory 463
Germain, Sophie 197, *197*
Germain's Theorem 198
German Chemical Society, Leibig Medal 417
Gerritsen, Carel Victor 270
Giant Sun and His Family 470
Gibson, Robert 338
Gilbert, Walter 285, 595
Gilbreth, Frank 199
Gilbreth, Lillian Evelyn 199, *199*
Giliani, Alessandra 1, 201
Gilman, Charlotte Perkins 270
Gilmer, Gloria Ford 202
Gilmore, Gerard 626
Glaser, Otto Charles 621
Glass, non-reflecting 47
Glater, Ruth Ann Bobrov 203
Glavnauk Prize 25
Gleason, Catherine Anselm 204, *205*
Gleditsch, Ellen 46, 206, *206*
Glover Award 246
Glusker, Jenny 244
Glutaric acid, synthesis of 325
Glycogen storage disorders 112, 114
Godeffroy, Caesar 132
Goeppert-Mayer, Maria 208, *208*
Gold Cross of Honor 572
Gold Medal of Science 235
Gold Star Medal 574
Gold, Thomas 36
Goldring, Winifred 211
Goldstine, Adele K. 212
Gonorrhea, treatment of 28
Goodall, Jane 183, 213, *213*
Goodman, Joseph W. 427
Goodman, Reuben 536
Gordan, Paul 418
Gorillas 183
Gorillas in the Mist 183, 185
Gosset, Thorold 562
Göttingen University 354
Gournia 228
Grandin, Temple 215
Granville, Evelyn Boyd 64, 164, 217, *217*
Grasses 86
Gravitational lensing 236
Gray, Mary W. 517

Great attractor 163
"Great Wall" of galaxies 196
Greening of India: Environmental Activism 533
Grenville-Wells, Judith 334
Griffith, Frederick 313
Grounds of Natural Philosophy 85
Groundwater Contamination in the United States 439
Group theory 412
Grout, Abel Joel 59
Growth hormones 611
Guarna, Rebecca 1
Guggenheim award 504
Guide to the Inverebrata in the Synoptic Collection in the Museum of Boston Society of Natural
History 529
Guillemin, Roger 631
Gunn, James E. 582
Gursky, Matt 85
Gutenberg, Beno 576
Guthrie, Mary Jane 219

H

Habicht, Paul 151
Hahn, Dorothy Anna 79, 221, *221*
Hahn, Hans 571
Hahn, Otto 209, 277, 382
Hall, Charles Martin 222
Hall, Julia Brainerd 222
Hall-Heroult Process 223
Halley's comet 323
Hamburger, Viktor 326
Hamilton, Alice 223, *224*
Hammett Award in Chemistry 604
Hammon, William McDowell 255
Handbook of Birds in the Western United States 24
A Handbook of the Living Primates 409
A Handbook of the Trees of California 144
Handbook on Nature Study 109
Handy Tables 264
Hardin, J. A. 551
Hardy, Legrand 477
Harold E. Edgerton Award 237
Harrison, Anna Jane 225, *225*
Hart, William B. 439
"Harvard standard regions" 320
"Harvard system" 76
Harvard University 3
  Department of Earth and Planetary Sciences 364
  William Cranch Bond Astronomer 77
Harvey, Ethel Browne 226
Harwood, Margaret 227
Hassler, Gerald L. 367
Hastings, E. G. 161
Hawes, Charles Henery 228
Hawes, Harriet Ann Boyd 228
Hawkes, Graham 141
Hawley, Steven Alan 487
Hayes, Ellen Amanda 229
Hazardous working conditions 223
Hazen, Elizabeth Lee 63, 230, *230*
Hazlett, Olive Clio 231
Heezen, Bruce 576
Heilbrunn, L. V. 636
Heinrich, Ferdinand 222
Hemophilia, treatment of 466
Henri, Victor 79
Henry Draper Catalogue of stellar spectra 76
Henry Draper Medal 76
Henry, Beulah Louise 232, *233*
Heredity 552
Herlihy, W. C. 394
Herophilus 6
Herrad of Landsberg 233
Herschel, Caroline Lucretia 234, *235*, 396
Herschel, William 234
The Herschels and Modern Astronomy 96
Hertzsprung, Ejnar 320
Herzfeld, Karl 209
Hesselink, Lambertus 427
Hessian flies 405
Hevelius, Elisabetha Koopman 236
Hevelius, Johannes 236
Hewish, Anthony 34
Hewitt, David 556
Hewitt, Jacqueline N. 236
Hewitt, John N. B. 542
Hexachlorobenzene 333
Hexamethylbenzene 333
Hibbard, Hope 238
Hicks, Beatrice 239, *239*
High Service Cross 417
High-energy physics 330
Hilbert, David 348, 414, 418, 571, 606
Hilbert's tenth problem 491
Hildebrand Award 282
Hildegard of Bingen 1, 234, 240, *240*
Hill, Ellsworth 87
Hille, Einar 218
Hispanic Achievement Award in Science 595
Hispanic Engineer National Achievement Award in College Education 595
Histology, animal 400
Hitchcock, Albert Spear 87
Hitchcock, Edward 340
Hitchings, George Herbert 154
Hobbes, Thomas 84
Hobby, Gladys Lounsbury 242, *242*
Hodgkin, Dorothy Crowfoot 243, *243*, 621
Hodgkin's disease 385
Hoffleit, Ellen Dorrit 245
Hogg, Helen Sawyer 247, *247*
Hogue, Mary Jane 248
Holley, Richard 284
Holmes, Mary Emilee 250
Holweck, Fernand 276
Home economics 484, 549
Home Studies in Nature 583
Honeybees 258
Hoobler, Gertrude Macy 345
Hooke, Robert 84
Hoover, Erna Schneider 250
Hoover, Herbert 251
Hoover, Lou Henry 251, *252*
Hopper, Grace Murray 252, *253*
Horstmann, Dorothy Millicent 255
Hortus Deliciarum 233
Hospice de la Maternité 307
Hôtel Dieu 306
Houghton, Chris 413
Houssay, Bernardo A. 112
Howard University, School of Human Ecology 294
Howell, John thomas 144
Hoyle, Fred 70
Hubbard, Ruth 256
Hubble Space Telescope 69
Huber, Francois 257
Huber, G. Carl 117
Huber, Marie Aimee Lullin 257
Huchra, John P. 196
Huckins, Olga Owens 83
Huggins, Margaret Lindsay Murray 96, 258
Huggins, William 258
Hughes, John 450
Hull House 224
Human metabolism, biochemical aspects 126
Human nerve cells 248
Humans, effect of acceleration and heat on 560
Humans, genetic diseases of 410
Humoral theory of disease 84
Humphrey, Tryphena 117
Hutchins, Ellen 259
Hutton, Charles 66
Hydantoins 222
Hyde, Ida H. 260, 466
Hydrazine resistojet 58
Hydrocarbons, unsaturated 78
Hydrodynamics 465
Hydrogen 441
Hyginus 6
Hyman, Libbie Henrietta 261, *261*
Hypatia of Alexandria 263, *263*
Hypersolids 562

I

Ichnographia nova contemplationum de sole 406

Ichthyosaurus 15
Illuminating Engineering Society 478
Image tubes 57
Immune system 509
Imuran 155
Inbreeding 288
Indian Women Scientist Association 477
Indigo 458
Industrial management 199
Industrial microbiology 376
Industrial poisons 223
Industrial Poisons in the United States 224
Industry Innovation Award in the Meat Industry 217
Infectious Diseases Society of America, Maxwell Finland Award 255
Influenzal meningitis 8
Inquiry into the Causes Preventing the Female Sex from Studying 158
Insecta 529
Insecticides, microbial 534
Insectivorous Plants 583
Insects, social 579
Instantons 589
Instantons and 4-Manifold Topology 590
Institut de France, Gold Medal Prix Extraordinaire 198
Institute für Neuroinformatick 349
Institute of Electrical and Electronic Engineers, Gruenwald Award 31
Institutions de physique 89
Instituto de Quimica Fisica 362
Instituzione analitiche ad uso della gioventu' italiana 5
Insulin 244
Interferon 279, 300
Intermediary metabolism 592
International Critical Tables (ITC) 79
International Institute of Biotechnology, Gold Medal Award 112
International Study Group on Ethnomathematics 202
International Union of Biorganic Chemists, Klaus Schwarz Medal 548
International Union of Crystallography 244, 333
International X-Ray Tables 334
Introduction to Botany, in a Series of Familiar Letters 599
An Introduction to the Natural History, in a Series of Familiar Letters 599
Inugsuk culture 129
Invariants 231
Invertebrate zoology 261
The Invertebrates 262
An Investigation of Stellar Motions 614
Invisible Seas 112
Irish Bird Protection Society 365
Iroquois, ethnology of 542
Irving, Roland D. 28
Is Peace Possible? 335
Isotopes 207
Iveronova, Valentina Ivanovna 265, *265*

J

J. Paul Getty Wildlife Conservation Prize 215
Jackson, Robert 163
Jackson, Shirley Ann 267, *267*
Jacobi, Mary Putnam 268
Jacobs, Aletta Henriette 270
Jacobs, Frederika 270
Jacobs, Merkel H. 375
Jamaican vomiting sickness 612, 613
James Flack Norris Award 80
Janovskaja, Sof'ja Aleksandrovna 271
Jeffreys, Harold 322
Jellyfish 130
Jemison, Mae Carol 272, *273*
Jenner, Edward 399
Jensen, J. Hans D. 208, 210
Jex-Blake, Sophia, 6, 28, 274, *274*
Jobling, J. W. 386
John Burroughs Medal 82
John W. Gardner Leadership Award 302
Johns Hopkins University 28
Johnson, Treat B. 222
Joliot-Curie, Frédéric 275
Joliot-Curie, Irène 113, 123, 275, *275*, 384
Jonas, Anna Isabel 295
Jones, Bernard 626
Jones, Dorothy Walker 100
Jones, Edith Irby 152
Jones, Mary Ellen 277
Jordan, David Starr 91, 149
Jordan, Lynda 278
Joseph, A. F. 243
Joullié, Madeleine M. 279
A Journey in Brazil 4
Just, Ernest Everett 635

K

Kabbala 110
Kafatos, Fotis 595
Kahn, Edgar A. 117
Kalmár, László 453
Kappers, C. U. Ariens 117
Karle, Isabella Lugoski 281, *281*
Karle, Jerome 281
Kasner, Edward 602
Kate Depew Strang Tumor Clinic 305
Katsnelson, A. A. 265
Kaufman, Joyce Jacobson 282
Kefauver-Harris Amendments 287
Keith, George 110
Keller, Elizabeth 284
Keller, Evelyn Fox 285
Keller, Joseph Bishop 285
Kelsey, Frances Oldham 286, *287*
Kepler, Johannes 56, 120, 562
Kerotakis 361
Kevlar 302, 303
King Leopold II Prize 444
King, Helen Dean 288
King, William 71
Kingsley, Mary Henrietta 289, *289*
Kinships of Animals and Man 404
Kirch, Gottfried 290
Kirch, Maria Margaretha Winkelmann 290
Kistiakowsky, Vera 292
Kittrell, Flemmie Pansy 293
Klein, Felix 308, 348, 414, 418, 606
Klug, Aaron 189
Knight, Margaret 294
Kniker, Hedwig 18
Knopf, Eleanora Bliss 295
Knowles, Matilda 26
Koch, Robert 510, 525
Kochin, Nikolai Evgrafovich 465
Koehl, Mimi A. R. 296
Koenenia 502
Köenigsberger, Leo 299
Kohlrausch, Friedrich 354
König, Arthur 308
Koshland, Marian Elliott 297
Koski, Walter S. 283
Kosok, Paul 483
Kossuth Prize 453
Kosterlitz, Hans 450
Kovalensky, Vladimir. 299
Kovalevskaya, Sonya Vasilievna 298, 324, 489, 520
Krill 379
Krim, Mathilde 300, *301*
Kwashiorkor 612
Kwolek, Stephanie Louise 302
Kyoto Prize in Basic Sciences 215

L

L'Esperance, Elise Depew Strang 305, *305*
L'origine de l'homme et des sociétés 499
L'vov, M. D. 325
La Constitution du monde:Natura rerum 500
Laboratory Directions in General Zoology 219
Laboratory Handbook for Dietetics, Feeding the Family 498
A Laboratory Outline of Neurology 116
Lachapelle, Marie-Louise Dugès 51, 306, *306*
Ladd-Franklin, Christine 307, *308*, 396, 414
A Lady's Life in the Rockies 41

LaFlesche, Francis 180
Laird, Elizabeth Rebecca 309, *310*
Lafrancais de Lalande, Marie-Jeanne Lafrancais de 310
Lalande, Joseph Jerome Lafrancais de 310, 323
Lamme, Benjamin 311
Lamme, Bertha Aranelle 311
Lamp, microwave-pumped 56
Lancefield system 312
Lancefield, Rebecca Craighill 312
Landau, Lev Davidovich 36
Lange, Erik 56
Langmuir, Irving 47, 621
Laplace, Pierre Simon 544
Lauer, Edward 117
Laura Leonard Prize 464
Lauritsen, Thomas 7
Lavoisier, Antoine-Laurent 89, 314
Lavoisier, Marie 314, *315*
Law of conservation of matter 314, 315
Lawrence, Ernest Orlando 622
Leadership and America's Future in Space 487
Leaflets of Western Botany 144
Leakey, Louis 183, 213, 316
Leakey, Mary 316, *317*
Leavitt, Henrietta Swan 178, 319, *319*, 564
Lectures in Natural Philosophy 66
Lectures to Young Ladies 455
Lederberg, Esther Miriam Zimmer 320, *321*
Lederberg, Joshua 320
Lee Hawley, Sr. Award for Arthritis Research 551
Lee, Tsung-Dao 622
Legend of the Stars 470
Legendre, Adrien-Marie 197
Lehmann, Inge 322
Leibniz, Gottfried 89
Leibniz, Gottfried Wilhelm von 109
Leidy, Grace 9
Lepaute, Nicole-Reine Étable de la Brière 323
Lermontova, Iulya Isevolodovna 324
Lerner, M. R. 551
Les Jumeaux D'Hellas 499
"Letter of the Crown and the Nature of the Creation by Mary the Copt of Egypt, The" 361
Leukemia 190
Leukemia, drug therapy for 155
Levi, Giuseppe 326
Levi-Montalcini, Rita 325, *326*
Lewis culture 329
Lewis, Edward B. 423
Lewis, Graceanna 327
Lewis, Margaret Adaline Reed 329
Lewis, Robert C. 345
Lewis, Warren Harmon 329
Libby, Leona Woods Marshall 330
Liber Compositae Medicinae 241
Liber Divinorum Operum Simplicis Hominis 241
Liber Scivias 240
Liber Simplicis Medicinae 241
Liber Subtilitatum Diversarum Naturarum Creaturarum 241
Liber Vitae Meritorum 241
Liberty Hyde Bailey Medal 367
Lichenes Boreali-Americani 119
Liddell, Dorothy 317
Lieve, Loretta 594
Life of a New England Boy 529
The Life of Newton 600
Light nuclei 6
Line divider 22
Linear algebra 231
Ling-Gerard electrode 466
Linnaeus, Carl 42, 358, 387
Lipmann, Fritz 277
Liposarcoma cell stains 476
Lippard, Stephen 604, 605
Lippincott, Sarah Lee 163
Liquids, superheated 437
Little, Arthur D. 438
Livestock behavior 215
Livestock Conservation Institute Award for Meritorious Service 217
Lloyd, Ruth Smith 331
Locke-Lewis solution 329
Locusts, 17-year 405
Loeb, Jacques 91
Logan, Martha Daniell 332
Logic, symbolic notation in 307
London Natural History Society 332
Long, Esmond R. 524
Longfield, Cynthia Evelyn 332
Lonsdale, Kathleen 333, *334*
Lorch, Lee 164
Lorentz, Hendrik Antoon 148
Lorises, Lemurs and Bushbabies 409
Lost comets 495
Lotz-method 181
Louis Empain Prize 127
Low, Barbara 244
Lubchenco, Jane 335
Lucid, Shannon Ann 337, *337*, 487
Lunar nomenclature 45
The Lung and Its Disorders in the Newborn Infant 20
Luzin, Nikolai Nikolaevich 25
Luzzi, Mundinus de 201
Lycra 303
Lyell, Charles 339
Lyell, Mary Elizabeth Horner 339
Lymann, Theodore 207
Lymphatic system 509, 510
Lyon, Mary Mason 79, 91, 340

M

M. Carey Thomas prize 511
MacGillavry, Caroline 363
Machinae Coelestis 236
Machine-tool industry 204
Mackay, James Townsend 259
MacKinnon, Annie Louis 348
Macklin, Madge Thurlow 343
MacLeod, Grace 344
MacMahon, Brian 556
Maddison, Ada Isabel 347
Magnetohydrodynamics (MHD) 624
Mahowald, Michelle Anne 349, *349*
Maison d'Accouchements 307
Makemson, Maud Worcester 350, *350*
Malaria, treatment of 531
Male and Female 381
Maling, Harriet Florence Mylander 351, *352*
Mall, Franklin P. 510
Malone-Mayes, Vivienne 352
Malta fever 161
Maltby, Margaret Eliza 61, 353
Manabrea, Luigi Federico 72
Mandl, Ines 355
Mandrell, Steven 254
Mangold, Hilde Proescholdt 356
Mangold, Otto 356
Manhattan Project 330, 474, 602
Manso, Eugenio Leira 10
A Manual for the Study of Insects 108
A Manual of Grasses of the United States 87
Manual of Injurious Insects, with Methods of Prevention and Remedy 431
Manzolini, Anna Morandi 357
Marcet, Francis 358
Marcet, Jane Haldimand 357
Margulis, Lynn 359
Maria Goeppert-Mayer Award 237
Maria Practica 361
Maria the Jewess 95, 360
Marie, Marie 206
Marine biotechnology 111
Mark I computer 253
Markovnikov, V. V. 325
Marks, Phoebe Sara. See Ayrton, Hertha
Marquette University, School of Education 202
Martin, Devin 349
Martineau, Harriet 358
Martinez-Carrera, Sagrario 362, *362*
Marvin, Thomas Crockett 364
Marvin, Ursula Baile 364
Maryland Academy of Sciences 455
Maryland Chemist Award 283

Mass spectrometry 170
Massachusetts Institute of Technology 93
Massee, George 468
Massy, Anne L. 365
Masters, Sybilla 366
Mathematical Association of America 202
Mathematical Association of America, Lester R. Ford Award 403
Mathematical biology 285, 620
Mathematical Excursions 389
Mathematical logic 271
Mathematical Theory of Compressible Fluid Flow 598
Mathematical Theory of Probability and Statistics 597
Mathias, Mildred Esther 367
Matijasevic, Yuri 492
Matrix theory 570
Mauchly, John 212, 253
Maunder, Annie Russell 368
Maunder, Edward Walter 368
Maupertuis, Pierre-Louis Moreau de 88
Maury, Antonia Caetana de Paiva Pereira 76, 135, 178, 369, *369*, 396
Maury, Carlotta Joaquina 369, 370
Max Planck Institute, Kraepelin Gold Medal 519
Max Planck Medal 385
Maximilian in Mexico 553
Maxwell, Martha Dartt 371
Mayer, Ferdinand 269
Mayer, Joseph E. 209
Mayflies 403
Mayr, Gustav 583
McClintock, Barbara 372, *373*
McCouch, Margaret Sumwalt 375
McCoy, Elizabeth 376
McDuff, Margaret 86
McGilll University 60
McIntosh, Charles 467
McNutt, Marcia Kemper 377
McPherson, William 79
McWhinnie, Mary Alice 378
Mead, Margaret 37, 380, *380*
Meara, Mary Angnes. See Chase, Agnes
The Mechanism of the Heavens 544
Mechanistic philosophy 84
Medical Council of India, Jubilee Research Award 476
Médicis, Mariede 579
Meitner, Lise 209, 382, *383*, 417
Meloney, Missy 123
Mémoires de Chimie 316
Memorial Hospital for Women and Children 554
Mendel, Gregor Johann 512, 552
Mendel, Lafayette B. 345
Mendeleev, D. I. 324
Mendenhall, Dorothy Reed 385
Meningitis 461
Menstruation 471
Menten, Maud Leonora 386
6-mercaptopurine (6MP) 155
Mercuriade 1
Merian, Maria Sibylla 387, *388*
Mering, Jacques 187
Merrill, Helen Abbot 389
Metabolism 126, 344, 550, 592, 611
Metamorphosis Insectorum Surinamensium 388
Métraux, Rhoda 381
Meurdrac, Marie 390
Mexia, Ynes 391
Mexianthus mexicanus 391
Mexico, pictographic works in 425
Meyer Medal 527
Meyer, R. A. 132
Michael, Arthur 393
Michael, Helen Abbott 392
Michaelis, Johann 520
Michaelis, Leonor 386
Michaelis-Menten kinetics 386
Microbial insecticides 534
Microbiology, industrial 376
Microfossils 17
Micrographia Stellarum Phases Lunae Ultra 300 406
Micrographia 84
Microorganisms, effect of radiation on 67
Microscope Teachings 600
Microwave-pumped lamp 56
Mid-Atlantic Ridge valley 575
Midwifery 306
Milk, pasteurization of 160
Milledge, Judith Grenville-Wells 334
Millikan, Robert A. 345
Millis, Cynthia Dominka 393
Millspaugh, Charles 87
Minerals, minimum daily requirements for 490
Minkowski, Hermann 418, 606
Minor, Jessie E. 524
Minority Access to Research Careers (MARC) program 618
Minority Biomedical Research Support (MBRS) program 618
Minority students, programs for 100
Mintz, Beatrice 394
Mitchell, Helen Swift 397
Mitchell, Maria 395, *396*, 608
Mittag-Leffler, Gosta 300
Modern Cosmogonies 96
Modular invariants 231
Molecular biology 320
Molecular orbitals 334
Mollusk fossils 433
Mollusks 339, 365
Mommaerts, Elizabeth 486
Monkeys and Apes 409
Monro, Alexander 578
Montagu, Mary Wortley 398, *398*
Moody, Agnes Mary Claypole 94, 400
Moore, Emmeline 401
Moore, R. L. 502
Moore, Ruth Ella 402
Morand, Jean 40
Morawetz, Cathleen Synge 402
More, Henry 110, 156
Moreau, Renatus 1
Morgan, Ann Haven 403, *404*
Morgan, Augustus de 71
Morgan, Paul W. 303
Morgan, Thomas Hunt 52, 91, 447, 553
Morning sickness 471
The Morning Star Rises 351
Morris, Margaretta Hare 405
Motor design 311
Mount Holyoke College 340
  chemistry program 78
  physics department 309
Movement and Mental Imagery 601
Mucopolysaccharide storage disorders 410
Mueller, Edith 565
Müller, G. E. 308
Muller, Hermann Joseph 18
Müller, Johann Heinrich 406
Müller, Maria Eimmart 406
Mulliken, Robert S. 80, 330
A Multiple Table of Astrophysical Interest 540
Münz-, Geld-, und Bergwerksgeschichte des russischen Kaiserthums von Jahren, 1700-1789 520
Murray, Margaret 33
Murray, Sandra 406
Murtfeldt, Mary Esther 407
Mutagenesis 18
Mycotoxins 534
Myia 577
The Mystery of Comets 496
Mystery on the Desert 483
Myths of Gender:Biological Theories about Women and Men 168
Myths of the Iroquois 542
Myxofibrosarcoma cell stains 476

N

Naegele, Franz Carl 307
Napier, John R. 409
Napier, Prudence Hero Rutherford 409
Naples Table Association Prize 510
Naples Table Association, Ellen Richards Research Prize 77
National Academy of Sciences, Benjamin Apthorp Gould Prize 496
National Academy of Sciences, Comstock Award 623

National Academy of Sciences, Henry Draper Medal 77, 135
National Academy of Sciences, Public Welfare Medal 482
National Association of Student Leaders, Woman of Distinction Award 32
National Council of Jewish Women, Woman of the Century Award 135
National Geographic Society Centennial Award 215
National Geographic Society, Hubbard Medal 577
National Hemophilia Foundation, Murray Thelin Award 467
National Hispanic Quincentennial Commission Pride Award 428
National Institutes of Health 548
National Inventors' Hall of Fame 155
National Medal of Science 70, 101, 116, 136, 327, 519, 551, 623
National Medal of Technology 147, 252
National Science Medal 623
National Society of Black Engineers, Outstanding Professor Award 31
National Tuberculosis Association, Trudeau Medal 511, 525
National Women's Hall of Fame 106, 155, 524
National Women's Hall of Fame, Emily Warren Roebling Award 32
Native American culture, study of 179
Natural childbirth 386
Natural History of Birds 328
The Natural History of the Primates 409
Natural History of the Primates 409
Nature Conservancy National Award 367
Nature study movement 109
Nature's Pictures 85
Nazca Lines 482
Needham, Dorothy Moyle 621
Needham, Joseph 621
Nepenthes northiana 421
Nerve cells 325
Nerve growth factor (NGF) 325
Neuberg, Carl 355
Neues Blumenbuch 388
Neufeld, Elizabeth F. 410, *410*
Neumann, Hanna 412, *412*
Neuroendocrinology 517
Neuroendocrinology 518
Neuromorphic engineering 349
Neurophysiology, computer technology in 159
Neurosecretory cells 518
Neutron spectrometer 330
Neutron stars 36
Neutrons, cold 330
New York Botanical Garden 59
New York Infirmary for Indigent Women and Children 44
Newborns, nervous system of 509
"Newcastle Circle" 84
Newly Exposed Geologic Features Within the '8000-Acre Grant' 529
Newson, Mary Frances Winston 354, 413
Newton, Isaac 88
Nice, Margaret Morse 414, *414*
Nicholas, John Spangler 429
Nicholson, John William 620
Nightingale, Dorothy Virginia 416
Nikolayev, Andrian 574
Nobel Prize for Theoretical Physics 208
Nobel Prize in Chemistry 243, 275
Nobel Prize in Physiology or Medicine 112, 153, 155, 325, 372, 423, 629, 631
Noddack, Ida Tacke 417
Noddack, Walter 417
Noether, Amalie Emmy 418, *418*, 521, 571, 606
Noether's Theorem 419
Nomex 303, 560
Nonchromosomal genetics 512
Norrish, Ronald G. W. 187
North, Marianne 420, *421*
Norwegian Women Academics Association 207
Nottebohm, Fernando 615
Nouvelles Observations sur les Abeilles 258
Novae 178
Novello, Antonia Coello 422
Nuclear fission 382, 384, 417
Nüsslein-Volhard, Christiane 423, *424*
Nutrition 550
Nutrition in Health and Disease 397
Nutrition Work with Children 490
Nuttall, George Henry Falkiner 425
Nuttall, Zelia Maria Magdalena 425
Nystatin 63, 230, 231

O

O'Shaughnessy, Tom 488
Observations upon Experimental Philosophy 84
Obstetrics 53, 386
Ochoa, Ellen 427, *427*
Odonata 332
Ogburn, William Fielding 380
Ogilvie, Ida H. 428
Ohio State University 311, 402
Okie, Susan 488
Old World Monkeys 409
Olduvai Gorge 316
Oligomycin 376
Oliver, Thomas 224
Olney Medal 575
The Omaha Tribe 180
On Diseases of Women 125
On Molecular and Microscopic Science 544
On the Conics of Apollonius 264
On the Connection of the Physical Sciences 544
On the Origin of Species 498
One of the Most Frequent and Least Known Causes of Abortion 51
One World or None 603
Onufriyenko, Yuri 338
Opiate receptors 450
Oppenheimer, Jane Marion 429
Optical Society of America, Edgar D. Tillyer Medal 478
"Order "Band of Honor" 265
Order of Friendship Medal 337
Order of Lenin 265, 574
Order of Merit 244
Order of the Crown of Belgium 443
Order of the Sun 484
Ordre National des Grandes Lacs 185
Organic molecules, synthesis of 222
Organic synthetic reactions 416
Organization for Tropical Studies 367
Organizer regions 356
The Origin and Development of the Lymphatic System 510
Ormerod, Eleanor Anne 430
Ornatu Mulierum 584
Oroonoko, or the History of the Royal Slave 34
Ortiz, Fernando 133
Orton, Edward 567
Osteodontornus 625
Osteology 578
Ostwald, Friedrich W. 464
Ouchterlony, Orjan 461
Our Stolen Future: Are We Threatening Our Fertility, Intelligence, and Survival? A Scientific Detective Story 102
Outlines of Experimental Physiology 260
Outstanding Educators of America Award 624
Outstanding Women in Science and Engineering Award 437
Oxidation 314, 315
Oxygen, identification of 314

P

Pacific cultures 129
Padmabhushan Award 476
Palade, George 452
Paleoneurology 144
Paleontological Research Institution 433
Paleontological Society 567
Paleontology, avian 625
Paleontology, tertiary 433
Palmer, Katherine Evangeline Hilton 433
Palmetto leaf, working system for 366
Palser, Barbara F. 434

Pap smear 305
Papanicolaou Award for Scientific Achievement 395
Papanicolaou, George 90
Paper bag production machine 294
Pappenheimer, Alwin M. 452
Parity 622, 623
Parker, Ivy May 434, *435*
Parsons, William 600
Partial differential equations 85
Particle physics 267
Passano Foundation Young Scientist Award 551
Passionibus Mulierum Curandorum 584
Patch, Edith Marion 436, *436*
Patent medicine 366
Patrick, Jennie R. 437, *437*
Patrick, Ruth 438, *439*
"Patterns of culture" theory 37, 38
Patterns of Culture 38
Patterns of Living in Puerto Rican Families 491
Patterson, Flora Wambaugh 440
Pauling, Linus 387, 621
Payne-Gaposchkin, Cecilia 441, *441*
Pearce, Louise 443
Peck, Annie Smith 444, *445*
Peckham, Elizabeth Gifford 445
Peckham, George Williams 445
Pediatric cardiology 569
Peebles, Florence 446
Peirce, Benjamin 608
Peirce, Charles Sanders 307
Pell, Alexander 606
Penicillin 242, 244
Penicillin: Meeting the Challenge 242
Pennington, Mary Engle 447, *448*
Penny Bank for Children 599
Perey, Marguerite Catherine 449, *449*
Perinatology 17
Period-luminosity relation 320
Perlmann, Gertrude 313
Pert, Candace Dorinda Bebe 450
Pesticides 559
Péter, Rózsa 453
Petermann, Mary Locke 451, *452*
Peters, George H. 227
Petrie, Willim Flinders 33
Petrie's Naqada Excavations, A Supplement 33
Peyrony, Elie 316
Phalamycin 64
Phelps, Almira Hart Lincoln 454
Philosophical and Physical Opinions 84
Philosophical Fancies 84
Philosophical Letters: or, Modest Reflections upon some Opinions in Natural Philosophy, maintained by several Famous and Learned Authors of this Age, Expressed by way of Letters 84
Phlogiston theory 315
Phospholipase A2 278
Photomicroscopy 182, 562
Phylogenetics 514
Phylon: A Journal of Race and Culture 133
Physica 241
Physical Geography 544
Physics, high-energy 330
Physiological optics 477
Phytoplankton 522
Pickering, Edward 76, 319, 369
Pickering, Edward C. 177, 607
Pickering-Fleming System 178
Pickett, Lucy Weston 456
Picotte, Susan LaFlesche 457, *457*
Pictographic works, Mexico 425
Pinart, Alphonse Louis 425
Pinckney, Charles 459
Pinckney, Elizabeth Lucas 458
Pine Barrens 583
Pipeline corrosion 434
Piscopia, Elena Cornaro 459
Pitelka, Dorothy Riggs 460
Pittman, Margaret 461
PLA2 278
Planck, Max 309
Plane plastic distortions 597
Planetary conic curves 229
Planets, elliptical orbits of 56
Plant ecology 489
Plant tissues 159
Plants, anatomy of 514
Plants, carnivorous 583
Plants, chemical classification of 392
Plants, effect of pollution on 203
Plasmid Reference Center 321
Plastids 166
Plate tectonics 575
Platonic solids 562
Platt, Julia Barlow 462
Playing with Infinity 453
Plesiosaurus 15
Pockel's point 464
Pockels, Agnes 463
Podokesaurus holyokensis 567
Poems and Fancies 84
Polar regions 379
Polio vaccine 255
Poliomyelitis 248
The Politics of Women's Biology 256
Pollution 203
Polonium 60, 122
Polubarinova-Kochina, Pelageya Yakovlevna 465
Polybromated biphenyls (PBBs) 393
Polymers 575
Polytechnic Institute of Brooklyn 355
Pontifical Academy of Sciences 327
Pool, Judith Graham 466
Pope Benedict XIV 5
A Popular Flora of Denver, Colorado 144
A Popular History of Astronomy during the Nineteenth Century 96
Porter, Rodney 452
Potter, Helen Beatrix 467, *468*
Power systems analysis 93
Practica Brevis 585
Practice of Obstetrics 307
Praeger, Robert Lloyd 26
Pregnancy 471
President's Medal of Freedom 83
Priestly, Joseph 315
Primack, Joel 163
Primates 409
Prince, Helen Walter Dodson 469
Principia mathematica 89
Principles of Philosophy 156
Principles of the Most Ancient and Modern Philosophy 109
Prix Bordin 300
Probability theory 598
Probability, Statistics and Truth 597
Problems in Fresh Water Fisheries 401
Proconsul africanus 317
Proctor, Mary 470
Prodromus Astronomiae 236
Profet, Margie 471
Project Head Start 618
Project Mercury space program 218
Project Vanguard space program 218
Proof, constructive method of 24
Propellants 58
Propositiones philosophicae 5
Prosser, Charles 567
Protactinium 383
Protecting Your Baby-to-Be 471
Protein structures 128
Proteins, formation of 284
Proteins, separation of 387
Protograph 233
Protozoa 460
Psychology 601
The Psychology of Management 199
Pterodactylus macronyx 15
Ptolemy 264
Pueblo indians 1
The Pueblo Indians of New Mexico, Their Land, Economy and Civil Organization 2
Pulmonary surfactant 19
Pulsars 34
Purinethol 155
Putnam, Frederic W. 179, 425
Pyrimethamine 155
Pythagoras 577

Q

Quality Education for Minorities Network, Giants in Science Award 165

Quark 186
Quasars 69
Quimby, Edith H. 473, *473*

R

Race: Science and Politics 38
"The Races of Mankind" 38
Radcliffe College 3, 442
Radcliffe Institute for Independent Study 68
Radioactive recoil 60
Radioactivity 60, 121
Radioactivity, artificial 275
Radioactivity, chemical 206
Radioactivity, effects of 532, 555, 564
Radioimmunoassay (RIA) 629
Radiology 473
Radiotherapy 473
Radium, half life of 207
Radon 60
Ramart-Lucas, Pauline 383
Ramey, Estelle R. 475, *475*
Ran Anomalscope 477
Ranadive, Kamal Jayasing 476
Rancho Los Tunas 367
Rand, Marie Gertrude 477
Randall, John T. 187
Rathbun, Mary Jane 478
Ratner, Sarah 479
Rats, breeding of 288
Ray, Dixy Lee 480, *480*
Reactions, organic synthetic 416
Reagents for Organic Synthesis 174
Recursive functions 453
Recursive Functions in Computer Theory 453
Reed cell 385
Rees, Mina S. 481, *481*
Refiguring Life: Metaphors of 20th Century Biology 286
Reflections on Gender and Science 286
Reiche, Maria 482, *483*
Reifenstein, Edward 36
Renal disease 166
Research Corporation Award 623
Resnick, Anna Fisher 338
Resnik Challenger Medal 58
Resnik, Judith 487
Resources and Industries of the United States 176
Respiration 314
Respiratory Distress Syndrome (RDS) 19
The Retreat from Parenthood 620
Revkevich, G. P. 265
Rhenium 417
Rhoades, Marcus 373
Ribonucleoproteins 550
Ribosomes, animal 451
Richards, Ellen H. 344
Richards, Ellen Swallow 396, 484
Richer, Leon 500
Richter, Charles F. 576
Ricketts Prize 541
Ride, Sally K. 338, 485, *486*
Right Livelihood Award 533
Riley, Charles v. 407
Ris, Hans 359
Rittenhouse Medal 248
Ritter, M. Catherine 477
Roberts, Dorothea Klumpke 488
Roberts, Edith Adelaide 489
Roberts, Lydia Jane 397, 490
Robeson, Paul 90
Robinson, Daisy Maude Orleman 493, *493*
Robinson, Julia 491, *492*
Rockefeller Public Service Award 537
Rocky Mountain Screech Owl 371
Roebling, Emily Warren 494
Roebling, Washington A. 494
Roemer, Elizabeth 495
Roman, Nancy Grace 496, *497*
Romana, Rancesca de 1
Roscoe, Henry 467
Rose, Mary Swartz 344, 498
Royal Astronomical Society 540
Royal Astronomical Society, Herschel Medal 36
Royal Danish Geodetic Institute 322
Royal Horticultural Society, Flora Medal 431
Royal Institution, Actonian Prize 96
Royal Order of the Lion 444
Royal Society of Edinburgh, Keith Award 19
Royal Society of London 84
Royal Society of London, Davy Medal 335
Royal Society of London, Hughes Medal 22
Royer, Clemence Augustine 498
Rubin, Vera Cooper 163, 500, *501*, 634
Rucker, Augusta 502
Rudin, Mary Ellen 502
Rudnick, Dorothea 504
Rudolphine Tables 120
Russell, Anna Worsley 505
Russell, Bertrand 620
Russell, Elizabeth Shull 506, *506*
Russell, Frederick Stratten 10
Russell, Henry Norris 442
Ruth Lyttle Satter Prize 86, 127
Ruth Sanger Medal 526
Rutherford, Ernest 60, 122, 134
Ryan, Francis J. 513

S

Sabin, Florence Rena 509, *509*, 602
Sagan, Carl 359
Sager, Ruth 512, *512*
Salerno school 584
Sandhouse, Grace Adelbert 514
Sargant, Ethel 514
Satellite observatories 496
Satellites, propulsion systems for 58
Savitch, Pavle 277, 384
Sawflies 514
Say, Lucy Way Sistare 515
Say, Thomas 515
Scarlet fever 131
Schafer, Alice T. 516
Schally, Andrew V. 631
Scharrer, Berta 517
Scharrer, Ernst 517
Schlesinger, Frank 27
Schlözer, Dorothea 519
Schneider, Richard C. 117
School of Salerno 1
Schoute, Pieter Hendrik 562
Schreiner, Olive 270
Schrödinger, Erwin 47
Schwartz, Robert 155
Scotchgard 530
Scott, Charlotte Angas 347, 414, 520, *521*
Scott, Roland 171
Scoville, Nick Z. 634
The Sea around Us 82
Seafloor spreading 575
Sears, Mary 522
Seaside Studies in Natural History 3
Seddon, Margaret Rhea 338, 487
Segel, Lee 285
Seibert, Florence Barbara 524, *524*
Seibert, Mabel 524
Seismology 322
Selenium biochemistry 547
Selove, Walter 7
Semi-conductor Physics 627
Semiconductors 12
Septra 155
Serjeantson, Susan Wyber 525
Sessions, Kate Olivia 527
Set theoretic topology 502
Seven Samurai project 163
Sewall, Lucy 274
Sewell, Seymour 576
Sex and Temperament in Three Primitive Societies 381
Sex roles 381
Shapley, Harlow 320, 369
Sharp, Lester 373
Shattuck, Lydia White 91, 527, *528*
Shaw, Peter 579
Sheep breeding 587
Sheldon, Jennie Arms 529
Sherman, Althea Rosina 415, 529
Sherman, Patsy O'Connell 530
Sherrill, Mary Lura 80, 345, 531, *531*
Shields, Lora Mangum 532

Shiva, Vandana 533
Shotwell, Odette Louise 534
Sickle-cell anemia 171
Siegemundin, Justine Dittrichin 535
Sigma Xi 109
Silbergeld, Ellen Kovner 536
Silent Spring 81, 83
Silicon retina 349
Simon, Dorothy Martin 537
Simpson, Joanne Malkus 538
Sitterly, Charlotte Emma Moore 540
Six Nations of the Iroquois federation 542
Skinker, Mary Scott 81
Sleeping sickness 443
Sloan Award 452
Sloan, Louise 478
Sloan-Kettering Institute 452
Slye, Maud 541, *541*
Small nuclear ribonucleoproteins 550, 551
Smallpox inoculation 398
Smith, Alexander 79
Smith, Clara E. 389
Smith, Erminnie Adele Platt 542
Smith, J. E. 259
Smith, Sam 530
Snedecor, George 115
Snethlage, Emilie 543
SnRNPs 550, 551
Snyder, Solomon 450
Social insects 579
Société Astronomique de France, Prix des Dames 489
Société d'Anthropologie 499
Society for the Advancement of Chicanos and Native Americans 595
Society of Economic Paleontologists and Mineralogists 18
Society of Women Engineers 239
Society of Women Engineers, Achievement Award 58, 137, 158, 180, 254, 281, 537, 560, 575, 610, 624
Society of Women Engineers, Upward Mobility Award 32
Society to Encourage Studies at Home 485
Soddy, Frederick 60, 122
Solar flares 469
Solid Physics 627
Somerville, Mary 71, 234, 358, 396
Somerville, Mary Fairfax 543, *544*
Sonduk (Queen of Silla) 545
Southwick, Mildred 490
Soviet Kosmos Award 430
Space engineering 537
Spalding, Effie Almira Southworth 546
Spallanzani, Lazzaro 30
Spectral lines, classification system for 369
Spectrophotometry, ultraviolet 78
Spectroscopy 456
Speculum 51
Spemann, Hans 356
Spiders 445
Spikes, Dolroes Richard 546
Squaloraja 15
Squibb Award in Chemotherapy 64
Stadtman, Thressa Campbell 547, *548*
Staelin, David 36
Stanley, Louise 549
Star formation 626, 634
The Stars Belong to Everyone 247
Stars of High Luminosity 442
Stars, bright 246
Stars, brightness of 320
Stars, cataloging system for 76, 177
Stars, double 609
Stars, evolution of 582
Stars, metal content of 69
Stars, variable 77, 178, 227, 245, 564, 565, 608, 615, 632
Statistical Mechanics 209
Statistical thermodynamics 147
Stearns, Genevieve 550
Stefani, Rosa 491
Steitz, Joan Argetsigner 550
Stellar atmospheres 615
Stellar hydrogen 441
Stellar spectra 613
Stephenson, Louisa 79
Stephenson, Marjory 333
Stetter, Georg 46
Stevens, Nettie Maria 52, 551, *552*
Stevenson, Sara Yorke 553
Steward, Susan Smith McKinney 554
Stewart, Alice M. 555
Stewart, Grace Anne 558, *558*
Stickel, Lucille Farrier 559
Stieglitz, Julius 79, 531
Still 361
Stillingfleet, Bemjamin 399
Stokes, Whitley 259
Stoll, Alice M. 560
Stone, Isabelle 561
Stories of Insect Life 407
Stories of Starland 470
Story, William 307
Stott, Alicia Boole 562
Strassmann, Fritz 209, 384, 417
Stratigraphic paleontology 195
Streptococcus, classification of 312
Streptomycin 242
Stress, endocrine aspects of 475
Strobell, Ella Church 182, 562
Stroud-Lee, F. Agnes Naranjo 563
Stuart, Miranda. See Barry, James
Studies in the Life History of the Song Sparrow 415
Submersible craft 142
Sugar metabolism 112
Sullivan, Kathryn 487
Sullivan, Kathryn D. 338
Sunspots 368, 632
Superheated liquids 437
Sur la natalité 499
Surface films 463
Surfactants 464
Susan Smith McKinney Steward Medical Society 90
Swain, Joseph 149
Swatow Chinese dialect 173
Swedish Academy of Sciences, Gregori Aminoff Prize 282
Swift, Homer 313
Swope, Henrietta Hill 227, 564
The Sycamore Trail 230
Syllogistic reasoning 307
Sylvester, J. J. 307
Symbiotic theory of evolution 359
Symonds, Catherine Addington 421
Synesius of Cyrene 263
Syphilis 28, 444
The System of the Stars 96
Systematic botany 143
Szkody, Paula 565

T

T. Duckett Jones Memorial Award 314
Tacconi, Gaetano 30
Tait, Peter Guthrie 607
Talbot, Mignon 567, *567*
The Tale of Peter Rabbit 467
Taren, James A. 117
Tarski, Alfred 492
Taussig, Helen Brooke 568, *568*
Taussky-Todd, Olga 570, *571*
Taxonomy of primates 409
Taylor, Charlotte de Bernier Scarbrough 572
Taylor, Clara Mae 344
Technetium 540
Tektite II Project 141
Teleost embryology 430
Telephones, switching system for 250
Telescope Teachings 600
Teller, Edward 208, 209
Tello, Julio 483
Tereshkova, Valentina 487, 573, *573*
Termites 579
Tertiary paleontology 433
Tertre de la Marche, Marguerite du 54
Tesoro, Giuliana Cavaglieri 574
Tevatron 147
Textbook of General Zoology 219
Thalidomide 286, 568
Tharp, Marie 575
Theano 577
Theodor Boveri: Life and Work of a Great Biologist 505
Theories of Organic Chemistry 221, 222

Theory and Application of Mathematics for Teachers 218
Theory of conic sections 264
Theory of endocrine disruption 102
Theory of flame propagation and quenching 537
Theory of Ground Water Movement 465
Thermodynamics, statistical 147
Thin films 561
Thiroux d'Arconville, Marie 578
Thomas, Vivian 569
Thompson, Caroline Burling 579
Thomson, J. J. 60
Thorvold Madsen Award 255
Through a Window 215
Tickenor, Anna 485
Tilghman, Shirley Marie Caldwell 580, *580*
Tilorone 279
Tinsley, Beatrice Muriel Hill 581
Tissue culture 329
Tissue regeneration 446
Tissue, elastic 355
Titchener, Edward Bradford 601
To Space and Back 488
Top quark 186
Topology 85
Torrey Botanical Club 59
Tower of the Moon and Stars 545
Townsend, Mary 328
Traité d'horlogerie 323
Traité Élémentaire de Chimie 315
Transduction 320, 321
Transonic flow 402
Transplantation antigens 525
Transposable genes 372
Transposition 374
Trashing the Planet 480
Treat, Mary Lua Adelia Davis 583
Treatise on Invertebrate Paleontology 195
Treatise on the Passions 156
Trematodes 375
Trimble, Henry 392
Trimethoprim 155
Trotula of Salerno 1, 125, 584
Trotula Major 584
Trotula Minor 584
Trueblood, Kenneth 244
Truswell, Elizabeth 585
Trypanosomiasis 444
Tryparsamide 443
Tuberculosis 510, 524
Tuberculosis Research Commission 305
Tumor chemotherapy 139
Tumors, development of 330
Turner, Dawson 259
Turner, H. H. 45
Turner, Helen Alma Newton 586
Tuscarora Rice 366
Two Hundred Queries . . . Concerning the Doctrine of the Revolution of Humane Souls 110
Tyler Ecology Award 438
Typewriter 233
Typhoid fever 94

U

U.S. Department of Agriculture 546
U.S. Department of Commerce 12
U.S. Department of Energy, Ernest O. Lawrence Award 147
U.S. Fish and Wildlife Service 92
U.S. Geological Survey 28
U.S. National Aeronautics and Space Administration 142
U.S. National Aeronautics and Space Administration Achievement Award 430
U.S. National Aeronautics and Space Administration Flight Medal 105
U.S. National Oceanic and Atmospheric Administration 142
U.S. Natural Reserve System 367
U.S. Surgeon General 151, 422
Uhlenbeck, Karen Keskulla 589, *589*
Ultraviolet spectrophotometry 78
Umbellifers 367
Umbrella 232
Under the Sea-Wind 82
Understanding Computers 254
Undulant fever 160
United Nations Environmental Program, Global 500 Award 534
United Nations Peace Medal 480
United Nations, Food and Agriculture Organization, Ceres Medal 587
United States. See U.S.
UNIVAC computer 253
University Museum, Pennsylvania 553, 554
University of Bologna 30
University of California at Berkeley 118
University of Missouri 225
University of Texas 353, 434
Upjohn Award 612
Uptake-reduction model 604
Urania Propitia 120
Uranium mining 532
Uranus, discovery of 235
Urea cycle 479
Urey, Harold 57, 101, 209
Urinalysis 189
Usachev, Yuri 338

V

Vaccines 461
Vaginal speculum 51
Van Helmont, Francis Mercury 110, 156
Van Hise, Charles R. 28
Van Lawick, Hugo 214
Van Straten, Florence Wilhelmina 591, *591*
Variable stars 178, 227, 245, 319, 441, 564, 565, 608, 615, 632
Variable Stars 442
Vassar College 395
Vassar, William 396
Veatch, Arthru Clifford 370
Velez-Rodriguez, Argelia 592, *592*
Vennesland, Birgit 592
Vera Barantzova 299
Verein Deutscher Ingenieure 205
Vigneaud, Vincent du 101
Villa-Komaroff, Lydia 594, *594*
Viruses 193
Vision 256, 307
Vitalistic philosophy 84, 109
Vitamin B-12 244, 547, 548
Vitamins 157, 174, 397
  recommended daily allowances 397
  minimum daily requirements for 346, 490
Voegtlin, Carl 138
Vold, Marjorie Jean Young 596
Vold, Robert D. 596
Voltaire, François-Marie Arouet de 88
Von Hofmann, A. W. 324
Von Humboldt, Alexander 396
Von Krosigk, Bernhard Frederick 291
Von Leibniz, Gottfried Wilhelm 156, 290
Von Mises, Hilda Geiringer 597
Von Mises, Richard 597
Vostok VI 574
Voyager space shuttle 488
Vyssotsky, Alexander 613

W

Wakefield, Priscilla Bell 599
Wald, Elijah 257
Wald, George 256
Wambacher, Herta 46
Warburg, Otto 593
Ward, Mary 600
Warner-Lambert Award for Distinguished Women in Science 537
Warren Triennial Prize 551
Washburn, Margaret Floy 601, *601*
Wasps 445
Wasps Social and Solitary 446
Water bath 361
Watson, James 187, 550, 551
Wavelet theory 127
Way, Katharine 602
Way-Wigner formula 603
Way-Wood systematics 603
Weather patterns 591
Weber, Heinrich Friedrich 151
Webster, A. G. 354
Weierstrass, Karl 299, 324

Weightlessness, physiological effects of 429, 430
Weinberg, Alvin 603
Weltfish, Gene 38
Wetterhahn, Karen Elizabeth 604, *604*
Wheeler, Anna Johnson Pell 605
Wheeler, John 603
Wheeler, R. E. M. 317
White House Initiative Faculty Award for Excellence in Science and Technology 55
White, John 244
Whiting, Sarah Frances 76, 259, 607
Whitney, Mary Watson 396, 608
Whooping cough vaccine 462
Widnall, Shelia Evans 609, *610*
Wiedersheim, Robert Ernst 463
Wiegold, Jim 413
Wieschaus, Eric F. 423, 424
Wigner, Eugene Paul 210, 603
Wild Flower Preservation Society of America 59
Wiley, Harvey W. 448
Wiley, Ida A. R. 444
Wilhelmi, Alfred Ellis 611
Wilhelmi, Jane Anne Russell 611
Wilker, Jonathan 605
Wilkins, Maurice 187, 550
Willard, Emma 454
William F. Meggers Award 540
Williams, Cicely Delphin 612
Williams, Emma T. R. 613
Williams, Heather 614
Willson, Lee Anne Mordy 615
Wilson Ornithological Society 415
Wilson, Edmund Beecher 91, 463, 552
Windaus, Adolf 157
Wiseman, John 576
"Witch of Agnesi" 5
Wolf Prize 410, 623
Woman's Medical College of Philadelphia 50
Women and Economics 270
Women and Labor 270
Women in Science and Engineering 292
Women in Science and Engineering Achievement Award 428
Women in Science and Engineering, Lifetime Achievement Award 281
Women in Science Project (WISP) 604
Women in Technology International Hall of Fame 32, 349
Women, anatomy of 578
Women's Hospital and Dispensary, Brooklyn, NY 554
Women's Medical Association of New York City 269
Women's Medical College of New York 44
Wonderful Metamorphosis and Special Nourishment of Caterpillars 388
Wood, Elizabeth Armstrong 617
Wood, Marion 603
Woods, Geraldine Pittman 617
Workman, Fanny Bullock 445
Wright, Jane Cooke 618, *619*
Wright, Sewall 506
Wrinch, Dorothy Maud 620
Wu, Chien-Shiung 292, 622, *622*
Wu, Y. C. L. Susan 624
Wundt, William 601
Wylde, Hildegarde Howard 625
Wyse, Rosemary Frances Gillian 626

X

X-ray crystallography 333, 617
X-ray diffraction 281
X-ray scattering, dynamic theory of 265
X rays, soft 309
Xide, Xie 627, *627*

Y

Yalow, Rosalyn Sussman 629, *629*
Yang, Chen Ning 622
Yang, Paul 85
Yates, Frank 587
Young, Anne Sewell 632
Young, Grace Chisholm 347, 354, 632, *633*
Young, James 267
Young, Judith Sharn Rubin 634
Young, Lai-Sung 86
Young, Roger Arliner 635
Young, William Henry 632

Z

Zakrzewska, Marie Elizabeth 44
Zanthoxylum blackburnia 42
Zephranthes treatae 583
Zhdanov, Stepanovich 266
Zinjanthropus 318
Zooplankton 10, 522
Zovirax 155
Zyloprim 155

Aerospace Engineering
Brill, Yvonne Claeys 58
Widnall, Shelia Evans 609
Wu, Y. C. L. Susan 624

Agriculture
Pinckney, Elizabeth Lucas 458

Alchemy
Cleopatra the Alchemist
Flammel, Perrenelle Lethas 177
Maria the Jewess 360

Anatomy
Biheron, Marie Catherine 39
Crosby, Elizabth Caroline 116
Giliani, Alessandra 201
Lewis, Margaret Adaline Reed 329
Lloyd, Ruth Smith 331
Manzolini, Anna Morandi 357
Sabin, Florence Rena 509
Thiroux d'Arconville, Marie 578

Animal Science
Grandin, Temple 215

Anthropology
Aberle, Sophie Bledsoe 1
Benedict, Ruth Fulton 37
Diggs, Irene 133
Fletcher, Alice Cunningham 179
Leakey, Mary 316
Mead, Margaret 380

Anthropology
DeLaguna, Frederica Annis 129

Aquatic biology
Moore, Emmeline 401

Archaeology
Bäumgartel, Elise Jenny 32
Hawes, Harriet Ann Boyd 228
Nuttall, Zelia Maria Magdalena 425
Peck, Annie Smith 444
Reiche, Maria 482
Stevenson, Sara Yorke 553

Astronomy
Aglaonice 4
Barney, Ida 27
Bell Burnell, Jocelyn Susan 34
Blagg, Mary 44
Brahe, Sophie 55
Cannon, Annie Jump 76
Clerke, Agnes Mary 95
Cunitz, Maria 120
Draper, Mary Ann Palmer 135
Dumée, Jeanne 138
Faber, Sandra M. 163
Fleming, Williamina Paton 177
Geller, Margaret Joan 196
Harwood, Margaret 227
Herschel, Caroline Lucretia 234
Hevelius, Elisabetha Koopman 236
Hoffleit, Ellen Dorrit 245
Hogg, Helen Sawyer 247
Huggins, Margaret Lindsay Murray 258
Hypatia of Alexandria 263
Kirch, Maria Margaretha Winkelmann 290
Lalande, Jeanne Amelie Harlay Lafrancaise de 310
Leavitt, Henrietta Swan 319
Lepaute, Nicole-Reine Étable de la Brière 323
Makemson, Maud Worcester 350
Maunder, Annie Russell 368
Maury, Antonia Caetana de Paiva Pereira 369
Mitchell, Maria 395
Müller, Maria Eimmart 406
Payne-Gaposchkin, Cecilia 441
Prince, Helen Walter Dodson 469
Proctor, Mary 470
Roberts, Dorothea Klumpke 488
Roemer, Elizabeth 495
Roman, Nancy Grace 496
Rubin, Vera Cooper 500
Swope, Henrietta Hill 564
Szkody, Paula 565
Tinsley, Beatrice Muriel Hill 581
Whiting, Sarah Frances 607
Whitney, Mary Watson 608
Williams, Emma T. R. 613
Willson, Lee Ann Mordy 615
Young, Anne Sewell 632
Young, Judith Sharn Rubin 634

Astrophysics
Burbidge, Eleanor Margaret 69
Douglas, Allie Vibert 134
Hewitt, Jacqueline N. 236
Sitterly, Charlotte Emma Moore 540
Wyse, Rosemary Frances Gillian 626

Aviation
Cobb, Geraldyn 97
Collins, Eileen Marie 105

Bacteriology
Hobby, Gladys Lounsbury 242
Lancefield, Rebecca Craighill 312
Moore, Ruth Ella 402
Pittman, Margaret 461

Biochemistry
Brown, Rachel Fuller 63
Cohn, Mildred Cohn 101
Cori, Gerty Theresa 112
Daly, Marie M. 126
Dayhoff, Margaret Oakley 128
Dyer, Helen M. 138
Elion, Gertrude Belle 153
Emerson, Gladys Anderson 157
Farr, Wanda Margarite Kirkbride 166
Hoobler, Gertrude Macy 345
Jones, Mary Ellen 277
Jordan, Lynda 278
Keller, Elizabeth 284
Lucid, Shannon Ann 337
Mandl, Ines 355
Neufeld, Elizabeth F. 410
Pert, Candace Dorinda Bebe 450
Petermann, Mary Locke 451
Ratner, Sarah 479
Seibert, Florence B. 524
Stadtman, Thressa Campbell 547
Stearns, Genevieve 550
Steitz, Joan Argetsinger 550
Vennesland, Birgit 592
Wetterhahn, Karen Elizabeth 604

Biology
Carson, Rachel Louise 81
Clark, Jamie Rappaport 92
Cobb, Jewel Plummer 99
Evans, Alice 160
Farquhar, Marilyn G. 166
Fausto-Sterling, Anne 168
Franklin, Rosalind Elsie 187
Friend, Charlotte 190
Fuller, A. Oveta 193
Harvey, Ethel Browne 226
Hazen, Elizabeth Lee 230
Hobby, Gladys Lounsbury 242
Hogue, Mary Jane 248
Hubbard, Ruth 256
Keller, Evelyn Fox 285
Koehl, Mimi A. R. 296
Margulis, Lynn 359
McCouch, Margaret Sumwalt 375
McCoy, Elizabeth 376
McWhinnie, Mary Alice 378
Moore, Emmeline 401
Murray, Sandra 406
Peebles, Florence 446
Ranadive, Kamal Jayasing 476
Robinson, Daisy Mause Orleman 493
Sager, Ruth 512
Scharrer, Berta 517
Sears, Mary 522
Shields, Lora Mangum 532
Stevens, Nettie Maria 551
Stroud-Lee, Agnes Naranjo 563
Thompson, Caroline 579
Tilghman, Shirley Marie Caldwell 580
Villa-Komaroff, Lydia 594
Wrinch, Dorothy Maud 620

Biomedical Research
Profet, Margie 471

Biophysics
Cohn, Mildren 101
Quimby, Edith H. 473
Stoll, Alice M. 560

Botanical Illustration
Barnes, Eileen 26
Blackwell, Elizabeth (G.B.) 42
Hutchins, Ellen 259
North, Marianne 420

Botany
Barnes, Eileen 26
Bodley, Rachel 50
Britton, Elizabeth Gertrude Knight 59
Chase, Agnes 86
Colden, Jane 104
Cummings, Clara Eaton 119
Eastwood, Alice 143
Esau, Katherine 159
Ferguson, Margaret Clay 172
Glater, Ruth Ann Bobrov 203
Hutchins, Ellen 259
Mathias, Mildred Esther 367
Mexia, Ynes 391
Michael, Helen Abbott 392
Murtfeldt, Mary Esther 407
Palser, Barbara F. 434
Roberts, Edith Adelaide 489
Sargant, Ethel 514
Shattuck, Lydia White 527
Spalding, Effie Almira Southworth 546
Wakefield, Priscilla Bell 599

Cancer Research
Ranadive, Kamal Jayasing 476

Cardiology
Taussig, Helen Brooke 568

Cartography
Tharp, Marie 575

Cell Biology
Murray, Sandra 406

Chemical Engineering
Patrick, Jennie R. 437

Chemistry
Anderson, Gloria L. 13
Benerito, Ruth Mary Roan 38
Blodgett, Katherine Burr 47
Bodley, Rachel 50
Carr, Emma Perry 78
Cleopatra the Alchemist 95
Fenselau, Catherine Clarke 170
Fieser, Mary Peters 174
Flammel, Perrenelle Lethas 177
Free, Helen M. 189
Fulhame, Elizabeth 192
Gleditsch, Ellen 206
Hahn, Dorothy Anna 221
Harrison, Anna Jane 225
Hodgkin, Dorothy Crowfoot 243
Joliot-Curie, Irène 275
Joullié, Madeleine M. 279
Karle, Isabella Lugoski 281
Kaufman, Joyce Jacobson 282
Kwolek, Stephanie Louise 302
Lavoisier, Marie 314
Lermontova, Iulya Isevolodovna 324
Maria the Jewess 360
Meurdrac, Marie 390
Michael, Helen Abbott 392
Nightingale, Dorothy Virginia 416
Noddack, Ida Tacke 417
Pennington, Mary Engle 447
Pickett, Lucy Weston 456
Richards, Ellen Swallow 484
Shattuck, Lydia White 527
Sherman, Patsy O'Connell 530
Sherrill, Mary Lura 531
Shotwell, Odette Louise 534
Simon, Dorothy Simon 537
Stanley, Louise 549
Tesoro, Giuliana Cavaglieri 574
Vold, Marjorie Jean Young 596

Computer Science
Easley, Annie J. 142
Hoover, Erna Schneider 250
Hopper, Grace Murray 252

Crystallography
Hodgkin, Dorothy Crowfoot 243
Iveronova, Valentina Ivanovna 265
Karle, Isabella Lugoski 281
Lonsdale, Kathleen 333
Martinez-Carrera, Sagrario 362
Wood, Elizabeth Armstrong 617

Cytogenetics
Stevens, Nettie Maria 551

Cytology
Foot, Katherien A. 182
Strobell, Ella Church 562

Ecology
Colborn, Theodore Emily Decker 102
Morgan, Ann Haven 403

Education
Bryan, Margaret 66
Carr, Emma Perry 78
Cumming, Elizabeth Bragg 118
Dalle Donne, Maria 125
Edwards, Cecile Hoover 145
Gilmer, Gloria Ford 202
Granville, Evelyn Boyd 217
Kittrell, Flemmie Pansy 293
Koshland, Marian Elliott 297
Kovalevskaya, Sonya Vasilievna 298
Lyon, Mary Mason 340
Malone-Mayes, Vivienne 352
Neumann, Hann 412
Phelps, Almira Hart Lincoln 454
Proctor, Mary 470
Ramey, Estelle R. 475
Spikes, Dolores Richard 546
Stone, Isabelle 561
Talbot, Mignon 567
Velez-Rodriguez, Argelia 592

Electrical Engineering
Baum, Eleanor 31
Ochoa, Ellen 427

Embryology
Harvey, Ethel Browne 226
Mangold, Hilde Proescholdt 356
Mintz, Beatrice 394
Oppenheimer, Jane Marion 429
Platt, Julia Barlow 462
Rudnick, Dorothea 504
Woods, Geraldine Pittman 617

Endocrinology
Wilhelmi, Jane Anne Russell 611

Engineering
Baum, Eleanor 31
Brill, Yvonne Claeys 58
Clarke, Edith 93
Colmenares, Margarita 106
Cumming, Elizabeth Bragg 118
Estrin, Thelma 159
Flügge-Lotz, Irmgard 181
Gilbreth, Lillian Evelyn 199
Gleason, Catherine 204
Hicks, Beatrice 239
Lamme, Bertha Aranelle 311
Mahowald, Michelle Anne 349
Ochoa, Ellen 427
Parker, Ivy May 434
Patrick, Jennie R. 437
Roebling, Emily Warren 494
Widnall, Shelia Evans 609
Wu, Y. C. L. Susan 624

Entomology
Comstock, Anna Botsford 108
Fielde, Adele Marion 173
Huber, Marie Aimee Lullin 257
Longfield, Cynthia Evelyn 332
Morris, Margaretta Hare 405
Murtfeldt, Mary Esther 407
Ormerod, Eleanor Anne 430
Patch, Edith Marion 436
Peckham, Elizabeth Gifford 445
Sandhouse, Grace Adelbert 514
Sheldon, Jennie Arms 529
Taylor, Charlotte de Bernier Scarbrough 572

Environmental Engineering
Colmenares, Margarita 106

Environmental Science
Colborn, Theodora Emily Decker 102
Shiva, Vandana 533

Epidemiology
Stewart, Alice M. 555

Ethnology
Fletcher, Alice Cunningham 179
Goodall, Jane 213
Smith, Erminnie Adele Platt 542

Exploration
Bird, Isabella Lucy 40
Kingsley, Mary Henrietta 289
Longfield, Cynthia Evelyn 332
Peck, Annie Smith 444

General Science
Hall, Julia Brainerd 222
Montagu, Mary Wortley 398
Royer, Clemence Augustine 498

Genetics
Auerbach, Charlotte 18
Bunting-Smith, Mary 67
King, Helen Dean 288
Krim, Mathilde 300
Lederberg, Esther Miriam Zimmer 320
Macklin, Madge Thurlow 343
McClintock, Barbara 372
Nüsslein-Volhard, Christiane 423
Russell, Elizabeth Shull 506
Sager, Ruth 512
Serjeantson, Susan Wyber 525
Steitz, Joan Argetsinger 550
Stevens, Nettie Maria 551
Turner, Helen Alma Newton 586

Geology
Applin, Esthr Richards 17
Bascom, Florence 28
Buckland, Mary 66
Fisher, Elizabeth F. 176
Gardner, Julia Anna 195
Holmes, Mary Emilee 250
Hoover, Lou Henry 251
Knopf, Eleanora Bliss 295
Lyell, Mary Elizabeth Horner 339
Marvin, Ursula Bailey 364
Ogilvie, Ida H. 428
Smith, Erminnie Adele Platt 542
Stewart, Grace Anne 558
Talbot, Mignon 567
Tharp, Marie 575

Geophysics
Lehmann, Inge 322
McNutt, Marcia Kemper 377

Horticulture
Sessions, Kate Olivia 527

Hydrology
Polubarinova-Kochina, Pelegeya Yakovlevna 465

Ichthyology
Eigenmann, Rosa Smith 149

Illustration
Barnes, Eileen 26
Blackwell, Elizabeth (G.B.) 42
Herrard of Landsberg 233
Hutchins, Ellen 259
Merian, Maria Sibylla 387
Müller, Maria Eimmart 406
North, Marianne 420
Potter, Helen Beatrix 467
Russell, Anna Worsley 505
Say, Lucy Way Sistare 515

Immunology
Koshland, Marian Elliott 297

Invention
Ayrton, Hertha 21
Henry, Beulah Louise 232
Knight, Margaret 294
Masters, Sybilla 366

Limnology
Patrick, Ruth 438

Logic
Ladd-Franklin, Christine 307
Péter, Rózsa 453

Marine biology
Alvariño, Angeles 10
Carson, Rachel Louise 81
Earle, Sylvia Alice 141
Harvey, Ethel Browne 226
McCouch, Margaret Sumwalt 375
McWhinnie, Mary Alice 378
Ray, Dixy Lee 480
Sears, Mary 522

Marine Ecology
Lubchenco, Jane 335

Marine geophysics
McNutt, Marcia Kemper 377

Marine Microbiology
Colwell, Rita R. 111

Marine Zoology
Rathbun, Mary Jane 478

Mathematics
Agnesi, Maria Gaëtana 5
Bari, Nina 24
Bozeman, Syliva Trimble 54
Browne, Marjorie Lee 64
Byron, Augusta Ada 71
Chang, Sun-Yung Alice 85
Daubechies, Ingrid 126
Falconer, Etta Zuber 164
Germain, Sophie 197
Gilmer, Gloria Ford 202
Goldstine, Adele K. 212
Granville, Evelyn Boyd 217
Hayes, Ellen Amanda 229
Hazlett, Olive Clio 231
Hypatia of Alexandria 263
Janovskaja, Sof'ya Aleksandrovna 271
Kovalevskaya, Sonya Vasilievna 298
Maddison, Ada Isabel 347
Malone-Mayes, Vivienne 352
Merrill, Helen Abbot 389
Morawetz, Cathleen Synge 402
Neumann, Hanna 412
Newson, Mary Frances Winston 413
Noether, Amalie Emmy 418
Piscopia, Ellen Cornaro 459
Polubarinova-Kochina, Pelageya Yakovlevna 465
Rees, Mina S. 481
Reiche, Maria 482
Robinson, Julia 491
Rudin, Mary Ellen 502
Schafer, Alice T. 516
Scott, Charlotte Angas 520
Somerville, Mary Fairfax 543
Spikes, Dolores Richard 546
Stott, Alicia Boole 562
Taussky-Todd, Olga 570
Theano 577
Uhlenbeck, Karen 589
Velez-Rodriguez, Areglia 592
Von Mises, Hilda Geiringer 597
Wheeler, Ann Johnson Pell 605
Wrinch, Dorothy Maud 620
Young, Grace Chisholm 632

Mechanical Engineering
Gleason, Catherine 204

Medical Botany
Blackwell, Elizabeth (G.B.) 42

Medicine
Abella 1
Agamede 2
Agnodice 6
Apgar, Virginia 15
Avery, Mary Ellen 19
Barry, James Miranda Stuart 27
Blackwell, Elizabeth (G.B.) 42
Blackwell, Elizabeth (U.S.A.) 43
Bocchi, Dorotea 49
Boivin, Marie Anne 51
Bourgeois, Louyse 53
Brown, Dorothy Lavinia 61
Canady, Alexa I. 75
Chinn, May Edward 90
Comnena, Anna 107
Dalle Donne, Maria 125
Dick, Gladys Henry 131
Elders, Minnie Jocelyn 151
Erxleben, Dorothea Christiana Leporin 158
Felicie, Jacoba 169
Ferguson, Angella Dorothea 171
Hamilton, Alice 223
Jacobs, Aletta Henriette 270
Jemison, Mae Carol 272
Jex-Blake, Sophia 274
Kelsey, Frances Oldham 286
Lachapelle, Marie-Louise Dugès 306
Mendenhall, Dorothy Reed 385
Novello, Antonia Coello 422
Pearce, Louise 443
Picotte, Susan LaFlesche 457
Robinson, Daisy Maude Orleman 493
Rucker, Augusta 502
Siegemundin, Justine Dittrichin 535
Steward, Susan Smith McKinney 554
Taussig, Heleln Brooke 568
Theano 577
Trotula 584
Williams, Cicely Delphin 612
Wright, Jane Cooke 618
Yalow, Rosalyn Sussman 629

Meteorology
Simpson, Joanne Malkus 538
Van Straten, Florence W. 591

Microbiology
Alexander, Hattie E. 8
Colwell, Rita R. 111
Evans, Alice 160
Friend, Charlotte 190
Fuller, A. Oveta 193
Hazen, Elizabeth Lee 230
Hobby, Gladys Lounsbury 242
McCoy, Elizabeth 376

Microscopy
Ward, Mary 600

Midwifery
Boivin, Marie Anne 51
Lachapelle, Marie-Louise Dugès 306
Siegemundin, Justine Dittrichin 535

Mineralogy
Schlözer, Dorothea 519

Molecular Biology
Tilghman, Shirley Marie Caldwell 580
Villa-Komaroff, Lydia 594

Mycology
Hazen, Elizabeth Lee 230
Patterson, Flora Wambaugh 440
Potter, Helen Beatrix 467

Natural Science
Agassiz, Elizabeth 3
Bailey, Florence Augusta Merriam 23
Barnes, Eileen 26
Bird, Isabella 40
Blackburne, Anna 41
Delap, Maude Jane 130
Dietrich, Amalie 132
Kingsley, Mary Henrietta 289
Lewis, Graceanna 327
Maxwell, Martha Dartt 371
Merian, Maria Sibylla 387
North, Marianne 420
Russell, Anna Worsley 505
Shattuck, Lydia White 527
Treat, Mary Lua Adelia Davis 583

Natural Philosophy
Bryan, Margaret 66
Cavendish, Margaret 83
Elizabeth of Bohemia 156
Herrad of Landsberg 233
Hildegard of Bingen 240

Neuroanatomy
Crosby, Elizabeth Caroline 116

Neurobiology
Levi-Montalcini, Rita 325

Neuromorphic Engineering
Mahowald, Michelle Anne 349

Neuroscience
Pert, Candace Dorinda Bebe 450
Platt, Julia Barlow 462

Neurosurgery
Canady, Alexa I. 75

Nuclear Physics
Ajzenberg-Selove, Fay 6

Nutrition
Edwards, Cecile Hoover 145
Emerson, Gladys Anderson 157

Kittrell, Flemmie Pansy 293
MacLeod, Grace 344
Mitchell, Helen Swift 397
Roberts, Lydia Jane 490
Rose, Mary Swartz 498

Obstetrics
Bourgeois, Louyse 53
Dalle Donne, Maria 125
Mendenhall, Dorothy Reed 385

Oceanography
Earle, Sylvia Alice 141
Sears, Mary 522

Ornithology
Bailey, Florence Augusta Merriam 23
Nice, Margaret Morse 414
Sherman, Althea Rosina 529
Snethlage, Emilie 543
Williams, Heather 614

Paleontology
Anning, Mary 14
Applin, Esther Richards 17
Edinger, Tilly 144
Gardner, Julia Anna 195
Goldring, Winifred 211
Leakey, Mary 316
Maury, Carlotta Joaquina 370
Palmer, Katherine Evangeline Hilton 433
Wylde, Hildegarde Howard 625

Palynology
Truswell, Elizabeth 585

Pathology
Claypole, Edith Jane 94
Farquhar, Marilyn G. 166
Hamilton, Alice 223
L'Esperance, Elise Depew Strang 305
Menten, Maud Leonora 386
Slye, Maude 541

Pediatrics
Avery, Mary Ellen 19
Ferguson, Angella Dorothea 171
Taussig, Helen Brooke 568

Petroleum Engineering
Parker, Ivy May 434

Pharmacology
Kelsey, Frances Oldham 286
Maling, Harriet Florence Mylander 351

Philosophy
Agnesi, Maria Gaëtana
Bocchi, Dorotea 49
Bryan, Margaret 66
Cavendish, Margaret 83
Conway, Anne Finch 109
Elizabeth of Bohemia 156
Herrad of Landsberg 233
Hildegard of Bingen 240
Hypatia of Alexandria 263
Theano 577

Physics
Ajzenberg-Selove, Fay 6
Ancker-Johnson, Betsy 11
Ayrton, Hertha 21
Bassi, Laura Maria 30
Blau, Marietta 45
Bramley, Jenny Eugenia Rosenthal 56
Brooks, Harriet 60
Châtelet, Gabrielle-Émilie du 88
Curie, Marie 121
Dresselhaus, Mildred Spiewak 136
Edwards, Helen T. 147
Ehrenfest-Afanaseva, Tatiana 147
Einstein-Marić, Mileva 150
Franklin, Canadian 186
Goeppert-Mayer, Maria 208
Iveronova, Valentina Ivanovna 265
Jackson, Shirley Ann 267
Jacobi, Mary Putnam 268
Joliot-Curie, Irène 275
Karle, Isabella Lugoski 281
Keller, Evelyn Fox 285
Kistiakowsky, Vera 292
Laird, Elizabeth Rebecca 309
Libby, Leona Woods Marshall 330
Maltby, Margaret Eliza 353
Meitner, Lise 382
Perey, Marguerite Catherine 449
Pockels, Agnes 463
Ride, Sally 485
Shiva, Vandana 533
Stone, Isabelle 561
Van Straten, Florence W. 591
Way, Katharine 602
Whiting, Sarah Frances 607
Wrinch, Dorothy Maud 620
Wu, Chien-Shiung 622
Xide, Xie 627
Yalow, Rosalyn Sussman 629

Physiology
Claypole, Edith Jane 94
Hyde, Ida H. 260
Lewis, Margaret Adaline Reed 329
Pool, Judith Graham 466
Ramey, Estelle R. 475

Primatology
Fossey, Dian 183
Napier, Prudence Hero Rutherford 409

Psychology
Ladd-Franklin, Christine 307
Rand, Marie Gertrude 477
Washburn, Margaret Floy 601

Radiation Chemistry
Curie, Marie 121

Radiobiology
Stroud-Lee, F. Agnes Naranjo 563

Scientific Illustration
Herrard of Landsberg 233

Space Flight
Collins, Eileen Marie 105
Jemison, Mae Carol 272
Lucid, Shannon Ann 337
Ochoa, Ellen 427
Ride, Sally 485
Tereshkova, Valentina 573

Statistics
Cox, Gertrude Mary 115
Turner, Helen Alma Newton 586

Surgery
Brown, Dorothy Lavinia 61
Canady, Alexa I. 75

Taxidermy
Maxwell, Martha Dartt 371

Toxicology
Millis, Cynthia Dominka 393
Silbergeld, Ellen Kovner 536

Vegetable Pathology
Patterson, Flora Wambaugh 440

Virology
Horstmann, Dorothy Millicent 255

Writing/Translation
Behn, Aphra 33
Bird, Isabella 40
Boivin, Marie Anne 51
Cavendish, Margaret 83
Châtelet, Gabrielle-Émilie du 88
Comnena, Anna 107
Comstock, Anna Botsford 108
Fausto-Sterling, Anne 168
Fieser, Mary Peters 174
Marcet, Jane Haldimand 357
Montagu, Mary Wortley 398
Phelps, Almira Hart Lincoln 454

Potter, Helen Beatrix 467
Siegemundin, Justine Dittrichin 535
Somerville, Mary Fairfax 543
Trotula 584
Wakefield, Priscilla Bell 599

Zoology
Boring, Alice Middleton 52
Carothers, E. Eleanor 77
Clapp, Cornelia 91
Eigenmann, Rosa Smith 149
Guthrie, Mary Jane 219
Hibbard, Hope 238
Hyman, Libbie Henrietta 261
King, Helen Dean 288
Massy, Anne L. 365
Moody, Agnes Mary Claypole 400
Morgan, Ann Haven 403
Peebles, Florence 446
Pitelka, Dorothy Riggs 460
Rucker, Augusta 502
Stickel, Lucille Farrier 559
Young, Roger Arliner 635

African American

Anderson, Gloria L. 13
Bozeman, Sylvia Trimble 54
Brown, Dorothy Lavinia 61
Browne, Marjorie Lee 64
Canady, Alexa I. 75
Chinn, May Edward 90
Cobb, Jewel Plummer 99
Daly, Marie M. 126
Diggs, Irene 133
Easley, Annie J. 142
Edwards, Cecile Hoover 145
Elders, Minnie Jocelyn 151
Falconer, Etta Zuber 164
Ferguson, Angella Dorothea 171
Fuller, A. Oveta 193
Gilmer, Gloria Ford 202
Granville, Evelyn Boyd 217
Jackson, Shirley Ann 267
Jemison, Mae Carol 272
Jordan, Lynda 278
Kittrell, Flemmie Pansy 293
Lloyd, Ruth Smith 331
Malone-Mayes, Vivienne 352
Moore, Ruth Ella 402
Murray, Sandra 406
Patrick, Jennie R. 437
Spikes, Dolores Richard 546
Steward, Susan Smith McKinney 554
Woods, Geraldine Pittman 617
Wright, Jane Cooke 618
Young, Roger Arliner 635

American

Agassiz, Elizabeth 3
Alexander, Hattie E. 8
Ancker-Johnson, Betsy 11
Anderson, Gloria L. 13
Apgar, Virginia 15
Applin, Esther Richards 17
Avery, Mary Ellen 19
Bailey, Florence Augusta Merriam 23
Barney, Ida 27
Bascom, Florence 28
Baum, Eleanor 31
Benedict, Ruth Fulton 37
Benerito, Ruth Mary Roan 38
Blackwell, Elizabeth 43
Blodgett, Katherine Burr 47
Bodley, Rachel 50
Boring, Alice Middleton 52
Bozeman, Syliva Trimble 54
Bramley, Jenny Eugenia Rosenthal 56
Brill, Yvonne Claeys 58
Britton, Elizabeth Gertrude Knight 59
Brown, Dorothy Lavinia 61
Brown, Rachel Fuller 63
Browne, Marjorie Lee 64
Bunting-Smith, Mary 67
Burbidge, Eleanor Margaret 69
Canady, Alexa I. 75
Cannon, Annie Jump 76
Carothers, E. Eleanor 77
Carr, Emma Perry 78
Carson, Rachel Louise 81
Chang, Sun-Yung Alice 85
Chase, Agnes 86
Chinn, May Edward 90
Clapp, Cornelia 91
Clark, Jamie Rappaport 92
Clarke, Edith 93
Claypole, Edith Jane 94
Cobb, Geraldyn 97
Cobb, Jewel Plummer 99
Cohn, Mildred Cohn 101
Colborn, Theodora Emily Decker 102
Colden, Jane 104
Collins, Eileen Marie 105
Colmenares, Margarita 106
Colwell, Rita R. 111
Comstock, Anna Botsford 108
Cori, Gerty Theresa 112
Cox, Gertrude Mary 115
Crosby, Elizabeth Caroline 116
Cumming, Elizabeth Bragg 118
Cummings, Clara Eaton 119
Daly, Marie M. 126
Daubechies, Ingrid 126
Dayhoff, Margaret Oakley 128
DeLaguna, Frederica Annis 129
Dick, Gladys Henry 131
Diggs, Irene 133
Draper, Mary Ann Palmer 135
Dresselhaus, Mildred Spiewak 136
Dyer, Helen M. 138
Earle, Sylvia Alice 141
Easley, Annie J. 142
Eastwood, Alice 143
Edinger, Tilly 144
Edwards, Cecile Hoover 145
Edwards, Helen T. 147
Eigenmann, Rosa Smith 149
Elders, Minnie Jocelyn 151
Elion, Gertrude Belle 153
Emerson, Gladys Anderson 157
Esau, Katherine 159
Estrin, Thelma 159
Evans, Alice 160
Faber, Sandra M. 163
Falconer, Etta Zumber 164
Farquhar, Marilyn G. 166
Farr, Wanda Margarite Kirkbride 166
Fausto-Sterling, Anne 168
Fenselau, Catherine Clarke 170
Ferguson, Angella Dorothea 171
Ferguson, Margaret Clay 172
Fielde, Adele Marion 173
Fieser, Mary Peters 174
Fisher, Elizabeth F. 176
Fleming, Williamina Paton 177
Fletcher, Alice Cunningham 179
Flügge-Lotz, Irmgard 181
Foot, Katherien A. 182
Fossey, Dian 183
Free, Helen M. 189
Friend, Charlotte 190
Fuller, A. Oveta 193
Gardner, Julia Anna 195
Geller, Margaret Joan 196
Gilbreth, Lillian Evelyn 199
Gilmer, Gloria Ford 202
Glater, Ruth Ann Bobrov 203
Gleason, Catherine 204
Goeppert-Mayer, Maria 208
Goldring, Winifred 211
Goldstine, Adele K. 212
Grandin, Temple 215
Granville, Evelyn Boyd 217
Guthrie, Mary Jane 219
Hahn, Dorothy Anna 221
Hall, Julia Brainerd 222
Hamilton, Alice 223
Harrison, Anna Jane 225
Harvey, Ethel Browne 226

Harwood, Margaret 227
Hawes, Harriet Ann Boyd 228
Hayes, Ellen Amanda 229
Hazen, Elizabeth Lee 230
Hazlett, Olive Clio 231
Henry, Beulah Louise 232
Hewitt, Jacqueline N. 236
Hibbard, Hope 238
Hicks, Beatrice 239
Hobby, Gladys Lounsbury 242
Hoffleit, Ellen Dorrit 245
Hogg, Helen Sawyer 247
Hogue, Mary Jane 248
Holmes, Mary Emilee 250
Hoobler, Gertrude Macy 345
Hoover, Erna Schneider 250
Hoover, Lou Henry 251
Hopper, Grace Murray 252
Horstmann, Dorothy Millicent 255
Hubbard, Ruth 256
Hyde, Ida H. 260
Hyman, Libbie Henrietta 261
Jackson, Shirley Ann 267
Jacobi, Mary Putnam 268
Jemison, Mae Carol 272
Jones, Mary Ellen 277
Jordan, Lynda 278
Joullié, Madeleine M. 279
Karle, Isabella Lugoski 281
Kaufman, Joyce Jacobson 282
Keller, Elizabeth 284
Keller, Evelyn Fox 285
Kelsey, Frances Oldham 286
King, Helen Dean 288
Kistiakowsky, Vera 292
Kittrell, Flemmie Pansy 293
Knight, Margaret 294
Knopf, Eleanora Bliss 295
Koehl, Mimi A. R. 296
Koshland, Marian Elliott 297
Kwolek, Stephanie Louise 302
L'Esperance, Elise Depew Strang 305
Ladd-Franklin, Christine 307
Lamme, Bertha Aranelle 311
Lancefield, Rebecca Craighill 312
Leavitt, Henrietta Swan 319
Lederberg, Esther Miriam Zimmer 320
Levi-Montalcini, Rita 325
Lewis, Graceanna 327
Lewis, Margaret Adaline Reed 329
Libby, Leona Woods Marshall 330
Lloyd, Ruth Smith 331
Lubchenco, Jane 335
Lucid, Shannon Ann 337
Lyon, Mary Mason 340
Macklin, Madge Thurlow 343
MacLeod, Grace 344
Mahowald, Michelle Anne 349
Makemson, Maud Worcester 350
Maling, Harriet Florence Mylander 351
Malone-Mayes, Vivienne 352
Maltby, Margaret Eliza 353
Mandl, Ines 355
Margulis, Lynn 359
Marvin, Ursula Bailey 364
Masters, Sybilla 366
Mathias, Mildred Esther 367
Maury, Antonia Caetana de Paiva Pereira 369
Maury, Carlotta Joaquina 370
Maxwell, Martha Dartt 371
McClintock, Barbara 372
McCouch, Margaret Sumwalt 375
McCoy, Elizabeth 376
McNutt, Marcia Kemper 377
McWhinnie, Mary Alice 378
Mead, Margaret 380
Mendenhall, Dorothy Reed 385
Merrill, Helen Abbot 389
Mexia, Ines 391
Michael, Helen Abbott 392
Millis, Cynthia Dominka 393
Mintz, Beatrice 394
Mitchell, Helen Swift 397
Mitchell, Maria 395
Moody, Agnes Mary Claypole 400
Moore, Emmeline 401
Moore, Ruth Ella 402
Morawetz, Cathleen Synge 402
Morgan, Ann Haven 403
Morris, Margaretta Hare 405
Murray, Sandra 406
Murtfeldt, Mary Esther 407
Neufeld, Elizabeth F. 410
Newson, Mary Frances Winston 413
Nice, Margaret Morse 414
Nightingale, Dorothy Virginia 416
Noether, Amalie Emmy 418
Novello, Antonia Coello 422
Nuttall, Zelia Maria Magdalena 425
Ochoa, Ellen 427
Ogilvie, Ida H. 428
Oppenheimer, Jane Marion 429
Palmer, Katherine Evangeline Hilton 433
Palser, Barbara F. 434
Parker, Ivy May 434
Patch, Edith Marion 436
Patrick, Jennie R. 437
Patrick, Ruth 438
Patterson, Flora Wambaugh 440
Payne-Gaposchkin, Cecilia 441
Pearce, Louise 443
Peck, Annie Smith 444
Peckham, Elizabeth Gifford 445
Peebles, Florence 446
Pennington, Mary Engle 447
Pert, Candace Dorinda Bebe 450
Petermann, Mary Locke 451
Phelps, Almira Hart Lincoln 454
Pickett, Lucy Weston 456
Picotte, Susan LaFlesche 457
Pinckney, Elizabeth Lucas 458
Pitelka, Dorothy Riggs 460
Pittman, Margaret 461
Platt, Julia Barlow 462
Pool, Judith Graham 466
Prince, Helen Walter Dodson 469
Proctor, Mary 470
Profet, Margie 471
Quimby, Edith H. 473
Ramey, Estelle R. 475
Rand, Marie Gertrude 477
Rathbun, Mary Jane 478
Ratner, Sarah 479
Ray, Dixy Lee 480
Rees, Mina S. 481
Richards, Ellen Swallow 484
Ride, Sally 485
Roberts, Dorothea Klumpke 488
Roberts, Edith Adelaide 489
Roberts, Lydia Jane 490
Robinson, Daisy Mause Orleman 493
Robinson, Julia 491
Roebling, Emily Warren 494
Roemer, Elizabeth 495
Roman, Nancy Grace 496
Rose, Mary Swartz 498
Rubin, Vera Cooper 500
Rucker, Augusta 502
Rudin, Mary Ellen 502
Rudnick, Dorothea 504
Russell, Elizabeth Shull 506
Sabin, Florence Rena 509
Sager, Ruth 512
Sandhouse, Grace Adelbert 514
Say, Lucy Way Sistare 515
Schafer, Alice T. 516
Scharrer, Berta 517
Sears, Mary 522
Seibert, Florence B. 524
Sessions, Kate Olivia 527
Shattuck, Lydia White 527
Sheldon, Jennie Arms 529
Sherman, Althea Rosina 529
Sherman, Patsy O'Connell 530
Sherrill, Mary Lura 531
Shields, Lora Mangum 532
Shotwell, Odette Louise 534
Silbergeld, Ellen Kovner 536
Simon, Dorothy Simon 537
Simpson, Joanne Malkus 538
Sitterly, Charlotte Emma Moore 540
Slye, Maude 541
Smith, Erminnie Adele Platt 542
Spalding, Effie Almira Southworth 546
Spikes, Dolores Richard 546
Stadtman, Thressa Campbell 547

Stanley, Louise 549
Stearns, Genevieve 550
Steitz, Joan Argetsinger 550
Stevens, Nettie Maria 551
Stevenson, Sara Yorke 553
Steward, Susan Smith McKinney 554
Stewart, Grace Anne 558
Stickel, Lucille Farrier 559
Stoll, Alice M. 560
Stone, Isabelle 561
Strobell, Ella Church 562
Stroud-Lee, F. Agnes Naranjo 563
Swope, Henrietta Hill 564
Szkody, Paula 565
Talbot, Mignon 567
Taussig, Heleln Brooke 568
Taussky-Todd, Olga 570
Taylor, Charlotte de Bernier Scarbrough 572
Tesoro, Giuliana Cavaglieri 574
Tharp, Marie 575
Thompson, Caroline 579
Tinsley, Beatrice Muriel Hill 581
Treat, Mary Lua Adelia Davis 583
Uhlenbeck, Karen 589
Van Straten, Florence W. 591
Velez-Rodriguez, Areglia 592
Vennesland, Birgit 592
Villa-Komaroff, Lydia 594
Vold, Marjorie Jean Young 596
Von Mises, Hilda Geiringer 597
Washburn, Margaret Floy 601
Way, Katharine 602
Wetterhahn, Karen Elizabeth 604
Wheeler, Ann Johnson Pell 605
Whiting, Sarah Frances 607
Whitney, Mary Watson 608
Widnall, Shelia Evans 609
Wilhelmi, Jane Anne Russell 611
Williams, Emma T. R. 613
Williams, Heather 614
Willson, Lee Ann Mordy 615
Wood, Elizabeth Armstrong 617
Woods, Geraldine Pittman 617
Wright, Jane Cooke 618
Wrinch, Dorothy Maud 620
Wu, Chien-Shiung 622
Wu, Y. C. L. Susan 624
Wylde, Hildegarde Howard 625
Yalow, Rosalyn Sussman 629
Young, Anne Sewell 632
Young, Judith Sharn Rubin 634
Young, Roger Arliner 635

Asian American
Chang, Sun-Yung Alice 85
Wu, Chien-Shiung 622
Wu, Y. C. L. Susan 624

Australian
Serjeantson, Susan Wyber 525
Truswell, Elizabeth 585
Turner, Helen Alma Newton 586

Austrian
Blau, Marietta 45
Hubbard, Ruth 256
Mandl, Ines 355
Meitner, Lise 382

Austro-Hungarian
Cori, Gerty Theresa 112
Einstein-Marić, Mileva 150
Taussky-Todd, Olga 570

Belgian
Daubechies, Ingrid 126

Byzantine
Comnena, Anna 107

Canadian
Brill, Yvonne Claeys 58
Brooks, Harriet 60
Douglas, Allie Vibert 134
Eastwood, Alice 143
Franklin, Melissa 186
Hogg, Helen Sawyer 247
Kelsey, Frances Oldham 286
Laird, Elizabeth Rebecca 309
Menten, Maud Leonora 386
Stewart, Grace Anne 558
Tilghman, Shirley Marie Caldwell 580
Vold, Marjorie Jean Young 596

Chinese
Chang, Sun-Yung Alice 85
Wu, Chien-Shiung 622
Wu, Y. C. L. Susan 624
Xide, Xie 627

Cuban
Velez-Rodriguez, Argelia 592

Danish
Lehmann, Inge 322
Brahe, Sophie 55

Dutch
Ehrenfest-Afanaseva, Tatiana 147
Jacobs, Aletta Henriette 270
Merian, Maria Sibylla 387

Egyptian
Cleopatra the Alchemist 95
Maria the Jewess 360

English
Anning, Mary 14
Ayrton, Hertha 21
Barry, James 27
Behn, Aphra 33
Bird, Isabella Lucy 40
Blackburne, Anna 41
Blackwell, Elizabeth 42
Blagg, Mary 44
Bryan, Margaret 66
Buckland, Mary 66
Burbidge, Eleanor Margaret 69
Byron, Augusta Ada 71
Cavendish, Margaret 83
Clerke, Agnes Mary 95
Conway, Anne Finch 109
Franklin, Rosalind Elsie 187
Fulhame, Elizabeth 192
Goodall, Jane 213
Herschel, Caroline Lucretia 234
Hodgkin, Dorothy Crowfoot 243
Huggins, Margaret Lindsay Murray 258
Jex-Blake, Sophia 274
Kingsley, Mary Henrietta 289
Leakey, Mary 316
Lonsdale, Kathleen 333
Lyell, Mary Elizabeth Horner 339
Maddison, Ada Isabel 347
Marcet, Jane Haldimand 357
Montagu, Mary Wortley 398
Moody, Agnes Mary Claypole 400
Napier, Prudence Hero Rutherford 409
North, Marianne 420
Ormerod, Eleanor Anne 430
Payne-Gaposchkin, Cecilia 441
Potter, Helen Beatrix 467
Proctor, Mary 470
Russell, Anna Worsley 505
Sargant, Ethel 514
Scott, Charlotte Angas 520
Somerville, Mary Fairfax 543
Stewart, Alice M. 555
Stott, Alicia Boole 562
Tinsley, Beatrice Muriel Hill 581
Wakefield, Priscilla Bell 599
Williams, Cicely Delphin 612
Wrinch, Dorothy Maud 620
Young, Grace Chisholm 632

French
Biheron, Marie Catherine 39
Boivin, Marie Anne 51
Bourgeois, Louyse 53
Châtelet, Gabrielle-Émilie du 88
Curie, Marie 121
Dumée, Jeanne 138
Flammel, Perrenelle Lethas 177
Germain, Sophie 197
Joliot-Curie, Irène 275

Lachapelle, Marie-Louise Dugès 306
Lalande, Jeanne Amelie Harlay Lafrancaise de 310
Lavoisier, Marie 314
Lepaute, Nicole-Reine Étable de la Brière 323
Meurdrac, Marie 390
Neumann, Hanna 412
Perey, Marguerite Catherine 449
Pockels, Agnes 463
Royer, Clemence Augustine 498
Stevenson, Sara Yorke 553
Thiroux d'Arconville, Marie 578

German
Ajzenberg-Selove, Fay 6
Auerbach, Charlotte 18
Bäumgartel, Elise Jenny 32
Cunitz, Maria 120
Dietrich, Amalie 132
Edinger, Tilly 144
Elizabeth of Bohemia 156
Erxleben, Dorothea Christiana Leporin 158
Flügge-Lotz, Irmgard 181
Goeppert-Mayer, Maria 208
Herrad of Landsberg 233
Herschel, Caroline Lucretia 234
Hildegard of Bingen 240
Kirch, Maria Margaretha Winkelmann 290
Mangold, Hilde Proescholdt 356
Müller, Maria Eimmart 406
Neumann, Hann 412
Nüsslein-Volhard, Christiane 423
Noddack, Ida Tacke 417
Noether, Amalie Emmy 418
Reiche, Maria 482
Scharrer, Berta 517
Schlözer, Dorothea 519
Siegemundin, Justine Dittrichin 535
Snethlage, Emilie 543

Greek
Agamede 2
Aglaonice 4
Agnodice 6
Hypatia of Alexandria 263
Theano 577

Hispanic American
Colmenares, Margarita 106
Mexia, Ynes 391
Ochoa, Ellen 427
Villa-Komaroff, Lydia 594

Hungarian
Einstein-Marić, Mileva 150
Péter, Rózsa 453

Indian
Shiva, Vandana 533
Ranadive, Kamal Jayasing Indian 476

Irish
Barnes, Eileen 26
Bell Burnell, Jocelyn Susan 34
Clerke, Agnes, Mary 95
Delap, Maude Jane 130
Huggins, Margaret Lindsay Murray 258
Hutchins, Ellen 259
Longfield, Cynthia Evelyn 332
Massy, Anne L. 365
Maunder, Annie Russell 368
Stott, Alicia Boole 562
Ward, Mary 600

Italian
Abella 1
Agnesi, Maria Gaëtana 5
Bassi, Laura Maria 30
Bocchi, Dorotea 49
Dalle Donne, Maria 125
Felicie, Jacoba 169
Giliani, Alessandra 201
Krim, Mathilde 300
Levi-Montalcini, Rita 325
Manzolini, Anna Morandi 357
Piscopia, Ellen Cornaro 459
Tesoro, Giuliana Cavaglieri 574
Trotula 584

Jamaican
Williams, Cicely Delphin 612

Jewish
Ajzenberg-Selove, Fay 6
Auerbach, Charlotte 18
Ayrton, Hertha 21
Blau, Marietta 45
Cohn, Mildred 101
Edinger, Tilly 144
Franklin, Rosalind Elsie 187
Glater, Ruth Ann Bobrov 203
Hubbard, Ruth 256
Hyman, Libbie Henrietta 261
Jacobs, Aletta Henriette 270
Kaufman, Joyce Jacobson 282
Keller, Evelyn Fox 285
Levi-Montalcini, Rita 325
Mandl, Ines 355
Maria the Jewess 360
Meitner, Lise 382
Noether, Amalie Emmy 418
Taussky-Todd, Olga 570
Tesoro, Giuliana Cavaglieri 574
Von Mises, Hilda Geiringer 597

Native American
Aberle, Sophie Bledsoe 1
Picotte, Susan LaFlesche 457
Shields, Lora Mangum 532
Stroud-Lee, Agnes Naranjo 563

Norwegian
Gleditsch, Ellen 206
Vennesland, Birgit 592

Polish
Curie, Marie 121
Hevelius, Elisabetha Koopman 236

Russian
Bari, Nina 24
Bramley, Jenny Rosenthal 56
Ehrenfest-Afanaseva, Titiana 147
Esau, Katherine 159
Iveronova, Valentina Ivanovna 265
Janovskaja, Sof'ya Aleksandrovna 271
Kovalevskaya, Sonya Vasilievna 298
Lermontova, Iulya Isevolodovna 324
Polubarinova-Kochina, Pelageya Yakovlevna 465
Tereshkova, Valentina 573

Scottish
Fleming, Williamina Paton 177
MacLeod, Grace 344
Somerville, Mary Fairfax 543
Wyse, Rosemary Frances Gillian 626

Spanish
Alvariño, Angeles 10
Martinez-Carrera, Sagrario 362

Swiss
Huber, Marie Aimee Lullin 257